SAGE
Premium
Video

BOOST COMPREHENSION. BOLSTER ANALYSIS.

- Management in Action **VIDEOS ILLUSTRATE FUNDAMENTAL MANAGEMENT CONCEPTS** using a variety of relatable scenarios and assessment questions to challenge students to apply their learning and analyze workplace situations.

- **BRIDGES BOOK CONTENT** with application and critical thinking.

- Includes short, auto-graded quizzes that **DIRECTLY FEED TO YOUR LMS GRADEBOOK**.

- Premium content is **ADA COMPLIANT WITH TRANSCRIPTS**.

- Comprehensive media guide helps you **QUICKLY SELECT MEANINGFUL VIDEO** tied to your course objectives.

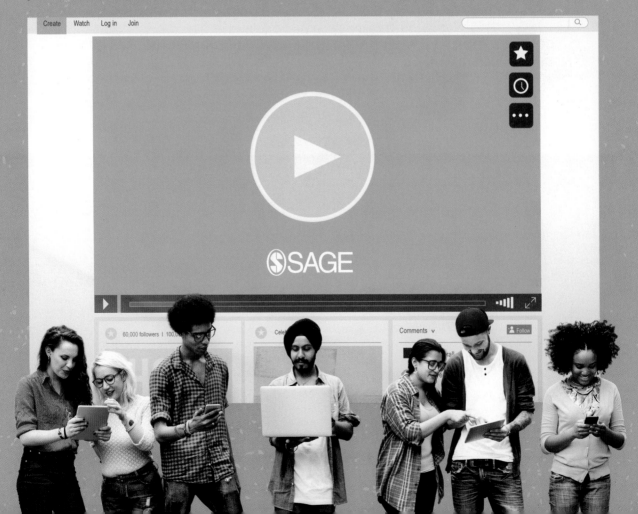

The Hallmark Features

A COMPLETE LEARNING PACKAGE

Using a three-pronged approach of concepts, applications, and skill development, Robert N. Lussier's *Management Fundamentals* provides students with a solid foundation of management concepts and skills that they can immediately put to use in their personal lives and at work.

- **IDEAS ON MANAGEMENT** opening cases and **END-OF-CHAPTER CASES** highlight contemporary topics and challenge students to apply course concepts.

- **SKILL BUILDERS** provide three types of focused exercises—Individual, Group, or Role-Play—that help students develop skills they can use today and in their future professional lives.

- **SELF-ASSESSMENTS** in each chapter allow students to gain insight into their knowledge of the management functions in the real world while also learning about their personal management styles.

MANAGEMENT
FUNDAMENTALS

8e

SAGE PUBLISHING: Our Story

We believe in creating fresh, cutting-edge content that helps you prepare your students to make an impact in today's ever-changing business world. Founded in 1965 by 24-year-old entrepreneur Sara Miller McCune, SAGE continues its legacy of equipping instructors with the tools and resources necessary to develop the next generation of business leaders.

- We invest in the right **authors** who distill the best available research into practical applications

- We offer intuitive **digital solutions** at student-friendly prices

- We remain permanently independent and fiercely committed to **quality, innovation, and learning.**

MANAGEMENT

FUNDAMENTALS

CONCEPTS, APPLICATIONS, AND SKILL DEVELOPMENT

8e

ROBERT N. LUSSIER

Springfield College

Los Angeles | London | New Delhi
Singapore | Washington DC | Melbourne

FOR INFORMATION:

SAGE Publications, Inc.
2455 Teller Road
Thousand Oaks, California 91320
E-mail: order@sagepub.com

SAGE Publications Ltd.
1 Oliver's Yard
55 City Road
London EC1Y 1SP
United Kingdom

SAGE Publications India Pvt. Ltd.
B 1/I 1 Mohan Cooperative Industrial Area
Mathura Road, New Delhi 110 044
India

SAGE Publications Asia-Pacific Pte. Ltd.
3 Church Street
#10-04 Samsung Hub
Singapore 049483

Acquisitions Editor: Maggie Stanley
Editorial Assistant: Alissa Nance
Content Development Editor: Lauren Holmes
Production Editor: Tracy Buyan
Copy Editor: Kim Husband
Typesetter: C&M Digitals (P) Ltd.
Proofreader: Lawrence W. Baker
Indexer: Judy Hunt
Cover Designer: Janet Kiesel
Marketing Manager: Amy Lammers

Printed in Canada

Library of Congress Cataloging-in-Publication Data

Names: Lussier, Robert N., author.

Title: Management fundamentals : concepts, applications, and skill development / Robert N. Lussier, Springfield College.

Description: 8e [edition]. | Thousand Oaks, Calif. : SAGE, [2019] | Includes bibliographical references and indexes.

Identifiers: LCCN 2017043147 | ISBN 9781506389394 (pbk. : alk. paper)

Subjects: LCSH: Management. | Supervision of employees.

Classification: LCC HD31.2 .L87 2019 | DDC 658—dc23
LC record available at https://lccn.loc.gov/2017043147

This book is printed on acid-free paper.

18 19 20 21 22 10 9 8 7 6 5 4 3 2 1

●●● Brief Contents

●●● Detailed Contents

Part I: The Global Management Environment

JONATHAN NACKSTRAND/AFP/Getty Images

David Ryder/Getty Images

Jan-Stefan Knick / EyeEm

Part II: Planning

Jason Alden/Bloomberg via Getty Images

Tim Boyle/Getty Images

SainPhoto by Chesnot/Getty Images

Chapter 6. Managing Change, Innovation, and Entrepreneurship

Part III: Organizing

Jasper Juinen/Bloomberg via Getty Images

Chapter 7. Organizing and Delegating Work

George Frey/Bloomberg via Getty Images

Spencer Platt/Getty Images

©iStockphoto.com/Cecilie_Arcurs

Part IV: Leading

©iStockphoto.com/Pixfly

Ascent Xmedia via Getty Images

Kevork Djansezian/Getty Images

Justin Sullivan/Getty Images

Chapter 13. Communication and Information Technology 422

Part V: Controlling

Courtesy of The Ranch Golf Club

Chapter 14. Managing Control Systems, Finances, and People 462

Russiavia/CreativeCommons https://creativecommons.org/licenses/by-sa/2.0/deed.en

Chapter 15. Operations, Quality, and Productivity

●●● Preface

In his book *Power Tools*, John Nirenberg asks, "Why are so many well-intended students learning so much and yet able to apply so little in their personal and professional lives?" Students want more than just an understanding of the concepts of management. They also want skills they can use in their everyday lives and at work. It's not enough to learn about management; they want to learn how to succeed in today's business environment. This is why I wrote this book.

If you look at the textbooks over time, they keep getting smaller as authors cut out material. When writing this eighth edition, I decided to set a higher standard. I've actually added more material while making the text more concise and completely updated it by adding more than 1,250 new references for a total of more than 2,600. I've also added more than 700 new company examples. Compare the contents to any major competitor, and you will find that, as reviewers consistently say, the real difference is that I offer superior quantity and quality application and skill-development options that engage millennials.

I personally developed the total package to have the following competitive advantages:

- A unique **"how-to-manage"** approach with a focus on personal advice on how to succeed in today's changing business environment of shared leadership
- Eight types of high-quality **application materials** using the concepts to develop critical-thinking skills
- Five types of high-quality **skill-building exercises** to develop management skills that can be utilized in students' professional and personal lives
- A **flexible** package—with all these features, instructors can design the course by selecting the features that meet their needs
- A **lower price** to students than major competitors

Designed to Meet a Variety of Learning Styles

Today's students need to be engaged, as the old primary lecture method is no longer effective. My text is very flexible and can be used with the traditional lecture method. But it also offers a wide range of engaging activities to select from that best meet the professor and student goals and preferred teaching/learning styles. Many of the specific learning preferences of millennials have been addressed in the book's overall approach, organization, and distinctive features.

- **Active Learning.** A design for active learning is addressed with a wide variety of application activities and skill-building tools that can be used immediately in their own lives.
- **Practical Approach.** Students are provided with **immediate feedback** and ongoing **self-assessment** opportunities found in the Work Application, Applying the Concept, and Self-Assessment features. Organizational tools such as **checklists**, summaries, and **"how-to"** instructions are integrated throughout.
- **Accessible Content.** Text material presents management concepts followed by application material so that students can break up the reading while applying the concepts and getting feedback. The boxed items are not just passively reading an example; they engage the student to come up with an answer. Content is **chunked** into easily digested segments to help students process new ideas and concepts.
- **Online Resources.** The text is accompanied by a password-protected **instructor website** and an open-access **student website** (see the following for more details). Also, while all the elements in the text are designed to be used by individuals, they can also be used in group settings, making *Management Fundamentals* an ideal text for *online courses*.

Integrated Three-Pronged Approach

As the title of this book implies, it involves a balanced, three-pronged approach to the curriculum:

1. A clear understanding of management **concepts**
2. The **application** of management concepts for critical thinking in the real world
3. The development of management **skills**

I wrote this text and its supporting ancillary package to support these three distinct but integrated parts. This text follows a management-functions approach covering all the traditional concepts and current topics. The applications develop students' critical-thinking skills as they require them to apply specific concepts to their own work experience (volunteer, part time, summer, or full time), to short situations, and to cases. In addition, this text meets the challenge of the AACSB (Association to Advance Collegiate Schools of Business) call for skills development. Since I wrote almost every exercise and application in the package, the material is completely integrated to create a seamless experience in the classroom or online.

The three key elements of concepts, applications, and skills are integrated throughout the chapters. However, they are identified clearly and are delineated in some detail for your reference in this preface and in Chapter 1. Recognizing the diverse needs of students and faculty, they can be used flexibly to fit any course. Instructors can create their course by using only features that fit with their objectives in class or online.

My goal is to make both students and instructors successful in and out of the classroom by providing learning features that not only teach about management but also help students succeed in the changing business environment.

Concepts

This text covers all key management topics and concepts. It is comprehensive in scope, as shown by the detailed **Learning Objectives** at the front of each chapter. Each outcome is reinforced and identified throughout the chapter. Key terms are highlighted in green to emphasize the vocabulary of management for students.

Current Management Issues

This text is not cluttered with extraneous boxes. Instead, current topics as described by the AACSB, such as globalization, diversity, technology, and ethics, are covered throughout the chapters, and each chapter ends with the section "Trends and Issues in Management" to apply each of these four topics as they relate to the chapter contents.

End-of-Chapter Material Reinforcement of Concepts

Each chapter ends with a **Chapter Summary** that reinforces every Learning Objective. A **Key Term Review** section enables the readers to quiz themselves on the definitions, making it an active glossary. In addition, each chapter includes an average of 13 **Review Questions** to support and reinforce the key concepts that appear in the chapters.

Applications

Powerful learning takes place when theory is put within the context of the real world. Using this text, students are challenged to apply the concepts they learn to actual business situations, especially as they have experienced them personally. Students must think critically as they apply specific concepts to their own work experience, short situations, and cases.

Ideas on Management Opening Cases

At the beginning of each chapter, information about an actual manager and organization is presented. The case is followed by four to eight questions to get students involved.

Throughout the chapter, the answers to the questions are given to illustrate how the organization actually uses the text concepts to create opportunities and solve problems through decision making. The students get a real-world example illustrated extensively throughout the chapter, beginning with the opening pages.

Real-World Examples

Company examples illustrate how businesses use the text concepts. There are more than 700 new examples, with an average of 47 per chapter. Text concepts come alive as students see how actual organizations use them to succeed. Companies featured include **Netflix**, **Uber**, **Airbnb**, **Google**, and **Apple**, among many others. The organization names are highlighted throughout the text in bold font.

Work Applications

Open-ended questions called Work Applications require students to explain how the text concepts apply to their own work experience; more than 160 of these are strategically placed throughout the text. Student experience can be present, past, summer, full-time or part-time employment, or volunteer work. The questions help students bridge the gap between theory and their real world.

Applying the Concept

Every chapter contains a series of three to six Applying the Concept boxes that require the student to determine the management concept being illustrated in a specific short example. There are 19 to 43 objective questions per chapter (and every question is new or revised in the eighth edition) for development of student critical-thinking skills.

Join the Discussion: Ethics and Social Responsibility Dilemmas

There are 40 ethical dilemma boxed items, with at least two to three included per chapter. Many of the dilemmas include information from companies such as **Gap** and **JetBlue Airways**. Each dilemma has two to four questions for critical thinking and possible class or online discussion.

End-of-Chapter Cases

Following the review and communication questions, students are presented with two cases of an actual manager or organization. **Case questions** require the student to apply management practices and concepts to the actual organization. Chapters 2 through 15 also include **cumulative case questions** that relate case material to concepts from prior chapters. Thus, students continually review and integrate concepts from previous chapters.

Skill Development

The difference between learning about management and learning to be a manager is the acquisition of skills. This text focuses on skill development so students can use what they learn in their personal lives and on the job. The skill material is integrated throughout the text, but instructors can choose how to incorporate the material into their classroom or online experience—individually or as groups, inside the class or as outside group projects.

Students can actually develop a skill that can be used on the job. The features listed in the following paragraphs include true skill building, such as step-by-step models, and skill-building exercises. Other features also support skill building, such as self-assessments and group exercises.

Step-by-Step Models

The book contains approximately 25 detailed sets of how-to steps for handling day-to-day management functions. They are integrated into the context of the chapter or skill-building exercise being taught. For example, models teach students how to set objectives and priorities, how to handle a complaint, and how to discipline an employee. This feature directly teaches students how to be managers.

Skill Builders

Chapters contain an average of three Skill Builders, all of which have been class tested to be the best found in any text on the market. Full support of more than 45 activities can be found in the Instructor's Manual, including detailed information, timing, answers, and so on. All exercises and their uses are optional in the classroom or online. There are three primary types of exercises:

1. Individual Focus: Around half are those in which participants are required to make individual decisions prior to or during class. These answers can be shared in class or online for discussion, or the instructor may elect to go over recommended answers.
2. Group Focus: Around a quarter are those in which participants discuss the material presented and may select group answers.
3. Role-Play Focus: Around a quarter are those in which participants are presented with a model and given the opportunity to use the model, usually in groups of two or three.

Self-Assessments

Scattered throughout the text are more than 25 Self-Assessments, with at least one per chapter. Students complete these assessments to gain personal knowledge. All information for completing and scoring the assessments is contained within the text. Many of the assessments are tied to exercises within the book, thus enhancing the impact of the activities.

Communication Skills

There are approximately 150 critical-thinking questions (an average of 10 per chapter) that can be used for class discussion and/or written assignments to develop communication skills.

New to the Eighth Edition

Having done a major revision of the seventh edition, in which 97% of the references were new, I thought this would be a quick minor revision. However, in adding more than 1,250 new references, I made several improvements in the text focusing on how to apply the concepts in one's personal and professional lives. Here they are:

- There is an average of 84 new references with a total of more than 175 per chapter. The theory comes primarily from Academy of Management articles.
- There are more than 700 new people's names, brands, and company examples, coming from *Business Week, Forbes, Fortune, The Wall Street Journal,* and others.
- New terms or concepts added to this new edition: ACBSP (Accreditation Council for Business Schools and Programs); IACBE (International Assembly for Collegiate Business Education; Go Suit; Mary Parker Follett; operations research, operations management, information management; Three Views of Ethics: utilitarianism, rights, and justice views; Golden Rule: Buddhism, Christianity, Confucianism, Hinduism, Judaism, Islam, Taoism; social enterprises; hybrid organizations; work integration social enterprises (WISEs); BCorp (benefits corporation); not-invented-here; Brexit; Trans-Pacific Partnership (TPP); IMF; Arguments for and Against Free Trade and the Future of Global Trade; Executive Orders; Generation Z characteristics; Glass Cliff; LGBT+; Fortune 50 Best Workplaces for Diversity; Attention Spans and Concentration and Smartphones;

frenemies; Our Resistance to Change—Habits; organizational entrepreneurs; opportunity cost; The Funding and Sales Pitch; SBA LINC (Leveraging Information and Networks to access Capital); informal organization chart; multiteam systems; Platform Organization; Fair Labor Standards Act of 1938; microlearning; e-learning companies; gratitude; habit; conflict of ideas; personal conflict; procrastination; perfectionism; time pressure; genomics; brain training; altercasting; bossless organization; self-leadership; followership; chatbots; cyberloafing; retentive listening; the performance success cycle; revenues vs. profits; profit margins; strategic cloud supply chains; third-party logistics providers (3PLS); dashboards.

- There is a second shorter end of chapter case for every chapter.
- More than half of the "Trends and Issues in Management" section has new updated material.
- All Applying the Concept questions have been changed. Four new boxes and 28 new questions have been added. There are more than 425 questions for an average of 29 per chapter.
- There is a new self-assessment (28 total) and skill-building exercise (47 total).
- Four of the opening cases are new, and all the others have been updated.
- Half of the end-of-chapter cases are new, and all the others have been updated. The cases replaced are in the Instructor's Manual for those who want to continue to use them.

The Test Bank continues to measure application and skill development, and the AACSB competencies tested are also identified.

Here are the changes for each chapter.

Chapter 1. Management and Its History

- There are 44 new current references in Chapter 1 for a total of 126 references.
- There are 12 new people and company/brand examples, including Sheryl Sandberg, COO of Facebook, Booker T. Washington, Starbucks, ACBSP (Accreditation Council for Business Schools and Programs), and IACBE (International Assembly for Collegiate Business Education.
- The opening case has been updated.
- There are two new sections with expanded discussion in the "Why Take Management" section to clearly state the skills that can be developed in one's personal life and professional lives as a manager or employee.
- The section What Does It Take to Be a Successful Manager subsection on AACSB has been expanded to now include ACBSP (Accreditation Council for Business Schools and Programs) and IACBE (International Assembly for Collegiate Business Education).
- All of the Applying the Concept boxes are changed with revised or new questions with a total of 28 application questions.
- There is a new Applying the Concept box 1-5, Matching History of Management People and Theories.
- There is a new Exhibit 1-9, Survey Results Comparing Large and Small Businesses Responses.
- There is a new Work Application question, 1-8.
- The jargon term Go Suit has been added to the Transitions to Management subsection.
- The Join the Discussion, Executive Compensation, has been updated with new references.
- In the History of Management section, the subsection Scientific Management now expands the discussion of Mary Parker Follett to include *integrative conflict resolution*.

- In the History of Management section, the Management Science subsection has been expanded to include operations research, operations management, and information management.
- The Trends and Issues in Management section now better identifies the trends in globalization, diversity, technology, ethics, and social responsibility.
- There is a new first short case at the end of the chapter.
- The second longer end-of-chapter case has been updated.
- Skill-Building Exercise 1-3, Careers, now includes reflecting on working for a small or large organization.

Chapter 2. The Environment: Culture, Ethics, and Social Responsibility

- There are 76 new current references in Chapter 2 with a total of 200 references.
- There are 68 new people and company/brand examples, including SpaceX, Mary Kay, Ben & Jerry's, Etsy, and Southwest Airlines.
- The chapter has been reorganized by moving the internal and external environments together in the first section. The discussion includes the same content but has been shortened a bit. Exhibit 2-3 has been deleted, as it is the center part of the new expanded Exhibit 2-3. This also changes some of the Learning Objectives and Work Application, Review Questions, and Communication Skills numbers.
- The opening case has been completely rewritten.
- The Organizational Culture section has been reorganized. The prior first subsection has been split into two level-two heads: Organizational Culture Artifacts and Organizational Culture Levels, Strength, and Health; the discussion of healthy and unhealthy cultures from prior editions has been added. The prior last two sections have been combined in the third level-two head: Managing and Changing Cultures and the Learning Organization. The Learning Organization subsection has been completely rewritten.
- In the Business Ethics section, a new subsection has been added, "Three Views of Ethics," to include a discussion of utilitarianism, rights, and justice views. The subsection "Caution" is now "Caution Against Escalation of Unethical Behavior" with expanded coverage.
- The "Methods to Help Ensure Ethical Behavior" subsection "Golden Rule" is more global in scope by stating that the following religions have a variation of the Golden Rule: Buddhism, Christianity, Confucianism, Hinduism, Judaism, Islam, and Taoism. There is also a new subtitle, "Application of Ethical Guides."
- In the Social Responsibility to Stakeholders section, there is a new subsection, "Social Entrepreneurs and Hybrid Organizations," that presents new terms: *social enterprises*, *hybrid organizations*, and *work integration social enterprises (WISEs)*.
- The new term *BCorp* (benefits corporation) has been added as a new subsection in the Social Responsibility to Stakeholders section.
- 2-2 Join the Discussion Ethics & Social Responsibility: Sex, Profanity, and Violence no longer has the word *TV* in the title because the discussion has been expanded to include portraying females as sex objects and violence against women in songs and music videos and in video games. Thus, questions 4 and 5 have been expanded.
- All of the Applying the Concept boxes are changed, 2-2 and 2-3 reversed, and all have revised or new questions with a total of 27 application questions.
- The Trends and Issues section has been revised with around 50% new material. The first two paragraphs discussing global issues have been combined and shortened. There is a new paragraph defining and discussing the sharing economy, and examples of new sustainability have been added.
- There is a new first short case at the end of the chapter.
- The second longer case is new.

Chapter 3. Managing Diversity in a Global Environment

- There are 167 new current references in Chapter 3 for a total of 216.

- There are 79 new people and company/brand examples including GM, Carrier, Airbnb, and United Nations.

- The chapter has been reorganized. The first section remains The Global Environment so that students understand its importance. However, the second section, Managing Global Business, has been moved to the end of the chapter, just before the trends and issues section, so that the flow of content goes to diversity, to global diversity, followed by how to manage a global business, which is often required in an international business class. The overall coverage of discrimination has been expanded, and the global coverage is a bit shorter.

- The chapter reorganization results in changes in numbering of the Learning Objectives, Work Applications, Applying the Concept, Review, and Communication Skills Questions.

- The opening case SHI is new.

- The first section, The Global Environment, has a new introduction covering the chapter topics and has a new paragraph to focus on making sure students understand how globalization does and will continue to affect them personally.

- The section "Ethnocentrism …" now includes the new topic "not-invented-here syndrome."

- In Self-Assessment 3-1, Nokia has been replaced with Pep Boys.

- In the section of Managing Foreign Trade, the subsection Trade Barriers now states that the trend is toward protectionism, and the subsection Trade Agreements now discusses Brexit and the possibility that the US will not be part of the Trans-Pacific Partnership (TPP). Also, the Exchange Rates subsection has been expanded to include the effects of Brexit and the strong US dollar in 2015–2016. Following Exchange Rates is a new subsection discussing the IMF.

- There is a new Applying the Concept box 3-1, Trade Barriers, in the section of Standard of Living and the Effects of Foreign Trade, the discussion of the effects of foreign trade has been rewritten to include three new subsections: Arguments for and Against Free Trade and the Future of Global Trade. The Big Mac index figures have been updated.

- In the section What Are Diversity and Inclusion?, the subsection Differences Between Valuing Diversity and Affirmative Action now states that it came from Executive Orders and provides the website www.us.gov for more information. In the U.S. Diversity subsection, the census population figures have been updated.

- In the Age and Generational Diversity and Management section, subsection Age now includes an example of age discrimination and discusses the aging population and shrinking work force. In the subsection Generational Differences, Generation Z characteristics are now presented. Exhibit 3-8 is now 3-6 and has been updated to 2017 information.

- The section Gender and Sexual Orientation Diversity and Management has been rewritten with new subheadings. Gender is now Sex, Gender, and Stereotypes and discusses how negative stereotypes about women lead to discrimination in promotions to management positions. There is a new subsection, Gender Discrimination and the Glass Ceiling, that provides updated facts supporting this reality, and the new term *glass cliff* has been added. There is also a new subsection, Promoting Gender Equality, discussing the benefits of gender equality and efforts to achieve it. In the last subsection, the + sign has been added to Sexual Orientation (LGBT+) to include other forms of sexual orientation.

- In the section Race and Ethnicity Diversity and Management, the representation of people of color and foreign born on the Fortune 500 list has been updated. The Fortune 50 Best Workplaces for Diversity has also been included.

- There is a new Applying the Concept box 3-2, Diversity Stereotypes, at the end of the Types of Diversity and Managing Diversity with six new questions.
- All of the Applying the Concept boxes are changed, with revised or new questions with a total of 34 application questions.
- The Trends and Issues section has been revised with around 50% new material.
- There is a new first short case at the end of the chapter.
- The second longer case is new.

Chapter 4. Creative Problem Solving and Decision Making

- There are 66 new current references in Chapter 4 for a total of 146.
- There are 57 new people and company/brand examples, including Under Armour, Converse, Jack Ma, Chairman Alibaba, and 3M Post-it Note.
- The opening case has been updated with more information on current CEO Mark Parker and Nike performance under his leadership through 2016.
- Join the Discussion Ethics & Social Responsibility 4-1, Avoiding Taxes, now includes information regarding President Trump's plan to cut corporate taxes with a new question 5.
- The section Big Data has been rewritten with new company examples including high- and low-cost big data services providers.
- All of the Applying the Concept boxes are changed, with a total of 22 application questions.
- The Trends and Issues section has been revised with around 50% new material.
- There is a new first short case at the end of the chapter.
- The second longer case is updated.

Chapter 5. Strategic and Operational Planning

- There are 82 new current references in Chapter 5 for a total of 179.
- There are 98 new people and company/brand examples, including Intelligentsia, Airbnb, HP, Anytime Fitness, Sears, Yankee Candle, and Pedigree.
- The opening case has been updated to state that Kevin Johnson took over as CEO for Starbucks in April 2017, and Schultz is executive chairman and is focusing on developing high-end coffee shops.
- The section Writing Effective Objectives has seven all-new company objective examples.
- There is a new Join the Discussion: Ethics and Social Responsibility box focusing on Wells Fargo's incentive system, with five questions for discussion.
- The Multitasking section has two new subheadings.
- The Trends and Issues section has been revised with around 50% new material.
- All of the Applying the Concept boxes are changed, with a total of 25 application questions.
- There is a first new short case at the end of the chapter.
- The second longer case is new.

Chapter 6. Managing Change, Innovation, and Entrepreneurship

- There are 123 new current references for a total of 212 references in Chapter 6.
- There are 71 new people and company/brand examples including Blockbuster, Travelocity, eHarmony, Angie's List, and *Shark Tank*.
- The opening case Apple, and questions and answers, are new.

- The first section, Innovation and Change, has been shortened a bit by dropping some of the older examples and replacing them with shorter and fewer examples.

- The subsection The Management Functions and Change is now The Management Skills and Functions and Change to include the management skills and it refers both back to Chapter 1.

- The subsection Discontinuous Change has been rewritten.

- The introduction to the Managing Innovation section has been rewritten with new references.

- The How to Overcome Resistance to Change section has a new subsection, Our Resistance to Change—Habits, with a focus on the need to change our attitude and habits to successfully make changes. The discussion focuses on personal and professional change.

- The major section Organizational Development contains the same contents, but more concisely.

- Self-Assessment 6-1, Entrepreneurial Qualities, has four new questions to improve this measure, and the 6-point scale is now a 5-point scale.

- In the Entrepreneurship subsection Entrepreneurs vs. Intrapreneurs, the new term *organizational entrepreneurs* has been added. The subsection Risk Taking by Entrepreneurs and Intrapreneurs now includes a discussion of opportunity cost and keeping your day job while starting a new venture.

- There is a new subsection, The Funding and Sales Pitch, giving entrepreneurs tips on pitching to investors and customers.

- The subsection Finance and Control the New Venture now includes the SBA LINC (Leveraging Information and Networks to access Capital) information with the link to view the online matchmaking of small business with SBA-approved lenders. The Trends and Issues section has been revised with more than 50% new material, with a focus on entrepreneurship diversity and statistics. All of the Applying the Concept boxes are changed, with a total of 25 application questions.

- There is a new first short case at the end of the chapter.

- The second longer case is new.

- There is a new skill-building exercise 6-4 Developing a New Habit.

Chapter 7. Organizing and Delegating Work

- There are 71 new current references for a total of 133 references in Chapter 7.

- There are 59 new people and company/brand examples, including CVS, Best Buy, Jones Counseling Center, Nest, DuPont, Sony, and Countrywide.

- The opening case is new.

- In the Organizational Design section, a discussion of the informal organization chart has been added.

- The subsection Challenges to New Organization has been rewritten with new references.

- The subsection Contemporary Organizational Designs—Teams has been rewritten and the new concept networks of teams called *multiteam systems* has been added. *Platform Organizations* connecting buyers and sellers in the shared economy has also been added as a bullet heading in this subsection.

- The Trends and Issues section has been revised with more than 50% new material.

- All of the Applying the Concept boxes are changed, with a total of 29 application questions.

- There is a new first short case at the end of the chapter.

- The second longer case is updated.

Chapter 8. Managing Teamwork

- There are 64 new current references for a total of 165 references in Chapter 8.
- There are 26 new people and company/brand examples, including Square and Twitter CEO Jack Dorsey, Formula 1, Disney, Bumble, H&M, and Marriott.
- The subsection How Cohesiveness Affects Group Performance has been rewritten based on current research.
- There is a new Applying the Concept box 8-2, Types of Group Structure, with five new questions.
- The Trends and Issues section has been revised.
- All of the Applying the Concept boxes are changed, with a total of 29 application questions.
- There is a new first short case at the end of the chapter.
- The second longer case is new.

Chapter 9. Human Resources Management

- There are 85 new current references for a total of 217 references in Chapter 9.
- There are 30 new people and company/brand examples, including Bill O'Reilly, Fox News, Lynda.com, Duolingo, King Arthur Flour, Virgin America, and FedEx.
- The Costco case has been updated with quantitative data.
- Exhibit 9-2, Federal Laws Related to HRM, has been changed to place more focus on the laws that apply to most organizations. The following laws related to specific organizations have been removed: Equal Employment Opportunity Law of 1972 (education and government), Civil Rights Act of 1991 (an amendment to CRA), Vocational Rehabilitation Act 1973 (federal contractors). The Fair Labor Standards Act of 1938 has been added as it applies to all organizations.
- Exhibit 9-3 Preemployment Inquiries now includes the new law that an employer can't ask the candidate how much they were paid on their last job.
- The section "Orientation" has been expanded to "Orientation Programs, Onboarding and Newcomer Socialization" to include these current terms in the heading.
- The ADIE Model is now a level-three heading.
- There is a new level-three heading, "Microlearning," under Training and Development to discuss microlearning offered through e-learning companies.
- The Trends and Issues section has been revised with more than 50% new material.
- All of the Applying the Concept boxes are changed, with a total of 43 application questions.
- There is a new first short case at the end of the chapter.
- The second longer case is updated.

Chapter 10. Organizational Behavior: Power, Politics, Conflict, and Stress

- There are 125 new current references for a total of 276 references in Chapter 10.
- There are 23 new people and company/brand examples, including tennis champion Venus Williams, motivational speaker Zig Ziglar, Zappos CEO Tony Hsieh, Steve Jobs of Apple, Nike, Castlight Healthcare, and Walmart.
- The Michael Jordan case has been updated.
- The "Thoughts and Self-Esteem" section now includes a discussion of gratitude and how to make positive thinking a habit.
- The "Big Five Personality Dimensions" section now includes research supporting the predictability of job success for each personality style.

- There is a new Applying the Concept Box 10.1, Big Five Personality Types, with five new questions.
- The Myers-Briggs Type Indicator (MBTI) section now includes a link to HumanMetrics (www.humanmetrics.com/cgi-win/jtypes2.asp) to take a more extensive free personality test.
- The "Managing Conflict" section has been reorganized into three sections as level-two headings. (1) Conflict, which now includes conflict of ideas, generally leads to changes that improve performance—functional conflict. Conversely, personal conflict tends to hurt relationships and decrease performance—dysfunctional conflict; (2) Conflict Management Styles; and (3) Initiating Conflict Resolution.
- In the "Stress" section, procrastination and perfectionism, time pressure, and smartphones have been added as "Causes of Stress" and "Stress Management" subsections.
- The Trends and Issues section has been revised with new material, including genomics and brain training.
- All of the Applying the Concept boxes are changed, with a total of 25 application questions.
- There is a new first short case at the end of the chapter.
- The second longer case is new.
- There is a new skill-building exercise 10-2, with five conflict situations requiring an initiating-conflict BCF statement.

Chapter 11. Motivating for High Performance

- There are 41 new current references for a total of 107 references in Chapter 11.
- There are five new people and company/brand examples: Google, Johnson & Johnson, GE, J&J, and Wells Fargo.
- The opening case has been updated.
- Applying the Concept box 11-2, Content Motivation Theories, now has a new fifth question (7–11) so that it is more challenging to select the recommended answer. Applying the Concept box 11-3, Process Motivation Theories, now has a new fourth question (12–15) so that it is more challenging to select the recommended answer.
- The "Goal Setting" section now includes a discussion of the importance of team goals.
- Applying the Concept box 11-4 and 11-5, Types of (16–20) and Schedules of Reinforcement (21–26), now has a new fifth question so that it is more challenging to select the recommended answer.
- The section "Combining the Motivation Process and Motivation Theories" now includes advice on how to be self-motivated.
- The "Giving Praise" section now includes the new term *altercasting*.
- The Trends and Issues section has been revised by deleting old material and including new ideas.
- All of the Applying the Concept boxes are changed, with a total of four new questions for a total of 26 application questions.
- There is a new first short case at the end of the chapter.
- The second longer case is updated.

Chapter 12. Leading With Influence

- There are 64 new current references for a total of 143 references in Chapter 12.
- There are 19 new people and company/brand examples, including Bill Gates of Microsoft, Barbara Bradley, Baekgaard co-founder and CEO of Vera Bradley, Martin Luther King Jr., Jeff Bezos of Amazon, and Intel.
- The opening case has been shortened and updated.

- The "Leaders Versus Managers" section now has two subheadings, "What's the Difference? and "Shared Leadership," to separate the two topics more clearly.
- The "Leadership Substitutes Theory" section is now "Leadership Substitutes" and includes three subheadings—"Leadership Substitutes Theory, "The Bossless Organization and Self-Leadership," and "Followership"—to include a discussion of the bossless organization, self-leadership, and followership.
- The "Leader-Member Exchange (LMX) Theory" section has been revised with a new subsection "Dyadic Relationships" with a new definition of LMX leaders focusing on developing positive dyadic relationship. The subsection "In-Groups and Out-Groups" still discusses the negative effects of having these two groups.
- Transactional leadership now states how it relates to LMX theory.
- The Trends and Issues section has been revised with more focus on research regarding diversity and leadership and less focus on ethics.
- All of the Applying the Concept boxes are changed with a total of four new questions for a total of 24 application questions.
- There is a new first short case at the end of the chapter.
- The second longer case is updated.

Chapter 13. Communication and Information Technology

- There are 94 new current references for a total of 203 references in Chapter 13.
- There are 41 new people and company/brand examples, including YouTube, Southwest Airlines, Clorox Brita, Weather Company, PayPal, and Pinterest.
- The opening case has been completely rewritten and now includes chatbots.
- The section "Information Technology, Systems, and Networks" has been completely updated with new facts, references, and company examples. The terms *the new night shift* and *cyberloafing* have been added.
- The "Receiving Messages" section now has a new level-two heading, "Retentive Listening," to discuss the need to concentrate and remember the message, and it presents how to advise for greater retention.
- The subsection "Calming the Emotional Person" has been rewritten and expanded to provide more detail on how to calm people and includes an example.
- The subsections "Giving Criticism" and "Getting Criticism" have been expanded to include ideas to keep in mind to help give and accept criticism.
- Applying the Concept Box 13-4, Response Styles, has two new questions.
- The Trends and Issues section has been revised, with more focus on research regarding diversity and leadership and less focus on ethics.
- All of the Applying the Concept boxes are changed, with a total of four new questions for a total of 26 application questions.
- There is a new first short case at the end of the chapter.
- The second longer case is updated.

Chapter 14. Managing Control Systems, Finances, and People

- There are 85 new current references for a total of 166 references in Chapter 14.
- There are 54 new people and company/brand examples, including Kimberly-Clark, GoDaddy, Dunkin Brands, Kraft Heinz, NBA basketball star LeBron James, and Snapchat.
- The opening case has been updated.
- Applying the Concept box 14-1 has a new question.
- In the "Control Systems Process," there is a new subsection, "The Performance Success Cycle," presenting a day-to-day approach to applying the control systems process.

- In the "Operating Budgets" section, the "increasing profits" subsection has been rewritten with new examples and has been moved down after the discussion of revenues and expenses. There is also a new subsection, "Revenues Versus Profit and Profit Margin," to introduce focusing on profits rather than revenues with higher profit margins.

- There is a new Applying the Concept box 14-3, Financial Statements, with six questions to assess an understanding of the accounts on the income statement and balance sheet.

- Applying the Concept box 14-3 is now 14-4, and a new question has been added.

- The Trends and Issues section has been updated with more than 50% new material, revised with more focus on research regarding diversity and leadership and less focus on ethics.

- All of the Applying the Concept boxes are changed, with a total of eight new questions for a total of 30 application questions.

- There is a new first short case at the end of the chapter.

- The second longer case is new.

Chapter 15. Operations, Quality, and Productivity

- There are 70 new current references for a total of 142 references in Chapter 15.

- There are 63 new people and company/brand examples including Helen's Homemade Ice Cream, Maytag, Teddy Bear Pools, Samsung Galaxy Note 7, Caterpillar, and Anheuser-Bush InBev.

- The Frito-Lay case has been updated.

- The "Supply Chain Management" section has been updated with new examples and two new subsections, "Supply Chain Management Services" to let readers know that UPS and FedEx are in the supply chain management business and "Strategic Cloud Supply Chains" to include the cloud with third-party logistics providers (3PLS).

- "The Balanced Scorecard" section is now "The Balanced Scorecard and Dashboards," including a new subheading "Dashboards" to state what they are and how they are used to monitor and increase productivity and help maintain a balanced scorecard.

- Applying the Concept box 15-3, Facility Layout, has a new question.

- The details of how to develop a PERT Network are beyond the scope of this book and therefore have been deleted from this edition.

- The Trends and Issues section has been revised with more than 90% new material.

- All of the Applying the Concept boxes are changed, with a total of 43 application questions.

- There is a new first short case at the end of the chapter.

- The second longer case is updated.

Digital Resources for the Instructor

Just as businesses must be integrated across functions and departments for success, text and ancillary material must also be integrated to create the optimum student learning experience. Many of our key supplements have been described to you as part of the support for our three-pronged approach to the management curriculum. The following paragraphs describe all elements of the text package, which are designed to create a successful classroom environment. The password-protected Instructor Teaching Site at **edge.sagepub.com/lussier8e** includes the following resources:

- **The Instructor's Manual**, written by the author, Robert N. Lussier, was designed to ensure that every faculty member would receive complete, integrated support for teaching. The manual contains the following for each chapter of the book: Work Application student sample answers, Review Questions and Communication Skills answers, Applying the Concept answers, and skill-builder ideas (including setup and timing). The instructor's manual also includes ideas on how to use the special features of the text in the classroom, with emphasis on creating an interactive learning environment.

- **A test bank** is available in Microsoft Word® format and ExamView format. The test bank is built on Bloom's taxonomy, the book's learning objectives, and AACSB (Association to Advance Collegiate Schools of Business) standards. Each question is tagged with this information, along with answer location and difficulty level. Containing multiple-choice, true/false, and essay questions for each chapter, the test bank provides you with a diverse range of prewritten options as well as the opportunity for editing any question and/or inserting your own personalized questions to effectively assess students' progress and understanding.

- Editable, chapter-specific **Microsoft PowerPoint® slides** offer you complete flexibility in easily creating a multimedia presentation for your course. The slides highlight essential content, features, and artwork from the book.

- **Experiential exercises and suggested activities** provide lively and stimulating learning opportunities to be used in or out of the classroom for groups or individuals.

- Links to engaging **video and multimedia resources** facilitate further exploration of key concepts.

- **Case notes** provide an essential reference for guiding discussion about the case studies in the book.

- **Sample syllabi** for semester and quarter courses provide suggested models for use when creating the syllabi for your courses.

- In-text **exhibits and models** are provided online to use in teaching aids such as PowerPoints, handouts, and lecture notes.

- All instructor materials and tools are easily integrated through **SAGE coursepacks**, which include pretests and posttests for each chapter, as well as video quizzes that make the Interactive eBook's premium videos assignable.

Digital Resources for Students

SAGE edge for Students helps students accomplish their coursework goals in an easy-to-use learning environment. Open-access resources at **edge.sagepub.com/lussier8e** include video and multimedia resources, mobile-friendly eFlashcards, and practice quizzes for students to use as they study each chapter.

Premium Video

Fully searchable, and with study tools such as highlighting, bookmarking, and note taking, the **Interactive eBook** for *Management Fundamentals* offers **embedded premium video**, as well as links to additional media resources, all from the same pages found in the printed text. The premium video includes videos licensed from *Wall Street Journal, Bloomberg*, and other sources, as well as **SAGE's exclusive Management in Action videos**, that help students apply key concepts to workplace scenarios. Each video has associated quiz questions tied to the book's learning objectives, assignable through the SAGE coursepacks. The Interactive eBook can be packaged with the text or purchased separately.

●●● Acknowledgments

The authorship of a publishing project of this magnitude is only one aspect of a complex process. Many hardworking individuals gave great effort to create this text and package. I wish to express my special gratitude to the fine people at SAGE Publications. Specifically, I would also like to thank my initial acquisitions editor, Patricia Quinlin, who truly believed in the value of my management text and knew it would be a valuable addition to the SAGE business list. Pat paved the way for my text to be published by SAGE, and I am forever grateful to her for that. I would like to thank my current editor, Maggie Stanley, content development editor Katie Ancheta, editorial assistant Alissa Nance, marketing manager Liz Thornton, production editor Tracy Buyan, and designer Janet Kiesel.

I would like to acknowledge that Herbert Sherman of Long Island University wrote six new end-of-chapter cases with the help of his graduate assistants, Hannah Walter and Naveed Ahmad, and updated nine end-of-chapter cases. Loren Kuzuhara of the University of Wisconsin wrote 15 new end-of-chapter cases for this edition.

I would also like to acknowledge the instructors who have developed digital resources for this edition and previous editions:

Jeffrey Anderson, Ohio University

Frank Armstrong, Ferris State University

Andreas Bechrakis, Miami Dade College

Eric S. Ecklund, Saint Francis University

Kristina Findley, George Fox University

Simona Ileana Giura, SUNY Oneonta

Joni A. Koegel, Cazenovia College

Vance Lewis, University of Texas, Dallas

Charles J. Mambula, Langston University

Michael Provitera, Barry University Miami

Lisa Sticca-Conrod, Johnson & Wales University

In addition, the reviewers of the project provided me with great ideas and inspiration for writing. The reviewers overwhelmingly confirmed the basic philosophical premise behind the book—teaching students how to be successful in today's business environment—and I am very grateful for their valuable input:

Carl Blencke, University of Central Florida

Charles J. Mambula, Langston University

Schuyler A. Banks, Erie Community College

Verl A. Anderson, Dixie State University

Violet Zlatar-Christopher, California State University, Northridge

David Biemer, Texas State University

Fereshteh Mofidi, Merritt College

Michael E. Cox, Ohio Christian University

Brian A. Bartel, Mid-State Technical College

Yi-Yu Chen, New Jersey City University

Callie Burnley, California State Polytechnic University, Pomona

Paula A. White, Independence University

Jeffrey Anderson, Ohio University

Simona Ileana Giura, SUNY Oneonta

Eric S. Ecklund, Saint Francis University

Robert Robertson, Independence University

Lauren Talia, Independence University

Cathy M. Littlefield, Peirce College

Joni A. Koegel, Cazenovia College

Jennifer Scott, Northcentral University

Diane D. Galbraith, Slippery Rock University

Lynn Klein, Chabot College

Violet Z. Christopher, Antelope Valley College; California State University, Bakersfield

Sheri Grotrian-Ryan, Peru State College

Callie Burnley, California State Polytechnic University, Pomona

Kevin Suber, Los Angeles Valley College

Linda Martinak, University of Maryland University College

HelenMarie Harmon, Indiana University Northwest

I hope everyone who uses this text enjoys teaching from these materials as much as I do.

Contact Me With Feedback

I wrote this book for you. Let me know what you think of it. More specifically, how can it be improved? I will respond to your feedback. If I use your suggestion for improvement, your name and college will be listed in the acknowledgments section of the next edition.

Robert N. Lussier
Springfield College
rlussier@springfieldcollege.edu

●●● About the Author

Robert N. Lussier is a professor of management at Springfield College and has taught management for more than 25 years. He is a prolific writer, with more than 444 publications to his credit. His articles have been published in the *Academy of Entrepreneurship Journal*, *Business Horizons*, *Entrepreneurship Theory and Practice*, *Family Business Review*, *Journal of Business Strategies*, *Journal of Management Education*, *Journal of Small Business Management*, *Journal of Small Business Strategy*, *SAM Advanced Management Journal*, and several others. He also has a human resources management textbook (with John Hendon) published by SAGE.

More than one million people globally have used his textbooks, earning him an unsurpassed national and international reputation as an author and keynote speaker. Dr. Lussier is the founder of Publish Don't Perish (**www.publishdonotperish.com**) and through contact, his *Publish Don't Perish: The Top Secrets to Get Published* book, and workshops has helped hundreds of institutions and individuals in 80 countries get published. His presentations inspire comments like: *"Bob explains complex business topics in an easy-to-understand language while keeping his audience engaged and spell-bound"* (Dr. Raj V. Mahto, professor, University of New Mexico).

Dr. Lussier also consults to a wide array of commercial and nonprofit organizations. In fact, some of the material in the book was developed for such clients as Baystate Medical Center, Coca-Cola, Friendly's Ice Cream, National Institute of Financial Education, Mead, Monsanto, Smith & Wesson, the Social Security Administration, the Visiting Nurse Association, and YMCAs.

Dr. Lussier holds a bachelor of science in business administration from Salem State College, two master's degrees in business and education from Suffolk University, and a doctorate in management from the University of New Haven.

Sara Miller McCune founded SAGE Publishing in 1965 to support the dissemination of usable knowledge and educate a global community. SAGE publishes more than 1000 journals and over 800 new books each year, spanning a wide range of subject areas. Our growing selection of library products includes archives, data, case studies and video. SAGE remains majority owned by our founder and after her lifetime will become owned by a charitable trust that secures the company's continued independence.

Los Angeles | London | New Delhi | Singapore | Washington DC | Melbourne

To my wife, Marie, and our six children:

Jesse, Justin, Danielle, Nicole, Brian, and Renee

Special thanks to Patricia Quinlin, my initial acquisitions editor,
for bringing this book to SAGE and for her valuable input to the contents

1 Management and Its History

● ● ● LEARNING OBJECTIVES

After studying this chapter, you should be able to:

1-1. Describe a manager's responsibility. PAGE 4

1-2. List the three skills of effective managers. PAGE 6

1-3. Explain the four management functions and the three management role categories. PAGE 8

1-4. Recall the hierarchy of management levels and describe the differences among the levels in terms of skills needed and functions performed. PAGE 11

1-5. Summarize the major similarities and differences between the classical and behavioral theorists. PAGE 17

IOM	## Ideas on Management

Ideas on Management
At Netflix

The idea of **Netflix** came to **Reed Hastings** when he was forced to pay $40 in overdue fines after returning a video well past its due date. Netflix was founded in 1997 by Hastings and **Marc Randolph**.

Hastings continues to run the company as founder and chief executive officer (CEO). He is a visionary that started three businesses. He started with DVD by mail and killed that business through streaming and then produced original content, such as the popular *House of Cards*. By 2017, Netflix had more than 39 million subscribers from 190 countries. Hastings was named *Fortune*'s Businessperson of the Year, and Netflix is ranked second among *Fortune*'s World's Most Admired Companies in the entertainment industry after **Disney**. So how did Hastings do it? We will answer the Ideas on Management (**IOM**) questions that follow throughout the chapter to give you a better understanding of how managers run successful companies.

IOM 1.   What resources does Netflix use to sell its entertainment?

IOM 2.   Which of Hastings's management skills has led to Netflix's success?

IOM 3.   What management functions are performed at Netflix?

IOM 4.   What level manager is Hastings, and which of his skills and functions are more important to Netflix's success?

You'll find answers to these **IOM** questions throughout the chapter. To learn more about Hastings and Netflix, visit www.netflix.com.

Source: Information for the case was taken from the Netflix website, www.netflix.com, accessed November 17, 2016; "World's Most Admired Companies," *Fortune* (March 1, 2016); "Businessperson of the Year," *Fortune* (2010).

You will find a box before all of the major sections with Learning Objectives to alert you to the sections that contain the important concepts you should know. The answer to the LO is provided in the section and summarized in the Chapter Summary at the end of the chapter.

Why Study Management?

As you will learn, applying management skills can help you succeed in both your personal life and your professional life. It's natural at this point to be thinking, "What can I get from this book?" or "What's in it for me?" These common questions are seldom asked or answered directly.[1] The short answer is that the better you can work with people—and this is what most of this book is about—the more successful you will be both personally and professionally.[2]

#1 Develop Skills You Can Use in Your Personal Life

Do you want to be happy? Well, happiness comes from our relationships.[3,4] Throughout this book, you can develop skills that can help you maintain and improve your personal relationships with family, friends, and coworkers. In just about every chapter, you can develop skills that can be used immediately in your personal lives. For example, at the end of this chapter in Skill Builder exercise 1-1, you will learn a technique to help you remember people's names, in the next chapter there are guides to ethical behavior, Chapter 4 presents a model that can help you make better decisions, Chapter 10 can improve your skills of resolving conflicts and managing your stress, and in Chapter 13 you can improve your communication skills. Here is a different tip from **Sheryl Sandberg, COO of Facebook.** If you want to be happier, have gratitude by focusing on the positive things in your life, not the negatives.[5]

American society tends to promote two isms that tend to lead to being unhappy. Individualism—being selfish by just looking out for yourself; take advantage of others for your own personal gain. Only do things that have something in it for me. Hedonism—don't do it if you don't feel like doing it; just do what makes you feel good. **Booker T. Washington** said, "Those who are happiest are those who do the most for others."[6] **B. C. Forbes** said, to be happy, strive to make others happy.[7] According to happiness expert **Sonja Lyubomirsky**, happy people are not as self-centered as unhappy people.[8] Making sacrifices for others brings happiness.[9] Do you know any selfish people? Do you like them? Are they really happy? Will they ever be happy? Are you happy?

#2 Develop Skills You Can Use as a Manager or Employee

Let's extend happiness and success to our professional lives. **LinkedIn** cofounder **Reid Hoffman** says job satisfaction and success come from relationships at work.[10] Former **Land O'Lakes** CEO **Jack Gherty** said that he became successful and that his company is doing so well because he focuses on helping other people win. CEO of **LinkAmerica Andrés Ruzo** says the more you give, the more you get back.[11] CEO of **XPRIZE Peter Diamandis** says the best way to become a billionaire is to help a billion people.[12]

As management guru **Henry Mintzberg** said, "No job is more vital to our society than that of a manager."[13] Positive manager–subordinate relationships are invaluable to organizational success.[14] If you are a manager or want to be a manager someday, you need good management skills to be successful,[15] and throughout this book, you will be given opportunities to develop your management skills.

But even if you are not interested in being a manager, you still need management skills to succeed in today's workplace. The old workplace, in which managers simply told employees what to do, is gone.[16] Today, employees want to be involved in management, and organizations are recruiting employees with people skills who can work effectively in teams and share in decision making and other management tasks.[17] At **Zappos**, they have even eliminated the term "manager" because they want employees to be self-managed.[18] Unfortunately, it has been said that new college grads lack the ability to manage or lead.[19]

This book can help you develop management skills that you can apply in your personal and professional lives. In this chapter, you will learn what management is all about, and we will begin the discussion of how you can develop your management skills.

manager The individual responsible for achieving organizational objectives through efficient and effective utilization of resources.

manager's resources Human, financial, physical, and informational resources.

What Is a Manager's Responsibility?

Managers and the Organizational Resources They Manage

A **manager** is responsible for achieving organizational objectives through efficient and effective utilization of resources. *Efficient* means doing things right so as to maximize the utilization of resources. *Effective* means doing the right thing in order to attain an objective. **Facebook** Chief Information Officer (CIO) **Timothy Campos** says his job is to use information technology (IT) to enable the efficiency and effectiveness of the company.[20] The **manager's resources** are human, financial, physical, and informational. The resources are listed in Exhibit 1-1.

Human Resources. Human resources are people, often referred to as human capital, and people are organizations' most valuable assets.[21] Managers are responsible for getting the job done through employees, so people are essential to organizational performance, as they are the ones to achieve the organizational objectives.[22] Throughout this book, we will focus on how managers work with employees to accomplish organizational objectives.

Financial Resources. It takes money to make money, and without proper finances, you don't have a business. Hastings invested $2.5 million in startup cash for **Netflix**.[23] Most managers have a budget stating how much it should cost to operate their department/store for a set period of time. In other words, a budget defines the financial resources available.

Physical Resources. Managers are responsible for making the products and services and keeping equipment in working condition and ensuring that necessary products, materials, and supplies are available when needed. **Amazon** has thousands of products in distribution centers around the world to provide fast delivery of its products.[24]

EXHIBIT 1-1   MANAGEMENT RESOURCES

Management Resources
Human
Financial
Physical
Informational

Informational Resources. We live in an information age,[25] and the new source of power is information.[26] You need information to set objectives and make decisions on how to allocate and use your resources to attain the objectives.[27] Information should be based on knowledge, and information should flow freely throughout the organization and between organizations.[28]

Resources and Performance. Managers have a profound impact on the performance of their organizations.[29] So how you acquire and manage the four resources affects organizational performance.[30] The level of organizational **performance** *is based on how effectively and efficiently managers utilize resources to achieve objectives.* Managers are responsible for and evaluated on how well they meet organizational strategies and objectives through utilization and control of resources.[31] Selecting the right resources—being effective—and using them efficiently results in high levels of performance.[32]

Netflix's (**IOM 1**) resource needs have changed over the years. People still remain critical to operating the entertainment, especially its original TV shows and movies. Hastings started Netflix with $2.5 million of his own money, and today membership subscriptions are its source of income. The entertainment content (TV and movies) and the Internet equipment used to stream it are critical physical resources. Getting information from subscribers on what they want to view (such as *House of Cards*) on Netflix is important to entertainment selection.

A Manager Interview

This interview with **Bonnie Castonguary**, a store manager for **Gap Inc.**, provides an overview of the manager's job and responsibility.

Q: What was your progression to your present job as store manager?

A: I started as a store manager in training. I replaced a woman on maternity leave as acting store manager, and then I had my first store. After a while, I was promoted to larger stores with more sales volume. A few years later, I was promoted to manager of [a] Gap outlet store....My next career advancement is to general manager....I would still be in one store, but I would assist the district manager by overseeing other stores in my district.

Q: Briefly describe your job.

A: **Gap Inc.**'s two-page "Position Overview Store Management" form, which also contains a detailed summary for each level of management, presents this general summary: "The Store Management team manages the sales, operations, and personnel functions of the store to ensure maximum profitability and compliance with company procedures. The Team includes Assistant Managers, Associate Managers, the Store Manager, and/or the General Manager."

Q: What do you like best about being a manager?

A: You don't have time to get bored on the job because you are always doing something different.

Q: What do you like least about being a manager?

WORK APPLICATION 1-1

Describe the specific resources used by a present or past boss. Give the manager's job title and department.

performance Means of evaluating how effectively and efficiently managers utilize resources to achieve objectives.

A: Dealing with difficult performance problems of employees and customers, and always being on call. When I'm not at work, I'm still on call when there are problems at the store. This could mean going to the store at 2:00 a.m. to shut off the alarm.

Q: What advice would you give to college graduates without any full-time work experience who are interested in a management career after graduation?

A: You need to be dedicated and hardworking. You must take great pride in your work. You have to be willing to take on a lot of responsibility. Remember, your employees are always looking to you to set the example; when you make a mistake (which you will do), it affects your staff. You have to be a self-starter. As a store manager, you have to motivate employees, but your boss is not around much to motivate you.

LO 1-2

List the three skills of effective managers.

What Does It Take to Be a Successful Manager?

Although managers' jobs vary, researchers generally agree on a set of qualities, skills, and competencies necessary to be a successful manager.

Management Qualities

WORK APPLICATION 1-2

Identify a specific manager, preferably one who is or was your boss, and explain what makes him or her successful or unsuccessful. Give examples.

Over the years, numerous researchers have attempted to answer the question "What does it take to be a successful manager?" In a *Wall Street Journal* Gallup survey, 782 top executives in 282 large corporations were asked, "What are the most important traits for success as a supervisor?"[33] Before you read what these executives replied, complete the Self-Assessment on management traits to find out if you have these qualities. It is said that self-awareness[34] and self-assessment[35] are crucial for improvement in the workplace. So you will have the opportunity to complete self-assessments in every chapter.

The executives in the Gallup survey identified integrity, industriousness, and the ability to get along with people as the three most important traits for successful managers.

Management Skills

Skills involve the ability to perform some type of activity or task. **Management skills** *include (1) technical, (2) interpersonal, and (3) decision-making skills.* Technical skills can be referred to as hard skills, whereas interpersonal and decision-making skills are often called soft skills, and the most sought-after skills in the job market are soft skills because organizations seek employees at all levels and positions who can communicate clearly, take initiative, problem solve and get along with coworkers.[36] Because management skills are so important, the focus of this book is on skill building. If you work at it, you can develop your management skills through this course.

WORK APPLICATION 1-3

Select a manager, preferably one who is or was your boss, and state the specific management skills he or she uses on the job.

Technical Skills. Technical skills *involve the ability to use methods and techniques to perform a task.* All employees need technical skills to perform their jobs. A manager may develop a budget (managerial job) using **Microsoft** Excel® (technical skill). Technical skills are more important for employees than for managers, and they vary widely from job to job; therefore, this course does not focus on developing these skills. Although technology is advancing, it is people with interpersonal skills working in teams who develop the technology.[37]

management skills The skills needed to be an effective manager, including technical, interpersonal, and decision-making skills.

technical skills The ability to use methods and techniques to perform a task.

interpersonal skills The ability to understand, communicate with, and work well with individuals and groups through developing effective relationships.

Interpersonal Skills. Interpersonal skills involve the ability to understand, communicate with, and work well with individuals and groups through developing effective relationships. Interpersonal skills are sometimes also referred to as human or people skills, as well as soft skills, and they are increasingly more important than technical skills.[38] If having good human relations is just common sense, then why doesn't everyone at work get along,[39] why do companies seek employees with good people skills,[40] and why are companies spending millions to develop employees' interpersonal skills?[41] The resources you need to get the job done are made available through relationships.[42] Sir **Richard Branson**, of **Virgin Group**, says, "You definitely need to be good with people to help bring out the best in people."[43] Several chapters focus on developing your interpersonal skills, especially the leadership section (Chapters 10–13).

1-1 SELF-ASSESSMENT

Management Traits

The following 15 questions relate to some of the qualities needed to be a successful manager. Rate yourself on each item by indicating with a number (1–4) how well each statement describes you.

1. The statement does not describe me at all.
2. The statement somewhat describes me.
3. The statement describes me most of the time.
4. The statement describes me very accurately.

_____ 1. I enjoy working with people. I prefer to work with others rather than working alone.

_____ 2. I can motivate others. I can get people to do things they may not want to do.

_____ 3. I am well liked. People enjoy working with me.

_____ 4. I am cooperative. I strive to help the team do well rather than to be the star.

_____ 5. I am a leader. I enjoy teaching, coaching, and instructing people.

_____ 6. I want to be successful. I do things to the best of my ability to be successful.

_____ 7. I am a self-starter. I get things done without having to be told to do them.

_____ 8. I am a problem solver. If things aren't going the way I want them to, I take corrective action to meet my objectives.

_____ 9. I am self-reliant. I don't need the help of others.

_____ 10. I am hardworking. I enjoy working and getting the job done.

_____ 11. I am trustworthy. If I say I will do something by a set time, I do it.

_____ 12. I am loyal. I do not do or say things to intentionally hurt my friends, relatives, or coworkers.

_____ 13. I can take criticism. If people tell me negative things about myself, I give them serious thought and change when appropriate.

_____ 14. I am honest. I do not lie, steal, or cheat.

_____ 15. I am fair. I treat people equally. I don't take advantage of others.

_____ TOTAL SCORE (add numbers on lines 1–15; the range of possible scores is 15–60)

In general, the higher your score, the better your chances of being a successful manager. You can work on improving your _integrity_ (items 11–15), _industriousness_ (items 6–10), and ability to get along with _people_ (items 1–5) both in this course and in your personal life. As a start, review the traits listed here. Which ones are your strongest and weakest? Think about how you can improve in the weaker areas—or, even better, write out a plan.

Decision-Making Skills. Clearly, the decisions you have made over your lifetime have affected you today. Organizations are seeking employees with conceptual critical thinking skills that can take initiative to solve problems.[44] Leadership decisions determine the success or failure of organizations,[45] so organizations are also training their people to improve their decision-making skills.[46] **Decision-making skills** _are based on the ability to conceptualize situations and select alternatives to solve problems and take advantage of opportunities._ You will develop your decision-making skills in Chapter 4.

Netflix (IOM 2) CEO Hastings doesn't do much technically, and he has good interpersonal skills to get employees to continually improve the business. However, the major skill leading to Netflix's success is Hastings's decision-making skill, as he conceptually understands how technology is affecting the entertainment industry and continues to create new business opportunities. The first important decision was to start Netflix as a mail-order DVD business to compete with Blockbuster; and Netflix essentially killed Blockbuster. The second key decision was to replace

decision-making skills The ability to conceptualize situations and select alternatives to solve problems and take advantage of opportunities.

1-1 APPLYING THE CONCEPT

Management Skills

Identify each activity as being one of the following types of management skills:

A. technical

B. interpersonal

C. decision making

_____ 1. The manager is working on fixing a broken machine.

_____ 2. The manager is sending an email letting the employees know they exceeded the sales goal.

_____ 3. The manager is scheduling which machines will produce each product next week.

_____ 4. The manager is trying to figure out a way to solve a problem.

_____ 5. The manager is giving an employee praise for a job well done.

EXHIBIT 1-2   MANAGEMENT SKILLS

Management Skills
Decision-Making Skills
Interpersonal Skills
Technical Skills

Thomas Imo/Photothek via Getty Images

Managers need to plan, organize, and monitor work to ensure employees achieve their objectives.

mail-order DVD rentals with streaming. More recently, Hastings decided to produce and stream original TV programs and movies.

To summarize, technical skills are primarily concerned with things, interpersonal skills are primarily concerned with people, and decision-making skills are primarily concerned with ideas and concepts. Review the management skills in Exhibit 1-2; then complete Applying the Concept 1-1.

AACSB Competencies

In addition to qualities and skills, the AACSB International (Association to Advance Collegiate Schools of Business) has established standards for accreditation of business schools; they were updated in 2016. The standards do not require any specific courses in the curriculum. Normally, the degree program includes learning experiences in such general-knowledge and skill areas as communication abilities, ethical understanding and reasoning abilities, analytic skills, interpersonal relations and teamwork, diverse and multicultural/global work environments, reflective thinking skills, and application of knowledge and skill development.[47] This book includes Applications and Skill Builders at the end of each chapter to foster the development of your management qualities, skills, and competencies. Each exercise identifies the area of development.

In addition to AACSB, this book also meets the core professional components of **ACBSP** (Accreditation Council for Business Schools and Programs),[48] and **IACBE** (International Assembly for Collegiate Business Education) standards.[49] AACSB, ACBSP, and IACBE standards can be classified within the tree management skills areas.[50]

LO 1-3

Explain the four management functions and the three management role categories.

What Do Managers Do?

Years of research have shown that essentially everything a manager does can be classified into one of the four management functions or as nonmanagerial work and by the managerial role being performed. Performing the management functions clearly is difficult real work, and managers may also perform employee tasks.

Management Functions

management functions
Planning, organizing, leading, and controlling.

The four **management functions** include *planning, organizing, leading, and controlling.* Managers perform the management functions through using organizational resources to achieve organizational objectives through others, usually in teams.[51] All of the Skill Builder exercises identify the management function skill being developed through the activity. Exhibit 1-3 lists the four functions of management.

MANAGEMENT IN ACTION
Core Management Skills

Planning—Based on Objectives. Planning is typically the starting point in the management process, and you should begin with a clear objective.[52] **Planning** *is the process of setting objectives and determining in advance exactly how the objectives will be met.* There is a relationship between planning and performance.[53] So before we do anything, we should have an objective stating the end result and then develop a plan for how to complete it.[54] You should also realize that the other three functions also focus on achieving your objectives. You will learn how to write effective objectives and plans in Part II: Planning (Chapters 4–6).

Organizing. Performance is based on how managers organize their resources.[55] **Organizing** *is the process of delegating and coordinating tasks and allocating resources to achieve objectives.* An important part of coordinating human resources is to assign people to various jobs and tasks. So we design our work to achieve our objectives.[56] An important part of organizing, sometimes listed as a separate function, is staffing. *Staffing* is the process of selecting, training, and evaluating employees.[57] You will learn how to organize in Part III: Organizing (Chapters 7–9).

EXHIBIT 1-3	**MANAGEMENT FUNCTIONS**

Management Functions
Planning
Organizing
Leading
Controlling

Leading. The ability to lead is an important skill for everyone, especially for managers, because leadership contributes to organizational success.[58] A survey found that 63% of companies screen new hires on the basis of leadership ability.[59] **Leading** *is the process of influencing employees to work toward achieving objectives.* Managers must communicate the objectives to employees and motivate them to achieve those objectives by developing positive relationships.[60] You will learn how to lead in Part IV: Leading (Chapters 10–13).

Controlling. Objectives will not be met without consistent monitoring.[61] You can't manage what you don't measure,[62] and sometimes you need to overcome obstacles to accomplish the objective.[63] **Controlling** *is the process of monitoring and measuring progress and taking corrective action when needed to ensure that objectives are achieved.* You will learn how to control in Part V: Controlling (Chapters 14–15).

Nonmanagement Functions. All managers perform the four functions of management as they get work done through employees. However, many managers perform nonmanagement, or employee, functions as well. For example, at **KFC** and **McDonald's** it is common for store managers to be cooking or waiting on customers at mealtimes, which is a nonmanagement function. Many managers are called working managers because they perform both management and employee functions.

Netflix's (**IOM 3**) managers are constantly implementing the four management functions. Managers set objectives and have to continuously plan the entertainment content to stream. When going from mail rental to online streaming, Netflix had to change its organizational structure, as Hastings delegated implementing the change and reallocation of resources. Managers need to consistently influence employees to achieve the objectives, and measuring and monitoring progress is needed to meet the objectives.

WORK
APPLICATION 1-4

Identify a specific manager, preferably one who is or was your boss, and give examples of how that person performs each of the four management functions.

planning The process of setting objectives and determining in advance exactly how the objectives will be met.

organizing The process of delegating and coordinating tasks and allocating resources to achieve objectives.

leading The process of influencing employees to work toward achieving objectives.

controlling The process of monitoring progress and taking corrective action when needed to ensure that objectives are achieved.

1-2 APPLYING THE CONCEPT

Management Functions

Indicate which type of function the manager is performing in each situation:

A. planning

B. organizing

C. leading

D. controlling

E. nonmanagement

_____ 6. The manager is encouraging an employee to get a college degree so she can become a manager.

_____ 7. The manager is conducting a job interview to select a new employee for a new open position in sales.

_____ 8. The manager is emptying his trash.

_____ 9. The manager is scheduling employee work hours for next week.

_____ 10. The manager is giving the workers a pep talk to motivate them to work hard to meet the production quota today with an absent employee.

_____ 11. The manager is conducting an employee's annual performance evaluation.

_____ 12. The manager is checking how many new computers have been produced so far today.

The Transition to Management—Managing People. Going from being an employee to being a manager is not an easy transition.[64] New managers often don't realize just how hard the job really is and how much more work managers do than employees, who constantly interrupt them, putting demands on their time. Because most new managers are used to doing nonmanagement functions, they often do the work for employees when their actual job is to train employees to do their job, help them improve their performance, and solve problems to make their jobs easier and less frustrating.

A current term for the transition is "go suit," defined as getting promoted to management—and forgetting your basic job skills once installed in an office.[65] This is because as a manager, you get the job done through employees, or your job is to manage people[66]—using interpersonal skills.[67] As a new manager, you will likely need to perform nonmanagement functions, but be sure to focus on planning, organizing, leading, and controlling to get the job done through people.

Management Roles

Managers have a set of distinct roles. A *role* is a set of expectations of how one will behave in a given situation. Henry Mintzberg identified 10 roles that managers play as they accomplish management functions. Mintzberg grouped these 10 roles into three **management role categories**:[68] *interpersonal, informational, and decisional roles* (see Exhibit 1-4).

Interpersonal Roles. When managers play interpersonal roles, they use their interpersonal skills as they perform management functions. Managers play the *figurehead* role when they represent the organization or department in ceremonial and symbolic activities. Managers play the *leader* role when they motivate, train, communicate with, and influence others. Managers play the *liaison* role when they interact with people outside of their unit to gain information and favors.

Informational Roles. When managers play informational roles, they use their interpersonal skills. Managers play the *monitor* role when they read and talk to others to receive information. Managers play the *disseminator* role when they send information to others. Managers play the *spokesperson* role when they provide information to people outside the organization.

WORK APPLICATION 1-5

Identify a specific manager, preferably one who is or was your boss, and give examples of how that person performs roles in each of the three management role categories. Be sure to identify at least one of the three or four roles in each category.

management role categories The categories of roles—interpersonal, informational, and decisional—managers play as they accomplish management functions

---

EXHIBIT 1-4   MANAGEMENT ROLES

Management Roles
Interpersonal—figurehead, leader, liaison
Informational—monitor, disseminator, spokesperson
Decisional—entrepreneur, disturbance handler, resource allocator, negotiator

1-3 APPLYING THE CONCEPT

Management Roles

Identify each of the managerial activities as part of one of the three role categories:

A. interpersonal role

B. informational role

C. decisional role

____ 13. The manager discusses next year's budget.

____ 14. The mayor is cutting the ribbon at the groundbreaking for the new town hall.

____ 15. The manager develops a new app that will be sold as an additional source of income.

____ 16. The manager is reading the monthly budget.

____ 17. The manager shows a new employee how to record her working hours.

Decisional Roles. When managers play decisional roles, they use their conceptual decision-making management skills. Managers play the *entrepreneur* role when they innovate and initiate improvements. Managers play the *disturbance-handler* role when they take corrective action during disputes or crisis situations. Managers play the *resource-allocator* role when they schedule, request authorization, and perform budgeting and programming activities, as when managers perform the *negotiator* role when they represent their department or organization during nonroutine transactions to gain agreement and commitment.

The Systems Relationship Among the Management Skills, Functions, and Roles

It is important to understand system interrelationships.[69] The management skills are interrelated, or have a systems effect.[70] For example, a first-line supervisor's technical skills will affect his or her interpersonal and decision-making skills and vice versa. A manager's skills also affect the implementation of the management functions and roles.

The management functions are not steps in a linear process. Managers do not usually plan, then organize, then lead, and then control. The functions are distinct yet interrelated. Managers often perform them simultaneously. In addition, each function depends on the others. For example, if you start with a poor plan, the objective will not be met even if things are well organized, led, and controlled. Or if you start with a great plan but are poorly organized or lead poorly, the objective may not be met. Plans without controls are rarely implemented effectively. Remember that the management functions are based on setting objectives (planning) and achieving them (through organizing, leading, and controlling).

How well a manager plays the various management roles is also affected by his or her management skills. The 10 management roles are also integrated with the management functions. Certain management roles are played when performing the different management functions.

Exhibit 1-5 *illustrates the interrelationship of management skills, functions, and roles.*

Differences Among Managers

As you will learn in this section, there are different levels of managers, and the importance of the skills and functions needed to perform the job varies by level. We will also discuss some of the differences between business sizes and managing for-profit companies and not-for-profit organizations.

LO 1-4

Recall the hierarchy of management levels and describe the differences among the levels in terms of skills needed and functions performed.

EXHIBIT 1-5   MANAGEMENT SKILLS, FUNCTIONS, AND ROLES

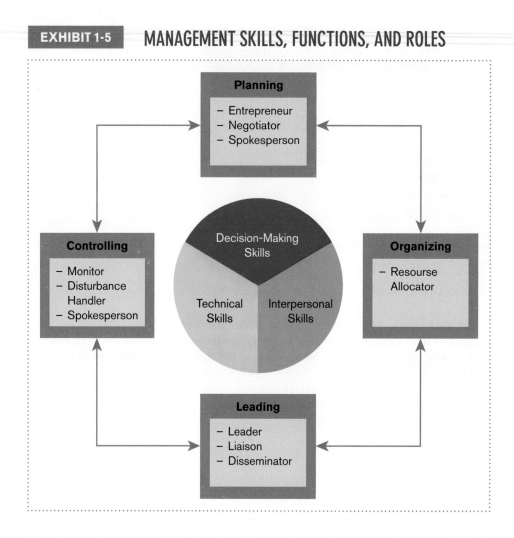

The Three Levels of Management

Managers differ in the level of management, and there are also nonpermanent managers called team leaders, as well as nonmanager operative employees. There are also different types of managers by level of management. Let's cover these concepts in this sequence.

The three **levels of management** are *top managers, middle managers, and first-line managers*. Job titles are given to help identify the level of management.[71] The three levels relate to each other as described here. See Exhibit 1-6 for an illustration of the three levels of management and operative employees.

Top Managers. Top managers—people in executive positions—have titles such as CEO, president, or vice president. Most organizations have relatively few top management positions. Top managers are responsible for managing an entire organization or major parts of it. They develop and define the organization's purpose, objectives, and strategies; for example, the new CEO of **Levis Strauss**, **Chip Bergh**, is charged with bringing the blue jeans pioneer back to its old glory.[72] They report to boards of directors or other executives and supervise the activities of middle managers.

Middle Managers. People in middle-management positions have titles such as sales manager, branch manager, or department head. Middle managers are responsible for implementing top management's strategy by developing short-term operating plans. They generally report to executives and supervise the work of first-line managers.

First-Line Managers. Examples of titles of first-line managers are team or crew leader, supervisor, head nurse, and office manager. These managers are responsible for implementing

levels of management Top managers, middle managers, and first-line managers.

middle managers' operational plans. They generally report to middle managers. Unlike those at the other two levels of management, first-line managers do not supervise other managers; they supervise operative employees.

Team Leader. This is a newer management position needed in organizations that focus on a team-based structure.[73] They are often called a project or program leader or task force or committee leader. The team leader facilitates team activities to achieve a goal rather than telling people what to do.[74]

Higher-level managers may also be team leaders who supervise a small group of people to achieve a goal. Nonmanagement operative employees may also be team leaders who manage a team until the goal is completed. The team leader is not usually a permanent management position and thus is not a level in the hierarchy of management. You will learn more about teams and how to lead them in Chapter 8.

Nonmanagement Operative Employees. Operative employees are the workers in an organization who do not hold management positions. They commonly report to first-line managers and possibly to team leaders. They make the products, wait on customers, perform repairs, and so on.

Types of Managers by Level. The three **types of managers** are general managers, functional managers, and project managers. Top-level and some middle managers are general managers because they supervise the activities of several departments that perform different activities. Middle and first-line managers are often business functional managers who supervise the completion of related tasks. Project managers are often team leaders.

Large corporations have multiple levels of management that serve different purposes to the organization. **Levi Strauss's CEO Chip Bergh** is a top manager who steered the company back to its position of prominence in American culture.

types of managers General managers, functional managers, and project managers.

EXHIBIT 1-6   ## MANAGEMENT LEVELS AND FUNCTIONAL AREAS

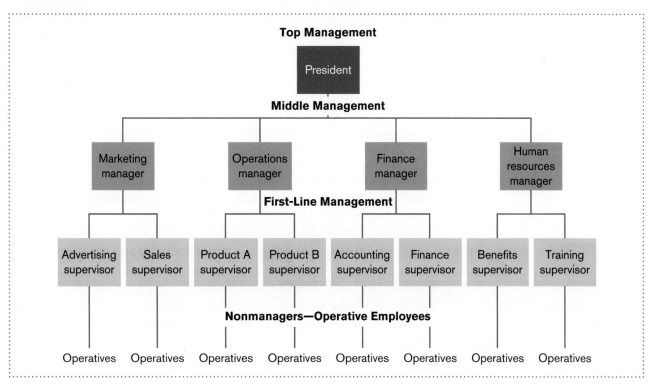

1-1 **JOIN THE DISCUSSION** ETHICS AND SOCIAL RESPONSIBILITY

Executive Compensation

In 2016, CEOs of S&P 500 Index companies received an average of $13.1 million in total compensation. In contrast, production and nonsupervisory workers earned only an average of $37,632–a CEO-to-worker pay ratio of 347 to 1. Some say top executives are being overpaid. Especially because some of the best-performing CEOs aren't the highest paid, and others get large raises even when the companies lose money. However, not everyone agrees. In capitalist countries, talented CEOs, like in pro sports, are entitled to fetch their price, as most compensation is geared toward results. Top executives should be paid multimillion-dollar compensation packages; after all, if it weren't for effective CEOs, companies would not be making the millions of dollars of profits they make each year. CEOs deserve a piece of the pie they help create.

1. Do executives deserve to make 335 times more than the average worker?

2. Is it ethical for managers to take large pay increases when laying off employees?

3. Is it ethical for managers to get pay raises when their companies lose money?

4. Are companies being socially responsible when paying executives premium compensation?

Sources: Information taken from the AFL-CIO's website at https://aflcio.org/paywatch, accessed October 18, 2017; J. S. Lublin, "Parsing the Pay and Performance of Top CEOs," *The Wall Street Journal* (June 25, 2015), B1.

The four most common *business functional* areas include marketing (sell the products and services), operations/production (make the product or perform the service), finance/accounting (maintain financial records), and human resources/personnel management (hire and compensate employees), as shown in Exhibit 1-6. We will discuss these functional areas in Chapter 7.

A project manager coordinates employees and other resources across several functional departments to accomplish a specific goal or task, such as developing and producing a new breakfast cereal for **Kellogg's** or a new aircraft at **Boeing**.

Differences in Management Skills and Functions

Differences in Management Skills. All managers need technical, interpersonal, and decision-making skills. However, the relative importance of these types of skills varies with the level of management. At all three levels of management, the need for interpersonal skills remains fairly constant. However, top-level managers have a greater need for decision-making skills, whereas first-line managers have a greater need for technical skills. Middle managers tend to need all three skills, but the mix required differs somewhat from organization to organization.

Differences in Management Functions. All managers perform the four management functions: planning, organizing, leading, and controlling. However, the time spent on each function varies with the level of management. First-line managers spend more time leading and controlling, middle-level managers spend equal time on all four functions, and top managers spend more time planning and organizing.

Exhibit 1-7 summarizes the primary skills needed and functions performed at each of the three management levels.

WORK APPLICATION 1-6

Identify the levels of management in a specific organization by level and title. Be sure to give the organization's name.

WORK APPLICATION 1-7

Identify which type of boss you have now or have had previously. If that person is or was a functional manager, be sure to specify the functional tasks of the department.

EXHIBIT 1-7   SKILLS NEEDED AND FUNCTIONS PERFORMED AT DIFFERENT MANAGEMENT LEVELS

Management Level	Primary Management Skills Needed	Primary Management Functions Performed
Top	Decision-Making and Interpersonal Skills	Planning and Organizing
Middle	Balance of All Three	Balance of All Four
First-Line	Technical and Interpersonal Skills	Leading and Controlling

1-4 APPLYING THE CONCEPT

Differences Among Management Levels

Identify the level of management in the following five instances:

A. top

B. middle

C. first-line

____ 18. Managers who report to executives.

____ 19. Managers who need technical skills more than decision-making skills.

____ 20. Managers who tend to spend more time planning and organizing.

____ 21. Managers who have operative employees reporting to them.

____ 22. Managers who take the long-term strategy and develop short-term operating plans.

Hastings is the CEO of **Netflix** (**IOM 4**), so he is a top-level manager. As discussed in **IOM 2**, Hastings has less need for technical skills and a greater need for decision-making skills. Hastings had responsibility for strategically planning how Netflix would change from rentals to streaming and developing original content. He also had to radically reorganize the company as it changed strategies.

Differences in Size and Profits

Large-Business Versus Small-Business Managers. Managers in large and small firms need the same skills and perform the same functions. However, generally, the larger the company, the more specialized the job. **Bonnie Castonguary** works for a large organization—**Gap Inc.** Her independent store resembles a small business, but it has the support of a large organization. Small businesses are important to economic growth,[75] even though they tend to have fewer resources.[76] Exhibit 1-8 lists some of the differences between large and small businesses. However, these are general statements; many large and small businesses share certain characteristics. Most large businesses, including **Starbucks**, **Google**, and **Apple**, started as small businesses and grew. Exhibit 1-9 presents survey results comparing small business (fewer than 500 employees) versus all companies (global average 12,000 employees).

EXHIBIT 1-8   DIFFERENCES BETWEEN LARGE AND SMALL BUSINESSES

Functions and Roles	Large Business	Small Business
Planning	Commonly have formal written objectives and plans with a global business focus.	Commonly have informal objectives and plans that are not written with a global focus.
Organizing	Tend to have formal organization structures with clear policies and procedures, with three levels of management. Jobs tend to be specialized.	Tend to have informal structures without clear policies and procedures, with fewer than three levels of management. Jobs tend to be more general.
Leading	Managers tend to be more participative, giving employees more say in how they do their work and allowing them to make more decisions.	Entrepreneurs tend to be more autocratic and want things done their way, often wanting to make the decisions.
Controlling	Tend to have more sophisticated computerized control systems.	Tend to use less sophisticated control systems and to rely more on direct observation.
Important management roles	Resource allocator	Entrepreneur and spokesperson

EXHIBIT 1-9   SURVEY RESULTS COMPARING LARGE AND SMALL BUSINESSES RESPONSES

Statement	Small Business Response Percentage*	Large Business Response Percentage*
My immediate manager is flexible when I need to take care of a personal or family matter.	91%	81%
The company supports me in achieving a reasonable balance between work and my personal life.	65%	60%
I believe the company will be successful over the next two to three years.	63%	72%
I have trust and confidence in the company's senior leadership team.	56%	63%
I believe my salary is fair, considering the pay of people doing similar work in other companies.	35%	49%
I plan to continue working for the company for more than five years.	36%	59%

*Percentage of employees who agreed with the statements

Source: Adapted from Korn Ferry's Hay Group Survey, Reported in *INC.* (November 2016), p. 44.

EXHIBIT 1-10   DIFFERENCES BETWEEN FOR-PROFIT AND NOT-FOR-PROFIT ORGANIZATIONS

Function	For-Profit	Not-for-Profit	
		Nongovernmental Organizations	Governmental Organizations
Ownership and Profits	The primary universal measure of performance is bottom-line profit. Owners are entitled to take profits out of the firm.	Organizations are mission driven; like all businesses, profits are the objective. However, any excess revenue remains in the organization. There are no individual owners.	Organizations are mission driven; however, unlike nongovernmental organizations, profits are not the goal. Ownership is an entity of a function of government.
Revenues	Raised primarily through sales.	Raised through donations, grants, memberships, and investments, as well as sales.	Raised through taxes, fees, and sales.
Staffing	Primarily all paid employees.	Both volunteer workers and paid employees.	Primarily all paid employees, with some entities relying on volunteers.

Source: Dr. Kathryn Carlson Heler, deceased professor, Springfield College, 2010. Used with permission.

WORK
APPLICATION 1-8

Would you prefer to work for a small or large business and a for-profit or not-for-profit organization?

Managers of For-Profit Versus Not-for-Profit Organizations. Is the manager's job the same in for-profit and not-for-profit organizations? Although some noteworthy differences exist (volunteers and fundraising), the answer is basically yes. All managers need management skills, perform management functions, and play management roles regardless of the organization type. **Bonnie Castonguary** works for a for-profit business, the **Gap**. Employees of the **American Red Cross** and the **YMCA** work for the public (not-for-profit) sector. Is the college you are attending for profit or not?

In the past, it was common to classify both nongovernmental and governmental organizations together into one group called not-for-profits. However, the current trend with globalization is to distinguish not-for-profit organizations into nongovernmental organizations (NGOs, such as **Doctors Without Borders**) and governmental organizations (**IRS**).

Exhibit 1-10 lists some of the differences between for-profit and not-for-profit organizations.

A Brief History of Management

LO 1-5

Summarize the major similarities and differences between the classical and behavioral theorists.

Organizational theorists say "History Matters."[77] There are two primary reasons you should be concerned about the history of management: to better understand current developments and to avoid repeating mistakes. Also, as you read the history, you will realize that today's organizations still use these management theories, as indicated by the chapters they are covered in. Early literature on management was written by management practitioners who described their experiences and attempted to extrapolate basic principles. More recent literature comes from researchers. There are different classifications of management approaches, or schools of management thought. In this section, you will learn about five management theories: the classical, behavioral, management science, systems, and contingency theories.

Classical Theory

The *classical theorists focus on the job and management functions to determine the best way to manage in all organizations.* In the early 1900s, managers began an organized approach to increasing performance by focusing on the efficiency of managing jobs. This focus later changed to a concern for managing departments and organizations. Scientific management stressed job efficiency through the development of technical skills, while administrative theory stressed rules and the structure of the organization.

Scientific Management. **Frederick Winslow Taylor** (1856–1915), an engineer known as the Father of Scientific Management, focused on analyzing jobs and redesigning them so that they could be accomplished more efficiently—which today is considered a technology goal.[78] As he searched for the best way to maximize performance, he developed "scientific management" principles, including the following:

1.   Develop a procedure for each element of a worker's job.
2.   Promote job specialization.
3.   Select, train, and develop workers scientifically.
4.   Plan and schedule work.
5.   Establish standard methods and times for each task.
6.   Use wage incentives such as piece rates and bonuses.[79]

Frank Gilbreth (1868–1924) and his wife **Lillian Gilbreth** (1878–1972) used time-and-motion studies to develop more efficient work procedures. Their work was popularized in a book titled *Cheaper by the Dozen* (and later two movies and a television comedy of the same name), which described their application of scientific management practices to their family of 12 children. When Frank died, the children ranged in age from 2 to 19 years old. Lillian continued her work as a consultant but changed the focus of her work to become a pioneer in industrial psychology. Lillian became a professor of management at Purdue University and is commonly referred to as the First Lady of Management.

Another person who made important contributions to scientific management was **Henry Gantt** (1861–1919). He developed a method for scheduling work over a period of time that is still widely used today. You will learn how to develop a Gantt chart in Chapter 15.

Administrative Theory. **Henri Fayol** (1841–1925) was a French engineer who is sometimes referred to as the Father of Modern Management. Fayol was a pioneer in the study of the principles and functions of management. He made a clear distinction between operating and managerial activities. Fayol identified five major functions of management: planning, coordinating, organizing, controlling, and commanding. In addition to his five management functions, Fayol developed 14 principles that are still used today.[80] Most principles-of-management textbooks are organized on the basis of the functions of management.

Two other contributors to administrative management are **Max Weber** (1864–1920) and **Chester Barnard** (1886–1961). Weber was a German sociologist who developed the

classical theorists Researchers who focus on the job and management functions to determine the best way to manage in all organizations.

©iStockphoto.com/shironosov

People are the most important resource that organizations have. **Mary Parker Follett**'s work, which focused on interactions between management and employees, still influences organizations today.

bureaucracy concept. The aim of his concept of bureaucracy was to develop a set of rules and procedures to ensure that all employees were treated fairly. Barnard studied authority and power distributions in organizations. He raised awareness of the informal organization—cliques and naturally occurring social groupings within formal organizations.

Mary Parker Follett (1868–1933) stressed the importance of people rather than engineering techniques. Follett contributed to administrative theory by emphasizing the need for worker participation, conflict resolution, and shared goals. She is best known for *integrative conflict resolution*: when all parties agree to a conflict resolution rather than one person dominates and wins and the other loses, and when there is no compromise where one party gives up something to get something because all parties win. The trend today is toward increasingly higher levels of employee participation. Barnard's and Follett's contributions led to the development of behavioral theory.

Many companies still use classical management techniques successfully today. **McDonald's** system of fast-food service is one good example of a company that uses these techniques. Managers at **Monsanto** also use classical techniques, such as time-and-motion studies and organization principles that you will learn about in Chapter 7. Large organizations that are downsizing to cut costs by laying off employees and becoming more efficient are using a classical management approach.

Behavioral Theory

The **behavioral theorists** *focus on people to determine the best way to manage in all organizations.* In the 1920s, management writers began to question the classical approach to management and changed their focus from the job itself to the people who perform the job. Like the classicists, behaviorists were looking for the best way to manage in all organizations. However, the behavioral approach to management stressed the need for human skills rather than technical skills.

Elton Mayo (1880–1949) pioneered the *human relations movement.* Mayo headed a group of Harvard researchers in conducting the Hawthorne studies, a landmark series of studies of human behavior in **Western Electric**'s Hawthorne plant (Cicero, Illinois) from 1927 to 1932. Like Taylor, Mayo wanted to increase performance; however, he viewed determining the best work environment as the means to this end. Mayo's research suggested that a manager's treatment of people had an important impact on their performance. In other words, treating people well and meeting their needs frequently results in increased performance. The *Hawthorne effect* refers to the phenomenon that just studying people affects their performance.[81] Abraham Maslow (1908–1970) developed the *hierarchy of needs theory.*[82] Maslow is one of the earliest researchers to study motivation, and motivation is still a major area of research. You will learn more about Maslow's hierarchy of needs and other motivation theories in Chapter 11.

Douglas McGregor (1906–1964) developed *Theory X* and *Theory Y.* McGregor contrasted the two theories based on the assumptions that managers make about workers. Theory X managers assume that people dislike work and that only if managers plan, organize, and closely direct and control their work will workers perform at high levels. Theory Y managers assume that people like to work and do not need close supervision. McGregor did not give specific details on how to manage; he suggested a reorientation in managerial thinking.[83] Behaviorists believed that happy employees would be productive. However, later research suggested that a happy worker is not necessarily a productive worker. As you can see, the classical and behavioral theories are very different, yet both kinds of theorists claim that their approach is the best way to manage in all organizations.

behavioral theorists
Researchers who focus on people to determine the best way to manage in all organizations.

The behavioral approach to management is still evolving and being used in organizations. The current term for studying people at work is the *behavioral science approach*, which draws from economics, psychology, sociology, and other disciplines. Most of the material in the chapters in Parts III and IV is based on behavioral science research. Managers all over the globe use behavioral sciences in dealing with people.

Management Science

The **management science theorists** *focus on the use of mathematics to aid in problem solving and decision making.* During World War II, a research program began to investigate the applicability of quantitative methods to military and logistics problems. After the war, business managers began to use management science (math) in three areas.

- **Operations research** emphasizes mathematical model building. Today these models are commonly called algorithms and are used with big data to better understand customers and how to promote products to increase sales. We will be discussing big data in Chapter 4 and other chapters.

- **Operations management** is a form of applied management science that uses quantitative techniques to help managers make decisions that can produce and improve goods and services more efficiently. Operations are covered in Chapter 15.

- **Information management**, or management information systems (MIS) or information systems (IS), provide access to data and information in a timely manner to transact business and make decisions. We discuss information management in Chapter 13.

The use of computers has led to an increase in the use of quantitative methods by managers all over the globe. Because management science stresses decision-making skills and technical skills, it is more closely aligned with classical management theory than with behavioral theory. You will learn more about management science in the chapters in Parts II and V. Management science is not commonly used in organizing and leading.

Integrative Perspective

The integrative perspective has three components: systems theory, sociotechnical theory, and contingency theory.

Systems Theory. The **systems theorists** *focus on viewing the organization as a whole and as the interrelationship of its parts.* In the 1950s, management theorists attempted to integrate the classical, behavioral, and management science theories into a holistic view of the management process. Systems theorists began by assuming that an organization is a system that transforms inputs (resources) into outputs (products and/or services).

According to **Ludwig von Bertalanffy**, **Margaret Mead**, **Harold Koontz**, **Daniel Katz and Robert Kahn**, **Peter Senge**, and others, the systems approach recognizes that an organization is an open system because it interacts with and is affected by the external environment.[84] For example, government laws affect what an organization can and cannot do, the economy affects the organization's sales, and so on. You will learn more about open systems and the organizational environment in Chapter 2.

According to **Russell Ackoff**, the commonly used classical approach to problem solving is a reductionist process. Managers tend to break an organization into its basic parts (departments), understand the behavior and properties of the parts, and add the understanding of the parts together to understand the whole. They focus on making independent departments operate as efficiently as possible. According to systems theorists, the reductionist approach cannot yield an understanding of the organization, only knowledge of how it works. Because the parts of a system are interdependent, even if each part is independently made to perform as efficiently as possible, the organization as a whole may not perform as effectively as possible. For example, all-star athletic teams are made up of exceptional players. But because such players have not played together as a team before, the all-star team may not be able

management science theorists Researchers who focus on the use of mathematics to aid in problem solving and decision making.

systems theorists Researchers who focus on viewing the organization as a whole and as the interrelationship of its parts.

| 1-5 | **APPLYING** THE CONCEPT |

Matching History of Management People and Theories

Identify the person or theory that helped develop the following six theory categories—Exhibit 1-11.

A. Classical theory

B. Behavioral theory

C. Management science

D. Systems theory

E. Sociotechnical theory

F. Contingency theory

_____ 23. Focused on the use of math to make decisions in operations management.

_____ 24. Elton Mayo, human relations movement

_____ 25. Eric Trist, focus on integrating people and technology

_____ 26. Henry Fayol, administrative theory

_____ 27. Russell Ackoff, focus on viewing the organization as a whole and as the interrelationship of its parts

_____ 28. Tom Burns and George Stalker, didn't believe there is one best management approach for all situations

to beat an average team in the league.[85] Systems theory stresses the need for conceptual skills in order to understand how an organization's subsystems (departments) interrelate and contribute to the organization as a whole. For example, the actions of the marketing, operations, and financial departments (subsystems) affect each other; if the quality of the product goes down, sales may decrease, causing a decrease in finances. Before managers in one department make a decision, they should consider the interrelated effects it will have on the other departments. The organization is a system (departments), just as the management process is a system (planning, organizing, leading, and controlling), with subsystems (parts of departments) that affect each other. So, in other words, when you have a problem to solve, do not break it into pieces; focus on the whole.

Today one of the major trends is toward total quality management (TQM) for continuous improvements, which takes a systems approach to management. You will learn more about TQM in Chapters 2 and 15.

Sociotechnical Theory. The **sociotechnical theorists** *focus on integrating people and technology.* Sociotechnical theory was formulated during the 1950s and 1960s by **Eric Trist**, **Ken Bamforth**, **Fred Emery**, and others.[86] They realized, as today's managers do, that a manager must integrate both people and technology. To focus on one to the exclusion of the other leads to lower levels of performance. Much of current behavioral science work is in agreement with sociotechnical theory.

Contingency Theory. The **contingency theorists** *focus on determining the best management approach for a given situation.* In the 1960s and 1970s, management researchers wanted to determine how the environment and technology affected the organization. **Tom Burns** and **George Stalker** conducted a study to determine how the environment affects a firm's organization and management systems. They identified two different types of environments: stable (where there is little change) and innovative (great changes). The researchers also identified two types of management systems: mechanistic (similar to bureaucratic classical theory) and organic (nonbureaucratic, similar to behavioral theory). They concluded that in a stable environment, the mechanistic approach works well, whereas in an innovative environment, the organic approach works well.[87]

Joan Woodward conducted a study to determine how technology (the means of producing products) affects organizational structure. She found that organizational structure did change with the type of technology. Woodward concluded that the mechanistic or classical approach worked well with mass-production technology (such as that of an automobile assembly line), whereas the organic or behavioral approach worked well with

sociotechnical theorists Researchers who focus on integrating people and technology.

contingency theorists Researchers who focus on determining the best management approach for a given situation.

| EXHIBIT 1-11 | COMPARING THEORIES | | | | |

Classical	Behavioral	Management Science	Systems Theory	Sociotechnical Theory	Contingency Theory
Attempts to develop the best way to manage in all organizations by focusing on the jobs and structure of the firm.	Attempts to develop a single best way to manage in all organizations by focusing on people and making them productive.	Recommends using math (computers) to aid in problem solving and decision making.	Manages by focusing on the organization as a whole and the interrelationship of its departments rather than on individual parts.	Recommends focusing on the integration of people and technology.	Recommends using the theory or the combination of theories that meets the given situation.

small-batch (custom-made) products and long-run process technology (such as that for refining crude oil).

These contingency theories may be historic, but they still influence present-day organizational structures. We will revise them in Chapter 7, "Organizing and Delegating Work."

Comparing Theories

Exhibit 1-11 reviews the theories covered in this chapter. Throughout this book, you will learn to take an integrative perspective using systems and contingency theories, combined with some management science, to ensure that you maximize development of your management skills. For example, Skill Builder 1-4 at the end of this chapter uses a contingency approach.

Managing the Old Versus New Workplace

In the old workplace, managers used an autocratic leadership style with a local domestic view, jobs were specialized and routinely performed by individuals, employees were homogeneous, and change was slow.[88] In the new workplace, managers use a more participative leadership style with a global view,[89] jobs are more flexible and performed by teams, employees are diverse, and change is rapid.[90] In today's global economy, managers are responsible for resources and lead employees in other countries in a virtual world.[91]

Knowledge Management and Learning Organizations. Today's leaders focus on learning and knowledge management, because the acquisition of knowledge and the ability to learn are important to organizational success.[92] Knowledge workers process information rather than physical goods.[93] **Knowledge management** *involves everyone in an organization in sharing knowledge and applying it to continuously improve products and processes. Learning is the process whereby knowledge is created through the transformation of experience. Knowledge sharing provides opportunities for mutual learning.*[94] *Learning organizations* have everyone engaged in identifying and solving problems, enabling change, and continuous improvement. Learning organizations also share knowledge through alliances with other organizations.[95] They share three characteristics: a team-based structure, participative management, and the sharing of information through knowledge management.[96]

Evidence-Based Management (EBM). Knowledge management is all about learning new things and applying the knowledge in order to improve.[97] It goes hand in hand with *evidence-based management*, which is the systematic use of the best available evidence to improve management practice.[98] EBM is about replacing hunches and guesswork with management practices that are supported through research.[99] It is sometimes referred to as best practices.[100] EBM has been defined as a process of using six As: Asking, Acquiring, Appraising, Aggregating, Applying, and Assessing.[101]

By ignoring EBM, billions of dollars are spent on ineffective management practices, to the detriment of employees and their families, communities, and the society at large.[102] As

knowledge management
Involving everyone in an organization in sharing knowledge and applying it continuously to improve products and processes.

suggested in EBM,[103] throughout this book, as discussed in the next section, you will learn about management and how to apply the knowledge to develop management skills based on EBM that you can use in your personal and professional lives. For more information on EBM, visit the **Center for Evidence-Based Management** (www.cebma.org).

Objectives of the Book

We all can get better,[104] or you can develop your management skills[105]—that is the major objective of this book. This book takes a "how-to" approach to management, as research has shown that knowledge is more likely to be implemented when it is acquired from learning by doing rather than from learning by reading, listening, or thinking.[106] As indicated by its subtitle, "Concepts, Applications, and Skill Development," this book uses a three-pronged approach, with these objectives:

- To teach you the important concepts of management
- To develop your ability to apply the management concepts through critical thinking
- To develop your management skills in your personal and professional lives

Recall that AACSB advocates learning, application of knowledge, and skill building.[107] The book offers some unique features to further each of these three objectives, as summarized in Exhibit 1-12.

Management Concepts

Throughout this book, you will learn management concepts based on EBM and see how they relate to organizational success, as well as to the difficulties and challenges managers face. Your knowledge of EBM concepts is vital to your success,[108] as EBM provides you with tools (concepts, theories, and models) to use on the job to improve your performance.[109] This book offers the seven features listed in Exhibit 1-12 to help you learn management concepts.

Application of Management Concepts

Understanding theory and concepts is essential before moving to the next level: applying the concepts, which requires critical thinking.[110] One of the criticisms of management education is the focus on teaching theory without the application to practice, called the knowing–doing gap and theory–practice gap.[111] We need to draw on concepts and theories,[112] and actually apply them.[113] As shown in Exhibit 1-12, this book offers seven features to help you develop critical-thinking skills. You will be given the opportunity to apply the concepts to your personal and professional lives in every chapter.

Development of Management Skills

Scholars agree that management education needs more emphasis on skills development.[114] The third and highest-level objective is to develop the management skills that you can use in your personal and professional lives as both a leader and a follower,[115] and thus AACSB wants skill development in the business curriculum.[116] Think about the EBM models in this book like proven cooking recipes. If you follow the step-by-step instructions, you will get consistently better results, as opposed to winging it on your own and potentially making mistakes.[117] This book offers four features to help you do so.

Practice. As with just about everything in life, you cannot become skilled by simply reading about or trying something once. Developing management skills takes persistence and practice.[118] The great **Green Bay Packers** football coach **Vince Lombardi** said that leaders are made by effort and hard work. If you want to develop your management skills, you must not only learn the concepts in this book but also practice with the applications and skill-building exercises.[119] Are you willing to change some of your behavior to develop habits of using the concepts of EBM? Will you commit today?[120]

EXHIBIT 1-12	FEATURES OF THIS BOOK'S THREE-PRONGED APPROACH AND TABLE OF CONTENTS

		Table of Contents

Features That Present Important Concepts	• Text discussions of management research
	• Step-by-step behavior models
	• Learning Outcomes
	• Chapter summaries and glossaries
	• Key Term Review
	• Review Questions
		I. THE GLOBAL MANAGEMENT ENVIRONMENT
		    1. Management and Its History
		    2. The Environment: Culture, Ethics, and Social Responsibility
		    3. Managing Diversity in a Global Environment
		II. PLANNING

Features That Help You Apply What You Learn	• Ideas on Management cases
	• Organizational examples
	• Work Applications
	• Applying the Concept
	• Cases
	• Videos
	• Join the Discussion: Ethics and Social Responsibility
		4. Creative Problem Solving and Decision Making
		    5. Strategic and Operational Planning
		    6. Managing Change, Innovation, and Entrepreneurship
		III. ORGANIZING
		    7. Organizing and Delegating Work
		    8. Managing Teamwork
		    9. Human Resources Management
		Appendix: Career Management and Networking

Features That Foster Skill Development	• Self-Assessments
	• Communication Skills
	• Behavior Modeling training
	• Skill Builder exercises
		IV. LEADING
		    10. Organizational Behavior: Power, Politics, Conflict, and Stress
		    11. Motivating for High Performance
		    12. Leading With Influence
		V. CONTROLLING
		    13. Communication and Information Technology
		    14. Managing Control Systems, Finances, and People
		    15. Operations, Quality, and Productivity

Flexibility. This book has so many features that it is unlikely that all of them can be covered in class during a one-semester course. Your instructor will select the features that best meet the course objectives and the amount of time available, but you may want to cover some or all of the other features on your own or with the assistance of others.

Organization of the Book

This book is organized into five parts, with Part I covering the introductory information and Parts II through V covering the four functions of management discussed in this chapter. Part II covers planning, Part III covers organizing, Part IV covers leading, and Part V covers controlling. See Exhibit 1-12 for the table of contents.

Trends and Issues in Management

Sorry, but there are no secrets to success. Research has shown that highly successful companies today can be the failures of tomorrow, such as **BlackBerry**. The only company listed on the original 12-corporation stock market index, the **Dow Jones Industrial Average (DJI)**, today is **GE**. In 2013, **Goldman Sachs**, **Nike**, and **Visa** replaced **Alcoa**, **Bank of America**, and **Hewlett-Packard**; and **Apple** replaced **AT&T** in 2015.[121] The highly successful companies are the ones that keep up with the latest trends and issues managers face. So we will end every chapter with a section to discuss some of the challenges managers face today.

So what are some of the current important trends and issues? To answer this question, a survey of CEOs of major corporations listed the top four: *globalization, technology* (which is moving two to three times faster than management and includes *big data*), *cybersecurity* (which is based on tech and also includes *privacy*), and a shift in economic power (again a global issue).[122]

With globalization, multinational corporations need to adapt to a *diversity* of cultures.[123] Even domestic companies have the challenge of diversity as the American workforce becomes increasingly diversified.[124] Because having a global mindset is important to career success,[125] in Chapter 3 we will discuss globalization and diversity; recall these are AACSB competencies.

Trust in business today is low due to ethical scandals.[126] *Ethics* is an AACSB competency. Also, society expects *corporate social responsibility*. Because ethics and social responsibility are so important, we cover these issues in Chapter 2, and in every chapter you will find the boxed item titled "Join the Discussion: Ethics & Social Responsibility."

As we bring this chapter to a close, you should realize the importance of studying management, what management is and the resources managers manage, the three skills and four functions of management, and some of the differences among managers. You should also understand a brief history of management, the objectives of the book, and some of the most important trends and issues facing managers today.

$SAGE edge™   edge.sagepub.com/lussier8e

Want a better grade?

Get the tools you need to sharpen your study skills. Access practice quizzes, eFlashcards, video and multimedia, and more at edge.sagepub.com/lussier8e.

Digital Resources

Learning Objective	Digital Resource
1-1. Describe a manager's responsibility.	▶ Management in Action: Core Management Skills*
	▶ Efficiency vs. Effectiveness
1-2. List the three skills of effective managers.	▶ Rational Decision Making
1-3. Explain the four management functions and the three management role categories.	▶ Required Management Skills*
1-4. Recall the hierarchy of management levels and describe the differences among the levels in terms of skills needed and functions performed.	▶ Four Functions of Management
1-5. Summarize the major similarities and differences between the classical and behavioral theorists.	🖥 Hawthorn Effect

* premium video available only in the interactive eBook

• • • CHAPTER SUMMARY

1-1. Describe a manager's responsibility.

A manager is responsible for achieving organizational objectives through efficient and effective use of resources. *Efficient* means doing things right, and *effective* means doing the right thing. The manager's

resources include human, financial, physical, and informational resources.

1-2. List the three skills of effective managers.

The three management skills are technical, interpersonal, and decision-making skills. Technical skills involve the ability to use methods and techniques to perform a task. Interpersonal skills involve the ability to understand, communicate with, and work well with individuals and groups through developing effective relationships. Decision-making skills are based on the ability to conceptualize situations and select alternatives to solve problems and take advantage of opportunities.

1-3. **Explain the four management functions and the three management role categories.**

The four management functions are planning, organizing, leading, and controlling. Planning is the process of setting objectives and determining in advance exactly how the objectives will be met. Organizing is the process of delegating and coordinating tasks and allocating resources to achieve objectives. Leading is the process of influencing employees to work toward achieving objectives. Controlling is the process of measuring and monitoring progress and taking corrective action when needed to ensure that objectives are achieved.

Managers play the interpersonal role when they act as figurehead, leader, or liaison. Managers play the informational role when they act as monitor, disseminator, or spokesperson. Managers play the decisional role when they act as entrepreneur, disturbance handler, resource allocator, or negotiator.

1-4. **Recall the hierarchy of management levels and describe the differences among the levels in terms of skills needed and functions performed.**

The three hierarchy levels are top managers (e.g., operations executive), middle managers (e.g., marketing manager), and first-line managers (e.g., accounting supervisor). Top managers have a greater need for decision-making skills than do first-line managers. Middle managers have a need for all three skills. First-line managers have a greater need for technical skills than do top managers.

1-5. **Summarize the major similarities and differences between the classical and behavioral theorists.**

Both classical and behavioral theorists wanted to find the best way to manage in all organizations. However, the classicists focused on the job and management functions, whereas the behaviorists focused on people.

• • • KEY TERMS

behavioral theorists, 18

classical theorists, 17

contingency theorists, 20

controlling, 9

decision-making skills, 7

interpersonal skills, 6

knowledge management, 21

leading, 9

levels of management, 12

management functions, 8

management role categories, 10

management science theorists, 19

management skills, 6

manager, 4

manager's resources, 4

organizing, 9

performance, 5

planning, 9

sociotechnical theorists, 20

systems theorists, 19

technical skills, 6

types of managers, 13

• • • KEY TERM REVIEW

Complete each of the following statements using one of this chapter's key terms:

1. A _____ is responsible for achieving organizational objectives through efficient and effective utilization of resources.

2. The _____ include human, financial, physical, and informational.

3. The level of organizational _____ is based on how effectively and efficiently managers utilize resources to achieve objectives.

4. _____ include technical, interpersonal, and decision-making skills.

5. _____ involve the ability to use methods and techniques to perform a task.

6. _____ involve the ability to understand, communicate, and work well with individuals and groups through developing effective relationships.

7. _____ are based on the ability to conceptualize situations and select alternatives to solve problems and take advantage of opportunities.

8. The four _____ include planning, organizing, leading, and controlling.

9. _____ is the process of setting objectives and determining in advance exactly how the objectives will be met.

10. _____ is the process of delegating and coordinating tasks and allocating resources to achieve objectives.

11. _____ is the process of influencing employees to work toward achieving objectives.

12. _____ is the process of monitoring progress and taking corrective action when needed to ensure that objectives are achieved.

13. The _____ include interpersonal, informational, and decisional.

14. There are three _____: top managers, middle managers, and first-line managers.

15. There are three _____: general, functional, and project.

16. The _____ focus on the job and management functions to determine the best way to manage in all organizations.

17. The _____ focus on people to determine the best way to manage in all organizations.

18. The _____ focus on the use of mathematics to aid in problem solving and decision making.

19. The _____ focus on viewing the organization as a whole and as the interrelationship of its parts.

20. The _____ focus on integrating people and technology.

21. The _____ focus on determining the best management approach for a given situation.

22. _____ involves everyone in an organization in sharing knowledge and applying it to continuously improve products and processes.

• • • REVIEW QUESTIONS

1. What are a manager's resources?

2. What are the three management skills?

3. What are the four functions of management?

4. What are the three management role categories?

5. What are the three levels of management?

6. What are the three types of managers?

7. What are the objectives of this book?

• • • COMMUNICATION SKILLS

The following critical-thinking questions can be used for class discussion and/or as written assignments to develop communication skills. Be sure to give complete explanations for all questions.

1. Are you interested in being a manager?

2. Why is it important to take this course in management?

3. Is it more important for managers to be efficient or effective? Can you improve both at the same time?

4. Is management ability universal? In other words, can a good manager in one environment (e.g., computers) also be effective in another (e.g., banking)?

5. Some people say the hard skills (technical, finance, quantitative analysis) are more important for managers than soft skills (interpersonal), and some say the opposite is true. What is your view?

6. Is your college professor a manager? Why or why not?

7. When a good employee is promoted to management, which management level is the promotion usually to, and how do the management skills and functions change with the job promotion?

8. When an employee is promoted to manager, do most organizations provide some type of training? Should they? Why or why not?

CASES

• • • Case 1-1   Joe Maddon, Manager of the Chicago Cubs

Joe Maddon has been the manager of the Chicago Cubs since 2015. In his first year, he exceeded the expectations of most analysts and fans by leading the team to an appearance in the National League Championship Series. In 2016, he broke the alleged "curse" that has hung over the team for more than 100 years and won the World Series against the Cleveland Indians in a thrilling seven-game series.

Although Joe Maddon is a "manager" of a baseball team rather than a traditional corporation, he is an excellent example of the key role that a manager plays in the effectiveness and success of any kind of team. First, he devotes significant time to developing strong relationships with his players through

open and honest communication on a regular basis. Second, he focuses not only on the outcome (i.e., to win) but also on the process by doing the things the "right way." Third, he likes to emphasize staying loose and having fun. He is known for creating t-shirts with humorous sayings on them, such as "Try Not to Suck." He also likes to hold "dress-up road trips" during which players wear crazy suits or onesies. By keeping things light and fun, Maddon believes that players will be more relaxed and perform better on the field. Fourth, Maddon believes in the "art of doing nothing." Rather than using a regimented approach to training and game preparation that is put into practice on a weekly basis, he encourages players to "just show up" for games. In fact, the Cubs take less formal batting practice than any other team in the league. Fifth, Maddon is an "outside-the-box" thinker who does not hesitate to make unconventional and risky decisions. For example, he has used pitchers like John Lackey as a pinch hitter in a key extra- innings situation with the game on the line. He has used pitchers to play field positions, and he rotates his position players to other positions. Maddon is willing to go against the grain if he feels that it can help the team win.

Joe Maddon's unconventional but highly effective management style has some key lessons for managers in other types of organizations. These include "instill a positive and upbeat attitude in the culture of the team," "stay loose and productive," "be old and new school" (i.e., be open to new approaches such as data analytics, but balance this with an emphasis on fundamentals), and "don't be the center of attention" (maintain a small ego and focus on the team as the key focus).

Discussion Questions

1. What types of resources does Joe Maddon control as the manager of the Chicago Cubs?

2. What types of management skills does Joe Maddon use as the manager of the Chicago Cubs?

3. How does Joe Maddon carry out the four management functions as the manager of the Chicago Cubs?

4. How does Joe Maddon apply contingency theory of management in his job as manager of the Chicago Cubs?

5. Would you like to work for a manager like Joe Maddon? Why or why not?

6. What is there to learn about how to be a good manager in a business organization based on studying coaches from the sports industry?

References

http://www.baseball-reference.com/bullpen/Joe_Maddon

https://blog.eosworldwide.com/blog/joe-maddon-management-guru

http://www.chicagotribune.com/sports/columnists/ct-cubs-joe-maddon-managerial-style-spt-0930-20160929-story.html

http://macalicomm.com/2015/10/11-brand-and-leadership-values-from-cubs-skipper-joe-maddon/

http://www.chicagobusiness.com/article/20151005/OPINION/151009931/leadership-lessons-from-the-dugout-courtesy-of-cubs-maddon

Case created by Loren Kuzuhara, University of Wisconsin–Madison.

••• Case 1-2   Jiffy Lube University

A leading provider of oil changes, Jiffy Lube doesn't expect to see its customers every day—but about every three months or 3,000 miles. The company boasts more than 2,100 outlets throughout North America that are mostly franchised. The rest of its locations are company-owned and operated. Besides oil changes, Jiffy Lube facilities provide maintenance services for air conditioning, fuel systems, and transmissions.(1)

Jiffy Lube focuses on its four key areas of preventative maintenance service: change, inspect, check/fill, and clean. "Jiffy Lube® strives to provide the highest quality service to each customer, and one of the best ways to accomplish this is by having some of the best technicians in the business. Jiffy Lube technicians are not just your standard technicians. Every Jiffy Lube service center employee is required to complete Jiffy Lube University℠, an award-winning training program so extensive that Jiffy Lube earned the distinction of being an Automotive Service Excellence (ASE) Accredited Training Provider."(2)

Jiffy Lube University℠ (JLU) combines state-of-the-art computer-based instruction, supervised on-the-job training and proficiency testing to help Jiffy Lube technicians become skilled in providing comprehensive preventive maintenance....The Jiffy Lube training program is so

thorough that it is recognized by the American Council on Education for college credit. And because Jiffy Lube is never satisfied with anything but the best, it won the American Society for Training and Development BEST Award—the training industry's most rigorous and coveted recognition."(3)

Problem: Retaining great employees and nurturing leadership. "Training is the foundation for achieving Jiffy Lube's business goals; it also is the cornerstone for attracting and retaining service center technicians and managers." According to Mauricio Quezada, director of operations, Finding ways to attract, retain, and train new leaders in the Jiffy Lube system is a key to long-term success.... "Knowing that most leadership positions are filled from internal promotions and that 45 percent of service center employees have a desire to continue their education, we developed two complementary initiatives."(4)

JLU developed a new Leadership curriculum for store managers. The three-day instructor-led training (ILT) course was developed using principles from top leadership and business books and insight from industry experts.... Following the interactive ILT class, students were asked to complete two further development steps:

1. **Leadership Simulation:** The successful completion of an innovative online simulation module, "A Day in the Life of a Store Manager," was required. The participant must resolve 32 real-life scenarios, earning points based on the quality of the response.

2. **180-day follow-up:** JLU also introduced an electronic online follow-up system to encourage service center employees to apply the learnings from class and to gain support from their supervisor. The system communicates to service center employees and their supervisor the day after class and again at 30, 60, 90, and 180 days following the session to assess their development as a leader as they continue to focus on learnings.

Some 1,549 students completed Leadership Training ILT classes in 2014, and an additional 1,400 completed the class in 2015. Managers who attend Leadership Training and engage in the follow-up system for the full 180 days have significantly higher customer service scores and car counts, plus lower rates of discounts and turnover than the system average.(5)

With this dedication to training, Jiffy Lube "surged to the top spot on the 2016 Training Top 125 and earned an additional victory lap with its fourth consecutive finish in the Top 5, making it eligible for induction into the Training Top 10 Hall of Fame in 2017."(6)

Discussion Questions

1. Which organizational resources did Jiffy Lube utilize? Explain.

2. How does Jiffy Lube University develop interpersonal skills?

3. Explain how the management training program supports the four management functions; *planning, organizing, leading,* and *controlling.*

4. Does using a simulator that looks at "situations" help or hurt management? Explain your answer.

5. What are the benefits to having Jiffy Lube University?

6. Would you like to attend Jiffy Lube University or a similar program for job training?

References

(1) Dun & Bradstreet Hoovers. (n.d.). Jiffy Lube International, Inc. Retrieved May 30, 2015, from http://www.hoovers.com/company-information/cs/company-profile.jiffy_lube_international_inc.45ccc685ae7303a1.html

(2) Jiffy Lube. (n.d.). Jiffy Lube technicians. Retrieved January 19, 2017, from https://www.jiffylube.com/about/technicians

(3) Ibid.

(4) Friefield, L. (n.d.). Jiffy Lube is leader of the pack. Retrieved January 19, 2017, from https://trainingmag.com/trgmag-article/jiffy-lube-leader-pack

(5) Ibid.

(6) Ibid.

Case created by Herbert Sherman, Hannah K. Walter, and Naveed Ahmad, Department of Management Sciences, School of Business Brooklyn Campus, Long Island University.

••• SKILL BUILDER 1-1: GETTING TO KNOW YOU

Objectives

1. To get acquainted with some of your classmates

2. To gain a better understanding of what the course covers

3. To get to know more about your instructor

Skills

The primary skills developed through this exercise are:

1. Management skill—interpersonal

2. AACSB competency—communication

3. Management function—leading

4. Break into groups of five or six, preferably with people you do not know. Have each member tell his or her name and two or three significant things about himself or herself. Then ask each other questions to get to know each other better.

5. Can everyone in the group address every other person by name? If not, have each member repeat his or her name. Then each person in the group should repeat the names of all the group members until each person knows everyone's first name.

Discussion

What can you do to improve your ability to remember people's names?

1. Elect a spokesperson for your group. Look over the following categories and decide on some specific questions you would like your spokesperson to ask the instructor from one or more of the categories. The spokesperson will not identify who asked the questions. You do not have to have questions for each area.

   - Course expectations. What do you expect to cover or hope to learn from this course?

   - Doubts or concerns. Is there anything about the course that you don't understand?

   - Questions about the instructor. List questions to ask the instructor in order to get to know him or her better.

2. Each spokesperson asks the instructor one question at a time until all questions have been answered. Spokespeople should skip questions already asked by other groups.

Apply It

What did I learn from this experience? How will I use this knowledge in the future?

••• SKILL BUILDER 1-2: COMPARING MANAGEMENT SKILLS

Objective

To better understand the importance of good management skills and functions

Skills

The primary skills developed through this exercise are:

1. Management skill—decision making
2. AACSB competency—analytic and application of knowledge
3. Management function—planning

Compare Your Supervisor's Management Skills

Recall the best supervisor or boss you ever worked for and the worst one you ever worked for. Compare these two people by writing brief notes in the chart below about each person's management skills and ability to perform the four management functions.

Management Skills and Functions		
Best Supervisor or Boss		**Worst Supervisor or Boss**
	Interpersonal (your relationship with the boss)	
	Decision Making	
	Planning	
	Organizing	
	Leading	
	Controlling	

Based on your own experiences with a good boss and a poor one, what do you believe are the key differences between good and poor managers?

Apply It

What did I learn from this exercise? How will I use this knowledge in the future?

••• SKILL BUILDER 1-3: CAREERS

Objective

To think about your career

Skills

The primary skills developed through this exercise are:

1. Management skill—decision making
2. AACSB competency—reflective thinking
3. Management function—planning

Discussion Questions

1. When you graduate, do you want to work for a small or large business in a for-profit or not-for-profit organization as an employee, manager, or entrepreneur?

2. Regarding a career plan, do you believe your answer will change with time? If yes, how?

Apply It

What did I learn from this exercise? How will I use this knowledge in the future?

_____

_____

_____

_____

_____

• • • SKILL BUILDER 1-4: MANAGEMENT STYLES

Note that this Skill Builder is based on leadership and can also be used with Chapter 12.

Objectives

1. To learn your preferred management style
2. To learn how to match a situation to an appropriate management style

Skills

The primary skills developed through this exercise are:

   a. Management skill—decision making

   b. AACSB competency—analytic

   c. Management function—leading

Self-Assessment of Your Preferred Management Style

Following are 12 situations. Select the one alternative that most closely describes what you would do in each situation. Don't be concerned with trying to pick the right answer; select the alternative you would really use. Circle a, b, c, or d. (Ignore the C _____ preceding each situation and the S _____ following each answer choice; these will be explained later.)

C _____ 1. Your rookie crew members seem to be developing well. Their need for direction and close supervision is diminishing. What do you do?

   a. Stop directing and overseeing performance unless there is a problem. S _____

   b. Spend time getting to know them personally, but make sure they maintain performance levels. S _____

   c. Make sure things keep going well; continue to direct and oversee closely. S _____

   d. Begin to discuss new tasks of interest to them. S _____

C _____ 2. You assigned Jill a task, specifying exactly how you wanted it done. Jill deliberately ignored your directions and did it her way. The job will not meet the customer's standards. This is not the first problem you've had with Jill. What do you decide to do?

   a. Listen to Jill's side, but be sure the job gets done right. S _____

   b. Tell Jill to do it again the right way and closely supervise the job. S _____

   c. Tell her the customer will not accept the job and let Jill handle it her way. S _____

   d. Discuss the problem and solutions to it. S _____

C _____ 3. Your employees work well together and are a real team; the department is the top performer in the organization. Because of traffic problems, the president has approved staggered hours for departments. As a result, you can change your department's hours. Several of your workers are in favor of changing. What action do you take?

   a. Allow the group to decide the hours. S _____

   b. Decide on new hours, explain why you chose them, and invite questions. S _____

   c. Conduct a meeting to get the group members' ideas. Select new hours together, with your approval. S _____

   d. Send out a memo stating the hours you want. S _____

C _____ 4. You hired Rahim, a new employee. He is not performing at the level expected after a month's training. Rahim is trying, but he seems to be a slow learner. What do you decide to do?

   a. Clearly explain what needs to be done and oversee his work. Discuss why the procedures are important; support and encourage him. S _____

   b. Tell Rahim that his training is over and it's time to pull his own weight. S _____

   c. Review task procedures and supervise his work closely. S _____

   d. Inform Rahim that his training is over and that he should feel free to come to you if he has any problems. S _____

C _____ 5. Padma has had an excellent performance record for the last five years. Recently you have noticed a drop in the quality and quantity of her work. She has a family problem. What do you do?

   a. Tell her to get back on track and closely supervise her. S _____

   b. Discuss the problem with Padma. Help her realize that her personal problem is affecting her work. Discuss ways to improve the situation. Be supportive and encourage her. S _____

   c. Tell Padma you're aware of her productivity slip and that you're sure she'll work it out soon. S _____

   d. Discuss the problem and solution with Padma and supervise her closely. S _____

C _____ 6. Your organization does not allow smoking in certain areas. You just walked by a restricted area and saw Joan smoking. She has been with the organization for 10 years and is a very productive worker. Joan has never been caught smoking before. What action do you take?

   a. Ask her to put the cigarette out; then leave. S _____

   b. Discuss why she is smoking and what she intends to do about it. S _____

   c. Give her a lecture about not smoking and check up on her in the future. S _____

   d. Tell her to put the cigarette out, watch her do it, and tell her you will check on her in the future. S _____

C _____ 7. Your employees usually work well together with little direction. Recently a conflict between Sue and Tom has caused problems. What action do you take?

a. Call Sue and Tom together and make them realize how this conflict is affecting the department. Discuss how to resolve it and how you will check to make sure the problem is solved. S _____

b. Let the group resolve the conflict. S _____

c. Have Sue and Tom sit down and discuss their conflict and how to resolve it. Support their efforts to implement a solution. S _____

d. Tell Sue and Tom how to resolve their conflict and closely supervise them. S _____

C _____ 8. Hector usually does his share of the work with some encouragement and direction. However, he has migraine headaches occasionally and doesn't pull his weight when this happens. The others resent doing Hector's work. What do you decide to do?

a. Discuss his problem and help him come up with ideas for maintaining his work; be supportive. S _____

b. Tell Hector to do his share of the work and closely watch his output. S _____

c. Inform Hector that he is creating a hardship for the others and should resolve the problem by himself. S _____

d. Be supportive but set minimum performance levels and ensure compliance. S _____

C _____ 9. Barbara, your most experienced and productive worker, came to you with a detailed idea that could increase your department's productivity at a very low cost. She can do her present job and this new assignment. You think it's an excellent idea. What do you do?

a. Set some goals together. Encourage and support her efforts. S _____

b. Set up goals for Barbara. Be sure she agrees with them and sees you as being supportive of her efforts. S _____

c. Tell Barbara to keep you informed and to come to you if she needs any help. S _____

d. Have Barbara check in with you frequently so that you can direct and supervise her activities. S _____

C _____ 10. Your boss asked you for a special report. Franco, a very capable worker who usually needs no direction or support, has all the necessary skills to do the job. However, Franco is reluctant because he has never done a report. What do you do?

a. Tell Franco he has to do it. Give him direction and supervise him closely. S _____

b. Describe the project to Franco and let him do it his own way. S _____

c. Describe the benefits to Franco. Get his ideas on how to do it and check his progress. S _____

d. Discuss possible ways of doing the job. Be supportive; encourage Franco. S _____

C _____ 11. Jean is the top producer in your department. However, her monthly reports are constantly late and contain errors. You are puzzled because she does everything else with no direction or support. What do you decide to do?

a. Go over past reports, explaining exactly what is expected of her. Schedule a meeting so that you can review the next report with her. S _____

b. Discuss the problem with Jean and ask her what can be done about it; be supportive. S _____

c. Explain the importance of the report. Ask her what the problem is. Tell her that you expect the next report to be on time and error free. S _____

d. Remind Jean to get the next report in on time without errors. S _____

C _____ 12. Your workers are very effective and like to participate in decision making. A consultant was hired to develop a new method for your department using the latest technology in the field. What do you do?

a. Explain the consultant's method and let the group decide how to implement it. S _____

b. Teach the workers the new method and supervise them closely as they use it. S _____

c. Explain to the workers the new method and the reasons it is important. Teach them the method and make sure the procedure is followed. Answer questions. S _____

d. Explain the new method and get the group's input on ways to improve and implement it. S _____

To determine your preferred management style, circle the letter you selected for each situation.

	Autocratic	Consultative	Participative	Empowering
1.	c	b	d	a
2.	b	a	d	c
3.	d	b	c	a
4.	c	a	d	b
5.	a	d	b	c
6.	d	c	b	a
7.	d	a	c	b

	Autocratic	Consultative	Participative	Empowering
8.	b	d	a	c
9.	d	b	a	c
10.	a	c	d	b
11.	a	c	b	d
12.	b	c	d	a
Totals	_____	_____	_____	_____

Now add up the number of circled items per column. The column with the most items circled suggests your preferred management style. Is this the style you tend to use most often?

Your management style flexibility is reflected in the distribution of your answers. The more evenly distributed the numbers, the more flexible your style. A total of 1 or 0 for any column may indicate a reluctance to use that style.

Learn More About Management Styles

According to contingency theorists, there is no best management style for all situations. Instead, effective managers adapt their styles to individual capabilities or group situations. Following is a discussion of how to use Model 1-1 (Situational Management); refer to it as you read about it.

MODEL 1-1 SITUATIONAL MANAGEMENT

Step 1. Determine the capability level of employees on a continuum from C1 to C4; follow the arrow left to right.

Step 2. Match the management style (S1A, S2C, S3P, S4E) with the employee capability level; follow the arrow down from the capability-level box to the management-style box.

Capability Level (C)

Employee Ability and Motivation to Perform the Task

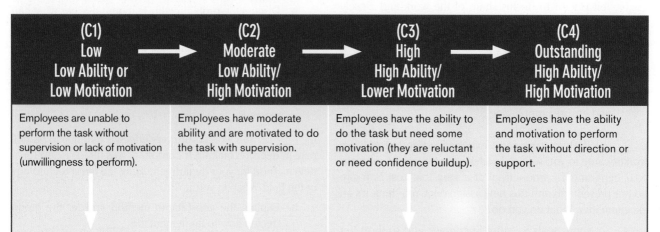

(C1) Low Low Ability or Low Motivation	(C2) Moderate Low Ability/ High Motivation	(C3) High High Ability/ Lower Motivation	(C4) Outstanding High Ability/ High Motivation
Employees are unable to perform the task without supervision or lack of motivation (unwillingness to perform).	Employees have moderate ability and are motivated to do the task with supervision.	Employees have the ability to do the task but need some motivation (they are reluctant or need confidence buildup).	Employees have the ability and motivation to perform the task without direction or support.

Management Style (S)

Directive and Supportive Behavior Manager Needs to Give Employee to Perform the Task

(S1A) Autocratic High Directive/ Low Supportive	(S2C) Consultative High Directive/ High Supportive	(S3P) Participative Low Directive/ High Supportive	(S4E) Empowerment Low Directive/ Low Supportive
Manager tells employees what to do and how to do it and closely oversees performance. Manager makes decisions without any employee input.	Manager sells employees on doing the task and oversees performance. Manager typically gets input from individual employees when making decisions.	Manager develops motivation by developing confidence. Manager typically has a group meeting to get employee input into decisions.	Manager assigns tasks and lets the employees do it on their own. Manager lets the employee or group make decisions.

1. **Manager–Employee Interactions.** Managers' interactions with employees can be classified into two distinct categories: directive and supportive.

- *Directive behavior.* The manager focuses on directing and controlling behavior to ensure that tasks get done and closely oversees performance.

- *Supportive behavior.* The manager focuses on encouraging and motivating behavior without telling the employee what to do. The manager explains things and listens to employee views, helping employees make their own decisions by building up confidence and self-esteem.

As a manager, you can focus on directing (getting the task done), supporting (developing relationships), or both.

2. **Employee Capability.** There are two distinct aspects of employee capability.

   - *Ability.* Do employees have the knowledge, experience, education, skills, and training to do a particular task without direction?

   - *Motivation.* Do the employees have the confidence to do the task? Do they want to do the task? Are they committed to performing the task? Will they perform the task without encouragement and support?

Employee capability may be measured on a continuum from low to outstanding. As a manager, you assess each employee's capability level and motivation.

   - *Low.* The employees can't do the task without detailed directions and close supervision. Employees in this category are either unable or unwilling to do the task.

   - *Moderate.* The employees have moderate ability and need specific direction and support to get the task done properly. The employees may be highly motivated but still need direction.

   - *High.* The employees have high ability but may lack the confidence to do the job. What they need most is support and encouragement to motivate them to get the task done.

   - *Outstanding.* The employees are capable of doing the task without direction or support.

Most people perform a variety of job tasks. It is important to realize that employee capability may vary depending on the specific task. For example, a bank teller may handle routine transactions easily but falter when opening new or special accounts. Employees tend to start working with low capability, needing close direction. As their ability to do the job increases, their managers can begin to be supportive and probably cease close supervision. As a manager, you must gradually develop your employees from low to outstanding levels over time.

3. **Four Management Styles.** The four situational management styles are autocratic, consultative, participative, and empowering.

   - An *autocratic style* is highly directive and less concerned with building relationships. The autocratic style is appropriate when interacting with low-capability employees. When interacting with such employees, give very detailed instructions describing exactly what the task is and when, where, and how to perform it.

Closely oversee performance and give some support. The majority of time with the employees is spent giving directions. Make decisions without input from the employees.

   - A *consultative style* involves highly directive and highly supportive behavior and is appropriate when interacting with moderately capable employees. Give specific instructions and oversee performance at all major stages of a task. At the same time, support the employees by explaining why the task should be performed as requested and answering their questions. Work on relationships as you explain the benefits of completing the task your way. Give fairly equal amounts of time to directing and supporting employees. When making decisions, you may consult employees, but retain the final say. Once you make the decision, which can incorporate employees' ideas, direct and oversee employees' performance.

   - A *participative style* is characterized by less directive but still highly supportive behavior and is appropriate when interacting with employees with high capability. When interacting with such employees, spend a small amount of time giving general directions and a great deal of time giving encouragement. Spend limited time overseeing performance, letting employees do the task their way while focusing on the result. Support the employees by encouraging them and building up their self-confidence. If a task needs to be done, don't tell them how to do it; ask them how they will accomplish it. Make decisions together or allow employees to make decisions subject to your limitations and approval.

   - An *empowering style* requires providing very little direction or support for employees and is appropriate when interacting with outstanding employees. You should let them know what needs to be done and answer their questions, but it is not necessary to oversee their performance. Such employees are highly motivated and need little, if any, support. Allow them to make their own decisions, subject to your approval. Other terms for empowerment are *laissez-faire* and *hands off.* A manager who uses this style lets employees alone to do their own thing.

Apply Management Styles

Return to the portion of the exercise in which you assessed your preferred management style. Identify the employee capability level for each item; indicate the capability level by placing a number from 1 to 4 on the line marked "C" before each item (1 indicates low capability; 2, moderate capability; 3, high capability; and 4, outstanding capability). Next, indicate the management style represented in each answer choice by placing the letter A (autocratic), C (consultative), P (participative), or E (empowering) on the line marked "S" following each answer choice. Will your preferred management style result in the optimum performance of the task?

Let's see how you did by looking back at the first situation.

C _____ 1. Your rookie crew members seem to be developing well. Their need for direction and close supervision is diminishing. What do you do?

a. Stop directing and overseeing performance unless there is a problem. S _____

b. Spend time getting to know them personally, but make sure they maintain performance levels. S _____

c. Make sure things keep going well; continue to direct and oversee closely. S _____

d. Begin to discuss new tasks of interest to them. S _____

- As a rookie crew, the employees' capability started at a low level, but they have now developed to the moderate level. If you put the number 2 on the C line, you were correct.

- Alternative a is E, the empowering style, involving low direction and support. Alternative b is C, the consultative style, involving both high direction and high support. Alternative c is A, the autocratic style, involving high direction but low support. Alternative d is P, the participative style, involving low direction and high support (in discussing employee interests).

- If you selected b as the management style that best matches the situation, you were correct. However, in the business world, there is seldom only one way to handle a situation successfully. Therefore, in this exercise, you are given points based on how successful your behavior would be in each situation. In situation 1, b is the most successful alternative because it involves developing the employees gradually; answer b is worth 3 points. Alternative c is the next-best alternative, followed by d. It is better to keep things the way they are now than to try to rush employee development, which would probably cause problems. So c is a 2-point answer, and d gets 1 point. Alternative a is the least effective because you are going from one extreme of supervision to the other. This is a 0-point answer because the odds are great that this approach will cause problems that will diminish your management success.

The better you match your management style to employees' capabilities, the greater are your chances of being a successful manager.

Apply It

What did I learn from this skill-building experience? How will I use this knowledge in the future?

Your instructor may ask you to do Skill Builder 1-4 in class in a group. If so, the instructor will provide you with any necessary information or additional instructions.

2

The Environment
Culture, Ethics, and Social Responsibility

••• LEARNING OBJECTIVES

After studying this chapter, you should be able to:

2-1. Explain the five internal environmental factors and how nine external environmental factors can affect the internal business environment. PAGE 38

2-2. Describe the three levels of organizational culture and their relationship to each other. PAGE 42

2-3. Explain why people use unethical behavior, why and how they justify their unethical behavior, and three factors that influence behavior to be ethical or unethical. PAGE 46

2-4. Identify four guides to ethical behavior and three things organizations should do to manage ethics. PAGE 50

2-5. Characterize the three levels of social responsibility and explain its relationship with sustainability. PAGE 53

IOM

Ideas on Management
at Amazon.com

You may know that **Amazon.com** sells just about anything you want to buy online, developed the *Kindle e-book reader* and *Kindle Fire* tablet computer, and offers Amazon Prime streaming and develops original shows like *Transparent* and *Catastrophe* to compete with **Netflix** and **HBO**. But do you know the following:

- In 2015, Amazon toppled **Walmart** to become the world's biggest retailer with a valuation of $272 billion. In 2016 it was estimated that it would sell 7.2 billion items.

- Amazon Web Services (AWS) developed cloud computing in its early stages and in 2015 had close to a 30% market share, compared to **Microsoft** (11%), **IBM** (7%), and **Google** (5%). Amazon gets around 67% of its operating profits from AWS.

- Amazon led to the decline in print news media and bookstores but also bought the ***Washington Post*** newspaper and plans to open as many as 400 bookstores.

- **Bezos** owns **Blue Origin**, which sent its *New Shepard* ship into space and brought the rocket back for future use, which can dramatically reduce the cost of bringing something big into orbit down to around $6 million to compete with **SpaceX**'s current cost of about $60 million with nonreturnable rockets.

- **Bezos** signed agreements to build rocket engines for **United Launch Alliance**, a partnership between **Boeing** and **Lockheed Martin**.

- **Bezos Expeditions** has very profitably invested in a variety of start-ups including **Twitter**, **Airbnb**, and **Uber**, and continues to get in on the ground floor of new up-and-coming ventures.

- Amazon is working on building a massive delivery network to decrease and possibly eliminate its need for **UPS** and **FedEx**. Amazon is working with air-cargo companies to lease airplanes and establish its own freight operations. Amazon has teamed up with **Air Transport Services**. It is also working on driverless bikes, ships, and trucks and drones to deliver packages.

- Amazon plans to sell more groceries through convenience stores and curbside pickup locations, plus same-day delivery.

- In 2017, Amazon acquired **Whole Foods** to expand further into selling groceries.

In 2016, **Jeff Bezos** was ranked number one on *Fortune*'s World's 50 Greatest Leaders and number two on the *Forbes* 400 Richest People lists with a net worth of $67 billion. Bezos is considered one of the all-time greatest entrepreneurs because he changed the way people buy books, the way we read them with e-book readers and tablets, and how many people shop—online. Plus, he is working on changing the way products are delivered and on space travel.

However, not everyone is a fan of Jeff Bezos and Amazon. There was an article in the *New York Times* depicting Amazon as a cutthroat environment that rewards cruelty and backstabbing and claimed it uses unethical practices. Bezos clearly stated that the article wasn't accurate.

IOM 1.   Who is Amazon's top manager, and what are the company's mission, major resource, systems process, and structure?

IOM 2.   How does the external environment affect Amazon?

IOM 3.   What type of culture does Amazon have?

IOM 4.   What does Amazon do to be ethical, socially responsible, and sustainable?

You'll find answers to these **IOM** questions throughout the chapter. To learn more about Amazon, visit www.amazon.com.

Sources: Information for the opening case was taken from the Amazon website, www.amazon.com, accessed November 29, 2016; "Forbes 400," *Forbes* (October 25, 2016): 192, 206; "The World's 50 Greatest Leaders," *Fortune* (April 1, 2016): 70–71; "Jeff Bezos," *Entrepreneur* (December 2015): 37; L. Rao, "A Leader With His Head in the Cloud," *Fortune* (July 1, 2015): 44–46; L. Stevens and G. Bensinger, "Amazon Seeks to Ease Ties With UPS," *The Wall Street Journal* (February 5, 2015): A1, A6; D. Leonard, "Will Amazon Kill FedEx?" *BusinessWeek* (August 31, 2016): 46–51; A. Vance, Jeff Bezos Just Ignited a New Space Race," *BusinessWeek* (December 7–13, 2015): 18–19; G. Bensinger and L. Stevens, "Amazon to Build Grocery Stores," *The Wall Street Journal* (October 12, 2016): A1; G. Bensinger and L. Stevens, "Amazon Takes Aim at UPS and FedEx," *The Wall Street Journal* (September 28, 2016): A1, A10.

The Environment

LO 2-1

Explain the five internal environmental factors and how nine external environmental factors can affect the internal business environment.

Organizations conduct business using their internal resources,[1] and how firms conduct business is affected by their external environment.[2] Thus, managers need to align the fit between their internal conditions and external environments[3] through continually monitoring both environments.[4] In this section, we begin with the internal followed by the external environment.

The Internal Environment

Organizations are groups of people working together for a common purpose.[5] They are created to produce products and/or services for customers using their resources. The organization's **internal environment** *includes the factors that affect its performance from within its boundaries.* They are called internal factors because they are within the organization's control, as opposed to external factors, which are outside the organization's control. The five internal environmental factors that we'll talk about in this section are presented in Exhibit 2-1. These five factors must be coordinated effectively and efficiently.[6]

internal environment Factors that affect an organization's performance from within its boundaries.

mission An organization's purpose or reason for being.

Mission. The late guru Peter Drucker said that, organizations need a clear purpose.[7] What is the ultimate shared purpose?[8] The organization's **mission** *is its purpose or reason for being.* It states why the firm exists and what greater good it serves.[9] What do you do?[10] "Here's who we are, here's what we do,"[11] and here's how we differ from our competitors.[12]

Here are some simple example mission statements **Snapchat** delivers disappearing photos, and **Ikea** sells nicely designed flat-pack furniture.[13] Here are two more formally stated missions.

- **Walmart**'s mission is to help people save money so they can live better.[14]
- The mission of **Springfield College** is to educate students in spirit, mind, and body for leadership in service to humanity by building upon its foundation of humanics and academic excellence.[15]

Companies don't always define their mission as we would expect. How would you say **Machine Zone** (a game of war), the **Giants** (a baseball team), **Domino's** (a pizza company), and **McDonald's** define their missions? "We're a technology company. We're really not a game company."[16] "We're a media and entertainment company, not just a sports team."[17] "We're in the delivery business."[18] "We're in the real estate business";[19] McDonald's real estate value is estimated to have topped $40 billion.[20]

The mission can change, such as at **Microsoft** going from delivering Windows and Office to "developing technology to help people live better lives and businesses run more efficiently."[21] IBM was a computer company. Today **CEO Ginni Rometty** says **IBM** is an enterprise innovation company.[22] The mission should also be relevant and known by all stakeholders,[23] especially employees, so they can stay focused on accomplishing the mission and goals.[24] **Stakeholders** are people whose interests are affected by organizational behavior, including employees, customers, and government. Stakeholders are listed in Exhibit 2-4 and discussed later.

The mission is an expression of the ends the organization strives to attain. The other internal environmental factors are considered the means to achieve the ends.[25] Exhibit 2-1 illustrates how all factors of the internal environment are means to achieving the organization's mission. Note that managers develop the mission and set objectives, but the managers are a means to an end. You are responsible for helping to achieve your organization's mission.

Management and Culture. Top-level managers are responsible for the organization's performance as they develop the visionary mission, strategies, and plans to achieve success.[26] Clearly, **FedEx** would not be the success it is today without its founder and CEO, **Frederick W. Smith**, nor would **Facebook** without **Mark Zuckerberg**.

An **organizational culture** *consists of the values, beliefs, and assumptions about appropriate behavior that members of an organization share.* The culture has to be based on the mission,[27] because firms need the right culture to achieve their mission.[28] Because culture is such an important part of management, we will discuss it in more detail after we have discussed the environment.

Resources. As stated in Chapter 1, organizational resources include human, financial, physical, and informational. Human resources (capital) is the most important,[29] because people develop and achieve the organization's mission and objectives through the other three resources.[30]

Structure. *Structure* refers to the way in which an organization groups its resources to accomplish its mission.[31] As discussed in Chapter 1, an organization is a system structured into departments such as finance, marketing, production, and so on. Each of these departments affects the organization as a whole, and each department is affected by the other departments. All of an organization's resources must be structured effectively to achieve its mission.[32] You will learn more about organizational structure in Chapter 7.

Systems Process. Organizations structure resources to transform inputs into outputs, primarily to make and deliver products and services,[33] such as a **Porsche** car or **FedEx** package. However, we all have a systems process to accomplish our tasks/job. The **systems process** *is the technology used to transform inputs into outputs to make and deliver products and services.* The systems process has four components:

1. *Inputs.* Inputs are an organization's resources that are transformed into products or services. At **FedEx**, the primary input is the millions of packages to be delivered worldwide daily.

2. *Transformation.* Transformation is the conversion of inputs into outputs. At FedEx, the packages (input) go to the hub (transformation), where they are sorted for delivery.

3. *Outputs.* Outputs are the products or services offered to customers. At FedEx, the packages are delivered to customers; the service of package delivery is FedEx's output.

4. *Feedback.* Feedback provides a means of control to ensure that the inputs and transformation process are producing the desired results. FedEx uses computers to gain feedback by real-time tracking of packages to help ensure that they are delivered on time.

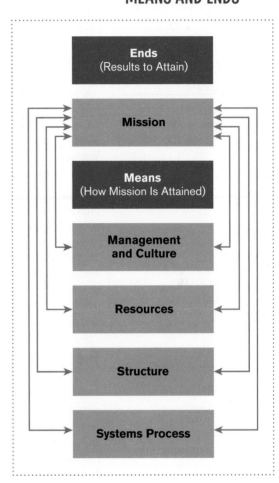

EXHIBIT 2-1

INTERNAL ENVIRONMENTAL MEANS AND ENDS

WORK
APPLICATION 2-1

For each work application in this chapter, use a different organization, or several different ones, for your examples.

State the mission of an organization, preferably an organization you work for or have worked for.

organizational culture The values, beliefs, and assumptions about appropriate behavior that members of an organization share.

systems process The method used to transform inputs into outputs to make and deliver products and services.

WORK
APPLICATION 2-2

Illustrate the systems process for an organization you work for or have worked for.

WORK
APPLICATION 2-3

Identify the quality and value of a product you purchased recently.

See Exhibit 2-2 for an illustration of the systems process. Note that technology is used to make and deliver products and services, and the technology often is not high tech. In fact, there are companies called low tech.

Quality is an important internal factor within the systems process. Customers determine *quality* by comparing a product's actual functioning to their requirements to determine value. *Customer value* is the perceived benefit of a product, used by customers to determine whether to buy the product. Customers don't simply buy a product itself. They buy the benefit they expect to derive from that product. Value is what motivates us to buy products.

Total quality management is the commonly used term for stressing quality within an organization. **Total quality management (TQM)** *is the process that involves everyone in an organization focusing on the customer to continually improve product value.* The two primary principles of TQM are (1) focusing on delivering customer value and (2) continually improving the system and its processes. The Japanese term for continuous improvement is *kaizen*. You will learn more about quality and TQM in Chapter 15. See Exhibit 2-3 for a review of the components of the internal environment.

Amazon's (**IOM 1**) top manager is still its founder, **Jeff Bezos**, who is the company's president, CEO, and chairman of the board. Amazon's mission is to be Earth's most customer-centric company for five primary customer sets: consumers, sellers, developers, enterprises, and content creators. In addition, it provides services, such as advertising services and cobranded credit card agreements.[34] Its primary resources are the Internet and its computer system and merchandise. Its primary retail systems process inputs are customer product orders that are transformed/filled and shipped to the customer, resulting in an output of sales that have created customer value. Amazon's primary structure is having a U.S. headquarters and subsidiaries in other countries.

The External Environment

The organization's **external environment** *includes the factors outside its boundaries that affect its performance.* Managers have very limited influence over what happens outside the organization. They need to continually align their internal environment with changes in the external environment,[35] which can result in changing the mission and organizational culture and shifting priorities and goals. The successful companies are the ones that keep changing.[36] It is also important to have good relationships with external stakeholders, because they provide access to resources.[37]

External Environmental Factors. The nine major external factors are listed in what follows. The first five are known as *task factors*, and the other four are known as *general factors*. Here, we briefly discuss how each external factor influences how you conduct business.

- **Customers.** Business success is based on customer relationships and providing the products customers want.[38] Without giving customers value, you don't have a business.
- **Competition.** Organizations must compete for customers. When a competitor changes prices, firms tend to match prices to keep customers. When competitors offer improved or better products, firms tend to do likewise.
- **Suppliers.** Organizations buy resources from suppliers. Therefore, a firm's performance is affected by suppliers.[39]
- **Labor Force.** The employees of an organization have a direct effect on its performance. Management recruits human resources from the available labor force outside its boundaries. Some jobs are easy to fill, whereas there is a shortage of some highly skilled workers.
- **Shareholders.** The owners of a corporation, known as *shareholders*, influence management.[40] They vote for the directors of the corporation, who hire and fire top management.
- **Society.** Our society, to a great extent, determines what are acceptable business practices.[41] Individuals and activist groups have formed to pressure business for changes.

total quality management (TQM) The process that involves everyone in an organization focusing on the customer to continually improve product value.

external environment The factors outside of an organization's boundaries that affect its performance.

2-1 APPLYING THE CONCEPT

The Internal Environment

EXHIBIT 2-2   THE SYSTEMS PROCESS

Identify the internal environmental factor underlying each statement.

A. management and culture

B. mission

C. resources

D. systems process

E. structure

_____ 1. "At **Dunkin Donuts** we sell donuts, but we make more money on real estate by renting our facilities to franchisees."

_____ 2. "The department of business under the School of A&S at **Springfield College** is going to be expanded to become the School of Management."

_____ 3. "After a six-month search, the board finally hired a new CEO from our competitor."

_____ 4. "At **Big Y** supermarkets we buy vegetables, cut them up, place them in bags, and sell them as salad."

_____ 5. "As the minimum wage continues to increase, **Wendy's** is buying machines to replace order takers."

- **Technology.** Technology has changed the speed and the manner in which organizations conduct and transact business, and they are often a major part of a firm's systems process.

- **The Economy.** No organization has control over economic growth, inflation, interest rates, foreign exchange rates, and so on, but they clearly affect business operations.

- **Governments.** National, state, and local governments all set laws and regulations that businesses must obey, and when they change, businesses must conform to the changed environment.[42]

In other words, to a large extent, businesses can't do whatever they want to do; the nine stakeholders, especially government, influence what they can and cannot do.[43] Just at the Federal level, US Federal regulatory agencies employ some 279,000 full-time employees, and regulatory activity cost $6.2 billion in 2016.[44] State and local laws and regulations vary; **DraftKing** was required by some state laws to stop fantasy sports games.[45] At the local level, there are some laws stating that you may need a license to start a business, where you can do business, and even regulations as to what type and size signs you can have and where you have to place them.

Dynamic Environments and Interactive Management. Organizational environments are becoming more dynamic, turbulent, complex, and competitive[46] as change takes place at an incredibly fast pace.[47] There is always the opportunity that someone will come out of nowhere and crush you. Today's managers need to adapt to changing conditions[48] to maintain the fit between the internal and external environments.[49] Management does so through *environmental scanning*—searching the environment for important events or issues that might affect the firm. But at the same time, change should be interactive. Focus on thriving, not simply surviving.

According to **Russell Ackoff**, unlike reactive managers (who make changes only when forced to by external factors) and responsive managers (who try to adapt to the environment by predicting and preparing for change before they are required to do so), interactive managers design a desirable future and invent ways of bringing it about.[50] They believe they are capable of creating a significant part of the future and controlling its effects on them. They try to prevent threats, not merely prepare for them, and to create opportunities, not merely exploit them. Rather than reacting or responding, interactive managers make things happen for their benefit and for that of their stakeholders. **Apple** was interactive when it created the

WORK
APPLICATION 2-4

Give an example of how one firm's competitors have affected that business.

WORK
APPLICATION 2-5

Give an example of how technology has affected one or more organizations, preferably one you work for or have worked for.

2-2 APPLYING THE CONCEPT

The External Environment

Identify which external environmental factor is referred to in each statement.

A. customers

B. competition

C. suppliers

D. labor force

E. shareholders

F. society

G. technology

H. the economy

I. governments

_____ 6. "The owners of the company will get to vote on its being acquired or staying independent."

_____ 7. "Are you going to close that sale to **Costco**?"

_____ 8. "If we don't get a 4% raise, the **Teamsters** union will go on strike at our company."

_____ 9. "Animal activist groups pressured the **Ringling Brothers** circus to the point that it will stop having elephant acts in 2018."

_____ 10. "**KFC** bought some bad chickens in China, and sales declined."

_____ 11. "Our company was going to be sold to **Sprint**, but the government said that would be in violation of antitrust laws."

_____ 12. "**Tesla** is working on software for its cars to be self-driven."

_____ 13. "**LinkedIn** and other social media websites took some of the traffic flow away from **Facebook**."

_____ 14. "Since the recession ended, we have had an increase in sales, but revenues are still not above prerecession levels."

Adam Glanzman/Getty Images

At the **New Balance** shoe factory, employees wear protective gear in compliance with government safety regulations.

first PC and changed how we listen to and buy music and how we use our phones.

Amazon (**IOM 2**) is customer driven. Selling products it does not make requires good suppliers. **Walmart** and **Alibaba** are competing to take its online customers,[51] and it is fighting with **Microsoft**, **IBM**, and **Google** over cloud services.[52] Amazon is a corporation with stockholders, and it has a global workforce. It has invested billions in technology. Amazon.com is affected by economic growth, inflation, interest rates, and foreign exchange rates in more than 100 countries, and it must meet their laws and regulations. As a business grows, the complexity of its internal and external environments increases.

As shown in Exhibit 2-3,[53] in the inner circle, a business has control of its five internal environmental factors, but it is influenced in the middle circle by its local nine external environmental factors[54] and in the outer circle by its global environment.[55] Imagine the complexity of **Xerox** conducting business in 160 countries[56] with different local external environments. In the next chapter, we will discuss conducting business in a global environment.

LO 2-2

Describe the three levels of organizational culture and their relationship to each other.

Organizational Culture

Organizational culture should be how the firm achieves its mission by living its values and beliefs on a daily basis.[57] The culture should cultivate people who care about each other and about their work.[58] Fostering the right organizational culture is one of the most important responsibilities of a chief executive, say **Google** cofounders.[59] Here are two examples of what CEOs are saying about organizational culture. **CEO/Founder Tory Burch**, of **Tory Burch LLC** (a $3 billion fashion empire), says, "Culture is everything."[60] MLB's **San Francisco Giants**

EXHIBIT 2-3   THE ORGANIZATIONAL ENVIRONMENT

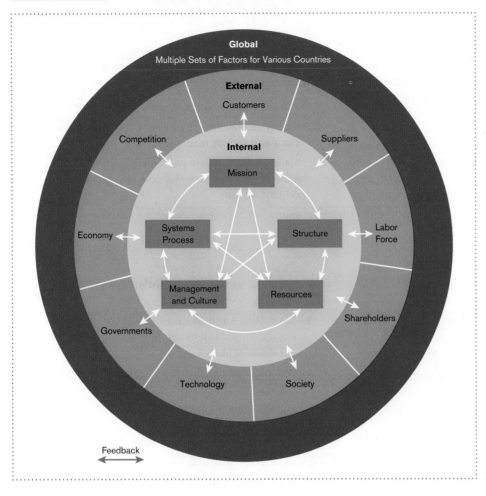

CEO **Larry Baer** says, "It's all about creating a culture."[61] Plus, in a survey of 3,300 executives, respondents stated that culture is even more important than leadership.[62]

Many firms, including **3M**, **USG**, and **Textron**, focus on developing an innovative culture.[63] **Under Armour founder and CEO Kevin Plank** says, "winning is a part of our culture—it's who we are. And culture is formed on habits."[64] **FedEx** has its people—Service—profit philosophy and its goal to ensure time-certain delivery.

In this section, we will discuss how employees learn organizational culture, the three levels of culture, strong and weak cultures, managing and changing cultures, and organizational learning.

Organizational Culture Artifacts

Learning the Organizational Culture Through Artifacts. Organizational culture is primarily learned through observing people and events. Simply, you watch and listen to people and learn the culture of what you should and shouldn't do. More complex, there are six artifacts of organizational culture, which are important ways that employees learn about it:

1. *Heroes,* such as founders **Sam Walton** of **Walmart** and **Herb Kelleher** of **Southwest Airlines**, and others who have made outstanding contributions to their organizations.

2. *Stories* are narratives,[65] and they are a good way to convey cultural knowledge.[66] They are often about founders and others who have made extraordinary efforts, such as **Sam Walton** visiting every **Walmart** store yearly. Public statements and speeches can also be considered stories.

2-1   JOIN THE DISCUSSION ETHICS & SOCIAL RESPONSIBILITY

Downsizing and Part-Time Workers

As firms struggle to compete in the global economy, many have downsized. *Downsizing* is the process of cutting resources to get more done with less and thereby increase productivity. In some firms, the positions formerly held by full-time employees are filled by part-time workers. Using part-time employees saves companies money because such employees do not receive any benefits (e.g., health insurance), in contrast to full-time employees, who are entitled to benefits. Walmart is known for maintaining a very high ratio of part-time to full-time employees as a way of keeping costs down. Walmart's employment policy is one of the reasons the chain can offer lower prices.

1. Is downsizing ethical and socially responsible?

2. Is using part-time employees rather than full-time ones ethical and socially responsible?

3. Would you be willing to pay higher prices at stores, such as Walmart, so that more full-time workers could replace part-time workers?

Michael Short/Bloomberg via Getty Images

Google is consistently rated one of the top companies to work for, in part because of its casual atmosphere that encourages employees to participate in discussions about company decisions.

WORK
APPLICATION 2-6

Identify the cultural heroes, stories, symbols, slogans, rituals, and ceremonies for an organization you are/were a member of.

3. *Slogans,* such as **McDonald's** Q, S, C, and V (or quality, service, cleanliness, and value).

4. *Symbols,* such as company logos, team mascots, plaques, pins, jackets, and so on. Winning a pink **Cadillac** at **Mary Kay**.

5. *Rituals,* such as a high-five, ringing a gong after making a deal, a chest bump, and so on.[67]

6. *Ceremonies,* such as awards dinners for top achievers at **GE**.

Organizational Culture Levels, Strength, and Health

Three Levels of Culture. The three **levels of culture** *are behavior, values and beliefs, and assumptions.* Exhibit 2-4 illustrates the three levels of culture.

1. **Behavior**—Behavior includes the observable things that people do and say or the actions employees take. Heroes, stories, slogans, symbols, rituals, and ceremonies are all part of behavior-level culture.

2. **Values and Beliefs**—Values represent the way people believe they ought to behave. Values and beliefs guide decision making and shape the behavior that results in level 1 culture. Although organizations use all six artifacts to convey the important values and beliefs, the slogan is critical to level 2 culture. A *slogan* expresses key values.

3. **Assumptions**—Assumptions are values and beliefs that are so deeply ingrained that they are considered unquestionably true and taken for granted. Because assumptions are shared, they are rarely discussed. They serve as an "automatic pilot" to guide behavior. Assumptions are often the most stable and enduring part of culture and are difficult to change.

Strong and Weak Cultures. Organizational cultural strength is characterized by a continuum from strong to weak. Organizations with strong cultures have employees who subconsciously know the shared assumptions; consciously know the values and beliefs; agree with the shared assumptions, values, and beliefs; and behave as expected. Organizations with many employees who do not behave as expected have weak cultures. In a strong culture, the group peer pressures nonconformists to behave as expected, including getting social loafers to do their share of the work.[68]

levels of culture Behavior, values and beliefs, and assumptions.

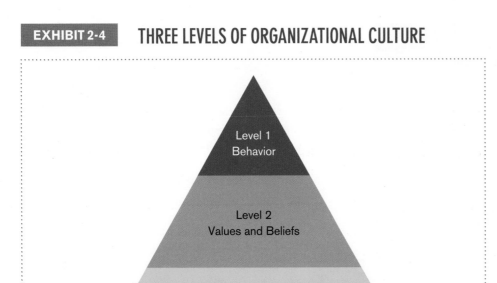

EXHIBIT 2-4   THREE LEVELS OF ORGANIZATIONAL CULTURE

Level 1
Behavior

Level 2
Values and Beliefs

Level 3
Assumptions

The primary benefits of a strong culture include easier communication and cooperation. Employees exhibit unity of direction, and consensus is easier to reach. The primary disadvantage is the threat of becoming stagnant and not changing when you should.

Healthy and Unhealthy Cultures. Organizational health is on a continuum from healthy to unhealthy. The continuum can also be thought of as positive or negative. A *healthy culture* has positive values that are implemented that contribute to success. Conversely, a culture can have unhealthy factors that are negative and hinder success and can lead to failure. Being on a continuum, a firm can have elements of both healthy and unhealthy cultures.

Two examples of unhealthy cultures are the following: **Wells Fargo Bank** was caught creating accounts for customers that they did not want, resulting in fees that they had to return. **VW** was caught devising software to lower emissions tests, resulting in large recalls and government fines. The VW CEO stated that its culture was flawed, as it tolerated rule breaking that allowed the deception to continue for a decade.[69]

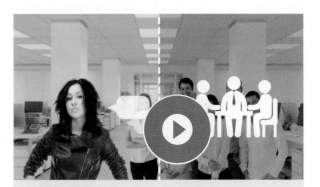

MANAGEMENT IN ACTION
Organizational Culture

Managing and Changing Cultures and the Learning Organization

Managing Organizational Culture. Strong, healthy cultures don't happen by accident, and it's not easy;[70] they are taught.[71] **Symbolic leaders** *articulate a vision for an organization and reinforce the culture through slogans, symbols, and ceremonies.* **Larry Page** of **Google** and **Jeff Bezos** of **Amazon** are often cited as examples of great symbolic leaders. Symbolic leaders manage, change, and merge cultures.

Organizational culture can be managed by drawing continual attention to its six artifacts. If any of these artifacts of a strong, healthy culture are missing or weak, top management can work to strengthen the culture. However, strengthening an organizational culture is not a program with a starting and ending date; it is an ongoing process.

2-3 APPLYING THE CONCEPT

Strong and Weak Cultures

Identify whether each statement reflects an organization with a strong or weak culture.

A. strong culture

B. weak culture

____ 15. "It's hard to know if I need to follow the ethics code because managers act unethically every now and then."

____ 16. "Oh no, do I really have to listen to the story about how the company founder Ted walked three miles in a snowstorm to deliver the package on time again?"

____ 17. "Everyone in the department acts differently, so I guess I can just be me rather than trying to act in a manner acceptable to others."

____ 18. "I started to tell this 'dumb blond' joke, and the other employees all gave me a dirty look, so I stopped."

____ 19. "When I walked around the department during my job interview, I realized I'd have to come to work in formal attire because all the women were wearing dresses or suits."

Changing Organizational Culture. Organizational cultures often need to be changed to ensure organizational success. However, changing cultures is not easy. **Wells Fargo** and **VW** are working to change the unhealthy parts of their cultures. **Satya Nadella** was hired as CEO and is working to change **Microsoft's** culture to inject urgency and speed, and Nadella told employees to embrace the new ways or leave.[72]

Learning Organizations. The learning organization is not a program with steps to follow. It's about managing and changing the culture to adapt to the ever-changing environment. A **learning organization** *has a culture that values sharing knowledge so as to adapt to the changing environment and continuously improve.* **IBM CEO Rometty** says that you can actually take any product or service and put learning inside of it. This is the current and future challenge for learning organizations because it will change the basis of a business.[73]

The learning organization is based on knowledge sharing to improve. Everyone you meet in your personal and professional life knows more about something than you do. So your job is to get them to pass that knowledge on to you so you can continually improve yourself.[74]

Amazon (**IOM 3**) is a learning organization with an informal but serious, very competitive culture—even serious about having fun. One of the many corporate mantras on display for workers reads "Work Hard, Have Fun, Make History." It is data driven with a bias for action. Amazon is obsessed with customers, continuous improvement of its website, and sophisticated fulfillment systems to get orders to customers reliably and quickly. Amazon strives to maintain a culture that allows people to create innovative solutions to the challenges it faces. It celebrates its success with informal and formal ceremonies, including picnics on the company lawn. **Jeff Bezos** is a hero, with stories often told about him. However, recall that Amazon has been accused of having an unhealthy, overly competitive, cutthroat culture that rewards cruelty and backstabbing, which Bezos denies.[75]

LO 2-3

Explain why people use unethical behavior, why and how they justify their unethical behavior, and three factors that influence behavior to be ethical or unethical.

learning organization An organization with a culture that values sharing knowledge so as to adapt to the changing environment and continuously improve.

Business Ethics

Dishonesty has become an accepted part of daily life for many people in their personal, government, and business lives.[76] Is there any wonder why the **Association to Advance Collegiate Schools of Business** (AACSB, introduced in Chapter 1) requires business ethics as part of the curriculum?[77] To improve ethics, business schools are improving their curriculum.[78] Because ethics is so important, we are going to discuss it in two separate sections. In this section, we first define business ethics and views of business ethics and discuss why people use unethical behavior and how they justify doing so. Next, we cover three factors

2-1 SELF-ASSESSMENT

How Ethical Is Your Behavior?

For this exercise, you will respond to the same set of statements twice. The first time you read them, focus on your own behavior and the frequency with which you behave in certain ways. On the line before each statement number, place a number from 1 to 4 that represents how often you do that behavior (or how likely you would be to do it):

1	2	3	4
Frequently			Never

The numbers allow you to determine your level of ethics. You can be honest, as you will not tell others in class your score. *Sharing ethics scores is not part of the exercise.*

Next, go through the list of statements a second time, focusing on other people in an organization that you work for now or one you have worked for. Place an *O* on the line after the number of each statement if you have observed someone doing this behavior; place an *R* on the line if you reported this behavior within the organization or externally: *O* = observed, and *R* = reported.

In College

_____ 1. _____ Cheating on homework assignments

_____ 2. _____ Cheating on exams

_____ 3. _____ Submitting as your own work papers that were completed by someone else

On the Job

_____ 4. _____ Lying to others to get what you want or to stay out of trouble

_____ 5. _____ Coming to work late, leaving work early, or taking long breaks/lunches and getting paid for them

_____ 6. _____ Socializing, goofing off, or doing personal work rather than doing the work that you are getting paid to do

_____ 7. _____ Calling in sick to get a day off when you are not sick

_____ 8. _____ Using an organization's phone, computer, Internet access, copier, mail, or car for personal use

_____ 9. _____ Taking home company tools or equipment for personal use without permission

_____ 10. _____ Taking home organizational supplies or merchandise

_____ 11. _____ Giving company supplies or merchandise to friends or allowing friends to take them without saying anything

_____ 12. _____ Applying for reimbursement for expenses for meals, travel, or other expenses that weren't actually incurred

_____ 13. _____ Taking spouse or friends out to eat or on business trips and charging their expenses to the organizational account

_____ 14. _____ Accepting gifts from customers/suppliers in exchange for giving them business

_____ 15. _____ Cheating on your taxes

_____ 16. _____ Misleading a customer to make a sale, such as promising rapid delivery dates

_____ 17. _____ Misleading competitors to get information to use to compete against them, such as pretending to be a customer/supplier

_____ 18. _____ Taking credit for another employee's accomplishments

_____ 19. _____ Selling more of a product than the customer needs in order to get the commission

_____ 20. _____ Spreading rumors about coworkers or competitors to make yourself look better so as to advance professionally or to make more sales

_____ 21. _____ Lying for your boss when asked or told to do so

(Continued)

(Continued)

_____ 22. _____ Deleting information that makes you look bad or changing information to make yourself look better

_____ 23. _____ Allowing yourself to be pressured, or pressuring others, to sign off on documents that contain false information

_____ 24. _____ Allowing yourself to be pressured, or pressuring others, to sign off on documents you haven't read, knowing they may contain information or describe decisions that might be considered inappropriate

_____ 25. _____ If you were to give this assessment to a coworker with whom you do not get along, would she or he agree with your answers? If your answer is yes, write a 4 on the line before the statement number; if your answer is no, write a 1 on the line.

After completing the second phase of the exercise (indicating whether you have observed or reported any of the behaviors), list any other unethical behaviors you have observed. Indicate if you reported the behavior, using *R*.

26. _____

27. _____

28. _____

Note: This self-assessment is not meant to be a precise measure of your ethical behavior. It is designed to get you thinking about ethics and about your behavior and that of others from an ethical perspective. All of these actions are considered unethical behavior in most organizations.

Another ethical aspect of this exercise is your honesty when rating your behavior. How honest were you?

Scoring: To determine your ethics score, add up the numbers for all 25 statements. Your total will be between 25 and 100. Place the number that represents your score on the continuum below. The higher your score, the more ethical your behavior.

25	30	40	50	60	80	90	100

Unethical   **Ethical**

that influence behavior that is ethical or unethical. In the next section, you will learn guides to ethical behavior and how to manage ethics. Let's begin by completing the Self-Assessment that follows to determine how ethical your behavior is.

Business Ethics and Justifying Unethical Behavior

What Are Ethics? Ethics *are the standards of right and wrong that influence behavior.* Right behavior is considered ethical, and wrong behavior is considered unethical. Honesty is ethical, which means lying, cheating, and stealing are unethical. Lying has long been identified as a critical unethical behavior.[79] We constantly have to make decisions that are ethical or unethical.[80]

Government laws and regulations are designed to govern business behavior. The **Sarbanes-Oxley Act** of 2002 was passed to tighten the laws affecting business ethics. However, ethics go beyond legal requirements to do the right thing even when we don't have to. It is not always easy to distinguish between ethical and unethical behavior, such as accepting a gift (ethical) versus taking a bribe (unethical).[81] But our objective is to help you know the difference.

Views of Ethics. Here are three ways to view ethics. However, we should try to implement them all based on the situation.

- *Utilitarian view* states that ethical decisions should be based on creating greater good for society (provide the greater good for the greatest number based on consequences/outcomes of actions).

ethics Standards of right and wrong that influence behavior.

- *Rights view* states that ethical decisions should respect and protect individual privileges (right to privacy, free speech).
- *Justice view* states that ethical decisions should be made to treat everyone fairly and impartially (don't discriminate, which we will discuss in the next chapter).

Why Do People Behave Unethically? Most people understand right and wrong behavior and have a conscience. So why do good people do bad things? Most people aren't simply good or bad. Of people, 1% will always be honest, 1% will always be dishonest, and 98% will be unethical at times, but just a little.[82] We respond to "incentives" and can usually be manipulated to behave ethically or unethically if we find the right incentives.[83] The incentive (or reason we are unethical at times) is usually for personal gain,[84] to avoid getting into trouble, and some people don't believe the rules apply to them.[85] Why did people at **Countrywide Financial** give mortgages to people whose homes would most certainly be repossessed?[86] Why did people at **Wells Fargo Bank** open accounts that customers didn't ask for? There were financial gains for doing so, and some employees feared losing their jobs if they didn't meet high quotas.

How Do People Justify Their Unethical Behavior? Few people see themselves as unethical. We all want to view ourselves in a positive manner.[87] Therefore, when we do behave unethically, we usually justify the behavior by *rationalizing* to ourselves that there was a good reason for the behavior.[88] Justification protects our *self-concept* so that we don't have to feel bad.[89] If we are only a little dishonest, we can still feel good about our sense of integrity.[90] Our memory tends to fade as we forget about unethical behavior, so we repeat it, and it can become a habit for some.[91]

Here are some common justifications for our unethical behavior.[92] *Everyone else does it*—we all cheat in college; everyone takes things home (steals). *I did it for the good of others or the company*—I cooked the books so the company looks good; we are not terrorists, but we are freedom fighters who bomb to help our cause. *I was only following orders*—my boss made me do it. *I'm not as bad as the others*—I only call in sick when I'm not sick once in a while. *Disregard for or distortion of consequences*—No one will be hurt if I inflate the figures, and I will not get caught. And if I do, I'll just get a slap on the wrist anyway.

Caution Against Escalation of Unethical Behavior. It is important to understand the subtlety of how unethical behavior can take hold of you. Today we live in a time of ethical confusion, with *relativism* saying there is no absolute truth or right or wrong—which contradicts itself by using an absolute. It's tempting to change the rules or truth and be unethical for personal gain, justifying the behavior by telling ourselves it's OK "to do whatever I want," "to do what works for me," or "to do what makes me feel good," which often leads to unethical behavior. The things we do repeatedly determine our character.[93]

Did the people at **Enron** and other companies start out planning to lie, cheat, and steal? Most didn't. What tends to happen is the company doesn't hit the target numbers, and the employees think "let's give inflated numbers this quarter, and we will make it up next quarter, and no one will know or get hurt in any way." The problem is, for several quarters the same thing happens so they get to the point of not being able or willing to admit their unethical/illegal behavior until they get caught. Little white lies are not little.[94] The subtlety creeps up on us because the more we engage in the unethical behavior, and especially if we don't get caught, the easier it is to be unethical. Everything tends to come out in due time anyway, so it's better if it happens early.[95] The moral of the story is don't take the first step that leads to escalation of unethical behavior.

Does Ethical Behavior Pay? Let's take a personal view. Recall from Chapter 1 that executives identified integrity as the most important management quality for success. Many companies seek integrity in job applicants and even test for ethics.[96] Also, recall our question "Do you want to be happy?" and that job satisfaction (happiness) comes from strong, rewarding relationships.[97] Relationships are based on trust,[98] and you get and keep friends and customers based on trust.[99] Unethical behavior that you justify might give you some type of short-term gain, but in the long run, you've sabotaged yourself.[100]

How? Because we usually eventually get caught being dishonest and lose people's trust—hurting our relationships, sometimes losing friends, and even going to jail (like **Bernie Madoff** for his Ponzi scheme). Victims of dishonesty often use counterproductive behavior and revenge tactics.[101] It can take years to build trust and only one lie to destroy it. How many friends do you have who are dishonest with you and take advantage of you for their own personal gain at your expense? Founder and **CEO Ray Dalio of Bridgewater** hedge fund says that being radically truthful and transparent pays off in excellent performance.[102] So yes, truth absolutely, unequivocally does matter.[103] At the end of the day, the truth is all that matters.[104]

Factors That Influence Behavior to Be Ethical or Unethical

If you want to have integrity, here are three things to realize that can influence your behavior in the right or wrong direction.

Personality Traits and Attitudes. In Chapter 10, you will learn more about personality. For now, you probably already realize that because of their personalities, some people have a higher level of ethics than others, as integrity is considered a personality trait. Related to personality is our attitude toward ethics. People with integrity intentionally use ethical behavior, whereas unethical people don't consider whether their behavior is ethical or not—"it's all about me." Some people are at the point that they don't even realize they are dishonest and don't see anything wrong with lying.[105]

Moral Development. A second factor affecting ethical behavior is *moral development*, which refers to distinguishing right from wrong and choosing to do the right thing.[106] People's ability to make ethical choices is related to their level of moral development.[107] Recall that 98% of us will be unethical at times, but just a little.[108] So we can be on different levels for different issues and situations. The three levels of personal moral development are preconventional, conventional, and postconventional.

WORK
APPLICATION 2-8

Give an example from an organization where you work or have worked of behavior at each of the three levels of moral development.

The Situation. A third factor affecting ethical behavior is the situation. In certain situations, it can be tempting to be unethical, such as when you are negotiating.[109] Unsupervised people in highly competitive situations are more likely to engage in unethical behavior for personal gain or to stay out of trouble. Unethical behavior occurs more often when there is no formal ethics policy or code of ethics and when unethical behavior is not punished, and even more so when managers ask and reward employees for using unethical behavior.[110] In other words, people are more unethical when they believe they will not get caught or they will be given rewards.[111] Unethical behavior is also more likely when performance falls below aspiration levels—recall the **Countrywide** and **Wells Fargo** examples.

People are also less likely to report unethical behavior (blow the whistle) when they perceive the violation as not being serious or when they are friends of the offender. It takes high moral responsibility to be a *whistle-blower.*

LO 2-4

Identify four guides to ethical behavior and three things organizations should do to manage ethics.

Methods to Help Ensure Ethical Behavior

We continue our discussion of ethics in this section by providing guides that will help you make ethical choices and describe how organizations can manage ethics to help ensure employees use ethical behavior.

Guides to Ethical Behavior

WORK
APPLICATION 2-9

Give at least two organizational examples of unethical behavior and the justification that was used in each instance.

If we are going to make business more ethical, we have to start with ourselves,[112] and we should lead the way for others by our example.[113] Are you an ethical person? The Self-Assessment earlier in this chapter will help you answer this question. Every day in your personal and professional lives, you face decisions in which you can make ethical or unethical choices. Doing the right things isn't always easy.[114] We can all develop our ethical character. Following are some guides that can help you make the right decisions.

2-4 APPLYING THE CONCEPT

Level of Moral Development

Identify each statement by its level of moral development.

A. preconventional level

B. conventional level

C. postconventional level

____ 20. Carl says to Lolo, "There is no big deal in telling lies to customers. We are helping them buy a good product."

____ 21. Sandy says, "I can't lie to customers because it is against my Christian religion; it is a sin to lie."

____ 22. Latavia says to John, "You're not selling as much as the rest of us. You really should lie to customers like we do. If the boss asks why you aren't selling as much as the rest of us, you better not tell him we lie, or you will be sorry."

Golden Rule. Are you familiar with the **Jewish** and **Christian** Biblical Golden Rule: "Do unto others as you want them to do unto you," or "Don't do anything to anyone that you would not want someone to do to you"? Most religions have a variation of the Golden Rule, including **Buddhism**, **Confucianism**, **Hinduism**, **Islam**, and **Taoism**). The most successful **National Basketball Association (NBA)** coach, **Phil Jackson**, said, "Much of my outlook in life is from a spiritual direction."[115] The workplace and world could change overnight if we all followed this one simple guide to our behavior.

Four-Way Test. Rotary International has a motto, "Service Above Self." This is a great motto to live by because helping others, as opposed to the "What can you do for me?" mentality, will improve relationships. Rotary developed a four-way test to guide one's thoughts and behavior in business transactions to live the motto. The four questions are (1) Is it the truth? (2) Is it fair to all concerned? (3) Will it build goodwill and better friendship? (4) Will it be beneficial to all concerned? When making a decision, if you can answer yes to these four questions, your potential course of action is probably ethical.

Stakeholders' Approach to Ethics. Under the **stakeholders' approach to ethics**, when making decisions, you try to create a win-win situation for all relevant stakeholders so that everyone benefits from the decision. Unfortunately, this is not always easy, because multiple stakeholders often have conflicting interests,[116] such as a layoff. However, as **Salesforce .com CEO Marc Benioff** says, to successfully manage a modern organization, you need to have multistakeholder dialogues.[117] You can ask yourself one simple question to help you determine if your decision is ethical from a stakeholders' approach: "Would I be proud to tell relevant stakeholders my decision?" If you would be proud to tell relevant stakeholders your decision, it is probably ethical. If you would not be proud to tell others your decision or you keep rationalizing it, or if you are trying to cover your tracks,[118] the decision may not be ethical. You can't always create a win for everyone, but you can try.

Discernment and Advice. Before you act, use an ethical guide to discern if the behavior is ethical or not. If you are unsure whether a decision is ethical, talk to your boss, higher-level managers, and other people with high ethical standards. If you are reluctant to ask others for advice on an ethical decision because you may not like their answers, the decision may not be ethical.

Application of Ethical Guides. Research shows that making a decision without using an ethical guide leads to less ethical choices. Using ethical guides at the point of making a decision helps keep you honest.[119] So if you want to maintain or improve your relationships, be ethical and get in the habit of using an ethical guide when making decisions. Are you willing to commit to doing so now?

stakeholders' approach to ethics Creating a win-win situation for all relevant stakeholders so that everyone benefits from the decision.

| 2-5 | **APPLYING** THE CONCEPT |

Ethical Approach

Identify each statement by its approach to making ethical decisions.

A. Golden Rule

B. four-way test

C. stakeholders' approach

D. discernment and advice

E. code of ethics

_____ 23. I try to treat people the way I want them to treat me.

_____ 24. Cindy, what do you think of my decision for handling this situation?

_____ 25. I'm a member of Rotary International, so I use its approach when I make decisions.

_____ 26. I follow the guidelines the company gave all of us to use to make sure I'm doing the right thing.

_____ 27. I try to make sure that everyone affected by my decisions gets a fair deal.

Managing Ethics

An organization's ethics are based on the collective behavior of its employees. If each individual is ethical, the organization will be ethical. Its management's job to help ensure that everyone in the firm uses ethical behavior. Some organizations take ethics very seriously and even compete to be listed in the World's Most Ethical Companies, including **Knights of Columbus** insurance and **Marriott**.[120] Here are three things managers should do to help ensure employees use ethical behavior.

Codes of Ethics and Training. Also called *codes of conduct*,[121] codes of ethics state the importance of conducting business in an ethical manner and provide moral standard guidelines (dos and don'ts) for ethical behavior.[122] Most large businesses have written codes of ethics, and many provide ethics training for employees. For an example, see **Deloitte**'s "Code of Ethics & Professional Conduct" at www2.deloitte.com.

Top Management Support and Example. Managers are ultimately responsible for the behavior of their employees,[123] and they need to lead by setting an ethical example, because employees tend to copy their behavior.[124] Many large corporations have ethics officers responsible for developing their ethics codes and developing and conducting this training. For example programs, visit **Lockheed Martin**'s website (www.lockheedmartin.com) and search for training programs.

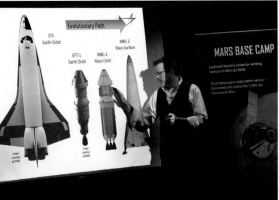

Enforcing Ethical Behavior and Whistle-Blowing. If employees are rewarded rather than punished for their unethical behavior, or if managers know about it and do nothing, both employees and managers are more likely to engage in unethical business practices.[125] But you need to be fair in judging and punishing the offender to avoid negative effects.[126]

As a means of enforcing ethical behavior, employees should be encouraged to become internal whistle-blowers. *Whistle-blowing* occurs when employees expose what they believe to be unethical behavior by their fellow employees. Whistle-blowing should begin internally, and information should go up the chain of command. If nothing is done, then the whistle-blower can go outside the organization as a last resort. According to the law and ethics, whistle-blowers should not suffer any negative consequences.

Lockheed Martin has a sophisticated program to manage ethics. The organization has ethics officers who create the ethics code and conduct ethics training for employees.

The Foreign Corrupt Practices Act (FCPA). The FCPA law bars U.S.-based or U.S.-listed companies from bribing foreign officials in exchange for business and requires them to keep accurate books and records. But it is sometimes hard to tell the difference between a legitimate business expense and a bribe. Thus, global companies need to clarify the difference in their code of ethics, top managers must set the example, and penalties for illegal behavior must be enforced. **GE** is known for taking pride in not paying bribes to gain business globally.

WORK
APPLICATION 2-10

Select a business and identify how it manages ethics.

Social Responsibility and Sustainability

Ethics and social responsibility are closely related, as being socially responsible is going beyond legal and economic obligations to do the right things and acting in ways that benefit stakeholders and society.[127] In this section, we'll discuss social responsibility to stakeholders, the levels of social responsibility, and sustainability.

LO 2-5

Characterize the three levels of social responsibility and explain its relationship with sustainability.

Social Responsibility to Stakeholders

What Is Social Responsibility? Social responsibility (SR) is often called *corporate social responsibility*, or CSR,[128] an umbrella term for exploring the responsibilities of business and its role in society.[129] SR is about doing good and doing no harm[130] and relationships with stakeholders.[131] When Google started, it had the motto, "Don't be evil."[132] **Social responsibility** *is the conscious effort to operate in a manner that creates a win-win situation for all stakeholders.* Notice we say making a "conscious effort." Why? Again, businesses can't always create a win-win for all their multiple stakeholders, because they often have conflicting objectives.[133]

Should Businesses Be Socially Responsible to Stakeholders? In the past, there was debate over this question. However, today, business is expected to improve the general welfare of society.[134] Major corporations have to be socially accountable because stakeholders, including customers, the media, and the public, are increasingly demand it.[135] Major corporations are expected to help solve the world's most challenging problems.[136] So again, if you run a business, you can't just do whatever you want to do. Like it or not, businesses have to be socially responsible.

Does It Pay to Be Socially Responsible? There is debate on the question of how SR affects corporate financial and economic performance.[137] But if it didn't benefit the company in some way, why would virtually all large public corporations have CSR programs? Some companies are using CSR as a strategy to increase profits.[138] Although it is difficult to measure the actual financial impact of CSR, in a study, companies considered to be highly socially responsible by **Forbes'** (including **American Express, F5 Networks, Ford, Peak Performer, PepsiCo, Pioneer Natural Resources, Southwest Airlines,** and **SVB Financial Group**) had an average return of 13.6% compared to 9.9% of those that have lower ratings of CSR.[139] Some companies with reputations for being SR have much larger profits than those that have poor reputations, including **Starbucks**, **Chipotle**, **Whole Foods**, and **Costco**.[140]

Blake Mycoskie opened a **TOMS** store in Venice, California, to further his buy-one-give-one mission to help provide shoes to children in need.

Social Entrepreneurs and Hybrid Organizations. There is growth in the number of *social entrepreneurs* who combine their concern for social issues with their desire for financial rewards.[141] Social entrepreneurs create *social enterprises* or hybrid organizations. *Hybrid organizations* pursue a social mission and sustain their operations through commercial activities through *work integration social enterprises (WISEs)*. The dual social and profit mission drives WISE social performance.[142]

   Blake Mycoskie founded **TOMS** shoes at age 29 to make money and help solve a social problem of children having no shoes to wear, resulting in blisters, sores, and infections. His business model is "With every pair you purchase, TOMS will give a pair of new shoes to a child in need. One for One." He wrote *Start Something That Matters* (2012) to guide others in helping society.[143] With a social mission, TOMS received lots of free publicity, and sales have increased, resulting in Mycoskie making lots of money for being SR.

social responsibility The conscious effort to operate in a manner that creates a win-win situation for all stakeholders.

The B Corp. B Corps (benefits corporation) are a new type of company that uses the power of business to solve social and environmental problems. B Corp is a title given to companies that meet the certification requirements. There are around 2,000 certified B Corps from 50 countries, including **Ben & Jerry's**, **Cabot**, **Etsy**, and **Patagonia**. For information on certification requirements, visit www.bcorporation.net.[144]

Responsibilities to Stakeholders. Here are some basic examples of how all companies need to be SR to their internal and external environmental stakeholders. Employees are the most valuable resource, and how the firm treats its employees is related to its performance.[145] Companies must provide *employees* with safe working conditions and with adequate pay and benefits. For *customers*, the company must provide safe products and services with customer value. For *society*, the company should improve the quality of life, or at least not destroy the environment. The company must compete fairly with *competitors*. The company must work with *suppliers* in a cooperative manner. It must abide by the laws and regulations of *government*. The company must strive to provide equal employment opportunities for the *labor force*. The company must provide *shareholders* with a reasonable profit.

WORK APPLICATION 2-11

Select a business and identify how it is socially responsible on a specific issue.

CSR Reporting. Virtually all of the *Fortune* 500 companies have formal CSR programs. Corporations are even measuring and assessing how well they meet their SR goals.[146] The measures are commonly called corporate social performance (CSP).[147] Visit your favorite large corporation's website, and you will most likely find a link stating how the firm engages in CSR; it is even included in most of the firm's annual reports, often called a *social audit* as its measure of social behavior.

2-2 JOIN THE DISCUSSION ETHICS & SOCIAL RESPONSIBILITY

Sex, Profanity, and Violence

The Federal Communications Commission (FCC) has the power to regulate television broadcasts. Advocates for more regulation (**Parents Television Council** and **Mediawatch**-UK) state that TV shows with violent acts, profanity, and sexual content should be shown later at night when children most likely will not be watching. For example, many *Seinfeld* episodes have sexual themes, and the show was not aired until 9:00 p.m., but now it's shown at all hours of the day. *Sex and the City, Jersey Shore, Keeping Up With the Kardashians*, and other shows with sexual content and violence are also shown at all hours.

Another related issue is that some advocates (both male and female) would like to stop or limit the portrayal of girls and women as sex objects and showing violence against them on TV and movies, in songs and music videos, and video games. They would like females to be portrayed as intellectuals that you would want to get to know as a person, not just as a sex object. Advocates believe that watching females portrayed as sex objects leads to a narrow view of the total person. Girls who aren't sexually attractive can have more negative self-perceptions, and boys can view girls simply as sex objects. Also, watching violence against females can lead to more violence against them.

However, advocates against regulation (**National Coalition Against Censorship**) don't want censorship at all, on the grounds that it violates free speech. They claim it's up to the parents and adults to restrict viewing TV and movies, listening to music and watching videos, and playing video games they don't approve of.

1. How does TV influence societal values? (Consider that many children watch as many as 5 hours of TV per day.)

2. Do TV shows that include sex and violence reflect religious and societal values?

3. Is it ethical and socially responsible to air TV shows with sexual content, profanity, and violence during hours when children are watching?

4. Is it ethical and socially responsible to portray women as sex objects and to show violence against them?

5. Should the FCC regulate the media, and if so, how far should it go? Should it make networks, music companies, and video games tone down the sex and violence or have greater restrictions on content?

Levels of Corporate Social Responsibility

Clearly, in today's society, the question is not whether business should be socially responsible but at what level of CSR the business should operate. Businesses do vary greatly in their social responsibility activities, based on the overall level of CSR at which they decide to operate.[148] Managers can choose to operate the business at one of three levels of CSR. The **levels of corporate CSR** are legal, ethical, and benevolent. However, a firm can be between levels or be on different levels for different issues. See Exhibit 2-5 for an illustration of the three levels.

Legal CSR. *Legal CSR* focuses on maximizing profits while obeying the law. In dealings with market stakeholders, these firms meet all of their legal responsibilities, such as fulfilling contract obligations and providing legally safe products while honoring guarantees and warranties. They do what it takes to beat the competition legally. **Philip Morris** and **Smith & Wesson** and other brands sell cigarettes and guns that are legal, but some question the ethics of the business.

Ethical CSR. *Ethical CSR* focuses on profitability and doing what is right, just, and fair. These companies do more than is required in dealing with market stakeholders. They meet reasonable societal expectations and exceed government laws and regulations. **CVS** voluntarily gave up selling legal cigarettes at an estimated cost of $2 billion a year.[149]

Benevolent CSR. *Benevolent CSR* focuses on profitability and helping society through philanthropy. These firms are *philanthropic*, giving gifts of money or other resources to charitable causes—often called giving back.[150] If you are attending a nonprofit college or university, the odds are that it receives money or other resources from companies, such as **Ford**, as part of its CSR programs. The founder of **Kenneth Cole Productions** says that giving as part of the journey to success makes the journey more meaningful.[151]

Let's face it: A company can't be benevolent if it is not making a profit[152]—you can't give away profits you don't make. **CVS** wouldn't have given up selling cigarettes if it wasn't profitable. In addition to giving corporate money, many rich entrepreneurs set up foundations and give their own money, such as the **Bill & Melinda Gates Foundation**, which gave away $1.55 billion in 2015.[153] **Facebook founder Mark Zuckerberg** plans to give away 99% of his Facebook stock, currently valued at $45 billion.[154] However, Mark and his wife **Priscilla Chang** are creating a limited-liability company rather than a foundation, which may become the new philanthropic model.[155]

A Situational Approach to CSR. Although firms have an overall guiding commitment to CSR, the level of CSR can and does vary based on individual issues. CSR has been called

---

EXHIBIT 2-5   # LEVELS OF CORPORATE SOCIAL RESPONSIBILITY

3. **Benevolent CSR.** Focus on profitability and helping society through philanthropy.

2. **Ethical CSR.** Focus on profitability and going beyond the law to do what is right, just, and fair.

1. **Legal CSR.** Focus on maximizing profits while obeying the law.

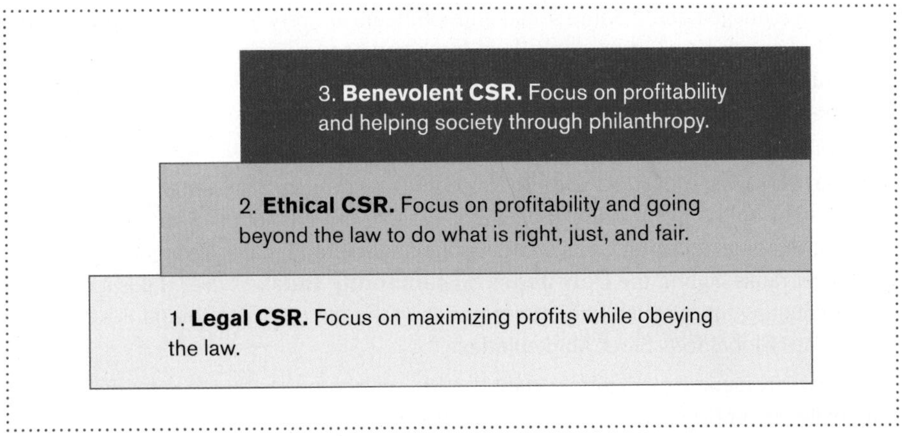

enlightened self-interest because firms will be motivated to engage in CSR activities when the benefits outweigh the costs.[156] However, each issue requires analysis, risk–reward considerations, and knowledge of how the stakeholder relations affect the overall health of the corporation.[157]

Amazon (IOM 4) is clearly on the benevolent level overall. However, it has been criticized for being only at the legal level (not being ethical) when it comes to not paying employees for the time it takes to get through the antitheft screen after their shifts in its warehouses, up to a half-hour per day. Employees even took Amazon to court to force it to pay, but the court said it doesn't have to pay, and it still refuses to do so.[158] Should Amazon move up to the ethical level and pay employees for that time?

Sustainability

What Is Sustainability? **Sustainability** *is meeting the needs of the present world without compromising the ability of future generations to meet their own needs.*[159] Society expects sustainability and for managers to use resources wisely and responsibly; protect the environment; minimize the amount of air, water, energy, minerals, and other materials used to produce the final goods we consume; recycle and reuse these goods to the extent possible rather than drawing on nature to replenish them; respect nature's calm, tranquility, and beauty; and eliminate toxins that harm people in the workplace and communities.[160] Thus, including sustainability in managing the business is being socially responsible.

Responsible leaders assess how to design products that will take advantage of the current environmental situation and how well a company's products perform with renewable resources.[161] *Sustainability* is now a business buzzword,[162] and based on the gravity of environmental problems, it is an important topic for all countries,[163] as is recognized by the AACSB.[164] Corporations are accepting the environment as an important external stakeholder.[165] The use of renewable energy is on the increase,[166] and sustainability standards are becoming the standard.[167]

What Is the Triple Bottom Line? Corporate sustainability requires managers to simultaneously address widely diverging but interconnected concern for the natural environment, social welfare, and economic prosperity of the firm.[168] Moving away from the single bottom line, SR managers are focusing on the triple bottom line, measuring profits, CSR, and environmental impact.[169] **Southwest Airlines** takes environmental awareness seriously and considers it part of its triple bottom line: profits, people, planet.[170] Some companies are using triple bottom-line accounting. Many corporations are addressing sustainability changes, and an important part of the reason is that it can pay to do so.[171] **Walmart** is saving billions in costs by reducing its environmental footprint.[172]

Sustainability Practices and Green Companies. Sustainability issues influence activities in the business world as organizations work to reduce their environmental impacts.[173] A *green company* acts in a way that minimizes damage to the environment. With the environmental problems such as air, water, and other forms of pollution, many new ventures have been created in green management.[174] Some social entrepreneurs are very interested in environmental issues and are starting businesses to help large companies become more sustainable.[175] **Pratt Industries** makes corrugated boxes using 100%-recycled paper, saving an estimated 50,000 trees a day, with an estimated company value of $3.4 billion.[176] With the trend toward online shopping and boxed delivery, Pratt is making an environmental impact.

Walmart is saving money by wasting less energy by putting solar panels on store roofs, using LED light bulbs, and making refrigerator cases more efficient.[177] **Unilever** is reducing its environmental footprint, as its sourcing of all agricultural materials went from 10% to 50%. Unilever ranks high in the **Dow Jones Sustainability Index**;[178] the DJSI is a family of indexes evaluating the sustainability performance of the largest 2,500 companies listed on the Dow Jones Global Total Stock Market Index.[179]

Sustainability management is important,[180] and a new corporate title has emerged—chief sustainability officer (CSO). CSOs are in charge of the corporation's environmental programs.

sustainability Meeting the needs of the present world without compromising the ability of future generations to meet their own needs.

Nearly all of the world's 150 largest companies have a sustainability officer with the rank of vice president or higher.[181] Some examples of organizations that have CSOs include **AT&T**, **DuPont**, and **Google**. Many companies, including **Intel**, are giving annual sustainability reports. Companies are helping each other develop sustainability best practices.[182]

Amazon (**IOM 4**) is considered an ethical company with a code of ethics. One of the many things it does to be socially responsible is to support and offer grants for more than 30 not-for-profit author and publisher groups that foster the creation, discussion, and publication of books. Amazon is also a green company that has reduced packaging and makes sure it is made from recycled materials that can be recycled again, and its headquarters was built to have eco-friendly buildings with **LEED (Leadership in Energy and Environmental Design)**–certified interiors and exteriors.

WORK
APPLICATION 2-12

Select a business and identify its sustainability practices.

Trends and Issues in Management

Clearly, today's businesses compete in a *global* external environment,[183] and multinational corporations (MNCs) have to manage their internal resources in each country to match the external stakeholders with different legal systems.[184] Think about the complexity of doing business in hundreds of countries globally with the same organizational culture. Even at the local level, businesses have to compete with MNCs, such as the local farmer who wants to sell produce to a national chain that is owned by an MNC that buys food from all over the world to provide fresh produce regardless of the season. Even jobs are increasingly becoming international.[185] You could work for a company with foreign ownership, be transferred overseas, have global suppliers, and compete with foreign MNCs. Globalization and cultural *diversity* are so important that we will discuss these issues in the topics of the next chapter and in the "Trends and Issues" section of every chapter.

Technology is so important that ***The Wall Street Journal*** newspaper has a section titled "Business & Tech." The trend of technology replacing employees will continue; **McDonald's** is now using huge touch-screen tablets to take your order and money.[186] CEO **Heidi Ganahl** of **Camp Bow Wow** plans to offer technology that can hold information to check the dogs in and out of camp, monitor dog exercise, and more.[187] Recall that we also have low tech, as **Amazon** is working on faster delivery by bicycle.[188]

The trend toward living in a *shared economy* will continue. The Uber and Airbnb business model is being copied by other companies, such as **BlaBlaCar** that connects long-distance drives with passengers going the same way; it's a carpooling business.[189] **SnapGoods** is a takeoff of **Taylor Rental** with individuals lending and borrowing assets.

We discussed *ethics*, but unethical leaders are under fire globally.[190] Trust in business is also low across countries,[191] including those in Europe and Asia.[192] We need to realize that ambiguous ethical standards is a global issue.[193] With specific country characteristics come varying ethical standards.[194] In some countries, giving bribes is illegal and considered unethical, whereas in others, it is the accepted way of doing business. Think of the complexity of dealing with ethics and having a common code of ethics when conducting business in 100 countries.

Our last issue is *CSR and Sustainability*, and the level does vary by country. MNCs are not just expected to act for the good of society in their home countries; they are expected to be good global corporate citizens.[195] The policy of business being neutral on social issues is changes, as more MNC are speaking up on and getting involved in social issues.[196] To be sustainable, **John Deere** has developed software to monitor soil moisture to avoid overwatering,[197] and **Farmobile** developed a tracker to monitor planting, spraying, and harvesting, then uses big *data* to curb costs and grow larger crops.[198] People are also working to develop technology so that we can drink the ocean,[199] filters large enough to clean the air of a city,[200] and systems to turn drilling waste water into clean electric energy.

The message of this chapter boils down to this: As a manager, you are going to have to manage the organization's internal environment (including its organizational culture) while interacting with its global external environment to create a win-win situation for stakeholders through ethical and socially responsible leadership while creating long-term sustainability.

$SAGE edge™   edge.sagepub.com/lussier8e

Want a better grade?

Get the tools you need to sharpen your study skills. Access practice quizzes, eFlashcards, video and multimedia, and more at edge.sagepub.com/lussier8e.

Digital Resources

Learning Objective	Digital Resource
2-1. Explain the five internal environmental factors and how nine external environmental factors can affect the internal business environment.	▶ Management in Action: Organizational Culture*
2-2. Describe the three levels of organizational culture and their relationship to each other.	▶ Suppliers
2-3. Explain why people use unethical behavior, why and how they justify their unethical behavior, and three factors that influence behavior to be ethical or unethical.	▣ Moral Development
2-4. Identify four guides to ethical behavior and three things organizations should do to manage ethics.	▶ Code of Ethics
2-5. Characterize the three levels of social responsibility and explain its relationship with sustainability.	▶ Social Responsibility*

* premium video available only in the interactive eBook

• • • CHAPTER SUMMARY

2-1. Explain the five internal environmental factors and how nine external environmental factors can affect the internal business environment.

Management refers to the people responsible for an organization's performance. Mission is the organization's purpose or reason for being. The organization has human, physical, financial, and informational resources to accomplish its mission. The systems process is the method of transforming inputs into outputs as the organization accomplishes its mission. Structure refers to the way in which the organization groups its resources to accomplish its mission.

Customers decide what products the business offers, and without customer value, there are no customers or business. *Competitors'* business practices often have to be duplicated in order to maintain customer value. Poor-quality inputs from *suppliers* result in poor-quality outputs without customer value. Without a qualified *labor force*, products and

services will have little or no customer value. *Shareholders*, through an elected board of directors, hire top managers and provide directives for the organization. *Society*, to a great extent, determines what are acceptable business practices and can pressure business for changes. The business must develop new *technologies*, or at least keep up with them, to provide customer value. *Economic* activity affects the organization's ability to provide customer value. For example, inflated prices lead to lower customer value. *Governments* set the rules and regulations that businesses must adhere to.

2-2. Describe the three levels of organizational culture and their relationship to each other.

Level 1 of culture is behavior—the actions employees take. Level 2 is values and beliefs. Values represent the way people believe they ought to behave, and beliefs represent if–then statements. Level 3 is assumptions—values and beliefs that are deeply ingrained as unquestionably true. Values, beliefs, and assumptions provide the operating principles that guide decision making and behavior.

2-3. Explain why people use unethical behavior, why and how they justify their unethical behavior, and three factors that influence behavior to be ethical or unethical.

People commonly use unethical behavior for personal gain or to avoid getting into trouble. People justify their behavior to protect their self-concept by rationalizing that there is a good reason for using the unethical behavior. The three factors that influence behavior are *personality traits and attitudes* (some people have more integrity), the *level of moral development* (preconventional, conventional, postconventional), and the *situations* (sometimes there is more incentive to be unethical).

2-4. Identify four guides to ethical behavior and three things organizations should do to manage ethics.

The four guidelines that help ensure ethical behavior are following the *Golden Rule* ("Don't do anything to anyone that you would not want someone to do to you"), answering the four questions of the *four-way*

test (Is it the truth? Is it fair to all concerned? Will it build goodwill and friendship? Will it be beneficial to all concerned?), trying to create a win-win situation for all relevant stakeholders so that everyone benefits from the decision with the *stakeholder's approach*, and using *discernment and advice* to consider if the behavior is ethical and asking others if it is. To manage ethics, organizations should develop *codes of ethics* and conduct *training*, top managers should support the code and *lead by example*, and the code should be *enforced* and violators punished by encouraging *whistle-blowing*.

2-5. Characterize the three levels of social responsibility and explain its relationship with sustainability.

Social responsibility is the conscious effort to operate in a manner that creates a win-win situation for all stakeholders. The three levels of social responsibility include legal (focus on maximizing profits while obeying the law), ethical (focus on profitability and going beyond the law to do what is right, just, and fair), and benevolent (focus on profitability and helping society through philanthropy). Social responsibility and sustainability are related because part of being socially responsible is maintaining or improving the firm's sustainability.

• • • KEY TERMS

ethics, 48
external environment, 40
internal environment, 38
learning organization, 46
levels of culture, 44

mission, 38
organizational culture, 39
social responsibility, 53
stakeholders' approach to ethics, 51
sustainability, 56

symbolic leaders, 45
systems process, 39
total quality management (TQM), 40

• • • KEY TERM REVIEW

Complete each of the following statements using one of this chapter's key terms:

1. The organization's _____ includes the factors that affect the organization's performance from within its boundaries.
2. The organization's _____ is its purpose or reason for being.
3. An _____ consists of the values, beliefs, and assumptions about appropriate behavior that members of an organization share.
4. The _____ is the technology used to transform inputs into outputs to make and deliver products and services.
5. _____ is a process that involves everyone in an organization focusing on the customer to continually improve product value.
6. The three _____ are behavior, values and beliefs, and assumptions.

7. _____ articulate a vision for an organization and reinforce the culture through slogans, symbols, and ceremonies.
8. A _____ has a culture that values sharing knowledge so as to adapt to the changing environment and continuously improve.
9. The organization's _____ includes the factors outside its boundaries that affect its performance.
10. _____ are the standards of right and wrong that influence behavior.
11. Using the _____, when making decisions, you try to create a win-win situation for all relevant stakeholders so that everyone benefits from the decision.
12. _____ is the conscious effort to operate in a manner that creates a win-win situation for all stakeholders.
13. _____ is meeting the needs of the present world without compromising the ability of future generations to meet their own needs.

• • • REVIEW QUESTIONS

1. What are the factors within the internal environment?
2. What are the components of the systems process?
3. How is quality determined, and why do people buy products?
4. What is the external environment?
5. What are the six artifacts of organizational culture?
6. What are the levels of culture?

7. What is a learning organization?
8. What are the levels of moral development?
9. How do people justify unethical behavior?
10. What is the stakeholders' approach to ethics?
11. What is social responsibility?
12. What are some ways in which businesses are going "green"?

• • • COMMUNICATION SKILLS

The following critical-thinking questions can be used for class discussion and/or as written assignments to develop communication skills. Be sure to give complete explanations for all questions.

1. Do you believe that most organizations focus on creating customer value?
2. Do you think that all organizations should use total quality management (TQM)? Explain your answer.
3. What is the relationship among management and mission, resources, the systems process, and structure? Which of these internal factors are ends, and which are means?
4. If you can't control the external environment, why be concerned about it anyway?
5. Which of the six artifacts, or important ways that employees learn about organizational culture, is the most important?

6. What is the difference between a strong and weak organizational culture, and which is preferable?
7. What is symbolic leadership? Is it important?
8. What is a learning organization? Should a manager create one?
9. Do you believe that ethical behavior will pay off in the long run?
10. Do you have your own guide to ethical behavior that you follow now? Will you use one of the guides from the text? If yes, which one and why?
11. Can ethics be taught and learned?
12. Do you believe that companies benefit from being socially responsible? Why or why not?
13. Do you believe that all businesses should go "green"? Why or why not?

CASES

• • • Case 2-1   Whole Foods Market

Whole Foods is a natural and organic foods retailer started by John Mackey and Renee Lawson in 1978. The company is headquartered in Austin, Texas. Today it operates 456 stores in the United States, Canada, and the United Kingdom and employs approximately 93,000 employees.

The mission statement of Whole Foods Market is:

> *"A dynamic leader in the quality food business. We are a mission-driven company that aims to set the standards of excellence for food retailers. We are building a business in which high standards permeate all aspects of our company. Quality is a state of mind at Whole Foods Market."*

The company's core values include a focus on the following: selling the highest quality natural and organic products available, satisfying, delighting, and nourishing our customers, supporting team member excellence and happiness, creating wealth through profits and growth, serving and supporting our local and global communities, practicing and advancing environmental stewardship, creating ongoing partnerships with our suppliers, and promoting the health of our stakeholders through healthy eating education.

The company has a variety of key strengths that it can leverage to achieve a competitive advantage in the future. First, it maintains a strong emphasis on the highest quality standards for all of its food and health products and customer service. Second, Whole Foods enjoys a strong brand reputation as being a good place to work as well as a great place to shop. Finally, the company has developed a highly motivated workforce that believes in its mission, is engaged, and is team oriented.

In terms of Whole Food's external environment, there are some additional key opportunities that are noteworthy. First, the company could export its business by opening retail stores in other countries. It could also expand its supply chain to a global level in order to obtain the highest-quality products for its customers. Finally, it could attempt to modify its pricing strategy to be more competitive with the growing number of retailers that are getting into the natural and organic foods market.

Whole Foods also places a strong emphasis on being an ethical and socially responsible company based on its core values of serving and supporting local and global communities and sustainability. The company's statement of its philosophy regarding sustainable agriculture includes the following principles:

> We respect our environment and recycle, reuse, and reduce our waste wherever and whenever we can;

> We are committed to greater production of organically and bio-dynamically grown foods to reduce pesticide use and promote soil conservation;

> We reduce waste and consumption of non-renewable resources. We promote and participate in recycling programs in our communities. We are committed to re-usable packaging, reduced packaging, and water and energy conservation.

> We encourage environmentally sound cleaning and store maintenance programs. In 2017, **Amazon** acquired Whole Foods. So only time will tell how Amazon will change Whole Foods.

Discussion Questions

1. What are the key internal environmental factors facing Whole Foods?

2. What are the key external environmental factors facing Whole Foods?

3. Describe the organizational culture at Whole Foods.

4. What does Whole Foods do to support being an ethical and socially responsible business?

5. Do you agree with Whole Foods' emphasis on being socially responsible and ethical in how it does business? Why or why not?

6. Is it a good or bad idea for Whole Foods to lower the quality standards for its food items so that it can reduce prices and potentially broaden the appeal of shopping there to a wider range of consumers?

References

http://www.makingafortune.biz/list-of-companies-w/whole-foods-market.htm
http://www.reuters.com/finance/stocks/companyProfile?symbol=WFM.O
http://www.wholefoodsmarket.com/company-info/whole-foods-market-history
http://panmore.com/whole-foods-market-swot-analysis-recommendations
http://www.wholefoodsmarket.com/mission-values
http://busn30-ethicalcompanies.weebly.com/whole-foods-market.html
http://www.wholefoodsmarket.com/mission-values/caring-communities

Case created by Loren Kuzuhara, University of Wisconsin–Madison.

• • • Case 2-2   Ride 'Em Cowboys: Wells Fargo and the Seattle City Council

This stagecoach likely makes a stop near you. Wells Fargo & Company owns Wells Fargo Bank, which is one of the largest banks in the US with more than 8,800 bank branches in 40-plus states. Community banking represents Wells Fargo's largest segment. Its wholesale banking arm handles corporate banking across the US and around the world; activities include investment banking and capital markets, securities investment, commercial real estate, and capital finance....The firm's three business segments are: Community Banking, serving consumers and small businesses; Wholesale Banking, whose clients include businesses with annual sales in excess of $5 million and financial institutions; and Wealth and Investment Management (formerly Wealth, Brokerage and Retirement), a provider of financial advisory services to clients, including ultra-high-worth families and individuals and their endowments and foundations through Abbot Downing.(1)

As a community bank, Wells Fargo asserts it takes its values very seriously.

> Our values should guide every conversation, decision, and interaction. Our values should anchor every product and service we provide and every channel we operate.(2)

Its values are embodied in its motto "Creating solutions for stronger communities" with its social responsibility priorities including diversity and social inclusion, economic empowerment and environmental sustainability. Two of its three principles, economic empowerment and environmental sustainability, are critical to its community outreach.

> Community reinvestment is an integral part of our culture. We understand that we can be no stronger, nor more successful, than the neighborhoods and communities where we do business.(3)

> We are committed to doing our part to accelerate the transition to a lower-carbon economy and reduce the impacts of climate change. We do this by increasing our operational efficiency; advancing clean technology; innovation; and other environmental solutions. We engage our customers, team members, suppliers, and community partners in our efforts to reduce waste, conserve resources, and support resilient communities.(4)

It came as a surprise to many when on February 7, 2017, the Seattle City Council voted to cut ties with banking giant Wells Fargo over its role as a lender to the Dakota Access pipeline project as well as other business practices. (Wells Fargo has said it is one of 17 firms involved in financing the pipeline and is providing $120 million of the $2.5 billion.) It also called out Wells Fargo for a number of enforcement orders issued against it in recent years. Regulators fined Wells Fargo $185 million after employees opened millions of customer accounts fraudulently to meet sales goals.

Seattle's measure came on the same day that the Army told Congress that it would allow the $3.8 billion Dakota Access oil pipeline to cross under a Missouri River reservoir in North Dakota, completing the disputed four-state project. The Standing Rock Sioux, whose reservation is just downstream from the pipeline's crossing, feared a leak would pollute the tribe's drinking water. Environmental activists across the country have called on a number of banks to stop financing the construction of the oil pipeline as well as on individuals to pull their money out of those banks.

Wells Fargo managed more than $3 billion of Seattle's operating account, processing everything from payroll and vendor payments to revenues collected from city business taxes to city fines. "While we are disappointed that the city has decided to end our 18-year relationship, we stand ready to support Seattle with its financial services needs in the future," said Tim Brown, Wells Fargo Middle Market Banking regional manager.

In the wake of this announcement, California and Illinois announced they would suspend some business relationships with the bank.(5)

Discussion Questions

1. Which external factors/stakeholders are addressed in this case?

2. What artifact(s) embody the culture and underlying values of Wells Fargo?

3. In this case, Wells Fargo's values and beliefs do not seem to match its behavior. Explain.

4. Given your answer to question 3, how would you characterize the firm's culture (strong or weak)?

5. Classify Wells Fargo's moral development as a firm within the context of this case. Indicate its level of development as per its stated values as well as its level of development given its actions in this case.

6. Using the Guide to Ethical Behavior, apply one of the guides to this case.

7. Given Wells Fargo's actions in this case, at what level of social responsibility would you classify it?

8. Given the movement toward evaluating a firm based upon the triple bottom line, how would you rate Wells Fargo?

Cumulative Case Questions

9. Tim Brown, Wells Fargo Middle Market Banking regional manager, expressed Wells Fargo's reaction to the Seattle City Council's actions as disappointing but stated that he and his firm stand ready to serve the Seattle community. Which of Mintzberg's management role categories was he enacting?

10. Was Tim Brown, Wells Fargo Middle Market Banking regional manager, the proper level manager to have expressed Wells Fargo's reaction to the Seattle City Council's actions?

References

(1) Hudspeth, C. (n.d.). Wells Fargo & Company. Hoovers. Retrieved February 15, 2017, from http://0-subscriber.hoovers.com.liucat.lib.liu.edu/H/company360/fulldescription.html?companyId=58450000000000

(2) Wells Fargo. (n.d.). The vision and values of Wells Fargo. Retrieved February 15, 2017, from https://www.wellsfargo.com/about/corporate/vision-and-values/

(3) Wells Fargo. (n.d.). Economic empowerment. Retrieved February 15, 2017, from https://www.wellsfargo.com/about/corporate-responsibility/economic-empowerment/

(4) Wells Fargo. (n.d.). Environmental sustainability. Retrieved February 15, 2017, from https://www.wellsfargo.com/about/corporate-responsibility/environment/

(5) Le, P. (2017, February 7). Seattle to cut ties with Wells Fargo over oil pipeline. Associated Press. Retrieved February 15, 2017, from https://www.yahoo.com/news/seattle-cut-ties-wells-fargo-over-oil-pipeline-234100575.html

Case created by Loren Kuzuhara, University of Wisconsin–Madison.

• • • SKILL BUILDER 2-1: ETHICS AND WHISTLE-BLOWING

Objective

To determine your level of ethics.

Skills

The primary skills developed through this exercise are:

1. Management skill—interpersonal

2. AACSB competencies—ethical understanding and reasoning abilities and reflective thinking skills and application of knowledge

3. Management function—leading

Preparing for Skill Builder 2-1

For this exercise, first complete Self-Assessment 2-1 in the chapter.

Discussion Questions

1. Who is harmed by and who benefits from the unethical behaviors in items 1 through 3?

2. For items 4 through 24, select the three (circle their numbers) you consider the most unethical. Who is harmed by and who benefits from these unethical behaviors?

3. If you observed unethical behavior but didn't report it, why didn't you report the behavior? If you did blow the whistle, what motivated you to do so? What was the result?

4. As a manager, it is your responsibility to uphold ethical behavior. If you know employees are doing any of these unethical behaviors, will you take action to enforce compliance with ethical standards?

5. What can you do to prevent unethical behavior?

6. As part of the class discussion, share any of the other unethical behaviors you observed and listed.

You may be asked to present your answers to the class or share them in small groups in class or online.

••• SKILL BUILDER 2-2: THE ORGANIZATIONAL ENVIRONMENT AND MANAGEMENT PRACTICES ANALYSIS

Objective

To determine an organization's environment, culture, ethics, social responsibility, and sustainability.

Skills

The primary skills developed through this exercise are:

1. Management skill—decision making
2. AACSB competencies—dynamics of the global economy, ethical understanding and reasoning abilities, multicultural and diversity understanding, and application of knowledge
3. Management function—planning

Preparing for Skill Builder 2-2

For this exercise, you will select a specific organization, preferably one you work for or have worked for, and answer the questions as they relate to the business you have selected. You may contact people in the organization to get your answers. Write your answers to all questions.

The Internal Environment

1. Identify the top managers and briefly discuss their leadership style.
2. State the organization's mission.
3. Identify some of the organization's major resources.
4. Explain the organization's systems process. Discuss how the organization ensures quality and customer value.
5. Identify the organization's structure by listing its major departments.

The External Environment

In answering this section's questions, be sure to state how each of these external factors affects the organization.

6. Identify the organization's target customers.
7. Identify the organization's major competitors.
8. Identify the organization's major suppliers.
9. What labor force does the organization primarily recruit from?
10. Does the organization have shareholders? Is its stock listed on one of the three major stock exchanges? If yes, which one?

Apply It

What did I learn from this experience? How will I use this knowledge in the future?

11. How does the organization affect society and vice versa?
12. Describe some of the past, present, and future technologies of the organization's industry. Is the organization a technology leader?
13. Identify the governments that affect the organization. List some of the major laws and regulations affecting the business.
14. Explain how the economy affects the organization.

Culture

15. Does the organization use all six artifacts to teach culture? Explain which are used and how.
16. Describe the culture at all three levels. Is it a strong or a weak culture?
17. Is the firm creating a learning organization? Explain why or why not.

Ethics

18. Does the organization have any guides to ethical behavior, such as a code of ethics? If yes, explain.
19. How does the organization manage ethics? Does it have a code of ethics? If so, what does the code cover? Does top management lead by good ethical example? Are ethical behaviors enforced? If so, how?

Social Responsibility

20. Is the organization socially responsible? If so, how?
21. What is the organization's overall level of CSR?

Sustainability

22. Does the organization use any sustainability practices? If yes, explain.

You may be asked to present your answers to the class or share them in small groups or online.

Apply It

What did I learn from this experience? How will I use this knowledge in the future?

• • • SKILL BUILDER 2-3: SMALL BUSINESS CORPORATE SOCIAL RESPONSIBILITY

Objective

To debate the value of social responsibility, including sustainability for a small business in your local community.

Skills

The primary skills developed through this exercise are:

1. Management skill—interpersonal and decision making
2. AACSB competencies—dynamics of the global economy, ethical understanding, reasoning abilities, and application of knowledge
3. Management function—planning

Preparing for Skill Builder 2-3

1. Select one of the three levels of CSR (1. legal, 2. ethical, 3. benevolent) you believe a small business in your community should operate on.
2. (a) Break into three groups based on the level of CSR you selected. (b) In your group, select a specific small business in your local community. (c) As a group, come up with a list of reasons why the business should operate at that level and why it should not operate at the other two levels. If your group selected benevolent, give specific things the business should do as part of its philanthropy program. (d) Select a spokesperson to present your list of answers to step c.

Conducting the Exercise in Class

1. The spokesperson from each group presents his or her list of answers to the class. Present from level 1 to 2 to 3.
2. After each presentation, or at the end of all three, the professor may lead a class debate, as other group members may challenge the level selected or specific issues listed, ask for further discussion, or give a summary.

Apply It

What did I learn from this experience? How will I use this knowledge in the future?

David Ryder/Getty Images

3 Managing Diversity in a Global Environment

••• LEARNING OBJECTIVES

After studying this chapter, you should be able to:

3-1. Contrast the classification of businesses in the global village, define ethnocentrism, and describe issues managers encounter through foreign trade. PAGE 68

3-2. Discuss diversity and inclusion and why they are important. PAGE 74

3-3. Describe the six major types of diversity groups and practices of managing diversity. PAGE 77

3-4. Compare and contrast the Hofstede national culture dimensions with Project GLOBE. PAGE 87

3-5. Rank the six forms that make a business a global one, in order from lowest to highest cost and risk. PAGE 89

IOM	Ideas on Management

Ideas on Management
at SHI International

You probably haven't heard of **Thai Lee** or the company she cofounded. But **SHI International** is the largest minority- and woman-owned business enterprise (MWBE) in the United States. It's made Thai Lee one of just 18 self-made female billionaires in the United States.

Lee was born in Thailand, spent most of her childhood in Korea, and moved to America in her teens to live with a family friend. Lee graduated from Amherst College and received her MBA from Harvard and gained experience working for **Procter & Gamble** and **American Express** in preparation for her college-planned plunge into entrepreneurship.

In 1989, Lee (and her cofounder husband—60/40% ownership each) bought a failing company with five employees and about as many customers and changed the name to Software House International. Under CEO Thai's management, she grew the company into the one of the biggest and best-regarded IT providers in the global economy, with more than $6 billion in sales. SHI has 17,500 customers including **Boeing, Johnson & Johnson**, and **AT&T**, serviced by 3,000 employees worldwide.

Building a private company without selling any stock to raise money for expansion and without any mergers or acquisitions would not have been possible without a strong and stable management structure. CEO Thai Lee says that the key to her success is her obsession with an organizational culture of keeping customers and employees happy. SHI empowers employees to solve customer problems while trying to make sure that everybody feels valued, because in this social compact they in turn create value.

IOM 1.   How is SHI's business classified in the global village?

IOM 2.   Is SHI ethnocentric, and is it involved in foreign trade?

IOM 3.   Does SHI promote workplace diversity and inclusion in the United States and globally?

IOM 4.   What global business practices does SHI practice, and which form of global business does it use?

You'll find answers to these **IOM** questions throughout the chapter. To learn more about SHI, visit www.shi.com.

Source: Information for this case was taken from SHI International website, accessed January 5, 2017; D. M. Ewalt, "The Modest Tycoon," *Forbes* (June 15, 2015): 77–80.

The Global Environment

Interacting effectively with a global diversity of people and managing a global company are what this chapter is all about. We start this chapter with an overview of globalization and international trade in this section, move from diversity in general to global diversity, and then discuss management of the global business.

As the title implies, we are expanding the external environment from the last chapter to be global. Globalization is one of the most vital business trends of the past 50 years,[1] as large corporations have employees from and conduct business all over the globe.[2] It is important to realize that no matter where you are, you live in and are affected by the global environment. Globalization may

LO 3-1

Contrast the classification of businesses in the global village, define ethnocentrism, and describe issues managers encounter through foreign trade.

require you to interact effectively with people from many different cultural backgrounds:[3] "as an employee" with coworkers, suppliers, and customers; "as a customer" in a local store; "as a student" in college; and "as a consumer" you use and buy products from other countries.

Think about the complexity of **FedEx**'s environment, delivering to more than 220 countries and territories worldwide.[4] Therefore, it has to follow the rules and regulations of different governments in countries with different economies, labor forces, societies, and so on. Refer to Chapter 2, Exhibit 2-3, for a review of the environment. Clearly, a global mind-set is a key standard for contemporary managers.[5] In this section, we classify businesses in the global village and discuss ethnocentrism, managing foreign trade, and how trade effects improves standards of living.

Classifying Businesses in the Global Village

WORK
APPLICATION 3-1

Classify a business you work for or have researched as domestic, international, or multinational. If the business is international or an MNC, list some of the countries in which it does business.

Let's begin with defining *global business* as the buying and selling of goods and services among different countries. The **global village** *refers to companies conducting business worldwide without boundaries.* The word *village* implies something small and emphasizes that the world, although very large, is becoming smaller through technology. Technology and the Internet have changed the way business is conducted in the global village. In its first 30 days, **Amazon.com** went global, recording sales in all 50 U.S. states and 45 other countries.[6]

Domestic and International Businesses. A *domestic business* conducts business in only one country. Most small businesses, like **Anthony's Pizza Place**, are domestic businesses. But most domestics will get equipment, material, supplies, and so forth that are made in other countries. An **international company** *is based primarily in one country but transacts business in other countries.* International companies commonly buy and sell products through importing and exporting. **Ferrari** cars are made in Italy and imported for sale by car dealers in other countries.

global village Refers to companies conducting business worldwide without boundaries.

international company An organization that is based primarily in one country but transacts business in other countries.

multinational corporation (MNC) An organization that has ownership in operations in two or more countries.

ethnocentrism Regarding one's own ethnic group or culture as superior to others.

Multinational Corporations (MNC). A **multinational corporation (MNC)** *has ownership in operations in two or more countries.* The MNC can have partial or full ownership of the operations—a separate independent business facility (factories or offices) in another country. Partial ownership comes commonly though buying stock in a foreign company or through a strategic alliance.

The foreign company is commonly referred to as a *foreign subsidiary or affiliate;* in essence, a *subsidiary* is a company owned and controlled by another company, making up a combined company, called the *holding company* or *parent company.* **FedEx** expanded globally by acquiring several other companies to deliver its packages to other countries globally. But companies can also have same-country subsidiaries. The parent company **PepsiCo**'s primary businesses include **Frito-Lay**, **Quaker**, **Pepsi-Cola**, **Tropicana**, and **Gatorade**, with operations in the United States and globally.[7]

There is also a *transnational company*, a type of MNC that eliminates artificial geographical barriers without having a real single national headquarters. **IBM** changed its structure from a country-based structure to industry groups to transcend boundaries. **SHI (IOM 1)** is a transnational MNC.[8]

Ethnocentrism Is Out and "Made in America" Is Blurred

Parochialism means having a narrow focus, or seeing things solely from one's own perspective. **Ethnocentrism** *is regarding one's own ethnic group or culture as superior to others.* Thus, a parochial view is part of ethnocentrism, which is a negative stereotype.[9] Another negative stereotype is the *not-invented-here (NIH)* syndrome, described as a negative attitude toward knowledge/technology/products from other external sources.[10]

Successful managers of large companies headquartered in the United States (including **Coca-Cola** and **Google** to name just two) are not ethnocentric and do not have a NIH attitude; they view themselves not simply as American companies but rather as companies conducting business in a global village. If MNCs can buy or make better or cheaper materials,

$SAGE edge™

Get the edge on your studies. **edge.sagepub .com/lussier8e**

- Take a quiz to find out what you've learned.
- Review key terms with eFlashcards.
- Watch videos that enhance chapter content.

parts, or products and make a profit in another country, they do so. **British Petroleum (BP)** has been doing business in the United States for more than 100 years, and BP supports more than 250,000 American jobs through all of its business activities.[11]

Many consumers subscribe to the idea behind "buy American," but few know the country of ownership or origin of the products they regularly buy. Look at the labels in your American **PVH Corp.** brand-name clothes including **Calvin Klein**, **Tommy Hilfiger**, and **IZOD**, and you will realize that most clothing is not made in America.[12] Did you know that the top three tuna fish brands are headquartered in the United States but not American owned? **Chicken of the Sea** and **Bumble Bee** are owned by **Union Frozen Products** of Thailand and **StarKist** by **Dongwon Enterprises** of South Korea.[13] Some **General Motors (GM)** and **Ford** cars are made in America with more foreign than American parts. **Toyota** and **Honda** make some cars in America with fewer parts coming from foreign companies. So which is "really" made in America?[14] The **Made in America Store** has a challenge stocking the store with fashionable only-American merchandise and hasn't been able to find any electric or electronic products because they are all made abroad.[15]

In addition to not knowing products are foreign, some people don't care where the products they buy come from; price is more important to them. Plus, some people prefer products, such as cars, made by foreign companies. Test your global knowledge of company and product country of ownership by completing Self-Assessment 3-1.

WORK
APPLICATION 3-2

Do you try to buy American products? Should you?

Managing Foreign Trade

Foreign trade is about conducting business with other countries, so managers need to understand trade barriers. **Netflix** wants to operate in 200 countries,[16] but it will face regulatory and trade barriers,[17] as **Facebook** is now facing in India.[18] Global managers also need to know about the World Trade Organization (WTO), trade agreements, and how exchange rates affect their profits at home. Here we discuss managing these foreign trade issues.

Trade Barriers. Overall, foreign trade benefits business and countries,[19] but it does create losers as well as winners,[20] and it can also hurt. For example, it is difficult for the United States to compete against China because of the large difference in labor costs. Also, some companies don't play fair through *dumping*. They sell products in one country at a high profit and sell in another country at a loss with the intention of driving out the competition. Thus, to help the domestic businesses compete with foreign companies at home, governments use *protectionism*—trade barriers to protect domestic companies and their workers from foreign competition. The first three are nontax barriers, and the last is a tax method. See Exhibit 3-1 for an illustration and what follows for definitions.

An *embargo* is a total ban on the importing of a product from one or more countries. This protects domestic companies and employees, as it stops foreign products from entering the home country. A *quota* sets a limit on the number or volume of a product that can be

---

3-1 JOIN THE DISCUSSION ETHICS & SOCIAL RESPONSIBILITY

Buy American

You most likely have heard the slogan "Buy American." Many labor unions urge Americans to buy products made in the United States, because that helps retain jobs for American workers. On the other hand, some Americans ask why they should buy American products if they cost more or their quality or style is not as good as that of foreign-made products. But as you've seen, it isn't always easy for consumers to know the country of ownership of many products they buy.

1. Is it ethical and socially responsible to ask people to buy American?

2. Is it ethical and socially responsible to buy foreign products?

3-1 SELF-ASSESSMENT

Country of Origin Ownership of Products

For each item, determine the country of origin. If your answer is the United States, place a check in the center column. If it's another country, write the name of the country in the right-hand column.

Product	United States	Other (list country)
1. Shell gasoline		
2. Nestlé hot cocoa		
3. Dove soap		
4. Pep Boys auto centers		
5. L'Oreal cosmetics		
6. Johnson & Johnson baby powder		
7. Burger King fast food		
8. Samsung televisions		
9. Bayer aspirin		
10. Bud Light beer		
11. Volvo cars		
12. AMC theaters		
13. Bentley cars		
14. Reebok sneakers		
15. Tide detergent		

1. Shell is owned by Royal Dutch Shell of the Netherlands. 2. Nestlé is headquartered in Switzerland. 3. Dove is a brand of Unilever, which is British. 4. Pep Boys is Japanese. 5. L'Oreal is French. 6. Johnson & Johnson is a U.S. company. 7. Burger King stock is controlled by Brazilian 3G Capital. 8. Samsung is South Korean. 9. Bayer is German. 10. Bud is owned by Anheuser-Busch InBev and is Belgian owned. 11. Volvo and 12. AMC are both Chinese owned. 13. Bentley is owned by Volkswagen of Germany. 14. Reebok is owned by German Adidas. 15. Tide is a brand of Procter & Gamble and is U.S. owned.
How many did you get correct?

imported or exported during a set period. This tends to decrease the supply of products, which tends to result in higher prices of the imported products, giving the home country an advantage over foreign competitors. *Subsidies* include government grants, loans, and tax breaks given to domestic companies. A grant is a gift that doesn't have to be paid back. Loans are usually set at below-market interest rates. Tax breaks allow the company to retain more of its revenues. Subsidies tend to lower the cost and price of domestic products to compete with foreign companies. A *tariff* is a direct tax on imports to make them more expensive. This tends to increase the price of exports, making them above or closer to the price of domestic products.

3-1 APPLYING THE CONCEPT

Trade Barriers

EXHIBIT 3-1

Identify the trade barrier exemplified by each statement.

A. embargo
B. quota
C. subsidies
D. tariff

____ 1. The Chinese government is giving grants to its domestic car business.

____ 2. The Japanese government will not let us export any cars.

____ 3. The Korean government is raising our prices by place a tax on our exported cars.

____ 4. The South African government will only let us export 100 cars a year.

Managers need to understand these four foreign trade barriers and how to use them at home and to help prevent them from being used against them in other countries. For more information on U.S. trade barriers, visit www.usa.gov. Today, capitalism is under attack,[21] as global protectionism is increasing,[22] and **President Trump** has threatened to increase U.S. protectionism.[23] Our next two topics discuss how countries facilitate global free trade with the help of the WTO.

World Trade Organization (WTO). Managers should know that if they are being treated unfairly in most other countries, the WTO can help them. Organizations and governments are working together to develop free trade among countries. Replacing the **General Agreement on Tariffs and Trade (GATT)**, the **World Trade Organization (WTO)** is an international organization dedicated to global free trade. It is a forum for governments to negotiate trade agreements. The WTO is a place for countries to settle trade disputes. It operates and enforces a system of trade rules. Essentially, the WTO is a place where its 164 member governments try to sort out the trade problems they face with each other. A WTO panel can order unfair practices stopped or allow the country claiming unfair practices to retaliate; it ruled that European governments gave unfair state subsidies to **Airbus**, giving it an advantage over U.S. **Boeing**.[24] The WTO also provides technical assistance and training for developing countries.[25] Visit www.wto.org for updated information about the World Trade Organization. Virtually all 164 WTO countries are members of one or more trade agreements administered by the WTO, our next topic.

Trade Agreements. If managers are seeking to expand sales overseas, it is important to know about trade agreements that their home country is part of, as these countries usually have fewer trade barriers to doing business with member countries, which generally makes them good opportunities for expansion. There are six major trade agreements around the globe: **North American Free Trade Agreement (NAFTA), Dominican Republic–Central America Free Trade Agreement (CAFTA-DR), Union of South American Nations (UNASUR), European Union (EU), Association of Southeast Asian Nations (ASEAN),** and **Asia-Pacific Economic Cooperation (APEC).** For a list of the countries in each trade agreement and more information on these trade agreements, see Exhibit 3-2 and visit their websites listed in the exhibit. Although not a trade agreement, many global companies are expanding in the **BRIC** (Brazil, Russia, India, and China) countries.[26]

In 2016, with the trend to protectionism, Britain voted to drop out of the EU (**Brexit**), which will also affect its U.S. trade,[27] and President Trump threatened protectionism. China is already moving to replace the United States as trade champion,[28] and Russia, Japan, and China are rushing to fill the trade gap.[29]

WORK APPLICATION 3-3

Give an example of how a domestic company benefits from trade barriers.

Lawrence Manning

Free trade helps increase the standard of living globally.

Since 2001, with the help of WTO, some dozen countries have been negotiating **The Trans-Pacific Partnership (TTP)**, but President Trump threatens vetoing a congressional bill to allow membership in TTP. However, that doesn't mean the United States will not join TTP. Trump stated that he believes the United States is not getting a fair deal with present trade agreements, but he may renegotiate some changes to TTP that will gain his support for U.S. membership. But Russia, China, and Japan are not waiting for the United States; they are maneuvering to lock in trade deals now.[30]

Exchange Rates. International managers need to understand exchange rates because they can affect their companies' profits at home. The *exchange rate* is how much of one country's currency you get for that of another country. Your own currency is considered strong when you get more of another country's currency than you give up in the exchange and weak when you get less. If you are an American traveling to other countries, a strong dollar gives you greater buying power, as you get more for your money.

However, when a U.S. business conducts foreign trade, the opposite is true. When the dollar is weak, foreign goods are generally priced higher to cover exchange-rate losses, making them more expensive in the United States, but when it is strong, foreign goods are less expensive. See Exhibit 3-3 for an example, realizing that currencies don't usually fluctuate dramatically,[31] but they can as they did in Britain.

With Brexit, the value of the British pound dropped by double digits (to a 31-year low against the U.S. dollar), giving it the exporting advantage, and resulted in the price of **Microsoft software** and **iPhones** rising.[32] On paper, the drop in the value of the pound cost **Anheuser-Busch InBev** $13 billion because it had to buy pounds to acquire **SAB-Miller** in October 2016.[33]

In 2015 and 2016, the value of the U.S. dollar was strong, putting a major drag on the U.S. economy, negatively affecting total sales and profits.[34] Companies that do a lot of their business in other countries are hurt by a strong currency. **Groupon** gets 35% of its revenues

EXHIBIT 3-2	TRADE AGREEMENTS	
Agreement	**Members**	**Website**
North American Free Trade Agreement (NAFTA)	3 North American countries (Canada, United States, Mexico)	www.naftanow.org
Dominican Republic–Central America Free Trade Agreement (CAFTA-DR)	6 beneficiary countries	www.caftadr.net
Union of South American Nations (UNASUR)	12 South American countries	www.unasursg.org
European Union (EU)–Maastricht Treaty of Europe	28 European member states	http://europa.eu
Association of Southeast Asian Nations (ASEAN)	10 Asian and Pacific Rim countries	www.asean.org
Asia-Pacific Economic Cooperation (APEC)	21 Pacific Rim countries	www.apec.org

outside North America and was hurt by the strong dollar that led to decreased profits, resulting in cutting 1,100 jobs globally, about 1 in 10 employees.[35] For current exchange rates, visit www.x-rates.com.

The International Monetary Fund (IMF). The IMF is an organization of 189 countries, working to foster global monetary cooperation, secure financial stability, facilitate international trade, promote high employment and sustainable economic growth, and reduce poverty around the world. The IMF's primary purpose is to ensure the stability of the international monetary system—the system of exchange rates and international payments that enables countries (and their citizens) to transact with each other. The Fund's mandate was updated in 2012 to include all macroeconomic and financial-sector issues that bear on global stability.[36] For more information on the IMF, visit its website, www.imf.org.

Standard of Living and the Effects of Foreign Trade

Standard of living refers to the level of wealth, comfort, material goods, and necessities available to a certain socioeconomic class in a certain geographic area. People in developed countries have a higher standard of living because they get paid more and have greater *purchasing power*—the relative cost of a product in different countries. The key to increasing the standard of living is to increase productivity—think about how modern farming has helped feed the world.

The *Economist* magazine produces the Big Mac index interactive currency-comparison tool to show the differences in purchasing power (how much you get for your money) across countries. For example, the average price of a Big Mac in the United States in July 2016 was $5.04; in China it was only $2.79 at market exchange rates. So the "raw" Big Mac index says that the yuan was undervalued by 45% at that time.[37] Visit www.economist.com/content/big-mac-index to compare the prices among several countries.

Arguments Against Free Trade. According to former **GE CEO Jeff Immelt**, globalization is being blamed for unemployment and wage inequality everywhere. There is a general sense that globalization must be somebody else's fault and that addressing it by being more competitive is not an option.[38] Unions, such as the **United Auto Workers (UAW)**, oppose free trade agreements, claiming that they cost U.S. jobs.[39] By far the major argument against free trade is loss of jobs followed by wage inequity.

Unlike in the United States where the government cannot have any ownership (even stock) of businesses because of conflict of interest, other countries, especially China, have *state-owned enterprises (SOEs)*. SOEs represent around 10% of global domestic product.[40] Thus, governments with SOEs have an incentive to use trade barriers to protect their self-interest in business profits that go to the government.[41]

WORK
APPLICATION 3-4

Would you be willing to pay more for the same product made domestically than abroad? For example, if Nike made sneakers in the United States and sold them for $125 and made them abroad and sold them for $100, which would you buy?

EXHIBIT 3-3   # EXCHANGE RATES

Suppose you are selling a product in China for 8,000 yuan. With an exchange rate of 8 yuan to 1 dollar, you get $1,000 (8,000 [yuan selling price] divided by 8 [8 yuan = $1]) for each product you sell. Suppose that this price and exchange rate give you a 25% profit margin. Now let's see what happens with the extreme fluctuations in exchange rates that sometimes occur:

If the exchange rate becomes 6 yuan to 1 dollar, the yuan is strong (and the dollar is weak). When you exchange the yuan for dollars, you get $1,333.33 (8,000 [yuan selling price] divided by 6 [6 yuan = $1]) for each product you sell.

Now let's make the dollar strong (and the yuan weak). If the exchange rate goes to 10 yuan to the dollar, you get $800 (8,000 [yuan selling price] divided by 10 [10 yuan = $1]).

You can either change your yuan selling price to maintain your 25% profit margin or make more or less based on the exchange rate. Now think about the complexity of **FedEx** doing business in more than 100 currencies.

Some argue with the fact that the United States imports more than we export. Since **NAFTA** went into effect on January 1, 1994, there has been an increase in imports of 133%, versus an increase in exports of 97%.[42] With NAFTA, some U.S. businesses moved production to Canada and Mexico—again causing loss of U.S. jobs. By far the United States' major argument against free trade is loss of jobs. Wage and standard of living inequity within and between countries are also concerns globally.

Arguments for Free Trade. First, others claim that although the United States imports more than it exports, Americans are better off since **NAFTA**. Most economists agree that the entire global economy and most people benefit as each country gains from foreign trade even when one country is more efficient at producing the goods traded.[43] To the loss of jobs, there are three rebuttals:

1. What destroys jobs is innovation and productivity. If you can think of any jobs that can be replaced by technology, like a kiosk for taking orders and collecting money at **McDonald's**, they probably will be.[44] Automation actually leads to more job creation.[45] The problem is that in free markets, there are winners and losers. Some jobs are eliminated, but the overall number of quality jobs increases.[46] But it is difficult for laid-off **GM** autoworkers to find equal employment in growing high-tech jobs at **Google**. There is actually a shortage of skill labor in the United States.

2. Protectionism leads to subsidizing less productive jobs at home. In 2016, President-elect **Trump** negotiated with **Carrier** to keep jobs in America. However, not all jobs were saved, and to keep them, tax breaks were given. Essentially, the jobs saved are in part being paid for by the government and by consumers, who will pay more for the products than if they were made at a lower cost overseas.

3. As discussed, the strong value of the U.S. dollar makes American goods less competitive globally. This leads to the loss of jobs, especially manufacturing exporters, which are the jobs the United States is trying to protect.[47]

Another argument is that trade barriers only lead to trade wars. If the United States increases protectionism, the Chinese government will retaliate, and both countries lose. Higher tariffs on Chinese goods can also hurt American manufactures that export and produce products in other countries.[48] The **IMF** forecast a slowing of global growth due to protectionism and weak trade.[49] The **WTO** director general said that protectionism is going to hurt countries, not solve their problems.[50]

The Future of Global Trade. Whether you agree with free trade or not, despite its recent setback, globalization remains an irreversible trend of our times.[51] Let's face it, just about every country needs trade to provide goods and services it doesn't have to maintain or increase its standard of living, and the only way most large MNCs can continue to grow sales and profits that increase jobs is through global trade. If you want to be a top-level manager, you better develop a global mind-set if you want to have a successful career.[52] **SHI (IOM 2)** is not ethnocentric, and it is involved in foreign trade. SHI has 30+ offices across the United States, Canada, United Kingdom, France, and Hong Kong.

LO 3-2

Discuss diversity and inclusion and why they are important.

Workplace Diversity and Inclusion

In this section, we discuss what diversity and inclusion are and answer the question, "Are they really important globally and in the United States?" In the next section, we explain the types of diversity and end by discussing how to manage diversity.

What Are Diversity and Inclusion?

Let's start by defining diversity and then show the progression going from a focus on affirmative action to diversity to inclusion. Next, we give U.S. diversity data and end with a discussion of discrimination, stating not only what diversity is but also what it isn't, followed by how the United States is truly diversified.

Diversity. When you are in class, at work, or just out in public somewhere, look around, and you will most likely see that people are both the same and different. **Diversity** *refers to the variety of people with different group identities within the same workplace.* Diversity and work aren't separate because we tend to judge the nature of workers by the gender, race, and other diversity of the people who do the work. Workplace diversity includes both employees and customers. See Exhibit 3-4 for a list of six major diversity group identities, which we will discuss shortly.

Differences Between Valuing Diversity and Affirmative Action. Diversity and affirmative action are sometimes thought to be the same—but they aren't. *Affirmative action* policies are designed to improve work outcomes for underrepresented groups by providing them with extra help in the employment process. It started in the United States as a Federal Executive Order back in the 1960s; for more information visit www.usa.gov. Some other countries have similar policies under different names.

Affirmative action plans have increased the number of women and minorities in several occupations and in management and thus help promote diversity at work.[53] Valuing diversity is broader in scope, as it doesn't focus simply on not discriminating against diverse groups and helping only some of them, sometimes at the expense of others through reverse discrimination. But valuing diversity still has a focus on accepting differences and on helping certain groups. Today, several firms, including **Twitter**, are setting targets as the key to diversity.[54]

From Valuing Diversity to Inclusion Focus. The terms *diversity* and *inclusion* are often used interchangeably, but they are different. Most organizations have moved from affirmative action to accepting differences to valuing diversity to inclusion[55]—valuing all types of diversity, which includes integrating everyone to work together while maintaining their differences.[56] **Inclusion** *is a practice of ensuring that all employees feel they belong as valued members of the organization.* An inclusive value system creates a sense of belonging: a feeling of being respected, being valued for who you are; feeling a level of supportive energy and commitment from others so that everyone can do their best work.[57]

Many organizations are now replacing the word *diversity* with the term *inclusion* to better reflect the shift away from diversity to inclusion. **Major League Baseball (MLB)** now has an Ambassador for Inclusion.[58] **Dun & Bradstreet**, **BellSouth**, **Frito-Lay**, **Home Depot**, **Procter & Gamble**, and many others now focus on inclusion.[59] On your present or past job, did you feel included as a valued member of the organization? Is your present or past place of work truly inclusive, or are there in-groups and out-groups and individuals?

Being Personally Inclusive. To be inclusive, we all need to *empathize* with everyone—put ourselves in their shoes and try to understand where they are coming from and accept them for who they are rather than reject them or try to make them into who we want them to be—just like us.[60] One thing we should realize is that "our way" of interacting with others (or doing things) is not the only one right style (or way of doing things). Are you truly open to letting people who are very different from you at work be who they are? Recall that being happy is about relationships, and firms are placing a top priority on recruiting employees who can work with and manage a diversity of employees.[61]

U.S. Diversity. We all know that there is diversity in cultures throughout the world. But do you realize that there are people from all over the globe living in America? The United States has cultural diversity at home as a country populated by immigrants. With the popularity of an American education and higher incomes, you will likely interact with people on campus and at work from other countries.[62]

According to the U.S. Census Bureau,[63] the U.S. population continues to grow slowly, with more than 325 million people (with a net gain of one person every 13 seconds), and it is

EXHIBIT 3-4	TYPES OF WORKFORCE DIVERSITY

Age and Generation
Gender and Sexual Orientation (LGBT+)
Race and Ethnicity
Disability and Ability
Religion
Other

diversity The variety of people with different group identities within the same workplace.

inclusion A practice of ensuring that all employees feel they belong as valued members of the organization.

EXHIBIT 3-5   U.S. POPULATION CHANGES 2013 TO 2060 (PROJECTED)

Population by Race	2013 Percentage of Total Population	2060 Estimated Percentage of Total Population
Native Hawaiian and Other Pacific Islander	0.2%	0.3% ↑
American Indian and Alaska Native	1.2%	1.5% ↑
Two or more races	2.4%	6.4% ↑
Asian	5.3%	8.2% ↑
Black or African American	13.2%	15% ↑
Hispanic of any race	17.1%	31% ↑ more than double
White (non-Hispanic)	62.6%	43% ↓

Sources: 2013 U.S. Census Bureau, accessed April 8, 2015; 2060 estimates reported in *The Wall Street Journal* (December 13, 2012): A3.

rapidly diversifying. The Caucasian population is decreasing, as there are more deaths than births. The population growth is coming from minorities, and Hispanics are now the largest minority group. Today, minority births are now the majority. One in 12 children (8%) born in the United States is the offspring of illegal immigrants, making those children U.S. citizens. By counties, in 2015, almost one-third of the population was of color, and in 370 counties across 36 states, less than half are Caucasian.[64] By around 2040, less than half of the total U.S. population will be Caucasian. By 2060, Caucasians are estimated to be 43% of the population, and one in three people will be Hispanic. See Exhibit 3-5 for population statistics.

Discrimination. As shown in Exhibit 3-4, there are six major types of diverse groups in the workplace, including others not listed, that often get differential or unfavorable treatment.[65] As you most likely already know, it is illegal to discriminate against most diversity groups. **Discrimination** *is illegal because it gives unfair treatment to diversity groups in employment decisions.*

Stereotyping, the mistaken generalization of the perceived characteristics of a diversity group to an individual, has negative consequences.[66] Through stereotyping, discrimination has numerous negative consequences, as it threatens one's identity, leading to decreased self-esteem and individual performance, conflict between individuals and groups, turnover, and harassment.[67] We need to break down stereotypes and assess each individual's qualifications for the job.[68] We will discuss the legal issues of discrimination in more detail in Chapter 9, "Human Resources Management."

We are more attached to our agenda and biases than we realize, because it is often subconscious.[69] We tend to view the world from our own self-focused viewpoint, with an *ethnocentric* view of our group.[70] We need to break away from our prejudices that cloud our position.[71] Like organizations, we need to develop a global mind-set[72] and go beyond accepting diversity to embracing inclusion to eradicate discrimination.[73]

Are Diversity and Inclusion Really Important?

Yes! Discrimination is illegal, and promoting diversity and inclusion creates equal opportunities for all employees, so it is the right thing to do.[74] But it is also beneficial to business. Why? There is a wealth of evidence that diversity helps teams and organizations perform better in terms of creativity, innovation, revenue, and profits.[75] If employees don't feel included, they generally will not place a high value on organizational membership and will not be as productive as those who do.[76] Think about this! Even if a company only wanted to hire and do business with Caucasians, do you really believe it could be successful or even survive? The global white population is decreasing, making diversity an important topic within the workplace.[77]

discrimination An illegal practice that gives unfair treatment to diversity groups in employment decisions.

People unconsciously think like and favor people of their own social groups, so having diverse employees can bring unique cultural sensitivity that appeals to a diverse customer base. People may complain about having to push a button on their phone to talk in English, but if you want diverse customers, you need employees who can speak their language. **Travelers Insurance** and **Airbnb**, along with other companies, say diversity is a business imperative, and train its people to be inclusive.[78]

Let's face it; like it or not, diversity is going to continue to grow. And again, the better you can work with diverse people, the greater are your chances of having a successful business career. So avoid ethnocentrism and develop your global mind-set.[79] Are you willing to commit to offering inclusion of diverse people into your homogeneous groups?

WORK
APPLICATION 3-5

Explain how diversity is important to your current or past workplace.

LO 3-3

Describe the six major types of diversity groups and practices of managing diversity.

Types of Diversity and Managing Diversity

Here we focus more on the challenges of managing a diverse workforce, breaking down stereotypes, and creating equal opportunities for all individuals. Part of the challenge comes from the fact that people tend to get along better with people in their own group. Do you tend to associate with people of your own age, gender, race/ethnicity, disability/ability, or religion? As a manager, you need to get everyone to work together. We discuss how to manage these diverse groups through inclusion.

Note that most diverse groups have legal protection against discrimination. While here we focus on diversity, we will discuss the laws that protect the legal rights of diverse groups in Chapter 9, "Human Resources Management."

Age and Generational Diversity and Management

Age. There is a wide range of age groups in the workplace, resulting in different diverse generations in the workplace. There is job discrimination against older workers.[80] **Hooters**, **Texas Roadhouse**, as well as other industries, have been accused of not hiring older, more qualified workers by selecting younger, more attractive, less experienced candidates.[81]

To promote age integration, employees and especially managers should understand stereotypes about older workers that are myths. Older employees have more company knowledge, show better judgment, care more about the quality of their work, and are less likely to quit, show up late, or be absent—which are very costly. They also have fewer injuries on the job and cost less in health care than younger workers with school-aged children. Other myths include, in general, that older workers can't learn new technologies, that they resist change, and that they are less productive, regardless of the type of job, than younger workers.[82]

3-2   JOIN THE DISCUSSION ETHICS & SOCIAL RESPONSIBILITY

Speaking English

The United States was once known as the "melting pot," as people from all over the world came to the country and adjusted to its culture. In the past, generally, immigrants had to learn English to get a job. Today, however, many organizations hire people who can't speak English, and they use translators and have policies written in multiple languages for these employees. Government agencies at the federal, state, and local levels are also providing translators and written materials in other languages.

1. Why are some organizations no longer requiring workers to speak English?

2. Should a worker be required to be able to speak English to get a job in the United States?

3. Is it ethical and socially responsible to (or not to) hire people who can't speak English and to provide translators and policies written in multiple languages?

Brooks Brothers makes and alters its clothes in New York City, and half the workers are 55 and older.[83]

So all members of the organization should realize that they tend to have negative stereotypes that are not based on facts about older workers. Managers should make decisions based on the individual's qualifications for the job to be done regardless of age. Negative stereotypes tend to break down as people get to know each other on a personal level, so be sure younger and older people work together. One thing Exhibit 3-6 is doing is creating younger and older worker peer mentors, in which they both teach each other new tricks.[84]

We should also realize that the global population is aging and will require more health care workers and fewer durable goods manufacturing workers, such as cars.[85] By 2060, the **United Nations** estimates that for every 100 people of working age, there will be 30 people who are 65 and older. That's more than double the ratio of old to young people today.[86] The working-age population will decline by 5% by 2050.[87] Thus, with a shortage of skilled workers and shrinking workforce, like it or not, businesses will need to employ more older workers.

Generational Differences and Management. For the first time in history, five generations are working side by side. Different values, experiences, styles, and activities can create misunderstandings and frustrations. To succeed, managers need to be aware of the similarities and differences among generations and how they prefer to be led.[88] The best way to understand this diversity and how to manage generational differences is by reading Exhibit 3-6. Do realize that there is no universally accepted list of differences and that these are generalizations based on research but that there are always exceptions to the guidelines presented. However, every 20 years, the generation with power and comfort tends to dislike the younger generation. Generations tend to start work being innovative but tend to become more similar as they get older. So there are more similarities between generations at the same age than there are differences.[89]

One thing to realize is that millennials are now dominating management positions in greater numbers. GenY is slowly changing business operations based on their preference for informal hierarchies, teamwork with shared decisions, social media sharing, more flexible work schedules with more vacations, snacks, texting, and earbuds. This trend will continue as they advance in management.[90]

Generation Z, born after 1996, make up almost a quarter of the U.S. population,[91] but they don't make up much of the full-time workforce, because in 2016 most of Gen Z was still in college.[92] Therefore, it is still early to include them in Exhibit 3-6. It's also fuzzy what distinguishes Gen Z from Gen Y. Gen Z is said to be an unprecedentedly diverse, Internet-obsessed, social media–optimized bunch—which also describes Gen Y. But Gen Z is still forming and growing into itself.[93] In a survey, around a third of college students think that being able to work remotely with a flexible schedule is a right, not a privilege.[94]

Here are some of the characteristics associated with Gen Z that have been identified by two generational experts.[95] Gen Z has been shaped by the recession, so they are thinking about college earlier in high school and view it as an investment, not an experience. They want steady paychecks. Gen Z has also been shaped by the personalization of media, streaming any song or TV show at any time. They expect to be more networked all the time and to customize things exactly to their preferences. When asked what makes them different, Gen Z said they were both more accepting and more rebellious. Gen Y wasn't very rebellious and had a shiny outlook on their future. Gen Z is more pragmatic and not happy about the systems they are inheriting.

EduardoP/CreativeCommons

In order to better support an aging workforce, many organizations are proving assistance such as kneepads to make older works more comfortable on the job.

Gender and Sexual Orientation Diversity and Management

Let's discuss each of these related categories of diversity.

Sex, Gender, and Stereotypes. The terms *sex* and *gender* are often used interchangeably, but they are different. *Sex* distinguishes biological males and females. *Gender* does include sex, but it also includes common behavioral characteristics, language used to describe gender, clothes, and other things used to refer to the genders, which are learned through social interactions generalized by sex, often referred to as *masculine* (he's tough; he's good at math) and *feminine* (she's nurturing; she's good at English). There are also negative terms used to pressure people into conforming to gender stereotypes (he's a sissy; she's a tomboy). We need to be aware of gender stereotypes and not judge others because they don't fit into our view of how males and females should look and act.

We also need to break stereotypes of the jobs men (doctor, policeman, fireman, mailman, serviceman, construction worker) and women (nurse, child care, teacher, secretary, hairdresser) should pursue. One thing we can do is stop using words that stereotype jobs and use gender-neutral terms—*police officer, firefighter, letter carrier, administrative assistant*, and so on. We need to look at the qualifications of the individual and not discourage people and, much worse, discriminate against them by not giving them jobs they are qualified to do.

Gender stereotypes about leadership tend to result in gender discrimination against women in management. Men are expected to possess qualities associated with leadership, such as assertiveness, confidence, and independence, whereas, women are expected to be helpful, nurturing, and kind. Women who behave with aggressive male leadership characteristics are often penalized and criticized as being bossy.[96] **COO Sheryl Sandberg,** who is given much of the credit for growing **Facebook,** says that America and the world are not comfortable with women in leadership roles.[97] To get more women into management roles, we have to address our culture's discomfort with female leadership.[98] Complete Self-Assessment 3-2 to determine your attitude about women advancing—be honest.

Gender Discrimination and the Glass Ceiling. Women make up about half of the U.S. workforce,[99] but they are only paid 77 cents on the dollar compared to men.[100] Women make less than men in all but two of the occupations for which the United States publishes data,[101] and highly educated women fare worst of all.[102] In highly prestigious jobs, women perform equally but are rewarded significantly lower than men in terms of salary, bonuses, and promotions.[103]

Although research supports equality of the sexes, research also reports that it is more difficult for women to advance.[104] Despite modest progress, women are underrepresented at every management level, and it starts with entry-level employees. Men are 30% more likely than women counterparts to be promoted into a managerial role.[105] Women are at a disadvantage when it comes to getting promoted to high-level management positions, especially women with children.[106]

The barriers to upward mobility in organizations are commonly called the **glass ceiling**—*the invisible barrier that prevents women and minorities from advancing to the top jobs in organizations.* In the 2016 ***Fortune 500*** listing of the largest American corporations, only 21 CEOs (4%) were women, down from 24 in 2015.[107] At the current pace of progress, we are more than 100 years away from gender equality in the C-suite.[108]

Women CEOs face extra pressures and scrutiny, as they must overcome the glass ceiling.[109] Women are also more likely than men to be promoted to CEO when the company is struggling or is in crisis (44% vs. 22%), placing them on the risky *glass cliff*—after years of climbing to the top, they are at risk to tumble and not make it back up again to that level if they are fired. No woman fired or pressured to resign has ever returned to be a CEO of a *Fortune 500* company, whereas 5 of 93 men regained a CEO position.[110]

Discrimination is considered the most significant factor in holding both women and minorities back from the top jobs.[111] The United States has the **Equal Employment Opportunity Commission (EEOC)** to handle legal charges of sex-based discrimination and

glass ceiling The invisible barrier that prevents women and minorities from advancing to the top jobs in organizations.

EXHIBIT 3-6   GENERATIONAL DIFFERENCES AND MANAGEMENT

Differences	Traditionalists	Baby Boomers	Generation X	Generation Y/Millennials
Birth year	1925–1945	1946–1964	1965–1980	1981–1996
Age group 2017	72+	53–71	37–52	21–36
Work ethic	Dedicated Pay your dues Work hard Age = seniority	Driven Work long hours to establish self-worth and identity and fulfillment	Balance Work smarter and with greater output, not work longer hours	Ambitious What's next? Multitasking Tenacity Entrepreneurial
Job wants	Recognition and respect for their experience Value placed on history/traditions Job security and stability Clearly defined rules/policies	Ability to "shine"/"be a star" Make a contribution Need clear and concise job expectations, and will get it done	Cutting-edge systems/tech Forward-thinking company Flexibility scheduling Input evaluated on merit, not age/seniority	Meaningful work with challenge, not boring More social, networked, participative teams, less hierarchical organizations Flexible schedules Evaluated on output, not input, on the work itself To be paid well
Career path	Keep same job with security	Job changing risky	Job changing is necessary	Doesn't need to be a straight line

How to Manage

	Traditionalists	Baby Boomers	Generation X	Generation Y/Millennials
	Consider engaging them as teachers, mentors, coaches When they retire, consider rehiring them as part-time project leaders and coaches	Boomers are burning out with today's workload and are not impressed with less ambitious Gen Xers or Ys Offer them flexibility, authority, and respect Challenge them to keep growing (in their own way)	Gen Xers don't want to burn out They think whiny Millennials need too much hand holding Manage them with a coaching style—feedback and credit for results Push them to keep learning just in time for every new project	Millennials feel that basics such as punctuality and dress code are less important They want fair and direct managers who are highly engaged in their personal development Get to know their capabilities and put them in roles that push their limits Treat them as professional colleagues, and they will act like professionals Keep them focused with speed, customization, and interactivity

Sources: Generations website, www.generations.com, accessed April 9, 2015; Generational Differences Chart, www.wmfc.org/uploads/GenerationalDifferencesChart .pdf, accessed April 9, 2015; R. Reuteman, "Millennials Are Taking Over the Work Force at a Rapid Clip: What's an Older Leader to Do?" *Entrepreneur* (March 2015): 43–48; C. Groden, "Five Things You Can Do to Attract Millennial Talent," *Fortune* (March 15, 2016): 182–183; K. Rockwood, "Blowing Up the Workweek," *INC.* (December 2016 / January 2017): 84–85.

a federal **Glass Ceiling Commission** to help eliminate the problem. However, as you just read, despite legislative remedies, they haven't made much progress.[112]

Promoting Gender Equality. Why? Less successful organizations show the greatest bias against women.[113] **Warren Buffett**, chairman of **Berkshire Hathaway**, says women are the key to America's prosperity and asks fellow males to get on board and fully employ the talent of all its citizens.[114] If women globally were offered the same economic opportunities as men, an estimated $28 trillion would be added to global gross domestic product by 2025.[115]

On the more optimistic side, women are gaining more seats on corporate boards of directors, one-fifth (20%) of all *Fortune 500* directors, and heading more boardroom committees

3-2 SELF-ASSESSMENT

Attitudes About Women and Minorities Advancing

Be honest in this self-assessment, as your assessment will not be accurate if you don't. Also, you should not be asked to share your score with others.

Answer the 10 questions below twice, once related to women and a second time related to minorities. Place the number 1 (*disagree*), 2, 3, 4, or 5 (*agree*) on the line before each statement for women and at the end of each statement for minorities.

5	4	3	2	1
Agree				Disagree

Women		Minorities
_____	1. Women/Minorities lack motivation to get ahead.	1. _____
_____	2. Women/Minorities lack the education necessary to get ahead.	2. _____
_____	3. Women/Minorities working has caused rising unemployment among white men.	3. _____
_____	4. Women/Minorities are not strong enough or emotionally stable enough to succeed in high-pressure jobs.	4. _____
_____	5. Women/Minorities have a lower commitment to work than white men.	5. _____
_____	6. Women/Minorities are too emotional to be effective managers.	6. _____
_____	7. Women/Minorities who are managers have difficulty in situations calling for quick and precise decisions.	7. _____
_____	8. Women/Minorities have a higher turnover rate than white men.	8. _____
_____	9. Women/Minorities are out of work more often than white men.	9. _____
_____	10. Women/Minorities have less interest in advancing than white men.	10. _____

Total

Women—To determine your attitude score toward women, add up the total of your answers on the lines before each statement and place it on the total line and on the following continuum.

10	20	30	40	50
Positive attitude				Negative attitude

Minorities—To determine your attitude score toward minorities, add up the total of your answers on the lines after each statement and place it on the total line and on the following continuum.

10	20	30	40	50
Positive attitude				Negative attitude

Each statement in Self-Assessment 3-2 is a negative attitude about women and minorities at work. However, research has shown all of these statements to be false; they are considered myths.

(28%), arguably the power positions, which could lead to more future diversity at the top.[116] Research also supports that female board representation is positively related to accounting returns.[117] **Melinda Gates, co-chair of the Bill and Melinda Gates Foundation,** is considered the most powerful advocate in the world with a singular focus on women and girls. *Forbes* called her "The First Woman of Women." Melinda says, "When you get women in roles of leadership, we make things happen."[118]

Self-made billionaire **Sheryl Sandberg**[119] is promoting making it safe to talk about gender in the workplace and helping women get into positions of power everywhere[120] through her Lean In organization; visit https://leanin.org for more information. More than 30,000 *Lean In Circles* from 154 countries are helping women pursue their ambitions.[121] In her bestselling book *Lean In: Women, Work, and the Will to Lead,* Sandberg suggests more women get into the higher-paying jobs in STEM (science, technology, engineering, and mathematics).[122] **GM CEO Mary Barra** an engineer role model for women in male-dominated industries, is also helping women advance everywhere; 25% of senior officers and 42% of GMs board are women.[123] The **Financial Women's Association (FWA)** is helping females advance to the C-suite and to become tomorrow's CEOs. For more information on FWA, visit http://fwa.org.

Author of *Unfinished Business* **Anne-Marie Slaughter** says that nothing is going to change for professional women in the realm of work, life, and family demands until men get on board. The so called "women's issues" of managing a career and family should be reframed as a "caring issue" for everyone. Most women with children state the importance of selecting and having a partner who can help balance the work–family load.[124] Close to half of American couples have dual-careers, yet men don't come close to shouldering half of the family responsibilities. One thing that does help, for those who can afford it, is to pay others to do tasks, like cleaning and lawn care, so that you have more family time. Unfortunately, a survey found that single parents are less happy than couples, no matter how they divided the labor.[125] Again, much of our happiness comes from relationships.

Sexual Orientation (LGBT+). LGBT is intended to emphasize a diversity of sexuality and gender identity-based cultures. LGBT refers to people who are lesbian, gay, bisexual, and transgender. There are other diversities including Q = for those who identify as queer or are questioning their sexual identity (LGBTQ); I = to include intersex people (LBGTI); and A = asexual (LBGTA). Putting them all together would be LGBTQIA. So LGBT+ is becoming more common. Although the **Supreme Court** legalized same-sex marriage, the **Civil Rights Act of 1964** doesn't mention sexual orientation protection. However, court cases are being tried on the bases that sexual orientation discrimination is inherently a form of sex discrimination, so the law might change.[126]

Regardless of the law, our beliefs, or religious attitudes, for a company to have true inclusion, it must include LGBT+s. To this end, most *Fortune* 500 companies provide nondiscrimination protection and provide same-sex partner benefits.[127] Over the years, the general population has become more accepting of LGBTs. **Apple** CEO **Tim Cook** came out stating he is gay, and **Major League Baseball's (MLB)** first Ambassador of Inclusion, **Billy Bean**, is a former baseball player who came out as gay after retirement and is now working for gay inclusion in sports.[128]

Many religions teach that we should not judge others, and it is generally not a good idea to promote our religious beliefs in corporate America. At least at work, we need to include LGBTs in our groups by avoiding *homophobia* (an aversion to homosexuals) and bias and discrimination based on a person's sexual orientation if we want to get along well with all people. The gender- and sexual-orientation–neutral terms replacing *husband* or *wife* and *boyfriend* or *girlfriend* are *significant other* and *partner*.

Race and Ethnicity Diversity and Management

Race and ethnicity are similar yet different. *Race* is a biological characteristic, such as skin color, that creates diverse group identities. *Ethnicity* is a social trait, such as cultural background, customs, or allegiances, again creating diverse groups. Most people identify themselves as part of a racial group; therefore, race diversity is an integral part of a country's culture. However, there is a slow trend of selecting more than one racial group. As discussed under the heading "U.S. Diversity" (page 75), the global white population is decreasing, and the other diverse groups are growing at a fast pace, so the United States is increasingly racially and ethnically diversified.[129]

Although companies with the most ethically diverse teams are 35% more likely to have returns above the national industry median,[130] minorities are stereotyped and discriminated against.[131] Black workers still make less than whites with the same college degrees.[132] Research also supports that blacks are at a disadvantage when they are evaluated in terms of their leadership ability, as they are negatively stereotyped, which leads to poorer prospects for career advancement.[133] Review Self-Assessment 3-2. How is your attitude toward minority advancement?

Research clearly supports that people of color (non-white of any race or ethnicity) clearly have the work ethic and intelligence to advance in organizations.[134] A survey found that black, Hispanic, and Asian women of color actually have a higher ambition to advance and to be promoted to top executive positions than do white women and men.[135] However, the glass ceiling is even more difficult for people of color to break. In 2016, only five (1%) African Americans were CEOs of *Fortune 500* companies (up from four in 2015),[136] and only three men were CEOs of *S&P 500* companies (down from seven in 2007).[137] **Ursula Burns**, who became the first and only black woman to head a *Fortune 500* company but stepped down as the **CEO of Xerox**, will continue as chair of the board but will not be included in the 2017 CEO list. To find out more about successful blacks, visit **Black Entrepreneurs & Executives** at www.blackentrepreneurprofile.com.

Foreign-born U.S. citizens are racially or ethnically diverse but can be white and are making the most progress in advancing in the American *Fortune 500*. In 2016, 73 CEOs were foreign born (up from 71 in 2015).[138] Indian-born woman CEO **Indra Nooyi** of **PepsiCo** is a role model to both women and minorities. Out of frustration with their advancement, some people of color and foreign-born Americans are choosing to start their own businesses. Nearly a third of America's 50 richest self-made women were born abroad. Like **SHI (IOM 3)** CEO Thai Lee, these executives and entrepreneurs built their fortunes after moving to the United States.[139]

To have equal opportunities for all, a good place to start is with simple statistics. Are the hiring, promoting, and quitting rates significantly different between the sexes and between whites and minorities? Differences don't necessarily mean discrimination, but you can take action to improve the numbers in diversity groups. Chief Diversity and Inclusion Officer (CDIO) **Danielle Brown** is studying the numbers and found equal pay is now working to improve minority advancement and retention at **Intel**.[140] To help promote diversity, Fortune has the *50 Best Workplaces for Diversity*. In 2016, the top three organizations were **Texas Health Resources**, **Delta Air Lines**, and **Navy Federal Credit Union**. They also have a list of the top 10 best places for African Americans, Hispanic and Latino, and Asian Americans to work.[141] For the complete up-to-date list, visit www.fortune.com/diversity.

Make sure selection and promotion criteria are clear and objective to help avoid racial bias. Training managers who make hiring and promotion decisions to understand the problem and to be objective is needed.[142] Businesses around the world realize that a diverse supplier base with minority business enterprises (MBEs) is a critical competitive advantage, as MBEs better connect with their own diverse customer bases, and in most cases minority suppliers offer better prices, service, and value. For more information on MBEs, visit the **National Minority Supplier Development Council (NMSDC)** at www.nmsdc.org. **BP** has a minority member as its director of supplier diversity, and she works with the NMSDC to find suppliers, as BP is committed to a more inclusive supply chain.

Disability and Ability Diversity and Management

Disabilities. Back in 1990, the Americans with Disabilities Act (ADA) defined a **disability** as *a mental or physical impairment that substantially limits one or more major life activities.* The law prohibits discrimination against people with disabilities (www.ada.gov) by treating them differently because of their disabilities. The ADA also requires companies to make

disability A mental or physical impairment that substantially limits an individual's ability.

reasonable accommodations so their facilities are accessible to people with disabilities to enable them to perform jobs.[143] Largely due to ADA and inclusion efforts, people with disabilities are getting more job opportunities. However, of the major types of diversity, they face the most discrimination. The percentage of people with disabilities who have jobs is not that high; they are disproportionately employed in low-status or part-time jobs with little chance for advancement, and they are more likely to live in poverty.

Negative stereotypes are myths, as studies have found that with reasonable accommodations, people with disabilities perform their jobs just as well as people without disabilities. **SAP** and **Freddie Mac** have found that autism can be a job skill, and they recruit individuals with autism for precision jobs, including debugging software and answering customer queries.[144]

To give equal opportunities to people with disabilities, the first thing we need to do is change our mind-set. Instead of looking for disabilities, look for *abilities*. For example, a person in a wheelchair is perfectly capable of performing most jobs that require the employee to sit. People with disabilities are good candidates for work-from-home jobs. We should actively recruit qualified workers with disabilities. Companies also need to provide reasonable accommodations; some don't cost anything, and others are not expensive.

Managers need to create and maintain an environment in which people with disabilities can feel comfortable disclosing their need for reasonable accommodations. Training can help get people without disabilities comfortable working with people who have disabilities. One thing to note is that people with disabilities are people first, so they prefer to be called people with disabilities, not disabled people.

Abilities. Although we just discussed focusing on abilities, we must also realize that we all have different abilities. Based on different levels of education, training, and experience, employees tend to have diverse knowledge, skills, and attitudes (KSAs). People in different functional areas of the company (operations, finance, marketing, human resources) tend to see things from their own departmental perspective and bring different contributions to the company. To maximize performance, companies are using teams and bringing in a variety of KSAs. They are breaking down the barriers of departments so that everyone focuses on improving company products and services and the process to run the business. You will learn how to manage teams in Chapter 8. So from the management perspective, we should focus on utilizing a person's expertise.[145]

Religious Diversity and Management

Although fewer people today attend organized religious services, many people identify themselves as belonging to a religion. Employers are required by law to make reasonable accommodations for employees' religious beliefs without undue hardship on the employer. "Undue hardship" is fairly clear. It involves having to pay premium wages or other costs to accommodate an employee's religious rights, defined as "all forms and aspects of religion." However, "reasonable accommodation" is ambiguous. With the increase in Muslim employees, companies face issues of how employees dress and when and where they pray. Some companies have made reasonable accommodations by changing dress codes and have set up prayer rooms and flexible work schedules to accommodate their Muslim employees as part of their inclusion focus.

Employers need to make it clear when offering jobs what the specific work hours will be and ask if the employee will commit to working those hours. Companies should also be willing to negotiate with employees and allow them flexibility in work schedules and to swap shifts or job dates with consenting colleagues. And employees should be allowed to take religious holidays off in place of other paid days off. Some employers allow employees to select which paid holidays they want to take. Although not associated with any formal religion, some companies encourage spirituality in the workplace as part of their inclusion efforts.

One thing managers do need to be cautious of in making accommodations is not giving special treatment to people that other employees will resent. If everyone doesn't feel equally included, or excluded, employees will not include the privileged into their groups, and performance can suffer.

WORK
APPLICATION 3-6

First, state the types of diversity that are evident where you work(ed). Next, describe how diversity has affected you personally by being discriminated against, including being unfairly treated through being criticized or excluded in some way for being different from others.

Other Types of Diversity and Management

There are all kinds of other ways that people are diverse in the workplace, so let's discuss just a few of them.

- **Weight.** Obesity in the United States is a problem that is on the increase. Overweight people are also known as *weight challenged*. Some jobs require physical tasks that legally restrict them, such as law enforcement officers having to be able to run a certain distance in less than a set time. However, for many jobs, a certain weight is not a legal requirement, but there is discrimination against this group. Again, inclusion means everyone is welcome who can do the job.

- **Personality.** There is also diversity in *personality*. Our behavior (what we say and do) is rooted in our personality. Have you ever had

MANAGEMENT IN ACTION
Religious Diversity and Management

a so-called personality conflict with anyone who irritates you? We do tend to prefer to associate with people with similar personalities, but again, inclusion means getting along with the jerks at work. You will learn about personality types and how to get along with this diversity in Chapter 10, "Organizational Behavior."

- **Attractiveness.** There are also differences in *physical attractiveness*. Let's face it: We all look different, and people in general tend to be nicer to the so-called good-looking people of both sexes, especially evidenced by males' behavior toward attractive females who dress to show it and like the attention they get. You don't find many high-level positions held by the people who try to get by on their looks. But like it or not, people are judged on how they dress, which is another type of diversity, and attire can affect career success. In business, when selecting people for jobs and promotions, we need to focus on the ability to do the job, not attractiveness.

- **Family.** One last diversity we will discuss is *family background*. If you are thinking, "What does family have to do with work?" think again. We don't leave our personal life at home when we go to work. You have probably realized that people from different family backgrounds (including socioeconomic upper and lower incomes) tend to behave differently at work based largely on how they were brought up; our behavior at work is clearly affected by our family life. People from higher incomes tend to have better social networks that led to good jobs, and people from lower income levels tend to have a more difficult time finding good jobs. One last time, we need to include everyone.

Managing Diversity Through Inclusion

We've already discussed ways to manage each of the major diverse groups by promoting diversity to create equal opportunities for all who recognize the value of each individual.[146] Although effective management of diversity remains an elusive goal,[147] as it is difficult to get a diversity of employees to get along at work, here we present approaches that apply to multiple diverse groups as well as all employees.

Diversity Policies and Practices. Inclusion must be part of every manager's job starting with the CEO down.[148] **CEO Lip-Bu Tan** says diversity is a top priority at **Cadence,** where 95% of its 6,500 employees state that Cadence is an inclusive workplace regardless of age, race, gender, or sexual orientation.[149] Companies need active policies and practices to promote diversity. The policies and practices should promote a diversity climate of inclusion that is part of the *organizational culture* (Chapter 2). Records of diverse group hiring and promoting should be kept, and efforts should be made to help these groups succeed in the workplace, often called a *diversity audit*.

3-2 APPLYING THE CONCEPT

Diversity Stereotypes

Identify the negative stereotype that tends to lead to discrimination.

A. Age and Generation

B. Gender and Sexual Orientation

C. Race and Ethnicity

D. Disability and Ability

E. Religious

F. Other

____ 5. They are too emotional and moody monthly to be good managers.

____ 6. It's not fair to let Muslims take extra breaks and have their own prayer room.

____ 7. I just don't feel comfortable around the guy with a missing leg.

____ 8. She's a dumb blond. The only reason Joe hired her is for her looks.

____ 9. You can't teach an old dog new tricks. Even though he has a lot less experience, teach him to run the new high-tech machine.

____ 10. You know those people just don't have the motivation to get a good education and advance.

In promoting diversity, be sure to follow all Equal Employment Opportunity (EEO) laws, treat group differences as important but not special, and tailor opportunities to individuals, not groups. You should have high standards and hire and advance the most qualified candidates. But given equal qualifications for the job, the diverse candidate (who in some cases will be a white male) can be given the job to support diversity. Make sure diverse employees have access to the same job training and other practices at work to have equal opportunities to advance. Also, have diversity training for all employees. Three practices that promote diversity follow.

Diversity Training. *Diversity training* teaches people how to get along better with diverse workers through inclusion. It helps diverse people to talk about bias and better understand each other by becoming aware of and more empathetic toward people different from themselves.[150] Training breaks down negative stereotypes and builds acceptance of differences, viewing people as individuals, and realizing that diversity improves teamwork and organizational performance. Training can last for hours or days. Most large companies offer diversity training. Would-be renters said that **Airbnb** hosts denied them lodging after identifying their race or sexual identity, so Airbnb took steps to promote inclusive lodging including requiring employee training.[151] Skill Builder 3-2 is an example of a diversity training exercise. For an online example of an exercise in awareness of attitudes and beliefs about diverse groups, see Self-Assessment 3-3.

Airbnb CEO Brian Chesky required employee training after renters alleged discrimination based on race and sexual identity.

Mentoring. *No one gets to the top alone.*[152] *Mentors* are higher-level managers who prepare high-potential people for advancement. Mentoring is a process that enhances management skills, encourages diversity, and improves productivity. Having mentors who are willing to work with you to develop your knowledge, abilities, and skills can help you in both your professional and your personal lives. Mentoring can be between people in different companies or at the same company, formal or informal. Most large corporations, including **Sun Microsystems**, **Intel**, and **Microsoft**, offer several internally developed formal mentoring programs for their employees.[153] Mentoring is especially recommended for women and minorities who want to advance to top-level positions because it can help them break into the "good old boy" networks that often make the selections for these jobs.[154]

Rather than providing mentors on premises, many MNCs today, such as **IBM**, are turning to online mentoring programs for global employee mentoring. With *e-mentoring*, employees typically fill out a profile, and the program's software matches them up with a mentor. Instead of getting together in person, the two meet and communicate electronically, such as via email and **Skype**.

Network Diversity Groups. *Network diversity groups* promote equality.[155] They have employees throughout the organization from a diverse group whose members share information about how to succeed in the company and how to help the company succeed, including **Cadence**.[156] **American Express** has been using these groups for more than 22 years. While some believe they can create division, others believe they are beneficial. **Frito-Lay** has a Latino employee network that provides management with very valuable feedback on marketing products to the Latino community.[157]

Global Diversity

Employees from different countries do not see the world in quite the same way because they come from different national cultures.[158] Understanding national culture is important because it affects nearly every aspect of human behavior,[159] making cultural sensitivity and important skill,[160] as is recognized by **AACSB** accreditation (Chapter 1 page 8). For the MNC, all of the workplace diversity exists, plus national culture as well.[161] Therefore, capability to manage such cultural diversity has become one of the most important skills for global leaders.[162] In this section, we discuss Hofstede's cultural dimensions, Project GLOBE, and how to handle international assignments.

Hofstede National Cultural Diversity

Back in the 1970s and 1980s, Geert Hofstede surveyed more than 116,000 **IBM** employees in 40 countries about their work-related values. He identified five cultural dimensions on a continuum in which employees differ (countries in parentheses are very high or low compared to other countries on the dimension).[163] These cultural dimensions continue to be studied.[164]

- *Power distance inequality versus power equality*—Power distance being distributed between levels of management down to employees can be more accepted (Russia and China) or rejected as employees want to participate in decisions that affect them (Denmark and Sweden).
- *Individualism versus collectivism*—Individualist cultures believe individuals should be self-sufficient with loyalty to themselves first and the group and company second (United States and Netherlands), whereas collectivism places the group and company first (Indonesia and China).
- *Assertiveness versus nurturing*—Assertive cultures are more aggressive and competitive, with a focus on achievement and material possessions (Japan and Germany), whereas nurturing cultures emphasize the importance of relationships, modesty, caring, and quality of life (Netherlands and France).
- *Uncertainty avoidance or acceptance*—Uncertainty-avoidance cultures like structure and security and are less likely to take risks (Japan and West Africa), whereas

LO 3-4

Compare and contrast the Hofstede national culture dimensions with Project GLOBE.

WORK
APPLICATION 3-7

Describe a company's policies and practices for promoting diversity, preferably a business you work(ed) for.

uncertainty-acceptance cultures are more comfortable dealing with the unknown and change and taking more risk (Hong Kong).

- *Long-term versus short-term orientation*—Long-term cultures look to the future and value thrift (China and Hong Kong), whereas short-term cultures focus on the past and present and immediate gratification (United States and Germany).

GLOBE

As Hofstede's research became dated, GLOBE confirmed his dimensions are still valid today and extended and expanded his five dimensions into nine, including hundreds of companies and more countries. Project GLOBE stands for *Global Leadership and Organizational Behavior Effectiveness*, which is an ongoing cross-cultural investigation of leadership and national culture. The GLOBE research team uses data from hundreds of organizations in more than 62 countries to identify nine dimensions in which national cultures are diverse. See Exhibit 3-7 for a list of the dimensions with examples of country ratings.[165] Notice that some of the GLOBE dimensions have the same or similar names as Hofstede's five dimensions. As shown, through cross-cultural comparisons, there are differences,[166] especially between Eastern and Western cultures.[167]

International Assignments

With increasing globalization and workforce mobility, there is a chance that you will be sent to another country to conduct business.[168] It may be a brief visit, or it can be an international assignment as an expatriate. **Expatriates** *live and work outside their native country.* It can be difficult to adjust to a different language, culture, and society[169] Being abruptly placed in a very different foreign country often leads to what is called *culture shock.* As a result, expatriates often unknowingly use inappropriate behaviors when they travel to foreign countries.

WORK APPLICATION 3-8

Give an example of cultural diversity you have encountered, preferably at work.

WORK APPLICATION 3-9

How do you feel about taking an international assignment? What countries would be appealing to you?

expatriates Individuals who live and work outside their native country.

EXHIBIT 3-7   **GLOBE DIMENSIONS**

Dimension	Low	Moderate	High
Assertiveness People are tough, confrontational, and competitive.	Switzerland New Zealand	Ireland Philippines	Spain United States
Future Orientation People plan, delaying immediate gratification to invest in the future.	Russia Argentina	Slovenia India United States	Netherlands Canada
Gender Differences People have great gender role differences.	Sweden Denmark United States	Brazil Italy	Egypt China
Uncertainty Avoidance People are uncomfortable with the unknown/ambiguity.	Bolivia Hungary	Mexico United States	Austria Germany
Power Distance People accept power inequality differences.	South Africa Netherlands United States	England France	Spain Thailand
Societal Collectivism Teamwork is encouraged (vs. individualism).	Greece Germany	Hong Kong United States	Japan Singapore
In-Group Collectivism People take pride in membership (family, team, organization).	Denmark New Zealand	Israel Japan United States	China Morocco
Performance Orientation People strive for improvement and excellence.	Russia Venezuela	England Sweden	Taiwan United States
Humane Orientation People are fair, caring, and kind to others.	Singapore Spain	United States Hong Kong	Indonesia Iceland

3-3 APPLYING THE CONCEPT

GLOBE Dimensions

Identify the dimension of cultural diversity exemplified by each statement.

A. assertiveness

B. future orientation

C. gender differences

D. uncertainty avoidance

E. power distance

F. societal collectivism

G. in-group collectivism

H. performance orientation

I. humane orientation

____ 11. The people in this country have one of the highest savings rates in the world.

____ 12. Managers throughout organizations in this country focus on getting the job done through teamwork.

____ 13. People in this country are known to be difficult to negotiate with.

____ 14. In some companies in this country, the male managers go around kissing the female employees good morning; and the women get the coffee for the male managers.

____ 15. The people in this country follow the football/soccer team closely as they take great satisfaction from watching their team in the World Cup.

____ 16. Managers place great importance on status symbols such as having the executive dining room, reserved parking spaces, and big offices.

____ 17. Managers don't really care about the safety of their employees and provide poor working conditions.

____ 18. Employees get nervous and stressed when they even hear that changes are coming.

____ 19. Employees focus on constant small changes to make the products and processes better.

Cultural values and beliefs are often unspoken and taken for granted, and even with a common language, accurate communication can be difficult.[170] We tend to expect people to behave as we do. However, to be successful in the global village, you need to be sensitive to other cultures[171] as you interact with people whose values and behaviors differ from your own.[172] One more time, you need to get along with others,[173] and to do so, you need to have a global mind-set.[174] In fact, companies seek employees who have intercultural competences[175] and those with multicultural backgrounds.[176]

MNCs, such as **IBM** and **EMC**, are also training managers and employees in local languages, customs, and business practices so they can be successful in the global market. Some people say that taking—or refusing—an international assignment affects career advancement, especially for top-level management. Whether you are asked to take an international assignment or not, as a global manager, you need to be flexible and adapt to other ways of behaving; you cannot expect others to change for you.[177] As stated, **SHI (IOM 4)** has a strong culture that focuses on making sure that "everyone" globally feels valued.

Managing Global Business

To manage a global business successfully, you need to understand the differences in practices between internationals and MNCs and the six forms of global business, which we discuss in this section. But first, if you are thinking why conduct business globally, and that countries should limit free trade, it's all about increasing sales and profits, resulting in an increasing standard of living. See Exhibit 3-8 for a view of global populations and U.S. importing and exporting partners. As you can see, in 2015, a U.S. MNC conducting business in China

LO 3-5

Rank the six forms that make a business a global one, in order from lowest to highest cost and risk.

EXHIBIT 3-8   WORLD AND U.S. POPULATION AND EXPORT AND IMPORT PARTNERS

Most Populous Countries	Top U.S. Export Partners	Top U.S. Import Partners
1. China 1,373,541,278	1. Canada $280.0 B	1. China $481.9 B
2. India 1,266,883,598	2. Mexico $236.4 B	2. Canada $295.2 B
3. United States 323,995,528	3. China $116.2 B	3. Mexico $294.7 B
4. Indonesia 258,316,051	4. Japan $62.5 B	4. Japan $131.1 B
5. Brazil 205,823,665	5. Germany $50.0 B	5. Germany $124.1 B

Source: U.S. Census, www.census.gov, accessed January 10, 2017.
Note: K = thousands, M = millions, B = billions.

and India increases its potential business from around 325 million Americans to more than 2.5 billion people. With a global total population of around 7.4 billion people, close to one-third of the people live in these two countries today.[178] However, the African population is growing fast; by 2050, some 2.5 billion people will be African. That will be double the current number and will grow to 25% of the world's total population.[179] Emerging markets are still the future, as some 3 billion people will enter the middle class by 2015, almost all of them in the developing world.[180]

Global Management Practices

The first thing we should realize is that the demands of corporate leadership are changing how leaders manage in the global village.[181] Managers can't use simple Western techniques in some countries, like China.[182] In fact, U.S. concepts are no longer held up as the dominant models, especially because managing is different in countries with government ownership of corporations (SOEs).[183] **Panasonic** blends Japanese tradition with American resourcefulness.[184] With globalization comes complex human exchanges, making interpersonal skills and problem solving increasingly important.[185]

The most notable global manager is **Carlos Ghosn**, who was the first CEO to head three Global 500 companies at once. From June 2013 to June 2016, Ghosn was chairman of Russia-based automobile manufacturer **AvtoVAZ**. Ghosn is also chairman and CEO of the **Renault-Nissan Alliance**, the strategic partnership overseeing Nissan and Renault through a unique cross-shareholding agreement. The Alliance, which includes AvtoVAZ and **Mitsubishi**, has held approximately 10% of the global market share since 2010, and as of 2016, it was the fourth-largest automobile group worldwide.[186] So through the alliance, Ghosn is also the chairman and/or CEO of three auto companies—Renault, Nissan, and Mitsubishi.

Both MNCs and small international companies compete in the global environment, and they have one thing in common but use different business practices based on size and resources.[187] Let's compare them next.

Think Globally, Act Locally. One thing internationals and MNCs have in common is thinking and integrating globally, but they adapt to local market needs in specific countries.[188] **Disneyland** castles are different in Hong Kong, Paris, Tokyo, and Shanghai to appeal to local families.[189] **McDonald's** sells the Big Mac in India, for example, but it is not made of beef, as in India it is not culturally acceptable to eat cows. With increasing country protectionism, global **GE** plans to be more localized to protect its business from trade barriers.[190]

Differences in Business Practices of Internationals and MNCs. For a list of differences, see Exhibit 3-9.

EXHIBIT 3-9   ## MANAGEMENT PRACTICES OF GLOBAL COMPANIES

- **Global Management Team.** Leading MNCs have top-level managers who are foreign nationals and subsidiaries managed by foreign nationals. Small businesses often can't afford to hire foreign managers, but some use consultants and agents.

- **Global Strategy.** In an MNC, there is one strategy for the entire company, not one per subsidiary. Worldwide coordination attains economies of scale but still allows a country manager to respond to local consumer needs and counter local competition.

- **Global Operations and Products.** MNCs have standardized operations worldwide to attain economies of scale, and they make products to be sold worldwide, not just in local markets. Small businesses can sell standard global products, but they commonly use contractors to make the products and for exporting.

- **Global Technology and R&D.** Technology is developed internally through large research-and-development (R&D) budgets, and they acquire small companies that develop the tech. Small businesses develop new technology with limited or no funds for R&D, and they are often quick to adopt others' new technology.

- **Global Financing.** MNCs search world markets to get the best rates and terms when borrowing and managing money. Small companies tend to only bank in their home country.

- **Global Marketing.** Products used to be developed in the home market and then brought to other countries later, which small companies still do, but the trend is toward global introduction of products. MNCs tend to have much larger marketing budgets to promote their products globally.

Managing Different Forms of Global Business

There are six forms of global business. Exhibit 3-10 presents these forms in order by cost and risk and indicates what types of companies tend to use them.

WORK
APPLICATION 3-10

Select a company and identify as many of its global management practices as you can.

3-3 JOIN THE DISCUSSION ETHICS & SOCIAL RESPONSIBILITY

File Sharing

Since the early 2000s, some peer-to-peer (P2P) file-sharing networks and services have been targeted by music companies and an industry watch group, the **Recording Industry Association of America (RIAA)**, which represents musicians, for copyright infringement and shut down. The music companies complain that they are losing profits and that musicians are losing royalties as people download music for free, which violates copyright law. The RIAA also expanded into lawsuits against individuals. Movies, software, and other copyrighted materials are also being illegally copied through file sharing (piracy).

According to the **International Federation of the Phonographic Industry,** piracy is a real problem, as 95% of all music downloads violate copyrights.(a) In many countries, because some governments don't have the desire or resources to enforce copyright laws, some governments even resist allowing companies to take legal action against companies and individuals.

1. Is it ethical and socially responsible for file-sharing companies to give people the means to download music, movies, or software for free?

2. Is it ethical and socially responsible for people to download music, movies, or software for free, which prevents recording, film, or software companies and artists from getting any royalties?

3. Is it ethical and socially responsible for countries to ignore and even resist enforcing copyright laws? Should all countries enforce copyright laws?

Reference

a. P. Sonne and M. Colchester, "France, the U.K. Take Aim at Digital Pirates," *The Wall Street Journal* (April 15, 2012): B1.

**WORK
APPLICATION 3-11**

Select a business and identify how it uses global sourcing and/or importing and exporting.

global sourcing Hiring others outside the organization to perform work worldwide.

licensing The process of a licensor agreeing to give a licensee the right to make its products or services or use its intellectual property in exchange for a royalty.

Global Sourcing. Global sourcing *is hiring others outside the firm to perform work worldwide.* It is also called *outsourcing* and *offshoring*, and it is expected to increase.[191] Global managers look worldwide for the best deal on materials/parts, labor, and so forth and a location (any country in the world) for producing their products and services.[192] Outsourcing saves money and better allocates global resources,[193] as it benefits everyone because countries specialize in what they can do better than others. **BMW**, **Honda**, and other automakers get their parts from all over the globe. There is a saying: "Do what you do best and outsource the rest." Apple buys its iPhone and Apple Watch computer chips from its greatest rival, Samsung.[194] As a global-minded manager, you will need to scan the world, not just your country, for the best deal. The other six methods of going global usually encompass global sourcing. Your college may use a global source to run its bookstore and dining hall.

Importing and Exporting. When *importing*, a domestic firm *buys* products from foreign firms and sells them at home. **Pier 1 Imports**' business revolves around searching the globe for foreign goods to sell at home. **GM** will become the first major auto maker to sell Chinese-made cars in the U.S.[195] When *exporting,* a domestic firm *sells* its products to foreign buyers, like **Amazon** did in its first month in business.[196] One myth about small businesses is that it is too difficult for them to go global, but in reality they account for a large percentage of exports.[197] The **U.S. Export-Import Bank (EXIM Bank)** helps businesses of all sizes go global. For more information, visit www.exim.gov. **FedEx** and **UPS** both offer a variety of services to help any-size business use global sourcing and importing and exporting.

Licensing and Franchising. Also known as *cooperative contracts,* internationals and MNCs use these two methods to go global. In **licensing**, a licensor agrees to give a licensee the right to make its products or services or use its intellectual property in exchange for a royalty. Under a global licensing agreement, the domestic individual or company licensor allows another foreign company licensee to make its product, sell its service, or use its

EXHIBIT 3-10   FORMS OF GLOBAL BUSINESS

Lowest Cost and Risk ⟶ Highest Cost and Risk				
Importing/ Exporting	Licensing and Franchising	Contracting	Strategic Alliances and Joint Ventures	Direct Investment

Characteristic of International Business ⟶ Characteristic of Multinational Corporations

Note that global sourcing can be used alone (at low cost/risk), but is commonly used in tandem with other global strategies.

intellectual property—brand name, trademark, a particular technology, a patent, or a copyright—in exchange for a royalty in a particular foreign market. **Apple** earns revenue by licensing its patented technology to other companies.

In **franchising**, *the franchisor licenses the entire business to the franchisee for a fee and royalties*. The franchiser provides a combination of trademark, equipment, materials, training, managerial guidelines, consulting advice, and cooperative advertising to the franchisee for an initial fee and a percentage of the revenues. Franchising is a global business. **KFC** was yielding 70% of its profits from China before separating into two companies in 2016.[198] In January 2017, **Subway** had 44,851 locations in 112 countries.[199] Several fast food restaurants, including **KFC, Burger King, Wendy's,** and **McDonald's,** are selling their company stores to franchisees.[200]

franchising An entrepreneurial venture in which a franchisor licenses a business to the franchisee for a fee and royalties.

Contracting. Contracting is similar to global sourcing, but it tends to be on a large scale. Global product sourcing commonly includes using materials and parts from other companies in the firm's product. Conversely, contracting is having the foreign company actually make the entire product for you. With global **contract manufacturing**, *a company has a foreign firm manufacture the products that it sells as its own.* **Nike** focuses on designing and marketing its products; it doesn't own any manufacturing facilities; virtually all of its

contract manufacturing Contracting a foreign firm to manufacture products a company will sell as its own.

3-4   APPLYING THE CONCEPT

Global Practices

Identify each practice as more likely to be used by large or small global companies:

A. large MNCs
B. small international companies

____ 20. Companies that develop a product in one country and then bring the product to other countries.

____ 21. Companies that only import and/or export to operate globally.

____ 22. Companies that have foreign nationals among their top-level managers.

____ 23. Companies that make their products in other countries.

____ 24. Companies that develop the latest technology through R&D.

Global companies often partner with contractors to produce goods or perform services.

©iStockphoto.com/GCShutter

products are made in foreign countries. **Levi Strauss & Co**. has been contracting its iconic jeans in China for more than 30 years.[201] **Foxconn** is a multinational Taiwanese electronics contract manufacturing company that makes products, including **Apple** iPhones and iPads. There is global *management contracting*, in which a company provides management services for a foreign firm. **Hilton** manages hotels and resorts for other companies globally.

Strategic Alliances and Joint Ventures. It is very difficult to go to a foreign country and operate a new venture on your own. Therefore, alliances and joint ventures (similar but different) are especially advantageous to smaller partners who want to go global but don't have the resources to operate on their own in a foreign country and for the partner who doesn't have the brand name or resources to expand domestically. A **strategic alliance** *is an agreement to share resources that does not necessarily involve creating a new company.* The two (or more) companies remain separate and independently controlled but share resources to sell products and services in other countries, to develop new or improved products and/or to build production facilities. Your college may have global strategic alliances, such as study-abroad programs. **Springfield College** offered its master's degree through an alliance with the **Health and Behavioral Sciences College**, using its facilities and some of its faculty in Israel. **SHI (IOM 4)** has strategic alliances with **Adobe, Autodesk, Dell, HP, Intel, Microsoft,** and others.

A **joint venture** *is created when two or more firms share ownership of a new company.* The two (or more) companies remain separate and independently controlled but share the ownership and control of the new company created through the partnership. **Starbucks** expanded to India through a joint venture with **Tata Global Beverages—Tata Starbucks.** The business model created and enforced in China is for foreign companies to have a Chinese partner. U.S. **GM** has 11 joint ventures in China.

Direct investment. Direct investment *is the building or buying of operating facilities in a foreign country.* It is also called *wholly owned affiliates* or *subsidiaries.* Foreign direct investment is on the increase,[202] as being local virtually eliminates foreign trade barriers.[203] Chinese-owned **Volvo Car Corp.** and German owned **Daimler** plan to build new factories in America.[204] Chinese SOE **Haler Group** bought **GE**'s appliance business,[205] and African-owned **Steinhoff International Holdings** acquired **Mattress Firm**[206] to break into the U.S. market.

Trends and Issues in Management

As you already know, we discussed two of the major trends and issues in this chapter, so we will keep it brief on global and diversity issues here. As discussed in Chapter 2, it is important to keep up with the rapid changes in the global business environment.[207] One quick tip for developing a *global* mind-set: Consider a study-abroad program while you are in college.[208] Let's combine *global, diversity,* and *technology.* **Facebook** has grown from a U.S. hangout for college students into a global community whose members are increasingly not American.[209] Although there is a call for more women and minorities to get STEM (science, technology, engineering, math) jobs, clearly there is a need for greater diversity in high-tech firms globally,[210] as women and minorities are hampered.[211] Their rate of advancing is even slower than in old-line businesses.[212]

Although there has been international trade since the beginning of the New World thousands of years ago, clearly *technology* in communications and travel, including shipping goods around the world (like with **UPS** and **FedEx**), has clearly accelerated the speed of globalization of business. But with doing business globally, companies face challenges in

---

WORK
APPLICATION 3-12

Select a business you buy from that has a global license or franchise.

WORK
APPLICATION 3-13

Select a business you buy from that used contract manufacturing to make your product.

WORK
APPLICATION 3-14

Select a business that uses strategic alliances, joint ventures, and/or direct investments globally.

strategic alliance An agreement to share resources that does not necessarily involve creating a new company.

joint venture Two or more firms sharing ownership of a new company.

direct investment The building or buying of operating facilities in a foreign country.

3-5 APPLYING THE CONCEPT

Forms of Global Business

Identify which activity or form of global business is described in each statement.

A. global sourcing

B. importing and exporting

C. licensing and franchising

D. contracting

E. strategic alliance and joint venture

F. direct investment

_____25. Springfield College offers a master's degree program in Israel at the Health and Behavioral Sciences College, which provides the facilities and administrative support.

_____26. Philips in France makes TVs using speakers from Japan.

_____27. Tires R Us in the United States buys tires from Bridgestone in Japan for retail sale.

_____28. Chinese Alibaba buys a warehouse in America to distribute online orders in the United States.

_____29. The American Children's Television Workshop gives a Chinese company the right to make its Sesame Street character puppets.

_____30. Whirlpool makes its appliances in its factory in Russia.

_____31. Dell assembles its computers in the United States and sells them online to people globally.

_____32. Costco has a Canadian company make some of its Kirkland brand items for sale in its U.S. stores.

_____33. Wilson Sporting Goods buys the rubber for tennis balls from Brazil.

_____34. McDonald's makes a deal with an Italian businessperson to open a McDonald's in Rome.

3-4 JOIN THE DISCUSSION ETHICS & SOCIAL RESPONSIBILITY

Bribes

An American businessperson working in a foreign country complained to a local telephone manager that the technician showed up and asked for a bribe before installing the phone. The businessperson refused, so the telephone worker left without installing the phone. The telephone company manager told the businessperson that the matter would be investigated, for a fee (bribe).

1. Is it ethical and socially responsible to pay bribes?

2. Should the businessperson have paid the bribe to get the phone installed?

cultural barriers to communications, as communication styles do vary between cultures.[213] We will discuss this in Chapter 13, "Communication and Information Technology."

Getting back to *ethics*, what is considered ethical does vary among countries, and the U.S. Foreign Corrupt Practices Act (Chapter 2) is confusing, not to mention that it is not globally accepted.[214] Hopefully, the FCPA or a similar law will have a trend of increased adoption globally. Does it pay to be ethical? **Volkswagen** created a $19.3 billion fund to cover the cost of its cheating on auto emissions. In addition, the unethical illegal scandal hurt its reputation, resulting in costly lost sales.[215]

Another important issue is *social responsibility*. As discussed in the last chapter, today's business leaders realize the importance of social responsibility including *sustainability*. Even though the laws and regulations on environmental safety and pollution vary greatly across the globe, businesses need to go beyond the law to the second level of corporate social responsibility to be ethical and preserve our natural environment to the best of their ability using the latest *technology* even though it may be more costly. **Volkswagen**'s unethical cheating on emissions resulted in more air pollution.

As we bring this chapter to a close, you should better understand the global environment including its three classifications of businesses and the importance of foreign trade. You should also realize the importance of workplace diversity and the six types of diverse groups and how to manage diversity through inclusion. This understanding should also expand to global diversity in working well with people from other country cultures, as well as considering some trends and issues facing managers regarding these topics. It is also important to know how to manage a global business with six global management practices and six forms of global business.

$SAGE edge™   edge.sagepub.com/lussier8e

Want a better grade?

Get the tools you need to sharpen your study skills. Access practice quizzes, eFlashcards, video and multimedia, and more at edge.sagepub.com/lussier8e.

Digital Resources

Learning Objective	Digital Resource
3-1. Contrast the classification of businesses in the global village, define ethnocentrism, and describe issues managers encounter through foreign trade.	▶ Ethnocentrism
3-2. Discuss diversity and inclusion and why they are important.	▶ Diversity and Inclusion*
3-3. Describe the six major types of diversity groups and practices of managing diversity.	▶ Diversity Management
3-4. Compare and contrast the Hofstede national culture dimensions with Project GLOBE.	▶ Management in Action: Religious Diversity and Management*
3-5. Rank the six forms that make a business a global one, in order from lowest to highest cost and risk.	▣ Global Market Entry Strategies

* premium video available only in the interactive eBook

••• CHAPTER SUMMARY

3-1. **Contrast the classification of businesses in the global village, define ethnocentrism, and describe issues managers encounter through foreign trade.**

Businesses are classified in three ways. A *domestic business* does business in only one country. An *international company* is based primarily in one country but transacts business in other countries. A *multinational corporation (MNC)* owns operations in two or more countries. *Ethnocentrism* is regarding one's own ethnic group or culture as superior to others. Foreign trade clearly can increase company profits and increase the standard of living in countries trading even if one country is more efficient at producing the goods. Managers may encounter *trade barriers* (embargos, quotas, subsidies, or tariffs) that can put them at a disadvantage in the

global village, but they may get help to overcome them with the aid of the *World Trade Organization (WTO)* and *trade agreements*. The *exchange rate* is how much of one country's currency you get for that of another country. Fluctuations in exchange rates can affect profits at home when conducting foreign trade. When your own currency is strong, it may decrease profits as you get less in exchange, and a weak home currency can increase profits as you get more in exchange.

3-2. **Discuss diversity and inclusion and why they are important.**

Diversity refers to the variety of people with different group identities within the same workplace. *Inclusion* is a practice of ensuring that all employees feel they belong as valued members of the organization. *Discrimination* is illegal because it gives unfair treatment to diversity groups in employment decisions. But promoting diversity and inclusion creates equal opportunities for all employees, so it is the right thing to do. It is also beneficial to business. The global white population is decreasing while the other races are growing at a fast pace, making developing and selling products and services to non-Caucasians critically important to survival and business growth. Diversity and inclusion can have positive effects on financial outcomes, as other races are creative at innovating and selling products and services to the growing diverse population.

3-3. Describe the six major types of diversity groups and practices of managing diversity.

There is diversity in (1) the range of *ages* and generational difference in the workplace, (2) gender and sexual orientation (LGBT), (3) different *races* and *ethnic* groups, (4) people with *disabilities* that substantially limit one or more major life activities and abilities to excel at some things, (5) people from different religions, and (6) several others including weight, personality, physical attractiveness, and family background, just to list a few. To manage diversity, companies cannot discriminate against any group and should promote equal opportunities for everyone. Practices that promote diversity include (1) *diversity training* to teach people how to get along better with diverse workers through inclusion, (2) higher-level manager *mentors* who prepare high-potential people for advancement, and (3) *network diversity groups* of employees throughout the organization from a diverse group who share information about how to succeed in the company.

3-4. Compare and contrast the Hofstede national culture dimensions with Project GLOBE.

The two are similar because they both measure cultural diversity among countries. Back in the 1970s and 1980s, Hofstede identified five dimensions of diversity (power distance inequality vs. power equality, individuality vs. collectivism, assertiveness vs. nurturing, uncertainty avoidance vs. uncertainty acceptance, and long-term vs. short-term orientation) using employees of one company, IBM, in 40 countries. GLOBE confirmed that Hofstede's five dimensions are still valid today and extended and expanded his five dimensions into nine (assertiveness, future orientation, gender differences, uncertainty avoidance, power distance, societal collectivism, in-group collectivism, performance orientation, and humane orientation), and the sample includes hundreds of companies from more than 60 countries. GLOBE is also an ongoing study.

3-5. Rank the six forms that make a business a global one, in order from lowest to highest cost and risk.

A business can become a global one by (1) participating in *global sourcing*, hiring others outside the firm to perform work worldwide; (2) *importing and exporting*, buying and selling products between countries; (3) *licensing*, in which the licensor agrees to give a licensee the right to make its products or services or use its intellectual property in exchange for a royalty, or *franchising*, in which the franchisor licenses the entire business to the franchisee for a fee and royalties; (4) *contract manufacturing*, in which a company has a foreign firm manufacture the products that it sells as its own; (5) forming a *strategic alliance*, an agreement to share resources that does not necessarily involve creating a new company, or a *joint venture*, created when two or more firms share ownership of a new company; or (6) making a *direct investment*, building or buying operating facilities in a foreign country. Global sourcing is the least costly and risky of these activities, and it can be a part of any of the others.

••• KEY TERMS

contract manufacturing, 93	expatriates, 88	international company, 68
direct investment, 94	franchising, 93	joint venture, 94
disability, 83	glass ceiling, 79	licensing, 92
discrimination, 76	global sourcing, 92	multinational corporation (MNC), 68
diversity, 75	global village, 68	strategic alliance, 94
ethnocentrism, 68	inclusion, 75	

••• KEY TERM REVIEW

Complete each of the following statements using one of this chapter's key terms.

1. The _____ refers to companies conducting business worldwide without boundaries.

2. An _____ is based primarily in one country but transacts business in other countries.

3. A _____ has ownership in operations in two or more countries.

4. _____ is regarding one's own ethnic group or culture as superior to others.

5. _____ is hiring others outside the firm to perform work worldwide.

6. In _____, a licensor agrees to give a licensee the right to make its products or services or use its intellectual property in exchange for a royalty.

7. In _____, the franchisor licenses the entire business to the franchisee for a fee and royalties.

8. With global _____, a company has a foreign firm manufacture the products that it sells as its own.

9. A _____ is an agreement to share resources that does not necessarily involve creating a new company.

10. A _____ is created when two or more firms share ownership of a new company.

11. _____ is the building or buying of operating facilities in a foreign country.

12. _____ refers to the variety of people with different group identities within the same workplace.

13. _____ is a practice of ensuring that every employee feels he or she belongs as a valued member of the organization.

14. _____ is illegal because it gives unfair treatment to diversity groups in employment decisions.

15. The _____ is the invisible barrier that prevents women and minorities from advancing to the top jobs in organizations.

16. A _____ is a mental or physical impairment that substantially limits one or more major life activities.

17. _____ live and work outside their native country.

● ● ● REVIEW QUESTIONS

1. How are businesses classified in the global village?

2. What are the four trade barriers?

3. What is the role of the World Trade Organization (WTO)?

4. What are the six major trade agreements?

5. Which country has the foreign trade advantage based on exchange rates?

6. What is the difference between diversity and affirmative action?

7. What is the glass ceiling?

8. When dealing with people with disabilities, what should be the focus?

9. What are three practices used to promote diversity?

10. What are the five dimensions of Hofstede's cultural diversity?

11. What is Project GLOBE?

12. What are the nine dimensions of Project GLOBE?

13. What is the difference between a license and a franchise?

14. What is the difference between a strategic alliance, a joint venture, and a direct investment?

15. What do international and multinational companies have in common?

16. If you were to start your own small business, would you most likely use contracting, strategic alliances, joint ventures, or direct investment?

● ● ● COMMUNICATION SKILLS

The following critical-thinking questions can be used for class discussion and/or as written assignments to develop communication skills. Be sure to give complete explanations for all questions.

1. How does globalization affect your life and that of your family and friends?

2. Should people in the United States make an effort to buy products made in America? If so, how should "made in America" be defined?

3. Should your home country drop all or some of its trade barriers?

4. Is the North American Free Trade Agreement (NAFTA) of more benefit or harm to the United States? Why?

5. Should there be one global trade agreement rather than the six major agreements?

6. Should countries with a trade deficit create barriers to trade to eliminate the deficit?

7. Overall, are the effects of foreign trade more positive or negative for your home country?

8. How does diversity affect you personally? Do you really value diversity?

9. What experience have you had with each of the diverse groups?

10. How can you improve your awareness and empathy for diverse groups?

11. Identify mentors you have had in your life (relatives, friends, teachers, coaches, managers) and how they helped you to succeed. Also, will you seek out a mentor(s) to help you advance in your career?

12. Should expatriates be given global cultural diversity training, and should their families get training, too?

13. Is it too difficult and time consuming to engage in global sourcing?

14. Are smaller international companies at a disadvantage when competing with large multinational corporations?

CASES

● ● ● Case 3-1   Marriott International

Marriott International is a leader in the hospitality industry with more than 3,200 lodging properties worldwide and a workforce of more than 146,000 employees working in 55 countries and territories. Its core values include: We Put People First, We Pursue Excellence, We Embrace Change, We Act with Integrity, and We Serve Our World. The company is particularly well known for its commitment to workforce diversity and inclusion. The emphasis on the importance of workforce diversity is reflected in the words of J.W. Marriott Jr., chairman and CEO:

> We are broadening how we think about global diversity and inclusion, reaching across cultural borders to compete for customers and talent worldwide. In this competitive marketplace, we must continue to embrace the unique talents and experiences of our employees— who speak more than 50 languages in 66 countries and territories—to help us meet the changing needs of our customers.

Marriott International has been recognized for its commitment to workforce diversity through various industry and business awards including 50 Best Workplaces for Diversity, 10 Best Workplaces for Latinos, 10 Best Workplaces for African Americans, and America's top corporations for lesbian, gay, bisexual, and transgender (LGBT) equality, where it earned a perfect 100% score on the 2016 Aon Best Employer in Asia Pacific.

Marriott focuses its diversity efforts on a holistic view that includes guests, associates, business owners, and suppliers in all of the places and communities in which it does business. For guests, the company offers its award-winning #LoveTravels campaign, which inspires guests to explore their personal passions and to celebrate their unique perspectives and experiences. For associates (employees), Marriott offers a variety of initiatives including the empowerment of its associates to champion diversity and drive inclusion, developing multicultural tools and resources that help managers further understand and build awareness about cultural differences, and engaging with organizations that support and provide opportunities for veterans and people with disabilities. With

its suppliers, Marriott has spent more than $4 billion to support the development of relationships with thousands of businesses owned by minorities, women, veterans, disabled people, and LGBT leaders around the globe. It is also an active corporate member of multinational organizations that support the development of diverse and historically excluded suppliers, such as the National Gay and Lesbian Chamber of Commerce and the Women's Business Enterprise. Finally, for business owners, Marriott runs an Ownership Educational Summit for diverse and women business owners to educate them on potential investment opportunities in the industry.

Discussion Questions

1. Why does Marriott International view diversity and inclusion as being important for its business success?

2. Which types of diversity and inclusion exist in Marriott International's workforce?

3. How do Marriott International's business practices not reflect an emphasis on affirmative action?

4. What business practices does Marriott International use to support workforce diversity and inclusion?

5. Do you think it is a good idea for companies like Marriott International to consider diversity issues when making hiring and promotion decisions, or should these decisions always be made based solely on who is the most qualified person for a job in terms of education, experience, and relevant knowledge and skills? Take a position and support it.

6. How important would it be to you to work for an employer that has an effective diversity program? Take a position and support it.

References

http://www.marriott.com/diversity/diversity-and-inclusion.mi

http://www.marriott.com/diversity/corporate-diversity.mi

http://www.marriott.com/diversity/cultural-diversity.mi

http://www.marriott.com/diversity/partners-in-diversity.mi

http://www.marriott.com/Multimedia/PDF/Corporate/DiversityFactSheet.pdf

http://www.diversityinc.com/marriott-international/

http://www.marriott.com/about/corporate-overview.mi

Case created by Loren Kuzuhara, University of Wisconsin–Madison.

● ● ● Case 3-2   Ford: Bringing It On Back From Mexico

You used to be able to buy a Ford in any color you wanted— as long as it was black! Today Ford Motor is one of the world's largest automakers and includes a staple of brands and models including the Ford Mustang, the F-Series pickup, Focus, Lincoln, Fiesta, and Taurus. Reflecting a growing global auto market, Ford launched 16 new vehicles globally in 2015, followed by 12 global products in fiscal 2016, including the new

F-Series Super Duty, Ford GT, and Lincoln Continental. It will add more electrified products for Ford and Lincoln, including the new Focus Electric. Through 2020, it has plans to invest $4.5 billion in electrified vehicle solutions.

Like many other carmakers, the company is also looking to emerging economies for growth, particularly Brazil, Russia,

India, and China, where cars sales are forecast to grow more rapidly than in mature markets. Ford has planned to build new plants in India, Thailand, and especially China to meet more demand in the region.(1)

Yet those plans quickly changed when President-Elect Donald Trump took to Twitter to criticize Ford's fellow U.S.-based competitor General Motors: "General Motors is sending Mexican made model of Chevy Cruze to U.S. car dealers-tax free across border. Make in U.S.A. or pay big border tax!"(2)

> It used to be cars were made in Flint and you couldn't drink the water in Mexico. Now the cars are made in Mexico, and you can't drink the water in Flint. That's not good." [Donald Trump was referring to the lead water crisis in the Michigan city.](3)

Ford immediately announced it would cancel its $1.6 billion plans to build a plant in San Luis Potosi, Mexico, and instead invest an additional $700 million to expand an existing plant in Michigan to make autonomous and electric vehicles. That came on the heels of another decision in November to keep production of some small SUVs at its plant in Kentucky. The move marks a departure for Ford, whose CEO Mark Fields said that it was very likely Ford would not change plans for its $1.6 billion factory. CEO Fields said that Trump's rhetoric was a factor in reversing his earlier decision, but one of several factors. "Ford is a global automaker, but our home . . . is right here in the United States," he said.(4)

Ford chairman Bill Ford Jr. said he spoke with President-elect Trump to tell him of the decision to invest in the United States and cancel the Mexico plant, according to Reuters. "We're also encouraged by the pro-growth policies that president-elect Trump and the new Congress have indicated that they will pursue," Ford president and CEO Mark Fields said in a statement.

He said the carmaker was influenced by promises of new tax and regulatory reforms and the prospect of keeping jobs at home.(5)

The Mexican government did not stand idly by. Mexico's economy ministry argued that investments in Mexico have helped keep jobs in the United States.

> The Mexican government regrets the decision of the Ford Motor Company to cancel the investment project in San Luis Potosi, and it has assured the return by the company of any expenditures made by the state government to facilitate this investment. The growth of the Ford Motor Company in North America, particularly in Mexico, is a strategy of competitiveness based on global value chains, in which North America competes with other world regions. The jobs generated in Mexico have contributed to keeping manufacturing jobs in the United States that would otherwise have disappeared in the face of Asian competition.(6)

Mexico's economy ministry argued that investments in Mexico have helped keep jobs in the United States. The minister also reiterated that Mexico was still in favor of a "modernization" of NAFTA that would "strengthen the competitive capacities of North America and of each of its members."(7)

Discussion Questions

1. How would you classify Ford Motor from the perspective of the global village?

2. What is the "buy American" effort and how does this consumer movement affect this case?

3. Assume that President Trump decided to take actions to limit car imports into the United States, what would we call these actions and what alternatives are available to him?

4. What is NAFTA and how does it affect this case?

5. What are the differing forms of managing a global business and which form(s) is (are) being addressed in this case?

6. Agree or disagree with Ford's decision to cancel its manufacturing plant in Mexico and build in the United States based upon the impact this decision may make on the U.S. standard of living.

Cumulative Case Questions

7. President-elect Trump's tweet about GM's moving its plant to Mexico demonstrate which managerial role(s)? (Chapter 1)

8. Which environmental factors (stakeholders) were effected by this case? (Chapter 2)

References

(1) Anderson, A. (n.d.). Ford Motor Company. Hoovers. Retrieved February 15, 2017, from http://0-subscriber.hoovers.com.liucat.lib.liu.edu/H/company360/fulldescription.html?companyId=10597000000000

(2) Noguchi, Y. (2017, January 3). Shaming firms that export jobs has worked for Trump so far. NPR. Retrieved February 15, 2017, from http://www.npr.org/sections/thetwo-way/2017/01/03/508078574/trump-has-gotten-action-so-far-by-shaming-firms-that-export-jobs

(3) Lovelace, B., Jr. (2017, January 3). Ford canceling plans for $1.6 billion plant in Mexico, investing $700 million in Michigan expansion instead. CNBC. Retrieved February 15, 2017, from http://www.cnbc.com/2017/01/03/ford-canceling-plans-for-16-billion-plant-in-mexico-investing-700-million-in-michigan-expansion-instead.html

(4) Noguchi, Y. (2017, January 3). Shaming firms that export jobs has worked for Trump so far. NPR. Retrieved February 15, 2017, from http://www.npr.org/sections/thetwo-way/2017/01/03/508078574/trump-has-gotten-action-so-far-by-shaming-firms-that-export-jobs

(5) Lovelace, B., Jr. (2017, January 3). Ford canceling plans for $1.6 billion plant in Mexico, investing $700 million in Michigan expansion instead. CNBC. Retrieved February 15, 2017, from http://www.cnbc.com/2017/01/03/ford-canceling-plans-for-16-billion-plant-in-mexico-investing-700-million-in-michigan-expansion-instead.html

(6) *Industry Week* (2017, January 3). Mexico "regrets" Ford decision to scrap new plant. Agence France-Presse. Retrieved February 15, 2017, from http://www.industryweek.com/trade/mexico-regrets-ford-decision-scrap-new-plant

(7) Ibid.

Case created by Herbert Sherman, Long Island University.

••• SKILL BUILDER 3-1: THE GLOBAL ENVIRONMENT, DIVERSITY, AND MANAGEMENT PRACTICES ANALYSIS

Objective

To better understand an organization's global environment, diversity, and practices that can help get a job candidate a position with the company.

Skills

The primary skills developed through this exercise are:

1. *Management skill*—conceptual decision making
2. *AACSB competencies*—dynamics of the global economy, reasoning abilities, and multicultural and diversity understanding
3. *Management function*—planning, organizing, leading, and controlling

For this exercise, select a company that does business globally, preferably one you would like to work for. You will most likely need to conduct some research to get the answers to the questions that follow.

1. How is the business classified in the global village?
2. What trade barriers has it had to deal with?
3. What countries does it conduct business in, and what trade agreements are these countries involved in?

4. Which of the methods for going global does the business use? Be sure to give examples of its global sources; names of any import or export partners; names of any companies to which it gives licenses or franchises; any contractors, strategic allies, or joint venture partner names; and any subsidiaries it has as direct investments.
5. What are its diversity groups and its policies and practices for promoting diversity?
6. Compare the company's nine GLOBE dimensions for five countries it does business with. Make a chart similar to Exhibit 3-9, "GLOBE Dimensions."
7. Does the company offer international assignments, and how does it train its expatriates and families?

You may be asked to pass in this assignment, present your answers to the class, and/or discuss your answers in small groups or online.

Apply It

What did I learn from this experience? How will I use this knowledge in the future?

••• SKILL BUILDER 3-2: DIVERSITY TRAINING

Objective

To become more aware of and sensitive to diversity.

Skills

The primary skills developed through this exercise are:

1. *Management skill*—decision making (conceptual, diagnostic, analytical, and critical-thinking skills are needed to understand diversity)
2. *AACSB competency*—multicultural and diversity understanding
3. Management function—organizing

Answer the following questions.

Race and Ethnicity

1. My race (ethnicity) is _____.
2. My name, _____, is significant because it means _____. [or] My name,_____, is significant because I was named after _____.
3. One positive thing about my racial/ethnic background is _____.
4. One difficult thing about my racial/ethnic background is _____.

Religion

5. My religion is _____. [or] I don't have one.
6. One positive thing about my religious background (or lack thereof) is _____.
7. One difficult thing about my religious background (or lack thereof) is _____.

Sex

8. I am _____ (male/female).
9. One positive thing about being (male/female) is _____.
10. One difficult thing about being (male/female) is _____.

Age and Generational

11. I am _____ years old.
12. One positive thing about being this age is _____.
13. One difficult thing about being this age is _____.

Other

14. One way in which I am different from other people is _____.
15. One positive thing about being different in this way is _____.

16.   One negative thing about being different in this way is ____.

Prejudice, Stereotypes, Discrimination

17.   If you have, and we all have, ever been prejudged, stereo- typed, or discriminated against, describe what happened.

You may be asked to discuss your answers in small groups or online to better understand people different from you.

Apply It

What did I learn from this experience? How will I use this knowledge in the future?

• • • SKILL BUILDER 3-3: CULTURAL DIVERSITY AWARENESS

Objective

To develop your awareness of cultural diversity.

Skills

The primary skills developed through this exercise are:

1.   *Management skill*—interpersonal
2.   *AACSB competency*—multicultural and diversity understanding
3.   Management function—leading

Procedure 1 (4–6 minutes)

You and your classmates will share your international expe- rience and nationalities. Start with people who have lived in another country; then move to those who have visited another country; and follow with discussion of nationality (e.g., I am half French and Irish but have never been to either

country). The instructor or a recorder will write the countries on the board until several countries/nationalities are listed or the time is up.

Procedure 2 (10–30 minutes)

You and your classmates will share your knowledge of cul- tural differences between the country in which the course is being taught and those listed on the board. This is a good opportunity for international students and those who have visited other countries to share their experiences. For exam- ple, in Spain most people have a two-hour lunch break and go home for a big meal and may take a nap. In Japan, people expect to receive and give gifts. You may also discuss cultural differences within the country.

Apply It

What did I learn from this experience? How will I use this knowledge in the future?

4 Creative Problem Solving and Decision Making

• • • LEARNING OBJECTIVES

After studying this chapter, you should be able to:

4-1. Discuss the relationship among objectives, problem solving, and decision making and their relationship among the management functions. PAGE 106

4-2. Describe when to use rational (maximizing) versus bounded rational (satisficing) decision making and group versus individual decision making. PAGE 110

4-3. Explain the difference between an objective and "must" and "want" criteria. PAGE 113

4-4. State the difference between creativity and innovation and identify five group techniques used to generate creative alternatives. PAGE 113

4-5. Compare quantitative techniques including big data, cost-benefit analysis, and intuition for analyzing and selecting an alternative. PAGE 119

4-6. Explain the importance of planning, implementing, and controlling decisions. PAGE 124

IOM

Ideas on Management
at Nike

Phil Knight ran track for coach **Bill Bowerman** at the University of Oregon in the 1960s. From that athletic alliance, they went on together to start the **Nike** corporation in 1972. Initially, the company imported track shoes from Japan, and Knight sold them out of his car at track meets. But the company soon began to design and market its own running shoes, taking market share from the top German brands **Adidas** and **Puma**. Today, **Under Armour** is also a tough competitor.

The NIKE Inc. (with **Jordan, Hurley,** and **Converse brands**) mission is to bring inspiration and innovation to every athlete in the world: If you have a body, you are an athlete. The mission reflects a key insight that Bill Bowerman had early in the company's history—that everyone is an athlete. This idea continues to drive Nike's business decisions and inform its marketing strategies.

Knight led Nike from a small partnership founded on a handshake to the world's largest footwear, apparel, and equipment company that is ranked in the top 100 of the ***Fortune*** *500* list, with 2016 profits of $3.2 billion, and it is ranked in the top 20 of the *Fortune World's Most Admired Companies.* He retired in 2015 with **Mark Parker** as chief executive officer (CEO) and **Jeanne Jackson** as president of product and merchandising. In 2016, Chairman Emeritus Knight was ranked in the top 20 on the ***Forbes*** *400 Richest People* list with a net worth of $25.5 billion.

Knight made a good decision in promoting Parker, an introverted sneaker designer, to CEO, as under his leadership Nike revenues and profits doubled, and its stock price jumped six-fold. In 2015, Mark Parker was the ***Fortune*** *Business Person of the Year.* Profits accelerated on high-margin direct-to-consumer sales and a batch of self-lacing sneakers that cost around $700 a pair.

IOM 1. Has Nike made any bad decisions?

IOM 2. What type of decision does Nike make to sign large endorsement contracts with young, unproven athletes, such as National Basketball Association (NBA) player LeBron James back in 2003?

IOM 3. What objectives does Nike meet through its star athlete endorsements?

IOM 4. How does Nike demonstrate creativity and innovation?

IOM 5. Does the amount of contracts given to young, unproven athletes pose a serious financial risk to Nike? Which techniques could Nike use to analyze the alternatives in contract decisions?

You'll find answers to these **IOM** questions throughout the chapter. To learn more about Nike, visit www.nike.com.

Sources: Case information and answers to questions within the chapter were taken from Nike's website at www.nike.com, accessed January 9, 2017; "World's Most Admired Companies," *Fortune* (March 1, 2016); *Forbes 400, The Top 20, Forbes* (October 25, 2016); "Largest U.S. Corporations—*Fortune 500,*" *Fortune* (June 15, 2016): F5; Fortune Business Person of the Year, *Fortune* December 2, 105): 95; K. Stock, "Movers, Nike," *BusinessWeek* (December 26–January 8, 2017).

Discuss the relationship among objectives, problem solving, and decision making and their relationship among the management functions.

Problem Solving and Decision Making: An Overview

Recall that decision making is one of the three critical management skills. Corporate recruiters want employees that like to solve problems[1] and have decision-making skills.[2] Decisions made by large corporate managers don't only affect their companies and employees—they have a profound impact on their stakeholders (Chapter 2).[3] Poor decisions cost **BP** billions of dollars and fishermen their businesses, as well as destroying wildlife and ecosystems. Almost every problem harbors opportunity.[4] Several businesses made profits by helping clean up the mess made by BP. **Google** has made billions over the years solving the problem of finding and organizing reliable information quickly through its search engine.

Michael Jordan wanted a sponsorship deal with **Adidas** when he went to the NBA, but executives said he wasn't tall enough and no one could relate to him.[5] As you most likely know, Nike made the right decision to sign Jordan. Nike also made a good decision leading to taking the NBA sponsorship away from **Reebok**—owned by Adidas.[6] **Nike** (**IOM 1**) has made some poor decisions too, such as buying **Umbro** for $484 million and selling the subsidiary in 2012 for only $225 million, a 46% loss.

Let's face it—we are not perfect decision makers, but we can improve our decision-making skills;[7] that is the objective of this chapter. In this section, we discuss problem-solving and decision-making interrelationships, as well as an exploration of your preferred decision-making style, and we end with the decision-making model steps.

Problem-Solving and Decision-Making Interrelationships

Problem solving and decision making are interrelated with each other and with objectives and the management functions. Here's how.

The Relationship Among Objectives, Problem Solving, and Decision Making. When you do not meet your objectives, you have a problem. The better you can develop plans that prevent problems before they occur, the fewer problems you will have, and the more time you will have to take advantage of opportunities and respond to competitive threats.[8]

problem The situation that exists whenever objectives are not being met.

problem solving The process of taking corrective action to meet objectives.

decision making The process of selecting a course of action that will solve a problem.

A **problem** *exists whenever objectives are not being met.* In other words, you have a problem whenever there is a difference between what is actually happening and what you want to happen. If the objective is to produce 1,500 units per day but the department produces only 1,490, a problem exists. **Problem solving** *is the process of taking corrective action to meet objectives.* **Decision making** *is the process of selecting a course of action that will solve a problem.* Decisions must be made when you are faced with a problem.[9] When something isn't working, fix it.[10] **McDonald's** has a problem with decreasing sales and made decisions to offer all-day breakfast and fresh baked goods.

The first decision you face when confronted with a problem is whether to take corrective action. Some problems cannot be solved, and others do not deserve the time and effort it would take to solve them. However, your job requires you to achieve organizational objectives. Therefore, you will have to attempt to solve most problems—this is what managers and employees get paid to do.

Get the edge on your studies. **edge.sagepub .com/lussier8e**

- Take a quiz to find out what you've learned.
- Review key terms with eFlashcards.
- Watch videos that enhance chapter content.

The Relationship Among the Management Functions, Problem Solving, and Decision Making. All managers perform the same four functions of management. While performing these functions, you must make decisions and solve problems. When *planning*, you first make decisions about objectives and when, where, and how they will be met. When *organizing*, you must make decisions about what to delegate and how to coordinate the department's resources. When staffing, you must decide whom to hire and how to train and evaluate employees. To *lead*, you must decide how to influence employees. To *control*, you must monitor progress and select methods to ensure that objectives are met and take corrective action when needed.

4-1 SELF-ASSESSMENT

Decision-Making Styles

Individuals differ in the way they approach decisions. To determine whether your decision-making style is reflexive, reflective, or consistent, evaluate each of the following eight statements using the scale below. Place a number between 1 (indicating "This behavior is common for me") and 5 (indicating "This behavior is not common for me") on the line preceding each statement.

1	2	3	4	5
This behavior is common for me.				**This behavior is not common for me.**

1. ____ Overall, I make decisions quickly.
2. ____ When making decisions, I go with my first thought or hunch.
3. ____ When making decisions, I don't bother to recheck my work.
4. ____ When making decisions, I gather little or no information.
5. ____ When making decisions, I consider very few alternative options.
6. ____ When making decisions, I usually decide well before any deadline.
7. ____ When making decisions, I don't ask others for advice.
8. ____ After making decisions, I don't look for other alternatives or wish I had waited longer.

____ Total score

To determine your style, add up the numbers you assigned to the statements; the total will be between 8 and 40. Note where you fall on the decision-style continuum.

8	20	30	40
Reflexive	**Consistent**		**Reflective**

Decision-Making Styles

How do you approach decisions?[11] Before learning about the three decision-making styles, determine your preferred style by completing Self-Assessment 4-1.

Reflexive Style. A reflexive decision maker likes to make quick decisions ("shooting from the hip") without taking the time to get the information that may be needed and without considering many alternatives. On the positive side, reflexive decision makers are decisive; they do not procrastinate. On the negative side, making quick decisions can lead to waste and duplication. **Samsung** rushed conclusions based on incomplete evidence. Rushing resulted in fires and other problems that led to recalls and discounting sales of its **Galaxy Note 7** phone,[12] and its mobile division profits plunged 96%.[13] If you use a reflexive style for important decisions, you may want to slow down and spend more time gathering information and analyzing alternatives.

Reflective Style. A reflective decision maker likes to take plenty of time to make decisions, gathering considerable information and analyzing several alternatives. On the positive side, the reflective type does not make hasty decisions. On the negative side, the reflective type may procrastinate, lose opportunities, and waste valuable time and other resources. The

WORK APPLICATION 4-1

Describe a situation in which a job objective was not met. Identify the problem created and the decision made in regard to this problem.

WORK APPLICATION 4-2

Give an example of a poor decision made by a manager performing a management function. Explain the management function and the problem created by the poor decision.

MANAGEMENT IN ACTION
Decision-Making Styles

reflective decision maker may be viewed as wishy-washy and indecisive. Even a correct decision is wrong when it is taken too late.[14] **Cisco** CEO **John Chambers** said, "Without exception, all of my biggest mistakes occurred because I moved too slowly."[15] If you constantly use a reflective style, you may want to speed up your decision making.

Consistent Style. In the fast-changing environment, making better decisions faster is important to success.[16] However, rushing decisions like **Samsung** can be costly. Thus, many organizations are slowing down decisions and taking the time to analyze data as consistent decision makers, including speedy, agile companies **Amazon, Facebook,** and **Google**.[17] Consistent decision makers tend to make decisions without either rushing or wasting time. They know when they have enough information and alternatives to make a sound decision. Consistent decision makers tend to have the best record for making good decisions. They tend to follow the steps in the decision-making model, which we present soon.

However, the consistent decision style can also result in failure. **Keurig Green Mountain** slowly developed the countertop **Kold Soda Maker** using its successful **K-cups** single-coffee-serve model, with **Coca-Cola** investing, but it resulted in insufficient sales and its discontinuing Kold. About a year after introducing Kold, **JAP Holdings**, a major global coffee player, bought the entire Keurig company.[18]

Following the steps in the decision-making model can aid in making better decisions.

decision-making model A six-step process for arriving at a decision that involves (1) classifying and defining the problem or opportunity, (2) setting objectives and criteria, (3) generating creative and innovative alternatives, (4) analyzing alternatives and selecting the most feasible, (5) planning and implementing the decision, and (6) controlling the decision.

The Decision-Making Model

Recall the importance of evidence-based management (EBM),[19] discussed in Chapter 1. So when making decisions, we want to avoid using *bad intuition*—a hunch, gut feeling, knowing, suspicion, or belief arrived at unconsciously without the use of a rational reasoning processes—also called winging it.[20] Be careful not to use this type of intuition, as you can be deceived into making a bad decision,[21] as you can have biases and false beliefs.[22] On the other side, EBM holds great promise for improved decisions and action, with commensurate benefits for organizations and stakeholders,[23] because EBM provides tools we can use in our personal and professional lives.[24]

Through years of research to determine how the most successful managers make decisions, a decision-making model has been developed, encompassing EBM.[25] The question isn't whether the model works; it's whether you will use the model when it is appropriate, which you will learn throughout this chapter. Following the steps in the model will not guarantee that you will make a good decision every time, like the **Keurig** example. However, using models will increase your chances of success in problem solving and decision making.[26]

The **decision-making model** is a six-step process for arriving at a decision and involves (1) classifying and defining the problem or opportunity, (2) setting objectives and criteria, (3) generating creative and innovative alternatives, (4) analyzing alternatives and selecting the most feasible, (5) planning and implementing the decision, and (6) controlling the decision. Notice that the steps do not simply go from start to finish (see Exhibit 4-1). At any step, you may have to return to a prior step to make changes. The remainder of this chapter discusses the details of the model so that you can develop your creative problem-solving and decision-making skills.

Thomas Barwick via Getty Images

4-1 APPLYING THE CONCEPT

Steps in Decision Making

Identify the step in the decision-making model represented by each statement.

step 1   step 4

step 2   step 5

step 3   step 6

_____ 1. "Tyson, what symptoms have you observed to indicate that a problem even exists?"

_____ 2. "That is a good idea, Mary, but how are you going to put it into action?"

_____ 3. "Good ideas, Tami and Carlos. Let's consider the odds of the success of each of your ideas."

_____ 4. "Now that we understand the problem, let's use the brainstorming technique to solve it."

_____ 5. "Eddie, is the machine still jamming, or has it stopped?"

_____ 6. "I don't understand what we are trying to accomplish here, Raj."

Classify and Define the Problem or Opportunity

Although it may seem surprising, it's true: Half the decisions made by managers fail to solve the problems they are aimed at;[27] outcomes fall short of their objectives.[28] The first step of the decision-making model is to classify and define the problem, which may sometimes take the form of an opportunity.[29] In this section, we discuss how to classify problems, select the appropriate level of participation, and determine the cause of problems, so we can determine the type of decision to make.

Classify the Problem

Problems may be classified in terms of the decision structure involved, the conditions under which a decision will be made, and the type of decision made using the decision-making model.

Decision-Making Structure. For **programmed decisions**, *those that arise in recurring or routine situations*, you should use decision rules or organizational policies and procedures to make the decision. So it is not necessary to follow all the steps of the model. Reordering inventory every time stock reaches a specified level and scheduling employees are examples of programmed decisions.

For **nonprogrammed decisions**, significant decisions that arise in nonrecurring and nonroutine situations, you should use the decision-making model. To be significant, a decision must be expensive and/or have major consequences for the department or organization. Selecting a new product to sell, entering new products, and opening a new facility are examples of nonprogrammed decisions. Upper-level managers tend to make more nonprogrammed decisions than lower-level managers do. Nonprogrammed decisions usually take longer to make than programmed decisions do. The decision structure continuum is illustrated in Exhibit 4-2.

Decision-Making Conditions. The three **decision-making conditions** *are certainty, risk, and uncertainty.* When making a decision

EXHIBIT 4-1   **THE DECISION-MAKING MODEL**

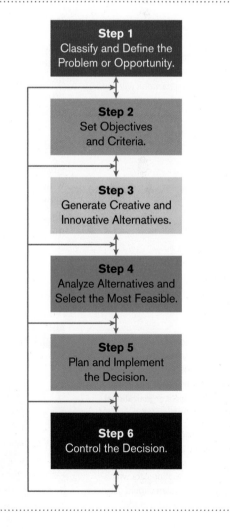

Step 1
Classify and Define the Problem or Opportunity.

Step 2
Set Objectives and Criteria.

Step 3
Generate Creative and Innovative Alternatives.

Step 4
Analyze Alternatives and Select the Most Feasible.

Step 5
Plan and Implement the Decision.

Step 6
Control the Decision.

under the conditions of *certainty*, you know the outcome of each alternative in advance, so you can usually take quick action.[30] When making a decision under conditions of *risk*, you do not know the exact outcome of each alternative in advance but can assign probabilities to each outcome. Under conditions of *uncertainty*, lack of information or knowledge makes the outcome of each alternative unpredictable,[31] so you cannot accurately determine probabilities.[32]

Entrepreneurs and upper-level managers tend to make more risky and uncertain decisions than lower-level managers do.[33] Although risk and uncertainty cannot be eliminated, they can be reduced with information—EBM.[34] Exhibit 4-3 illustrates the continuum of decision-making conditions.

Select the Appropriate Level of Participation

When a problem exists, you must decide who should participate in solving it. Do you want to make the decision yourself or use a team?[35] Today's employees want to have a voice in decisions,[36] the trend is using teams,[37] especially when the decision affects them directly,[38] and a group can often solve problems better than individuals.[39] Thus, the major question is not whether managers should allow employees to participate but when and how this should be done. When making decisions, you should use the management style appropriate to the situation. In Skill Builder 4-2, you will be given the opportunity to use the situational decision-making model to help you select the appropriate level of participation in 12 situations.

For now, realize that even though the trend is toward group decision making, it does have disadvantages and is not always better than individual decision making.[40] Exhibit 4-4 lists the potential advantages and disadvantages of involving groups in decision making. The key to success when using groups is to maximize the advantages while minimizing the disadvantages. In general, for a significant nonprogrammed decision with high risk or uncertainty, use group decision making. For a programmed decision with low risk or certainty, use individual decision making.

Define the Problem

After you have classified the problem, you or the group must define it clearly and accurately, which requires conceptual skills as part of decision making. Because of time pressures, managers often hurry. Rushing to solve a problem that is not correctly defined often leads to a decision that does not solve the problem—haste makes waste. An important part of defining the problem is to distinguish symptoms from cause.

EXHIBIT 4-2 | **DECISION STRUCTURE CONTINUUM**

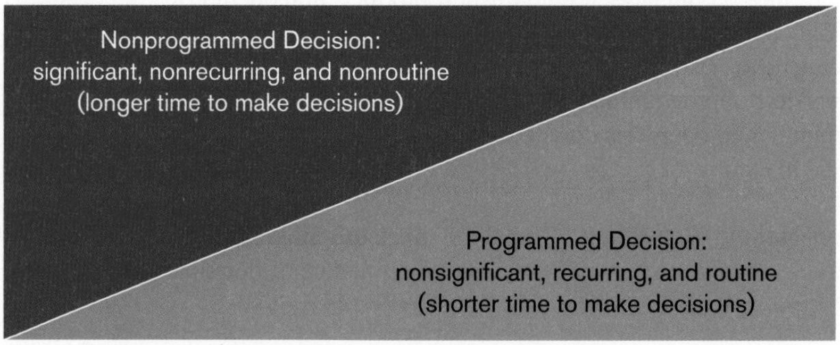

Nonprogrammed Decision:
significant, nonrecurring, and nonroutine
(longer time to make decisions)

Programmed Decision:
nonsignificant, recurring, and routine
(shorter time to make decisions)

4-2 APPLYING THE CONCEPT

Classify the Problem

Classify the problem in each statement according to the structure and condition under which the decision must be made.

A. programmed, certainty

B. programmed, uncertainty

C. programmed, risk

D. nonprogrammed, certainty

E. nonprogrammed, uncertainty

F. nonprogrammed, risk

_____ 7. Aden has to decide if he should invest in a new company in a brand-new industry.

_____ 8. Tinna, a manager in a department with high turnover, must hire a new employee.

_____ 9. When Sean graduates from college, he will buy an existing business rather than work for someone else.

_____ 10. Ron is making a routine decision, but being new, he has no idea what the outcome will be.

_____ 11. Sam, a small business owner, has had a turnaround in business; it's now profitable. She wants to keep the excess cash liquid so that she can get it quickly if she needs it. How should she invest it?

_____ 12. Erica, a purchasing agent, must select new cars for the business. This is the fifth time in five years she has made this decision.

Distinguish Symptoms From the Cause of the Problem. Think of this as a cause-and-effect/symptoms relationship. Begin by asking the right questions and listing the observable and describable occurrences (symptoms) that indicate a problem exists. Only after doing this can you determine the cause of the problem. If you eliminate the cause, the symptoms should disappear. For example, Sam has been an excellent producer. However, in the last month, Sam has been out sick or late more times than he was in the past two years. What is the problem? If you say "absenteeism" or "lateness," you are confusing symptoms and causes. They are symptoms of the problem, but they don't tell you "why" the problem has occurred. If you don't eliminate the cause of the problem, the symptoms will reappear. **McDonald's** sales and profits are down. Its not being profitable is a symptom. The real question is "What is the cause of the decline in sales and profits?" Two possible causes are the societal change to healthier food and increased competition from **Chick-fil-A** and **Chipotle** and others, which weren't competitors years ago.

Decision-Making Types—Rational Versus Bounded Rational Decisions

There are two primary types of decisions that can be made using the decision-making model in Exhibit 4-1: rational (or maximizing) decisions and bounded rational (satisficing) decisions.[41] Both tend to be considered consistent styles because the decision is neither so fast as to ignore information nor so slow as to miss opportunities.

EXHIBIT 4-3   CONTINUUM OF DECISION-MAKING CONDITIONS

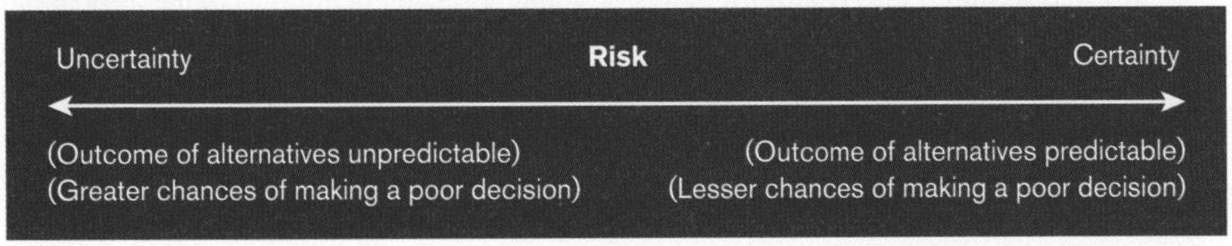

Uncertainty	Risk	Certainty
(Outcome of alternatives unpredictable) (Greater chances of making a poor decision)		(Outcome of alternatives predictable) (Lesser chances of making a poor decision)

EXHIBIT 4-4	POTENTIAL ADVANTAGES AND DISADVANTAGES OF USING GROUP DECISION MAKING

Potential Advantages	Potential Disadvantages
1. *Better-quality decisions.* Groups usually do a better job of solving complex problems than the best individual in the group.	1. *Wasted time and slower decision making.* It takes longer for a group to make a decision, and employees are not on the job producing.
2. *More information, alternatives, creativity, and innovation.* A group of people usually has more of these important factors.	2. *Satisficing.* Groups are more likely than individuals to select a quick alternative, especially when group meetings are not run effectively.
3. *Better understanding of the decision.* When people participate, they understand why the decision selected was the best alternative.	3. *Domination and goal displacement.* One group member or a subgroup may control the group decision with the goal of personal gain.
4. *Greater commitment to the decision.* People involved in making a decision have increased commitment to implementing the decision.	4. *Conformity.* Group members may feel pressured to go along with the group's decision without questioning it out of fear of not being accepted.
5. *Improved morale and motivation.* Participation is rewarding and personally satisfying.	5. *Groupthink.* It occurs when members withhold different views to appear as though they are in agreement. This nullifies the advantage of diversity.
6. *Good training.* Participation trains people to work in groups.	6. *Social loafing.* Team members may withhold their effort and fail to perform their share of the work.

WORK
APPLICATION 4-5

Define a problem in an organization you work for or have worked for. Be sure to clearly distinguish the symptoms from the causes of the problem.

Rational Maximizers Versus Bounded Rational Satisficers. Psychologists have identified two types of decision makers. *Maximizers* tend to make *rational decisions*, taking their time and weighing a wide range of options before choosing. *Satisficers* (blending *satisfy* and *suffice*) tend to make *bounded rational decisions* and would rather be fast than thorough; they prefer to quickly choose the option that fills the minimum criteria.[42] They both follow rational procedure analysis;[43] which one best describes you, or are you somewhere in between?

When to Use Each Decision Style. Knowing when to use each decision style can improve your decision making.

- *Maximizing* with the *rational decisions.* The more complex and nonprogrammed the decision, the higher the degree of risk and uncertainty, and the more significant the decision outcome, the greater the need to spend time as a *maximizer* conducting research with the aid of the decision-making model to make a *rational* decision. When **Nike (IOM 2)** signs young unproven athletes to million-dollar endorsement deals, such as it did with LeBron James, it is making a nonprogrammed decision under the condition of high risk to uncertainty.

- *Satisficing* with the *bounded rational decisions.* Often due to time pressure, cost and availability of information, and cognitive inability to process too much information, managers make satisficing decisions.[44] The more programmed the decision, the more certain the outcomes of the decision, and the less important the decision outcome, the less research and use of the decision-making model needed to make a satisficing decision.

- *Combining styles* with participation. Nothing suggests that either style results in making bad decisions more often. Also, when making group decisions, it is good to have people using both these styles to balance speed and quality.[45] The difference is more about the speed and alternatives considered in decision making.

Exhibit 4-5 puts together the concepts from this section to help you better understand how to classify problems or opportunities and select the most appropriate decision type to use. Note that each part/box is on a continuum, and most decisions will lie somewhere between the two ends of the continuum.

Set Objectives and Criteria

Generally, with simple programmed decisions, the objectives and the criteria have been set. Therefore, you need not complete steps 2 through 4 of the decision-making model. However, with nonprogrammed decisions, you should follow all the steps in the decision-making model. Therefore, the second step for the individual or group facing such a decision requires setting objectives and developing criteria. **Nike**'s (**IOM 3**) objective in signing athletes to endorse its products is to make a profit by generating sales revenues that greatly exceed the cost of the endorsement.

Setting Objectives. Setting clear objectives gets you to focus on the final result you want to accomplish.[46] Objectives drive decisions, and they must state what the decisions should accomplish—whether they will solve a problem or take advantage of an opportunity. Teams are good at setting objectives.[47] You'll learn how to set effective objectives in Chapter 5.

Setting Criteria. You should also specify the criteria for choosing an alternative solution to a problem, as they set the level of performance. **Criteria** *are the standards that an alternative must meet to be selected as the decision that will accomplish the objective.* Having multiple criteria helps to maximize the decision. You should distinguish "must" and "want" criteria. "*Must*" criteria have to be met in order for an alternative to be acceptable, whereas "*want*" criteria are desirable but not necessary for the alternative to be acceptable. With satisficing, you stop with the first acceptable alternative; with maximizing, you seek to select the best possible option.

Suppose a regional manager faces the problem that a **Pizza Hut** store manager has quit and a new manager must be hired. The objective is to hire a store manager by next month. The "must" criteria are that the person have a college degree and a minimum of five years' experience as a store manager. The "want" criterion is that the person should be a minority group member. The regional manager wants to hire a minority employee but will not hire one who does not meet the "must" criteria. We will discuss criteria again later in this chapter.

When selecting a new employee, managers weigh criteria such as candidates' experience and education.

Weighing Criteria. Some criteria are more important than others. But all the "must" criteria are essential, so they each get equal weight at the top rating, say 10 points. However, the "want" criteria can be weighted by importance. For example, in buying a car, a "must" criterion could be a price of under $15,000 or a specific brand—**Ford** Mustang. "Want" criteria can be weighted, such as low mileage (8), good gas mileage (6), blue (4), and so on. You could get technical and develop a mathematical calculation chart for the "want" criteria—such as using the **Kepner-Tregoe** method. But if you are not mathematically inclined to do so, it is a good idea to give the want criteria weights to keep in mind when analyzing alternations—step 4 of the decision-making model.

Generate Creative and Innovative Alternatives

After the problem is defined and objectives and criteria are set, you generate possible alternatives for solving the problem or exploiting the opportunity (step 3 of the decision-making model). Usually, many possible ways exist to solve a problem. Without alternatives from

LO 4-3

Explain the difference between an objective and "must" and "want" criteria.

WORK APPLICATION 4-6

Identify some of the qualification criteria (college degree, years of experience, etc.) for jobs at an organization you work for or have worked for. Distinguish any "must" and "want" criteria.

criteria The standards that an alternative must meet to be selected as the decision that will accomplish the objective.

LO 4-4

State the difference between creativity and innovation and identify five group techniques used to generate creative alternatives.

EXHIBIT 4-5   CONTINUA FOR CLASSIFYING A PROBLEM

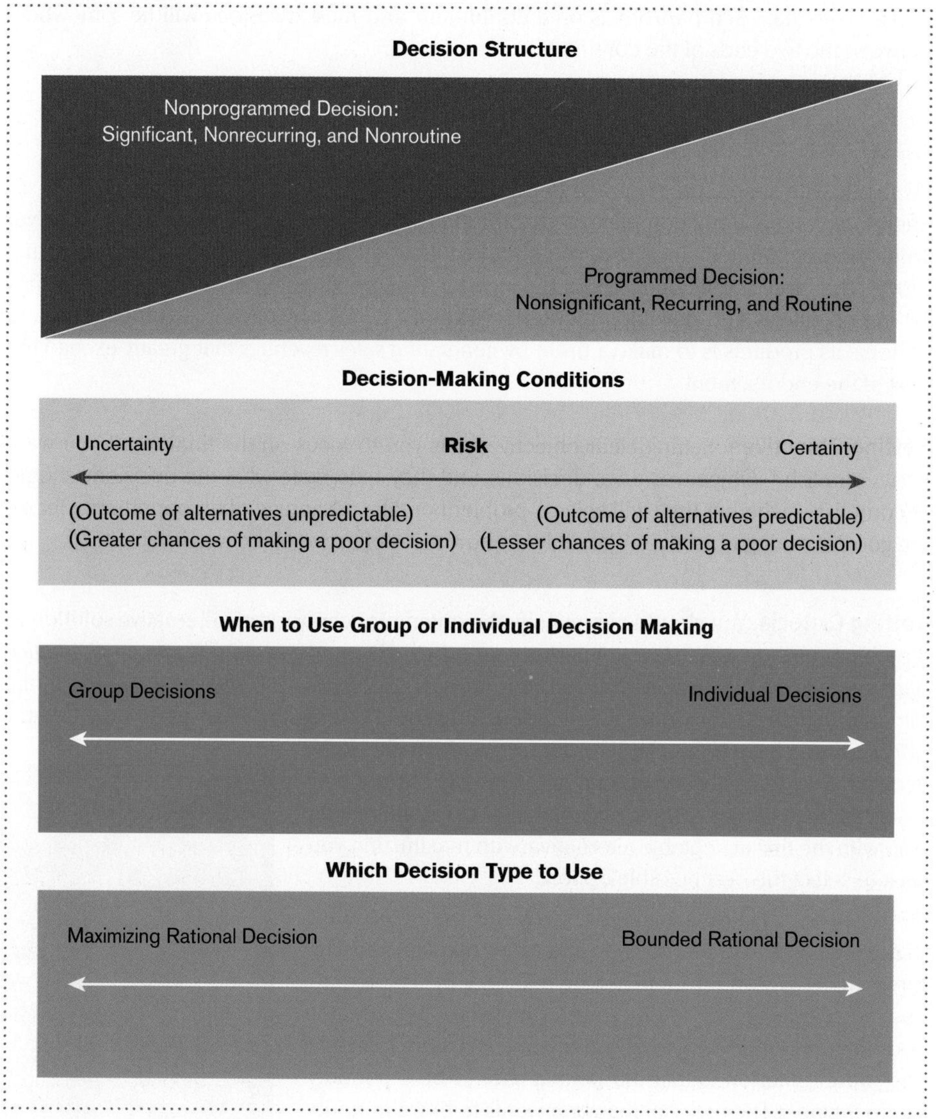

Decision Structure

Nonprogrammed Decision:
Significant, Nonrecurring, and Nonroutine

Programmed Decision:
Nonsignificant, Recurring, and Routine

Decision-Making Conditions

Uncertainty   **Risk**   Certainty

(Outcome of alternatives unpredictable)   (Outcome of alternatives predictable)
(Greater chances of making a poor decision)   (Lesser chances of making a poor decision)

When to Use Group or Individual Decision Making

Group Decisions   Individual Decisions

Which Decision Type to Use

Maximizing Rational Decision   Bounded Rational Decision

multiple sources,[48] you don't have to make a decision, and you should write your alternatives down—visual people like decision trees.

With programmed decision making, the alternative is usually determined by a policy. However, with nonprogrammed decision making, time, effort, and resources are needed to come up with new creative and innovative ideas. So ask others to offer ideas.[49] In this section, you will read about creativity and innovation, as companies such as **GE** and **3M** love to say they innovate. We also discuss five group techniques for generating creative alternatives and viewing the alternatives with decision trees.

Creativity and Innovation

From Creativity to Innovation. Creativity *is a way of thinking that generates new ideas.* Creativity is the driver that leads to innovation.[50] It's about seeing things through a different lens,[51] often called thinking outside the box, and coming up with novel and useful ways to solve problems or come up with opportunities.[52] **Innovation** *is the implementation of a new idea.* Two important types of innovation are *product innovation* (new things such as goods/services) and *process innovation* (new ways of doing things). Creativity is needed,

creativity A way of thinking that generates new ideas.

innovation The implementation of a new idea.

4-1 JOIN THE DISCUSSION ETHICS & SOCIAL RESPONSIBILITY

Avoiding Taxes

Many large corporations have an objective to pay less in taxes and are using corporate *tax loopholes* to avoid paying taxes. **Walmart** and **Apple** are such companies. **Apple** CEO **Tim Cook** was quoted in the press as defending Apple's tax-avoiding practices, which saved $44 billion in offshore income from 2009 to 2012. Apple also has three Irish subsidiaries that claim to have no residence anywhere for tax purposes.(1)

It is not known just how many corporations are engaging in these kinds of activities. What is known, though, is that as these corporations continue taking advantage of corporate tax laws, the more taxes ordinary families and small businesses pay.

The U.S. federal corporate tax rate is the highest in the world, as high as 35% in early 2017, and most states and some local governments also impose taxes on corporate profits. **President Trump** said he wants tax cuts, which would give less incentive to move jobs overseas and keep money in America. However, others claim that large, profitable corporations should

pay high taxes to help fund social programs, and the tax rate should not be cut.

1. Although it is legal, is it ethical for Apple, Walmart, and other corporations to take advantage of tax loopholes to avoid paying taxes?
2. If you became CEO of one of these corporations, would you continue to take advantage of the tax loopholes? Why or why not?
3. As an individual, do or will you take advantage of tax loopholes or pay more taxes than legally required by law?
4. What is the government's role and responsibility regarding tax loopholes? What should the government do?
5. Should the corporate tax rate be cut? If so, by how much?

Note

1. Staff, "Don't Blame Apple for Keeping Its Money," *BusinessWeek* (May 27–June 2, 2013): 12.

---

but essentially useless if not implemented.[53] After years of making juice and discarding the leftover cranberry skins, an employee at **Ocean Spray** came up with the idea of turning them into a consumer snack like Craisins.

Unfortunately, many employees come up with great ideas, but managers fail to implement them. So employees give up trying to improve products and processes; they even hide creative knowledge.[54] Conversely, managers who ask for employees' ideas, reward them for sharing, and innovate get improved managerial effectiveness through increased performance.[55] Creativity obviously leads to innovation, but it can be costly,[56] and there is always the risk of failure,[57] like with the **Kold Soda Maker**.

Creativity and Innovation Killers. There are barriers to changing and trying something different. But success only comes from taking some risks and innovating.[58] In Chapter 6, you will learn how to overcome these barriers and manage change. For now, while thinking and working with a group to solve problems or take advantage of new opportunities, you'll want to be on guard against the kinds of responses that can block creativity and stop innovation,[59] such as the following:

- "It is impossible.""It can't be done."
- "We've never done it.""Has anyone else tried it?"
- "It won't work in our department (company/industry)."
- "It costs too much.""It isn't in the budget."
- "Let's form a committee and have lots of meetings."

If group members say and think something is impossible, they will not try to be creative. If you think about or anyone makes such statements, your job is to remind yourself and the group to focus on generating ideas, the more offbeat the better. So keep a positive, can-do attitude.

The Creative Process. The image of the creative type, like **Steve Jobs** of **Apple**, is over-rated. Everyone has creative capability, and you can become more creative. If not, why do **Coca-Cola**, **OMRON**, **Pitney Bowes**, and **Shiseido** all have training programs that empha-size creativity for their employees? One thing that helps creativity is to simply give people time and space to think, which they do at **Tumblr**.[60]

The three stages in the **creative process** *are (1) preparation, (2) incubation and illumina-tion, and (3) evaluation* (see Exhibit 4-6). As with the decision-making model, you may have to return to prior stages as you work through the creative process.

1. *Preparation.* First, you must define the problem by getting others' opinions, feelings, and ideas, as well as the facts. Look for new angles, use imagination and invention, and don't limit yourself to the boundaries of past thinking. Generate as many possible solu-tions as you can think of without making a judgment.

2. *Incubation and illumination.* After generating alternatives, take a break; sleep on the prob-lem. Creativity seems to happen outside the "ordinary groves of thought and action."[61] During the incubation stage, as your subconscious works on the problem, you may gain an insight into the solution—*illumination.*[62] Illumination can also happen while working on the problem; it is sometimes referred to as the "Aha, now I get it" phenomenon.

3. *Evaluation.* Before implementing a solution, you should evaluate the alterna-tive to make sure the idea is practical. A good approach is to become the devil's advocate. With the **devil's advocate approach,** *group members focus on defend-ing a solution while others try to come up with reasons the solution will not work.* Using the devil's advocate approach usually leads to more creativity as the idea is improved upon.

Engineer **Arthur Fry** of **3M** developed a new glue that was extremely weak (prepara-tion), so the company called it a failure and decided not to use it. However, Fry sang in a church choir and put little pieces of paper in the hymnal to mark the songs. The problem was the paper often fell out. While listening to a sermon, he had an illumination to use his weak glue to solve the problem. The **Post-it** note was invented and became a great success, and even today with all the electronic technology, it still sells well.[63]

Using Information to Generate Alternatives. Successful managers, such as **Amazon's Jeff Bezos** and **Google's Sergey Brin**, use facts, data, information, and knowledge to make decisions, and they are more creative and innovative.[64] However, when generating alternatives, the question for many managers is "How much information and how many alternatives do I need, and where should I get them?" There is no simple answer. The more significant the decision, generally, the more information and/or alternatives you need. However, if you get too much information or have too many alternatives, the decision becomes too complex, and the best alternative may not be selected. So data should be your tool, not your master.[65]

Using Technology to Generate Alternatives. Technology, especially the Internet, has shown considerable potential for assisting with problem solving and decision making, as it provides so much data instantly. **Two Sigma Investments** uses computers to trawl the sea of data for stock picks, including **Twitter**.[66] However, when using the Internet to make decisions, one must be careful due to the amount of false information posted on the web. Technology is also used to generate creative alternatives in groups.

Nike (**IOM 4**) has a team of 50 research scientists developing new technology to improve the performance of athletes using its products, such as its featherweight **Flyknit** sneakers.[67] Nike continues to innovate the fashion looks of its sports footwear, apparel, and equipment with new materials, colors, and designs and star athletes to endorse them. Nike also offers customizing your own shoes and apparel under the NIKEiD option at its website.

creative process The approach to generating new ideas that involves three stages: (1) preparation, (2) incubation and illumination, and (3) evaluation.

devil's advocate approach Group members focus on defending a solution while others try to come up with reasons the solution will not work.

Using Groups to Generate Creative Alternatives

Creativity can thrive in small groups,[68] so there is a trend today toward using groups to develop creative ideas and make decisions.[69] A big advantage to using a group is members' ability to combine and improve creative ideas.[70] It also helps creativity to get out of the routine, so get away to change the scene like they do at **The Land of Nod** company.[71] Five of the more popular group creativity techniques are illustrated in Exhibit 4-7.

Brainstorming. Brainstorming *is the process of suggesting many possible alternatives without evaluation.* When brainstorming ideas, follow these guidelines. Include diverse people.[72] The group is presented with a problem and asked to develop as many solutions as possible. Members should be encouraged to make wild, extreme suggestions. You should also build on suggestions made by others. Everyone should have an equal voice. No criticizing others' ideas,[73] and none of the alternatives should be evaluated until all possible alternatives have been presented,[74] **Microsoft** used brainstorming to choose "**Bing**" as the name of its search engine.[75]

Research has also shown that we are more creative when walking, so with small groups, some companies are holding *walking brainstorming* sessions.[76] Using technology, a newer form of brainstorming is electronic *e-brainstorming*. People use computers to generate alternatives. Participants synchronously send ideas without getting together. People who are far apart geographically can brainstorm this way, and the number of participants does not have to be limited.

Synectics. Synectics *is the process of generating novel alternatives through role playing and fantasizing.* Synectics focuses on generating novel ideas rather than a large quantity of ideas. At first, the group leader does not even state the exact nature of the problem so that group members avoid preconceptions.

Nolan Bushnell, founder of **Chuck E. Cheese's**, wanted to develop a new concept in family dining, so he began by discussing leisure activities generally. Bushnell then moved to leisure activities having to do with eating out. The idea that came out of this synectic process was a restaurant–electronic game complex where families could entertain themselves while eating pizza and hamburgers.

Nominal Grouping. Nominal grouping is the process of generating and evaluating alternatives using a structured voting method. This process usually involves six steps:

1. *Listing.* Each participant generates ideas in writing.
2. *Recording.* Each member presents one idea at a time, and the leader records these ideas where everyone can see them. This continues until all ideas are posted.
3. *Clarification.* Alternatives are clarified through a guided discussion, and any additional ideas are listed.
4. *Ranking.* Each employee rank orders the ideas and identifies what he or she sees as the top three; low-ranked alternatives are eliminated.
5. *Discussion.* Rankings are discussed for clarification, not persuasion. During this time, participants should explain their choices and their reasons for making them.
6. *Vote.* A secret vote is taken to select the alternative.

EXHIBIT 4-6   STAGES IN THE CREATIVE PROCESS

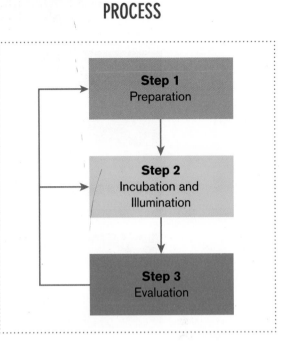

WORK APPLICATION 4-7

Give an example of how you or someone else solved a problem using the stages in the creative process. Be sure to list the steps and note whether illumination came during incubation or while working on the problem.

WORK APPLICATION 4-8

Give examples of organizational problems for which brainstorming, nominal grouping, consensus mapping, or the Delphi technique would be appropriate techniques.

brainstorming The process of suggesting many possible alternatives without evaluation.

synectics The process of generating novel alternatives through role playing and fantasizing.

nominal grouping The process of generating and evaluating alternatives using a structured voting method.

EXHIBIT 4-7   GROUP DECISION-MAKING TECHNIQUES THAT FOSTER CREATIVITY AND INNOVATION

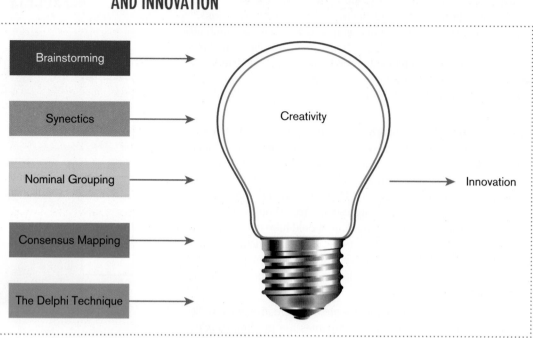

Nominal grouping is appropriate to use in situations in which groups may be affected by disadvantages (Exhibit 4-4) of domination, goal displacement, conformity, and groupthink, because it minimizes these effects.

Consensus Mapping. Consensus mapping *is the process of developing group agreement on a solution to a problem.* If a consensus cannot be reached, the group does not make a decision. Consensus mapping differs from nominal grouping because there can be no competitive struggle ending in a vote that may force a solution on some members of the group. The Japanese call this approach *ringi.* Consensus mapping can be used after brainstorming by categorizing or clustering ideas in the process of trying to agree on a single solution. A major benefit is that because any solution chosen is the group's, members generally are more committed to implementing it. However, consensus can't always be reached, and leaders can't always wait for consensus and must make decisions themselves.

The Delphi Technique. The *Delphi technique* involves using a series of confidential questionnaires to refine a solution. Responses on the first questionnaire are analyzed and resubmitted to participants on a second questionnaire. This process may continue for five or more rounds before a consensus emerges. Managers commonly use the Delphi technique for technological forecasting, such as projecting the next Internet breakthrough and its effect on a specific industry. By knowing what is to come, managers can make creative decisions to plan for the future.

Upper-level managers commonly use synectics and the Delphi technique for a specific decision. Brainstorming, nominal grouping, and consensus mapping techniques are frequently used at the departmental level with work groups.

Decision Trees

consensus mapping
The process of developing group agreement on a solution to a problem.

After you come up with alternative problem solutions, you may want to make a decision tree, as it can help you visualize the alternatives you are considering.[77] A *decision tree* is a diagram of alternatives. The diagram gives a visual picture of the alternatives, which makes it easier

4-3 APPLYING THE CONCEPT

Using Groups to Generate Alternatives

Identify the most appropriate group technique for generating alternatives in each situation.

A. brainstorming

B. synectics

C. nominal grouping

D. consensus mapping

E. Delphi technique

____ 13. Management wants to expand the business by offering a new product but doesn't know what to offer.

____ 14. Management wants to project future trends in the social media industry as part of its long-range planning.

____ 15. Management at a video game maker wants to develop a new game. It calls in a consultant, who is leading groups of employees and children to come up with ideas together.

____ 16. A department is suffering from morale problems, and the manager doesn't know why or how to improve morale.

____ 17. A department is getting new computers, and everyone has to get the same type: either desktop, laptop, or tablet. The manager doesn't know which type to select for her 25 employees.

for some people to analyze them. Decision trees are also especially helpful when you face information overload.

Carolyn Blakeslee started ***Art Calendar*** (a business magazine for visual artists) dedicated to helping artists make a living doing what they love. Blakeslee started *Art Calendar* as a part-time business in a room in her house. But as the business grew, it became more than a full-time job. She wanted to have it all—to meet financial goals and devote time to her family and create her own artwork. Like many small business owners, she had to make a decision. Her choices are diagrammed in a decision tree in Exhibit 4-8. Blakeslee decided to expand her business—to work full time and hire professional help. But she later decided to sell the company magazine, now called ***Professional Artist***.[78]

Analyze Alternatives and Select the Most Feasible

Notice that in the decision-making model in Exhibit 4-1, generating and analyzing alternatives and selecting the most feasible are two different steps (steps 3 and 4). This is because generating and evaluating alternatives at the same time tends to lead to satisficing and wasting time discussing poor alternatives rather than moving to maximizing. So only after you gather evidence-supported alternatives[79] is it time to analyze them, and *analytical thinking* is an important skill job recruiters are looking for in job candidates.[80] **Adidas** hired **Herbert Hainer** as CEO because he is known for his analytical approach with the task of solving the problem of decreasing market share to **Nike** and **Under Armour**.[81] You want to select the "best" alternative.[82] But notice we said *select* the most feasible, because some options may not be practical. You have limited resources and just can't afford some options, or the cost may be too high for the expected return. The CEO of **Priceline** says that sometimes it is harder to decide what you're not going to do,[83] especially when analyzing opportunities instead of problems.

In evaluating alternatives, think forward and try to predict the possible outcome of each action on your stakeholders that will be affected by the decision.[84] Don't forget to consider the ethics of each alternative.[85] Be sure to compare alternatives to the objectives and criteria set in step 2 of the decision-making process. In addition, compare each alternative to the others.

LO 4-5

Compare quantitative techniques including big data, cost-benefit analysis, and intuition for analyzing and selecting an alternative.

EXHIBIT 4-8   ## DECISION TREE

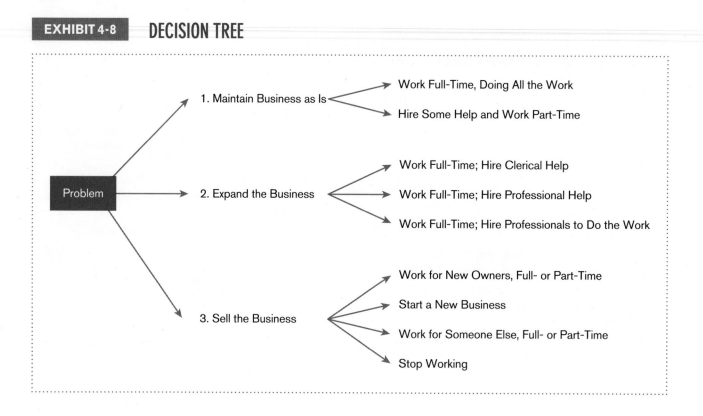

This section presents quantitative and qualitative approaches that are commonly used to analyze alternative solutions: quantitative techniques, big data, and cost-benefit analysis and intuition.

Quantitative Techniques

As you read in Chapter 1, one of the five approaches to management is management science, which uses math to aid in problem solving and decision making. Quantitative techniques professionalize decision making by using math in the objective analysis of alternative solutions. The **MLB Oakland Athletics Billy Beane** became a celebrity (did you see the movie *Moneyball?*) by popularizing the use of statistics to make baseball decisions.[86]

You may not be expected to compute the math for all types of quantitative techniques. However, if you know when to use these techniques, you can seek help from specialists within or outside the organization. If you are interested in the actual calculations, you should take courses in quantitative analysis.

Break-Even Analysis. Break-even analysis allows calculation of the volume of sales or revenue that will result in a profit. The break-even point occurs at the level at which no profit or loss results. If a **Stop & Shop** store buys a carpet cleaner for $300 and rents it for $25 a day, how many times does it have to rent it to break even? If you said 12, you are correct.

Many companies today realize that good decisions often hinge on gathering relevant data and performing good data analysis.

Capital Budgeting. Capital budgeting is used to analyze alternative investments in assets that will be used to make money, such as machines to make products and equipment to provide a service like a lawn mower. Capital budgeting is used for *make-or-buy, fix-or-replace, upgrade-replacement,* and *rent/lease-or-buy* decisions. The payback approach allows the calculation of the number of years it will take to recover the initial cash invested. Another approach computes the *average rate of return*. It is appropriate when the yearly returns differ. A more sophisticated approach, *discounted cash flow*, takes into account the time value of money. It assumes that a dollar today is worth more than a dollar in the future. Organizations including **AMF**, **Kellogg's**, **Procter & Gamble**, and **3M** use discounted cash flow analysis.

Linear Programming. Optimum allocation of resources (time, money, space, material, equipment, and employees) is determined using linear programming (LP). Companies primarily use LP for programmed decisions under conditions of certainty or low risk, but LP is also widely applied to product-mix decisions. **Lear Siegler** uses LP when determining work flow to optimize the use of its equipment. **FedEx** and **UPS** use LP to determine the best sequence of deliveries to minimize costs for their trucking fleets.

Queuing Theory. Queuing theory focuses on waiting time. An organization can have any number of employees providing service to customers. If the organization has too many employees working at one time, not all of them will be waiting on customers, and the money paid to them is lost. If the organization has too few employees working at one time, it can lose customers who don't want to wait for service, which results in lost revenue. Queuing theory, which helps the organization balance these two costs, is used by retail stores to determine the optimum number of checkout clerks and by production departments to schedule preventive maintenance. **Kaiser Permanente** uses queuing theory to help doctors' offices reduce waiting times for patients.

Probability Theory. Probability theory enables the user to make decisions that take into consideration conditions of risk. You assign a probability of success or failure to each alternative. Then you calculate the expected value, which is the payoff or profit from each combination of alternatives and outcomes. The calculations are usually done on a payoff matrix by multiplying the probability of the outcome by the benefit or the cost. Probability theory is used to determine whether to expand facilities and to what size, to select the most profitable investment portfolio, and to determine the amount of inventory to stock. Using probability theory, hedge fund investors are providing movie financing to major film studios, such as **Walt Disney** and **Sony Pictures**, using computer-driven investment simulations to pick movies with the right characteristics to make money. Have you ever used a simple probability, such as I have a 75% chance of winning or getting the job or sale?

Big Data

You should realize that big data is also a quantitative technique that is used with or rapidly replacing the other quantitative techniques. Data scientists are in demand.[87] *Fortune* 500 executives are all talking about big data.[88]

What Is Big Data? Big data *is the analysis of large amounts of quantified facts to aid in maximizing decision making.* The quantitative analysis is commonly done through algorithms and their related sophisticated software. **Jack Ma, Chairman of Alibaba,** says, "Data will become the biggest production material in the future."[89] Executives must transform into math machines,[90] because whoever has the most exact data—and knows how to use it—wins today.[91] Data-driven businesses make faster decisions and are more profitable than companies with low reliance on data.[92]

Using big data with the help of data crunchers like **Gauss & Neumann** and **Google Analytics** can be expensive, but big data can be used by small business at no or low cost. Google Analytics does have a free version, and for $100 or less per month, **Wicked Reports, ClicData, Graphly,** and **SumAll** can provide reports of information telling you what is working and what isn't from websites and social media.[93]

WORK
APPLICATION 4-9

Give examples from an organization you work for or have worked for of decisions that might appropriately be analyzed using the quantitative techniques.

big data The analysis of large amounts of quantified facts to aid in maximizing decision making.

4-4 APPLYING THE CONCEPT

Selecting Quantitative Methods

Select the appropriate quantitative method to use in each situation.

A. break-even analysis

B. capital budgeting

C. linear programming

D. queuing theory

E. probability theory

_____ 18. Burger King manager Tania wants to even the workload in her fast-food restaurant. At times, employees hang around with no customers to wait on; at other times, they have long waiting lines.

_____ 19. Taylor Rental manager Matthew wants to know how many times a bounce house will have to be rented out to recoup the expense of adding it to the rental list.

_____ 20. Machine shop manager Henry is scheduling which products to make on which machines next week.

_____ 21. Kandeeda, a lawn care services sole owner/operator, must decide whether to repair her old truck or to replace it with a new one.

_____ 22. Shawn wants to invest money in commodities futures to make a profit.

How Is Big Data Used? It can reveal patterns and opportunities that 99% of businesspeople would miss.[94] The math department is the hottest new function because it provides the big data to the operation, marketing, accounting, and other functional departments.[95] Big data is being used in all industries to improve operations and marketing.[96] **Harklinikken** (Danish for hair clinic) founder **Lars Skjoth** uses his algorithm and tonics to prevent and stop hair loss.[97] **Domino's Pizza** uses big data to customize marketing, select locations, and manage staffing.[98] **GE** uses big data in operations to make its products and in the maintenance of its assets to keep them running longer at a lower cost. **United Airlines** uses big data to decide where to fly, how often, how many people to carry, and how big or small a plane.[99] **Taco Bell** and **Pizza Hut** are using apps to take orders and payment to improve service and increase sales.[100] **Apple** and **Google** are collecting big data in a race to predict what future products and services you will buy.[101]

Do you believe those big-hit music artists and songs just happen by chance? **Alex White** brought data analysis to the music industry, forecasting which artists were on the brink of stardom and which songs would be hits before they were released, and now he is using big data to help predict best-selling books with **Next Big Book**.[102] Have you ever been online and received customized ads for products you bought in the past or are likely to buy or ads telling you it's time to reorder? That's big data.

Cost-Benefit, Pros and Cons, and Intuition

Decision making is not simple trust data-versus-gut decisions.[103] Quantitative techniques including big data are objective mathematical approaches to comparing alternatives. However, there are times when management science approaches alone don't work well, and data is a tool for enhancing intuition,[104] or data and intuition are commonly used together,[105] as discussed here. The leader who truly understands the numbers will make the best gut decisions.[106]

Cost-Benefit Analysis. When making decisions, it is helpful to use a cost-benefit analysis.[107] It compares the cost of implementing a decision to the benefits received. Although we should still use EBM,[108] sometimes you can't put a number on a cost and/or benefit. You may be able to tell me how much you paid for tuition, but how much did you lose in income while you were in college and not working? Plus, the benefits of your education are surely more than the pay you get for a job—how do you put a price on these? How do you put a price on a human life, and how should you compare the cost of adding extra safety features to the benefits of fewer "potential" accidents? In such cases, *cost-benefit analysis* is considered a mixed technique for comparing the cost and benefit of each alternative course of action using subjective judgment along with some quantitative math. *Judgment* is the cognitive process of drawing conclusions using a rational reasoning process in reaching a decision.[109] So cost-benefit should be a mix of EBM information and judgment.[110] Even with big data, in the fast-changing global environment, managers tend to use some judgment.[111]

Pros and Cons. With pros-and-cons analysis, you identify the advantages, which can be considered the benefits, and the disadvantages, which can be considered the costs, of each alternative. **Ben Franklin** is said to have used pros-and-cons analysis. Franklin would draw a line down the middle of a piece of paper. On one side he would list the pros and on the other the cons of whatever he was considering.

Intuition. Recall that we suggested not using bad intuition, winging it without using the decision-making model and EBM information. However, when using the decision-making model, it is appropriate to use good intuition by selecting an alternative based on your experience and rational judgment.[112] Many successful entrepreneurs suggest listening to your voice of intuition.[113] When you have dealt with a recurring problem calling for a programmed decision and it comes up again, you can act quickly with what seems to be limited information when in fact it is based on good intuition. Intuition can also be used with nonsignificant nonprogrammed decisions with low risk, but it is also used to some extent with the decision-making model to complement the other techniques.

Exhibit 4-9 compares the three major approaches to analyzing and selecting alternatives. Although the exhibit seems to have three distinct types, they are actually on a continuum. Regardless of the method used to analyze alternatives, the one selected must meet the criteria established in step 2 of the decision-making model. If none of the alternatives meets the criteria, you have two options: (1) return to step 2 and change the criteria for the best alternative or (2) return to step 3 and generate more alternatives.

Multimillion-dollar endorsement contracts may seem like a lot to offer to star athletes. However, contract amounts are paid over several years, and **Nike (IOM 5)** has more than $3 billion in profits yearly. The contracts also include clauses that specify how they may be ended if things don't work out. So, relatively speaking, endorsement contracts are not a great

EXHIBIT 4-9   CONTINUUM OF ANALYSIS TECHNIQUES

Quantitative Techniques	Mixed Technique	Qualitative Technique
Break-even Capital budgeting Linear programming Queuing theory Probability theory Big data	Cost-benefit analysis	Intuition
Decision is objective, based primarily on math	Decision is based on some objective EBM information and/or math along with subjective judgment	Decision is based on experience and subjective judgment
Used for making significant nonprogrammed decisions under the condition of uncertainty and risk	Used for making significant nonprogrammed decisions under the condition of uncertainty and risk	Used for making nonsignificant programmed decisions under the condition of certainty and low risk
Follows all steps of decision-making model	Follows all steps of decision-making model	May skip steps of decision-making model
Commonly a group decision	Commonly a group decision	Commonly an individual decision

financial risk for Nike. Nike can use quantitative break-even analysis in making contract decisions, as Nike managers know the cost and can figure the sales needed to break even on contracts, and they are using big data. Cost-benefit analysis is also applied in making contract decisions, as there is a cost to having a competitor contract with the athletes, thereby causing Nike to potentially lose sales and market share.

LO 4-6

Explain the importance of planning, implementing, and controlling decisions.

Plan, Implement the Decision, and Control

The final two steps in the decision-making model involve planning and implementing the decision (step 5) and controlling (step 6). Unfortunately, decisions will be made but not implemented,[114] and a major cause is not developing a detailed plan to achieve the objective of the decision. Have you ever made a New Year's resolution, which is a decision, but didn't succeed, like to lose weight and exercise more? So once the decision is made, everyone needs to commit to meeting its objective[115] (step 2 of the decision-making model), and this requires giving support and getting the necessary resources[116] and coordinating them with current resources.[117]

After making a decision, you develop a plan of action with a schedule for implementation. (You will learn the details of the planning process in the next chapter.) The plan needs to be clearly communicated so that everyone can do his or her part to achieve the objective.[118] (You will learn about communication in Chapter 13.) After a decision has been made and plans developed, the plans must be implemented—you need to take action to achieve your objective.[119] In implementing a decision, it is likely to be necessary to delegate assignments to others. (You will learn about delegating in Chapter 7.)

Control methods should be developed while planning to measure and monitor decision outcomes.[120] Checkpoints should be established to determine whether the chosen alternative is solving the problem. If not, corrective action may be needed.[121] (You will learn about control methods in Chapters 14 and 15.) If you are not on track to achieve the objective, you don't want to give up too soon and lose the desired outcome, but you also don't want to get caught in the escalation of commitment.[122]

When we will not admit that we made a bad decision, we are in the process known as *escalation of commitment*.[123] We tend to maintain commitment to losing courses of action, even in the face of bad news, by wasting more resources, called *throwing good money after bad*.[124] Why? Because we don't like to lose something once we have it, and we don't like to admit we made a mistake, even to ourselves. Do you know anyone who will never admit to making a mistake? The pain of losing outweighs the joy of winning. It's called *loss aversion*. When you make a poor decision, you should admit the mistake and try to rectify it quickly. Go back over the steps in the decision-making model. **Target** went global, for the first time opening stores in Canada, but it was a major misstep, as after losing billions in investment it shut down.[125] You also need to learn from your mistakes by building intuition so you don't repeat them. On the positive side, poor decisions and failure can often be fixed[126] and may even lead to new opportunities;[127] recall the **3M** Post-it note.

WORK
APPLICATION 4-10

Give examples from an organization where you work or have worked of decisions that might appropriately be analyzed using cost-benefit analysis and intuition.

Once a decision is made, managers need to plan its implementation.

Trends and Issues in Management

We live in a *global* village. The **World Economic Forum** provides detailed assessments of the productive potential of 139 nations worldwide in its annual "Global Competitiveness Report"[128] (for a copy, visit http://www3.weforum.org/docs/gcr/2015-2016/Global_Competitiveness_Report_2015-2016 .pdf). As discussed in Chapter 3's section on Project GLOBE, people around the globe are different, and people from different cultures don't necessarily make decisions the same way.

Managers in some countries (such as the United States) are more oriented to problem solving, whereas those in others (such as Thailand and Indonesia) tend to accept things the way they are. Culture influences the selection of problems to solve, the depth of analysis, the importance placed on logic and rationality, and the level of participation in decision making. Thus, in high-power-distance cultures (most Latin American countries and the Philippines), where decisions are more autocratic, participation is not acceptable. In lower-power-distance cultures (the United States, Ireland, Australia, and Israel), there is greater use of participation in decision making.

Decision-making styles also often vary based on time orientation *globally*. In some countries, decisions are made more quickly than in others. In countries that are less time conscious, such as Egypt, decision styles are more reflective than in time-conscious countries like the United States, where decision styles are more reflexive. In countries where managers use participative decision making, decisions take longer than in countries where managers use autocratic decision making. Japanese managers, for example, for whom decision making involves high levels of participation, often take longer to make decisions than U.S. managers do.

Globalization also brings *diversity*, which can help in problem solving and decision making, as it really helps creativity as you understand how to rethink a problem or reanalyze a situation.[129] **Hikmet Ersek**, **Western Union** CEO, says that if you listen to people whether they are from the United States, Spain, or Brazil, whether they are rich or poor, white or black, male or female, they help you grow and innovate.[130]

Big data is being collected and used *globally*.[131] With more than 3.2 billion social networking users, 3.9 billion active e-mail users, and 400 million tweets a day, the rise of social media has generated vast amounts of big data content[132] that is being used as discussed in this chapter. People are also posting their problems on social media and getting personal information to aid in their decision making globally.[133]

Technology can help you think about problems and how to solve them or create opportunities,[134] such as using *big data*. However, *big data* can be misread and lead to poor, costly decisions. Even though **Coca-Cola** made a bad decision to replace Coke with New Coke and brought Coke back years ago, **PepsiCo** made the same poor decision. Pepsi spent two years surveying consumers, conducting taste tests, and tinkering with soft drink recipes using sucralose sweetener to improve Diet Pepsi taste and sales. But it misread what customers wanted. To fix the poor decision, it brought back Diet Pepsi with aspartame.[135]

Along with big data come the issues of *privacy* and *security*. People question their privacy using websites like, **Google**, **Facebook**, and **LinkedIn** and are concerned about how these companies are using (and possibly selling) their data. As you may know, hackers broke into companies' data files, including **Yahoo**! and **Home Depot**, and stole customer information. States challenged **RadioShack**'s plan to auction customer data.[136] If it is legal, is the sale *ethical*? Are you concerned?

Clearly, when it comes to making decisions, we need to be *ethical*[137] and *socially responsible* globally,[138] and not simply go by the big data numbers.[139] We need to be honest in reporting statistical data and not fix the data to support the decisions we want to make.[140] Some question the ethics and accuracy of using algorithms to manage people, such as when making hiring, promoting, and firing decisions.[141]

We need to balance economics and *sustainability* of the environment,[142] so don't abuse your power.[143] Be a responsible leader;[144] use the ethical guides (Chapter 2). *Technology* and *big data* can also help with environmental *sustainability* problems, such as sewage treatment plants, and in China, where they are turning the sea into fresh water.[145] **Bayer** and **Monsanto** are collecting big data that helps farmers increase productivity while helping to preserve our natural resources to feed the world.[146]

$SAGE edge™ edge.sagepub.com/lussier8e

Want a better grade?

Get the tools you need to sharpen your study skills. Access practice quizzes, eFlashcards, video and multimedia, and more at edge.sagepub.com/lussier8e.

Digital Resources

Learning Objective	Digital Resource
4-1. Discuss the relationship among objectives, problem solving, and decision making and their relationship among the management functions.	▶ Management in Action: Decision-Making Styles*
4-2. Describe when to use rational (maximizing) versus bounded rational (satisficing) decision making and group versus individual decision making.	▶ Maximizing vs. Satisficing
4-3. Explain the difference between an objective and "must" and "want" criteria.	▶ SMART Objectives
4-4. State the difference between creativity and innovation and identify five group techniques used to generate creative alternatives.	▶ Creativity and Innovation*
4-5. Compare quantitative techniques including big data, cost-benefit analysis, and intuition for analyzing and selecting an alternative.	▯ Cost-Benefit Analysis
4-6. Explain the importance of planning, implementing, and controlling decisions.	▯ Planning Strategies

* premium video available only in the interactive eBook

• • • CHAPTER SUMMARY

4-1. Discuss the relationship among objectives, problem solving, and decision making and their relationship among the management functions.

Managers are responsible for setting and achieving organizational objectives. When managers do not meet objectives, a problem results. When a problem exists, decisions must be made about what, if any, action must be taken.

When managers perform the functions of planning, organizing, leading, and controlling, they make decisions and solve problems.

4-2. Describe when to use rational (maximizing) versus bounded rational (satisficing) decision making and group versus individual decision making.

The more complex and nonprogrammed the decision, the higher the degree of risk and uncertainty, and the more significant the decision outcome, the greater the need to spend time as a *maximizer* conducting research with the aid of the decision-making model to make a *rational* decision.

The more programmed the decision, the more certainty of the outcomes of the decision, and the less important the decision outcome, the less research and use of the decision-making model needed to make a *bounded rational* (satisficing) decision. The greater the need to maximize, the greater the need to use group decision making. With a group, it is good to have a mix of maximizers and satisficers to increase the speed and quality of the decision. Simple satisficing decisions can be made by an individual.

However, this is a general guide; there may be exceptions to the rule.

4-3. Explain the difference between an objective and "must" and "want" criteria.

An objective is the result you want to achieve when making a decision. "Must" criteria are the requirements that an alternative must meet to be selected. "Want" criteria are desirable but are not necessary for the alternative to be selected. "Want" criteria should also be weighted by their level of importance to achieving the objective.

4-4. State the difference between creativity and innovation and identify five group techniques used to generate creative alternatives.

Creativity is a way of thinking that generates new ideas. Innovation is the implementation of new ideas for products and processes. Five techniques for generating creative alternatives include brainstorming, synectics, nominal grouping, consensus mapping, and the Delphi technique. Decision trees can also be used as a visual aid for generating alternatives.

4-5. Compare quantitative techniques including big data, cost-benefit analysis, and intuition for analyzing and selecting an alternative.

Quantitative techniques (break-even, capital budgeting, linear programming, queuing, and probability theories) including *big data* (the analysis of large amounts of quantified facts to aid in maximizing *decision making*) are objective management science approaches using math to select the alternative with the highest value.

Cost-benefit analysis compares the cost of implementing a decision to the benefits received. It is commonly used when some of the cost and/or benefits can't be quantified. Cost-benefit tends to be used by a group that mixes evidence-based information/math and subjective judgment.

Intuition is based on experience and subjective rational judgment. It is commonly used by individuals with recurring problems calling for a programmed decision under the condition of certainty.

4-6. Explain the importance of planning, implementing, and controlling decisions.

Decisions are of no value to the company unless there is a plan stating how the objective of solving the problem will be achieved, and a plan that is not implemented is also of no value. The implementation of the plan must also be controlled to measure and monitor the progress of achieving the objective. Based on control, the decision maker must also not give up too soon and lose the benefits or get caught in the escalation of commitment and throw good money after bad.

••• KEY TERMS

big data, 121
brainstorming, 117
consensus mapping, 118
creative process, 116
creativity, 114
criteria, 113

decision making, 106
decision-making conditions, 110
decision-making model, 108
devil's advocate approach, 116
innovation, 114
nominal grouping, 117

nonprogrammed decisions, 110
problem, 106
problem solving, 106
programmed decisions, 110
synectics, 117

••• KEY TERM REVIEW

Complete each of the following statements using one of this chapter's key terms.

1. A _____ exists whenever objectives are not being met.

2. _____ is the process of taking corrective action to meet objectives.

3. _____ is the process of selecting a course of action that will solve a problem.

4. The steps of _____ include (1) classifying and defining the problem or opportunity, (2) setting objectives and criteria, (3) generating creative and innovative alternatives, (4) analyzing alternatives and selecting the most feasible, (5) planning and implementing the decision, and (6) controlling the decision.

5. For _____, which are recurring or routine, the decision maker should use decision rules or organizational policies and procedures.

6. For _____, which are significant, nonrecurring, and nonroutine, the decision maker should use the decision-making model.

7. The three _____ are certainty, risk, and uncertainty.

8. _____ are the standards that an alternative must meet to be selected as the decision that will accomplish the objective.

9. _____ is a way of thinking that generates new ideas.

10. _____ is the implementation of a new idea.

11. The three stages in the _____ are (1) preparation, (2) incubation and illumination, and (3) evaluation.

12. With the _____, group members focus on defending a proposed solution to a problem while others try to come up with criticisms of why the solution will not work.

13. _____ is the process of suggesting many possible alternatives without evaluation.

14. _____ is the process of generating novel alternatives through role playing and fantasizing.

15. _____ is the process of generating and evaluating alternatives using a structured voting method.

16. _____ is the process of developing group agreement on a solution to a problem.

17. _____ is the analysis of large amounts of quantified facts to aid in maximizing decision making.

• • • REVIEW QUESTIONS

1. What is the relationship among the management functions, problem solving, and decision making?

2. Why is it necessary to determine the decision structure and decision-making conditions?

3. What is the current trend concerning the use of groups to solve problems and make decisions?

4. Is a decrease in sales and/or profits a symptom or a cause of a problem?

5. Would a maximum price of $1,000 to spend on a stereo be an objective or a criterion?

6. Is there really a difference between creativity and innovation?

7. What is the major difference between nominal grouping and consensus mapping?

8. Why are generating and analyzing alternatives separate steps in the decision-making model?

9. What quantitative techniques are commonly used to compare alternatives?

10. When is the cost-benefit analysis commonly used?

11. When is intuition commonly used?

• • • COMMUNICATION SKILLS

The following critical-thinking questions can be used for class discussion and/or as written assignments to develop communication skills. Be sure to give complete explanations for all questions.

1. Are problem solving and decision making really all that important? How do you rate your decision-making ability?

2. Which potential advantage and disadvantage of group problem solving and decision making do you think arises most frequently?

3. Are creativity and innovation really important to all types of businesses? Is it important to evaluate a creative idea before it becomes an innovation?

4. What is the role of intuition in decision making? Should managers use more objective or subjective intuition techniques when making decisions?

5. Have you ever used any of the techniques for analyzing and selecting an alternative? If so, which one(s)?

6. Should managers be ethical in their decision making? If so, how should ethics be used in decision making?

7. Have you or someone you know experienced escalation of commitment? If so, explain.

8. Do men and women make decisions differently?

9. Have you ever made a decision with information that was not timely, of good quality, complete, and/or relevant? If so, was the decision a good one? Why or why not?

CASES

• • • Case 4-1   Toyota Motor Corporation

Toyota Motor Corporation is a leading, global manufacturer of motor vehicles. It has seven key operating principles that drive what the company does and how it does it:

- Honor the language and spirit of the law of every nation and undertake open and fair business activities to be a good corporate citizen of the world.

- Respect the culture and customs of every nation and contribute to economic and social development through corporate activities in their respective communities.

- Dedicate our business to providing clean and safe products and to enhancing the quality of life everywhere through all of our activities.

- Create and develop advanced technologies and provide outstanding products and services that fulfill the needs of customers worldwide.

- Foster a corporate culture that enhances both individual creativity and the value of teamwork, while honoring mutual trust and respect between labor and management.

- Pursue growth through harmony with the global community via innovative management.
- Work with business partners in research and manufacture to achieve stable, long-term growth and mutual benefits, while keeping ourselves open to new partnerships.

The company consists of three business units: automotive operations, financial services, and all others. The company was started by Kiichiro Toyoda in 1937 and is headquartered in Toyota, Japan. The company has a workforce of more than 348,000 employees, and it sells its vehicles in 190 countries and regions. The company has won many industry awards including most trusted brand, longest-lasting vehicles, and best overall value.

Toyota has established itself as an industry leader in quality, reliability, and efficiency in its automotive operations. Its methods for product development, production, and operations have served as the benchmark for others in the industry. One set of practices that has enabled Toyota to achieve a sustainable competitive advantage is the Toyota eight-step problem-solving process that it deploys throughout its global operations. The steps include the following:

- Step 1: Clarify the problem
- Step 2: Break down the problem
- Step 3: Set the target
- Step 4: Analyze the root cause
- Step 5: Develop countermeasures
- Step 6: Implement countermeasures
- Step 7: Monitor results and process
- Step 8: Standardize and share success

Clarifying the problem (step 1) involves Toyota management and employees working in teams to obtain direct experience with the problem for themselves to understand the nature of the problem. Breaking down the problem (step 2) focuses on further analyzing the problem and decomposing it into subproblems that are more specific and manageable. Setting the target (step 3) involves Toyota management and workers agreeing to challenging goals for solving a problem (e.g., reducing defects) as well as mapping out a plan and timeline for achieving the objectives. Analyzing the root cause (step 4) refers to collecting empirical data to understand the underlying causes of a problem. This step is typically helpful in terms of identifying multiple causes of the problem. Developing countermeasures (step 5) focuses on teams of Toyota managers and workers brainstorming specific solutions to remove the root causes of a problem.

Implementing countermeasures (step 6) is the actual deployment of the selected countermeasure. Monitoring results and process (step 7) is based on a process called Plan-Do-Check-Act (PDCA) that supports the effective implementation and continuous improvement of a countermeasure. Basically, PDCA involves implementing a countermeasure, evaluating its effectiveness, modifying the countermeasure to further improve it, and then implementing that countermeasure as a cyclical process. Standardizing and sharing success (step 8) focuses on "institutionalizing" the new practice or process into Toyota's overall production and operational system. This could involve redesigning a process, changing rules and policies, job redesign, and realigning the culture of the organization. This also involves communicating the new practices or processes to others in the Toyota organization so that they may also learn from the success of the change and obtain guidance about how they can achieve similar results.

The decision-making and problem-solving process used at Toyota Motor Corporation has enabled it to produce some of the most popular and reliable vehicles in their respective market segments including the Camry sedan and the RAV4 sport utility vehicle.

Discussion Questions

1. How does Toyota address both decision making and problem solving in its operations?
2. How does Toyota's approach to decision making and problem solving address the four management functions?
3. How does Toyota apply the six-step decision-making process model in its operations?
4. How does Toyota use groups to support decision making and problem solving?
5. What do you think of Toyota's 8-Step Problem Solving Model? Do you think you could use it at any of the employers where you have held part-time jobs or internships as a student? Why or why not?
6. Do you think that it would be better for Toyota to use a more informal approach to decision-making and problem solving so that management and workers have more flexibility to address issues they face in performing their jobs? Why or why not?

References

http://www.kaizen-news.com/eight-steps-practical-problem-solving/
http://www.toyota-global.com/company/profile/overview/
http://money.cnn.com/quote/profile/profile.html?symb=TM
https://hbr.org/2008/06/the-contradictions-that-drive-toyotas-success
http://www.toyota.com/awards/

Case created by Loren Kuzuhara, University of Wisconsin–Madison.

• • • Case 4-2   Was Target Missing the Mark With Fashion Designer Clothing?

Target, or as many refer to, "Tar-zhay," was once known for its super chic, affordably priced, designer clothing that targeted

middle-class consumers. The fashion-forward discount chain was based around the consumer expectation to "expect more, pay less." Unfortunately for Target, it only focused on the "pay less" part during the recent recession.(1) Realizing its mistake, Target has committed to revitalizing the mantra of expect more, pay less by working with such famous designers as Jason Wu, Lilly Pulitzer, Marimekko, Missoni, Phillip Lim, Prabal Gurung, and Zac Posen.

"Target has recently teamed up with Victoria Beckham for a capsule collection to be released in the spring of 2017. Victoria Beckham for Target will include more than 200 items, including tops and bottoms for women, plus corresponding styles for girls, toddler and baby. Beckham's line will range in price from $6 to $70, with most articles costing under $40. Items will be offered in sizes XS–3X for women and NB–XL for girls, toddler and baby. The collection will be available Apr. 9 through Apr. 30, 2017, or while supplies last. Select pieces will also be sold online for global shoppers via VictoriaBeckham.com."(2)

The question everyone is asking, though, is, can Target keep pace with the consumer demands for these designer products? Why are they asking this question?

In 2011, when internationally known designer Missoni launched a collection at Target, the unanticipated high traffic unintentionally caused its website to crash. The Target website and designer merchandise were unavailable for a half day while the company worked to restore the website from the high-volume crash.(3)

Believing it had learned from its prior mistake, Target decided to collaborate with Lilly Pulitzer—the first big designer that it brought back to shelves after abandoning its original mantra. This limited-edition collection excited many consumers, giving Target hope that it would attract previous consumers and capture the attention of many new ones. Lilly Pulitzer is a high-end luxury designer known for its colorful American resort wear.

Lilly Pulitzer at Target did create quite the hype, attracting its typical middle-class target market and the upper-class Lilly Pulitzer loyalist. Everyone, including Target, was excited for the high-end line to be available for a fraction of its typical price. On April 19, 2015, the limited-time capsule collection launched.(4)

Its objective worked as planned—and yet it was still not prepared for its success. Eager consumers on Target's website at midnight were utterly disappointed to learn the site had crashed due to an overwhelmingly high volume of traffic. As a result, during points in the launch, Target decided to deactivate the website.(5) Lucky consumers who had the ability to navigate and shop the site were disappointed when they went to check out and merchandise was no longer available. Consumers who went to shop in brick-and-mortar stores lined up outside Target locations prior to opening with hundreds of others seeking out the Lilly Pulitzer line. Consumers scrambled in to get their hands on any of the apparel, accessories, or home goods that became available. Merchandise in stores lasted minutes—five minutes to be exact in one Michigan location.(6)

The overall consumer feeling regarding Lilly Pulitzer at Target was disappointment. Many who sought out the highly anticipated collection did not have access to the merchandise online or in stores. What should have been a revitalization of the "Tar-zhay" image resulted in an inconsistent shopping experience. A collaborative collection that was intended to run for weeks lasted only a few minutes. However, consumers, also known as "the lucky ones," who were able to purchase the merchandise were extremely satisfied by the design and quality of the items.(7)

It is then not surprising that in 2016, when the Finnish designer Marimekko collection hit the stores, customers waited several hours outside the store before its opening in order to make sure to get first grabs at the collection. Many waiting were wondering if Target was going to run into the same problems that it had with the Pulitzer collection. An employee said to a reporter that it was expected that Target would run out of inventory at the end of the day.(8)

Target invested countless hours into its limited-edition designer collaborations, only to see them falter when actually launched in stores and online. Though the products are well received, the shopping experience and impression they leave on consumers is not a positive one. So what went wrong with these prior designer collections? Was the culprit inventory control or rather how Target launched the product lines or both? If Target plans to fulfill the mantra of "expect more, pay less," will it have learned from prior experiences and give consumers what they "really really want" from Victoria Beckham's collection or will consumers just be saying "Goodbye"?(9)

Discussion Questions

1. Explain the objective, decision, and problem when Target collaborated with Lilly Pulitzer and other designer firms.

2. When Target deactivated its website, what type of decision did it make? Explain.

3. How could Target have utilized steps 4–6 in the decision-making model with its inventory to have a more successful launch?

4. Did Target use the Delphi Technique? Elaborate.

5. If you were in charge of operations for these collaborations, what type of decisions would you have made during the creation and launch of these lines?

6. Did Target make the right decision by collaborating with Lilly Pulitzer and other designers to revitalize the "Tar-zhay" image?

7. Do you think Lilly Pulitzer Company was satisfied by this outcome?

Cumulative Case Questions

8. Please rate the customer value on a scale of 1 (low) to 10 (high) with regard to the Lilly Pulitzer collection and other designer collections at Target. (Chapter 2)

9. Was Target's management ultimately effective during this launch? (Chapter 1)

10. What type of managers were used heavily on this project? Distinguish their responsibilities. (Chapter 1)

11. Did Lilly Pulitzer enter a licensing contract with Target? (Chapter 3)

References

(1) Lilly Pulitzer ® at Target. Only at Target and only for a limited time. (n.d.). Retrieved June 6, 2015, from http://www.target.com/c/lilly-pulitzer-for-target-brand-shop/-/N-4ymap 2

(2) Johnson, Z. (2016, October 20). Victoria Beckham for Target coming in spring 2017: All the details. Retrieved January 24, 2017, from http://www.eonline.com/news/803343/victoria-beckham-for-target-coming -in-spring-2017-all-the-details

(3) Clifford, S. (2011, September 13). Demand at Target for fashion line crashes web site. Retrieved June 6, 2015, from http://www.nytimes.com/2011/09/14/business/demand-at-target-for-fashion-line-crashes-web-site.html?_r=0

(4) Grinberg, E. (2015, April 20). Lilly Pulitzer for Target causes shopping frenzy. Retrieved June 6, 2015, from http://www.cnn.com/2015/04/19/living/feat-lilly-pulitzer-target/

(5) Ziobro, P. (2015, April 19). Lilly Pulitzer: Target website, apps overwhelmed by demand. Retrieved June 6, 2015, from http://wasnews.com/i/Lilly-Pulitzer-Target-Website-Apps-Overwhelmed-by-Demand-for-Lilly-Pulitzer

(6) Grinberg, E. (2015, April 20). Lilly Pulitzer for Target causes shopping frenzy. Retrieved June 6, 2015, from http://www.cnn.com/2015/04/19/living/feat-lilly-pulitzer-target/

(7) Wahba, P. (2015, April 21). Target admits Lilly Pulitzer line was supposed to have lasted weeks. Retrieved June 6, 2015, from http://fortune.com/2015/04/21/target-lilly-pulitzer/

(8) Raddatz, K. (2016, April 17). Target unveils new Marimekko clothing line. Retrieved January 24, 2017, from http://minnesota.cbslocal.com/2016/04/17/target-unveils-new-marimekko-clothing-line/

(9) Bing. (n.d.). Spice Girls top songs. Retrieved January 24, 2017, from https://www.bing.com/search?q=spice+girl+songs&form=EDGEAR&qs=P-F&cvid=f3577829834d485abd973e6a5596820d&pq=spice+girl+songs

Case created by Herbert Sherman, Hannah K. Walter, and Naveed Ahmad, Long Island University.

● ● ● SKILL BUILDER 4-1: MAKING A DECISION USING THE DECISION-MAKING MODEL

Select a problem or opportunity that you now face. Remember, a problem exists when objectives are not being met—when there is a difference between what is happening and what you want to happen. The problem or opportunity may be from any facet of your life—work, college, sports, a relationship, a purchase to be made in the near future, where to go on a date, and so on. Use the decision-making model outline that follows to solve your problem or take advantage of the opportunity.

Objective

To improve your ability to make decisions.

Skills

The primary skills developed through this exercise are:

1. *Management skill*—decision making (conceptual, diagnostic, analytical, critical thinking, and quantitative reasoning)

2. *AACSB competency*—analytic skills and application of knowledge

3. *Management function*—primarily planning (but decisions are made when organizing, leading, and controlling)

Step 1. Classify and Define the Problem or Opportunity

Decision structure. Do you need to make a programmed or a nonprogrammed decision?

Decision condition. Are you facing a condition of uncertainty, of risk, or of certainty?

Decision-making type. Is a rational or bounded rational decision appropriate? (Continue to follow all steps in the decision-making model even if a bounded rational decision is appropriate.)

Select the appropriate level of participation. Should the decision be made by an individual or a group? (If a group decision is appropriate, use a group for the following steps in the model. But remember to maximize the advantages and minimize the disadvantages of group decision making.)

Define the problem. List the symptoms and causes of the problem (or opportunity); then write a clear statement of it.

Step 2. Set Objectives and Criteria

Write down what is to be accomplished by the decision and the standards that any alternative must meet to be selected as the decision that will accomplish the objective. (Specify "must" and "want" criteria if appropriate for the decision.)

Objective: Criteria ("must" and "want")

Step 3. Generate Creative and Innovative Alternatives

What information do you need? (Remember that information must be timely, of good quality, complete, and relevant to be useful.) Will you use any technology?

If you are working with a group, will brainstorming, nominal grouping, or consensus mapping be used?

List your alternatives (at least three); number them. If a decision tree will be helpful, make one.

Step 4. Analyze Alternatives and Select the Most Feasible

Is a quantitative or cost-benefit (pros and cons) analysis appropriate? Choose a method and complete your analysis.

Step 5. Plan and Implement the Decision

Write out your plan for implementing the decision. Be sure to state the controls you will use to make sure you know if the decision is working. How can you avoid escalation of commitment?

Step 6. Control the Decision

After implementing the decision, make notes about progress in solving the problem or taking advantage of the opportunity.

Indicate any need for corrective action, and if you need to, return to prior steps in the decision-making model.

Apply It

What did I learn from this experience? How will I use this knowledge in the future?

Your instructor may ask you to do Skill Builder 4-1 in class in a group. If so, the instructor will provide you with any necessary information or additional instructions.

• • • SKILL BUILDER 4-2: USING THE SITUATIONAL DECISION-MAKING MODEL

Objective

To determine the appropriate level of participation using the decision-making model.

Skills

The primary skills developed through this exercise are:

1. *Management skill*—decision making (conceptual, diagnostic, analytical, critical thinking, and quantitative reasoning)

2. *AACSB competency*—analytic skills and application of knowledge

3. *Management function*—primarily planning (but decisions are made when organizing, leading, and controlling)

Preparation (Individual and/or Group)

In this exercise, you will learn how to use the situational decision-making model. Chapter 1's Skill Builder 1-4 discussed the situational management model. Now you will learn an extension of the model to use when deciding which style to use when solving problems and making decisions. Selecting the appropriate level of participation style includes two steps: (1) diagnose the situation, and (2) select the appropriate style.

Step 1: Diagnose the Situation. The first step is to diagnose the situational variables, which include time, information, acceptance, and employee capability level. See Model 4-1 for a list of variables. The top half summarizes step 1. Note that we use the term *supervisor* to represent a manager or group leader of any type overseeing the decision.

Time You must determine if there is enough time to include the group in decision making. If there is not enough time, use the autocratic style, and ignore the other three variables—they are irrelevant if there is no time. If time permits, consider the other three variables and select the style without considering time. *Time*, however, is a relative term. In one situation, a few minutes may be considered a short time period, while in another, a month or more may be a short period of time.

Information The more information you have to make the decision, the less need there is to use participation, and vice versa. If you have all the necessary information to make a decision, there is no need to use participation. If you have little information, you need to get it through participation.

Acceptance If you make the decision alone, will the group implement it willingly? The more the team will like the decision, the less need there is to use participation, and vice versa.

Employee Capability The leader must decide if the group has the ability and willingness to be involved in problem solving and decision making. The more capable the employees, the higher the level of participation, and vice versa. Realize that a group's capability level can change from situation to situation.

Step 2: Select the Appropriate Supervisory Style for the Situation. After considering the four variables, you select the appropriate style for the situation. In some situations, all variables suggest the same possible style, while other cases indicate conflicting styles. For example, you may have time to use any style and may have all the information necessary (autocratic); employees may be reluctant (consultative or participative); and the capability may be moderate (consultative). In situations in which conflicting styles are indicated for different variables, you must determine which variable should be given more weight. In the given example, assume it was determined that acceptance was critical for successful implementation of the decision. Acceptance takes precedence over information. Realizing that employees have a moderate capability, the consultative style would be appropriate. See the bottom half of Model 4-1 for an explanation of how the decision is made using each of the four situational supervisory styles.

Applying the Situational Decision-Making Model

We will apply the model to the following situation:

Ben, a supervisor, can give one of his employees a merit pay raise. He has a week to make the decision. Ben knows how well each employee performed over the past year. The employees really have no option but to accept getting or not getting the pay raise, but they can complain to upper management about the selection. The employees' capability levels vary, but as a group, they have a high capability level under normal circumstances.

Step 1: Diagnose the Situation.

       time   information   acceptance   capability

Ben, the supervisor, has plenty of time to use any level of participation. He has all the information needed to make the decision (autocratic). Employees have no choice but to

MODEL 4-1

Step 1: Diagnose the Situation

Variable	Use of Style
Time	No = S-A ----stop----------- Yes = any style continue
Information	All = S-A Some = S-C Little = S-P or S-E
Acceptance	Accept = S-A Reluctance = S-C Reject = S-P or S-E
Capability	Low = S-A Moderate = S-C High = S-P Outstanding = S-E

Step 2: Select the Appropriate Style for the Situation

Autocratic (S-A)

The supervisor makes the decision alone and announces it after the fact. An explanation of the rationale for the decision may be given.

Consultative (S-C)

The supervisor consults individuals or the group for information and then makes the decision. Before implementing the decision, the supervisor explains the rationale for the decision and sells the benefits to the employees. The supervisor may invite questions and have a discussion.

Participative (S-P)

The supervisor may present a tentative decision to the group and ask for its input. The supervisor may change the decision if the input warrants a change. Or the supervisor may present the problem to the group for suggestions. Based on employee participation, the supervisor makes the decision and explains its rationale.

Empowerment (S-E)

The supervisor presents the situation to the group and describes limitations to the decision. The group makes the decision. The supervisor may be a group member.

accept the decision (autocratic). And the group's level of capability is normally high (participative).

Step 2: Select the Appropriate Style for the Situation. There are conflicting styles to choose from (autocratic and participative):

The variable that should be given precedence is information. The employees are normally capable, but in a situation like this, they may not be capable of putting the department's goals ahead of their own. In other words, even if employees know which employee deserves the raise, they may each fight for it anyway. Such a conflict could cause future problems. Some of the possible ways to make the decision are as follows:

- *Autocratic (S-A).* The supervisor would select the person for the raise without discussing it with any employees. Ben would simply announce the decision and explain the rationale for the selection after submitting it to the payroll department.

- *Consultative (S-C).* The supervisor would consult the employees as to who should get the raise. Ben would then decide who would get the raise. He would announce the decision and explain the rationale for it. The supervisor may invite questions and discussion.

- *Participative (S-P).* The supervisor could tentatively select an employee to get the raise but be open to change if an employee or group convinces him that someone else should get the raise. Or Ben could explain the situation to the group and lead a discussion of who should get the raise. After considering their input, Ben would make the decision and explain the rationale for it.

- *Empowerment (S-E).* The supervisor would explain the situation and allow the group to decide who gets the raise. Ben may be a group member. Notice that this is the only style that allows the group to make the decision.

Selection: The autocratic style is appropriate for this situation because Ben has all the information needed, acceptance is not an issue, and capability is questionable.

Following are 10 situations calling for a decision. Select the appropriate problem-solving and decision-making style. Be sure to use Model 4-1 when determining the style to use. On the time, information, acceptance, and capability lines, place S-A, S-C, S-P, or S-E, as indicated by the situation. Based on your diagnoses, select the one style you would use. Note that style on the line preceding the situation.

S-A = Autocratic   S-C = Consultative   S-P = Participative
S-E = Empowerment

1. You have developed a new work procedure that will increase productivity. Your boss likes the idea and wants you to try it within a few weeks. You view your employees as fairly capable and believe that they will be receptive to the change.

    _____ time _____ information _____ acceptance _____ capability

2. The industry of your product has new competition. Your organization's revenues have been dropping. You have been told to lay off 3 of your 10 employees in two weeks. You have been the supervisor for over one year. Normally, your employees are very capable.

    _____ time _____ information _____ acceptance _____ capability

3. Your department has been facing a problem for several months. Many solutions have been tried, but all have failed. You have finally thought of a solution, but you are not sure of the possible consequences of the change required or of acceptance by the highly capable employees.

    _____ time _____ information _____ acceptance _____ capability

4. Flextime has become popular in your organization. Some departments let each employee start and end work when he or she chooses. However, because of the cooperative effort of your employees, they must all work the same eight hours. You are not sure of the level of interest in changing the hours. Your employees are a very capable group and like to make decisions.

    _____ time _____ information _____ acceptance _____ capability

5. The technology in your industry is changing so fast that the members of your organization cannot keep up. Top management hired a consultant, who has made recommendations. You have two weeks to decide what to do. Your employees are normally capable, and they enjoy participating in the decision-making process.

    _____ time _____ information _____ acceptance _____ capability

6. A change has been handed down from top management. How you implement it is your decision. The change takes effect in one month. It will personally affect everyone in your department. Your employees' acceptance is critical to the success of the change, but they are usually not too interested in being involved in making decisions.

    _____ time _____ information _____ acceptance _____ capability

7. Your boss called you on the telephone to tell you that someone has requested an order for your department's product with a very short delivery date. She asked you to call her back in 15 minutes with the decision about taking the order. Looking over the work schedule, you realize that it will be very difficult to deliver the order on time. Your employees will have to push hard to make it. They are cooperative and capable and enjoy being involved in decision making.

    _____ time _____ information _____ acceptance _____ capability

8. Top management has decided to make a change that will affect all your employees. You know the employees will be upset because it will cause them hardship. One or two may even quit. The change goes into effect in 30 days. Your employees are very capable.

    _____ time _____ information _____ acceptance _____ capability

9. You believe that productivity in your department could be increased. You have thought of some ways that may work, but you are not sure of them. Your employees are very experienced; almost all of them have been in the department longer than you have.

    _____ time _____ information _____ acceptance _____ capability

10. A customer has offered you a contract for your product with a quick delivery date. The offer is open for two days. Meeting the contract deadline would require employees to work nights and weekends for six weeks. You cannot require them to work overtime. Filling this profitable contract could help get you the raise you want and feel you deserve. However, if you take the contract and don't deliver on time, it will hurt your chances of getting a big raise. Your employees are very capable.

    _____ time _____ information _____ acceptance _____ capability

Preparation: You should have completed the 10 situations from the preparation.

Experience: You will try to select the recommended problem-solving and decision-making style in the 10 preparation situations.

Procedure 1 (5–12 minutes)

The instructor reviews Model 4-1 and explains how to use it for selecting the appropriate supervisory style for situation 1 of the exercise preparation.

Procedure 2 (12–20 minutes)

Break into teams of two or three. Apply the model to situations 2 through 5 as a team. You may change your original answers. The instructor goes over the recommended answers and scoring for situations 2 through 5. Do not continue on to situation 6 until after the instructor goes over the answers to situations 2 through 5.

In the same teams, select problem-solving and decision-making styles for situations 6 through 10. The instructor will go over the recommended answers and scoring.

Apply It

What did I learn from this experience? How will I use this knowledge in the future?

Your instructor may ask you to do Skill Builder 4-2 in class in a group. If so, the instructor will provide you with any necessary information or additional instructions.

5 Strategic and Operational Planning

••• LEARNING OBJECTIVES

After studying this chapter, you should be able to:

5-1. Describe how strategic planning differs from operational planning. PAGE 137

5-2. Explain the reason for conducting an industry, competitive, and company situation analysis. PAGE 140

5-3. List the parts of an effective written objective and its must and want criteria. PAGE 145

5-4. Discuss the four corporate-level grand strategies and the three growth strategies. PAGE 148

5-5. Summarize the three business-level adaptive and competitive strategies. PAGE 151

5-6. Identify the operational functional strategies, contrast standing plans and single-use plans, describe the value of a time log analysis, and explain how to effectively multitask. PAGE 153

5-7. Explain the importance of implementing and controlling strategies. PAGE 162

IOM

Ideas on Management
at Starbucks

Howard Schultz was working in a local **Starbucks**, named after the quiet and right-minded character from Herman Melville's *Moby Dick*. Its logo is also inspired by the sea, featuring a twin-tailed siren from Greek mythology. The idea that transformed the local coffee retailer into a global brand came to Schultz on a visit to Italy. Observing the popularity of espresso bars there, he thought of introducing the coffee bar concept back in the United States. Schultz later bought Starbucks. From the beginning, Starbucks set out to be a different kind of company, one that not only celebrated coffee and the rich tradition but that also brought a feeling of connection. Its mission is to inspire and nurture the human spirit—one person, one cup, and one neighborhood at a time. Today, Starbucks connects with millions of customers every day with exceptional products and more than 24,000 retail stores in 70 countries.

But it hasn't been all smooth sailing for Starbucks. Schultz stepped down as CEO in 2000, and the company had problems, so Schultz came back as CEO in 2008 to get the company back on its growth track, and revenues more than doubled to more than $19 billion. On April 3, 2017, **Kevin Johnson** took over as CEO for Starbucks global business and operations. Schultz became executive chairman to focus on retail innovation and accelerating growth of Starbucks ultra-premium retail formats to build high-end coffee shops that will charge as much as $12 a cup. Schultz is attempting to refresh the brand and revolutionize the way Americans consume coffee, as Starbucks has been facing increased competition from specialty roasters such as **Stumptown** and **Intelligentsia**, as well as **Dunkin' Donuts** introducing more cold-brewed coffee. Schultz is such a great leader that he was named Businessperson of the Year by *Fortune*.

IOM 1. What are some of Starbucks's strategic and operational plans?

IOM 2. What are Starbucks's mission statement and competitive advantage?

IOM 3. What long-range goals has Starbucks established?

IOM 4. What is the corporate-level grand strategy and primary growth strategy at Starbucks?

IOM 5. What types of adaptive and competitive business-level strategies does Starbucks currently employ?

IOM 6. What type of functional and operational plans does Starbucks have?

You'll find answers to these **IOM** questions throughout the chapter. To learn more about Starbucks, visit www.starbucks.com.

Sources: Information for this case was taken from www.starbucks.com, accessed January 23, 2017; R. M. Murphy, "The 2011 Businessperson of the Year," *Fortune* (December 12, 2011): 87–95; J. Jargon, "Starbucks CEO Turns Focus to Pricier Brew," *The Wall Street Journal* (December 2, 106): A1, A6.

Strategic and Operational Planning

Recall from Chapter 1 that planning is the process of setting objectives and determining in advance exactly how the objectives will be met—or objectives lead to better plans.[1] There is an old saying: "When you fail to plan, you plan to fail." Some managers complain that they don't have time to plan, yet planners do better than nonplanners. Research supports these statements,[2] as there is a link between planning and performance.[3]

LO 5-1

Describe how strategic planning differs from operational planning.

This chapter focuses on improving your planning skills in your personal and professional lives. In this section, we explore planning dimensions, strategic versus operational planning and strategies, and the strategic planning process. Before we begin, complete Self-Assessment 5-1 to determine how well you plan.

Planning Dimensions

Having a plan makes it far more likely you will actually achieve the objectives,[4] and planning has several dimensions. Exhibit 5-1 summarizes the five planning dimensions. Note that upper-level and some middle-level managers spend more time developing strategic, broad/directional, long-range, single-use plans for the organization.[5] Other middle-level and all lower-level managers, in contrast, spend more time specifying how the strategic plans will be accomplished by developing operational, narrow/specific, short-range plans and implementing standing plans (policies, procedures, and rules). Success companies push forward via careful planning.[6] Throughout this chapter, we explore these five planning dimensions.

Strategic Versus Operational Planning and Strategies

Strategic Versus Operational Planning. There are two types of plans. **Strategic planning** *is the process of developing a mission and long-range objectives and determining in advance how they will be accomplished.* **Operational planning** *is the process of setting short-range objectives and determining in advance how they will be accomplished.*

As shown in Exhibit 5-1, differences between strategic planning and operational planning are primarily the time frame and management level involved. *Long term* generally means that it will take longer than one year to achieve the objective. Strategic plans are commonly developed for five years and reviewed and revised every year so that a five-year plan is always in place,[7] such as at **Domino's. Ferrari** has an ambitious five-year growth plan to unlock the value of its sports-car brand.[8] Conversely, operational plans have short-term objectives that will be met in one year or less.

At **Starbucks (IOM 1)**, the decisions to expand by opening new stores and now upscale coffee shops, going into overseas markets, and selling its products in grocery stores are all examples of strategic, long-term planning. Operational plans at Starbucks include short-term objectives developed for individual stores, such as an annual sales forecast or marketing plan for a specific location developed by a store manager or regional manager.

Strategic and Operational Strategies. A **strategy** *is a plan for pursuing a mission and achieving objectives.* Strategic thinking is important, as it was ranked fifth as a skill that employers value.[9] Strategic and operational types of plans include three *planning levels*: corporate, business, and functional. Each of these levels of planning requires strategies, which should be stated simply.[10] The corporate and business levels are part of strategic planning, and the functional level is part of operational planning.

A *corporate strategy* is the strategic plan for managing multiple lines of business. In essence, there is more than one business within the corporation. A *business strategy* is the strategic plan for managing one line of business. Functional strategies are part of operational planning. A *functional strategy* is the operational plan for managing one area of a business.

strategic planning The process of developing a mission and long-range objectives and determining in advance how they will be accomplished.

operational planning The process of setting short-range objectives and determining in advance how they will be accomplished.

strategy A plan for pursuing a mission and achieving objectives.

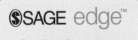

Get the edge on your studies. **edge.sagepub .com/lussier8e**

- Take a quiz to find out what you've learned.
- Review key terms with eFlashcards.
- Watch videos that enhance chapter content.

| EXHIBIT 5-1 | PLANNING DIMENSIONS |

Management Level	Type of Plan	Scope	Time	Repetitiveness
Upper and Middle	Strategic	Broad/Directional	Long Range	Single-Use Plan
Middle and Lower	Operational	Narrow/Specific	Short Range	Standing Plan

5-1 SELF-ASSESSMENT

Effective Planning

Indicate how well each statement describes your behavior by placing a number from 1 (*does not describe me*) to 5 (*describes me*) on the line before the statement.

5	4	3	2	1
Describes me				**Does not describe me**

____ 1. I have a specific result to accomplish whenever I start a project of any kind.

____ 2. When setting objectives, I state only the result to be accomplished; I don't specify how the result will be accomplished.

____ 3. I have specific and measurable objectives; for example, I know the specific grade I want to earn in this course.

____ 4. I set objectives that are difficult but achievable.

____ 5. I set deadlines when I have something I need to accomplish, and I meet the deadlines.

____ 6. I have a long-term goal (what I will be doing in 3–5 years) and short-term objectives to get me there.

____ 7. I have written objectives stating what I want to accomplish.

____ 8. I know my strengths and weaknesses, am aware of threats, and seek opportunities.

____ 9. I analyze a problem and alternative actions rather than immediately jumping right in with a solution.

____ 10. I spend most of my day doing what I plan to do rather than dealing with emergencies and trying to get organized.

____ 11. I use a calendar, appointment book, or some form of "to-do" list.

____ 12. I ask others for advice.

____ 13. I follow appropriate policies, procedures, and rules.

____ 14. I develop contingency plans in case my plans do not work out as I expect them to.

____ 15. I implement my plans and determine if I have met my objectives.

Add up the numbers you assigned to the statements to see where you fall on the continuum below.

75	65	55	45	35	25	15
Effective Planner						**Ineffective Planner**

Don't be too disappointed if your score isn't as high as you would like. All of these items are characteristics of effective planning. Review the items that did not describe you. After studying this chapter and doing the exercises, you can improve your planning skills.

Exhibit 5-2 illustrates the relationship between strategic planning and operational planning and their three planning levels. We will discuss the various types of corporate, business, and functional strategies in separate sections later. The plans at the three levels must be coordinated through the strategic planning process, and adapt to changing environments.[11]

The Strategic Planning Process

You need to plan carefully before making a strategic move,[12] and following the five steps helps. The steps in the *strategic planning process* are illustrated in Exhibit 5-3. Notice that the process is not simply linear; it does not proceed through steps 1 through 5 and then end. As the arrows indicate, you may need to return to prior steps and make changes as part of an ongoing process. Strategic planning may sound intimidating or unnecessary, but without it,

WORK APPLICATION 5-1

Give an example of a strategic objective and an operational objective from an organization you work for or have worked for.

WORK APPLICATION 5-2

Does a business you work for or have worked for have one or multiple lines of business? List the line(s).

EXHIBIT 5-2   # STRATEGIC AND OPERATIONAL PLANNING AND STRATEGIES

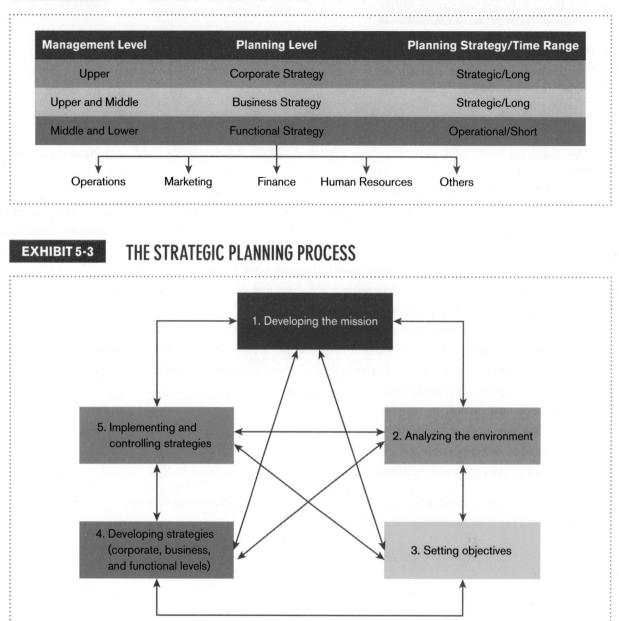

Management Level	Planning Level	Planning Strategy/Time Range
Upper	Corporate Strategy	Strategic/Long
Upper and Middle	Business Strategy	Strategic/Long
Middle and Lower	Functional Strategy	Operational/Short

Operations   Marketing   Finance   Human Resources   Others

EXHIBIT 5-3   # THE STRATEGIC PLANNING PROCESS

1. Developing the mission

5. Implementing and controlling strategies

2. Analyzing the environment

4. Developing strategies (corporate, business, and functional levels)

3. Setting objectives

you may miss big opportunities.[13] The major headings throughout the rest of this chapter list the steps in the strategic planning process.

LO 5-2

Explain the reason for conducting an industry, competitive, and company situation analysis.

Developing the Mission and Analyzing the Environment

In this section, we discuss the first and second steps of the strategic planning process.

The Mission

Recall our discussion of the mission statement in Chapter 2 stating that the mission is a business's purpose or reason for being, and we'll be brief here. Developing the mission is the first step in the strategic planning process. However, after analyzing the environment, managers should reexamine the mission and values to see if they need to be changed as the environment changes.[14] To this end, **United Parcel Service (UPS)** has a new slogan to redefine itself as "United Problem Solvers" to reflect its new emphasis on providing global supply chain services.[15] The mission is the foundation of the other four steps in the strategic planning process. The **Starbucks** (**IOM 2**) corporate mission is "to inspire and nurture the human spirit—one person, one cup and one neighborhood at a time."

A mission is often based on or also creates a *vision* that defines where the company is headed in inventing its future and why. It contains the expectations the organization strives to achieve. Top management needs to articulate a compelling vision so clear that it can be seen almost as a movie in one's head.[16] However, it's not easy, as companies including **Airbnb** struggled to define its mission and brand, and **Twitter** to define a clear vision[17]

United Parcel Service (UPS) uses the slogan "United Problem Solvers" to encourage its employees to achieve the organization's goal.

Analyzing the Environment

The second step of the strategic planning process is analyzing the environment to keep up with changes[18] that require changes in strategy[19] and to realign the firm's resource base in response to changes in the environment.[20] It is also known as situation analysis. A **situation analysis** *focuses on those features in a company's environment that most directly affect its options and opportunities.* This analysis has three parts: industry and competitive situation analysis, company situation analysis, and identification of a competitive advantage. It is important to do a good analysis, because managers tend to mis-specify what they actually face. Keep in mind that companies with multiple lines of business must conduct an environmental analysis for each line of business.

Industry and Competitive Situation Analysis. Industries vary widely in their makeup, competitive situation, and growth potential. Determining the position of an industry requires answering questions such as these: "How large is the market?" "What is the growth rate?" "How many competitors are there?" According to **Michael Porter**, competition in an industry is a composite of five competitive forces that should be considered in analyzing the competitive situation.[21] **UPS** is struggling with profitability as giant e-tailers like **Amazon.com** command bigger discounts for deliveries and are delivering goods, so it is focusing on other higher-margin services.[22] Exhibit 5-4 shows a competitive analysis for Starbucks explaining each of the five forces. Note that you start in the middle.

Company Situation Analysis. A company situation analysis is used at the business level to determine the strategic issues and problems that need to be addressed through the next three steps of the strategic planning process. A complete company situation analysis has five key parts, listed in Exhibit 5-5:

1. *Assessment of the present strategy based on performance.* This assessment can be a simple statement or a more complex comparison of performance indicators (market share, sales, net profit, return on assets, and so on) over the last five years.

2. *SWOT analysis. An organization's internal environmental strengths and weaknesses and external environmental opportunities and threats are determined through a* **SWOT analysis**. (SWOT stands for *strengths, weaknesses, opportunities*, and *threats.*) In the critical tool SWOT analysis,[23] the internal environmental factors analyzed for *strengths* and *weaknesses* are management and culture, mission, resources, systems, process, and structure. The external environmental (Chapter 2) factors analyzed for *opportunities* and *threats* are customers, competitors, suppliers, and so on. Essentially how you make or lose money.[24] Exhibit 5-6 outlines a SWOT analysis for Starbucks. You can find a SWOT analysis for the ***Fortune*** *100 companies* at its website Fortune.com.[25]

WORK
APPLICATION 5-3

Conduct a simple five-force competitive analysis for a company you work for or have worked for. Use Exhibit 5-4 as an example.

situation analysis An analysis of those features in a company's environment that most directly affect its options and opportunities.

SWOT analysis A determination of an organization's internal environmental strengths and weaknesses and external environmental opportunities and threats.

EXHIBIT 5-4   STARBUCKS'S FIVE-FORCE COMPETITIVE ANALYSIS

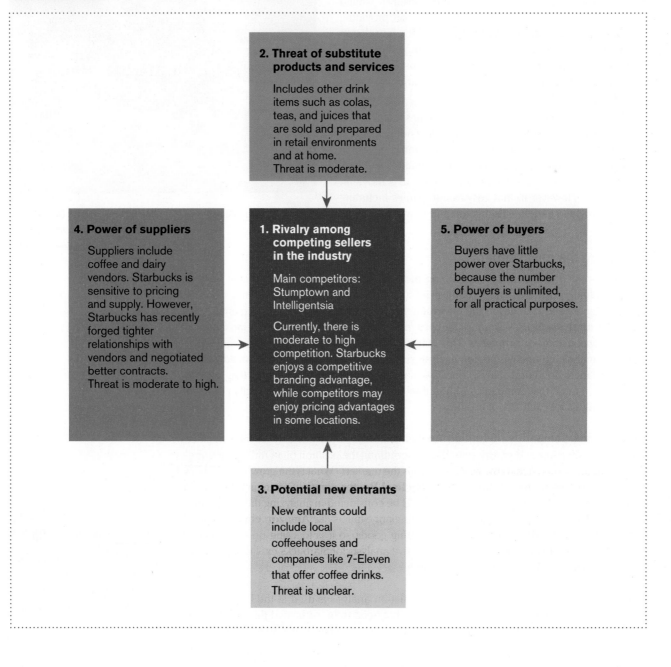

3. *Assessment of competitive strength and identification of competitive advantage.* In assessing competitive strength, you compare the *critical success factors* for a business to those of each major competitor. Critical success factors are the few major things that the business must do well to be successful. We will discuss competitive advantage shortly.

4. *Conclusions concerning competitive position.* How is the business doing compared to its competition? Are things improving or slipping?

5. *Determination of the issues and problems that need to be addressed through the strategic planning process.* Based on the results of the first four parts of the company situation analysis, what needs to be done in the future to improve the business's competitive position?

EXHIBIT 5-5   PARTS OF A COMPANY SITUATION ANALYSIS

1. Assessment of the present strategy based on performance → 2. SWOT analysis → 3. Assessment of competitive strength and identification of competitive advantage → 4. Conclusions concerning competitive position → 5. Determination of the issues and problems that need to be addressed through the strategic planning process

EXHIBIT 5-6   SWOT ANALYSIS FOR STARBUCKS

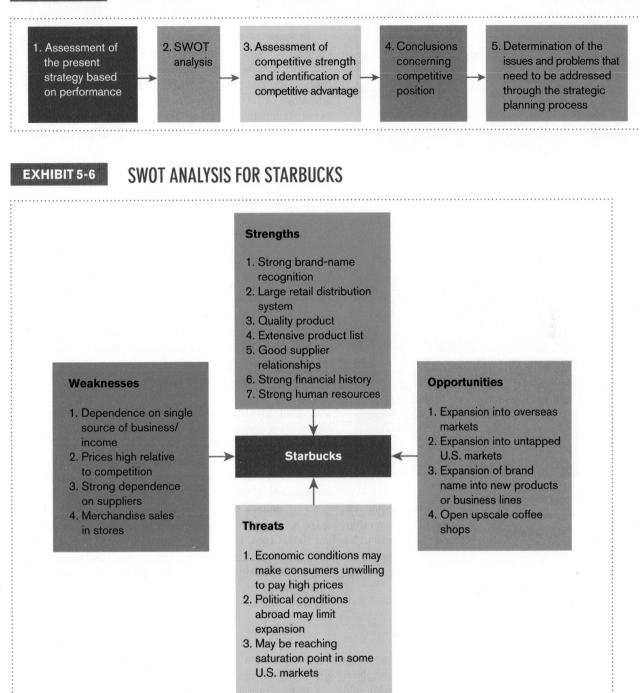

Strengths
1. Strong brand-name recognition
2. Large retail distribution system
3. Quality product
4. Extensive product list
5. Good supplier relationships
6. Strong financial history
7. Strong human resources

Weaknesses
1. Dependence on single source of business/income
2. Prices high relative to competition
3. Strong dependence on suppliers
4. Merchandise sales in stores

Starbucks

Opportunities
1. Expansion into overseas markets
2. Expansion into untapped U.S. markets
3. Expansion of brand name into new products or business lines
4. Open upscale coffee shops

Threats
1. Economic conditions may make consumers unwilling to pay high prices
2. Political conditions abroad may limit expansion
3. May be reaching saturation point in some U.S. markets

Competitive Advantage

A **competitive advantage** *specifies how an organization offers unique customer value.* It answers the questions, "What makes us different from and better than the competition?"[26] and "Why should a person buy our products or services rather than those of our competitors?"[27] A company has to have answers to these questions to have a competitive advantage and succeed in business,[28] and it has to sustain the advantage against competitors.[29] A firm may identify a competitive advantage in the process of assessing its competitive strength. Many companies say their people are their advantage.[30] **Starbucks's (IOM 2)** competitive

MANAGEMENT IN ACTION
Analyzing the Environment

Domino's model of quick ordering and delivery has become a process that many other pizza delivery companies benchmark.

advantage is its relaxed coffee house environment where friends can meet that offers free Wi-Fi, high-quality coffee, and other products.

Two aspects of a company's competitive advantage are core competency and benchmarking. A *core competency* is what a firm does well. By identifying core competencies, managers can oversee the creation of new products and services that take advantage of the company's strengths. **TGI Fridays** determined its core competency to be selling and managing franchisees, not operating restaurants. So it will sell most of its 200-plus U.S. and UK company-owned restaurants to franchisees.[31]

Benchmarking is the process of comparing an organization's products or services and processes with those of other companies. In benchmarking, you try to find out about other products and processes, through competitive intelligence, and copy them or improve upon them legally and ethically. Most benchmarking takes place within an industry. The Internet is an excellent source of information for benchmarking.

Pizza Hut, **Papa John's**, and **Little Caesars** copied **Domino's** delivery. However, looking at noncompetitors can provide good ideas that create a competitive advantage. Other restaurants now have delivery. **Uber** and **Airbnb** have inspired copycats and other types of businesses.[32] **Ford** is expanding its car-sharing service for its customers who want to rent out their Fords when they aren't using them.[33]

Changing Strategies. After managers have evaluated the organization and the competition by completing the situation analysis, they should go back and review the mission and its vision to see if they need to be changed. Remember that situation analysis is an ongoing process, referred to as *scanning the environment*. It tells what is going on in the external environment that may require change to continually improve customer value. **Netflix** changed its business model from shipping DVDs to streaming to making TV shows to stream.[34] **Amazon** offering cloud services has hurt **IBM, Cisco, HP**, and others sales of expensive data-center equipment, resulting in these companies focusing more on offering cloud and other services. Instead of selling software outright, **Microsoft** and **Oracle** are shifting to a cloud subscription model.[35]

LO 5-3

List the parts of an effective written objective and its must and want criteria.

benchmarking The process of comparing an organization's products and services and processes with those of other companies.

objectives Statements of what is to be accomplished that are expressed in singular, specific, and measurable terms with a target date.

Setting Objectives

After developing a mission and completing a situation analysis, you are ready for the third step in the strategic planning process: setting objectives that flow from the mission to take advantage of opportunities and address problems identified through the situation analysis. In this section, we discuss goals and objectives, writing objectives, criteria for effective objectives, and management by objectives (MBO).

You should be able to distinguish between goals and objectives. *Goals* state general, broad targets to be accomplished. **Objectives** *state what is to be accomplished in specific and measurable terms with a target date.* Recall that objectives are end results; they do not state how they will be accomplished—that's the plan.[36] **Starbucks**'s (**IOM 3**) long-range goal is to continue to expand globally; it also has a goal of being environmentally responsible, with more eco-conscious stores on a global scale from the design stage right through to construction and operations. Can you see how goals should be translated into objectives so that you can determine if the goal and objective have been achieved?

Writing Effective Objectives

Successful people are goal oriented,[37] and many have daily goals.[38] What are your objectives? In a survey of CEOs, the second-biggest challenge facing leaders today is staying focused, and setting objectives helps.[39] To help ensure that you will meet your objectives, it is a good idea to write them down and keep them someplace where they are constantly visible.[40] You will practice setting objectives in Skill Builder 5-1.

Max E. Douglas, Indiana State University, developed a model that is helpful in writing effective objectives. One variation on Douglas's model is shown in Model 5-1, with some examples of corporate strategic objectives shown following the model.

Criteria for Objectives

As the model for writing objectives implies, an effective objective conforms to three "must" criteria: It expresses a *specific* and *measurable* result, and it sets a *date* for achieving that result. It should also have a single result—or don't put multiple objectives together. Another similar way of writing objectives is called *SMART goals*—specific, measurable, attainable, realistic, and timely. Let's discuss the parts of Model 5-1, or the criteria that needed to be met in the model. Note that as shown in Exhibit 5-7, the top or first three are "must" criteria, as they are required for writing effective objectives, whereas the bottom or last three are "want" criteria because it can't be known if they are met by reading the objective.

Difficult but Achievable (Realistic). A number of studies show that individuals perform better when given difficult but achievable (realistic) objectives rather than objectives that are too difficult (don't try) or too easy (do the minimum).[48] So set bold objectives,[49] but be aware that too difficult an objective can lead to unethical behavior to achieve it to attain the reward for doing so[50]—like at **Enron** and **Wells Fargo**.

WORK APPLICATION 5-5

State one or more goals of an organization you work for or have worked for.

MODEL 5-1   OBJECTIVE WRITING

The Model

(1) *To* + (2) Action Verb + (3) Specific and Measurable Result + (4) Target Date

Corporate Objectives using the Model

McDonald's: (1) To (2) increase (3) the percentage of franchised units to 90% (4) by 2018.[41]

Apple: (1) To (2) build (3) a car (4) by year-end 2019.[42]

Starbucks: To open 1,400 stores in China by 2019.[43]

Anheuser-Busch InBev: To increase revenues to $100 billion by 2020.[44]

Tesla: To increase annual sales to 500,000 vehicles by 2020.[45]

GM: To sell 2 million cars a year through 2030.[46]

Ford: To sell driverless cars without steering wheels or pedals by 2021.[47]

EXHIBIT 5-7   CRITERIA THAT OBJECTIVES SHOULD MEET

Specific. Vague objectives fail.[1] So objectives should state the exact level of performance desired.[2] Specific objectives lead to focuses on achieving them.[3]

Ineffective Objective	To maximize profits in 2020 (How much is "maximize"?)
Effective Objective	To earn a net profit of $1 million in 2020

Measurable. If you are to achieve objectives, you must be able to observe and measure progress regularly to determine if the objectives have been met.[4]

Ineffective Objective	Perfect service for every customer (How is "perfect service" measured?)
Effective Objective	To attain an "excellent" satisfaction rating from 90% of customers surveyed in 2020

Target Date. A specific date should be set for accomplishing the objective. When people have a deadline, they usually try harder to get a task done on time than when they are simply told to do it when they can.

Ineffective Objective	To become a millionaire (by when?)
Effective Objective	To become a millionaire by December 31, 2020

It is also more effective to set a specific date than to give a time span, because it's too easy to forget when a time period began and should end.

Somewhat Effective	To double international business to $5 billion annually within five years
Effective Objective	To double international business to $5 billion annually by year-end 2019

Note, however, that some objectives are ongoing and do not require a stated date. The target date is indefinite until it is changed.

Somewhat Effective	To be number one or two in world sales in all lines of business–**GM**
Effective Objective	To have 25% of sales coming from products that did not exist five years ago–**3M**

1. H. Mitchell, "What's the Best Way to Stick With a Resolution?" *The Wall Street Journal* (December 23, 2014): D1, D2.
2. R. Bachman, "The Week Resolutions Die," *The Wall Street Journal* (January 20, 2015): D1, D4.
3. M. Dorf, "Long-Distance Leadership," *Entrepreneur* (March 2015): 19.
4. H. Ibarra, "The Way to Become a Strategic Executive," *The Wall Street Journal* (February 23, 2015): R7.

5-1   JOIN THE DISCUSSION ETHICS & SOCIAL RESPONSIBILITY

Objectives

Objectives should be difficult but achievable. However, **Wells Fargo & Co.** is considered to have created objectives that were too difficult and led to bank employees feeling pressured by the quotes and managers' pressure to meet the objective. The pressure resulted in employees creating new accounts that customers never asked for to either keep their jobs or to get more sales commissions resulted in overdraft fees for customers. The government imposed a fine of $185 million, and **CEO John Stumpf** retired.

Mary Mack, head of **Community Banking,** was charged with coming up with a new incentive system that didn't result in unethical or illegal activities of its 100,000 retail-bank employees at some 6,000 U.S. branches. Mack said Wells Fargo won't abandon cross-selling, or efforts to sell multiple products to individual households, which was seen as contributing to the misconduct.

1. If you were a manager at Wells Fargo, would you pressure employees?

2. Would you fire employees who didn't meet the difficult quotas?

3. As an employee, would you give in to the pressure and use unethical/illegal practices to meet the quotas in order to keep your job?

4. As an employee, would you use unethical practices to exceed the quotas in order to make more money?

5. Would your answers to questions 3 and 4 change if you knew that it was common practice of your coworkers to use these techniques and encourage you to do the same things? How about if there was peer pressure to also use the tactics?

Source: A. Andriotis and E. Glazer, "Wells Pushed Overdraft Services," *The Wall Street Journal* (October 11, 2016): C1, C2; E. Glazer, "Can She Save Wells Fargo's Branches?" *The Wall Street Journal* (October 20, 2016): C1, C2.

Participatively Set. Groups that participate in setting their objectives generally outperform groups with assigned objectives; participation helps members feel they have a shared destiny. CEOs say they do at least get input when setting company objectives.[51] You should use the appropriate level of participation for the employees' capabilities (Chapters 1 and 4).

Acceptance and Commitment. If objectives are to be met, you need to get buy-in,[52] or people must accept them and be committed to achieve them. If employees do not commit to an objective, then even if it meets all the other "must" and "want" criteria, it may not be accomplished. So you want to get people thinking and believing "I can do that" to motivate them to achieve the objective.[53]

Management by Objectives (MBO)

Management by objectives (MBO) is the process in which managers and their employees jointly set objectives for the employees, periodically evaluate performance, and reward according to the results, and it is used at firms including **GE**[54] and **Springfield College**.[55] At **Google**, every employee has objectives, and every other employee can see them.[56] MBO is also referred to as work planning and review, goals management, goals and controls, and management by results.

MBO has three steps:

Step 1. Set individual objectives and plans. You set objectives with each individual employee. The objectives are the heart of the MBO process and should meet the "must" and "want" criteria. They should be based on achieving the company and team objectives.[57]

Step 2. Give feedback and evaluate performance. Communication is the key factor in determining MBO's success or failure. Thus, you and your employees must meet frequently to review progress. The frequency of evaluations depends on the individual and the job performed.

Step 3. Reward according to performance. Employees' performance should be measured against their objectives. Employees who meet their objectives should be rewarded through recognition, praise, pay raises, promotions, and so on. We will discuss motivating employees with rewards in Chapter 11 and measuring performance in Chapter 14.

WORK APPLICATION 5-6

Using the model for writing objectives, write one or more objectives for an organization you work for or have worked for, making sure they meet the "must" criteria.

management by objectives (MBO) The process in which managers and their employees jointly set objectives for the employees, periodically evaluate performance, and reward according to the results.

5-1 APPLYING THE CONCEPT

Objectives

For each objective, state which "must" criterion is not met.

A. single result

B. specific

C. measurable

D. target date

_____ 1. To be perceived as the highest quality hotel in the Tri-State by the end of 2020

_____ 2. To write objectives next week

_____ 3. To double profits in Mexico

_____ 4. To sell 10% more nachos and 5% more beer at the hockey game on February 20, 2018

_____ 5. To increase sales in 2020

LO 5-4

Discuss the four corporate-level grand strategies and the three growth strategies.

Corporate-Level Strategies

Once you've set an objective, you need to develop a plan to achieve it.[58] In more detail, after the mission has been developed, the situation analysis has been completed, and objectives have been set, you move on to the fourth step of the strategic planning process: developing strategies at the corporate, business, and functional levels. In this section, we discuss corporate strategies, which are shown in Exhibit 5-8. Recall that to have a corporate strategy, the parent corporation must have subsidiary or business unit companies (companies within one company). So a corporate strategy allocates and coordinates resources among its different business units.

Grand Strategy

Multibusiness MNCs are the most prevalent form of business around the globe, and they need a grand strategy.[59] A **grand strategy** *is an overall corporate strategy for growth, stability, or turnaround and retrenchment, or for some combination of these.* Each grand strategy aligns with different objectives. Let's discuss each separately.

Growth. With a *growth strategy*, the company makes aggressive attempts to increase its size through increased sales, including **Google**, **Facebook**, and **Twitter**. **Apple** seeks new growth beyond its iPhone.[60] The 24-hour fitness club **Anytime Fitness** hit the 3,000-unit milestone faster than **Subway**, **McDonald's**, or **Dunkin" Donuts**.[61] **Starbucks** (**IOM 4**) has a growth strategy.

Stability. With a *stability strategy*, the company attempts to hold and maintain its present size or to grow slowly. Many smaller companies are satisfied with the status quo, but large MNCs are expected to keep growing. Rather than increasing its size aggressively, the company attempts to balance growth and profits. The **WD-40 Company** produces WD-40 lubricant. The company pursues a strategy of stability, as it has "slowly" added products over the years, including **Spot Shot**, **X-14**, **2000 Flushes**, **Lava**, **WD 40 Bike**, **3-In-One**, and **Carpet Fresh**.[62]

Turnaround and Retrenchment. A *turnaround strategy* is an attempt to reverse a declining business as quickly as possible. A *retrenchment strategy* is the divestiture or liquidation of assets. These strategies are listed together because most turnarounds include retrenchment. Turnaround strategies generally attempt to improve cash flow by increasing revenues, decreasing costs, reducing assets, or combining these strategies to realign the firm with its external environment.[63] Companies currently pursuing a turnaround strategy include

WORK
APPLICATION 5-7

State the grand strategy for an organization you work for or have worked for.

grand strategy An overall corporate strategy for growth, stability, or turnaround and retrenchment, or for some combination of these.

EXHIBIT 5-8   GRAND AND GROWTH STRATEGIES

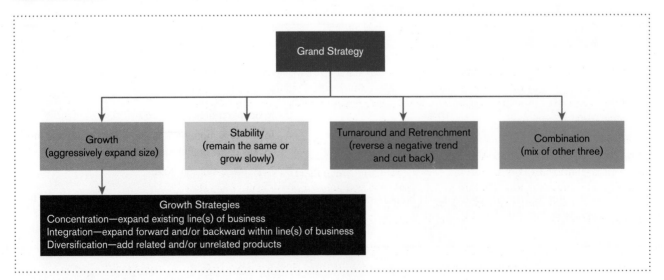

Coca-Cola,[64] **Levi Strauss**,[65] and **McDonald's**[66] in the United States. Emerging from its second bankruptcy, **Sbarro** plans to make a comeback by opening stand-alone pizzerias.[67] Led largely by a female management team, **Best Buy** completed a difficult turnaround and is now profitable.[68]

Companies currently pursuing a retrenchment strategy include retail stores hurt by online sales including **Limited** closing all 250 stores, **Walmart** planning to close 269 stores,[69] **Gap** will close a quarter of its U.S. stores,[70] and **Sears** closing stores and selling its **Craftsman** brand.[71] **Procter & Gamble (P&G)** is selling 116 of its 166 (70%) brands.[72] **Citigroup** sold or shut retail operations in more than half the 50 countries, reduced the number of U.S. branches by more than 62%, losing 69 million customers.[73]

A *spinoff* is a form of retrenchment in which a corporation sets up one or more of its business units as a separate company rather than selling it. **KFC** spun off its China stores, and **Xerox** split into two companies.

Combination. Corporations may pursue growth, stability, and turnaround and retrenchment for their different lines of business or areas of operations, which are considered business-level strategies, discussed shortly, but they tend to have one overall corporate strategy.

A diversification strategy at the corporate level entails selling a variety of products and/or services. **Samsung** sells electronics and appliances, but it also operates an amusement park in South Korea.

Growth Strategies

Most large MNCs have growth strategies, and that is a major reason they are global MNCs. A company that wants to grow has three major options. These **growth strategies** *are concentration, backward and forward integration, and related and unrelated diversification.*

Concentration. With a *concentration strategy,* the organization grows aggressively in its existing line(s) of business. **Starbucks (IOM 4)** has a concentration growth strategy to continue to open new stores globally, as do most franchisors. **Subway** has the most stores in America (around 27,000), followed by **McDonald's** (around 13,000), and **Dunkin' Donuts** (around 8,500), but the global leader by far is **7-Eleven** (around 60,000), followed by Subway (around 45,000), and McDonald's (around 36,500).[74]

Integration. With an *integration strategy,* the organization enters a new line or lines of business related to its existing one(s) on a continuum as follows:

Raw Materials, Farms	Manufacturing	Retail, Wholesale	Customer
←Backward Integration	←	→	Forward Integration→

Forward integration occurs when the organization enters a line of business closer to the final customer. **Apple** (manufacturing) has engaged in forward integration by opening **Apple Stores** (retail), thus bypassing traditional retailers, with **Google** and **Microsoft** following its lead.

Backward integration occurs when the organization enters a line of business farther away from the final customer. **Delta Airlines** (retail service) bought a refinery (manufacturing) to lower its jet-fuel costs. **Coca-Cola** (primarily makes the concentrate) bought several of its bottling and distribution manufacturers, moving toward customers with a growth strategy, but is now selling them, moving backwards with a retrenchment strategy.[75] **Starbucks (IOM 4)** has important alliances with its coffee suppliers globally.

Diversification. With a *diversification strategy,* the organization goes into a related or unrelated line of products.[76] **Nike** used *related (concentric) diversification* when it diversified from

growth strategies Strategies a company can adopt in order to grow: concentration, backward and forward integration, and related and unrelated diversification.

sports shoes to sports clothing and then to sports equipment. **General Mills** (cereal) has stayed with the food industry with **Green Giant** and **Haagen-Dazs**.[77] **Starbucks** (**IOM 4**) selling its products in grocery stores was a related diversification strategy.

Virgin has pursued an unrelated (conglomerate) diversification since its existence, owning 42 ventures including **Virgin Atlantic** (air travel), **Virgin Casino**, **Virgin Hotels**, and **Virgin Mobile**.[78] **Google** (search engine) diversified to music subscriptions, **Nexus** tablets, **Google Glass**, and many others.[79] **Jarden** owns **Rawlings** sports**, Mr. Coffee**, **Crock-Pot**, **Marmot** sleeping bags, **Yankee Candle**, and most recently **Jostens** high school memorabilia.[80] Did you know that **Mars** candy is also in the pet-care industry? Its brands include **Pedigree**, **Iams**, **Royal Canin**, and more recently **VCA**.[81]

Merger and Acquisition Growth Strategy. Companies can also pursue a common MNC growth strategy by means of mergers and acquisitions, commonly referred to as M&As,[82] and 2015 was a record year.[83] Companies engage in M&As to decrease competition, to compete more effectively with larger companies, to realize economies of size, to consolidate expenses, and to achieve access to markets, products, technology, resources, and management talent.[84]

A **merger** *occurs when two companies form one corporation.* The new company name is often a combination of the merged businesses. **Anheuser-Busch** and **InBev** merged to create **Anheuser-Busch InBev**, creating the leading global beer brewer.

An **acquisition** *occurs when one business buys all or part of another business.* One business becomes a part of an existing business. **Google** bought **Motorola** to get into mobile devices and hardware, including the **Droid** line of smartphones, to promote its **Android** software to compete against **Apple**. **Facebook** acquired **FriendFeed** and **Instagram**. **Microsoft** acquired **LinkedIn** for $26.2 billion.[85] **Marriott** bought **Starwood Hotels**, giving it 30 lodging brands with more than 1 million rooms.[86] **Starbucks** (**IOM 4**) acquired companies over the years; more recent ones include **La Boulange** and **Evolution Fresh**.

The terms *merger* and *acquisition* are commonly used interchangeably. However, with a true merger, owners of stock in each company get new shares in the new combined company under its new name, and with a true acquisition, stock owners in the acquired company get shares in its purchaser stock. When **Google** acquired **YouTube**, its stock owners got Google shares. Despite their popularity,[87] M&As often don't lead to greater coordination,[88] and M&As have a dismal track record, as half the deals eventually divest.[89] Five years after the merger that created **United Continental Holdings** airlines, a new **CEO, Oscar Munoz**, was brought in because the merger has been poorly managed and he needs to solve the integration problems.[90]

merger Occurs when two companies form one corporation.

acquisition Occurs when one business buys all or part of another business.

APPLYING THE CONCEPT

Growth Strategies

Identify the type of growth strategy described by each statement.

A. concentration

B. related diversification

C. forward integration

D. unrelated diversification

E. backward integration

____ 6. PepsiCo's Sprite soda buys lemon and lime groves.

____ 7. Dell Computer starts making printers.

____ 8. Home Depot acquires a tool manufacturer to make its own brand-name tools.

____ 9. Facebook buys Toys "R" Us.

____ 10. Apple opens a new Apple store in a mall.

____ 11. Tesla starts opening its own dealerships to sell its cars.

____ 12. New Age Diamond Mines starts to cut its stones into diamond shapes for jewelry.

____ 13. Pizza Hut opens one of its fast-food restaurants in China.

____ 14. Netflix acquires a small upscale restaurant in New York.

____ 15. Boeing buys the Johnson Custom Jets company.

| 5-2 | **JOIN THE DISCUSSION** ETHICS & SOCIAL RESPONSIBILITY |

Insider Trading

Insiders are people who have confidential information about upcoming events that will affect the price of a stock. It is common for the price of a stock to go up when investors learn that the company is negotiating a merger or acquisition of another company. Insiders are not supposed to buy or sell any stock they have confidential information about or to tell anyone this information to avoid illegal profit from stock dealing. This process, known as "tipping," is illegal. However, many government public officials have access to insider information and legally get rich from tipping.

1. If you were "tipped" by an insider, would you buy/sell the stock?

2. What are the implications of using insider information? Is anyone hurt by the practice? If yes, who is hurt, and how are they hurt?

3. Without using insider information, some speculators try to predict which companies are likely to merge or be acquired and buy stock options. This is a legal way of making money, but is it ethical?

4. Is it ethical for government officials to use insider information to make money?

Portfolio Analysis

Business portfolio analysis *is the corporate process of determining which lines of business the corporation will be in and how it will allocate resources among them.* A business line, also called a strategic business unit (SBU), is a distinct business having its own customers that is managed independently of other businesses within the corporation. What constitutes an SBU varies from company to company, but it can be a division, a subsidiary, or a single product line. **PepsiCo** started with just **Pepsi** and went on to acquire a business portfolio including **Frito-Lay**, **Tropicana**, **Gatorade**, and **Quaker Oats** SBUs—or PepsiCo has multiple companies within a company with a growth grand strategy.

The primary objective of *corporate portfolio management (CPM)* is to make strategic decisions about the allocation of resources among SBUs. A popular approach to CPM is to create a **Boston Consulting Group (BCG)** Growth-Share Matrix for each line of business or product line as a business strategy. A BCG matrix contains four cells: *Cash cows* generate more resources than they need, so the profits are used to fund question marks and stars. *Question marks* are entries into new businesses. *Stars* are question marks that succeed. *Dogs* are doing poorly and are usually sold or liquidated. Exhibit 5-9 shows a BCG matrix for **Starbucks**. With the focus on the **iPhone**, **Apple MacBook Pro** computer division employees and its customers feel neglected (cash cows) without any support and good updates,[91] and the **Kia** division has similar views, as **Hyundai** makes Kia stagger its new-models to avoid head-on competition.[92]

A company in a single line of business cannot conduct a business portfolio analysis. However, it should perform a *product portfolio analysis.* **McDonald's** started by offering a simple hamburger and fries. Over the years, the company introduced new products, such as the Big Mac and salads, that started as a question mark, became a star, and then joined the hamburger and fries as a cash cow. McDonald's introduced pizza and the Angus Burger as question marks, but rather than becoming stars, they became dogs and were dropped from most restaurants.

Business-Level Strategies

Each line of business must develop its own mission, analyze its own environment, set its own objectives, and develop its own strategies. For the organization with a single line of products, corporate and business strategies are the same, so we are still in the fourth step of the strategic planning process. In this section, we discuss adaptive and competitive strategies.

WORK
APPLICATION 5-8

Identify any growth strategies used by an organization you work for or have worked for. Be sure to identify the type of growth strategy and note if any mergers, acquisitions, joint ventures, or strategic alliances were used.

business portfolio analysis The corporate process of determining which lines of business the corporation will be in and how it will allocate resources among them.

LO 5-5

Summarize the three business-level adaptive and competitive strategies.

EXHIBIT 5-9   BCG GROWTH SHARE MATRIX FOR STARBUCKS

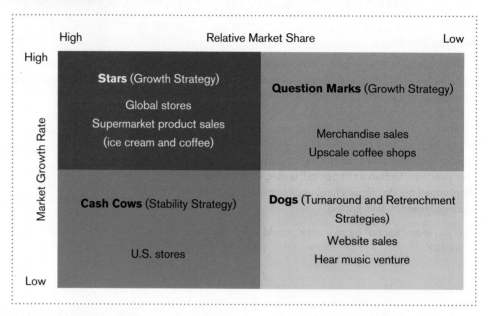

Adaptive Strategies

Adaptive strategies emphasize adapting to changes in the external environment and entering new markets as means of increasing sales.[93] The **adaptive strategies** *are prospecting, defending, and analyzing.* Each adaptive strategy reflects a different objective.[94] Exhibit 5-10 indicates the different rates of environmental change, potential growth rates, and corresponding grand strategy for each adaptive strategy.

Prospecting Strategy. The *prospecting strategy* calls for aggressively offering new products and services and/or entering new markets in pursuit of opportunities.[95] The prospecting strategy resembles the grand strategy of growth, and prospecting firms tend to be the most successful.[96] It is often used by smaller companies that want to grow fast, like **Groupon**, which was one of the fastest-growing startup prospectors of all times.[97] **Starbucks (IOM 5)** continues to open new upscale coffee shops as a prospector.

Defending Strategy. The *defending strategy* calls for staying with the present product line and markets and maintaining or increasing customers slowly in new markets. It is often used by large established companies that want to protect their dominance,[98] like **Coca-Cola** keeping its number-one position against archrival **Pepsi**. The defending strategy resembles the grand strategy of stability.

Analyzing Strategy. The *analyzing strategy* calls for a midrange approach between prospecting and defending. Analyzing resembles the combination grand strategy. Analyzing involves moving into new market areas at a cautious, deliberate pace and/or offering a core product

adaptive strategies Overall strategies for a line of business, including prospecting, defending, and analyzing.

EXHIBIT 5-10   ADAPTIVE STRATEGIES

Adaptive Strategy	Rate of Environmental Change	Potential Growth Rate	Corresponding Grand Strategy
Prospecting	Fast	High	Growth
Analyzing	Moderate	Moderate	Combination
Defending	Slow	Low	Stability

group and seeking new opportunities. Analyzers also commonly imitate their rivals' prospecting actions through the use of benchmarking.[99] **Domino's** was the prospector offering pizza delivery first. **Pizza Hut** was the analyzer waiting to see if delivery would be successful, and when it was, Pizza Hut copied Domino's. **Miller** was the first to offer a successful lite beer, so **AB** came out with Bud Light, and it eventually became the best-selling light beer.

Competitive Strategies

Michael Porter identified three effective business *competitive strategies:* differentiation, cost leadership, and focus.[100]

WORK
APPLICATION 5-9

Identify the adaptive strategy used by an organization you work for or have worked for. Be sure to describe how it used the strategy.

Differentiation Strategy. With a *differentiation* strategy, a company stresses its competitive advantage over its competitors,[101] focusing on being sufficiently distinctive.[102] Differentiation strategy somewhat resembles the prospecting strategy and tends to lead to being able to charge higher prices than competitors,[103] such as **Apple** over **Samsung** smartphones. **Starbucks**'s (**IOM 5**) competitive strategy is differentiation, as it focuses on coffee houses with upscale buyers willing to pay higher prices than at **Dunkin' Donuts** and **McDonald's**. **Nike**, **Ralph Lauren**, **Calvin Klein**, and others place their names and logos on the outside of their products to differentiate them. **Coca-Cola** uses differentiation with its scripted name logo and contour bottle.

The distinct look of a **Coca-Cola** label is part of the company's differentiation strategy.

Cost Leadership Strategy. With a *cost leadership* strategy, the company stresses lower prices to attract customers. To keep its prices down, it must have tight cost control and efficient low-cost systems processes. Growth demands high volume, and high volume demands low prices. **Walmart** and **Target** have had success with this strategy, **Southwest** has hung up its low-cost jersey, as its costs are close to those of **Delta**, **United**, and **American Airlines** competitors as it has grown to be the largest carrier of domestic fliers in the United States.[104] **Allegiant**, **Spirit**, and **JetBlue** have become today's low-cost carriers.[105]

Focus Strategy. With a *focus strategy*, the company targets a specific regional market, product line, or buyer group. Within a particular target segment, or market niche, the firm may use a differentiation or cost leadership strategy. With a focus strategy, smaller companies can often compete with MNCs by not competing head on based on price. **Asics** successfully competes with much larger **Nike** and **Adidas** by focusing primarily on the running shoe market.[106] *Ebony* and *Jet* magazines target African Americans, and **Rolex** watches have a market niche of upper-income people. **Right Guard** deodorant is aimed at men and **Secret** at women.

Porter doesn't recommend trying to combine differentiation and cost leadership because it is rarely successful, as the company gets stuck in the middle. Remember that the various grand and adaptive strategies complement one another. Managers select the appropriate strategy based on the mission, situation analysis, and objectives.

Operational-Level Planning

So far in this chapter, we have discussed long-range, external, competitive strategic planning; we are at the last part of the fourth step of the planning process. After selecting the strategy, you need to develop plans to achieve the desired outcomes. Recall that poor planning leads to not achieving objectives.[107] But don't make the plans too complex, for keeping plans simple gets better results.[108] In this section, we discuss short-range operational planning, including functional strategies, standing and single-use plans, contingency plans, time management, and multitasking.

Functional Strategies

The functional departments of a company must develop internal strategic plans for achieving the mission and objectives. **Functional strategies** *are strategies developed and implemented*

LO 5-6

Identify the operational functional strategies, contrast standing plans and single-use plans, describe the value of a time log analysis, and explain how to effectively multitask.

functional strategies Strategies developed and implemented by managers in marketing, operations, human resources, finance, and other departments.

Noam Galai/WireImage

Adaptive Strategies

Identify the type of strategy represented in each statement.

A. prospecting

B. defending

C. analyzing

____ 16. Dell pioneers a laptop-powered computer that can be folded up to the size of a smartphone.

____ 17. Domino's used this strategy after Pizza Hut started to copy delivering pizza.

____ 18. This is the primary strategy of Walmart in the saturated U.S. market as the number of dollar stores increased.

____ 19. When McDonald's came out with a new Angus Burger to compete with Burger King's successful Angus Burgers, it was using this strategy.

____ 20. 7-Eleven expands globally by opening stores in Vietnam.

---

by managers in marketing, operations, human resources, finance, and other departments of a company.

Marketing Strategy. The marketing department has the primary responsibility for knowing what the customer wants, or how to add customer value, and for defining the target market. Marketing focuses on the four *P*s: product, promotion, place, and price. The marketing department makes decisions about which products to provide, how they will be packaged and advertised, where they will be sold and how they will get there, and how much they will be sold for.

Operations Strategy. The operations (or production) department is responsible for systems processes that convert inputs into outputs of products or services for its customers. Operations focuses on quality and efficiency in producing the products that marketing determines will provide customer value. (You will learn more about operations in Chapter 15.)

Finance Strategy. The finance department has at least two functions: (1) financing the business activities by raising money through the sale of stock (equity) or bonds or through loans (debt) and paying off the debt and dividends (if any) to shareholders, and (2) keeping records of transactions, developing budgets, and reporting financial results (income and cash flow statements and balance sheet). (You will learn more about finance in Chapter 14.)

Human Resources Strategy. The human resources (HR) department is responsible for working with all the other functional departments in the areas of recruiting, selecting, training, evaluating, and compensating employees. (You will learn more about HR in Chapter 9.)

Other Functional Strategies. Based on the type of business, any number of other departments will also need to develop a strategy, such as information technology (IT) and research and development (R&D).

WORK APPLICATION 5-10

Identify one functional area of an organization you work for or have worked for. What was its operational strategy?

Standing Plans Versus Single-Use and Contingency Plans

Depending on how repetitive they are, plans may be either *standing plans*, which are made to be used over and over again to ensure repeated behavior for handling routine issues,[109] or *single-use plans*, which are made to be used only once (nonrepetitive). Most strategic plans are single use, whereas operational plans are more often standing plans. Exhibit 5-11 illustrates the different types of standing and single-use plans.

EXHIBIT 5-11   STANDING PLANS VERSUS SINGLE-USE PLANS

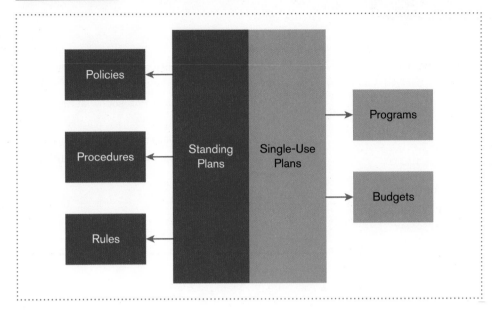

Standing Plans. Operational objectives may be accomplished by following standing plans, which save planning and decision-making time. **Standing plans** *are policies, procedures, and rules developed for handling repetitive situations.* Their purpose is to guide employees' actions in day-to-day decision making.[110]

Policies *provide general guidelines to be followed when making decisions.* Companies should develop formal policies,[111] as they serve as guides for employee behavior in their relationships with stakeholders.[112] Here are a few examples of policy statements: "The customer is always right." "We produce high-quality goods and services." "We promote employees from within." Notice that policy statements are intentionally general guides; you use your discretion in implementing them. As a manager, your daily decisions will be guided by policies.

A **procedure** *is a sequence of actions to be followed in order to achieve an objective.* Procedures may also be called *standard operating procedures (SOPs)* or *methods.* Procedures can be formal or informal and are more specific than policies,[113] as they establish routine ways of doing things consistently.[114] Procedures ensure that all recurring, routine situations are handled in a consistent, predetermined manner,[115] such as making products, purchasing, taking inventory, settling grievances, and so forth.

Rules *state exactly what should or should not be done.* Policy routines can lead to establishing rules for greater consistency of behavior,[116] as employees have no discretion on how to implement rules and regulations designed to govern their behaviors.[117] These are examples of rules: "No smoking or eating in the work area." "Everyone must wear a hard hat on the construction site." Violating rules usually subjects a person to penalties that vary in severity according to the seriousness of the violation and the number of offenses,[118] and everyone should be treated fairly.[119]

Single-Use Plans. Single-use plans *are programs and budgets developed for handling nonrepetitive situations.* Single-use plans, unlike standing plans, are developed for a specific purpose and probably will not be used again in the same form. However, a single-use plan may be used as a model for a future version of the program or budget. A corporate- or business-level strategy is usually a single-use plan, such as a turnaround strategy, that can result in new standing plans.

A *program* describes a set of activities and is designed to accomplish an objective over a specified time period. A program may have its own policies, procedures, budget, and so forth. It might take several years or less than a day to complete a given program. Examples include the development of a new product or expansion of facilities.

WORK APPLICATION 5-11

Give an example of a policy, a procedure, and a rule from an organization you work for or have worked for.

standing plans Policies, procedures, and rules developed for handling repetitive situations.

policies General guidelines to be followed when making decisions.

procedure A sequence of actions to be followed in order to achieve an objective.

rules Statements of exactly what should or should not be done.

single-use plans Programs and budgets developed for handling nonrepetitive situations.

5-4 APPLYING THE CONCEPT

Identifying Plans

Identify the type of plan exemplified by each statement.

A. policy

B. procedure

C. rule

D. program

E. budget

____ 21. A helmet must be worn on the football field.

____ 22. Forms for a leave of absence must be filled out, approved, and signed by the supervisor and submitted to the HR office one month in advance of the planned leave.

____ 23. We follow the "Humanics Philosophy" at Springfield College.

____ 24. We will make a driverless car within five years.

____ 25. Here is an Excel sheet describing how much I need to run my division next year.

A *budget* is the funds allocated to operate a unit for a fixed period. When that time has passed, a new budget is needed. Developing a budget requires planning skills rather than accounting and mathematical skills. When developed, a budget is a planning tool, and when implemented, it is a control tool. We discuss budgeting in Chapter 14.

Contingency Plans. No matter how effectively you plan, there will be times when unexpected events (crisis) prevent you from achieving your objectives.[120] Things that go wrong are often beyond your control in an uncertain changing environment.[121] When the uncontrollable occurs, you should be prepared with a backup, or contingency, plan. **Contingency plans** *are alternative plans to be implemented if uncontrollable events occur.* If a key employee calls in sick, another employee fills in to do the job. Construction work is usually contingent on the weather. If it's nice, employees work outside; if it is not, they work indoors.

To develop a contingency plan, answer three questions: What might go wrong? How can I prevent it from happening? If it does occur, what can I do to minimize its effect? The answer to question 3 is your contingency plan. With good contingency plans, you can prevent problems and solve them quickly and effectively. **BP** was criticized for not having an effective contingency plan in place after one of its oil rigs in the Gulf of Mexico exploded, ultimately resulting in the worst oil spill in history. BP could have saved billions of dollars in fixing a disaster that could have been avoided in the first place with an effective contingency plan.

When developing contingency plans, ask everyone involved what can go wrong and what should be done if it does go wrong. Also ask others within and outside the organization who have implemented similar plans. They may have encountered problems you haven't thought of, and they may have good contingency plans to suggest.

Starbucks's (**IOM 6**) functional strategies for marketing, operations, finance, and human resources are critical to its success in implementing its growth grand strategy. Opening each new Starbucks store requires a single-use plan; each store is somewhat different. However, standing plans for the store-opening process are also in place. Starbucks also has extensive policies, procedures, and rules to operate each store in a consistent manner. Finally, opening stores and operating them require contingency plans.

Time Management

Our time is valuable.[122] Do you ever feel like there is never enough time?[123] Or that you have so much to do but so little time?[124] Time is measured objectively, but how we spend our time is subjective, as we tend to waste time.[125] *Time management* refers to techniques that enable

---

WORK APPLICATION 5-12

Give an example of a program you were involved in at work.

WORK APPLICATION 5-13

Describe a situation in which a contingency plan is appropriate. Explain the plan.

WORK APPLICATION 5-14

Review your time log to identify your three biggest time wasters. How can you cut down or eliminate these time wasters?

contingency plans Alternative plans to be implemented if uncontrollable events occur.

us to get more done in less time with better results. Time management skills will have a direct effect on your productivity and career success.[126] The focus here is on improving your time management skills, as we can gain an hour a day.[127]

Analyzing Time Use With a Time Log. The first step to successful time management requires using a time log, because most of us don't know how we waste our time.[128] A *time log* is a daily diary that tracks your activities and enables you to determine how you spend (and waste) your time each day. Exhibit 5-12 gives an example you can use as a template to develop your own time logs. You should keep track of your time every day over a period of one or two typical weeks. Try to keep the time log with you throughout the day. Fill in the Description column for each 15-minute time slot, if possible, describing what you did. If you are technically inclined, there are software programs for PCs and apps for smartphones that will track your time and use of these devices.[129]

After completing your time logs, analyze the information and find time consumers you can eliminate. Write notes in the Evaluation of Time Use column of the log, using the following abbreviations:

- Determine how much time you are spending on your high-priority (HP) and low-priority (LP) responsibilities. How do you spend most of your time?
- Identify areas where you spend too much time (TT) and where you do not spend enough time (NT).
- Identify major interruptions (I) and distractions (D) like text, email, social media, and crisis situations (C) that keep you from doing what you want to get done. Our biggest time waster is unnecessary interruptions, which cost the U.S. economy more than $997 billion a year.[130] How can you eliminate them? How about turning off all the electronic devices you don't need (and the noises they make) until you complete important tasks?[131] Do you have effective contingency plans?

A Time Management System. Do you sometimes find yourself looking at your schedule and wondering when you'll find the time to do everything you need to do? If so, a time management system may help. The time management system has a proven record of success and is used by thousands. Try it.

There are four key components of the time management system: (1) *Priorities.* There usually isn't enough time to do everything, but there is time to do the most important things. Employees confessed to wasting about 40% of their time at work doing unimportant or downright irrelevant things.[132] Don't confuse being busy doing lots of activities with making progress on the important priorities.[133] Focus on your most important priorities (which are often fewer than you think),[134] doing them well, and eliminating essentially everything else.[135] So assign a priority to each task, and do the most important thing first (without unnecessary interruptions)[136]—make it a rule. Try to get at least 90 minutes of uninterrupted time a day.[137] (2) *Objectives.* Set weekly objectives using the objectives model. (3) *Plans.* Develop operational plans to meet your objectives. (4) *Schedules.* Schedule each week and workday, and follow it.[138] Time management systems all boil down to developing a plan and sticking to it as much as possible. The *time management system* involves the following three steps. Refer to Exhibit 5-12 for the template for each step.

Step 1. Plan each week. Fill in a plan for the upcoming week using the "Weekly Planner" form. One caution: Planning too much is frustrating and causes stress when you cannot get everything done, so be realistic and focus on what you get done, not what is left to do that is less important anyway.[139]

Step 2. Schedule each week. Scheduling helps you avoid distractions and focus on your priorities.[140] Start scheduling by filling in already-committed time slots, such as regular weekly meetings. Then schedule controllable events. Most managers should leave about 50% of the week unscheduled to accommodate unexpected events. Your job or schoolwork may require more or less unscheduled time.

Step 3. Schedule each day. Your schedule is in essence a to-do list. Leave your daily schedule flexible. Remember that if you are working on a high-priority item and you find yourself facing a lower-priority task, let it wait unless it is a true emergency. This will help you control interruptions and distractions.

To-Do Lists. The time management system described here works well for managers who have to plan for a variety of nonrecurring tasks. For managers and employees who deal primarily with routine tasks, a to-do list that prioritizes items may work quite well. We will discuss using a to-do list in Chapter 7. For now, realize that procrastination generally leads to more stress and can cause poor-quality work done late or at the last minute, as well as problems in relationships, jobs, finances, and health.[141] So put the task on your to-do list and, as **Nike** says, "Just Do It!"

EXHIBIT 5-12	TIME MANAGEMENT TOOLS

DAILY TIME LOG

Daily Time Log for Day _____ Date _____		
Starting Time	Description	Evaluation of Time Use
8:00		
8:15		
8:30		
8:45		
9:00		
9:15		
9:30		
9:45		
10:00		
(etc., to ending time)		

WEEKLY PLANNER

Plan for the week of _____

Objectives:

Activities	Priority	Time Needed	Day to Schedule
Total time for the week			

WEEKLY SCHEDULE

Schedule for the week of _____					
Time	Mon.	Tues.	Wed.	Th.	Fri.
8:00					
8:15					
8:30					
8:45					
9:00					
(etc., to ending time)					

DAILY SCHEDULE

Schedule for the day of _____

Time
8:00
8:15
8:30
8:45
9:00
(etc., to ending time)

Forms similar to those in Exhibit 5-12 can be purchased in any number of formats, including in electronic form such as your email, websites, and apps. Some are free, and some charge.

Time Management Techniques. Self-Assessment 5-2 contains 49 time management techniques arranged by management function. Planning and controlling are placed together because they are so closely related. Select and, more importantly, implement the items that will help you get more done in less time.

Multitasking

Multitasking is the practice or capability of handling more than one task at a time. In our e-world, people are multitasking more today than ever. Complete Self-Assessment 5-3 to get an idea of your use of multitasking and how it affects you.

WORK APPLICATION 5-15

How would you assess your use of multitasking in your personal life? In your professional life? How can you improve?

Multitasking, the Brain, and Decreased Productivity. "Simply put, multitasking is a fantasy."[142] Why? Although you may not want to believe it, research has shown that the human brain is not actually capable of doing two thinking (cognitive) tasks at the same time.[143] Think of it as a single-screen TV. You can't watch two shows at once, but you can flip back and forth, missing some of each show; the more shows you watch, the more you miss of each one. Time is lost when switching between tasks, and the time loss increases with the complexity of the task. When people multitask things that require thinking, either at the same time or alternating rapidly between them, errors go way up, and it takes far longer to get the jobs done than if they were done sequentially.[144]

Research has shown that most people, even those who think they are good at it, are not good at multitasking. You may think you are accomplishing two tasks at once, but you're not. When you're talking on the phone and writing an e-mail simultaneously, you are switching back and forth—and each time you switch, it takes time for the brain to figure out where it left off on that task, slowing performance by 50% or more.[145] Long before multitasking was popular, the late great **Peter Drucker** said that if you watch highly productive people, they do one thing at a time.

Attention Spans and Concentration. These are important skills for getting high-priority tasks completed, yet employers today say that young job applicants have short attention spans and can't concentrate for very long. Why? One of the problems with high levels of multitasking is that it undermines our attention spans by decreasing our ability to concentrate for any length of time. With things binging and bonging and tweeting at you, you don't think. Daily workplace interruptions and distractions, such as texts, phone calls, apps, or the arrival of email or social media alerts undermine our minds' chief productivity tool—our ability to pay attention.[146] A major reason we get distracted and lose our ability to pay attention is the separation of the use of our eyes and mind—they need to work together to concentrate at all.[147]

Smartphones. Smartphones are supposed to save time, but they actually prove to do the opposite. Why? Because they lead to wasting time multitasking. The average person looks at their smartphone 221 times per day, or over three hours—that's about every four minutes.[148] How long can you go without looking at your smartphone? Try it. If you really want to get those important priorities completed faster and better, avoid multitasking.[149] Shut off your phone and other distractions and do one important thing at a time.[150]

Effective Multitasking. Yes, I know you're not giving up multitasking. So how can you multitask effectively? The first step is to recognize that the entire process is, essentially, a form of time management[151] and that many of the time management techniques listed in Self-Assessment 5-2 can be applied to multitasking—especially stopping interruptions and distractions. Here are some suggestions.

- ***Know when it is appropriate.*** Realize that certain thinking tasks, like reading, require your undivided attention. When your full attention should be on a single complex or important task, multitasking is not appropriate and will likely affect the quality

WORK
APPLICATION 5-16

From the time management techniques listed in Self-Assessment 5-2, choose the three most important ones you should be using. Explain how you will implement each technique.

of your work. Save multitasking for noncomplex tasks that do not require thinking with undivided attention.

- ***Limit distractions and interruptions.*** Around 45% of the time, we are self-interrupting.[152] You can save time by turning off all the electronics you don't need to perform the task you are working on.[153] Stay on track for a set amount of time, such as a half or full hour. Only after the set time can you check for texts, emails, and so forth. Music and especially TV are distracting and can overtax the brain. If you need background sounds to overcome distracting noise, try music that you don't really like or dislike, so you can ignore it, like classical music or ocean sounds, or you can wear noise-canceling headphones.

5-2 SELF-ASSESSMENT

Time Management Techniques

Following is a list of 49 ideas that can be used to improve your time management skills. Place a check mark in the appropriate box for each item.

Planning and Controlling Management Functions	1 = should do	2 = could do	3 = already doing	4 = doesn't apply to me
1. Use a time management system.	☐	☐	☐	☐
2. Use a to-do list and prioritize the items on it. Do the important things rather than the seemingly urgent things.	☐	☐	☐	☐
3. Get an early start on top-priority items.	☐	☐	☐	☐
4. Do only high-priority items during your best working hours (prime time); schedule unpleasant or difficult tasks during prime time.	☐	☐	☐	☐
5. Don't spend time performing unproductive activities to avoid or escape job-related anxiety. It doesn't really work; get the job done.	☐	☐	☐	☐
6. Throughout the day, ask yourself, "Should I be doing this now?"	☐	☐	☐	☐
7. Plan before you act.	☐	☐	☐	☐
8. Plan for recurring crises to eliminate crises (contingency planning).	☐	☐	☐	☐
9. Make decisions. It is better to make a wrong decision than to make none at all.	☐	☐	☐	☐
10. Schedule enough time to do the job right the first time. Don't be too optimistic about the amount of time it takes to do a job.	☐	☐	☐	☐
11. Schedule a quiet hour to be interrupted only by true emergencies. Have someone take messages or ask people who call then to call you back.	☐	☐	☐	☐
12. Establish a quiet time for the entire organization or department. The first hour of the day is usually the best time.	☐	☐	☐	☐
13. Schedule large blocks of uninterrupted (emergencies-only) time for projects and so forth. If this doesn't work, hide somewhere.	☐	☐	☐	☐
14. Break large (long) projects into parts (periods).	☐	☐	☐	☐
15. Before abandoning a scheduled item to do something unscheduled, ask yourself, "Is the unscheduled event more important than the scheduled event?" If not, stay on schedule.	☐	☐	☐	☐
16. Do related activities (for example, making and returning calls, writing letters and memos) in the same time slot.	☐	☐	☐	☐

Organizing Management Function	1 = should do	2 = could do	3 = already doing	4 = doesn't apply to me
17. Schedule time for unanticipated events and let people know the time. Ask people to see or call you only during this time unless it's an emergency. Answer mail and do routine things while waiting for people to contact you. If people ask to see you—"Got a minute?"—ask whether it can wait until your scheduled time.	☐	☐	☐	☐
18. Set a scheduled time, agenda, and time limit for all visitors, and keep on topic.	☐	☐	☐	☐
19. Keep a clean, well-organized work area/desk.	☐	☐	☐	☐
20. Remove all non–work-related or distracting objects from your work area/desk.	☐	☐	☐	☐
21. Do one task at a time.	☐	☐	☐	☐
22. When paperwork requires a decision, make it at once; don't read through the paperwork again later and decide.	☐	☐	☐	☐
23. Keep files well arranged and labeled with an active and inactive file section. When you file an item, put a throwaway date on it.	☐	☐	☐	☐
24. Call rather than write or visit, when appropriate.	☐	☐	☐	☐
25. Delegate someone else to write letters, memos, and so forth.	☐	☐	☐	☐
26. Use form letters and form paragraphs in word-processing software.	☐	☐	☐	☐
27. Answer letters (memos) on the letter itself.	☐	☐	☐	☐
28. Have someone read and summarize things for you.	☐	☐	☐	☐
29. Divide reading requirements with others and share summaries.	☐	☐	☐	☐
30. Have calls screened to be sure the right person handles each call.	☐	☐	☐	☐
31. Plan before calling. Have an agenda and all necessary information ready; take notes on the agenda.	☐	☐	☐	☐
32. Ask people to call you back during your scheduled unexpected time. Ask about the best time to call them.	☐	☐	☐	☐
33. Have a specific objective or purpose for every meeting you conduct. If you cannot think of an objective, don't have the meeting.	☐	☐	☐	☐
34. Invite to meetings only the necessary participants, and keep them only as long as needed.	☐	☐	☐	☐
35. Always have an agenda for a meeting, and stick to it. Start and end as scheduled.	☐	☐	☐	☐
36. Set objectives for travel. List everyone you will meet with. Call the attendees or send them agendas, and have a file folder for each with all necessary data for your meeting.	☐	☐	☐	☐
37. Combine and modify activities to save time.	☐	☐	☐	☐

(Continued)

(Continued)

Leading Management Function	1 = should do	2 = could do	3 = already doing	4 = doesn't apply to me
38. Set clear objectives for subordinates and make sure they know what they are accountable for; give them feedback and evaluate results often.	☐	☐	☐	☐
39. Don't waste others' time. Don't make subordinates wait idly for decisions, instructions, or materials, at meetings, and so on. Conversely, wait for a convenient time to speak to subordinates or others, rather than interrupting them and wasting their time.	☐	☐	☐	☐
40. Train your subordinates. Don't do their work for them.	☐	☐	☐	☐
41. Delegate activities in which you do not need to be personally involved, especially nonmanagement functions.	☐	☐	☐	☐
42. Set deadlines earlier than the actual deadline.	☐	☐	☐	☐
43. Use the input of your staff. Don't reinvent the wheel.	☐	☐	☐	☐
44. Teach time management skills to your subordinates.	☐	☐	☐	☐
45. Don't procrastinate; do it.	☐	☐	☐	☐
46. Don't be a perfectionist—define acceptable and stop there.	☐	☐	☐	☐
47. Learn to stay calm. Getting emotional only causes more problems.	☐	☐	☐	☐
48. Reduce socializing, but don't become antisocial.	☐	☐	☐	☐
49. Communicate well. Don't confuse employees.	☐	☐	☐	☐

LO 5-7

Explain the importance of implementing and controlling strategies.

Implementing and Controlling Strategies

Strategic change is difficult, but failure to change strategies to keep up with environmental changes can lead to severe consequences.[154] The fifth and final step of the strategic planning process involves implementing and controlling strategies to ensure that the mission and objectives, at all three levels, are achieved; it's about taking action.[155] Top and middle managers are more involved with the planning, whereas the lower-level functional managers and employees implement the operational strategies on a day-to-day basis. Successful implementation of strategies requires effective and efficient support systems throughout the organization.[156] Although strategic planning usually goes well, implementation is often a problem.[157] One reason is that strategic plans often end up buried in bottom drawers; no action is taken to implement the strategy. So you need to have the right people doing the right things[158]—taking action to implement specific plans.[159] Throughout Chapters 6 through 13, you will learn how to organize and lead so as to implement strategies.

As strategies are being implemented, they must also be controlled. *Controlling* is the process of monitoring progress and taking corrective action when needed to ensure that objectives are achieved (Chapter 1). You need to overcome the barriers that will try to prevent you from achieving your objectives.[160] Another important part of controlling is staying within the budget when appropriate or changing it when necessary to meet changes in the dynamic environment. You will develop your change management skills in the next chapter and controlling skills in Chapters 14 and 15.

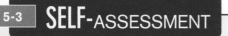

5-3 SELF-ASSESSMENT

Multitasking

Identify how frequently you experience each statement.

1	2	3	4	5
Not frequently				**Frequently**

_____1. I have a hard time paying attention; my mind wanders when I'm listening to someone or reading.

_____2. I have a hard time concentrating; I can't do just one work/homework task for an hour or longer.

_____3. I continually check my texts, phone, email, online/Facebook, and so on while doing work/homework.

_____4. I feel stress if I'm not checking screens regularly.

_____5. I'm easily bored, distracted, or interrupted while doing work/homework.

Add up your score (5 to 25) and place it here: _____. On the continuum below, mark the point that represents your total score.

1	5	10	15	20	25
Effective Planner					**Ineffective Planner**

Trends and Issues in Management

As discussed in Chapters 2 and 3, with *globalization* and its *diversity*, business becomes more complex. MNCs like **GE** doing business in more than 100 countries have to develop strategic plans in all the countries. With the wide diversity in the global village, MNCs must develop different strategies to appeal to the variety of cultures to meet local customs to satisfy customer needs. We also need to be culturally sensitive to ways we conceptualize, use, and control time in different countries.[161]

The prior global strategic focus was to go it alone and compete head on. Today, the strategic trend is to be more collaborative with alliances.[162] Forming alliances (friends) with competitors (enemies) is called being *frenemies*. **Steve Jobs** and **Bill Gates** were among the first to be called frenemies, as **Microsoft** helped **Apple** develop operating systems and software. **Google** has been coproducing its **Nexus** line of phones with **Android** partners, such as **HTC**, **Samsung**, **Motorola**, and **LG**, sold alongside those companies' own models.[163] **GM** has had an alliance with **Isuzu** for decades and will sell Japanese-made Isuzu trucks in the United States under its **Chevrolet** brand.[164] The rise of robot cars is forcing alliances between automakers, including **BMW**, and tech companies, including **Google** and **Apple**, and **GM** invested $500 million in **Lyft** for a 9% ownership of the ride-sharing company.[165]

Technology is critical to competing in the global market. *Big data* is very important to focus strategies because it divides the total market into unique niche markets to better meet unique diverse customer needs.[166] Companies using big data have greater quality and speed of executing their strategies because it helps in developing specific action plans to meet objectives.[167]

Companies that use big data may see the market more clearly, giving them an advantage over competitors.

Another trend is to include customers and suppliers in strategic planning and communicating growth plans to the external environmental stakeholders.[168] An ongoing issue of MNCs is market share and fighting to be the best seller, such as **Pepsi** wanting to overtake **Coke** globally or **Ford** going after **GM** for market leadership in the United States. What do you think is the bestselling beer in the world? If you said **Bud Light** or **Bud**, you're wrong; they are numbers three and four. The two sales leaders are Chinese **Snow** and **Tsingtao**.[169]

Recall that we focused on a low-tech time management system, and as stated, there is a lot of software and apps to help you manage your time, including the **Roll-A-Goal** app (it monitors your time as you progress on a task and gives you an estimated time at your current pace of when you should finish) and **Workflow** app (it programs routine tasks and turns them into buttons for your phone's home screen, thus transforming many potentially tedious activities into simple, one-touch operations).

Although we didn't discuss *ethics* within the chapter topics, it is not an afterthought, as it fits better here, and we discussed the need to use ethics guides whenever you make decisions in Chapter 4. So while selecting strategies and planning, implementing, and controlling them, be sure to be ethical at all stages—maintain your moral standards.[170] **Subway** settled a class-action lawsuit accusing it of coming up short on its six-inch and foot-long subs.[171] Did Subway intentionally cheat customers, or was it an accident? Do the right things, and be responsible for what you don't do right.[172]

Companies are using *social responsibility* strategically to gain a competitive advantage.[173] Part of ethics and corporate social responsibility (CSR) is being a good global corporate citizen through *sustainability* efforts.[174] **Unilever** puts environmental and social goals prominently at the center of its strategy in 190 countries and is making it pay.[175]

Having read this chapter, you should understand the importance of effective planning and recognize the five planning dimensions and the differences between strategic and operational plans. You should understand the five steps in strategic planning and be able to develop a mission, analyze the environment, set effective objectives using a model, develop corporate-level and business-level strategies and operational-level plans, and implement and control strategies. You should understand operational strategies; know the four functional areas, the difference between standing and single-use plans, and how to use a time management system; have techniques to improve your time management; and know when and when not to multitask.

$SAGE edge™   edge.sagepub.com/lussier8e

Want a better grade?

Get the tools you need to sharpen your study skills. Access practice quizzes, eFlashcards, video and multimedia, and more at edge.sagepub.com/lussier8e.

Digital Resources

Learning Objective	Digital Resource
5-1. Describe how strategic planning differs from operational planning.	Strategic vs. Operational Planning
5-2. Explain the reason for conducting an industry, competitive, and company situation analysis.	Management in Action: Analyzing the Environment*
5-3. List the parts of an effective written objective and its must and want criteria.	SMART Goals
5-4. Discuss the four corporate-level grand strategies and the three growth strategies.	Integration Strategy*

Learning Objective	Digital Resource
5-5. Summarize the three business-level adaptive and competitive strategies.	▶ Porter's Generic Strategy
5-6. Identify the operational functional strategies, contrast standing plans and single-use plans, describe the value of a time log analysis, and explain how to effectively multitask.	▣ Effective Multitasking Strategy
5-7. Explain the importance of implementing and controlling strategies.	▶ Strategy Monitoring and Controlling

* premium video available only in the interactive eBook

• • • CHAPTER SUMMARY

5-1. Describe how strategic planning differs from operational planning.

The primary differences concern the time frame and the level of management involved. Strategic planning involves developing a mission and long-range objectives and plans; operational planning involves short-range objectives and plans. Upper-level managers develop strategic plans, and middle- and lower-level managers develop operational plans. The strategic planning process includes developing a mission, analyzing the environment, setting objectives, developing strategies (corporate, business, and functional levels), and implementing and controlling strategies.

5-2. Explain the reason for conducting an industry, competitive, and company situation analysis.

The industry and competitive situation analysis is used to determine the attractiveness of an industry. It is primarily used at the corporate level to make decisions regarding which lines of business to enter and exit and how to allocate resources among lines of business.

The company situation analysis is used at the business level to determine the issues and problems that need to be addressed through the strategic planning process.

5-3. List the parts of an effective written objective and its must and want criteria.

The parts of the objective are (1) *to* + (2) action verb + (3) singular, specific, and measurable result to be achieved + (4) target date. The must criteria need to be part of the objective and include being specific, measureable, and with a target date. The want criteria are desirable but not part of the objective and include being difficult but achievable, being participatively set,

and having acceptance and commitment. When reading an objective, one can determine if the must criteria are met but not if the want criteria are met.

5-4. Discuss the four corporate-level grand strategies and the three growth strategies.

The four corporate-level strategies include growth, stability, turnaround, and retrenchment. With a *growth* strategy, the firm aggressively pursues increasing its size. With a *stability* strategy, the firm maintains the same size or grows slowly. With a *turnaround* strategy, the firm attempts a comeback; with *retrenchment*, it decreases in size. With a combination strategy, two or more of the three strategies are used for different lines of business.

The three growth strategies include concentration, integration, and diversification. With a *concentration* strategy, the firm grows aggressively in its existing line(s) of business. With *integration*, the firm grows by entering *forward* or *backward* line(s) of business. With *diversification*, the firm grows by adding *related* or *unrelated* products and/or services.

5-5. Summarize the three business-level adaptive and competitive strategies.

The three adaptive strategies are prospecting, defending, and analyzing. With the *prospecting* strategy, the firm aggressively offers new products or services and/ or enters new markets. With the *defending* strategy, the firm stays with its product line and markets and aggressively tries to stop prospectors from taking its customers. With the *analyzing* strategy, the firm moves into new markets cautiously and/or offers a core product group and seeks new opportunities; analyzers commonly copy the successful strategies of prospectors. The three competitive strategies include differentiation, low cost, and focus. The *differentiation* strategy stresses developing a clear competitive advantage. The *low-cost* strategy stresses keeping prices low. The *focus* strategy targets a specific regional market, product line, or buyer group; it develops a niche to better meet the needs of its target customers than the mass marketers.

5-6. Identify the operational functional strategies, contrast standing plans and single-use plans, describe the value of a time log analysis, and explain how to effectively multitask.

The four major *functional area strategies* include marketing, operations, finance, and human resources. *Standing plans* are policies, procedures, and rules developed for handling repetitive situations, whereas *single-use plans* are programs and budgets developed for handling one-time nonrepetitive situations. The value of a time log is that it allows one to determine how time is wasted so that it can be eliminated or decreased to improve productivity. To effectively multitask, use it only with noncomplex tasks that do not require thinking with undivided attention, and limit distractions and interruptions.

5-7. Explain the importance of implementing and controlling strategies.

Strategies are of no value to the company unless it has plans stating how the objectives will be achieved, and a plan that is not implemented is also of no value. The implementation of the strategic plan must also be controlled to measure and monitor the progress of achieving the objective. Based on control, management must also not give up too soon and lose the benefits or get caught in the escalation of commitment and throw good money after bad.

• • • KEY TERMS

acquisition, 150
adaptive strategies, 152
benchmarking, 144
business portfolio analysis, 151
competitive advantage, 144
contingency plans, 156
functional strategies, 153
grand strategy, 148

growth strategies, 149
management by objectives (MBO), 147
merger, 150
objectives, 144
operational planning, 138
policies, 155
procedure, 155
rules, 155

single-use plans, 155
situation analysis, 141
standing plans, 155
strategic planning, 138
strategy, 138
SWOT analysis, 141

• • • KEY TERM REVIEW

Complete each of the following statements using one of this chapter's key terms:

1. _____ is the process of developing a mission and long-range objectives and determining in advance how they will be accomplished.

2. _____ is the process of setting short-range objectives and determining in advance how they will be accomplished.

3. A _____ is a plan for pursuing a mission and achieving objectives.

4. A _____ focuses on those features in a company's environment that most directly affect its options and opportunities.

5. Through a _____, the organization's internal environmental strengths and weaknesses and external environmental opportunities and threats are determined.

6. _____ specifies how an organization offers unique customer value.

7. _____ is the process of comparing the organization's products or services and processes with those of other companies.

8. _____ state what is to be accomplished in specific and measurable terms with a target date.

9. _____ is the process in which managers and their employees jointly set objectives for the employees, periodically evaluate performance, and reward according to the results.

10. _____ is the overall corporate strategy of growth, stability, or turnaround and retrenchment, or for some combination of these.

11. _____ include concentration, backward and forward integration, and related and unrelated diversification.

12. A _____ occurs when two companies form one corporation.

13. An _____ occurs when one business buys all or part of another business.

14. _____ is the corporate process of determining which lines of business the corporation will be in and how it will allocate resources among them.

15. _____ include prospecting, defending, and analyzing.

16. _____ are developed and implemented by managers in marketing, operations, human resources, finance, and other departments.

17. _____ are policies, procedures, and rules developed for handling repetitive situations.

18. _____ provide general guidelines to be followed when making decisions.

19. A _____ is a sequence of actions to be followed in order to achieve an objective.

20. _____ state exactly what should or should not be done.

21. _____ are programs and budgets developed for handling nonrepetitive situations.

22. _____ are alternative plans to be implemented if uncontrollable events occur.

• • • REVIEW QUESTIONS

1. What are the five planning dimensions?

2. What are the two types of plans?

3. Is there a difference between a plan and a strategy?

4. Which planning levels and their strategies are part of strategic planning?

5. What are the steps in the strategic planning process?

6. What is the relationship between the mission statement and developing strategies?

7. Why is a company situation analysis part of the strategic planning process?

8. What is the writing objectives model?

9. What criteria should an objective meet?

10. What are the grand strategies?

11. What is the difference between a merger and an acquisition?

12. What are the adaptive strategies?

13. What is the relationship between grand strategies and adaptive strategies?

14. What are the competitive strategies?

15. What are the common functional strategy areas?

16. What is the difference between standing plans and single-use plans?

17. Explain the use of a time log.

18. List and briefly describe the three steps in the time management system.

19. Explain what multitasking is and how to practice it effectively.

• • • COMMUNICATION SKILLS

The following critical-thinking questions can be used for class discussion and/or as written assignments to develop communication skills. Be sure to give complete explanations for all questions.

1. Why are strategic and operational planning important?

2. Should all businesses have corporate, business, and functional strategies?

3. Should a mission statement be customer focused?

4. Should all businesses formally analyze the environment?

5. Should all businesses have a competitive advantage?

6. Is it ethical to copy other companies' ideas through benchmarking?

7. Are both goals and objectives necessary for a business?

8. Is it important to write objectives?

9. As a manager, would you use management by objectives (MBO)?

10. Which growth strategy would you say is the most successful?

11. Why would a business use a focus strategy rather than trying to appeal to all customers?

12. Give examples of functional departments other than those mentioned in the text.

CASES

• • • Case 5-1   FedEx Corporation

Federal Express Corporation, now known as FedEx, was started in 1971 by Frederick W. Smith, an entrepreneur who recognized the need for a company that could deliver documents overnight. The company is headquartered in Memphis, Tennessee, and it maintains a workforce of more than 290,000. The company provides transportation, e-commerce, and business services in more than 220 countries through a portfolio of businesses including FedEx Express, TNT Express, FedEx Ground, FedEx Freight, and FedEx Services. FedEx's main competitors include UPS and DHL along with various smaller, local delivery providers. The company is known for being a great place to work at, as it has frequently made *Fortune* magazine's list of the Best Companies to Work For. It accomplishes this through the use of annual employee surveys (The Survey Feedback Action Program), evaluations of leadership potential (The Leadership Evaluation and Awareness Program), and a Reward and Recognition Program (e.g., Golden Falcon and Bravo Zulu! Awards).

The mission of the company is as follows:

> FedEx Corporation will produce superior financial returns for its shareowners by providing high value-added logistics, transportation and related business services through focused operating companies. Customer requirements will be met in the highest quality manner appropriate to each market segment served. FedEx will strive to develop mutually rewarding relationships with its team members, partners and suppliers. Safety will be the first consideration in all operations. Corporate activities will be conducted to the highest ethical and professional standards.

The company's strategic objectives are to:

- Achieve 10%-plus operating margin
- Increase EPS 10% to 15% per year
- Grow profitable revenue
- Improve cash flows
- Increase ROIC
- Increase returns to shareowners

In terms of corporate strategies, FedEx focuses on growth in the following areas:

- Grow internationally
- Grow our supply chain capabilities
- Grow through e-commerce and technology
- Grow through new services and alliances

One core competency for the company is its ability to use the planning process to support continuous improvement and innovation in all aspects of its operations. Technology has been a major focus of the company's planning efforts. This has resulted in a variety of industry-leading innovations, including the first automated customer service center that includes the COSMOS (Customer Operations Service Master Online System), real-time package tracking, and the Command and Control satellite-to-ground-level operations system that enables the company to deliver packages based on the

fastest and safest routes possible. It manages the interface between more than 750 customer service stations and 500 air traffic and traffic hubs around the world. This enables the company to coordinate inbound and outbound aircraft and thousands of delivery vehicles to ensure the smooth and efficient delivery of packages to their destinations. Other examples of how FedEx's superior operational planning process has led to the creation of innovative technological solutions include the SuperTracker devices that are used by drivers to track and retain detailed information about all packages and the APEC Tariff Database that is used to expedite global delivery of packages through the creation of an integrated information source for the specific tariff and customs requirements of most countries.

Discussion Questions

1. How does FedEx engage in both strategic and operational planning?
2. Conduct a SWOT analysis of FedEx. Based on this analysis, what can you conclude about the company?
3. What is FedEx's competitive advantage?
4. What are the human resources functional strategies used at FedEx?
5. Do you think it is beneficial for organizations to engage in a strategic planning process? Why or why not?
6. Think about a student organization you have been involved with or a part-time job or internship you have held. Did this organization have a competitive advantage? If so, what was it?

References

http://money.cnn.com/quote/profile/profile.html?symb=FDX

http://investors.fedex.com/company-overview/fedex-express/strategy/default.aspx

http://fedexworldwide-ray.blogspot.com/2011/09/strategic-planning.html

http://investors.fedex.com/company-overview/mission-and-goals/default.aspx

http://www.marketing91.com/marketing-mix-of-fedex/

https://www.thehrdigest.com/implementing-best-hr-practices-makes-fedex-great-place-work/

http://investors.fedex.com/company-overview/mission-and-goals/default.aspx

https://opsmgt.edublogs.org/2014/09/30/operations-at-fedex-ground/

https://www.ukessays.com/essays/business/strategic-management-methods-used-by-fedex-business-essay.php

http://www.fedex.com/ma/about/overview/innovation.html

http://marketingdawn.com/swot-analysis-of-fedex-corporation/

http://www.casestudyinc.com/hr-best-practices-at-fedex-best-company

http://www.casestudyinc.com/hr-best-practices-at-fedex-best-company

Case created by Loren Kuzuhara, University of Wisconsin–Madison.

••• Case 5-2   The Not-So-Friendly Skies: Air Canada's Plan of Attack on U.S. Markets

Air Canada is Canada's largest airline and the largest provider of scheduled passenger services in the Canadian market, the Canada–U.S. transborder market, and the international market to and from Canada. In 2016, Air Canada together with its Air Canada Express regional partners

carried more than 45 million passengers, offering direct passenger service to more than 200 destinations on six continents. Air Canada is a founding member of Star Alliance™, providing the world's most comprehensive air transportation network.(1)

Air Canada has been pursuing a multifaceted growth strategy designed to generate revenue from new and existing sources and reduce personnel expenses. The company has been aggressively investing in technologies that enhance services to customers, including creating a Web-based reservation system and self-service check-in and adding entertainment systems to seatbacks and in-flight wireless Internet services (for a fee). It has also been bolstering its capacity to international destinations in the United States, Europe, and Asia. The airline also leverages its membership in the Star Alliance, which extends its network of destinations to 1,160 airports in 181 countries.

Air Canada serves about 178 destinations, primarily in Canada and the United States but also in the Asia/Pacific region and Europe. Together with regional affiliate Jazz, the carrier operates a fleet of about 330 aircraft from hubs in Calgary, Montreal, Toronto, and Vancouver. It extends its network as part of the Star Alliance global marketing group, which is led by United Continental and Lufthansa. (The alliance allows the airlines to sell tickets on one another's flights.) Besides its passenger business, Air Canada also hauls cargo and offers ground handling and travel arrangement services.(2)

With these powerful numbers as a backdrop, Air Canada is launching an all-out assault to the south. In May of 2017, the airline launches new service to a half dozen U.S. cities, including smaller markets such as Memphis and Savannah, Georgia. These will further expand a global route map that stretches from Algiers to Reykjavik and Taipei to Tel Aviv. The airline is also scouting Africa for future destinations.(3)

> Every time an American flies up on us they go "Oh my God, you're the best-kept secret. How did we not know about this?" That is what's music to my ears. [Ben Smith, Air Canada's president of passenger airlines.](4)

For Air Canada, this aggressive tactic comes with some hazards. Carriers like Delta Air Lines Inc. are notoriously sharp-elbowed when it comes to turf scuffles, and Emirates has the ability to throw on huge capacity as needed simply by moving the service to its superjumbo Airbus A380. In other words, Air Canada may be running a liability of being squeezed. The carrier is nowhere near the size of the American behemoths to the south, most of which do not take kindly to losing passengers to anyone. Long-haul flying typically commands higher fares and thus a more lucrative customer base, placing it among the more fiercely contested segments in air travel.(5)

> I don't know when, but there will be a reaction by the U.S. carriers at some point when the supply of seats gets too high. In the short term, the U.S. carriers are probably focusing on some other markets as a group—Los Angeles, Orlando, San Francisco—but once they stop focusing on that, you might start to see some competitive response to Air Canada. For now, it is not on their radar screen. They have bigger fish to fry, such as the Middle East carriers. [Ben Smith, Air Canada's president of passenger airlines.](6)

If Warren Buffett, considered by many an investment guru, is any weather vane of corporate performance, bet on the U.S. industry firms winning the airlines war. Back in November of 2016, he or one of his portfolio managers (Ted Weschler and Todd Combs) heavily purchased three airline stocks: American Airlines, Delta Airlines, and United Continental Holdings Inc.(7)

Yet even if Air Canada wins this battle, it could lose the war. Industry analysts have noted that profitability comes hard to an industry in which price wars are rampant and customer loyalty a myth.

> The airline industry has . . . very, very, very low incremental cost per seat with enormous fixed costs. The temptation to sell that last seat at a very low price is very high and sometimes it's very hard to distinguish between that seat and the last seat. It's labor-intensive and capital-intensive and largely [a] commodity-type business.(8)

That same Warren Buffett who invested in three U.S. airlines has traditionally detested airline stocks, famously saying in 2002, "If a capitalist had been present at Kitty Hawk back in the early 1900s, he should have shot Orville Wright."

Discussion Questions

1. Air Canada's launching new services to a half dozen U.S. cities could be categorized as what type of plan?

2. What environmental factors has Air Canada taken into account with its planned expansion into the United States? What might it have overlooked?

3. Which industry factors negatively affect the profitability of this industry?

4. Assume that Air Canada performed a SWOT analysis before it adopted the grand strategy of growth. What would have been the general results of that analysis to support growth?

5. Air Canada is expanding its operation. What actions has it taken to increase its core competencies in providing air services?

6. Air Canada has stated that it will launch new service to a half dozen U.S. cities by May 2017, including smaller markets such as Memphis and Savannah. What is missing from these goals to make them effective objectives?

7. What specific growth strategy(ies) is Air Canada utilizing?

8. Which adaptive strategy seems to best fit Air Canada's decision to expand into markets that are more international?

9. Michael Porter defined three competitive strategies—which one best fits Air Canada?

Cumulative Case Questions

10. What type of resources would be needed to support Air Canada's expansion plans (Chapter 1)?

11. What international trade agreement(s) appear(s) to allow Air Canada to easily expand into the United States (Chapter 3)?

12. Decisions are made under conditions of either certainty, risk, or uncertainty. Which condition best describes Air Canada's decision to expand into the U.S. market (Chapter 4)?

References

(1) Air Canada Corporate Communications. (2017, February). Air Canada corporate profile. Retrieved February 23, 2017, from https://www.aircanada.com/ca/en/aco/home/about/corporate-profile.html

(2) Gallo, R. (n.d.). Air Canada. Retrieved February 23, 2017, from http://0-subscriber.hoovers.com.liucat.lib.liu.edu/H/company360/fulldescription.html?companyId=157623000000000

(3) Bachman, J., & Domesco, F. (2017, February 15). Air Canada's plan of attack flies over America. Bloomberg News. Retrieved February 23, 2017, from http://montrealgazette.com/business/local-business/aerospace/air-canadas-plan-of-attack-flies-over-america

(4) Ibid.

(5) Ibid.

(6) Ibid.

(7) LaFon, H. (2016, November 14). Warren Buffett reports buying 3 airline stocks, cuts Walmart. Gurufocus.com. Retrieved February 23, 2017, from http://finance.yahoo.com/news/warren-buffett-reports-buying-airline-220611830.html

(8) Ibid.

Case created by Herbert Sherman, Long Island University.

• • • SKILL BUILDER 5-1: WRITING OBJECTIVES

For this exercise, you will first work at improving ineffective objectives. Then you will write nine objectives for yourself.

Objective

To develop your skill at writing objectives.

Skills

The primary skills developed through this exercise are:

1. *Management skill*—decision making (setting objectives is the first step to planning)
2. *AACSB competencies*—communication abilities, analytic skills, and application of knowledge.
3. *Management function*—planning (both strategic and operational)

Part 1

Indicate which of the "must" criteria each of the following objectives fails to meet and rewrite the objective so that it meets all those criteria. When writing objectives, use the following model:

> *To* + action verb + specific and measurable result + target date

1. To improve our company image by the end of 2020

   Criteria not met:

   Improved objective:

2. To increase the number of customers by 10%

   Criteria not met:

   Improved objective:

3. To increase profits during 2020

   Criteria not met:

   Improved objective:

4. To sell 5% more hot dogs and soda at the baseball game on Sunday, June 14, 2021

   Criteria not met:

   Improved objective:

Part 2

Write three educational, three personal, and three career objectives you want to accomplish using Model 5-1, Objective Writing. Your objectives can be short term (something you want to accomplish today) or long term (something you want to have accomplished 20 years from now) or in between those extremes. Be sure your objectives meet the criteria for effective objectives.

Apply It

What did I learn from this experience? How will I use this knowledge in the future?

• • • SKILL BUILDER 5-2: THE STRATEGIC PLANNING PROCESS AT YOUR COLLEGE

This exercise enables you to apply the strategic planning process to your college or university as an individual and/or group.

Objective

To develop your planning skills.

Skills

The primary skills developed through this exercise are:

1. *Management skill*—decision making (conceptual, diagnostic, analytical, and critical thinking)

2. *AACSB competencies*—communication abilities, analytic skills, reflective thinking skills, and application of knowledge

3. *Management function*—planning (strategic)

Step 1. Developing the Mission

1. What is the mission statement of your university/college or school/department?

2. Is the mission statement easy to remember?

3. How would you improve the mission statement?

Step 2. Analyzing the Environment

1. Conduct a five-force competitive analysis, like that in Exhibit 5-4.

2. Complete a SWOT analysis, like that in Exhibit 5-6.

3. Determine the competitive advantage of your university/college or school/department.

Step 3. Setting Objectives

What are some goals and objectives of your university/college or school/department?

Step 4. Developing Strategies

1. Identify your university/college's or school/department's grand, adaptive, and competitive strategies.

_____

_____

2. Where would you place your program/major on the BCG growth-share matrix?

_____

_____

_____

_____

Step 5. Implementing and Controlling Strategies

How would you rate your university/college's or school/department's strategic planning? How could it be improved?

Apply It

What did I learn from this experience? How will I use this knowledge in the future?

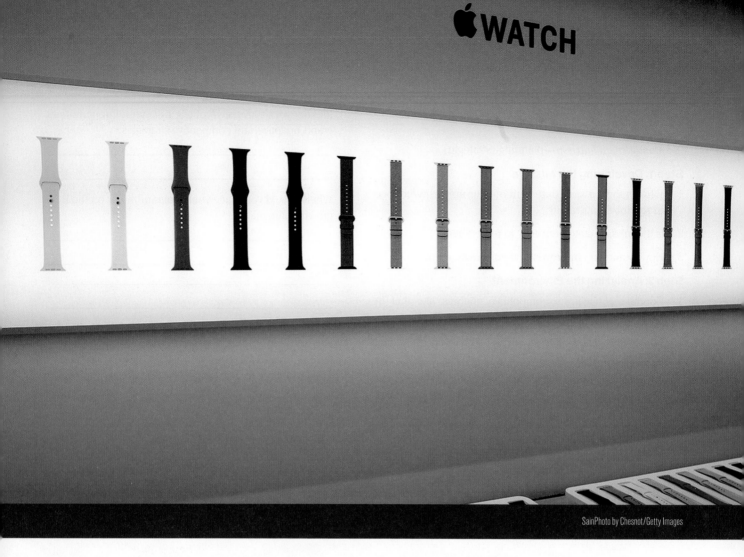

SainPhoto by Chesnot/Getty Images

6 Managing Change, Innovation, and Entrepreneurship

• • • LEARNING OBJECTIVES

After studying this chapter, you should be able to:

6-1. Identify the forces for change, the types of change, and the forms of change. PAGE 173

6-2. Contrast managing innovation during incremental and discontinuous change in terms of approach, goals, and strategy. PAGE 177

6-3. List the reasons employees resist change and suggest ways of overcoming such resistance. PAGE 179

6-4. Define organizational development and identify the steps in the Lewin and comprehensive change models. PAGE 185

6-5. Compare an entrepreneur and an intrapreneur and discuss the entrepreneurial process. PAGE 189

IOM	# Ideas on Management

Ideas on Management
at Apple

Together with **Apple cofounder Steve Wozniak**, **Steve Jobs** helped popularize the personal computer in the late 1970s and is credited with bringing cheap, easy-to-use computers and later other devices to the masses. In December 1980, Apple Computer became a publicly traded corporation. During Jobs's tenure as CEO, Apple's product and service lineup grew to include the Mac, MacBook Pro, MacBook Air, iPod, iPhone, iPad, and iTunes, among others. Unfortunately, Jobs's health deteriorated, and **COO Tim Cook** was promoted as CEO six weeks before Jobs passed away on October 5, 2011.

Under Cook's leadership, the iPad Mini, Apple Watch, updated iPhones, Apple Pay, and lots of apps have been added to the Apple product mix, and it is developing the driverless iCar. Although Apple has sold more than a billion iPhones, sales have slowed, and its Apple Watch failed to fill the void. Apple reported its first quarterly decline in revenues in 13 years in 2016. But don't expect Apple to have a retrenchment strategy.

In 2016, Apple had nine consecutive years with the title **Fortune**'s Most Admired Companies, and it remained the world's largest company by market value. Its $53 billion in net income was greater than the combined earning of technology giants **Facebook**, **Google**'s **Alphabet**, and **Microsoft**. Yes, Apple actually made more money than these three companies together, but can it keep up this lead? Cook said that Apple has been through cycles before, and this one will pass. He was correct, as Apple's revenue rose to a record $78.4 billion in the next quarter. There are a billion active devices out there, and Apple will continue to add services as a growth strategy.

IOM 1.   What types of changes has Apple made over the years?

IOM 2.   How is Apple committed to innovation?

IOM 3.   What type of resistance to change does Apple face?

IOM 4.   How does Apple use organizational development (OD)?

IOM 5.   Is Apple entrepreneurial?

You'll find answers to these **IOM** questions throughout the chapter. To learn more about Apple, visit www.apple.com.

Sources: Information for this case and answers within the chapter are taken from Apple's website at www.apple.com, accessed January 30, 2017; A. Lashinsky, "Exclusive Q&A: Apple CEO Tim Cook," *Fortune* (March 1, 2016): 119–122; D. Wakabayashi, "Apple Sinks on iPhone Stumble," *The Wall Street Journal* (April 27, 2016): A1, A2; K. Stock, "Briefs: Sour Apple," *BusinessWeek* (May 2–8, 2016): 25; S. Russolillo, "How Apple's Tim Cook Is Faring," *The Wall Street Journal* (August 22, 2016): C1; T. Mickle, "Apple Breaks Losing Streak, as Sales of iPhones Shine," *The Wall Street Journal* (February 1, 2017): A1, A10,

••• CHAPTER OUTLINE

Innovation and Change

The Innovation and Change Interrelationship and Risk

Forces for Change

Types of Change

Forms of Change

Managing Innovation

Innovative Organizational Structures and Cultures

Managing Innovation During Incremental and Discontinuous Change

Managing Change

Stages in the Change Process

Resistance to Change

How to Overcome Resistance to Change

A Model for Identifying and Overcoming Resistance to Change

Organizational Development

Change Models

Organizational Development Interventions

Entrepreneurship

New Venture Entrepreneurs and Intrapreneurs

The Entrepreneurial Process

Trends and Issues in Management

Innovation and Change

Progress is impossible without change,[1] change is faster than ever,[2] and the period between 2015 and 2020 is poised to redefine virtually every facet of how we live and work.[3] Thus, company recruiters seek employees with the skill of adaptability to change.[4] In this section, we discuss the innovation and change interrelationship and risk, the forces for change, and types and forms of change.

LO 6-1

Identify the forces for change, the types of change, and the forms of change.

The Innovation and Change Interrelationship and Risk

Creativity, Innovation, and Change. Recall from Chapter 4 that *creativity* is a way of thinking that generates new ideas and that creativity can lead to innovation. *Innovation* is the implementation of a new idea. So creativity has been established as a fundamental driver that serves as a basis for individual, group, and organizational pursuits of innovative efforts.[5] But creativity doesn't count until it is implemented through innovation.[6] **Apple** (**IOM 1**) comes up with lots of creative ideas but only implements a few. Two important types of innovation are *product innovation* (new things goods/services) and *process innovation* (new ways of doing things). Thus, all innovations require some changes to be made in the organization. **Organizational change** *is alterations of existing work routines and strategies that affect the whole organization.*

Taking Risk. All companies have to take risk and deal with uncertainty in the results of their decisions to start and continue to compete in business.[7] Innovation requires risks,[8] and successfully fast-growing companies are greater innovative risk takers,[9] as they take advantage of opportunities.[10] Innovative **Under Armour** CEO **Kevin Plank** said, "Part of the formula for success in our business is making a big bet."[11]

Failing to Take Risk. Unfortunately, failing to take risks and change with the dynamic environment can lead to a decline in business.[12] **IBM** has been criticized for being too slow to innovate, resulting in declined revenues, as it has strong competition in cloud computing services in **Amazon** and **Google**, where it should be dominating. Lack of innovation is why **Ginni Rometty** (ranked #1 in *Fortune*'s Most Powerful Women) got the CEO position and is working to get IBM to be more risk taking and innovative.[13] Without innovation, your company can become a dinosaur.[14]

Forces for Change

Here are three forces that lead to changes in business; businesses must adapt to these changing conditions.

The Environment. As you saw in Chapters 2 and 3, an organization interacts with its internal and external global environments, and these factors require adaptive change in an organization,[15] and the environment is becoming increasingly global, dynamic, complex, and competitive.[16] Sometimes change is required from within, and other times it is mandated by the external environment.[17] When **Google** acquired **YouTube**, it required changes internally to coordinate the business units and to adapt to a changing environment with competition from **Facebook** and others.

An important external factor includes keeping up with competitors' innovations. Ever hear of a BlackBerry? The name **BlackBerry** was used interchangeably with the early term "smartphone" as it dominated sales, but it failed to innovate and lost market share to **Samsung** and **Apple**, and in 2016 it stopped making phones.[18]

Technology Cycles. A *technology cycle* begins with the birth of a new technology and ends when it is replaced by a newer, substantially better technology. The **Ford** Model T car replaced the horse-drawn carriage. The vinyl record (**RCA** record player) was replaced by the cassette (**Sony** Walkman), then the CD (**GPX** CD player/boom box), and now we transition to online purchasing, including **Apple** iTunes (MP3/iPod to iPhone) and to streaming. It takes time to go through a technology cycle, but through the transition, there are usually many improvements that change the performance of the product, often going through generations.

Next Generation. The technology cycle is different from the *next generation*, such as 3G to 4G, because it allows the old technology to still work with the new technology. **Microsoft** updates its Office software and Xbox, but it allows the older-generation documents and games to be used with the new generation. People often prefer the next generation to a new technology cycle because there is less need to change, as they don't like to have to lose the old technology and pay for the new technology.

The Management Skills and Functions and Change. Change requires conceptual skills to understand the problems associated with changing environments and to make decisions (Chapter 1) to adapt, effectively implementing the management functions (Chapter 1) to make the changes.[19] Most plans that managers develop require changes. When managers organize and delegate tasks, they often require employees to make some changes in their regular routines. When managers hire, orient, train, and evaluate performance, change is required. Leadership calls for influencing employees, often to change in some way, and control may require the use of new methods or techniques to ensure the objective is met.

Types of Change

Types of change refer to what actually changes within the organization. The four **types of change** are *changes in strategy, in structure, in technology, and in people.* Because of the systems effect, you need to consider the repercussions of a change in one variable (type of change) on the others and plan accordingly. As you read about each type of change, you will understand the interrelationship of the systems effect. See Exhibit 6-1 for a list of the changes.

Changes in Strategy. Changes in the environment often require changes in strategy. You'll recall from Chapter 5 that an organization may change its strategy (at the corporate, business, and/or functional level). **IBM** changed its strategy over the years, moving away from being a hardware computer manufacturer, selling its PC line of business to Chinese **Lenovo**, and offering more services through the cloud.

Changes in Structure. *Structure* refers to how the organization is departmentalized into work units. Structure commonly follows strategy. **Google** changed its structure, creating a parent company, **Alphabet Inc.**, with **Google Inc**. now just one of the business divisions.[20] We will discuss structure in Chapter 7.

Changes in Technology. Recall from Chapter 2 that the *systems process* is the technology used to transform inputs into outputs, and the technology doesn't have to be high tech. So *technology* is the essential part of the systems process, and how we do our jobs does change. The Internet and smartphones have clearly changed the way we live and work.[21] With the fast pace of changes in technology, which is moving two to three times faster than management,[22] you need to be flexible and develop new products quickly,[23] such as **Netflix** (Chapter 1).

Changes in People. Organizations can't change without changes in people by adopting new behaviors.[24] A change in team membership is a common type of people change. When tasks change with technology, people's *skills* and *performance* must change. So you need to view learning as a career-long, life-long process to advance, and happiness is about behavior change.[25] A change in organizational *culture* (Chapter 2) is also considered a people change. People develop and implement strategy and structure. People also create, manage, and use technology; therefore, people are the most important resource.[26] Change in other variables will not be effective without people.[27]

WORK
APPLICATION 6-3

Give one or more examples of a type of change you experienced in an organization you work for or have worked for.

types of change Changes in strategy, in structure, in technology, and in people.

EXHIBIT 6-1   **TYPES OF CHANGES**

Strategy	Structure	Technology	People
The corporate, business, and functions strategies change over time (Chapter 5).	How the organization as a whole and its departments and jobs change over time (Chapter 7).	How the firm transforms inputs into outputs can change (Chapters 13–15).	Employees can change their attitudes and behavior and develop skills that change their performance (Chapters 8–14).

6-1 APPLYING THE CONCEPT

Types of Change

Identify the type of change in each statement:

A. strategy

B. structure

C. technology

D. people

_____ 1. "Jane, we need to purchase the new machine to speed up production."

_____ 2. "Usain, we are improving our smartphones by making the battery life longer."

_____ 3. "Tauna, did you hear we are implementing a retrenchment strategy by laying off 2,500 employees?"

_____ 4. "Karl, we are going to have to focus on retaining our existing customers to stop losing them to Amazon."

_____ 5. "Mo, I'd like you to get a college degree so you can advance into management positions with us."

Neilson Barnard/Getty Images for Tiffany & Co

Tiffany & Co. started as a stationery company, but after 16 years, it became a jewelry retailer, an example of discontinuous change.

incremental change Continual improvement that takes place within the existing technology cycle.

discontinuous change A significant breakthrough in technology that leads to design competition and a new technology cycle.

Forms of Change

Change also takes one of two broad forms—incremental or discontinuous[28]—and there is a technology adoption curve.

Incremental Change. Incremental change *is continual improvement that takes place within the existing technology cycle.* Companies innovate by lowering costs and improving performance of existing products and services.[29] **Samsung** continues to improve its smartphones with new models.

Discontinuous Change. Discontinuous change is a significant breakthrough in technology that leads to design competition and a new technology cycle, such as mobile connectivity and apps.[30] Disruptive technology requires the disruptive companies to make radial changes or go out of business.[31] **Western Union** started in 1851 as a telegraph service, which was disrupted by long distance calls and the Internet. Today, it's the largest international money-transfer MNC.[32]

The *innovator's dilemma* occurs when new technologies cause great firms to fail—**BlackBerry** phones. **Netflix** disrupted **Blockbuster** in-store DVD rentals with its mail-order DVDs; then it changed to streaming video content and making it. **Travelocity**, **Orbitz**, and others disrupted the travel agent–based model, causing many small travel agencies to close.

The **Apple** iPhone and **Samsung** Galaxy smartphones are discontinuing individual purchases, for many people, of CDs, iPods, radios, watches and stopwatches, alarm clocks, flashlights, printed news and books, audio recorders, cameras and video cameras, GPS devices, calculators, pedometers, and others.[33] It's better to be the disrupter than the disrupted.[34] How would you like to be the CEO of any company making one of these products?

Tesla is making incremental changes to electric cars, whereas **Uber** is disrupting taxi and public transportation,[35] and **Airbnb** disrupts travel accommodations.[36] If you don't abandon yesterday, you can't create tomorrow.[37] It often requires cannibalizing how the company does business—like at Netflix.[38] **Amazon** disrupted bookstores, then disrupted its own mail-order model with Kindle e-readers.[39]

Technology Adoption Curve. Also called the *Diffusion of Innovations*, the technology adoption curve illustrates how people adopt new technology within a bell-shaped curve. See Exhibit 6-2 for an illustration. The percentages refer to the percent of buyers within that cycle of the adoption curve, and note that sales don't take off until the majority start to buy the product or service. With communications technology, the speed of going through the adoption curve to the next disruptive technology cycle is accelerating.[40]

Apple (**IOM 1**) continues to take risks as it creates innovative new products, as it competes in a competitive dynamic environment. Apple continues to have a growth strategy, as it acquires more companies but is expanding its services, such as Apple Pay, Apple Music, and apps. Apple is also changing its structure, as it built a new headquarters to get a lot of people back together again in 2017. Apple focuses on hiring curious people who want to explore technology to make great products that help people in some way. Apple helped bring new technologies to the PC and tablets, music, and more recently with smartphones with the highly successful iPhone, and the smart multifunction Apple Watch is disrupting the simple time watch.

Managing Innovation

CEOs of **Fortune 500** companies listed "the rapid pace of technology change as their single biggest challenge,"[41] saying we are all technology companies now.[42] Thus, global executives say innovation is extremely important to their growth strategies,[43] as they constantly seek opportunities to improve and develop new products.[44] What's **IBM**? **CEO Ginni Rometty** says, "It's an enterprise innovation company."[45] Staying innovative over time is a major challenge.[46] **Siemens** has remade half its product offerings in just the past decade to stay relevant.[47] Many companies have innovation officers, as management is crucial for innovation success.[48] In this section, we discuss organizational structures and cultures that stimulate innovative change and how to manage innovation during incremental and discontinuous change.

Innovative Organizational Structures and Cultures

Innovative Structures. Formal organizational structures are needed to coordinate internal activities,[49] but structural rigidities[50] and bureaucracy[51] can kill or slow creativity and innovation. CEOs say it's so hard to get stuff done with speed and agility.[52] Organizations that stimulate innovation are commonly structured as flat organizations with limited bureaucracy, have a generalist division of labor, coordinate with cross-functional teams, and are flexible. They challenge the status quo to continually improve,[53] as they don't stress following standing plans (Chapter 5). They use small team structures.[54] Use of informal authority is common, and authority is decentralized. We will discuss these structures in Chapter 7.

Many innovative organizations set up *skunkworks projects*. A skunkworks project is one typically developed by a small and loosely structured group of people who research and

LO 6-2

Contrast managing innovation during incremental and discontinuous change in terms of approach, goals, and strategy.

EXHIBIT 6-2   **THE TECHNOLOGY ADOPTION CURVE**

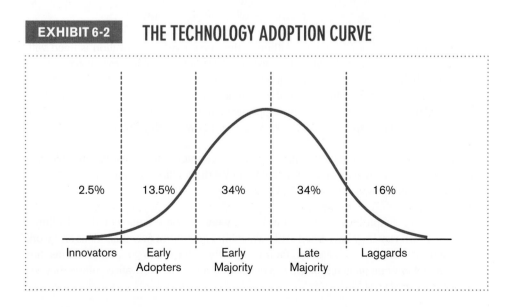

| 2.5% | 13.5% | 34% | 34% | 16% |

Innovators | Early Adopters | Early Majority | Late Majority | Laggards

Online High School

There are high schools, including National High School, offering online courses and diplomas. They tend to be attractive to individual-sport athletes, such as tennis players, golfers, and skaters, because they allow flexibility to train, travel long distances to compete, and do coursework in between. Online courses also allow students to work at their own pace. Unlike public school, students pay to earn credits and don't have face-to-face, in-person contact with peers and teachers. Some of the online high schools are for-profit businesses making lots of money.

1. How do you feel about high school students missing the experience of attending traditional classes and socializing with their peers?

2. How do you feel about students paying to earn a high school diploma online when they can earn one for free at a public school?

3. Is it ethical and socially responsible to offer a for-profit online high school?

develop a project primarily for the sake of radical innovation. A skunkworks project often operates with a high degree of autonomy and is often undertaken in secret with the understanding that if the development is successful, then the product will be designed in the usual process. **Apple**, **Lexus**, and **Michelin** are just a few companies that successfully use skunkworks projects to develop new products. At **Google X** (its secret lab), incremental changes aren't good enough; the company really strives to innovate for discontinuous technology breakthroughs, such as **Google Glass** and its driverless car.[55]

Innovative Cultures. Recall from Chapter 2 that top managers need to develop a strong culture and model it.[56] CEOs of **Aetna**, **Salesforce**, and **Yahoo** all say that creating the right culture is the central challenge for surviving technology-driven change and innovation.[57] Employees need to take ownership in pride in being part of an innovative culture.[58] The successful organizations encourage creativity and innovation;[59] 94% of **Cadence** employees say they have exciting opportunities to innovate.[60]

Organizations known to have strong innovative cultures include **3M**, **Amazon.com**, **Google**, and **LG Electronics**. **Apple** CEO Tim Cook (**IOM 2**) brags about Apple's culture of innovation. Such organizations develop structures that match and become a part of their innovative cultures. The new practices become part of the existing culture or lead to a change in culture.[61] Such cultures commonly have the following characteristics:

- *Encouragement of Risk Taking.* Although the curvy road to innovation is lined with failures, risking failure is what we do to succeed.[62] Getting employees to voice creative ideas helps lead to innovation.[63] Innovative cultures encourage and reward employees for taking risks without fear of punishment if they fail, such as with skunkworks. **NetApp** has developed a strong supportive culture that fosters innovation because employees can experiment and take risks; they know that their ideas are heard.[64]

A method of encouraging risk taking is through encouraging *intrapreneurs*,[65] people who start a new line of business for an existing company. We discuss the difference between entrepreneurs and intrapreneurs later in this chapter.

- *Flexibility.* Employees are more innovative when they are empowered to do things their own way. They have a sense of ownership and control over their ideas and work, and they can make changes to their work without having to get permission, as they are not micromanaged. **Google** has developed a flexible innovative culture that will take care of itself.[66]

Part of being flexible is letting employees work on ideas that don't seem practical or related to the business. **Google** is working on stretchable electronics, an invisible helmet, delivery drones, and self-driving cars.[67]

- *Open systems.* With an open system, you seek innovation from within and outside the firm. Many companies today are turning to their customers, suppliers, and others in their supply chain for innovation. **Microsoft** came up with the name **Bing** based on suggestions from within and outside the firm. **Starbucks** sponsored an online contest in which customers could submit ideas on how to reduce paper cup consumption. Starbucks provided $20,000 in cash prizes to customers with the most innovative ideas.[68]

Managing Innovation During Incremental and Discontinuous Change

Almost every problem harbors opportunity. It's the creative people who have the vision to see the opportunity and turn it into an innovation.[69] Let's discuss the difference in managing these two forms of change, which also are presented in Exhibit 6-3.

Managing Innovation During Incremental Change: The Compression Approach. It is called the *compression approach* because it is used in more certain environments during incremental change. The goal is to lower costs and incrementally improve performance and functions of the existing dominant design. The general strategy is to continue to improve the existing technology as rapidly as possible, moving to the *next-generation* technology while still allowing the use of the old technology; this is called *generational change*. The compression approach uses a series of planned steps to avoid wasted time and delays between steps of generational change. **Apple** (**IOM 2**) continues to incrementally improve its **Mac**, **iPad**, **iPhone**, and **Apple Watch**.

Managing Innovation During Discontinuous Change: The Experimental Approach. It is called the *experimental approach* because it is used in more uncertain environments during discontinuous change. The goal is to make significant improvements in performance and to establish a new dominant design, creating the next technology cycle. The general strategy is to build something new, different, and substantially better, causing a breakthrough in technology to begin a new technology cycle that leaves the old technology obsolete. With the uncertainty, companies compete to establish the new dominant design to become the market leader. **Ginni Rometty** was selected **CEO of IBM** to change its slow, risk-avoidance culture to an innovative one. Her repeated mantra is, "the key is to always disrupt ourselves."[70]

As stated, **Apple** (**IOM 2**) disrupted multiple industries. Even during down cycles, Apple continues to invest in research and development (R&D) to be creative and develop innovative products. Apple doubled its R&D spending since 2013, but it still spends a smaller portion of revenues than any other big U.S. tech company. Based on the percentage of revenues spent on R&D, Apple (3.5%) actually innovates for significantly less than **Google** (15%), **Facebook** (21%), and **Qualcomm** (22%).[71]

Managing Change

As we've discussed, managing innovation is essential to business success, and an important part of successful innovation is managing change[72] with the appropriate strategies.[73] Companies need to respond to changes in the competitive environment.[74] Any company that fails to change its business model[75] and embrace change will be overtaken by it.[76] Of the original *Fortune* **500** companies, only 65 still exist today. That's an 87% failure rate. Why? Because they didn't change with the times.[77] As part of **IBM**'s turnaround strategy, CEO **Ginni Rometty** has three rules: (1) Don't protect the past, (2) never be defined by your product, and (3) always transform yourself.[78] As the world changes, if we don't change, somebody will replace us pretty soon. Need we say that managing change is a critical skill to develop? In this section, we discuss stages in the change process and resistance to change and how to overcome it, and we present a model for identifying and overcoming resistance to change.

WORK
APPLICATION 6-4

Does an organization you work for or have worked for have any of the characteristics of innovative structure and cultures? Overall, does the organization have a creative culture?

WORK
APPLICATION 6-5

Does an organization you work for or have worked for compete in a more incremental or discontinuous change environment?

LO 6-3

List the reasons employees resist change and suggest ways of overcoming such resistance.

EXHIBIT 6-3   MANAGING INNOVATION

	Incremental Change	Discontinuous Change
Approach	Compression	Experimental
Environment	More certain	Uncertain
Goals	To lower costs and incrementally improve performance and functions of the existing dominant design	To make significant improvements in performance and to establish a new dominant design, creating the next technology cycle
Strategy	To continue to improve the existing technology as rapidly as possible, moving to the next-generation technology while still allowing the use of the old technology	To build something new and different, a substantially better breakthrough in technology, to begin a new technology cycle that leaves the old technology obsolete

Stages in the Change Process

People tend to go through four distinct stages when facing change. The four **stages of the change process** are *denial, resistance, exploration, and commitment.*

1. *Denial.* Changes are often difficult to understand or accept. So when people first hear that change is coming, they may deny that it will affect them. Managers at **Research in Motion (RIM)** most likely denied that **BlackBerry** would lose its cell phone market leadership position.

2. *Resistance.* Once people get over the initial shock and realize that change is going to be a reality, they often resist the change. People, including managers at **RIM**, often doubt there really is a need for change.

3. *Exploration.* When the change begins to be implemented, employees explore the change, often through training, and ideally they begin to better understand how it will affect them. Managers at **RIM** realized they were behind in smartphone technology and worked on innovations to catch up with competitors but couldn't.

4. *Commitment.* Through exploration, employees determine their level of commitment to making the change a success. Commitment is necessary to implement the change, but some employees continue to resist the change. Managers at **RIM** realized the actual threat to its BlackBerry too late for a turnaround. It also came out late with the **PlayBook** tablet, and it lost $1 billion in unsold inventory after giving up on tablets.[79]

stages of the change process Denial, resistance, exploration, and commitment.

6-2 APPLYING THE CONCEPT

Innovative and Noninnovative Cultures

Identify the type of organizational culture described in each statement.

A. innovative culture

B. noninnovative culture

____ 6. "Howie, I tried to develop a better-tasting cola, but people like the old taste better. However, my boss gave me a very sincere thanks for trying."

____ 7. "Carol, why is our boss so autocratic—always telling us all the details of how to do a new task without our input?"

____ 8. "Heidy, does your boss focus on having you follow the rules too?"

____ 9. "Sheen, our supervisor lets us do our jobs any way we want to, so long as we meet our objectives."

____10. "Tip, when we come up with a creative idea, we have several levels of management that have to approve the innovation."

EXHIBIT 6-4   STAGES IN THE CHANGE PROCESS

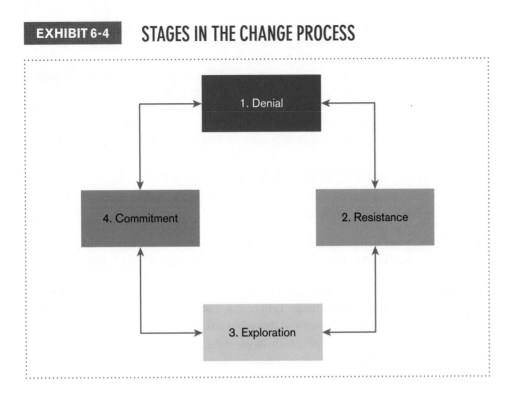

Exhibit 6-4 illustrates the four-stage change process. Notice that the stages are in a circular formation because change is an ongoing process, not a linear one. People can regress, as the arrows show.

Resistance to Change

Let's face it. As stated by **J.C. Penney's chairman Michael Ullman**, "only a baby with a wet diaper likes change."[80] We don't want to change our habits and routines.[81] Some people deliberately try to kill good ideas[82] and others to beat the system for their advantage as they attempt to block change efforts.[83] Why do employees resist change, and how do managers overcome resistance to change? As shown in Exhibit 6-5, employees resist change for six major reasons:

- **Uncertainty.** Uncertainty tends to make us react defensively by denying the need for change and allows us to rationalize that we don't really need to change. Fear of the unknown outcome of change often brings *fear of potential failure.* We often get anxious and nervous and resist change in order to cope with these feelings. But don't be afraid to try new things.

- **Learning anxiety.** For many of us, the prospect of learning something new produces anxiety—*learning anxiety.* We realize that new learning may make us temporarily incompetent and may expose us to rejection by valued groups.

- **Self-interest.** We tend to resist change that threatens our own self-interest.[84] We are commonly more concerned about our best interests than about the interests of the organization even when failure to change can have severe consequences.

- **Fear of loss.** Change creates winners and losers. With change, jobs may possibly be lost. Change may involve an economic loss as a result of a pay cut. A change in work assignments or schedules may create a loss of social relationships.

- **Fear of loss of control.** Change can also result in an actual or perceived loss of power, status, security, and especially control. We may resent the feeling that our destiny is being controlled by someone else.

- *Successful Habits.* When we are successful, we tend to think change is not needed—like **BlackBerry**. Even when we do change, we can fall back into old habits that have worked in the past.[85] **Microsoft** Windows for PCs was highly successful for some 25 years, but it was too slow to develop mobile cell phone software like **Google's Android**, and the **Apple iOS** is taking sales away from laptop sales that use Windows. Microsoft also acquired **Nokia**, which once was the tech leader that held 40% of the handheld devices, to offer its smartphones. But as you likely know, it was a bad decision, as Microsoft couldn't turn around Nokia to its former glory days as the tech leader.[86]

How to Overcome Resistance to Change

Let's start by discussing our own resistance to change followed by overcoming others' resistance to change.

Our Resistance to Change—Habits. Do you really like your daily routine disrupted?[87] Are you bound by your habits of repetition?[88] If you can't change your mind and embrace change, you cannot change anything.[89] So the aim is to cultivate a mind-set that embraces change in ourselves and others.[90] Easier said than done, right? Well, the first step is to realize we need to take a positive attitude about change. Let's face it, if we know we have to make a change, resisting it doesn't help—so accept it and move forward.

Have you ever wondered why people do illogical things? It helps to realize that our brains cling to habit at the exclusion of all else, including common sense. Or our feelings and habits overrule common sense. So to make, a change we have to change our thoughts and habit, or make the change a habit to make it successful.[91] The reason most people don't keep their New Year's resolution is they don't make it a habit. If you say you will exercise more but don't make a scheduled time to work out (routine habit), you won't work out. Developing a habit takes conscious planning and effort—schedule time to work out and, as **Nike** says, Just Do It. A habit has three parts, and here are three examples listed A through C.

1. **Cue**. A. Running shoes left near your bed. B. Phone dings. C. Feel sad.
2. **Routine**. A. Run first thing in the morning. B. Check your phone. C. Eat and/or drink.
3. **Reward**. A. Endorphin rush, feel good about yourself and healthier, weight loss and more energy, healthy breakfast. B. Words with the caller. We crave the ding and the rush of endorphins it promises—that is why most people are addicted to their phones and have to multitask (Chapter 5). C. Temporary escape from sadness, which often doesn't work and can lead to other problems and bad habits.

MANAGEMENT IN ACTION
Managing Change

Think about it. What is your usual attitude about and level of resistance toward change? Are there any good habits you should develop, or bad self-destructive ones you should drop/replace? Will you work at being more positive about accepting change and consciously develop habits to succeed? Skill Building Exercise 6-4, Developing a New Habit, can help.

Others' Resistance to Change. Here we focus primarily on overcoming others' resistance to change, but these tips can also apply to ourselves. Companies do create new habits with changes. They are commonly called procedures and rules for completing new tasks (Chapter 5).

You need to overcome resistance to implement change. Change projects rarely claim the substantial success that is intended,[92] but as shown in Exhibit 6-5, there are seven major things you can do, in addition to changing your attitude and habits, to help overcome resistance to successfully make changes:

- ***Develop a positive trust climate for change.*** Develop and maintain good human relations. Make employees realize you have their best interests in mind and develop a culture of mutual trust.[93] Encouraging employees to suggest changes and implementing their ideas are important parts of continuous improvement.

- ***Plan.*** Implementing changes successfully requires good planning. You need to identify the possible resistance to change and plan how to overcome it. View change from the employees' position. Set clear objectives so employees know exactly what the change is. Develop small, simple, nonthreatening steps so that employees can think, "I can do that."[94] The next four tips should be part of your plan.

- ***Clearly state why the change is needed and how it will affect employees.*** Changes can be difficult to understand, so employees want and need to know why the change is necessary and how it will affect them, both positively and negatively—especially with successful habits that need to be changed. So you need to communicate clearly what you want to do. Employees need to understand why the new, changed method is more legitimate than the existing method of doing things. Be open and honest with employees. Giving employees the facts as far in advance as possible helps them to overcome fear of the unknown.

- ***Create a win-win situation.*** We have a desire to win. The goal of human relations is to meet employee needs while achieving organizational objectives. Be sure to answer the other parties' unasked question, "What's in it for me?" When people can see how they benefit, or at least minimize their loss, they are more willing to change. If the organization is going to benefit by the change, so should the employees when possible.

- ***Involve employees.*** To create a win-win situation, involve employees. A commitment to change is usually critical to its successful implementation. Employees who participate in developing changes are more committed to them than employees who have changes dictated to them. It helps if you phrase your own ideas as if an employee said them.

- ***Provide support and evaluation.*** Employees need to know that managers are there to help them cope with the changes. You need to make the learning process as painless as possible by providing training and other support. Managers must also provide feedback and evaluation during the learning process to increase the employees' efficiency and effectiveness in implementing the change.

- ***Create urgency.*** When you decide on a change, you have to move fast. Many people procrastinate making changes. A feeling of urgency is the primary driver toward

EXHIBIT 6-5   RESISTANCE TO CHANGE AND WAYS TO OVERCOME RESISTANCE

Resistance to Change	Overcoming Resistance
Uncertainty	Change attitudes about change and habits Develop trust climate for change
Learning anxiety	Plan
Self-interest	State why change is needed and how it will affect employees
Fear of loss	Create a win-win situation
Fear of loss of control	Involve employees
Successful habits	Provide support and evaluation Create urgency

Nokia, once a leading brand in cellular phones, did not change fast enough to keep up with competitors. Because it resisted adapting to market needs, Nokia lost its leadership position among cell phone companies.

taking action. If something is perceived as urgent, it is given a high priority and is usually done immediately. It appears that **BlackBerry** and **Nokia** didn't create urgency or implement the other six tips effectively to make the necessary changes to maintain market leadership.

Apple (**IOM 3**) faces resistance to change from customers for two major reasons. First, Apple offers new innovative products. As shown in Exhibit 6-2, the Technology Adoption Curve, it takes time to get large sales volume. Apple prices its products higher than most competitors. Apple tends to overcome the resistance by offering attractive easy-to-use products, with the famous global Apple brand name and logo—many people have to have the prestigious Apple, not the low-price model. Apple is ranked first on the Fortune World's Most Admired Companies.[95]

A Model for Identifying and Overcoming Resistance to Change

Before making changes, you should anticipate how others will react. Resistance to change varies in its intensity, source, and focus.[96]

Intensity. People have different attitudes toward change. Some thrive on it; some are upset by it; many resist it at first but gradually accept it. As a manager of change, you must anticipate whether resistance will be strong, weak, or somewhere in between. Intensity will be lower if you use the seven methods for overcoming resistance to change.

Sources. There are three major sources of resistance to change:

1. *Facts.* The facts (provable statements) about an impending change are often circulated through the grapevine—but people tend to use facts selectively to prove their point. Facts used correctly help to overcome fear of the unknown.
2. *Beliefs.* Facts can be proved; beliefs cannot. Beliefs are subjective opinions that can be shaped by others. Our beliefs lead us to think that a change is correct or incorrect or good or bad. Differences in perception can cause resistance to change.
3. *Values.* Values are what people believe are worth pursuing or doing. What we value is important to us and influences our behavior. Values pertain to right and wrong and help establish priorities. Values are also related to religion and ethics.

Focus. There are three major focuses of resistance to change:

1. *Self.* People naturally want to know, "What's in it for me? What will I gain or lose?" When the facts of change have a negative effect on employees, creating a perceived loss, employees resist the change.
2. *Others.* After considering what's in it for them and concluding that a change does not affect them, people tend to consider how the change will affect their friends, peers, and colleagues. If employees analyze the facts and believe that a change will affect others negatively, they may be resistant to the change.
3. *Work environment.* The work environment includes the physical setting, the work itself, and the climate. People like to be in control of their environment, and they resist changes that take away their control.

Model 6-1 is a resistance matrix with examples of each area of resistance. Once you have identified the probable resistance to change, you can work at overcoming it. Note that the intensity of resistance can be strong, moderate, or weak for each of the nine matrix boxes. In Skill Builder 6-2, you will use the resistance matrix to identify the source and focus of change.

MODEL 6-1   RESISTANCE MATRIX

Sources of Resistance: Facts, Beliefs, and Values

1. Facts about self	4. Beliefs about self	7. Values pertaining to self
• I have never done the task before. • I failed the last time.	• I'm too busy to learn it. • I'll do it, but don't blame me if it's wrong.	• I like the way I do my job now. Why change? • I like working in a group.
2. Facts about others	5. Beliefs about others	8. Values pertaining to others
• She has the best performance record in the department. • Other employees told me it's hard to do.	• He just pretends to be busy to avoid extra work. • She's better at it than I am; let her do it.	• Let someone else do it; I do not want to work with her. • I like working with him. Don't cut him from our department.
3. Facts about the work environment	6. Beliefs about the work environment	9. Values pertaining to the work environment
• We are only paid $10 an hour. • It's over 100 degrees.	• This is a lousy job. • The pay here is too low.	• I don't care if we meet the goal or not. • The new task will make me work inside. I'd rather be outside.

Intensity (high, medium, or low for each box)

Organizational Development

Organizational development is the commonly used method of managing planned change through change agents.[97] **Organizational development (OD)** *is the ongoing planned process of change used as a means of improving performance through interventions.* The human resources management department (discussed in Chapter 9) is usually responsible for OD throughout an organization. The **change agent** *is the person responsible for implementing an organizational change effort.* So the change agent is very important and runs an OD intervention.[98] The change agent may be a member of the organization or a hired consultant. CEO **Steve Easterbrook** calls himself a change agent dedicated to turning **McDonald's** into a modern progressive burger company.[99]

Implementing the environmental SWOT analysis (Chapter 5), changes should be made to reduce and eliminate the firm's *weaknesses* while taking advantages of *opportunities* and overcoming *threats* through mobilizing its *strengths*. In this section, we discuss change models and OD interventions.

Change Models

Models provide steps to follow to help implement planned organizational change. Two popular change models used by organizations today are Lewin's change model and a more comprehensive model for change.

Lewin's Change Model. Kurt Lewin developed a technique for changing people's behavior, skills, and attitudes. You can think of it like taking an ice cube and melting it back to water and refreezing it into another shape.[100] Lewin's change model consists of the three steps listed in Exhibit 6-6. The model presents a change–stability paradox, going from *unfreezing*— recognizing the need for change—to *moving*—implementing the change—to *refreezing*— make change a habit. Lewin's model works well with incremental changes, but the comprehensive model tends to work better for discontinuous change.[101]

A Comprehensive Change Model. The model consists of five steps, as shown in Exhibit 6-6. In the first step, you need to clearly state the objective (using the model in Chapter 5) of the

LO 6-4

Define organizational development and identify the steps in the Lewin and comprehensive change models.

WORK
APPLICATION 6-7

Describe the intensity, source, and focus of the resistance to change you identified in Work Application 6-6.

organizational development (OD) The ongoing planned process of change used as a means of improving performance through interventions.

change agent The person responsible for implementing an organizational change effort.

EXHIBIT 6-6   CHANGE MODELS

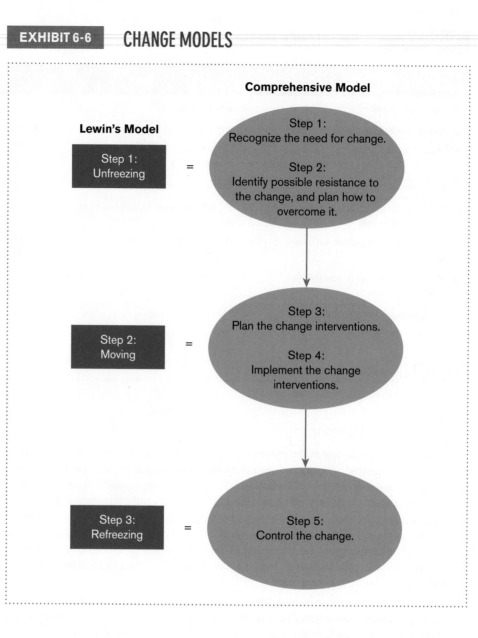

needed change, and the last step is really implemented throughout the change process to monitor the process toward the change to ensure the objective of the change is achieved. Let's move on to discuss the interventions the change agent can use (step 3) to make the change.

Organizational Development Interventions

OD interventions *are specific actions taken to implement specific changes.* Although there are many types, we discuss the nine OD interventions listed in Exhibit 6-7.

- **Training and Development.** Training and development are listed first because they focus on the individual, and the other interventions often include some form of training. Training is the process of developing skills, behaviors, and attitudes to be used on the job. Virtually every organization provides some type of training. You will learn about training in the next chapter.

- **Sensitivity Training.** Sensitivity training takes place in a group of 10 to 15 people. The training sessions have no agenda. People learn about how their behavior affects others and how others' behavior affects theirs. So the focus is on individual behavior in a group. Although popular in the 1960s, it is not commonly used in business today.

OD interventions Specific actions taken to implement specific changes.

| EXHIBIT 6-7 | OD INTERVENTIONS AND THEIR FOCUS |

OD Intervention	Individual Focus	Group Focus	Organization Focus
1. Training and Development	X		
2. Sensitivity Training	X		
3. Team Building		X	
4. Process Consultation		X	
5. Forcefield Analysis		X	
6. Survey Feedback		X	X
7. Large-Group Intervention			X
8. Work Design	X	X	X
9. Direct Feedback	X	X	X

- **Team Building.** Team building is probably the most widely used OD technique today[102]—the topic of Chapter 8. **Team building** *is an OD intervention designed to help work groups increase structural and team dynamics and performance.* It is widely used as a means of helping new or existing groups improve their effectiveness in setting objectives, planning, problem solving and decision making, and developing open, honest working relationships based on trust and an understanding of group members. Team-building programs vary in terms of agenda and length, also depending on team needs and the change agent's skills.

- **Process Consultation.** Process consultation is often part of team building, but it is commonly used as a separate, more narrowly focused intervention. **Process consultation** *is an OD intervention designed to improve team dynamics.* Team building may focus on the process of getting a job itself done, but process consultation focuses on how people interact as they get the job done—work together. The ultimate objective of team dynamics is to train the group so that process consultation becomes an ongoing team activity. You will learn more about team dynamics in Chapter 8.

- **Forcefield Analysis.** Forcefield analysis is particularly useful for small-group (4 to 18 members) problem solving. **Forcefield analysis** *is an OD intervention that diagrams the current level of performance, the forces hindering change, and the forces driving toward change.* The process is to list the hindering and driving forces to make the desired change. Exhibit 6-8 represents a possible forcefield analysis for **Dell** losing market share. After developing the diagram, group members develop strategies for maintaining or increasing the driving forces and for decreasing the hindering forces.

- **Survey Feedback.** Collecting feedback is one of the oldest and most popular OD techniques at the department, division, and organizational levels. Companies want to know how their employees and customers feel about them,[103] and they agree they should conduct surveys more than once a year.[104] **Survey feedback** *is an OD intervention that uses a questionnaire to gather data to use as the basis for change.* If you have ever filled out a professor/course assessment form or a restaurant or any service form in person, by phone, or online, you have participated in survey feedback. The change agent develops a survey designed to identify problems and areas for improvement and, based on the survey results, recommends planned change improvements.

One popular organization development technique is to have employees provide survey feedback about the company, then use the feedback to inform improvements within the company.

team building An OD intervention designed to help work groups increase structural and team dynamics and performance.

process consultation An OD intervention designed to improve team dynamics.

forcefield analysis An OD intervention that diagrams the current level of performance, the forces hindering change, and the forces driving toward change.

survey feedback An OD intervention that uses a questionnaire to gather data to use as the basis for change.

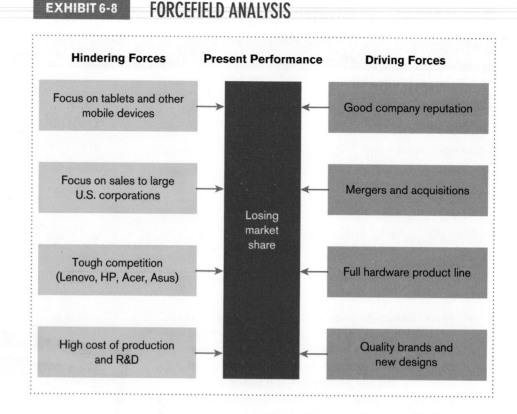

EXHIBIT 6-8   FORCEFIELD ANALYSIS

Hindering Forces	Present Performance	Driving Forces
Focus on tablets and other mobile devices		Good company reputation
Focus on sales to large U.S. corporations	Losing market share	Mergers and acquisitions
Tough competition (Lenovo, HP, Acer, Asus)		Full hardware product line
High cost of production and R&D		Quality brands and new designs

- **Large-Group Intervention. Large-group intervention** *is an OD technique that brings together participants from all parts of the organization, and often key outside stakeholders, to solve problems or take advantage of opportunities.* Large-group interventions often include 50 to 500 people and may last for days. A major difference between large-group interventions and the other OD interventions is the focus on functional diversity and inclusion of key stakeholders. When developing a new product, a company might convene a large group of people in product development, engineering and research and development (R&D), marketing, production, and service from within the firm and also customers and suppliers, who would meet to analyze the new product in an effort to ensure its success.

- **Work Design.** As we will discuss in Chapter 7, *work design* refers to organizational structure. Work can be designed as an individual job, as a job for a group to perform, or by departmentalization. Job enrichment is commonly used to change jobs to make them more interesting and challenging, which leads to innovation.

- **Direct Feedback. Direct feedback** *is an OD intervention in which the change agent makes a direct recommendation for change.* In certain situations, especially those involving technology changes, the most efficient intervention is to have a change agent make a direct recommendation for a specific change. The trend today is to use more *outside consultants* as change agents.[105]

large-group intervention An OD technique that brings together participants from all parts of the organization, and often key outside stakeholders, to solve problems or take advantage of opportunities.

direct feedback An OD intervention in which the change agent makes a direct recommendation for change.

Apple (**IOM 4**) uses OD interventions. For new employees, it provides many robust learning opportunities through training and development and in-depth mentoring programs. Apple also uses team building with its employees and feedback from both employees and customers. CEO Cook says that much of Apple success is based on teamwork. It considers and debates a lot of new products but offers a lot fewer. Even though it is developing the iCar, it may not actually sell it, and if it does sell the iCar, it will utilize contract manufacturers, like with its computers and phones. Apple may just sell the technology to other driverless car manufacturers.

6-3 APPLYING THE CONCEPT

OD Interventions

Identify the appropriate OD intervention for the change described in each statement.

A. training and development

B. sensitivity training

C. team building

D. process consultation

E. forcefield analysis

F. survey feedback

G. large-group intervention

H. work design

I. direct feedback

____ 11. "Connie, when we install the new software, who is going to learn to run it?"

____ 12. "Francesco, what intervention will we use to prepare our employees to put the product together as a group rather than each person continuing to produce one part of it?"

____ 13. "Liza, are you sure this intervention will work? Our team has a lot of conflict that is affecting how we get along as we complete the job."

____ 14. "Hanna, what intervention can we use to make jobs more interesting and challenging for our employees?"

____ 15. "Kent, our employees are often rude to each other. What intervention can we use to make them better understand how their behavior affects their coworkers?"

____ 16. "Candy, is there an intervention we can use with a small group to figure out things that are holding us back from getting a higher product quality rating and what we can do to improve quality?"

____ 17. "Jordan, I think we could benefit from using intervention that gets lots of employees from many departments and our key suppliers to discuss ideas on improving productivity."

____ 18. "Winona, we need an intervention that can identify the employee morale problems so we can change the situation."

____ 19. "Tony, I've been hearing a lot about social media marketing. Should we try it?"

Entrepreneurship

Entrepreneurs are a driving force for innovation and change worldwide.[106] America was founded, quite literally, by entrepreneurs.[107] Interest in entrepreneurship is on the increase, as are college programs, because these skills can be developed.[108] Entrepreneurs have certain traits that help them to succeed.[109] Complete Self-Assessment 6-1 to discover whether you have entrepreneurial qualities. In this section, we discuss new venture creation by entrepreneurs and intrapreneurs and the entrepreneurial process.

New Venture Entrepreneurs and Intrapreneurs

When people think of entrepreneurship, they often tend to think of small businesses. However, in the global business environment, organizations of all types and sizes are becoming more entrepreneurial.[110] **Major League Baseball's (MLB) San Francisco Giants** CEO **Larry Baer** says that every day is a fight to be entrepreneurial.[111]

New Ventures. A **new venture** *is a new business or a new line of business.* When **Jeff Bezos** started **Amazon.com** to sell books, it was a new business venture; when it offered customers cloud computing services, it was a new line of business. In either case, new ventures bring about innovation and change.

Entrepreneurs Versus Intrapreneurs and Franchisees. Entrepreneurs commonly start new small-business ventures. **Intrapreneurs** commonly start a new line of business within a larger organization. They are also called *corporate entrepreneurs* and *organizational entrepreneurs.*[112]

LO 6-5

Compare an entrepreneur and an intrapreneur and discuss the entrepreneurial process.

WORK APPLICATION 6-8

Give an example of one or more OD interventions used in an organization that you work for or have worked for.

new venture A small business or a new line of business.

entrepreneur Someone who starts a small-business venture.

intrapreneur Someone who starts a new line of business within a larger organization.

Entrepreneur **Raymond Berry** worked full time while he founded **White Lion Brewing Company.**

In essence, intrapreneurs commonly start and run small businesses within large organizations, often as separate business units. Franchisees (Chapter 3), such as **Subway** and **McDonald's** shop owners, are important in entrepreneurship, as they create new ventures. However, they are under the direction of a franchisor. So they are not considered real entrepreneurs or intrapreneurs by some, as they are kind of an external intrapreneur creating a duplicate business.

Entrepreneurship Activities. Entrepreneurship activities include creating new products or processes, entering new markets, or creating new business ventures and organizations or productivity techniques[113]—developing or improving a product, speeding up manufacturing, or delivering existing products to the customer in a new faster way. So without being an entrepreneur, you can engage in entrepreneurial activities by being creative and innovative. But no new venture is started without entrepreneurial activities, and existing businesses seek employees with entrepreneurial behavior skills.[114] The number of colleges teaching students how to be entrepreneurial is increasing.[115]

Small-Businesses Entrepreneurs. The legal definition of *small* varies by country and by industry. In the United States, the **Small Business Administration (SBA)** establishes small-business size standards on an industry-by-industry basis.[116] According to the U.S. **Department of Labor (DOL)**, a small business employs fewer than 100 workers, and a *small to medium-size enterprise (SME)* employs fewer than 500 workers.[117] For our purposes, we blend the two definitions: A **small business** *is a business that is independently owned and operated, with a small number of employees and relatively low volume of sales.* Small business is important because more than 90% of U.S. businesses are small businesses,[118] and they are important to economic growth because as much as 80% of new jobs are created by small businesses.[119] They also provide valuable products and services to consumers and to large businesses.[120]

Don't forget that almost all large businesses started small. **Michael Dell** founded **Dell Computer** and **Mark Zuckerberg**, with others, started **Facebook** in their college dorm rooms. **Steve Jobs** and **Steve Wozniak** started **Apple** in the Jobs family garage.

Large Business Intrapreneurs. Both the **SBA** and the **DOL** define a large business as employing 500 or more workers. Large businesses are clearly trying to be more entrepreneurial,[121] as they are creating innovative cultures and getting all employees to think like owners.[122] So large businesses that innovate and change have an *entrepreneurial orientation.*[123] Major corporations spend billions of dollars on intrapreneurship, which is often called *internal corporate ventures.*[124] **3M** and **GE** are well known for encouraging *entrepreneurship activities and intrapreneurship.* One of 3M's goals is to have 25% of sales coming from products that did not exist five years ago. GE developed **FastWorks** to roll out products faster and cheaper.[125]

Risk Taking by Entrepreneurs and Intrapreneurs. To be successful at anything requires taking calculated risks, and one of the important traits of entrepreneurs is that they are risk takers.[126] Starting a new business is risky, as there is a high failure rate, with around half of new businesses surviving less than five years.[127] So clearly, starting a new venture involves risk taking. Entrepreneurs are concerned about failure, but they don't let fear of failing stop them.[128] The risk of entrepreneurship is much greater than that of intrapreneurship.

Entrepreneurs don't actually get a real paycheck; they get profits or losses. They commonly risk personal assets, as they finance part or all of their business and run the risk of losing their investment.[129] Some entrepreneurs have lost their life savings, retirement investments, homes, cars, and other assets. As an entrepreneur, everything costs something. Are you willing to pay those costs to start a new venture?[130] **Matt Macinnis** quit his high-level marketing job working for **Steve Jobs** at **Apple** to start **Inkling**, providing a platform for publishing interactive textbooks and manuals.[131]

small business A business that is independently owned and operated with a small number of employees and relatively low volume of sales.

6-1 **SELF**-ASSESSMENT

Entrepreneurial Qualities

Have you ever thought about starting your own business? This exercise gives you the opportunity to determine whether you have entrepreneurial qualities. Each item below presents two statements describing opposite ends of a spectrum of attitudes or behavior. Below each pair of statements is a five-point scale. After reading the two statements for each item, circle the number that best represents where you see yourself on the spectrum.

1. I have a strong desire to be independent, to do things my way, and to create something new.				I like following established ways of doing things.
5	4	3	2	1
2. I enjoy taking reasonable risks.				I avoid taking risks.
5	4	3	2	1
3. I avoid making the same mistakes twice.				I often repeat my mistakes.
5	4	3	2	1
4. I can work without supervision.				I need supervision to motivate me to work.
5	4	3	2	1
5. I seek out competition.				I avoid competition.
5	4	3	2	1
6. I enjoy working long, hard hours.				I enjoy taking it easy and having plenty of personal time.
5	4	3	2	1
7. I am confident in my abilities and don't fear failing.				I lack self-confidence and fear failing.
5	4	3	2	1
8. I need to be the best and to be successful.				I'm satisfied with being average.
5	4	3	2	1
9. I have a high energy level.				I have a low energy level.
5	4	3	2	1
10. I like the challenge of solving problems.				I don't like to deal with problems.
5	4	3	2	1
11. I don't give up when things don't go my way.				I give up easily.
5	4	3	2	1
12. I look for ways to improve things.				I don't like to change things.
5	4	3	2	1

Scoring: Add up the numbers below your check marks. The total will be between 12 and 60. Note where your score fits on the continuum of entrepreneurial qualities below.

60	**50**	**40**	**30**	**20**	**12**
Strong					Weak

Entrepreneurship is clearly not for everyone. Generally, the higher/stronger your entrepreneurial score, the better your chance of being a successful entrepreneur. However, simple paper-and-pencil surveys are not always good predictors. If you had a low score but really want to start a business, you may be successful. But realize that few people have all the typical entrepreneurial qualities.

A very important risk consideration is the choice of being an entrepreneur rather than a paid employee—*opportunity cost*.[132] Often, you cannot go back if the business fails. You risk job security with a dependable salary and benefits for potential profits, which usually take a few years to earn and may never come.[133] Common leveraging advice is not to quit your day job before your business is started[134] with proven profit potential and you can pay your bills without your salary.

Raymond Berry, founder of **White Lion Brewing Company**, Springfield, Massachusetts, started the company while working full-time; utilizing the contract brewing concept mitigated the company's start up risk. The advantage of contract brewing gave the brand the opportunity to scale up production without investing in hard assets from the outset. It also allowed Berry to keep his day job. Berry noted, "It was a balancing act that cannot be underestimated; you never want to be in a position where both roles are suffering due to lack of a time commitment. Expect to work double the hours just to stay ahead of your job and company."

To support a growing demand for its products,. Berry determined White Lion wanted to have greater control over its sales and production and that led to a transition from a full-time job to being a full-time entrepreneur. Berry states, "I was realizing I was more of a detriment to the growth and success of White Lion because I was not 100% vested." In fact, many investors will not even entertain investing in a business that has its principal officer not working full time. It is not easy when you are used to a consistent paycheck and you become an entrepreneur and don't get a paycheck— you really only get business profits or losses, and your actual income can do down. Timing is key, but eventually a decision has to be made to quit your day job to grow your company.[135]

On the other hand, intrapreneurs commonly have no risk of personal investment, as the large business provides the financing, and if the venture fails, they can usually return to their prior job or a similar one. Intrapreneurs also maintain their salary and often get a raise and/ or part of the profits. However, like entrepreneurs, intrapreneurs usually work long hours. Because entrepreneurs take greater risks than intrapreneurs, their reward (like their loss) is usually greater, as all the profits are theirs.

The Entrepreneurial Process

Starting a new business is a challenging process requiring continuous action by the entrepreneur.[136] The *entrepreneurial process* includes selecting the new venture, planning the new venture, funding the new venture, and controlling the new venture. Entrepreneurship is all about recognition and exploitation of venture opportunities.[137] Because opportunity is so important to the entrepreneurial process, let's start by discussing opportunity, followed by the four steps of the process illustrated in Exhibit 6-9.

Opportunity Recognition and Exploitation. In line with entrepreneurial orientation,[138] opportunity identification is a core element in entrepreneurship.[139] Where do entrepreneurs find opportunities? They solve problems[140] as they make things faster, cheaper, and better. In a survey of fast-growing companies, 64% said they took an existing product or service and made it better, whereas 35% said they created a new product or service.[141] Highly successful entrepreneurs come up with products and services people are eager to have.[142]

**WORK
APPLICATION 6-9**

Are you interested in being an entrepreneur or an intrapreneur? What business would you like to start?

EXHIBIT 6-9   THE ENTREPRENEURIAL PROCESS

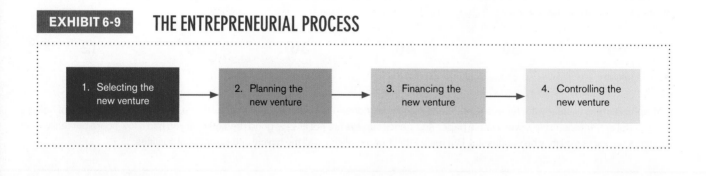

1. Selecting the new venture → 2. Planning the new venture → 3. Financing the new venture → 4. Controlling the new venture

JOIN THE DISCUSSION ETHICS & SOCIAL RESPONSIBILITY

Virtual Internships

You are familiar with the traditional internship model, in which a student works at an organization to gain experience and perhaps a full-time job after graduation. With today's Internet technology, more and more companies are hiring virtual interns, who work from their college computers. Virtual interns do a variety of tasks, including secretarial work, software and website development, and information technology (IT) projects. Most virtual interns never even set foot inside the organization's facilities.

Entrepreneurs **Nataly Kogan** and **Avi Spivack** cofounded **Natavi Guides**, a New York small business, in 2002, to publish guidebooks for students. Natavi hires virtual interns to write stories and locates people by posting openings with career offices at more than 30 universities nationwide. Kogan

estimates that Natavi saved $100,000 in overhead during the first year in business by not having to furnish office space, computers, and other equipment to interns.

1. What are the benefits of virtual internships to employers and to interns?
2. Should a student be given college credit for a virtual internship, or should he or she receive only pay without credit—a part-time job?
3. Is it ethical and socially responsible to use interns instead of regular employees?
4. Will the use of virtual interns become the norm, or will the practice fade?

We actually have lots of opportunities in our lives.[143] Lots of people say they would like to be entrepreneurs—how about you? Many of us have creative ideas for a new business, but very few of us actually take the risk and exploit the opportunity and start an innovative new venture.

Entrepreneurs don't only find opportunities, they create opportunities.[144] Here are examples of created opportunity recognition and exploitation. **Uber** and **Airbnb** are making travel cheaper than taking a taxi and staying in a hotel while giving people an opportunity to share their resources and make some money. **Roadie** is getting college students and other travelers to earn some extra pocket money by delivering packages on the way to where they're already going at a lower cost than **FedEx** and **United Parcel Service (UPS)**.[145] Social media such as **eBay** have created a platform offering business opportunities to individuals to create small businesses.

Selecting the New Venture. The first step to entrepreneurship is usually to select the new venture or the industry in which the business will compete—what type of business do you want to start? **Sandy Lerner,** co-founder of **Cisco**, says you have to offer a real product or service that fills a real need.[146] **Rhonda Abrams,** entrepreneurial consultant and author, says, It's almost impossible to beat the big guys at their own game, and by trying to sell everything to everybody. Instead, use a niche strategy.[147]

When selecting the new venture, you should have a *competitive advantage* (Chapter 5). Why should a person buy your product rather than the competitor's? If you don't have an answer, you may not be able to get enough customers to have a successful business. **Virgin** CEO **Sir Richard Branson**'s advice is don't start a business unless you are radically different from the competition.

A related concept is *first-mover advantage*, which refers to offering a unique customer value before competitors do so. **Pizza Hut** had a competitive advantage for chain pizza restaurant dining. When **Domino's** started, it did not compete directly with restaurants; it made free delivery its competitive advantage, gaining the first-mover advantage over competitors. But free delivery was easily duplicated, so Domino's lost much of its competitive advantage. However, you don't have to be a first mover to be successful. The **iPhone** and **Google** search engine weren't the first to market; they offered better products and grew. **Facebook** started with a niche strategy exclusively for college students and took market share from **MySpace** and **Friendster** and grew by appealing to a broader audience.[148] Today, Facebook has other niche competitors, such as **LinkedIn** focusing on business careers.

Before you rush off to start a new venture, you need to assess your chances of success.[149] Through marketing research, you investigate the competition and select products based on your competitive advantage. You also need to forecast sales to determine profit potential.[150] **Brian Chesky, cofounder of Airbnb**, says to keep this in mind: "When you're starting a company, it never goes at the pace you want . . . You start, you build it, and you think everyone's going to care. But no one cares, not even your friends."[151] So it takes passion and presence to succeed. Don't quit.[152] In Skill Builder 6-3 at the end of the chapter, you will select a new venture.

Planning the New Venture. After you select a new business venture, you need a plan to start it—going from intentions to entrepreneurial behavior.[153] A **business plan** *is a written description of a new venture—its objectives and the steps for achieving them.* Yes, there are successful businesses that didn't start with a business plan. But you should plan carefully before making a move into business.[154] Research supports that having a business plan is a distinguishing factor between successful and failed small businesses in multiple countries.[155]

Two very important questions to answer in the plan are "How do I make a profit?" and "When will the venture be profitable?"[156] Freebies may get you customers, but if you don't make a profit, you have a hobby, not a business. **Google** gives you a free search but makes money on ads. How do **NBC**, **ABC**, and other TV networks make money? They primarily make money (their business is) selling ads. The TV shows are the method of getting the viewers, and the more viewers, the more they can charge for the ads—think Super Bowl. **eHarmony** and **Angie's List** primarily sell subscriptions to their services. Although it ran into a growth problem, **Groupon** started out as highly successful, as it got its cut of the sale when the coupon was bought; and **Airbnb** gets fees paid by both hosts who rent their homes through the site and travelers who stay in those houses.[157] So you need to clearly state your *financials*—how you take in revenue, how you can pay your bills, and if you will be profitable, and by when. Two other important questions are "What resources do I need to start and run the business?" and "How will I get them?"[158]

Taking time to develop a business plan is crucial for survival and success.[159] For several example business plans, visit the U.S. **Small Business Administration (SBA)** website (www.sba.gov). The SBA is an excellent source of help with selecting a new business, planning it, and growing it. There are also several business-planning software programs that walk you through the process, such as **Business Plan Pro** (www.businessplanpro.com), which costs $99.95 or $159.99,[160] and **Enloop**, whose free program automatically writes your customized business plan, proves your idea, and forecasts the success of your business (www.enloop.com).[161]

The Funding and Sales Pitch. The business plan should be condensed into a clear, concise business pitch commonly called the elevator pitch, and your pitch should tell your story. The *elevator pitch* is an entrepreneur's one-minute explanation of the business and is directed at anyone who might want to provide funding for the startup. Without a good pitch, you may not get funding.[162]

Research based on the pitches made on the TV show *Shark Tank* found that the pitches with the following criteria had greater chances of getting funding.[163] So know your financials, nod and smile, be interactive (let them touch or play with stuff), and tell your story or journey about why you started the business.

The second pitch should be based on the elevator pitch, but it has a different purpose—sales. Without revenue, you don't have a business. So entrepreneurs need to develop a passion for selling. You have to persuade potential customers to buy your product. Your pitch should focus on what your product can do for the customer (better, faster, cheaper), and people react more to a fear of losing out than the pleasure of gains.[164] Yes, there is lots of rejection in sales, but success is the ability to realize you can't win them all, and it's the ability to go from failure to failure without losing your enthusiasm. Really believing in your product and being passionate keep you going.

business plan Written description of a new venture, describing its objectives and the steps for achieving them

Finance and Control the New Venture. You may have heard the expression "It takes money to make money." Before you can start the new venture, you need to answer these two questions: "Where do I get the money to acquire the resources to start and run by company?"[165] "Do I need capital from outside investors?"[166] In a survey of successful entrepreneurs, with multiple answer options, 78% said startup money came from savings, 29% said credit cards, 22% said family loans, and only 5% said bank loans; almost 50% started with less than $5,000.[167] However, a common mistake is starting without enough capital,[168] as most entrepreneurs underestimate the startup cost and operating expenses of the firm. It is recommended that you double your best estimate of the time and money you think you'll need.[169]

You usually need a good business plan to borrow money from lenders and investors. But you don't necessarily have to borrow money if you can get customers to finance your early growth, using models like **Costco** starting with an annual membership fee.[170] Many businesses are also started at home, and in a survey, close to 60% of entrepreneurs' first office was at home.[171] To help finance a business, many entrepreneurs, called hybrid entrepreneurs, including **Ray Berry** starting **White Lion**, keep their jobs until the business is doing well enough to quit and go full time. Another option is that some couples have one person working full time paying all the household bills, while the other focuses on getting the business to the point of being profitable.

When financing a startup or growing the venture, you have two options: debt (some type of loan you must repay with interest) versus equity (giving others part ownership and you must share your profits). Try to pay off debt as soon as possible,[172] and you need to be careful not to give away too much ownership equity (stock) in your company because if you do, you can get fired from the very venture you started. This happened to cofounders **Steve Jobs** at **Apple** and **Andrew Mason** at **Groupon**. **Bill Gates** didn't raise any venture capital to start **Microsoft**,[173] and when he sold stock, he kept controlling interest in his company. **Facebook cofounder Mark Zuckerberg** had a special new class of nonvoting shares that would allow him to maintain control of the company.[174]

The **SBA** has **LINC (Leveraging Information and Networks to access Capital)** "Connecting Borrowers with SBA Approved Lenders" to help small businesses find financing by providing an online matchmaking tool for small businesses and potential lenders beyond local options. Lenders provide free financial advice and specialize in microlending, smaller loans and real estate financing, and other financial products. For more information visit sba.gov/tools/linc.[175]

The last step in the entrepreneurial process is based on your business plan. Once you get the new venture up and running, how do you keep it on track? One way is hard work. In a survey of highly successful entrepreneurs, 42% said they worked some 80 hours a week, and 37% didn't take a paycheck for at least the first year.[176] We will discuss controlling in Chapters 14 and 15, but remember that planning (Chapter 5) is an ongoing process.

Steve Jobs was clearly an exceptional entrepreneur cofounding **Apple** (**IOM 5**). Jobs revolutionized at least six industries: personal computers (Apple PC), animated movies (**Pixar**), music (iPods and iTunes), phones (iPhone), tablet computing (iPad), and digital publishing (**iStudio Publisher**).[177] But he did get fired from Apple, largely because he sold so much stock that he lost management control to the board of directors. However, he rose from failure to acquire Pixar, which he sold to **Disney** and became its largest shareholder. So his net worth from Disney stock was much greater than from his Apple shares. Jobs moved on to start another computer company, which he sold to Apple, and part of the deal was for him to work for Apple. He later was asked to return to his old CEO position and turned Apple around in the 1990s to the success it maintained through his death in 2011. Today, Apple is still strongly influenced by Jobs's legacy and remains entrepreneurial offering new and improved products and services.

Trends and Issues in Management

With 95% of the world's consumers outside of the United States, *global* trade is critical to MNC growth.[178] To this end, **Apple** is planning to manufacture its products in India to boost its sales there.[179] Around 84% of global executives believe that *innovation* is extremely important to their growth strategy,[180] and culture influences creative innovations.[181] Organizational culture is related to national culture, and both cultures influence a firm's entrepreneurial orientation.[182] Although it is well known that small businesses create jobs and economic growth and that most governments offer assistance to small businesses[183] (similar to the U.S. SBA), only 10% of the adult population is involved in entrepreneurial activities in high-income countries. Thus, there is a need for further entrepreneurship education and training.[184]

There is *diversity* in entrepreneurship activity. Let's start with *gender*. Although there are few women making it to the top of MNCs (Chapter 3), women are making strides in business ownership. More males start businesses than females, but neither gender has a higher failure rate.[185] Women in the United States are starting businesses at almost four times the rate of men, but women also encounter discrimination as entrepreneurs, as they continue to face challenges accessing capital and other obstacles to growth.[186] Despite the lack of diversity in tech companies, including **Google**,[187] women-led private tech companies outperform men-led companies. So people are questioning, "Will the next **Steve Jobs** be a woman?"[188]

On the *global* scale, in almost every country, there are more men than women entrepreneurs.[189] But there are an estimated 126 million *women* starting or running new businesses in 67 countries. However, entrepreneurial activity varies widely across countries. In Pakistan, only 1% of business owners are women, whereas 40% of the business owners in Zambia are female.[190] In the United States, 36% of the business owners are women.[191]

More women are starting new ventures in traditional male-dominated industries, including **Buffalo Wild Wings**. When **founders Sally Smith** and her **chief financial officer (CFO) Mary Twinem** pitched the company's initial public offering, investors kept asking, "How can two women run a sports bar and grill?" **Brianna Wu** dared to venture into video games for females as an independent by developing **Giant Spacekat** starring kick-ass female characters from her home near Boston, and she was actually driven from her apartment by death threats.[192]

There is also U.S. diversity by *race*. Nearly a third of America's 50 richest self-made women were born abroad.[193] Of course, there are lots of successful black entrepreneurs. **Michael Jordan** is an entrepreneur, as is principal owner and chairman of the **National Basketball Association's (NBA) Charlotte Hornets**. **Jay-Z** and **Beyoncé** are just singers? Think again. Jay-Z has owned nightclubs, basketball teams, and other entrepreneurial trinkets, and his latest venture is **Tidal** to compete with **Spotify**.[194] Beyoncé cofounded ready-to-wear fashion line **House of Deréon** in 2004 with her mother, and eight years later, Beyoncé launched **shop.beyonce.com**.[195]

Age and *education* diversity also exist. Many millennials want to be and are entrepreneurs,[196] including **Snapchat's** cofounders **Evan Spiegel** and **Bobby Murphy**, who turned down a $3 billion acquisition offer from **Facebook**.[197] The elderly also start businesses, like sixth-grade dropout **KFC founder Colonel Sanders**. Although there are highly successful entrepreneurial school dropouts, many of them (64% in a survey) do recommend getting a college degree before starting a business.[198] Also, large corporations, including **Burger King**[199] and Chinese **Alibaba**,[200] are promoting younger college grads to run the business.

On the *technology* front, clearly the Internet has created opportunities for entrepreneurs to start new ventures from anywhere,[201] including from home, with very limited financial capital, and they are also getting free promotion for their businesses with the use of social media. Today, everything is mobile.[202] There are five billion phones, 40% of which are Web enabled, and in another five years, it will be 6 billion and 60%.[203] Some *big data* is collected through the survey OD intervention, as *apps* are used for employee surveys.[204] However, as discussed, people resist change. Ten years ago experts said sales of printed books would fall, as e-books would disrupt this industry. They were wrong, as sales of physical books have risen for the past three years in the United States.[205] Are you reading a softcover book or e-book?

Needless to say, entrepreneurs need to be *ethical* and *socially responsible*, and *social entrepreneurs* are starting new *social ventures* with a social mission[206] and the goal of changing the world while making a profit.[207] Some entrepreneurs, called *social entrepreneurs*, seek the opportunity to help society while making a profit.[208] They say doing good is good business.[209] **Blake Mycoskie** founded **TOMS** shoes to make money and help solve a social problem of children in Argentina having no shoes to wear, resulting in blisters, sores, and infections. His business model is "With every pair you purchase, TOMS will give a pair of new shoes to a child in need. One for One."[210] **Maxine Bédat**'s retail startup **Zady** donates a portion of each purchase to launching microbusinesses in the developing world.[211] Although you can't own and take profits from a not-for-profit organization, you can start one and get your board to pay you a good salary. **Sal Khan** started **Khan Academy** and later quit his finance job to devote himself to the tutorials.[212]

Again, corporations are being more socially responsible with *sustainability* efforts, such as **Energizer** introducing its EcoAdvanced batteries—the world's first AA battery made with 4% recycled batteries.[213]

From this chapter, you should understand the importance of managing innovation and change and how to manage it using OD interventions. Understanding the contributions of entrepreneurs to innovation is also important, as is the entrepreneurial process of creating new ventures that contribute social and economic growth.

$SAGE edge™   edge.sagepub.com/lussier8e

Want a better grade?

Get the tools you need to sharpen your study skills. Access practice quizzes, eFlashcards, video and multimedia, and more at **edge.sagepub.com/lussier8e**.

Digital Resources

Learning Objective	Digital Resource
6-1. Identify the forces for change, the types of change, and the forms of change.	▶ Disruptive Innovation
6-2. Contrast managing innovation during incremental and discontinuous change in terms of approach, goals, and strategy.	▶ How to Manage Disruptive Innovation
6-3. List the reasons employees resist change and suggest ways of overcoming such resistance.	▶ Management in Action: Managing Change*
6-4. Define organizational development and identify the steps in the Lewin and comprehensive change models.	🖥 Lewin 3-Step Change Model
6-5. Compare an entrepreneur and an intrapreneur and discuss the entrepreneurial process.	▶ Successful Entrepreneurs*

* premium video available only in the interactive eBook

• • • CHAPTER SUMMARY

6-1. Identify the forces for change, the types of change, and the forms of change.

The external environments, new technology cycles, and internal management functions are forces for change. The four types of change include strategy, structure, technology, and people. Two major forms of change are incremental and discontinuous change.

6-2. Contrast managing innovation during incremental and discontinuous change in terms of approach, goals, and strategy.

The *compression approach* is used in more certain environments during incremental change, whereas the *experimental approach* is used in more uncertain environments during discontinuous change. The *goal* during incremental change is to lower costs and incrementally improve performance and functions of the existing dominant design, whereas the goal during discontinuous change is to make significant improvements in performance and to establish a new dominant design, creating the next technology cycle. The general *strategy* used during incremental change is to continue to improve the existing technology as rapidly as possible, moving to the next-generation technology while still allowing the use of the old technology, whereas the strategy during discontinuous change is to build something new and different, a substantially better breakthrough in technology, to begin a new technology cycle that leaves the old technology obsolete.

6-3. List the reasons employees resist change, and suggest ways of overcoming such resistance.

Employees resist change because of fear of the unknown, learning anxiety, self-interest, and fear of economic loss or loss of power, status, security, or control. These forms of resistance can be overcome by establishing a positive trust climate for change, planning, clearly explaining the need for the change, pointing out how individual employees will benefit from the change, involving employees, and providing support

and evaluation for employees during the change and creating urgency.

6-4. Define organizational development and identify the steps in the Lewin and comprehensive change models.

Organizational development (OD) is the ongoing planned process of change used as a means of improving performance through interventions. The Lewin model steps are (1) unfreezing, (2) moving, and (3) refreezing. The steps in the comprehensive model are (1) recognize the need for change, (2) identify possible resistance to the change and plan how to overcome it, (3) plan the change interventions, (4) implement the change interventions, and (5) control the change.

6-5. Compare an entrepreneur and an intrapreneur and discuss the entrepreneurial process.

Entrepreneurs commonly start a new small-business venture, whereas intrapreneurs commonly start a new line of business within a large organization, or they tend to run a smaller business within a large organization. The *entrepreneurial process* includes selecting the new venture, planning the new venture, funding the new venture, and controlling the new venture.

• • • KEY TERMS

business plan, 194

change agent, 185

direct feedback, 188

discontinuous change, 176

entrepreneur, 189

forcefield analysis, 187

incremental change, 176

intrapreneur, 189

large-group intervention, 188

new venture, 189

OD interventions, 186

organizational change, 174

organizational development (OD), 185

process consultation, 187

small business, 190

stages of the change process, 180

survey feedback, 187

team building, 187

types of change, 175

• • • KEY TERM REVIEW

Complete each of the following statements using one of this chapter's key terms.

1. _____ are alterations of existing work routines and strategies that affect the whole organization.

2. The _____ are changes in strategy, structure, technology, and people.

3. _____ is continual improvement that takes place within the existing technology cycle.

4. _____ is a significant breakthrough in technology that leads to design competition and a new technology cycle.

5. The _____ are denial, resistance, exploration, and commitment.

6. _____ is the ongoing planned process of change used as a means of improving performance through interventions.

7. The _____ is the person responsible for implementing an organizational change effort.

8. _____ are specific actions taken to implement specific changes.

9. _____ is an OD intervention designed to help work groups increase structural and team dynamics and performance.

10. _____ is an OD intervention designed to improve team dynamics.

11. _____ is an OD intervention that diagrams the current level of performance, the forces hindering change, and the forces driving toward change.

12. _____ is an OD intervention that uses a questionnaire to gather data to use as the basis for change.

13. _____ is an OD technique that brings together participants from all parts of the organization, and often key outside stakeholders, to solve problems or take advantage of opportunities.

14. _____ is an OD intervention in which the change agent makes a direct recommendation for change.

15. A _____ is a new business or a new line of business.

16. _____ commonly start a new small-business venture.

17. _____ commonly start a new line of business within a large organization.

18. A _____ is a business that is independently owned and operated for profit, with a small number of employees and relatively low volume of sales.

19. A _____ is a written description of the new venture—its objectives and the steps for achieving them.

• • • REVIEW QUESTIONS

1. How do the management functions relate to change?

2. What is the difference between a change in strategy and a change in structure?

3. List the four areas of technology change.

4. What are the two forms of change?

5. What are the characteristics of an innovative culture?

6. What are the two approaches to managing innovation?

7. What are the four stages in the change process?

8. What are the five major reasons employees resist change?

9. What are the three major sources and focuses of resistance to change?

10. Explain the difference between team building and process consultation.

11. State the difference in the use of forcefield analysis and survey feedback.

12. What is a new venture, and who starts it?

13. How do you define *small business*?

14. What are competitive and first-mover advantages?

• • • COMMUNICATION SKILLS

The following critical-thinking questions can be used for class discussion and/or as written assignments to develop communication skills. Be sure to give complete explanations for all questions.

1. How does the systems effect relate to the four types of change?

2. Which type of change is the most important?

3. Do you believe that organizational change today is more slow/incremental (calm-water canoeing) or radical (whitewater rafting)?

4. Do you consider yourself to be a creative and innovative person? Why or why not?

5. Would you prefer to work during a time of incremental or discontinuous change?

6. Which stage of the change process is the most difficult to overcome?

7. Which of the five reasons for resisting change do you believe is most common?

8. Which of the seven ways to overcome resistance to change do you believe is the most important?

9. Does creating urgency really help to get people to change? Give at least one example to support your position.

10. As a manager, which, if any, OD interventions would you use?

11. Would you rather work for a small or large business? Why?

CASES

• • • Case 6-1   Chobani

Chobani LLC, is a producer and marketer of Greek yogurt. The company was founded in 2005 by Hamdi Ulukaya, an immigrant from Turkey, who recognized the lack of options for high-quality yogurt in the United States. The company is headquartered in Norwich, New York, and it employs approximately 2,000 employees. It operates two manufacturing plants—its original facility in central New York and a second new state-of-the-art facility in Twin Falls, Idaho.

The mission of the company is "To provide better food for more people. We believe that access to nutritious, delicious yogurt made with only natural ingredients is a right, not a privilege. We believe every food maker has a responsibility to provide people with better options, which is why we're so proud of the way our food is made." Chobani's core values are integrity, craftsmanship, innovation, leadership, people, and giving back.

The company's beginning in 2005 occurred when Hamdi Ulukaya discovered a notice about an old Kraft yogurt factory in South Edmeston that was closed. He decided to obtain a business loan in order to purchase it. Between 2005 and 2007, Ulukaya worked with four former Kraft employees and yogurt master Mustafa Dogan to develop the recipe for Chobani Greek Yogurt. Between 2007 and 2009, the company started to sell its yogurt in local grocery stores including Stop and Shop and ShopRite. By 2010, Chobani Greek yogurt became the best selling Greek yogurt in the United States. The company pursued global expansion by entering Australia in 2011 and the United Kingdom in 2012. In 2013, the company opened its international headquarters in Amsterdam, and Hamdi Ulukaya was named the Ernst and Young World Entrepreneur of the Year.

Chobani has achieved its success in large part due to its ability to innovate in its product lineup. For example, in 2016, it launched a new line of yogurt drinks, more flavors of its Flip mix-in product, and even a concept café in Manhattan.

The company also created a food incubator program that is designed to provide resources, expertise (e.g., brand and marketing, packaging and pricing), and funding to small, young companies that have promising ideas for new natural foods that they aspire to develop.

Although Hamdi Ulukaya has been extremely successful in his founding and establishment of Chobani, he has recognized that there are some key lessons learned from his experience as the head of a young but very successful and industry-leading company. These include the importance of hiring people with functional experience such as marketing, supply chain, logistics, operations, and quality control, as they were essential to the smooth operation of the company. In addition, remembering to respect the competition and not to underestimate it is critical, as Chobani's two main competitors, Dannon and Yoplait, launched their own Greek yogurt lines, and they were able to win back some of Chobani's market share over time.

Discussion Questions

1. What types of changes is Chobani planning to establish itself as a company?

2. How does Chobani possess an innovative structure and culture?

3. How does Chobani manage change effectively?

4. How did Hamdi Ulukaya engage in the entrepreneurial process in establishing Chobani?

5. Think about managing change at a personal level. Why is it so hard for so many people to change their behavior or way of thinking? Are these personal challenges to managing change also relevant to managing change in organizations?

6. What can you learn from Hamdi Ulukaya about what is needed to become a successful entrepreneur?

References

http://www.globaladvisors.biz/inc-feed/20170213/why-chobani-is-one-of-the-most-innovative-companies-of-2017/

http://www.pymnts.com/news/retail/2016/chobani-and-the-surprising-innovative-world-of-yogurt/

http://www.chobani.com/core/wp-content/uploads/2013/04/Chobani-Media-Kit-2013.pdf

http://www.chobani.com/blog/2013/06/chobani-founder-and-ceo-hamdi-ulukaya-named-ernst-young-world-entrepreneur-of-the-year-2013/

http://www.chobanifoodincubator.com

http://blog.gocatalant.com/5-success-lessons-entrepreneurs-can-learn-from-chobani/

https://www.wsj.com/articles/at-chobani-rocky-road-from-startup-status-1431909152

http://www.chobani.com/history

http://www.bloomberg.com/research/stocks/private/snapshot.asp?privcapId=51756380

Case created by Loren Kuzuhara, University of Wisconsin–Madison.

• • • Case 6-2   Sir Richard Branson in the Pilot Seat: Flying High With Virgin Airlines

Sir Richard Branson is the slightly eccentric founder of U.K.–based Virgin Group, which consists of more than 400 companies around the world, including airlines Virgin Atlantic and Virgin America, wireless company Virgin Mobile, and the international health club Virgin Active.(1)

Richard Branson is well known as the guru of entrepreneurship. You could call him a change agent in his own company, since he is always inspiring everyone who works for him to look for industries they can enter and provide the spark for a discontinuous change on the way business is done in that industry.

Branson started his first business when he was 16 and, in 1972, opened a chain of record stores, Virgin Records, that kick-started his Virgin brand globally. His business ventures have included a vodka line, financial services brand, a private 74-acre island for rent, and even a soft drink line, Virgin Cola.

Branson believes his main goal is to change industries—not just keep them the same. He feels that trying to change industries makes employees want to achieve more than what competitors have ever achieved in their industry.

If you read enough of Branson's books and articles in entrepreneurship magazines, you will realize he brings his eccentric behavior to classic organizational change concepts such as leadership, building teams, managing the change process, creating discontinuous change in industries, and being willing to take a risk and developing your organization. Branson is a little like that eccentric, wacky uncle who comes over to visit once a year—except he runs more than 400 companies and is one of the richest men in the world after starting his empire from scratch.

Branson often writes about what it was like when he started his business. In an interesting twist, he wrote about what he learned as a small entrepreneur and how those lessons are still being applied to his modern-day business empire.

So what are the lessons he learned that he still applies? What are the similarities between managing one business and managing 400 businesses? Are any of these lessons applicable to other business owners?

1. Surround yourself with good people no matter what size your business is.
2. If you treat your employees right, they will treat your customers right, and sustained profits will follow.
3. Launch a new business with the same energy and enthusiasm as you did with your first business—it will help create momentum.
4. You have to win customers away from your competitors. You have to surprise and delight customers by offering something different.
5. You have to experience failures, changing your business along the way. It takes experience to properly change your internal management structure to match external opportunities to work with new partners and start new businesses.
6. Although making decisions with your gut is important, Branson now uses teams of people to analyze data about economic, consumer, and population trends while looking for new products and opportunities. He believes that the education and health care industries are looking for opportunities to work with successfully branded companies.(2)

He recently updated his list based upon his discussions and observations with the top entrepreneurs who run multibillion-dollar operations—household-name businesses like Apple, Microsoft, Google, and Amazon. He has come to realize that there are five distinctive traits for any successful entrepreneur:

Takes Calculated Risks

The luckiest people in business are those that are prepared to take the greatest risks. We can all create our own luck by taking the necessary risks to open the door to change, progression, and success.

Learns From Failure

Every successful entrepreneur has learned from failure. Nobody gets everything right the first time. Business is like a giant game of chess—you have to learn quickly from your mistakes. Successful entrepreneurs do not fear failure; they learn from it and move on.

Sees the Bigger Picture

When we began Virgin, I did not see it as an end in itself, a noun; I saw it as the beginning of a whole range of services, an adjective. Successful entrepreneurs take an idea and let it fly.(3)

Delegates Wisely

To see the bigger picture, an entrepreneur needs to learn how to delegate effectively. It's a fairy tale to think that you can do everything by yourself—it's vital to the success of your business that you learn to hand off those things that you aren't able to do well.

Communicates Effectively

Communication makes the world go round. It facilitates human connections and allows us to learn, grow and progress. It is not just about speaking or reading but understanding what is being said—and in some cases what is not being said. I believe that communication is the most important skill any entrepreneur can possess.(4)

Global competition driven by technological change, the fluctuating political landscape, terrorism, and social media are pressuring Virgin to change. Will Branson continue to be the change agent of the Virgin Group or become a reactor to change?

Discussion Questions

1. Is the pressure for Richard Branson to change Virgin's business strategy coming from the internal or external environment?
2. In order to better compete with its rivals, should Virgin focus on a change in strategy, structure, technology, or people?
3. Is Virgin in the denial, resistance, exploration, or commitment stage when it enters new industries?
4. Is Virgin an innovative company?
5. Is Virgin currently at the unfreezing, moving, or refreezing stage of the Lewin model?
6. Which of the following organizational development interventions could Virgin most benefit from?
7. Use the five steps of the comprehensive change model to explain Virgin's business strategy.

Cumulative Case Questions

8. Discuss Richard Branson's management functions in implementing Virgin's strategy (Chapter 1). Richard Branson does a great job with all four functions—he plans to enter new businesses, he motivates his employees to be creative, he is an inspiring leader and entrepreneur, and he controls his businesses; otherwise the businesses will be divested for poor performance (such as Virgin Records).
9. What external environmental factors were most influential in Virgin changing its business strategy (Chapter 2)? Branson is very good at appealing to consumers with lower prices (such as Virgin Mobile with no long-term contracts), while the global economy has had slow financial growth. Branson does a good job of taking advantage of changes in technology in industries such as music, cell phone service, and airline service.
10. What type of grand strategy is Virgin pursuing (Chapter 4)? Virgin is always using a grand strategy of growth. His entrepreneurial inclinations have him looking for opportunities to work with successfully branded companies

while trying to reshape industry landscapes in order to find the next big product, service or market.

References

(1) Branson, R. (2013, September 16). Richard Branson on the secret of Virgin's sustained success. *Entrepreneur*. Retrieved August 24, 2015, from http://www.entrepreneur.com/article/228382#ixzz2fXCblflp

(2) Ibid.

(3) Branson, R. (2017, January 30). Five skills and abilities that entrepreneurs share. Retrieved February 2, 2017, from https://www.virgin.com/richard-branson/5-skills-and-abilities-successful-entrepreneursshare

(4) Ibid.

Case created by Herbert Sherman, Long Island University.

● ● ● SKILL BUILDER 6-1: IDENTIFYING RESISTANCE TO CHANGE

Objective

To improve your skill at identifying resistance to change.

Skills

The primary skills developed through this exercise are:

1. *Management skill*—decision making (conceptual, diagnostic, analytical, and critical-thinking skills are needed to understand resistance to change)

2. *AACSB competency*—analytic skills and application of knowledge

3. Management function—organizing

Preparing for Skill Builder 6-1

Below are 10 statements made by employees who have been asked to make a change on the job. Identify the source and focus of their resistance using Exhibit 6-5. Because it is difficult to identify intensity of resistance on paper, skip the intensity factor. However, when you deal with people on the job, you need to identify the intensity. Place the number of the box (1–9) that best represents the resistance on the line in front of each statement.

_____ 1. "But we never did the job that way before. Can't we just do it the same way as always?"

_____ 2. The tennis coach asked Jill, the star player, to have Rashida as her doubles partner. Jill said, "Come on, Rashida is a lousy player. Ria is better; don't break us up." The coach disagreed and forced Jill to accept Rashida.

_____ 3. The manager, Winny, told Marco to stop letting everyone in the department take advantage of him by sticking him with extra work. Marco said, "But I like my coworkers, and I want them to like me, too. If I don't help people, they may not like me."

_____ 4. "I can't learn how to use the new computer. I'm not smart enough to use it."

_____ 5. The police sergeant asked Chris, a patrol officer, to take a rookie cop as her partner. Chris said, "Do I have to? I broke in the last rookie. He and I are getting along well."

_____ 6. An employee asked Loc, the manager, if she could change the work-order form. Loc said, "That would be a waste of time; the current form is fine."

_____ 7. Diane, an employee, is busy at work. Her supervisor tells her to stop what she is doing and begin a new project. Diane says, "The job I'm working on now is more important."

_____ 8. "I don't want to work with that work team. It has the lowest performance record in the department."

_____ 9. A restaurant worker tells the restaurant manager, "Keep me in the kitchen. I can't work in the bar because drinking is against my religion."

_____ 10. "But I don't see why I have to stop showing pictures of people burning in a fire to help get customers to buy our smoke detector system. I don't think it's unethical. Our competitors do it."

Apply It

What did I learn from this experience? How will I use this knowledge in the future?

● ● ● SKILL BUILDER 6-2: MANAGING CHANGE AT YOUR COLLEGE

Objective

To better understand the need for change, resistance to change, and how to overcome resistance.

Skills

The primary skills developed through this exercise are:

1. *Management skill*—decision making (organizing requires conceptual skills)

2. *AACSB competencies*—analytic skills, reflective thinking skills, and application of knowledge

3. *Management function*—organizing

Preparing for Skill Builder 6-2

As an individual, group, or class, select a change you would like to see implemented at your college. Answer the following questions and conduct a forcefield analysis.

1. State the change you would like to see implemented.

2. State which of the four types of change it is.

3. Identify any possible resistance(s) to the change.

4. Select strategies for overcoming the resistance(s).

5. Conduct a forcefield analysis for the change. Write the present situation in the center and the forces that hinder

the change and the forces that can help get the change implemented, using Exhibit 6-8 as an example.

Hindering Forces   Present Situation   Driving Forces

Apply It

What did I learn from this experience? How will I use this knowledge in the future?

• • • SKILL BUILDER 6-3: SELECTING A NEW VENTURE

Objective

To develop a simple business plan idea.

Skills

The primary skills developed through this exercise are:

1. *Management skill*—decision making
2. *AACSB competency*—analytic and application of knowledge
3. *Management function*—planning

Select Your New Venture

Would you like to be your own boss? Have you given any thought to running your own business someday? For this exercise, you will think of a new venture you would like to start someday. The new venture can be entrepreneurial or intrapreneurial. With either approach, don't be concerned about financing the business. At this stage, you are only selecting a new venture. If you select intrapreneurship, you don't have to be working for the organization for which you would like to start a new venture. Provide information about your potential business in the following list. Give all of the topics some thought before writing down your final answers.

1. Company name (or line of business)
2. Products (goods and/or services)
3. Target market (potential customer profile)
4. Mission statement (Chapters 2 and 5)
5. Environment competitive analysis (Chapter 5, five forces, and SWOT)
6. Competitive advantage (Will you have a first-mover advantage?)
7. Possible location of business (home, mall, downtown, near college, etc.)
8. The issues and problems that need to be addressed through strategic planning

Apply It

What did I learn from this skill-building experience? How will I use this knowledge in the future?

Your instructor may ask you to do Skill Builder 6-3 in class in a group. If so, the instructor will provide you with any necessary information or additional instructions.

• • • SKILL BUILDER 6-4: DEVELOPING A NEW HABIT

Objective

To develop a new habit.

Skills

The primary skills developed through this exercise are:

1. *Management skill*—decision making
2. *AACSB competency*—analytic and application of knowledge
3. *Management function*—planning

Develop a New Habit

It is important to understand the contents of the subsection "Our Resistance to Change—Habits" on page 182. Realizing the importance of having a positive attitude and thoughts about a change, select a new habit you want to develop, such as (A.) better study habits or (B.) losing weight. Now set an objective, for example, to study nine hours a week or to lose five pounds by June 30. Next develop a cue, routine, and reward like the examples below.

1. **Cue**. A. Set a schedule of study in your appointment book/calendar to remind you it's time to study. B. Put a note about diet on fridge.
2. **Routine**. A. Study on Sunday, Monday, and Wednesday from 6:00 to 9:00. B. Drink water (no sugar/diet drinks) and no snacks—eating between meals.
3. **Reward**. A and B. Feel better about yourself. A. Better grades. B. Special snack on Sunday. Lower weight resulting in looking and feeling better.

Let's be honest. We will most likely slip and miss a study session or cheat on our diet. The question is, how do you handle the slip? Are you going to give up and go back to your old habits, or will you get back to your new routine? Caution—once you slip, and the more often you slip, the easier it is to go back to your old habits.

Apply It

What did I learn from this experience? How will I use this knowledge in the future?

7 Organizing and Delegating Work

••• LEARNING OBJECTIVES

After studying this chapter, you should be able to:

7-1. Explain the difference between mechanistic and organic organizations and the environments in which they are more effective. PAGE 206

7-2. Contrast formal and informal authority, centralized and decentralized authority, and line and staff authority. PAGE 210

7-3. Define what an organization chart is, list the four aspects of a firm that it shows, and describe the four traditional departmentalization designs. PAGE 212

7-4. Discuss the two multiple forms of departmentalization and five contemporary designs. PAGE 215

7-5. Classify each of the nine job designs under the three job design option categories. PAGE 219

7-6. Explain how to set priorities by answering three priority-determination questions, and list the four steps in the delegation process. PAGE 222

| IOM | # Ideas on Management
at Tesla Motors |

Tesla Motors intends to supercharge the public's passion for electric vehicles. Founded in 2003, the company designs, manufactures, and markets high-performance, technologically advanced electric cars and powertrain components. Tesla sells two models: the Model S, a saloon, and the Model X, an SUV, which are among the world's top-selling electric cars. The fuel-efficient, fully electric vehicles recharge their lithium-ion batteries from an outlet and, depending on a driver's speed, are capable of approaching 300 miles per charge. Tesla is gearing up for the launch of the Model 3, an affordable family sedan, in 2018. Tesla **CEO Elon Musk** founded **PayPal** and runs **SpaceX** and **SolarCity**. Tesla operates through 208 stores and service locations. Its rapidly expanding supercharger network counts 4,749 superchargers at 751 supercharger stations. North America accounts for nearly 50% of sales, followed by Norway (9%) and China (8%), and other areas (35%). In late 2016, Tesla made its most important acquisition to date when it purchased SolarCity in a deal valued at $2.6 billion. By combining Tesla's new electric vehicles with SolarCity's newest solar products, the companies expect to lower hardware costs, reduce installation costs, and improve their manufacturing efficiency.

Tesla Motors, Inc. has an organizational structure that supports continuous business growth. The organizational structure takes a traditional form, considering the company has limited approach to its production facility development. As a major producer of fully electric automobiles, Tesla uses its corporate structure to facilitate extensive control of the organization. The company also maximizes its ability to implement new strategies and manage its operational activities through its organizational structure.

Global Hierarchy. The most significant characteristic of Tesla's corporate structure is global hierarchy. Global hierarchy involves offices that oversee domestic and international operations. In Tesla's organizational structure, the following offices direct and represent the global hierarchy:

1. Chairman & Chief Executive Officer

2. Chief Financial Officer

3. Chief Technology Officer

4. Vice President—Vehicle Engineering

5. Vice President—Powertrain Operations

6. Vice President—North America Sales

7. Chief Designer

8. Vice President—Manufacturing

9. Vice President—Autopilot Hardware Engineering

10. Vice President—Worldwide Services & Deliveries

11. General Counsel

Minimal Regional Divisions. This characteristic of the corporate structure focuses on the extent of divisions in Tesla's automotive business. These divisions are used to implement different strategies and marketing campaigns and to organize financial records and reports. Tesla's organizational structure has the following divisions, mainly used for financial reporting:

1. United States

2. China

3. Norway

4. Other

Tesla Motors, Inc. benefits from its organizational structure in terms of effective control of global operations. Another advantage is the ease of implementing new strategies throughout the organization. Also, the minimal regional divisions support not just financial reporting and analysis but also possible future regionalization of strategies and tactics in the automotive business. These advantages empower Tesla to use its organizational structure for further international growth. However, a disadvantage of Tesla's corporate structure is the rigidity that limits rapid adjustment in the organization. For example, global centralization is a structural characteristic that limits the ability of overseas offices to readily respond to issues they experience in their respective regional markets.

Sources: Information for this case was taken from: M. Geldhill (n.d.). "Tesla Inc." *Hoovers.* Retrieved July 3, 2017, from http://0-subscriber .hoovers.com.liucat.lib.liu.edu/H/company360/fulldescription.html?companyId=15931000000000; P. Meyer. (Feb. 21, 2017). "Tesla Motors, Inc.'s Organizational Structure, Characteristics." Panmore Institute. Retrieved July 3, 2017, from http://panmore.com/ tesla-motors-inc-organizational-structure-characteristics-analysis

Herbert Sherman contributed to the Ideas on Management feature in this chapter.

IOM 1.   Where is Tesla on the mechanistic and organic continuum?

IOM 2.   Is Tesla more centralized or decentralized?

IOM 3.   What is Tesla's organizational design?

IOM 4.   Given Tesla's organizational design, how does the company design employees' jobs?

IOM 5.   What delegation issues does Tesla face with its regional divisions?

IOM 6.   How is Tesla using technology to run its business?

IOM 7.   How is Tesla implementing its values and demonstrating its social responsibility?

IOM 8.   Have you taken a ride in a Tesla and/or thought about owning one?

You'll find answers to these **IOM** questions throughout the chapter. To learn more about Tesla, visit www.tesla.com.

Get the edge on your studies. edge.sagepub .com/lussier8e

- Take a quiz to find out what you've learned.
- Review key terms with eFlashcards.
- Watch videos that enhance chapter content.

LO 7-1

Explain the difference between mechanistic and organic organizations and the environments in which they are more effective.

Organizational Considerations and Principles

Managers design formal structures to organize a company's resources,[1] and structure influences innovative entrepreneurial orientation[2] (Chapter 6). Organizing, the second function of management, is defined as the process of delegating and coordinating tasks and resources to achieve objectives (Chapter 1). When designing an entire organization, there are some things to consider and principles to follow. These are the topics of this section.

Organizational Considerations

Here are some things to consider and questions to answer when organizing the entire company.

Mechanistic Versus Organic Organization and the Environment. As the structure of the firm must align with the environment in which it operates,[3] overall there are two major forms of organization that are more effective in different environments—stable and dynamic[4] (Chapter 3). **Mechanistic organizations** *are bureaucratic, focusing on following procedures and rules through tight controls and having specialized jobs, with decisions being made by*

mechanistic organizations
Bureaucratic organizations, focusing on following procedures and rules through tight controls and specialized jobs, with top managers making decisions.

EXHIBIT 7-1   ORGANIZING QUESTIONS

Questions for Managers	Chapter Topic
To whom should departments and individuals report?	Chain of command; organization chart (pp. 207, 212)
How many individuals should report to each manager?	Span of management (p. 208)
How should we subdivide the work?	Division of labor (p. 208)
How do we get everyone to work together as a system?	Coordination (p. 208)
At what level should decisions be made?	Centralization vs. decentralization of authority (p. 210)
How do we organize to meet our mission and strategy?	Departmentalization (p. 214)

top managers. This model tends to work well in stable environments, in which uniformity and the traditional command and control are important.[5] Conversely, **organic organizations** *are flexible, with minimal focus on procedures and rules, broadly defined jobs, and decisions made at lower levels.* This model tends to work well in the current trend of more dynamic environments.[6]

Although there are two forms, they are really on a continuum between being mechanistic and being organic. Many companies are organized somewhere between the two extremes but can be more identified overall with one form or the other. It is also common for some parts like manufacturing to be mechanistic, whereas research, design, and marketing are organic. **Tesla (IOM 1)** is closer to the mechanistic side of the continuum, as Tesla organizational structure takes a traditional form, considering the company has limited approach to its production facility development. Tesla uses its corporate structure to facilitate extensive control of the organization.

Strategy, Size, and Technology. As discussed in Chapter 5, companies develop strategies, and thus, company organizational structure must be designed to achieve the strategic objectives.[7] As companies change strategies to align with the external environment, they tend to change their structure.[8] With innovative growth strategies in a dynamic environment, organic structures tend to work well, whereas with a stability strategy in a stable environment, mechanistic structures tend to work well (see Chapter 1). Generally, the larger the firm, the more mechanistic it becomes, but highly innovative companies can be organic. Companies that use mass-production technology tend to use a more mechanistic organization, whereas firms with more custom-made products tend to be organic. But again, most companies are between the two extremes.

Organization Questions. There are at least six questions that you need to answer when organizing. The questions are listed in Exhibit 7-1. The answers are discussed in more detail in the indicated topic sections of this chapter.

Principles of Organization

Exhibit 7-2 lists the organizational principles generally followed by companies that we discuss in this section. Note that not all companies follow all of the guidelines. You will learn that there is a difference in their use by organic and mechanistic organizations.

Unity of Command and Direction. The principle of *unity of command* requires that each employee report to only one boss. When there are two bosses, you can often get two conflicting messages. Recalling the importance of being goal oriented and setting objectives[9] (Chapters 1 and 5), the principle of *unity of direction* requires that all activities be directed toward the same objectives. Unity of command and direction is more closely enforced in mechanistic organizations than in organic ones.

Chain of Command. *Chain of command*, also known as the *Scalar Principle*, is the clear line of authority from the top to the bottom of an organization, forming a hierarchy,[10] which

organic organizations Flexible organizations with minimal focus on procedures and rules, broadly defined jobs, and decisions made at lower levels.

EXHIBIT 7-2	PRINCIPLES OF ORGANIZATION

- Unity of command and direction
- Chain of command
- Span of management (flat and tall organizations)
- Division of labor (specialization, departmentalization, integration)
- Coordination
- Balanced responsibility and authority
- Delegation
- Flexibility

WORK APPLICATION 7-1

Follow the chain of command from your present position (or one you held in the past) to the top of the organization. Start by identifying anyone who reported to you; then list your boss's title, your boss's boss's title, and so on up to the top manager's title.

WORK APPLICATION 7-2

Identify your boss's span of management, or your own if you are or were a manager. How many levels of management are there in your organization? Is it a flat or a tall organization?

span of management The number of employees reporting to a manager.

responsibility The obligation to achieve objectives by performing required activities.

authority The right to make decisions, issue orders, and use resources.

is illustrated in the organization chart.[11] All members of the firm should know whom they report to and who, if anyone, reports to them. The chain of command is clearer and more closely followed in mechanistic organizations.

Span of Management. The **span of management** (or span of control[12]) *refers to the number of employees reporting to a manager.* The fewer employees supervised, the smaller or narrower the span of management, and vice versa. The trend is to increase the span.[13] The span of management in an organization is related to the number of its organizational levels, which determines its organizational height. In a *tall organization*, there are many levels with narrow spans of management. In a *flat organization*, there are few levels with wide spans of management. Mechanistic organizations tend to be taller. In recent years, many organizations have flattened[14] by cutting out layers of management, including **Zappos**, which eliminated all managers.[15] **ContextMedia** has 12 department heads creating a management team as the only layer of management in the 160-person company.[16]

Division of Labor. With *division of labor,* employees have specialized jobs. Related functions are grouped together under a single boss. Employees generally have specialized jobs in a functional area such as accounting, production, or sales. Mechanistic organizations have a greater division of labor.

Coordination. *Coordination* and collaboration ensure that all departments and individuals within an organization work together,[17] and coordination increases both team and firm performance.[18] **Paul Lawrence** and **Jay Lorsch** coined the terms *differentiation* and *integration.*[19] *Differentiation* refers to the need to break the organization into departments, and *integration* refers to the need to coordinate the departmental activities,[20] it's a balancing act.[21] Coordination is generally easier in mechanistic organizations that have formal structures that facilitate coordination.[22]

Balanced Responsibility and Authority. With balanced responsibility and authority, the responsibilities of each individual in the organization are clearly defined in mechanistic firms. Each individual is also given the authority necessary to meet these responsibilities and is held accountable for meeting them.[23]

Responsibility *is the obligation to achieve objectives by performing required activities.* When objectives are set, the people responsible for achieving them should be clearly identified. Managers are responsible for the performance of their units. We need to take responsibility for our behavior,[24] and don't deny or blame others for our actions when justly criticized.[25]

Authority *is the right to make decisions, issue orders, and use resources.* You should be given responsibility and authority for achieving objectives. The CEO is responsible for the results of the entire organization and delegates authority down the chain of command to the lower-level managers, who are responsible for meeting operational objectives.

Accountability is the evaluation of how well individuals meet their responsibilities. Managers are accountable for everything that happens in their departments. As a manager, you delegate responsibility and authority to perform tasks, but you should realize that you can never delegate "your" accountability.

Delegation. Delegation *is the process of assigning responsibility and authority for accomplishing objectives.* Responsibility and authority are delegated down the chain of command. Delegation is important to success[26] and will be covered in detail later in this chapter. But for now, you should realize that delegation only takes place when you give an employee a new task. If tasks are already part of employees' job and you ask them to do a task, it's not delegation. Delegating tends to be used more often in organic organizations, as jobs are not as clearly defined and employees are expected to do a wider variety of tasks.

Start-up organizations often use organic structures that allow for more flexibility.

Flexibility. Employees in mechanistic organizations focus on following company rules;[27] they fear getting into trouble for breaking or bending the rules. Organic organization employees are allowed to be more flexible and make exceptions to the procedures and rules to create customer satisfaction.[28] Employees are expected to be flexible and come up with quick solutions to problems.[29] With flexibility comes accountability for producing results.[30] Are you willing to be flexible and seize unexpected opportunities?[31]

Authority

In this section, you will learn about formal and informal authority, levels of authority, centralized and decentralized authority, and line and staff authority.

WORK
APPLICATION 7-3

Does an organization you work for or have worked for emphasize following the standing procedures or being flexible? Explain your answer.

delegation The process of assigning responsibility and authority for accomplishing objectives.

7-1 APPLYING THE CONCEPT

Principles of Organization

Identify which organizational principle or principles are represented by each statement.

A. unity of command and direction

B. chain of command

C. span of management

D. division of labor

E. coordination

F. balanced responsibility and authority

G. delegation

H. flexibility

_____ 1. "Tom told me to use his computer to get some information for him. But when I got to the computer, it was turned off, and when it booted up, I didn't have Tom's password, so I couldn't get the information."

_____ 2. "Tonya handles all the accounts receivable transactions, and Ed does all the accounts payable transactions."

_____ 3. "I know it will be difficult to supervise 19 employees reporting to you, Brenda, but after cutting two managers, we all have to take on more employees."

_____ 4. "He is a good customer, Helen, so make him happy. Ignore the rule and give him a cash refund without the sales receipt."

_____ 5. "To make your job more interesting, Sean, I'm going to assign a new task to you."

_____ 6. "My department manager, Rick, tells me to do one thing, but my project manager, Betty, tells me to do something else at the same time. Whom should I listen to?"

_____ 7. "I need Carlos to do some research for me, but as a middle manager, I can't give an operative employee a direct order to do it. I have to have my supervisor, Chris, give Carlos the assignment for me."

_____ 8. "The ambulance is on the way. Anita, call Dr. Rodriguez and have her get to emergency room A in 10 minutes. Aaron, prepare emergency room A. Juan, get the paperwork ready."

LO 7-2

Contrast formal and informal authority, centralized and decentralized authority, and line and staff authority.

Formal and Informal Authority and Scope and Levels of Authority

It is helpful to distinguish authority from power, to distinguish between formal and informal authority, and to understand the scope and level of your authority for a given task.

Authority Versus Power. Managers hold positions of power and authority,[32] but authority is different from power structure;[33] power is broader in scope. The organization gives managers and employees formal authority to do the job, and managers are given positions of hierarchical power.[34] However, *power* is the ability to influence others. So you can be a manager without any real power, and you can have power without being a manager. We will discuss power in Chapter 10.

Formal and Informal Authority. *Formal authority* (or structure) is based on the specified relationships among employees. It is the sanctioned way of getting the job done. The organization chart (see LO 7-3) illustrates formal authority and shows the lines of authority. *Informal authority* arises from the patterns of relationships and communication that evolve as employees interact and communicate.[35] It is the unsanctioned way of getting the job done. Formal authority is common in mechanistic organizations, whereas informal authority is more accepted in organic organizations.

Scope of Authority. The *scope of authority* is a hierarchy that narrows as it flows from the top down through the organization.[36] A president has more authority than a vice president, who has more authority than a manager. Responsibility and authority are delegated[37] and flow down the organization, whereas accountability flows up the organization, as Exhibit 7-3 illustrates.

EXHIBIT 7-3   SCOPE OF AUTHORITY

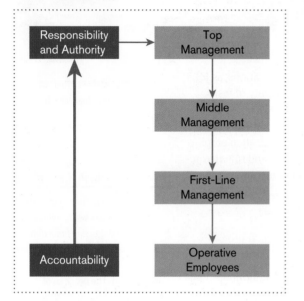

Levels of Authority. The **levels of authority** *are the authority to inform, the authority to recommend, the authority to report, and full authority.*

WORK
APPLICATION 7-4

Identify and explain your level of authority for a specific task in an organization.

1. *The authority to inform.* You inform your supervisor of possible alternative actions. The supervisor has the authority to make the decision.

2. *The authority to recommend.* You list alternative decisions/actions, analyze them, and recommend one action. However, you may not implement the recommendation without the boss's OK. The boss may require a different alternative if he or she does not agree with the recommendation. Committees are often given authority to recommend.

3. *The authority to report.* You may freely select a course of action and carry it out. However, afterward you must report the action taken to the boss.

4. *Full authority.* You may freely make decisions and act without the boss's knowledge. However, even people with full authority may consult their bosses for advice.

WORK
APPLICATION 7-5

Describe the type of authority (centralized or decentralized) used in an organization you work for or have worked for.

levels of authority The authority to inform, the authority to recommend, the authority to report, and full authority.

centralized authority Important decisions are made by top managers.

decentralized authority Important decisions are made by middle and first-line managers.

Centralized and Decentralized Authority

The major distinction between centralized and decentralized authority lies in who makes the important decisions.[38] With **centralized authority**, *important decisions are made by top managers.* With **decentralized authority**, *important decisions are made by middle and first-line managers.* Decentralization pushes authority and accountability further down the line.[39] It contrasts controlling versus empowering employees.[40]

Which type of authority works best? There is no simple answer, as it depends on the situation. The major advantages of centralization are control and reduced duplication of work. The major advantages of decentralization are efficiency and flexibility. Mechanistic organizations tend to use centralized authority, whereas organic ones tend to use decentralized authority. **Tesla (IOM 2)** is more centralized and uses this type of organizational structure to effectively control its global operations. The minimal regional divisions support not just financial reporting and analysis but also possible future regionalization of strategies and tactics in the automotive business. These advantages empower Tesla to use its organizational structure for further international growth. **Berkshire Hathaway** has more than 60 operating units, and each one has its own decentralized authority.[41]

Authority is a continuum, with centralized authority at one end and decentralized authority at the other. Most organizations lie somewhere between the two extremes but can be classified overall. On the continuum, **McDonald's** is closer to being centralized; however, it is now giving regional managers the authority to offer new food items to meet local consumer tastes and preferences.[42] The key to success seems to be having the right balance between the two extremes. **Gap** now realizes it has to change faster with fashion trends, so it is now more decentralized.[43]

Micromanagement. Micromanagement *is a management style generally used as a negative term for when a manager closely observes or controls the work of his or her employees.* They are also called old-fashioned bossy managers.[44] Rather than giving general instructions on tasks and then devoting time to supervising larger concerns, the micromanager monitors and assesses every step of a business process and avoids delegation of decisions. Allowing employees to make decisions and act without having to get permission all the time clearly increases the speed of getting the job done. Micromanagers need to learn to trust employees and delegate more.[45] **Cofounder and CEO Jeff Greenfield** of **C3 Metrics** says that since he stepped back from being a micromanager, he has time to focus on long-term strategic thinking and has pursued opportunities that have grown the business.[46] Micromanaging is more common with centralized authority.

Line and Staff Authority

There are differences between line and staff authority, and staff can be generalist or specialist.

Line Versus Staff Authority. Line authority *is the responsibility to make decisions and issue orders down the chain of command.* **Staff authority** *is the responsibility to advise and assist other personnel.* Line managers are primarily responsible for achieving the organization's objectives and directly bringing revenue into the organization, and staff people provide them with services that help them do that. Operations and marketing are usually line departments. Human resources management, public relations, and data processing are almost always staff departments. The line departments are internal "customers" of the staff departments.

WORK
APPLICATION 7-6

Identify one or more line and staff positions in an organization you work for or have worked for. Also, indicate whether the staff positions are general staff or specialist staff.

micromanagement A management style generally used as a negative term for when a manager closely observes or controls the work of his or her employees.

line authority The responsibility to make decisions and issue orders down the chain of command.

staff authority The responsibility to advise and assist other personnel.

7-1 | ## JOIN THE DISCUSSION ETHICS & SOCIAL RESPONSIBILITY

Breaking the Rules

Suppose you are a sales rep for a major pharmaceutical company. You get paid by commission, so the more drugs you sell to doctors, the more money you make. You know that sales reps in your company have been visiting doctors and telling them that if they prescribe your company's medication, they will receive 5% of the sales revenues. This arrangement can bring in thousands of dollars each year for both the sales reps and the doctors. You know the names of a few sales reps who are allegedly giving these kickbacks, but you are not sure how many sales reps are involved. You also don't know if sales managers know about the kickbacks or are receiving payments from the reps.

1. Is it unethical to be flexible and break the law against kickbacks?

2. Why are kickbacks illegal? Who benefits from kickbacks, who gets hurt by them, and how?

3. What would you do in this situation? (Would you start giving kickbacks yourself? Blow the whistle on sales reps to their managers? Blow the whistle to an outside source like the government or the media? Do nothing?)

EXHIBIT 7-4   TYPES AND LEVELS OF AUTHORITY

Formal Versus Informal Authority	Level of Authority	Centralized Versus Decentralized	Line Versus Staff Authority
• Formal: sanctioned way of doing job • Informal: unsanctioned	1. Inform: present alternatives to boss 2. Recommend: present alternatives and suggest one to boss 3. Report: take action and tell boss after 4. Full: take action and don't tell boss	• Centralized: top managers make decisions • Decentralized: middle and first-line managers make decisions	• Line: issue orders • Staff: assist and advise line and other staff

General and Specialist Staff. *General staff* work for only one manager and help the manager in any way needed. *Specialist staff* help anyone in the organization who needs it. Human resources, accounting, public relations, and maintenance offer specialized advice and assistance. Line managers use the services of staff departments such as printing and human resources. Exhibit 7-4 reviews types and levels of authority. Mechanistic organizations tend to have more specialized staff than do organic organizations.

LO 7-3

Define what an organization chart is, list the four aspects of a firm that it shows, and describe the four traditional departmentalization designs.

organization chart A graphic illustration of an organization's management hierarchy and departments and their working relationships.

Organizational Design

Strategic management (Chapter 5) is about selecting activities to engage in and how to configure them,[47] and top-level managers create and design formal structures for the entire firm.[48] *Organizational design* is the internal structure of an organization, or the arrangement of positions in the organization into work units or departments and the interrelationships among them. As you'll learn in this section, organizational design is illustrated in the organization chart and is determined by the type of departmentalization.

Organization Chart

Formal authority is illustrated in the formal structure of an organization (org) chart.[49] An **organization chart** *is a graphic illustration of the organization's management hierarchy and*

7-2   APPLYING THE CONCEPT

Authority

Identify the type of authority referred to in each statement.

A. formal

B. informal

C. centralized

D. decentralized

E. line

F. staff

_____ 9. "I like your creative idea for a new product. I'll talk to the boss, and if Jamal likes it, he'll let us present the idea to his boss, Ginna."

_____ 10. "When I recommend good sales rep job candidates to the marketing manager, I get angry when Sam does not hire them."

_____ 11. "Everyone throughout the organization is encouraged to share information and knowledge with everyone else to get the job done."

_____ 12. "Hu, it's time to stop making pencils and start making pens."

_____ 13. "Being a manager here is great because we have the autonomy to run the department the way we want to."

_____ 14. "Don't forget—don't take any action until you check with me for my approval first."

EXHIBIT 7-5   ORGANIZATION CHART

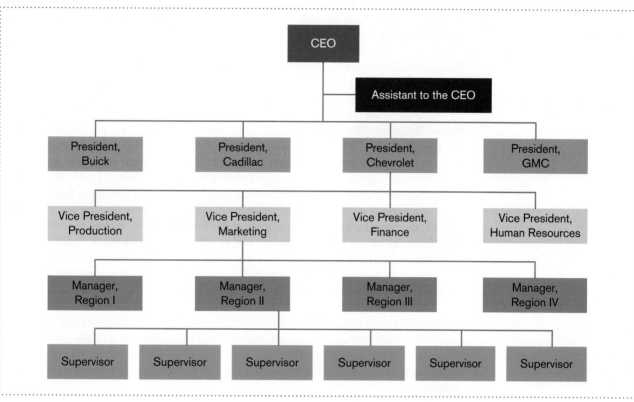

departments and their working relationships. Each box represents a position within the organization, and each line indicates the reporting relationships and formal lines of communication.

Exhibit 7-5, an adaptation of **GM**'s organization chart, illustrates four major aspects of such a chart:

- **The level of management hierarchy.** The org chart is a top-down structure[50] showing the levels of management.[51] At GM, the CEO and division presidents are top management, the vice presidents and managers are middle management, and the supervisors are first-line management.

- **Chain of command.** By following the vertical lines, you can see who reports to whom, as the GM division presidents report to the CEO. Within each division, vice presidents report to a president. The managers report to a vice president, and supervisors report to a manager. The assistant to the CEO is a general staff person, and the finance and human resources departments include specialist staff.

- **The division and type of work.** GM divides work by type of automobile: Buick, Cadillac, Chevrolet, and GMC (trucks). Each vice president within a division is responsible for a function, and the managers serve as linking pins coordinating the divisions' work.[52]

- **Departmentalization.** An organization chart shows how the firm is divided into permanent work units. GM is organized primarily by product divisional departmentalization.

You should also realize what an organization chart doesn't show, including day-to-day activities performed. A typical firm has three org charts: the formal one on paper discussed here, the real informal one in terms of knowing who to talk to and politics and influence (discussed in Chapter 10), and the org chart that the firm wants to be to perform better.[53]

Traditional Departmentalization

Departmentalization *is the grouping of related activities into units.* Traditional departmentalization tends to have a simple structure. Departments may have either an internal or an external focus, as discussed here.

Functional Departmentalization. Functional departmentalization capitalizes on functional expertise,[54] as it involves organizing departments around essential internal input activities, such as making/selling and financing products and services. It can also be called *process departmentalization* when the focus is on work or customer flow, such as at a **Registry of Motor Vehicles (RMV)** with departments to "flow" you through the process of getting or renewing your driver's license or auto registration. Functional departmentalization is illustrated in the top left portion of Exhibit 7-6. The functional approach is the form most widely used by small organizations, including **Table Group** consultants.[55] Large organizations tend to use external focused departmentalization, our next three structures. **Tesla (IOM 3, part 1)** possesses a global hierarchy that is functional in nature in that it has the following officers directing the entire operation of the firm: chairman & chief executive officer, chief financial officer, chief technology officer, vice president—vehicle engineering, vice president—powertrain operations, vice president—North America sales, chief designer, vice president—manufacturing, vice president—autopilot hardware engineering, vice president—worldwide services & deliveries and general counsel.

Product (Service) Departmentalization. Product (service) departmentalization involves organizing departments around goods (or services). Companies with multiple products commonly use product departmentalization. Retail chains like **CVS** and **Best Buy** use product departmentalization within their stores. The org chart at the bottom left of Exhibit 7-6 is by product.

Customer Departmentalization. Customer departmentalization involves organizing departments around the needs of different types of customers. The product or service may be the same or slightly different, but the needs of the customer warrant different marketing approaches. **SAGE Publications** focuses on selling books to different customer groups: research books, textbooks, journals, and reference books.[56] Some not-for-profit organizations use it, such as **Jones Counseling Center**, offering individual, family, and drug/alcoholic counseling. The org chart at the top right in Exhibit 7-6 illustrates customer departmentalization.

departmentalization The grouping of related activities into units.

Territory (Geographic) Departmentalization. Territory (geographic) departmentalization involves establishing separate units in each area in which the enterprise does business.

EXHIBIT 7-6 **TYPES OF TRADITIONAL DEPARTMENTALIZATION**

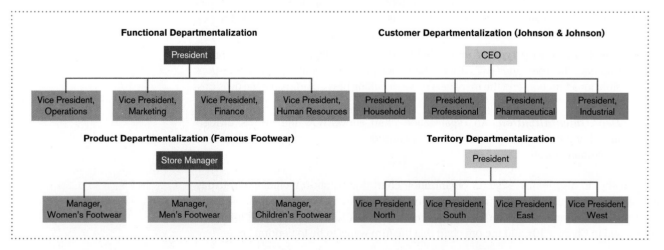

Functional Departmentalization
- President
  - Vice President, Operations
  - Vice President, Marketing
  - Vice President, Finance
  - Vice President, Human Resources

Customer Departmentalization (Johnson & Johnson)
- CEO
  - President, Household
  - President, Professional
  - President, Pharmaceutical
  - President, Industrial

Product Departmentalization (Famous Footwear)
- Store Manager
  - Manager, Women's Footwear
  - Manager, Men's Footwear
  - Manager, Children's Footwear

Territory Departmentalization
- President
  - Vice President, North
  - Vice President, South
  - Vice President, East
  - Vice President, West

Virtually all MNCs, including **Ford** and **Coca-Cola**, have some form of territory structure. The org chart at the bottom right of Exhibit 7-6 is by territory. **Tesla (IOM 3, part 2)** is expanding fast globally, so it is secondarily departmentalized by territory—United States, China, Norway, and other.

Contemporary Organizational Design

In this section, we expand on organizational design to using multiple departmentalization and contemporary issues and designs.

Multiple Departmentalization

Many organizations, particularly large, complex ones, use several types of departmentalization to create a hybrid structure.[57] Any mixture of types can be used. For example, some organizations have functional departments within a manufacturing facility, but sales are departmentalized by territory, with separate sales managers and salespeople in different areas.

Matrix Departmentalization. *Matrix departmentalization* combines functional and product departmentalization. With matrix departmentalization, an employee works for a functional department and is also assigned to one or more products or projects. The major advantage of matrix departmentalization is flexibility. It allows the enterprise to temporarily organize for a project. The major disadvantage is that each employee has two bosses—a functional boss and a project boss—which violates the unity-of-command principle and makes coordination difficult.

MANAGEMENT IN ACTION
Traditional Departmentalization

LO 7-4
Discuss the two multiple forms of departmentalization and five contemporary organizational designs.

EXHIBIT 7-7   **MATRIX DEPARTMENTALIZATION**

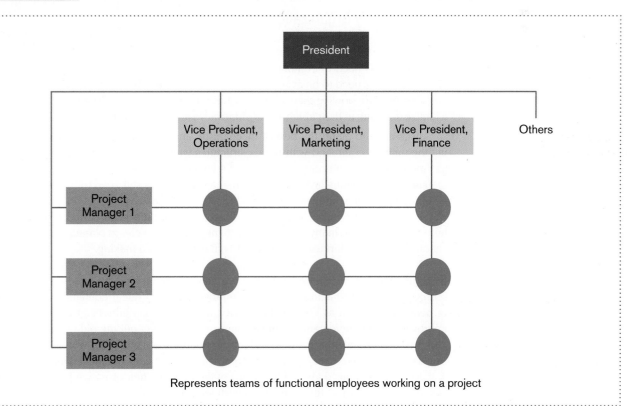

Represents teams of functional employees working on a project

Justin Sullivan/Getty Images

Home Depot uses functional organizational structure at the global level and also uses geographic divisions.

WORK
APPLICATION 7-7

Draw a simple organization chart for an organization you work for or have worked for. Identify the type of departmentalization and staff positions, if any.

Professor Lussier became a two-time intrapreneur at **Springfield College**—first when he started a consulting business and later when he opened a branch in Israel. He had split responsibilities, with a department chair supervisor for teaching for both ventures and the dean supervisor for starting and managing the consulting business and branch. The use of matrix departmentalization will continue to increase as a contemporary design.[58] Exhibit 7-7 illustrates a matrix structure.

Divisional Departmentalization. As part of the corporate-level grand strategy (Chapter 5), a **divisional structure** is *based on semiautonomous strategic business units.* It is sometimes called multidivisional or M-form.[59] In essence, this structure creates coordinated companies within a company with their own departmentalization, which may be different. Divisional structure is common for large, complex global businesses that offer related goods and services. **PepsiCo** uses divisional departmentalization for its **Pepsi** beverages, **Tropicana** juice, **Gatorade** sport drinks, **Frito-Lay** snacks, and **Quaker Oats** cereal and granola bars. These and other PepsiCo-brand products are sold through six global divisions based on territory departmentalization.[60] **Smith & Wesson** restructured by adding new divisions for outdoor sporting goods as a growth diversification strategy (Chapter 5) to add to its firearms division.[61]

The *conglomerate* (holding company) *structure* is based on autonomous profit centers. Companies with unrelated diversified business units use the conglomerate structure. Top management focuses on corporate-level strategy business portfolio management (Chapter 5) to buy and sell lines of business without great concern for coordinating divisions. **Berkshire Hathaway** owns more than 60 operating units with no companywide budgeting or strong central controls for a conglomerate with 340,000 employees.[62] **Google** created a parent[63] or holding company called **Alphabet**.[64] It restructured to separate its core businesses from its newer unrelated businesses, such as **Nest**, **Google Life Sciences**, and **Fiber**.[65]

Contemporary Organizational Issues and Designs

Challenges to New Organization. Staying innovative (Chapter 6) over time is challenging,[66] as organizations need to continually redesign their structures to align with environmental changes.[67] MNCs need to be agile and change quickly today, but sound mechanistic bureaucracy features are slowing them down.[68] **Amazon**, **Facebook**, and **Google** are successful to a large extent due to their ability to stay innovative and change quickly.[69]

MNCs need to blend the best of mechanistic and organic advantages. They are breaking the unity of command with matrix structures while keeping unity of direction, as they use more informal authority and bypass the chain of command and increase the span of management by cutting layers of middle management. Jobs still need to be specialized, but employees are being empowered more through decentralized authority to do the job their way as managers delegate more responsibility. **McDonald's** restructured to minimize its bureaucracy with too many layers of management, redundancies in planning and communication, competing priorities, and barriers to efficient decision making.[70]

Reengineering. *Reengineering* is the fundamental rethinking and radical redesign of business processes to achieve dramatic improvements in critical contemporary measures of performance, such as cost, quality, service, and speed. As defined, it's about radical big improvement, not incremental change. You start by throwing out the old organization chart and methods and reengineer new, radically better ways of getting the work done. **Michael Porter** says we need to reengineer the U.S. national health care system and its organizations. It needs to be organized around the needs of the patient—not insurance, health care facilities, and doctors.[71] An entire company, department, or job can be reengineered.

divisional structure Departmentalization based on semiautonomous strategic business units.

Digital-marketing firm **Fathom**'s CEO **Scot Lowry** shredded his organization chart and reorganized everyone into teams dedicated to specific accounts and listed himself at the bottom of the new chart.[72] **Founder and CEO Tony Hsieh** reengineered **Zappos.com** into what he calls *holacracy*. Hsieh eliminated all management positions and dropped the hierarchy of people into a hierarchy of purpose to foster collaboration. It has multiple circles. There's a general company circle. Then each circle has roles in it and subcircles. Each circle and each role has its own purpose. Employees can fill multiple roles in multiple circles, and they are free to move around different circles to work on different projects.[73]

Contemporary Organizational Designs. Here are five commonly used designs. Note, however, that MNCs are still departmentalized by the six structures we presented already. The five contemporary organizational designs we present here are generally embedded within the existing departmentalization but change the structure, and they are not shown on an organization chart unless the organization is reengineered to do so.

- *Team Organization.* Many companies are organizing based on teams, and networks of interdependent teams that pursue shared goals are called *multiteam systems*.[74] Team members are commonly viewed as leaders, as they participate in self-management.[75] **Zappos**'s circles are essentially teams. You will learn about work teams later in this chapter and Chapter 8, titled "Managing Teamwork." **General Foods, P&G, Sherwin-Williams**, and the **University of Oregon Ducks** football coaching staff[76] have all developed team structures.

- *Network Organization.* *Networks* are *boundaryless* interrelationships among different organizations.[77] A network firm may be viewed as a central hub surrounded by a network of outside specialists that change as needed. Networks create multiple kinds of relationships,[78] as firms share information and resources.[79] Networks use cross-functional and cross-firm teams.[80] **Facebook** and **Google's** power comes from the size of their partnership networks.[81] These two firms partner and compete in different lines of business, and are so-called *frenemies*. Modular and virtual organizations are types of boundaryless networks.

- *Modular Organization.* **Nike** and **Reebok** design and market their footwear and outsource manufacturing to contractors that change over time. Some companies, including **Dell** and **RCA**, either purchase products ready made or buy all the parts and only assemble the product.

- *Virtual Organization.* A *virtual organization* is a continually evolving network of contingent workers (temporary, freelance, or contract—not full-time employees) and companies that unite temporarily to exploit specific project opportunities or to attain strategic advantages. **Second Life** hired contingent programmers to develop its software to create a virtual world of colorful online avatars. Unlike the more stable modular organization, the virtual organization has no central hub; it's more like a potluck dinner, as each independent worker or company selects which companies it wants to network with to meet a specific objective.

- *The Learning Organization.* As discussed in Chapter 2, work is becoming more based on knowledge.[82] In a learning organization, everyone in the firm is engaged in identifying and solving problems to continuously improve and achieve the firm's objectives through knowledge sharing within and outside the firm.[83] There is no agreement about how the learning organization looks or operates, and you don't see it on an organization chart.

- *Platform Organization.* One of the newest structures is platforms that are used to connect buyers and sellers.[84] Platforms utilize the shared economy. **Uber** connects riders and drivers, and **Airbnb** connects renters and home owners through the use of sophisticated technology.

Visa is facing discontinuous innovation (Chapter 6) from virtual currencies such as **Bitcoin** and alternative online-payments systems like **PayPal** that can bypass credit cards and

7-3 APPLYING THE CONCEPT

Departmentalization

Identify the type of departmentalization illustrated by each organization chart.

a. functional

b. product (service)

c. customer

d. territory (geographic)

e. matrix

f. divisional

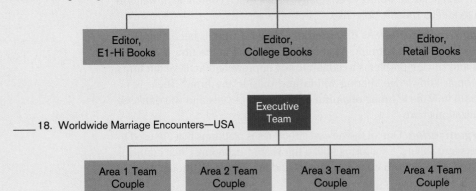

_____ 15. Procter & Gamble (P&G)

CEO

Beauty Care Division | Household Care Division | Health & Well-Being Division

Market Development

Global Business Services

Corporate Functions

_____ 16. Chicago Consulting

President

Manager, Strategic Planning

Manager, Training and Development

Manager, Marketing Research

_____ 17. Digital Age PC

President

Editor, E1-Hi Books

Editor, College Books

Editor, Retail Books

_____ 18. Worldwide Marriage Encounters—USA

Executive Team

Area 1 Team Couple

Area 2 Team Couple

Area 3 Team Couple

Area 4 Team Couple

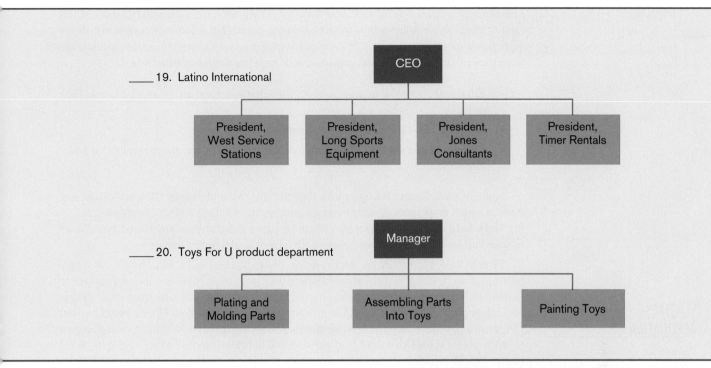

_____ 19. Latino International

_____ 20. Toys For U product department

new methods for enabling mobile phone transactions. Thus, **Visa** is fighting for survival as the world's largest payment system by creating a team-based, network-learning organization partnering with frenemies **Apple Pay** and **Google Wallet** by giving them and other developers of payment systems, such as **Square Inc.** (which helps small businesses accept cards), access to Visa's systems. Visa is also investing in firms like **LoopPay Inc.** (whose software allows customers to store credit card data on their phones).[85]

As discussed in this section, firms are changing the way they organize. Complete Self-Assessment 7-1 to determine your organizational preference. Knowing your preference can help in job searching.

Job Design

Job or work design is about doing what must be done to accomplish objectives.[86] Tasks or activities to be performed by organizations are grouped into functional departments, and the tasks are further grouped into jobs for each employee with a job title to describe responsibilities.[87] **Job design** _is the process of identifying tasks that each employee is responsible for completing._ Job design is crucial because it affects job satisfaction and productivity.[88] **Tesla** (**IOM 4**), as a major producer of fully electric automobiles, uses its corporate structure to facilitate extensive control of the organization including job design. Tesla, given its traditional organizational structure with minimal regional divisions, designs jobs focusing upon the individual work the employee performs within their specific functional area (i.e., manufacturing versus worldwide services and delivery) regardless of his or her physical location.

As we will discuss in this section, jobs may be simplified, or they may be expanded. You can use work teams and a job characteristics model to design jobs.

Job Simplification

Job simplification is the process of eliminating or combining tasks and/or changing the work sequence to improve performance, making jobs more specialized. It is based on the

Lyft functions as a platform organization, connecting drivers and customers.

LO 7-5

Classify each of the nine job designs under the three job design option categories.

job design The process of identifying tasks that each employee is responsible for completing.

organizing principle of division of labor and Taylor's scientific management (Chapter 1). The idea behind job simplification is to work smarter, not harder. A job is broken down into a work-flow process to improve it.[89] It creates steps (flowchart), and employees analyze the steps to see if they can eliminate, combine, or change the sequence of activities.

- **Eliminate.** Does the task, or parts of it, have to be done at all? If not, don't waste time doing it.
- **Combine.** Doing similar things together often saves time.
- **Change sequence.** Often, a change in the order of doing things results in a lower total time.

Simplification doesn't have to make the job repetitive and boring. **GE** has Workout sessions at which employees present ideas for eliminating pointless tasks.[90] Companies including **McDonald's** and **Costco** stopped requiring paper signatures for small credit card sales to speed up service and eliminate paperwork, as well as electronic signatures.

Uber's (**IOM 4**) primary job design for its drivers is job simplification, as the job is simply to pick up clients and drive them to where they want to go following the mapped route. Related to its drivers, a very important part of Uber's organizational structure is that drivers are not employees. They are contingent independent contractors, so Uber doesn't have to give them a paycheck with the legal requirements of paying and withholding multiple types of employment taxes. Drivers get paid per ride, and they are responsible for paying the taxes on the 1099-MISC (Miscellaneous Income) form received from Uber for the tax year. The IRS gets a copy, so don't even think about not paying taxes if you get a 1099 from any firm.

Job Expansion

Job expansion is the process of making jobs less specialized. Jobs can be expanded through rotation, enlargement, and enrichment. The trend is toward organic structure, giving employees more job autonomy.[91]

Job Rotation. Job rotation involves performing different jobs in some sequence, each one for a set period. For example, employees making cars on a **GM** assembly line might rotate so that they get to work on different parts of the production process for a set period, which is used in teams.[92] Many organizations develop conceptual skills in management trainees by rotating them through various departments, including **Bank of America** and **Target**.

Related to job rotation is *cross-training*, so employees learn to perform different jobs so they can fill in for those who are not on the job. **Jumpstart:HR** consulting company's CEO **Joey Price** says you need at least two people trained on every single function.[93] As skills increase, employees become more valuable to the organization.

Job Enlargement. Job enlargement involves adding tasks to broaden variety. Although you can add more variety of tasks to a highly repetitive, boring job, once the new tasks are mastered, the job is still rather boring. **AT&T, Chrysler, GM,** and **IBM** have used job enlargement.

Job Enrichment. Job enrichment *is the process of building motivators into the job itself to make it more interesting and challenging.* The goal is to get employees fully engaged at work so they are satisfied and productive.[94] Job enrichment works for jobs of low motivation potential and employees who are ready to be empowered to do meaningful work. A simple way to enrich jobs is to delegate more responsibility to employees to make a job satisfying. **Monsanto, Motorola,** and the **Travelers Companies** have successfully used job enrichment.

To enrich jobs, firms are using more *flexible work arrangements*, including

- *telecommuting,* in which employees work remotely, connected to the office through the Internet;
- *flextime,* in which employees can select their working hours within certain hours;

WORK
APPLICATION 7-8

Describe how a job at an organization you work for or have worked for could be simplified. Be sure to specify if you are eliminating, combining, or changing the sequence of the job.

job enrichment The process of building motivators into a job to make it more interesting and challenging.

| 7-1 | **SELF**-ASSESSMENT |

Organizational Preference

Individuals differ in the type of organizations in which they prefer to work. To determine your organizational preference, evaluate each of the following 12 statements, using the scale below. Place a number from 1 (*I disagree*) to 5 (*I agree*) that represents your level of agreement with the statement.

5	4	3	2	1
I agree				I disagree

_____ 1. I prefer having just one boss telling me what to do rather than multiple people.

_____ 2. I prefer to just perform my job rather than being concerned about organizational objectives and being involved in setting them.

_____ 3. I prefer knowing the reporting relationship, who is whose boss, and working through proper channels rather than just working directly with a variety of people based on the situation.

_____ 4. I prefer to get information from my boss rather than multiple sources.

_____ 5. I prefer having a clear job description so I know just what I need to do at work rather than the ambiguity of not being sure and doing whatever needs to be done.

_____ 6. I prefer being a specialist rather than a generalist.

_____ 7. I prefer doing my own thing that contributes to the organization rather than coordinating the work I do with that of others in teams.

_____ 8. I prefer to make excuses and blame others rather than accept responsibility for my shortcomings.

_____ 9. I prefer having my boss make decisions for me at work rather than making my own decisions.

_____ 10. I prefer routine at work rather than being delegated new tasks to perform.

_____ 11. I prefer having job security rather than knowing I could be let go.

_____ 12. I prefer that people get promoted based primarily on seniority rather than based on performance.

_____   Total

Scoring: To determine your preference, add up the numbers you assigned to the statements; the total will be between 12 and 60.

   The higher your score, the more you prefer to work in a traditional organizational structure, often referred to as mechanistic. The lower your score, the more you prefer to work in a contemporary organizational structure, often called organic. Review your answers knowing that the opening statement applies to traditional organizations and the opposite statement (after "rather than") applies to contemporary organizations. Most firms tend to be organized somewhere between the two extremes.

- *compressed workweek,* in which employees work more hours per day and fewer days per week—commonly four 10-hour days, allowing a three-day weekend; and

- *job sharing,* in which two or more employees split one full-time job—commonly two working half the shift each.

Job Characteristics Model. The Job Characteristics Model (JCM) was developed by **Richard Hackman** and **Greg Oldham** to be a method that uses a complex model to guide the job designer to make the job more interesting and challenging based on the job itself (core job dimensions), the characteristics of the employee doing the job (critical psychological states), and the employee's interest in having an enriched job (employee growth-need strength). Correctly used, jobs designed with the JCM have been found to increase motivation, increase job satisfaction, and improve job results.[95] Due to its complexity and need for training to use the JCM correctly, which is beyond the scope of this book, it tends to be used by consultants, such as **YourCoach**, or large organizations with a JCM specialist, such as **GE**.

Work Teams

The traditional approach to job design has been to focus on individual jobs. But the trend is toward designing jobs for work teams—or, to be more accurate, teams are redesigning members' jobs. Having teams design their own jobs is a form of job enrichment. Two common types of work teams used to design jobs are integrated teams and self-managed teams.

Integrated Work Teams. *With integrated work teams,* the manager is primarily responsible for job design of team members, and the manager can use job simplification or job expansion. Teams are used at **Boeing** and **HP**.

Self-Managed Work Teams. *Self-managed work teams* are assigned a goal, and the team members plan, organize (design their jobs), lead, and control to achieve the goal. Usually, self-managed teams operate without a designated manager; the team is both manager and worker. Teams commonly elect their own members and evaluate each other's performance. **W. L. Gore and Associates**, **3M**, and more recently **Zappos** have used self-managed work teams.

Exhibit 7-8 reviews the job design options we have discussed, and it clearly answers LO 7-5.

Organizing Yourself and Delegating

Now that you understand how organizations and jobs are designed, it's time to learn how to organize yourself by setting priorities and delegating work. Productivity isn't about how many brutal hours you work; it's about how effective you are at accomplishing the important things (priorities) and delegating effectively so you don't burn out.[96] You need to prioritize results over busywork[97] and hours worked.[98] But do realize that you must work and manage within the organizational structure.[99]

Successful managers are effective at using judgment to set priorities[100] and delegating work.[101] Recall that planning entails setting objectives and that organizing is the process of delegating and coordinating resources to achieve objectives. Thus, prioritizing objectives is

7-4   APPLYING THE CONCEPT

Job Designs

Identify which job design technique is exemplified in each statement.

A. job simplification
B. job rotation
C. job enlargement
D. job enrichment/Job Characteristics Model
E. work teams

____ 21. "Elan, I'd like you to learn how to run the monthly budget reports so that you can fill in for Kramer while he is on vacation."

____ 22. "I'd like you to work together to come up with ways to improve how your jobs get done."

____ 23. "Jamal, would you like me to delegate a new task to you to make your job more challenging?"

____ 24. "When you travel, you will be given $25 per meal, so you no longer need to provide a receipt."

____ 25. "Waneta, I want your job to be less repetitive. So you will be trained to add a couple new tasks to your job responsibility."

| EXHIBIT 7-8 | JOB DESIGN OPTIONS | |

Job Option Category	Job Design	Intended Results
Job Simplification	Eliminate tasks	Stop doing task to save time and effort
	Combine tasks	Do related tasks together to save time and effort
	Change task sequence	Do tasks in different order to save time and effort
Job Expansion	Job rotation	Learn how to do—and then perform—different jobs
	Job enlargement	Add more different tasks to a job to provide variety
	Job enrichment	Build motivators into the job itself to make it more interesting and challenging
	Job Characteristics Model	Enrich jobs with the use of a complex model
Work Teams	Integrated	The manager gets the job done through managing the team
	Self-managed	The team gets the job done through self-management

important, because some objectives are more important than others.[102] As a manager, you get the work done by delegating it to employees.[103] Start by completing Self-Assessment 7-2 on prioritizing to determine what is important to you personally (your values).

Setting Priorities

Prioritizing is about figuring out the few key things that are most important in your role and accomplishing them rather than doing less important busywork.[104] As a manager, you'll be faced with several tasks to get done at any given time. How you select the priority order in which these tasks will be completed will affect your success.[105] To prioritize successfully, make a to-do list of tasks that you must perform and then assign each task a priority;[106] then focus on accomplishing only one task at a time to avoid errors and save time (time management and multitasking; see Chapter 5).

Managers understand which objectives to prioritize in order to allocate resources accordingly and delegate tasks appropriately.

Priority-Determination Questions.[107] As a manager, answer "yes" or "no" to the following three priority-determination questions about each task that needs to be completed:

1. *Do I need to be personally involved because of my unique knowledge or skills?* Often, you are the only one who can do the task; if so, then you must be involved.

2. *Is the task my responsibility, or will it affect the performance or finances of my department?* You must oversee the performance of your department and keep finances in line with the budget.

3. *When is the deadline—is quick action needed?* Should you work on this activity right now, or can it wait? The key is to start the task soon enough so that you will meet the deadline.

Assigning Priorities. After answering the three questions, you can assign a high, medium, or low priority to each activity to determine the level or sequence for completion[108]:

- ***Delegate (D) priority:*** If the answer to question 1 is no, the task is delegated, and it is not necessary to answer questions 2 and 3. However, planning how to delegate the task now becomes a priority.

- **High (H) priority:** Assign the task a high priority if you answer yes to all three questions. Try not to have too many *H*s, because you will lose focus on what is really important.[109]
- **Medium (M) priority:** Assign the task a medium priority if you answer yes to question 1 but no to one of the remaining two questions.
- **Low (L) priority:** Assign the task a low priority if you answer yes to question 1 but no to both questions 2 and 3.

The Prioritized To-Do List. Exhibit 7-9 is a prioritized to-do list that you can copy and use on the job. Follow these steps when using the prioritized to-do list:

1.   *Write the task* that you must perform on the task line.
2.   *Answer the three priority-determination questions* by placing a *Y* (yes) or *N* (no) in the relevant column. Also place the deadline and time needed to complete the task in the relevant column. The deadline and time needed are used with lower-level priorities that change into high priorities as the deadline approaches. You may want to write in the deadline for starting the task rather than the completion deadline.
3.   *Assign a priority* to the task by placing the letter *D* (delegate), *H* (high), *M* (medium), or *L* (low) in the priority column. The top left of the prioritized to-do list shows how to determine priority based on the answers to the priority-determination questions. If you write *D*, set a priority on when to delegate the task.
4.   *Determine which task to complete now.* You may have more than one high-priority task, so follow the rule of "Do the most important thing first." When all high priorities are completed, go to medium-priority tasks, followed by low-priority tasks.

EXHIBIT 7-9   PRIORITIZED TO-DO LIST

Assigning a Priority		1. Do I need to be personally involved because of my unique knowledge or skills?	2. Is the task my responsibility, or will it affect the performance or finances of my department?	3. When is the deadline—is quick action needed?	Deadline/time needed	Priority (D, H, M, L)
(D) Delegate priority	(N) No to question 1					
(H) High priority	(YYY) Yes to all three questions					
(M) Medium priority	(YNY or YYN) Yes to question 1 and No to question 2 or 3					
(L) Low priority	(YNN) Yes to question 1 and No to questions 2 and 3					
Task						

7-2 SELF-ASSESSMENT

Personal Priorities

Rate how important each of the following is to you on a scale from 0 (*not important*) to 100 (*very important*). Write the number you choose on the line to the left of each item.

0	10	20	30	40	50	60	70	80	90	100

Not Important   Somewhat Important   Very Important

____ 1. An enjoyable, satisfying job

____ 2. A high-paying job

____ 3. A good marriage

____ 4. Meeting new people, attending social events

____ 5. Involvement in community activities

____ 6. My relationship with God, my religion

____ 7. Exercising, playing sports

____ 8. Intellectual development

____ 9. A career with challenging opportunities

____10. Nice cars, clothes, home, etc.

____11. Spending time with family

____12. Having several close friends

____13. Volunteer work for not-for-profit organizations

____14. Meditation, quiet time to think, pray, etc.

____15. A healthy, balanced diet

____16. Educational reading, self-improvement TV programs, etc.

Below, copy the number you assigned to each of the 16 items in the space next to the item number; then add the two numbers in each column.

Professional	Financial	Family	Social	Community	Spiritual	Physical	Intellectual
1. _____	2. _____	3. _____	4. _____	5. _____	6. _____	7. _____	8. _____
9. _____	10. _____	11. _____	12. _____	13. _____	14. _____	15. _____	16. _____
Totals _____	_____	_____	_____	_____	_____	_____	_____

The higher the total in any area, the higher the value you place on that particular area. The closer the totals are in all eight areas, the more well rounded you are. Think about the time and effort you put into your top three values. Are you putting in enough time and effort to achieve the level of success you want in each area? If not, what can you do to change?

Update the prioritized to-do list and add new tasks. As time passes, the medium- and low-priority tasks become high-priority tasks. There is no set rule for how often to update, but do it at least daily. As new tasks come up, be sure to add them to your to-do list and prioritize them. In doing so, you will avoid the tendency to put off a high-priority task to work on a lower-level task. The so-called emergencies and urgent things can often wait.

Every day, **IBM CEO Ginni Rometty** asks herself if she only did the things that only she could do. If she did things others could do, she wasted time and should have delegated those things.[110] You should also delegate things you are not good at or really can't do.[111] Complete Skill Builder 7-1 at the end of this chapter to develop your skill at setting managerial priorities using a prioritized to-do list.

Delegating

Delegation is the process of assigning responsibility and authority for accomplishing objectives. Telling employees to perform tasks that are part of their job design is issuing orders, not delegating. Delegating refers to giving employees new tasks. The new task may become part of a redesigned job, or it may simply be a one-time assignment.

Benefits of and Obstacles to Delegating. When managers delegate, they benefit by having more time to perform high-priority tasks,[112] and they can spend more time away from the job and the work gets done.[113] Successful managers delegate to draw on others' abilities to get the job done,[114] so they accomplish more things like growing the business.[115] Delegation trains employees and improves their self-esteem;[116] it is a means of enriching jobs.

Unfortunately, there are some obstacles to delegation, as managers become used to doing things themselves. They don't want to give up power and fear that employees will fail to accomplish the task or will show them up.[117] Managers might believe that they can perform the task more efficiently than others.[118] You should realize that delegating is an important management skill; don't let these or other obstacles stop you from delegating.

Delegation Decisions. Successful delegation is often based on selecting what to delegate and to whom to delegate. Exhibit 7-10 suggests what to delegate and what not to delegate, because knowing what to delegate is important to your success.[119]

Tesla delegates the responsibility of sales and vehicle services to its 208 stores and services locations throughout North America, China, Norway, and its other locations. The primary issue of delegation faced by **Tesla (IOM 5)** is that although it has regional offices, its global centralization is a structural characteristic that limits the ability of overseas offices to readily respond to issues they experience in their respective regional markets.

The Delegation Process. After determining what to delegate and to whom, you must plan for and delegate the tasks. Most managers haven't been taught how to delegate successfully, so they aren't good at it and are reluctant to delegate, but they realize its importance and their own need for improvement.[120] Delegating tasks quickly without details may seem expedient,

WORK
APPLICATION 7-11

List three to five tasks you must complete in the near future and prioritize them using Exhibit 7-9.

WORK
APPLICATION 7-12

Describe an obstacle to delegation or a sign of delegating too little that you have observed.

| EXHIBIT 7-10 | WHAT TO DELEGATE AND WHAT NOT TO DELEGATE |

What to Delegate	What Not to Delegate
• Tasks you don't need to do; priority-determination question 1 • Tasks you don't like to do that are appropriate to delegate • Things you are not good at or others can do better • Tasks that develop employees—job enrichment; even if you can do the task better, you will not have to do it at all, and you can do more important things • Tasks associated with solving employees' problems; help them learn to solve their own problems by delegating making the decision to them • Technical matters and routine tasks like paperwork	• Anything that you need to be involved with because of your unique knowledge or skill; priority-determination question 1 • Personnel matters (evaluating, disciplining, firing) • Confidential matters • Projects or tasks in crisis • Activities delegated to you personally

| **MODEL 7-1** | THE DELEGATION PROCESS |

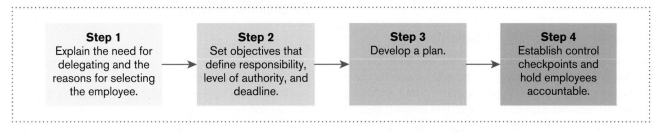

| Step 1
Explain the need for delegating and the reasons for selecting the employee. | → | Step 2
Set objectives that define responsibility, level of authority, and deadline. | → | Step 3
Develop a plan. | → | Step 4
Establish control checkpoints and hold employees accountable. |

but it tends to result in the task not being done the way you wanted or needed it done to meet your objective.[121] If you follow the steps in Model 7-1 and explained here, you will improve your delegation skills.

Step 1. Explain the need for delegating and the reasons for selecting the employee. It is helpful for an employee to whom you delegate a task to understand why the assignment must be completed and to realize the importance of the task. Telling employees why they were selected should make them feel valued. Don't use the "it's a lousy job, but someone has to do it" approach. Be positive; make employees aware of how they may benefit from the assignment. If step 1 is completed successfully, employees should be motivated, or at least willing, to do the assignment.

Step 2. Set objectives that define responsibility, level of authority, and deadline. The objectives should clearly state the result the employee is responsible for achieving by a specific deadline (use Model 5-1, "Objective Writing," in Chapter 5, page 145).

Define the level of authority the employee has. Does the employee *inform* you, *recommend* action for you to take, do the task and *report* it, or have *full* authority to just do it without your approval?

Setting clear deadlines (e.g., Tuesday, May 22, by 2:00 p.m.) is critical because it creates pressure to get the job done.[122] Saying "Do it when you have time" is not a deadline, and having no established deadline leads to procrastination or the task not getting done.

On a personal note, if you can't meet a deadline, tell your manager or customer as soon as you know it—don't surprise the person at the deadline, and be sure to set a new realistic deadline, and meet it.[123] If you want to impress your boss and get good performance reviews that can lead to raises and promotions, follow **Professor Lussier**'s motto: "I don't meet deadlines—I beat deadlines."

Step 3. Develop a plan. Once the objectives and deadline are set, a plan is needed to achieve them. The level of autonomy for developing the plan to accomplish the task should be based on the employee's capability level. (Refer to Skill Builder 1-4, "Management Styles," and Model 1-1, "Situational Management," in Chapter 1 for details on selecting the management style appropriate for the employee's capability level.) Make sure instructions for completing the task are clear; writing them down helps.

Step 4. Establish control checkpoints and hold employees accountable. For simple, short tasks, a deadline without control checkpoints is appropriate. However, when tasks have multiple steps and/or will take some time to complete, it is often advisable to check progress at predetermined times (control checkpoints). This approach builds information flow into the delegation system from the start. You and the employee should agree on how (text, email, phone call, visit, or detailed report) and when (daily, weekly, or after specific steps are completed but before going on to the next step) the employee will provide information regarding the assignment. When establishing control, consider the employee's capability level. Don't *micromanage* unless the employee really needs you to frequently check up on their progress. The higher the capability, the less frequent the

7-2 JOIN THE DISCUSSION ETHICS & SOCIAL RESPONSIBILITY

Delegating Destroying Documents

Arthur Andersen, a consulting company, was taken to court for destroying evidence that could have been used in court to support allegations of illegal activities. Arthur Andersen destroyed evidence related to the auditing of **Enron** to protect both companies from being found guilty of engaging in illegal business practices. Arthur Andersen claimed that it was not trying to destroy incriminating evidence but was simply destroying records, which is done periodically. Destroying documents is, in fact, routine. The key question is this: "What is being destroyed, and why is it being destroyed?"

1. Is it ethical and socially responsible to delegate the task of destroying documents that may potentially be used as evidence of wrongdoing?

2. What would you do if your boss asked you to destroy documents and you thought the goal was to cover up evidence of wrongdoing by the firm? (Would you just do it? Say nothing but neglect to do it? Question your boss's motives? Look closely at what you were asked to destroy? Check with your boss's boss to make sure it's OK to do it? Tell the boss you will not do it? Tell the boss to do it him- or herself? Blow the whistle to an outside source?)

3. If you were charged with destroying evidence, do you believe it would be a good defense to say, "I was only following orders"?

checks (again, use Model 1-1). All parties involved should note the control checkpoints on their calendars.

The four steps of the delegation process are summarized in Model 7-1. In Skill Builder 7-3 at the end of this chapter, you will practice using the delegation process so you can develop your delegation skills.

Trends and Issues in Management

We are living through a radical shift in how business is organized in the US and *globally*. Many MNCs engage in nearly continuous restructuring. MNCs are spinning-off into separate companies (**HP, Time-Warner, DuPont, Alcoa, Abbott Labs, Sony, Kodak)**, going private (**Dell**), radically restructuring (**GM, GE**), or going out of business (**Blockbuster, Borders, Circuit City, Lehman, Countrywide**).[124] Also, recall that there are differences in Western and Eastern countries.[125] Some country governments own companies, state-owned enterprises (SOEs), creating unique hybrid organizational structures different from the U.S. MNC. More than 10 percent of the world's largest MNCs are SOEs.[126]

Being a global MNC clearly brings a wide *diversity* of people and challenges we discussed in Chapter 3. **Facebook** embraces inclusion and actually prefers younger workers. The majority of its 8,000 workers are millennials under 30, and the company has crafted management techniques around them. **Google** and **Apple** prefer youth as well, with a median age of 30 and 31, compared to Facebook's 28 years.[127]

Tesla (**IOM 6**) is making a disruptive change through *technology* by designing, manufacturing, and marketing high-performance, technologically advanced electric cars and powertrain components. The fuel-efficient, fully electric vehicles recharge their lithium-ion batteries from an outlet, and, depending on a driver's speed, are capable of approaching 300 miles per charge. Other technological advances in the automotive industry include **Ford**'s self-driving cars and its use of *big data* from sensor-equipped cars of 650 employee volunteers to better inform its ride-sharing pilots in cities around the globe.[128] **Google** is also working on driverless cars, but it is also developing flying cars. There are working prototypes of the Terrafugia TF-X, E-volo Volocopter, and AeroMobil 3.0 and others.[129]

Facing a fast-changing, turbulent environment and the need to continually innovate, **Coca-Cola, GE, IBM, Tyco,** and others want to be more entrepreneurial and are reorganizing to be more flexible.[130] *Big data* are being used to create learning organizations, as data create knowledge that is easily shared and helps coordination and collaboration among network teams internally and externally.[131] Big data are also helping to flatten organizational structures through decentralized authority by pushing decisions all the way down the hierarchy; some call big data the "new middle manager."[132]

As always, with all management functions, managers must be *ethical and socially responsible* as good global citizens when they use authority, design organizational structures, and create jobs. **Tesla (IOM 7) CEO Elon Musk** wanted to create a vehicle that is not only environmentally sustainable and fashionable but also affordable for the middle-income family. That is why the firm is gearing up for the launch of the Model 3, an affordable family sedan, in 2018. Also, have you taken a ride in a **Tesla (IOM 8)** and/or thought of owning one?

Having completed this chapter, you should understand the differences between mechanistic and organic organizations and the principles of organization, authority, departmentalization, job design, and how to set priorities and delegate tasks.

WORK
APPLICATION 7-13

Select a manager you work for or have worked for and analyze how well he or she implements the four steps of delegation. Which steps does the manager typically follow and not follow?

ⓈSAGE edge™   edge.sagepub.com/lussier8e

Want a better grade?

Get the tools you need to sharpen your study skills. Access practice quizzes, eFlashcards, video and multimedia, and more at edge.sagepub.com/lussier8e.

Digital Resources

Learning Objective		Digital Resource
7-1.	Explain the difference between mechanistic and organic organizations and the environments in which they are more effective.	▶ Mechanistic vs. Organic Organizations*
7-2.	Contrast formal and informal authority, centralized and decentralized authority, and line and staff authority.	▶ Centralized vs. Decentralized Authority
7-3.	Define what an organization chart is, list the four aspects of a firm that it shows, and describe the four traditional departmentalization designs.	▶ Management in Action: Traditional Departmentalization*
7-4.	Discuss the two multiple forms of departmentalization and five contemporary designs.	▶ Divisional Structure*
7-5.	Classify each of the nine job designs under the three job design option categories.	▤ Job Rotation & Job Enrichment
7-6.	Explain how to set priorities by answering three priority-determination questions, and list the four steps in the delegation process.	▶ Delegation

* premium video available only in the interactive eBook

• • • CHAPTER SUMMARY

7-1. Explain the difference between mechanistic and organic organizations and the environments in which they are more effective.

Mechanistic organizations are bureaucratic, focusing on following procedures and rules through tight controls, and have specialized jobs, with decisions being made by top managers. Conversely, *organic organizations* are flexible, with minimal focus on procedures and rules, and have broadly defined jobs, with decisions being made at lower levels. Mechanistic organization tends to be effective in stable environments, whereas organic organization tends to work well in dynamic environments.

7-2. Contrast formal and informal authority, centralized and decentralized authority, and line and staff authority.

Formal authority involves sanctioned relationships and ways of getting the job done, whereas informal authority involves unsanctioned relationships and ways of getting the job done. With centralized authority, top managers make important decisions; with decentralized authority, middle and first-line managers make important decisions. Line authority gives responsibility to issue orders down the chain of command, whereas staff authority gives responsibility to advise and assist others.

7-3. Define what an organization chart is, list the four aspects of a firm that it shows, and describe the four traditional departmentalization designs.

An organization chart is a graphic illustration of the organization's management hierarchy and departments and their working relationships. It shows the level of management hierarchy, chain of command, division and type of work, and departmentalization. *Functional departmentalization* focuses on internal activities performed within the organization, such as operations, marketing, finance, and human resources, or process of work flow. There are three types of external departmentalization. *Product/service departmentalization* creates separate units for the various same *products/services* it offers all its customers. *Customer departmentalization* creates units to make products/services that meet the unique customer group needs. *Territory departmentalization* creates units for the geographical areas in which the organization does business.

7-4. Discuss the two multiple forms of departmentalization and five contemporary designs.

A matrix departmentalization commonly combines functional and product departmentalization, and employees work for a department and project manager. A divisional structure is based on semiautonomous strategic business units, or companies within a company. *Team organizations* create group units. *Network organizations* are boundaryless interrelationships among different organizations and include modular and virtual organizations. *Modular organization* firms focus on what they do best, outsource the rest to other companies, and coordinate their activities. A *virtual organization* is a continually evolving network of contingent workers and companies that unite temporarily to exploit specific project opportunities or to attain strategic advantage. The *learning organization* design focuses on continuous improvement through sharing knowledge throughout internal and external networks.

7-5. Classify each of the nine job designs under the three job design option categories.

Job simplification options are used to make jobs faster and easier with more specialization by *eliminating* or *combining* tasks and/or *changing* the *sequence* of work. **Job expansion** options are used to make jobs less specialized through employee *job rotation* to perform more jobs, *job enlargement* by providing more variety, and/or *job enriching* to make the job more interesting and challenging; and jobs can be enriched by using the *Job Characteristics Model*. **Work team** job design options include using an *integrated team* with a manager or *self-managed teams* that share the management of job designs.

7-6. Explain how to set priorities by answering three priority-determination questions, and list the four steps in the delegation process.

A manager first answers "yes" or "no" to the three priority-determination questions: (1) Do I need to be personally involved because of my unique knowledge or skills? (2) Is the task my responsibility, or will it affect the performance or finances of my department? (3) When is the deadline—is quick action needed? Depending on the answers to these questions, the manager delegates the task or assigns it a high, medium, or low level of priority. The steps in the delegation process are (1) explain the need for delegating and the reasons for selecting the employee; (2) set objectives that define responsibility, level of authority, and deadline; (3) develop a plan; and (4) establish control checkpoints and hold employees accountable.

••• KEY TERMS

authority, 208
centralized authority, 210
decentralized authority, 210
delegation, 209
departmentalization, 214
divisional structure, 216

job design, 219
job enrichment, 220
levels of authority, 210
line authority, 211
mechanistic organizations, 206
micromanagement, 211

organic organizations, 207
organization chart, 212
responsibility, 208
span of management, 208
staff authority, 211

••• KEY TERM REVIEW

Complete each of the following statements using one of this chapter's key terms.

1. _____ are bureaucratic, focusing on following procedures and rules through tight controls, and have specialized jobs, with decisions being made by top managers.

2. _____ are flexible, with minimal focus on procedures and rules, and have broadly defined jobs, with decisions being made at lower levels.

3. The _____ refers to the number of employees reporting to a manager.

4. _____ is the obligation to achieve objectives by performing required activities.

5. _____ is the right to make decisions, issue orders, and use resources.

6. _____ is the process of assigning responsibility and authority for accomplishing objectives.

7. The _____ are the authority to inform, the authority to recommend, the authority to report, and full authority.

8. With _____, important decisions are made by top managers.

9. With _____, important decisions are made by middle and first-line managers.

10. _____ is a management style generally used as a negative term for when a manager closely observes or controls the work of his or her employees.

11. _____ is the responsibility to make decisions and issue orders down the chain of command.

12. _____ is the responsibility to advise and assist other personnel.

13. An _____ is a graphic illustration of an organization's management hierarchy and departments and their working relationships.

14. _____ is the grouping of related activities into units.

15. A _____ departmentalizes based on semiautonomous strategic business units.

16. _____ is the process of identifying tasks that each employee is responsible for completing.

17. _____ is the process of building motivators into a job to make it more interesting and challenging.

••• REVIEW QUESTIONS

1. What is the difference between unity of command and unity of direction?

2. What is the relationship between the chain of command and the span of management?

3. What do the terms *differentiation* and *integration* mean?

4. What is the difference between responsibility and authority?

5. Can accountability be delegated?

6. How does the scope of authority change throughout an organization, and what is the flow of responsibility, authority, and accountability?

7. What is the difference between general staff and specialist staff?

8. What type of authority is needed to make decisions and issue orders down the chain of command?

9. What does an organization chart show? What doesn't it show?

10. What is the difference between product and customer departmentalization?

11. What type of organizations commonly use functional departmentalization?

12. What is the difference between a network structure and a virtual organization?

13. What is job design, and why is it necessary?

14. What is the difference between an integrated work team and a self-managed work team?

15. Why is the strength of employees' need for growth important to the Job Characteristics Model?

16. Why is it important to update priorities on a to-do list?

17. As a simple guide, what one question can a manager ask to determine what and what not to delegate?

18. Why is each of the four steps in the delegation process necessary?

● ● ● COMMUNICATION SKILLS

The following critical-thinking questions can be used for class discussion and/or as written assignments to develop communication skills. Be sure to give complete explanations for all questions.

1. Does formal organizational structure really matter? In other words, shouldn't management just focus on getting the work done?

2. How is division of labor (specialization of jobs) used in the medical profession and in schools? How does the restaurant industry use specialization?

3. Is centralized or decentralized authority better?

4. As firms grow, should they have division of labor and add staff positions? Give examples with your answer.

5. Historian Alfred Chandler suggested that structure should follow strategy. Should a firm develop the strategy first and then develop the organization structure? Why or why not?

6. Matrix departmentalization violates the unity-of-command principle. Should companies not use matrix departmentalization?

7. What impact does technology have on organizational structure?

8. Why has there been a trend toward more team, network, virtual, and learning organizations? Is this a fad, or will it last?

9. When focusing on jobs, is it better to use job simplification or job expansion?

10. Are setting priorities and delegating really all that important?

CASES

● ● ● Case 7-1   AT&T

The foundation for what is now AT&T was laid in 1876 when Alexander Graham Bell invented the telephone. This led to the creation of the Bell Telephone Company in 1877 and the opening of the first telephone exchange network in 1878. Additional growth in establishing networks in major U.S. cities continued between 1877 and 1885 under license from the Bell Telephone Company. In 1885, the American Telephone and Telegraph Company was established as a subsidiary of the American Bell Telephone Company with a charter to build the nation's first long-distance network between New York and Philadelphia.

AT&T made some significant changes to its structure through the acquisition of computer manufacturer NCR Corporation in 1991 and McCaw Cellular Communications, the nation's largest wireless phone service, provider in 1994. In 2000, the company restructured itself into a family of businesses consisting of AT&T (AT&T Business and AT&T Consumer), AT&T Wireless, and AT&T Broadband. Subsequent to this reorganization, the company continued its acquisitions-focused strategy through the purchase of DirecTV in 2015 and Time Warner in 2016.

Today, AT&T's strategy is to transform itself from a telecommunications firm into a media and entertainment powerhouse that can produce and distribute its own content. The company's current structure has four operating units: Business Solutions, Entertainment and Internet Services, Consumer Mobility, and International. It is headquartered in Dallas, Texas, and employs more than 283,000 people. The company's mission is: "Connect people with their world, everywhere they live, work and play . . . and do it better than anyone else." Its vision is called "Connect to Good" to leverage connections to build a better tomorrow for its business and for the benefit of its customers, employees, suppliers, and communities.

A major component of AT&T's strategy for achieving its mission is leveraging technology. John Donovan, chief strategy officer and president for technology and operations, commented that in order for the company to develop the kind of network it wants, it will need to use the next-generation wireless network called 5G, but it will also need the AT&T workforce to acquire new knowledge and skills, to do it rapidly, and to do so on an ongoing basis. He told the company's workforce that they needed to adapt to the challenges associated with change by envisioning a different set of circumstances and then to persevere in getting there.

The learning and development function at AT&T plays a key role in ensuring that the workforce possesses the knowledge and skills needed to adapt to all of the changes taking place in the company and its use of technology to drive cutting-edge innovations. First, the learning strategy is developed to directly align with the strategies of the overall company based on meetings among business unit leaders, the corporate strategy and development group, the company's CEO, and learning and development leaders. The strategy team gives each business an action plan for achieving its objectives, and then the learning and development group creates a learning plan within each of these action plans. Second, all learning programs are pilot-tested, evaluated, and modified as needed before they are made available to the rest of the workforce. Finally, learning programs are facilitated by a mixture of AT&T leaders and outside subject matter experts to ensure that participants learn from the most knowledgeable individuals.

AT&T invests heavily in its workforce to provide a culture and work environment in which they can thrive and be rewarded for contributing to the success of the company. Employees enjoy opportunities to have fun through community service and celebrations of personal milestones and work achievements. They are also empowered to work on projects of strategic importance to the company's future.

Discussion Questions

1. To what degree does AT&T possess the characteristics of a mechanistic versus an organic organization?

2. Describe the type of departmentalization that exists in AT&T's organizational design.

3. How is AT&T a learning organization?

4. How does AT&T address job design issues for various positions in the company?

5. If you could design the ideal job for yourself, what would it look like? What would be the most important aspects of this ideal job for you? Why?

6. Have you ever worked for an organization that is a "learning organization"? Do you feel that it was a better place to work because it was a learning organization? Why or why not?

References

https://www.nytimes.com/2016/02/15/technology/atts-strategy-is-one-part-innovation-one-part-inspiration.html?_r=0

http://www.fiercetelecom.com/telecom/at-t-reorganizes-operating-segment-into-4-divisions-but-analysts-say-plan-lacks-performance

http://about.att.com/content/dam/csr/2025-goals/2025-ATT-Goals-PDF-Overview.pdf

http://about.att.com/content/dam/snrdocs/dtv/DTV_Fact_Sheet.pdf

http://about.att.com/sites/company_profile

http://att.jobs

http://www.clomedia.com/2013/05/20/att-the-marriage-of-business-and-learning/

http://about.att.com/content/dam/snrdocs/dtv/DTV_Infographic.pdf

https://www.theofficialboard.com/org-chart/att

http://newswire.telecomramblings.com/2012/04/att-earns-top-marks-for-learning-development/

http://blogsitusjob.blogspot.com/2011/07/job-enlargement.html

https://www.corp.att.com/history/milestones.html

https://www.bloomberg.com/news/articles/2016-10-05/at-t-said-to-turn-to-media-acquisitions-as-video-ambitions-grow

Case created by Loren Kuzuhara, University of Wisconsin–Madison.

• • • Case 7-2   Zappos: Strategic Reengineering or a Path to Structural Failure?

Complacency is a word nonexistent in the vocabulary of Zappos CEO Tony Hsieh. Since joining the firm as an investor in 1999 and as CEO in 2000, Hsieh has built Zappos into a market leader through largely nonconventional corporate methods.

Hsieh's staunch commitment toward building a corporate culture of happiness has led to many of Zappos' quirky practices. Perhaps the most notable is a hiring process that measures an applicant's weirdness and humility and offers a $2,000 pay-to-quit severance option to any new hire who feels he or she doesn't fit the Zappos culture.(1) The company's unique approach to business has delivered results. In its 16 years of operation, Zappos has transformed from an upstart firm struggling to secure funds to stay afloat into the number-one online shoe retailer.(2)

How has Zappos developed its competitive advantage in the marketplace? By creating a structure that fosters employee and customer happiness above all, Hsieh has focused on removing organizational barriers that threaten the firm's strong corporate culture.

Front-line call-center representatives are given full authority to make decisions on customer calls. Zappos does not track call times or mandate representatives to read from scripts, a departure from typical industry call-center procedure. (3) Zappos does not have detailed policies on how to handle each customer service scenario; rather, representatives have autonomy to deal with each situation as they deem appropriate. Hsieh recalls a story in which a customer service representative received a phone call from a woman whose husband died in an automobile accident and needed assistance with returning boots she had ordered for him just days prior.(4) The following day, the customer received a delivery of flowers—the Zappos representative who handled her call ordered for the flowers to be sent at the company's expense without asking for supervisor consent.(5) Hsieh noted, "At the funeral, the widow told her friends and family about the experience. Not only was she a customer for life, but so were those 30 or 40 people at the funeral." (6)

Even with the authority given to front-line representatives, prior to 2015, Zappos operated through a largely traditional, hierarchical organizational structure that included functional positions and a chain of command. The firm's structure included line managers, middle managers, and upper-level strategic managers including a VP of finance and VP of merchandise.(7) Managers at Zappos had responsibilities similar to those of their peers in firms with traditional organizational structures including human resource management, overseeing and approving decisions, budgeting, and professional development of employees.(8) Zappos also provides extensive employee development for entry-level employees. The expectation is that these employees, with the training and mentorship offered by the firm, will become senior leaders within five to seven years.(9)

Despite Zappos's sustained success, Hsieh has continually strived to enable the firm to reach its "desired state of self-organization, self-management, increased autonomy, and increased efficiency." (10) In 2013, Hsieh announced the firm would eliminate its structure and job titles, including those of managers, and adopt an organization management system known as holacracy. Holacracy is a management structure in which "circles" of employees of equal privilege work autonomously in temporary functional roles, which they may move in and out of as needed.(11) These fluid teams can adapt organically to changing company needs through employee-led "governance" meetings.(12) Circles can dissolve as goals are met, and new circles that overlap with others can develop as new needs and projects arise.(13) Here, rather than organizational structure determining work flow, the work itself determines the necessary hierarchical structure and composition of the circle.(14)

In 2015, in a memo to the firm's 1,500 employees, Hsieh reiterated his commitment to the new self-managed, self-organized structure of the firm. To accelerate the process and fully convert to the new structure, Hsieh offered each employee a pay-to-quit severance package that included three months' salary.(15) Two hundred ten, or 14% of the company's employees accepted the offer,(16) well above the firm's normal 1% attrition rate.(17) Approximately 300 firms have adopted holacracy as an organizational structure since its creation 10 years ago, but none were as large as Zappos at the time of implementation.(18) Critics of the self-management and self-organization approach note that the lack of a clear structure and authority leads to confusion and creates an obscure career path for its employees.(19)

Was the move to reengineer the organization through the elimination of formal structure and titles prudent in light of Zappos's sustained success as a market leader? Can a large, established organization such as Zappos successfully succeed without a formal organizational structure? Should other organizations consider such a change? Time will tell if the reorganization of Zappos will prove to be fruitful and if other organizations will also reject the norm of a traditional structure, but one thing is clear about Zappos and its strategic leader Tony Hsieh—complacency is not an option.

Discussion Questions

1. Is Zappos a mechanistic or organic organization? How so?

2. From the perspective of authority, is Zappos more centralized or decentralized? Specify characteristics of the firm to support your answer.

3. Explain how the move to a self-managed, self-organized structure from a hierarchical structure was a form of reengineering.

4. Can Zappos be characterized as a learning organization? Why or why not?

5. How has Zappos used job enrichment to its advantage?

6. How do self-managed work teams factor into the new structure of Zappos?

Cumulative Case Questions

7. Explain the role of organizational culture at Zappos. Can it be characterized as strong or weak (Chapter 2)?

8. How did strategic planning factor into Zappos CEO Tony Hsieh's decision to move to a new organizational structure? What explanation can you offer for the change considering Zappos's continued success in its previous structure (Chapter 5)?

9. Search online for updates on Zappos's structural transition. Using the information in the case and the updates you find online, how have the firm's employees responded to this change? Use the four stages of the change process to explain how people tend to react to change (Chapter 6).

References

(1) Zappos website. Retrieved May 27, 2015, from http://about.zappos.com/it-true-zappos-offers-new-hires-2000-quit

(2) Hoovers website. Retrieved May 24, 2015, from http://0-subscriber.hoovers.com.liucat.lib.liu.edu/H/company360/fulldescription.html?companyId=112806000000000&newsCompanyDuns=098716132

(3) Chafkin, M. (2009, May 1). The Zappos way of managing. *Inc.* Retrieved May 25, 2015, from http://www.inc.com/magazine/20090501/the-zappos-way-of-managing.html

(4) Ibid.

(5) Ibid.

(6) Ibid.

(7) Zappos website. Retrieved May 27, 2015, from http://www.zappos.com/d/about-zappos-monkeys

(8) Feloni, R. (2015, April 15). Zappos CEO Tony Hsieh to employees: Embrace self-management or leave by the end of the month. *Business Insider.* Retrieved May 25, 2015, from http://www.businessinsider.com/tony-hsieh-self-management-memo-to-zappos-employees-2015-4

(9) Chafkin, M. (2009, May 1). The Zappos way of managing. *Inc.* Retrieved May 25, 2015, from http://www.inc.com/magazine/20090501/the-zappos-way-of-managing.html

(10) Feloni, R. (2015, April 15). Zappos CEO Tony Hsieh to employees: Embrace self-management or leave by the end of the month. *Business Insider.* Retrieved May 25, 2015, from http://www.businessinsider.com/tony-hsieh-self-management-memo-to-zappos-employees-2015-4

(11) Ibid.

(12) Bernstein, E. (2014, November 28). Flat organizations like Zappos need pockets of privacy. *Harvard Business Review.* Retrieved May 25, 2015, from https://hbr.org/2014/11/flat-organizations-like-zappos-need-pockets-of-privacy

(13) Ibid.

(14) Ibid.

(15) Snyder, B. (2015, May 8). 14% of Zappos' staff left after being offered exit pay. *Fortune.* Retrieved May 27, 2015, from http://fortune.com/2015/05/08/zappos-quit-employees

(16) Ibid.

(17) Denning, S. (2015, May 23). Is holacracy succeeding at Zappos? *Forbes.* Retrieved May 27, 2015, from http://www.forbes.com/sites/stevedenning/2015/05/23/is-holacracy-succeeding-at-zappos/

(18) Silverman, R. E. (2015, May 20). At Zappos, banishing the bosses brings confusion. *The Wall Street Journal.* Retrieved May 27, 2015, from http://www.wsj.com/articles/at-zappos-banishing-the-bosses-brings-confusion-1432175402

(19) Kraemer, H. (2015, May 29). Want to banish bureaucracy? There's a better way than Zappos' "holacracy." *Forbes.* Retrieved May

30, 2015, from http://www.forbes.com/sites/forbesleadershipforum/2015/05/29/want-to-banish-bureaucracy-theres-a-better-way-than-zappos-holacracy/

Case created by Herbert Sherman, Hannah K. Walter, and Naveed Ahmad, Long Island University.

••• SKILL BUILDER 7-1: SETTING PRIORITIES

Objective

To improve your skill at setting priorities.

Skills

The primary skills developed through this exercise are:

1. *Management skill*—decision making (setting priorities is based on conceptual skills)

2. *AACSB competencies*—analytic skills and reflective thinking skills

3. *Management function*—organizing (resources and time)

Preparing for Skill Builder 7-1

For this exercise, assume that you are the first-line manager of a production department in a large company. Read the to-do list containing 10 tasks that accompanies this exercise and assign priorities to each task by following the steps below. (Note: The 10 tasks have been numbered for you. When you make a to-do list for your own tasks, we recommend that you not number them.)

1. Answer the three priority-determination questions by placing a *Y* for yes or *N* for no in the columns labeled 1, 2, and 3. Because you are not the top manager of this department, do not fill in the deadline/time-needed column.

2. Assign a priority to the task by placing the letter *D* (delegate), *H* (high), *M* (medium), or *L* (low) in the priority column. Use the list at the top left to determine the priority based on the answers to the priority-determination questions.

3. Determine which task to complete first. You may have more than one high priority, so select the most important one to do first.

Apply It

What did I learn from this experience? How will I use this knowledge in the future?

Prioritized To-Do List		Priority-Determination Questions				
		1	2	3		
(D) Delegate priority	(N) No to question 1	1. Do I need to be personally involved because of my unique knowledge or skills?	2. Is the task my responsibility, or will it affect the performance or finances of my department?	3. When is the deadline—is quick action needed?	*Deadline/time needed*	*Priority (D, H, M, L)*
(H) High priority	(YYY) Yes all three questions					
(M) Medium priority	(YNY or YYN) Y to Q1, N Q2 or 3					
(L) Low priority	(YNN) Yes Q1 and No Q2 and 3					
Task						
1. Tom, the sales manager, tells you that three customers stopped doing business with your company because your products have decreased in quality. As production manager, it is your job to meet with the production crew and determine how to solve this problem.						
2. Your secretary, Michele, tells you that there is a salesperson waiting to see you. He does not have an appointment. You don't do any purchasing.						
3. Molly, a vice president, wants to see you to discuss a new product to be introduced in one month.						
4. Tom, the sales manager, sent you a memo stating that the sales forecast was incorrect. Sales are expected to increase by 20% starting next month. Inventory must be increased to meet the unexpected sales forecast.						

(Continued)

(Continued)

Prioritized To-Do List	Priority-Determination Questions				
	1	2	3		
5. Dan, the personnel director, sent you a memo informing you that one of your employees has resigned. Your turnover rate is one of the highest in the company.					
6. Michele tells you that someone named Bob Furry called while you were out. He asked you to return his call but wouldn't state why he was calling. You don't know who he is or what he wants.					
7. Phil, one of your best workers, wants an appointment to tell you about an incident that happened in the shop.					
8. Tom calls and asks you to meet with him and a prospective customer for your product. The customer wants to meet you.					
9. John, your boss, calls and asks to see you about the decrease in the quality of your product.					
10. In the mail, you got a note from Randolf, the president of your company, and an article from *The Wall Street Journal*. The note says FYI (for your information).					

●●● SKILL BUILDER 7-2: ORGANIZATIONAL STRUCTURE AT YOUR COLLEGE

This exercise enables you to apply the organizing concepts discussed in the chapter to your college or university as an individual and/or group.

Objective

To better understand organizational structures.

Skills

The primary skills developed through this exercise are:

1. *Management skill*—decision making (organizing requires conceptual skills)
2. *AACSB competencies*—analytic skills and reflective thinking skills—organizing (at all levels of the organization)
3. Management function

Preparing for Skill Builder 7-2

Your professor will select the university, college, school, or department level of analysis for this exercise. Based on the level,

answer the following questions to analyze the organization. You may need to interview some administrators or faculty members to get answers.

1. Refer to Exhibit 7-2. How are the principles of organization followed? (Be sure to include the span of management and division of labor.)
2. Identify line and staff positions. Is authority centralized or decentralized?
3. What type of departmentalization is used? Draw a simple organizational chart.
4. Describe the job design of faculty members.
5. Identify some of the current priorities and types of assignments delegated.

Apply It

What did I learn from this experience? How will I use this knowledge in the future?

●●● SKILL BUILDER 7-3: DELEGATING

Objective

To develop delegating skills.

Skills

The primary skills developed through this exercise are:

1. *Management skill*—decision making (organizing requires assigning work through delegation)

2. *AACSB competencies*—analytic skills and reflective thinking skills
3. Management function—organizing

Preparing for Skill Builder 7-3

Before beginning this exercise, review the text material on delegating.

Procedure

Work in groups of three. Each person in the group will role-play delegating one of the following three tasks to another member of the group, following the steps described in the text (explaining, setting objectives, and developing a plan). The third group member will observe and evaluate the delegation of the task; an evaluation form appears at the end of this exercise. Members then switch roles for the second task and again for the third. By the end of the exercise, each person in the group will have delegated a task, received an assignment, and observed the delegation of a task. (Note that in the real world, the process would not end with the delegation of the task. As a manager, you would establish control checkpoints to ensure that the task was completed as required.) After each person in the group has delegated a task, the group should discuss how effectively he or she delegated.

Delegation Task 1

Delegator: You are a college student with a paper due in three days. You have handwritten 20 pages, but they must be typed. You don't type well, so you have decided to hire someone to do it for you. The going rate is $1.50 per page. Be sure to include the course name, paper title, special typing instructions, and so on. Assume that you are meeting the typist for the first time and that he or she doesn't know you.

Receiver of the assignment: Assume that you are willing to do the job.

Delegation Task 2

Delegator: You are the manager of a fast-food restaurant. In the past, you have set workers' schedules, and your policy has been to continually vary them. You have decided to delegate the scheduling to your assistant manager. This person has never done any scheduling but appears to be very willing and confident about taking on new responsibility.

Receiver of the assignment: Assume that you are interested in doing the scheduling if the manager delegates the task.

Delegation Task 3

Delegator: You own and manage your own business. You have eight employees, one of whom is the organization's secretary. The secretary presently uses an old desktop computer, which needs to be replaced. You can afford to spend up to $1,000 for a new computer. Because the secretary will use the new machine, you believe that this employee should be involved in or maybe even make the decision. The secretary has never purchased equipment for the company, and you believe the person will be somewhat insecure about the assignment.

Receiver of the assignment: Assume that you are able to do the job but are somewhat insecure.

Evaluation Form

Each group should use three copies of this form: one for the observer, one for the person filling the role of delegator, and one for the person filling the role of receiver of the assignment. (The three forms should be labeled somehow, perhaps with *O* for observer, *D* for delegator, and *R* for receiver.) As one person in the group is delegating a task, the observer checks the steps that the delegator accomplishes. On another copy of the form, the delegator of the task checks those steps he or she believes are accomplished. On the third copy of this form, the receiver of the assignment checks those steps the delegator accomplishes. (When group members change roles for the next delegation task, they should exchange evaluation forms so that each person has the form appropriate to his or her role.) Discuss the questions below after each delegation situation. (The discussion should focus on any discrepancies between the evaluations of the three group members.)

Did the receiver of the assignment clearly understand what was expected and how to follow the plan?

How could the delegation be improved?

Apply It

What did I learn from this experience? How will I use this knowledge in the future?

Did the delegator follow these steps in Model 7-1, "The Delegation Process"?	Delegation Task		
	1	2	3
Step 1. Explain the need for delegating and the reason for selecting the employee.			
Step 2. Set an objective that defines responsibility and level of authority, and set a deadline.			
Step 3. Develop a plan—was it effective?			
Step 4. Were there any checkpoints, and was the person held accountable?			

••• SKILL BUILDER 7-4: JOB SIMPLIFICATION

Objective

To improve your skills at job simplification.

Skills

The primary skills developed through this exercise are:

1. *Management skill*—decision making (organizing requires designing jobs)

2. *AACSB competencies*—analytic skills and reflective thinking skills

3. Management function—organizing

Preparing for Skill Builder 7-4

For this exercise, you will use job simplification for your morning routine by following the steps below.

1. Make a flowchart by listing exactly what you do every morning from the time you get out of bed until the time you get to school/work in step-by-step order. Be sure to number each step and to list each activity separately. (For example, don't just write "Go to the bathroom," but list each activity you do while in the bathroom to prep for the day—shower, shave, brush teeth, comb hair, etc.)

2. At the end of the day (or whenever you have some free time), do a job simplification analysis of your flowchart to see if there are any activities you can eliminate, combine, and/or change the sequence of.

3. Based on your analysis, develop a new flowchart that eliminates, combines, and/or changes the sequence of the tasks you typically perform every morning.

4. Consciously follow the steps of your new flowchart until it becomes routine.

Apply It

What did I learn from this experience? How will I use this knowledge in the future?

8 Managing Teamwork

••• LEARNING OBJECTIVES

After studying this chapter, you should be able to:

8-1. Contrast groups and teams, and explain the group performance model. PAGE 242

8-2. Discuss the five components of group structure. PAGE 243

8-3. Define the six components of group process, and describe how they are used to maximize team performance. PAGE 248

8-4. Describe the four major stages of group development, and identify the appropriate leadership style usually associated with each. PAGE 252

8-5. Indicate how to develop groups into teams. PAGE 255

8-6. Explain how to plan a meeting, conduct it, and handle problem members during the meeting. PAGE 257

Ideas on Management
at W. L. Gore & Associates

W. L. Gore & Associates is a materials science company focused on discovery and productive innovation, with more than 2,000 patents worldwide. By using proprietary technologies with the versatile polymer polytetrafluoroethylene (PTFE), Gore offers 124 products through these product divisions: Consumer Products, Cables & Cable Assemblies, Electronic Components & Electrochemical Materials, Fabrics, Fibers, Filtration, Medical, Pharmaceutical & Biopharmaceutical, Sealants, and Venting.

You may wear clothing with GORE-TEX® (a waterproof, breathable, windproof fabric) or use Glide® dental floss, and you most likely have heard music played on its Elixir® guitar strings. You may have enjoyed static-free cell phone calls courtesy of the Gore SnapSHOT®, and one of its newest products, GORE® Acoustic Vent, lets you drop your cell phone in the water without any damage. Also, more than 40 million innovative Gore medical devices have been implanted, saving and improving the quality of lives worldwide.

The company was founded by **Wilbert L. (Bill) and Genevieve (Vieve) Gore** back in 1958, and they developed a strong corporate culture, long before *culture* became a buzzword, that still exists today. Much of Gore's innovative success comes from the power of its small, self-managing teams' organizational structure, described by Bill Gore as a "latticework" of strong interconnected talents woven together like a tapestry.

Today, Gore has annual sales of around $3 billion. It remains a privately held company, but its more than 10,000 employees globally are also part owners of the enterprise through the Associate stock plan. Gore has offices in more than 25 countries, with manufacturing operations in the United States, Germany, the United Kingdom, China, and Japan. It is also one of the few manufacturing technology-driven companies with a woman CEO, **Terri Kelly**. But Kelly doesn't like the term *CEO* because she views her most important job as empowering the individual. Gore is a *Fortune* 100 Best Companies to Work For all-star, having appeared on the list every year since 1998. As an early innovator in team structure and human resource practices, it has long been studied and replicated as a model for best practices.

IOM 1. How does W. L. Gore & Associates benefit from the use of groups and teams?

IOM 2. How does W. L. Gore's lattice structure facilitate teamwork?

IOM 3. How is group process managed at W. L. Gore?

IOM 4. What programs are in place at W. L. Gore to foster group development?

IOM 5. How does W. L. Gore ensure productive meetings?

IOM 6. What technology change was Gore slow to adopt?

You'll find answers to these **IOM** questions throughout the chapter. To learn more about W. L. Gore, visit www.gore.com.

Sources: Information for this case was taken from the W. L. Gore & Associates website at http://www .gore.com, accessed April 10, 2017; R. E. Silverman, "Who's the Boss? There Isn't One," *The Wall Street Journal* (June 20, 2012): B1, B8; D. Roberts, "A Latticework of Workers," *Fortune* (March 5, 2015): 130–134.

EXHIBIT 8-1   GROUPS VERSUS TEAMS

Characteristics	Group	Team
Size	Two or more; can be large	Small number, often 5 to 12
Leadership	One clear leader making decisions	Shared leadership
Jobs	Members perform one clear job; individual members do one independent part of a process and pass it on to the next person to do the next part.	Members share job responsibility by performing many interdependent tasks with complementary skills; the team completes an entire process.
Accountability and Evaluation	The leader evaluates individual members' performance.	Members evaluate each other's individual performance and group performance.
Rewards	Members are rewarded based on individual performance only.	Members are rewarded for both individual and group performance.
Objectives	Organizational	Organizational and those set by the team
Level of Autonomy		
Group Management-Directed	Semiautonomous	Team Self-Directed

LO 8-1

Contrast groups and teams, and explain the group performance model.

group Two or more members, with a clear leader, who perform independent jobs with individual accountability, evaluation, and rewards.

team A small number of members, with shared leadership, who perform interdependent jobs with both individual and group accountability, evaluation, and rewards.

group performance model Group performance is a function of organizational context, group structure, group process, and group development.

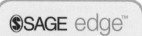

Get the edge on your studies. **edge.sagepub.com/lussier8e**

- Take a quiz to find out what you've learned.
- Review key terms with eFlashcards.
- Watch videos that enhance chapter content.

Groups and Teams and Performance

Refer to Chapter 4, Exhibit 4-4, for the list of advantages and disadvantages of using groups and when it is appropriate to use a group to make decisions. As discussed in the last chapter, companies are adopting team-based organizational designs[1] and relying on team creativity to innovate (Chapter 6).[2] Teamwork skills are based on your ability to work well with others (interpersonal skills, Chapter 1) by developing relationships.[3] **AACSB's** (Chapter 1) necessary competencies include team skills,[4] as the ability to work collaboratively is an important skill company recruiters seek in job applicants.[5] In this section, we discuss the differences between groups and teams, some factors that affect group performance, and the effects of organizational context on performance. First, complete Self-Assessment 8-1 to determine how much of a team player you are.

Groups and Teams

Although the terms *group* and *team* are used interchangeably, a distinction can be made between them. A **group** has two or more members, with a clear leader, who perform independent jobs with individual accountability, evaluation, and rewards. A **team** has a small number of members, with shared leadership, who perform interdependent jobs with individual and group accountability, evaluation, and rewards. Group managers are also called *directive leaders* and team leaders *empowering leaders*.[6] All teams are groups, but not all groups are teams.

Distinctions between groups and teams and their levels of autonomy are presented in Exhibit 8-1. As shown at the bottom of the exhibit, groups and teams are on a continuum; it's not always easy to make a clear distinction. The terms *management-directed, semiautonomous,* and *self-managed* (or *self-directed*) are commonly used to differentiate along the continuum. Management-directed is clearly a group, self-directed is clearly a team, and semiautonomous is between the two. *Mechanistic organizations*, like **McDonald's**, tend to use management-directed groups, whereas more *organic organizations* (Chapter 7), like **Zappos** and **Google**, use more self-directed teams. **Square** and **Twitter CEO Jack Dorsey** says that he focuses on building teams.[7]

The Group Performance Model

The performance of groups is based on four major factors. According to the **group performance model**, *group performance is a function of organizational context, group structure, group process, and group development.* Team members tend to be more engaged than group members,

8-1 SELF-ASSESSMENT

Are You a Team Player?

Rate each of the following statements by placing a number from 1 (*does not describe me*) to 5 (*describes me*) on the line. Use the scale below.

5	4	3	2	1
Describes me				Does not describe me

____ 1. I focus on what I accomplish during team projects.

____ 2. I don't like to compromise.

____ 3. I depend on myself to get ahead.

____ 4. I prefer to work alone rather than in a group when I have a choice.

____ 5. I like to do things my way.

____ 6. I do things myself to make sure the job gets done right.

____ 7. I know that teams do better when each member has a particular contribution to make.

____ 8. I'm more productive when I work alone.

____ 9. I try to get things done my way when I work with others.

____ 10. It bothers me if I can't get the group to do things my way.

Add the numbers you assigned to the statements, and place the total on the continuum below.

50	45	40	35	30	25	20	15	10
Individual								Team Player

and engaged teams grow profits three times faster than disengaged ones.[8] The group performance model is illustrated in Exhibit 8-2. A number of overall organizational and environmental factors affect how groups function and their level of performance.[9] These organizational context factors have been discussed in prior chapters and are listed in the exhibit. The other three factors affecting group performance are covered in detail in the following sections.

Groups and teams are the backbone of organizations because of the systems effect: Each group's/department's performance is affected by at least one other group, and each department affects the performance of the total organization.[10] So through this chapter and the rest of the book, you can improve important teamwork skills and your ability to develop and build teams.[11]

Group Structure

Group structure dimensions include *group type, size, composition, leadership,* and *objectives.* Each of these five components of group structure is described in this section. A major challenge of group work is that it always implies some form of coordination within a group/department and among the firm's various teams.[12] As shown in Exhibit 8-2, you have got to get the group structure right to maximize team performance.

The organizational structure is a contemporary design at **Gore** (**IOM 1**). It has no rigid hierarchy, as it is a team-based, networking, learning organization as described in Chapter 5.

WORK
APPLICATION 8-1

Consider your present job or a past job. Did you work in a group or a team? Explain, using each of the six characteristics in Exhibit 8-1. Note: You may want to select one job and use it to answer the work applications throughout this chapter.

LO 8-2

Discuss the five components of group structure.

group structure dimensions
Group type, size, composition, leadership, and objectives.

8-1 APPLYING THE CONCEPT

Group or Team

Identify each statement as characteristic of a group (A) or a team (B).

A. a group

B. a team

____ 1. "Sharon, I'd rather just get paid for my own output. I make more money with this current bonus system because I sell more than the rest of the sales reps."

____ 2. "Cindy, I get the assembled product from Tina; then I paint it and send it to Jamal for packaging."

____ 5. "There are ten people in my department, and we get along well, Jose."

____ 6. "Our boss is great, Hanna. She lets us all participate in decisions."

____ 5. "Supervisor Kim is the only one who conducts employee performance appraisals in our department."

____ 6. "Your department has goals, Eddy; we don't. But we have been told to do the best we can to accomplish the company mission statement."

EXHIBIT 8-2   ## GROUP PERFORMANCE MODEL

Group Performance Is a Function of:			
Organizational Context	**Group Structure**	**Group Process**	**Group Development**
Environment (Chapters 2 and 3)	Type	Roles	Forming
Mission (Chapters 2 and 5)	Size	Norms	Storming
Strategy (Chapter 5)	Composition	Cohesiveness	Norming
Culture (Chapter 2)	Leadership	Status	Performing
Structure (Chapter 7)	Objectives	Decision making	Terminating
Systems processes (Chapters 1 and 15)		Conflict resolution	

Gore has a strong network of partners. Managers are called leaders who oversee teams and divisions. Teams in its "latticework" structure set objectives and are responsible for achieving them. Team members select new members, and twice each year, team members rank each other based on who is adding the most value to the company, which affects individual pay raises. In addition, Gore rewards all associates (they are not called employees) with profit sharing and stock options.

Group Types

Some of the **group types** are *formal or informal, functional or cross-functional,* and *command or task.*

Formal or Informal Groups. *Formal groups,* such as departments and their smaller sub-parts, are created by an organization as part of its formal structure. All employees have formal group membership, and the higher in the organization, the more formal groups the manager is a member of. *Informal groups* are not created by the organization as part of the formal structure. Members join together voluntarily because of similar interests and develop social structures.[13] Employees form network communities.[14]

Functional or Cross-Functional Groups. The members of *functional,* or vertical, *groups* perform jobs within one limited area. A work unit or department is a functional group. The members of *cross-functional,* or horizontal, *groups* come from different areas and possibly different levels of an organization, and they are on the increase[15] largely because they help

group types Formal or informal, functional or cross-functional, and command or task.

specialized departments understand and coordinate with other departments, such as having marketing give input to product design engineering to ensure the product meets customer demands.[16] **ArcelorMittal** steel company has cross-functional teams review and monitor product innovation and **Suburban Hospital** to coordinate patient health care. Generally, the higher the management level, the more cross-functional the responsibility.

Companies create lots of small teams, but they have to link them to have a common shared consciousness to achieve the organization's mission and objectives.[17] Ideally, all functional groups coordinate their activities through the aid of the managers, who are responsible for linking the activities together.[18] Exhibit 8-3 illustrates functional and cross-functional groups with managers acting as linking pins.

©iStockphoto.com/Rawpixel

Technology makes it easier for virtual teams to work together effectively. Globalization means that the need for global virtual teams will increase, especially for multinational corporate employees.

Command or Task Groups. Command groups *consist of managers and the employees they supervise.* People are usually hired to be a part of a command group, such as **Formula 1** racing teams that spring into action during pit stops. Command groups are distinguished by department membership as functional or cross-functional. In Exhibit 8-3, the president and the vice presidents are a cross-functional command group, whereas each vice president and the managers reporting to him or her form a functional command group. **Task groups** *consist of employees selected to work on a specific objective.* There are two primary types of task groups: task forces and standing committees.

A *task force*, or *ad hoc committee*, is a temporary group formed for a specific purpose. *Project teams,* which use a matrix structure (Chapter 7), are a form of task group in which employees have a functional boss and work with cross-functional departments as needed. **Microsoft** used this type of team to create the **Surface** tablet. The purpose of the task force highlighted in Exhibit 8-3's oval shapes is to select three top candidates to present to the board of directors as potential replacements for the current president, who will retire in six months. This task force has members from all the functional areas in the company.

A *standing committee* is a permanent task group that works on continuing organizational issues, such as the **University of New Mexico** tenure and promotion committee. Membership on standing committees is often rotated every year so that new ideas are brought to the group. For example, membership may be for three years, with one third of the committee replaced every year.

There are a couple of major differences between a command group and a task group. Command group members tend to be from the same functional area, whereas task groups are often cross-functional. In addition, everyone in an organization belongs to a command group, but employees may never be a member of a cross-functional task group. Generally, the higher the level of management, the more time is spent in task groups and their meetings.

Global Virtual Teams. The members of **global virtual teams** *are physically located in different places but work together as a team.* Advances in information and telecommunications technologies are allowing new ways of structuring, processing, and distributing work and overcoming the barriers of distance and time.[19] MNCs developing new global products, such as **GE, Disney,** and **Google,**[20] and those with 24/7/365 tech support, such as **HP** and **IBM,** and small businesses, such as **N2 Publishing** and **Bumble** online dating service, have global virtual teams.[21]

Group Size

There Is No Ideal Group Size. There is no clear agreement on the ideal number, as it varies depending on the purpose, situation, and type of work performed. Groups tend to be larger than teams, and size is the span of management (Chapter 7).[22] At **Titeflex**, teams of 6 to 10 people manufacture fluid- and gas-holding systems. **Johnsonville Foods** uses self-managed

WORK
APPLICATION 8-2

Identify task groups used in an organization you work for or have worked for. Specify whether each group is a task force or a standing committee.

command groups Groups that consist of managers and the employees they supervise.

task groups Employees selected to work on a specific objective.

global virtual teams Teams whose members are physically located in different places but work together as a team.

8-2 | APPLYING THE CONCEPT

Types of Group Structure

EXHIBIT 8-3 | FUNCTIONAL AND CROSS-FUNCTIONAL GROUPS

Identify the dimension of the group structure exemplified in each statement.

A. formal group

B. informal group

C. functional group

D. cross-functional group

E. task force

F. standing committee

G. global virtual team

7. "Hank, don't forget we have a Skype meeting with our England and German engineers at 6:00 our time today."

8. "Suzan, I just got elected to serve a three-year term on the budgeting group."

9. "Juanita, some of our department members are going skiing next Sunday. Want to join us?"

10. "Kirsten, will you serve on the search group to select the new software program?"

11. "Kent, our group consist of our sales manager and seven sales reps."

teams of around 12. **Amazon** CEO **Jeff Bezos** uses the "two-pizza rule" to guide team size. If it takes more than two pizzas to feed the team, it's too big.[23]

A group that is too small limits ideas and creativity. The workload is not distributed over enough members. On the other hand, a group that is too large tends to be too slow and less innovative, and not everyone gets to participate.[24] With 20 or more members, reaching a consensus slows down.[25] In large groups, *freeriding* (also called *social loafing*) is also a problem, as members rely on others to carry their share of the workload.[26]

Connections: Five- to Nine-Member Relationships and Performance. Our short-term memory works best in holding between five and nine items—or seven plus or minus two (think telephone numbers and zip codes). Groups of less than five often break into pairs or trios, and with more than nine, team communications break down. Why? Most of us are good at staying in contact with five or six others, but it's difficult with 12 or more. The larger the group, the more connections (or people to talk to) we have, and the harder it is to have effective communications. Effective teams are based on good relationships, and as the number of team members grows, relationships degrade quickly as shown here.

2 members = 1 connection	16 members = 256 connections
4 members = 6 connections	32 members = 1,024 connections
6 members = 15 connections	1,500 members = 2.25 million connections

So having five to nine members generally provides the best relationships and performance.[27] Even with social media networks, like **Facebook** and **LinkedIn**, we don't have the time or the bandwidth to continually maintain hundreds of close, really personal connections.[28]

How Size Affects Management. The appropriate leadership style may depend on group size. The larger the size, the more formal or autocratic the leadership needs to be to provide direction. Managers tend to be more informal and participative when they have smaller teams. Generally, participation is more equal in groups of around five. This is why teams are small. The larger the group (department), the greater the need for formal and structured plans, policies, procedures, and rules.

Management Implications. Usually, managers have no say in the size of their command groups. However, if you have a large department, you can break this larger group into teams of five to nine. As the chair of a committee, you may be able to select the group size. Remember that people are more willing to express their opinions, concerns, and ideas in smaller groups. In doing so, keep the group size appropriate for the task, and be sure to get the right group composition.[29]

Group Composition

Group composition *is the mix of members' skills and abilities.* Recall from Chapter 3 that diversity provides group benefits, but it is tough to get it right.[30] Regardless of type and size, group or team performance is affected by the composition.[31] Without the right mix of skills and abilities, a group will not perform at high levels.[32]

Management Implications. One of the most important group leadership functions is to attract, select, and retain the best people for the job. When selecting group or team members, be sure to include diverse individuals. You want members with complementary skills rather than people with the same skills.[33] Cross-functional teams are likely to provide diversity and complementary skills. **Tory Burch,** fashion designer and CEO, recommends surrounding yourself with excellent people who bring a lot of skills.[34]

Group Leadership and Objectives

Leadership. To a large extent, the leader determines group structure and the success of the team.[35] Exhibit 8-1 pointed out that the leadership style is different in groups and teams, as team leaders share the responsibility[36] as they empower the team members.[37] The quality of team leadership, whether from the formal leaders or other team members (like you), is becoming increasingly important as it affects team performance.[38] You will learn more about group and team leadership and managing teams throughout this chapter.

Objectives. In Chapter 5, you learned the benefits of setting objectives; they apply to both individuals and groups, and teams set their own objectives. In groups, however, the objective is commonly very broad—usually to fulfill the mission.

Management Implications. Part of a leader's responsibility is to be sure the size and composition of a group or team is appropriate for the situation. Realize that in both formal and informal groups and teams, there are official and unofficial leaders who influence each other and the members.[39] As a group or team leader or as a member with leadership skills, be sure that the group or team has clear objectives.

In summary, group structure dimensions include group type, size, composition, leadership, and objectives. Exhibit 8-4 reviews group structure dimensions. How associates work at **Gore (IOM 2)** sets them apart. It is a *team-based, flat lattice organization.* There are no traditional

WORK
APPLICATION 8-3

Identify a group or team you belong to and describe its size, composition, leadership, and objectives.

group composition The mix of members' skills and abilities.

8-1 JOIN THE DISCUSSION ETHICS & SOCIAL RESPONSIBILITY

Team Players

JetBlue Airways is not structured around teams. However, teamwork skills and attitudes are important to the success of JetBlue. In fact, JetBlue screens job candidates extensively to make sure that they are team players.

1. Is it necessary to be a team player to be a successful employee at JetBlue?

2. Is it ethical and socially responsible of JetBlue to reject job candidates because they are considered not to be team players?

EXHIBIT 8-4   DIMENSIONS OF GROUP STRUCTURE

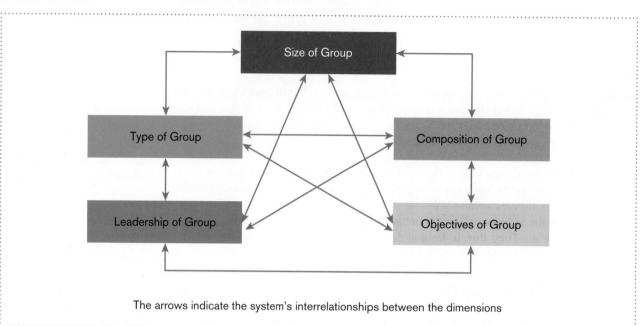

The arrows indicate the system's interrelationships between the dimensions

organizational charts, no chains of command, and no predetermined channels of communication. It's been called the bossless company. How does this work? Associates are hired for general work areas. With the guidance of their sponsors (not bosses), associates commit to projects that match their skills. Everyone can earn the credibility to define and drive projects. Sponsors help associates chart a course in the organization that will offer personal fulfillment while maximizing their contribution to the enterprise. Leaders may be appointed, but more often, leaders emerge naturally by demonstrating special knowledge, skill, or experience that advances a business objective.

LO 8-3

Define the six components of group process, and describe how they are used to maximize team performance.

Group Process

Group process *refers to the patterns of interactions that emerge as members perform their jobs.* Group process is also called *group dynamics.*[40] It is about how members get along, not how they do their work. Relationships affect our behavioral interactions in groups,[41] and group process affects team performance.[42] **Group process dimensions** *are roles, norms, cohesiveness, status, decision making, and conflict resolution.* These components are discussed in this section.

Group Roles

Job and group roles are different,[43] and they can change.[44] *Job roles* are shared expectations of how group members will fulfill the requirements of their position—what you do to get the job done—whereas group roles are the roles used through group process—how you interact as you work. For high levels of performance, roles should be integrated.[45]

Classifying Group Roles. The three primary **group roles** *are group task roles, group maintenance roles, and self-interest roles.*

Group task roles are played by members who do and say things that directly aid in the accomplishment of the group's objectives.[46] Task roles are often said to be structuring, job centered, production oriented, task oriented, or directive, such as "John, turn on the ignition switch to see if the engine starts now."

group process The patterns of interactions that emerge as members perform their jobs.

group process dimensions Roles, norms, cohesiveness, status, decision making, and conflict resolution.

group roles Group task roles, group maintenance roles, and self-interest roles.

Group maintenance roles are played by members who do and say things to develop and sustain the group process with cooperative behavior to benefit others or the entire team.[47] Terms used to describe maintenance roles include employee centered, relationship oriented, and supportive, such as "Hydria, you did a great job fixing that engine."

Self-interest roles are played by members who do and say selfish things (often hidden agendas) that help themselves at the expense of other members or the entire group.[48] People with narcissistic personalities often only seek personal gain,[49] and self-centered people are less happy than those who look out for others.[50] Are you and your coworkers just looking out for yourselves—"What's in it for me?"—or the team?

How Roles Affect Group Performance. To be effective, a group must have members who play task roles and maintenance roles while minimizing self-interest roles. Groups that have only task role players may suffer performance problems because they do not deal with common conflict between members effectively[51] and because the job will be boring if there is no maintenance. On the other hand, groups that have a great time but do not have members playing task roles will not get the job done. Any group whose members are mostly playing self-interest roles will not produce to its fullest potential.

Management Implications. If you are a manager or team member, you should be aware of the roles the group members play. If no member is playing the task or maintenance role required at a given time, you should play the role. As the manager, you should also make the group aware of the need to play these roles and the need to minimize self-interest roles. Try to create a win-win situation by balancing personal and organizational interest.[52] Later in the chapter, you will learn about group development and how the leader should use task and maintenance roles to help the group develop.

Group Norms

In addition to policies, procedures, and rules, all groups form their own unwritten norms that determine what is socially accepted as appropriate behavior.[53] Rules are formally established by management or by the group itself.[54] Norms are not developed by management or explicitly agreed to by a group; they develop as members interact.[55] Norms are also called unspoken rules of a group that shape behavior and attitudes.[56] **Norms** *are expectations about behavior that are shared by members of a group.*

How Norms Develop. Norms develop spontaneously as the members of a group interact and compare themselves to the other members. For example, the group decides, without ever actually talking about it, what is an acceptable level of work. If the group members develop a shared expectation that a certain level is desirable, members will produce it. For example, the military has the **Uniform Code of Military Justice (UCMJ)**, Article 134, stating that indecent language should not be used. However, some members and groups develop the norm of breaking the rule and swearing. Most of us want to be liked and fit in with the group, so we tend to follow group norms,[57] even when we disagree with the behavior.[58] What have you done to fit in, or when didn't you try to stop group members from doing unethical or illegal behaviors? Norms can change over time to meet the needs of the group.

How Groups Enforce Norms. If a group member does not follow a norm, the other members try to enforce compliance—in other words, *peer pressure.*[59] As we have all faced group pressure, we can understand how it is a powerful influence over our behavior. For example, if Sal works at more than the accepted level of performance, other members may kid or ridicule him. If Sal continues to break the norm, members might take his tools or supplies and even damage his work to slow down his production. Sal could be considered an outsider of the group.

Management Implications. Be aware that we tend to adjust our behaviors to try to match that of our team norms, so be careful not to be led into illegal or unethical behavior. Research at **Google** found that who you put on a team is less important than having positive norms, such as everyone talks in meetings and feels safe sharing ideas without being judged.[60] So you should be

WORK APPLICATION 8-4

Identify members of a group or team you have been on and state the primary group role each played in the group.

WORK APPLICATION 8-5

Identify at least two norms that developed in a group/team of which you were a member. Explain how you knew they were norms and how the group enforced those norms.

norms Expectations about behavior that are shared by members of a group.

8-2 JOIN THE DISCUSSION ETHICS & SOCIAL RESPONSIBILITY

Norms

Group members influence each other's behavior through the development and enforcement of norms—that is, essentially through peer pressure. In general, this process is positive, as it helps get the job done. On the other side, complying with illegal or unethical norms can lead to disasters, as it did at Enron.

1. Should employees be able to "do their own thing" without group enforcement of norms?

2. Is it ethical and socially responsible for groups to develop and enforce norms? If yes, what type of ethical standards should a group have?

aware of group norms and work toward maintaining and developing positive norms and try to eliminate negative norms. Managers should be positive role models of desired norms,[61] and they should confront groups with negative norms and try to work out solutions to make them positive.

Group Cohesiveness

The extent to which members of a group abide by and enforce the group norms depends on the degree of loyalty and cohesiveness. **Group cohesiveness** *is the extent to which members stick together.* The more cohesive the group, the more it sticks together—bonds—as a team.

Factors Influencing Cohesiveness. Six factors influence group cohesiveness: The stronger the agreement with and commitment to the achievement of the group's *objectives* and the more *success* it has at achieving its objectives, the higher the cohesiveness of the group. Generally, the smaller the group *size*, the more *homogeneous* the group members, and the more equal the level of *participation* among members, the higher the cohesiveness. Generally, teams that *compete* against external teams tend to be more cohesive than those with members who compete against each other.

How Cohesiveness Affects Group Performance. Cohesiveness clearly affects team performance.[62] **Great Place to Work** found three important factors contribute to team success in its **World's 25 Best Multinational Workplaces**, which include **H&M**, **Marriott**, and **Google**.[63] First, these companies have a culture of having fun together. Second, everyone is

WORK
APPLICATION 8-6

Identify the level of cohesiveness in a group or team of which you are or have been a member.

group cohesiveness The extent to which members stick together.

8-3 APPLYING THE CONCEPT

Roles

Identify the type of role exemplified in each statement.

A. task

B. maintenance

C. self-interest

_____ 12. "I want to hear Karin's idea before we make this decision."

_____ 13. "So do we all understand the objective? Any questions?"

_____ 14. "We tried your idea before you came to work here, Sandy. It did not work then, so it won't work now. Let's just do it my way."

_____ 15. "We are getting sidetracked talking about TV shows we like to watch."

_____ 16. "Tolo's idea is better than mine. Let's implement her idea instead of mine."

included; members like to be together, as they care for each other. Last, they cooperate and behave according to the group norms. So team members play both task and maintenance roles, and no one plays self-interest roles as they all work for the success of the team.

Management Implications. As a team member or leader, you should strive to develop cohesive groups that exhibit a high level of productivity. It is important to have fun, care for each other, and cooperate.[64] So play maintenance roles to make sure all team members feel welcome, respected, and valued for their contribution. Try to avoid having members break into cliques of insiders that exclude outsiders[65]—you've seen it, haven't you? Implement the six factors above that help develop team cohesiveness by helping the team set and achieve objectives. Try to keep the team size small, get everyone to participate, focus more on external competition, and be sure to be inclusive to maximize diversity as discussed in Chapter 3.

Status Within the Group

Status hierarchies develop in teams.[66] The more respect, prestige, influence, and power a group member has, the higher the status within the group.[67] **Status** *is the perceived ranking of one member relative to other members in the group.* It's common to strive for high status within the group.[68]

The Development of Status. Status is based on several factors, including members' performance, job title, wage or salary, seniority, knowledge or expertise, interpersonal skills, appearance, education, race, age, sex, and so on. A group is more willing to listen to a high-status member and to overlook such a member's breaking of the norms. High-status members also have more influence on the development of the group's norms and the decisions made by the group. Lower-status members' ideas are often ignored, and they tend to copy high-status members' behavior and to agree with their suggestions in order to be accepted.[69]

An individual may develop high status among their peers based on their performance, skill set, seniority, knowledge, and other factors. A high-status individual has more influence over others in their group, giving them the ability to greatly affect group performance.

How Status Affects Group Performance. High-status members have a major impact on a group's performance.[70] In a command group, the boss is usually the member with the highest status. The leader's ability to manage affects the group performance. Other high-status members also affect performance. If high-status members support positive norms and high productivity, chances are the rest of the group will, too. To help break down management and employee status so that teams better share leadership, companies including **Facebook** downplay titles and any status symbols of management, such as executive dining rooms and parking spaces.

Another important factor influencing group performance is status congruence. *Status congruence* is the acceptance and satisfaction members receive from their group status. Members who are not satisfied with their status may not be active participants of the group.[71] They may physically or mentally escape from the group and not perform to their full potential. Or they may cause group conflict as they fight for a higher status level.

Management Implications. To be effective, you need to have high status within a command group.[72] As the manager, maintain good human relations with the group, particularly with the high-status informal leaders, to be sure that they endorse positive norms and objectives. Be aware of and try to prevent conflicts that may be the result of lack of status congruence. Ideally, status should be about equal among group members. But in reality, be sure to listen to and include low-status members in the group process to ensure cohesiveness so they are not outsiders of the group.[73]

Decision Making and Conflict Resolution

The decisions made by groups and teams have a direct effect on performance.[74] Recall from Chapter 4, Exhibit 4-4, that there are advantages and disadvantages to group decision making.

WORK
APPLICATION 8-7

Recall a group of which you were a member. List each member, including you, and identify each person's level of status within the group. Explain why each member had the level of status you identified.

status The perceived ranking of one member relative to other members in a group.

In groups, decision-making authority is held by the manager, whereas in teams, decision-making authority is held by the members through empowerment. Shared-decision making is the trend.[75] However, the level of participation in a decision should be based on the decision, as discussed in Chapter 4's Skill Builder 4-2 using Model 4-1, "Situational Decision Making." Also, for group decisions to be successfully implemented, the group must unify behind the decision, even if some members vigorously disagree with it.

Conflict is common in groups and teams, and unresolved conflicts can have a negative effect on performance.[76] Conflict of ideas can help team performance, but personal conflicts tend to hurt relationships and performance. Unresolved conflict often leads to members' withdrawal from the group process and hurts cohesiveness. So you need to prevent disruptive conflicts and resolve conflicts to maintain productive working relationships.[77] In Chapter 10, you will develop your skills at resolving conflict.

At **Gore** (**IOM 3**), sponsors help new associates understand and carry out their roles within the team, learn the norms, fit in, gain status, handle conflict, and be an active part of team decision making. Gore plays down status differences with its philosophy that "we have no managers and employees; we are *all* associates working as a team."

If you understand and develop group process skills, you will be a more effective member, leader, and manager. Exhibit 8-5 summarizes the six dimensions of group process.

LO 8-4

Describe the four major stages of group development, and identify the appropriate management style usually associated with each.

Stages of Group Development and Management Styles

It is generally agreed that all groups go through the same stages of development identified by **Bruce Tuckman**.[78] This has been called the team development process[79] and cycle.[80] The **stages of group development** are *forming, storming, norming, performing, and termination.* As groups grow and change, so should the ways in which they are managed. In this section, we discuss the five stages of group development and an appropriate management style for each stage, as illustrated in Model 8-1.

Stage 1. Forming—Autocratic Management Style

stages of group development Forming, storming, norming, performing, and termination.

The *forming stage*, also known as the *orientation stage,* is characterized by a low development level. When people first form a group, they tend to have moderate to high commitment to group membership. However, because they have not worked together, they often do not have the competence to do the job as a team.

8-4   APPLYING THE CONCEPT

Group Process

Identify the dimension of the group process exemplified in each statement.

A. roles

B. norms

C. cohesiveness

D. status

E. decision making

F. conflict resolution

_____ 18. "You're late, Sue. Everyone else was on time, so we started without you. Be on time for the next meeting."

_____ 19. "What does this topic have to do with solving the problem we are working on?"

_____ 20. "We do have occasional differences of opinion, Jon. But you will find out that we really get along well and enjoy working together."

_____ 21. "Let's stop the discussion and select one of these three insurance packages."

_____ 22. "That's a tough one. Go ask Kennedy; she knows more about the program than any of us."

_____ 23. "Every time there is a disagreement, Aden tries to get the members to work out the problem."

EXHIBIT 8-5 **DIMENSIONS OF GROUP PROCESS**

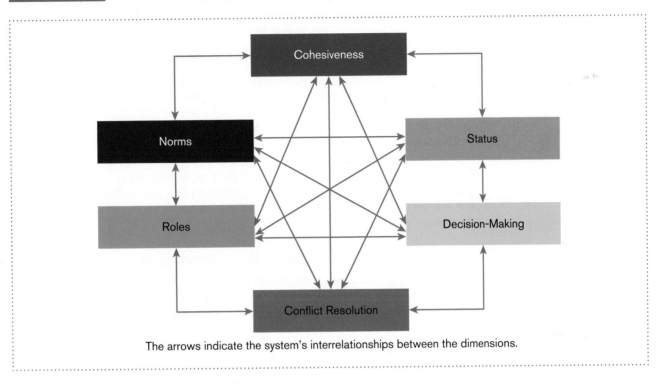

The arrows indicate the system's interrelationships between the dimensions.

MODEL 8-1 **STAGES OF GROUP DEVELOPMENT AND MANAGEMENT**

Stage of Group Development	Forming	Storming	Norming	Performing
Level of Group Development	1. Low	2. Moderate	3. High	4. Outstanding
Management Style	Autocratic	Consultative	Participative	Empowering
Management Behavior	High Directive[1] Low Supportive[2]	High Directive High Supportive	Low Directive High Supportive	Low Directive Low Supportive

Competence

Commitment

[1] Directive behavior is using a group task role.
[2] Supportive behavior is using a group maintenance role.

During forming, members have concerns about the structure, leadership, and objectives of the group. Note that command groups are rarely started with all new members but that a change in membership generally does change group process and can affect group development and performance. This stage is more characteristic of task groups that have clear beginnings. Group process issues include anxiety over how members will fit in (status), what will be required of them (roles and norms), what the group will be like (cohesiveness), how decisions will be made, and how members will get along (conflict). These structure and process issues must be resolved if the group is to progress to the next stage of development.

Autocratic Management Style. During the forming stage, the appropriate management style is usually autocratic; that is, a manager tells group members what to do and how to do it and closely oversees their performance. It is a management-directed group. When a group first comes together, you need to spend most of the time directing the group by playing a task role of helping the group clarify its objectives, providing clear expectations of members. But low support doesn't mean none, so you also allow some time for group members to start to get to know one another, playing the maintenance role.

Stage 2. Storming—Consultative Management Style

The *storming stage*, also known as the *dissatisfaction stage*, is characterized by a moderate development level. As members work together for some time, they tend to become dissatisfied with the group. Members start asking such questions as these: "Why am I a member?" "Is the group going to accomplish anything?" "Why don't other group members do what is expected?" Often the task is more complex and difficult than anticipated; members become frustrated and have feelings of incompetence. However, the group does develop some competence to perform the task.

During the dissatisfaction stage, the group needs to work on resolving its structure and process issues before it can progress to the next stage of development. Groups can get stuck in this stage of development by not developing a workable group process; in that case, members may never progress to being satisfied with the group and performing as a team.

Consultative Management Style. During the storming stage, the appropriate management style is usually consultative; that is, you as the manager are highly directive and oversee group members' performance playing the task role, but at the same time, you are highly supportive, including their input, playing the maintenance role, and encouraging members to continue to work toward objectives.

Stage 3. Norming—Participative Management Style

The *norming stage*, also called the *resolution stage*, is characterized by high development. With time, members often resolve the differences between their initial expectations and the realities of objectives, tasks, skills, and so forth. As members develop competence, they often become more satisfied with the group as they develop friendships. Members learn to work together as they attain a group structure and process with acceptable leadership, norms, status, cohesiveness, and decision making. During periods of conflict or change, the group needs to resolve these issues.

Commitment can vary from time to time as the group interacts. If the group does not deal effectively with group process issues, the group may regress to stage 2 or continue fluctuating in commitment and competence. If the group is successful at developing a workable group structure and process, it will move to the next stage.

Participative Management Style. During the norming stage, the appropriate management style is usually participative: You and the group members share decision making. Once group members know what to do and how to do it, there is little need to give directives. The group needs you to play a maintenance role.

When commitment varies, it is usually because there is some problem in the group's process, such as a conflict. You need to focus on maintenance behavior to get the group through the issue(s) it faces. If you continue to provide task directives that are not needed, the group can either become dissatisfied and regress or remain at this level.

Stage 4. Performing—Empowerment Management Style

The *performing stage*, also called the *production stage*, is characterized by outstanding development. At this stage, commitment and competence do not fluctuate much. The group works as a team, with high levels of satisfaction. The group maintains its effective group structure and process. The fact that members are very productive helps lead to positive feelings. The group structure and process may change with time, but the issues are resolved quickly and easily; members are open with each other.

Empowerment Management Style. During the performing stage, the appropriate management style is usually empowering—you give group members the authority to do their task in their own way and to make decisions on their own. It is now a self-directed team. Groups that develop to this stage have members who play the appropriate task and maintenance roles; you do not need to play either type of role unless there is a problem, because the group has effective shared leadership, though not all have equal status and power.

Stage 5. Termination

Command groups do not usually reach the *termination stage*, also called the *adjourning stage*, unless there is some drastic reorganization. However, task groups do terminate. During this stage, members experience feelings about leaving the group, but there is no need for a management style.

Changes in Group Development and Management Style

Different groups make it to different levels of development. However, to help ensure that groups develop, employees can be trained in group process skills. Teams tend to develop to higher levels than groups. As a leader or member of a group or team, be aware of the development stage and use the appropriate management style to help it develop to the desired productivity level.

As a manager, you need to change your leadership behavior to help the group progress through all stages of development. Two key variables in each stage of group development are competence (work on the task) and commitment. These two variables do not progress in the same manner. Competence tends to continue to increase over time, whereas commitment tends to start high, drop off, and then rise. This pattern is illustrated in Model 8-1; the appropriate leadership style and leadership behavior for each stage of development is shown at the bottom. In Skill Builder 8-2 at the end of this chapter, you will develop your ability to identify group development stages and to match the appropriate management style to various real-world situations.

Gore (IOM 4) has ongoing teams that need to take in new members, so new hires get a sponsor responsible for newcomers' success. Associates serve on multiple teams; thus, Gore seeks associates who are good team players and leaders who play the needed task and maintenance roles for group success. So the team, not the manager, takes the team through the stages of group development.

Developing Groups Into Teams

As Exhibit 8-1 points out, groups and teams are different. Among businesses today, the trend is toward the empowerment of teams, because teams can be more productive than groups.[81] As a manager, it's your job to build great teams,[82] but it's not easy to mold a group of employees with different skills and personalities into a functioning and successful team.[83] In this section, we discuss training, explore the difference between a group manager and a team leader, and discuss using recognition and rewards to develop groups into teams.

WORK
APPLICATION 8-8

Recall a group from a present or past job. Identify the group's stage of development and the leadership style. Did the leader use an appropriate style? Explain what could be done to improve the group's structure and/or process.

LO 8-5

Indicate how to develop groups into teams.

Training and Team Leadership

Managers and employees can be trained to become better team players and leaders.[84] But you can't rush the change process, which we discuss before training.

Managing Change and Group Development. Recall from Chapter 6 that it is difficult to manage change. You can't take an organization or group and turn it into a team overnight. You need to carefully take the team through the stages of development, changing management styles to make the transition from group to team, or you will have problems.

Zappos moved quickly to a bossless self-managed team structure called **holacracy** in mid-2015. In resistance to the change, 210 of the company's 1,500 employees (14%) quit,[85] and the company is still working on perfecting this new arrangement.[86] Model 8-1, "Stages of Group Development and Management," says you can't successfully jump from using an autocratic style, telling employees what to do and how, to an empowerment style and leave them alone to figure it out on their own. Should Zappos have changed more slowly through the stages of team development?

Training. Organizations offer ongoing training to benefit both employees and the organization.[87] People can be trained to improve their interpersonal skills and become better team players and leaders.[88] If they are to function as a team, the manager and members need training in group process skills, as you are being trained in this chapter. That is why **AACSB** encourages developing team-building skills.[89] Consulting firms, including **HolacracyOne**, train employees to become teams.[90]

An organizational development (OD) team-building program (Chapter 6) is also very helpful in turning groups into teams with the help of a change agent.[91] **John Bunch** is leading **Zappos**'s transition to holacracy teamwork.[92] As part of team building, firms have employees engage in nonwork activities to get to know each other better.[93] **Indeed** has regular get-together socials at work and occasional trips to help member cohesiveness.[94] Part of formal training is to understand the difference between being a group manager and being a team leader.

WORK
APPLICATION 8-9

Think about the leadership style of a present or past boss. Did that person behave as a group manager or as a team leader? What made you classify the person this way?

Group Managers Versus Team Leaders. The roles of the group manager (directive leadership) and team leader (empowering leadership) are different.[95] The group manager takes responsibility for performing the four functions of management (Chapter 1). **Team leaders** *empower members to take responsibility for performing the management functions and focus on developing effective group structure and group process and on furthering group development.* Team leaders often don't have the word *management* in their title, such as at **Zappos**. Each of its 300 circles has a "lead link," not circle manager, who is similar to a project manager with limited authority.[96] To make the transition, group managers need the attitude of understanding that they are not more important than the rest of the team and that they need to be a team member.[97]

The Management Functions. Let's discuss team leadership, realizing that a group doesn't develop into a team overnight; team development is a gradual process, not a light switch.[98]

- *Leading.* Most teams do identify a specific person as the leader, but the leader shares this responsibility. You don't focus on telling others what to do and assigning individuals to do it. You focus on developing group structure and process. Bring the team up to the performing stage of development, changing management styles with the level of development.

- *Planning.* To convert a group into a team, you must empower the members to set objectives, develop plans, and make decisions. Involve members and make sure that they know the objectives, accept them, and are committed to achieving them.

- *Organizing and Staffing.* The important part of organizing and staffing a team is the participation of its members in selecting, evaluating, and rewarding members. Jobs on a team are interchangeable and are assigned by the members as they perform dependent parts of the entire process.

team leaders Empower members to take responsibility for performing the management functions and focus on developing effective group structure and group process and on furthering group development.

- ***Controlling.*** You help the team set the standards and develop positive norms. As you move from being a group to being a team, members are responsible for monitoring progress, taking corrective action, and performing quality control.

Team Rewards and Recognition

Individuals should be rewarded and recognized, but for teams to succeed, the organizational structure needs to reward and recognize team cooperation rather than focusing on internal competition between individuals. Good team players should get praise, pay raises, promotions, and other rewards and recognition for their work. Incentives need to be tied to performance. The challenge is to correctly balance individual and teamwork compensation and recognition with the level of individual and team performance. One of the problems at **Zappos** was that employees, and especially managers, feared pay cuts and uncertain future compensation and couldn't see any career path with holacracy.[99] Here are three ways that employees can be rewarded and recognized for teamwork.

- ***Nonfinancial.*** Being part of a successful team is satisfying, as it provides opportunity for personal development and to help teammates grow, as well as providing enjoyable relationships. So being part of a satisfying team helps motivate employees to be good team players. The company can also have formal and informal meetings or awards ceremonies to recognize team accomplishments with lunches/dinners, cookouts/barbecues, plaques/certificates, T-shirts/jackets/coffee mugs, and so forth.
- ***Skill-Based Pay.*** Employees are paid for learning additional skills or knowledge they need to perform multiple jobs within a team and to share knowledge with other team members. Skill-based pay works well with self-managing teams performing complex tasks.
- ***Gainsharing and Profit Sharing.*** Employees share the financial gains through increasing productivity, decreasing costs, and improving quality. We will talk more about pay systems in Chapter 9.

WORK
APPLICATION 8-10

Give examples of team rewards and recognition where you work(ed).

LO 8-6

Explain how to plan a meeting, conduct it, and handle problem members during the meetings.

Managing Meetings

James David Powers, founder of **J.D. Powers,** says meetings are critical to team success.[100] As businesses use more teams, meetings are taking up an increasing amount of time for all employees,[101] or teams live in meetings.[102] There are an estimated 11 million meetings each day in the United States, and workers spend at least six hours per week in meetings.[103] Unfortunately, many people don't like meetings,[104] some even dread going to meetings,[105] and most people believe there are too many meetings.[106] Why do employees feel this way?

Participants say about half of the meetings are ineffective, unnecessary, and a waste of time.[107] Author and consultant **Stanley Bing** said that "yesterday I had so many meetings that I didn't get to any of my priority to-do items."[108] Committees have been called a body that keeps minutes and wastes hours. Some of the best managers can't seem to run effective meetings. But after completing this section, you will know how to plan a meeting, conduct it, and handle problem people during meetings. You can also improve meetings by suggesting improvements that you will learn now.

Google cofounder Larry Page gave employees clear guidelines about effective meetings, noting that meetings should have limited attendees who should all contribute to the discussion and one decision maker. Here, Google **CEO Sundar Pichai** meets with four colleagues in his office.

Brooks Kraft LLC/Corbis via Getty Images

Planning Meetings

The quality of both leaders' and members' preparation for a meeting has a direct effect on the meeting; in other words, planning pays off.[109] Unprepared managers tend to conduct unproductive meetings. **Sproxil founder Ashifi Gogo** says to avoid bad meetings.[110] There

EXHIBIT 8-6   MEETING PLAN

Meeting Element	Description	Example
Time	List meeting date, meeting place (unless the team always meets in the same place), and time (both beginning and ending times).	November 22, 2019, Gold Room, 9–10 A.M.
Objectives	State the objective or purpose of the meeting. (Note: Objectives may be listed with agenda items, as shown in agenda item 1 below, rather than as a separate section, but wherever they are listed, they should be specific.)	1. To narrow down the choices of computer systems to two out of six possibilities 2. To get an update on the Venus Project and proposed process change
Participation and assignments	List the assignment for the entire team, or if individual members have different assignments, list each person's name and assignment. (Assignments may be listed as agenda items, as shown in agenda items 2 and 3.)	All members should have read the six enclosed brochures about computer systems before the meeting. Be ready to discuss your preferences.
Agenda	List each item to be covered in the meeting, in order of importance, with an approximate time limit.	1. Discussion of new computer systems; narrow down the choices to two out of six possibilities; 45 minutes 2. Venus Project report (Ted); 5 minutes 3. Presentation on proposed change in production process (Karen); 5 minutes. (Discussion will take place at our next meeting, after team members have had a chance to give the proposal some thought.)

are at least six areas in which planning is needed. A written copy of the plan should be sent to members prior to the meeting. See Exhibit 8-6 for a sample meeting plan.

Objectives. The first thing to ask yourself is, Do we need this meeting, and why? You need everyone to understand why the meeting is important[111] or what they're going to accomplish in a meeting. So, before calling a meeting, clearly define its purpose and set objectives to be accomplished during the meeting. **Google CEO Larry Page** pushes managers to outline clear goals before scheduling a meeting. So if you don't have clear objectives, don't have a meeting. Some meetings are just informational, so send the information via email to all members instead of meeting.

MANAGEMENT IN ACTION

Planning Meetings

Participants and Assignments. Limit attendees,[112] as too many people at a meeting slows things down and wastes the time of people who don't need to attend.[113] **Google** CEO Page limits most meetings to 10 attendees. Meetings run longer when people haven't prepared well for them. So participants should know in advance what is expected of them so they know what they are supposed to do at the meeting.[114] If any preparation is expected (read material, do some research, make a report, and so forth), attendees should have adequate advance notice to prepare.

Agenda. Every formal meeting needs an agenda distributed beforehand.[115] The agenda tells the members what is expected and how the meeting will progress.[116] It should identify the activities that will take place in order to achieve the objective. Team members may also submit agenda items. Having a set time limit for each agenda item helps keep the group on target; needless discussion and getting off the subject are common at meetings.[117] However, you may need to be flexible and allow more time. Agenda items that require action should have objectives listed with them.

Soulcycle founder Melanie Whelan says that when you set priorities on the things that will move your team forward, you're going to have an impact.[118] So place agenda items in order of priority.[119] Then, if the group does not have time to cover every item, the least important items will be carried forward to the next meeting.

Date, Place, and Time. Get team members' input on which days of the week and times of the day are best for meetings, but before lunch is usually the most productive time.[120] When members are close, it is better to have more frequent, shorter meetings focusing on one or a few items. However, when members have to travel, fewer, longer meetings are needed. Yes, it is very important to start and end meetings on time to avoid wasting everyone's time.[121]

Be sure to select an adequate place for the meeting and plan for the physical comfort of the group. Seating should allow eye contact for small discussion groups,[122] and enough time should be allocated so that the members do not have to rush. If reservations are needed for the meeting place, make them far enough in advance to get a proper meeting room.

Meetings are typically scheduled for 30 to 90 minutes, as longer than this reduces the quality of decision making,[123] but they shouldn't run for longer than it takes to accomplish the objectives. However, companies do hold multiple-day meetings, often off site, as they can solve problems and spark creativity.[124] **Zappos** had a three-day orientation for its holacracy program, but some workers looked confused or bored.[125]

Leadership. The leaders' primary role is to facilitate discussion.[126] However, the leader should determine the appropriate management style for the meeting based on the group's development stage, and different agenda items may need to be handled differently. For example, some items may simply call for disseminating information, but others may require a discussion, vote, or consensus; still other items may require a report from a member. An effective way to develop group members' ability is to rotate the role of the group moderator/leader for each meeting. At **Indiana University Alumni Association** staff meetings, members take turns running meetings.[127]

Technology. Let's discuss technology trends and issues here. Email has eliminated the need for some meetings. Ongoing chat rooms and project-sharing tools can also take the place of meetings and are especially useful with virtual teams with members from around the globe in different time zones.[128] Some companies, including **McDonald's**, are having more conference telephone calls. Other companies are having more online meetings.[129] **Johnson & Johnson** and others are using more videoconferencing/**Skype**, as the meeting software is getting better and costs are dropping. These techniques save travel costs and time, and they may result in better and quicker decisions. However, meetings via technology will never be as effective as interacting face to face,[130] so meet in person when feasible.

There is also tech that can help you plan, run, and follow up on meetings, such as smartphone app **Meeting Minutes Pro** that allows you to organize meetings and keep track of results without a slew of follow-up emails.[131] Digital dry-erase boards are available for use during meetings, such as **SMART kapp** ($889), a new **Bluetooth**-connected board that instantly shares meeting notes with team members from anywhere on any device (smartphone) and allows you to save notes before erasing them. Team members most commonly use **Evernote**, **Google** Keep, or **Microsoft** OneNote software file sharing, via a simple click of an app or link.[132] Unfortunately, some employees bring tech gadgets (such as smartphones) to meetings, but they use them to do other things not related to the meeting, such as checking emails, sending personal texts, and actually taking calls. This can distract members and reduce the effectiveness of the meeting—or class. Some organizations are banning their use during meetings[133] (class)—but some will take a tech break during the meeting.

Conducting Meetings

Starting and ending meetings on time is important,[134] because waiting for late members penalizes the members who are on time and develops a *norm* for coming late. You also don't want team members to be late for their next important activity. About 37% of meetings start and end late, which tends to put members in a bad mood, feeling frustrated, disrespected or insulted, which tends to hurt creativity and performance.[135]

The First Meeting. At its first meeting, a team is in the forming stage. A recommended sequence is introductions, objectives, and role assignments including leader, timelines, and contact information exchange[136] (which can be done through including it on the agenda, which you send to all members in a contact group email). Tell members you will be starting and ending the meeting on time, and time will not be spent catching up late members on the meeting.[137] During or following this procedure, schedule a break that enables members to interact informally. If members find that their social needs will not be met, dissatisfaction may occur quickly.

The Three Parts of Meetings. Meetings should have the following three parts:

1. *Identify objectives.* Begin by reviewing progress to date, the group's objectives, and the purpose or objective for the specific meeting. Recorded minutes are usually approved at the beginning of the meeting. For most meetings, a secretary should be appointed to take minutes.

2. *Cover agenda items.* Stick to the agenda and keep the discussion on track to ensure you achieve the objectives. Be sure to cover agenda items in priority order. Try to keep to the approximate times—**Google Ventures** actually uses a time clock that goes off when the time is up[138]—but be flexible. If the discussion is constructive and members need more time, give it to them.

3. *Summarize and review assignments.* The leader should summarize what took place during the meeting, what the meeting accomplished, or progress toward objectives so members know time wasn't wasted,[139] and review all of the assignments given during the meeting so members know what to do.[140] The secretary and/or leader should record all action plan assignments, as is done at **Danna-Gracey** insurance agency and **Renaissance Learning** software. If there is no accountability and follow-up on assignments, members may not complete them.

At **Gore** (IOM 5), every associate is part of one or more teams, so all associates attend team meetings scheduled as needed. Sponsors also make sure that newcomers have opportunities to sit in on important meetings with other teams to better understand the systems effect of their projects and products and to learn how Gore operates.

©iStockphoto.com/LuckyBusiness

Wanderers tend to change the subject and complain. Meeting leaders need to make sure that the discussion remains focused and productive.

Handling Problem Members

Employees help the team and organization through "*voice*"—the expression of constructive opinions, concerns, or ideas about work-related issues that lead to improved work and group processes and innovation,[141] which is important to effective teamwork.[142] However, certain personality types can cause the group to be less efficient than it could be. So let's identify six problem types you will most likely encounter in meetings and how to keep them productive.

Silent Type. Some employees choose silence over voice, and for others, it's part of their personality.[143] In either case, to be fully effective, all group members should participate. If members are silent, the group does not get the benefit of their input. You need to hear from everyone to make sure the team is moving ahead together.

It is your responsibility to encourage silent members to participate without being obvious or overdoing it. You can draw them out by asking them in advance for a specific contribution and/or use the "*round robin*" rotation method, in which all members take turns giving their input. To build up silent members' confidence, call on them with questions they can easily answer. **Zappos** teams emphasize that each member is entitled to his or her opinion and is encouraged to voice whatever is on his or her mind during meetings.[144]

If you are a silent type, try to participate more often. Realize that speaking up is hard to do for many people[145] and that women may be more likely to be silent at meetings because they are more attentive to what people are feeling or thinking and more sensitive to group dynamics. Come to meetings prepared, knowing what you want to say (you can practice your delivery), and bring notes. Know when to stand up for your views and be assertive; trust yourself, and take risks, because you and your ideas are as good as or better than others.

Talker. Talkers have something to say about everything, and they tend to ramble. They like to dominate the discussion. However, if they do, the other members do not get to participate. The talker can cause intragroup problems such as low cohesiveness and conflicts. A second type of talker is the people who have a private conversation during the meeting.

It is your responsibility to slow talkers down, not to shut them up. Do not let them dominate the group. Interrupt people talking to each other (crosstalking) to keep it a team meeting. You can gently interrupt the talker and present your own ideas or call on other specific members to present their ideas. The rotation method can be effective with talkers because they have to wait their turn. **Zappos** has a no-crosstalking rule, and interruptions are forbidden.[146]

If you tend to be a talker, try to slow down. Give others a chance to talk and do things for themselves. Good leaders develop others' ability in these areas.

Wanderer. Wanderers distract the group from the agenda items; they tend to change the subject and often like to complain.

It's your responsibility to keep the group on track. Don't let them wander; stay focused on the agenda. Be kind, thank each member for the contribution, and then throw a question out to the group to get it back on track.

If you tend to be a wanderer, try to be aware of your behavior that disrupts the team and stay on the subject at hand.

Bored Member. Your group may have one or more members who are not interested/engaged in the meeting discussion.[147] The bored person may be preoccupied with other issues and not pay attention or participate in the group meeting. Bored members may also feel superior and overestimate their value to the team.[148]

Attention spans are dwindling,[149] so if you don't involve members every few minutes, they will tune you out.[150] Look for nonverbal clues of boredom and engage the team member. Assign the bored member a task such as recording ideas on the board or recording the minutes. Call on bored members; bring them into the group. If you allow them to sit back, things may get worse, and others may decide not to participate either.

If you tend to be bored, try to find ways to help motivate yourself. Work at becoming more patient and in control of behavior that can have negative effects on other members. Realize that if you are multitasking during the meeting (text/email/work), you will seem disengaged even if you are paying attention. This behavior nonverbally says, "This person/work is more important than you." Some members, especially old ones, will believe you are not interested in them and the team or that you are being disrespectful and insulting them.[151] If you are addicted to your phone, you may want to shut it off and put it out of sight during the meeting. It may even be required for this reason; it is **The Esquire Guy** rule when conducting business meetings for ***Esquire*** magazine.[152]

Arguer. Like the talker, the arguer likes to be the center of attention. Arguers enjoy arguing for the sake of arguing rather than helping the group. They turn things into a win-lose situation, and they cannot stand losing. They can also be negative, arguing that others' ideas will not work.[153]

Resolve conflict, but not in an argumentative way. Do not get into an argument with arguers; that is exactly what they want to happen. If an argument starts, bring others into the discussion. If an argument becomes personal, cut it off. Personal attacks only hurt the group. Keep the discussion moving on target.

If you tend to be an arguer, strive to convey your views in an assertive, positive way rather than in a negative, aggressive manner. Challenge ideas, not the people themselves; don't make it personal. Listen to others' views and be willing to change if they have better ideas.[154]

Social Loafer. To succeed, it is important that all members contribute to the team's task[155] without social loafers that are also called *free loaders*.[156] Based on foundational research by **Max Ringlemann**,[157] social loafers (Chapter 4) are selfish slackers who withhold their effort and fail to perform their share of the work.[158] If you have done any team-based class projects, you likely have seen slackers who contribute poor, little, or no work but want the same grade as everyone else who did the work.

Following all the previously mentioned meeting guidelines helps, especially giving clear individual assignments. Don't let the group develop norms that allow social loafing, and use peer pressure to get group members to do their work. Confront social loafers assertively; you will learn how to use the conflict resolution model in Chapter 10. When necessary, threaten to go to the boss. If these methods do not work, go to the supervisor (professor or boss) and explain the situation, stating the specific behavior and that you and the group have tried to resolve the problem, but the social loafer refuses to perform to standards.

If you have tendencies toward social loafing, realize that social loafing is unethical because you have a negative impact on individuals and the group.[159] Everyone wants to be on a successful team, and that success comes from everyone doing their share of the work. So if you want to be on a good team with high levels of performance, you need to pitch in and help develop positive norms of equal participation.

Working With Group Members. Whenever you work in a group, do not embarrass, intimidate, or argue with any members, no matter how much they provoke you. Don't belittle others in meetings, and don't let members belittle others. If you do, the group will perceive them as martyrs and you as a bully. If problem members do not respond to the preceding techniques, confront them individually outside of the group. Get them to agree to work in a cooperative way.

WORK
APPLICATION 8-11

Recall a meeting you had recently attended. Did you receive an agenda prior to the meeting? How well did the leader conduct the meeting? Give ideas on how the meeting could have been improved. Did the group have any problem members? How well did the leader handle them?

8-5 APPLYING THE CONCEPT

Problematic Group Members

Identify the problem type described in each statement.

A. silent type

B. talker

C. wanderer

D. bored member

E. arguer

F. social loafer

_____ 24. Clarita asks if anyone heard about their manager and the new guy she's dating.

_____ 25. "Tony, this looks like you just rushed through it to get it down without concern for giving us really good data for our team presentation."

_____ 26. Sonia is usually reluctant to give her ideas, and when she does and is challenged, Sonia backs down easily.

_____ 27. Chris enjoys challenging members' ideas and getting them emotional so they will let him get his own way.

_____ 28. Kim is always first or second to give her ideas. She is always elaborating in detail on others' ideas as well.

_____ 29. Sean, one of the usually active group members, is sitting back quietly today for the first time. The other members are doing all the discussing and volunteering for assignments.

Trends and Issues in Management

Globalization and *cultural diversity* (see discussion of GLOBE dimensions in Chapter 3) go hand in hand and create opportunities and challenges.[160] So what issues does a manager need to understand when leading global virtual teams? *Group structure* types of groups and size are not major issues; however, composition skills and abilities do vary, so managers need to draw on the strengths globally when selecting team members to innovate[161] and span boundaries globally.[162] Proper leadership does vary with cultural power distance, as some cultures are more and less accepting of the use of autocratic versus participative management styles, which also affects if the manager or team develops the team objectives.

Getting a global team to have effective *group process* is also challenging, as individualism versus collectivism (societal/in-group) affects playing group roles (individualists play more self-interest roles), norms (collectivists are more conformist), cohesiveness (easier with collectivists but challenging when mixing), decision making (collectivists like consensus), and conflict resolution (less with collectivists). Cultural power distance also affects team acceptance of status and preferred management style.

It is also more challenging to take a group through the *stages of group development* and to *develop groups into teams* with culturally diverse members. *Meetings* can be planned and conducted the same way, but leadership should vary with power distance preferences, and managers face more problem members during meetings in individualist cultures (more arguers and social loafers), as members from collectivist cultures are more cooperative.

Research supports a positive relationship between *diversity* and firm performance. However, more diverse teams reported lower levels of satisfaction, trust, and cooperation. Why? Diversity brings more innovation, but we also prefer to work with people who are like us.[163] How diverse are your close friends at work and away? So the challenge is to be sensitive to inclusion (Chapter 3). One point about *age diversity* is that younger workers accept the norm of interrupting your personal interaction to answer texts email/calls, whereas older workers reject this norm and think it's rude.[164]

Gore (**IOM 6**) was slow to adopt the use of internal *technology*—iPhones and iPads and workflow apps—and using them to become more connected to help teams move faster and communicate better. But thanks to millennials, they are catching up.

Needless to say, we have to be *ethical* and *socially responsible* in our human relations as both team members and leaders. The **University of Cambridge** in the United Kingdom is adopting a more "ethical" approach to investing its multibillion-dollar endowment fund. It established a team, including three students, to devise rules to ensure that half of the investments made by the endowment are socially responsible.[165]

As we bring this chapter to a close, you should understand the growing use of teams in business settings and how to develop groups into teams. You should know that team performance is based on organizational context, group structure (type, size, composition, leadership, and objectives), group process (roles, norms, cohesiveness, status, decision making, and conflict resolution), and group development (orientation, dissatisfaction, resolution, production, and termination). You should also know how to run and participate in effective meetings and how to handle problem members.

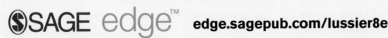

$SAGE edge™   **edge.sagepub.com/lussier8e**

Want a better grade?

Get the tools you need to sharpen your study skills. Access practice quizzes, eFlashcards, video and multimedia, and more at edge.sagepub.com/lussier8e.

Digital Resources

Learning Objective	Digital Resource
8-1. Contrast groups and teams, and explain the group performance model.	▶ Group versus Teams
8-2. Discuss the five components of group structure.	▶ Cross Functional Teams
8-3. Define the six components of group process, and describe how they are used to maximize team performance.	▶ Group Cohesiveness
8-4. Describe the four major stages of group development, and identify the appropriate leadership style usually associated with each.	▤ 4 Stage Group Development Model
8-5. Indicate how to develop groups into teams.	▶ Team Building
8-6. Explain how to plan a meeting, conduct it, and handle problem members during the meeting.	▶ Management in Action: Planning Meetings*

* premium video available only in the interactive eBook

••• CHAPTER SUMMARY

8-1. Contrast groups and teams, and explain the group performance model.

The major areas of difference are size, leadership, jobs, accountability and evaluation, rewards, and objectives. A group is two or more members, with a clear leader, who perform independent jobs and experience individual accountability, evaluation, and rewards. A team has a small number of members, with shared leadership, who perform interdependent jobs and experience both individual and group accountability, evaluation, and rewards.

According to the group performance model, group performance is a function of organizational context, group structure, group process, and group development.

8-2. Discuss the five components of group structure.

Group types include formal or informal, functional or cross-functional, and command (managers and their employees) or task groups (task force and ongoing standing committees). There is no ideal *group size*, as size varies depending on the purpose, situation, and type of work performed; but having five to nine members generally provides the best relationships and performance. *Group composition* is the mix of members' skills and abilities needed to perform the task. *Group leadership* affects performance and can be more autocratic or shared based on the situation but tends to be more formal as the size increases from a team to a group. Groups and teams need to accomplish *objectives* that can be set by the manager or the team.

8-3. Define the six components of group process, and describe how they are used to maximize performance.

Group roles include task roles played to get the job done, maintenance roles played to develop and sustain the group process, and self-interest roles played for personal gain at the expense of others. *Norms* are unspoken rules that are expectations about behavior that are shared by group members. *Cohesiveness* is the extent to which members stick together. *Status* is the perceived ranking of group members. *Decision making* refers to the level of participation used to make group decisions. *Conflict resolution* refers to how well the group deals with conflict.

To maximize group performance, both task and maintenance *roles* should be played (and the self-interest role minimized), positive productive *norms* should be developed, every member should be respected and included for *status* and *cohesiveness*, *decisions* should be made using the appropriate level of participation, and *conflicts* should be resolved to maintain cohesive group process.

8-4. Describe the four major stages of group development, and identify the appropriate management style usually associated with each.

(1) *Forming* is characterized by a low development level. The appropriate management style is generally *autocratic*. (2) *Storming* is characterized by a moderate development level. The appropriate management style is generally *consultative*. (3) *Norming* is characterized by a high development level. The appropriate management style is generally *participative*. (4) *Performing* is characterized by an outstanding development level. The appropriate management style is generally *empowerment*.

8-5. Indicate how to develop groups into teams.

To develop a group into a team, it is important to gradually take the team through the stages of group development by changing management styles. During the transition, team members can be trained to become better team players and leaders as the team takes on more responsibility for planning, organizing/staffing, leading, and controlling the group process. The team-building organizational development technique and social events can be used with non-work activities to help members get to know one another on a more personal level to help break down status differences and develop team cohesiveness.

8-6. Explain how to plan a meeting, conduct it, and handle problem members during the meeting.

Meetings should begin with a review of the purpose and objectives for the meeting. During the meeting, agenda items should be covered in priority order. The meeting should end with a summary of what took place and assignments to be completed for future meetings.

Problem members include the *silent* (engage them in the conversation), *talker* (slow them down), *wanderer* (keep them on track), *bored* (keep them engaged), *arguer* (don't argue with them), and *social loafer* (get them to do their work). Calling on members and having a norm of everyone sharing helps handle problem members during meetings.

••• KEY TERMS

command groups, 245
global virtual teams, 245
group, 242
group cohesiveness, 250
group composition, 247
group performance model, 242

group process, 248
group process dimensions, 248
group roles, 248
group structure dimensions, 243
group types, 244
norms, 249

stages of group development, 252
status, 251
task groups, 245
team, 242
team leaders, 256

••• KEY TERM REVIEW

Complete each of the following statements using one of this chapter's key terms.

1. A _____ is two or more members, with a clear leader, who perform independent jobs with individual accountability, evaluation, and rewards.

2. A _____ is a small number of members, with shared leadership, who perform interdependent jobs with both individual and group accountability, evaluation, and rewards.

3. In the _____, group performance is a function of organizational context, group structure, group process, and group development.

4. _____ are group type, size, composition, leadership, and objectives.

5. _____ include formal or informal, functional or cross-functional, and command or task.

6. _____ consist of managers and the employees they supervise.

7. _____ consist of employees selected to work on a specific objective.

8. Members of _____ are physically located in different places but work together as a team.

9. _____ is the mix of members' skills and abilities.

10. _____ is the patterns of interactions that emerge as members perform their jobs.

11. _____ include roles, norms, cohesiveness, status, decision making, and conflict resolution.

12. _____ include group task roles, group maintenance roles, and self-interest roles.

13. _____ are expectations about behavior that are shared by members of a group.

14. _____ is the extent to which members stick together.

15. _____ is the perceived ranking of one member relative to other members in a group.

16. The _____ are forming, storming, norming, performing, and termination.

17. _____ empower members to take responsibility for performing the management functions and focus on developing effective group structure and group process and on furthering group development.

••• REVIEW QUESTIONS

1. Which are usually larger, groups or teams?

2. Which level of management has the most influence over organizational context?

3. Is there an ideal group size?

4. Why is diversity important to group composition?

5. Why are objectives important to groups?

6. How do groups enforce norms?

7. Which type of group tends to terminate, and which does not?

8. Are the four functions of management important to both groups and teams?

9. Why is it important to keep records of meeting assignments?

10. Describe the six types of problem members in meetings. How does each cause a problem to the group?

••• COMMUNICATION SKILLS

The following critical-thinking questions can be used for class discussion and/or as written assignments to develop communication skills. Be sure to give complete explanations for all questions.

1. Is it really worth making a distinction between groups and teams? Why or why not?

2. Which part of the group performance model is the most important to high levels of performance? Why?

3. Select any type of group (work, school, sports) you belong or have belonged to. Explain how each of the group's five structure components affects or did affect its performance.

4. Select any type of group (work, school, sports) you belong or have belonged to. Explain how each of the group's six group process components affects or did affect its performance.

5. Are most team leaders really capable of determining the stage of group development and using the appropriate leadership style for the situation? Why or why not?

6. Based on your experience with meetings and what you have read and heard from others, which part of planning a meeting is most lacking?

7. Which type of group problem member is most annoying to you? Why? How can you better work with this type of group member in the future?

CASES

••• Case 8-1   Ritz-Carlton Hotels

The Ritz-Carlton Hotel Company was established by president and founding father Colgate Holmes along with four business partners in 1983. At that time, the only existing Ritz-Carlton hotel was located in Boston. By 1992, the company had opened 22 additional hotels in the United States. By 1998, the company was acquired by Marriott International. Today, Ritz-Carlton Hotels is based in Chevy Chase, Maryland, operates more than 90 luxury hotels in 30 countries and territories, and employs more than 40,000 people.

The Credo

- The Ritz-Carlton is a place where the genuine care and comfort of our guests is our highest mission.

- We pledge to provide the finest personal service and facilities for our guests, who will always enjoy a warm, relaxed, yet refined ambiance.

- The Ritz-Carlton experience enlivens the senses, instills well-being, and fulfills even the unexpressed wishes and needs of our guests.

The Motto

At the Ritz-Carlton, "We are Ladies and Gentlemen serving Ladies and Gentlemen." This motto exemplifies the anticipatory service provided by all staff members.

Service Values

1. I build strong relationships and create Ritz-Carlton guests for life.

2. I am always responsive to the expressed and unexpressed wishes and needs of our guests.

3. I am empowered to create unique, memorable, and personal experiences for our guests.

4. I understand my role in achieving the Key Success Factors, embracing community footprints, and creating the Ritz-Carlton mystique.

5. I continually seek opportunities to innovate and improve the Ritz-Carlton experience.

6. I own and immediately resolve guest problems.

7. I create a work environment of teamwork and lateral service so that the needs of our guests and each other are met.

8. I have the opportunity to continuously learn and grow.

9. I am involved in the planning of the work that affects me.

10. I am proud of my professional appearance, language, and behavior.

11. I protect the privacy and security of our guests, my fellow employees, and the company's confidential information and assets.

12. I am responsible for uncompromising levels of cleanliness and creating a safe and accident-free environment.

In order to ensure the effective implementation of its legendary service philosophy, the Ritz-Carlton emphasizes the importance of teamwork at all of its properties. In particular, teamwork is emphasized in service value #7—I create a work environment of teamwork and lateral service so that the needs of our guests and each other are met. Lateral service means that all Ritz-Carlton employees must support each other in realizing the hotel's mission. Sometimes this may involve performing duties and responsibilities that are not part of their job, such as assisting a guest with his/her luggage, obtaining a bottle of shampoo or soap from housekeeping for a guest, or providing a recommendation for a good local restaurant or show to see for a guest.

The company uses a variety of practices to support lateral teamwork, including the following:

- Managers foster a culture that supports teamwork through the effective modeling of desired behaviors and recognizing those who practice lateral teamwork;

- Employees provide informal training on what their coworkers need to do to provide lateral teamwork and how they need to do it;

- Employees complete formal training on teamwork as well as participate in team-building activities;

- Employees team up with each other (e.g., concierge and the hotel's restaurant manager) when doing so will enhance a guest's experience;

- Managers incorporate lateral teamwork into the professional development plans of employees so that they can see how lateral teamwork can enhance their ability to grow and advance at a personal and professional level.

Discussion Questions

1. What types of groups/teams are used at the Ritz-Carlton Hotels?

2. How are roles defined in order to support teamwork at the Ritz-Carlton Hotels?

3. Evaluate the performance of teams at the Ritz-Carlton Hotels in terms of the six dimensions of a team process.

4. How does the Ritz-Carlton develop teams?

5. What can you learn about how to work more effectively in group projects in classes, based on the things that the Ritz-Carlton does to promote teamwork in their hotels?

6. Why is teamwork so important to organizations like the Ritz-Carlton? Do you agree with its focus on teams as opposed to the individual efforts and contributions of its associates? Why or why not?

References

http://ritzcarltonleadershipcenter.com/tag/teamwork/

http://ritzcarltonleadershipcenter.com/2015/03/encourage-teamwork/

http://ritzcarltonleadershipcenter.com/2016/02/dos-and-donts-of-teamwork-and-lateral-service/

http://www.ritzcarlton.com/content/dam/the-ritz-carlton/brand/community-foot prints/pdfs/MOD4PowerTeamwork.pdf

http://www.ritzcarlton.com/en/about/factsheet

http://www.ritzcarlton.com/en/about/history

http://www.marriott.com/ritz-carlton-careers/history.mi

http://www.ritzcarlton.com/en/about/gold-standards

Case created by Loren Kuzuhara, University of Wisconsin–Madison.

● ● ● Case 8-2   Saving Lives Together: Partnering and Teamwork at Medtronic

Medtronic is a medical device company headquartered in Dublin, Ireland. Its operational headquarters is in Fridley, Minnesota. Medtronic is the world's largest standalone medical technology development company. Medtronic operates in more than 140 countries, employs more than 85,000 people, and has more than 53,000 patents.(1)

Medtronic ended fiscal 2016 on a promising note with fourth-quarter earnings and revenues both surpassing the Zacks Consensus Estimate. The consolidated company demonstrated strong segmental performances, reflecting successful integration and achievement of synergy targets. All four major business groups contributed to solid top-line growth on above-market revenue growth that, according to

the company, highlighted sustainability across groups and regions. It was expected that the solid growth trend would successfully continue in the United States, as would the healthy global acceptance of its advanced therapies. Apart from product innovation, the company is currently focusing on geographical diversification of its businesses.(2)

When asked how the firm has become so successful over the years, CEO Omar Ishrak stated,

How can we collectively find solutions that will guide the industry toward value-based care? Collaborative partnerships …are key to driving value-based healthcare….That's why we are partnering with health systems and providers to combine our capabilities with their expertise to change the way we work together to achieve the best outcomes.(3)

Teamwork, both outside and within the firm, seems to be one of the distinctive competencies of Medtronic that fuels their competitive advantage. For example, the company is working with leading healthcare thinkers and practitioners such as *Harvard Business Review*, creating conversations and initiating collaboration to support value-based healthcare around the world. This has included HBR webinars featuring global healthcare experts discussing key information and promising approaches to address pressing issues in healthcare. A recent example is "The Case for Bundled Payments in Health Care" featuring Robert S. Kaplan and Michael E. Porter.(4) Medtronic has also teamed up with Fitbit to continue its goal of transforming diabetes management. By combining activity data from Fitbit wearable technology along with Medtronic's sensor and glucose data, Medtronic can provide patients and physicians with information to help manage their disease.(5)

You cannot have good relations with external partners unless you nurture teamwork within the firm, according to the firm's human resource management department.

> Excellent managers realize that it takes an active, engaged and motivated workforce to achieve desired financial targets, as well as engender patient and referring physician loyalty.... [This starts with] developing a team [which] is essential because employees tend to flourish when they have co-workers whom they can count on for support.(6)

Therefore, when Medtronic needed a way to give high-potential employees a sense of teamwork under pressure, it turned to simulation technology. The company incorporated a team-based leadership simulation from Enspire Learning into its Emerging Leader Program (ELP) that created insights on personal leadership styles that allowed employees to see their own blind spots and learn from their own mistakes in a meaningful way. It also allowed emerging leaders to practice cross-functional teamwork that deals with ambiguity under time pressure, communication across the enterprise, and making strategic trade-offs.

The simulation creates teams of eight or nine participants who immerse themselves in a dynamic, competitive marketplace in which they compete against three other teams. Participants have their laptop connected to the simulation online and play a unique role on the leadership team of a virtual company. The interface allows each participant to manage a pool of virtual employees, move projects through the virtual company's product development pipeline, check marketplace reports, and receive company announcements in their inbox. This technology lets each participant play an important role in the development of the company and be held accountable for his or her decisions as an individual, as well as a team. Participants must communicate with their team members to ensure everyone's individual decisions adhere to the team's overall business strategy. Part of the game includes job rotation—just as participants learn how to effectively play their roles, they receive an e-mail in their inbox notifying them of a corporate reorganization, in which the CEO suddenly may be reassigned as a director-level employee or vice versa.

Through interactive debriefs and reflection periods, participants identify individual leadership and management styles and learn how to balance personal and organizational objectives, build effective teams, solve complex business problems collaboratively, define a clear strategic vision, and implement their vision in the face of adverse events. Working closely with fellow Medtronic employees in the simulation also helps participants forge strong relationships across departments, offering networking opportunities for the participants.(7)

How effective is this training? More than 90% of participants responded "agreed" or "strongly agreed" to the statements that they received significant value from participating in the simulation and that the experience increased their ability to work more effectively as part of an organization and team. As one participant noted,

> It was great to think about the big picture. I feel so cut off from many parts of the organization in my day-to-day job that this will help me continue to see and think about higher-level decisions.(8)

Discussion Questions

1. Looking at the simulation described in this case, are employees playing the simulator part of a group or a team?

2. Having a partnership with Harvard Business Review (HBR) and Fitbit creates what types of groups?

3. Agree or disagree with the size of the simulation teams relative to performance.

References

(1) Medtronic. (n.d.). Facts and statistics—Medtronic. Retrieved March 1, 2017, from http://www.medtronic.com/us-en/about/facts-stats.html

(2) Zacks Investment Research. (2016, May 31). Medtronic (MDT) beats Q4 earnings & revenue estimates. Retrieved March 1, 2017, from https://www.zacks.com/stock/news/218923/medtronic-mdt-beats-q4-earnings-amp-revenue-estimates

(3) Medtronic. (n.d.). About Medtronic. Retrieved March 1, 2017, from http://www.medtronic.com/us-en/about.html

(4) Medtronic. (n.d.). Medtronic and *Harvard Business Review*. Retrieved March 1, 2017, from http://www.medtronic.com/us-en/transforming-healthcare/aligning-value/harvard-business-review-advancing-value-based-healthcare.html

(5) Medtronic. (2017, February 23). Medtronic and Fitbit. Retrieved March 1, 2017, from http://www.medtronic.com/us-en/about.html

(6) Woodcock, E. (2014, May 30). Morale—Twelve steps to success. Retrieved March 1, 2017, from https://professional.medtronic.com/rm/pmr/hr/NHCP-PM-TWELVE-STEPS-HR#.WZ3N7j6GOUk

(7) Friefield, L. (n.d.). Medtronic, Inc.: Simulating high-potential teamwork and medical device usage. *Training*. Retrieved March 1, 2017, from https://trainingmag.com/content/medtronic-inc-simulating-high-potential-teamwork-and-medical-device-usage

(8) Ibid.

Case created by Herbert Sherman, Hannah K. Walter, and Naveed Ahmad, Long Island University.

• • • SKILL BUILDER 8-1: COMPARING TEAMS

Objectives

To use your experience to better understand what makes teams successful and to better contribute to team performance.

Skills

The primary skills developed through this exercise are:

1. *Management skill*—interpersonal (teamwork)
2. *AACSB competency*—analyzing (within groups)
3. *Management function*—leading (in groups)

Preparation

Select the best and worst group (work, school, sports, club, etc.) of which you are/were a member and answer the following questions:

1. What was it about the best group that made you select it? Be sure to incorporate the chapter's discussion on groups and teams in your answer.

2. What was it about the worst group that made you select it? Be sure to incorporate the chapter's discussion of teams and groups in your answer.

Procedure

In groups of five to seven, share your answers to the Preparation questions, and identify the three major factors making a group the best and worst.

Apply It

What did I learn from this exercise? How will I use this knowledge in the future?

• • • SKILL BUILDER 8-2: MANAGEMENT STYLES IN GROUP SITUATIONS

Objective

To determine appropriate leadership styles in group situations.

Skills

The primary skills developed through this exercise are:

1. *Management skill*—interpersonal (teamwork)
2. *AACSB competency*—analyzing (preferred group leadership style)—teamwork
3. *Management function*—leading (in groups)

Assess Your Preferred Team Management Style

Following are 12 situations. Select the one alternative that most closely describes what you would do in each situation. Don't be concerned with trying to select the right answer; select the alternative you would really use. Circle a, b, c, or d. (Ignore the D ____ and the S ____ following each answer choice; these will be explained later.)

1. Your group works well together; members are cohesive and have positive norms. They maintain a fairly consistent level of production that is above the organizational average, as long as you continue to play a maintenance role. You have a new assignment for them. To accomplish it, you would: D ____

   a. Explain what needs to be done and tell the group members how to do it. Oversee them while they perform the task. S ____

   b. Tell the group members how pleased you are with their past performance. Explain the new assignment, but let them decide how to accomplish it. Be available if they need help. S ____

   c. Tell the group members what needs to be done. Encourage them to give input on how to do the job. Oversee task performance. S ____

   d. Explain to the group what needs to be done. S ____

2. You have been promoted to a new supervisory position. The group you supervise appears to have little talent to do the job, but the members do seem to care about the quality of the work they do. The last supervisor was fired because of the group's low productivity level. To increase productivity, you would: D ____

   a. Let the group members know you are aware of their low production level, but let them decide how to improve it. S ____

   b. Spend most of your time overseeing group members as they perform their jobs. Train them as needed. S ____

   c. Explain to the group members that you would like to work together to improve productivity. Work together as a team. S ____

   d. Tell the group members how productivity can be improved. With their ideas, develop methods and make sure they are implemented. S ____

3. Your department continues to be one of the top performers in the organization. The members work well as a team. In the past, you generally let them take care of the work on their own. You decide to: D ____

   a. Go around encouraging group members on a regular basis. S ____

   b. Define members' roles and spend more time overseeing performance. S ____

   c. Continue things the way they are; leave them alone. S ____

d. Hold a meeting. Recommend ways to improve and get members' ideas as well. After agreeing on changes, oversee the group to make sure it implements the new ideas and does improve. S ____

4. You have spent much of the past year training your employees. However, they do not need you to oversee production as much as you used to. Several group members no longer get along as well as they did in the past. You've played referee lately. You: D ____

   a. Have a group meeting to discuss ways to increase performance. Let the group members decide what changes to make. Be supportive. S ____

   b. Continue things the way they are now. Supervise the group members closely and be the referee when needed. S ____

   c. Leave the group members alone to work things out for themselves. S ____

   d. Continue to supervise closely as needed, but spend more time playing a maintenance role; develop a team spirit. S ____

5. Your department has been doing such a great job that it has increased in size. You are surprised at how fast the new members were integrated. The team continues to come up with ways to improve performance. Because it has grown so large, the department will be moving to a larger location. You decide to: D ____

   a. Design the new layout and present it to the group to see if the members can improve on it. S ____

   b. Allow the group to design the new layout. S ____

   c. Design the new layout and put a copy on the bulletin board so employees know where to report for work after the move. S ____

   d. Hold a meeting to get employee ideas on the layout of the new location. After the meeting, think about their ideas and finalize the layout. S ____

6. You are appointed to head a task group. Because of the death of a relative, you had to miss the first meeting. At the second meeting, the group seems to have developed objectives and some ground rules. Members have volunteered for assignments that have to be accomplished. You: D ____

   a. Take over as a strong leader and change some ground rules and assignments. S ____

   b. Review what has been done so far and keep things as they are. However, you take charge and provide clear direction from now on. S ____

   c. Take over the leadership, but allow the group to make the decisions. Be supportive and encourage them. S ____

   d. Given the group is doing so well, leave and do not attend any more meetings. S ____

7. Your group was working at, or just below, standard. There has been a conflict within the group, and as a result, production is behind schedule. You: D ____

   a. Tell the group how to resolve the conflict. Then closely supervise to make sure people do what you say and production increases. S ____

   b. Let the group work it out. S ____

   c. Hold a meeting to work as a team to come up with a solution. Encourage the group members to work together. S ____

   d. Hold a meeting to present a way to resolve the conflict. Sell the members on its merits, ask for their input, and follow up. S ____

8. Your organization allows flextime. Two of your employees have asked if they can change work hours. You are concerned because the busy work hours need adequate coverage. The department is very cohesive with positive norms. You decide to: D ____

   a. Tell them things are going well; we'll keep things as they are now. S ____

   b. Hold a department meeting to get everyone's input, then reschedule their hours. S ____

   c. Hold a department meeting to get everyone's input; then reschedule their hours on a trial basis. Tell the group that if there is any drop in productivity, you will go back to the old schedule. S ____

   d. Tell them to hold a department meeting. If the department agrees to have at least three people on the job during the busy hours, they can make changes, giving you a copy of the new schedule. S ____

9. You have arrived 10 minutes late for a department meeting. Your employees are discussing the latest assignment. This surprises you because, in the past, you had to provide clear direction, and employees rarely would say anything. You: D ____

   a. Take control immediately and provide your usual direction. S ____

   b. Say nothing and just sit back. S ____

   c. Encourage the group to continue but also provide direction. S ____

   d. Thank the group for starting without you and encourage them to continue. Support their efforts. S ____

10. Your department is consistently very productive. However, occasionally the members fool around, and someone has an accident. There has never been a serious injury. You hear a noise and go to see what it was. From a distance, you can see Sue sitting on the floor, laughing, with a ball made from company material in her hand. You: D ____

    a. Say and do nothing. After all, she's OK, and the department is very productive; you don't want to make waves. S ____

b. Call the group members together and ask for suggestions on how to keep accidents from recurring. Tell them you will be checking up on them to make sure the behavior does not continue. S ____

c. Call the group members together and discuss the situation. Encourage them to be more careful in the future. S ____

d. Tell the group members that's it; from now on you will be checking up on them regularly. Bring Sue to your office and discipline her. S ____

11. You are at the first meeting of an ad hoc committee you are leading. Most of the members are second- and third-level managers from the marketing and financial areas; you are a supervisor from production. You decide to start by: D ____

a. Working on developing relationships. Get all group members to feel as though they know each other before you talk about business. S ____

b. Going over the group's purpose and the authority it has. Provide clear directives. S ____

c. Asking the group to define its purpose. Because most of the members are higher-level managers, let them provide the leadership. S ____

d. Providing both direction and encouragement. Give directives and thank people for their cooperation. S ____

12. Your department has done a great job in the past. It is getting a new computer system. You have been trained to operate the computer, and you are expected to train your employees to operate it. To train them, you: D ____

a. Give the group instructions and work with people individually, providing direction and encouragement. S ____

b. Get the group members together to decide how they want to be instructed. Be very supportive of their efforts to learn. S ____

c. Tell the group members it's a simple system. Give them a copy of the manual and have them study it on their own. S ____

d. Give the group members instructions. Then go around and supervise their work closely, giving additional instructions as needed. S ____

Scoring

To determine your preferred leadership style, follow these steps:

1. Circle the letter you selected for each situation.

2. Add up the number of circled items per column. The column with the most circled items represents your preferred style.

The more evenly distributed the numbers are among the four styles, the more flexible you are at leading groups. A total of 0 or 1 in any column may indicate a reluctance to use that style. Is your preferred leadership style the same as your preferred management style (Chapter 1)?

	Autocratic	Consultative	Participative	Empowerment
1.	a	c	b	d
2.	b	d	c	a
3.	b	d	a	c
4.	b	d	a	c
5.	c	a	d	b
6.	a	b	c	d
7.	a	d	c	b
8.	a	c	b	d
9.	a	c	d	b
10.	d	b	c	a
11.	b	d	a	c
12.	d	a	b	c
Totals	_____	_____	_____	_____

••• SKILL BUILDER 8-3: ASSIGNING APPROPRIATE MANAGEMENT STYLES TO GROUP SITUATIONS

Objectives

To help you understand the stages of group development and to select the appropriate leadership styles for group situations.

Preparation

You should understand the stages of group development and have completed assessment of your leadership style.

Step 1. Determine the level of development of the group in each of the 12 situations. Place the number (1, 2, 3, or 4) on the line marked D at the end of the situation.

1 = forming stage

2 = storming stage

3 = norming stage

4 = performing stage

Step 2. Identify the leadership style described in each answer choice. Place the letter A, C, P, or E on the line marked S following each answer choice.

A = autocratic

C = consultative

P = participative

E = empowering

Step 3. Now circle the letter of the answer choice that represents the leadership style that is most appropriate for the level of development for the group in each situation.

See Model 8-1 for an illustration of the four levels of development and their leadership styles.

Apply It

What did I learn from this experience? How will I use this knowledge in the future?

Your instructor may ask you to do part of Skill Builder 8-3 in class as a group. You may be instructed, for example, to break into teams to assign stages of development and leadership styles to each situation, or you may be asked to discuss the reasons behind your stage and style decisions.

••• SKILL BUILDER 8-4: GROUP PERFORMANCE

Note: This exercise is designed for class groups that have worked together for some time. (Five or more hours of prior work are recommended.)

Objectives

To gain a better understanding of group structure, process, and development and of meetings and how they affect group performance.

Skills

The primary skills developed through this exercise are:

1. *Management skill*—interpersonal (teamwork)

2. *AACSB competency*—analyzing a group—teamwork

3. *Management function*—leading (in groups)

Answer the following questions as they apply to your class group/team.

1. Using Exhibit 8-1, would you classify your members as a group or a team? Why?

Group Structure

2. What type of group/team are you (formal/informal, functional/cross-functional, command/task)?

3. Assess the size of your group/team (too large, too small, ideal).

4. What is the group/team composition?

5. Is there a clear leader or leaders? If so, who is or are the leaders?

6. Does your group/team have clear objectives?

7. List some ways in which group structure could be improved to increase group performance.

Group Process

8. List each group member, including yourself, and the major role(s) each plays.

9. Identify at least three group norms. Are they positive or negative? How does the group enforce them?

10. How cohesive is your group (very cohesive, moderately cohesive, minimally cohesive)?

11. List each group member, including you, in order of status.

12. How are decisions made in your group/team?

13. How is conflict resolved in your group/team?

14. List some ways in which group process could be improved to increase group performance.

Group Development Stage

15. At what stage of development is your group/team? Explain.

16. List some ways in which your group/team can move to a higher level of development to increase group performance.

Meetings

17. List some ways in which your meetings could be improved to increase group performance.

18. Does your group have any problem members? What can be done to make them more effective?

Apply It

What did I learn from this experience? How will I use this knowledge in the future?

Your instructor may ask you to continue Skill Builder 8-4 in class by discussing your answers to the questions with other members of your class group. You may also be asked to do a team-building exercise by jointly making specific recommendations about ways in which your team can improve its performance.

Spencer Platt/Getty Images

9 Human Resources Management

• • • LEARNING OBJECTIVES

After studying this chapter, you should be able to:

9-1. List the four parts of the human resources management process, define *harassment* and *sexual harassment*, and discuss the importance of understanding employment law. PAGE 275

9-2. Explain the role of strategic human resources planning and the need for conducting a job analysis including its two parts. PAGE 282

9-3. Discuss the two parts of attracting employees. PAGE 282

9-4. Describe the three parts of developing employees. PAGE 288

9-5. Summarize the role of compensation in retaining employees, and indicate three methods of employment separation. PAGE 295

| IOM | # Ideas on Management
at Costco Wholesale |

Costco Wholesale is a membership warehouse club, dedicated to bringing its members the best possible prices on quality brand-name merchandise. Its goal has been to boost sales while cutting long-term costs so that it can pass those savings along to members; it gives 80% to 90% back to members. Costco became the first company ever to grow from zero to $3 billion in sales in less than six years.

While many brick-and-mortar stores' sales are declining, due largely to online shopping, Costco continues to grow, with only 3% of its sales coming from e-commerce. Today, it has thousands of employees working in more than 725 locations in nine countries with revenues exceeding $119 billion from its 81-plus million members.

Cofounder Jim Sinegal points to his employees as the key to Costco's success. Based on this philosophy, Costco is one of the most impressive employers in the world when it comes to the treatment of its retail employees, with higher pay and better benefits through its human resource management process for its employees. This helps keep Costco's employee turnover rate remarkably low for the retail industry. Costco starting hourly pay is above $11.50, with an average of $22 per hour. Its turnover is about 10%, compared with the industry norm of 55%.

IOM 1. How does Costco view its human resources management process?

IOM 2. What types of recruiting methods does Costco use?

IOM 3. How does Costco use its compensation and benefits package to retain employees?

IOM 4. What is Costco's attitude toward organizational labor?

You'll find answers to these **IOM** questions throughout the chapter. To learn more about Costco, visit www.costco.com.

Sources: Information for this case was taken from Costco's website at http://www.costco.com, accessed May 8, 2017; J. Kell, "Dancing in the Aisles," *Fortune* (December 15, 2015): 26.

The Human Resources Management Process

Recall from Chapter 1 that business success is based on four resources (human, financial, physical, and information) and that people are the most important resource.[1] Thus, how an organization manages its people is critical,[2] as it gives the firm a competitive advantage.[3] Thus, firms compete with effective human resources management (HRM) processes to attract and retain the best employees to increase productivity.[4] However, finding and keeping the best employees is a challenge even for the most famous companies.[5] To effectively manage people, the organization needs to be proficient in all four parts of the HRM process. The **human resources management process** *involves planning for, attracting, developing, and retaining employees.* It is also known as the *staffing process.* Exhibit 9-1 illustrates the process; each of the four parts of the process is discussed in this chapter. Notice the arrows used to illustrate the systems effect. For example, planning and compensation affect the kinds of employees an organization can attract; labor relations affect planning; job analysis affects training; and so on.

LO 9-1

List the four parts of the human resources management process, define *harassment* and *sexual harassment*, and discuss the importance of understanding employment law.

human resources management process Planning for, attracting, developing, and retaining employees.

Costco (IOM 1) cofounder Jim Sinegal knew from the start that if employees were treated right, including being offered good pay and benefits and chances for promotion, the company's HRM costs would easily be recouped. Its satisfied employees are motivated to work hard and produce more, and the increased productivity more than exceeds the cost of attracting, developing, and compensating new employees. This explains why Costco's turn-over rate is one of the lowest in the retailing industry.

We'll begin our examination of the HRM process with a discussion of the HRM department, which is responsible for carrying out the HRM process, and of the legal environment, as the law affects all four functions of the HRM process.

The Human Resources Department

Human resources (HR) is one of the four major functional departments in an organization. It is a staff department that advises and assists all the other departments in the organization. In organizations large enough (usually about 100 or more employees) to have a separate human resources department, the department performs each of the four functions of the HRM process.

RJP. We are not trying to scare you away from a career in HRM, but let's do a little reality check (realistic job preview, or RJP) so you have a better idea of HRM work before we get into this chapter.[6] Some people consider a career in HRM because they "like working with people." Well, in most jobs, you have to work with people (Chapter 8). Many HR jobs require maintaining records, auditing, or controlling. Record-keeping activities such as tracking attendance, sick and vacation time, payroll, benefits, safety, and so on have to be done by the HR department. Much of the time is spent working with all types of forms—getting job applicants and employees to fill them out and keeping track of all this paperwork, which is becoming more electronic. Much of this record keeping is needed to be in compliance with government laws and regulations that require regular reports that need to be completed and sent in on time. The more entry level the job, usually the more time that is spent record keeping. Also, when compared to all the jobs a company has to fill, the percentage of HRM jobs is small, and the jobs are often filled by employees already working in other jobs within the firm.

Generally, the smaller the firm, the wider the job responsibilities within the HRM department, and vice versa in a larger firm. If you are interested in an HR career, look at Exhibit 9-1, and as we progress through this chapter, think about your interest in working in each of the four areas.

Outsourcing. Outsourcing is becoming more common in business (Chapter 3). Many firms, especially small businesses, are outsourcing most or parts of their HRM functions. Outsourcing payroll and benefits lets the company focus on the more important activities of attracting and developing employees.[7] So outsourcing is decreasing some HR jobs within organizations, but it is creating the need for more jobs within HRM consulting firms, which creates new venture opportunities and HR careers. **Jim Dryfus** was laid off from his HRM job with **Hersey** and went on to start his own consulting firm, **Dryfus and Associates**.[8]

SHRM. The largest professional association for HRM is the **Society for Human Resource Management (SHRM)**. Its work is dedicated primarily to two areas—advocacy for national HR laws and policies for organizations and training and certification of HR professionals in a number of specialty areas. It also provides members with a place to network and learn from their peers as well as a vast library of articles and other information on HR management. Anyone thinking about a career in human resources should consider joining. Student memberships are inexpensive.[9] For more information, visit www.shrm.org.

HRM for All. It is a myth that HRM is only the responsibility of the HR department. The HR department is primarily responsible for developing employment policies, procedures, and rules, but it is the line managers and employees who implement the standing plans. As a manager or employee (especially in self-managed teams), you need HRM knowledge and

| EXHIBIT 9-1 | THE HUMAN RESOURCES MANAGEMENT PROCESS |

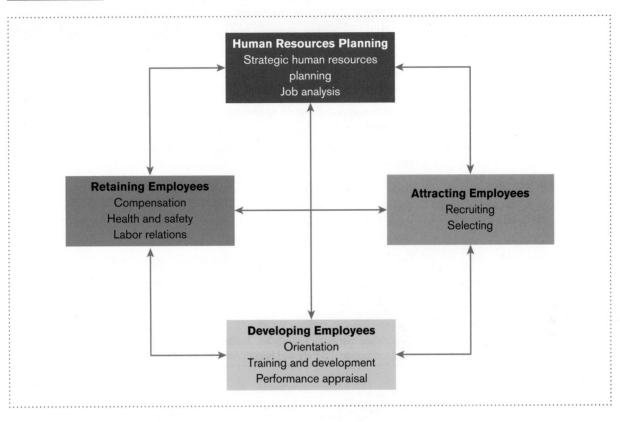

skills. For example, (1) *planning*: if you break an employment law, you could get the company sued and yourself fired and even face criminal charges, and you may have to help develop a job description; (2) *attracting*: you may be asked to recruit new employees and interview them; (3) *developing*: you should help orient new employees, may train them, and may even evaluate their performance; and (4) *retaining*: your relationships will influence employees to stay or leave the firm, and you need to follow health and safety regulations so you don't get hurt or hurt other employees, customers, or anyone else who can be hurt by your actions.

WORK
APPLICATION 9-1

Describe the kinds of interactions you have had with the human resources department of an organization you work for or have worked for.

The Legal Environment

The external environment, especially the competitive and legal environment, has a major impact on HRM practices. Organizations are not completely free to hire, promote, or fire whomever they want. The HRM department usually has the responsibility of seeing that the organization complies with the law.

Federal Laws Related to HRM. Some of the major federal laws and regulations affecting employment in U.S. companies are presented in Exhibit 9-2.[10] The **Equal Employment Opportunity Commission (EEOC)** minority guidelines identify Hispanics, Asians, African Americans, Native Americans, and Alaska natives as minorities protected under the CRA; the act also protects disadvantaged young people, disabled workers, and persons older than 40 years of age. Although the law protects women from discrimination in employment, they are not considered to be a statistical minority because they make up half of the population; in some work situations, women are a majority.[11]

The EEOC is responsible for enforcing equal opportunity laws. It has 53 district, field, area, and local offices across the nation, and it operates a toll-free line (1-800-669-4000) around the clock to provide information on employee rights. For more information on federal employment law, visit www.eeoc.gov.

EXHIBIT 9-2   FEDERAL LAWS RELATED TO HRM

Law	Description
Equal Employment Opportunity	
Title VII of the Civil Rights Act (CRA) of 1964	Prohibits discrimination on the basis of race, religion, color, sex, or national origin in all areas of the employment relationship
Age Discrimination in Employment Act (ADEA) of 1967 (amended 1978, 1984)	Prohibits age discrimination against people older than 40 and restricts mandatory retirement
Americans with Disabilities Act (ADA) of 1990	Requires employers to provide "reasonable accommodations" to allow disabled employees to work
Compensation and Benefits	
Fair Labor Standards Act (FLSA) of 1938	The FLSA introduced the 40-hour work week, established a national minimum wage, guaranteed "time-and-a-half" for overtime in certain jobs, and prohibited most employment of minors in "oppressive child labor."
Equal Pay Act (EPA) of 1963	Requires that men and women be paid the same for equal work
Family and Medical Leave Act (FMLA) of 1993	Requires employers with 50 or more employees to provide up to 12 weeks unpaid leave for family (childbirth, adoption) or medical reasons
Health and Safety	
Occupational Safety and Health Act (OSHA) of 1970	Establishes mandatory safety and health standards in organizations; regulated by the Occupational Safety and Health Administration (OSHA)

Ignorance of employment law is no excuse for breaking the law, so it is important to know the legal requirements. Violation of the law, including harassment and sexual harassment, can lead to being investigated by the EEOC or to becoming a defendant in a costly civil or criminal lawsuit.

State and Local Government Employment Laws. No matter what state you operate in, you must follow the federal laws. However, all of the states and some cities have additional laws that must be followed, such as the minimum wage laws. You can't pay less than the federal minimum, but the state and even some cities will require a higher minimum wage. There are far too many differences to discuss, but as an HRM professional, you will need to know these laws, in addition to federal law. Getting back to record keeping and paperwork, you need to do so for various state and local government agencies, usually on different forms in various formats.

Preemployment Inquiries. On a job application or during an interview, no member of an organization can ask illegal discriminatory questions. The two major rules of thumb to follow include: (1) Every question asked should be job related, or don't ask it. When developing questions, you should have a job-related purpose for using the information. (2) Any general question that you ask should be asked of all candidates. Exhibit 9-3 lists what can and cannot be asked during the selection process.

You most likely have heard that you can't discriminate in hiring, but this is not completely true because you can legally discriminate if there is a bona fide occupational qualification for the specific job. A **bona fide occupational qualification (BFOQ)** *is one that may be discriminatory but is reasonably necessary to normal operation of a particular organization.* For example, a BFOQ for a job teaching Jewish religion classes could require that the person selected be a practicing Jew, but it could not be a BFOQ to teach math or English in a Jewish school.

The trend today is to hire the most qualified person for the job without consideration of the diversity groups he or she belongs to. However, when candidates are equal in qualifications, minorities and women tend to get the job when they are underrepresented in the

bona fide occupational qualification (BFOQ) An occupational qualification that may be discriminatory but that is reasonably necessary to normal operation of a particular organization.

workplace. But white males may also be underrepresented such as in nursing and elementary school teaching.

Harassment and Sexual Harassment and Workplace Romance

As discussed in Chapter 3 with diversity, sex discrimination is illegal, and so is sexual harassment.[12] It is illegal, so let's discuss two types here.

Harassment. Harassment is a form of employment that is unwelcome conduct that is based on race, color, religion, sex (including pregnancy), national origin, age (40 or older), disability, or genetic information. Petty slights, annoyances, and isolated incidents (unless extremely serious) will not rise to the level of illegality. Harassment becomes unlawful where (1) enduring the offensive conduct becomes a condition of continued employment or (2) the conduct is severe or pervasive enough to create a work environment that a reasonable person would consider intimidating, hostile, or abusive.[13] The HR department is responsible for helping ensure that no one is harassed at work and for keeping records.

Sexual Harassment. According to the EEOC, sexual harassment is a form of sex discrimination that includes unwelcome sexual advances, requests for sexual favors, and other verbal or physical conduct of a sexual nature. This conduct constitutes sexual harassment when it explicitly or implicitly affects an individual's employment, unreasonably interferes with an individual's work performance, or creates an intimidating, hostile, or offensive work environment.[14]

Keeping it simple, *sexual harassment* is any unwelcomed behavior of a sexual nature. There are two major types. *Quid pro quo sexual harassment* occurs when sexual consent affects job outcomes, such as getting a job or assignment or promotion, or keeping one's job. *Hostile work environment sexual harassment* occurs when unwelcomed sexual behavior creates an intimidating and offensive workplace for anyone. By far the most common offense is men sexually harassing women, but women also are the harassers, and same-sex harassment also takes place at work. Sexual harassers can be fired, such as **Bill O'Reilly** from **Fox News** after being accused of sexual harassment, even though he denied it.

WORK
APPLICATION 9-2

Have you or has anyone you know been asked discriminatory questions during the preemployment process? If yes, please explain the situation in language acceptable to all.

9-1 APPLYING THE CONCEPT

Legal or Illegal Questions

Using the two major rules of thumb for preemployment inquiries and Exhibit 9-3, identify whether each question can or cannot be asked during a job interview.

A. legal (can ask)

B. illegal (cannot ask during preemployment)

_____ 1. How do you feel about unions?

_____ 2. What is your age?

_____ 3. Did you ever get arrested for stealing on the job?

_____ 4. Do you own your own car?

_____ 5. Tell me if you have any form of disability.

_____ 6. Do you belong to the Jewish Community Center, the Knights of Columbus, or other similar organizations?

_____ 7. Do you have proof that you are legally eligible to work in the United States?

_____ 8. Can you speak any foreign languages?

_____ 9. What is your marital status: single, married, or divorced?

_____ 10. I like children; do you have any?

_____ 11. I see that you are applying for a truck driver position with us at U.S. Freight Delivery. Are you a member of the Teamsters?

_____ 12. What is your sexual orientation—straight or homosexual?

_____ 13. How did you like your prior jobs? Did you file a lawsuit against an employer?

_____ 14. Where do you live now, and how long have you resided there?

_____ 15. Have you ever tested positive for a sexually transmitted disease, HIV, or AIDS?

EXHIBIT 9-3   PREEMPLOYMENT INQUIRIES

Topic	Can Ask . . .	Cannot Ask . . .
Name	Current legal name and whether the candidate has ever worked under a different name	Maiden name or whether the person has changed his or her name
Address	Current residence and length of residence there	Whether the candidate owns or rents his or her home, unless one or the other is a BFOQ
Age	Whether the candidate's age is within a certain range (if required for a particular job; for example, an employee must be 21 to serve alcoholic beverages); if hired, can ask for proof of age	How old are you? What is your date of birth? Can you provide a birth certificate? How much longer do you plan to work before retiring?
Sex	Candidate to indicate sex on an application if sex is a BFOQ	Candidate's sexual identity
Marital and Family Status	Whether candidate can adhere to the work schedule; whether the candidate has any activities, responsibilities, or commitments that may hinder him or her from coming to work	Specific questions about marital status or any question regarding children or other family issues
National Origin, Citizenship, or Race	Whether the candidate is legally eligible to work in the United States, and whether the candidate can provide proof of status if hired	Specific questions about national origin, citizenship, or race
Language	What languages the candidate speaks and/or writes; can ask candidate to identify specific language(s) if these are BFOQs	What language the candidate speaks when not on the job or how the candidate learned the language
Criminal Record	Whether the candidate has been convicted of a felony; if the answer is yes, can ask other information about the conviction if the conviction is job related	Whether the candidate has ever been arrested (an arrest does not prove guilt); for information regarding a conviction that is not job related
Height and Weight	Whether the candidate meets BFOQ height and/or weight requirements and whether the candidate can provide proof of height and weight if hired	Candidate's height or weight if these are not BFOQs
Religion	If candidate is of a specific religion, if religious preference is a BFOQ	Candidate's religious preference, affiliation, or denomination if not a BFOQ
Credit Rating	For information if a particular credit rating is a BFOQ	Unless a particular credit rating is a BFOQ
Education and Work Experience	For information that is job related	For information that is not job related
References	For names of people willing to provide references or who suggested the candidate apply for the job	For a reference from a religious leader
Military Record	For information about candidate's military service that is job related	Dates and conditions of discharge from the military; draft classification; National Guard or reserve unit of candidate
Organizations	About membership in job-related organizations, such as unions or professional or trade associations	About membership in any non–job-related organization that would indicate candidate's race, religion, or the like
Disabilities	Whether candidate has any disabilities that would prevent him or her from performing the job being applied for	General questions about disabilities
Past Salary/Pay	For determining prior employments	How much the candidate was paid on the job

Note: BFOQ = bona fide occupational qualification

HRM Sexual Harassment and Romance Policies. Most large firms have written policies defining sexual harassment and how to report violations;[15] some also have policies regarding romance at work. Why? Sexuality at work detracts from productivity.[16] Employee dating is rarely a private matter, especially between a supervisor and subordinate. Romance can be disruptive to other employees, triggering questions about fairness and favoritism, and can disrupt team cohesiveness. A competent female can be stereotyped as simply the "boss's girl-friend."[17] Romance by both genders sometimes leads to sexual harassment once the relationship ends.[18] Inappropriate relationships can topple careers, and allegations of unwanted attention or favoritism can cost companies millions and land businesses in the headlines for all the wrong reasons, including the abrupt departure of **Chief Operating Officer (COO) Keith Rabois** from mobile-payment company **Square Inc.** after being accused of sexual harassment, even though he claims the relationship was consensual. To help avoid these problems, many companies have workplace relationship policies.[19] If you work for a company with such policies, be sure to follow the rules, and you may want to think twice about a romantic relationship at work.

Verbal Warning and Reporting Violations. Some behavior is clearly harassment the first time, such as unwelcome requests for quid pro quo and touching in private areas, and should be reported, or at least employees should be given a verbal warning threatening to report the harassment if it happens again. But other behaviors are not clearly harassment, such as telling racial, religious, or sexual jokes and being asked out on a date. Therefore, if someone does something that offends you, you should tell him or her that you find it offensive or harassing and ask him or her not to do it again. Repeated unwelcome offenses become sexual harassment that you should report, even if you are not the victim.

If the firm has a sexual harassment policy, it will state how to report a violation. If not, it is generally recommended to complain first to the HR department, and if the problem is not resolved within a reasonable time for investigation, you can threaten to take your case to the EEOC, and if that doesn't work or you believe it is a waste of time, take your case to the EEOC; visit its website for instructions. Some victims get a lawyer and sue for monetary damages.

HR develops the policies, investigates the allegations to determine the accuracy of the violation, and does the paperwork and record keeping. Managers need to help prevent violations and are commonly required to report any suspicions of harassment to the HR department, and they and coworkers are commonly interviewed during investigations of reported violations.

WORK
APPLICATION 9-3

Have you or has anyone you know been harassed at work? If yes, please explain the situation in language acceptable to all.

9-2 APPLYING THE CONCEPT

Sexual Harassment

Indicate which kind of behavior is described in each statement.

A. sexual harassment: (1) quid pro quo or (2) hostile work environment

B. not sexual harassment

____ 16. Cindy tells her assistant Jose that if he goes to a motel with her, she will recommended him for a promotion.

____ 17. Marisol drops some cookie crumbs in Henry's lap and immediately brushes them off with her hand and gives his privates a gentle squeeze that causes him to jump up in surprise.

____ 18. Sue and Karly both hung up pictures of nude men and women on the walls near their desks, in view of other employees who walk by.

____ 19. Billy Bob tells his coworker Jane an explicitly sexual joke, even though twice before Jane said she doesn't want to hear dirty jokes.

____ 20. Kelly typically puts her hand on Tim's shoulder as she talks to him, and Tim is comfortable with it.

____ 21. Adam, the supervisor of the production department, tells subordinate Carleen that he thinks she is sexy and that he'd like to take her out.

Brianna Soukup/Portland Press Herald via Getty Images

LO 9-2

Explain the role of strategic human resources planning and the need for conducting a job analysis including its two parts.

Human Resources Planning

In this section, we discuss the first HRM process: HR planning and job analysis.

Strategic Human Resources Planning

Managers realize the need to hire and manage good people,[20] and they are increasingly recognizing that they must strategically manage their human capital—employees.[21] Thus, the trend is toward strategic human resources management.[22] The job of strategic HRM is planning to provide the right kinds of people in the right quantity with the right skills and human capital characteristics[23] and personal traits that fit the organizational culture,[24] at the right time,[25] because gaps in staffing cause a variety of problems.[26]

There needs to be a direct link between strategic HRM and company strategy (Chapter 5).[27] If the strategy is growth, then you need a plan to hire employees,[28] and fast-growing companies recruit people to innovate.[29] **Cisco Systems** grew from a small staff to 70,000 employees. E-commerce firm **Alibaba** grew too fast to 30,000 employees and had to freeze hiring.[30] If the strategy is retrenchment, then there will be layoffs, like at **McDonald's**. **Strategic human resources planning** *is the process of staffing the organization to meet its objectives.* At retailers like **L.L. Bean** and **Walmart**, thousands of employees are hired for the Christmas holiday season and let go shortly after; same thing goes for recreational businesses like New England's **Mount Snow** and **BlueGreen Beach Resorts**.

L.L. Bean, aiming to downsize its workforce by 10%, has offered early retirement packages to hundreds of employees. This human resource plan will allow the company to invest in expansion and automation.

WORK APPLICATION 9-4

Complete a job analysis for a job you hold or held; write a simple job description and job specifications.

WORK APPLICATION 9-5

Were you given a realistic job preview during a job interview? Explain.

strategic human resources planning The process of staffing the organization to meet its objectives.

job description Identifies the tasks and responsibilities of a position.

job specifications Identify the qualifications needed by the person who is to fill a position.

Job Analysis

Before you begin to search for a new employee, you need to conduct a job analysis.[31] *Job analysis* is the process of determining what the position entails (job description) and the qualifications needed (job specifications) to staff the position. The job analysis also results in a job title for the position.

The **job description** *identifies the tasks and responsibilities of a position.* The job description should identify skills needed[32] and give you and the applicant a clear understanding of the expectations in performing the job[33] so that everyone "really" knows what the position entails.[34] It is often called a *realistic job preview (RJP)*. Some managers think their job is to paint a rosy picture,[35] but research shows that making the job sound better than it really is just disappoints the new employee, who often quits, so you just end up with turnover problems.[36] Exhibit 9-4 shows a sample job description.

Based on the job description, you determine job specifications. **Job specifications** *identify the qualifications needed by the person who is to fill a position.* The job specifications identify the types of people needed. So it's not about getting someone; you need to get the right person who matches the job you want done.[37] The job analysis should be periodically updated as the job and qualifications to do the job change in a dynamic business environment.[38]

The Occupational Information Network (O*NET) is an excellent source of HR help.[39] O*NET OnLine has detailed descriptions of the world of work for use by job seekers, workforce development and HR professionals, students, researchers, and more. To learn more, visit www.onetonline.org.[40] HR is responsible for conducting the job analysis, and you can get copies of job descriptions, which usually include a job specification, from O*NET and use them as is or revise them for your specific job. HR keeps copies; distributes them to department hiring managers, recruiters, advertisers, and job candidates; and does all the paperwork to keep track of them.

LO 9-3

Discuss the two parts of attracting employees.

Attracting Employees

After hiring needs have been determined and jobs analyzed, the HR department generally recruits people, and two-thirds of MNCs say talent acquisition has the greatest impact on

EXHIBIT 9-4   JOB DESCRIPTION

DEPARTMENT: Plant Engineering

JOB TITLE: Lead Sheet Metal Specialist

JOB DESCRIPTION:

Responsible for the detailed direction, instruction, and leading of sheet metal department personnel in the construction and repair of a wide variety of sheet metal equipment. Receives verbal or written instructions from foreperson as to sequence and type of jobs or special methods to be used. Allocates work to members of the group. Directs the layout, fabrication, assembly, and removal of sheet metal units according to drawings or sketches and generally accepted trade procedures. Obtains materials or supplies needed for specific jobs according to standard procedures. Trains new employees, as directed, regarding metalworking procedures and safe working practices. Checks all work performed by the group. Usually makes necessary contacts for the group with supervision or engineering personnel. May report irregularities to higher supervision but has no authority to hire, fire, or discipline other employees.

performance.[41] In a survey, attracting and retaining skilled employees was the biggest challenge companies faced.[42] **First American CEO Dennis Gilmore** says that the company's success is based on its ability to attract and keep the best workers.[43] How do you attract good employees[44] who have the ability to do the job and fit the organizational culture?[45] You'll find out in this section and also learn about the selection process and how to conduct an interview.

Recruiting

Recruiting *is the process of attracting qualified candidates to apply for job openings.* Attracting applicants is important because people need to know about your job opening before they can apply.[46] Note that recruiting is not about getting lots of applications,[47] it's about attracting qualified candidates[48] for job and organizational culture fit.[49] You don't want to waste your time reviewing unqualified applications.[50] Recruiting can be conducted internally and externally, and external hiring is on the increase.[51] Exhibit 9-5 lists possible recruiting sources. It is critical to select the right recruiting source for the specific job.[52]

- *Internal Recruiting/Mobility.* *Internal recruiting* involves filling job openings with current employees. There are two types. There are horizontal or lateral transfers that are common today, and there are vertical moves called *promotions from within.* However, many firms just use the *promotion from within* term for both, but a new term to cover both is *internal mobility.*[53] At **Scripps Health**, three-quarters of all job openings are filled by existing employees.[54]

recruiting The process of attracting qualified candidates to apply for job openings.

EXHIBIT 9-5   RECRUITING SOURCES

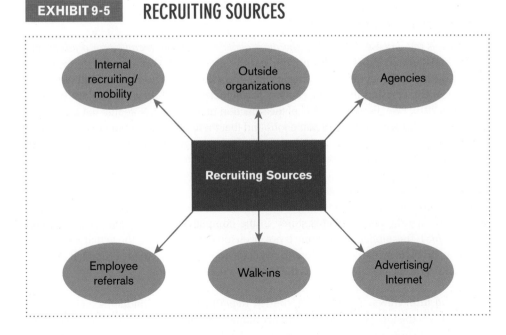

- **Employee referrals.** Employees may be encouraged to refer external friends and relatives to apply for positions. A survey found it to be the favorite recruiting method.[55] It is based on *networking*, and more people get jobs through networking than all the other methods combined.[56]

- **Walk-ins.** Without actually being recruited, good candidates may come to an organization "cold" and ask for a job. But most professionals send a résumé and cover letter asking for an interview.

- **Outside organizations.** Recruiting takes place at high schools, vocational/technical schools, colleges, professional associations, career conferences, and trade and job fairs. Many schools offer career planning and placement services to aid students and potential employers. Educational institutions are good places to recruit entry-level people who have little or no prior experience.

- **Agencies.** There are three major types of agencies: (1) *Temporary agencies*, such as **Kelly Services**, provide part- or full-time help for limited periods. (2) *Public agencies* are nationwide state employment services. They generally provide job candidates to employers at no cost or very low cost. (3) *Private employment agencies* are privately owned and charge a fee for their services. *Executive recruiters* are sometimes referred to as "headhunters." They specialize in recruiting managers and/or those with specific high-level technical skills, such as engineers and computer experts, charging the employer a large fee.

- **Advertising/Internet.** A simple help-wanted sign in the window is an advertisement. Newspapers are good places to advertise most positions, but professional and trade magazines may be more suitable for specific professional recruiting. Companies also use some direct mail, radio, and TV. Many employers and people look for work online. Several websites, such as **Indeed.com**, **Monster.com**, and **CareerBuilder. com**, provide job listing opportunities. At low or no cost, companies are also using social media, including **LinkedIn**, **Facebook**, and **Foursquare**, and are even using **Twitter** to "tweet" job ads.[57] **Zappos** stopped posting many jobs online in favor of a free membership program.[58]

WORK
APPLICATION 9-6

Identify the recruiting source used to hire you for your current job or one of your previous jobs.

Costco (**IOM 2**) is committed to internal recruiting and promoting from within the company, but it also uses external recruiting by employee referrals and hiring walk-ins for primarily entry-level positions. The majority of its managers started out at entry-level positions in Costco's warehouses, learned the business, and moved up within the company. Costco believes that promoting from within ensures equal promotional opportunities for motivated individuals, and this is one of the reasons Costco has such a loyal workforce.

The Selection Process

Selection *is the process of choosing the most qualified applicant recruited for a job.* Hiring can be stressful and expensive,[59] and you want to create equal opportunity for everyone, seeking diversity, without discriminating in violation of the CRA law.[60] Even though the speed of business is increasing, the hiring process has actually slowed down to 63 days, up from 42 days in 2010.[61] We discuss six parts of the selection process next. Note that not all parts of the selection process are used for some jobs and that there is no set sequence of steps to be followed in the selection process. **Airbnb** has a 10–key stage process for hiring.[62] However, you can think of the parts as a set of hurdles to get through to get the job.

Application Form. The recruited candidates are typically asked to complete an application or, for professional jobs, a résumé, but in either case, today online applications are often required so that the information is stored in the company's *human resources information system (HRIS)*. The application/résumé is not given too much weight in the actual selection.[63] Its primary use is to screen applications to select the top candidates to proceed. Or it gets you in the door so you can sell yourself as the best candidate for the job.

Screening Interviews. Specialists in the HR department often conduct screening interviews to select the top candidates who will continue in the selection process. This step helps

selection The process of choosing the most qualified applicant recruited for a job.

save line managers, who select the person, time when there are large numbers of job applicants. Many organizations, including **Nike** and **PricewaterhouseCoopers**, use computers to conduct screening interviews. **Google** is known for having between 4 and 12 grueling screening interviews.[64] To save time and travel expenses, companies, including **Airbnb**, are conducting screening interview via **Skype** and other programs.[65]

Testing. Testing helps place people in the right jobs,[66] as they can be used to predict job success, as long as the tests meet EEOC guidelines for *validity* (people who score high on the test do well on the job, and those who score low do not do well on the job) and *reliability* (if people take the same test on different days, they will get approximately the same score each time).[67] Some of the major types of tests include achievement tests, aptitude tests, personality tests, interest tests, and physical exams. Drug use and testing for the use of illegal drugs are on the increase in the United States.[68] Although marijuana is legal in some states, buying, growing, and/or selling it is against federal law. So even if the state you are applying for a job has legalized the use of marijuana, some MNCs will not hire you if you test positive for it during a drug test.

One trend in testing is to have candidates perform actual work for the company for free as part of the selection process. Unpaid internships are a kind of test that may result in a job.[69] Eight of the top 10 U.S. companies administer testing for some positions.[70] Online personality testing is on the increase as an estimated 60% to 70% of U.S. applicants take them, especially for customer service jobs; test users include **Dialog Direct**, **Lowe's**, **McDonald's**, and **Xerox**.[71]

Large firms often test through assessment centers. **Assessment centers** *are places job applicants undergo a series of tests, interviews, and simulated experiences to determine their potential.* Hospitality company **Delaware North** uses customized assessment. At **Great Western Bank**, job candidates for a teller job sit before a computer, which asks them to make change, respond to tough customers, and sell products that customers don't ask for. These tests and simulated experiences help select the best candidates.[72]

As job applications come in, managers screen the candidates by reviewing their applications and résumés.

Suzanne Kreiter/The Boston Globe via Getty Images

WORK
APPLICATION 9-7

Identify which selection methods were used in the process of selecting you for a job you have now or one you held in the past. If a test was used, specify the type of test.

assessment centers Places job applicants undergo a series of tests, interviews, and simulated experiences to determine their potential.

9-3 APPLYING THE CONCEPT

Recruiting Sources

Select the major recruiting source(s) that should be used for each of the job openings described.

A. internal recruiting/mobility

B. employee referrals

C. walk-ins

D. outside organizations

E. agencies

F. advertising/Internet

_____ 22. "Shane, Robert is taking a three-week paternity leave, so please recruit a replacement for him."

_____ 23. "Wauneta, our first-line supervisor Henry is retiring in two months. What recruiting method should we use to replace him?"

_____ 24. "Oh, by the way, Sonata, do you know anyone who could fill the administrative assistant position in your department?"

_____ 25. "We need a new sales rep. Sales Manager Carlos likes to hire young people without experience in order to train them to sell using our unique approach, so please recruit for the position ASAP."

_____ 26. "We need a person to perform routine cleaning services in a couple of weeks, but we have no budget, Lee Ann. Can you please pick someone coming in looking for a job?"

_____ 27. "Hi, Lena. Please go online and see if you can get us some applications for the software engineer job opening."

9-1   JOIN THE DISCUSSION ETHICS & SOCIAL RESPONSIBILITY

Homeless Workers

Andre Jehan, Pizza Schmizza founder of the Northwest chain, has an unusual way of recruiting and selecting workers. Homeless people are given pizza slices and soda and sometimes a couple of dollars to carry a sign that reads "Pizza Schmizza paid me to hold this sign instead of asking for money." Jehan believes he is helping the homeless, saying that carrying the signs has been a win-win situation, as the homeless, many of whom have mental illness or other problems that keep them from being able to hold a job, don't feel embarrassed or exploited;

they look forward to the work and food. However, Donald Whitehead of National Coalition for the Homeless says Jehan is exploiting the homeless.

1. Is Jehan exploiting the homeless?
2. Is it ethical and socially responsible to give homeless people food for carrying signs?

Source: G. Williams, "Will Work for Pizza," *Entrepreneur*, http://www.entrepreneur.com/article/65058, accessed May 8, 2017.

Background and Reference Checks. References aren't given much weight in the selection because you rarely get a negative reference for legal reasons.[73] But background checks are needed to verify the honesty of the applicant throughout the selection process, as nearly 1 in 10 checks disclose some form of adverse information.[74] If the background and references are OK, applicants usually proceed in the process, but if caught lying, such as stating qualifications they don't actually have, they are eliminated. Many companies today conduct an online search for job candidates, and if they find unprofessional things (like pictures of a sexual nature, drunkenness, drug use, etc.), they reject candidates.

Interviewing. The interview is usually the most heavily weighted step in the selection process.[75] The interview gives the candidate a chance to learn about the job and organization and you a chance to assess things about a candidate that can't be obtained from the other steps, such as the candidate's ability to communicate and his or her personality, appearance, and motivation. An important criterion includes whether or not the person will fit within the organizational culture.[76] Assessing these traits is subjective, so it requires accurate judgment.[77] A trend to help ensure selecting the best fit is to include trusted employees in the interview process.[78] You will learn how to prepare for and conduct a job interview later in this section.

WORK APPLICATION 9-8

What types of job interviews have you experienced?

Hiring. Based on the preceding, you compare the candidates and decide who is the best suited for the job. Diversity should be considered when selecting a candidate.[79] The candidate is contacted and offered the job. If the candidate does not accept the job or accepts but leaves after a short time, the next-best candidate is offered the job. Upon hiring, HR fills out the paperwork, including legal forms for government agencies. Hiring the right person for the job is not easy; even **Gap founder Don Fisher** said he only hired the right person about half of the time.[80]

WORK APPLICATION 9-9

Identify the types of questions you were asked during a job interview.

The focus of this chapter is on hiring others. On a personal note, **Broadcom CEO Scott McGregor** says not to post anything anywhere, or let anyone else post anything, that you wouldn't want your parents—or a job recruiter—to see.[81] Before applying for a job, do a search on yourself and remove anything unprofessional, and make sure your phone message and email address are professional as well. Also, the appendix to this chapter (page 310) gives personal career advice. Take a few minutes to determine how ready you are to progress in your own career by completing Self-Assessment 9-1, "Career Development."

Selection Interviewing

As a manager, you will likely need to know how to conduct a job interview to select people to work for you. So this part of the section can help you. You can practice this skill in Skill Builder 9-1.

9-1 SELF-ASSESSMENT

Career Development

Indicate how accurately each statement describes you by placing a number from 1 (*does not describe me*) to 5 (*describes me*) on the line before the statement.

5	4	3	2	1
Describes me				Does not describe me

_____ 1. I know my strengths, and I can list several of them.

_____ 2. I can list several skills that I have to offer an employer.

_____ 3. I have career objectives.

_____ 4. I know the type of full-time job that I want next.

_____ 5. My written job objective clearly states the type of job I want and the skills I will use on the job.

_____ 6. I have analyzed help-wanted ads or job descriptions and determined the most important skills I will need to get the type of full-time job I want.

_____ 7. I have or plan to get a part-time job, summer job, or internship related to my career objectives.

_____ 8. I know the proper terms to use on my résumé to help me get the full-time job, part-time job, or summer internship I want.

_____ 9. I understand how my strengths and skills are transferable, or how they can be used on jobs I apply for, and I can give examples on a résumé and in an interview.

_____ 10. I can give examples (on a résumé and in an interview) of suggestions or direct contributions I made that increased performance for my employer.

_____ 11. My résumé focuses on the skills I have developed and on how they relate to the job I am applying for rather than on job titles.

_____ 12. My résumé gives details of how my college education and the skills I developed in college relate to the job I am applying for.

_____ 13. I have a résumé that is customized to each part-time job, summer job, or internship I apply for rather than one generic résumé.

Add up the numbers you assigned to the statements and place the total on the continuum below.

65	39	13
Career ready		In need of career development

Types of Interviews and Questions. Exhibit 9-6 shows the types of interviews and questions. One thing to keep in mind is the need to develop a set of consistent questions to ask all candidates so that you can objectively compare them to select the most qualified.

Preparing for and Conducting the Interview. Completing the interview preparation steps shown in Model 9-1 and following the five steps of the interview in Model 9-2 will help you improve your interviewing skills.

Career planning and networking to get jobs are discussed in the appendix to the chapter.

EXHIBIT 9-6   TYPES OF INTERVIEWS AND QUESTIONS

Interviews

Structured interview: All candidates are asked the same list of prepared questions.
Unstructured interview: Has no planned questions or sequence of topics.
Semistructured interview: The interviewer has a list of questions but also asks unplanned questions.

Questions

Closed-ended questions: "Do you have a Class 1 license?" "Can you work 9 to 5?"
Open-ended questions: "Why do you want to be a computer programmer for our company?" "Tell me about yourself."
Hypothetical questions: "What would the problem be if the machine made a ringing sound?" "What would you do if . . . ?"
Behavioral questions: "How would you respond to a customer who swore at you?" "Give me an example of how you successfully calmed a loud, angry customer."
Probing questions: The probe is not planned; it is used to clarify the candidate's response to an open-ended or hypothetical question. "What do you mean by 'it was tough'?" "What was the dollar increase in sales you achieved?"

MODEL 9-1   INTERVIEW PREPARATION STEPS

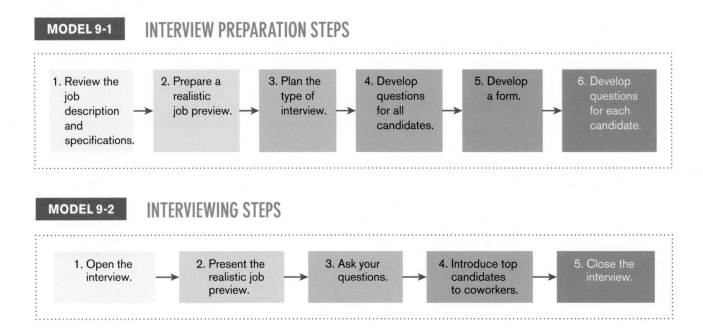

1. Review the job description and specifications. → 2. Prepare a realistic job preview. → 3. Plan the type of interview. → 4. Develop questions for all candidates. → 5. Develop a form. → 6. Develop questions for each candidate.

MODEL 9-2   INTERVIEWING STEPS

1. Open the interview. → 2. Present the realistic job preview. → 3. Ask your questions. → 4. Introduce top candidates to coworkers. → 5. Close the interview.

WORK APPLICATION 9-10

Identify the steps that were used when you were interviewed for a job.

Problems to Avoid. Don't rush; don't stereotype—get to know each individual; don't hire people who are your clones—recall the benefits of diversity (Chapter 3); don't consider just one or two positive or negative things—review the candidate's entire set of qualifications.

Selecting the Candidate. After all interviews are completed, compare each candidate's qualifications to the job specifications to determine who would be the best fit for the job. Again, get coworkers' impressions of each candidate, because they will have to work with them and can judge if they fit the culture.

LO 9-4

Describe the three parts of developing employees.

Developing Employees

After employees have been hired, they must be developed[82]—oriented, trained, and evaluated, which is a big expense for companies of all sizes.[83] So we discuss it in this section. **Unilever CEO Paul Polman** says that one of the most important things a company can do is invest in human capital.[84] Developing employees significantly enhances the firm's stock of human capital while reducing the costs of recruiting and selecting external new hires.[85] So for people to really be the organization's most valuable resource, they need to be developed.[86]

Orientation Programs, Onboarding, and Newcomer Socialization

Orientation *is the process of introducing new employees to the organization and their jobs.* Initiating new hires successfully into the team is critical to their individual success and the team's.[87]

Orientation Programs. Orientation programs are developed by the HRM department that have some form of personnel policy handbook, which HR managers discuss and give to employees or have online. People are socialized by institutions,[88] and firms want to create a sense of belonging for newcomers quickly.[89] Although orientation programs vary in formality and content, five important elements should be included: (1) description of organization and department functions, (2) specification of job tasks and responsibilities, (3) explanation of standing plans, (4) a tour, and (5) introduction to coworkers.

Onboarding and Newcomer Socialization. The trend is to call orientation *onboarding*,[90] and firms including **iCracked** cellphone repair share the mission multiple times.[91] *Newcomer socialization* refers to the process through which new employees acquire the knowledge, skills, behaviors, and attitudes required for effective participation in the firm.[92] Onboarding is about *socializing* new hires and developing relationships,[93] because if people don't feel like they are accepted into the team, they tend to quit.[94] Socialization is ranked more important than the formal HRM department orientation.[95] Recall the importance of cultural fit and group process cohesiveness (Chapter 8). It is important for new hires to know whom to go to for information and help,[96] so a very important part of onboarding is for the new hire to have an informal mentor,[97] whose role is to make sure socialization is successful.

On-the-job training allows employees to learn how to face challenges in their new position under the guidance of more experienced employees.

Training and Development

Employees have to be taught how to perform a new job and to update skills with changes in technology.[98] We hope you aren't thinking, "I can't wait to be done with college studies," because as **PepsiCo CEO Indra Nooyi** says, never stop learning; the strongest leaders are lifelong students.[99] Ongoing learning benefits both employees and firms—learning organizations (Chapters 2 and 7).[100]

The ADIE Model. A popular approach to training and development is the use of the ***ADIE model.*** You Assess training needs, Design the training, Implement it, and Evaluate results.

Training Versus Development. Training and development are different processes. **Training** *is the process of teaching employees the skills necessary to perform a job.* Today, having diverse skills enables employees to perform a variety of task.[101] Training typically addresses the technical skills of nonmanagers. **Development** *is ongoing education to improve skills for present and future jobs.* With the increasing use of teams, companies are conducting leadership development,[102] including **Unilever,**[103] and **General Electric (GE), IBM,** and **Johnson & Johnson** are well known for their great leadership programs. GE trained 40,000 employees in FastWorks methodology.[104] Electronic design company **Cadence** provides 60 hours of annual training and development.[105] But much of what is taught through development isn't used on the job.[106] Be honest. How many of the developmental skills you have learned through this course are you actually using in your personal and professional lives? It's tough to implement new skill because we don't like to change our habits.

Off-the-Job and On-the-Job Training. As the name implies, *off-the-job training* is conducted away from the work site, often in some sort of classroom setting. A common method

WORK APPLICATION 9-11

Recall an orientation you experienced. Which elements did it include and exclude? Briefly describe the orientation.

orientation The process of introducing new employees to the organization and their jobs.

training The process of teaching employees the skills necessary to perform a job.

development Ongoing education to improve skills for present and future jobs.

MODEL 9-3   JOB INSTRUCTIONAL TRAINING STEPS

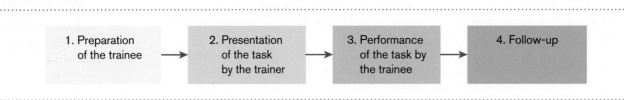

| 1. Preparation of the trainee | → | 2. Presentation of the task by the trainer | → | 3. Performance of the task by the trainee | → | 4. Follow-up |

is vestibule training. **Vestibule training** *develops skills in a simulated setting.* For example, many large retail stores like **Target** and **Walmart** have training rooms where new employees learn how to run cash registers and other equipment. The training is usually conducted by a training specialist.

On-the-job training (OJT) is done at the work site with the resources the employee uses to perform the job. The manager or an employee selected by the manager usually conducts the training. Many firms, including **IBM**, **Ford**, and **NASA,** are using developmental assignment to facilitate on-the-job learning.[107] Most large organizations conduct some training off the job, whereas small companies tend to use OJT.[108]

Job Instructional Training. Because of its proven record of success, job instructional training (JIT) is a popular training method used worldwide. Teaching by demonstration is supported by evidence-based management.[109] JIT has four steps, presented in Model 9-3. You essentially (1) explain the task objective, (2) demonstrate how to do the task, (3) watch employees perform the task and correct as needed until they can do the task on their own, and (4) tell them whom to see if they have any questions or need help, and keep an eye on them in case they need more training.

WORK
APPLICATION 9-12

Identify which steps of JIT your trainer used to train you for a present or past job. Was the training conducted on or off the job?

vestibule training Training that develops skills in a simulated setting.

9-4   APPLYING THE CONCEPT

Training and Development Methods

To select the most appropriate training method for each situation, use the letters ranging from A to J in the second column, "AC 9-4," of Exhibit 9-7.

____ 28. I'm delegating to you the task of calculating the company's turnover rate last year compared to the last five years, and I need your report tomorrow.

____ 29. You need to train employees to cover for each other when they are not on the job being absent or on vacation.

____ 30. You want to conduct a diversity training program to improve the relationship between diverse group members so they better understand each other.

____ 31. You will like the course because you get information on a company and do an analysis to improve its performance by answering questions.

____ 32. Now I'm going to show you how to run the machine.

____ 33. The HR department needs to develop a method to developing interpersonal and decision-making skills

for managers all over the United States and three other countries that allows them to get the training on their own whenever they can get it done.

____ 34. You will be running a company by filling out these forms and getting quarterly results on your performance; the most important measure of success is stock price.

____ 35. There has been a large increase in the number of employee complaints. You need to develop a training program that will improve supervisors' ability to resolve complaints.

____ 36. Your company is growing fast and hiring lots of new employees who must learn several rules and regulations before they can start their jobs.

____ 37. You have new employees whom you must train to handle the typical daily tasks and problems that may come up that they will have to handle on the job.

EXHIBIT 9-7   TRAINING AND DEVELOPMENT METHODS

Skills Developed	AC 9-4	Methods	Description
Technical skills	A	Written material, lectures, videotapes, question-and-answer sessions, discussions, demonstrations (JIT)	The trainer gives material, talks, shows a video (which usually has written material and talk), asks if trainees have any questions and answers them, leads a discussion, or shows trainees how to perform a task.
	B	Programmed learning	The trainee uses a software program by reading material and then is tested by being asked to select a response to each question or problem and is given feedback on the response.
	C	Job rotation	Employees are trained to perform different jobs. Job rotation can also develop trainees' conceptual skills.
	D	Projects	Trainees are given special assignments, such as developing a new product or preparing a report. Certain projects may also develop trainees' interpersonal skills and conceptual skills.
Interpersonal skills	E	Role-playing	Trainees act out situations that might occur on the job with minimum guidance from trainers. It is best used when there is no single correct way to handle a situation, such as identifying feelings and developing empathy.
	F	Behavior modeling	Trainees observe how to perform a task correctly (by watching either a live demonstration or a videotape). Trainees role-play the observed skills and receive feedback on their performance. Trainees develop plans for using the observed skills on the job.
Decision-making skills	G	Cases	The trainee is presented with a simulated situation and asked to diagnose and solve the problems involved. The trainee usually must also answer questions about his or her diagnosis and solution.
	H	In-basket exercises	The trainee is given actual or simulated letters, memos, reports, and so forth that would typically come to the person holding the job. The trainee must determine what action each item would require and must assign priorities to the actions.
	I	Management games	Trainees work as part of a team to "manage" a simulated company over a period of several game "quarters" or "years."
	J	Interactive videos	No trainer is needed, as trainees can view videotapes online 24/7/365 that present situations requiring interpersonal and/or conceptual and decision-making skills.

Note: The column labeled "AC 9-4" is for use with Applying the Concept 9-4, "Training and Development Methods."

Microlearning. With the decline in attention spans, one of the trends is to keep lessons short. Among e-learning companies that offer microlearning formats are **Grove**, **Udemy**, and **Lynda.com** for corporate-skills training and **Duolingo** for language skills. Most produce or distribute a mix of video and interactive lessons that take under five minutes to complete and include a quiz. Lessons are available to users whenever they want to access them online or via smartphones.[110]

Training and Development Methods. Exhibit 9-7 lists various commonly used training methods, many of which can be used as part of JIT. The training methods are grouped on the basis of the primary skills developed (Chapter 1). However, some of the technical methods can be combined. The trend is to have more active involvement of participants and offer online simulation training and development.

WORK
APPLICATION 9-13

Explain the training methods used to teach you how to perform your present job or a past job.

MANAGEMENT IN ACTION
Performance Appraisal

Performance Appraisal

After you have hired and trained employees, you must evaluate how well employees perform their jobs so they know how they are doing, so it is an important part of the manager's job.[111] Through performance management,[112] managers need to be evaluated for current performance and potential promotions.[113] **Performance appraisal** *is the ongoing process of evaluating employee performance.* In a mechanistic organization, managers perform subordinate evaluations, but in organic self-managing team structures, peers also evaluate each other, as is done at **Zappos**.[114] In some cases, the evaluation is expanded to everyone the employees come into contact with, including other departments, customers, and suppliers through *360-degree feedback.*

The Performance Appraisal Process. Exhibit 9-8 illustrates the performance appraisal process. Note the connection between the organization's mission and vision and objectives and the performance appraisal process that measure how well strategic objectives are met. Even though formal performance appraisal reviews are only conducted once a year by 77% of surveyed companies, they should be ongoing, as our definition states. Employees need regular feedback on their performance, so use coaching.[115] Coaching is a development tool that involves ongoing giving of praise for a job well done to maintain performance or taking corrective action when standards are not met.[116]

The HR department develops that process, but it's primarily the managers' job to conduct the evaluations, and both need to document and keep records of the assessments. **Robert Graham CEO Michael Buckley** does it the old-fashioned way with a file folder for each of his direct reports,[117] but there are software programs to track performance that should be used during the formal review. In Chapter 14, we will discuss coaching and discipline.

You Get What You Reinforce. One thing you should know is that people will generally do what they are rewarded for doing (good work) and avoid what they are punished for doing (breaking rules). Here is a realistic example that happens. If you say you want good-quality products, and you focus on punishing workers for not meeting production quotas, and you don't reward employees who do quality work and punish those who don't, employees will meet the quotas and skimp on quality to do so. Tax services firm **Ryan LLC** says to reward results, not looking busy and hours worked.[118] Reinforcement is a motivation theory that we will discuss in detail in Chapter 11.

Standards and Measurement Methods. To effectively assess performance, you need to have clear expectation standards,[119] and methods to objectively measure performance.[120] The formal performance appraisal often involves the use of a standard form developed by the HR department to measure employee performance. Exhibit 9-9 explains the commonly used performance appraisal measurement methods and displays them on a continuum based on their use in administrative and developmental decisions. A combination of the methods is usually superior to any one method used by itself, as critical incidents should be used with all the other methods.

The success of performance appraisal does not lie in the method or form used; it depends on your interpersonal coaching skills. An important part of your job is to make sure that your employees know what the standards are and how they are performing through ongoing coaching. If you give an employee an average rather than a good rating, you should be able to clearly explain why. The employee should understand what exactly needs to be done during the next performance period to get the higher rating. With clear standards and coaching, you can minimize disagreements over performance during the formal performance appraisal.

performance appraisal The ongoing process of evaluating employee performance.

EXHIBIT 9-8 THE PERFORMANCE APPRAISAL PROCESS

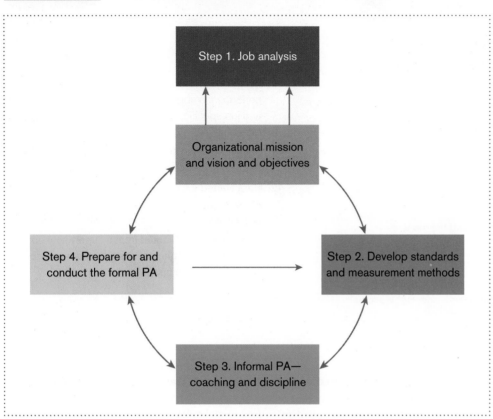

EXHIBIT 9-9 PERFORMANCE APPRAISAL MEASUREMENT METHODS

The ***Critical Incidents File*** is a coaching performance appraisal method in which a manager keeps a written record of positive and negative performance of employees throughout the performance period.

Management by Objectives (MBO) is a process in which managers and employees jointly set objectives for the employees, periodically evaluate performance, and reward according to the results.

The ***Narrative Method*** requires a manager to write a statement about the employee's performance. The system can vary. Managers may be allowed to write whatever they want, or they may be required to answer questions about the employee's performance. The narrative method is often combined with another method.

Behaviorally Anchored Rating Scale (BARS) is a performance appraisal method combining the rating scale and the critical incidents file. It is more objective and accurate than either method used separately. Rather than having ratings of excellent, good, average, and so forth, the form has several statements that describe the employee's performance, from which the manager selects the best one. Standards are clear when a good BARS is developed.

The ***Rating Scale*** is a performance appraisal checklist on which a manager simply rates the employee's quantity of work, quality of work, dependability, judgment, attitude, cooperation, and initiative.

Ranking is a performance appraisal method that is used to evaluate employee performance from best to worst. Under the ranking method, the manager compares an employee to other employees rather than to a standard measurement. An offshoot of ranking is the forced distribution method, which is similar to grading on a curve. Predetermined percentages of employees are placed in various performance categories, for example: excellent, 5%; above average, 15%; average, 60%; below average, 15%; and poor, 5%. Note that it is good to use informally when making administrative decisions, but as an overall system, it can cause problems. Former **GE CEO Jack Welch** used it. **Dell** tried forced ranking, and it turned good employees into politicians, bad employees into backstabbers, and colleagues into enemies and destroyed collaboration—so Dell dropped using it.[a]

a. R. Karlgaad, "Do Jerks Always Win?" *Forbes* (December 29, 2014): 44.

9-5   APPLYING THE CONCEPT

Performance Appraisal Methods

Select the performance appraisal method (see Exhibit 9-9) that is most appropriate for the given situation.

A. critical incidents file

B. management by objectives (MBO)

C. narrative method

D. behaviorally anchored rating scales (BARS)

E. rating scale

F. ranking

_____ 38. Bonnie Sue is not performing her job well.

_____ 39. Kasandra wants to use an assessment system for developing each employee.

_____ 40. Managers and employees have complained that the one existing appraisal form does not work well for different types of employee jobs. Usain has decided to hire an HRM professional to develop a performance appraisal system that is more objective and job specific, with forms for various employee groups.

_____ 41. Samantha asked you for a letter of recommendation for a job she applied for at another company.

_____ 42. Indra started a small company and now has a dozen employees. She wants to develop one performance appraisal form that you can use with all employees.

_____ 43. John has been promoted from a supervisory position to a middle-management position and needs to select his replacement.

Developmental and Evaluative Performance Appraisal Interviews. Extending Exhibit 9-9, there are two types of performance appraisal (PA): developmental and evaluative. A *developmental performance appraisal* is used to make decisions and plans for performance improvements. An *evaluative performance appraisal* is used to make administrative decisions about such issues as pay raises, transfers and promotions, and demotions and terminations. The evaluative PA focuses on the past, whereas the developmental PA focuses on the future. They are related because a developmental PA is always based on an evaluative PA. However, the primary purpose of PA should be to help employees continuously improve their performance.

When a developmental and an evaluative PA are conducted together (which they commonly are), the appraisal is often less effective as evaluation crushes development, especially when the employee disagrees with the evaluation.[121] Most managers are not good at being a judge and a coach at the same time. Therefore, separate meetings make the two uses clear and can help you be both a judge and a coach. To help you prepare for and conduct an evaluative PA interview, see Model 9-4; see Model 9-5 for developmental PA interviews.

Being Evaluated. On a personal note, you may not agree at all with your boss's assessment, but your supervisor's evaluation will affect your pay raises and promotions. But when you get evaluated by your boss, here is some good advice on things not to do.[122] Try not to get angry and raise your voice, because your boss will become angry and mistrustful of you. Don't deny mistakes and not meeting the boss's performance expectations, especially when your boss has a critical incidents file, because your boss will doubt your credibility. Don't make excuses and blame others, because your boss will lose respect for you.

What can you do? Take responsibility for not meeting your boss's expectations. The best thing to do is calm down and have a separate developmental session with your boss. During the meeting, tell your boss you want to improve and get a higher-level assessment the next time. Get your boss to very clearly state exactly what needs to be improved, develop a plan to improve, and agree that if you meet the expectations, you will get a higher assessment the next time. Document your agreement in writing, and both of you sign it.

If you don't want to follow this advice, or it doesn't work, you can find another job that may better utilize your skills and provide better job satisfaction. Here is a lesson that some people learned the hard way. If you complain to your boss's supervisor about your boss (going over

MODEL 9-4 THE EVALUATIVE PERFORMANCE APPRAISAL INTERVIEW

MODEL 9-5 THE DEVELOPMENTAL PERFORMANCE APPRAISAL INTERVIEW

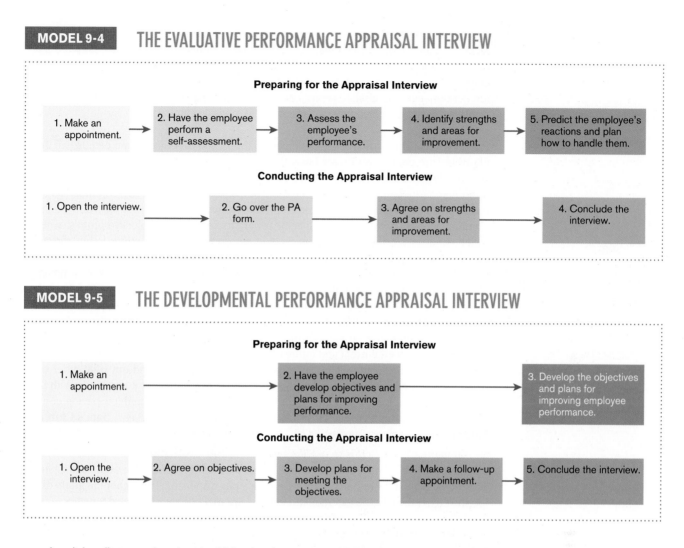

your boss's head), remember that the higher-level manager most likely promoted your boss because he or she meets the supervisor's expectations, and you will most likely only cause your boss to dislike and distrust you all the more. Some people are vengeful, and your boss can make your life even more miserable at work.

Retaining and Separating Employees

An organization must have HRM systems to retain good and separate (also called terminate) poor employees. Discussions of retention and separation commonly use the term *turnover*— employees leaving the firm. When you spend the time, effort, and money (cost) to attract and develop employees, it is costly to replace them,[123] and productivity suffers when you don't have needed workers and during their development.[124] Although retention is critical, managers list turnover among their most important challenges.[125]

W. L. Gore prides itself in its very low 3% voluntary turnover rate.[126] **Marriott Hotels' Bill Marriott** says that a seasoned workforce does a better job and costs less.[127] Think about the cost to **Zappos** of losing 14% of its employees.[128] What do the best companies, including **Google**, do to attract and retain the best workers? They foster strong, rewarding relationships among their employees.[129] **King Arthur Flour** says it has thrived for more than 225 years because it treats its employees well.[130] In this section, we discuss compensation, health and safety, labor relations, and separating employees, all of which affect retention and separation.

Compensation

Compensation *is the total of an employee's pay and benefits.* Compensation is an important part of the HRM process because it affects both attracting and retaining employees.[131] An important

LO 9-5

Summarize the role of compensation in retaining employees, and indicate three methods of employment separation.

compensation The total of an employee's pay and benefits.

overall compensation decision is pay level. *Pay level* reflects top management's choice to be a high-, medium-, or low-paying organization. Low-paying firms may save money on pay, but the savings can be lost to the high of turnover as employees leave for better jobs; but good pay alone will not retain good employees.[132] Giving *pay raises* is commonly done once a year with the performance appraisal. However, companies including **Google**, **Facebook**, **Evolv**, and **Zulily** are giving more frequent pay raises to help motivate employees to stay.[133]

Pay Systems. There are three general pay methods, and an organization can use all three. (1) *Wages* are paid on an hourly basis. (2) *Salary* is based on time—a week, a month, or a year. A salary is paid regardless of the number of hours worked. (3) *Incentives* are pay for performance. Incentives include piece rate (pay based on production), commissions (pay based on sales), merit raises (the more productive workers get paid more), and bonuses. Common types of bonuses[134] are a specific reward for reaching an objective, profit sharing in which employees get a part of the profits, and company stock and options to buy the stock at below market value. The use of pay for performance rather than hours worked is the trend today.[135] The HR department develops pay systems including benefits and pay determination and keeps records in compliance with laws.

Pay Determination. A difficult decision is how much to pay each employee. It is very important to determine an amount that is within your budget but at the same time high enough to retain your current and future employees. External approaches include using data from industry sources and using pay averages.[136] It's common to find out what other organizations pay for the same or similar jobs and set pay levels that are comparable. With high turnover and increased competition to recruit new workers, traditional low-paying companies, including **Walmart** (which loses about 500,000 store workers a year), **Sam's Club**, and **McDonald's** are increasing starting pay and giving raises to stem turnover.[137]

An internal approach is to use job evaluation. **Job evaluation** *is the process of determining the worth of each job relative to the other jobs within the organization.* Organizations commonly group jobs into pay grades, creating a pay dispersion. The higher the grade of the job, the higher the pay. The external and internal approaches are often used together.

Benefits. *Benefits* are various nonwage compensations provided to employees in addition to their normal wages or salaries. Legally required benefits include *workers' compensation* to cover job-related injuries, *unemployment compensation* to provide for employees who are laid off or terminated, *Medicare* for health insurance, and *Social Security* for retirement. The employer generally pays all of the workers' and unemployment compensation and matches the amount the government takes out of each employee's pay for Social Security.

job evaluation The process of determining the worth of each job relative to the other jobs within the organization.

9-2   # JOIN THE DISCUSSION ETHICS & SOCIAL RESPONSIBILITY

College Sports Agents

The National Collegiate Athletic Association (NCAA) continues to penalize college sports teams because their athletes receive cars, cash, clothing, and other gifts from sports agents. NCAA rules allow agents to meet with college athletes. However, they forbid these students from entering into contracts—including oral deals—with agents or accepting gift incentives to sign contracts later. The idea is to ensure fair play and to shield amateurs until they are done with school.

The number of hours that student athletes put into collegiate sports, however, coupled with the millions of dollars that some major universities earn from the performance of their student athletes, has sparked a debate as to whether these student athletes deserve monetary compensation, despite the fact that they are still students and are playing at an amateur (not professional) level.

1. Is it ethical and socially responsible for college athletes to accept gift incentives from sports agents?

2. Do you think the NCAA should change its rules and allow college athletes to get paid?

Most employers are also required by law to provide some time off for medical reasons and to care for a sick family member or to care for a new child under the *Family and Medical Leave Act.*

Commonly offered optional benefits include health insurance; paid sick days, holidays, and vacations; and pension plans. Optional benefits can be paid in full by employers or split between employee and employer. Other benefits less commonly offered include dental and life insurance, membership in fitness centers, membership in credit unions, and tuition reimbursement for education.

Offering health insurance benefits helps to attract and retain employees, and it is a major concern for both employees and employers,[138] especially with the still unknown changes and effects of the Affordable Care Act (ACA). The cost of a family health care yearly plan is more than $17,000.[139] Due to the rising cost of health care, many companies have cut back on this benefit by increasing employees' share of the cost and increasing copayments.

A strong benefits package can reduce turnover. **Ikea** offers four months of paid parental leave to all employees who have been with the company for a year or longer.

Benefits are expensive, costing employers 25 to 35% of employee compensation.[140] Some companies minimize full-time workers (using more part-time workers and contractors) to avoid having to pay any benefits; everyone hired at **Sid Simone Solutions** is an independent contractor.[141] Author Robert Lussier is a contractor for SAGE Publishers. **Uber** has thousands of drivers, but they are contractors and don't get any benefits. Some companies are outsourcing work from employees to contractor companies, such as **Virgin American**. **Google** parent **Alphabet** has roughly equal numbers of outsourced workers and full-time employees.[142] Companies such as **FedEx** are also reclassifying their current employees as contractors to cut costs, as they continue to do essentially the same work.[143]

To help attract and retain the best workers, some companies offer generous benefits. **Google** is well known for its generous benefits, including free gourmet food all day long, free gyms and massages, and generous parental leave, and dogs are welcome at work.[144] **L.L. Bean** gives employees discounts of 33% to 40% on company-made items, and it increased its tuition reimbursement from $2,750 to $5,250 per year.[145] **Starbucks** will reimburse tuition cost for online degrees from **Arizona State University**.[146]

Many corporations offer "*cafeteria-style*," or *flexible, benefit plans* to their employees. These plans let employees select the benefits that best meet their needs up to a preset dollar value. A common approach is for one member of a couple to select health insurance and the other to decline it and use the funds for other benefits.

Employees say that retirement benefits are very important for feelings of loyalty— retention.[147] Regardless of your age, think *retirement*, right now.[148] There are sayings, pay yourself first, and retirement should always be your top payment priority.[149] Most people aren't saving or are not saving enough for retirement.[150] A word of advice for the young: start saving for retirement in your 20s. If your employer offers a retirement account, such as a 401(k) plan, start one as soon as you can. Ask the HR staff if the company will match the money you put into your retirement plan, and go to the max to take advantage of free money. Matching dollar for dollar is a 100% return on your investment.

Would you like to be a millionaire? If you start putting away $2,000 a year (with or without a match) in your early 20s, such as in a low-fee stock index fund,[151] with competent professional help, you can be a millionaire by the time you retire at age 67. Besides, if you start your retirement account with your first job, you will never miss the money. Plus, with deferred taxes, less than the amount put into retirement is taken out of your pay.

If you are past your 20s, the longer you wait to fund a retirement account, the less you will have when you retire. The general rule is to put away 10% to 15% of your gross income into retirement,[152] and even more if you are older. It's also a lot less stressful and can bring happiness knowing you have financial security.[153] Don't think, "I can't afford to put money away today." Think, "I can't afford to lose compound savings and give away matching funds; and I don't want to have to work well into my senior years and live on Social Security."

WORK
APPLICATION 9-14

Describe the compensation package offered by your present or past employer.

Michael Nagle/Bloomberg via Getty Images

Work–Life Balance and Benefits. In analyzing the needs of the workforce, work–life balance is high on the list of issues facing both employers and employees.[154] Thus, work–life balance is a perpetually hot topic, with 40% of full-time American workers logging more than 50 work hours a week.[155] Connectivity technology advances like the smartphone have blurred the line between the workday and off hours.[156] People say these technologies help them do the job, but they end up working more hours, as some 44% of Internet users regularly perform some job tasks outside of work.[157] On the other side, employees are using company electronic devices for personal use during work hours, such as social media and shopping.[158]

Although some men are getting more involved in child care,[159] and both men and women say balancing work and family life difficulties deters them from seeking executive roles,[160] work–life balance is especially difficult for women because of gender family responsibility inequity.[161] Family-friendly practices, such as onsite child-care, relate to low absenteeism.[162] Some companies, including **Campbell Soup** and **Lowe's**, are providing family-friendly practices, employee assistance programs, seminars, and workshops on how to better balance work and life. For more information and help, visit the **Families and Work Institute** website www.familiesandwork.org.

Businesses are increasingly using *flexible work practices (FWPs)*, allowing employees control over when, where, or how much they work because it improves work–life balance and job satisfaction and lowers stress.[163] Flexibility focus should be on work performed, not set hours worked.[164] Flexible practices by **Ryan LLC** resulted in a decrease in voluntary turnover from 18.53% to 10.33%.[165] Here are some of the most common FWPs ranked by firm use: control over when to take breaks, gradual return after childbirth or adoption, paid time off for family or personal needs, flexible starting and quitting times, choice of whether to work overtime, option to work longer hours on fewer days, ability to work from home on occasion, and ability to work from home regularly. Research supports that people who work from home are happier and more productive.[166] However, less than 3% of full-time employees work remotely.[167] Smaller companies offer more of these flexibilities than do larger firms.[168]

Costco (**IOM 3**) is able to retain employees with a lower turnover rate than most retailers by offering its workers higher-than-average wages and better benefits with opportunities for advancement through promotion from within. A higher percentage of its U.S. employees, including part-time workers, received health care and other benefits compared to those of **Walmart** and **Target**.

Health and Safety

Workplace safety is a concern for all companies, but especially in more dangerous industries with higher death rates ranked such as construction; transportation and warehousing; agriculture, forestry, fishing, and hunting; professional and business services; and manufacturing.[169] Most accidents such as plane crashes,[170] and 98% of truck accidents,[171] are caused by human error. To help protect employees, companies must meet safety standards set by the **U.S. Occupational Safety and Health Administration (OSHA)**, maintain records of injuries and deaths due to workplace accidents, and submit to onsite inspections; visit www.osha.gov for more information. Those who do not comply are subject to citations and penalties, usually in the form of fines. You may save a few bucks skimping on safety, but it can be very costly, like at **BP** for the Gulf oil spill.

Employees are concerned about safety.[172] The HR department commonly has responsibility for ensuring the health and safety of employees and needs to develop policies and rules to provide a safe environment for all groups.[173] It works closely with the other departments to enforce safety rules and maintains health and safety records. Employee-owned **PCL Construction** boasts a safety record five times better than the national average.[174] A growing area of safety concern is workplace incivility and violence.[175] As a manager, you should know the safety rules, be sure your employees know them, and enforce them to prevent accidents and acts of violence.

Unions and Labor Relations

labor relations The interactions between management and unionized employees.

A *labor union* is an organization that represents employees in collective bargaining with the employer over wages, benefits, and working conditions. **Labor relations** *are the interactions*

9-3 JOIN THE DISCUSSION ETHICS & SOCIAL RESPONSIBILITY

Sweatshops

Nike and many other companies have been criticized for using contract manufacturing with sweatshops that employ workers for very low wages and in poor working conditions. In many countries where much of today's manufacturing takes place, there are few or no health and safety regulations. Some employees get hurt and die on the job. People complain that the United States is losing jobs overseas to companies that are exploiting people.

However, others argue that most Americans don't want these jobs and that U.S. companies are helping people in other countries by giving them jobs. Thus, these companies are raising the standard of living in other countries and keeping prices down at home.

1. In your opinion, are companies that hire sweatshop workers helping these workers or exploiting them?

2. Should a global company compensate all employees at the same rates, or should compensation be based on the cost of doing business and the cost of living in a given country?

3. Is it possible for a company to apply the same health and safety standards that it follows in the United States to its operations in other countries and still compete globally with companies that don't apply such standards?

4. Is it ethical and socially responsible to contract work with sweatshops?

5. What, if anything, should be done about sweatshops?

between management and unionized employees. Labor relations are also called *union–management relations* and *industrial relations.* Unions are a source of recruitment and retention. Union membership has been steadily declining in the United States for several decades.[176] It is currently stagnated at around 11%.[177] Here is a breakdown by industry: construction (14.7% of all workers are unionized), manufacturing (10.5%), retail (5%), health care (3.8%), and finance (1.6%).[178] Therefore, most businesses do not have labor relations as part of their HR process.

The National Labor Relations Act (also known as the Wagner Act after its sponsor) established the **National Labor Relations Board (NLRB)**, which oversees labor relations in the United States by conducting unionization elections, hearing unfair labor practice complaints, and issuing injunctions against offending employers. For more information about the NLRB, visit www.nlrb.gov. Under **President Trump**'s administration, the government is expected to be less inclined to help unionization than it was under **President Obama**'s.[179]

The Union-Organizing Process. There are typically five stages in forming a union, as shown in Exhibit 9-10.

Collective Bargaining. Collective bargaining *is the negotiation process resulting in a contract between employees and management that covers employment conditions.* The most common employment conditions covered in contracts are compensation, hours, and working conditions, but a contract can include any condition that both sides agree to. To overcome the higher cost of union members, some businesses have developed a two-tier pay so that new hires get less pay and benefits. During the **United Auto Workers'** (UAW with 140,000 members) negotiation with **General Motors (GM)**, **Ford**, and **Fiat Chrysler**, this was on the UAW's list of things to get rid of.[180] Plus, with its great health benefits package, called a "Cadillac" plan, the UAW is upset about its health benefits being cut and taxed under Obamacare.[181]

To avoid a strike or a lockout (a refusal by management to let employees work) and to handle *grievances* by either side, collective bargainers sometimes agree to use neutral third parties, called mediators, from the **Federal Mediation and Conciliation Service (FMCS)**. (For more information about the FMCS, visit www.fmcs.gov.) A *mediator* is a neutral party that helps management and labor settle their disagreements. In cases in which management and employees are not willing to compromise but do not want to call a strike or a lockout, they may call in an arbitrator. An *arbitrator* is different from a mediator in that the arbitrator

collective bargaining The negotiation process resulting in a contract between employees and management that covers employment conditions.

EXHIBIT 9-10   THE UNION-ORGANIZING PROCESS

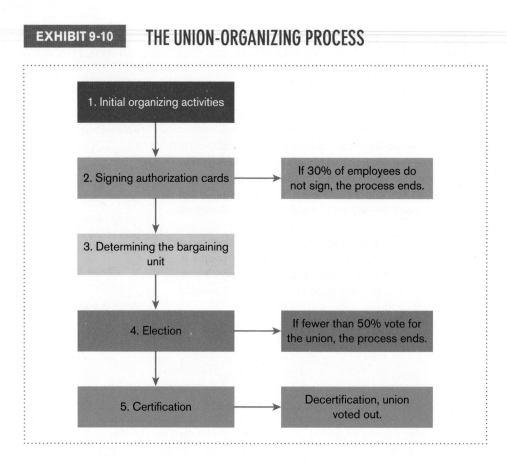

makes a binding decision, one to which management and labor must adhere. The services of an arbitrator are more commonly used to settle employee grievances than to deal with impasses in collective bargaining.

The majority of **Costco** (**IOM 4**) locations are not unionized, but some former **Price Club** locations in California and the northeastern United States are staffed by Teamsters union members. The nonunion locations have revisions to their Costco Employee Agreement every three years concurrent with union contract ratifications in locations with collective bargaining agreements. Only remotely similar to a union contract, the *Costco Employee Agreement* sets forth such things as benefits, compensations, wages, disciplinary procedures, paid holidays, bonuses, and seniority. The employee "agreement" is subject to change by Costco at any time and offers no absolute protection to the workers.

Separating Employees

Employment is terminated for three primary reasons comprising collective turnover: (1) attrition, (2) firings, and (3) layoffs. Attrition is voluntary turnover, but firing and layoffs are not. For all three reasons, turnover increases and performance often decreases.[182] With attrition and firing, employees often need to be replaced, and sometimes layoffs of one type of work result in increased workers in other jobs. Again, calling for strategic HRM to manage turnover effectively.[183]

Attrition. Attrition occurs when employees leave for other jobs, elect to stop working for a time, or retire. Employees lost through attrition often need to be replaced. Retirement is an ongoing issue that the HR staff needs to anticipate, and some companies are retaining employees by offering retirees part-time positions. Employees who leave voluntarily are often interviewed so that managers can find out their reasons for leaving. The *exit interview*, usually conducted by someone from the HR department, can help identify problem areas that lead to turnover and can be used to help retain good employees. One of the key reasons employees leave is that they do not feel that they are part of, or accepted and appreciated by, the manager and team (Chapter 8) they work with.[184]

Firing. Reasons for termination should be spelled out in the company's HR employee manual based on avoiding wrongful discharge. *Wrongful discharge* is a legal doctrine that requires employers to have a job-related reason for terminating employees, including violation of rules and poor performance. To validate job-related reasons for firing employees, you should go by the book and have documentation—build a written record that includes any warnings issued to the employee and performance reviews—in case there is future litigation.

Managers are sometimes hesitant to terminate employees who can't do the job to standards,[185] but retaining them is not fair to other employees, who often get stuck doing extra work and resent them—hurting group cohesiveness. Also, people who want to do a good job but can't usually are not happy. Fired employees are often devastated but often go on to find jobs that better match their skill set, and they are grateful that they were fired and have greater job satisfaction. In fact, many highly successful people have been fired during their career, including **Steve Jobs** from **Apple**; yes, he was fired from the company he cofounded.

Layoffs/Downsizing. Employees can also lose their jobs due to company layoffs or downsizing based on a retrenchment strategy (Chapter 5). Layoffs usually occur because of poor economic conditions, organizational problems, or mergers and acquisitions. Most large companies try to be ethical and socially responsible during layoffs, and the HR department offers *outplacement services* to help employees find new jobs and give *severance pay* to provide some money while the person conducts a job search.

Downsizing, although a popular practice in the U.S. corporate world, has been called one of the most ineffective and expensive methods of reducing a workforce. Morale usually drops, and companies tend to end up losing more employees than they bargained for due to a surge in voluntary turnover after the downsizing initiative begins, and it is usually the better employees who voluntarily leave for other jobs.

Trends and Issues in Management

Global companies' HRM becomes much more complex, as it has to follow different legal employment rules and regulations. Talent acquisition and retention are major challenges for MNC as they compete for talent worldwide.[186] Attracting and developing methods also vary by country and culture. Compensation salary and benefit cost vary widely; in some countries, health care is provided solely by the government. Firing and layoffs are more and less difficult in various countries. Another global trend is decreasing numbers of full-time employees by replacing them with contractors, and the laws do vary.

Sorry to say, but American women face bias in the workplace, as more than 50% have personally experienced *gender* discrimination, and women are paid less than men.[187] *Ethnic* minorities also continue to face employment discrimination.[188] *Millennials*, who now dominate the workforce, are the hardest generation to retain,[189] as they won't stay at a job they don't like. Around 50% of millennials say having a "job you enjoy" is extremely important to them, compared to just 38% of baby boomers.[190] They will leave if they don't feel valued and respected and if they don't like their boss.[191] HRM practices are changing to help retain employees, like **Facebook** managers being told that performance reviews should be 80% focused on strengths.[192]

The driver of HR information systems is *technology* and *big data*.[193] Hiring and firing decisions are increasingly being affected by algorithms; it's like *Moneyball* for HR.[194] **Google** uses testing with *qDroid* algorithmic questions scored using behaviorally anchored rating scales for selecting employees.[195] The job application process through payroll and benefits has been automated with powerful big-data tools and inexpensive online software;[196] cloud software by **Zenefits** and others is cutting HR jobs.[197] Companies including **Walmart**, **Credit Suisse**, and **Box** are even using big data to understand why employees stay and leave so they can predict who is likely to quit so they can warn managers to take action to retain them.[198]

United Technologies is using big data to enhance flight safety,[199] and **Daimler** is developing self-driving trucks to eliminate drivers and increase safety.[200] Technology also brings a dark side, as sexual harassment has also gone online with "*textual harassment*" including pictures through **Snapchat**.[201] HR records and monitoring of employees bring *privacy* issues,[202] and HR records are being *cyberattacked*.[203] Companies are also using social media websites, including Facebook and LinkedIn, to recruit candidates. Walmart is using social media to get information on union-organizing efforts to help prevent unionization.[204]

Yes, *technology*, including robots, is being used to replace people in the factory and office.[205] However, technology creates new jobs, and the American **Fortune 500** employ 27.9 million people worldwide, and they continue to increase their use of tech and hiring.[206] Even as technology wipes out jobs, companies continue to recruit people with good interpersonal skills, as it takes people and teamwork to innovate the tech.[207]

Employers not only need to be *ethical and socially responsible* throughout the HRM process; they also need to hire honest people, and they are giving honesty tests to help avoid hiring unethical people.[208] Although it is legal to reclassify employees as contractors, some question if it is an ethical decision, and **Uber** and **FedEx** have faced legal challenges for misclassification of workers in the United States,[209] and Uber in the United Kingdom.[210] Although you want to hire for organizational culture fit, you need to be careful to ethically promote diversity by avoiding national cultural biases.[211]

Having read this chapter, you should understand the human resources management processes of (1) obeying the law and planning for (2) attracting—recruiting and selecting; (3) developing—orientation, training and development, and performance appraisals; and (4) retaining and separating employees.

$SAGE edge™   edge.sagepub.com/lussier8e

Want a better grade?

Get the tools you need to sharpen your study skills. Access practice quizzes, eFlashcards, video and multimedia, and more at edge.sagepub.com/lussier8e.

Digital Resources

Learning Objective	Digital Resource
9-1. List the four parts of the human resources management process, define *harassment* and *sexual harassment*, and discuss the importance of understanding employment law.	Roles and Functions of HR
9-2. Explain the role of strategic human resources planning and the need for conducting a job analysis including its two parts.	Job Analysis
9-3. Discuss the two parts of attracting employees.	Interviewing Employee
9-4. Describe the three parts of developing employees.	Management in Action: Performance Management and Appraisal*
9-5. Summarize the role of compensation in retaining employees, and indicate three methods of employment separation.	Compensation and Employee Retention*

* premium video available only in the interactive eBook

••• CHAPTER SUMMARY

9-1. List the four parts of the human resources management process, define *harassment* and *sexual harassment*, and discuss the importance of understanding employment law.

The four parts of the HRM process are (1) planning for, (2) attracting, (3) developing, and (4) retaining employees. *Harassment* is unwelcome conduct that is based on race, color, religion, sex (including pregnancy), national origin, age (40 or older), disability, or genetic information. *Sexual harassment* is essentially any unwelcomed behavior of a sexual nature. There are two major types. *Quid pro quo* sexual harassment occurs when sexual consent affects job outcomes, such as getting a job or assignment or promotion or keeping one's job. *Hostile work environment* sexual harassment occurs when unwelcomed sexual behavior creates an intimidating and offensive workplace for anyone. It is important to understand employment law, because violations can result in costly civil and criminal lawsuits.

9-2. Explain the role of strategic human resources planning and the need for conducting a job analysis including its two parts.

The role of the HR plan is to staff the organization to meet its strategic objectives. If the strategy is growth, the HRM department plans to increase hiring, and if the strategy is retrenchment, it plans to decrease current employment. Job analysis is necessary because it is the basis for attracting, developing, and retaining employees. The job description identifies the tasks and responsibilities of a position, whereas job specifications identify the qualifications needed by the person who is to fill the position.

9-3. Discuss the two parts of attracting employees.

The two parts are recruiting and selecting job candidates. Recruiting is the process of attracting qualified

candidates to apply for job openings. There are six major sources used in recruiting: internal recruiting/mobility, employee referrals, walk-ins, outside organizations, agencies, and advertising/Internet. The selection process can include having candidates complete application forms, be interviewed one or more times, take tests, and submit to background and reference checks, leading to hiring.

9-4. Describe the three parts of developing employees.

Orientation is the process of introducing new employees to the organization and their jobs. *Training and development* are related but different. Training is the process of teaching employees the skills necessary to perform a job. Development is ongoing education to improve skills for present and future jobs. There are two types of *performance appraisals*. A developmental performance appraisal is used to make decisions and plans for performance improvements. An evaluative appraisal is used to make administrative decisions, including decisions about pay raises, transfers, promotions, demotions, and separation.

9-5. Summarize the role of compensation in retaining employees, and indicate three methods of employment separation.

Generous compensation helps to attract and retain good employees. If employees are not satisfied with their compensation, they may leave for better jobs, creating turnover. Separation takes place for three reasons: *attrition*, in which employees voluntarily stop working; *firing*, in which employees are terminated due to breaking rules or not performing to standard; and *layoffs/downsizing*, in which retrenchment strategies result in separating employees.

••• KEY TERMS

assessment centers, 285
bona fide occupational qualification (BFOQ), 278
collective bargaining, 299
compensation, 295
development, 289

human resources management process, 275
job description, 282
job evaluation, 296
job specifications, 282
labor relations, 298
orientation, 289

performance appraisal, 292
recruiting, 283
selection, 284
strategic human resources planning, 282
training, 289
vestibule training, 290

••• KEY TERM REVIEW

Complete each of the following statements using one of this chapter's key terms.

1. The _____ consists of planning for, attracting, developing, and retaining employees.

2. A _____ allows discrimination where it is reasonably necessary for normal operation of a particular organization.

3. _____ is the process of staffing the organization to meet its objectives.

4. The _____ identifies the tasks and responsibilities of a position.

5. _____ identify the qualifications needed by a person who is to fill a position.

6. _____ is the process of attracting qualified candidates to apply for job openings.

7. _____ is the process of choosing the most qualified applicant recruited for a job.

8. _____ are places job applicants undergo a series of tests, interviews, and simulated experiences to determine their potential.

9. _____ is the process of introducing new employees to the organization and their jobs.

10. _____ is the process of teaching employees the skills necessary to perform a job.

11. _____ is ongoing education to improve skills for present and future jobs.

12. _____ develops skills in a simulated setting.

13. _____ is the ongoing process of evaluating employee performance.

14. _____ is the total of an employee's pay and benefits.

15. _____ is the process of determining the worth of each job relative to the other jobs within the organization.

16. _____ are the interactions between management and unionized employees.

17. _____ is the negotiation process resulting in a contract between employees and management that covers employment conditions.

••• REVIEW QUESTIONS

1. List the two major rules of thumb to follow during pre-employment inquiries.

2. What is a bona fide occupational qualification (BFOQ)?

3. What is a job analysis?

4. What are the types of internal recruiting?

5. What are the stages in developing employees?

6. What is the difference between training and development?

7. What is vestibule training?

8. How often should performance appraisals be conducted?

9. How is compensation used to both attract and retain employees?

10. What types of organizations have labor relations?

11. What is the difference between a mediator and an arbitrator?

••• COMMUNICATION SKILLS

The following critical-thinking questions can be used for class discussion and/or as written assignments to develop communication skills. Be sure to give complete explanations for all questions.

1. Why do you think that most organizations do not employ state-of-the-art human resources management (HRM) practices?

2. What is your opinion of the use of bona fide occupational qualifications (BFOQs)?

3. What is your opinion of using promotions from within as a recruiting source?

4. Do you agree that the job interview should be the primary criterion for selection?

5. What is the most common problem to avoid during interviewing?

6. If you work as a manager for a company with a human resources (HR) department, does this mean that you don't have to orient and train employees? Explain.

7. What is your view of performance appraisals? How can they be improved?

8. What pay system do you prefer? Why is this your preference?

9. Why don't most employees realize how expensive benefits are and how much they contribute to compensation cost?

10. Are unions greedy because they expect workers to receive more than they are worth, or is management greedy because it takes excessive salaries and gives too large a share of the profits to the owners?

CASES

••• Case 9-1   Boston Consulting Group

The Boston Consulting Group was founded by Bruce Henderson in 1963. Henderson was known as a brilliant strategic thinker who emphasized the importance of challenging the status quo to enable organizations to achieve and sustain competitive advantage.

The mission of the Boston Consulting Group is: "We go deep to unlock insight and have the courage to act. We bring the right people together to challenge established thinking and drive transformation. We work with our clients to build the capabilities that enable organizations to achieve sustainable advantage. We are shaping the future. Together." The foundation for the realization of this mission is core values such as: clients come first, the strategic perspective, value delivered, and expanding the art of the possible.

In order to maintain its reputation as a leading management consulting firm, Boston Consulting Group invests a lot of time and resources in its human resources practices to attract, develop, and retain the best and brightest consultants in the industry. The firm has been included on *Fortune* magazine's list of Best Companies to Work For since 2007. In 2017, it was ranked number three on this list. Some of the HR practices that contributed to this high ranking include paid time off for volunteer work, college tuition reimbursement, unlimited sick days, and compressed work schedules. In terms of the work itself, associates have the opportunity to work on high-level projects with senior executives at leading companies.

Competition for jobs at Boston Consulting Group is intense. The firm holds on-campus college recruiting events at targeted, elite universities including attendance at career fairs and running workshops on various topics related to strategy and consulting. One of the most effective recruiting methods the firm sponsors is the annual Strategy Cup competition that is held at locations around the world such as Belgium and Hungary. This competition gives undergraduate and graduate students the opportunity to work in teams to help an actual client to solve a critical business problem.

Candidates who are selected for interviews typically participate in initial on-campus screening interviews that include questions such as:

- Why do you want to go into consulting?
- What are your long-term goals?
- What motivates you?

Candidates who make it through to the next level of consideration are invited for an office visit. It is common for the firm to use a "case interview" that assesses the candidates' analytical and problem-solving abilities. These cases may focus on a wide range of business problems including driving revenue growth and developing a distribution strategy.

Boston Consulting Group associates receive numerous opportunities for professional development including access to an online learning portal that contains more than a thousand learning classrooms. More than 400 internal trainers facilitate a wide range of creative and engaging learning programs to enhance client relationship-building and consulting skills, as well as subject matter and functional expertise. These programs provide opportunities for peer–peer learning between associates from around the world.

Discussion Questions

1. What kinds of practices at Boston Consulting Group have enabled it to make *Fortune* magazine's list of the Best Companies to Work For?

2. Evaluate the recruiting strategies that Boston Consulting Group uses to attract talent. Are they effective? Why or why not?

3. Evaluate the selection process that Boston Consulting Group uses to determine the best job candidates for its position openings. Is it effective? Why or why not?

4. Evaluate the training and development strategies that Boston Consulting Group uses to enhance the capabilities of its workforce.

5. Do you agree with the consideration that Boston Consulting Group is one of the best companies to work for? Why or why not?

6. Can you think of anything that Boston Consulting Group does not do for its workforce that you believe would make it an even better company to work for? Why?

References

https://www.bcg.com/en-us/about/heritage/default.aspx

http://beta.fortune.com/best-companies/the-boston-consulting-group-3

https://www.bcg.com/en-us/default.aspx

https://www.glassdoor.com/Interview/Boston-Consulting-Group-Associate-Interview-Questions-EI_IE3879.0,23_KO24,33.htm

https://www.bcg.com/careers/path/consulting/learning-development.aspx

https://www.bcg.com/careers/events/default.aspx

https://www.bcg.com/en-us/careers/path/consulting/practice-interview-cases.aspx

Case created by Loren Kuzuhara, University of Wisconsin–Madison.

• • • Case 9-2   People Operations: Using Data Analytics to Bolster Female Retention at Google

Google's success is based on its high quality human resources. The company generally emphasizes smartness and excellence among its employees. Google's human resource management also includes carefully selected strategies, methods, and techniques for recruitment and selection, and for the retention of high quality workers. The firm's recruitment practices and selection process ensure an adequate workforce. The retention programs at Google are designed to retain excellent employees. These programs also attract employees to the firm. The company is now one of the best places to work. This popularity and positive perception indicates the success of the firm's human resource management in recruitment, selection, and employee retention.(1)

Rather than a human resources office, Google refers to its department as people operations.

> In people operations (also known as human resources), they "find them, grow them, and keep them"—bringing the world's most innovative people to Google and building programs that help them thrive.(2)
>
> Google's compensation packages are the main HRM tool that the company uses for retaining high-quality human resources. The company's compensation packages are competitive and above average. For example, Google provides high salaries and wages. In addition, employees get free meals and other incentives and benefits. The typical design of the company's offices emphasizes fun and creativity, which attract and retain creative and innovative workers. Google's human resource management uses coaching and mentoring to retain and develop employees with leadership potential.(3)

Human resources managers are faced with many daily decisions on how best to handle new and current employee situations. Whether recruiting the next great Googler, refining core programs, developing talent, or simply looking for ways to inject more fun into the lives of Googlers, they bring a data-driven approach that is reinventing the human resource field. As Prasad Setty from people operations said, "We make thousands of people decisions every day—who we should hire, how much we should pay them, who we should promote, who we should let go of. What we try to do is bring the same level of rigor to people decisions that we do to engineering decisions. Our mission is to have *all* people decisions be informed by data."(4)

Yet despite working at Google being a dream job for many, women were leaving Google. The company, known for its happy employees, asked why. Google used its analytical skills to study the problem and found that its maternity leave plan did not match the working mothers' needs and the newborns they were now caring for. Google's maternity policy previously allowed for 12 weeks of fully paid and vested leave. A more flexible plan was created that allowed new mothers to take a more reasonable amount of time off. The new maternity plan offered biological mothers 18 to 22 weeks of paid maternity leave to better match the significant development that occurs in children in the 12- to 18-month-old range.(5)

> When Google increased paid maternity leave from 12 to 18 wks., the rate at which new mothers quit fell 50% #paidleave https://t.co/48iT6qAjX7
>
> —Susan Wojcicki (@SusanWojcicki)
> January 27, 2016

It may sound counterintuitive, but the research—and Google's own experience—shows a generous paid maternity leave actually increases retention. When women are given a short leave, or they're pressured to be on call, some decide it's just not worth it to return.(6)

Discussion Questions

1. Which human resources management process was likely the most important for Google?
2. What aspect of Google's HRM practices affected female recruitment, selection, and retention the most?
3. Does Google practice effective strategic human resources planning?
4. From reading the case, does it seem that Google gets most of its employees from internal or external recruiting?
5. How did Google change its human resources management process regarding maternity leave?

Cumulative Case Questions

6. Explain how changes in the external environment resulted in changes in the internal environment at Google (Chapter 3).
7. What type of strategy is Google currently pursuing (Chapter 5)?
8. How did Google manage diversity in the case (Chapter 3)?

References

(1) Lombardo, J. (2017, January 28). Google's HRM: Recruitment, selection, retention. Panmore Institute. Retrieved February 1, 2017, from http://panmore.com/google-hrm-recruitment-selection-retention

(2) Grant, R. (2015, March 2). Silicon Valley's best and worst jobs for new moms (and dads). *The Atlantic.* Retrieved June 1, 2015, from http://www.theatlantic.com/technology/archive/2015/03/the-best-and-worst-companies-for-new-moms-and-dads-in-silicon-valley/386384/

(3) Lombardo, J. (2017, January 28). Google's HRM: Recruitment, selection, retention. Panmore Institute. Retrieved February 1, 2017, from http://panmore.com/google-hrm-recruitment-selection-retention

(4) Manjoo, F. (2013, January 21). The happiness machine. *Slate.* Retrieved August 25, 2017, from http://www.slate.com/articles/technology/technology/2013/01/google_people_operations_the_secrets_of_the_world_s_most_scientific_human.html

(5) Grant, R. (2015, March 2). Silicon Valley's best and worst jobs for new moms (and dads). *The Atlantic.* Retrieved June 1, 2015, from http://www.theatlantic.com/technology/archive/2015/03/the-best-and-worst-companies-for-new-moms-and-dads-in-silicon-valley/386384/

(6) Truong, A. (2016, January 28). When Google increased paid maternity leave, the rate at which new mothers quit dropped 50%. *Quartz.* Retrieved February 1, 2017, from https://qz.com/604723/when-google-increased-paid-maternity-leave-the-rate-at-which-new-mothers-quit-dropped-50

Case created by Herbert Sherman, Hannah K. Walter, and Naveed Ahmad, Long Island University.

••• SKILL BUILDER 9-1: SELECTING A TENNIS COACH

Objectives

To perform a job analysis and to develop skills in employment interviewing.

Skills

The primary skills developed through this exercise are:

1. *Management skill*—decision making (conceptual, diagnostic, analytical, and critical-thinking skills are needed to select an employee)
2. *AACSB competencies*—communication abilities and analytic skills
3. *Management function*—organizing (staffing)

Recruiting

You are in your first year as athletic director at a high school. The tennis coach position is open, and you must fill it. The compensation for the job is set in the budget; the coach is to be paid in one lump sum at the end of the season. The salary is competitive with the pay of other tennis coaches in the area.

Because you have no recruiting budget, you do some internal recruiting and contact some athletic directors in your area to spread the word about the opening. You recruit three candidates for the coaching position. Following are descriptions of their qualifications:

- *Candidate A* has been a history teacher at your school for 10 years. This person was the tennis coach for two years. It's been five years since this person coached the team. You don't know why the candidate stopped coaching or how good a job was done. Candidate A never played competitive tennis. However, someone told you that the candidate plays regularly and is pretty good. You guess the teacher is about 35 years old.

- *Candidate B* works as a supervisor on the 11 P.M.-to-7 A.M. shift for a local business. This candidate has never coached before. However, the person was a star player in high school and college. Candidate B still plays in local tournaments, and you see the name in the local newspaper now and then. You guess this candidate is about 25 years old.

- *Candidate C* has been a basketball coach and physical education teacher at a nearby high school for the past five years. The person has a master's degree in physical education. You figure it will take the person 20 minutes to get to your school. Candidate C has never coached tennis but did play on the high school team. The candidate plays tennis about once a week. You guess the person is about 45 years old.

Preparing for the Interviews

Follow the six interview preparation steps in Model 9-1. (You can skip step 1, as there is no job description or specifications.) Because there are only three candidates, you have decided to interview them all.

Conducting the Interviews

During the in-class part of this exercise, you will conduct a job interview. Be sure to bring your written list of questions to class.

- *Procedure 1* (5–10 minutes). Break into groups of five or six, pass the lists of questions around to the other members, and discuss them. You may make changes to improve your list. For example, you may want to add some questions you had not thought of.

- *Procedure 2* (30–80 minutes). Each person elects to play the role of one of the three job candidates. While playing the role, you may use your real name but assume that you have the qualifications described earlier. Ad lib as necessary. Another member of the group plays the role of interviewer, and the third person is the observer. The interviewer uses the questions devised earlier to conduct the interview. The observer gives feedback at the end of the interview, and the group members discuss how the interview could be improved. After the discussion, group members switch roles: A different group member plays another job candidate, and another group member acts as interviewer. Again, discuss the interview once it is completed before switching roles for a third time.

- *Procedure 3.* Each member of the group selects the candidate for the job; members of the other groups will do the same. The class can discuss the reasons for choosing a particular candidate.

Apply It

What did I learn from this experience? How will I use this knowledge in the future?

● ● ● SKILL BUILDER 9-2: JOB INSTRUCTIONAL TRAINING

Objective

To improve your skill at conducting training using the JIT model.

Skills

The primary skills developed through this exercise are:

1. *Management skills*—technical (to do the task) and interpersonal (to communicate and motivate the person to do the task)
2. *AACSB competency*—communication abilities
3. *Management function*—organizing (training and development)

Preparing for Skill Builder 9-2

For Skill Builder 9-2, you will prepare to conduct a training session in which you will use the steps of the job instructional training (JIT) process outlined in the text and illustrated in Model 9-3.

Select a task: Begin by selecting a task or a skill that you are familiar with but that other class members may not know how to do. It should be a task or a skill that you can teach someone else in about 10 minutes (for example, how to knit, an athletic technique, the basics of some computer software, the rules of a card game, how to perform a magic trick, or the like).

Set objectives: *Write down your objectives for the training session.*

Prepare for training: Write a description of your training session, making sure that it follows the steps in the JIT process. Your plan should include a description of how you will measure and evaluate your training results. The training itself will be conducted in class. Plan to bring to class anything you'll need for your training (knitting needles and yarn, a deck of cards, or whatever).

Apply It

What did I learn from this experience? How will I use this knowledge in the future?

• • • SKILL BUILDER 9-3: HIRING A PROFESSOR AT YOUR COLLEGE

Objective

To develop your understanding of the hiring process.

Skills

The primary skills developed through this exercise are:

1. *Management skill*—decision making (conceptual, diagnostic, analytical, and critical-thinking skills are needed to select an employee)
2. *AACSB competencies*—analytic skills and reflective thinking skills
3. *Management function*—organizing (staffing)

Preparing for Skill Builder 9-3

For Skill Builder 9-3, you will use the concepts discussed in the chapter to answer the following questions on how you would go about hiring a new professor to teach at your college. You should do some research to help you do the following four things.

1. Write a brief job description and job specifications for an opening to teach this and other related courses.
2. Write a list of questions that you will ask the candidates during the job interview.
3. What methods would you use to evaluate the professor's teaching performance?
4. How much does the position pay, and what are the benefits?

Apply It

What did I learn from this experience? How will I use this knowledge in the future?

Appendix: Career Management and Networking

• • • LEARNING OBJECTIVES

After studying this appendix, you should be able to:

A-1. List the five steps in career planning.
PAGE 311

A-2. Identify the five steps in the networking process. PAGE 314

A-3. Describe a one-minute self-sell and its three parts. PAGE 315

Career Management

Career success is probably on your mind, as it is important to both work and life satisfaction. A *career* is a sequence of related job positions, involving increasing responsibility and increased compensation and held over a lifetime. Career success depends on hard work and planning. Remember that you must take the responsibility for managing your career; you can't simply rely on others to give you jobs, raises, and promotions. This appendix will help you with your career by discussing career planning and development and getting a job. If you have not completed Self-Assessment 9-1, "Career Development," in Chapter 9, do so now (see page 287).

Career Planning and Development

There is a difference between career planning and career development. **Career planning** *is the process of setting career objectives and determining how to accomplish them.* **Career development** *is the process of gaining skill, experience, and education to achieve career objectives.*

Most colleges offer career-planning services that can help you. The career-planning counselor's role is not to find you a job but to help you set realistic career objectives and plans. The *career-planning model* steps in what follows can help you develop your own career plan. Skill Builder A-1 will guide you in the use of these steps to develop your own career plan.

Step 1. Self-assessment. Who are you? What are your interests, values, needs, skills, experience, and competencies? What do you want to do during your career? The key to career success is to determine what you do well, what you enjoy doing, and how to find a job that combines your interests and skills. If you aren't sure what your interests are, your college career center may have a test to help match you with a job. You can also take a test online at some websites.

Step 2. Career preferences. Others can help you get a job, but you are responsible for selecting your career. Based on your self-assessment, you must decide what you want from your job and career and prioritize these preferences. What motivates you?

Some of the things you should consider as you think about your career preferences are (1) what industry you want to work in, (2) what size organization you want to work for, (3) what type of job(s) you want in your career and which functional areas interest you (production/operations, marketing, finance, human resources, and so on), (4) what city, state, or country you want to work in, and (5) how much income you expect when you start your career and 5 years and 10 years after that.

Once you have thought about these preferences, read about the career areas that interest you. Talk to people in your school's career-planning office and to people who hold the types of jobs you are interested in. (This is called networking, and we discuss networking in more detail later in this appendix.) Determine the requirements and qualifications you need to get a job in the career that interests you. Participating in an internship or fieldwork and taking on a part-time job and/or a summer job in your field of interest can help you land the job you want after graduation.

Step 3. Career objectives. You need to set goals and act on them. Set short- and long-range objectives, using the planning guidelines discussed in Chapter 5.

LO A-1

List the five steps in career planning.

career planning The process of setting career objectives and determining how to accomplish them.

career development The process of gaining skill, experience, and education to achieve career objectives.

Step 4. Plan. Develop a plan that will enable you to attain your objectives. This is where career development fits in. You must determine what skills, experience, and education you need in order to progress from your current level to your career goal. But be open to taking advantage of unplanned opportunities.

Step 5. Control. Review your objectives, check your progress at least every few months, and change and develop new objectives and plans. Update your résumé as you improve your skills and experience. Having a good career coach or mentors can help you get a job and advance through career stages.

Getting a Job

Based on your career plan, you prepare a résumé and cover letter for each job, research the organization, and prepare for the interview. But let's start with some pre–job search considerations.

Pre–Job Search Considerations. These ideas can help you.

- *Search Yourself.* Many employers will look you up on the Internet, so before you start looking for a job, research your online reputation and take down any unprofessional things.

- *Phone Message.* You may also get calls from employers, so make sure your phone messages are businesslike; skip the music and sound professional.

- *Job Selection.* Make sure you get a job that is in your field that will add experience you need to progress in your career. Avoid taking any job just to have a job, because your experience can move you in a direction with experience you don't want that can even actually hurt your chances of getting into your chosen career.

- *Jobs While Searching.* If you are thinking, "Well, I need money," here are three options to help get you to the job you really want. (1) Work for a temporary agency. This can give you some experience and get you into some organizations you may want to work for that could lead to networking and a full-time job. Agency staff commonly help improve résumés. (2) Be a substitute teacher. In most states, you don't need to be a certified teacher, and in some states, you don't even need to have completed your college degree. Temping and subbing can be tough, but you can earn money, and you can easily take days off from temping, and when subbing, you are done with work early enough to get to job interviews as you search for the job in your field that you really want to progress to in your career. (3) If you know you want to work for a specific organization, do an internship or take an entry-level job to get your foot into the door. If you do a good job, you may be able to move up through a promotion from within to the job you really want.

- *Target Your Search Using Keywords.* Don't simply send out hundreds of generic résumés. Select jobs you want and customize your résumé and cover letter to match the job. In the objective, state the company name and title of the job you want. Most large companies scan résumés for keywords. To increase your chances of being in the interview pile, you need to carefully read the job description and use the exact words in your résumé, and don't vary the terms for variety. After selecting the targeted job, your entire résumé should focus on letting the employer know that you can do the job.

Résumé and Cover Letter. Your résumé and the cover letter you send with it are your introduction to the organization you wish to work for. If the résumé is messy or contains mistakes, you may not get an interview. The cover letter should be short—one page or less. Its purpose is to introduce your résumé and to request an interview. The résumé should also be short; one page is recommended, unless you have extensive education and experience. Exhibit A provides a sample résumé. Note that the objective lists a specific job and company, so again target your search by listing the job and the company for each and every job you apply for. Skill Builder A-2 will give you practice in preparing a résumé.

WORK
APPLICATION A-1

What career development efforts are you making?

- ***Accomplishments.*** When listing internships and other work experience, volunteer work, and sports on your résumé, be sure to focus on accomplishments and skills that can be used on the job you are applying for. Show leadership skills and initiative.

- ***Transferable Skills.*** When you are applying for a professional job unrelated to prior jobs, no one cares that you mowed lawns or bussed tables. Describe the skills you learned that can be used to do the job you are applying for, such as communication and leadership skills. Explain how you dealt with customers.

- ***Critique.*** Have your résumé reviewed for improvements (especially correcting errors) by multiple people, such as the career center staff, professors, family and friends, and especially people in your career field.

- ***Use Résumés for All Jobs.*** Note that presenting a résumé when you are applying for part-time or summer employment or an internship can give a positive impression that makes you stand out from the competition to get the job.

- ***Finding Jobs.*** Research shows that most jobs are filled through networking,[1] so we will discuss how to network in detail in the next major section. Larger company websites have a link for "careers"—opportunities and job listings—and you can apply online. Many colleges offer seminars in job-search strategies. Help-wanted ads in newspapers and online job-search services (such as www.indeed.com, www.monster.com, and www.career builder.com) are common places to research jobs, and www.collegerecruiter.com focuses on internships and entry-level jobs for recent college grads. You can also post your résumé online and create a profile on career-related networking sites, such as **LinkedIn**, and participate in discussion boards to develop online relationships that can lead to a job.

- ***Employer Information/Research.*** Before you go to an interview, you should research the organization. You want to determine as much about the organization as you can, such as knowing something about the products and/or services it offers, the industry and its trends, and its profits and future plans. One place to find this information is the organization's website. Essentially all employer websites will give detail on their products and services, and corporations should have an annual report providing the other information you want to bring up in the interview.

The Interview—Tips. Your résumé and your references can get you an interview, but how you perform during the interview usually determines whether you get the job. During the interview, you need to convince the person that you can do the job and that you are a good fit for the job, department, and firm culture. Here are some tips related to interviewing, and there are more tips in the follow-up section:

- Don't show up more than 10 minutes early; respect the interviewer's time and just hang around until near interview time.

- It is vital to make a very positive first impression, so your attire and appearance should be appropriate for the job.

- Offer a firm handshake and make direct contact, and use eye contact throughout the interview.

- Answer the questions directly with details but without long-winded, useless information.

- Your best bet is to wait until you're offered the job before talking about compensation. And you should have done your research to know what the salary range is, because interviewers may ask you how much you expect. But you can try to avoid making the first offer by asking them what the salary range is or what the company has budgeted for the position.

- After the interview, evaluate your own performance; make some notes on what you did and did not do well.

- Send a thank-you letter/email to the interviewer, adding anything you forgot to say, stating your interest and the most important reasons you should get the job, and closing by saying that you look forward to hearing from the interviewer. Enclose/attach a copy of your résumé.

- Wait at least a week before checking on your candidacy, because the firm may need to interview more candidates, and it takes time to do a background and reference check. A good method is to ask the interviewer when you can expect to find out if you will be offered the job, and wait until a day after that to follow up.

- Only call the person at the office, and leave a message if you get voice mail.

- If you know that you did not get the job, ask the interviewer why and how you can improve. You may or may not be told, but an honest answer can be helpful in preparation for future interviews.

**WORK
APPLICATION A-2**

*Which specific ideas on getting
a job do you plan to use?*

Career Services. Many college career-planning services offer workshops on job searching, résumé writing, and how to interview for a job. Some provide the chance to go through a mock interview that is videotaped so that you can evaluate yourself afterward. If your career-planning office offers this service, take advantage of it, because you have to nail the interview.

Helpful Websites. At MyPerfectResume (www.myperfectresume.com) you can create a résumé and cover letter, and get tips to improve your interview and job searching skills.[2] College students and recent grads can use www.CollegeRecruiter.com to find internships, entry-level jobs, and careers.[3] Career Rookie (www.CareerRookie.com) provides internships, part-time jobs, and entry level careers.[4] Geared more for the experienced person, you can search for jobs on www.indeed.com, www.monster.com, www.careerbuilder.com, and others. If you want to work for a specific organization, go to its website and find the link with titles like "career opportunities."

LO A-2

Identify the five steps in the
networking process.

Networking

Networking *is the process of building relationships for the purpose of career building and socializing.* We'll begin by discussing the importance of networking, and then we'll outline the five steps of the networking process.[5]

The Importance of Networking

Networking is about marketing yourself to attain help achieving your career objectives. You have most likely heard the statement "It's not what you know; it's who you know that's important." Networking results in more interviews than mass sending of résumés that often end in rejection.

There are many reasons, in addition to getting a job, to develop your networking skills:

- To get a job
- To learn how to perform better at your job
- To advance within an organization
- To stay current in your field
- To maintain mobility
- To get advice and resources to start and to grow a business
- To develop personal and professional relationships

The Networking Process

networking The process
of developing relationships
for the purpose of career
building and socializing.

When you need any type of help, whom do you turn to? Networking sounds easy, and people tend to think that it should come naturally. However, the reality is that networking is a learned skill that just about everyone struggles with at one time or another. Although the same networking process is used for both job searches and broad career development, this discussion focuses more on the job search. So when you are looking for a job, get the word out. Tell everyone you know you are looking for work—in person, by phone, and online.

Step 1. Perform a self-assessment and set objectives. Based on your self-assessment, in networking, you set narrower objectives. For example, your own networking objectives might include "get a mentor," "determine the expertise, skills, and requirements needed for [a specific job]," and "get feedback on my résumé and job and/or career preparation so that I can be ready to move into [a specific job]."

Step 2. Create your one-minute self-sell. Create a brief statement about yourself to help you accomplish your goal. A **one-minute self-sell** *is an opening statement used in networking that quickly summarizes your history and career plan and asks a question.* If it is to take 60 seconds or less, your message must be concise, but it also needs to be clear and compelling. It gives the listener a sense of your background, identifies your career field and a key result you've achieved, and tells the listener what you plan to do next and why. It also should stimulate conversation.

WORK
APPLICATION A-3

Write a networking objective.

LO A-3

Describe a one-minute self-sell and its three parts.

- *History.* Start with a summary of the highlights of your career to date. Briefly describe the jobs or internships you've held and any relevant courses, certification, and other qualifications you have.

- *Plans.* Identify the career you are seeking, the industry you prefer, and a specific function or role. You can also mention names of organizations you are targeting and state why you are looking for work.

- *Question.* Finally, ask a question to encourage two-way communication. The question will vary, depending on the person you hope to network with and the goal of your one-minute self-sell. For example, you might ask one of the following questions:

  "What areas might offer opportunities for a person with my experience?" "In what other fields can I use these skills or this degree?" "Are there other positions in your organization where my skills could be used?" "What do you think of my career goals? Are they realistic, given my education and skills?" "Do you know of any job openings in my field?"

In your one-minute self-sell, be sure to clearly separate your history, your plans, and your question, and customize your question based on the contact you are talking to. Consider the following example:

Hello. My name is Will Smith. I am a senior at Springfield College, graduating in May with a major in marketing, and I have completed an internship in the marketing department at the Big Y supermarket. I'm seeking a job in sales in the food industry. Can you give me some ideas of the types of sales positions available in the food industry?

Practice delivering your self-sell to family members and friends, and get feedback from them to improve it. The more opportunities you find to use this brief introduction, the easier it becomes. Skill Builder A-3 will give you the opportunity to practice your one-minute self-sell.

Step 3. List your potential network contacts. You should build a network before you need it, so start today. Chances are you have already been involved in networking with **Facebook** or other websites (and don't forget to develop a profile at **LinkedIn** and/or another professional website), so use it along with other networking methods to get a job. Begin with people you know, your primary contacts; look through your email contact address book. It is a good idea to set up a separate email account for professional networking.

Your goal is to create a list of professional and personal contacts. Professional contacts include colleagues (past and present); members of trade or professional organizations and alumni associations; vendors, suppliers, or managers from current or past jobs; and mentors. On a personal level, your network includes relatives, neighbors, friends, and even personal service providers (your doctor, dentist, insurance agent, stock broker, accountant, or hairstylist).

Ask your primary contacts for secondary contacts you can network with. You'll want to continually update and add to your list as you get referrals from others. You will discover that your network grows exponentially.

Next, expand your list to include people you don't know. How do you do this? Make a point to go where people gather: meetings of the Chamber of Commerce or college alumni clubs,

WORK
APPLICATION A-4

Write a one-minute self-sell to achieve the networking objective you wrote for Work Application A-3.

one-minute self-sell An opening statement used in networking that quickly summarizes your history and career plan and asks a question.

EXHIBIT A   RÉSUMÉ

Will Smith
10 Oak Street
Springfield, MA 01118
(413) 555-3000 / wsmith@aol.com

Objective

Hardworking self-starter seeks sales position at New England Wholesale Foods

Education

Springfield College, Springfield, MA

B.S. Marketing, GPA: 3.4, May 2019

Experience

Big Y Supermarket

100 Cooley St., Springfield, MA 01118, supervisor Fred Fry (413) 782-8273

Marketing Internship Spring Semester 2019

- Helped with the weekly newspaper ad inserts and suggested a layout change that is currently being used
- Worked directly for the store manager on a variety of tasks and projects including Big Data research to better understand customers

Eblens

732 Boston Rd., Springfield, MA 01118, supervisor Julie DeSata (413) 783-0982

Salesperson September to May 2012–2013, 2013–2014

- Sold clothing and footwear to a diverse mix of customers
- July Employee of the Month for having the highest sales volume

Eastern Landscaping

10 Center St., Springfield, MA 01109, supervisor John Fotier (413) 782-7439

Landscaper May 2009–August 2011

- Developed communication skills by interacting with customers and resolving complaints
- Helped get two new customers, which resulted in a 5% increase in sales

Honors and Interests

- Dean's Scholarship: Recipient of academic scholarship for academic achievement excellence
- Basketball: Member of the Springfield College basketball team; captain senior year
- Kappa Delta Pi Honor Society

---

college reunions, trade shows, and career fairs. There are e-groups and chat rooms for all types of interests; seek these out and participate. Get more involved with professional associations; many have special student memberships, and some even have college chapters. To develop your career reputation, become a leader, not just a member, in whatever civic/social/religious organizations you join. Volunteer to be on committees or boards, to give presentations, and so on. When you give a speech, you are instantly networking with everyone in the audience.

Step 4. Conduct networking interviews. Consult your list of potential network contacts and set up a networking interview to begin meeting your objective. It may take many interviews to meet a goal, such as getting a job. You may have to begin with an informational interview—a phone call or (preferably) a meeting that you initiate to gain information from a contact who has hands-on experience in your field of interest. In such a situation (in contrast to a job interview), you are the interviewer, so you need to be prepared with specific questions to ask the contact regarding your targeted career or industry.

You'll find that if you ask, many people will agree to talk to you for 15 or 20 minutes. These meetings can be most helpful, especially if you can talk to someone within an organization you'd like to join or in an industry you are targeting. Leave a business card and résumé so that the person can contact you in case something comes up. During the interview, be sure to do the following:

- Establish rapport—thank the person for talking with you.
- Deliver your one-minute self-sell, even if the interviewer already heard it.
- Ask your prepared questions, such as "What do you think of my qualifications for this field?" "With your knowledge of the industry, what career opportunities do you see in the future?" "What advice do you have for me as I begin my career?"
- Get additional contacts for your network. You might ask a question like "If you were exploring this field, who else would you talk with?" Most people can give you three names; if you are offered only one, ask for others. Add the new contacts to your network list and plan to interview them. (When contacting new people, be sure to mention who referred you to them.)
- Ask your contact how you might help him or her.

Follow up the interview with a thank-you note and a status report, and enclose your résumé; a handwritten personal note is best, but email will do for less relevant contacts.

Step 5. Maintain your network. It is important to keep members of your network informed of your career progress. Saying "Thank you" to those who helped you along the way will strengthen your business relationships; providing updated information about yourself will increase the likelihood of getting help in the future. It is also a good idea to notify everyone in your network that you are in a new position and to provide contact information. Networking doesn't stop once you've made a career change. Make a personal commitment to continue networking in order to be in charge of your career development. Go to trade shows and conventions, make business contacts, and continue to update, correct, and add to your network list. Computer software is available that can help you manage your networking.

Networking is not only about getting help; it's also about helping others, especially those in your network. You will be amazed at how helping others can help you. Try to contact everyone on your network list at least once a year and find out what you can do for him or her. Send congratulations on recent achievements.

Reid Hoffman, founder of **LinkedIn,** is the guru of networking, and he is in constant contact with his network he calls his tribe. He wrote the book on networking, with **Ben Casnocha,** *The Start-Up of You* (Crown, 2012), and there are great excerpts in "The Real Way to Network" and "Three Degrees of Reid Hoffman"; both articles are in *Fortune* (February 6, 2012, pp. 23–32).

• • • APPENDIX SUMMARY

A-1. List the five steps in career planning.

The steps in the career planning model are (1) completing a self-assessment, (2) determining your career preferences, (3) setting objectives, (4) developing a plan, and (5) controlling the plan.

A-2. Identify the five steps in the networking process.

The steps in the networking process are (1) performing a self-assessment and setting objectives, (2) creating a one-minute self-sell, (3) developing a list of potential network contacts, (4) conducting networking interviews, and (5) maintaining the network.

A-3. Describe a one-minute self-sell and its three parts.

A one-minute self-sell is an opening statement used in networking that quickly summarizes (1) a person's history and (2) career plan and (3) asks a question to start a conversation.

• • • KEY TERMS

career development, 311   networking, 314
career planning, 311   one-minute self-sell, 315

• • • KEY TERM REVIEW

Complete each of the following statements using one of this appendix's key terms.

1. _____ is the process of setting career objectives and determining how to accomplish them.

2. _____ is the process of gaining skill, experience, and education to achieve career objectives.

3. _____ is the process of building relationships for the purpose of career building and socializing.

4. The _____ is an opening statement used in networking that quickly summarizes your history and career plan and asks a question.

• • • SKILL BUILDER A-1: CAREER PLANNING

Objective

To develop a career plan.

Skills

The primary skills developed through this exercise are:

1. *Management skill*—decision making (developing career plans)

2. *AACSB competency*—reflective thinking (as you take charge of your career)

3. *Management function*—planning

Preparing for Skill Builder A-1

Answering the following questions will help you develop a career plan. Use additional paper if needed. If your instructor asks you to do this exercise in class, do not reveal anything about yourself that you prefer not to share with classmates.

Step 1. Self-Assessment

A. Write two or three statements that answer the question, "Who am I?"

B. Write about two or three of your major accomplishments. (They can be in school, work, sports, or hobbies.) List the skills it took to accomplish each one.

C. Identify skills and abilities you already possess that you can use in your career (for example, skills related to planning, organizing, communicating, or leading).

Step 2. Career Preferences

A. What type of industry would you like to work in? (List as many as interest you.)

B. What type and size of organization do you want to work for?

C. List in priority order, beginning with the most important, the five factors that will most influence your job/career decisions (examples are opportunity for advancement, challenge, security, salary, hours, location of job, travel involved, educational opportunities, recognition, prestige, environment, coworkers, boss, responsibility, and variety of tasks).

D. Describe the perfect job.

E. What type of job(s) do you want during your career (marketing, finance, operations, personnel, and so forth)? After selecting a field, select a specific job (for example, salesperson, manager, or accountant).

Step 3. Career Objectives

A. What are your short-term objectives for the first year after graduation?

B. What are your intermediate-term objectives (the second through fifth years after graduation)?

C. What are your long-range objectives?

Step 4. Developing an Action Plan to Help You Achieve Your Objectives

Be sure to state deadlines for each action you plan to take.

• • • SKILL BUILDER A-2: RÉSUMÉ

Objective

To develop a résumé.

Skills

The primary skills developed through this exercise are:

1. *Management skill*—interpersonal (as you communicate your job qualifications)

2. *AACSB competency*—reflective thinking skills (as you take charge of your career), communication (of your qualifications)

3. *Management function*—leading (communication)

Preparing for Skill Builder A-2

Now that you have a career plan, create a résumé that reflects your plan. For help, visit your college career center and/or a résumé-building website such as www.resume.com or www.livecareer.com/resume-builder.

Before finalizing your résumé, improve it by using the following assessment procedure.

Résumé Assessment

1. Could a reader understand, within 10 seconds, what job you are applying for and that you are qualified for the position on the basis of skills, experience, and/or education?

2. Does the résumé include an objective that clearly states the position being applied for (such as sales rep)?

3. Does the résumé list skills or experience that support the claim that you can do the job? (For example, if you don't have sales experience, does the résumé list skills developed on other jobs, such as communication skills? Or does it indicate that you have product knowledge or point out that you enjoy meeting new people and that you are able to easily converse with people you don't know?)

4. If education is a major qualification for the job, does the résumé list courses you've taken that prepared you for the position applied for?

5. Does the résumé clearly list your accomplishments and contributions you made during your job experiences to date?

• • • SKILL BUILDER A-3: NETWORKING SKILLS

Objective

To develop your networking skills.

Skills

The primary skills developed through this exercise are:

1. *Management skill*—interpersonal (as you communicate your job qualifications)

2. *AACSB competency*—reflective thinking skills (as you take charge of your career), communication (of your qualifications)

3. *Management function*—leading (communication)

Preparing for Skill Builder A-3

Review the appendix section on the networking process, and complete the following steps.

1. Perform a self-assessment and set objectives. List two or three of your accomplishments, and set an objective—for example, to learn more about career opportunities in your major or to get an internship or a part-time, summer, or full-time job.

2. Practice the one-minute self-sell that you wrote for Work Application A-4.

3. Develop your network. List at least five people to be included in your network, preferably individuals who can help you achieve your objective.

4. Conduct a networking interview. To help meet your objective, select one person from your network list to interview (by phone if it is not possible to meet in person) for about 20 minutes. Write questions to ask during the interview.

Source: This exercise was developed by Andra Gumbus, Associate Professor, College of Business, Sacred Heart University. © Andra Gumbus, 2002. It is used with Dr. Gumbus's permission.

©iStockphoto.com/Pixfly

10 Organizational Behavior
Power, Politics, Conflict, and Stress

• • • LEARNING OBJECTIVES

After studying this chapter, you should be able to:

10-1. Define *behavior* and *organizational behavior* (OB), state the goals of OB, and explain the relationship between thoughts and self-confidence and self-esteem. PAGE 322

10-2. Describe each of the Big Five personality dimensions. PAGE 323

10-3. Explain the perception and attribution processes, and describe five perception biases. PAGE 327

10-4. Recall how attitudes affect job satisfaction and how employee and managerial attitudes affect employee performance. PAGE 331

10-5. List the six OB foundations, summarize how to shape your own and your management foundations, and discuss managing diversity in three critical foundations. PAGE 334

10-6. Discuss the relationship between organizational power and politics and their importance to organizational performance. PAGE 335

10-7. Identify the four parts of the negotiation process, define the five conflict management styles, state how to initiate a conflict resolution, and explain the stress tug-of-war. PAGE 341

IOM | Ideas on Management

From Michael Jordan and the NBA's Hornets

Michael Jordan (MJ) is the most recognizable athlete of all time, holding several **National Basketball Association (NBA)** records and several endorsement deals including **Gatorade, Hanes,** and of course **Nike**; Jordan gear still dominates basketball shoe sales. MJ is the first athlete to become a professional team owner and billionaire. He is a successful businessman, owning a motor-sports team and several restaurants. But he hasn't left NBA basketball. In 2010, Jordan acquired a majority stake in the NBA's **Charlotte Hornets** for $175 million, and in 2013, he increased his share of ownership to 90%. MJ is also part owner of **Sportrader**, a company that feeds data to sports-betting platforms. He splits his time jetting in his custom-designed **Gulfstream G450** between Charlotte and Florida, with stops in Las Vegas.

Jordan has a passion for golf and has played with pros including **Tiger Woods, Dustin Johnson,** and **Fred Couples**; his best score is 69. He takes his one set of clubs with him wherever he goes. He hosts the annual **Michael Jordan Celebrity Invitational** golf tournament to raise money for charity at the exclusive **Shadow Creek Golf Course** in Las Vegas, where he has played more than 100 times.

IOM 1. What failure did Michael Jordan (MJ) face in his early basketball career, and how did he deal with it?

IOM 2. How would you describe MJ's personality?

IOM 3. How would you describe MJ's attitude?

IOM 4. What type of power does MJ have?

IOM 5. Are negotiations, resolving conflict, and managing stress important to MJ?

IOM 6. What ethical controversy did MJ face as a basketball player back in 1993?

You'll find answers to these **IOM** questions throughout the chapter. To learn more about MJ, do an Internet search for information on the NBA's Hornets, or visit www.nba.com and select Hornets.

Sources: Information for this case was taken from K. Stock, "Briefs," *BusinessWeek* (November 2–8, 2015): 26; J. Reinsdorf, "Newcomer Michael Jordan," *Forbes* (March 23, 2015): 151; S. Gummer, "Michael Jordan," *Fortune* (June 13, 2011): 38.

Organizational Behavior (OB)

Let's start this chapter by defining OB and its goals, the foundations of individual behavior, and how thoughts and self-confidence and self-esteem affect behavior.

Goals of OB

Behavior, OB, Its Goals. Behavior is simply the things people do and say, or our actions. **Organizational behavior** (OB) *is the study of actions that affect performance in the workplace.* Would you like to be able to better understand and explain why people do and say the things they do? Would you like to predict what

LO 10-1

Define *behavior* and *organizational behavior* (OB), state the goals of OB, and explain the relationship between thoughts and self-confidence and self-esteem.

they will do next and to influence their behavior? A theory answers these questions. The goal of OB theorists is to understand, explain, predict, and influence behavior to improve performance.[1] Recall (Chapter 1) that interpersonal skills (our ability to get along with others) are important to success.[2] How we behave with others determines our OB skills, which companies value.[3]

The Foundations of Individual Behavior. The foundations include our thoughts, self-confidence, self-esteem, personality, perception, and attitudes—the topics of the first five sections. However, these foundations are not observable. You can only observe individuals' actions and try to explain and predict their behavior based on your understanding of the foundations.[4] It's about reading people. Relationships are great, but they are challenging,[5] and OB skills help you develop and maintain good relationships. **Racecar champion Mario Andretti** has an uncanny knack of being able to work with and read people.[6]

Thoughts and Self-Esteem

We'll start with self-esteem and then discuss how your thoughts affect your self-confidence and self-esteem, and finish with using self-talk to improve your self-esteem.

Self-Esteem. *Self-esteem* is about your overall view of yourself.[7] Do you like or dislike yourself? Are you a winner or a loser? How do you treat yourself?[8] Our self-esteem clearly affects our behavior.[9] We are not born with high or low self-esteem; it is influenced by our past experience and our thoughts of self-confidence and self-doubt. Stop comparing yourself to others—there will always be someone who is better at something than you are—and never put yourself down.[10] Focus on your own abilities and skills and your successes. Forget your failures; we all have them.

Self-Confidence Versus Self-Doubt. *Self-confidence* is about believing you can do a specific task; it is also called *self-efficacy* and *self-concept*.[11] It is an "I can do this" attitude and is typically believed to be a quality of leadership.[12] And it needs to be based on realistic experience and skill, or it's extreme irrational overconfidence.[13] Self-doubt leads to fear—of rejection, failure, or taking a risk. *Self-doubt* is our negative thoughts;[14] it holds us back more than our ability and resources.[15] **Fishs Eddy's Julie Gaines** says to be successful, you need to project self-confidence.[16] Founder and **CEO Rod Lewis** of **Lewis Energy** says you can't be overconfident, but you have to believe in your ability.[17] **Leyla Seka** said she had to overcome her self-doubt to advance to a vice president (VP) position at software provider **Salesforce**.[18] Founder **Tory Burch** of **Tory Burch** fashions said that gaining the confidence to really believe in herself was a big factor in her success.[19]

Thoughts. Think of the last time you told yourself something critical or negative. Then think of the last compliment or positive thought you had. We tend to have too many negative thoughts and think about them over and over.[20] This needs to stop, because our *thoughts* determine most of our feelings and behavior, or our thoughts cause our behavior and performance and affect our self-confidence and self-esteem.[21] Science confirms that what you think is what you get.[22] Again, as **Henry Ford** said, if you think you will succeed or fail, you are correct. Have you ever shot a basketball at the hoop (or done some other task) thinking you were going to miss? What usually happens? You can improve your self-esteem by using more positive thoughts,[23] and that is what this section is all about. When you change your thoughts[24] and make the new thoughts habits,[25] you change your life.

Optimism helps to overcome self-doubt;[26] it is the opposite of pessimism, and it is often considered to be a personality trait. Optimistic people believe that things will go well, and they tend to generally have less stress, are happier and more confident, and have higher levels of performance than pessimistic people. Are you an optimist or a pessimist? Optimism is based on positive thinking, and research supports that it increases performance,[27] and the **Ohio State** football team trains its players to use the power of positive thinking.[28] Are you a happy person? Do you want to be happy? **ESPN** sports announcer **Lou Holtz** says, "You choose to be happy or sad" (and optimistic or pessimistic). "Happiness is nothing more than a poor memory of the bad things that happen to us."[29]

organizational behavior The study of actions that affect performance in the workplace.

Get the edge on your studies. **edge.sagepub.com/lussier8e**

- Take a quiz to find out what you've learned.
- Review key terms with eFlashcards.
- Watch videos that enhance chapter content.

Gratitude is powerful.[30] Grateful people are happier, healthier, and less stressed. Ungrateful people tend to be dissatisfied with what they do have and are never satisfied because no matter how much they get, it is never enough.[31] So, if you aren't grateful with what you have now, you may never be happy. Focus on the positive of what you do have, appreciate it, and be happier.

Improving Self-Confidence and Self-Esteem With Self-Talk. The way to improve your self-confidence and self-esteem is to change your thoughts through positive self-talk. You do talk to yourself, don't you? Self-talk is a subset of thinking in which you make comments, set reminders, and give yourself advice.[32] As motivational speaker **Zig Ziglar** said, "no Stinking Thinking."[33] Use positive self-talk to psych yourself up. *Visualizing* your success is also commonly used along with self-talk. Tennis champion **Venus Williams** says, "How you talk to people and how you talk to yourself, has got to be positive.[34]

Successful self-talk is based on positive affirmation statements, such as "You can do this, Tom; it's easy"; not "I can't do it; it's too hard." Or "Jean, you enjoy going to work/class and learning"; not "I hate work/school." Note that it is recommended to call yourself by name or *you*, rather than *I*, because your thoughts seem more objective and get better results. To develop your self-talk and other OB foundation skills, complete Skill Builder 10-3.

Thoughts actually create strong neural circuits in your brain, so you need to practice a new thought over and over.[35] Like all the skills you can develop through reading this book, you have to consciously practice every day until the skill becomes a habit. One simple technique is to be aware of your thoughts, and if you start having self-doubt, stop and change to positive, optimistic thoughts.[36] So to make positive thinking a *habit*,[37] the (1) cue is negative thoughts, the (2) routine is change to positive thoughts, and the (3) reward is feeling more self-confident and happier. You can also just use positive self-talk throughout the day.

Michael Jordan (IOM 1) failed to make the varsity basketball team at **Emsley A. Laney High School**, but he didn't get discouraged and quit. It motivated him to work even harder to improve, and he came back the next season with strong self-confidence and self-esteem, thinking optimistically that he was going to make the team, and he did. Where would MJ be today if he had given in to self-doubt and quit his basketball career in high school? MJ has also had a lot of failure as a pro; he said, "I've missed more than 9,000 shots in my career. I've lost almost 300 games. Twenty-six times I've been trusted to take the game-winning shot and missed. I've failed over and over and over again in my life. And that is why I succeed." Can you bounce back from failure and succeed?

Personality

Why are some people outgoing and others shy, some loud and others quiet, some warm and others cold, some aggressive and others passive? The answer: personality characteristics.[38] **Personality** *is a combination of behavioral, mental, and emotional traits that define an individual.* We all have our own personality, and our personality is a primary influence on how we behave,[39] including how we make decisions (Chapter 4).[40]

In this section, we begin by explaining how personalities develop and influence careers. There are many personality classification methods,[41] and we will discuss three of them. We first present the single-traits classification, followed by the popular Big Five personality dimensions,[42] and end with brief coverage of the Myers-Briggs Type Indicator (MBTI).

Personality Development and Careers

Personality is based on genetics and environmental factors, or it's about 50% innate and 50% learned. Your basic personality is developed by age 5, thus making parents and child-care providers important in the early years of life, but your personality does change as you age, and you can speed up the change, like improving your self-esteem, but it isn't easy and takes work.[43] Your family, friends, school, and work relationships influence your personality.

Our personality influences the types of careers we choose, such as being people oriented like social workers and teachers or task oriented like accountants and computer programmers.

LO 10-2

Describe each of the Big Five personality dimensions.

personality A combination of behavioral, mental, and emotional traits that define an individual.

Personality is a predictor of job performance.[44] Personality and job fit are so important that companies including **Lowe's** and **McDonald's** give job applicants a personality test.[45] Why? These tests meet the goal of OB because they help to explain and predict job performance.[46]

Steve Jobs was creative and chose a career path of entrepreneurship by cofounding **Apple** with **Steve Wozniak** and went on to purchase the Computer Division from **George Lucas** and establish **Pixar**. But he was known for having a poor personality, or he was called a jerk.[47] He was harsh, cruel, and insulting, and he would publicly humiliate employees and even lie.[48] People were scared of Steve Jobs.[49] Although Jobs was highly successful, would you want him for your boss? If he wasn't charismatic and a founding CEO, he might never have risen to CEO, and don't forget that he was fired from Apple because he couldn't get along with his replacement CEO and board members. Conversely, Jobs's replacement CEO **Tim Cook** is well liked and viewed as a great manager, and Apple is doing well under his different personality style.

Single Traits of Personality

Here are some of the single traits that make up one's personality. One that we already discussed is *optimism*.

Locus of Control. Locus of control is a trait that lies on a continuum between believing that control over one's destiny is external and believing that it is internal. *Externalizers* believe that they have no control over their fate and that their behavior has little to do with their performance. *Internalizers* believe that they control their fate and that their behavior has a direct effect on their performance; they tend to have high self-esteem and self-confidence.[50] Internalizers have been shown to have higher levels of performance. Who do you believe is responsible for your destiny?

Risk Propensity. Risk propensity lies on a continuum from risk taking to risk avoiding. Former **NetApp** CEO **Tom Georgens** says, to be successful, you have to take calculated risks;[51] entrepreneurs have a risk-taking propensity.[52] Organizations with risk-avoiding managers often go out of business because they do not keep up with changes in their industries.

Entrepreneurial Types. Entrepreneurs have different personality traits and characteristics.[53] It takes a lot of self-confidence[54] and self-control (positive thoughts, emotions, gratitude, and avoiding harmful habits)[55] to become an entrepreneur. Entrepreneurial types have been classified as follows:[56] *hustlers* (go-getting sales types), including **Mary Kay Ash**, founder of **Mary Kay**; *innovators* (looking for creative ideas), including **Sir Richard Branson**, founder of the **Virgin** companies; *machines* (quiet, diligent doers), including founders **Larry Ellison** of **Oracle** and **Bill Gates** of **Microsoft**; *prodigies* (stoic, brilliant recluses), including founders **Elon Musk** of **Tesla** and **Larry Page** of **Google**; and *visionaries* (planning the future), including cofounder of **Facebook Mark Zuckerberg**.

Machiavellianism. Machiavellianism is a trait based on the belief that the ends can justify the means and power should be used to reach desired ends. People with this trait are also called *narcissist* because they manipulate others for selfish personal gain,[57] and they are so self-centered that they lack empathy or concern for others.[58] *High Machs* play the self-interest role (Chapter 8), and their unethical behavior often hurts others, the department, and the organization.[59]

The Big Five Personality Dimensions

The use of the Big Five personality dimensions puts multiple traits together to form what is often called a personality profile.[60] It is said that all individual traits can be placed in one of the five dimensions. The Big Five is also called the *Five-Factor Model*[61] and is abbreviated to *OCEAN* (openness, conscientiousness, extraversion, agreeableness, and neuroticism).[62] Before reading about the Big Five, complete Self-Assessment 10-1, "Personality Profile," to better understand your own personality.

Extroversion. Extroversion is measured along a continuum between extrovert and introvert. *Extroverts* tend to be social, talkative, and assertive and willing to take charge. *Introverts* tend to be less social, quiet, nonassertive, and less willing to take charge. Founder of **HVF**, **Affirm**,

10-1 SELF-ASSESSMENT

Personality Profile

Using the scale below, rate each of the 25 statements according to how accurately it describes you. Place a number from 1 (*not like me*) to 7 (*like me*) on the line before each statement. There are no right or wrong answers, so be honest, and you will really increase your self-awareness.

7	6	5	4	3	2	1
Like me			Somewhat like me			Not like me

_____ 1. I enjoy meeting new people.

_____ 2. I am concerned about getting along well with others.

_____ 3. I have good self-control; I don't get emotional and get angry and yell.

_____ 4. I'm dependable; when I say I will do something, it's done well and on time.

_____ 5. I try to do things differently to improve my performance.

_____ 6. I feel comfortable speaking to a diverse mix of people (different ages, races, genders, religions, intelligence levels, etc.).

_____ 7. I enjoy having lots of friends and going to parties.

_____ 8. I perform well under pressure.

_____ 9. I work hard to be successful.

_____10. I go to new places and enjoy traveling.

_____11. I am outgoing and initiate conversations rather than shy and hesitant to approach others.

_____12. I try to see things from other people's points of view.

_____13. I am an optimistic person who sees the positive side of situations (the cup is half full).

_____14. I am a well-organized person.

_____15. When I go to a new restaurant, I order foods I haven't tried.

_____16. I am willing to go talk to people to resolve conflicts rather than say nothing.

_____17. I want other people to like me and view me as very friendly.

_____18. I give people lots of praise and encouragement; I don't put people down and criticize.

_____19. I conform by following the rules of an organization.

_____20. I volunteer to be the first to learn and do new tasks at work.

_____21. I try to influence other people to get what I want.

_____22. I enjoy working with others more than working alone.

_____23. I view myself as being relaxed and secure rather than nervous and insecure.

_____24. I am considered to be credible because I do a good job and come through for people.

_____25. When people suggest doing things differently, I support them and help bring change about; I don't make statements like "It won't work," "We never did it this way before," "No one else ever did this," or "We can't do it."

To determine your personality profile, (1) in the blanks below, place the number from 1 to 7 that represents your score for each statement. (2) Add up each column—your total should be a number from 5 to 35. (3) On the number scale, circle the number that is closest to your total score. Each column in the chart represents a specific personality dimension.

Extroversion		Agreeableness		Adjustment		Conscientiousness		Openness to Experience	
	35		35		35		35		35
	30		30		30		30		30
_____ 1.	25	_____ 2.	25	_____ 3.	25	_____ 4.	25	_____ 5.	25
_____ 6.	20	_____ 7.	20	_____ 8.	20	_____ 9.	20	_____10.	20
_____11.	15	_____12.	15	_____13.	15	_____14.	15	_____15.	15
_____16.	10	_____17.	10	_____18.	10	_____19.	10	_____20.	10
_____21.	5	_____22.	5	_____23.	5	_____24.	5	_____25.	5
_____ Total		_____ Total		_____ Total		_____ Total		_____ Total	

The higher the total number, the stronger the dimension that describes your personality. What are your strongest and weakest dimensions? To better understand the Big Five, read each of the five statements describing each dimension consecutively—read 1, 6, 11, 16, and 21, and then do the same for the other four dimensions.

and **Glow Max Levchin** says, "I'm an introvert, and talking to people all the time is exhausting for me."[63] It is helpful for managers to have complementary traits, including **Google** extrovert **Eric Schmidt** and introvert **Larry Page** and **Facebook** extrovert **Sheryl Sandberg** and introvert **Mark Zuckerberg**.[64] But most people aren't on the very ends of the continuum, and some people are in the middle and are called *ambiverts*. Some highly successful business founders and CEOs are ambiverts, including **Virgin** companies' **Sir Richard Branson** and **Microsoft**'s **Bill Gates**.[65] Extroversion is a good predictor of success in jobs requiring social skills[66] (such as sales) and leadership.[67]

Agreeableness. Agreeableness lies on a continuum between easy and difficult to work with. *Agreeable* people are considered to be nice and good-natured—cooperative, flexible, polite, tolerant, forgiving, and trusting. *Disagreeable* people are the opposite, making them difficult to work with. **Apple CEO Tim Cook** tends to be agreeable but knows how to say no without being too negative, whereas Jobs actually called people and their ideas stupid.[68] Agreeableness is a good predictor of success in jobs requiring cooperative teamwork[69] and leadership.[70]

Emotionalism. Emotionalism is on a continuum between emotional stability and instability. Emotionally *stable* people are calm and in control of their behavior; they are secure and positive. The commonly used term *emotional intelligence* (EI) describes people who have good interpersonal skills.[71] *Unstable* people are neurotics who are angry, depressed, anxious, nervous, insecure, and excitable—they can get out of control and display their emotions negatively, such as by yelling.[72] *Neurotics* can be very charming and use flattery to influence others, but they are poor losers and can display negative emotions toward others when they don't get their way,[73] like **Apple**'s **Steve Jobs**. Neurotics often seek management positions,[74] such as U.S. **president Donald Trump**. They are predictably self-destructing and cause organizational problems.[75]

Agreeableness and emotionalism tend to go together, as agreeable people tend to be in control of their emotions and disagreeable people tend to be neurotics who get out of control.[76] **Apple**'s Jobs and **Microsoft**'s **Bill Gates** were frenemies, as they helped each other while competing in business. As stated, Jobs could be a disagreeable neurotic, whereas Gates is considered to be agreeable with EI. When Jobs would get upset and yell insults at Gates, Gates would not get emotional and yell back; he would remain very calm and speak softly until Jobs calmed down to continue a rational conversation.

Conscientiousness. The conscientiousness continuum goes between responsible/dependable and irresponsible/undependable. *Conscientious* people are responsible/dependable, hardworking, persistent, organized, consistent, and achievement oriented. *Unconscientious* people are irresponsible, so you can't depend on them. **Dwayne "the Rock" Johnson** says success isn't about greatness; it's about consistency—consistent hard work.[77] To realize your dreams, you need to work harder than others.[78] Conscientiousness is an overall good predictor of job success,[79] and effective leaders are conscientious,[80] including **Facebook chief operating officer (COO) Sheryl Sandberg**.[81]

Openness. Also called "open to experience," openness lies on a continuum between being willing to try new things and not being willing to do so.[82] People who are *open to experience* tend to be receptive to new ideas and willing to change; they are curious and broad minded, with a tolerance for ambiguity. People who are *closed to experience* want to stay with the status quo. Openness is a good predictor of job success in creative and innovative jobs.[83] Successful leaders are open to change.[84] **BlackBerry** was not open to change until it was too late and will most likely never be a major player in mobile technology again.

Michael Jordan (IOM 2) appears to be more of an extrovert—that is, agreeable and emotionally stable—which has led to his popularity for endorsements. He obviously would

Jason Alden/Bloomberg via Getty Images

Sheryl Sandberg has gotten strong results while solving complex problems as chief operating officer at **Facebook**. She demonstrates a high level of conscientiousness that is critical to leadership.

10-1 APPLYING THE CONCEPT

Big Five Personality Types

Identify the personality type indicated by each comment.

A. extroversion

B. agreeableness

C. adjustment

D. conscientiousness

E. openness

_____ 1. "I really like working with Tanya because she always comes through with good work."

_____ 2. "I really like working with Tyson because he is so cooperative. We get along great."

_____ 3. "I really like working with Tianna because she always comes up with creative ideas during meetings."

_____ 4. "I really like working with Timmy because he is so easy to have a conversation with."

_____ 5. "I really like working with Terri because she isn't a drama queen like some of the other employees who make a big deal of little things."

not have been a superstar basketball player without being conscientious, and he is open to experience, as he owns a motor-sports team and several restaurants that are unrelated to basketball and the **NBA**.

The Myers-Briggs Type Indicator (MBTI)

Our third and most complex personality classification method is the Myers-Briggs Type Indicator (MBTI). The MBTI model of personality identifies your personality preferences. It is based on your four *preferences* (or inclinations) for certain ways of thinking and behaving. Complete Self-Assessment 10-2 to get an idea of your MBTI personality preference. For a more extensive free 64-question assessment of your personality type, visit **HumanMetrics** www.humanmetrics.com/cgi-win/jtypes2.asp. You can also discover suitable careers for your personality type and better understand your communication and learning styles.[85] Note that MBTI doesn't have strong academic research support for its validity, but it is commonly used in business, so we include it.

Perception

Our personality affects how we perceive things, as well as our attitudes and behavior.[86] Why do some people view a behavior or decision as ethical while others do not?[87] The answer often lies in perception.[88] Perception refers to a person's interpretation of reality. It is important to realize that perceptions, right or wrong, affect behavior and performance, because behavior is the product of or is based on perception.[89]

LO 10-3

Explain the perception and attribution processes, and describe five perception biases.

The Perception and Attribution Processes

The Perception Process. Perception *is the process of selecting, organizing, and interpreting environmental information.* No two people ever perceive—and thus ever experience—anything exactly the same way. Have you ever done a task or watched a movie with someone, and you enjoyed it but the other person didn't? Our perception of our self/ability affects our decisions and behavior.[90] One factor that determines how you select, organize, and most importantly interpret information is your own internal environment, including your behavioral foundations of your thoughts, self-confidence and self-esteem, personality, and attitudes. Or your thoughts reveal the perception you have of yourself, which in turn affects your behavior. If you have negative thoughts because you perceive yourself to be a loser, you will lack self-confidence and have poor self-esteem, often leading to destructive self-behavior and low levels of performance.

A second factor that influences the perception process is the information available from the external environment. Organizational practices influence employee perceptions of

perception The process of selecting, organizing, and interpreting environmental information.

10-2   SELF-ASSESSMENT

Your MBTI Personality Preference

Classify yourself on each of the four preferences by selecting the one statement that best describes you:

1. *Where you focus your attention*—**Extrovert or Introvert**

   _____ I'm outgoing and prefer to deal with people, things, or situations—the outer world. (E)
   _____ I'm shy and prefer to deal with ideas, information, explanations, or beliefs—the inner world. (I)

2. *How you take in information*—**Sensing or Intuitive**

   _____ I prefer facts to have clarity, to describe what I sense with a focus on the present. (S)
   _____ I prefer to deal with ideas, and look into unknown possibilities with a focus on the future. (N)

3. *How you make decisions*—**Thinking or Feeling**

   _____ I prefer to make decisions based on objective logic, using an analytic and detached approach. (T)
   _____ I prefer to make decisions using values and/or personal beliefs, with a concern for others. (F)

4. *How you prefer to organize your life*—**Judging or Perceiving**

   _____ I prefer my life to be planned, stable, and organized. (J)
   _____ I prefer to go with the flow, to maintain flexibility, and to respond to things as they arise. (P)

Place the four letters of preferences here _____ _____ _____ _____

There are 16 combinations, or personality preferences, often presented in the form of a table. Remember, this indicates *preferences* only. You may also use the other traits that you did not select.

ISTJ	ISFJ	INFJ	INTJ
ISTP	ISFP	INFP	INTP
ESTP	ESFP	ENFP	ENTP
ESTJ	ESFJ	ENFJ	ENTJ

Completing Self-Assessment 10-2 gives you an idea of the types of questions included in the MBTI. There are actually multiple forms of the MBTI for various uses. For more information on the 16 personality types, and to complete a more detailed 64-question assessment based on the MBTI for free, visit HumanMetrics (www.humanmetrics.com/cgi-win/jtypes2.asp). You will obtain your four-letter type formula, along with the strengths of preferences and the description of your personality type. You will also discover careers and occupations most suitable for you, as well as gain an understanding of your communication style of your type.

Think about your friends and family and the people you work with. What MBTI type are they?

WORK APPLICATION 10-1

Identify a present or past boss's personality; refer to the personality traits in Self-Assessment 10-2.

WORK APPLICATION 10-2

Give three examples of how you (or a manager you know) have used the attribution process at work.

attribution The process of determining the reason for someone's behavior and whether that behavior is situational or intentional.

management and the firm.[91] The more factual and accurate the information received, the closer the perception may be to reality. If a good employee quits because he or she is mistreated, or if he or she only perceives mistreatment, the result is still the loss of a good employee.[92] So what people know or don't know isn't important—all that really matters is their perception.[93]

The Attribution Process. We make attributions when we infer causes about particular outcomes,[94] which affects behavior.[95] Recall that the OB foundations, especially perception, can't be observed. We can only see the behavior and make an attribution of the actions.[96] **Attribution** *is the process of determining the reason for someone's behavior and whether that behavior is situational or intentional.* Situational behavior is either accidental or out of the control of the individual, whereas intentional behavior is done on purpose. People tend to attribute their own success to their intentional behavior and blame failures on situational factors out of their control.[97]

Your response to someone else's behavior will be determined in part by whether you attribute the behavior to situational factors or intentional factors. So attribution is about making judgments,[98] and it can help meet the goal of OB by explaining the reason for an employee's behavior and predicting future behavior.[99] The attribution process is illustrated in Exhibit 10-1.

| EXHIBIT 10-1 | THE ATTRIBUTION PROCESS |

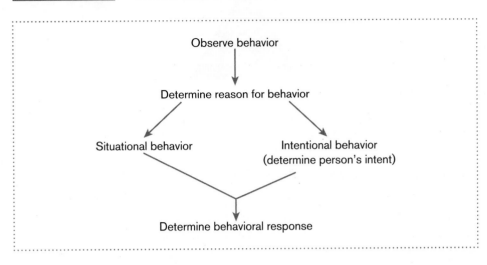

For example, suppose that Eduardo, a manager, observes an employee, Pat, coming to work late. If Eduardo has observed that Pat is often late, he might conclude that Pat's lateness is intentional and that she doesn't care about being on time. In that case, Eduardo would probably decide to discipline Pat. However, if Pat is late only once, Eduardo might determine that her lateness was situational—the result of car problems, traffic, or the like—and take no action.

Bias in Perception

We all have bias.[100] Different people may perceive the same behavior differently because of perception biases listed:

Selectivity. Selectivity refers to people's tendency to screen information in favor of their desired outcome. People will sometimes make great efforts to find information that supports their point of view and ignore information that does not. In other words, people only see and hear what they want to.

Here is a different spin on selectivity. If you ask couples or coworkers how much they each contribute to the relationship and work, the total far exceeds 100%. Try asking if you want to find out. Why? We tend to selectively see how busy we are and all the things we do and fail to see how busy others are and what they do.[101] Let's try to get out of our own little world and see all sides of the issue and how much others are actually doing.

Frame of Reference. Frame of reference refers to seeing things from your own point of view. Employees often view management decisions differently than managers do, especially management versus unions during contract negotiations. Do you always see things the same as your boss and parents? Try to see things from others' perspective and create a win-win situation so that all parties get what they want, based on their perceptions. Some organizations are conducting frame-of-reference training to help overcome this bias.[102]

Stereotyping. Stereotyping is the process of making generalizations about the behavior of a group and then applying the generalities to one individual. People form stereotypes about race/nationality, religion, sex, age, and so forth. Stereotyping a person can lead to perception errors, because not all individuals from a particular group possess the same traits or exhibit the same behaviors. Negatively stereotyping an individual can also affect that person's self-perception in a negative way. Try not to negatively stereotype others; get to know them as individuals.

Expectations. Expectation refers to seeing or hearing what we anticipate. Read the phrase in the triangle shown:

Did you read the word *the* twice? Or, like most people, did you read what you expected, only one *the*? Many people, especially those who know each other well, often do not really

WORK
APPLICATION 10-3

Give an example of a situation that you and someone else experienced together but perceived differently. Which of the biases in perception might explain the difference in perception?

listen to each other. They simply hear what they expect to hear. So let's try to give people our full attention.

The "Like Me" Assumption. The "like me" assumption is the process of believing that others perceive things as you do because they are similar to you or that your behavior makes sense. Remember to value diversity. What you believe to be logically the best way to do something may not be perceived as being logical from others' perspective. Don't expect others to accept your ideas and behave as you do, and don't judge others' behavior as wrong just because it is different from yours.

Perception Congruence

Let's discuss perception congruence and dissonance and how to improve it.

Perception Congruence Versus Dissonance. *Perception congruence* simply means that all parties perceive a situation in the same way. Due to bias, we often have trouble achieving perception congruence. One area that is often not in congruence (*perception dissonance*) is our perception of our own behavior and performance.[103] Why? Because few people want to view themselves as a jerk or poor performer, so we tend to perceive our abilities inaccurately and distort recollections of past behavior,[104] or we rationalize and use attribution and blame it on situational factors outside of our control.[105] Our misperception is actually a defense mechanism to protect our self-esteem.[106]

Narcissists in reality tend to be jerks, with overinflated self-esteem that highly overrates their performance.[107] They are so self-centered and oblivious to others that they don't realize they are in perception dissonance. However, most workers are blissfully unaware of how they come across and how it costs them.[108]

The Importance of Your Personal Perception Congruence. Recall from Chapter 1 that relationships are the key to business success and personal happiness. Not realizing how others see you or not caring about your behavior and performance leads to bad behavior and spoiled relationships (personal and professional). When others sense you're clueless or just don't care, it can undermine your status and credibility, which can also hurt your career progression.[109] So understanding yourself as others see you is important to success.[110]

Improving Perception Congruence. How closely do you think your self-perceptions of your behavior and performance would match those of your coworkers, boss, and family? Would you like to have better relationships and a better career? If so, here are some suggestions for changing yourself, not others.[111] The first step is self-awareness. When you interact with others, watch how they react to your behavior; don't just listen to what is said. Watch their nonverbal communications to know what they are really thinking of you. If you are doing or saying something that gets a negative reaction, stop the behavior. You can also observe others who are jerks and not use any of their negative behavior, and watch well-respected people and copy their behavior.

If your boss criticizes you, do you try to be objective about your shortcomings and really try to improve so that the two of you have perception congruence, or do you disagree and defend your performance and not change? Return to Chapter 9's discussion of developmental performance appraisal for ideas on how to come to an agreement on performance and how to meet the boss's expectations and get a higher review.

10-2 APPLYING THE CONCEPT

Perception Bias

Identify the perception bias indicated by each comment.

A. selectivity

B. frame of reference

C. stereotyping

D. expectations

E. "like me" assumption

_____ 6. Hank, I know you're a good worker, but I can't give you the assignment again. You should understand that I have to be fair to everyone in the department.

_____ 7. Shawn, I thought you were my friend and that you would back me on this.

_____ 8. Jamal, your point is weak. Don't you understand that my idea is much better?

_____ 9. The new guy Kit is a tall black man, so I guess I should talk about basketball with him.

_____ 10. I usually know what Conroy is going to say at meetings. He is so predictable.

A more difficult approach to take for most people, because they are going to hear some things they don't agree with and don't really want to hear, is to ask trusted people how their behavior comes across and how they can improve. As suggested in Self-Assessment 10-1, you can have others give you their perception of your personality traits by taking the self-assessment so you can compare the scores they give you with your own scores. Once you calm down without denying the scores and trying to get them to change their answers, you can discuss how you can improve your behavior and performance.

Attitudes

Attitudes *are positive or negative evaluations of people, things, and situations.* They are judgments and are based on perceptions.[112] In this section, we discuss how attitudes are formed and the way they affect behavior and job satisfaction, followed by how employees' and managers' attitudes affect performance.

Attitude Formation, Behavior, and Job Satisfaction

Attitude Formation. Our internal OB foundations of our thoughts, self-esteem, personality, and perception all affect our attitudes and behavior. Externally, family, friends, teachers, coworkers, bosses, the mass media, and so on affect your attitudes. Before you signed up for this course, you may have read the course description, talked to students who completed it to find out more about the course, and thought about your interest in the course. Based on what you read and heard and your interest in the subject, you may have started this course with a particular attitude. People generally find what they are looking for, so if you had a positive attitude coming into the course, you probably like it—and vice versa. Perceptions and attitudes are biased.[113] However, attitudes can be changed. Has your attitude toward this course become more positive or negative? What were the primary factors that formed your present attitude toward this course?

Attitudes and Behavior. Attitudes often affect behavior.[114] People with opposite attitudes toward a person, job, course, event, or situation often behave differently. People's attitudes toward you may affect your behavior.[115] Do you behave differently with people who like you than with those who don't? What is your attitude about whether or not people like you? Do you try to get people to like you?

Attitudes and Job Satisfaction. *Job satisfaction* is a person's attitude toward the job. Although there has long been a debate over the expression that a happy worker is a productive worker,

LO 10-4

Recall how attitudes affect job satisfaction and how employee and managerial attitudes affect employee performance.

attitudes Positive or negative evaluations of people, things, and situations.

10-3 SELF-ASSESSMENT

Job Satisfaction

Select a present or past job. Identify your level of satisfaction by placing a check mark at the appropriate position on the continuum for each determinant of job satisfaction.

Personality		
I have positive self-esteem.	_____	I *do not* have positive self-esteem.
Work itself		
I enjoy doing the tasks I perform.	_____	I *do not* enjoy doing the tasks I perform.
Compensation		
I am fairly compensated.	_____	I am *not* fairly compensated.
Growth and Upward Mobility		
I have the opportunity to learn new things and get better jobs.	_____	I have *no* opportunity to learn new things and get better jobs.
Coworkers		
I like and enjoy working with my coworkers.	_____	I *do not* like and enjoy working with my coworkers.
Management		
I believe that managers are doing a good job.	_____	I *do not* believe that managers are doing a good job.
Overall Job Satisfaction		
When determining your overall job satisfaction, you cannot simply add up a score based on the above six determinants, because they are most likely of different importance to you. Thus, think about your job and the above factors, and rate your overall satisfaction with your job.		
I am satisfied with my job (high level of satisfaction).	_____ 7 6 5 4 3 2 1	I am dissatisfied with my job (low level of satisfaction).

---

there is support for the idea of a positive relationship between job satisfaction and **citizenship behavior**—*employee efforts that go above and beyond the call of duty.*[116] Studies have also found that dissatisfied employees are more apt to break the rules, to be absent, and to leave, all of which are costly and decrease productivity.[117] So organizations do strive for employee job satisfaction.[118] **Google** strives to keep employees happy because it helps productivity.[119] Also, job satisfaction can affect our satisfaction off the job, as we tend to take our jobs home with us, which affects our behavior and work–life balance (Chapter 9).[120] Women are more likely than men to be satisfied with their entry-level career, but the opposite is true at senior levels, as women hit the glass ceiling.[121]

Job satisfaction is generally measured along a continuum from satisfied/positive/high to dissatisfied/negative/low. Complete Self-Assessment 10-3 to find out your own level of job satisfaction. You can have an overall high level of job satisfaction and not like some aspects of your job; this is common. Think about a job you have or had. What did you like and not like so much about it? Do relationships at work affect your job satisfaction?

Oftentimes, it's the small hassles that throw us off and cause us to develop negative attitudes.[122] So don't focus on the negative part of your job. Let it go and focus on the positive, optimistic side of what you like about your job to maintain your job satisfaction.

WORK
APPLICATION 10-4

Give an example of how your attitude affected your performance at work.

citizenship behavior Employee efforts that go above and beyond the call of duty.

How Employee and Managerial Attitudes Affect Employee Performance

How Employees' Attitudes Affect Performance. Attitude is a major factor in determining performance. Conscientiousness is a good predictor of job performance, so companies recruit employees with good attitudes because they are more conscientious. **J. W. Marriott Jr.**, president of **Marriott International**, stated, "We have found that our success depends more upon employee attitude than any other single factor." The founding CEO **Jessica Herrin** of social retailer **Stella & Dot** says, "It's all about attitudes,"[123] and founding CEO **Tom Gimbel** of **LaSalle Network** says that you have to keep an upbeat attitude to succeed.[124]

Jessica Herrin, CEO of Stella & Dot, center, credits her company's success to a positive attitude among employees.

The Self-Fulfilling Prophecy. Recall our discussion about how our thoughts affect our behavior. Well, they also affect our attitudes. We tend to live up to or down to our attitudinal expectations of ourselves. Thinking with a negative "I can't do it" attitude tends to lead to a *self-fulfilling prophecy* of failure because of lack of effort. After failing, some people will actually say, "I told you I couldn't do it!" Ever been there, done that? Do you try harder at the things you like than the things you don't like to do? If you take a negative or a positive attitude toward a person, thing, or situation, how does it affect your behavior and performance?

Attitudes Are Contagious. Not only can employees' attitudes have an effect on their own performance, but they can also have an effect on the performance of their coworkers. Since employees usually have to work in cooperation with each other, other employees may pick up on negative attitudes of coworkers and adopt them as their own.[125] Do you like to be around negative people who are always complaining about someone or something? Avoid being around them as much as you can so they don't bring you down with them. If you catch yourself being a complainer, stop and turn it around, focus, and talk about the positive things at work and in your life.

Therefore, having a positive attitude is an important determinant of both individual and organizational performance. When "good" managers realize they misjudged new hires' attitude, or it turns bad, they talk to them about it and try to get them to realize how their attitude is affecting them and others, and the new hires try to change their attitude to be more positive; if they don't, the managers fire them to avoid this problem. However, "poor" and especially abusive managers will always have employees with negative attitudes who may also mistreat their coworkers and customers.[126] What is your attitude toward working? To succeed, develop and maintain a positive work attitude.[127]

How Managers' Attitudes Affect Employee Performance. The **Pygmalion effect** *is the theory that managers' attitudes toward and expectations and treatment of employees largely determine their performance.* Various studies have supported this theory, as managers have the ability to affect employee performance.[128] Let's discuss treatment and then expectations. Managers who have negative attitudes toward employees and are abusive (hostile verbal and nonverbal behavior, excluding physical contact) tend to cause negative employee attitudes and job dissatisfaction that leads to lower levels of performance.[129] The expectations part of the theory is that employees live up or down to fulfill expectations of managers about themselves.[130] Thus, if managers expect employees to be productive and successful and treat them accordingly, employees react by being productive, or vice versa.[131]

Unfortunately, some managers negatively stereotype their employees as having low ability or willingness to work. This negative attitude leads to low expectations and not treating employees with respect. The employees see and do as their managers expect. These managers' expectations lead to the *self-fulfilling prophecy* of low-performing employees. As a manager, if you create win-win situations by expecting high performance and treating employees as capable, you will get the best performance from them.

Don Feria/Getty Images for Stella & Dot

WORK
APPLICATION 10-5

Think of someone who really expected you to perform well (or poorly) and treated you as if you would do well (or poorly), which strongly affected your success (or failure). Explain how the Pygmalion effect influenced your performance.

Pygmalion effect The theory that managers' attitudes toward and expectations and treatment of employees largely determine their performance.

If you have ever seen **Michael Jordan** (**IOM 3**) interviewed or playing basketball, you have most likely observed his positive, winning attitude. His positive attitude is reflected in his nice smile that has helped him win endorsement contracts.

LO 10-5

List the six OB foundations, summarize how to shape your own and your management foundations, and discuss managing diversity in three critical foundations.

Shaping OB Foundations

As stated, you can change your own six individual OB foundations: thought, self-confidence, self-esteem, personality, perceptions, and attitudes. Here we expand to shaping your employees' OB. But it is not easy; it takes conscious effort and work, and it is usually easier to shape yourself than others.

We use the term *shape* rather than *change* because most of us don't need a major disruptive change (only the narcissists, but they don't get it), just some incremental change (Chapter 6), tweaking, or fine tuning to continuously improve behavior to increase performance.

Shaping Your OB Foundations

Would you like to be happier, have better relationships, and progress during your career? Let's face it—the jerks at work aren't going to change. Are you willing to shape your behavior and make a conscious effort to change? You can complete Skill Builder 10-3, "Improving Your OB Foundations," to shape your behavior. Let's review the foundations and think of areas in which you can shape behavior.

The pillar that holds up (or affects) all the other OB foundations is your *thoughts*. As we already covered, you can train your brain to have positive thoughts and feel happier every day.[132] Positive optimistic thoughts lead to higher levels of both *self-confidence* and *self-esteem*. Need any shaping here? A successful *personality* is to be conscious, agreeable, open, and emotionally stable, as emotional intelligence is important to good relationships. You don't have to be an extrovert, but do match your personality to your career. How is your *perception* of your behavior and performance? Do you have biases? Do you and your boss agree? Happiness is based largely on *attitudes;* do you need a perception or attitude adjustment?

Shaping Your Management OB Foundations

Let's be honest here. If your employees *think* you're a jerk with an unpleasant *personality*, their *perception* of you is that you're a bad boss, and they have negative *attitudes* toward you, how truly successful do you really think you will be? Narcissists are sometimes referred to as a crazy boss.[133] Yes. **Steve Jobs** was a successful jerk, but don't forget that his behavior led to several talented people leaving **Apple**; maybe the company would have been even more successful if he had been nicer—we will never know. Plus, he also got fired from Apple by the directors because he couldn't get along with people. How do you know if your employees think you're a bad boss? It's all about *perception congruence*, so you may want to revisit that section.

The old-school, hard-nosed boss is obsolete.[134] Why? Because millennials, who now dominate the workforce, and the younger Generation Y workers will not work for a bad boss, and the hard-nosed boss may be fired and right behind them leaving the company. This entire book focuses on helping you to be a good manager, but your OB foundations clearly affect how you manage. So if you are a hard-nosed boss, you may want to work on your individual OB foundations. Next, we discuss how to manage diverse foundations to shape behavior and performance.

Managing Diverse Employee OB Foundations

Managers clearly supervise employees with a diversity of individual OB foundations. So here are some ideas on managing the diversity. The first step is to hire people with good OB foundations and then to continually coach your employees to improve. As stated, *thoughts* affect all of the other OB foundations, so they are the first critical foundation to work on. You can't control employees' thoughts, but you can help them to be more optimistic and supportive to help build their *self-confidence*, which in turn builds more positive *self-esteem*.

Work to build and maintain positive *personality profiles*, and don't hire or do get rid of *narcissists* if you can. If not, beware of their tactics. Don't let them manipulate and deceive you or others with their charm and compliments, and be cautious about listening to them gossip to discredit coworkers to win your favor and get what they want. If they realize that you are on to them and that they can't get away with being Machiavellian, they may leave.[135]

Remember that it's not reality that matters; it's employees' *perceptions*. Do a good job of seeing things from the employees' side, and do a good job of communicating the facts of what you are doing and why to help them to perceive the situation as you do. A second critical area to work on is *perception congruence* of employee job performance. To obtain it, give employees constant feedback on your perception of their performance with specific things they need to do to improve. If an employee is performing below standard and doesn't improve, document it and terminate him or her.

It is easier to hire a person with a good *attitude* than to change it, so carefully consider attitudes when selecting employees. If employees have a negative attitude about something, point it out to them and help them realize that it is having a negative effect on their and others' behavior and performance and coach them to change. Don't let poor attitudes spread.[136] A third critical OB foundation is to implement the *Pygmalion effect*. You need to have a positive attitude and high expectations and treat employees like they are winners so they have an "I can do it" attitude to get high levels of performance, which also builds their *self-confidence* and *self-esteem*.

Using Chapter 1's Model 1-1, "Situational Management," can aid you in matching employees' capability levels with the management style that provides the needed directive and supportive behavior needed to assist employees in performing tasks successfully and improve their capability level. In Chapter 13, we expand the model to focus on communications. In Chapter 14, you will learn how to use a coaching model that can help maintain and improve performance.

Organizational Power and Politics

LO 10-6

Discuss the relationship between organizational power and politics and their importance to organizational performance.

Based on an internal focus of individual OB foundations, we move to a more external focus of OB topics, including power, organizational politics, negotiation, conflict, and stress. Realize that our OB foundations are internal, and they affect how we deal with these external interactions. For example, narcissists want to gain and use power and politics for personal gain,[137] whereas agreeable personality types have less interest in power. In this section, we discuss power and politics. There is a relationship between power and politics,[138] so let's begin by explaining it.

The Relationship Between Organizational Power and Politics

Whether you have a positive or negative attitude toward power and organizational politics, they are a reality of organizational life that is important to performance. Organizations have power structures[139] as a source of power,[140] and colleges prepare students for powerful positions.[141] For our purposes, **power** *is the ability to influence others' behavior.* **Politics** *is the process of gaining and using power.* Power and politics are often viewed negatively because some people abuse them using unethical behavior.[142] But power and politics in and of themselves are neither good nor bad; it's how they are used.

Managers need ethical power and politics to meet organizational objectives. Recall (Chapter 1) that leadership is the process of influencing employees to work toward achieving objectives, so power and politics go hand in hand with leadership. The fundamental concept in social science is power, in the same way energy is the fundamental concept in physics.[143]

Let's admit it—we all have a desire for influence,[144] as we try to influence people at work and off the job to get what we want every day. Unless you always just go along with doing whatever others want you to do. This comes naturally, and there is nothing wrong with looking out for your self-interest, so long as you are not narcissistic to get your way at the expense of others. Recall that looking out for others and even putting their needs ahead of your own is the foundation of good relationships and happiness.

power The ability to influence others' behavior.

politics The process of gaining and using power.

A positive way to view politics is to realize that it is simply a medium of exchange.[145] Like money, it is simply a means of getting what we want—meeting objectives. In most economies, money is the medium of exchange; in an organization, politics is the medium of exchange—if you do this for me, I will do that for you. Let's move on to providing details of power, then politics.

Power

Here we discuss the sources and types of power and how to increase your power without taking it away from others.

Sources of Power. You don't have to be a manager to have power, as some employees actually have more influence over other employees than the manager does. You do not actually have to use power to influence others. Often it is the perception of your power rather than actual power that influences others. Status within the team gives power (Chapter 8).[146] Having power influences our OB foundations, especially perceptions and attitudes,[147] and from personality types come power.[148] People have different needs for power[149] (which we discuss in the next chapter); some want it, and others don't. But the trend is to give employees more power through shared leadership,[150] and power does shift in teams.[151]

There are two sources of power influencing behavior: one's position and one's person. *Position power* is derived from top management and is delegated down the chain of command.[152] It gives formal authority (Chapter 7).[153] The supervisory relationship affects employee attitudes, behaviors, job satisfaction and performance.[154] *Personal power* is derived from followers, based on an individual's behavior. Charismatic people tend to be leaders and have personal power. Therefore, personal power can be gained or lost based on positive or negative behavior. It is best to have both position power and personal power.

Types of Power. There are different types of power. The seven types of power are presented in Exhibit 10-2.

- *Coercive power* use involves threats and/or punishment to influence compliance. Out of fear of negative outcomes, employees often do as their boss requests. However, abusive power often leads to employee retaliation of negative behavior and lower performance.[155] *Bullying* tends to be about gaining power for personal gain[156] and is common with narcissists.[157] Group members may use coercive power to enforce norms[158] (Chapter 8). Coercive power is appropriate to use in maintaining discipline when enforcing rules.

- *Connection power* is based on the user's relationship with influential people. You rely on the use of contacts or friends who can influence the person you are dealing with. The right connections can give power, or at least the perception of power. If people know you are friendly with people in power, they are more apt to do as you request.

- *Reward power* is based on the user's ability to influence others by providing something of value to them. In a management position, reward power involves the use of positive reinforcement or incentives, such as praise, recognition, pay raises, and

| EXHIBIT 10-2 | SOURCES AND TYPES OF POWER |

Position Power						Personal Power
Coercive	Connection	Reward	Legitimate	Referent	Information	Expert

JOIN THE DISCUSSION ETHICS & SOCIAL RESPONSIBILITY

Following Orders

Officers in the armed forces tend to use legitimate power with troops. Military recruits are conditioned to follow orders without questioning authority. In fact, it is a crime for a military member to willfully disobey any lawful order. However, many military officers issue unlawful orders to recruits and expect them to obey them.

1. Is it ethical and socially responsible to teach people in the military or any other organization to follow orders without questioning authority?

2. What would you do if your boss gave you an unethical/unlawful order?

3. Is following orders a good justification for conducting unethical/unlawful practices?

promotions, to influence others' behavior. With peers, you can give complements and exchange favors or give them something of value.

- **Legitimate power** is based on the user's position power in the organization. Legitimacy is generalized assumptions of desirability or appropriateness of behavior.[159] It is important so that employees will tend to feel that they ought to do what the boss says.[160] Day-to-day manager–employee interactions are based on legitimate power.

- **Referent power** is based on the user's personal source of power relationships with others. When asking another person to do something, you would express it as a request rather than as an order. Referent power is often used by people who have little or no position power; it is also used in teams in which leadership is shared.

- **Information power** is based on others' need for data. Information is the new source of power, not money.[161] Managers rely on information, which is usually but not always related to the job. Some assistants have more information and are more helpful in answering questions than the managers they work for. An important part of the manager's job is to convey information. Employees often come to managers for information on what to do and how to do it.

- **Expert power** is based on the user's skill and knowledge. Being an expert gives you power. Being an expert makes other people more convinced to trust and respect you. When your expertise is valued, so are your ideas and leadership.[162] Thus, employees with expert power are often promoted to management positions.

How to Increase Your Power. You can increase your power without taking power away from others. Increasing your power builds your career and helps you get ahead. To have *coercive power*, you usually need to have a management job with formal authority. To increase your *connection power*, network (Chapter 9 Appendix) with people who have power and use political behavior. Being a manager gives you *reward* and *legitimate power*, but you can also give praise (you will learn how in Chapter 14) and use political behavior. To increase your *referent power*, develop your interpersonal skills and make efforts to gain others' confidence and trust. To increase your *information power*, know what is going on in the organization, and serving on committees gives you a chance to increase both information power and connection power. To increase your *expert power*, participate in training and educational programs, keep up with the latest technology, and volunteer to be the first to learn something new.

Using Power

Michael Jordan (IOM 4) has position power as the owner of a motor-sports team, several restaurants, and the majority of the **NBA's Hornets**. Being called the greatest basketball player ever, holding several records, he clearly has expert power. His outgoing personality and

WORK
APPLICATION 10-6

Identify the type(s) of power usually used by your current boss or a previous boss. Was there any type(s) of power that this person used only rarely?

WORK
APPLICATION 10-7

Which of the suggestions for increasing your power are the most relevant to you? Explain.

APPLYING THE CONCEPT

Using Power

Identify the appropriate type of power to use in each situation.

A. coercive

B. connection

C. reward or legitimate

D. referent

E. information or expert

____ 11. You have to get an important customer order shipped today, and Sonia is not working to standard again. Sonia claims that she does not feel well and cannot afford to take time off, so she can't get much work done today.

____ 12. Ari, one of your best workers, is currently not doing as good a job as usual. You think Ari has a personal problem affecting her work.

____ 13. A new, expensive robot machine is now available that can increase your department productivity. Major purchases must be approved by a committee, and its decisions tend to be influenced by politics.

____ 14. Amita has talked to you about getting ahead and has asked you to help prepare her for a supervisor position when the next opportunity opens.

____ 15. Samuel is not wearing a required safety vest again, saying it is too hot.

charm also give him personal power, and he has lots of powerful connections. Who would pass up the opportunity to meet with MJ?

Organizational Politics

Like power, politics can be abused, so it must be used to help the organization achieve objectives.[163] According to **Zappos CEO Tony Hsieh**, the real organization chart isn't drawn on paper; it is knowing who to talk to and politics and influence to get the job done.[164] At **City Winery**, the managers set objectives and openly talk about office politics.[165] Political skills come into play when using power. Whether you have a positive or negative attitude toward politics, politics is a reality of organizational life, and it pays to have political skills.[166] The amount and importance of politics vary from organization to organization. However, larger organizations tend to be more political, and the higher the level of management, the more important politics becomes.[167] **Facebook CEO Mark Zuckerberg** received political coaching to help win over directors to create a new class of nonvoting shares that would allow him to maintain control of the company he cofounded.[168] You cannot meet your objectives without the help of others, including people and departments over which you have no authority, so you need to use political skills.[169] Begin by determining your own political behavior by completing Self-Assessment 10-4.

Political Behavior

- Networking *is the process of developing relationships for the purpose of career building and socializing.* It's about developing mutually beneficial relationships.[170] Successful managers spend more time networking than do average managers.[171] Refer to the Appendix to Chapter 9 for details on how to network.

  Reciprocity *involves the mutual exchange of favors and privileges to accomplish objectives.* The process of reciprocity is also referred to as *social exchange theory.*[172] Managers and employees and colleagues form relationships that have mutual obligation and reciprocity.[173] It's the usually unspoken "I owe you" (IOU). It goes like this: "You have power where I don't, so do me this favor and I will pay you back at a later date." Helping others is the driver of success.[174] As **Zig Ziglar** says, "You can have everything in life you want, if you will just help enough other people get what they want."[175] Reciprocity can also be negative when driven by retaliation and retribution.[176]

  reciprocity The mutual exchange of favors and privileges to accomplish objectives.

  coalition A network of alliances that help achieve an objective.

- A **coalition** *is a network of alliances that help achieve an objective.* Reciprocity is used to achieve ongoing objectives, whereas coalitions are developed for achieving a specific objective. Many decisions made in organizations are actually made by coalitions before a formal meeting and approval. For example, Rajesh has an idea for a new service to be offered by his company. By himself, Rajesh has no authority to offer a new service. To begin building a coalition, he might first go to his boss or bosses. Rajesh would present the idea to his boss and get approval to gain wider support. He would then try to get peers and people at other levels as allies. Walking into the meeting to make the decision, Rajesh knows he has management support and that the service will be offered. Narcissists are good at developing coalitions.[177]

Successfully navigating organizational politics not only requires understanding the type of power you have but also how others in the organization use their power.

Guidelines for Developing Political Skills. It is natural, especially for young people, to take a purely rational approach to a job without considering politics. But many business decisions are nonrational, based primarily on power and politics. If you want to climb the corporate ladder, or at least avoid getting thrown off it, you should develop your political skills. Review the 10 statements in Self-Assessment 10-4 on political behavior and the three political behaviors just discussed, and consciously increase your use of any or all of these behaviors. The guidelines in Exhibit 10-3 and discussed here can also help you develop your political skills.

10-4 SELF-ASSESSMENT

Use of Political Behavior

Beside each statement, write the number of the choice that best describes how often you use the particular behavior on the job (or how often you imagine you will use it once you are employed).

| 1 = rarely | 2 = seldom | 3 = occasionally | 4 = frequently | 5 = usually |

_____ 1. I get along with everyone, even those considered to be difficult to get along with.

_____ 2. I avoid giving my personal opinions on controversial issues, especially when I know others don't agree with them.

_____ 3. I try to make people feel important by complimenting them.

_____ 4. I compromise when working with others and avoid telling people they are wrong.

_____ 5. I try to get to know the key managers and find out what is going on in all the organizational departments.

_____ 6. I dress the same way as the people in power and take on the same interests (watch or play sports, join the same clubs, etc.).

_____ 7. I purposely seek contacts with higher-level managers so that they will know my name and face.

_____ 8. I seek recognition and visibility for my accomplishments.

_____ 9. I get others to help me get what I want.

_____10. I do favors for others and ask them for favors in return.

To determine your level of political behavior, add the 10 numbers you selected as your answers. The total will range from 10 to 50. The higher your score, the more political behavior you use. Place your score on the continuum below.

50	40	30	20	10
Nonpolitical				Political

EXHIBIT 10-3   POLITICAL BEHAVIORS AND GUIDELINES FOR DEVELOPING POLITICAL SKILLS

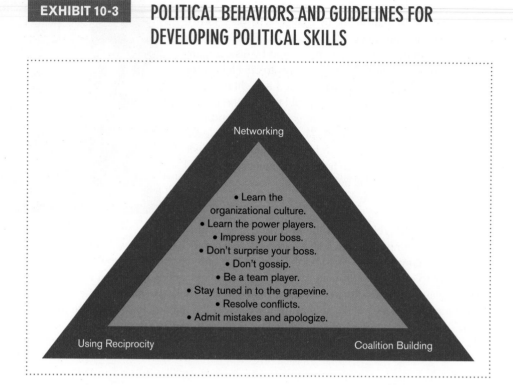

- ***Learn the organizational culture*** and find out what it takes to succeed in your job and to advance, and don't be afraid to ask. Use political behavior to get noticed and to promote yourself without looking like a braggart, but be sure to use methods that are considered appropriate and ethical within the organizational culture.

- ***Learn the power players***—your boss. Find out who those people are in your organization, and find opportunities to get to know them using political behavior. And always remember that your boss is a key player for you, regardless of your personal feelings toward him or her. Your manager's *perception* of you will shape your career success. To get raises and promotions, you need to have a good working relationship with your boss. If you are not getting top performance evaluations, as we discussed in Chapter 9 and earlier in this chapter, talk to your boss and develop a plan to get them.

- ***Impress your boss*** by delivering more than you are asked to do. Get to know what your boss expects from you and do it, and don't be afraid to ask. Beating deadlines, arriving at work early and staying later when needed, and volunteering for more work are all ways to impress a boss and get top performance evaluations (Chapter 9).

- ***Don't surprise your boss*** if you are having a work problem, such as being behind schedule; never wait until the deadline to tell your boss. Tell leaders the awkward truth.[178] Let your boss (or customer) know as early as possible and set a new deadline.[179]

- ***Don't gossip*** like the narcissist "backstabbers"—people who like to make others look bad by spreading negative gossip about them.[180] Follow the old rule "If you can't say something nice about somebody, don't say anything at all." Watch out for narcissists, because they will start making negative comments about the boss, and if you join in, they will likely tell the boss on you. Forgive? Forget? Not likely. If your boss finds out you said negative things, you can lose trust, and it will most likely hurt your relationship and chances for a top performance evaluation.

- ***Be a team player,*** supporting your group or team by taking responsibility for shared goals.[181] One way to help you get what you want is to phrase your own ideas as if someone else has said them. "It's like Jamal was saying ... [your idea]" or "Building on Tina's thoughts ... [your idea]."[182] Refer to Chapter 8 for details on how to be a good team player.

WORK
APPLICATION 10-8

Give an example of how you used political behavior to achieve an organizational objective.

- *Stay tuned in to the grapevine* to find out what is going on. It can help you to learn the organizational culture and identify key players to include in your coalitions. Your grapevine should include a network of people within and outside your organization.

- *Resolve conflicts.* Following the preceding guidelines can help you avoid a political fight. However, if you are suddenly left out of the information loop or if your coworkers or boss start treating you differently, find out why. Managing and resolving conflict is discussed in more detail later in the chapter.

- *Admit mistakes and apologize.* We all make mistakes, so admit them, especially to your boss. Defending and justifying mistakes and behavior that hurt others damages relationships, and can lead to lower performance evaluations. However, an apology to a boss is more than just saying "I'm sorry." You need to acknowledge what you've done, solve it for the future, then make some assurance that it won't happen again.[183] With colleagues, friends, and family, a sincere apology can go a long way in maintaining and repairing damaged relationships.[184] If you don't believe you did anything wrong, but your behavior hurt someone, an apology doesn't mean you need to accept blame but that you are sorry for causing pain.[185] Saying "I'm sorry" can sometimes transform a relationship from venom to honey.[186] So apologize quickly and move on.

WORK
APPLICATION 10-9

Which of the suggestions for developing political skills is the most relevant to you?

Negotiation, Conflict, and Stress Management

Like power and politics, negotiation and conflict skills are an important part of interpersonal skills based on our individual OB foundations,[187] and how we deal with them affects stress.[188] OB behavior of power and politics is often used during negotiations and conflict, which can be stressful. You should realize that negotiation and conflict are not about being unethical for personal gain[189] or being a *narcissist* and deceiving people to create an "I win and you lose" situation.[190] They are about building trust so that everyone gets a good deal.[191] In this section, you will learn how to negotiate, resolve conflicts, and better manage your stress.

LO 10-7

Identify the four parts of the negotiation process, define the five conflict management styles, state how to initiate a conflict resolution, and explain the stress tug-of-war.

Negotiating

You have to negotiate in both your personal and your professional life. *Negotiating* is a process in which two or more parties in conflict attempt to come to an agreement—a deal. If there is a set "take it or leave it" deal, such as retail prices, there is no negotiation. Also, not all negotiations end with an agreement. Acquisitions require sophisticated negotiating, and **Facebook cofounder Mark Zuckerberg** is a good negotiator and personally handled the **Instagram** acquisition.[192]

10-4 | APPLYING THE CONCEPT

Political Behavior

Identify the political behavior in each situation as

A. effective

B. ineffective

____ 16. Juanita has to drop off daily reports at a certain office by noon. She brings them in around 10:00 on Monday and Wednesday so that she can run into some higher-level managers who meet at that time near the office. On the other days, Juanita drops the reports off around noon on her way to lunch.

____ 17. Ronnie signed up to play on the company softball team that includes some higher-level managers.

____ 18. Hoang told his boss's boss about a mistake her boss made yesterday.

____ 19. Romeo avoids socializing so that he can be more productive on the job.

____ 20. Juliet sent copies of a report that she wrote to three higher-level managers.

MANAGEMENT IN ACTION

Negotiating

Negotiation is often a *zero-sum game* in which one party's gain is the other party's loss.[193] For example, every dollar less that you pay for a car is your gain and the seller's loss. Ideally, all parties should believe they got a good deal.[194] Not everyone is born a great negotiator, but the skill can be developed. Following the steps in the negotiation process can help you develop your negotiation skills; Model 10-1 uses evidence-based management (EBM).[195] The *negotiation process* has three, possibly four, steps: plan, negotiate, possibly postpone, and finally come to an agreement or no agreement.[196] These steps are summarized in Model 10-1 and discussed here. In the course of actual negotiations, you may have to make slight adjustments to the steps in the process.

Plan the Negotiation. Success or failure in negotiating is usually based on preparation. Planning has four steps:

Step 1. Research the other party or parties to the negotiation. Try to find out what the other parties want, what they will and will not be willing to give up, and what they expect in return.[197] Know what your deal is really worth before you negotiate.[198]

Step 2. Set objectives. Based on your research, what can you expect—what is your objective?[199] You have to identify the one thing you must come away with. You want to set three objectives, or levels: First, set a specific lower limit that you are unwilling to give up, and you must be willing to walk away from negotiations if you can't get it. Second, set a target objective that represents what you believe is fair. Last, set an opening objective that is more than you actually expect but that you may achieve. Remember that the other party is probably also setting these kinds of objectives. The key to successful negotiation is for each person or party to achieve something between the minimum objective and the target objective. This creates a fair deal or a win-win situation.

Step 3. Try to develop options and trade-offs. In some negotiating situations, you may find that you are in a position of power to achieve your target objective. For example, when negotiating prices with a supplier or applying for jobs, you may be able to quote other

---

MODEL 10-1 **THE NEGOTIATION PROCESS**

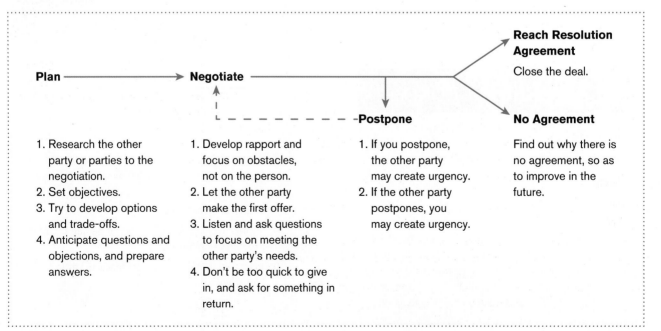

Plan ——————→ Negotiate —————————————————→ **Reach Resolution Agreement**

Close the deal.

- - - - - - - - - →**Postpone**

No Agreement

1. Research the other party or parties to the negotiation.
2. Set objectives.
3. Try to develop options and trade-offs.
4. Anticipate questions and objections, and prepare answers.

1. Develop rapport and focus on obstacles, not on the person.
2. Let the other party make the first offer.
3. Listen and ask questions to focus on meeting the other party's needs.
4. Don't be too quick to give in, and ask for something in return.

1. If you postpone, the other party may create urgency.
2. If the other party postpones, you may create urgency.

Find out why there is no agreement, so as to improve in the future.

prices or salary offers and get the other person to beat them. If you have to give up something or cannot get exactly what you want, be prepared to ask for something in return.[200]

Step 4. Anticipate questions and objections, and prepare answers. Very likely the other party to negotiations will want an answer to the unasked question, "What's in it for me?" Focus on how the negotiations will benefit the other party; speak in terms of "you" and "we" rather than "I." There is a good chance that the other person will raise objections.[201] Unfortunately, not everyone will be open about his or her real objections. Thus, you need to listen and ask questions to find out what is preventing an agreement.[202]

Negotiate. Face-to-face negotiations are generally preferred because you can see the other person's nonverbal behavior (discussed in Chapter 13) and better understand objections.[203] However, negotiations by telephone and written negotiations work, too. It will help to keep the following four steps in mind as you negotiate.

Step 1. Develop rapport and focus on obstacles, not on the person. Open with small talk. How long you wait before getting down to negotiations will depend on the particular situation and the other party's style. Stay calm and do not become adversarial.[204] Never attack the other party's personality or use negative statements such as "You're being unfair." If people perceive that you are pushing them into something, threatening them, or belittling them, they will not trust you and will be unlikely to come to an agreement with you.[205]

Step 2. Let the other party make the first offer—most of the time. Letting the other party make the first offer often gives you the advantage, because if the other party offers you more than your target objective, you can close the agreement.[206] Of course, the other party may pressure *you* to make the first offer. If so, you can counter with a question such as "What do you expect to pay, or what is the pay range?" or "What is a reasonable price?"

Step 3. Listen and ask questions to focus on meeting the other party's needs. When you give people what they want, they tend to give you what you want.[207] Create an opportunity for the other party to disclose reservations and objections. Determining whether the objection is a "want" criterion or a "must" criterion (Chapter 4) will help you decide how to proceed. To help protect yourself from the other party lying or withholding important information you should know,[208] you can ask, "Is there something important that you know about this deal you haven't told me?"

Negotiating is not just about getting what you want; it's also about giving others what they want so you both get a good deal.

Step 4. Don't be too quick to give in, and remember to ask for something in return. You want to satisfy the other party without giving up too much yourself. If you are giving something, you ought to get something.[209] Remember not to go below your minimum objective, and be prepared to walk away if that minimum can't be met. Recall your planned trade-offs. For example, if the other party asks for a lower price, ask for a concession such as a large-volume sale to get it, or a longer delivery time, a less popular color, and so on. If you can't get your salary, ask for extra vacation time or a lower medical payment or larger retirement matching benefit.

Postpone. When there doesn't seem to be any progress, it may be wise to postpone negotiations.

If the other party is postponing, you can try to create urgency. In doing so, remember that people will do more to avoid a loss than to score a win. Suppose the other party says, "I'll get back to you." You may try to create urgency by saying, for example, "This product is on sale, and the sale ends today." However, honesty is the best policy. Or, if you have other options, you can use them to create urgency, such as by saying, "I have another job offer pending. When will you let me know if you want to offer me the job?"

If you want to postpone, the other party may try to create urgency. If you are not satisfied with the deal or want to shop around, tell the other party you want to think about it. You may also need to check with your manager or someone else, which simply may be for advice, before you can finalize the deal. If the other party is creating urgency, be sure the urgency is real; don't be pressured into agreeing to something you are not satisfied with or may regret later. If you do want to postpone, give a specific time that you will get back to the other party.

Agreement or No Agreement. Once you have come to an agreement, put things in writing, if appropriate. It is common to follow up on an agreement with a letter/email of thanks that restates the agreement. Also, after the deal is reached, stop selling it. Change the subject to a personal one and/or leave, depending on the other party's preferred negotiation style.

No Agreement. There will be times when you simply will be unable to come to an agreement or make a sale. Rejection, refusal, and failure happen to us all; in negotiating, you need to be thick skinned. The difference between the "also-rans" and the "superstars" lies in how they respond to the failure. If you cannot close a deal, analyze the situation and try to determine how you can improve in the future.

Skill Builder 10-1 develops negotiation skills.

Conflict

A **conflict** *exists whenever people are in disagreement and opposition*. You are in conflict when you get aggravated at someone[210] or when someone does something that bothers you,[211] and conflict is part of every relationship[212] and every social system.[213] You don't want to avoid it; you want to manage it effectively to maintain and improve relationships,[214] because if you don't, you can hurt feelings, kill important relationships, and damage your career.[215] Thus, conflict management is an important skill in your personal and professional lives.[216] Here we discuss the psychological contract and functional and dysfunctional conflict, five conflict management styles, how to initiate a conflict resolution, and how to respond to and mediate conflict resolutions.

The Psychological Contract—Reasons for Conflict. All human relations rely on the psychological contract because people want to have their expectations met.[217] The *psychological contract* is composed of the implicit expectations of each party. You have a set of expectations about what you will contribute to the organization and what it will provide to you. Often we are not aware of our expectations until they have not been met. *Conflict* arises when the psychological contract is broken,[218] which happens for two primary reasons: (1) We fail to make explicit our own expectations and fail to inquire into the expectations of others. (2) We assume that others have the same expectations that we hold. As long as people meet our expectations, everything is fine; when they don't meet our expectations, we are in conflict. Thus, it is important to share information and communicate expectations assertively. After all, how can you expect others to meet your expectations when they don't know what they are? And it's really hard for people to know that they're bugging you if you don't tell them, says **HotelTonight** CEO **Sam Shank**.[219]

Functional and Dysfunctional Conflict. People often think of conflict as "fighting" and view it negatively, which it can be.[220] However, conflict can be positive or negative.[221] *Conflict of ideas* generally leads to changes that improve performance—functional conflict. Conversely, *personal conflict* tends to hurt relationships and decrease performance—dysfunctional conflict.

Functional conflict *exists when disagreement and opposition support the achievement of organizational objectives* Functional conflict can decrease complacency and reveal inefficiencies. This, in turn, can lead to a more positive work environment, increase employee creativity, and enhance motivation, morale, and performance. Have you ever heard coworkers complain to the boss or about each other's performance behind each other's back? Well, the **National Football League**'s **(NFL)** successful **Seattle Seahawks** don't do it; they have a culture of confronting each other about play performance.[222] Tennis doubles players

conflict A situation in which people are in disagreement and opposition.

functional conflict A situation in which disagreement and opposition support the achievement of organizational objectives.

Bob and Mike Bryan say the key to their success is that they get mad and yell at each other about a bad play—and then get over it and act like nothing ever happened.[223]

On the other hand, conflict that prevents the achievement of organizational objectives is negative, or *dysfunctional*, conflict. Dysfunctional conflict is often personal and can bring about many negative outcomes within an organization, including damaged relationships, decreased productivity, revenge, avoidance, and aggression. At **AIG Insurance, CEO Bob Benmosche** and **Chairman Harvey Golub** continually had personal conflicts. To end the conflict, Benmosche said that one of them had to go. The board had to pick one of them—Golub was forced to resign.[224] The same thing happened with **Steve Jobs** at **Apple**, but Jobs was fired.

The longer you wait to deal with conflict, the harder it is to keep it from being dysfunctional. Executives at **Common Forms** waited to discuss when to come out with the company's new tax e-filing app; it was delayed two weeks, and they all agreed they wished they had confronted the issue sooner.[225]

Conflict Management Styles

When you are faced with conflict, you have five conflict management styles to choose from. The five styles, along with concern for your own and others' needs; passive, aggressive, and assertive behavior; and win-lose combinations, are presented in Exhibit 10-4 and are discussed in what follows. Some advantages and disadvantages and the appropriate use of each conflict management style (there is no one best style) are also discussed. Also, realize that personality affects how people respond to conflict. *Agreeable* personality types are more willing to collaborate, whereas *narcissists* are more likely to use force to get their way.

- *Avoiding conflict style,* users attempt to passively ignore conflict rather than resolve it. When you avoid a conflict, you are being unassertive and uncooperative. People avoid conflict by refusing to take a stance, by mentally withdrawing, or by physically leaving. A lose-lose situation results because the conflict is not resolved.

Avoiding can lead to building frustration and blowing up at the person—passive-aggressive behavior, which often results in ongoing arguments, and the conflict is never resolved.[226] So don't let emotions build up; confront others early and stay calm.[227] However, there are times when it is best to avoid an argument over a trivial matter that may hurt your relationship, and when you don't have time, avoid it until you have the time to resolve the conflict.

EXHIBIT 10-4   CONFLICT MANAGEMENT STYLES

• *Accommodating conflict style,* users attempt to resolve conflict by passively giving in to the opposing side. When you use this style, you are being unassertive but cooperative. You attempt to satisfy the needs of others but neglect your own needs by letting others get their own way by doing something you really don't want to do. A win-lose situation is created.

You may like being a follower and maintaining relationships by doing things other people's way, but it is counterproductive when you have a better solution. An overuse of accommodating tends to lead to people taking advantage of you, and the type of relationship you try to maintain is usually lost anyway. We often have to accommodate our bosses, especially when they use a forcing style.

• *Forcing conflict style,* users attempt to resolve conflict by using aggressive behavior to get their own way—narcissists use this style. You are uncooperative and aggressive; you do whatever it takes to satisfy your own needs. Some managers commonly use their position power to force others to do what they want them to do. Forcers use authority, threaten, intimidate, and call for majority rule when they know they will win. Forcers commonly enjoy dealing with avoiders and accommodators.

WORK
APPLICATION 10-10

Think of one of your present or past bosses and give examples of the conflict management style that person used most often.

Overuse of this style leads to hostility, poor relationships, and resentment toward its user. But when the boss is right, like enforcing rules or openly challenging the manager's authority, it should be used.

• Users of the *negotiating conflict style,* also called the *compromising style,* attempt to resolve conflict through assertive give-and-take concessions. When you use the negotiating style, you are moderate in assertiveness and cooperation. An "I win some and you win some" situation is created through compromise.

Compromise may lead to counterproductive results, such as suboptimum decisions. An overuse of this style leads to game playing in which people ask for twice as much as they need in order to get what they want. However, in true negotiation situations, already discussed, it should be used, as well as when the issues are complex and critical and there is no simple and clear solution.

Users of the *collaborating conflict style,* also called the *problem-solving style,* assertively attempt to resolve conflict by working together with the other person to find a solution

10-5 APPLYING THE CONCEPT

Conflict Management Styles

Identify the most appropriate conflict management style to use in each situation.

A. avoiding style

B. accommodating style

C. forcing style

D. negotiating style

E. collaborating style

_____ 21. Usain is over budget for labor this month. The store currently is not busy, so he asks Erica, a part-time employee, to leave work early. Erica tells him she doesn't want to go because she needs the money.

_____ 22. Kendra joined a committee that she has no real interest in to make contacts. At a meeting, she makes a recommendation that is opposed by narcissist Kirkland, who is using a forcing style.

_____ 23. Deanna is on a task force that has to select a new high-tech machine. The four alternatives will all do the job, but team members disagree about the brand, price, and service.

_____ 24. Jessica is the sales manager. Competent sales rep Hemet is trying to close a big sale. The two are discussing the next sales call, and they disagree on the strategy to use to close the sale.

_____ 25. Donald is on his way to an important meeting and running a little late. As he leaves the office, at the other end of the work area he sees Bonita socializing instead of working.

acceptable to all parties. When you use the collaborating approach, you are being assertive and leading to an "I win some and I lose some" situation. For example, two police officers in a patrol car each like different music. If for half the shift they each listen to the music they like, they are negotiating. However, if there is a third station they both like and agree to listen to, this is a collaboration.

Collaborating tends to lead to the best solution to the conflict. However, it takes more skill, effort, and time to resolve conflict. There are situations in which it is difficult to come up with an agreeable solution or when a forcer prevents its use.

If you have problems using the avoiding and accommodating styles when appropriate, work at giving in to others by saying or doing nothing or by going along with others' way of doing things. For most people, the two most difficult styles to develop are the negotiating and collaborating styles. Thus, you already learned how to negotiate, and in the next subsection, you will learn how to resolve conflicts using the collaborative style.

Initiating Conflict Resolution

An initiator is a person who confronts another person(s) in order to resolve conflict. The conflict can be of ideas or personal. Let's face it—some people do things that annoy us.[228] Your objectives should be to change the specific behavior, which may be your own, without hurting your relationship. The way you express conflict will influence perceptions and reactions, changing the way the conflict process unfolds, and subsequently outcomes.[229] Model 10-2, "**The Collaborative Conflict Resolution Model**," is evidence based (EBM)[230] and can help you meet the objective of changing behavior by effectively initiating a conflict resolution.

Step 1. State the problem in terms of behaviors, consequences, and feelings (in a BCF statement). The **BCF statement** describes a conflict in terms of behaviors (B), consequences (C), and feelings (F) in a way that maintains ownership of the problem. What does "maintaining ownership of the problem" mean? Think about it: If you don't smoke and a smoker lights a cigarette, who has the problem? Since the smoker enjoys it, the problem is yours. Maintaining ownership of the problem means being collaborative by expressing it without

- *judging* the behavior as right or wrong, because you can't influence people when you are judging them.[231] "You shouldn't leave this place a mess."

- *assigning blame* about who is right or wrong.[232] Your behavior may be directly or indirectly contributing to the conflict (there are always two sides to every story). "This is all your fault."

- *threatening* the other person.[233] Threats should be a last, not first, option. "If you do it again, I'm going to tell the boss on you."

WORK
APPLICATION 10-11

Which one of the five conflict management styles do you tend to use most often? Explain.

collaborative conflict resolution model A conflict resolution model that calls for (1) stating the problem in a BCF statement, (2) getting the other party to acknowledge the problem or conflict, (3) asking for and/or presenting alternative resolutions to the conflict, and (4) coming to an agreement.

BCF statement A statement that describes a conflict in terms of behaviors, consequences, and feelings in a way that maintains ownership of the problem.

MODEL 10-2   THE COLLABORATIVE CONFLICT RESOLUTION MODEL

INITIATOR	RESPONDER	MEDIATOR
Step 1. State the problem in terms of behaviors, consequences, and feelings (in a BCF statement).	*Step 1.* Respond as appropriate to the initiator's statement of the problem, using your own BCF statements.	*Step 1.* Bring the conflicting parties together and help them resolve the conflict by coaching them as they follow the steps in the model.
Step 2. Get the other person to acknowledge the problem or conflict.	*Step 2.* Acknowledge the problem or conflict.	*Step 2.* Remain neutral, focusing on how the conflict is affecting work.
Step 3. Ask for and/or present alternative resolutions to the conflict.	*Step 3.* Discuss alternative resolutions to the conflict.	*Step 3.* Address behavior, not personalities.
Step 4. Come to an agreement.	*Step 4.* Come to an agreement.	*Step 4.* Encourage the parties to clarify their statements and responses.
		Step 5. Follow up to make sure the parties carry out the actions they agree to in step 4.

- *telling* the person what to do. Do you like people telling you what to do? Or don't start with a solution? Notice that is steps 3 and 4. "Next time, ask me first."

- *using inappropriate wording.* [234] Don't say, "You never/always/constantly do it."

Do you like people to confront you by judging, blaming, threatening, or telling you what to do? These statements are not collaborative and only make people defensive and emotional, and you can end up arguing rather than resolving the conflict.

Don't confront people because you don't like their personality;[235] you're not going to change it. There really is no such thing as a personality conflict; it's about specific things people do and say that bother you. So construct a short BCF statement. For example, "When you smoke around me (B), I have trouble breathing and become nauseous (C), and I feel ill and stressed (F)." Note that you can vary the sequence if the situation warrants it. Because how you initiate the conflict is so important to how it unfolds leading to its resolution,[236] Skill Builder 10-2 will help you develop effective BCF statements.

After planning your BCF statement, think of some possible solutions you might suggest in step 3. Be sure your ideas take into consideration the other person's point of view. Put yourself in his or her position—use empathy.[237] If you were the other person, would you like the solutions you have thought of? And don't be surprised if the other person comes up with things you do that bother him or her, and again you are collaborating, so you need to be open to changing.

Step 2. Get the other person to acknowledge the problem or conflict. After stating your BCF, let the other person respond. If the other person doesn't understand or acknowledge the problem, repeat your statement in different terms, if necessary. Stay calm and don't argue.

Step 3. Ask for and/or present alternative resolutions to the conflict. Next, ask the person how the conflict might be resolved. If he or she acknowledges the problem but seems unwilling to resolve it, appeal to common goals. Try to make the other person realize how he or she, the team, the department, or the company might also benefit from a solution to this conflict.

Step 4. Come to an agreement. Determine what specific actions you will each take to resolve the conflict. Perhaps the person will agree not to smoke in your presence now that he or she knows how it affects you. Clearly state whatever actions you each agree to.

Skill Builder 10-3 will give you a chance to practice initiating a conflict resolution using the model.

Responding to and Mediating Conflict Resolution

Responding to Conflict Resolution. In the role of responder, you have a responsibility to contribute to successful conflict resolution when someone confronts you with a problem. You should keep in mind the "Responder" steps in the middle of Model 10-2.

Mediating Conflict Resolution. Frequently, parties in conflict cannot resolve their dispute alone. In these cases, a mediator may be used.[238] A **mediator** *is a neutral third party who helps resolve a conflict.* As a manager, you may be called upon to serve as a mediator between two or more employees or groups of employees. In this case, remember that you should be a mediator, not a judge. Get the employees to resolve the conflict themselves, if possible. Remain impartial unless one party is violating company policies, and follow the "Mediator" steps on the right in Model 10-2.

When bringing conflicting employees together, focus on how the conflict is affecting their work. Discuss the issues by addressing specific behavior, not personalities. If a person says, "We cannot work together because of a personality conflict," ask him or her to identify the specific behavior that is the root of the conflict. The discussion should make the employees aware of their behavior and of how its consequences are causing the conflict.

WORK
APPLICATION 10-12

Describe a conflict in which you used (or should have used) a BCF statement.

mediator A neutral third party who helps resolve a conflict.

If the conflict cannot be resolved by mediation, an arbitrator may be used as a follow-up. An **arbitrator** *is a neutral third party who resolves a conflict by making a binding decision.* The arbitrator is like a judge whose decision must be followed. However, the use of arbitration should be kept to a minimum because it is not a collaborative conflict style.

Managers should be aware of employees' stress. While functional stress can lead to high productivity, minimal or excessive stress can lead to lower performance.

Stress

Stress *is the body's reaction to environmental demands.* This reaction can be emotional and/or physical. Stress levels are on a continuum from low to high. All of the chapter topics can cause stress and negative attitudes, including a lack of *work–life balance.*[239] But stress is an individual perception matter. Some people are better at handling stress than others. In the same situation, one person may be very comfortable and stress free while another is stressed out. Here we discuss functional and dysfunctional stress, causes of job stress, how to manage stress, and the stress tug-of-war analogy.

Functional and Dysfunctional Stress. With no or low stress, people tend to just take it easy and waste time, and performance is lower, which is *dysfunctional.* An optimal level of stress, like a deadline, is *functional* because it helps improve performance; it is also called *eustress.*[240] However, beyond a certain point, stress stops being helpful and becomes *dysfunctional* because it hurts performance. It can also lead to *burnout,* a constant lack of interest and motivation to perform one's job.[241] Burnout can cause mental and physical health problems including colds, weight gain, sleep dysfunction, heart disease, depression, ulcers and other stomach problems, and back, neck, and shoulder pain.[242]

Causes of Job Stress. Here are nine common causes of job stress:

- **Personality type.** The *Type A personality* is characterized as fast moving, hard driving, time conscious, competitive, impatient, and preoccupied with work.[243] The *Type B personality* is the opposite of Type A. In general, people with Type A personalities experience more stress than people with Type B personalities. Complete Self-Assessment 10-5 to determine your personality type as it relates to stress.

- **Organizational culture.** Cultures that are like Type As are more stressful.

- **Organizational change.** Changes can be stressful, especially if they are discontinuous.

- **Management behavior.** The manager (bad boss) is often a cause of stress put on employees.[244]

- **Type of work.** Some types of work are more stressful than others.

- **Interpersonal relations.** Conflicts among coworkers can be very stressful.

- **Procrastination and perfectionism.** Intentionally delaying getting the task done despite foreseeable negative future consequences is procrastination. Perfectionism can be a form of procrastination in getting started and finishing, and it adds stress and waste time when little improvements delay task completion.[245]

- **Time pressure.** The time pressure of a deadline can help motivate competing the task,[246] but too much time pressure of deadlines can be very stressful.[247]

- **Smartphones.** Recall from Chapter 5 that smartphones are actually more of a time waster than saver, as the average person stares at his or her phone 221 times per day. Repeatedly checking your phone, especially after work hours, can be stressful. Constantly looking at your phone creates eyestrain, and looking down puts stress on your neck and shoulders, which can cause long-term problems.[248]

arbitrator A neutral third party who resolves a conflict by making a binding decision.

stress The body's reaction to environmental demands.

PeopleImages via Getty Images

10-5 SELF-ASSESSMENT

Personality Type and Stress

Identify how frequently each item applies to you at work or school. Place a number from 1 (*rarely*) to 5 (*usually*) on the line before each statement.

5 = usually	4 = often	3 = occasionally	2 = seldom	1 = rarely

_____ 1. I enjoy competition, and I work/play to win.

_____ 2. I skip meals or eat fast when there is a lot of work to do.

_____ 3. I'm in a hurry.

_____ 4. I do more than one thing at a time.

_____ 5. I'm aggravated and upset.

_____ 6. I get irritated or anxious when I have to wait.

_____ 7. I measure progress in terms of time and performance.

_____ 8. I push myself to work to the point of getting tired.

_____ 9. I work on days off.

_____10. I set short deadlines for myself.

_____11. I'm not satisfied with my accomplishments for very long.

_____12. I try to outperform others.

_____13. I get upset when my schedule has to be changed.

_____14. I consistently try to get more done in less time.

_____15. I take on more work when I already have plenty to do.

_____16. I enjoy work/school more than other activities.

_____17. I talk and walk fast.

_____18. I set high standards for myself and work hard to meet them.

_____19. I'm considered a hard worker by others.

_____20. I work at a fast pace.

_____ Total

Add up the numbers you assigned to all 20 items. Your score will range from 20 to 100. Indicate where your score falls on the continuum below.

100	90	80	70	60	50	40	30	20

Type A   Type B

The higher your score, the more characteristic you are of the Type A personality. The lower your score, the more characteristic you are of the Type B personality.

Stress Management

Stress management is the process of eliminating or reducing stress. Many organizations today are making stress a priority through training employees in stress management because it improves the bottom line.[249] Here are eight stress management techniques you can use to decrease stress:

- *Time management.* Generally, people with good time management skills experience less job stress.[250] Refer to Chapter 5 for details on time management.

- *Relaxation.* It is important that you relax to help yourself unwind. Finding a hobby or activity you enjoy, taking a vacation, laughing, and performing relaxation exercises (see Exhibit 10-5) are all ways in which you can relax. Religious practices also combat stress, as nearly 100 studies found a positive association between religious involvement and better health, longevity, incomes, and happiness.[251]

- *Sleep.* A good night's sleep makes you more productive.[252] Recent research found that 7 hours of sleep a night is the best amount of sleep to function the next day—not 8; and skimping on a full night's sleep, even by 20 minutes, impairs performance and memory the next day. But too much sleep is associated with diabetes, obesity, and cardiovascular disease. Of course, not everyone is average, and some people need more sleep than others.[253] A lack of sleep can even cause brain damage,[254] and it also makes you more selfish and emotional, and you are more likely to get into arguments and hurt relationships.[255]

- *Nutrition.* Good health is essential to everyone's performance, and nutrition is a major factor in health.[256] Eating a well-balanced breakfast provides the body with nutrients to help cope with stress all day. Too often people turn to cigarettes, alcohol/drugs, caffeine (coffee/energy drinks), junk food, and too much sleep to "manage" stress. While these may provide short-term relief, they often create other long-term problems. The general rule is to limit your intake of white bread, flour, and sugar, as well as processed foods including fried foods. Artificial sweeteners, like in coffee and diet soda, may not have sugar or calories, but they do increase your risk of developing diabetes and other health problems.[257]

- *Exercise.* Staying fit can reduce the production of stress hormones.[258] Physical exercise is an excellent way to improve health while releasing stress.[259] Virtually any form of exercise can act as a stress reliever, such as fast walking or jogging, biking,

EXHIBIT 10-5   ## RELAXATION TECHNIQUES

Head and Neck	Back and Core	Legs and Feet	Shoulders and Arms
Forehead: Wrinkle forehead by trying to make eyebrows touch hairline; hold for 5 seconds.	**Back:** Lie on back on the floor or a bed and arch back up off the floor while keeping shoulders and buttocks on the floor; tighten for 5 seconds.	**Thighs:** Press thighs together and tighten for 5 seconds.	**Shoulders:** Lift shoulders up to ears and tighten for 5 seconds.
Eyes, nose: Close eyes tightly for 5 seconds.	**Stomach:** Suck in and tighten stomach muscles for 5 seconds.	**Feet, ankles:** Flex feet with toes pointing up as far as possible and hold position for 5 seconds.	**Upper arms:** Bend elbows and tighten upper arm muscles for 5 seconds.
Lips, cheeks, jaw: Draw corners of mouth back tightly in a grimace; hold for 5 seconds.	**Hips, buttocks:** Tighten buttocks for 5 seconds.	**Toes:** Curl toes under and tighten for 5 seconds; then wiggle toes to relax them.	**Forearms:** Extend arms out against an invisible wall and push forward with hands for 5 seconds.
Neck: Drop chin to chest; then slowly rotate head without tilting it back.			**Hands:** Extend arms to front; then clench fists tightly for 5 seconds.

swimming, weight lifting, and playing sports. You are more likely to stick with it if you perform an exercise you enjoy. Exercising with a partner helps.

- **Positive thinking.** People with an optimistic personality and attitude generally have less stress than pessimists.[260] As discussed, you become what you think, and you can become more positive and optimistic.

- **Support network.** Talking to others in a support network can help reduce stress. Develop a network of family, friends, and peers you can go to for help with your problems. But don't be a whiner that people want to avoid.

- **Cut back smartphone checking.** Stop your addiction to constantly looking at it. Set a time limit of frequency of checking it (such as every half hour), or better yet shut it off for an extended period when you can, especially when you have a high priority task to complete. When looking at it, hold it higher to help avoid neck and shoulder stress.[261] Also, place your other screens (computer monitor, TV) higher so you look up a bit to help offset your downward pressure.

- **Others.** Take time for yourself[262] and reward yourself.[263] Stop procrastinating;[264] deal with your most unpleasant tasks early in the day.[265] As **Nike** says, just do it! Also, stop wasting time trying for perfection and using it as an excuse to procrastinate doing the next task. Define perfection within a reasonable time, and finish it. When given unrealistic deadlines, try to negotiate for more time.

WORK
APPLICATION 10-13

When experiencing stress at school or work, identify which of the stress management techniques you believe you can put into practice.

You don't need to use all of the stress management techniques to help deal with stress. Select some that you enjoy and make them a habit.

The Stress Tug-of-War. Think of stress as a tug-of-war with you in the center, as illustrated in Exhibit 10-6. On the left are causes of stress trying to pull you away from functional stress toward dysfunctional stress. On the right are stress management techniques you use to keep yourself in the center. If the stress becomes too powerful, it will pull you off center. The functional stress turns into dysfunctional stress, and as a result, your performance suffers. The stress tug-of-war is an ongoing game. On easy days, you move to the right, and on overly tough days, you move to the left. Your main objective is to stay in the center.

Owning several businesses, **Michael Jordan** (**IOM 5**) had to do lots of negotiating to start the new ventures and to get people to run them for him. Obviously, as in any organization, as a manager, MJ has to deal with conflict daily. If you have watched MJ play basketball, you realize he is good at dealing with stress.

Trends and Issues in Management

People do think differently nationally and internationally, but thoughts do affect behavior *globally*. The Big Five personality dimensions do apply globally, as traits can be classified into one

---

10-2 **JOIN THE DISCUSSION** ETHICS & SOCIAL RESPONSIBILITY

Obesity

Being overweight places stress on the body, and poor nutrition contributes to obesity. Obesity is on the increase, and it is a major contributor to the rising cost of health care. Health officials are trying to persuade Americans to lose weight. The government has released public service ads to convince people to get in shape and eat right.

1. Is there prejudice and discrimination against obese people at work?

2. Is it ethical and socially responsible for the government to try to get people to lose weight through ads and other methods?

3. What is the reason for the increase in obesity in the United States? Are restaurant owners and other food marketers responsible for the obesity problem, or are consumers at fault?

EXHIBIT 10-6   THE STRESS TUG-OF-WAR

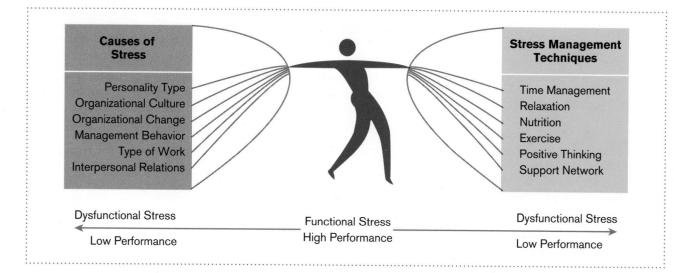

of the five dimensions. Perceptions and attitudes also vary. As discussed in Chapter 3, there are differences in the GLOBE dimensions, including assertiveness and the use of political behavior being low in Switzerland and high in the United States. There is diversity in gender differences being low in the United States but high in China. People in the United States tend to dislike power distance, whereas in Thailand it is accepted, and America is more individualistic and confrontational than Japan, which is more collectivist. With international negotiations, Americans need to realize that in many countries, especially Asian countries, negotiators are more ceremonial and are much slower to reach a deal. They often want to get to know and trust you over time. So you may need to be patient in order to close a foreign deal.

Gender and minority differences do exist. Women and minorities are often stereotyped as not being as competent as white men. Men are often perceived to be competent until shown otherwise, whereas women and minorities have to prove they are competent.[266] Research supports that across 62 cultural regions worldwide, in general, men have higher levels of attachment avoidance and seek to avoid negative emotions and conflict more than women. Women tend to like to talk through problems, whereas men want to solve them and move on.[267] We all have biases in perception and only want to accept *data* that supports what we think.[268]

People do have different perceptions and attitudes toward *technology*. Although technology keeps wiping out jobs, interpersonal skills are critical to technology jobs, as it is teams of people that create technology.[269] To help deal with stress and improve health, companies are developing *genomics* technology.[270] Employee wellness firms and insurers (**Castlight Healthcare**) are working with companies (**Walmart**) to mine big data to improve employee health and keep health care costs down.[271] **Oscar Insurance** is pushing wearable technology. Customers can request a plastic, **Bluetooth**-enabled **Misfit Flash** pendant for free and wear it to keep track of daily activity and sleep.[272] The **Apple** Watch is enabled with more than 10 sensors to monitor health and fitness signs. **Kaiser Permanente** insurance, the **Mayo Clinic**, and **Memorial Sloan Kettering Cancer Center** are working with Apple to build apps that work with Apple's offerings, including **HealthKit**, which channels information from various devices to doctors.[273] *Brain training* devices offered by **Melon, Emotiv Insight, Melomind, iFocusBand**, and **Narbis** consists of wearable gadgets that promise to monitor or stimulate your brain to make you calmer, more focused—perhaps even smarter.[274]

We need to be *ethical* and *socially responsible* in our relationships, and it can be tempting to abuse power and politics to force others we are in conflict with to give us what we want. But honesty is the best policy. Why are there usually two versions of the events leading to the same conflict? Are people lying? Sometimes, but the difference is often based on perception biases, especially selectivity, as we tend to remember our side of the story.[275] Negotiations often leave room for morally iffy gamesmanship.[276]

Michael Jordan (IOM 6) faced ethical issues back in 1993 when he was a basketball player. During the Bulls' playoff run, controversy arose when Jordan was seen gambling in Atlantic City, New Jersey, the night before a game against the New York Knicks. In that same year, he admitted to having to cover $57,000 in gambling losses. MJ stated that his gambling was under control and didn't jeopardize his financial situation, which today is apparent, as he owns multiple businesses.

Having read this chapter, you should understand the foundations of individual behavior: thoughts, self-confidence, self-esteem, personality, perception, and attitude. You should also understand the role that power and politics play in organizations. You should be able to negotiate and manage and resolve conflicts properly. Finally, you should understand the causes of stress and how to minimize it.

$SAGE edge™   edge.sagepub.com/lussier8e

Want a better grade?

Get the tools you need to sharpen your study skills. Access practice quizzes, eFlashcards, video and multimedia, and more at edge.sagepub.com/lussier8e.

Digital Resources

Learning Objective	Digital Resource
10-1. Define *behavior* and *organizational behavior* (OB), state the goals of OB, and explain the relationship between thoughts and self-confidence and self-esteem.	▶ Organizational Behavior
10-2. Describe each of the Big Five personality dimensions.	▶ Big 5 Personality Traits
10-3. Explain the perception and attribution processes, and describe five perception biases.	▶ Stereotyping of Gender in Workplace*
10-4. Recall how attitudes affect job satisfaction and how employee and managerial attitudes affect employee performance.	▶ Job Satisfaction and Attitudes
10-5. List the six OB foundations, summarize how to shape your own and your management foundations, and discuss managing diversity in three critical foundations.	▶ Visual Perception
10-6. Discuss the relationship between organizational power and politics and their importance to organizational performance.	▣ Power and Politics
10-7. Identify the four parts of the negotiation process, define the five conflict management styles, state how to initiate a conflict resolution, and explain the stress tug-of-war.	▶ Negotiation* ▶ Management in Action: Negotiating*

* premium video available only in the interactive eBook

● ● ● CHAPTER SUMMARY

10-1. **Define *behavior* and *organizational behavior* (OB), state the goals of OB, and explain the relationship between thoughts and self-confidence and self-esteem.**

Behavior is the things we do and say, or our actions. *OB* is the study of actions that affect performance in the workplace. The *goal of OB theorists* is to understand, explain, predict, and influence behavior to improve performance. Thoughts affect behavior and what happens to people, so thoughts also affect self-confidence to perform a specific task, and overall self-esteem is influenced by thoughts.

10-2. **Describe each of the Big Five personality dimensions.**

Extroversion lies on a continuum between extrovert and introvert; *agreeableness* between easy and difficult to work with; *emotionalism* between stability and instability; *conscientiousness* between responsible/dependable and irresponsible/undependable; and *openness to experience* between willing to try new things and not being willing to do so.

10-3. **Explain the perception and attribution processes, and describe five perception biases.**

Perception is the process of selecting, organizing, and interpreting environmental information. *Attribution* is the process of determining the reason for someone's behavior and whether that behavior is situational or intentional. Situational behavior is either accidental or out of the control of the individual, whereas intentional behavior is done on purpose. Five biases to perception include *selectivity*, using information to support desired outcomes; *frame of reference*, seeing things from one's own point of view; *stereotyping*, using generalizations about a group to judge individuals; *expectations*, hearing what we anticipate; and the *"like me" assumption*, believing others perceive things as we do and that our way is the best.

10-4. **Recall how attitudes affect job satisfaction and how employee and managerial attitudes affect employee performance.**

Job satisfaction is a person's positive or negative attitude toward the job. Generally, people with positive attitudes about their jobs have higher levels of job satisfaction, and vice versa. Employees' job attitudes tend to lead to living up or down to their performance expectations through the *self-fulfilling prophecy*. Through the *Pygmalion effect*, managers' attitudes toward and expectations and treatment of employees largely determine their performance. Having employees with positive "I can do this" attitudes with managerial support leads to higher levels of performance.

10-5. **List the six OB foundations, summarize how to shape your own and your management foundations, and discuss managing diversity in three critical foundations.**

The six OB foundations are thought, self-confidence, self-esteem, personalities, perceptions, and attitudes. To continuously improve your own behavior and performance in each of the foundation areas, you need to make a conscious effort and work at it. To shape your management behavior, you need to realize that the OB foundations affect how you manage employees and to continually work on them. Employees have a diversity of OB foundations, and managers need to hire for these positive foundations and avoid hiring people with poor foundations. Also, managers need to continually work with employees to improve their OB foundations. Three critical foundations to work on begin with employee thoughts because they affect all the other foundations. A second critical foundation is perception congruence of employee performance, and third is to implement the Pygmalion effect, because these foundations also affect the other OB foundations.

10-6. **Discuss the relationship between organizational power and politics and their importance to organizational performance.**

Power is the ability to influence others' behavior. *Politics* is the process of gaining and using power; it is a medium of exchange. Like money, power and politics in and of themselves are neither good nor bad. They are simply means of getting what we want—meeting objectives. Leadership is the process of influencing employees to work toward achieving objectives, so power and politics go hand in hand with leadership because power and politics are the means used to achieve organizational objectives.

10-7. **Identify the four parts of the negotiation process, define the five conflict management styles, state how to initiate a conflict resolution, and explain the stress tug-of-war.**

The negotiation process includes (1) planning for the negotiation, (2) conducting the negotiation, (3) possibly postponement, and (4) reaching an agreement or not.

The five conflict management styles include (1) The user of the *avoiding conflict style* attempts to passively ignore conflict rather than resolve it. (2) The user of the *accommodating conflict style* attempts to resolve the conflict by passively giving in to the other party. (3) The user of the *forcing conflict style* attempts to resolve conflict by using aggressive behavior to get his or her own way. (4) The user of the *negotiating conflict style* attempts to resolve conflict through assertive give-and-take concessions. (5) The user of the *collaborating conflict style* assertively attempts to resolve conflict by working together with the other party to find an acceptable solution.

The steps in the initiating conflict resolution model are: Step 1. State the problem in terms of behaviors, consequences, and feelings (in a BCF statement), *Step 2.* Get the other person to acknowledge the problem or conflict, *Step 3.* Ask for and/or present alternative resolutions to the conflict, and *Step 4.* Come to an agreement.

In the stress tug-of-war, you are in the center, where stress is functional and performance is high. On your left are the causes of stress trying to pull you off center. On your right are the stress management techniques you use to keep yourself in the center. If the causes of stress pull you off center, the stress turns dysfunctional, and as a result, your performance decreases. If there is an absence of stress, performance is also decreased.

••• KEY TERMS

arbitrator, 349
attitudes, 331
attribution, 328
BCF statement, 347
citizenship behavior, 332
coalition, 338

collaborative conflict resolution model, 347
conflict, 344
functional conflict, 344
mediator, 348
organizational behavior, 321
perception, 327

personality, 323
politics, 335
power, 335
Pygmalion effect, 333
reciprocity, 338
stress, 349

••• KEY TERM REVIEW

Complete each of the following statements using one of this chapter's key terms.

1. _____ is the study of actions that affect performance in the workplace.
2. _____ is a combination of behavioral, mental, and emotional traits that define an individual.
3. _____ is the process of selecting, organizing, and interpreting environmental information.
4. _____ is the process of determining the reason for someone's behavior and whether that behavior is situational or intentional.
5. _____ are positive or negative evaluations of people, things, and situations.
6. _____ refers to employee efforts that go above and beyond the call of duty.
7. The _____ is the theory that managers' attitudes toward and expectations and treatment of employees largely determine their performance.
8. _____ is the ability to influence others' behavior.
9. _____ is the process of gaining and using power.
10. _____ is the process of developing relationships for the purpose of career building and socializing.

11. _____ involves the mutual exchange of favors and privileges to accomplish objectives.
12. A _____ is a network of alliances that help achieve an objective.
13. A _____ exists whenever people are in disagreement and opposition.
14. _____ exists when disagreement and opposition support the achievement of organizational objectives.
15. A _____ describes a conflict in terms of behaviors, consequences, and feelings in a way that maintains ownership of the problem.
16. The _____ calls for (1) stating the problem in a BCF statement, (2) getting the other party to acknowledge the problem or conflict, (3) asking for and/or presenting alternative resolutions to the conflict, and (4) coming to an agreement.
17. A _____ is a neutral third party who helps resolve a conflict.
18. An _____ is a neutral third party who resolves a conflict by making a binding decision.
19. _____ is the body's reaction to environmental demands.

••• REVIEW QUESTIONS

1. What are the Big Five personality dimensions?
2. What are five biases in perception?
3. What are the determinants of job satisfaction? Are they of equal importance to everyone?

4. What are the seven types of power?

5. Can managers order that power and politics in an organization be abolished? If yes, should they?

6. Why should you learn the organizational culture and identify power players where you work?

7. How do you know when you are in conflict?

8. What is the difference between functional and dysfunctional conflict, and how does each affect performance?

9. What does it mean to "maintain ownership of a problem"?

10. What is the difference between a mediator and an arbitrator?

11. What are the characteristics of a Type A personality?

12. What are six stress management techniques?

• • • COMMUNICATION SKILLS

The following critical-thinking questions can be used for class discussion and/or as written assignments to develop communication skills. Be sure to give complete explanations for all questions.

1. Does personality really play a part in your personal and professional happiness and success? Can you change your personality? If so, how?

2. Why do most people use attribution rather than ask people why they do and say the things they do? How often do you use attribution rather than asking people? Why?

3. Does the Pygmalion effect really work? Why or why not?

4. What is your attitude toward power and politics in organizations? Should power and politics be changed, and if so, how?

5. Which of the guidelines for developing political skills do you think is most important? Why?

6. What are the most relevant points you learned about negotiation that you didn't already know and use? Will you follow the steps in the negotiation process in future negotiations?

7. Which of the conflict management styles do you tend to use most often? Why?

8. How much stress do you have in your life? When do you tend to have more stress, and what is or are the major cause or causes of the stress?

9. Which of the stress management techniques listed in the text do you use currently? Can you think of or do you use any other stress management techniques that are not listed in the text?

CASES

• • • Case 10-1   GlaxoSmithKline

GlaxoSmithKline is a global healthcare company that operates in three business sectors: pharmaceuticals, vaccines, and consumer healthcare. The company was incorporated in 1999 and is headquartered in the United Kingdom. Its mission is: "To help people to do more, feel better, live longer." The company's primary business objectives are to increase growth, reduce risk, and improve long-term financial performance. These objectives translate into strategic priorities to grow a balanced global business, deliver more products of value, simplify the operating model, and be a responsible business. The company's core values are patient focus, integrity, respect for people, and transparency. GlaxoSmithKline is also a very socially responsible company—it maintains a strong commitment to four key areas: Health for All, Our Behavior, Our People, and Our Planet.

The company's commitment to "Our People" includes an emphasis on creating a healthy and safe work environment for all of its employees through the offering of preventive healthcare services, counseling services, coaching, and "resilience" workshops that are designed to help employees to manage stress more effectively and to function in a dynamic, complex, global, and challenging work environment.

The first Resilience Program was launched in 2001. After four years in operation, the program resulted in a 60% reduction in work-related behavioral health issues and a 29% decline in work days lost due to mental health issues. The success of the initial Resilience Program led to the creation of a Team Resilience program that encouraged employee work groups to identify and reduce or eliminate job and situational stressors such as workload and management practices that can undermine job performance.

Today, GlaxoSmithKline offers a portfolio of Energy and Resilience Programs for employees that include:

- Energy for Performance—A workshop for individuals emphasizing work/life balance and emotional well-being.

- Personal Resilience. A workshop for individuals to better manage work-related and personal stressors.

- Team Resilience. A workshop for empowering teams to take a collaborative approach toward wellness and stress management.

These workshops are also supported by occupational health physicians and nurses who employees have access to if they have questions or concerns.

The results from the Energy and Resilience programs have been overwhelmingly positive:

- Participation in the Energy for Performance Programs was positively associated with an employee's sense of empowerment.

- Team Resilience program resulted in an 80% decrease in workplace pressures, a 25% drop in work/life conflict, and a 21% increase in satisfaction with GSK as an employer.

- The Personal Resilience program was associated with improvement in 7 out of 10 indices, including: tiredness, anxiety, anger, relaxed, positive attitude, employee engagement, and self-management.

- An assessment of the Energy for Performance Program found that 31% of respondents reported "significant to very significant" improvement in physical, emotional, mental, and spiritual capacity 12 months after the workshop.

The Energy and Team Resilience programs have also received a number of awards such as the Alliance for Work Life Progress's Work-Life Innovative Excellence Award in 2006.

Discussion Questions

1. What types of job stressors are likely to exist in the GlaxoSmithKline work environment?

2. What are the benefits of the Energy and Resilience programs for GlaxoSmithKline as a company in terms of functional versus dysfunctional stress?

3. What are the benefits of the Energy and Resilience programs for GlaxoSmithKline employees in terms of functional versus dysfunctional stress?

4. Which of the stress management strategies discussed in this chapter are likely to be addressed by the Team Resilience program?

5. Do you think that work stress is a growing problem in the workplace these days? Why or why not?

6. What would you do if you were a manager and one of your employees was showing signs of high stress and burnout?

References

http://www.businessinsurance.com/article/20080622/STORY/100025211?template=printart

http://www.gsk.com/en-gb/careers/working-at-gsk/employee-health-safety-and-well-being/

http://us.gsk.com/en-us/responsibility/our-people/working-at-gsk/improving-health-safety-and-resilience/

http://us.gsk.com/en-us/careers/working-at-gsk/employee-health-safety-and-well-being/

http://us.gsk.com/en-us/about-us/

http://www.reuters.com/finance/stocks/companyProfile?symbol=GSK

Case created by Loren Kuzuhara, University of Wisconsin–Madison.

• • • Case 10-2   Changing Times: Has IBM (I've Been Moved) Become TTMJ (They Took My Job)?

International Business Machines (IBM) bets that cognition is the ignition for growth. The company, the world's top provider of computer products and services, is increasingly investing in its cognitive computing system, Watson. The artificial intelligence system helps customers in a wide range of business analyze massive amounts of data to make better decisions. The company's information technology, business services, and software units are now among the largest in the world. While it has moved from hardware to a large degree, the company maintains industry-leading enterprise server and data storage products lines. IBM is transforming its operations as it deals with a rapidly changing technology environment....

As the company works to reposition itself to capitalize on data, analytics, and cloud computing (all parts of its cognitive initiatives), among other areas, its revenue has dropped for four consecutive years. In 2015 sales were off 12% from 2014, falling to $81.7 billion from $92.8 billion. Revenue slipped in all of its segments. Its two biggest businesses, Global Technology Services and Global Business Services, posted the biggest drops, 10% and 12%, respectively.

The company saw a boost in profit in 2015, posting net income of $13.7 billion, 10% higher than 2014. A lower loss on discontinued operations in 2015 from 2014 helped increase the profit.

Cash flow from operations improved a hair to $17 billion in 2015 from $16.9 billion in 2014. (1)

Financial woes have required strategic repositioning of IBM, which has had some negative side effects. Turmoil has befallen the ranks of IBM's existing work force as reports of "resource actions" (i.e., layoffs) continue to surface. A reading of the "Watch IBM" Facebook page shows clearly that worries continue.... Douglas A. McIntyre wrote, "It's a simple question, presumably with a simple answer. How many of its American employees has International Business Machines Corp. fired in the past year? Or two? Or five?" (2)

Robert X. Cringley cuts to the heart of the matter for many long-term IBM employees.

> The IBMers I hear from, and there are lots of them, are generally either pissed-off or scared. But it's frankly far too late to save the IBM they remember. That company has been gone for years.... That has to be a kick in the head to all the IBM old-timers who had been waiting for the axe to fall no matter how good they were at their jobs.... The best they can hope for is a little clarity and leverage concerning the terms under which they are being shown the door.... IBM used to be able to count on its size, its people, its loyal customers, but all of those are going

or gone. Apple or Google could buy IBM with cash on hand, so it's no longer the *Big Kahuna*. IBMers of yore are all gone and for the current breed, it is just another job.(3)

Rather than directly responding to criticism of past practices, IBM CEO Ginni Rometty has said Big Blue will hire 25,000 professionals in the United States and invest $1 billion in the training and development of those employees over the next four years. Rometty said IBM would make 6,000 of those hires in 2017, yet there seems to be a shift away from the tradition of a highly educated workforce.(4)

…in many other cases, new collar jobs may not require a traditional college degree. In fact, at a number of IBM's locations spread across the United States, as many as one-third of employees don't have a four-year degree. What matters most is that these employees—with jobs such as cloud computing technicians and services delivery specialists—have relevant skills, often obtained through vocational training.—Ginni Rometty(5)

Even with the shift in personnel, and naysayers abound, IBM continues to create break-through technology. A team of IBM researchers just created the world's smallest magnet using a solitary atom. Furthermore, they packed it with one bit of digital data for good measure. Future applications of this discovery could allow people to store 1,000 times more information in the same amount of space. For a more practical illustration of the scale, IBM says a system using the tiny magnets could potentially hold the entire iTunes music library—that is *35 million* songs—on a drive the size of a credit card.(6)

Discussion Questions

1. Describe the impact of job layoffs and job "moves" on the current workforce's self-esteem and self-confidence.

2. Use the concept of locus of control to explain the opinion that all the IBM old-timers have been waiting for the axe to fall no matter how good they were at their jobs.

3. Using attribution theory, describe the two main differing perspectives on IBM's future as described in the case.

4. Robert X. Cringely sees IBM as dying (from the article title), while IBM CEO Ginni Rometty views IBM as strong

and growing. These differing viewpoints illustrate what perceptual principle?

5. Your attitude toward IBM may have been affected by reading this case. Why might that attitude influence your future dealings with IBM products, services, and employees?

6. What types of power did IBM CEO Ginni Rometty demonstrate in this case?

7. The "Watch IBM" Facebook page may be considered what form(s) of political behavior?

8. What factors might cause old-time IBM employees to feel job stress?

Cumulative Case Questions

9. Describe how IBM's shift to a vocational workforce will affect the firm's culture (Chapter 2).

10. What type of planning encompasses IBM's shift from being a top provider of computer products and services to investing in its cognitive computing systems (Chapter 5)?

11. What types of changes are described in this case (Chapter 6)?

12. What human resources management processes are addressed in the case (Chapter 9)?

References

(1) Green, T. (n.d.). International Business Machines, Corporation. Hoovers. Retrieved March 9, 2017, from http://0-subscriber.hoovers.com.liucat.lib.liu.edu/H/company360/fulldescription.html? companyId=10796000000000

(2) Wral, R. S. (2017, January 26). As another reorg hits, IBM employee turmoil grows despite CEO's pledge to add 25,000 jobs. Wral@TechWire. Retrieved March 9, 2017, from http://wraltechwire.com/ ibm-employee-turmoil-grows-even-as-ceo-promises-25-000-jobs/16470366/#vtmZ2e-3iCezz7 163.99

(3) Cringley, R. X. (2016, March 8). What's happening at IBM (it's dying). I, Cringley. Retrieved March 9, 2017, from http://www.cringely.com/2016/03/08/whats-happening-at-ibm/

(4) Lawson, S. (2016, December 14). IBM's plans to hire 25,000 U.S. workers aren't new. Computerworld. Retrieved March 9, 2017, from http://www.computerworld.com/article/3150527/it-industry/ibms-plans-to-hire-25000-us-workers-arent-new.html

(5) Rometty, G. (2016, December 13). We need to fill "new collar" jobs that employers demand: IBM's Rometty. USA Today. Retrieved March 9, 2017, from http://www.usatoday.com/story/tech/columnist/2016/12/13/we-need-fill-new-collar-jobs-employers-demand-ibms-rometty/95382248/

(6) Williams, B. (2017, March 8). IBM researchers made a magnet with a single atom—then stuffed digital data into it. Mashable. Retrieved March 9, 2017, from http://mashable.com/2017/03/08/ibm-atom-magnet-data-storage/#.zZoVuWQM5qY

Case created by Herbert Sherman, Long Island University.

••• SKILL BUILDER 10-1: CAR DEALER NEGOTIATION[a]

Preparing for Skill Builder 10-1

Before beginning Skill Builder 10-1, read and be sure you understand the text discussion of the negotiation process.

Objective

To develop your understanding of power and to build negotiation skills.

Skills

The primary skills developed through this exercise are:

1. *Management skill*—interpersonal (negotiation)

2. *AACSB competencies*—communication abilities and analytic skills

3. *Management function*—leading (through influencing others)

Experience

You will be the buyer or seller of a used car.

Procedure 1 (1–2 minutes)

Pair off and sit facing your partner so that you cannot read each other's confidential sheet. Pairs should be as far apart as possible so they cannot overhear other pairs' conversations. If there is an odd number of students in the class, one student will be an observer or work with the instructor. Decide who will be the buyer and who will be the seller of the used car.

Procedure 2 (1–2 minutes)

The instructor will give a confidential sheet to each buyer and seller. (These do not appear in this book.)

Procedure 3 (5–6 minutes)

Buyers and sellers read their confidential sheets and jot down some plans (what your basic approach will be, what you will say) for the negotiation.

Procedure 4 (3–7 minutes)

Negotiate the sale of the car. You do not have to buy or sell the car. After you make the sale or agree not to sell, read your partner's confidential sheet and discuss the experience.

Integration (5–7 minutes)

Answer the following questions:

1. What type of plan was appropriate for this situation?
2. Which type of power was most relevant in helping you to negotiate the car deal?
3. Did you experience any stress as a result of this exercise (faster heart rate, perspiration, anxiety, tension, or pressure)?

4. Did you set a lower limit, target, and opening price?
5. Did you imply that you had other options and/or develop trade-offs?
6. Did you anticipate questions and objections and prepare answers?
7. Did you develop rapport and focus on obstacles rather than on the person?
8. Did you let the other party make the first offer?
9. Did you listen and ask questions to focus on meeting the other party's needs?
10. Were you quick to settle for less than your target price and/or ask for something in return for giving concessions?
11. Did you reach a sales agreement?
12. If you did reach a sales agreement, which price did you receive?

Apply It

What did I learn from this experience? How will I use this knowledge in the future?

a. The Car Dealer Negotiation confidential information is from A. G. Woodside, Tulane University. The Car Dealer Game is part of a paper, "Bargaining Behavior in Personal Selling and Buying Exchanges," presented by Dr. Woodside at the Eighth Annual Conference of the Association for Business Simulation and Experiential Learning (ABSEL): Orlando, Florida, 1980. It is used with Dr. Woodside's permission.

• • • SKILL BUILDER 10-2: MAKING BCF CONFLICT STATEMENTS

Objective

To improve your ability to initiate conflict resolution with positive BCF statements.

Skills

The primary skills developed through this exercise are:

1. *Management skill*—interpersonal (conflict management)
2. *AACSB competencies*—communication abilities and analytic skills, interpersonal relations, and application of knowledge.
3. *Management function*—leading (through influencing others)

Below are five conflict situations. Write the BCF statement you would use to resolve the conflict. Remember the goal of resolving the conflict while maintaining human relations.

1. A coworker has asked you to go out after work for the second time. The first time you gave an excuse for not being able to go, but you really don't want to go out with this person. What would you say?

B _____

_____

C _____

_____

F _____

_____

2. A coworker keeps coming to your work area to socialize. You have been talking as long as the person wants to. But it is affecting getting your work done, and you have had to stay late. What would you say?

B _____

_____

C _____

_____

F _____

_____

3. A coworker has been taking it easy and not doing his share of the work on your two-person assignment. You have had to do more than your share, and you don't want it to continue. What would you say?

B _____

_____

C _____

_____

F _____

_____

4. A coworker has continued to interrupt another coworker friend of yours as she speaks. It is upsetting you, and you have decided to talk to the interrupter privately about it. What would you say?

B _____

_____

C _____

_____

F _____

_____

5. A coworker is playing music loud for the third time. You don't like the music, and it affects your ability to concentrate. You haven't said anything, but you plan to now. What would you say?

B _____

_____

C _____

_____

F _____

_____

Procedure (5–30 minutes)

Select one option:

1. The instructor goes over possible answers to the five situations.

2. The instructor asks students for their BCF statements to the situations, followed by giving possible answers.

3. Break into groups of two or three, and together come up with a BCF statement, followed by the instructor's going over the recommended answers. Discuss the possible consequences of each alternative response in the situation. Would it help or hurt human relations and performance? How?

- *Conclusion:* The instructor leads a class discussion and/or makes concluding remarks.

- *Apply It:* What have I learned from this experience? How will I use this knowledge in the future?

• • • SKILL BUILDER 10-3: INITIATING CONFLICT RESOLUTION

Objective

To develop your skill at initiating conflict resolution.

Skills

The primary skills developed through this exercise are:

1. *Management skill*—interpersonal (conflict management)

2. *AACSB competencies*—communication abilities and analytic skills

3. *Management function*—leading (through influencing others)

During class, you will be given the opportunity to role-play a conflict you are facing or have faced in order to develop your conflict resolution skills. Students and workers have reported that this exercise helped prepare them for successful initiation of conflict resolution with roommates or coworkers. Fill in the following information:

1. Other party/parties (you may use fictitious names):

_____

2. Describe the conflict situation: List pertinent information about the other party (i.e., relationship to you, knowledge of the situation, age, and background):

_____

3. Identify the other party's possible reaction to your confrontation. (How receptive will he or she be to collaborating? What might he or she say or do during the discussion to resist change?)

_____

4. How will you overcome the resistance to change?

_____

5. Following the steps in the collaborative conflict resolution model, write out your BCF statement.

_____

Apply It

What did I learn from this experience? How will I use this knowledge in the future?

• • • SKILL BUILDER 10-4: IMPROVING YOUR OB FOUNDATIONS

Objective

To develop a plan for improving your OB foundations of personality and attitudes.

Skills

The primary skills developed through this exercise are:

1. *Management skill*—interpersonal (personal motivation)
2. *AACSB competency*—reflective thinking skills
3. *Management function*—leading

We can all improve certain aspects of our personalities and attitudes. Review your responses to Self-Assessment 10-1, "Personality Profile" (page 325). Of the traits listed, choose one you'd like to work on improving, or a negative attitude, as a way of increasing your job performance and satisfaction. For example, suppose you decided that you needed to develop a more optimistic and positive attitude and that to do so, you would work on thinking and talking more positively. You might write the following specific steps for accomplishing your plan:

- I will be aware of what I say and will focus on the positive rather than the negative. I will tell myself, for example, "I'm getting a lot done today, so I can do it" rather than "I'll never meet this deadline," or "I'm losing weight" rather than "I'm too fat" or "I need to lose weight."

- If I do find myself saying something negative to myself or to someone else, I will immediately stop and rephrase the statement in a positive manner.

- I will let friends and coworkers know that I am working on being more positive and ask for their help. I will ask them not only to point out when I'm being negative but also to reinforce me when they observe a more positive attitude from me.

Zig Ziglar recommends that if you really want to be more positive about your situation (at work, in school, in your family, in a romantic relationship, etc.), you need to focus on the good side, not dwell on the negative. To do so, write out a list of everything you like about the situation. Then write down some positive affirmations, such as "I have a positive attitude"; "I enjoy my job/school"; "I like Fred." Every morning and evening, while looking in the mirror, read your list. You may also record your list and play it. Do this for a month, and you and others will see a changed, more positive personality and attitude.

Here are some specific steps you might list for yourself if you wanted to develop a more extroverted personality: *I will say hi to people before they say hi to me. I will attend a party at which I don't know many people, and I will approach people first to talk to them. I will go to class early (or stay after class) once a week and approach someone I don't know, or don't know well, and talk to that person for a few minutes before (or after) class.* You can also follow Ziglar's recommendation and write a positive affirmation for yourself, such as "I enjoy meeting new people."

Ascent Xmedia via Getty Images

11 Motivating for High Performance

IOM	# Ideas on Management

Ideas on Management
at Market America® and Shop.Com

Market America's UnFranchise® Business is a proven plan with clear vision and strength, enabling Independent Shop Consultants to earn residual income, which can lead toward financial security. It was started back in 1992 by **JR Ridinger** based on the multilevel marketing (MLM) business model. MLM is based on the company getting entrepreneurial people to sell its products and bring in people under them to make a percentage of their sales. MLM is used by **Avon**, **Amway**, **Tupperware**, and others. But what makes Market America different? In 2011, it acquired **SHOP.com** to become the first to integrate the Internet, e-commerce, and social media to create a new business model to challenge **Amazon.com**. It sells hundreds of exclusive Market America branded products and services, with more than 40 million additional products/services through affiliates and direct partners operating globally in the United States, Canada, Mexico, Australia, Hong Kong, Taiwan, United Kingdom, Spain, and Singapore.

The company has generated more than $7.3 billion in accumulated retail sales, and its independent entrepreneurs have earned more than $3.8 billion in commissions and retail profits. But why is the company so successful? In a feature article in *BusinessWeek*, this was the opening: "The true story of how **JR and Loren Ridinger** amassed an outrageous fortune, won celebrity friends (Kim Kardashian, Eva Longoria, Jennifer Lopez, etc.), and turned their company into a global Internet sales empire by selling their most valuable asset: Themselves."

Plenty of people are good at selling stuff, but JR has the gift of motivating others through being able to sell belief—the belief that you can succeed if you follow his system and make that commitment and that you can change your life. JR has created more than 300 millionaires.

JR is a strong believer in the saying that "you become what you think about all the time" (we discussed it in Chapter 10). At a conference for new recruits, to help motivate people to think positively with an "I can do it" attitude and get rid of the negative thinking, JR actually stuck his head in an oversized prop toilet.

IOM 1. What does Market America do to motivate its distributors, and how does this affect performance?

IOM 2. How does Market America meet its distributors' content motivation needs?

IOM 3. How does Market America meet its distributors' process motivation needs?

IOM 4. How does Market America use reinforcement theory to motivate its distributors?

IOM 5. Does the Market America UnFranchise® business model for motivation work in other countries?

IOM 6. Are there any ethical issues in Market America's multilevel marketing business model?

You'll find answers to these **IOM** questions throughout the chapter. To learn more about Market America and SHOP.com, visit www.marketamerica.com and www.shop.com.

Source: Information for this case and answers within the chapter were taken from the Market America website at http://www.marketamerica.com, accessed May 27, 2017; K. T. Greenfield, "You Too Can Live the Dream," *BusinessWeek* (June 27–July 3, 2011): 67–74.

••• CHAPTER OUTLINE

Motivation and Performance

What Is Motivation, and How Does It Affect Performance?

An Overview of Three Major Classes of Motivation Theories

Content Motivation Theories

Hierarchy of Needs Theory

ERG Theory

Two-Factor Theory

Acquired Needs Theory

Process Motivation Theories

Equity Theory

Goal-Setting Theory

Expectancy Theory

Reinforcement Theory

Types of Reinforcement

Schedules of Reinforcement

Combining the Motivation Process and Motivation Theories

Motivating Employees With Rewards and Recognition

How Each of the Motivation Theories Uses Rewards and Recognition

Reward and Recognition Programs

Giving Praise

Trends and Issues in Management

LO 11-1

Illustrate the motivation process, and explain the performance formula and how to use it.

Motivation and Performance

Great leaders, including **Martin Luther King Jr.**, **Mahatma Gandhi**, **Winston Churchill**, and **Mother Teresa** have motivated followers to do good deeds.[1] You may recall that power, politics, and leadership are about influencing employees to achieve organizational objectives. Well, managers need to be able to motivate employees to work at achieving those objectives,[2] so good managers are good motivators.[3] But company recruiters also value self-starters,[4] with the skill of self-motivation and drive to succeed.[5] This chapter is all about theories to better understand, explain, and predict how to motivate yourself and others. In this section, we discuss what motivation is and how motivation affects performance. You will also get an overview of three major classes of theories of motivation.

What Is Motivation, and How Does It Affect Performance?

From a business perspective, **motivation** is the willingness to achieve organizational objectives or to go above and beyond the call of duty (organizational citizenship behavior, or OCB).[6] Managers' behavior does influence employees' OCB.[7] Many firms, including **Engagient**, are using the term *employee engagement* when referring to motivation/OCB.[8] Engagement results in increased employee productivity, customer satisfaction, and profitability.[9] Unfortunately, only 32% of U.S. workers said they are engaged,[10] and an unengaged worker costs an organization approximately $3,400 for every $10,000 in annual salary.[11] Clearly, managers need to take action to motivate OCB.[12] Some companies are setting goals to increase engagement including **Nationwide Insurance**.[13]

Motivational Effort. Motivational *effort* is needed to achieve objectives, and effort has three parts. *Initiation of effort* refers to how much effort to exert (What level of performance will I go for?). *Direction of effort* refers to where to put effort (Do I do job A or B?). *Persistence of effort* refers to how long effort will be forthcoming (Do I keep pushing or let up?). What is your motivational effort for this course?

People want to gain something for their effort. Recall from Chapter 1 that managers need to answer the usually unasked question, "What's in it for me?" Understanding that people are motivated by self-interest helps us understand how and why they are motivated and to predict their behavior. So, as managers look out for their own self-interest, they need to look out for their employees' interest while meeting organizational objectives.[14]

The Motivation Process. Through the **motivation process**, *employees go from need to motive to behavior to consequence to satisfaction or dissatisfaction*. For example, you are thirsty (need) and have a desire (motive) to get a drink. You get a drink (behavior) that quenches your thirst (consequence and satisfaction). Satisfaction is usually short-lived. Getting that drink satisfied you, but soon you will need another drink. For this reason, the motivation process is a feedback loop.

A need or want motivates behavior. However, needs and motives are complex; people don't always know what their needs are or why they do the things they do. Understanding needs will help you understand behavior. You cannot observe motives, but you can observe behavior and infer the motive through the attribution process (Chapter 10).

The Role of Expectations in Motivation and Performance. Recall from Chapter 10 that our thoughts lead to self-confidence to perform a task and meet an objective. We tend to put forth more motivational effort when we believe we will succeed. You will live up or down to your own expectations—the *self-fulfilling prophecy*. You become what you think about, so be positive, confident, and optimistic.

How managers treat employees affects their behavior,[15] so *leader–member exchange (LMX)* affects employee motivation and performance.[16] Employees tend to live up or down to their managers' expectations. Recall the *Pygmalion effect* in which managers' attitudes toward and expectations and treatment of employees largely determine their performance. We tend to be more motivated to put in the effort to live up to good managers' belief in our ability to succeed. **Walmart founder Sam Walton** said, "High expectations are the key to everything."

motivation The willingness to achieve organizational objectives or to go above and beyond the call of duty (organizational citizenship behavior).

motivation process The process of moving from need to motive to behavior to consequence to satisfaction or dissatisfaction.

SAGE edge™

Get the edge on your studies. **edge.sagepub.com/lussier8e**

- Take a quiz to find out what you've learned.
- Review key terms with eFlashcards.
- Watch videos that enhance chapter content.

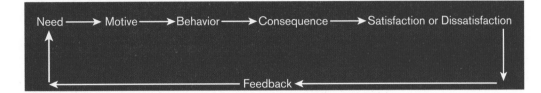

Motivation and the Performance Formula. Generally, a motivated employee will put forth more effort than an unmotivated one to do a good job; motivation does affect performance.[17] However, performance is not simply based on motivation.[18] Three interdependent factors determine the level of performance attained and are expressed as a **performance formula**:

$$performance = ability \times motivation \times resources$$

For maximum performance, all three factors must be high. When performance is not optimum, you must determine which performance factor needs to be improved. The key to success is to figure out what you like to do (*motivation*), what you are good at doing (*ability*), and what *resources* you need to achieve your goals—such as a college degree. **Tom Mitchell**, cofounder of **MVP Performance Institute**, says that passion translates to high performance.[19] Both **Chief Executive Officer (CEO) Warren Buffett** of **Berkshire Hathaway** and **CEO Mary Barra** of **General Motors (GM)** give this career advice: If you do something you are passionate about, you will be successful.[20]

Market America's (**IOM 1**) primary means of affecting performance is to create self-motivation by making each distributor his or her own boss. In terms of the performance formula, the real focus of UnFranchise® is on motivation; you don't have to be intelligent (the model provides *ability* with a proven system), and there is a very low financial *resource* fee to start your business. It's all about being *motivated* to get out there and sell, sell, sell—which only succeeds with people who are motivated to be entrepreneurs. Market America's structure is based on the UnFranchise® business model in which people have all the benefits of a franchise but do not have to pay a franchise fee. Additionally, instead of paying the franchisor a royalty, the company pays commissions and retail profits from sales through individual SHOP.com websites and referral networks. Customers get paid for shopping, and UnFranchise® owners earn commissions and retail profits, resulting in an ongoing income.

An Overview of Three Major Classes of Motivation Theories

It has been said that nothing is as practical as a good theory, and motivation theories have found numerous applications in organizations.

performance formula
Performance = ability × motivation × resources.

11-1 **APPLYING** THE CONCEPT

The Performance Formula

Identify the factor contributing to low performance in the following five situations.

A. ability

B. motivation

C. resources

____ 1. "Usain, it's not my fault the machine broke, and now we are behind schedule."

____ 2. "Betty Lou went on a sales call, but when she went online, our company website was down, resulting in no sale."

____ 3. "Butch, I know you are trying hard, but you aren't meeting your sales quotas. We have to let you go."

____ 4. "Too bad Latoya does not seem to like doing her work and just does the minimum to keep her job."

____ 5. "John Boy makes more sales calls than the other five reps, but he has the lowest sales."

____ 6. "I know Mark is bright and could get all As, but he doesn't seem to realize that grades are important to getting a good job."

Recall that a theory helps us to understand, explain, and predict behavior. However, there is no single universally accepted theory of how to motivate people. In this chapter, we discuss three major classes of motivation theories and show how you can use them to motivate yourself and others. Exhibit 11-1 lists the major motivation theories. After studying all of these theories and seeing them put together, you can select one theory to use, use several theories in developing your own approach, or apply the theory that best fits the specific situation.

Content Motivation Theories

Leaders who want to motivate employees should do so by focusing on meeting follower needs, not their own needs.[21] Motivation comes from how you engage with people on their terms.[22] When employees are asked to meet objectives, they think, but usually do not say, "What's in it for me?" The key to achieving organizational objectives is to understand what others need and meet their needs.[23] As you create a win-win situation, you need to sell the benefits that meet employees' needs to the employees.

content motivation theories Theories that focus on identifying and understanding employees' needs.

Content motivation theories *focus on identifying and understanding employees' needs.* While being fair to all, consider individual needs.[24] In this section, we describe and discuss the application of four content motivation theories: hierarchy of needs theory, ERG theory, two-factor theory, and acquired needs theory.

Hierarchy of Needs Theory

hierarchy of needs theory Theory that proposes that employees are motivated by five levels of needs: physiological, safety, social, esteem, and self-actualization.

The **hierarchy of needs theory** *proposes that employees are motivated by five levels of needs: physiological, safety, social, esteem, and self-actualization.* **Abraham Maslow** developed this theory in the 1940s.[25] People have five levels of needs, listed here in hierarchical order from lowest to highest:

| EXHIBIT 11-1 | MAJOR MOTIVATION THEORIES |

Class of Motivation Theories	Specific Theory (Creator)
Content motivation theories focus on identifying and understanding employees' needs.	**Hierarchy of needs theory** proposes that employees are motivated by five levels of needs: physiological, safety, social, esteem, and self-actualization. (Maslow)
	ERG theory proposes that employees are motivated by three needs: existence, relatedness, and growth. (Alderfer)
	Two-factory theory proposes that employees are motivated by motivators (higher-level needs) rather than by maintenance factors (lower-level needs). (Herzberg)
	Acquired needs theory proposes that employees are motivated by their need for achievement, power, and affiliation. (McClelland)
Process motivation theories focus on understanding how employees choose behaviors to fulfill their needs.	**Equity theory** proposes that employees are motivated when their perceived inputs equal outputs. (Adams)
	Goal-setting theory proposes that achievable but difficult goals motivate employees. (Locke)
	Expectancy theory proposes that employees are motivated when they believe they can accomplish a task and the rewards for doing so are worth the effort. (Vroom)
Reinforcement theory proposes that the consequences of their behavior will motivate employees to behave in predetermined ways. (Skinner)	**Types of Reinforcement**
	Positive reinforcement is offering attractive consequences (rewards) for desirable performance to encourage the continuation of that behavior.
	Avoidance reinforcement is threatening to provide negative consequences for poor performance to encourage desirable behavior.
	Punishment is providing an undesirable consequence (punishment) for an undesirable behavior to prevent the behavior.
	Extinction is the withholding of reinforcement for a particular behavior.

- *Physiological needs.* These are people's basic needs for air, water, food, shelter, sex, and relief from or avoidance of pain.
- *Safety needs.* Once they satisfy their physiological needs, people are concerned with safety and security.
- *Social needs.* After establishing safety, people look for love, friendship, acceptance, and affection.
- *Esteem needs.* After they meet their social needs, people focus on acquiring status, self-respect, recognition for accomplishments, and a feeling of self-confidence and prestige.
- *Self-actualization needs.* The highest-level need is to develop one's full potential. To do so, people seek growth, achievement, and advancement.

The idea of fulfilling a dream such as managing a business can be a powerful motivator.

Motivating Employees With Hierarchy of Needs Theory. Today, a manager's critical task is to show sensitivity to employees' needs.[26] Managers should meet employees' lower-level needs so that those needs will not dominate the employees' motivational process. So meet lower-level needs first and then focus on meeting higher-level needs. Although the hierarchy of needs is not supported by research, businesses do in fact attempt to meet these needs, as shown in Exhibit 11-2.

Working with **Market America (IOM 2a)** allows people to meet many needs. Earning money allows them to satisfy physiological needs. Because the job involves a minimum of risk, people's safety needs are met. Customer contact and meetings satisfy some of people's social needs. The job itself offers great growth potential and thus may satisfy some distributors' esteem needs. Finally, being the boss allows people to have control over the work experience, which may help them meet self-actualization needs.

ERG Theory

A well-known simplification of the hierarchy of needs theory, the **ERG theory**, *proposes that employees are motivated by three needs: existence, relatedness, and growth.* **Clayton Alderfer** reorganized Maslow's hierarchy of five types of needs into three needs: existence (physiological and safety needs), relatedness (social), and growth (esteem and self-actualization). Alderfer agreed with Maslow that unsatisfied needs motivate individuals, and he theorized that more than one need may be active at one time.[27]

Motivating Employees With ERG Theory. To apply ERG theory, you must determine which employee needs have been met and which have not been met or have been frustrated, and then you must plan how to meet the unsatisfied needs.

Two-Factor Theory

In the 1950s, **Frederick Herzberg** classified two sets of needs that he called *factors.*[28] Herzberg combined lower-level needs into one classification he called *maintenance factors* and higher-level needs into one classification he called *motivators.* The **two-factor theory** *proposes that employees are motivated by motivators rather than by maintenance factors.* Maintenance factors are also called *extrinsic motivators*, because the motivation comes from outside the job. Motivators are called *intrinsic motivators* because the motivation comes from the work itself.[29] Complete Self-Assessment 11-1 to find out what motivates you.

Based on their research, Herzberg and his associates disagreed with the traditional view that satisfaction and dissatisfaction were at opposite ends of a single continuum. Instead, they proposed two continuums: one for maintenance factors and one for motivators. The continuum for maintenance factors runs from not dissatisfied to dissatisfied. The continuum for motivators runs from satisfied to not satisfied, as illustrated in Exhibit 11-3.

WORK APPLICATION 11-1

Describe how your needs at each of Maslow's levels are addressed by an organization you work for now or were addressed by one you worked for in the past.

WORK APPLICATION 11-2

Recall a present or past job; were you dissatisfied or not dissatisfied with the maintenance factors? Were you satisfied or not satisfied with the motivators? Identify the specific maintenance factors and motivators, and explain your response.

ERG theory Theory that proposes that employees are motivated by three needs: existence, relatedness, and growth.

two-factor theory Theory that proposes that employees are motivated by motivators rather than by maintenance factors.

EXHIBIT 11-2 **HOW MANAGERS MOTIVATE BASED ON MASLOW'S HIERARCHY OF NEEDS THEORY**

Self-Actualization Needs
Organizations help employees meet their self-actualization needs by providing them with opportunities for skill development, the chance to be creative, promotions, and the ability to have complete control over their jobs.

Esteem Needs
Organizations meet employees' esteem needs with pay raises, recognition, challenging tasks, participation in decision making, and opportunity for advancement.

Social Needs
Organizations meet employees' social needs by providing them with the opportunity to interact with others, to be accepted, and to have friends. Many organizations schedule employee parties, picnics, trips, and sports teams.

Safety Needs
Organizations meet employees' safety needs by providing safe working conditions, job security, and fringe benefits (medical insurance/sick pay/pensions).

Physiological Needs
Organizations meet employees' physiological needs by providing adequate salaries, work breaks, and safe working conditions.

Herzberg contended that addressing maintenance factors will keep employees from being dissatisfied, but it will not make them satisfied or motivate them. For example, if employees are dissatisfied with their pay (a maintenance factor) and they get a raise, they will no longer be dissatisfied. However, before long, employees will get accustomed to the new standard of living and become dissatisfied again. They will need another raise to avoid becoming dissatisfied again. This becomes a repeating cycle.

Motivating Employees With Two-Factor Theory. Organizations need to ensure that employees are not dissatisfied with maintenance factors and then focus on motivating them through their jobs. **Dow Chemical CEO Andrew Liveris** says that people can be bought with their pockets, but to get their full motivated effort they have to be passionate about what they are doing.[30] One thing that has changed over the years is that many of the successful young companies including **Google** and **Facebook** are focusing on making the workplace a fun place to go to.[31] **Southwest** former **CEO Herb Kelleher** developed a culture of having fun at work back in the late 1970s. In a survey, 95% of **Camden** apartments employees said it was a fun place to work.[32]

Employees are more motivated when they feel they are doing meaningful work.[33] One successful way to motivate employees is to build challenges and opportunities for achievement into their jobs. *Job enrichment,* the Job Characteristics Model, and delegating (discussed in Chapter 7) can be effective motivators.

Market America (**IOM 2b**) allows people to operate their own businesses. In terms of the two-factor theory, the focus of this organization is on motivators that allow distributors to meet their high-level needs for esteem and self-actualization. Maintenance factors are not directly addressed.

EXHIBIT 11-3   HERZBERG'S TWO-FACTOR THEORY

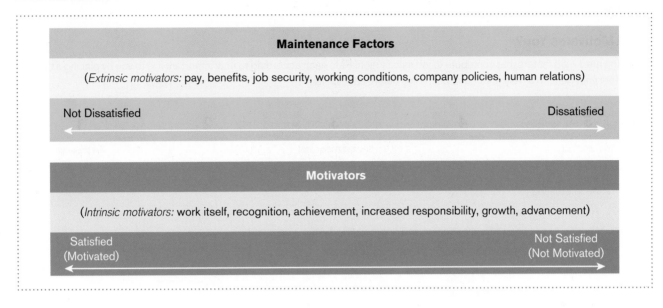

Acquired Needs Theory

The **acquired needs theory** *proposes that employees are motivated by their needs for achievement, power, and affiliation.* It is also called learned needs and three-needs theory. **David McClelland** does not have a classification for lower-level needs.[34] His affiliation needs are the same as Maslow's social and relatedness needs, and his power and achievement needs are related to esteem, self-actualization, and growth.

Unlike the other content theories, the acquired needs theory holds that needs are based on personality and are developed and learned as people interact with the environment. All people possess the needs for achievement, power, and affiliation, but to varying degrees. One of the three needs tends to be dominant in each individual and motivates his or her behavior. Before learning more about each need, complete Self-Assessment 11-2 to determine your profile.

The Need for Achievement (n Ach). People with a high need for achievement tend to want to take personal responsibility for solving problems. They are goal oriented, and they set moderate, realistic, attainable goals. They seek challenge, excellence, and individuality; take calculated, moderate risks; desire concrete feedback on their performance; and are willing to work hard. Companies recruit people who are motivated to succeed on the job.[35] One of the things they look for on a résumé (Chapter 9 and accompanying Appendix) is achievement.

The Need for Power (n Pow). People with a high need for power (Chapter 10) have a take-charge attitude. They tend to want to control the situation, to influence or control others, to enjoy competition in which they can win (they do not like to lose), and to be willing to confront others.

The Need for Affiliation (n Aff). People with a high need for affiliation tend to seek close relationships with others, to want to be liked by others, to enjoy social activities, and to seek to belong. They like to interact with other people rather than being alone.

The Manager Acquired Needs Profile. Managers tend to have a high n Pow, followed by a high need for n Ach, and a low n Aff. People with a high n Aff tend to avoid management because they tend to have a low n Pow and like to be one of the group rather than its manager, who needs to evaluate and discipline others. Not everyone wants to be a manager. Do you? Being promoted to manager is being turned down by some, including at **Morgan Stanley**.[36]

acquired needs theory Theory that proposes that employees are motivated by their needs for achievement, power, and affiliation.

11-1   SELF-ASSESSMENT

What Motivates You?

Following are 12 job factors that contribute to job satisfaction. Rate each according to how important it is to you by placing a number from 1 (*not important*) to 5 (*very important*) on the line before each factor.

5	4	3	2	1
Very important		Somewhat important		Not important

____ 1. An interesting job I enjoy doing

____ 2. A boss who treats everyone the same regardless of the circumstances

____ 3. Getting praise and other recognition and appreciation for the work that I do

____ 4. A job that is routine without much change from day to day

____ 5. The opportunity for advancement

____ 6. A nice job title regardless of pay

____ 7. Job responsibility that gives me freedom to do things my way

____ 8. Working conditions (safe environment, cafeteria, etc.)

____ 9. The opportunity to learn new things

____ 10. An emphasis on following company rules, regulations, procedures, and policies

____ 11. A job I can do well and succeed at

____ 12. Job security for life

Indicate below how you rated each factor.

Motivating Factors	Maintenance Factors
1. ____	2. ____
3. ____	4. ____
5. ____	6. ____
7. ____	8. ____
9. ____	10. ____
11. ____	12. ____
____ **Total points**	____

Add each column vertically. Are motivators or maintenance factors more important to you?

Motivating Employees With Acquired Needs Theory. People have different needs profiles and must be motivated and led differently. To motivate employees with a high n Ach, give them nonroutine, challenging tasks with clear, attainable objectives. Give them fast and frequent feedback on their performance. To motivate employees with a high n Pow, give them greater autonomy, letting them plan and control their jobs as much as possible. Try to include them in decision making, especially when the decision affects them. To motivate employees

11-2 **SELF**-ASSESSMENT

Acquired Needs

Indicate how accurately each of the 15 statements describes you by placing a number from 1 (*not like me*) to 5 (*like me*) on the line before each statement.

5	4	3	2	1
Like me		Somewhat like me		Not like me

_____ 1. I enjoy working hard.

_____ 2. I enjoy competing and winning.

_____ 3. I enjoy having many friends.

_____ 4. I enjoy a difficult challenge.

_____ 5. I enjoy being in a leadership role.

_____ 6. I want other people to like me.

_____ 7. I want to know how I am progressing as I complete tasks.

_____ 8. I confront people who do things I disagree with.

_____ 9. I enjoy frequently getting together socially with people.

_____ 10. I enjoy setting and achieving realistic goals.

_____ 11. I try to influence other people so that I get my way.

_____ 12. I enjoy belonging to many groups and organizations.

_____ 13. I enjoy the satisfaction of completing a difficult task.

_____ 14. In a leaderless situation, I tend to step forward and take charge.

_____ 15. I enjoy working with others more than working alone.

To determine your dominant need, write the number you assigned to each statement in the table below. Add up the total of each column, which should be between 5 and 25 points. The column with the highest score is your dominant need.

Achievement	Power	Affiliation
1. _____	2. _____	3. _____
4. _____	5. _____	6. _____
7. _____	8. _____	9. _____
10. _____	11. _____	12. _____
13. _____	14. _____	15. _____
Total points: _____	_____	_____

with a high n Aff, be sure to let them work as part of a team. They derive satisfaction from the people they work with more than from the task itself. Delegate responsibility for orienting and training new employees to them.

11-2 APPLYING THE CONCEPT

Content Motivation Theories

Identify the theory behind each of the following statements on how to motivate employees.

A. hierarchy of needs theory

B. ERG theory

C. two-factor theory

D. acquired needs theory

_____ 7. "Carl, at **Google**, we created a culture where we work hard, but it's a fun place to work."

_____ 8. "Stanley, already offering good salaries and benefits, our HR staff is recommending that we have more social events so employees can get to know each other better to promote more motivated teamwork."

_____ 9. "Harry, here at Pets R Us Animal Clinic, we focus on hiring people who love animals and want to come to work to take care of them."

_____ 10. "Edwina, I know I like to micromanage, but I'm working at giving some of my employees more autonomy in their jobs."

_____ 11. "Mookie, a five-step sequence of needs is too complex. That's why I like this other one with three needs better."

WORK
APPLICATION 11-3

Explain how your need for achievement, power, and/ or affiliation has affected your motivation on the job.

LO 11-3

Compare the three process motivation theories.

process motivation theories Theories that focus on understanding how employees choose behaviors to fulfill their needs.

Market America (**IOM 2c**) helps distributors meet all three acquired needs. It provides support so that they can achieve their goal of successfully running their own business, they have the power to be in control, and they can develop an affiliation with customers and other distributors.

Exhibit 11-4 compares the four content motivation theories. Read left to right by row to see how each of Maslow's needs is classified under the other three theories.

Process Motivation Theories

Process motivation theories *focus on understanding how employees choose behaviors to fulfill their needs.* Content motivation theories focus simply on identifying and understanding employees' needs. Process motivation theories go a step further and attempt to explain how and why we choose to try to satisfy needs in different ways, the mental process we go through as we understand situations (perception), and how we evaluate our need satisfaction. In this section, we discuss equity theory, goal-setting theory, and expectancy theory.

EXHIBIT 11-4   A COMPARISON OF FOUR CONTENT MOTIVATION THEORIES

Hierarchy of Needs (Maslow)	ERG Theory (Alderfer)	Two-Factor Theory (Herzberg)	Acquired Needs Theory (McClelland)
Self-actualization	Growth	Motivators	Achievement and power
Esteem	Growth	Motivators	Achievement and power
Social	Relatedness	Maintenance factors	Affiliation
Safety	Existence	Maintenance factors	(Not addressed)
Physiological	Existence	Maintenance factors	(Not addressed)
Needs must be met in a hierarchical order.	Needs at any level can be unmet simultaneously.	Maintenance factors will not motivate employees.	Motivating needs are developed through experience.

Equity Theory

Let's face it, we are not all equal, but we want to be treated fairly,[37] with mutually beneficial relationships.[38] Employees' perception of being treated fairly affects their attitude and performance.[39] So we need to be honest and fair to develop trusting relationship to motivate others.[40] When managers are unfair and abusive, they can demotivate employees and hurt performance.[41]

Equity theory was popularized by **J. Stacy Adams**.[42] **Equity theory** *proposes that employees are motivated when their perceived inputs equal outputs.* We compare our inputs (effort, experience, seniority, status, intelligence, and so forth) and outputs (praise, recognition, pay, benefits, promotions, increased status, supervisor's approval, etc.) to those of relevant others. A relevant other could be a coworker or a group of employees from the same or different organizations.

Notice that the definition says that employees compare their *perceived* (not actual) inputs to outputs (as covered in Chapter 10). Equity may actually exist. However, if employees believe that they are not being treated fairly, they will change their behavior, attempting to create equity. Inequity perceptions hurt attitudes, commitment, and cooperation, thereby decreasing individual, team, and organizational performance.[43] It is also used as a justification for unethical behavior.[44]

Motivating Employees With Equity Theory. Using equity theory in practice can be difficult, because you don't know the employees' reference groups and their views of inputs and outcomes. However, managers can help control employee perceptions of fairness by following the perception congruence advice in Chapter 10. The theory does offer some useful general recommendations:

1. Managers should be aware that equity is based on perception, which may not be correct. Managers should not play favorites but instead should treat employees equally but in unique ways.

2. Rewards should be equitable. Employees producing at the same level should be given equal rewards. Employees who perceive they are working harder than others, and/or for less pay, may decrease performance. It helps to know who the comparison person or group is to know if equity does exist.[45]

3. High performance should be rewarded, but employees must understand the inputs needed to attain certain outputs. When using incentive pay, managers should clearly specify the exact requirements to achieve the incentive. A manager should be able to state objectively why one person got a higher merit raise than another.

Market America's (**IOM 3a**) UnFranchise® business model treats all distributors with equity. Owners have unlimited potential, as the more time and effort (inputs) they put into their business, the more potential rewards (outputs) they can reap. However, not everyone is cut out for sales, and some people who start as independent distributors drop out or stay at this level rather than advancing to become UnFranchise® owners.

Goal-Setting Theory

The first step in self-motivation is knowing what you want to accomplish.[46] Recall (Chapter 5) that our first step to planning (means) anything should be to set objectives (ends),[47] and having deadlines[48] and measuring and evaluating performance based on objectives[49] helps motivate goal achievement. That's why **Johnson & Johnson** gives bonuses based on revenue, profits, and other metrics.

Goal-setting theory, developed by **Edwin Locke** and later validated with **Gary Latham**, is currently the most researched approach to work motivation.[50] The **goal-setting theory** *proposes that achievable but difficult goals motivate employees.* Or as Latham puts it, higher specific goals lead to higher levels of performance.[51] Goals influence the way we think, feel, and behave;[52] they help structure our effort toward achieving the goal.[53] That's why **GE** develops "stretch goals."[54]

Recall from Chapter 1 that setting goals is the starting point of the management functions. Goal-setting theory suggests that setting difficult but achievable goals can motivate employees to excel.

Lou Holtz—motivational speaker, **ESPN** college football analyst, and former football coach of the national championship winner **University of Notre Dame** and the **University of South Carolina**—stated that the three keys to success are a winning *attitude*, positive *self-esteem*, and setting a *higher goal*. Holtz said, "Of all my experiences in managing people, the power of goal setting is the most incredible."[55]

With the increasing use of team structures,[56] people must work together to set and achieve collective goals.[57] One of the key drivers of effective team outcomes is the motivation of team members.[58] So leaders need to motivate both individuals and teams.[59]

Motivating Employees With Goal-Setting Theory. Here is what not to do and what to do.

1. Don't set easy goals, because most employees will just do the minimum.
2. Don't simply tell employees to do their best, because they most likely will not perform well and will use the excuse that they did their best when they really didn't.
3. For goals to be motivational, they must be difficult but achievable with employee commitment to get employees motivated to push hard (stretch) to reach the goal.
4. Refer to Chapter 5 for how to set objectives using the model that will motivate yourself and others.

WORK
APPLICATION 11-5

Give an example of how goal(s) affected your motivation and performance or that of someone you work with or have worked with.

Market America (**IOM 3b**) relies heavily on goal-setting theory. One of its company goals is to take on **Amazon.com** as a top location for one-stop Internet shopping. Goal setting is one of "the Basic 5" steps for success at Market America. Distributors are taught to set business and personal goals—both short term and long term. They are then encouraged to develop a detailed plan of what they must do each year, each month, each week, and each day to achieve their goal(s).

Expectancy Theory

Expectancy theory is based on **Victor Vroom**'s formula: motivation = expectancy × instrumentality × valence.[60] The **expectancy theory** *proposes that employees are motivated when they believe they can accomplish a task and the rewards for doing so are worth the effort.*

Three important variables in Vroom's formula determine motivation:

1. *Expectancy* refers to the person's *perception* of his or her ability (probability) to accomplish an objective. Generally, the higher one's expectancy, the better the chance for motivation. When employees do not believe that they can accomplish objectives, they will not be motivated to try. What is your expectancy grade for this course?
2. *Instrumentality* refers to the perception of the relationship between performance and the outcome/reward that will actually be gained. Generally, the higher one's expectation for a positive outcome, the better the chance for motivation. Do the low odds of winning the lottery's big prize motivate you to buy tickets?
3. *Valence* refers to the value a person places on the outcome. Generally, the higher the value (importance) of the outcome, the better the chance of motivation. Are you motivated to apply for a minimum-wage job?

Motivating Employees With Expectancy Theory. Following are some keys to using expectancy theory successfully:

expectancy theory Theory that proposes that employees are motivated when they believe they can accomplish a task and the rewards for doing so are worth the effort.

1. Clearly define objectives and the performance needed to achieve them.
2. Tie performance to rewards. High performers should be rewarded more than low performers.

11-3 APPLYING THE CONCEPT

Process Motivation Theories

Identify the theory behind each of the following statements on how to motivate employees.

A. equity theory

B. goal-setting theory

C. expectancy theory

____ 12. "Tony, I do agree that you do exceptional work. So I will request the raise you want with HR."

____ 13. "Shelby, I talked to all of my employees so I would know what is important to them. Now I can offer rewards that will motivate them when they perform a task well."

____ 14. "Tyson, my style is to delegate tough tasks that my employees can do, and I tell them exactly what I want them to do, with a tough deadline."

____ 15. "Lolo, you have to realize that we are overbooked and everyone else is working tomorrow, so you have to work."

---

3. Be sure rewards have value to employees. Get to know employees as individuals. Letting employees speak (called *employee voice*) about the rewards they want and giving them results in higher levels of motivation and performance.[61]

4. Make sure employees believe that you will do what you say you will.

Market America (IOM 3c) focuses on attracting people who have the expectancy that they can succeed at running their own business, and it provides the business model to help them succeed. Valence does vary for these people, but most UnFranchise® owners are seeking their own business so that they can achieve financial independence and the freedom to determine how to spend their time.

Reinforcement Theory

B. F. Skinner contended that in order to motivate employees, there is no need to identify and meet needs. Instead, you need to understand the relationship between behaviors and their consequences and then reinforce desirable behaviors and discourage undesirable

WORK APPLICATION 11-6

Give an example of how expectancy theory has affected your motivation or someone else's you work with or have worked with. Be sure to specify the expectancy and the valence.

LO 11-4

Explain the four types and two schedules of reinforcement.

11-1 JOIN THE DISCUSSION ETHICS & SOCIAL RESPONSIBILITY

Academic Standards

The academic credit-hour system was set up many years ago to ensure that there would be some standardization across colleges throughout the country and that academics and employers had the same understanding of the workload that a college student had carried to earn a degree. The credit-hour system was based on the assumption that a student would spend 2 hours of preparation for each hour of in-class time. So a student taking five classes should spend 15 hours per week in classes and about 30 hours preparing for classes, or a total of about 45 hours a week—which is a full-time schedule.

1. How many hours outside of class, on average, do you and other students you know spend preparing for class each week?

2. Are college professors today assigning students 2 hours of preparation for every hour in class? If not, why do you think they have dropped this standard?

3. Are students who are essentially doing part-time work (that is, attending classes but doing little academic work outside of class) during college being prepared for a career after graduation (with a 40- to 60-hour workweek)?

4. Is it ethical and socially responsible for professors to drop standards and for colleges to award degrees for doing less work than students did 5, 10, or 20 years ago?

behaviors.[62] People respond to consequences and will behave as you want them to if you find the right incentives.[63] On a personal note, by changing our behavior through developing new habits, we can change our lives.[64]

The **reinforcement theory** *proposes that the consequences of their behavior will motivate employees to behave in predetermined ways.* It's about teaching and learning behavior, and it is also called *operant conditioning* and is used to shape behavior (Chapter 10). Employees learn what is and is not desired behavior as a result of the consequences for specific behaviors, which they engage in to meet their needs and self-interest. Former White House chief of staff **Donald Rumsfeld** puts it this way: If you make something more (or less) attractive, people will do more (or less) of it.[65] In this section, we discuss two important concepts used to modify behavior (the types of reinforcement and the schedules of reinforcement) and how to motivate using reinforcement.

Types of Reinforcement

The four types of reinforcement are positive (reward), avoidance (negative), punishment, and extinction. The first two tend to encourage desirable behavior. Punishment is a consequence that tends to discourage undesirable behavior, whereas extinction eliminates a targeted behavior. **Microsoft chairman John Thompson** says that managers need to say, "This is what we do and do not do, and here is the behavior that will be rewarded and punished,"[66] and that is what they do at **Johnson & Johnson**.[67]

Positive Reinforcement. Positive reinforcement generally works better than punishment, especially when training employees. One method of encouraging desirable behavior is to offer attractive consequences (*rewards*). For example, an employee who arrives on time for a meeting is rewarded by thanks from the supervisor. If desirable behavior is not positively reinforced, it may decrease or even be eliminated (extinction). For example, if employees' high performance is ignored by management, the employees may stop making extra effort, thinking, "Why should I do a good job if I'm not rewarded in some way?" In teams, it can result in *social loafing*.[68]

Avoidance Reinforcement. Avoidance reinforcement is also called *negative reinforcement*. Like positive reinforcement, avoidance reinforcement is used to encourage continued desirable behavior; in this case, the reinforcement occurs because the behavior prevents a negative consequence (instead of leading to a positive one). For example, an employee arrives at meetings on time to avoid the negative consequence of a reprimand. With avoidance reinforcement, it's the threat of a negative consequence that controls behavior.

Punishment. Punishment involves the actual use of a negative consequence to decrease undesirable behavior. For example, an employee who arrives late for a meeting is reprimanded. Other means of punishment include fines, demotions, and taking away privileges. (Note that rules for avoidance, which are designed to get employees to avoid certain behaviors, are not punishment in and of themselves; punishment is only given if a rule is broken.) Using punishment may reduce the targeted behavior, but it may also cause other undesirable behavior, such as lower productivity or theft or sabotage,[69] and it is ineffective for motivating employees to work harder because you can't force people to be engaged and use OCB.[70]

Extinction. Extinction (like punishment) is applied in an attempt to reduce or eliminate a behavior. Unlike punishment, however, which is the active application of a negative consequence, extinction involves withholding reinforcement when an undesirable behavior occurs. For example, a manager can withhold a pay raise or might ignore an employee who arrives late for a meeting. However, extinction often doesn't work, because ignoring problems usually only leads to more problems, such as lateness.

Schedules of Reinforcement

An important consideration in using positive reinforcement to control behavior is when to reinforce performance. The two major reinforcement schedules are continuous and intermittent.

reinforcement theory Theory that proposes that the consequences of their behavior will motivate employees to behave in predetermined ways.

11-4 APPLYING THE CONCEPT

Types of Reinforcement

Identify the theory behind each of the following statements on how to motivate employees.

A. positive/reward

B. avoidance/negative

C. punishment

D. extinction

____ 16. "Helen, for being late again, next time we have overtime, I'm not going to give you extra hours."

____ 17. "Chet, I know we can make more money by fixing prices, but it is illegal, so I'm not going to do it."

____ 18. "Avi, I really appreciate your staying late tonight to finish this project."

____ 19. "Sharron, you know the rule is that we dock your pay if you come in late. No excuses."

____ 20. "I was hoping that Heidi would stop being mean to Jake, but it has been going on for a week now, so I guess I'm going to have to talk to her about it."

Continuous Reinforcement. With a continuous schedule of reinforcement, each and every desired behavior is reinforced. Examples of this approach include the use of a machine with an automatic counter that lets the employee know, at any given moment, exactly how many units have been produced; the payment of a piece rate for each unit produced; a commission for every sale; or a compliment from the manager for every positive customer report. Continuous reinforcement is better for sustaining desired behavior; however, it is not always possible or practical.

Intermittent Reinforcement. With intermittent reinforcement schedules, reinforcement is given based on the passage of time or amount of output. When the reinforcement is based on the passage of time, an *interval* schedule is being used. When reinforcement is based on output, a *ratio* schedule is being used. Ratio schedules are generally better motivators than interval schedules. When electing to use intermittent reinforcement, you have four alternatives, but ratio tends to be a better motivator:

1. *Fixed-interval schedule.* Consequences follow a behavior after a set time—for example, giving a paycheck every week or breaks and meals at the same time every day.

2. *Variable-interval schedule.* Consequences follow a behavior after different times—for example, giving praise only now and then, and quarterly reports varying in the number of days in a quarter.

3. *Fixed-ratio schedule.* Consequences follow a specific number of behaviors—for example, giving a bonus after workers produce at a standard rate.

4. *Variable-ratio schedule.* Consequences follow a different number of behaviors—for example, giving praise only for exceptional performance.

Motivating With Reinforcement. Following are some general guidelines:

1. Make sure employees know what behavior is expected and reinforced. Set clear, effective objectives.

2. Select appropriate rewards. A reward to one person could be considered a punishment by another. Let your employees know what's in it for them for achieving desirable behavior.

3. Select the appropriate reinforcement and schedule.

4. Do not reward mediocre or poor performance.

5. Look for the positive and give praise regularly rather than focusing on the negative and criticizing. Make people feel good about themselves (the Pygmalion effect, Chapter 10).

6. Do things *for* your employees instead of *to* them, and you will see productivity increase.

11-5 APPLYING THE CONCEPT

Schedules of Reinforcement

Identify the theory behind each of the following statements on how to motivate employees.

A. continuous incremental schedules

B. fixed-interval

C. variable-interval

D. fixed-ratio

E. variable-ratio

_____ 21. "Anita, congratulations. You made the most computer chips again this week, making you the high-income earner for the fourth month in a row since we started this new piece rate system."

_____ 22. "Thanks. Anton. You really hustled to get that shipment out on time today."

_____ 23. "Tom, I just closed another sale. I'm looking forward to a nice commission check this week."

_____ 24. "Katie, you need to work fast so we can meet our quarterly sales goal and get a share of the profits."

_____ 25. "Hillary, I look forward to getting out of working on Monday mornings to attend our weekly department meeting."

_____ 26. "Kyle, I want to continue being paid monthly, and I like February better than the months with 31 days."

MANAGEMENT IN ACTION

Schedules of Reinforcement

Market America (IOM 4) uses positive reinforcement with a continuous schedule, as each and every sale results in compensation. There are business meetings, and distributors are reinforced with praise and other recognition for accomplishments. Distributors share success stories, testimonials, voicemail tips, audiotapes, and books.

Combining the Motivation Process and Motivation Theories

Motivation is important, but you may be wondering: How do these theories fit together? Is one the best? Should I try to pick the correct theory for a given situation? People want a theory of total motivation, so that is what this section is all about. The groups of theories are complementary; each refers to a different stage in the motivation process or answers a different question. Content motivation theories answer this question: "What needs do employees have that should be met on the job?" Process motivation theories answer another question: "How do employees choose behavior to fulfill their needs?" Reinforcement theory is not concerned about meeting needs; it answers a different question: "What can managers do to get employees to behave in ways that meet the organizational objectives?"

LO 11-5

Contrast content, process, and reinforcement theories.

WORK
APPLICATION 11-7

Give a few examples of the types of reinforcement and the schedules used at a present or past job.

In the first section of this chapter, you learned that the motivation process moves from need to motive to behavior to consequence to satisfaction or dissatisfaction. The motivation process becomes a little more complex when we incorporate the motivation theories in the form of answers to the preceding questions, as illustrated in Exhibit 11-5. Note that step 4 loops back to step 3 because, according to reinforcement theory, behavior is learned through consequences. Step 4 does not loop back to steps 1 or 2 because reinforcement theory is not concerned with needs, motives, or satisfaction; it focuses on getting employees to behave in certain ways through consequences provided by managers. Also, note that step 5 loops back to step 1, because meeting needs is an ongoing and never-ending process. Finally, be aware that, according to the two-factor theory, step 5, satisfaction or dissatisfaction, is not on one continuum but on two separate continua (satisfied to not satisfied or not dissatisfied to dissatisfied), based on the level of need being met (motivator or maintenance factor).

On a personal note, successful careers are usually based on two factors: knowing what you like to do and doing what you are good at. Recall that you become what you think about,

EXHIBIT 11-5   THE MOTIVATION PROCESS AND THE MOTIVATION THEORIES

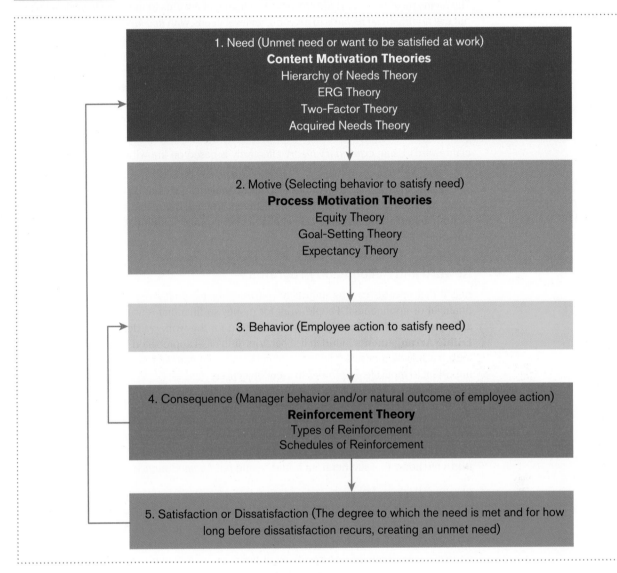

1. Need (Unmet need or want to be satisfied at work)
Content Motivation Theories
Hierarchy of Needs Theory
ERG Theory
Two-Factor Theory
Acquired Needs Theory

2. Motive (Selecting behavior to satisfy need)
Process Motivation Theories
Equity Theory
Goal-Setting Theory
Expectancy Theory

3. Behavior (Employee action to satisfy need)

4. Consequence (Manager behavior and/or natural outcome of employee action)
Reinforcement Theory
Types of Reinforcement
Schedules of Reinforcement

5. Satisfaction or Dissatisfaction (The degree to which the need is met and for how long before dissatisfaction recurs, creating an unmet need)

or what you think is what you get.[71] To be self-motivated, you need to have a positive attitude about yourself (self-concept) and your job. A starting place to self-motivation is knowing what you need and want (content motivation theories) so that you can better understand what motivates you (process motivation theories). When you know your own motivations, you make better decisions.[72] Based on your wants, set objectives and develop new habits using cues, new changed behavior, and rewards (reinforcement theory).[73]

Motivating Employees With Rewards and Recognition

Managers need to take action to motivate employee OCB.[74] However, what motivates one person may not motivate another, so it is important to know people as individuals to engage them.[75] However, it's not easy, because managers are expected to treat employees uniformly and consistently while considering individual needs and sometimes making exceptions—that can be perceived as unfair by others.[76]

To answer "What's in it for me?" companies develop motivational systems that include rewards and recognition[77] that will create a motivational climate[78] and culture.[79] This section begins by stating how the motivation theories use rewards and recognition, followed by a discussion of reward and recognition programs and giving praise.

LO 11-6

Identify some of the rewards and recognitions organizations use to motivate employees.

How Each of the Motivation Theories Uses Rewards and Recognition

The *hierarchy of needs* and *ERG theories* use financial rewards to meet the lower-level needs but use nonfinancial rewards to meet higher-level needs. With *two-factor theory*, maintenance needs are primarily met financially, and motivators are met nonfinancially. *Acquired needs* rewards vary with need. People with high n Ach seek achievement and can be motivated to achieve goals with both types of rewards. The n Pows tend to provide both, because having power is a nonfinancial reward, but as people gain power, they often get pay raises. The n Affs' needs are met primarily through relationships.

People want *equity* in both their pay and their treatment, which includes recognition. With *goal-setting theory*, people can be motivated to meet goals with both financial and nonfinancial rewards. Using *expectancy theory* effectively is based on knowing what people value as rewards, which can be either or both depending on the individual.

Again, *reinforcement theory* doesn't focus on meeting needs, and although the focus is on giving a positive reward, it also gives punishment instead. The rewards (or punishment) can be both financial and nonfinancial with either continuous or intermittent reinforcement. Pay does affect performance.[80]

Reward and Recognition Programs

Recall that rewards can be internally (intrinsic) or externally (extrinsic) focused and be financial or nonfinancial. People work for money, so financial rewards are critical, but just as important are relationships[81] and recognition for the work we do.[82] In an exit interview, **Edible Arrangements** found that separators didn't feel appreciated.[83] Money talks, but non-cash rewards do motivate.[84] So both financial and nonfinancial rewards and recognition are important to motivate employees to meet objectives.

Types of Rewards and Recognition. People respond to incentives,[85] and rewards and recognition are motivational incentives,[86] so they are also called *incentive systems*. Some of the many types of rewards and recognition include *good compensation and flexible work schedules*[87] (Chapter 9)—for example, **FlexJobs** director of employer outreach **Kristin Thomas** works the hours that suit her from home[88]—and *pay for performance*.

Flexible Work and Parents. Companies are paying closer attention to the needs of working parents and being more flexible with their work hours. Women with children under 18 spend twice as much time as men on child care.[89] Do you recall our discussion of work–life balance? Well, some say you can't balance work and life, so *work–life integration* is the new normal. People think little of a workout at noon and a conference call at 9 p.m. More than 75% of high-earning women do personal things during work hours and business after hours. **Google** product manager **Eileen Hiromura** has two kids, and they visited her at the office Wednesday, and she came to work at 10:30 on Friday because she took them to the dentist. She comes home for dinner almost every night but does work after the kids go to bed and writes reports on Saturdays.[90]

11-2 JOIN THE DISCUSSION ETHICS & SOCIAL RESPONSIBILITY

Using Reinforcement Theory

Reinforcement theory has been used successfully to maintain and increase performance by many companies globally. However, its use does have critics who claim that it manipulates employees and that it is the carrot-and-stick approach to motivation.

1. Does reinforcement motivate you?

2. Is reinforcement effective (does it serve to motivate) in today's global economy?

3. Is the use of reinforcement theory ethical and socially responsible or manipulative?

Pay for Performance. Many companies offer *pay for performance* including *bonuses* (usually additional money for meeting objectives), *profit sharing* (creating a pool of monies to be disbursed to employees by taking a stated percentage of a company's profits), and *stock options* (giving employees the right to buy a specified number of a company's shares at a fixed price for a specified time, which are a major part of top executive compensation).

Frequency of Rewards and Recognition. The frequency is on the increase. **Google**, **Facebook**, **Zulily**, and **Evolv** find that giving quarterly raises is a better motivator than giving them annually.[91] Motivational consulting firm **Globoforce** recommends sharing the wealth and giving small rewards. When the firm wants to reinforce certain behavior, you should give 80% to 90% of employees some reward every year. To show appreciation, small prizes of around $100 work as well as larger ones, such as tickets to a game/play/movie and gift certificates for dinner or to stores. The VP of human resources at **Intuit** says, "I've never seen bigger awards get as much bang for the buck."[92]

Many organizations use reward and recognition programs because they have been successful in motivating employees to perform at high levels.

Most firms have an annual convention or meeting of some kind that includes giving rewards. But **Globoforce** found that companies get the best results with weekly rewards. Five percent of employees should get an award every week so that employees don't forget about the program. Small awards all the time are a way to constantly tell employees management appreciates their efforts.[93]

Departmental Rewards and Recognition. You can even give your own rewards and recognition to your department employees. A good way to start is to give small spot rewards based on performance. When **Intuit** acquired **Paycycle**, **Jennifer Lepird** spent several weeks working long hours integrating the new employees into Intuit's salary structure. The acquisition team manager sent her a handwritten note of recognition with a gift certificate reward. Lepird was thrilled that somebody took the time to recognize her effort.[94] Would you like to be surprised with a $50 gift certificate to your favorite restaurant?

Giving Praise

Giving praise is a form of reward,[95] and praise works better than criticism.[96] Giving praise is simply complimenting the achievements of others to motivate them to perform a task or to encourage repeat performance. Giving a person a compliment is a great way to open a conversation and get to know him or her,[97] and it's a good way to influence people—called *ingratiation*.[98] You can also use *altercasting*—you characterize the person as a certain type of person in order to encourage him or her to behave in a desired manner. "Shawn, I know you're a good writer and know the test, will you please write the report?" People want to rise to the occasion.[99]

It cost you nothing to give praise, involves very little effort, and produces a lot in return.[100] Unfortunately, managers often don't realize how important giving recognition is, and they get so busy that they neglect to give praise. When was the last time your boss thanked or praised you for a job well done? When was the last time your boss complained about your work? If you are a manager, when was the last time you praised or criticized your employees? What is the ratio of praise to criticism?

Authors of *The One Minute Manager* **Ken Blanchard** and **Spencer Johnson** developed a technique for feedback that involves giving one minute of praise; so keep praise short and look the person in the eye. You don't have to be a manager to give praise. When was the last time you told your boss, a coworker, or a friend or family member he or she did a good job? Don't go a day without giving praise. Model 11-1 shows the steps in the **giving praise model.**

WORK
APPLICATION 11-8

Select an organization that you work for or have worked for and briefly describe its rewards and recognition.

giving praise model A four-step technique for providing feedback to an employee: (1) Tell the employee exactly what was done correctly; (2) tell the employee why the behavior is important; (3) stop for a moment of silence; and (4) encourage repeat performance.

MODEL 11-1 GIVING PRAISE

1. Tell the employee exactly what was done correctly. → 2. Tell the employee why the behavior is important. → 3. Stop for a moment of silence. → 4. Encourage repeat performance.

Step 1. Tell the employee exactly what was done correctly. Be very specific and descriptive. "Mia, I just overheard you deal with that customer's complaint. You did an excellent job of keeping your cool; you were polite. That person came in angry and left happy."

Step 2. Tell the employee why the behavior is important. Briefly state how the organization and/or person benefits from the action. Also, tell the employee how you feel about the behavior. "One dissatisfied customer can cause hundreds of dollars in lost sales. It really made me proud to see you handle that tough situation the way you did."

Step 3. Stop for a moment of silence. Being silent is tough. The rationale for the silence is to give the employee the chance to feel the impact of the praise.

Step 4. Encourage repeat performance. You may also make some physical gesture, if both parties feel comfortable with physical contact: "Thanks, Mia, keep up the good work" (while giving a thumbs-up or shaking hands).

When it is difficult to give face-to-face praise, it can also come in the form of a *phone call/ Skype* and *written communication* following the giving praise model. Email works, but it is said that a *handwritten note* is more personal and powerful.

Trends and Issues in Management

There is a new term called *cultural intelligence (CQ*—similar to IQ), including cognitive, motivational, and behavioral dimensions of multicultural competence.[101] The motivation theories you have studied were developed largely in North America. As organizations become *global*, you must be aware of the *cultural* impact on theoretical generalizations. **Geert Hofstede** and the **GLOBE** research (Chapter 3) support these findings.[102] The intrinsic motivation provided by the satisfaction of higher-level needs tends to be more relevant in developed countries than in developing countries, in which most people are on a lower level of the hierarchy of needs. The term *self-actualization* has no literal translation in some Chinese dialects. Even in developed countries, the level of needs on which people focus varies. In the United States, people tend to be motivated by higher-level needs of self-actualization and esteem; in Greece and Japan, security is more important; and in Sweden, Norway, and Denmark, people are more concerned with social needs. McClelland's need for achievement is more predominant in the United States than elsewhere. Thus, this need has limited use as a motivator outside of the United States and Canada, unless managers are willing to try to instill it in employees.

One major *cultural* difference that affects motivation in businesses is that between *individualistic and collective societies*. Individualistic societies (the United States, Canada, Great Britain, Australia) tend to value individual accomplishment. Collective societies (China, Japan, Mexico, Singapore, Venezuela, Pakistan) tend to value group accomplishment and loyalty. Cultural differences suggest that self-actualization, achievement, and esteem needs tend to be met through group membership in Japan and China and through individual accomplishments in the United States.

Expectancy theory holds up fairly well cross-culturally, because it is flexible. It allows for the possibility that there may be differences in expectations and valences across cultures. For example, social acceptance may be of higher value than individual recognition in collective societies. However, incentive systems have to vary based on laws and the characteristics of country cultures.[103] **Market America** (**IOM 5**) started in the United States, but it has international operations in both individual- and collective-culture countries. Market America is confident that its UnFranchise® approach will work with anyone who wants to be an entrepreneur anywhere in the world.

Perks help,[104] but the real key to motivation is interpersonal relationships; employees are more engaged where relationships thrive.[105] And this is especially true of younger workers, as there is *generational diversity* in what motivates employees (Chapter 3).[106] Millennials and Generation Y (younger) employees are more likely than Generation X and baby boomers (older) to leave a job they don't like and a boss they don't like.[107] They are also more concerned about flexible work schedules and work–life integration. So managers need to show they care about these employees, who tend to need more frequent feedback and encouragement than older workers to keep motivated.

Motivational methods should be *ethical*. You have to be careful that incentives don't lead to unethical behavior, like at **Wells Fargo**. At **Market America** (**IOM 6**), and for all businesses, the ethical concern about multilevel marketing (MLM) is that many people start their entrepreneurial venture and don't make any money. According to the **Consumer Awareness Institute**, an MLM watchdog group, in a study of 400 MLM companies, more than 99% of people lose money. **JR Ridinger** says that is not the case at Market America and that what you get out of his business is what you put into the business. People who don't succeed are not motivated and didn't work the system as instructed, so they don't change their lives.

As we close this chapter, you should have a better understanding of the relationship between motivation and performance. You should also know the four different content motivation theories, three process motivation theories, reinforcement theory, and how these motivation theories affect the motivation process. Finally, you should have better knowledge of employee reward and recognition programs and about motivation theories in a global generationally diverse context.

$SAGE edge™   **edge.sagepub.com/lussier8e**

Want a better grade?

Get the tools you need to sharpen your study skills. Access practice quizzes, eFlashcards, video and multimedia, and more at edge.sagepub.com/lussier8e.

Digital Resources

Learning Objective	Digital Resource
11 1. Illustrate the motivation process, and explain the performance formula and how to use it.	▶ The Puzzle of Motivation
11-2. Compare the four content motivation theories.	▶ Two Factor Theory
11-3. Compare the three process motivation theories.	▣ Expectancy Theory
11-4. Explain the four types and two schedules of reinforcement.	▶ Management in Action: Schedules of Reinforcement*
11-5. Contrast content, process, and reinforcement theories.	▣ Reinforcement Theory
11-6. Identify some of the rewards and recognitions organizations use to motivate employees.	▶ Intrinsic Rewards*

* premium video available only in the interactive eBook

• • • CHAPTER SUMMARY

11-1. **Illustrate the motivation process, and explain the performance formula and how to use it.**

Employees go through a five-step process to meet their needs, beginning with a need that motivates behavior that leads to a consequence and satisfaction or dissatisfaction on meeting the need, and there is feedback throughout the process. Note that this is a cyclical process, because needs recur. The performance formula proposes that performance is based on ability, motivation, and resources. For maximum performance, all three factors must be high. When performance is not optimum, managers need to determine which factor of the performance formula is weak and take appropriate action to correct the problem.

11-2. **Compare the four content motivation theories.**

The similarity among the four content motivation theories is their focus on identifying and understanding employees' needs. The theories identify similar needs but differ in the way they classify the needs. *Hierarchy of needs theory* classifies needs by five levels as physiological, safety, social, esteem, and self-actualization needs. *ERG theory* proposes existence, relatedness, and growth needs. *Two-factor theory* proposes that employees are engaged by motivators (higher-level needs) rather than by maintenance factors (lower-level needs). *Acquired needs theory* includes achievement, power, and affiliation needs; it includes no lower-level needs.

11-3. **Compare the three process motivation theories.**

The similarity among the three process motivation theories is their focus on understanding how employees choose behaviors to fulfill their needs. However, they are very different in how they perceive employee motivation. Equity theory proposes that employees are motivated when their perceived inputs equal outputs. Goal-setting theory proposes that achievable but difficult goals motivate employees. Expectancy theory proposes that employees are motivated when they believe they can accomplish the task and the rewards for doing so are worth the effort.

11-4. **Explain the four types and two schedules of reinforcement.**

Positive reinforcement is rewarding desirable behavior. *Avoidance reinforcement* (also called negative reinforcement) is the use of the threat of a negative consequence to prevent undesirable behavior; the negative consequence is not used as long as the behavior is desirable. *Punishment* is the actual use of a negative consequence to decrease undesirable behavior. *Extinction* is the withholding of reinforcement in order to reduce or eliminate (extinguish) a behavior. The two schedules of reinforcement include *continuous*, in which every behavior is reinforced; and *intermittent* in which reinforcement is given based on the passage of time (interval) or output (ratio).

11-5. **Contrast content, process, and reinforcement theories.**

Content motivation theories focus on identifying and understanding employees' needs. *Process motivation* theories go a step further to understand how employees choose behavior to fulfill their needs. *Reinforcement theory* is not concerned about employees' needs; it focuses on getting employees to do what managers want them to do through the consequences provided for their behavior. The use of rewards is the best means of motivating employees.

11-6. **Identify some of the rewards and recognitions organizations use to motivate employees.**

To motivate employees, organizations use good compensation packages with incentives, flexible work schedules, and pay for performance (bonuses, profit sharing, and stock options). Giving praise is also a quick and no-cost motivator.

• • • KEY TERMS

acquired needs theory, 371
content motivation theories, 368
equity theory, 373
ERG theory, 369
expectancy theory, 376

giving praise model, 383
goal-setting theory, 375
hierarchy of needs theory, 368
motivation, 366
motivation process, 366

performance formula, 367
process motivation theories, 374
reinforcement theory, 378
two-factor theory, 369

• • • KEY TERM REVIEW

Complete each of the following statements using one of this chapter's key terms.

1. _____ is the willingness to achieve organizational objectives or to go above and beyond the call of duty (organizational citizenship behavior).

2. The _____ is the process of moving from need to motive to behavior to consequence to satisfaction or dissatisfaction.

3. The _____ is performance = ability × motivation × resources.

4. _____ focus on identifying and understanding employees' needs.

5. The _____ proposes that employees are motivated by five levels of needs: physiological, safety, social, esteem, and self-actualization.

6. _____ proposes that employees are motivated by three needs: existence, relatedness, and growth.

7. _____ proposes that employees are motivated by motivators rather than by maintenance factors.

8. _____ proposes that employees are motivated by their needs for achievement, power, and affiliation.

9. _____ focus on understanding how employees choose behaviors to fulfill their needs.

10. _____ proposes that employees are motivated when their perceived inputs equal outputs.

11. _____ proposes that achievable but difficult goals motivate employees.

12. _____ proposes that employees are motivated when they believe they can accomplish a task and the rewards for doing so are worth the effort.

13. _____ proposes that the consequences of their behavior will motivate employees to behave in predetermined ways.

14. The steps in the _____ are as follows: (1) Tell the employee exactly what was done correctly; (2) tell the employee why the behavior is important; (3) stop for a moment of silence; and (4) encourage repeat performance.

● ● ● REVIEW QUESTIONS

1. How is the performance formula used by managers?

2. What are the three major classes of motivation theories?

3. What are the four content motivation theories?

4. What do the *E*, *R*, and *G* stand for in ERG theory?

5. What are the two factors in Herzberg's two-factor theory?

6. What is the role of perception in equity theory?

7. Does the goal-setting theory really motivate employees?

8. What are the two variables of the expectancy theory?

9. What are the two schedules of reinforcement?

10. Is there a relationship among the three major classifications of motivation theories?

● ● ● COMMUNICATION SKILLS

The following critical-thinking questions can be used for class discussion and/or as written assignments to develop communication skills. Be sure to give complete explanations for all questions.

1. Do people really have diverse needs?

2. What is motivation, and why is it important to know how to motivate employees?

3. Do you agree that managers' attitudes and expectations affect employee motivation and performance? Explain your answer.

4. Do you agree with the performance formula? Will you use it on the job?

5. Which of the four content motivation theories makes the most sense to you? Why?

6. Which of the three process motivation theories makes the most sense to you? Why?

7. What reinforcement methods have been used to get you to go to work and to be on time?

8. Reinforcement theory is unethical because it is used to manipulate employees. Do you agree with this statement? Explain your answer.

9. Which motivation theory makes the most sense to you? Explain why.

10. What are the major methods and techniques you plan to use on the job as a manager to increase motivation and performance?

CASES

● ● ● Case 11-1   The Walt Disney Company

The Walt Disney Company was incorporated in 1995. It operates in four business segments including Media Networks, Parks and Resorts, Studio Entertainment, and Consumer Products and Interactive Media. The company is headquartered in

Burbank, California, and maintains a workforce of 195,000 people worldwide. The mission of the Walt Disney Company is: "To be one of the world's leading producers and providers of entertainment and information. Using our portfolio of brands to differentiate our content, services and consumer products, we seek to develop the most creative, innovative and profitable entertainment experiences and related products in the world." Four core values provide the foundation to support the achievement of the company's mission—safety, courtesy, the show (performing according to a role's requirements) and efficiency. To provide a world-class experience for all of the guests who visit Disney theme parks, the company translates these four core values into specific service practices for its case members (employees):

Safety

- I practice safe behaviors in everything I do
- I take action to always put safety first
- I speak up to ensure the safety of Others

Courtesy

- I project a positive image and energy
- I am courteous and respectful to Guests of all ages
- I go above and beyond to exceed Guest expectations

Show

- I stay in character and perform my role in the show
- I ensure my area is show-ready at all times

Efficiency

- I perform my role efficiently so Guests get the most out of their visit
- I use my time and resources wisely

Effective leadership is critical for motivating Disney cast members to provide the desired level of guest experience at its theme parks. The four core values have been linked to specific leader practices referred to as Disney Leader Basics:

- I lead with a positive attitude and demonstrate commitment to Cast Members
- I know and manage my operation and teach it to Cast Members
- I recognize and hold Cast Members accountable for delivering The Four Keys Basics

In addition, Disney leaders motivate cast members by articulating a vision for how to achieve the mission of the company in a way that is consistent with its four core values. Storytelling is an essential part of putting this principle into practice. Closely related to this is an emphasis on purpose before task so that cast members understand why they are performing their job duties. Finally, leaders need to focus on concrete actions that are consistent with Disney's mission and values so that they provide a strong model for cast members.

The Walt Disney Company places a strong emphasis on cast member recognition as a means to motivate and engage them. The company has more than 180 recognition programs. Some examples of these programs include the following:

- Lifetime Spirit of FRED Award that was created from the name of an employee who personified the Disney values: Friendly, Resourceful, Enthusiastic, and Dependable. Recipients are given a miniature Mickey Mouse statue.

- WOW! Cards—Staff use brightly colored, trifold thank-you notes to recognize fellow staff members for their help.

- Eliminate the Negative—Disney recognizes cast members who are service minded and people oriented by inviting them to serve as facilitators for training programs for new cast members. The program reinforces the Disney culture in the trainers.

- Disney expects its leaders to be coaches and to give its people regular developmental feedback to help them grow at a personal and professional level. Managers' job performance is formally evaluated based on their financial/technical skills, but also on their ability to lead people.

Discussion Questions

1. How does the Disney Company use Alderfer's ERG theory of motivation to motivate its workforce?

2. How does the Disney Company use the expectancy theory of motivation to motivate its workforce?

3. How does the Disney Company use reinforcement theories of motivation to motivate its workforce?

4. How does the Disney Company use recognition to motivate its workforce?

5. If you worked at Disney Company, would its recognition programs be effective in motivating you? Why or why not?

6. What do you think are the factors that motivate workers the most today? Why?

References

https://thewaltdisneycompany.com/about/

https://thewaltdisneycompany.com

http://www.reuters.com/finance/stocks/companyProfile?symbol=DIS.N

http://www.weigniteit.com/pdfs/Ignite-Core-Values.pdf

http://disneyatwork.com/disneys-four-keys-to-a-great-guest-experience/

https://disneyinstitute.com/blog/2014/03/leadership-lessons-from-walt-disney-how-to-inspire-your-team/252/

https://www.forbes.com/sites/georgebradt/2015/05/20/disneys-best-ever-example-of-motivating-employees/#338e2ce0144b

http://www.meetingsnet.com/corporate-meetings/motivation-matters-disneys-magic-recognition

https://www.helpscout.net/blog/disney-customer-experience/

Case created by Loren Kuzuhara, University of Wisconsin–Madison.

••• Case 11-2   Clif Bar & Company: Creating a Sustainable World Through Employee Engagement

We're working to run a different kind of company: The kind of place we'd want to work, that makes the kind of food we'd like to eat, and that strives for a healthier, more sustainable world—the kind of world we'd like to pass on to our children. And those aren't just words. They're our mission statement. —Kit Crawford(1)

Clif Bar & Company is a leading manufacturer of natural, organic energy foods and has found a successful market niche with its Clif and Luna branded bars.(2) Whether for hiking, mountaineering, or snacking on the go, those who have shopped for energy food products are likely familiar with the Clif Bar. With its distinctive brown packaging featuring an image of a rock climber scaling a mountainside, the Clif Bar has become synonymous with energy bar and is the company's flagship product.

A family-owned business at its outset, the Clif Bar was born out of the quest to find a better-tasting energy bar.(3) Twenty-three years later and now boasting a staff of more than 300, Clif Bar still approaches its employees with the family-like, people-first attitude that led to its success. Ranked in Fortune's top 25 best places to work,(4) Clif Bar has found ways to keep employees throughout the company engaged.

Employee Engagement. Founder and CEO Gary Erickson's vision is "If I want to keep employees passionate and engaged, I've got to let them go, to make sure they have time to live their lives, have adventures in the world, and come back refreshed."(5)

So a workout with a personal trainer in the middle of a workday? No problem. Need a three-day weekend or rather work from home once a week? Sure thing. Last-minute babysitter cancellation? On-site day care is available. These are a few of the employee perks at Clif Bar & Company. In line with the company's focus on nutrition and healthy lifestyles, Clif Bar reimburses employees up to $1,500 per year for biking or walking to work. (6) Every seven years, employees become eligible for a paid six-week sabbatical in addition to any vacation time accrued.

Beyond the unique perquisites, surveys indicated that 92% of Clif Bar employees felt as though their work usually carried meaningful responsibility within the company.(7) Management has also been known to entrust employees with a high level of responsibility without the fear of being micromanaged. Questions, feedback, comments, ideas, and information sharing is encouraged and valued and can be communicated in a free and transparent manner with both managers and others within the organization. Professional development is encouraged and fostered—88% of Clif Bar's surveyed employees felt as though they received the training and development necessary to further their careers.(8)

Purpose is baked into the Clif Bar brand. The company's founders, Gary Erickson and Kit Crawford, turned down a lucrative buyout offer because they felt they could do better creating a company with purpose. Thanks to an authentic approach to being a responsible business and an impressive array of benefits aimed at fostering not only work–life balance but work–life integration, 90% of employees at Clif Bar participate in the CLIF® CORPS volunteer program, and 98% are proud of where they work. When you consider that 70% of people in the United States are not engaged in their jobs, it is clear that this company is doing something right. "Purpose drives performance. If we can get people circled around a bigger purpose, performance will improve and ultimately drive efficiency."(9)

As a result, Clif Bar employees are proud of their accomplishments and the impact they have within the organization, in the community, and on the company's reputation. (10) For many, the company's values and culture align with their own. It is more than just a job; rather, employees feel a deeper sense of meaning can be derived from the opportunity to have a positive influence on both the company and the community while building a sustainable work–life balance.(11)

Clif Bar & Company's employee-centric position has proven successful. Over the previous decade, Clif Bar has reported a 20% compound annual growth rate and an employee turnover ratio of 3%.(12) Word has gotten out about the company—in the span of one year, 7,700 job applications were received for a mere 114 new and available positions.(13) Clearly, Clif Bar & Company's people-first strategy has helped forge its path toward sustainable employee engagement.

Discussion Questions

1. How does Herzberg's two-factor theory apply to Clif Bar & Company's employee engagement and motivation techniques? Name the case's extrinsic and intrinsic factors.

2. Does Vroom's expectancy theory support Clif Bar & Company's policies? Why or why not?

3. Are Clif Bar & Company's methods sustainable, long-term motivators for its employees? Be sure to use theory from the chapter to support your answer.

4. Drawing from your experiences and preferences, would perks and fringe benefits similar to those that Clif Bar offer be an effective motivator for you? Would the company's development and job enrichment opportunities be a motivator for you? Why or why not?

5. What types of organizations can Clif Bar's engagement and motivation techniques be applied in? In what organizations won't they work? Why or why not?

Cumulative Case Questions

6. How does organizational culture apply to the case (Chapter 2)?

7. Which of the four grand strategies is Clif Bar & Company utilizing (Chapter 5)? Search online to find current information on the company's business decisions to inform your answer.

8. In what ways does human resource management support Clif Bar's employee engagement techniques (Chapter 9)?

References

(1) Crawford, K. (2017). A different type of company. Retrieved February 1, 2017, from http://www.clifbar.com/who-we-are

(2) Hoovers website. http://0-subscriber.hoovers.com.liucat.lib.liu.edu/H/company360/fulldescription.html?companyId=59746000000000

(2) Ibid.

(3) Mangalindan, J. (2014, September 18). Clif Bar climbs to the top of America's workplaces. *Fortune*. Retrieved June 11, 2015, from http://fortune.com/2014/09/18/clif-bar-top-of-americas-workplaces/

(4) Ibid.

(5) Great Place to Work website. http://reviews.greatplacetowork.com/clif-bar-co

(6) Mangalindan. J. (2014, September 18). Clif Bar climbs to the top of America's workplaces. *Fortune*. Retrieved June 11, 2015, from http://fortune.com/2014/09/18/clif-bar-top-of-americas-workplaces/

(7) Great Place to Work website. http://reviews.greatplacetowork.com/clif-bar-co

(8) Ibid.

(9) Palkovsky, N. (2016, June 17). Clif Bar, Kohler, Pixar, Timberland share the "secret sauce" of employee engagement. Retrieved February 1, 2017, from http://www.sustainablebrands.com/news_and_views/organizational_change/nicole_palkovsky/clif_bar_kohler_pixar_timberland_share_secret_

(10) Great Place to Work website. http://reviews.greatplacetowork.com/clif-bar-co

(11) Ibid.

(12) Mangalindan, J. (2014, September 18). Clif Bar climbs to the top of America's workplaces. *Fortune*. Retrieved June 11, 2015, from http://fortune.com/2014/09/18/clif-bar-top-of-americas-workplaces/

(13) Ibid.

Case created by Herbert Sherman, Hannah K. Walter, and Naveed Ahmad, Long Island University.

● ● ● SKILL BUILDER 11-1: GIVING PRAISE

Objective

To develop the skill of giving praise to motivate people to higher levels of performance.

Skills

The primary skills developed through this exercise are:

1. *Management skill*—leadership (motivating others)

2. *AACSB competency*—communication abilities

3. *Management function*—leading

Think of a job situation in which you did something well, deserving of praise and recognition. For example, you may have saved the company some money, you may have turned a dissatisfied customer into a happy one, and so on. Imagine yourself in a management position, and write out the praise you would give to an employee for doing what you did.

Briefly describe the situation:

Step 1. Tell the employee exactly what was done correctly.

Step 2. Tell the employee why the behavior is important.

Step 3. Stop for a moment of silence. (Count to 5 silently.)

Step 4. Encourage repeat performance.

Apply It

What did I learn from this experience? How will I use this knowledge in the future?

● ● ● SKILL BUILDER 11-2: SELF-MOTIVATION

Objective

To better understand what motivates you.

Skills

The primary skills developed through this exercise are:

1. *Management skill*—leadership (motivating yourself)

2. *AACSB competency*—reasoning abilities

3. *Management function*—leading

Review the two Self-Assessment exercises. What did you learn about yourself? How can you improve your self-motivation so that you can be more successful?

Apply It

What did I learn from this experience? How will I use this knowledge in the future?

Kevork Djansezian/Getty Images

12 Leading With Influence

Ideas on Management
From Elon Musk, Visionary Leader

Elon Musk is a South Africa–born Canadian American (citizen 2002) entrepreneur, investor, engineer, inventor, and influential leader. According to *Forbes*, "Elon Musk has inherited Steve Jobs's mantle as the cult favorite CEO. And his electric car company Tesla has grabbed Apple's "creative crown" as the most innovative company.

In 2002, Musk sold **PayPal** for $165 million and became founder and CEO of **SpaceX** (Space Exploration Technologies). **Tesla Motors** (electric cars) was cofounded in 2003, and in 2004, Musk helped raise capital and took an active role within the company and became CEO in 2008. Musk provided the initial concept and financial capital for **SolarCity** (the largest installer of solar panels), which was cofounded in 2006 by his cousins **Lyndon and Peter Rive** with Musk as chairman. Musk is also backing a radical new intercity mass-transportation concept called Hyperloop. As a multibillionaire, why is Musk working so hard? As a global leader, he wants to change the world. As you will find out in this chapter, it's been a bumpy road, as he is changing transportation on earth and space.

IOM 1. Is trust important to Musk's success, is he a manager or leader, and what other new ventures did Musk start before SpaceX?

IOM 2. What leadership traits does Musk have, and what major problems did these traits help him overcome, especially in 2008?

IOM 3. Which behavioral leadership styles does Musk use?

IOM 4. Which situational leadership styles does Musk use?

IOM 5. What type of contemporary leader is Musk?

IOM 6. What trends is Musk setting?

You'll find answers to these **IOM** questions throughout the chapter. To learn more about the three companies, visit www.spacex.com, www.teslamotors .com, and www.solarcity.com.

Source: Information for this case was taken from J. Dyer, H. Gregersen, and N. Furr, "Tesla's Secret Formula," *Forbes* (September 7, 2015): 91–118.

Leadership Theories

Leadership is a topic of great interest to both scholars and managers,[1] and leadership is ranked in the top five skills companies value in new hires.[2] Why? Because leadership is an important factor contributing to organizational success.[3] In this section, we discuss leadership and trust, the difference between leadership and management, and an overview of the four major classifications of leadership theories.

Leadership and Trust

Let's start by discussing the importance of leadership, move on to its development, and end with trust.

The Importance of Leadership. As defined in Chapter 1, *leadership* is the process of influencing employees to work toward achieving objectives.

LO 12-1

Compare the four classifications of leadership theories.

Recall (Chapter 10) that *power* and *politics* are also about influencing. Founding CEO of **City Winery Michael Dorf** says there is no way his company could have grown without great managers.[4] It takes people skills to be an effective leader,[5] and we will talk about leadership at all levels throughout this chapter. But here let's focus on the importance of top management leadership, because it is commonly believed that success or failure is based on top management leadership. Do you believe **Apple** would be the company it is today without its cofounder **Steve Jobs**, or would Microsoft be **Microsoft** without **Bill Gates**?

Berkshire Hathaway CEO **Warren Buffett** is best known as the investment guru, but his management record is just as good. Buffett has more than 60 operating units; he buys companies and turns them around and makes good companies even better.[6] After a century of mismanagement, the new owner of **Major League Baseball's (MLB) Chicago Cubs, Tom Ricketts,** provided the resources and empowered his top managers—President of Baseball Operations **Theo Epstein** (credited with turning the **Red Sox** team roster into winners) and President of Business Operations **Crane Kenney**—with the shared leadership to excel into a winning team.[7]

Leaders who cultivate a trusting environment create room for employees to help each other without worrying about their own safety within the organization.

Conversely, if a company is not performing well or the CEO can't get along with the board, the CEO—and even founding CEOs, including **Steve Jobs** from **Apple**, **Andrew Mason** from **Groupon**, and **George Zimmer** from **Men's Wearhouse**—can be fired by the board of directors.[8]

Leadership Development. There are two age-old leadership questions: "Are leaders born or made?" and "Can leadership skills be developed?" The first question is actually kind of a trick question because the answer is both, and part of the answer to question 1 answers question 2. We are all born with different levels of natural leadership ability, but research shows that leadership skills can be developed.[9] Teaching leadership theories (as we do in this chapter) contributes to developing leaders' skills.[10] Over the past 50 years or so, leadership has been one of the most widely taught subjects in business schools around the globe.[11] Also, business sections of bookstores are full of books on the latest leadership gimmicks and fads.[12] Unfortunately, most are not based on scientific research like the theories you will learn in this chapter.

If leadership skills can't be developed, why would colleges offer management and leadership courses and companies (including **GE** and **Apple**, just to name a few) spend millions on training and development programs, especially leadership development? **IBM** wants its human resources (HR) department to focus on leadership development.[13] **Unilever** recently invested heavily in a new training facility for leadership development.[14] **McKinsey** consulting firm itself is a leadership factory, whose alumni have become CEOs of **American Express**, **AT&T**, **Boeing**, **IBM**, and dozens of other companies.[15]

In a survey, companies were asked to agree or disagree with the following statements; here is the percentage of "agree" answers.[16]

- My company screens external candidates on the basis of leadership ability—77% agreed.
- My company devotes significant resources to leadership development—63% agreed.
- My company is effective at building a leadership pipeline—71% agreed.
- My company evaluates employees on their leadership potential—87% agreed.

The Importance of Trust in Leadership. Recall that happiness and success in our personal and professional lives are based on our relationships. Good relationships are based on trust.[17] Do you have good relationships with people you can't trust? Employees' trust in managers affects their motivation to engage in organizational citizenship behavior (OCB).[18] A survey

©iStockphoto.com/PeopleImages

12-1 SELF-ASSESSMENT

Your Trustworthiness

For each statement, select the frequency with which you use, or would use, the behavior at work. Be honest; that's part of trustworthiness.

1	2	3	4	5
Almost always				Almost never

_____ 1. I tell the truth; I tell it like it is.

_____ 2. When I make a commitment to do something, I do it.

_____ 3. I strive to be fair by creating a win-win situation for all parties.

_____ 4. I do the task to the best of my ability.

_____ 5. I volunteer to help others when I can, and I seek help when I need it.

_____ 6. I am humble; I don't brag about my accomplishments.

_____ 7. When I make a mistake, I admit it rather than try to cover it up or downplay it.

_____ 8. I don't overcommit to the point of breaking commitments.

_____ 9. I practice what I preach and walk the talk; I don't say one thing and do another.

_____ 10. I treat coworkers—both friends and others—fairly.

_____ 11. I stand by, protect, and save face for coworkers.

_____ 12. When someone tells me something in confidence, I don't tell anyone else.

_____ 13. I say only positive things, or nothing, about coworkers; I don't gossip.

_____ 14. I am viewed by coworkers as being collaborative rather than competitive.

Place the numbers (1 to 5) you recorded for the situations on the lines below. Total each by column; then add the totals of the four columns and place the grand total on the continuum (14–70) below the totals.

Integrity	Competence	Consistency	Loyalty
_____ 1	_____ 4	_____ 8	_____ 11
_____ 2	_____ 5	_____ 9	_____ 12
_____ 3	_____ 6	_____ 10	_____ 13
	_____ 7		_____ 14
_____ total	_____ total	_____ total	_____ total

14	20	30	40	50	60	70
Trustworthy						Untrustworthy

The lower your score, the more trustworthy you perceive yourself to be. To validate your score, you can have friends and coworkers complete the assessment and compare scores. If you have any high scores, you may want to work at changing the behavior to be more trusting.

- *Integrity* is being honest. It is the most important dimension;[19] without it, you will not be trusted. To have integrity, don't lie, cheat, or steal from others, and be fair by creating a win-win for everyone.
- *Competence* is getting the task done. Know your strengths and limitations and don't commit to doing something you can't deliver on. Competent people admit their mistakes and apologize when they don't deliver as expected.
- *Consistency* is predictability in competence. Always keep your commitments. If you say you will do something, be sure to actually deliver.
- *Loyalty* is looking out for others' interests. Good friends even go to the point of putting others' needs before their own. No narcissistic backstabbing and taking advantage of others. If someone tells you something in confidence (a secret), don't tell others. Don't gossip negatively about others, because people will assume you gossip about them to others too.

revealed that 74% of engaged employees trust their manager, while only 14% don't trust their boss.[20] Would you go above and beyond what is expected (work harder) for a boss you don't trust? In turn, managers need to be able to trust employees.[21] Trustworthiness is based on at least four dimensions, listed in what follows with tips on improving it. But before reading, complete Self-Assessment 12-1 to find out how trustworthy you are.

Leaders Versus Managers

What's the Difference? People tend to use the terms *manager* and *leader* interchangeably. However, managers and leaders differ.[22] Leading is one of the four management functions (planning, organizing, leading, and controlling). Thus, management gives position power and is broader in scope than leadership, but leadership is critical to management success.[23] A manager can have this position without being a true leader. There are managers—you may know of some—who are not leaders because they do not have the trust and ability to influence others. There are also good leaders who are not managers. An informal leader, an employee group member, is a case in point. You may have been in a situation in which one of your peers had more influence than the manager/coach. So leadership doesn't have to be an aspect of a title; you can be an informal leader, be a peer leader, and play a leadership role in a team when you influence others to do something.[24]

Apple's **Steve Jobs** was viewed as a leader in his ability to influence others to make great products, but he was not viewed as a good manager. **Chief Operating Officer (COO) Tim Cook** did most of the management at Apple, and as CEO today, he is viewed as both a good manager and a good leader.[25] In fact, Cook was given the title The World's Greatest Leader by ***Fortune*** in 2015.[26]

Shared Leadership. Today, leadership is a serial emergence of both official and unofficial leaders as part of a simultaneous, ongoing, mutual influence process,[27] as in participative leadership[28]. Hence all leadership is shared leadership; it is a matter of degree—sometimes it is shared completely, and other times leadership is not shared at all.[29] So you don't have to be a manager to be a leader, and as we have stated repeatedly, leadership is being shared today, so everyone is expected to lead when the need arises.[30] Unfortunately, it has been said that new college grads lack the ability to manage and lead.[31] Therefore, this book focuses on helping you develop both these skills.

Elon Musk (**IOM 1**) needed to have the trust of people to lend him money and invest in his business ventures. Would you lend money or invest in a business with a guy you didn't trust? Musk is both a manager as CEO of **SpaceX** and **Tesla** and a leader to influence people within and outside his companies. Musk started his serial entrepreneurial career as a college student, buying a 10-bedroom frat house and using it as an unofficial nightclub. In 1995, with trust and leadership skills, Musk and his brother, Kimbal, started web software company **Zip2** and sold it to **Compaq Computer**. Musk cofounded **X.com** in March 1999, merged it with **Confinity**, changed the name to **PayPal** in 2001, and sold it to **eBay** in 2002.

An Overview of Four Major Classifications of Leadership Theories

There are four major classifications of leadership theories. All four theories have the same goal of determining what it takes to be an effective leader. However, their focus is different, as shown in the first column of Exhibit 12-1. We present the theories in the next four major sections in their historical development progressing from trait to behavioral to situational to contemporary leadership theories. After centuries of inquiry, leadership theory has been stated as underdeveloped, so the leadership evolution continues.[32]

LO 12-2

Describe leadership trait theory, and explain its inconclusive findings.

Leadership Trait Theory

The development of leadership theory began with trait theory, so we begin this section with a discussion of traits and personality and then discuss problems with the theory and current thinking.

EXHIBIT 12-1   MAJOR LEADERSHIP THEORIES

Class of Leadership Theories	Specific Theories
Trait Theory attempts to determine a list of distinctive characteristics that account for leadership effectiveness.	**Trait theory leadership style** is based on the leader's personal traits and characteristics.
Behavioral Leadership Theories attempt to determine distinctive styles used by effective leaders. *Leadership style* is the combination of traits, skills, and behaviors managers use in interacting with employees.	**Basic leadership** styles include autocratic, democratic, and laissez-faire. **Two-dimensional leadership styles** are four possible leadership styles that are based on the dimensions of job structure and employee consideration. **Leadership Grid®** identifies the ideal leadership style as incorporating a high concern for both production and people.
Situational Leadership Theories attempt to determine the appropriate leadership styles for particular situations using models.	**Contingency leadership model** is used to determine if leadership style is task or relationship oriented and if the situation matches the style. **Leadership continuum model** is used to determine which of seven styles of leadership, on a continuum from autocratic (*boss centered*) to participative (*employee centered*), is best for a given situation. **Path-goal model** is used to determine employee objectives and to clarify how to achieve them using one of four leadership styles. **Normative leadership model** is a time-driven or development-driven decision tree used in selecting one of five leadership styles based on seven questions/variables to maximize a decision in a given situation. **Situational Leadership® model** is used to select one of four leadership styles that match the employees' maturity level in a given situation. **Substitutes for leadership** are characteristics of the task, of subordinates, or of the organization that replace the need for a leader.
Contemporary Leadership Theories attempt to determine how effective leaders interact with, inspire, and support followers.	**Leader-Member Exchange** **Visionary leaders** create an image of the organization in the future that provides direction for setting goals and developing strategic plans. **Charismatic leaders** inspire loyalty, enthusiasm, and high levels of performance. **Transformational leaders** bring about continuous learning, innovation, and change. **Transactional leaders** make social exchanges to get the job done. **Servant leaders** help others by placing their needs ahead of self. **Authentic leaders** develop open, honest, trusting relationships.

Traits and Personality

Early leadership studies were based on the assumption that leaders are born, not made. (Recall that, today, research supports the opposite.) Researchers wanted to identify a set of characteristics or traits that distinguished leaders from followers or effective leaders from ineffective ones. **Leadership trait theorists** *attempt to determine a list of distinctive characteristics that account for leadership effectiveness.* Researchers analyzed physical and psychological traits, such as appearance, aggressiveness, self-reliance, persuasiveness, and dominance in an effort to identify a set of traits that all successful leaders possessed.

Recall from Chapter 10 that your personality is made up of traits,[33] and thus, personality is an important part of trait theory because personality affects a leader's behavior.[34] Extroverts[35] and narcissists[36] tend to seek leadership roles, as do people motivated by a need for power, whereas people seeking affiliation don't (Chapter 11). **Uber founder and former CEO Travis Kalanick** received more press for being a jerk than he did for being an excellent CEO.[37]

leadership trait theorists Theorists who attempt to determine a list of distinctive characteristics that account for leadership effectiveness.

Let's apply personality to Elon Musk and how it affects his success. On the Big Five, **Elon Musk** (IOM 2) seems to be more introverted, as he can be shy and awkward in person. Like a lot of engineers, he will pause while searching for exact phrasing and wander down a scientific rabbit hole without offering any lay translations along the way. He expects you to keep up; there is no small talk. Musk wants people to agree with him; he is very contentious, can be emotional and drive some people away, and is clearly open to new experience such as starting disruptive innovations.

On the single trait front, Musk is a great optimist, with incredible conviction, perseverance, and persuasiveness, and he risks everything to make his companies succeed. Just about everyone said **SpaceX** and **Tesla** didn't have a chance to survive. In fact, SpaceX had three major failed launches, but Musk didn't give up. But by the time SpaceX figured out how to succeed, it was going broke, and Tesla was still losing money. In 2008, Musk was very close to bankruptcy of both companies. He begged and borrowed money from anyone who would trust him to succeed.

Musk's big breakthrough came when **NASA** gave him a space contract. However, he didn't have enough to fund both businesses. Should he put all his efforts into one of the businesses and let the other go? Out of desperation, Musk had a failed negotiation of selling **Tesla** to **Google** with his friend **Larry Page**. But Musk came through with more funding, and SpaceX is now profitable, but in 2015, Tesla lost $167 million in the first quarter. Who else but Elon Musk could go through all this and turn failure into success?

Inconclusive Findings and Current Thinking

If researchers could have come up with a universal list of traits, managers could select only leaders possessing all the traits and predict that they would succeed as leaders. Unfortunately, the theory didn't work because, in 70 years, more than 300 trait studies were conducted. However, no one was able to compile a universal list of traits that all successful leaders possess. In all cases, there were exceptions, such as the trait of being tall, and the great French leader **Napoleon** was short. People also questioned whether traits such as assertiveness and self-confidence were developed before or after one became a leader.

The Ghiselli Study. Edwin Ghiselli conducted probably the most widely publicized trait study. He studied more than 300 managers from 90 different businesses in the United States and published his results in 1971.[38] He concluded that certain traits are important to effective leadership, though not all of them are necessary for success. Ghiselli identified the following six traits, in order of importance, as being significant traits for effective leadership: (1) *supervisory ability*—getting the job done through others (basically, the ability to perform the four functions of management you are studying in this course), (2) *need for occupational achievement*, (3) *intelligence*, (4) *decisiveness*, (5) *self-assurance*, and (6) *initiative*.

Current Thinking. Organizations continue to hire and train for traits that contribute to their success. Recall from Chapter 10 the increasing use of personality tests. **General Electric (GE)** says integrity, vision, decision making, and the ability to motivate are critical traits for leaders.[39] Author **Geoff Colvin** says that the most important thing about a leader is not skills but traits.[40] **Unilever** says it can teach basic functional skills (accounting, operations), but it is difficult to develop traits. Publishing listings of important leadership traits and qualities continues.[41] Some of the contemporary leadership theories include traits. So current thinking is that traits are important to leadership, but there is no one universally accepted list.

Ethics and Spirituality in the Workplace. Personality, morals, values and other traits do affect a leader's use of ethical or unethical behavior—or *moralized leadership*.[42] Managers who use unethical behavior and encourage employees to be unethical do tend to influence employee behavior—bad apples. But as discussed in Chapter 2, businesses are encouraging ethical behavior and social responsibility because it is the right thing to do and it pays.[43] Companies are developing ethical cultures.[44]

WORK
APPLICATION 12-1

Of Ghiselli's six traits, which does your boss possess? Are there any that she or he does not possess?

JOIN THE DISCUSSION ETHICS & SOCIAL RESPONSIBILITY

Dilbert

Through his cartoon character Dilbert, **Scott Adams** makes fun of managers. Adams distrusts top-level managers and has said that leadership is really about manipulating people to get them to do something they don't want to do when there may not be anything in it for them. Adams says that we may be hung up on leadership as part of our DNA. Apparently, we have always sought to put somebody above everybody else.

1. Do you agree with Adams that leadership is basically manipulation?
2. Do we really need leaders?
3. Is it ethical and socially responsible to make fun of managers?

Related to ethics and values is spirituality. People are looking for meaning in life and at work. Organizations are offering programs to help employees and managers find this meaning. For example, many organizations are offering programs that focus on helping employees understand more about their values, spiritual principles, and sense of purpose. Some companies even have corporate chaplains. Consultants, including **Edgewalkers International** (https://edgewalkers.org) founded by **Judi Neal**, offer materials and packaged and custom programs to all types of organizations.[45]

Former **National Basketball Association (NBA)** coach **Phil Jackson** of national champions the **Chicago Bulls** and **Los Angeles Lakers** says that much of his outlook comes from his spiritual direction.[46] Evangelist **Billy Graham** identified four main character traits as personal qualities of leadership: (1) *integrity*, (2) *personal security*, (3) *sense of priority*, and (4) *vision*. **Zig Ziglar**, a best-selling author who trained people to be successful, and **Peter Lowe**, who conducted success seminars all over the world, both say that proper emphasis on the spiritual aspects of life is extremely important to success. Research has shown that people who attend church regularly make more money, have better health, are happier with their jobs and family life, and have a much lower divorce rate. Ziglar stated, "In short, they get more of the things that money can buy and all of the things that money can't buy."[47] Of course, not all successful leaders are spiritual.

Leading teams requires leaders to interact with all team members. Behavioral leadership theory sheds insight on how a leader's actions influence outcomes.

STRINGER/AFP/Getty Images

Behavioral Leadership Theories

In the continuing quest to find the best leadership style for all situations, by the late 1940s, most leadership research focused on the behavior of leaders rather than on analyzing their traits. **Behavioral leadership theorists** *attempt to determine distinctive styles used by effective leaders.* Recall that **Douglas McGregor** developed Theory X and Theory Y (Chapter 1). Complete Self-Assessment 12-2 to determine your leadership behavior according to Theory X and Theory Y. In this section, we discuss the basic leadership styles, two-dimensional leadership styles, and the Leadership Grid®.

Basic Leadership Styles

Leadership style *is the combination of traits, skills, and behaviors managers use in interacting with employees.* Note that behavioral theorists focus on the leaders' behaviors. However, behaviors are based on traits and skills, and the leader's behavior affects others' behavior.[48]

In the 1930s, before behavioral theory became popular, research was conducted by **Kurt Lewin** and associates at the **University of Iowa** on the managerial leadership

LO 12-3

Compare behavioral two-dimensional leadership styles and the Leadership Grid®, and identify its inconclusive findings.

behavioral leadership theorists Theorists who attempt to determine distinctive styles used by effective leaders.

leadership style The combination of traits, skills, and behaviors managers use in interacting with employees.

12-2 SELF-ASSESSMENT

Theory X and Theory Y Leadership Behavior

Beside each of the following 10 statements, place the letter (*U, F, O,* or *S*) that best describes what you would do as a manager. There are no right or wrong answers.

Usually (U)	Frequently (F)	Occasionally (O)	Seldom (S)

_____ 1. I would set the objectives for my department alone rather than include employees' input.

_____ 2. I would allow employees to develop their own plans rather than develop them myself.

_____ 3. I would delegate several tasks I enjoy doing to employees rather than do them myself.

_____ 4. I would allow employees to make decisions to solve problems rather than make them myself.

_____ 5. I would recruit and select new employees alone rather than use employees' input.

_____ 6. I would orient and train new employees myself rather than have employees do it.

_____ 7. I would tell employees only what they need to know rather than give them access to anything they want to know.

_____ 8. I would spend time praising and recognizing employees' work efforts rather than just giving criticism.

_____ 9. I would set several controls for employees to ensure that objectives are met rather than allow employees to set their own controls.

_____ 10. I would frequently observe my employees to ensure that they are working and meeting deadlines rather than leave them alone.

To better understand your own behavior toward employees, score your answers. For items 1, 5, 6, 7, 9, and 10, give yourself one point for each *U*, two points for each *F*, three points for each *O*, and four points for each *S*. For items 2, 3, 4, and 8, give yourself one point for each *S*, two points for each *O*, three points for each *F*, and four points for each *U*. Total all points. Your score should be between 10 and 40.

Theory X and Theory Y are on opposite ends of a continuum. Most people's behavior falls somewhere between the two extremes. Place a check on the continuum where your score falls.

Theory X Behavior				**Theory Y Behavior**
10	**20**	**30**	**40**	**40**
(More Autocratic)				**(More Participative)**

The lower your score, the stronger your Theory X behavior, and the higher your score, the stronger your Theory Y behavior. A score of 20 to 30 could be considered balanced between the two theories. Your score may not be an accurate measure of how you would behave in an actual managerial position. However, it should help you anticipate how you are likely to behave.

WORK
APPLICATION 12-2

Recall a present or past boss. Which of the four leadership styles created by Ohio State's version of the two-dimensional leadership model did your boss use most often? Describe your boss's behavior.

two-dimensional leadership styles Four possible leadership styles that are based on the dimensions of job structure and employee consideration.

style. The studies identified three basic leadership styles:[49] *autocratic* (similar to Theory X behavior), *democratic* (similar to Theory Y behavior), and *laissez-faire* (a leave-employees-alone approach).

Two-Dimensional Leadership Styles

Two-dimensional leadership styles are four possible leadership styles that are based on the dimensions of job structure and employee consideration.

Structuring and Consideration Styles. In 1945, the Personnel Research Board of **The Ohio State University** began a study to determine effective leadership styles.[50] In the process, researchers developed an instrument known as the Leader Behavior Description

EXHIBIT 12-2   THE OHIO STATE UNIVERSITY AND THE UNIVERSITY OF MICHIGAN TWO-DIMENSIONAL LEADERSHIP STYLES

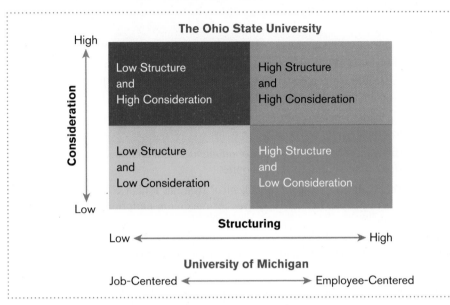

Questionnaire (LBDQ). Respondents to the questionnaire perceived leaders' behavior on two distinct dimensions:

1. *Structuring*—the extent to which the leader takes charge to plan, organize, lead, and control as the employee performs the task. This dimension focuses on getting the job done.

2. *Consideration*—the extent to which the leader communicates to develop trust, friendship, support, and respect. This dimension focuses on developing relationships with employees.

Job-Centered and Employee-Centered Styles. At approximately the same time as **The Ohio State University** studies began, the **University of Michigan**'s Survey Research Center initiated its own leadership studies.[51] This research identified the same two dimensions, or styles, of leadership behavior as the Ohio research. However, the Michigan researchers called the two styles *job centered* (analogous to structuring) and *employee centered* (analogous to consideration).

Using Two-Dimensional Leadership Styles. When interacting with employees, the manager can focus on getting the job done through directing (structuring, or job-centered behavior) and/or through developing supportive relationships (consideration, or employee-centered behavior). Combinations of the two dimensions of leadership result in the four leadership styles illustrated in Exhibit 12-2.

The **Ohio State** and **University of Michigan** leadership models are different in that the University of Michigan places the two leadership behaviors at opposite ends of the same continuum, making it one-dimensional with two styles. The Ohio State University model considers the two behaviors independent of one another, making it two-dimensional with four styles.

The Leadership Grid®

Robert Blake and **Jane Mouton** developed the Managerial Grid, which Blake and **Anne Adams McCanse** later transformed into the Leadership Grid.[52] The Leadership Grid® builds on the Ohio State and Michigan studies. It is based on the same two leadership dimensions that they called "concern for production" and "concern for people." The **Leadership Grid®**

Leadership Grid® A model that identifies the ideal leadership style as incorporating a high concern for both production and people.

identifies the ideal leadership style as incorporating a high concern for both production and people. A questionnaire is used to measure a manager's concern for people and production on a scale from 1 to 9, 1 being low concern and 9 being high concern. Five major leadership styles are highlighted on the grid:

- (1, 1) The leader with an *impoverished management style* has low concern for both production and people.
- (9, 1) The leader with an *authority-compliance management style* has a high concern for production and a low concern for people.
- (1, 9) The leader with a *country club management style* has a high concern for people and a low concern for production.
- (5, 5) The leader with a *middle-of-the-road management style* has balanced, medium concern for both production and people.
- (9, 9) The leader with a *team management style* has a high concern for both production and people. This leader strives for maximum performance and employee satisfaction.

According to Blake, the team leadership style is the most appropriate style to use in all situations.

Elon Musk (IOM 3) could be considered somewhat of a team leader. His success comes largely from his behavior of conviction and passion to convince people to work with and for him with a rare combination of mental skills: a deep understanding of technological possibility, strong design instinct, a clear grasp of the economic ecosystem surrounding a potential product, and an uncanny ability to enter the head of a future customer who doesn't know about the product yet, to work together to create innovative, disruptive new products. Like **Steve Jobs**, his behavior has been known to drive people crazy (and out of the company), getting them to develop and deliver his visionary products.

Like with trait theory's inconclusive finding, behavioral theories couldn't find one style that researchers agreed was the one best style to use in all situations. However, today, we know that a leader's behavior affects employees[53] and that leaders use different behavioral approaches to influence employees,[54] especially if they want to achieve OCB.[55] Founder of **Lolly Wolly Doodle Brandi Temple** says that most advances she has made in leadership skills came from observing other leaders' behavior.[56] The contemporary leadership theories we discuss later are based on behavior.

WORK
APPLICATION 12-3

Recall a present or past boss. Which of the five major Leadership Grid styles did your boss use most often? Describe your boss's behavior.

12-1 APPLYING THE CONCEPT

The Leadership Grid®

Identify the leadership style described in each of the five situations.

A. impoverished (1, 1)

B. authority-compliance (9, 1)

C. country club (1, 9)

D. middle-of-the-road (5, 5)

E. team (9, 9)

_____ 1. The employees dislike the manager, but the department is one of the top performers.

_____ 2. The manager's department has the low-producing employees with a low level of morale. Yet he doesn't do anything to improve the department.

_____ 3. The manager has the top performers and also has the highest morale.

_____ 4. The manager is friends with everyone and they get along great, but the productivity level is one of the lowest in the company.

_____ 5. The manager has been evaluated as having adequate morale and an average productivity level.

Situational Leadership Theories

LO 12-4

State the primary difference between the contingency leadership model and the other four situational leadership models.

Both trait and behavioral leadership theories were attempts to find the best leadership style in all situations. In the 1960s, it became apparent that no single leadership style is appropriate in all situations. Situational leadership theory is also called *contingency theory*, because how leaders behave is contingent on the situation.[57] Today's managers are getting to know employees and motivating and influencing them as individuals based on situational principles.[58] But it is not easy, as managers are expected to treat followers uniformly and consistently while considering individual needs and sometimes making exceptions.[59] Thus, leaders need to use situational control.[60] Thus, **situational approaches to leadership** *attempt to determine appropriate leadership styles for particular situations.* **Hewlett-Packard (HP) CEO Meg Whitman** says that she is a big believer in situational leadership.[61] In this section, we discuss some of the most popular situational theories shown in Exhibit 12-1, which are called models.

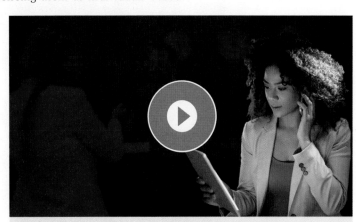

MANAGEMENT IN ACTION
Contingency Leadership Model

Contingency Leadership Model

In 1951, **Fred E. Fiedler** began to develop the first situational approach to leadership—the contingency theory of leader effectiveness.[62] Fiedler believed that one's leadership style reflects one's personality and remains basically constant. That is, leaders do not change styles. The **contingency leadership model** *is used to determine if leadership style is task or relationship oriented and if the situation matches the style.*

situational approaches to leadership Theories that attempt to determine appropriate leadership styles for particular situations.

contingency leadership model A model used to determine if leadership style is task or relationship oriented and if the situation matches the style.

Leadership Style. The first step is to determine whether your leadership style is task or relationship oriented. To do so, you fill in what Fiedler called the Least Preferred Coworker (LPC) scale. The LPC essentially answers this question: "Do you use a more task-oriented or relationship-oriented leadership style in working with others?"

Situational Favorableness Decision Tree. After determining leadership style, you determine situational favorableness. *Situational favorableness* refers to the degree to which a situation enables you to exert influence over followers. The more control you have over followers, the more favorable the situation. The three variables that determine situational favorableness are as follows:

1. *Leader–Follower Relations.* Is the relationship between you and followers good or poor?

2. *Task Structure.* Is the task structured (repetitive/routine) or unstructured (not repetitive)?

3. *Position Power.* Do you have position power?

Tony Avelar/Bloomberg via Getty Images

Steve Jobs, the late CEO of **Apple,** was a job-centered executive whose leadership was instrumental to Apple's success. Jobs focused more on tasks than on relationships.

After determining your leadership style, you can answer the three questions pertaining to situational favorableness by following a decision tree to discover the best leadership style to a given situation. Exhibit 12-3 shows the decision tree.

EXHIBIT 12-3   CONTINGENCY LEADERSHIP MODEL

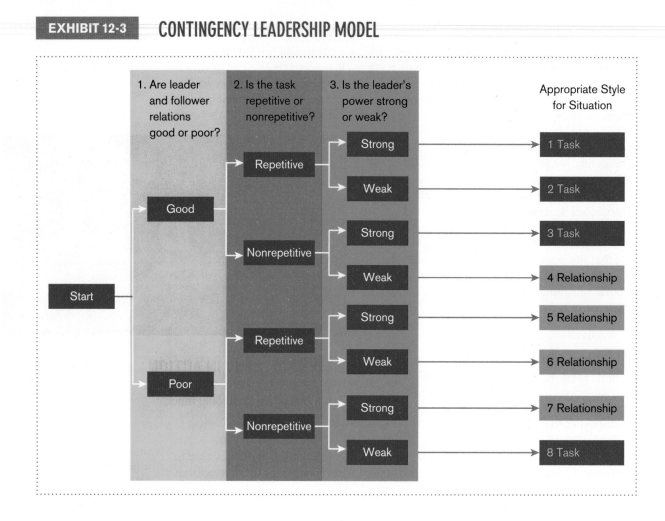

WORK
APPLICATION 12-4

Classify your present or past boss's preferred style as task or relationship oriented. Think of a specific situation at work and use the contingency model to determine the appropriate style to use for this situation. Did the boss use the appropriate style?

Matching the Situation to the Leadership Style. If your preferred leadership style is the one indicated by the decision tree, you match and do nothing. If, however, your preferred leadership style is not ideal for the given situation, then the situation must be changed to match your leadership style. You can change your relationship, the repetitiveness of the task, or your power.

One of the major *criticisms* of contingency theory is that it's often difficult to change a situation. Critics say that when a manager's leadership style does not match the situation, the style should be changed. All the other situational leadership theories disagree with changing the situation to match your leadership style; they advocate changing your leadership style to match the situation.

Leadership Continuum Model

leadership continuum model A model used to determine which of seven styles of leadership, on a continuum from autocratic (*boss centered*) to participative (*employee centered*), is best for a given situation.

Robert Tannenbaum and **Warren Schmidt** developed a model of leadership that focuses on who makes the decisions. They viewed leadership behavior on a continuum from autocratic (*boss centered*) to participative (*employee centered*). The continuum includes seven major styles from which a leader can choose. Exhibit 12-4 lists the seven styles.[63] The **leadership continuum model** *is used to determine which of seven styles of leadership, on a continuum from autocratic (*boss centered*) to participative (*employee centered*), is best for a given situation.* Before selecting one of the seven leadership styles, the leader must consider the following three variables: the *leader's preferred style,* the *followers' preferred style for the leader,* and *the situation.*

12-2 APPLYING THE CONCEPT

Contingency Leadership Theory

Using Exhibit 12-3, determine the appropriate leadership style under the given conditions. Place the letter *A* or *B* on the first line and the situation number (between 1 and 8) on the second line.

A task-oriented situation 1, 2, 3, 8

B. relationship-oriented situation 4, 5, 6, 7

____ 6. Nyota gets along well with her employees, who make water bottles, and she is in control of her department.

____ 7. Ted, the chair of a committee charged with recommending ways to increase organizational performance, is highly regarded by the volunteer members from a variety of departments.

____ 8. Usain oversees the assembly of mass-produced containers. He determines rewards and punishments and is viewed as a hard-nosed boss.

____ 9. Lakesha is a manager from the corporate planning staff; she helps departments plan. She is viewed as being a dreamer who doesn't understand the company's various departments. Employees tend to be rude in their dealings with Lakesha.

____ 10. John is a manager who oversees the processing of canceled checks for a bank. He is well liked by the employees and enjoys hiring and evaluating his employees' performance.

____ 11. Carly, the principal of a school, assigns teachers to classes and other various duties. She hires and decides on tenure appointments. The school atmosphere is tense.

____ 12. Aarti is well liked by her employees, who make all kinds of websites to customer specifications, and Aarti makes the hiring, promoting, discipline, and firing decisions.

____ 13. Juan's employees, who manufacture cardboard boxes, think he is a jerk and tend to ignore what he says because his boss does their evaluations and determines pay raises.

EXHIBIT 12-4   THE LEADERSHIP CONTINUUM

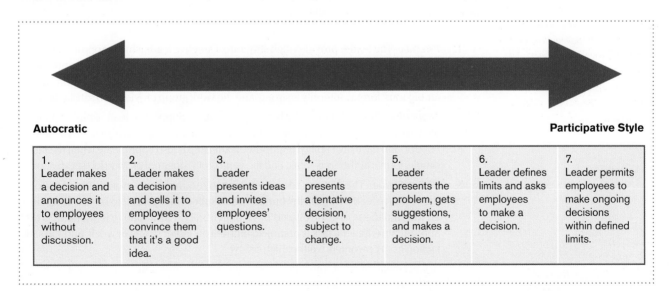

1. Leader makes a decision and announces it to employees without discussion.	2. Leader makes a decision and sells it to employees to convince them that it's a good idea.	3. Leader presents ideas and invites employees' questions.	4. Leader presents a tentative decision, subject to change.	5. Leader presents the problem, gets suggestions, and makes a decision.	6. Leader defines limits and asks employees to make a decision.	7. Leader permits employees to make ongoing decisions within defined limits.

Autocratic ← → **Participative Style**

Source: Adopted from Robert Tannenbaum and Warren Schmidt, "How to Choose a Leadership Pattern," *Harvard Business Review* (May/June, 1973).

12-3 APPLYING THE CONCEPT

Leadership Continuum

Refer to Exhibit 12-4 and indicate the leadership style exemplified in each statement by placing its number (between 1 and 7) on the lines below.

_____ 14. "I've made the vacation schedule. Let me know which week you want to take off."

_____ 15. "I'd like your suggestion on how to resolve this, but I'll choose a solution and implement it."

_____ 16. "I selected you to serve on the task force, but you don't have to if you don't want to."

_____ 17. "Please take this letter to the mail room for me right away."

_____ 18. "I just thought of a way to improve performance and make our jobs easier. You're going to think it's a great idea."

_____ 19. "You decide how to deal with this problem. You don't need me."

_____ 20. "Receipts for business meals under $50 are no longer needed. Any questions?"

WORK APPLICATION 12-5

Using the leadership continuum model, identify your boss's most commonly used leadership style. Now recall a specific situation in which this leadership style was used. Would you say this was the most appropriate leadership style in that situation? Explain.

WORK APPLICATION 12-6

Identify your boss's most commonly used path-goal leadership style. Now recall a specific situation in which this style was used. From the perspective of the path-goal model, was this the most appropriate leadership style based on the situational factors? Explain.

path-goal model A model used to determine employee objectives and to clarify how to achieve them using one of four leadership styles.

Path-Goal Model

Robert House developed the path-goal leadership model. The **path-goal model** *is used to determine employee objectives and to clarify how to achieve them using one of four leadership styles.* The model focuses on how leaders influence employees' perceptions of their goals and the paths they follow toward goal attainment.[64] As shown in Exhibit 12-5, the path-goal model uses situational factors to determine the leadership style that affects goal achievement through performance and satisfaction.

Situational Factors. *Subordinate* situational factors are (1) authoritarianism (the degree to which employees defer to leaders and want to be told what to do and how to do the job), (2) locus of control (Chapter 10), and (3) ability (the extent of employees' ability to perform tasks to achieve goals).

Environmental situational factors are (1) task structure (repetitiveness in the job), (2) formal authority (leader's power), and (3) work group (the extent to which coworkers contribute to job satisfaction).

Leadership Styles. Based on the situational factors, a leader can select the most appropriate of the following leadership styles:

1. *Directive.* The leader provides high structure. Directive leadership is appropriate when subordinates want authoritarian leadership, have an external locus of control, and have low ability. Directive leadership is also appropriate when the task is complex or ambiguous, formal authority is strong, and the work group provides job satisfaction.

2. *Supportive.* The leader provides high consideration. Supportive leadership is appropriate when subordinates do not want authoritarian leadership, have an internal locus of control, and have high ability. Supportive leadership is also appropriate when the task is simple, formal authority is weak, and the work group does not provide job satisfaction.

3. *Participative.* The leader considers employee input when making decisions. Participative leadership is appropriate when subordinates want to be involved, have an internal locus of control, and have high ability. Participative leadership is also appropriate when the task is complex, authority is either strong or weak, and job satisfaction from coworkers is either high or low.

4. *Achievement-oriented.* The leader sets difficult but achievable goals, expects subordinates to perform at their highest level, and rewards them for doing so. In essence, the leader provides both high structure and high consideration. Achievement-oriented leadership is appropriate when subordinates are open to authoritarian leadership,

EXHIBIT 12-5   A SUMMARY OF PATH-GOAL FACTORS AND STYLES

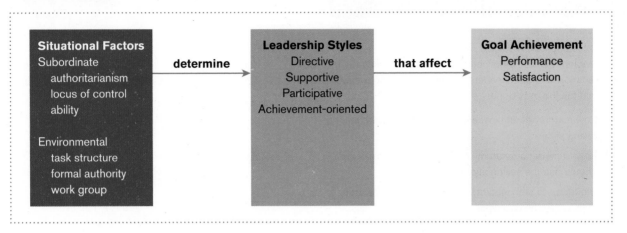

Situational Factors		Leadership Styles		Goal Achievement

Subordinate
  authoritarianism
  locus of control
  ability
 	
Environmental
  task structure
  formal authority
  work group
	determine →	Directive
		Supportive
		Participative
		Achievement-oriented
			that affect →	Performance
				Satisfaction

have an external locus of control, and have high ability. Achievement-oriented leadership is also appropriate when the environmental task is simple, authority is strong, and job satisfaction from coworkers is either high or low.

Normative Leadership Model

Victor Vroom and his colleagues at **Yale University** developed participative decision-making models that integrate leadership and decision-making processes.[65] It is called *normative* because the model tells users which leadership style to use for their given situation. The model uses decision trees like Fiedler's model in Exhibit 12-3, but it is much more complex. There are actually two versions of the model called time-driven and development-driven based on the decision being made; plus it has seven questions to answer to select one of five leadership styles Vroom calls decide, consult individual, consult group, facilitate, and delegate.

The normative leadership model is popular in the academic community because it is based on research with more than 100,000 managers.[66] Vroom now has an electronic model. However, the model is not very popular with managers, who find it cumbersome to have to decide which version of the model to use and follow a seven-question decision tree every time they have to make a decision. Therefore, we don't include the models.

Situational Leadership® Model

Paul Hersey and **Ken Blanchard** developed the Situational Leadership® model.[67] The **Situational Leadership® model** *is used to select one of four leadership styles that match the employees' maturity level in a given situation.* Their model identifies four leadership styles, expanding the **Ohio State** model in Exhibit 12-2 so that the user can select the leadership style that matches the situation.

To select a leadership style, you determine the followers' maturity level. "Maturity level" refers to the level of employee development (competence and commitment) or readiness to do the job (ability and willingness). If employee maturity is low, you use a *telling style*, giving employees explicit directions about how to accomplish a task. If employee maturity is moderate to low, you use a *selling style*, explaining decisions to gain understanding. If employee maturity is moderate to high, you use the *participating style* to facilitate decision making among subordinates. And if employee maturity is high, you use a *delegating style*, giving employees responsibility for decisions and their implementation.

Situational Leadership® model A model used to select one of four leadership styles that match the employees' maturity level in a given situation.

ARIE KIEVIT/AFP/Getty Images

Museum employees move a painting. The situational leadership model suggests that, based on the employees' experience and the complexity of the task, the manager's leadership style should change.

Situational Leadership Styles

For each of the following situations, identify the maturity level of the employee and the leadership style the manager should use so that the job gets done.

A. Low maturity of employee: The manager should use the telling style.

B. Low to moderate maturity of employee: The manager should use the selling style.

C. Moderate to high maturity of employee: The manager should use the participating style.

D. High maturity of employee: The manager should use the delegating style.

_____ 21. Candy's job is to clean off the tables quickly after dinners leave. Candy is on her phone again.

_____ 22. George has never written a formal report, but you know he can do it with your encouragement and with minimum help from you.

_____ 23. You told Shinji exactly how to do a job. However, he deliberately ignored your directions again. So the job is not done correctly.

_____ 24. Rookie Milani's training is progressing well, so you have decided to teach her a new task.

Hersey has used a baseball metaphor to explain how this model helps managers. Hersey says that he can't give you the way to hit a home run every time at bat, but the model can help you increase your batting average. Likewise, this book with all its various models cannot teach you all the details of how to lead in every situation, but the theories and models presented here can help you increase your leadership skills and managerial success.

Comparing Leadership Models

The behavioral and situational leadership models we've discussed are all based on two dimensions of leadership, shown in Exhibit 12-2. However, as you've seen, different authors use different terms for what are basically the same dimensions. Exhibit 12-6 provides a comparison of the behavioral and situational leadership models and uses *direction* and *support* to describe these two dimensions of leadership. The columns in the exhibit are headed "High Direction/Low Support," "High Direction/High Support," and so on. The terms that appear below these headings have basically the same meanings as the column headings. Note that back in Chapter 1, we already learned how to use Model 1-1, "Situational Management," which was developed by **Robert Lussier** and is based on the other contingency models, so we don't discuss it again here, but we do add it to the comparison at the bottom of Exhibit 12-6.

In contrast to what Fiedler advocated with his contingency leadership model, **Elon Musk (IOM 4)** does change his leadership style as necessary to focus on tasks or relationships. For example, Musk is task oriented, being personally involved in every aspect of product design, but is more relationship oriented when it comes to other CEO responsibilities where he relies more on other managers to run other parts of the business. Musk also has lots of networking relationships that he taps into when he needs help and money.

Leadership Substitutes Theory

Leadership Substitutes Theory. The leadership theories and models that have been discussed so far assume that some leadership style will be effective in each situation. **Steven Kerr** and **John Jermier** argued that certain situational variables prevent leaders from affecting subordinates' attitudes and behaviors.[68] **Substitutes for leadership** *are characteristics of the task, of subordinates, or of the organization that replace the need for a leader.* These characteristics can also neutralize the effect of leadership behavior. That is, the following may substitute for or neutralize leadership by providing direction and/or support: *characteristics of the task, subordinates, and the organization.* For routine *tasks* with highly skilled *subordinates* in mechanistic structured *organizations*, employees don't need supervisory instructions. Today, with shared leadership in teams, there is less need for a manager.

WORK APPLICATION 12-8

Identify the one leadership theory or model you prefer. State why.

---

substitutes for leadership Characteristics of the task, of subordinates, or of the organization that replace the need for a leader.

| **EXHIBIT 12-6** | A COMPARISON OF BEHAVIORAL AND SITUATIONAL LEADERSHIP MODELS |

	High Direction/ Low Support	High Direction/ High Support	Low Direction/ High Support	Low Direction/ Low Support
Behavioral Leadership Theories				
Basic Leadership Styles	Autocratic	Democratic		Laissez-faire
The Ohio State University Model (Exhibit 12-2)	High structure/Low consideration	High structure/High consideration	Low structure/High consideration	Low structure/Low consideration
University of Michigan Model (Exhibit 12-2)	Job centered			Employee centered
Leadership Grid	Authority-compliance (9, 1)	Team (9, 9)	Country club (1, 9)	Impoverished (1, 1)
		Middle of the road (5, 5)		
Situational Approaches to Leadership				
Contingency Leadership Model (Exhibit 12-3)	Task		Relationship	
Leadership Continuum Model (Exhibit 12-4)	Style 1	Styles 2 and 3	Styles 4 and 5	Styles 6 and 7
Path-Goal Model (Exhibit 12-5)	Directive	Achievement oriented	Supportive	Participative
Normative Leadership Model	Decide	Consult	Facilitate	Delegate
Situational Leadership Model	Telling	Selling	Participating	Delegating
Situational Management (Model 1-1)	Autocratic	Consultative	Participative	Empowerment

The Bossless Organization and Self-Leadership. Leadership is no longer about bossing or being in control.[69] There is a trend towards the *bossless organization*. **Barbara Bradley Baekgaard**, cofounder and CEO of **Vera Bradley**, says, "I hate the word 'boss.' We work with someone, not for someone."[70] **Zappos** reorganized into a bossless structure.[71] Without a boss, you need to lead yourself. The concept of *self-leadership* appears in the literature.[72]

Followership. Followership is becoming more popular.[73] Although "followership" has been called the new buzzword in the business news and popular press,[74] **Harvard professor Barbara Kellerman** has done research on *followership*.[75] Some companies are saying that they have too many leaders and too few followers, so they are now training employees in followership. Followership is about taking responsibility for shared goals, being a self-starter, and telling leaders the truth when they mess up.[76]

Contemporary Leadership Theories

As presented, leadership theories progressed from focusing on traits to behavior to the situation. Today, researchers try to put these theories together. **Contemporary leadership theories** *attempt to determine how effective leaders interact with, inspire, and support followers.* In this section, we discuss seven contemporary leadership theories that have a lot in common, with a heavy focus on behavior.

WORK
APPLICATION 12-9

Could the characteristics of the task, subordinates, or the organization substitute for your present or a past boss? In other words, is your boss necessary? Explain.

contemporary leadership theories Theories that attempt to determine how effective leaders interact with, inspire, and support followers.

LO 12-5

Define the seven contemporary leadership theories.

Leader-Member Exchange (LMX) Theory

Dyadic Relationships. Leader-member exchange (LMX) theory is based on social exchange relationships between leaders and their followers.[77] LMX's core contribution is its explicit emphasis on the unique dyadic relationships that develop between leaders and each of their subordinates rather than on the general effects of leader traits and behaviors.[78] LMX effective **leader-member exchange (LMX) leaders** *create positive relationships with each individual.* The current focus on LMX is developing positive relationships.[79] Big Four accounting firm **KPMG CEO Lynne Doughtie** says relationships are important in business,[80] and leadership is about building relationships to influence all members of your relational system.[81] As you have been learning throughout this book, our personal and professional happiness and success are based on relationships.

In-Group and Out-Group. Past LMX research focused on in and out groups. Have you ever been in a group in which the leader liked you and you were a member of the in-group (favorites, cliques), or have you ever been in the out-group, like most of us at some time or another? Then you have experienced negative LMX grouping. Not surprisingly, the members of the in-group get better assignments, receive higher performance ratings, have greater job satisfaction, and often have higher-level performance—recall the Pygmalion effect (Chapter 11). Leadership is about bringing out the best in people,[82] but putting them in out-groups doesn't do that. Back in Chapter 3, we discussed the importance of inclusion, and in Chapter 8, we covered the importance of group process and how it affects team performance. Clearly, leaders who develop in- and out-groups will not have group cohesiveness; they create status differences between members, and they create more conflict. LMX leaders sometimes end up with the two groups fighting for power and using unethical politics. So we need to be inclusive in developing positive relationships with everyone without creating any out-groups. The national champion **NBA Golden State Warriors** basketball team's success is based on inclusion. Forward **Marreese Speights** said, "We support every guy that steps on the court, whether it's 30 minutes or two minutes. Everyone gets the same love."[83]

Getting back to politics (Chapter 10), when you get a job, often your manager will believe you should be with the in-group. If there is a clear in- and out-group, you should be able to recognize the members, as the out-group tends to try to recruit new members to their coalition. Belonging to the in-group has its career benefits. As discussed in Chapter 9, you may want to get top evaluation ratings from your boss; if so, figure out what you need to do to succeed. Consultant **Jack Welch** says that it is important to know what the boss really thinks of you, but he says that only 5% to 10% of us know.[84] Are you willing to ask? If you slip into the out-group based on performance, are you willing to confront your boss to agree on what it will take to get a top rating and do it?

Visionary and Charismatic Leaders

Visionary and charismatic leadership is often associated with top-level strategic management.[85] Leadership tends to stress the role of charismatic individuals in setting compelling visions to which all organizational members are expected to subscribe.[86] But a leader can be both or just one or the other, or neither.

Visionary Leaders. *Entrepreneur* editor-in-chief **Amy Cosper** says that great leaders inspire and create meaningful, lasting opportunities and new ways of thinking. They believe in change and impact the future.[87] **Visionary leaders** *create an image of the organization in the future that provides direction for setting goals and developing strategic plans.* They believe they are capable of creating a significant part of the future and controlling its effects on them. Professor **Russ Ackoff** says that visionary leaders try to prevent threats, not merely prepare for them, and to create opportunities, not merely exploit them. They envision a desirable future and invent ways of bringing it about.[88] The vision creates shared purpose.[89]

Steve Jobs was a visionary leader who instigated a cultural revolution, at both **Apple** and **Pixar**, by developing disruptive, innovative products and services.[90] **Michael Dell** had the vision of selling customized PCs directly to customers and disrupted the industry business model of

WORK
APPLICATION 12-10

Describe the type of leader you want to be.

leader-member exchange (LMX) leaders Leaders who create in-groups and out-groups based largely on being similar to them and/or competency.

visionary leaders Leaders who create an image of the organization in the future that provides direction for setting goals and developing strategic plans.

selling PCs through retail stores. Other companies *benchmarked* his vision. There are moralized leaders.[91] **Martin Luther King Jr.** had a vision of equality for all that was expressed well with vivid imagery in his "I Have a Dream" speech.[92] Today you can go online and buy personalized M&M's® printed and pictured with whatever you want, directly from the **Mars** company (www.mymms.com) delivered to your door.[93] **Elon Musk** has a vision of taking passengers to Mars.[94] Visionary leadership is part of *strategic leadership*, as the vision is implemented through strategy.[95]

Charismatic leaders like **Malala Yousafzai**, Nobel Peace Prize winner and UN Messenger of Peace, have a strong influence on others. People are often willing to work hard to help a charismatic leader's vision become a reality.

Charismatic Leaders. Charismatic leaders *inspire loyalty, enthusiasm, and high levels of performance.* Their confident, dynamic personal traits and behavior enable them to develop strong relationships with followers they may not even know personally, giving them strong influence over followers' behavior and performance.[96] Charismatic leaders articulate a clear vision that is based on strongly held values, model those values, communicate high performance expectations, and display confidence in followers' ability to achieve the vision. Followers in turn trust charismatic leaders, are loyal to them, and are inspired to work hard to accomplish the leader's vision, goals, and strategy. The term *charismatic* has been applied to many leaders, from **John F. Kennedy** and **Mother Teresa** to **Martin Luther King Jr. Apple**'s **Steve Jobs**'s success was largely attributed to his incredible charisma, which often enabled him to inspire tremendous loyalty and overcome seemingly insurmountable obstacles.[97] Jobs was called a pied piper of charisma by his frenemy **Bill Gates** of **Microsoft**.[98] Many studies have reported that charismatic leaders have a strong effect on performance and that charismatic leadership skills can be developed.[99]

Transformational and Transactional Leaders

Transformational leadership tends to come from top management, whereas transactional leadership is more associated with lower levels of management, but both affect performance,[100] and the two are commonly compared.[101]

Transformational Leaders. Transformational leaders *bring about continuous learning, innovation, and change.* Transformational leaders are good at overcoming resistance to change. They are motivational,[102] as transformers gain acceptance of the mission and group's purpose and motivate followers to go beyond (transcend) their own self-interest for the good of the organization and group. Transformational leaders make their followers feel like a vital part of the firm and understand how their jobs fit with the vision or understand how to make the vision become a reality. Many charismatic leaders are also visionary and transformational leaders, but not all.[103] Transformational leaders are especially needed in firms with growth strategies competing in dynamic environments.

Jeff Bezos founded **Amazon** and transformed the way people buy books. Then through his e-reader he transformed how many people read books, as well as popularized tablets. Bezos has also made it possible to buy just about anything through Amazon online through various devices include simply asking Alexa. Alexa is an intelligent personal assistant developed by Amazon, made popular by the Amazon Echo and the Amazon Echo Dot devices. Amazon stock was the first ever to sell for more than $1,000.[104]

Transactional Leadership. Transactional leadership *is a leadership style based on social exchange.* The exchange involves the principle that "you do this work for me and I'll give this reward to you, and I'll punish you if you don't." Transactional leaders promote stability rather than change and are described as task and reward oriented, structured, and passive. Transactional leadership occurs mostly among middle and first-line managers, but some top-level managers are transactional. Recall that LMX leadership is based on social exchange,[105] and organizational politics (Chapter 10) is based on reciprocity,[106] or transactional relationships.

charismatic leadership A leadership style that inspires loyalty, enthusiasm, and high levels of performance.

transformational leaders Leaders who bring about continuous learning, innovation, and change.

transactional leadership A leadership style based on social exchange.

Servant and Authentic Leaders

People want leaders, but they reject self-serving inauthentic leaders.[107] These two theories are in an earlier stage of development than the others. **Pope Francis** is considered to be charismatic, and he has criticized capitalism calling for MNCs to focus less on profits and more on being authentic servants to people globally.

Servant Leadership. Servant leaders are good stewards of the organization's interests.[108] **Servant leaders** *focus on helping others by placing their needs ahead of self-interest.* This is the act of true friendship. Servant leadership is based on the premise that leaders who are best able to motivate followers are those who focus on prioritizing the fulfillment of followers' needs ahead of self-interest. It is a positive approach to OB (Chapter 10). Serving others leads to strong relationships, with followers becoming fully engaged in OCB and higher levels of performance.[109]

Servant leaders understand that leadership is never about you—it's about them.[110] Best-selling leadership author **Jim Clemmer** says to turn your organizational hierarchy upside down.[111] Managers should be focusing on helping employees do their jobs, not the other way around. Servant leaders are asking, "What can I do to help you do your job? What do you need from me?"

Authentic Leadership. Authentic leaders *develop open, honest, trusting relationships.* Authentic leaders emphasize building legitimacy through honest relationships with followers, seeking their input (voice) to improve performance.[112] They lead by example.[113] One of the problems with authentic leadership is that the very act of trying to be an authentic leader undercuts the possibility of achieving it.[114]

People look for authenticity and often spot a phony,[115] such as when a narcissist is nice to you just to get something from you.[116] The question is, how different is your behavior in the various roles you play and in your relationships from who you actually are? If you are too different, your nonauthentic behavior will likely cause relationship and other problems.[117] Keep it simple. As former **NBA** coach **Phil Jackson** says, "You have to be true to yourself as a leader."[118]

Recall the importance of relationships in our personal and professional lives. We can only be on our best behavior for so long before we reveal our true selves. Do you understand the need for unselfish authentic behavior?

Elon Musk (IOM 5) is clearly a visionary, charismatic, and transformational leader, as he had a clear vision of space travel since childhood, as he dreamed about rocket ships and space travel. It took charisma to get people to lend and invest in his multiple entrepreneurial ventures and recruit top aeronautics engineers to help him build his space rocket and to keep motivated after three failures. Although Musk has some good working relationships, he is not commonly considered an LMX or servant leader, but he is a very authentic leader as he is not afraid to be himself.

Trends and Issues in Management

The demands of leadership are changing as *globalization* makes the manager's job more complex.[119] Consultant **Jack Welch** says that increased *technology* and globalization has changed leadership; you can't use simple Western techniques.[120]

Like the motivation theories (Chapter 11), the leadership theories were developed primarily in the United States and can't be generalized to all countries. Americans tend to try to influence with the use of rational, logical ideas, whereas some cultures, like Arabs, stress spirituality and religion and others even superstition. Therefore, it is important to provide cultural training before sending employees on international assignments.

Recall our ongoing discussion of GLOBE starting back in Chapter 3. People from various *country cultures* do have different expectations of their leaders. Therefore, situational leadership applies and needs to be expanded globally, as one of the important variables to add to selecting the leadership style is cultural expectations of the leader. Leaders need to use good

servant leaders Leaders who focus on helping others by placing their needs ahead of self-interest.

authentic leaders Leaders who develop open, honest, trusting relationships.

judgment, especially in ambiguous situations.[121] However, GLOBE researchers found that people around the globe generally do want leaders with a vision and plans to guide them, so visionary and transformational leadership do tend to have global generalizability. Charisma also tends to be idealized across cultures.[122]

Many *Fortune* 500 firms reported that they currently lack effective global leaders, with 85% agreeing that their company did not have an adequate number of globally competent executives.[123] Women can help, as current research reported that women demonstrated strong global leadership profiles in regard to passion for diversity, intercultural empathy, and diplomacy—or they know how to work well with people from different parts of the world.[124] But women are being held back.[125] As discussed, *women and minorities* are negatively stereotyped, and few make it to the top levels of management. Part of the reason for *gender diversity* leadership issues in the United States is due to gender-specific societal roles and behavior expectations. Men are expected to possess agentic qualities (assertiveness, confidence, and independence) and to engage in behaviors that are congruent with a leader role. Women, on the other hand, are expected to possess communal qualities (helpfulness, nurturance, kindness) and to engage in behaviors that are incongruent with a leader role. Thus, there tends to be a bias against women that sets the stage for over-emergence of male leaders.[126]

In the United States, Latinos are often stereotyped and underestimated; **LinkAmerica founder and CEO Andres Ruzo** says, "I ask people to judge me by my actions, not my accent."[127] Due to stereotyping, women and minorities have more difficulty influencing others. **Facebook chief operating officer (COO) Sheryl Sandberg** says that women's ideas are not received as openly as men's, and they are frequently interrupted. Also, men are often viewed as confident and having leadership qualities, whereas women exhibiting the same type of behavior are viewed as bossy and territorial.[128] Research is mixed on whether men and women lead differently. What do you think? Check out Join the Discussion 12-2.

On the **Fortune** World's 50 Greatest Leaders list (it's not limited to business execs), 7 of the top 20 (35%) are women.[129] More women are breaking the glass ceiling in male-dominated fields, such as accounting. **KPMG** has its first woman CEO in **Lynne Doughtie**, who advocates for women and suggests networking to build relationships to help you advance; diversity is a top priority at KPMG.[130] However, women are not making much progress in the high-tech "[Silicon] Valley of the Boys."[131] Google[132] and Intel[133] are working on it, but they have a long way to go.

As our ongoing discussion shows, *generational differences* exist. Recall our ongoing emphasis on the importance of good relationships.[134] Millennials want to have a good relationship with their boss, and if they don't, they tend to leave.[135] While baby boomers didn't expect to be friends with the boss, it was discouraged. Millennials who had parents as friends expect it. Consultant **Jack Welch** puts it this way for managers: Why wouldn't you want to hang out with your employees? You selected them![136]

On the *tech* front, leaders who make decisions based on Big Data are more successful than those who don't.[137] Arguably, no one else has driven *sustainability* and green technology

12-2 JOIN THE DISCUSSION ETHICS & SOCIAL RESPONSIBILITY

Leadership and Gender

Are there differences in the leadership styles of men and women? Some researchers say that women tend to be more participative, relationship-oriented leaders and men more task oriented. However, others say that men and women are more alike as leaders than different and are equally effective.

1. Is it ethical and socially responsible to say that people of a particular gender make better leaders?
2. Do you think men and women lead in the same way?
3. Are men or women more ethical and socially responsible as leaders?
4. Would you prefer to have a man or a woman as boss?

as much as Elon Musk, or made as much money doing it.[138] The major trends that **Elon Musk (IOM 6)** is leading are technology-driven space travel and broadening the world we live and do business in (**SpaceX**), and striving for sustainable energy with electric cars (**Tesla**) and solar power (**SolarCity**). Tesla continuously improves its battery life.[139]

Leaders globally have come under fire for their *unethical* behavior.[140] **Uber Technologies** has been called "ethically challenged."[141] Although not usually considered a theory, the term *ethical leadership* is being used today, and the term *responsible leadership* is being used to describe managers who actively pursue *corporate social responsibility* (CSR) initiatives.[142]

As we bring this chapter to a close, you should understand the four major classifications of leadership: trait theory, behavioral theories (basic, two-dimensional, Leadership Grid), situational leadership theories (contingency, continuum, path-goal, normative, situational leadership), and contemporary leadership theories (LMX, visionary, charismatic, transformational, transactional, servant, and authentic leaders). You may want to give some thought to and answer this question. What kind of leader do you want to be, and what kind of behaviors can you model to earn respect and trust while influencing others?[143]

$SAGE edge™   edge.sagepub.com/lussier8e

Want a better grade?

Get the tools you need to sharpen your study skills. Access practice quizzes, eFlashcards, video and multimedia, and more at edge.sagepub.com/lussier8e.

Digital Resources

Learning Objective	Digital Resource
12-1. Compare the four classifications of leadership theories.	▶ Situational Leadership*
12-2. Describe leadership trait theory, and explain its inconclusive findings.	🖥 Leadership Traits
12-3. Compare behavioral two-dimensional leadership styles and the Leadership Grid®, and identify its inconclusive findings.	▶ Leadership Grid
12-4. State the primary difference between the contingency leadership model and the other four situational leadership models.	▶ Management in Action: Contingency Leadership Model*
12-5. Define the seven contemporary leadership theories.	▶ Charismatic Leadership

* premium video available only in the interactive eBook

••• CHAPTER SUMMARY

12-1. Compare the four classifications of leadership theories.

All four theories have the same goal of determining what it takes to be an effective leader; however, their focus is different. Trait theorists try to find a list of distinctive characteristics that account for leadership effectiveness. Behavioral theorists try to determine distinctive styles used by effective leaders and the one leadership style that is best in all situations. Situational theorists try to find the appropriate leadership style for various situations and believe that the best leadership style varies from situation to situation. Contemporary theorists try to determine how effective leaders interact with, inspire, and support followers.

12-2. Describe leadership trait theory, and explain its inconclusive findings.

Leadership trait theorists attempt to determine a list of distinctive characteristics that account for leadership effectiveness. In more than 70 years and 300 studies, researchers could not find a list of traits that successful leaders possessed, as there were always exceptions, as some great leaders did not possess all of the listed traits.

12-3. Compare behavioral two-dimensional leadership styles and the Leadership Grid®, and identify its inconclusive findings.

Both theories use basically the same two dimensions of leadership, although they give them different names. The major difference is that two-dimensional leadership theory has four major leadership styles (high structure/low consideration, high structure/high consideration, low structure/high consideration, low structure/low consideration), whereas the Leadership Grid® identifies five major leadership styles (impoverished, authority-compliance, country club, middle-of-the-road, and team). Both theories attempt to find the one best leadership style for all situations, but the findings are inconclusive as most researchers don't agree that there is one best leadership style.

12-4. State the primary difference between the contingency leadership model and the other four situational leadership models.

With the contingency leadership model, users first determine their preferred leadership style as task or relationship oriented. If their preferred style matches their situation, the leader takes no action. However, if their preferred style doesn't match the situation, Fiedler recommends changing the situation, not the leadership style. With the leadership continuum model, path-goal model, normative leadership model, and situational leadership model, users analyze the situation based on the model variables and select the appropriate style to use in their given situation. So these models recommend changing the leadership style, not the situation.

12-5. Define the seven contemporary leadership theories.

Leader-member exchange (LMX) leaders create in-groups and out-groups based largely on being similar to them and/or competency. *Visionary leaders* create an image of the organization in the future that provides direction for setting goals and developing strategic plans. *Charismatic leaders* inspire loyalty, enthusiasm, and high levels of performance. *Transformational leaders* bring about continuous learning, innovation, and change. *Transactional leadership* is a leadership style based on social exchange. *Servant leaders* focus on helping others by placing their needs ahead of self-interest. *Authentic leaders* develop open, honest, trusting relationships.

• • • KEY TERMS

authentic leaders, 412
behavioral leadership theorists, 399
charismatic leadership, 411
contemporary leadership theories, 409
contingency leadership model, 403
leader-member exchange (LMX) leaders, 410

leadership continuum model, 404
Leadership Grid®, 401
leadership style, 399
leadership trait theorists, 397
path-goal model, 406
servant leaders, 412
situational approaches to leadership, 403

Situational Leadership® model, 407
substitutes for leadership, 408
transactional leadership, 411
transformational leaders, 411
two-dimensional leadership styles, 400
visionary leaders, 410

• • • KEY TERM REVIEW

Complete each of the following statements using one of this chapter's key terms.

1. _____ attempt to determine a list of distinctive characteristics that account for leadership effectiveness.

2. _____ attempt to determine distinctive styles used by effective leaders.

3. _____ is the combination of traits, skills, and behaviors managers use in interacting with employees.

4. _____ are four possible leadership styles that are based on the dimensions of job structure and employee consideration.

5. The _____ identifies the ideal leadership style as incorporating a high concern for both production and people.

6. _____ attempt to determine appropriate leadership styles for particular situations.

7. The _____ is used to determine if leadership style is task or relationship oriented and if the situation matches the style.

8. The _____ is used to determine which of seven styles of leadership, on a continuum from autocratic (*boss centered*) to participative (*employee centered*), is best for a given situation.

9. The _____ is used to determine employee objectives and to clarify how to achieve them using one of four leadership styles.

10. The _____ is used to select one of four leadership styles that matches the employees' maturity level in a given situation.

11. _____ are characteristics of the task, of subordinates, or of the organization that replace the need for a leader.

12. _____ attempt to determine how effective leaders interact with, inspire, and support followers.

13. _____ create in-groups and out-groups based largely on being similar to them and/or competency.

14. _____ create an image of the organization in the future that provides direction for setting goals and developing strategic plans.

15. _____ inspire loyalty, enthusiasm, and high levels of performance.

16. _____ is a leadership style that brings about continuous learning, innovation, and change.

17. _____ is a leadership style based on social exchange.

18. _____ focus on helping others by placing their needs ahead of self-interest.

19. _____ develop open, honest, trusting relationships.

• • • REVIEW QUESTIONS

1. What is leadership, and why is it important?

2. What are the three parts of leadership style?

3. What are the two determinants of leadership and the four possible leadership styles according to The Ohio State University and University of Michigan studies?

4. What are the five major leadership styles identified on the Leadership Grid®?

5. What are the two leadership styles identified by the contingency leadership model?

6. What are the two styles of leadership at either end of the leadership continuum model?

7. What are the four leadership styles identified by the path-goal leadership model?

8. What are the five leadership styles identified by the normative leadership model?

9. What are the four leadership styles identified by the Situational Leadership® model?

10. What are the three substitutes for leadership?

11. What is the difference between transformational and transactional leadership?

• • • COMMUNICATION SKILLS

The following critical-thinking questions can be used for class discussion and/or as written assignments to develop communication skills. Be sure to give complete explanations for all questions.

1. Peter Drucker said it's not worth pointing out the differences between a leader and a manager. Do you agree? Why or why not?

2. What traits do you think are most important in a leader?

3. Should spirituality be allowed in the workplace? Should spirituality be encouraged in the workplace? Why or why not?

4. Based on Self-Assessment 12-2, is your behavior more Theory X or Theory Y? How do you feel about your score? Will you make any changes?

5. The Ohio State University and University of Michigan two-dimensional leadership styles identified in the 1940s haven't changed much over the years, as they are still being taught and used today. However, the way we conduct business today is very different from the way it was conducted in the 1940s. Do you think it is time for a revolutionary approach to leadership styles? If so, please provide some suggestions/ideas.

6. Today, the Leadership Grid® is still being taught in colleges and by consultants to be used by managers. Do you agree that the team leadership style is the best leadership style for use in all situations? Why or why not?

7. What situational approach to leadership do you prefer? Why?

8. What percentage of top leaders would you say are really visionary, charismatic, and/or transformational? (Your answers can change for each of the three leadership theories.)

9. Do you believe that men and women lead differently?

CASES

• • • Case 12-1   Brad Smith, CEO at Intuit

Intuit, Inc. was incorporated in 1993 by founder Scott Cook. It develops business and financial management solutions for consumers, small businesses, and accounting professionals. Some of its most popular products are the Quickbooks application for small businesses and TurboTax for income tax preparation. It is headquartered in Mountain View, California, and it has a workforce of approximately 7,900 employees. The mission of Intuit is "Powering prosperity around the world."

The CEO of Intuit is Brad Smith, who joined the company in 2003 in a leadership role overseeing the Accountant Central community. This led to other leadership positions in the Consumer Tax Group and then senior vice president and general manager of the company's small business division. In 2008, he was promoted to his current position as chief executive officer and then as chairman of the board of directors in 2016.

Since assuming the role of CEO, Brad Smith has demonstrated that he is a highly effective leader in helping Intuit to realize its mission and potential for growth and success. His belief is that the most important thing that a leader needs to do is to foster a strong corporate culture that supports and reinforces the company's mission and values. This is done by communicating the purpose of the company (i.e., its mission) to members of the company across all levels in the organizational hierarchy. Smith also believes that leaders need to create a work environment in which employees' ideas are valued and considered as much as one's own. Other leadership practices that Smith likes to put into practice include building an environment for "doers" that focuses on action and getting things done and holding regular meetings with employees to promote open communication and discussion of key ideas.

Smith's leadership style emphasizes the importance of inspiring and encouraging employees to take advantage of every opportunity to move into areas where they have little or no experience or expertise and where they are forced to rely on the "power of inquiry and learning" to be successful.

"The ability to learn, adapt and execute is critical," he says.

Instilling an entrepreneurial spirit into the Intuit culture is a critical concern in order to encourage "out-of-the-box" thinking, risk taking, and innovation. Smith believes that you need to remove barriers to innovation and get out of the way. "Idea Jams" and unstructured sessions give teams of employees the opportunity to collaborate on new ideas to solve customer problems.

Other examples of Brad Smith's effective leadership style include but are not limited to:

- When he assumed the role of CEO, he spent time in small groups with more than 300 of the company's customer-facing employees in order to obtain feedback from them about what they felt were opportunities and threats facing the company.

- He has a reputation for engaging in unconventional behaviors such as wearing a suit of armor or an Elvis costume to motivate his team to achieve a challenging goal.

Discussion Questions

1. How can Brad Smith's effectiveness as CEO of Intuit be explained from a trait theory of leadership perspective?

2. How can Brad Smith's effectiveness as CEO of Intuit be explained from a path-goal theory of leadership?

3. How can Brad Smith's effectiveness as CEO of Intuit be explained from a transformational leadership theory perspective?

4. How can Brad Smith's effectiveness as CEO of Intuit be explained from a servant leadership perspective?

5. Do you think that Brad Smith is a good leader? Why or why not?

6. What do you think are the most important things that you can learn from Brad Smith's leadership style about how to become a more effective leader yourself?

References

https://www.intuit.com/company/executives/brad_smith/

http://www.reuters.com/finance/stocks/companyProfile?symbol=INTU.O

http://observer.com/2016/01/intuit-ceo-the-most-important-job-of-a-ceo/

https://www.intuit.com/company/

https://www.intuit.com/company/profile/

https://www.intuit.com/company/executives/brad_smith/

https://www.forbes.com/sites/davidkwilliams/2012/06/25/growing-a-company-qa-with-brad-smith-intuit-ceo-remove-the-barriers-to-innovation-and-get-out-of-the-way/#51d2d6ba1ff5

http://www.success.com/article/corner-office-brad-smith

https://www.nytimes.com/2014/04/13/business/brad-smith-of-intuit-follow-the-fastest-beat-of-your-heart.html

Case created by Loren Kuzuhara, University of Wisconsin–Madison.

• • • Case 12-2   Tim Cook Polishing Steve Jobs's Apple: Really?

Apple is the company and case of our lifetime. Its story is full of adventure, entrepreneurship, teamwork, legends, and leadership. The story has been told in books, most recently and successfully *Steve Jobs* by Walter Isaacson. The book was turned into a movie starring Ashton Kutcher as Steve Jobs, and the firm's history, and more specifically his departure and returning to the firm, has become common knowledge as well as management folklore.

Much has been made of Jobs's notorious micromanaging of his employees and his aggressive and demanding personality, and people who have worked for Jobs over the years have had mixed reactions to his leadership style. Some call him temperamental, aggressive, tough, intimidating, and very demanding. He was known to verbally attack people who were not meeting goals and expectations. Many employees have admitted a fear of encountering Jobs while riding in the elevator, "afraid that they might not have a job when the doors opened"— a practice that became known as "getting Steved." Yet employees who performed to expectations were well rewarded. Many who feared him also had great respect for him, as he inspired loyalty, enthusiasm, and high levels of performance through continuous learning, innovation, and change. Many people believe that the reason Apple has had its continued, incredible turnaround since the late 1990s was due to the return of Steve Jobs's role as leader of the company. However, Jobs's health deteriorated, and everyone wondered what would happen when he passed away. Tim Cook was inserted as CEO while Jobs was still alive.

Passing the torch from the entrepreneur that started a business to a person hired into the business can be very difficult. Settling into the role of CEO in 2011 in a firm that once took on the personality of its temperamental leader Steve Jobs, Tim Cook radiated tranquility in its hallways, a reflection of his "calm Southern demeanor."(1) Commonly stopping to chat or take selfies with employees, Cook's easygoing and polite personality has trickled through the corporate ethos. (2) A quieter leader than his predecessor, Cook is also said to be more thoughtful and data driven in his decisions. Cook has also added new talent to Apple with a workforce that has nearly doubled since his appointment.(3) Yet there seemed to have been a price paid for a less dynamic environment, a less vigorous firm.

Under Tim Cook's watch, Apple introduced an iPad Mini. Although it was successful, it was not the breakout hit expected of Apple products. Jobs himself once said he did not like the mini devices that other companies sold to try to beat the original larger-size iPad. In response, Apple stock languished. By the summer of 2013, Apple's stock was down by as much as 40% from its record high due to concerns over lack of new products.(4)

The most difficult moment in Cook's tenure was when the new Apple Maps app for the iPhone was released and did not work correctly. Cook took over for his lower-level executive. His first move was to fire the Apple executive. His second move was to issue a public apology to iPhone owners.

With a lineup of mature products, Apple's stakeholders were looking to Cook for the type of innovation that was once common during the Jobs era. Apple's release of the iPhone 6 and 6 Plus brought the firm into the large-screen smartphone market that was previously dominated by Android phones from firms such as Samsung and Motorola, yet market and expert response to the product was disappointing.

Even though this is Apple's first attempt at building large phones, it's not breaking new ground—in fact, it feels more like the company is catching up than innovating.(5)

Cook's biggest leap toward innovation was bringing the Apple Watch to market, a new product category for the firm. To make the Apple Watch a reality, Cook decided to reorganize the way Apple operated. Previously, Apple was split into specialized groups devoted to hardware, software design, marketing, and finance, working independently and sharing minimal cross-functional information.(6) Under Cook, these lines have been blurred through the formation of interdisciplinary teams. In an effort to boost collaboration and improve product design and functionality, engineers now sit with marketing and finance staff in product road map meetings.(7) The result? The Apple Watch was on pace to surpass the iPhone in first-year sales(8) yet sales of the new Apple Watch plunged by 90% since its opening week.(9)

> Is this a sign Apple have once again lost their way without Steve Jobs? …Apple have always pushed the envelope in the past, dropping the floppy drive, dropping legacy ports in favor of the then relatively new USB, alienating nearly all previously available accessories, and dropping the optical drive. With product lines bloating and innovation a thing of the past, how long can Apple live off the halo effect of the past? Where are they going?(10)

Yet Cook seems to have proven the pundits wrong. With 6 years of CEO experience under his belt, Cook's imprints can be seen throughout the firm. The shift in culture, an expanding employee base, and new product lines can be attributed to Tim Cook's new vision and healthier firm performance. "The Company posted all-time record quarterly [4th quarter, 2016] revenue of $78.4 billion and all-time record quarterly earnings per diluted share of $3.36. These results compare to revenue of $75.9 billion and earnings per diluted share of $3.28 in the year-ago quarter."(11)

Cook has heard the critics and thinks Apple is primed for sustainable success. "Innovation is alive and well…. If there were any doubts, I think that they should be put to bed."(12)

Discussion Questions

1. Would you consider Steve Jobs a leader, a manager, or both?

2. Would you consider Tim Cook a leader, a manager, or both?

3. Would Ghiselli say that Steve Jobs or Tim Cook have the traits of a successful leader?

4. Which basic leadership style—autocratic, democratic, or laissez-faire—would Jobs's critics say he used? What style is Cook?

5. Could you make a case for the Ohio State leadership style of high structure/low consideration or low structure/high consideration in analyzing Jobs's versus Cook's leadership style?

6. Using the University of Michigan leadership style model, was Jobs/Cook job centered or employee centered?

7. Which Leadership Grid® style—(1, 1) impoverished, (9,1) authority-compliance, (1,9) country club, (5,5) middle-of-the-road, or (9, 9) team—would Jobs's and Cook's critics say they used?

8. Was Steve Jobs a charismatic leader?

9. Was Jobs considered a transformational or transactional leader?

10. Is Tim Cook considered a transformational or transactional leader?

11. Which contingency leadership style, task oriented or relationship oriented, would Jobs's and Cook's critics say they use?

12. Did leadership play a role in the change in performance at Apple with and without Steve Jobs as CEO?

13. Would you have liked to work for Steve Jobs? Why or why not?

14. Would you like to work for Tim Cook? Why or why not?

Cumulative Case Questions

15. Was Steve Jobs or Cook an entrepreneur (Chapter 6)? Why or why not?

16. What external environment factor did Apple change for the business and general economy (Chapter 3)?

17. What decision-making model is used at Apple when selecting new products and transitions (Chapter 4)?

18. What is the strategic level of planning of this case, and what strategy is Apple using (Chapter 5)?

19. Why do you think Cook moved the structure of the organization from one that was divided by function, to one that was cross-functional (Chapter 7)?

References

(1) Stone, B., & Satariano, A. (2014, September 17). Tim Cook interview: The iPhone 6, the Apple watch, and remaking a company's culture. *BusinessWeek.* Retrieved June 6, 2015, from http://ezproxy.cul.columbia .edu/login?url=http://search.proquest.com.ezproxy.cul.columbia.edu/ docview/1615699124?accountid=10226

(2) Ibid.

(3) Ibid.

(4) Ibid.

(5) Molen, B. (2014, September 16). iPhone 6 and 6 Plus review: Bigger and better, but with stiffer competition. Engadget. Retrieved February 2, 201, from https://www.engadget.com/2014/09/16/iphone-6-and-6-plus-review/

(6) Stone, B., & Satariano, A. (2014, September 17). Tim Cook interview: The iPhone 6, the Apple watch, and remaking a company's culture. *BusinessWeek.* Retrieved June 6, 2015, from http://ezproxy.cul.columbia .edu/login?url=http://search.proquest.com.ezproxy.cul.columbia.edu/ docview/1615699124?accountid=10226

(7) Olsen, P. (2015, May 8). Apple Watch looks set to outpace the iPhone in year-one sales. *Forbes.* Retrieved June 10, 2015, from http:// www.forbes.com/sites/parmyolson/2015/05/08/apple-watch-looks- set-to-outpace-the-iphone-in-year-one-sales/

(8) Stone, B., & Satariano, A. (2014, September 17). Tim Cook interview: The iPhone 6, the Apple watch, and remaking a company's culture. *BusinessWeek.* Retrieved June 6, 2015, from http://ezproxy.cul.columbia .edu/login?url=http://search.proquest.com.ezproxy.cul.columbia.edu/ docview/1615699124?accountid=10226

(9) Arends, B. (2015, July 8). Opinion: Apple Watch sales plunge 90%. Marketwatch. Retrieved February 2, 2017, from http://www.marketwatch.com/ story/apple-watch-may-not-be-ticking-with-customers-2015-07-07

(10) Royal, S. (2017, January 24). Apple without Steve Jobs again: What's next? Retrieved February 2, 2017, from http://lowendmac.com/2017/ apple-without-steve-jobs-again-whats-next/

(11) Huguet, K. (2017, January 31). Apple reports fourth quarter results. Apple press release. Retrieved February 2, 2017, from http://www.apple.com/ newsroom/2017/01/apple-reports-record-first-quarter-results.html

(12) Stone, B., & Satariano, A. (2014, September 17). Tim Cook interview: The iPhone 6, the Apple watch, and remaking a company's culture. *BusinessWeek.* Retrieved June 6, 2015, from http://ezproxy.cul.columbia. edu/login?url=http://search.proquest.com.ezproxy.cul.columbia.edu/ docview/1615699124?accountid=10226

Case created by Herbert Sherman, Hannah K. Walter, and Naveed Ahmad, Long Island University.

● ● ● SKILL BUILDER 12-1: THE SITUATIONAL LEADERSHIP® MODEL

Objective

To better understand situational leadership.

Skills

The primary skills developed through this exercise are:

1. *Management skill*—interpersonal (leaders need good people skills to influence others)

2. *AACSB competency*—analytic skills

3. *Management function*—leading (through influencing others)

Think of a situation from a present or past job that required a boss to show leadership. Describe the situation in enough detail so that others can understand it and determine the maturity level of the employees.

For your situation, determine the maturity level of the follower(s) and select the situational leadership style appropriate for the situation (low, telling; moderate to low, selling; moderate to high, participating; high, delegating).

Apply It

What did I learn from this experience? How will I apply this knowledge in the future?

••• SKILL BUILDER 12-2: THE SITUATIONAL MANAGEMENT MODEL

Refer to Chapter 1, Skill Builder 1-4, "Management Styles," on pages 30–32 to complete this exercise.

13 Communication and Information Technology

••• LEARNING OBJECTIVES

After studying this chapter, you should be able to:

Ideas on Management
at Facebook

Facebook's mission is to give people the power to share and make the world more open and connected. People use Facebook to stay connected with friends and family, to discover what's going on in the world, and to share and express what matters to them. Facebook is about two fundamental ideas.

First, it's a directory, which is where it gets its name. Its first 10 years were about taking down barriers to let new groups of people come onto Facebook. It has nearly 2 billion social networking users—that's 27% of the world's 7.4 billion people. Second, it's a medium for expressing your experience to somebody else. Messenger and WhatsApp provide intimate, high-frequency communications with people you care about. If you move up, you have groups and events, which are about communicating with hundreds or thousands of people at a time, and you can move up to news feed and **Instagram** for an even higher scale of audience. People also watch more than 1 billion hours of videos and other content on **YouTube** daily, on pace to eclipse TV. And depending on where you look in the world, you have people using these things in different ways. **Mark Zuckerberg**, with his college roommates and fellow Harvard University computer science students, founded Facebook back in 2004. Facebook went public with its initial public offering (IPO) in 2012. Clearly, CEO Mark Zuckerberg's leadership was a major factor in Facebook's success. He was named **Fortune** Businessperson of the Year in 2016 and stated that Facebook will continue to develop artificial intelligence and virtual reality in the company's 10-year road map. In 2016, Facebook was developing **chatbots**, similar to **Apple**'s Siri and **Amazon**'s Alexa, as a fresh alternative to smartphone apps to combine popular text-messaging programs and burgeoning artificial-intelligence techniques to connect business partners with Messenger and WhatsApp users.

IOM 1. What types of organizational communication are possible, and which information technology does Facebook use?

IOM 2. Can social networking sites such as Facebook be a type of communication between individuals and companies? Why or why not?

IOM 3. Which communication barriers are more common when using Facebook?

IOM 4. Which transmission channels are commonly used with Facebook?

IOM 5. When using a social networking site such as Facebook, which part of the message-sending process can be the most difficult to accomplish?

IOM 6. How can you analyze information from messages received on Facebook?

IOM 7. What have critics of Facebook said about it?

You'll find answers to these **IOM** questions throughout the chapter. To learn more about Facebook, visit www.facebook.com.

Sources: Information for this case and answers within the chapter were taken from Facebook's website at http://www.facebook.com, accessed June 7, 2017; J. Krim, "Here's What Facebook Sees in the Mirror," *The Wall Street Journal* (October 27, 2015): R8; "The Fast Tech 25," *Forbes* (June 13, 2017): 48; A. Lashinsky, "Businessperson of the Year," *Fortune* (December 1, 2016): 65–72; J. Nicas, "YouTube Notches Global Video Milestone," *The Wall Street Journal* (February 28, 2017): B1, B5; R. McMillan, "Facebook Focuses on Smarter Chatbots," *The Wall Street Journal* (April 18, 2016): B5.

LO 13-1

Explain the three ways communication flows through organizations.

Organizational Communication

Communication *is the process of transmitting information and meaning.* From Chapter 1, communication is important to management: skills, roles, and functions. Communications is the foundation of interpersonal skills,[1] and it is a transferable skill.[2] From Chapters 10 through 12, recall that leadership is about influencing others, which is based on communication skills.[3] Think about the jerks you have to deal with. Well, a major reason you think they are jerks is their poor communication skills.[4] HR professionals rated interpersonal-communication skills as the most valuable knowledge, skill, or ability for career success.[5] However, companies say that communication and other soft skills are difficult to find in job applicants.[6]

There are two major types, or levels, of communication: organizational and interpersonal. That is, communication takes place among organizations and among their units or departments, and communication takes place among individuals. Both companywide and individual communications are vital. In this section, we discuss organizational communication. In the next section, we focus on information technology; the rest of the chapter presents interpersonal communication. Organizational communication flows up, down, and sideways,[7] or formally in vertical and horizontal directions and informally through the grapevine.[8] Exhibit 13-1 illustrates these aspects of organizational communication.

Vertical Communication

Hierarchical structures create vertical communication.[9] **Vertical communication** *is the flow of information both downward and upward through the organizational chain of command.* It is also called *formal communication* because information that flows this way is recognized as the officially sanctioned information.

Downward Vertical Communication. When top-level management creates a vision and makes decisions or creates policies and procedures, these are often communicated down the chain of command to employees.[10] Downward communication occurs when higher-level managers tell those below them what to do and how to do it. The delegation process occurs via downward communication.

Upward Vertical Communication. When employees send a message to their bosses, they are using upward communication. Upward communication is vital, as it gives employees participation in management decisions and improving performance.[11] To help facilitate upward communication, many organizations have adopted an open-door policy that allows employees to feel at ease in going to managers.

Horizontal Communication

Horizontal communication *is the flow of information between colleagues and peers.* It is formal communication, but it does not follow the chain of command; instead, it is multidirectional. Horizontal communication is needed to coordinate within a department, among team members, and among different departments. When the manager of the marketing department communicates with the manager of the production department or other departments, horizontal communication takes place. Most employees spend more time communicating with peers than with managers. Organizations are becoming flatter and more horizontal (Chapter 7) to facilitate this flow of communications, including at **Basecamp**.[12]

Grapevine Communication

The **grapevine** *is the informal flow of information in any direction throughout an organization.* It is informal communication because it is not official or sanctioned by management. The information is often called rumors and gossip. Grapevine information can begin with anyone in the organization and can flow in any direction. Employees complain, talk about sports and news events, discuss work-related matters such as layoffs and personnel changes, and whisper secrets about coworkers through the grapevine. The maker of video games **Half-Life** and **Portal** says that the grapevine tends to be used by, and contribute to, cliques.[13] **Whole Foods CEO John Mackey** says it uses transparency to help eliminate gossipy speculation.[14]

WORK
APPLICATION 13-1

Give an example of vertical (upward and downward), horizontal, and grapevine communication at a company where you work or have worked.

communication The process of transmitting information and meaning.

vertical communication The flow of information both downward and upward through the organizational chain of command.

horizontal communication The flow of information between colleagues and peers.

grapevine The informal flow of information in any direction throughout an organization.

EXHIBIT 13-1   ORGANIZATIONAL COMMUNICATION

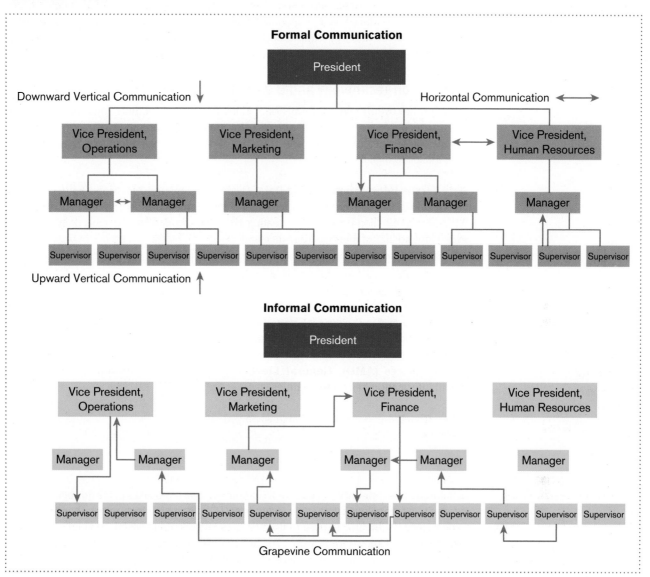

13-1 APPLYING THE CONCEPT

Communication Flow

Identify the form of communication flow occurring for each statement.

A. vertical downward

B. vertical upward

C. horizontal—identify as between (1) peers or (2) departments

D. grapevine

_____ 1. "Bubba, I just sold products to two new customers who want to set up charge accounts. Please rush the credit check so we can increase business."

_____ 2. "Paul, please take this package to the mailroom and have it sent out FedEx overnight for me."

_____ 3. "Tomas, have you heard about the president and his secretary?"

_____ 4. "Kyra, will you please hold this so we can get it straight and finish the job?"

_____ 5. "Arjun, here is the report you asked me to do. Check it, and I'll make any changes you want."

LO 13-2

Discuss information technology and how IT is used, describe the three primary types of information systems, and list the five components of an information network.

Information Technology, Systems, and Networks

The new source of power is information.[15] Information technology has made it much cheaper and easier to conduct business globally,[16] but it takes people communicating to develop and implement technology.[17] In this section, we discuss how organizations use technology to communicate.

Information Technology and Big Data

Today we are overrun with information.[18] Many firms have computer information systems and an executive who oversees all aspects of information technology. Generally, this executive has the title of chief information officer (CIO). CIOs are playing a major role in moving firms from analog to digital business.[19]

Data Versus Information and Big Data. *Data* are unorganized facts and figures, whereas *information* is data converted into a form that helps people make decisions and do their jobs. With close to 4 billion e-mail users creating 100 billion work-related e-mails daily, managers spend around 28% of their workday on e-mail.[20]

Big Data refers to having a very large data set, which is made possible through technology. Big Data has launched a boom industry in data analytics and science.[21] Data are used to run statistical analysis to find relationships between variables and predict outcomes, such as which product customers will buy, which become information used to make decisions. Employers seek young employees that can create and analyze data and sell their ideas, and companies want their employees to share information.[22] Big Data is transforming the way companies do business, including **Starwood Hotels**, **Advanced Micro Devices (AMD)**, **General Electric (GE)**, **Visa**, and **United Technologies**.[23] Useful information has three qualities:

- Timely—current and available when you need it
- Relevant—suited to the situation, accurate, complete but concise
- Understandable—easy to comprehend

Information Technology (IT) Defined. Communication often takes place through the use of information technology. *Information technology (IT)* refers to the technology (hardware, operating systems, and software) used to store, process, and distribute useful data and information. **Walmart** is well known for its use of IT.[24] **Southwest Airlines** says a planned upgrade of its IT system could boost annual profits $500 million by 2020.[25]

13-1 JOIN THE DISCUSSION ETHICS & SOCIAL RESPONSIBILITY

The Grapevine

The grapevine is commonly used to spread rumors and gossip. Most grapevine information is harmless and informs employees of what is going on in the firm. However, some, especially talk regarding work-related matters and coworkers, can destroy trust and sabotage productivity.

1. Have you or has anyone you know been hurt by rumors or gossip? Explain the situation and how you or the other person was hurt.

2. Do rumors and gossip help or hurt individuals and the organization?

3. Is it ethical and socially responsible to spread rumors and gossip?

4. Should employees gossip and spread rumors when they are not sure of the accuracy of the information they are spreading?

5. How should managers handle rumors and gossip?

Using IT. To use IT, you generally need hardware (PCs, laptops, digital device tablets, and smartphones), an operating system (Windows, Android, or iOS), and software (Microsoft Office or Messenger apps). At work, desktop and laptop running Windows remain the most commonly used IT devices.[26] Software lives in our pockets (smartphone), runs our cars and homes, and dominates our waking lives.[27] Here is how IT is used.

- *The Internet* is a global collection of computer networks linked together to exchange data and information, and the *World Wide Web (WWW)* is a segment of the Internet in which information is presented in the form of Web pages.

- Nearly everything in our world is powered by data.[28] Today we're connecting so many different digital devices (cars, manufacturing equipment, etc.) that there is a new term for it: the *Internet of things (IoT)*, and it is changing how we receive information.[29] Abbreviated *IoT*, it is an ecosystem of all types of devices connected through the Internet.[30] There will be an estimated 26 billion Internet-connected objects by 2020.[31] IoT is really about services. **HP** sells Office Jets and **Clorox** Brita unit sells smart pitchers that offers Wi-Fi–enabled reordering of its own ink and water filters.[32] **IBM** will invest $3 billion over the next four years in an IoT unit that will help its partners, such as broadcaster **Weather Company**, gather and analyze data collected from cars, jets, weather stations, and smart appliances.[33]

- *Electronic commerce (e-commerce)* consists of the buying and selling of products and services over electronic systems, typically the Internet. Exhibit 13-2 illustrates the various types of e-commerce. **Amazon.com** is a leading retail e-commerce company that has contributed to retailers filing for Chapter 11 bankruptcy protection and closing of stores at **RadioShack**, **Sears**, **Kmart**, **J.C. Penney,** and others.[34] Today, many of the business-to-business (B2B) transactions are being done through *machine-to-machine (M2M)* without human interaction, such as automatic inventory.[35] Advertisers will pay more than $50 billion to search giant **Google** for clicks that deliver potential customers to their Web pages (B2C).[36] **Uber** and **Airbnb** success has led to benchmarking businesses and the rapid growth of peer-to-peer (P2P) moneymaking opportunities,[37] also making P2P payments quick and easy through **PayPal** and other payment services to consumers.[38]

- The trend toward *wireless communication* continues, as people are becoming increasingly mobile. E-commerce is also being called *mobile commerce (m-commerce)*, as wireless handheld devices such as smartphones and personal digital assistants (PDAs) are being used to conduct business. Have you bought anything using your cell phone? With tablets and smartphones and apps, you don't have to lug around a laptop to conduct business on the road.[39] In 2015, 21% of Millennials (ages 18–34) accessed the Internet only through mobile devices,[40] and the numbers continue to grow.

Informal communication in the workplace is sometimes good, but it should not turn to gossip. Gossip can damage trust within an organization and distract employees from their work.

The idea behind *cloud computing* is that companies store data and software on the Internet, then access it and run it all over the Web from their office computers, which thereby don't need as much storage space or as much expensive software. Cloud-computing customers do not own the physical infrastructure where they store their data and software, instead avoiding capital expenditure by renting usage from a third-party provider. They consume resources as a service and pay cloud providers, including **Amazon**, **Microsoft**, **IBM**, **Google**, and others, only for resources that they use.[41] With cloud-based software and storage, it becomes easier to use mobile devices to conduct business.[42] According to the Internet of Things Consortium, if it weren't for cloud computing, there would be no IoT. Director of Cloud and Computer Electronics at **HIS** Jagdish Rebello says, "The role of the cloud is to take data from multiple devices and multiple applications and to combine that information into something an enterprise or person can use to make decisions."[43]

Facebook (IOM 1) can send information throughout an organization, as well as individually, horizontally, vertically, and through the grapevine, but its primary information technology channel used is the Internet, which can be accessed wirelessly.

The Dark Side of the Internet and Cell Phones. On the personal negative side of IT, recall that smartphones keep people connected to the office, *blurring work–life balance*.[44] Mobile devices make it easy to stay connected, as employees check work in the evening and/or on the weekends, and these numbers will continue to increase with what is being called "*the new night shift*" as employees log back on or never log off.[45]

Although technology is supposed to increase productivity, people *lose time* every day due to interruptions and distractions that deteriorate workers' ability to concentrate. As discussed in Chapter 5, people multitasking by constantly checking their screens decreases the speed at which they can get their work done—as multitasking is a myth, because you can't concentrate on two thinking tasks at the same time.

With 83% of employees admitting to accessing work computers for personal use,[46] every day employees are *doing personal work on the job*, contacting friends and family and visiting websites such as **Facebook** or **LinkedIn** and shopping at **Amazon.com**. This "cyberloafing" cost U.S. business as much as $85 billion a year, so companies are monitoring employee computer use and email to try to stop the abuse.[47] But with monitoring comes the question

EXHIBIT 13-2   E-COMMERCE

Business-to-Business (B2B)

Ford ◄—— (B2B) ——► Firestone

Ford buys tires from **Firestone**.

Business-to-Employee (B2E)

Business/Database ◄—— (B2E) ——► Employees

UPS drivers get electronic orders to pick up packages along their routes and send electronic information to businesses for tracking deliveries.

Business-to-Customer (B2C)

Amazon.com ◄—— (B2C) ——► John Smith

Amazon.com sells a book and a computer to John Smith.

Peer-to-Peer (P2P)

Employee ◄—— (P2P) ——► Employee

An **Apple** employee in the United States electronically contacts an Apple employee in China to find out why an iPod order is behind schedule.

Customer-to-Customer (C2C)

eBay (online auctions)

↑↓

John Smith ◄—— (C2C) ——► Jean Jones

John Smith buys a watch from Jean Jones and sells a car to Jones through **eBay**.

13-2 JOIN THE DISCUSSION ETHICS & SOCIAL RESPONSIBILITY

Should Personal Cell Phones Be Banned at Work?

As discussed, employees are wasting a lot of time at work using either their companies' computers or their own personal cell phones. To help prevent employees from wasting time, organizations are monitoring the use of their technology and banning personal cell phones at work.

1. Is it ethical and socially responsible for employees to use company time and perhaps its technology for personal use? Should employees get paid for doing personal things at work?

2. Is it ethical and socially responsible for companies to monitor employee use of their technology? Should they monitor?

3. Is it ethical and socially responsible for companies to ban the use of employee personal technology on the job? Should they ban personal cell phones at work?

of employee privacy and legal issues. Many employees are getting around the issue of using company IT by using their personal cell phones, so some companies are developing policies and even banning the use of personal technology at work.[48] In a survey, 23% of recent graduates said they wouldn't take a job if they couldn't use their cell phones for personal calls/texts.[49] Would you?

Privacy and Cybersecurity. With the increasing collection of Big Data come privacy concerns.[50] Back in 2010, **Facebook** was accused of selling data and not protecting its users' privacy and had to change its policies.[51] In a survey, CEOs were asked to list their greatest challenge, and 72% said technology innovation, followed by 66% stating cybersecurity.[52] As a result, companies were expected to spend some $76.9 billion on information security in 2015, and many companies have managers with titles like chief information security officer at **Yahoo**,[53] which had 1 billion accounts compromised in the Yahoo hack.[54] Some **Apple** apps were infected with malware that transmitted information about users' devices.[55]

Leaks, theft, and sabotage by employees have become major cybersecurity problems. The number-one source of cybercrime is not external hackers; it's the organization's own employees,[56] so companies are monitoring employees to neutralize insider threats.[57] **Dell** offers SecureWorks cybersecurity services to help prevent internal and external cybercrime.[58] **Stroz Friedberg** developed cybersecurity Scout to spot insider threats before they happen by reading employee email to identify disgruntled workers that could commit fraud or embezzle, steal intellectual property or other data, sabotage the IT system, or become violent.[59]

Types of Information Systems

Like any system, an information system has input, transformation, and output. Information systems (IS) have data as input, and they transform the data into information to help employees do their jobs and make decisions. These systems are used to communicate with employees throughout organizations and on the interpersonal level. Here are three primary types of IS.

Transaction Processing Systems (TPS). *Transaction processing systems* are used to handle routine and recurring business matters. Organizations use TPS to record accounting transactions, such as accounts receivable and payable and payroll. Most large retail organizations use scanners to record sales transactions at the checkout counter. Banks process checks and deposits and record credit card transactions. Stockbrokers buy and sell stock for clients.

Management Information Systems (MIS). *Management information systems* transform data into the information employees need to do their work. The information provided by MIS is commonly used for making routine decisions. Real-time tracking is done on MIS, such as with **FedEx** and **UPS** packages.

EXHIBIT 13-3   INFORMATION NETWORK

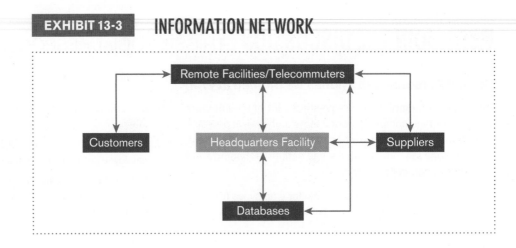

Decision Support Systems (DSS). *Decision support systems* use managers' insights in an interactive computer-based process to assist in making nonroutine decisions. They use decision rules, decision models, and comprehensive databases. DSS are more flexible than MIS. However, a decision support system can interact with an MIS by applying mathematical operations to the information available in the MIS. These data manipulations allow managers to evaluate the possible effects of alternative decisions.

Information Networks

How do you get employees to communicate and coordinate work when they are all over the map?[60] *Information networks* apply IT to connect all employees of an organization to each other, to suppliers, to customers, and to databases. Information networks are used to integrate information systems and, at many organizations, to find information, and to solve problems. New apps and cloud-based tools are turning global workers into hives of collaboration and connecting companies with their customers as never before.[61] **GHD**'s 8,500 employees collaborate on **Riverbed's 3D apps** to move massive digital files across continents as if they're working side by side.[62] Exhibit 13-3 illustrates the components of an information network. As you can see, much of the network is based on machine-to-machine (M2M) communications, which will eventually make up 50% of all data transmitted over the Internet.[63]

Facebook's (**IOM 2**) social networking has proved to be a type of communication in that individuals can connect to one another via the Internet, and companies are also using social networking to recruit new people to hire and as promotional tools for their products. Facebook is now offering business services and is also being used as a source of data to be included in its Big Data analysis for use in decision making.

LO 13-3

List the four steps in the interpersonal communication process and the nine barriers to communication.

WORK
APPLICATION 13-2

Give an example of a message that might be transmitted in a work setting. Be sure to illustrate the four steps in the communication process, state the channel, and note if feedback was given.

The Interpersonal Communication Process and Communication Barriers

We now turn to interpersonal communications, or one-on-one and small-group communications. Communication is the most important skill employers seek in new hires,[64] and companies, including **Deloitte Consulting**, expect new hires to arrive with communication skills and business acumen.[65] It's your job to make communications easier for the other person.[66] Exhibit 13-4 illustrates the communication process, which is discussed next, followed by barriers that interfere with interpersonal communications and how to overcome them.

The Interpersonal Communication Process

The **communication process** takes place between a sender who encodes a message and transmits it through a channel and a receiver who decodes it and may give feedback.

EXHIBIT 13-4   THE COMMUNICATION PROCESS

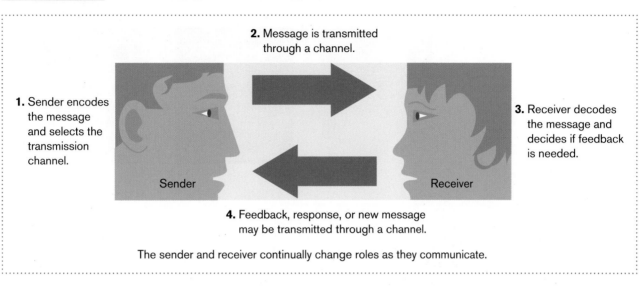

2. Message is transmitted through a channel.

1. Sender encodes the message and selects the transmission channel.

3. Receiver decodes the message and decides if feedback is needed.

Sender

Receiver

4. Feedback, response, or new message may be transmitted through a channel.

The sender and receiver continually change roles as they communicate.

Stage 1. The sender encodes the message and selects the transmission channel. The *sender* of the message is the person who initiates the communication. The *message* is the information and meaning communicated. **Encoding** *is the sender's process of putting the message into a form that the receiver will understand.* The message is transmitted through a **communication channel**—*the means or medium by which a message is transmitted;* the *three primary channels are oral, nonverbal, and written.*

Stage 2. The sender transmits the message. After the sender encodes the message and selects the channel, he or she transmits the message through the channel to the receiver(s).

Stage 3. The receiver decodes the message and decides if feedback is needed. The person receiving the message decodes it. **Decoding** *is the receiver's process of translating a message into a meaningful form.* The receiver interprets the meaning of the message and decides if feedback, a response, or a new message is needed.

Stage 4. Feedback: A response or a new message may be transmitted. After the receiver decodes the message, he or she may give feedback to the sender, or the sender may request feedback to ensure mutual understanding of the message. Even though communication is taking place, if the sender and receiver are not on the same page, the message may not have been transmitted with mutual understanding. So the role of feedback is to ensure mutual understanding of the message. You should realize that the roles of sender and receiver can be changed during a communication exchange.

After covering barriers, we devote the next four major sections to channel selection and sending, as well as receiving and responding to messages.

Communication Barriers

Exhibit 13-5 depicts a number of common barriers to communication.

Perception. As messages are transmitted, receivers perceive them and translate them so that they make sense to them. Recall perception (Chapter 10) bias as we interpret messages differently[67] and that often our biases can lead to two versions of the same story.[68] *Semantics* and *jargon* can be communication barriers, because the same word often means different things to different people.

communication process The process that takes place between a sender who encodes a message and transmits it through a channel and a receiver who decodes it and may give feedback.

encoding The sender's process of putting the message into a form that the receiver will understand.

communication channel The means or medium by which a message is transmitted; the three primary channels are oral, nonverbal, and written.

decoding The receiver's process of translating a message into a meaningful form.

EXHIBIT 13-5   ## MAJOR COMMUNICATION BARRIERS

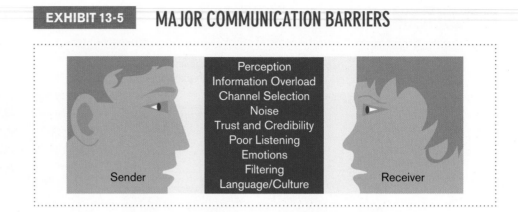

Sender

Perception
Information Overload
Channel Selection
Noise
Trust and Credibility
Poor Listening
Emotions
Filtering
Language/Culture

Receiver

To overcome perception problems, strive for *perception congruence* (Chapter 10), as you need to consider how the other person will most likely perceive the message, and try to encode and transmit it appropriately. Be careful not to use jargon with people who are not familiar with the terminology, especially people from countries with different cultures.

Information Overload. There is a limit to the amount of information people can understand at any given time. It is a common problem because we are often presented with too much information to comprehend in a short time.

To minimize information overload, send messages in a quantity that the receiver can understand. When sending an oral message, do not talk for too long without checking to be sure the receiver understands the message as you intended.

Channel Selection. Use of an inappropriate channel can result in missed communication. For example, most young people like to text, but many older ones don't text.

Before sending a message, give careful thought to selecting the most effective channel. We discuss channel selection in the next section.

Noise. Noise is anything that interferes with message transmission that disturbs or confuses the receiver. A machine or people may make noise that makes it difficult to hear, the sender may not speak loud enough for the receiver to hear well, or radio/TV or a phone call may distract the receiver, causing interpretation errors.

To overcome noise, consider the physical surroundings before transmitting a message. Try to keep noise to a minimum. If possible, stop the noise or distraction or move to a quiet location.

Trust and Credibility. When receivers do not trust senders[69] or do not believe senders know what they are talking about, they are reluctant to accept the message.

To improve trust, follow the guidelines in Chapter 12. To gain and maintain credibility, get the facts straight before you communicate, and send clear, correct messages.

Poor Listening. People usually hear what the sender is saying, but often they do not listen to the message or understand what is actually being transmitted. Poor listening is sometimes the result of not paying attention[70] or other distractions, like your phone and texting.[71]

One method to help ensure that people listen to your message involves getting their full attention and questioning them and having them paraphrase the message back to you. When listening, follow the listening tips presented later in this chapter, and put your phone away.[72]

Emotions. Everyone has emotions, and emotions can interfere with communication and make it difficult for people to be objective and to listen.

13-2 APPLYING THE CONCEPT

Communication Barriers

Identify the communication barrier indicated by each statement.

A. perception

B. information overload

C. channel selection

D. noise

E. trust and credibility

F. not listening

G. emotions

H. filtering

I. language/culture

_____ 6. "Ramzie, can you tell me what Juan is talking about? I can't understand him."

_____ 7. "Jose, you shouldn't be upset, so just calm down."

_____ 8. "So, Deondre, do you understand?" She doesn't respond (thinking, "You just went through 14 steps, and I was lost back on step 2").

_____ 9. "Yes, Billy Jean. We are right on schedule" (meanwhile thinking, "We are actually behind, but we'll catch up").

_____ 10. "Kasandra, I said I'd do it in a little while. It's only been 10 minutes, so why do you expect it to be done by now?"

_____ 11. "Paul, you don't know what you are talking about. I'll keep doing it my way."

_____ 12. "Ronnie, I don't like texting back and forth, so please call me."

_____ 13. "Eliana, how many times do I have to tell you to stop using your personal phone at work when you are waiting on customers?"

_____ 14. "Joe, please shut the loud music off. We need to talk about your incident with Karlton."

When communicating, remain calm and be careful not to make others emotional through your behavior. Later in this chapter, you will learn how to calm an emotional employee.

Filtering. *Filtering* is the process of altering or distorting information to project a more favorable image. At companies like **Enron**, people often don't start out planning to cheat. When they don't make the numbers, they cook the books, thinking, "Next period we will catch up, and no one will ever know or get hurt." After a few periods, they realize they can't catch up and fear telling the truth until it is too late. Some people lie, but don't, because the truth will catch up with you and you will lose trust and credibility, and you could even end up in jail.

To help eliminate filtering, treat errors as a learning experience rather than as an opportunity to blame and criticize employees. Don't set goals that are too difficult, with high rewards for achieving them (or punishment or failing to), because you give people incentives to filter, like what happened at **Wells Fargo**. You will learn about criticism later in this chapter.

Language/Culture. Recall that we have diversity (Chapter 3) in the United States, and even more so in the global village, and people who come from different cultures and speak different languages need to communicate, which can be difficult with cultural barriers.[73] Even if you can speak the same language, commonly English, cultural differences in verbal, nonverbal, and written messages have a tendency to be misunderstood, especially between Westerners and Easterners.[74] There are more than 6,000 spoken languages in the world; how many can you do business in?[75] If you can't communicate in the same language, you will encounter a major barrier.

So international communication effectiveness (ICE) in the workplace is important.[76] If you can speak the same language, you need to have intercultural sensitivity and be very careful to make sure your message is received as intended by getting feedback.[77] If you can't speak the other party's language, you need interpreter and translation help, such as by hiring people who can translate and/or by using the services of **Niki's Int'l Ltd.** in more than 350 languages.[78] Being multilingual increases career opportunities.

WORK
APPLICATION 13-3

Give two examples of different communication barriers you encountered at work. Explain how each barrier could have been overcome.

Facebook (IOM 3) can have information overload, as some people post tons of information that not even their friends want to know, which also results in poor listening, as people tune them out. Language and culture exist within countries but become more of a barrier with international communications.

LO 13-4

State the major advantages and disadvantages of oral and written communication and a general guide to channel selection.

Message Transmission Channels

When encoding a message, you should give careful consideration to selecting the channel.[79] Channels include oral, nonverbal, and written forms.[80] Exhibit 13-6 lists the major message transmission channels.

Oral Communication

Although texting is increasing in popularity, recruiters say oral communication skills are more important.[81] Here we discuss the five most common channels for oral communication. The major advantages of oral communication are that it is usually easier and faster than written communication and it encourages feedback. The disadvantage is that there is usually no record of such communication. In the global village, video communications/**Skype** often replace face-to-face meetings and presentations.[82] Try not to say "um" or other annoying things when using oral communications.

- *Face-to-face conversations* are important.[83] A spokesperson for **Mutual of America** insurance says, "There's a feeling you get when you talk face-to-face, not face-to-website." It is the appropriate channel for delegating tasks, coaching,[84] disciplining, and developing and maintaining good interpersonal relations.

  Telephone conversations are the appropriate channel for quick exchanges of information and for checking up on something; phone calls often save managers from having to travel. Face-to-face and phone conversations are more effective and faster than email/text and responding back and forth multiple times. Relationships matter,[85] so have some conversations.[86] A word on privacy: companies have the technology to listen to your personal calls on your own smartphone on their premises.[87]

- *Voice mail* is most commonly used to leave messages for people who are unable to answer the phone and sometimes in place of written messages. Voice mail is appropriate for sending short messages containing information that need not be in written form, and texting is more popular today.

- *Meetings are common today* (Chapter 8). The most common type of meeting is the brief, informal get-together of a manager with two or more employees. Meetings are appropriate for coordinating employee activities, delegating a task to a group, and resolving employee conflicts.

EXHIBIT 13-6   MESSAGE TRANSMISSION CHANNELS

Oral Communication	Nonverbal Communication	Written Communication
Face-to-face conversations	Setting	Email/text
Meetings	Body language	Memos
Presentations	Facial expressions	Letters
Telephone conversations	Vocal quality	Reports
Voice mail messages	Gestures	Faxes
	Posture	Bulletin boards
	Posters (pictures)	Posters (words)
		Newsletters

- ***Presentations*** are common in the workplace today,[88] and few skills are more important.[89] Be sure to (1) begin your presentation with a purpose statement and an overview of the main points to be covered, (2) discuss your main points in the detail necessary to get the message across, and (3) summarize the purpose, main points, and any action required of the audience.[90] The use of *PowerPoint (PP)* is popular. However, the audience should be looking at you, not reading the PP slides. Flashy slides can actually distract from your message. Don't simply read your PP presentation; the slides should just be an outline to help you talk to the audience about your topic points. The key to developing your presentation skills is preparation and practice. You also need to watch your nonverbal communication to add to, not distract from, you and your message.[91]

Presentation skills are among the most valuable skills to have in today's workplace. Practice and preparation are the keys to delivering a successful presentation.

Nonverbal Communication

Every time you talk to someone face to face, you also use nonverbal communication.[92] **Nonverbal communication** *consists of messages sent without words.* It includes the *setting* of the communication (physical surroundings) and *body language.* The impact of any face-to-face communication is dependent on body language, which includes (1) facial expressions[93] (eye contact and a wink or a smile, a frown, or a dirty look), (2) vocal quality[94] (not the words used but the way they are said—calmly or urgently, fast or slowly, softly or loudly), (3) gestures[95] (such as moving the hands, pointing and signaling, and nodding the head), and (4) posture[96] (sitting up straight or slouching, leaning back or forward, crossing arms and/or legs). One of the weaknesses of writing (email/text) and the phone is you lose most of the nonverbal communications.[97]

To make communication effective, make sure your body language, tone of voice, and word choice project a calm, professional demeanor.[98] Be aware of your nonverbal communication and make sure it is consistent with your oral communication. When your oral communication conflicts with your nonverbal communication, people tend to give more weight to the nonverbal communication—actions speak louder than words. If your manager says, "I care about you" but treats you poorly, which will you believe?

You also want to be aware of other people's nonverbal communication because it reveals their feelings and attitudes toward you and the communication. Listen to what people say and don't say;[99] read between the lines.

Remember to be positive and optimistic. Acting happy can make it so—improve your mood.[100] When talking to people, use nonverbal communication to convey openness to messages. Smile, face the person, and use appropriate eye contact for three to five seconds; lean forward a bit and gesture frequently to convey that you are listening and are interested.[101] Do not cross your arms or legs (signs of being closed to communication), and speak in a pleasant, calm tone of voice.[102]

A harsh tone of voice or a nasty look can be more effective than words. **Lovie Smith** was the head coach of the **National Football League's (NFL) Chicago Bears**. When Smith got mad, he stared straight ahead in silence. His players called it "the Lovie Look" and said it was more frightening—and more of a warning to play better—than his yelling angry words like other coaches.

Written Communication

With today's technology, we write all the time, and our words last forever.[103] Nothing can reveal your communication weaknesses more clearly than poorly written letters, reports, emails, texts, and so on. In a survey, more than half of respondents said they would never hire someone who can't communicate in writing.[104] The major advantages of written

WORK
APPLICATION 13-4

Give an example of an oral message and a written message you received at work, and specify the channel of each.

nonverbal communication
Messages sent without words.

communication are that we are more accurate and honest when we deliver news over email. It allows people to absorb the news without immediate responses (and to think about our reply), and it provides a record of what was communicated. The major disadvantages are that it usually takes longer, you lose nonverbal signals, and it hinders feedback. Below are sources of written communications.

- **Email/text** is often the channel that transmits all of the following.
- **Memos** are commonly used to send intraorganizational messages.
- **Letters** are commonly used to communicate with people outside of the organization.
- **Reports** are used to convey information, evaluation, analysis, and/or recommendations to management or colleagues.
- **Bulletin board and blog notices** usually supplement other forms of communication. Many companies today have electronic bulletin boards and blogs for their employees to post on.
- **Posters (or signs)** are commonly used as reminders of important information, such as a mission statement or safety instructions. Posters can also be nonverbal, or graphic, communication. An example is the universal symbol that bans or forbids some activity: a picture of what you are not supposed to do, circled and with a line through it.
- **Newsletters** are used to convey general information to all employees.

Written communication is appropriate when detailed instructions are required, when something needs to be documented, for formal or official messages (especially those containing facts and figures), and when there is a need to give a number of people the exact same information.

Here are a few writing tips. Use the active voice—for example, "we made the product" instead of "the product was made by us"—and be brief and clear.[105] Make sure to have a subject that gives an overview of the message that encourages reading it,[106] specify a call to action (an objective or statement of what you want),[107] and respond with simple, direct answers.[108]

Combining Channels

Nonverbal communication and oral communication are almost always combined. You can also combine oral and written communication (as in a presentation) or even oral, nonverbal, and written communication. Using combined channels is appropriate when the message is important and you want to ensure that employees attend to and understand it. You can send an email message to give the receiver time to think about it, then follow up with a personal visit or telephone call to talk about it.[109] Managers often formally document a face-to-face meeting, particularly in a disciplinary situation. However, don't be redundant and inefficient.[110] For example, some managers send out an agenda and simply tell people what it says during the meeting, wasting several employees' time, when a simple email would be more efficient.

Facebook (IOM 4) involves using nonverbal (pictures), oral (video), and written communication. Users can post pictures; in 2015, Facebook's video traffic skyrocketed;[111] and users can post messages on their own and others' walls (written communication). Facebook includes other forms of written communication such as text messaging and three instant messaging apps as well as traditional email. Facebook also wants to be your home page on your cell phone.

Selecting the Message Transmission Channel

Media richness refers to the amount of information and meaning conveyed through a channel. The more information and meaning, the "richer" the channel. Face-to-face communication is the richest channel because it allows the sender and receiver to take full advantage of both oral and nonverbal communication. The telephone is less rich than talking face to

13-3 APPLYING THE CONCEPT

Channel Selection

For each of the communication situations, select the most appropriate channel for transmitting the message.

Oral Communication

A. face-to-face

B. meeting

C. presentation

D. telephone

Written Communication

E. email/text

F. memo

G. letter

H. report

I. bulletin board, poster, newsletter

____ 15. Shawn is late again, and you need to take some action.

____ 16. "Christine, I need some statistics. Can you please run the numbers and get them to me by 1:00 today?"

____ 17. Katniss is applying to colleges and asked you for a recommendation.

____ 18. Janie is running a few minutes late for a meeting and wants her punctual boss to know she is on her way.

____ 19. Timmy is a drug sales rep and is meeting with a group of doctors to pitch a new cancer drug.

____ 20. Esther in HR came out with a new policy and wants to inform employees internally of the change.

____ 21. Kenny is waiting for an important FedEx and wants to know if it is in the mailroom yet.

____ 22. Tony's employees have been leaving the lights on in the break room when no one is in it, so he decided to send a message to them to shut them off.

____ 23. Carolyn needs to explain to her 12 employees how to fill out a new form.

face because most nonverbal cues are lost when you cannot see facial expressions and gestures. All forms of oral communication are richer than written communication because oral communication allows transmission of at least some nonverbal cues, which are lost with written messages.

It's important to select the most appropriate channel of transmission for any message.[112] As a general guide, use oral channels for sending difficult and unusual messages, written channels for transmitting simple and routine messages to several people or messages that contain facts and figures or detailed instructions, and combined channels for important messages that recipients need to attend to and understand.

Sending Messages

Every time we talk, we are sending messages.[113] Words make a difference,[114] as poor wording drains money due to miscommunication.[115] An important part of a manager's job is to give instructions, which is sending a message. Have you ever heard a manager say, "This isn't what I asked for"? When this happens, it is usually the manager's fault. You must take 100% of the responsibility for ensuring that your messages are transmitted clearly. This section discusses the processes of planning and sending messages and how to properly check the receiver's understanding of the message.

Planning the Message

The vast majority of messages you send and receive in the workplace are quite simple and straightforward and need minimal planning, because they are routine. However, sometimes the message you need to transmit is difficult, unusual, or especially important. As noted earlier, for these kinds of messages, the richer the channel, the better. Before sending a message, answer these questions:

LO 13-5

Name the five steps in the process of sending face-to-face messages, and describe paraphrasing and why it is useful.

- **What?** What is the goal of the message? What specific action do you want to achieve?[116]
- **Who?** Determine who should receive the message.
- **How?** Plan how you will encode the message so that it will be understood. Select the appropriate words and channel(s) for the audience and situation. *Words*—Have you ever heard "Sticks and stones will break my bones, but words will never hurt me"? Well, it's not true—derogatory words do hurt. This statement is used as a defensive response to hide the hurt caused by the words. So even if you believe society has gone overboard with political correctness, select your words carefully so you don't offend people and hurt relationships. Note that people have been forced to quit or retire for making derogatory comments, and business has been lost.
- **When?** When will the message be transmitted? Timing is important.
- **Where?** Decide where the message will be transmitted (setting).

The Message-Sending Process

As noted earlier, oral channels are richer than other channels, and face-to-face, oral communication is best when the message you must transmit is a difficult or complex one. When sending a face-to-face message, follow these steps in the **message-sending process** listed in Model 13-1. For step 1, start with small talk, then state your objective, transmit the details, be sure to check understanding, and, last, get a commitment to make sure the objective will be met and follow up to make sure it is.

Model 13-1 lists the five steps in the message-sending process.

Checking Understanding: Feedback

Feedback *is information that verifies a message.* The best way to get feedback is to ask for it.[117] Questioning, paraphrasing, and inviting comments and suggestions are all means of obtaining feedback that check understanding. **Paraphrasing** *is the process of restating a message in one's own words.* If the receiver of the message can answer the question or paraphrase the message, communication has taken place.

The Common Approach to Getting Feedback on Messages and Why It Doesn't Work. The most common approach to getting feedback is to send the entire message and then ask, "Do you have any questions?" Feedback usually does not follow because people tend not to ask questions.

After we send a message and ask if there are questions, we often make another common error. We assume we are good communicators and that if no one asks a question, the communication is complete.[118] In reality, recipients may have misunderstood the message. When this occurs, the result is often wasted time, materials, and effort.

How to Get Feedback on Messages. Use the following four guidelines when seeking feedback on messages.

WORK APPLICATION 13-5

Recall a specific task that a boss assigned to you. Identify which steps in the face-to-face message-sending process he or she did and did not use.

WORK APPLICATION 13-6

Recall a past or present boss. How effective was this person at getting feedback? Was the boss open to feedback and aware of nonverbal communication? Did the boss ask questions and ask you to paraphrase?

message-sending process A process that includes (1) developing rapport, (2) stating your communication objective, (3) transmitting your message, (4) checking the receiver's understanding, and (5) getting a commitment and following up.

feedback Information that verifies a message.

paraphrasing The process of restating a message in one's own words.

MODEL 13-1   THE MESSAGE-SENDING PROCESS

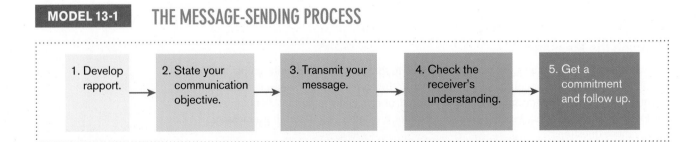

| 1. Develop rapport. | 2. State your communication objective. | 3. Transmit your message. | 4. Check the receiver's understanding. | 5. Get a commitment and follow up. |

- **Be open to feedback.** Effective feedback providers are open to listening to others and to changes.[119] There are no dumb questions, so invite questions. When someone asks a question, be responsive and patiently answer and explain things clearly. If people sense that you get upset if they ask questions, they will not ask.

- **Be aware of nonverbal communication.** Make sure that your nonverbal communication encourages feedback. For example, if you say, "I encourage questions" but you look at people as though they are stupid or you act impatient when they do ask, people will learn not to ask questions. You must also read nonverbal communication accurately. For example, if you are explaining a task to an employee and he or she has a puzzled expression, the employee is probably confused but may not be willing to say so. In such a case, you should stop and clarify things before going on.

- **Ask questions.** You have to ask good questions to get good answers.[120] When you send messages, you should know whether recipients understand the messages before taking action. Direct questions about the specific information you have given will indicate if the receiver has been listening and whether he or she understands enough to give an appropriate reply. If the response is not accurate, you need to repeat the message, giving more examples or elaborating further.

- **Paraphrase.** The most accurate indicator of understanding is paraphrasing. How you ask the receiver to paraphrase will affect his or her attitude. For example, saying, "Tell me what I just said so that I can be sure you will not make a mistake as usual" would probably result in defensive behavior or an error by the employee. Consider these examples of proper requests for paraphrasing:

"Now tell me what you are going to do so that we will be sure we are in agreement."

"Would you tell me what you are going to do so that I can be sure that I explained myself clearly?"

Notice that the second statement takes the pressure off the employee. The sender is asking for a check on his or her own ability, not that of the employee. These types of requests for paraphrasing should result in a positive attitude toward the message and the sender. They show concern for the employee and for communicating effectively.

The most difficult part of the message-sending process to accomplish when using **Facebook (IOM 5)** is checking the receiver's understanding. This is difficult with posted messages because you do not know if the receiver has even read a message if he or she doesn't respond. Thus, it is impossible to give feedback if you do not know if all the receivers have read the message or not.

Welcoming questions and asking questions will allow you to receive constructive feedback on messages you send.

Receiving Messages

The third step in the communication process requires the receiver to decode the message and decide if feedback is needed. This section discusses the process of receiving messages.

LO 13-6

Identify and explain the three parts of the process of receiving messages and active listening.

The Message-Receiving Process

The **message-receiving process** *includes listening, analyzing, and checking understanding.* The parts of the message-receiving process are illustrated in Model 13-2.

Listening. *First you have to listen,*[121] as it is an important part of communications.[122] **Estée Lauder president Jane Lauder** says that leadership is about listening.[123] If we are asked, "Are you a good listener?" most of us would say yes. However, we are naturally poor listeners,[124] because we don't remember what was said.[125] To find out how good you are, complete Self-Assessment 13-1 to determine the level and the quality of your listening skills.

message-receiving process A process that includes listening, analyzing, and checking understanding.

MODEL 13-2   THE MESSAGE-RECEIVING PROCESS

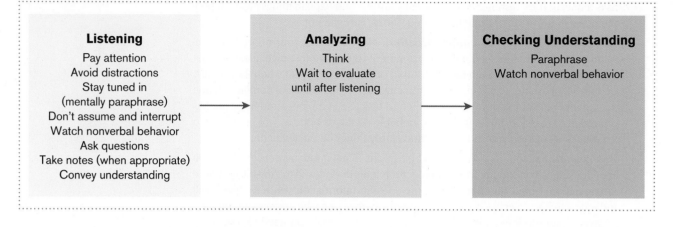

Note that in Model 13-2 under "Listening," there are eight tips to better listening. To implement the first three, shut off your phone and other distractions; concentration is key.[126] Ever hear the advice that we should "listen more and talk less"?[127] Former **Assurant CEO Robert Pollock** says that you learn more when your mouth is closed and your ears are open,[128] and **Western Union CEO Hikmet Ersek** says that if you listen to people, they make you grow.[129] Serial entrepreneur **Norm Brodsky** put it bluntly: "Shut up and listen."[130] We'll discuss active listening shortly.

Analyzing. *Analyzing* is the process of thinking about, decoding, and evaluating the message. As the speaker sends the message, you should be doing two things:

- *Thinking.* Use the speed of your brain positively by mentally repeating or paraphrasing, organizing, summarizing, reviewing, and interpreting what is being said often.

- *Waiting to evaluate until after listening.* You should first listen to the entire message without perception bias (Chapter 10), and then come to your conclusions.[131]

When analyzing information on **Facebook (IOM 6)**, you have to read the message carefully; think about the message, whether it is a written message, a video, or a nonverbal message such as a picture; evaluate the message; shape an opinion; and then formulate questions if you have any in order to get a better understanding.

Checking Understanding. *Checking understanding* is the process of giving feedback. After you have listened to the message (or while listening if it's a long message), check your understanding of the message by doing two things:

- *Paraphrasing/questioning.* Give feedback by paraphrasing the message back to the sender, and ask questions if you don't understand something.

- *Watching nonverbal behavior.* As you speak, watch the other person's nonverbal communication. If the person does not seem to understand what you are talking about, clarify the message before finishing the conversation.

Do you talk more than you listen? Ask your boss, coworkers, or friends, who will give you an honest answer. Regardless of how much you listen, if you follow the guidelines discussed in this section, you will become a better listener. Review items 1, 4, 5, 6, 9, 12, 13, 14, and 15 in Self-Assessment 13-1, which are the statements that describe good listening skills. Effective listening requires responding to the message to ensure mutual understanding.

13-1 SELF-ASSESSMENT

Listening Skills

For each statement, select the response that best describes how often you actually behave in the way described. Place the letter *A, U, F, O,* or *S* on the line before each statement.

A = almost always	U = usually	F = frequently	O = occasionally	S = seldom

_____ 1. I like to listen to people talk. I encourage others to talk by showing interest, smiling, nodding, and so forth.

_____ 2. I pay closer attention to people who are more similar to me than to people who are different from me.

_____ 3. I evaluate people's words and nonverbal communication ability as they talk.

_____ 4. I avoid distractions; if it's noisy, I suggest moving to a quiet spot.

_____ 5. When people interrupt me when I'm doing something, I put what I was doing out of my mind and give them my complete attention.

_____ 6. When people are talking, I allow them time to finish. I do not interrupt, anticipate what they are going to say, or jump to conclusions.

_____ 7. I tune people out who do not agree with my views.

_____ 8. While another person is talking or a professor is lecturing, my mind wanders to personal topics.

_____ 9. While another person is talking, I pay close attention to the nonverbal communication so I can fully understand what he or she is trying to communicate.

_____ 10. I tune out and pretend I understand when the topic is difficult for me to understand.

_____ 11. When another person is talking, I think about and prepare what I am going to say in reply.

_____ 12. When I think there is something missing from or contradictory in what someone says, I ask direct questions to get the person to explain the idea more fully.

_____ 13. When I don't understand something, I let the other person know I don't understand.

_____ 14. When listening to other people, I try to put myself in their position and see things from their perspective.

_____ 15. During conversations, I repeat back to the other person what has been said in my own words to be sure I understand what has been said.

If people you talk to regularly answered these questions about you, would they have the same responses that you selected? To find out, have friends fill out the questions using *you* (or your name) rather than *I*. Then compare answers.

To determine your score, give yourself 5 points for each *A*, 4 for each *U*, 3 for each *F*, 2 for each *O*, and 1 for each *S* for statements 1, 4, 5, 6, 9, 12, 13, 14, and 15. For items 2, 3, 7, 8, 10, and 11, the scores reverse: 5 points for each *S*, 4 for each *O*, 3 for each *F*, 2 for each *U*, and 1 for each *A*. Write the number of points on the lines next to the response letters. Now add your total number of points. Your score should be between 15 and 75. Note where your score falls on the continuum below. Generally, the higher your score, the better your listening skills.

15	20	25	30	35	40	45	50	55	60	65	70	75

Poor listener   Good listener

Retentive Listening

Hearing what people are saying is nice, but it's not enough. *Retentive listening* is not just about hearing what is said, which most of us can do; it's really about remembering the message, which takes concentration. How's your memory?[132] Business communications usually requires taking appropriate action based on the message. How can we take action if we don't understand or remember the message?

Frank Felberbaum, president of **Memory Training Systems,** says that to understand and remember the message, we have to concentrate. We remember what we see better than what we hear. The primary reason we get distracted and lose our ability to pay attention and remember things is the separation of the use of our eyes and mind. When they are not working together as a team, we cannot concentrate at all.[133] Think about this. If you are listening to someone talking as you check your phone (or look somewhere else), what happens? Loss of concentration. Can you see how multitasking kills concentration and memory?

So to maximize listening, you need to look the person in the eye and concentrate with your mind on what they say. If your eyes are looking but your mind is wandering, bring it back. Try repeating what the person is saying word for word as they speak. Active listening can help you concentrate and remember messages.

WORK
APPLICATION 13-7

Refer to Self-Assessment 13-1. What is your weakest listening skill? Give an example of how your listening skills have had an impact on you at work.

Active Listening

As you know, the message-receiving process is not a simple linear process. We listen, analyze, and check understanding constantly as we have a conversation, as well as change from receiver to sender of messages. So the best way to receive messages is to be an active listener.[134] *Active listening* puts the three parts of the message-receiving process together by using verbal and nonverbal communications to show the sender that the receiver is fully engaged and cares about the sender as a person. Thus, it fosters good human relationships.

Active listeners follow the eight guidelines of listening listed in Model 13-2. Here is a little more detail. Active listeners look for signs that the other person wants to talk; they ask open-ended questions like "How is it going?" and encourage the person to elaborate. They lean forward and nod their head, look at the person and make eye contact, and ask questions and paraphrase to ensure they understand what the person is saying and means.[135] Active listeners use reflective responses, which are discussed in the next section.

LO 13-7

Define five response styles, describe how to deal with emotional people, and discuss guides to giving and receiving criticism.

Responding to Messages

The fourth and last step in the communication process is responding to the message. However, not all messages require a response, but with oral communication, the sender often expects a response. In this section, we discuss five response styles, how to deal with emotions, and how to give and receive criticism.

Response Styles

As a sender transmits a message, how we respond directly affects the communication progression.[136] Our comments can encourage or cut off the conversation, and they can help the sender keep calm or get emotional.[137] Five typical response styles are shown in Exhibit 13-7 along with stating when they are appropriate for the situation. But before you can respond appropriately, you need to understand what the person needs from you.[138] Suppose an employee voices the following complaint to her supervisor:

"You supervise me so closely that you disrupt my ability to do my job."

We will consider how a manager might respond to this complaint using each response style.

Advising. *Advising responses* provide evaluation, personal opinion, direction, or instructions. Advising tends to close or limit discussion or direct the flow of communication away from the sender to the receiver. Being quick to give advice may stop people from discussing what is really on their mind, and they may not even need or want your advice. So it is best to only give advice when asked for it. But rather than simply telling people what to do, help them figure out their own solution to problems. Say something like, what do you think is a good solution, or what action are you thinking about taking?[139]

| **EXHIBIT 13-7** | FIVE TYPICAL RESPONSE STYLES |

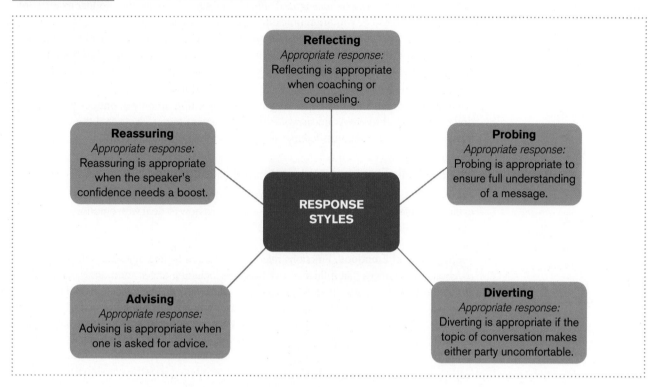

A manager's advising response to the employee's complaint might be "You need my directions to do a good job, since you lack experience" or "I disagree. You need my instructions, and I need to check your work." Note that in this situation, the employee did not ask for advice, but it was given anyway.

Diverting. *Diverting responses* switch the focus of the communication to a new message—in other words, they change the subject. Like advising, diverting tends to redirect, close, or limit the flow of communication. Diverting responses used during the early stages of receiving the message may cause the sender to feel that the message is not worth discussing or that the other party's message is more important, but there are times when it is best to change the subject to avoid conflict.

A manager's diverting response might be "You've reminded me of a manager I once had who. . . ."

Probing. Probing responses ask the speaker to give more information about some aspect of the message. Probing can be useful when you need to get a better understanding of the situation. Effective managers ask good questions for clarity to ensure they understand the message.[140] When probing, "What?" questions are preferable to "Why?" questions. After probing, responses in other styles are often needed.

A manager's probing response might be "What do I do to cause you to say this?" Note that "Why do you feel this way?" is *not* an appropriate probing response.

Reassuring. Reassuring responses are given to reduce the intensity of the emotions and give confidence associated with the message.[141] Essentially you're saying, "Don't worry, everything will be OK" or "You can do it."

A manager's reassuring response might be "Don't worry, I will not be supervising you so closely for much longer" or "Your work is improving, so I may be able to provide less direction soon."

WORK
APPLICATION 13-8

Recall two oral messages you received and your responses to them. Identify your response style, and give examples of responses you might have given using two other response styles.

Reflecting. Reflecting responses *paraphrase the message and communicate understanding and acceptance to the sender.* When reflecting, be sure *not* to use the sender's exact words, or the person may feel you are mimicking. Reflecting in your own words leads to the most effective communication and the best human relations.[142] As the communication progresses, it may be appropriate to change to other response styles. However, sometimes people just want someone to listen to what is going on with them—not give them advice, solve their problem, or talk about the other person.[143]

A manager's reflecting response might be "My checking up on you annoys you?" or "You don't think I need to check up on you—is this what you mean?" Note that these responses allow the employee to express feelings and to direct the communication.

Dealing With Emotions and Emotional Intelligence

Our emotions affect our attitudes, behavior, relationships, and performance. So we should explore emotions[144]—our own and others'—and learn how to deal with emotions using emotional intelligence. Let's do so here.

Today's View of Emotions. Emotions refer to our state of feeling that results in physical and psychological changes that influence our behavior, including anger, annoyance, boredom, disappointment, distrust, fear, happiness, and sadness. Our brain can't be logical/rational and highly emotional at the same time, and bad decisions are common when emotions run high.[145] But the old attitude of leaving your emotions at the door when you come to work has changed, because we can't turn off our emotions. Today, rationality isn't about getting rid of emotions; it's about analyzing them and taking them into consideration when making calm decisions.[146] Today's effective leaders are empathic.[147] Recall that businesses want passionate (positive emotional) employees.

Using Emotional Intelligence (EQ). Understanding and dealing with emotions (yours and those of others) depends on one's level of emotional intelligence. *Emotional intelligence* has five dimensions:[148] (1) self-awareness, or understanding your own emotions; (2) self-management, the ability to manage your own emotions; (3) self-motivation, the ability to persist through failure and setbacks; (4) empathy, the ability to understand others' emotions and to see things from their perspective; and (5) social skills that allow one to handle others' emotions.

One's level of emotional intelligence is also called one's *emotional quotient*, or EQ (to parallel the notion of intelligence quotient, or IQ). Some companies give EQ tests, and they can

reflecting responses Responses that paraphrase a message and communicate understanding and acceptance to the sender.

13-4 APPLYING THE CONCEPT

Response Styles

Identify the response style exemplified in each statement.

A. advising

B. diverting

C. probing

D. reassuring

E. reflecting

Administrative Assistant:	Carl, do you have a minute to talk?
Boss:	Sure, what's up, Mary?
AA:	Are you aware of all the swearing people do in the operations department? It carries through these thin walls into my work area. It's disgusting.

Boss:

____ 24. "Why don't you talk to them about it?"

____ 25. "It seems like you find swearing offensive."

____ 26. "What specific swears are they saying?"

____ 27. "No. I didn't know. But I'll look into it for you."

____ 28. "Just ignore the swearing. Don't let it bother you."

____ 29. "Did you see the new training video yet?"

____ 30. "So, Mary, you don't like swearing—is that it?"

be part of personality tests. It has been said that you need an IQ, EQ, and "I got a clue" to succeed. We want to deal with our emotions and help others deal with their emotions using our EQ,[149] which we will discuss, but we need to understand feelings first.

Acknowledge Feelings: Control Behavior. Feelings refer to the conscious subjective experience of our emotions. It doesn't really matter what people know or don't know; what counts is what they feel.[150] When dealing with your emotions and other people's, keep the following in mind:

MANAGEMENT IN ACTION
Emotional Intelligence

- Feelings are subjective; they tell us people's attitudes and needs.
- Feelings are usually disguised as factual statements. For example, when people are hot, they tend to say "It's hot in here" rather than "I feel hot." When they are bored, they tend to say "This topic is boring" rather than "I'm feeling bored by this topic."
- Most important: Feelings are neither right nor wrong.

Although we've recommended controlling our thoughts to be positive,[151] you cannot choose your feelings or really control them. However, we can control how we express feelings through controlling our behavior, which is commonly called controlling our emotions.[152] For example, if Rachel, an employee, says "You *!!" (pick a word that would make you angry) to Latoya, her manager, Latoya will feel its impact. However, Latoya has a choice about how she responds. She can express her feelings in a calm manner, or she can yell back, give Rachel a dirty look, write up a formal reprimand for Rachel's personnel file, and so on.

Managers should encourage people to express their feelings in a positive way, but they can't allow employees to go around yelling at, swearing at, or intimidating others. Avoid getting caught up in others' emotions. Staying calm when dealing with an emotional person works much better than getting emotional, too, as we discuss next.

Your Emotions and Behavior. We should use our EQ and be aware of our feelings but stay in control of our behavior so it doesn't hurt relationships. It only takes seconds to say something that hurts others, but it can take years to heal the wounds. Sometimes no response is the best response, or a postponed response after you calm down.[153] If you get a message that upsets you, don't reply in anger, because you may have misunderstood it; or the other person may not have meant it the way it sounds to you—*perception incongruence* and *attribution* (Chapter 10).

Some people don't intend to be hurtful; their behavior just comes across that way out of their ignorance of good human relations skills. Others may not even realize their behavior upsets you.[154] Have you ever been passive-aggressive,[155] gotten angry at someone and yelled about his or her behavior and the person didn't have a clue as to why you were upset? Does getting upset and yelling help the relationship or fix the problem? Angry outbursts hurt your health,[156] and you may regret responding in anger, and your revenge will likely hurt your relationship.[157] If you can control your negative emotional responses, you will have better relationships and be a more effective leader.[158]

Yes. Do confront people about their behavior that upsets you, but wait until you are calm to respond,[159] and follow the steps in resolving conflicts in Chapter 10. Recall that a sincere apology helps rekindle relationships.[160] Even if you believe you did nothing wrong or you were right, you can just say, "Sorry I yelled at [upset] you!" But don't follow up with a "But you ..." and justify your behavior because it really takes away the apology, and it can lead to an argument focused on placing blame rather than fixing your relationship. Again, focus on the conflict BCF (the behavior that upset you, its consequences to you and your relationship, and your feelings about it).

Calming the Emotional Person. We have to realize that we can't order people to change emotions, because it is physiologically impossible when overstressed or angry. Thus, telling a person to calm down or relax doesn't work; it often has the opposite effect by increasing the feelings.[161] So *never* make condescending statements such as "It's no big deal," "You shouldn't be angry," "Don't be upset." Telling someone to "Just sit down and be quiet" may get them to shut up and show them who is boss, but effective communication will not take place. The problem will still exist, and your relations with the employee will suffer because of it, as will your relations with others who see or hear about what you said and did.

We can't be both highly emotional and highly rational—feelings win. So the best way to calm someone is to be an empathic listener.[162] Show empathy and acknowledge the emotional feeling with open-ended reflective comments, like "You're upset because you didn't get the assignment, it that it?"[163] Let them get it out—express the feeling. After emotions are calm, you can rationally discuss the issue. However, don't encourage people to vent because research supports that venting actually makes us angrier and its unhealthy.[164] Focus on solving problems, not complaining about them. And as discussed, be optimistic, focus on the positive and be happier.

Empathic listening is one aspect of emotional intelligence. If you really want to understand where the other person is coming from, you need to see things from his or her perspective.

Compassion and Reflective Empathic Responding. We want people to care about us and help us in our time of need. To be a friend in a time of need, talk less and listen more.[165] *Compassion* is about helping others deal with their emotional situations, especially their hurts or pains. A **Kronos** survey found that 40% of respondents listed compassion as one of the most important attributes of a good manager,[166] and companies seek this trait in new hires.[167]

To help with compassion, we need empathy[168]—the ability to understand or feel what another person is experiencing emotionally from his or her *frame of reference* (Chapter 10). Exceptional leaders are empathetic—they hear and understand where their employees are coming from.[169] When we communicate bad news, we should be compassionate and show empathy.[170] **Western Union CEO Hikmet Ersek** says to put yourself in the other person's shoes and listen;[171] active listening helps.[172] **Empathic listening** *is understanding and relating to another's feelings*. The empathic responder deals with feelings, content, and the underlying meaning being expressed in the message.

Don't argue with emotional people or try to talk them out of their feelings—feelings are not right or wrong. Instead, encourage them to express their feelings in a positive way. Empathically let them know that you understand how they feel. Do not agree or disagree with the feelings; simply identify them verbally. Paraphrase the feeling to the person. Use statements such as these: "You were *hurt* when you didn't get the assignment." "You *resent* Chani for not doing her share of the work; is that what you mean?" "You are *doubtful* that the job will be done on time; is that what you're saying?" After you make an empathic response, most employees will feel free to open up and tell you what's going on.

After you deal with emotions, you can proceed to work on content (solving problems). It may be wise to wait until a later time if emotions are very strong. Sometimes people simply need to vent their emotions, so just listening actively to others' feelings is often the solution.

Criticism

While it's not something we look forward to, giving and getting criticism is necessary if we want to see continuous improvement.[173] Regardless of the role you are in, there are ways to give and receive criticism effectively.

Giving Criticism. An important part of leadership is to provide constructive criticism by giving feedback on things that can be improved and issues that can be avoided. Firms, including hedge fund **Bridgewater**, developed a "culture of candor" that encourages criticism to improve everyone's performance.[174] Feedback is best received when given with empathy in the spirit of helping others[175] and coming from a person who is trusted and respected.[176]

WORK
APPLICATION 13-9

Recall a situation in which a manager had to handle an emotional employee. Did the manager follow the guidelines for calming an emotional person? Did the manager use reflective, empathic responses?

empathic listening Understanding and relating to another's feelings.

So never put the person down using words like *never* and *always* and saying "You're doing it wrong" ("You're wrong") or "You don't know what you're doing/talking about." Criticism should not be about the person, and it must be something the person can actually change. It should have two parts.

1. Criticism should state the *specific* behavior that can be improved.
2. It should *specify* the improved behavior (which may need to be taught).

Chapter 14's section on coaching will provide more details on how to accomplish this task.

Getting the Person to Ask for Criticism. By far the best way to give criticism is to get the other person to ask for it without putting him or her down. Show genuine concern for them.[177] Here's how. Don't say, "You're doing that wrong. Let me show you how to...." Do say, "Would you like me to show you a way to do that task faster and easier?" How would you respond to each of these statements?

Criticizing the Boss. Criticism that moves upward is a different matter. Even when bosses ask, they usually don't want to hear personal criticism. If your boss asks you in a meeting for feedback on how good a manager he or she is or how he or she can improve, it may sound like the ideal opportunity to unload your complaints—but in such a situation, the first rule of thumb is to never publicly criticize anyone, especially your boss, even if specifically asked to do so. You are better off airing criticism to your boss in private and only if you know he or she really wants to hear it, will accept it, and will actually change behaviors. Don't criticize your boss behind his or her back, either; bosses often find out about it. Again, venting isn't good for us.[178]

Getting Criticism. Criticism from your boss, peers, or employees is painful—the truth can hurt.[179] People do not really enjoy being criticized, even when it is constructive, and many people handle it poorly—how good are you at accepting criticism and changing to improve? However, it is important to keep three things in mind:

*   more often than not, your boss and others want to help you succeed—they are helping you improve.
*   don't take it personally. It's not really about you as a person, it's about a specific behavior you can change to improve. Let's admit it—we can all improve—through criticism. Even if you disagree, there is usually some truth about your performance that you can improve. Psychologist **Michael Woodward** says, "Look for the nugget of value."[180]
*   keep the phrase "no pain, no gain" in mind when it comes to criticism. If you want to improve your chances of having a successful career, seek honest feedback and use it to improve your performance.[181]

Performance appraisals are a formal system of giving criticism; refer to Chapter 9 for tips on accepting criticism under the heading "Being Evaluated" (page 294). Finding out what your boss really thinks about your performance can be scary, but it is the best way to find out how to improve your performance that will lead to the highest performance reviews, raises, and promotions.[182] Let go of ego-defensive behavior.[183] When you get criticism from anyone whether you ask for it or not, view it as an opportunity to improve, stay calm (even when the other person is emotional), and don't get defensive, deny something you did, or blame others.[184] If you do (and it is hard not to when you feel attacked), the person will stop giving feedback, and you will not improve your performance. Apologies help, but you need to change to improve.[185]

Recall from Chapter 10 that **Apple**'s **Steve Jobs** could get very emotional and yell negative personal criticisms when he wasn't getting his way but that **Microsoft**'s **Bill Gates** was very successful in negotiating with Jobs because he didn't yell insults back. Gates stayed calm, spoke softly, and calmed Jobs down and then continued focusing on conducting business; this is how he closed multiple beneficial company deals between the two *frenemies*.

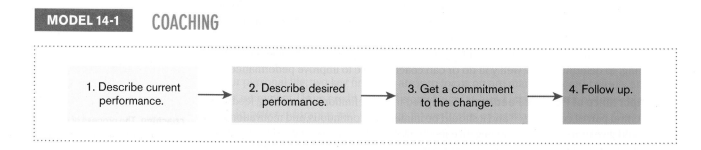

Coaching includes making sure employees are trained to the best of their ability, motivated to perform well, and have the resources they need to succeed.

Determining Corrective Coaching Action. When an employee is not performing up to potential, even when acceptable standards are being met, the first step is to determine why, using the performance formula: performance = ability × motivation × resources (Chapter 11).

When ability is holding back performance, training is needed. When motivation is lacking, motivational techniques, such as giving praise, may help. Talk to the employee to try to determine why motivation is lacking, and develop a plan together. If motivation does not work, you may have to use counseling or discipline, which will be discussed later. When resources are lacking, work to obtain them.

Pete Clark is unique, as he spent several years managing his own **Jiffy Lube** franchises and coaching high school baseball and football and college football teams before managing **The Ranch** (**IOM 6**). Pete says there are more similarities than differences among running a Jiffy Lube business, directing The Ranch Golf Club, and coaching sports. The focus is the same: high-quality service. You have to treat the customer or player right. Pete uses the same "3 *Is*" coaching philosophy at all three: You need *intensity* to be prepared to do the job right, *integrity* to do the right thing when no one is watching, and *intimacy* to be a team player. If one person does not do the job right, everyone is negatively affected. In business and sports, you need to strive to be the best. You need to set and meet challenging goals. Pete strongly believes in being positive and developing a supportive working relationship, which includes sitting down to talk and really listening to the other person.

The Coaching Model. Coaching should be viewed as a way to provide ongoing feedback to employees about their job performance. However, ask managers what they tend to put off doing, and they'll likely say advising weak employees that they must improve their performance. Many managers are hesitant to confront employees, even to the point of jarred nerves and sleepless nights. Procrastinators hope that the employees will turn around on their own, only to find—often too late—that the situation gets worse. Part of the problem is that managers don't know how to coach or are not good at coaching. Thus, Model 14-1 presents a four-step coaching model, and the steps are described after.

Step 1. Describe current performance. Using specific examples, describe the current behavior that needs to be changed, focusing on improving, not on wrong behavior.

For example, don't say, "You are picking up the box wrong." Say, "Billie, there is a more effective way of picking the box up off the floor than bending at the waist."

Step 2. Describe desired performance. Tell the employees exactly what the desired performance is in detail. Show how they will benefit from following your advice.

For example: *Ability*—"If you squat down and pick up the box using your legs instead of your back, it is easier, and there is less chance of injuring yourself. Let me demonstrate for you." *Motivation*—"Why should you squat and use your legs rather than your back to pick up boxes?"

MODEL 14-1   COACHING

| 1. Describe current performance. | → | 2. Describe desired performance. | → | 3. Get a commitment to the change. | → | 4. Follow up. |

14-1 SELF-ASSESSMENT

Coaching

For each of the following 15 statements, select the response that best describes your actual behavior or what you would do when coaching others to improve performance. Place the number 5 (*describes my behavior*), 4, 3, 2, or 1 (*does not describe my behavior*) on the line before each statement.

(More Autocratic)   **(More Participative)**

5	4	3	2	1

Describes my behavior   Does *not* describe my behavior

_____ 1. I know when to coach, counsel, and discipline people.

_____ 2. I don't try to be a psychological counselor or offer advice to solve personal problems, but I do refer people who need help to professionals.

_____ 3. I deal with mistakes as a learning opportunity rather than a reason to place blame and punish.

_____ 4. I make sure people are clear about my expectations rather than let them guess.

_____ 5. I take action to make sure people do at least the minimum rather than let them perform below standard.

_____ 6. I maintain a relationship with people when I coach them rather than let coaching hurt our relationship.

_____ 7. I coach soon after the incident rather than wait for a later time to talk about it.

_____ 8. I focus on showing concern for people and helping them improve performance for their own benefit rather than to get what I want done.

_____ 9. I show people how they can benefit by taking the action I suggest rather than just tell them what to do.

_____ 10. I offer very specific suggestions for improving rather than say general things like "You're not doing a good job" or "You need to do better."

_____ 11. I don't use words like *always* and *never* when talking about what the person does that needs to be improved. For example, I would say, "You were late twice this week," not "You're always late" or "You're never on time."

_____ 12. I focus on the behavior that needs to be improved rather than on the person. For example, I would say, "Why not set an earlier time to get to work—say, 7:45 instead of 8:00?" not "Why can't you be on time?"

_____ 13. I walk around and talk to people to help them improve rather than wait for them to come to me.

_____ 14. I feel comfortable giving people feedback rather than feeling uncomfortable or awkward.

_____ 15. I coach differently depending on the problem rather than always the same way.

_____ Total score

To determine your coaching score, add up the numbers for your 15 answers (between 15 and 75) and place the score on the total score line and on the following continuum.

75	70	60	50	40	30	20	15

Effective   Not effective
coaching   coaching

WORK
APPLICATION 14-12

How would you rate your present or past boss's coaching ability? Explain your answer using critical incidents.

Step 3. Get a commitment to the change. When dealing with an *ability* issue, it is not necessary to get employees to verbally commit to the change if they seem willing to make it. However, if employees defend their way and you're sure it's not as effective, explain why your proposed way is better. If you cannot get the employees to understand and agree, get a verbal commitment.[107] This step is also important for *motivation* issues, because if people are not willing to commit to the change, they will most likely not make the change.[108] Simply telling employees what to do doesn't always work, but asking questions to get the employee to say "yes, I will do it" improves their commitment to the desired behavior.[109]

For example: *Ability* lacking—the employee will most likely be willing to pick up boxes correctly, so skip this step. *Motivation* lacking—"Will you squat rather than use your back from now on?"

Step 4. Follow up. Remember that some employees do what managers *inspect* (imposed control), not what they *expect*. You should follow up to ensure that employees are behaving as desired.

When dealing with an *ability* issue, if the person was receptive and you skipped step 3, say nothing. However, watch to be sure that the activity is done correctly in the future. Coach again, if necessary. For a *motivation* problem, make a statement that you will follow up and that there are possible consequences for repeat performance.

For example: *Ability*—say nothing, but observe. *Motivation*—"Billie, picking up boxes with your back is dangerous; if I catch you doing it again, I will take disciplinary action."

Management by Walking Around

As a leader, you help people, and MBWA is one way to do so. Physically walking around actually helps in the development of creative ideas.[110] We also remember what we see better than what we hear.[111] **Management by walking around (MBWA)** *has three major activities: listening, teaching, and facilitating.* By *listening*, you find out what's getting in the way or slowing employees down; by *teaching*, you coach to improve; and by *facilitating*, you remove the stumbling blocks preventing employees from improving performance.

Sam Walton, deceased founder and CEO of **Walmart**, was a great believer in MBWA. Walton would visit every one of his stores every year. He would unexpectedly go into a store and walk up to customers and employees and talk to them about improving Walmart, writing notes on a little pad he carried around with him. Today, Walmart has too many stores for the CEO to visit every store annually. But, true to the philosophy, top executives are required to visit stores every year.[112] When **Angela Ahrendts** took the senior vice president of retail and online stores job at **Apple**, rather than send an email to introduce herself, she personally visited more than 100 stores to talk to employees and customers personally.[113]

Feedback is critical to success at **The Ranch** (**IOM 7**), as it tells the Clarks whether the players and diners are getting quality service and how to improve. The Clarks and employees are accepting of criticism because they realize that the only way to improve is to listen and make changes. In fact, **Pete and Korby Clark** spend much of their time at The Ranch managing by walking around, as they listen to employees, teach them how to improve through coaching, and help them satisfy golfers' requests. They also ask people about their experience, listening for suggestions for improvements and facilitating good ideas. The Clarks set clear objectives and have regular meetings with employees to get and give feedback on how The Ranch is progressing toward meeting its objectives.

Counseling

When coaching, you are fine-tuning performance; with counseling and disciplining, you are dealing with a problem employee who is not performing to standards or is violating standing plans. Problem employees have a negative effect on performance. Good human resource management (Chapter 9) skills can help you avoid hiring problem employees, but you will most likely have to confront problem employees as a manager.

management by walking around (MBWA) A type of supervision in which the three major activities are listening, teaching, and facilitating.

Problem Employees. Recall from Chapter 13 that how people feel determines how they behave,[114] so emotions often lead to performance-related problems from counterproductive work behavior.[115] Problem employees do poor-quality work, they don't get along with coworkers, they display negative attitudes, and they frequently don't show up for work, or they come late. There are four types of problem employees: Some employees do not have the *ability* to meet the job performance standards and should be transferred or terminated. There are employees who do not have the *motivation* to meet job performance standards or intentionally *violate standing plans* and often need discipline. There are also employees who have performed well in the past but have a job-related or personal *problem* negatively affecting their performance who may need counseling. It is not always easy to distinguish between the types of problem employees. Therefore, it is often advisable to start with coaching, move to counseling, and change to discipline if the problem persists.

Managers can direct employees who have personal problems to see help through the company's employee assistance program (EAP) to resolve issues that are affecting performance.

Management Counseling. When most people hear the term *counseling*, they think of psychological counseling or psychotherapy. That type of sophisticated help should not be attempted by a noncounseling professional such as a manager.[116] Instead, **management counseling** *is the process of giving employees feedback so they realize that a problem is affecting their job performance and referring employees with problems to the employee assistance program.*

Most managers do not like to hear the details of personal problems. Doing so is not a requirement. Instead, your role as a manager is to help employees realize that they have problems and that those problems affect their work. Your job is getting the employee back on track. You should not give advice on how to solve personal problems, such as a relationship difficulty. When professional help is needed, you should refer the employee to the human resources department for professional help through the employee assistance program.

EAP. The **employee assistance program (EAP)** *has a staff of people who help employees get professional assistance in solving their problems.* Most large businesses have an EAP to help solve employees' personal problems. EAPs are valuable employee interventions that have savings of about $4 for every $1 spent of these programs,[117] so they are more of an investment than an expense.

To make the referral, you could say something like "Are you aware of our employee assistance program? Would you like me to set up an appointment with Jean in the HR department to help you get professional assistance?" However, if job performance does not return to standard, discipline is appropriate, because it often makes the employee realize the seriousness of his or her problem and the importance of maintaining job performance. Some time off from work, with or without pay, depending on the situation, often helps the employee deal with the problem.

The Importance of Confronting Problem Employees. A manager's first obligation is to the organization's performance rather than to individual employees. Therefore, it is your job to confront problem employees. Not taking action with problem employees because you feel uncomfortable confronting them, because you feel sorry for them, or because you like them does not help you or the employee. Not only do problem employees negatively affect their own productivity, but they also cause more work for you and other employees.[118] Problem employees lower employee morale, as others resent them for not pulling their own weight. Team members may use clan control to pressure problem employees to perform to norms and standards. Thus, it is critical to take quick action with problem employees.

WORK
APPLICATION 14-13

Identify a problem employee you observed on the job. Describe how the person affected the department's performance.

management counseling The process of giving employees feedback so they realize that a problem is affecting their job performance and referring employees with problems to the employee assistance program.

employee assistance program (EAP) A benefit program staffed by people who help employees get professional assistance in solving their problems.

Disciplining

Coaching, which includes counseling, should generally be the first step in dealing with a problem employee. However, if an employee is unwilling or unable to change, a rule has been broken,[119] or misconduct behavior is used,[120] discipline is necessary. You don't have to be liked to be an effective manager (or worker); sometimes you have to be the bad guy.[121]

Workplace Deviance and Discipline. Deviance is negative voluntary behavior of problem employees that violates significant organizational norms, threatens the well-being of the organization, and is costly. Deviant behavior includes rudeness, stealing, violence, vandalism, frequently withholding effort, showing up late, leaving early, and absence from work. It's the manager's job to enforce the rules,[122] and you need to enforce them consistently,[123] without favoritism,[124] so you may have to discipline your friends. **Discipline** *is corrective action to get employees to meet standards and standing plans.*

The major objective of discipline is to change behavior. Secondary objectives may be to (1) let employees know that action will be taken when standing plans or performance requirements are not met and (2) maintain authority when challenged using coercive power.[125] Exhibit 14-8 lists eight guidelines for effective discipline. Narcissistic employees often cause problems,[126] and so do narcissistic abusive supervisors.[127] Generally, abusive supervisors have more discipline problems than do nonabusive supervisors.[128]

The human resources department handles many of the disciplinary details and provides written disciplinary procedures. These procedures usually outline grounds for specific sanctions and dismissal, based on the violation.

Progressive Discipline. Punishment usually varies with the severity of the violation.[129] Many organizations have a series of progressively more severe disciplinary actions.[130] The progressive disciplinary steps are (1) oral warning, (2) written warning, (3) suspension, and (4) dismissal. If problem employees don't change behavior, they should be fired to avoid more problems.[131] All four steps are commonly followed for minor violations, such as being late for work or excessive absenteeism.[132] For more important violations, such as stealing, steps may be skipped. Be sure to document each step.[133]

The Discipline Model. The steps in the discipline model should be followed when employees must be disciplined. The five steps are presented here and summarized in Model 14-2.

Step 1. Refer to past feedback. Begin the interview by refreshing the employee's memory. If the employee has been coached/counseled about the behavior or if he or she has clearly broken a known rule, state that.

For example: *Prior coaching*—"Billie, remember my telling you about the proper way to lift boxes with your legs?" *Rule violation*—"Billie, you know the safety rule about lifting boxes with your legs."

discipline Corrective action to get employees to meet standards and standing plans.

EXHIBIT 14-8   GUIDELINES FOR EFFECTIVE DISCIPLINE

A. Clearly communicate the standards and standing plans to all employees.
B. Be sure that the punishment fits the crime.
C. Follow the standing plans yourself.
D. Take consistent, impartial action when the rules are broken.
E. Discipline immediately, but stay calm and get all the necessary facts before you discipline.
F. Discipline in private.
G. Document discipline.
H. When the discipline is over, resume normal relations with the employee.

14-4 APPLYING THE CONCEPT

Guidelines for Effective Discipline

Identify which guideline is being followed—or not being followed—in the following statements. Use the guidelines in Exhibit 14-8 as the answers. Place the letter of the guideline (A–H) on the line before its statement.

_____ 22. "Katrina gave me a written warning for talking back to her again. She even made me sign it before putting it in my permanent record file."

_____ 23. "Sandy, as part of orientation, you need to learn the rules. The computer program will teach them to you and give you a test to make sure you understand them."

_____ 24. "Joel got on my case again, so I'll be getting the silent treatment again."

_____ 25. "Jose, that's not fair; you shouldn't dock my pay for coming in late just once."

_____ 26. "Tony, that's enough. Come into my office so that we can discuss your behavior."

_____ 27. "Did you see that? Chris really lost it and yelled at Erin."

_____ 28. "VP Karl comes back from break late all the time; why can't we?"

_____ 29. "When I come in a couple of minutes late, Edwardo reprimands me. But when attractive Wauneta does it, he never reprimands her."

_____ 30. "You're lucky, Jill. Professor Davidson didn't take attendance today, so you weren't marked absent."

Step 2. Ask why the undesired behavior was used. Giving the employee a chance to explain the behavior is part of getting all the necessary facts before you discipline. If you used prior coaching and the employee committed to changing the behavior, ask why the behavior did not change.

For example: *Prior coaching*—"Two days ago, you told me that you would use your legs rather than your back to lift boxes. Why are you still using your back?" *Rule violation*—"Why are you breaking the safety rule and using your back rather than your legs to lift the box?"

Step 3. Give the discipline. If there is no good reason for the undesirable behavior, give the discipline. The discipline will vary with the stage in the disciplinary progression.

For example: *Prior coaching*—"Because you have not changed your behavior, I'm giving you an oral warning." *Rule violation*—"Because you have violated a safety rule, I'm giving you an oral warning."

Step 4. Get a commitment to change and develop a plan. Try to get a commitment to change. If the employee will not commit, make note of the fact in the critical incidents file or use the procedures for a written warning. If a plan for change has been developed in the past, try to get the employee to commit to it again. Or develop a new plan if necessary.

14-3 JOIN THE DISCUSSION ETHICS & SOCIAL RESPONSIBILITY

Disciplining Ethical Behavior

Unfortunately, some employees are rewarded for being unethical, while others are disciplined for being ethical. For example, some auto repair shops pay a commission for work done, so mechanics are paid more if they get customers to buy parts and services they don't need. Mechanics who have a below-average number of repairs may be considered underachievers and may be pressured, through discipline, to perform unneeded repair work. Similarly, those in the medical field may push unnecessary tests or even treatments.

1. Have you ever been in or known of a situation in which people were rewarded for being unethical and disciplined for being ethical? If so, describe the situation.

2. Is it ethical and socially responsible for firms to establish controls that reward unethical behavior and discipline ethical behavior to make more money?

MODEL 14-2   DISCIPLINING

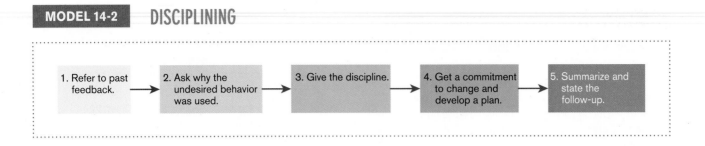

For example: *Prior coaching or rule violation*—"Will you lift with your legs from now on?" "Is there a way to get you to remember to use your legs instead of your back when you lift?"

Step 5. Summarize and state the follow-up. Summarize the discipline and state the follow-up disciplinary action to be taken. Part of follow-up is to document the discipline. At the written warning and suspension stages, get the employee's signature. If necessary, take the next step in the discipline model: dismissal.

For example: *Prior coaching or rule violation*—"So you agree to use your legs instead of your back when you lift. If I catch you again, you will be given a written warning, which is followed by a suspension and dismissal if necessary."

Handling Complaints

You need to understand what the other person needs,[134] but no matter how hard you try to do a good job and to satisfy all employees' and customers' needs, complaints will arise. A *complaint* is an expression of dissatisfaction with a situation, often coupled with a request for change. When you handle a complaint, don't just quickly dismiss it;[135] you need to be responsive[136] as you are using damage control.[137]

However, if you have problem employees with a bad attitude who are never happy and always complaining to everyone, they can drag others down with them,[138] so it is best to discipline and fire them to avoid ongoing problems.[139] There are also some customers who cause more problems than the value of the business they provide, so let them do business elsewhere.

Handling Employee Complaints. Not handling employee complaints effectively can create resentment, low morale, low productivity, and increased turnover. So it is advisable to have an open-door policy that allows employees to feel free to come to you with a complaint. Try not to take complaints personally as a reflection on you or your leadership ability. Even the best managers have to deal with complaints. Do not become defensive, talk down to the complainer, minimize the complaint, or try to talk the person out of the complaint.[140]

There are five steps summarized in Model 14-3 that you should take when an employee comes to you with a complaint. First, if you are talking, they are hearing you, and it's not about

WORK
APPLICATION 14-14

Review the discipline guidelines in Exhibit 14-8. Identify any guidelines your present or past boss did not follow.

MODEL 14-3   STEPS IN ADDRESSING EMPLOYEE COMPLAINTS

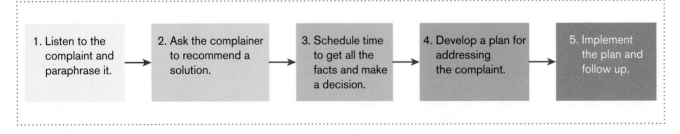

| MODEL 14-4 | STEPS IN ADDRESSING CUSTOMER COMPLAINTS |

1. Admit the mistake and apologize. → 2. Ask for, and agree on, a solution. → 3. Implement the solution quickly. → 4. Prevent future complaints.

you.[141] So you have to listen to their case.[142] If you can't paraphrase the complaint, you usually can't resolve it. Second, complainers often have a good solution; but just because you ask doesn't mean you have to do it. Third, you may need to get some facts and talk to someone, including other employees involved in the complaint and your boss, before you can make a decision. Fourth and fifth, without a plan and implementation and follow-up, nothing will change. You need to address the current complaint, but you usually also need to take action so that it doesn't happen again.[143]

Handling Customer Complaints. Handling a customer complaint is critical because customer satisfaction is the major goal of many organizations. Dissatisfied customers often complain to friends, and with increasing use of the Internet, this often results in lost customers and loss of future sales. On the positive side, complaints provide feedback that can be used to improve your products and services.[144]

The steps for handling customer complaints are listed in Model 14-4. First, by admitting the mistake and apologizing, you calm emotions and drop defensiveness.[145] Second, customers often have solutions that are easier and less costly than what you may recommend. The faster the resolution, the better the odds of satisfying and keeping the customer. Last, avoid repeating mistakes for this and all other customers by taking corrective action where needed.[146]

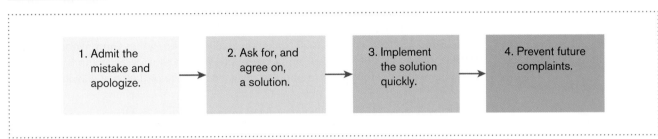

MANAGEMENT IN ACTION
Handling Complaints

Trends and Issues in Management

Financial systems and controls[147] and *corporate governance* vary widely *globally*.[148] Following the global financial crisis and bankruptcy of **Enron** and **WorldCom**, new laws were passed to establish better controls in large corporations. The United States passed the *Sarbanes-Oxley Act*, and some other countries, including Australia and Italy, passed similar laws. Most multinational corporations (MNCs), including **DuPont** and **GE**, have established strong governance. Growing numbers of the best-performing companies are "*asset light*," accomplishing fast global growth with relatively little financial or physical capital. **Amazon**, **Alphabet**, and **Facebook** use little of it relative to their size, while **Uber** and **Airbnb** use practically none.

In addition, *technology* can make any capital more efficient, thus, making human capital even more important.[149] Technology algorithm software is being used to manage people in making hiring, promoting, and firing decisions and giving coaching tips tailored to managers' own style and how they need to hear feedback. Companies developing and using "people analytics" include **Cisco, Deloitte, hiQ Labs, IBM, eBay**, and **GE**.[150] Hedge funds are making fortunes using data analysis to select stocks to buy and sell.[151] Getting back to **The Ranch**, golf is being data driven as technology tracks every shot on every hole. **ShotLink** technology has 600 data points, allowing pro golfer **Gary Woodland** and others to visualize their games like never before. Woodland says, "ShotLink is a statistics coach providing information to improve my game; it's one of the most valuable tools in my bag."[152]

There is *diversity* by age. Millennials like regular feedback, so give them lots of coaching[153] and lots of praise to make sure they feel appreciated.[154] In contrast to the past, companies are promoting younger workers faster. There is a growing number of millennial CEOs aged 50 and younger at companies including **McDonald's, Harley-Davidson, Microsoft, Cisco, Aqua America**, and **21st Century Fox**. Millennials are bringing different leadership styles, as they tend to be more tech savvy, take more risk, react faster to sudden business shifts, spend more time wooing and keeping younger employees, are more concerned about work–life balance and give employees more flexible work options, and focus more on keeping products and services relevant for the rising millennials, 75% of the workforce, than do the older CEOs they are replacing.[155]

To help women and minorities advance, some companies including **J&J, Intel, Pinterest, Twitter**, and **BASF** are setting quantitative objectives for advancement and tying those numbers to pay.[156] Although *gender* doesn't drive financial success, in general, women and men are diverse in how they plan for retirement and invest financially. Men tend to be more confident in their investments and take more risk. Women are more conservative and goal directed and more likely than men to participate in employer-sponsored retirement plans and save a greater percentage of their income.[157]

Unfortunately, *unethically*/illegally manipulating the numbers led to the global financial crisis and is still going on today.[158] Many corporations are reporting inflated income,[159] and **Toshiba** overstated profits by $1.9 billion over seven years, more than four times the initial estimate.[160] Although not illegal, some question the ethics of a U.S. corporation moving its headquarters overseas (inversion), such as **Snapchat** did to lower tax expenses, and is **Apple** unfairly paying too little tax on its overseas income?[161] On a personal note, be careful what you e-mail, tweet, or post on social media **Facebook** and **LinkedIn**, because it has the potential to be ethically or financially problematic to you and your firm.[162] Some people are writing fake poor product reviews that can hurt competitors financially and fake positive reviews for financial gain. Some companies including **Amazon** have gone to court to unmask fake reviewers.[163]

Again, companies must have *socially responsible* leaders,[164] and **Pope Francis** wrote a 181-page encyclical asking governments and MNCs of the world to be caretakers of *sustainability*.[165] The pontiff also denounced the inequalities of capitalism as he addressed the **U.S. Congress**, calling for changes in the greed for money and asking the government and MNCs to provide more aid to the poor of the world.[166] However, some critics claim the pope should not be writing about capitalism and the environment, whereas others say the pope is concerned about the poor of the world, and they are in need of financial help, and they tend to pollute the least but are affected the most. *What do you think?*

As we bring this chapter to a close, you should be able to establish systems controls (preliminary, concurrent, rework, and damage controls), use the control systems process (set objectives and standards, measure performance, compare performance to standards, and reinforce or correct performance), and use control methods (constant, periodic, and occasional) to achieve organizational objectives. You should also understand the budgeting process (operating, capital expenditure, and financial budgets) and contents of financial statements (income statement, balance sheet, and cash flow statement). You should also be able to manage by walking around and coach, counsel, discipline, and handle employee and customer complaints using behavioral models 14-1, 14-2, 14-3, and 14-4.

⑤SAGE edge™   edge.sagepub.com/lussier8e

Want a better grade?

Get the tools you need to sharpen your study skills. Access practice quizzes, eFlashcards, video and multimedia, and more at edge.sagepub.com/lussier8e.

Digital Resources

Learning Objective	Digital Resource
14-1. List the four stages of the systems process and describe the type of control used at each stage.	▶ Organization Control System
14-2. Identify the four steps in the control systems process, and describe the differences among the three categories of control frequency.	▣ Steps in Control Systems Process
14-3. Discuss the three parts of the master budgeting process, and compare bonds and stock.	▶ Management Counselling*
14-4. Explain the relationship between coaching, management counseling, and discipline.	▶ Management in Action: Handling Complaints*

* premium video available only in the interactive eBook

••• CHAPTER SUMMARY

14-1. List the four stages of the systems process and describe the type of control used at each stage.

The first stage of the systems process is inputs. Preliminary control is designed to anticipate and prevent possible input problems. The second stage is the transformation process. Concurrent control is action taken to ensure that standards are met as inputs are transformed into outputs. The third stage is outputs. Rework control is action taken to fix an output. The fourth stage is customer/stakeholder satisfaction. Damage control is action taken to minimize negative impacts on customers/stakeholders due to faulty outputs. During the four stages, feedback is used to improve upon the process to continually increase customer satisfaction.

14-2. Identify the four steps in the control systems process, and describe the differences among the three categories of control frequency.

The steps in the control systems process are (1) set objectives and standards, (2) measure performance, (3) compare performance to standards, and (4) correct or reinforce, with a feedback loop for continuous improvement. Controls vary based on the frequency of their use. Constant controls (self-control, clan control, and standing plans) are in continuous use. Periodic

controls (regular meetings and reports, budgets, audits) are used on a regular fixed basis, such as once a day or week. Occasional controls (observation, exception principle, special reports, project control) are used on a sporadic basis when needed.

14-3. Discuss the three parts of the master budgeting process, and compare bonds and stock.

The three parts of the master budget are (1) the *operating budget*, which includes forecasted revenues and expenses for the year; (2) the *capital expenditures budget*, which includes all planned major asset investments that will generate revenues; and (3) *financial budgets and statements*, which include the income statement (revenues – expenses = profits), the balance sheet (assets = liabilities + owner equity), and the cash flow statement (money received and paid). The budgeted pro forma statements project the next year's financial results, whereas the actual statements report past performance for the specified period of time. *Bonds and stock* are similar in that they are both used to raise money for the business. But they are different because when a company sells bonds, it must pay back the bond holders plus the rate of interest specified. In contrast, if the company sells stock, it never has to pay back the stockholders because they become part owners of the company. The sale of both results in cash being added to the asset section of the balance sheet, but bonds are part of the liabilities section, whereas stock is part of the owner's equity section.

14-4. Explain the relationship between coaching, management counseling, and discipline.

Coaching is the process of giving motivational feedback to maintain and improve performance. *Management counseling* is the process of giving employees feedback so they realize that a problem is affecting their job performance and referring employees with problems to the employee assistance program.

Discipline is corrective action to get employees to meet standards and standing plans. The three are related because the manager starts by coaching to fine-tune performance. However, if there are problem employees who are not meeting expectations, counseling or discipline is used. Counseling is commonly used when employees have personal problems, whereas discipline is used when employees will not meet work performance standards or break rules. If employees don't meet expectations with counseling help, discipline is used. The discipline is based on the severity of the violation, and progressive discipline leading to firing may be used.

• • • KEY TERMS

budget, 472

capital expenditures budget, 474

coaching, 477

concurrent control, 464

control frequency, 469

control systems process, 466

critical success factors, 468

damage control, 464

discipline, 482

employee assistance program (EAP), 481

financial statements, 475

management audit, 470

management by walking around (MBWA), 480

management counseling, 481

operating budgets, 472

preliminary control, 464

rework control, 464

standards, 467

• • • KEY TERM REVIEW

Complete each of the following statements using one of this chapter's key terms.

1. _____ is designed to anticipate and prevent possible problems.

2. _____ is action taken to ensure standards are met as inputs are transformed into outputs.

3. _____ is action taken to fix an output.

4. _____ is action taken to minimize negative impacts on customers/stakeholders due to faulty outputs.

5. _____ The steps are (1) set objectives and standards, (2) measure performance, (3) compare performance to standards, and (4) correct or reinforce.

6. _____ measure performance levels in the areas of quantity, quality, time, cost, and behavior.

7. _____ are the limited number of areas in which satisfactory results will ensure successful performance, achieving the objective/standard.

8. Categories of _____ include constant, periodic, and occasional.

9. The _____ analyzes the organization's planning, organizing, leading, and controlling functions to look for improvements.

10. A _____ is a planned quantitative allocation of resources for specific activities.

11. The _____ include the revenue and expense budgets.

12. The _____ includes all planned major asset investments.

13. The three primary _____ are the income statement, balance sheet, and cash flow statement.

14. _____ is the process of giving motivational feedback to maintain and improve performance.

15. _____ has three major activities: listening, teaching, and facilitating.

16. _____ is the process of giving employees feedback so they realize that a problem is affecting their job performance and referring employees with problems to the employee assistance program.

17. The _____ has a staff of people who help employees get professional assistance in solving their problems.

18. _____ is corrective action to get employees to meet standards and standing plans.

••• REVIEW QUESTIONS

1. Why is damage control important?

2. Why should you focus on preliminary and concurrent types of control rather than on rework and damage control?

3. Who are the primary customers/stakeholders for the outputs of the operations, marketing, human resources, finance, and information functional areas/departments?

4. What are the five areas of performance that standards measure?

5. Why is measuring performance important to an organization?

6. What is shown in a performance report?

7. What is the role of reinforcement in the control systems process?

8. What are the three constant control methods, the three periodic control methods, and the four occasional control methods?

9. What are the three steps in the master budgeting process?

10. Why is the capital expenditures budget the most important budget?

11. What is the difference between financial statements and financial budgets?

12. What is the objective of coaching?

13. How do managers commonly demotivate employees?

14. What is the performance formula, and how is it used with coaching?

15. What are the three activities of management by walking around, and what is the role of facilitating?

16. What are the differences among coaching, counseling, and disciplining?

••• COMMUNICATION SKILLS

The following critical-thinking questions can be used for class discussion and/or as written assignments to develop communication skills. Be sure to give complete explanations for all questions.

1. Recall a personal event that you had to help conduct, such as a party, shower, or wedding. Identify preliminary, concurrent, rework, and damage controls, as well as feedback. What did you learn from the experience and the textbook discussion that can help you to plan and control better in the future?

2. Apply the control systems process to your college education. What are your major objectives and standards? How do you measure and compare performance to your objectives and standards? What current and future corrective action have you taken? Do you reinforce your performance when meeting goals? If so, how?

3. Employees tend to resist control and sometimes break the rules. Give examples of things you or others have done to resist controls.

4. How does your professor in this course use controls to reduce and/or eliminate cheating on tests and other assignments?

5. How confident are you in your ability to develop budgets and read financial statements? What experience have you had in developing budgets and reading financial statements?

6. Do you feel that managers should spend more time on coaching and MBWA techniques? Explain.

7. Which of the eight discipline guidelines is most relevant to you personally? Explain.

8. Can the need for discipline be reduced? If so, how?

CASES

••• Case 14-1   General Electric

General Electric Company (GE), incorporated in 1892, is a global industrial conglomerate. The company operates in the following business segments: power, renewable energy, oil & gas, aviation, healthcare, transportation, energy, connections and lighting, and capital, in approximately 180 countries. It is headquartered in Boston, Massachusetts, and employs 333,000 people worldwide.

GE's mission is "To usher in the next industrial era and to build, move, power, and cure the world." Its vision is to focus on businesses that connect to its core competencies and in which it is a market leader. The company also intends to exit businesses that are either not in alignment with its core values or in which the company is underperforming and not likely to improve its competitive position.

General Electric has maintained its reputation as being a great company to work for because of its commitment to the development of its associates. Up until 2005, General Electric had used a traditional "forced distribution" rating scheme that required managers to spread out performance ratings on a competitive basis, with the bottom 10% of employees facing disciplinary action or termination. Between 2005 and 2015, the forced ranking component of the system was eliminated, but what remained was a traditional performance evaluation process with a single meeting between managers and direct reports to discuss performance issues and provide feedback. In 2016, General Electric decided to completely overhaul its performance evaluation process and redesign it as a performance management system that relied on a coaching process that provided ongoing feedback for direct reports. By setting up short-term goals and having ongoing growth conversations with direct reports that are not tied to compensation, managers believe that anybody can rise to the occasion and learn to be a successful performer in their job.

The new performance management system at General Electric uses a mobile app called PD@GE that enables managers to set short-term performance goals with their direct reports. Once these are in place, managers are expected to use a coaching process that involves frequent conversations called "touchpoints" to assess how well direct reports are progressing toward their goals on an ongoing basis. In addition, the most important element of the new performance management process is not the mobile app itself but rather the ongoing coaching sessions and the conversations that occur within them. Specifically, the touchpoint (coaching) sessions focus on taking a positive and constructive approach to providing performance feedback, and the issue of performance-based pay increases is not typically part of these conversations. At the end of each year, managers and their direct reports still complete a formal summary report that is then used as the basis for merit pay increases, promotional opportunities, and job performance improvement plans for the coming year.

Discussion Questions

1. How does coaching serve as a control system at General Electric?

2. How is coaching built into the performance management process at General Electric?

3. How does the performance management process at General Electric address providing positive feedback and corrective action for workers with performance issues?

4. How does the performance management system at General Electric apply the coaching process model?

5. Do you agree with General Electric's decision to eliminate its traditional performance evaluation system? Why or why not?

6. What do you think of the PD@GE mobile app that General Electric uses as part of its performance management process? Is it effective? Why or why not?

References

http://www.reuters.com/finance/stocks/companyProfile?symbol=GE.N

http://marketrealist.com/2016/02/general-electrics-mission-vision-strategy/

https://hbr.org/2015/08/ges-real-time-performance-development

https://hbr.org/2016/10/the-performance-management-revolution

https://www.fastcompany.com/3054547/six-companies-that-are-redefining-performance-management

https://www.wsj.com/articles/ge-re-engineers-performance-reviews-pay-practices-1465358463

http://blog.impraise.com/360-feedback/how-ge-renews-performance-management-from-stack-ranking-to-continuous-feedback-360-feedback

http://blog.hreonline.com/2016/07/27/farewell-to-performance-ratings-at-ge/

Case created by Loren Kuzuhara, University of Wisconsin–Madison.

••• Case 14-2   Figures Do Not Lie but Liars Figure: The "Searing" Truth

If you are looking for Sears, do not look for their catalogs. In the world of retail, Sears Holdings is an appliance giant. In addition to home appliances, the company is a leading retailer of tools, as well as lawn and garden, fitness, and automotive repair equipment. With 1,672 retail stores across the United States, Sears Holdings operates through subsidiaries Sears, Roebuck and Co. and Kmart, offering proprietary Sears brands including Kenmore, Craftsman, and DieHard. Beyond retail, Sears Holdings is the largest provider of home installation and product repair services in the United States. In 2014, Sears Holdings spun off Lands' End and reduced its once majority stake in Sears Canada to just 12% as it sought to raise cash to overcome struggling store sales. In 2017, the company agreed to sell its Craftsman tool brand to Stanley Black & Decker for $900 million.(1)

The once great retail giant though is in serious trouble. Declining store sales and mounting losses have plagued Sears Holdings for the past several years as the popularity of e-commerce and fierce competition from other big box retailers has been growing. In fiscal 2016, Sears Holdings' net revenues decreased by 19% due to a drop in revenues from all segments (and a drop of $2.1 billion associated with Sears Canada, which was de-consolidated in October 2014).

Kmart's revenues declined due to having fewer stores in operation, which accounted for approximately $1.1 billion of the decline and a drop in comparable store sales driven by declines in the consumer electronics, apparel, grocery and household and drugstore categories. The revenues from Sears Domestic segment decreased due to a drop in comparable store sales of 11.1%, which accounted for $1.2 billion of the decline, and the effect of having fewer full-line stores in operation, which accounted for $433 million of the decline. The company's net loss decreased by 33% in fiscal 2016, mainly due to a decline in selling and administrative expenses, related to decreases in payroll and advertising expenses and the absence of expenses of $603 million from Sears Canada and $77 million from the Lands' End business.(2)

Sears has been losing money while closing stores and selling assets in order to stay solvent for quite a while. The company has injected almost $12 billion in liquidity from 2012 to 2016 to fund ongoing operations given material declines in internally generated cash flow; the company's "cash burn" was $1.6 billion in 2016 and projected to hit $1.8 billion in 2017.(3) The firm is having increasing difficulty in paying its bills.

CEO Eddie Lampert has reacted to the firm's negative performance by developing a strategic plan including "a restructuring program designed to streamline operations, improve operating performance, and deliver cost reductions of at least $1 billion on an annualized basis. Some of these savings are new, while others come from an already underway plan to close 108 Kmart and 42 Sears's stores.

> Lampert also promised to further lower costs or generate cash by leveraging the company's real estate through potential in-store partnerships, subdivisions, and reformatting to support digital sales. In addition, the CEO reiterated plans to evaluate strategic options for the Kenmore and DieHard brands as well as the Sears Home Services and Sears Auto Centers businesses; this could mean a sale, partnership, or joint venture for any of the properties.(4)

Sears can survive for a while by selling off assets, but that doesn't increase sales.… In order for Sears to have a long-term future, it needs to return to profitability. That's something its CEO cites as a goal, but aside from cutting its cash loss in Q4, there have been few signs that Lampert's vision for a company with fewer physical stores and a robust online presence (through its ShopYourWay app) will work. The chain saw comparable-store sales decline by 10.3% in Q4—a terrible sign for a company that has been working on a turnaround for years.(5)

On February 7, 2017, the stock fell 13%. Why? A sudden surge in the cost of insuring Sears's bonds was rooted in the same frustration that stockholders had been suffering for years; it seems to be a simple matter of the company not selling enough of the right merchandise at the right price in the right way at the right time. If bond and stockholders are to be believed, the end is near for Sears.(6)

Discussion Questions

1. Control systems consist of preliminary controls, concurrent controls, rework controls, and damage controls. This case deals with what type(s) of control systems.

2. Which functional controls system(s) are directly addressed in this case?

3. Which functional control systems are indirectly addressed in this case?

4. Which step in the control system process does Sears Holdings appear to be implementing?

5. The controls discussed in this case fall into which one of the three control frequencies?

6. Most of the financial information described in this case can be found using which financial control tools?

7. Given what you have read in this case, what is your likelihood of investing in Sears stock and/or bonds?

Cumulative Case Questions

8. What factors in the external environment of Sears seem to have negatively affected its performance (Chapter 2)?

9. What does the statement "a simple matter of the company not selling enough of the right merchandise at the right price in the right way at the right time" imply from a planning perspective (Chapter 5)?

10. Sears has planned to close 150 stores. What challenges does this pose to its human resources department (Chapter 9)?

11. Given Sears's continuing decline, what do you think would be the impact on employee motivation and job performance (Chapter 11)?

12. CEO Eddie Lampert's development of a strategic plan to counter Sears's decline would be an example of what class of leadership theories (Chapter 12)?

References

(1) Hampton, S. (n.d.). Sears Holdings Corporation. Hoovers. Retrieved March 7, 2017, from http://0-subscriber.hoovers.com.liucat.lib.liu.edu/H/company 360/fulldescription.html?companyId=137766000000000

(2) Ibid.

(3) Kline, D. (2017, February 15). Can Sears really cut its way to survival? The Motley Fool. Retrieved March 7, 2017, from https://www.fool.com/investing/2017/02/15/can-sears-really-cut-its-way-to-survival.aspx

(4) Ibid.

(5) Ibid.

(6) Brumley, J. (2017, February 8). Why the end looks near for Sears. Investor Place. Retrieved March 7, 2017, http://investorplace.com/2017/02/sears-holdings-corp-shld-stock-already-insolvent/#.WL79M4WcGUk

Case created by Herbert Sherman, Long Island University.

••• SKILL BUILDER 14-1: BOLTON CONTROL SYSTEM

Objective

To improve your skill at developing a control system for an organization/department.

Skills

The primary skills developed through this exercise are:

1. *Management skill*—decision making (conceptual, diagnostic, analytical, critical-thinking, and quantitative-reasoning skills are needed to develop a control system for a business)

2. *AACSB competency*—analytic skills

3. *Management function*—controlling

Situation

Marie Bolton owns and operates the Bolton Clerical Employment Agency. As the name indicates, her agency focuses on providing clerical employees to its business clients. It has a file of clerical employees looking for jobs or better jobs. When employers place job orders with the agency, the agency recruiter tries to find a person who fits the job specifications. The agency sends possible candidates to the employer. The employment agency charges the employer a fee only when one of its referred candidates is hired by the company. The fee is based on the employee's first-year salary. The average fee paid by employers is $1,000.

Each agency recruiter gets 35% of the fee charged as a salary. Pay is 100% commission. Refunds are made if the person placed does not stay on the job for three months.

Marie has two employees called recruiters. With only two employees, Marie is also a full-time recruiter. She does the management functions in addition to recruiting.

Marie has no formal control methods because her two recruiters are very competent professionals who are paid only by commission; she places minimal restrictions on them. Marie is somewhat satisfied with the way her business is operating. However, through a professional association, she found out that her business is not doing as well as the average employment agency. Being competitive by nature, Marie does not want to be below average.

Marie has asked you to set up a control system to help her improve her agency's performance. She has provided you with the following performance report, comparing her agency's figures to those of the average agency. The professional association forecasts that revenues for next year will not increase for the industry.

Performance Information Report for Last Year

	Bolton	Average
Placement revenue (refunds deducted, not taxes)	$230,000	$250,000
Recruiter commissions paid	$80,500	$87,500
Refunds	$8,000	$10,000
Number of placements	230	250
Number of company interviews	*	1,000
Number of full-time recruiters (including owners who recruit)	3	3

*Bolton does not keep records of the number of candidates it sends to companies for interviews.

Procedure

Identify the systems process for Bolton by identifying its primary inputs, transformation process, outputs, and customers/stakeholders.

Inputs	Transformation Process	Outputs	Customers/Stakeholders

Identify major types of control for each stage of the systems process.

Preliminary	Concurrent	Rework	Damage

To set up a control system for Bolton, follow the steps in the control systems process.

Step 1. Setting Objectives and Standards

Marie's objective is to earn $250,000 in revenue for the next year, which is the industry average. Establish standards for the year that will enable Marie to reach her objective.

Quantity. Quantity of interviews per recruiter: ____

Quantity of placements per recruiter: ____

Calculate the number of additional interviews needed to meet the standard per recruiter: ____

Calculate the percentage increase: ____%

Quality. State the dollar value of acceptable refunds per recruiter: $____

State the corresponding number of refunds: ____

Time. State the time period in which the quantity and quality standards should be met: ____

Cost. State the cost based on commissions per recruiter: $____

Behavior. Identify any behaviors employees should change to help them meet the standards.

Step 2. Measuring Performance

What are the critical success factors for employment agencies? Have you identified the critical success factors within your standards? If not, rework them. How often should Marie measure performance, and what methods of control should she use?

Time frequency for measuring performance: ____

Quantity of interviews per recruiter for time period: ____

Quantity of placements per recruiter for time period: ____

List specific control methods to use:

Step 3. Comparing Performance to Standards

How should Marie compare her agency's performance to her new standards?

Step 4. Correcting or Reinforcing

What type of corrective action should Marie take if standards are not being met, or what type of reinforcement if they are?

Assume that Bolton does exactly meet the standard. Calculate the rate of productivity for Bolton's past performance (average agency): ____

1. Calculate the rate of productivity for the new performance standard: ____

2. Is there a change in productivity? ____ yes ____ no

3. If yes, by what percentage did it increase or decrease? ____

4. Base the inputs on recruiter commissions only.

5. Calculate the past commission per employee (average agency): ____

6. Calculate the new commission per employee: ____

7. What percentage pay increase do recruiters get? ____

8. Do profits increase when the new standards are met? ____

9. How do you think the employees will react to your proposed control system? Do you think they will resist the control? Why or why not?

Apply It

What did I learn from this exercise? How will I use this knowledge in the future?

Your instructor may ask you to do Skill Builder 14-1 in class in a group. If so, the instructor will provide you with any necessary information or additional instructions.

• • • SKILL BUILDER 14-2: COACHING

Objective

To develop your skill at improving performance through coaching.

Skills

The primary skills developed through this exercise are:

1. *Management skill*—interpersonal (coaching takes communication skills to motivate employees)

2. *AACSB competency*—communication ability (to resolve performance problems)

3. *Management function*—controlling

Procedure 1 (2–4 minutes)

Break into groups of three. Make some groups of two if necessary. Each member selects one of the following three situations in which to be the manager and a different one in which to be the employee. In each situation, the employee knows the standing plans; he or she is not motivated to follow them. You will take turns coaching and being coached.

Three Problem Employee Situations

1. Employee 1 is a clerical worker. The person uses files, as do the other 10 employees in the department. The employees all know that they are supposed to return the files when they are finished so that others can find them when they

need them. Employees should have only one file out at a time. The supervisor notices that Employee 1 has five files on the desk, and another employee is looking for one of them. The supervisor thinks that Employee 1 will complain about the heavy workload as an excuse for having more than one file out at a time.

2. Employee 2 is a server in an ice cream shop. The employee knows that the tables should be cleaned up quickly after customers leave so that new customers do not have to sit at dirty tables. It's a busy night. The supervisor finds dirty dishes on two of this employee's occupied tables. Employee 2 is socializing with some friends at one of the tables. Employees are supposed to be friendly; Employee 2 will probably use this as an excuse for the dirty tables.

3. Employee 3 is an auto technician. All employees at the garage where this person works know that they are supposed to put a paper mat on the floor of each car so that the carpets don't get dirty. When the service supervisor got into a car Employee 3 repaired, the car did not have a mat, and there was grease on the carpet. Employee 3 does excellent work and will probably make reference to this fact when coached.

Procedure 2 (3–7 minutes)

Prepare for coaching to improve performance. Below, each group member writes an outline of what he or she will say when coaching Employee 1, 2, or 3, following the steps below:

1. Describe current performance.

2. Describe desired performance. Get a commitment to the change.

3. Follow up.

Procedure 3 (5–8 minutes)

Role-Playing. The manager of Employee 1, the clerical worker, coaches him or her as planned. (Use the actual name of the group member playing Employee 1.) Talk—do not read your written plan. Employee 1, put yourself in the worker's position. You work hard; there is a lot of pressure to work fast. It's easier when you have more than one file. Refer to the workload while

being coached. Both the manager and the employee will have to ad lib. The person not playing a role is the observer. He or she makes notes on the observer form that follows. Try to make positive comments and point out areas for improvement. Give the manager alternative suggestions about what he or she could have said to improve the coaching session.

Observer Form

1. How well did the manager describe current behavior?

2. How well did the manager describe desired behavior? Did the employee state why the behavior is important?

3. How successful was the manager at getting a commitment to the change? Do you think the employee will change?

4. How well did the manager describe how he or she was going to follow up to ensure that the employee performed the desired behavior?

Feedback. The observer leads a discussion of how well the manager coached the employee. (This should be a discussion, not a lecture.) Focus on what the manager did well and how the manager could improve. The employee should also give feedback on how he or she felt and what might have been more effective in getting him or her to change. Do not go on to the next interview until you are told to do so. If you finish early, wait for the others to finish.

Procedure 4 (5–8 minutes)

Same as procedure 3, but change roles so that Employee 2, the server, is coached. Employee 2 should make a comment about the importance of talking to customers to make them feel welcome. The job is not much fun if you can't talk to your friends.

Procedure 5 (5–8 minutes)

Same as procedure 3, but change roles so that Employee 3, the auto technician, is coached. Employee 3 should comment on the excellent work he or she does.

Apply It

What did I learn from this experience? How will I use this knowledge in the future?

• • • SKILL BUILDER 14-3: DISCIPLINING

Objective

To develop your ability to discipline an employee.

Skills

The primary skills developed through this exercise are:

1. *Management skill*—interpersonal (discipline requires communication skills to motivate employees to improve)

2. *AACSB competency*—communication ability (to resolve performance problems)

3. Management function—controlling

Procedure 1 (2–4 minutes)

Break into groups of three. Make some groups of two if necessary. Each member selects one of the three situations from Skill Builder 14-2. Decide who will discipline Employee 1, the clerical worker, Employee 2, the ice cream shop server, and Employee 3, the auto technician. Also select a different group member to play the employee being disciplined.

Procedure 2 (3–7 minutes)

Prepare for the discipline session. Write a basic outline of what you will say to Employee 1, 2, or 3; follow the steps in the discipline model below.

1. Refer to past feedback. (Assume that you have discussed the situation before, using the coaching model.)

2. Ask why the undesired behavior was used. (The employee should make up an excuse for not changing.)

3. Give the discipline. (Assume that an oral warning is appropriate.)

4. Get a commitment to change and develop a plan.

5. Summarize and state the follow-up.

Procedure 3 (5–8 minutes)

Role-Playing. The manager of Employee 1, the clerical worker, disciplines him or her as planned. (Use the actual name of the group member playing the employee.) Talk—do not read your written plan. Employee 1, put yourself in the worker's position. You work hard; there is a lot of pressure to work fast. It's easier when you have more than one file. Both the manager and the employee will need to ad lib.

The person not playing a role is the observer. He or she makes notes on the observer form that follows. For each of the following steps, try to make a statement about the positive aspects of the discipline and a statement about how the manager could have improved. Give alternative things the manager could have said to improve the discipline session. Remember, the objective is to change behavior.

Observer Form

1. How well did the manager refer to past feedback?

2. How well did the manager ask why the undesired behavior was used?

3. How well did the manager give the discipline?

4. Did the manager get a commitment to change? Do you think the employee will change his or her behavior?

5. How well did the manager summarize and state the follow-up? How effective will the follow-up be?

Feedback. The observer leads a discussion of how well the manager disciplined the employee. The employee should also give feedback on how he or she felt and what might have been more effective in getting him or her to change. Do not go on to the next interview until you are told to do so. If you finish early, wait until the others finish or the time is up.

Procedure 4 (5–8 minutes)

Same as procedure 3, but change roles so that Employee 2, the ice cream server, is disciplined. Employee 2, put yourself in the worker's position. You enjoy talking to your friends, and you're supposed to be friendly to the customers.

Procedure 5 (5–8 minutes)

Same as procedure 3, but change roles so that Employee 3, the auto technician, is disciplined. Employee 3, put yourself in the worker's position. You are an excellent technician. Sometimes you forget to put the mat on the floor.

Apply It

What did I learn from this experience? How will I use this knowledge in the future?

••• SKILL BUILDER 14-4: HANDLING COMPLAINTS

Objective

To develop experience and skills in resolving complaints.

Skills

The primary skills developed through this exercise are:

1. *Management skill*—interpersonal (handling complaints requires people skills)

2. *AACSB competency*—communication abilities

3. *Management function*—leading (through working with others)

In this activity, you will role-play handling a complaint. To begin, think of a complaint—one you actually presented to a manager, one that was presented to you, one you heard about, or one you have made up. Write down details about the situation and the complaint, including any pertinent information that will help someone else play the role of the complainer (relationship to manager, knowledge level, years of employment, background, age, etc.).

The class will be divided into groups of three. One person in each group plays the role of the manager who must handle the complaint. This person gives his or her written complaint description to the person who is to present the complaint. The two ad lib the situation. A third person observes the role-play and evaluates how the complaint is handled, writing comments on the observer form that follows. After each role-play, group members should discuss how effectively the complaint was handled based on the observer's comments. After the discussion, group members switch roles and do another role-play until each group member has had a chance to play each role.

Observer Form

Observe the role-play to determine whether the person playing the role of manager followed the steps below. Try to note something positive the person does at each step of the process as well as some ways the person might improve his or her handling of complaints. Be specific and descriptive in your comments, and be prepared to suggest alternative behaviors when discussing how the person might improve.

Step 1. How well did the manager listen? Was the manager open to the complaint? Did the manager try to talk the employee out of the complaint? Was the manager defensive? Did the manager get the full story without interruptions? Did the manager paraphrase the complaint?

Positive behavior:

Ways to improve:

Step 2. Did the manager ask the complainer to recommend a solution? How well did the manager react to the suggested solution? If the solution could not be used, did the manager explain why?

Positive behavior:

Ways to improve:

Step 3. Did the manager schedule time to get all the facts and/or make a decision? Was it a reasonable length of time? Did the manager set a specific time to get back to the person?

Positive behavior:

Ways to improve:

Step 4. Did the manager and the employee develop a plan?

Positive behavior:

Ways to improve:

Apply It

What did I learn from this experience? How will I use this knowledge in the future?

15 Operations, Quality, and Productivity

● ● ● LEARNING OBJECTIVES

After studying this chapter, you should be able to:

15-1. Discuss why operations and products are important, and contrast manufacturing and service operations. PAGE 499

15-2. Compare the differences among operations systems with respect to tangibility of products, levels of customer involvement, operations flexibility, and management of resources and technology. PAGE 502

15-3. Explain the four facility layouts in terms of their level of customer involvement and flexibility, and give an example of the type of industry that would use each of the four facility layouts. PAGE 506

15-4. Describe the three planning schedules, supply chain management, and quality control. PAGE 509

15-5. Recall how to measure productivity and list three ways to increase it. PAGE 518

IOM

Ideas on Management
at Frito-Lay

In the 1930s, **Elmer Doolin** founded the **Frito Company** and **Herman Lay** founded **H. W. Lay Company**, each borrowing around $100 to start his business. In 1961, the Frito and Lay companies merged to form **Frito-Lay Inc.** In 1965, Frito-Lay merged with **Pepsi-Cola** to create **PepsiCo**, and Frito-Lay is a wholly owned subsidiary of PepsiCo Inc., earning more than half of PepsiCo revenues, and today it lists 30 brands on its website.

PepsiCo's chief executive officer (CEO) is **Indra Nooyi**, the only Indian woman to head a *Fortune* 500 company. Nooyi is ranked on the *Fortune* 50 Most Powerful Women and *Forbes* World's 100 Most Powerful Women lists. Nooyi is prescient, well disciplined, and a notoriously demanding boss, but she wouldn't ask anyone to do anything she wouldn't do herself. Nooyi is considered a good strategist and years ago understood the need to meet consumers' changing preference for healthier snacks and drinks, although customers still want salty, fatty snacks, too. Frito-Lay continues to face the challenges of transforming the company to a healthy image, but almost half of PepsiCo business now comes from "guilt-free" snacks and drinks.

Frito-Lay is the world's leading snack food company that thinks globally and acts locally. To ensure that its products are developed to satisfy the taste preferences of people in various countries around the world, Frito-Lay has acquired foreign operations and brands through direct investment. Nooyi has doubled sales from overseas to the point that international sales are about half of the company's revenues. The reasons Frito-Lay is so successful include aggressive marketing, an extensive distribution system, operating discipline to control consistent quality, and new product innovation.

IOM 1. How would Frito-Lay's operations systems be classified?

IOM 2. How would Frito-Lay's operations systems be described in terms of design?

IOM 3. How does Frito-Lay manage its operations systems and supply chain?

IOM 4. How does Frito-Lay control quality?

You'll find answers to these **IOM** questions throughout the chapter. To learn more about Frito-Lay, visit www.fritolay.com.

Sources: Information for this case was taken from the Frito-Lay North America Inc. website at http://www.fritolay.com, accessed June 21, 2017; K. Stock, "Movers," *BusinessWeek* (February 20–March 5, 2017): 11; Staff, "The 50 Most Powerful Women," *Fortune* (2015), http://fortune.com/most-powerful-women/, accessed June 21, 2017; Staff, "The World's 100 Most Powerful Women," *Forbes.com*, accessed June 21, 2017; J. Reingold, "Indra Nooyi Was Right. Now What," *Fortune* (June 15, 2015): 246–253.

Operations

As discussed, organizations develop missions and cultures (Chapter 2) and strategies (Chapter 5), and they must fit together.[1] Also, businesses have four primary functional area strategies—marketing, financing, human resources, and operations. In this chapter, we focus on operations. The head of operations is commonly called the chief operations officer (COO) and commonly works closely with the CEO. **Apple**'s **COO Tim Cook** was responsible for

LO 15-1

Discuss why operations and products are important, and contrast manufacturing and service operations.

operations and helped CEO **Steve Jobs** manage Apple, resulting in Cook replacing Jobs as CEO.[2] **Sheryl Sandberg** is COO of **Facebook**. In this first section, we discuss what operations and products are and then differences between manufacturing and service operations.

Operations and Products

Recall Exhibit 2-2, "The Systems Process" (Chapter 2, page 41), and its inclusion of controls in Exhibit 14-1 (Chapter 14, page 465). Well, this is what operations is all about. **Operations** *is the function concerned with transforming resource inputs into product outputs.* A **product** *is a good, a service, or a combination of the two.* Without a product, you don't have a business. Because the mission of all organizations revolves around providing products, the operations department is a primary focus of performance. Recall that technology (Chapter 6) is simply the method the firm uses to transform inputs into outputs. Complete Self-Assessment 15-1 to determine if you are more technically or intuitively inclined.

Operations must effectively use resources[3] (Chapter 1), especially physical resources, to make and deliver products.[4] Operations is important because if you don't have a good product developed through effective operations that change with the environment, you won't have a business. The for-profit **Corinthian Colleges** Inc. was accused of poor operations that led to its bankruptcy, negatively affecting hundreds of thousands of its students.[5]

Note that we use the broader term *product* to include both goods and services, whereas some refer to products as only goods or services. Many organizations' products have both, such as a **Ford** dealership that sells autos and services them as well. **Verizon** and **T-Mobile** will sell you a phone and service plan. Many firms have multiple products that are clearly goods or services, such as **Amazon** selling retail goods and cloud computer services, and the iPhone that **Apple** wants you to use to buy things with its Apple Pay.[6] *Customer service,* the service provided to the customer before, during, and after the purchase, is important.[7]

Manufacturing and Service Operations

Manufacturing and service operations are similar because they are both used to produce products, but they are also different, as discussed here.

Manufacturing. Manufacturing operations are used to transform inputs into tangible (physical) output products, such as this book, *Management Fundamentals*. Manufacturing remains important for the U.S. economy. However, only 10% of private-sector workers are employed by manufacturers, versus 25% back in 1980, but many other companies depend on services for the delivery (**St. Johnsbury Trucking** and **FedEx**), and sales (**Sears** and **Costco**) of products.[8] Some 63,000 factories closed since 2000 largely due to the high cost of labor in the United States versus other countries. **Keen Footwear** said to stay in business it was forced to move production of shoes to China. Small businesses struggle to manufacture in the United States, not only due to the prohibitive cost but also because there are not many U.S. contract manufacturers, and few that will even make parts and products for them.[9]

On the bright side, there have been hints of a U.S. manufacturing comeback,[10] called *inshoring.* **Ford**, **Toyota**, **Apple**, and **Whirlpool** are bringing some jobs back, and **Walmart** (called a U.S. manufacturing job killer) has pledged to buy an additional $250 billion worth of American-made products over the next 10 years.[11] However, no one expects the United States to make many of the $500 billion a year in household products that are currently imported.[12] In a survey, 90% of respondents said they have a favorable opinion of domestically manufactured products.[13] **STIHL** outdoor power tool manufacturer says that inshoring is a hot topic, but it prides itself on its products being built in the United States and sold worldwide since 1927.[14]

Services. Service operations use inputs to provide intangible (nonphysical) product services. The transformation is not as clear as with goods, such as **Uber** using drivers with their cars as "inputs" to "transform" by transporting riders to their "output" destination. What is the transformation process at your college? Give up? The administration brings the "inputs" of faculty, students, and education systems; the "transformation" is student education, and its "outputs" are its graduates.

operations The function concerned with transforming resource inputs into product outputs.

product A good, a service, or a combination of the two.

15-1 SELF-ASSESSMENT

Technical Inclination

For each of the following 10 statements, select the number for the statement that best describes you on a continuum from 1 (*describes me*) to 3 (*does not describe me*).

1	2	3
Describes me	Somewhat	Does not describe me

____ 1. I enjoy solving problems rather than just doing so because I have to.

____ 2. I take a logical, rational approach to solving problems rather than using feelings and hunches as to what is the best solution.

____ 3. I enjoy improving on things and processes that already exist, more so than trying to come up with disruptive innovation.

____ 4. I make decisions based on facts rather than on feelings and hunches.

____ 5. I prefer assignments that are well structured regarding what to do and how to do it rather than open to doing whatever I want to do.

____ 6. I'm good at organizing rather than being unorganized.

____ 7. My feelings and moods tend to be consistent rather than fluctuating based on what is happening.

____ 8. I'm more of a conformist rather than nonconforming and disregarding policies.

____ 9. I'm good at concentrating for 30 minutes or more rather than having my mind wander to distractions—such as checking my phone/email.

____ 10. I'm good at monitoring progress toward objectives rather than not setting objectives and monitoring progress.

Add up the points and place your total on the line below that represents your technical inclination.

10	20	30
Technical		**Intuitive**

As with all the self-assessments, there is no right or wrong score, but if you are more technically inclined, a career in operations may be of interest to you.

The United States is a service-oriented economy,[15] as services account for 77% of private-sector outputs.[16] **Starwood Hotels** says that its competitive advantage is its superior operations that provide guests with a better experience.[17] **General Electric (GE)** is increasing productivity by using Big Data technology to transform how it delivers services for its customers,[18] as 9% of U.S. imports and 18% of exports are being delivered digitally, especially in the finance fields.[19]

What Are Some of the Other Differences Between Manufacturing and Service Operations? Take a look at Exhibit 15-1. It lists the ways operations are classified, designed, and managed. In the first column, as stated, manufacturing operations make tangible goods versus intangible services, but both types of operations can have different levels of customer involvement, flexibility, and use of technology. In the second column, both types of operations have product mix and designs, a facility layout and location, and many services needed to plan capacity. In the last column is where there are more differences. Both can use planning

EXHIBIT 15-1	HOW OPERATIONS SYSTEMS ARE CLASSIFIED, DESIGNED, AND MANAGED	

Classifying Operations Systems	Designing Operations Systems	Managing Operations Systems
Tangibility of products	Product mix and design	Planning schedules and project management
Level of customer involvement	Facility layout	Inventory control
Operations flexibility	Facility location	Materials requirement planning (MRP)
Resources and technology management	Capacity planning	Supply chain management
		Quality control

schedules and have projects and need to provide a quality product. However, inventory control, materials requirement planning (MRP), and supply chain management are usually less relevant in service operations. In the next three sections, we progress through classifying, designing, and managing operating systems with limited future explanation of the differences between manufacturing and service operations.

LO 15-2

Compare the differences among operations systems with respect to tangibility of products, levels of customer involvement, operations flexibility, and management of resources and technology.

Classifying Operations Systems

In this section, we discuss how operations systems can be classified by the tangibility of products, level of customer involvement, operations flexibility, and management of resources and technology.

Tangibility of Products

The *tangibility of products* refers to whether the products are tangible, intangible, or mixed.

Tangible Products. Manufactured *goods*, such as **Kia** automobiles and **Hewlett-Packard (HP)** computers, are *tangible products*. **GameStop** sells games on CDs in its more than 6,000 stores, but some predict the company will greatly downsize like **Best Buy** or fail like **Blockbuster** DVD movie rentals losing customers to **Netflix** and music stores losing to **iTunes** and other streaming services.[20] What do you think?

WORK
APPLICATION 15-1

Describe the operations process from the major product where you work or have worked, and be sure to specify if it was manufacturing or service operations.

Intangible Products. *Services*, such as **Cost Cutters** haircuts, **Belmont Dry Cleaning**, and **Ryan Legal** advice, are *intangible products*.

Mixed Products. *Mixed products* are made up of both tangible and intangible products. Major appliance retail stores like **Manny's** (and **Best Buy** electronics with its **Geek Squad**) not only sell appliances but also offer extended warranties and service what they sell.

Level of Customer Involvement

It is important to view operations from the customer's perspective. The level of **customer involvement** refers to the amount of input from customers, which determines whether operations are make to stock, assemble to order, or make to order.

customer involvement The amount of input from customers, which determines whether operations are make to stock, assemble to order, or make to order.

Make-to-Stock (MTS) Operations. *Make-to-stock operations* produce products with a common design and price in anticipation of demand. Therefore, there is a low level of customer involvement. Most goods that you see in retail stores are from make-to-stock operations. While most services, such as **Sue Nails** manicures, cannot be made to stock, some, such as scheduled transportation on **Southwest** airline flights, can.

15-1 APPLYING THE CONCEPT

Level of Customer Involvement

Identify each product by its level of customer involvement.

A. make-to-stock

B. assemble-to-order

C. make-to-order

_____ 1. Chocolate ice cream in a sugar cone at Helen's Homemade Ice Cream

_____ 2. TheaterSeat Store chairs with subwoofer speakers

_____ 3. UPS delivers a package from Walmart to a customer

_____ 4. A Dell laptop at a Best Buy store

_____ 5. A massage at Cannon Ranch Resort & Spa

_____ 6. A bag of Smart Food popcorn by Frito-Lay

Assemble-to-Order (ATO) Operations. *Assemble-to-order operations* produce a standard product with some customized features. Some services and goods, such as those built with optional features, can be produced only after the receipt of an order. Therefore, there is a moderate level of customer involvement. Relatively expensive goods, such as Honda automobiles, **IBM** mainframe computer systems, and **Berkline Furniture**, are commonly assembled to order. Services can also be assembled to order. Standard training consulting packages and accounting and legal services can be customized to fit the needs of an organization.

Make-to-Order (MTO) Operations. *Make-to-order operations* are carried out only after an order has been received from a specific customer. Here, there is a high level of customer involvement. Many services, such as **Goodyear** auto repair and **Mercy Medical Center** services, have to be made to order. Some goods, such as **Hong Kong Grand** custom clothing and **Dell** computers, are also made to order. Recall **PillPack** combining multiple prescription drugs in separate wrappers printed with the date and time to take them.[21]

Some companies provide a mixture of customer involvement, including **General Motors (GM)** making cars to stock and custom orders and **Mars** making stock candy and printing custom sayings on its M&M's.

Operations Flexibility

Operations flexibility *refers to the amount of variety in the products an operation produces, which determines whether the products are produced continuously, repetitively, in batches, or individually.* Flexibility is based on product volume (how many units of one product are produced) and variety (how many different products the operation produces). The trend is toward more flexible manufacturing to allow customization.[22]

Continuous Process Operations (CPO). Continuous process operations produce outputs that are not in discrete units, such as **National Grid** electricity and **Exxon** gas sold at a service station. CPOs have little to no variety, and high-volume, continuous process operations are the least flexible of the operations systems. Therefore, they are used for MTS goods.

Repetitive Process Operations (RPO). *Repetitive process operations* (RPOs) produce outputs in an assembly line structure, having each unit follow the same path, such as **Chrysler** automobiles. All kinds of consumer and industrial goods are RPO outputs. Some services can also be assembly line oriented, such as a **Jiffy Lube** automatic car wash. RPOs are primarily used for MTS or ATO goods.

operations flexibility The amount of variety in the products an operation produces, which determines whether products are produced continuously, repetitively, in batches, or individually.

15-2 APPLYING THE CONCEPT

Flexibility of Operations

Identify the operations system that would be used to produce each product.

A. Continuous process operations (CPO)

B. Repetitive process operations (RPO)

C. Batch process operations (BPO)

D. Individual process operations (IPO)

E. Project process operations (PPO)

_____ 7. A Maytag washing machine built in the United States

_____ 8. A swimming pool installed by Teddy Bear Pools

_____ 9. The asphalt delivered for the driveway at a new house

_____ 10. Packages of Kirkland white, whole wheat, and rye breads

_____ 11. The library replacement Learning Commons built at Springfield College

Batch Process Operations (BPO). *Batch process operations* (BPOs) produce different outputs with the same resources, such as a **Maytag** stove being used to cook and bake all kinds of different products and **Johnson CPA** providing a variety of accounting services. **Fine** wood furniture maker uses the same people and machines to make dining room tables and chairs, desks, and bedroom dressers. Batch process operations are primarily used for MTS or ATO goods.

Individual Process Operations (IPO). *Individual process operations* (IPOs) produce outputs to customer specifications, just as **Thompson Graphic Design** does. They have high variety and low volume and so are used for MTO goods and services. In manufacturing, IPOs are known as *job shops.* Used by service organizations like **Bay State Medical** health care, IPOs have the most flexibility.

Project Process Operations (PPO). *Project process operations* (PPOs) have low volume and high variety. Commonly completed by sending the resources to the customer's site rather than working on the project at the seller's facilities, PPOs are used, for example, in the general contracting and construction industry by **Chapdelaine & Sons** builders and remodelers of fine homes. Consulting services often blend individual process with project process operations: A client gives the consultant a project to complete, and the work may be divided between the two sites, like building a website.

Resources and Technology Management

Recall that **technology** *is the process used to transform inputs into outputs.* So technology affects the way your firm operates.[23] Important operations decisions concerning the management of resources and technology include how labor and capital intensive the operations to make the product will be and how the customer will be served.

Intensity. In *capital-intensive operations,* machines do most of the work. Manufacturing companies that use continuous and repetitive operations processes (such as utilities, refineries converting oil into gasoline, and steel companies) are generally capital intensive. These companies tend to use high levels of technology.

In *labor-intensive operations,* human resources do most of the work. Organizations that use individual process operations tend to be labor intensive. Education and consulting, as well as personal services such as haircutting, auto repair, accounting, and legal services, tend to be very labor intensive. Due to the lower cost of labor in developing economies, many firms have their products manufactured overseas,[24] such as most **Apple** iPhones being made in China.

Some manufacturing firms use a *balance of capital and labor* in batch and individual process operations, because it takes skilled workers to use flexible machines. So a balance is in the middle of the continuum between capital and labor intensity.

technology The process used to transform inputs into outputs.

With the increasing costs of labor, largely due to the increasing minimum wage, and lowering cost of technology, companies are replacing workers with technology. You most likely have seen or used machines that dispense drinks at **KFC**, or the iPad that takes your order and payment at **Chili's** and **Applebee's**.[25] **McDonald's**, **Panera Bread**, and others are in the process of converting stores to include computerized kiosks to take your order and pay for your meals, as well as customize your orders.[26]

Ways of Serving Customers. Customers can be served by people, machines, or both. **Bank of America** provides service via tellers, automated teller machines, the Internet, and the telephone. Another consideration is where customers will be served. Today, some banks will send a loan officer to your home or office to take a mortgage loan application; others will do it over the phone and Internet. **Ford**, like many businesses, relies on intermediaries—a network of dealers—to serve and sell to customers.

Multiple Classifications

Exhibit 15-2 shows the four criteria for classifying operations systems. Notice that the focus on the left side of the exhibit is on manufacturing goods, while the focus on the right side is on providing services. However, it is not always easy to classify an organization's operations system, either because it falls at some intermediate point on the continuum or because it encompasses more than one type of operation.

Self-checkout machines are an example of automation that replaces labor costs.

EXHIBIT 15-2	CLASSIFYING OPERATIONS SYSTEMS

Tangibility of Products

Tangible ←――――――――――――――――――――――――→ Intangible

| Goods | Mixed Products | Services |

Level of Customer Involvement

Low ←――――――――――――――――――――――――→ High

| Make-to-Stock | Assemble-to-Order | Make-to-Order |

Operations Flexibility

Inflexible–high volume, low variety ←――――――――――――――――――――――――→ Flexible–high variety, low volume

| Continuous Process Operations | Repetitive Process Operations | Batch Process Operations | Individual and Project Process Operations |

Resources and Technology Management

Developers and users of technology— higher level of technology commonly used   Users of technology— lower level of technology commonly used

Capital-Intensive ←――――― Balanced Intensive ―――――→ Labor-Intensive

Frito-Lay (IOM 1) offers tangible goods produced through MTS operations. It uses a repetitive process for its high-volume products and a batch process for its lower-volume products. A batch process is also used for different-sized portions of the same product. Frito-Lay's resources are balanced in intensity, as its manufacturing plants and trucks are expensive, but it also has thousands of well-paid employees delivering the snacks. Customer service is important, and that is why Frito-Lay makes frequent deliveries and stocks shelves for store customers.

LO 15-3

Explain the four facility layouts in terms of their level of customer involvement and flexibility, and give an example of the type of industry that would use each of the four facility layouts.

Designing Operations Systems

Recall the importance of managing resources.[27] No matter what type and size of business you manage, you have to select products and design them, organize your operations facility layout to make your products, and select an operations facility location and how much product to produce (capacity). These are the operations design decisions we discuss in this section.

Product Mix and Design

Based on the organization's mission and objectives, top-level managers select the product mix and diversification.[28] The *product mix* includes the number of product lines, the number of products offered within each line, and the mixture of goods and services within each line. **Coca-Cola** has been criticized for failing to diversify away from a few core products, as sales have fallen in recent years as more people are replacing sugary drinks with water.[29] **Gap** can't figure out what shoppers want to wear.[30]

WORK
APPLICATION 15-2

Using Exhibit 15-2, identify the operations system where you work or have worked based on product tangibility, customer involvement, flexibility, and resources.

Amazon sells at least 1,800 products.[31] Ever heard of **Heinz** 57 varieties? Heinz acquired Kraft to expand its food product mix, and 98% of U.S. homes have a least one of its products.[32] **Jay-Z** expanded beyond rapping to start record companies, clothing companies, nightclubs, **National Basketball Association (NBA)** basketball teams, and more recently **Roc Nation** and **Tidal**.[33]

But not all increases to product mix are successful. **Microsoft** missed the opportunity to crack the mobile software market despite spending billions, and decided to acquire hardware **Nokia**'s handset business for $9.4 billion, which was unsuccessful as it wrote off a loss of $7.6 billion.[34] **McDonald's** started in 1948 with 9 menu items, and the number increased to 121 in 2014, but sales are down and service is slower, so it is cutting back.[35] It made the strategic decision to stop chasing healthier customers and focus on improving the quality of its food to retain existing customers and regain lapsed ones.[36]

Product design refers to new or improved product development. Manufacturing and design drive each other. If you lose one, you lose the other.[37] So let's now focus on design.

Quality Is a Virtue of Design. The throughput stages, shown in Exhibit 15-3, must be well coordinated and controlled, because well-designed, high-quality products tend to be more profitable.[38] As you can see, the first stage is to design the product. **Genichi Taguchi** advocated designing quality into each product. Hence, he emphasized quality as a virtue of design. "*Quality is a virtue of design*" means that if products are well designed, there will be fewer operations problems, the product will be easier to sell, and servicing the product will be less costly—less damage control through recalls to fix problems.

EXHIBIT 15-3	THROUGHPUT STAGES

Keurig Green Mountain recalled 7.2 million coffee machines after about 90 injuries from users being sprayed with scalding hot water.[39] Even though **Apple** is well known for its designs, it too has problems. Within hours of a new release, couriers start bringing defective returns from Apple's retail stores to headquarters so a team of engineers can quickly fix problems.[40]

Balancing Time-Based Competition and Design. Speed and agility are buzzwords, especially at **Amazon**, **Facebook**, and **Google**.[41] *Time-based competition refers* to the use of strategies to increase the speed with which an organization goes from creativity to delivery. The time required to complete this process is called throughput time (Exhibit 15-3). With globalization, the speed of competition has increased, and the winners are the companies that adapt the fastest.

Being first to market gives a competitive advantage,[42] and while companies need to increase innovation and speed products to market, they also need to have quality products to succeed. Many companies are now differentiating between development speed and launching speed, and both need to be done correctly for the company to succeed.[43] Rushing through the design process can lead to operations problems that can't be easily fixed. **Honda** had recalls and said it had been introducing models too quickly.[44]

Samsung rushed its Galaxy Note 7 to beat the new **Apple** iPhone but made a costly mistake.[45] The Note 7 burst into flames, leading to its recall and then discontinuation that led to its mobile division's profits plunging 96% from a year earlier.[46] The Note 7 eventually cost Samsung more than $6 billion and its global lead in smartphone sales.[47] Samsung and Apple are actually frenemies, as Samsung is a manufacturer, whereas Apple uses contract manufacturers, so some iPhones have Samsung computer chips.[48]

Facility Layout

Your operations should be designed to achieve your objectives.[49] *Facilities* are the physical resources used in the operations process. The building, machines, furniture, and so on are part of the facility. **Facility layout** *refers to the spatial arrangement of physical resources relative to each other.* The type of facility layout selected is based on the classification of the operations system and the product design.

- With *product layout*, the product must follow a set assembly-line sequence to be produced.

- In contrast, with a *process layout* in a retail store, you don't have to go up and down every aisle; you can just go to the one department that has what you want to buy.

- The idea behind *cellular layout* is to place things around you so you can easily get to them. Think of your kitchen. Would you want your sink, stove, fridge, counter, and cabinets all in an assembly-line layout rather than a circular one? Operations in a restaurant include food preparation that takes place in the kitchen, not the dining area. Office work areas, especially with *L*-shaped desks, tend to be cellular layouts so employees don't have to waste time by constantly getting up to go get things.

- With *fixed-position* layout, you have to go to the customer to do the work—you can't say, "Bring your lawn over, and I will mow it."

Exhibit 15-4 compares the four types of layouts with respect to their level of customer involvement and flexibility of operations, notes businesses that tend to use this layout, and provides an illustration of each systems process.

Facility Location and Capacity Planning

Location is the physical geographic site of facilities. The facility location must be determined based on the classification of the operations system and the organization's product mix, layout requirements, and capacity planning. Major factors that are considered when making the location decision include cost; proximity to inputs, customers, and/or competitors; availability of transportation; access to human resources; and number of facilities.

facility layout The spatial arrangement of physical resources relative to each other—operations use product, process, cellular, or fixed-position layouts.

EXHIBIT 15-4 FACILITY LAYOUT

Product layout is associated with make-to-stock (MTS) and assemble-to-order (ATO) levels of customer involvement and relatively inflexible repetitive process operations (RPO) or continuous process operations (CPO). Product layout is commonly used in all types of assembly-line manufacturing businesses.

Process, or functional, layout is associated with a make-to-order (MTO) level of customer involvement and flexible individual process operations (IPO). Process layout is commonly used in retail and health care businesses offering multiple products.

Cellular layout is associated with MTS and ATO levels of customer involvement and relatively flexible batch process operations (BPO). Cellular layout is commonly used in restaurant food preparation businesses and all types of office work areas.

Fixed-position layout is associated with MTO and ATO levels of customer involvement and flexible project process operations (PPO). Fixed-position layout is commonly used in construction-type industries in which the business must go to the customer.

Facility location selection is critical, but with so many factors to weigh, it often goes wrong.[50] **General Mills** and **Pillsbury** are both located in Minneapolis, Minnesota, where they can get easy access to grains for processing into their products. Coming out of liquidation, **Hostess** snacks streamlined production by paring the number of bakeries and increasing warehouses in strategic locations and upgrading them with larger ovens and robots that pack Twinkies into boxes.[51] The Chinese **Zhejiang Geely Holdings**–owned Swedish **Volvo** subsidiary will start making cars in the United States in 2018.[52] **Amazon** has fast product delivery with 123 fulfillment centers worldwide.[53]

Another part of the facility decision is capacity planning. **Capacity** *is the amount of products an organization can produce.* How many rooms should a **Holiday Inn** build? Should an **Outback** restaurant have 50 or 100 tables, and what capacity should the **BMW** 3 Series have?

It's a balancing act. On a weekend night and during a period of economic growth, you don't want to lose business, but you don't want empty tables weekdays and production lines idle during slow economic times. Automakers, including **GM** and **Toyota**, tend to have overcapacity even in China,[54] **Walt Disney Parks** is working on ways to spread out attendance

WORK
APPLICATION 15-3

Identify the facility layout used where you work or have worked. Draw the physical arrangement of the facilities.

capacity The amount of products an organization can produce.

15-3 APPLYING THE CONCEPT

Facility Layout

Identify the facility layout that would be used to produce each product.

A. product

B. process

C. cellular

D. fixed-position

____ 12. A man walks into a Target store to buy some t-shirts.

____ 13. Meals being made at TGI Fridays restaurants

____ 14. A Camaro car being built in a GM plant

____ 15. A lawn being cut by A&M Landscaping

____ 16. A woman comes to Yale Hospital to have an operation.

throughout the year so it can accommodate demand and avoid bursting at the seams. For the first time in 60 years, it is considering charging different prices when it is busier and slower.[55]

Frito-Lay (**IOM 2**) has expanded its convenience-food product mix in recent years. It is also focusing on health and wellness by making snacks with less fat, sugar, sodium, and calories. It has removed trans fats from its products and is offering baked versions of multiple products. Frito-Lay uses product and cellular layouts to make the snacks, and it has around 30 facility locations in the United States, with flexible capacity to meet fluctuating demand and optimize production and distribution.

Managing Operations Systems and the Supply Chain

After internal operations systems have been designed to align with the external environments,[56] they must be managed efficiently and effectively for success.[57] The principles of organization (Chapter 7) must be used. In this section, we discuss planning schedules and project management, inventory control, materials requirement planning, supply chain management, and quality control.

LO 15-4

Describe the three planning schedules, supply chain management, and quality control.

Planning Schedules and Project Management

Using visual project management scheduling tools is important, as we remember what we see better than what we hear.[58] So here we discuss scheduling and three techniques—the planning sheet, the Gantt chart, and the PERT network—which are often designed for specific projects.

15-1 JOIN THE DISCUSSION ETHICS & SOCIAL RESPONSIBILITY

Factory Conditions

Many companies in the past, including **Gap**, have been criticized for not monitoring factory conditions. To address the criticism, the firm set standards for its manufacturers and developed a thorough factory inspecting system. Gap's vendor compliance officers (VCOs) inspect factories around the world and check compliance with Gap factory standards. These standards include suppliers not employing anyone under the age of 14 and factories not permitting physical or nonphysical abuse. Gap will terminate its business relationship or require the factory to implement a corrective action plan if this code is violated. In

fact, since 2003, Gap has closed some 200 factories due to persistent or severe violations of standards.

1. Is it ethical and socially responsible for Gap to revoke contracts, causing poor workers to lose their jobs?

2. Is it ethical and socially responsible to Gap's stockholders to pay higher labor costs than necessary, thus possibly reducing profits and their dividends?

Source: Information taken from the Gap Inc. website at http://www.gap.com, accessed July 15, 2015.

Priority scheduling increases efficiency by evaluating the sequence in which products will be produced and making adjustments as necessary.

routing The path and sequence of the transformation of a product into an output.

priority scheduling The continuing evaluation and reordering of the sequence in which products will be produced.

planning sheet A scheduling tool that states an objective and lists the sequence of activities required to meet the objective, when each activity will begin and end, and who will complete each activity.

Scheduling. *Scheduling* is the process of listing activities that must be performed to accomplish an objective; the activities are listed in sequence, along with the time needed to complete each one. Scheduling answers the planning questions: "Which employees will make which products?" "When, how, and where will they be produced?" "How many of each will be produced?"

An important part of scheduling is routing. **Routing** *is the path and sequence of the transformation of a product into an output.* UPS developed routing software that it calls Orion to shave miles off of drivers' delivery routes and expects annual savings of $300 million to $400 million.[59]

Priority scheduling *is the continuing evaluation and reordering of the sequence in which products will be produced.* The method of priority scheduling depends on the layout used. Three simple methods are used to schedule operations:

- First come–first served. Jobs are scheduled in the order in which they are received. This method is common in service organizations.
- Earliest due date. The job with the earliest promised delivery date is scheduled first.
- Shortest operating time. Jobs that take the least amount of time are scheduled first.

Many organizations use a combination of the three methods.

The Planning Sheet. Planning sheets state an objective and list the sequence of activities required to meet the objective, when each activity will begin and end, and who will complete each activity. The planning sheet in Exhibit 15-5 shows the transformation process for a monthly marketing letter, which is mailed to 300 potential customers. It is commonly used with simple, singular tasks to be accomplished.

EXHIBIT 15-5   PLANNING SHEET

Objective: To mail a personalized form letter to all target clients by the 15th of each month.

Responsible: Latoya/Joel | **Starting date:** 1st of each month

Due date: 15th of each month | Priority: High

Control checkpoints: 7th and 12th of each month

Activities	Start		End	Who
1. Type letter on computer.	1st		2nd	Latoya
2. Deliver letter to printer.	3rd	or	4th	Joel
3. Print letters on company stationery.	5th		6th	printer
4. Pick up letters at printer.	6th	or	7th	Joel
5. Use mail merge to type names and addresses on letters and envelopes.	7th		9th	Joel
6. Sign each letter.	9th	or	10th	Latoya
7. Fold each letter and put in an envelope.	10th		11th	Joel
8. Bundle letters to meet bulk mailing specifications.	12th		13th	Joel
9. Deliver to U.S. Postal Bulk Mail Center.	13th			Joel
10. Mail letters.	14th	or	15th	U.S. Mail

EXHIBIT 15-6   GANTT CHART (ORDERS BY WEEK)

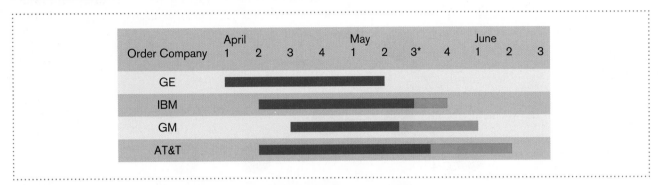

Order Company	April 1	2	3	4	May 1	2	3*	4	June 1	2	3
GE											
IBM											
GM											
AT&T											

Gantt Chart. Gantt charts *use bars to graphically illustrate a schedule and progress toward the objective over a period.* The different activities to be performed are usually listed vertically, with time shown horizontally. The resources to be allocated, such as people or machines, are also commonly shown on the vertical axis. Gantt charts, like planning sheets, are appropriate when independent sequential steps are needed to accomplish the objective. The Gantt chart has an advantage over the planning sheet in that it places progress toward the objective on the chart as a control technique.

Another important advantage of the Gantt chart over the planning sheet (and PERT, discussed in what follows) is that it can show multiple projects on one chart. This helps in prioritizing and scheduling project activities that use the same resources.

Exhibit 15-6 illustrates a Gantt chart for multiple orders in an operations department. Each bar extends from the start time to the end time, with the shaded portion indicating the part completed to date. Using the chart, you can see at a glance how orders are progressing. If you become aware that a project is behind schedule, you can take corrective action to get it back on schedule. If today is day 1 of week 3 in May, the end of the shaded portion of the bar will be directly under the second 3 if the project is exactly on schedule. What is the status of each of the four projects on the chart in Exhibit 15-6?

Performance Evaluation and Review Technique (PERT). Multiple activities are considered to be independent when they can be performed simultaneously; they are considered to be dependent when one must be completed before the next activity can begin. Planning sheets and Gantt charts are useful tools when the activities follow each other in a dependent series. However, when some activities are dependent and some are independent, PERT (critical path) is more appropriate. **PERT** *is a network scheduling technique that illustrates the dependence of activities.* Exhibit 15-7 shows a PERT network.

15-4 APPLYING THE CONCEPT

Scheduling Tools

Select the most appropriate scheduling tool for each situation.

A. planning sheet

B. Gantt chart

C. PERT network

_____ 17. You want a tool to schedule the making of five products on three different types of machines.

_____ 18. You want a tool for building a new restaurant.

_____ 19. You want a tool to develop a procedure for a new method of reporting accidents.

_____ 20. You want to use a tool to develop procedures for opening and closing the retail store.

_____ 21. You want to use a tool to schedule training classes in different rooms.

_____ 22. You want to use a tool for building a new submarine.

EXHIBIT 15-7   PERT NETWORK

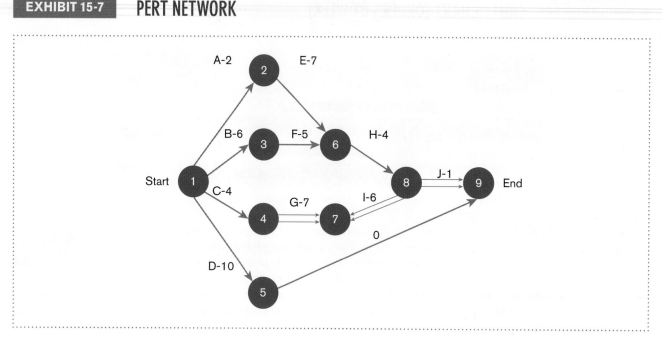

WORK APPLICATION 15-6

Give an example of a project in an organization for which you work or have worked that would be appropriate to schedule using a Gantt chart.

WORK APPLICATION 15-7

Give an example of a project in an organization for which you work or have worked that would be appropriate to schedule using a PERT network.

The key components of PERT are activities, events, times, and the critical path. With complex projects, it is common to have multiple activities represented as one event. For example, in automobile production, building the engine would be an event that requires multiple activities to complete. Time can be measured in a variety of ways (seconds, minutes, hours, days, weeks, months, years, etc.) to determine the critical path. The **critical path** *is the most time-consuming series of activities in a PERT network.* The critical path is important to know because it determines the length of time needed to complete a project. It is shown by the double lines in Exhibit 15-7. Any delay in the steps in the critical path will delay the entire project. The cost of each activity is sometimes shown with the time.

To summarize, planning sheets and Gantt charts are commonly used to develop procedures for routine standing plans, whereas PERT is commonly used for single-use program plans for a complex project with dependent activities. However, all three types of schedules can be used for either standing or single-use plans.

Inventory Control

Based on your product mix, an important question is "How do I know how much of each product I should have in inventory?"[60] **Inventory** *is the stock of materials held for future use.* Thus, inventory is a resource needed to transform inputs into outputs. Inventory control, also called *materials control,* is an important responsibility of the operations manager.

Inventory control *is the process of managing raw materials, work in process, finished goods, and in-transit goods.* Exhibit 15-8 illustrates how inventory control fits into the systems process.

critical path The most time-consuming series of activities in a PERT network.

inventory The stock of materials held for future use.

inventory control The process of managing raw materials, work in process, finished goods, and in-transit goods.

- *Raw Materials.* Raw materials are input materials that have been received but have not yet been transformed in any way by the operations department, such as eggs at a restaurant or steel at an automaker.
- *Work in Process.* Work in process is material that has had some transformation but is not yet an output, such as an egg that is being cooked or a car on the assembly line.
- *Finished Goods.* Finished goods are transformed outputs that have not yet been delivered to customers, such as cooked eggs sitting on a plate waiting to be served to a customer or a car sitting at the factory waiting to be shipped to a dealer.

- *In-Transit (Pipeline) Goods.* In-transit goods are finished goods being delivered to the customer, such as eggs being carried to the table by a server or cars being delivered by truck to the dealer.

It is difficult to balance demand for your products with manufacturing. In 2017, automakers including **Ford**, **Fiat Chrysler**, and **Toyota** continued to make vehicles (*raw material* and *work in process*) even though sales declined, resulting in swelling (*finished goods*) inventory (less *in-transit*), which usually leads to discount prices and lower profit margins to help sales. The average turnover time to sell a car slowed to 70 days.[61]

Retailing and Services Inventory. Retail inventory control, including *purchasing*, is concerned almost exclusively with finished goods for resale as is. **Walmart** is telling its 10,000 suppliers that it wants them to pay for storing their inventory in its warehouses.[62] Some retailers, such as **Amazon** and **L.L. Bean**, with online sales, do have in-transit inventory.

Most service organizations deal only with the finished-goods inventory they create by providing the service. An auto repair shop service like **Goodyear** and **Firestone** will have tires and parts inventory to use in fixing cars. Some services have in-transit inventory—for example, accounting statements and legal documents are often delivered to clients.

Just-in-Time (JIT) Inventory. The objective of inventory control is to have the correct amount of all four types of inventory available when and where they are needed while minimizing waste and the total cost of managing and storing inventory. To accomplish this objective, many organizations now use JIT. **Just-in-time (JIT) inventory** *is a method by which necessary parts and raw materials are delivered shortly before they are needed.* **Toyota** was a pioneer in lean manufacturing, including JIT inventory management.

Materials Requirement Planning (MRP)

In short, it's about production planning to determine the material requirements to meet the production schedule.[63] **Materials requirement planning (MRP)** *is a system that integrates operations and inventory control with complex ordering and scheduling.* MRP involves developing a process for ordering raw materials and components at the right time and in the right quantity so that they arrive shortly before their scheduled transformation into outputs and appropriate work in process is ready as needed. JIT is part of inventory control, which is part of MRP. MRP is becoming more important as retailers are placing smaller orders with less lead time.

MRP is commonly used by firms that have different delivery systems and lead times. **Lockheed Martin**, **Texas Instruments**, and **Westinghouse** all use MRP because they need hundreds of parts in vastly different quantities, with arrival times that vary from hours to

WORK
APPLICATION 15-8

Identify the type of inventory and how it is controlled where you work or have worked.

just-in-time (JIT) inventory A method by which necessary parts and raw materials are delivered shortly before they are needed.

materials requirement planning (MRP) A system that integrates operations and inventory control with complex ordering and scheduling.

EXHIBIT 15-8   **INVENTORY CONTROL WITHIN THE SYSTEMS PROCESS**

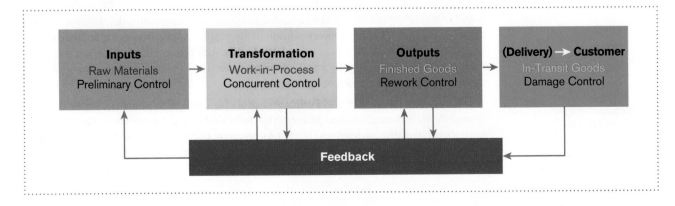

months. Coordinating and controlling such a complex system is virtually impossible for any manager. However, MRP software can manage such a system fairly easily. Today MRP technology can forecast consumer behavior and track inventory both outbound and inbound.[64]

Enterprise Resource Planning (ERP). *Enterprise resource planning* (ERP) takes MRP a step further, as it collects, processes, and provides information about a firm's entire enterprise. Ordering, product design, production, purchasing, inventory, distribution, human resources, receipt of payments, and forecasting of future demand are incorporated into one network system. For example, anyone with access can check the current inventory, a sales rep can enter an order and see what the actual delivery date will be, and an engineer can see how a decision about product design will affect production schedules and resource needs. **SAP** ERP software, as well as software by other companies, makes ERP possible.

Economic Order Quantity (EOQ). The *economic order quantity* (EOQ) is the optimal quantity of a product to order, determined on the basis of a mathematical model. The more often you order, the higher the ordering cost—but if you order less often, your holding cost goes up. By using the EOQ, you can minimize ordering and holding costs without running out of stock. Calculating EOQs is a part of MRP.

Supply Chain Management

Supply chain management (SCM) is now recognized as a key strategic discipline as it has a major impact on every part of every business,[65] and SCM jobs will grow at nearly twice the rate of many other professions.[66] Thus, every business needs to manage its supply chain well.[67] **Supply chain management** *is the process of coordinating all the activities involved in producing a product and delivering it to the customer.* Recall our focus on the importance of relationships. Well, customer relationships and supplier relationships form the critical links in a supply chain.[68] SCM is used to speed up the throughput process to win time-based competition. **Michael Dell**, who started **Dell Computers** in his college dorm room, was a pioneer in creating mass customization by developing innovative global SCM.

To provide high-quality products at the lowest cost, SCM starts with forecasting demand for a product and then moves on to planning and managing supply and demand, acquiring materials, scheduling and producing the product, warehousing, controlling inventory, distributing the product, and delivering it. The final stage involves customer service. SCM focuses heavily on purchasing and inventory control. Raw materials, including component parts, are expensive for many manufacturers. Thus, keeping inventory costs down while ensuring that good-quality materials are available when needed is important in the supply chain.

Federal-Mogul Holdings produces hundreds of thousands of auto parts and spent $100 million to upgrade its supply chain from end to end. It handles 400 million parts annually, so it's much more about distribution and getting those parts where they need to be in half the time. Federal-Mogul moved the entire company onto **SAP** SE enterprise software internally while using a combination of computer software to build a customer website. It opened additional warehouses with robotic systems that allow it to have all its products in one location using 100,000 square feet that used to take 400,000 square feet in multiple locations.[69]

Supply Chain Management Services. With the growth in online sales, deliveries are on the increase, and managing the delivery portion of the supply chain is becoming an increasingly important part of doing business using **UPS**, **FedEx**, **USPS**, and others to deliver packages. **Amazon** is working to drop UPS and others by delivering its packages to customers as part of its plan to take direct control of global shipping.[70]

When you think of **UPS** and **FedEx**, you probably think of shipping packages. But they provide services throughout the entire supply chain to businesses of all sizes, especially small firms, focusing mainly on logistics.[71] UPS is focusing more on its profitable SCM services. With its trademarked slogan "United Problem Solvers," UPS will help any size business throughout the supply chain from figuring it out to getting it done.[72]

supply chain management The process of coordinating all the activities involved in producing a product and delivering it to the customer.

Strategic Cloud Supply Chains. Rather than build and maintain in-house IT portals, firms now use cloud-based *third-party logistics providers (3PLS)*, such as **GT Nexus**. This software-as-a-service technology plugs suppliers, distributors, and customers into a single platform in cyberspace. These complex global networks read market signals in real time, pivot swiftly, and implement design changes that reflect what works now, not last year or quarter. GT Nexus has 27,000 customers including **Levi's** and **Columbia Sportswear**. **Adidas** uses its platform to fulfill individual orders for custom-made sneakers, and **Caterpillar** cut costs by $150 million by purging inefficiencies and shaved three days off its production cycle.[73]

The field of SCM has a professional association: the Council of Supply Chain Management Professionals (CSCMP). To learn more about SCM and the CSCMP, visit www.cscmp.org.

Radio-Frequency Identification (RFID) Technology. *Radio-frequency identification (RFID)* is an automatic identification method, relying on storing and remotely retrieving data using devices called RFID tags. An RFID tag is an object that can be stuck on or incorporated into a product, animal, or person for the purpose of identification using radio waves. These tags are so small they can be placed anywhere, even in paper. RFID is used in SCM to improve the efficiency of inventory tracking and management. RFIDs have changed how fashion retail chain **Zara** operates its stores. Zara uses RFID to keep better track of its stock and replenish its clothing racks more quickly, as it gives management greater visibility, knowing exactly where each garment is located.[74]

Frito-Lay (**IOM 3**) plans and schedules the production and delivery of its products. Its raw materials include tons of potatoes, corn, cheese, and many other ingredients, which it buys on a JIT basis from suppliers to make the products (work in process and finished goods inventory) that are shipped to customers. It offers JIT inventory to most of its customers, as it restocks shelves frequently so that many customers carry no stored inventory at all—it's all on the shelves. Within its SCM program, Frito-Lay uses ERP to integrate all its business-to-business (B2B) and electronic data interchange (EDI) activities with those of suppliers and customers. When products are delivered and sold, data are sent in real time so that supply, production, and inventory information can be adjusted quickly for effective inventory control.

Quality Control

Companies work hard to develop and maintain a quality image,[75] as many of the most profitable firms focus on quality status products with higher prices,[76] such as **Apple**. **Quality control** *is the process of ensuring that all types of inventory meet standards.* As you can tell by the definition, quality control and inventory control overlap. The top row in Exhibit 15-8 shows the systems process steps, the second row shows the four inventory stages, and the third row shows the four types of quality control. Quality control is just as important for goods as it is for services; it applies to the scrambled eggs in a **Denny's** restaurant as well as to the **M3** car produced by **BMW**.

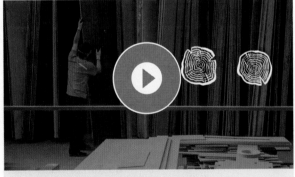

MANAGEMENT IN ACTION
Supply Chain Management

W. Edwards Deming. After being rejected by American companies that didn't see the need to increase quality, in the 1950s, W. Edwards Deming went to Japan to teach quality and is credited with being instrumental in turning Japanese industry into an economic world power. In fact, the highest Japanese award for quality is the *Deming Prize*. Deming said that improving quality would automatically improve productivity and called for a focus on customer value and continuous improvement. He directed managers' attention to the fact that most quality problems—up to 90%—are not the fault of employees; rather, the system is to blame. Deming developed the world-famous 14 points to improve quality, which are still

quality control The process of ensuring that all types of inventory meet standards.

implemented worldwide today. For more information and his 14 points, visit the **Deming Institute**, which he founded, at https://deming.org.

The 80–20 Rule. Joseph Juran stated that 20% of the reasons for out-of-control performance cause 80% of the quality problems. He called this the **Pareto principle**, more commonly known as the 80–20 rule. When performance is out of control, first look at the usual "vital few" reasons (20%), and most of the time (80%) they will have a standing-plan solution. Have you ever noticed how manufacturers commonly have a place in the product manual for troubleshooting that says, "If you have a problem, try 1, 2, 3, 4"?

Quality Assurance. *Quality assurance* requires that you "build in" quality; you cannot "inspect it in." As emphasized by **Genichi Taguchi**, recall that quality is a virtue of design, and from Chapter 14 remember that the quality focus should be on preliminary and concurrent control, not rework and damage control. **Philip B. Crosby** popularized the concepts "quality is free," "do it right the first time," and "zero defects" in the late 1970s. Crosby believed that it was possible and necessary to measure the costs of poor quality in order to combat the notion that quality was expensive.

The High Cost of Poor Quality and Errors. Businesses need to prevent quality problems, because errors can be very expensive.[77] **BP** failed to fix known quality problems that resulted in deaths in the *Deepwater Horizon* disaster. BP deferred repairs that were a critical factor in the Gulf of Mexico explosion. BP may have saved money by skimping on quality repairs, but it wasn't worth it. Rather than spend possibly thousands to prevent the accident, BP paid $18.7 billion in penalties to the U.S. government, and the total cost was around $54 billion. The cost exceeds all the profits it has earned since 2012.[78]

Japanese **Takata** Corp. supplied faulty airbags that killed 11 people and injured roughly 180 others in the United States.[79] There are an estimated 64 million vehicles with faulty Takata airbags in at least 18 models, resulting in the largest and longest recall in U.S. history.[80] Takata pleaded guilty to providing misleading test reports and will pay $1 billion. In addition, law firm **Motley Rice** is representing clients in a class-action lawsuit against Takata.[81] Takata went bankrupt, with 65% of the airbags not replaced.[82]

You Get What You Reward. Although not a total quality management (TQM) guru, **Steven Kerr** contributed indirectly to TQM by popularizing the idea that "you get what you reward." In other words, if you want people to do a quality job, you have to develop a system that really rewards employees for doing a quality job and punishes those who don't (reinforcement theory, Chapter 11). Based on past quality problems at **GM** that were essentially ignored, resulting in costly litigation, the new **CEO Mary Barra** fired at least seven high-level executives and 15 others, and Barra is changing the culture to place a greater focus on rewarding quality assurance.[83]

Customer Quality Service Control. Exhibit 15-9 lists five rules that will help ensure quality customer service. If you follow these rules, you will increase your chances of developing effective human relations skills and ensuring a high-quality product for your customers. And remember that everyone you deal with is a customer—yes, even the jerks you work with.

Total Quality Management (TQM). As defined in Chapter 2, *total quality management (TQM)* is the process that involves everyone in an organization focusing on the customer to continually improve product value. The four major TQM principles are (1) focus on delivering customer value, (2) continually improve systems and processes, (3) focus on managing processes rather than people, and (4) use teams to continually improve. Even small improvements to old products can lead to much bigger breakthroughs.[84]

TQM is much broader in scope than quality control because part of its core value is to make it the job of everyone in the organization to improve quality. Under quality control, the operations department is solely responsible for setting and accepting or rejecting a product's quality.

EXHIBIT 15-9	FIVE RULES OF CUSTOMER HUMAN RELATIONS

1. Put people before things.
2. Always be nice—no matter how busy you are.
3. Take your time with people.
4. Be polite; say "please," "thank you," and "you're welcome."
5. Don't discriminate with your service (treat everyone well).

The International Organization for Standardization (ISO). The **International Organization for Standardization (ISO)** *certifies firms that meet set quality standards.* Both manufacturing and service businesses can apply for ISO certification to improve their management systems and operational control. JIT and TQM are part of ISO 9000 certification, as organizations must document policies that address quality management, continuous improvement, and customer satisfaction. Most multinational corporations have ISO 9000 certification, and they require the suppliers they do business with to be certified in order to ensure the quality of materials used. For more information on ISO 9000 and other certifications, visit www.iso.org.

American Society for Quality (ASQ). The American Society for Quality (ASQ) is the global voice of quality, as it is a community of people passionate about quality who use their ideas and expertise to make our world work better. Like ISO certifying companies, ASQ certifies people as quality professionals. *ASQ certification* is a formal recognition by ASQ that an individual has demonstrated a proficiency within and comprehension of a specific body of knowledge. For more information on ASQ, visit www.asq.org.

WORK
APPLICATION 15-9

Explain quality control in an organization where you work or have worked.

WORK
APPLICATION 15-10

Are any of the gurus' quality contributions used where you work or have worked? Explain how.

Six Sigma. Six Sigma is used to eliminate defects/errors. It is a concurrent control with the goal of having 99.99966% of deviations corrected before they result in defects in final product outputs, or it shoots for only 3.4 defects or mistakes per million operations. *Sigma* is a letter from the Greek alphabet used to represent a statistical measure of deviations from a standard, so it is a statistical measure, not a number of rules to follow.[85] Six Sigma enforces process standardization and efficiency improvement throughout a firm. It can reduce costs, rejects, lead times, and capital spending while raising employee skill levels and strengthening overall financial results.[86] **Motorola** invented Six Sigma in 1987, and **GE** popularized it in the 1990s. But Six Sigma is not just for manufacturing.[87] The financial industry, including **MassMutual Insurance** and **Bank of America**, uses it to process millions of error-free financial transactions.

The money saved by skimping on quality control can be very costly and can damage a company's reputation in both the short and long term. It can even be harmful to employees and customers.

Statistical Quality Control. *Statistical quality control* is a management science technique that uses a variety of statistical tests based on probability to improve the quality of decision making. The most common test is statistical process control, a standard TQM technique that is part of Six Sigma. *Statistical process control (SPC)* aids in determining whether quality is within an acceptable standard range. It is called a process control because it is concurrent; quality is measured and corrected during the transformation process.

An example of an SPC chart for 16-ounce bags of Lay's Potato Chips is shown in Exhibit 15-10. As long as the bags of chips weigh between 15.80 and 16.20 ounces, the machine continues to produce them. However, if the measured weight goes out of this range, as it did at 10:00, the machine stops and is adjusted so as to produce the desired mean weight of 16 ounces, as shown at 10:30.

International Organization for Standardization (ISO) An organization that certifies firms that meet set quality standards.

JOIN THE DISCUSSION ETHICS & SOCIAL RESPONSIBILITY

Social Accountability International

Social Accountability International, or SAI (www.sa-intl.org), is a U.S.-based nonprofit organization dedicated to the development, implementation, and oversight of voluntary verifiable social accountability standards. SAI works to improve workplaces and combat sweatshops through the expansion and further development of the current international workplace standards. SAI gets key stakeholders to develop consensus-based voluntary standards and promotes understanding and implementation of standards worldwide. Like ISO 9000 certification, SA8000 certification verifies compliance of qualified organizations with international workplace standards.

1. Should global multinationals eliminate sweatshops by having SA8000-certified facilities?

2. Should global multinationals require all their suppliers to get SA8000 certification?

3. How might working toward SA8000 certification affect cost, revenues, and profits?

Frito-Lay (IOM 4) is very concerned about the quality of its products. It uses TQM to make sure that all of its ingredients (potatoes, corn, cheese, etc.) are of consistent quality and uniformly combined in its manufacturing plants so that each product always tastes the same. Packing supplies are also important so that products remain fresh until the expiration date on the package. Frito-Lay is ISO 9000 certified and requires its manufacturing suppliers to be certified, too. As illustrated in Exhibit 15-10, Frito-Lay uses SPC to ensure quality.

LO 15-5

Recall how to measure productivity and list three ways to increase it.

Productivity and the Balanced Scorecard

Recall the need for speed to compete,[88] as change continues hitting faster,[89] the reality is that large company bureaucracy is actually slowing down most business activities, such as decision making, hiring, and the time it takes to make a sale.[90] So much to do, so little time—how is your personal productivity?[91] Yes, productivity can be increased.[92] Today, productivity hinges less on physical stamina and more on emotional health,[93] so productivity isn't about how many hours you work; it's more about how mentally alert and focused you are when working.[94]

EXHIBIT 15-10   ## STATISTICAL PROCESS CONTROL CHART FOR 16-OUNCE BAGS OF LAY'S POTATO CHIPS

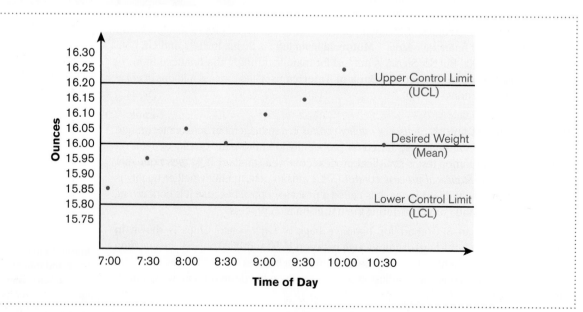

Do you believe smartphones have increased productivity? Although people are busier, in general, smartphones have done nothing to improve productivity.[95] Phones are often a distraction keeping you from getting your work done. Recall from Chapter 5 that multitasking, or doing two or more thinking tasks simultaneously, actually decreases your productivity level.[96]

As a manager, you need to understand how to measure and increase productivity, because what gets measured gets done.[97] In this section, we discuss how productivity affects wages and the standard of living, measuring and increasing productivity, and the balanced scorecard that is a method of increasing productivity.

How Productivity Affects Wages and the Standard of Living

Employees would like to get paid more. However, if they are paid more without producing more, a company must cut costs and/or raise product prices to offset the additional wage cost in order to maintain profits, which tends to happen when the minimum wage is increased. This causes inflation. Increased productivity drives wage increases and raises living standards.[98] So the only real way to increase our wages and standard of living is to increase productivity.[99]

Some people complain that technology is taking away jobs, but technology has been a net job creator. Historically, technology creates more jobs than are destroyed.[100] What destroys jobs is innovation and productivity.[101] The problem is technology creates winners and losers, and people don't like losing jobs. Companies invest in ways to increase productivity,[102] such as technology to replace employees as wages rise including at fast-food restaurants, including **McDonald's** replacing workers with kiosk machines to take orders and payment. So some people at McDonald's lose their jobs, while jobs are created to design, manufacture, install, and maintain the kiosks. Also, by increasing productivity, prices we pay for our products can be maintained or lowered. On a related idea, some people want to protect American jobs through protectionism, such as embargos, quotas, and tariffs on imports. Sounds good, but research supports that free trade means more job winners than losers. Also, protecting inefficient companies leads to higher costs and product prices.[103]

Unfortunately, productivity was down in early 2015, and the trend has been weak or down[104] since the last recession in 2009.[105] At *Fortune* 500 companies, employment is up, but productivity declined in 2016,[106] or employee costs have actually increased without them getting a raise, which results in making giving raises less possible. The more productive you are for an organization, the more you can get paid. Virtually everyone and every country would like to increase their standard of living, so is it any wonder why increasing productivity is so important on the individual, department, company, and national levels?

Increasing productivity, and therefore producing more goods and/or services, is the best way to increase our wages and standard of living.

Measuring and Increasing Productivity

As stated, if you can't measure it, you can't manage it. Measuring productivity can be complex, but it doesn't have to be. Here is a simple yet realistic approach for you to use on the job.

Calculating Productivity. **Productivity** *is a performance measure relating outputs to inputs.* In other words, productivity is measured by dividing the outputs by the inputs. Suppose a trucking company wants to measure productivity of a delivery. The truck traveled 1,000 miles and used 100 gallons of gas. Its productivity was 10 miles to the gallon:

$$\frac{\text{Output}}{\text{Input}} = \text{Productivity}$$

$$\frac{1{,}000 \text{ miles}}{100 \text{ gallons}} = 10 \text{ mpg}$$

productivity A performance measure relating outputs to inputs.

The inputs can be in a variety of forms. In the preceding example, the inputs were gallons of gas. Inputs could also be labor hours, machine hours, number of workers, the cost of labor, and so on. It is also measured by how much can be produced in an hour of work.[107] So productivity is often referred to as the output per hour of labor.[108]

Following is another fairly simple example, involving measuring the productivity of an accounts payable department:

Step 1. Select a base period, such as an hour, day, week, month, quarter, or year. In this example, we will use a week.

Step 2. Determine how many bills were sent out during that period (outputs). The records show that 800 bills were sent out.

Step 3. Determine the cost of sending out the bills (inputs). Determining cost can become complicated if you include overhead, depreciation, and so forth. In this instance, calculate cost based on direct labor charges for three employees who are each paid $10 per hour. They each worked 40 hours during the week, or a total of 120 hours. The total cost is $10 per hour times 120 hours, or $1,200.

Step 4. Divide the number of outputs (bills) by the inputs (labor costs) to determine the productivity rate of .67 (800 ÷ $1,200 = .67). Performance is usually stated as a ratio (in this case, .67:1) or as a percentage (67%). It can also be stated as a labor cost per unit. To determine the labor cost per unit, reverse the process and divide the input by the output. In this case, it cost $1.50 to send out each bill ($1,200 ÷ 800).

Here are some other methods of measuring productivity. Which company is the most productive when using inputs of number of employees and outputs as annual revenue? Here is a comparison of some of the top companies' revenues per employee calculations: **Netflix** ($2,514,690), **Apple** ($1,969,179), **Google** ($1,228,172), **Microsoft** ($677,570), and **LinkedIn** ($321,700).[109] How does U.S. automakers' productivity compare on profit per vehicle sold? **GM** makes $713 per car, **Fiat Chrysler** $849, and **Ford** $994; in contrast, Japanese **Toyota** makes more than twice as much at $2,132 per vehicle.[110]

Calculating Productivity Percentage Changes. The .67 productivity rate is set as the base standard. The next week, the accounting department again sent out 800 bills, but because of machine problems, concurrent corrective action of having employees work overtime was needed to meet the standard output, at an additional cost of $100. The productivity rate went down to .62 (800 ÷ $1,300). The labor cost per unit went up to $1.63 ($1,300 ÷ 800). To determine the percentage change, use this formula:

$$
\begin{array}{lr}
\text{Current productivity rate} & 62 \\
-\,\text{Base standard productivity rate} & -67 \\
\hline
\text{Change} & 5 \\
\end{array}
$$

There was a 7.46% decrease in productivity. Note that it is not necessary to use the decimals on .67 and .62 in this calculation. Also, when the current productivity rate is less than the standard, there is a decrease in productivity, but it is not necessary to use a negative number.

Production Versus Productivity. It is important to calculate productivity rather than just production output, because it is possible to increase production but decrease productivity, and you can decrease production and have a drop in productivity,[111] as you can lose economies of scale. If the accounts payable department sends out 850 bills (production) but uses 10 hours of overtime to do so (time-and-a-half at $15 per hour × 10 hours = $150), productivity has decreased from .67 to .63 (850 ÷ 1,350). In other words, if you measure only output production and it increases, you can be fooled into thinking you are doing a better job when, in reality, you are doing a worse job.

Productivity Comparisons. Productivity measures are more meaningful when they are compared to other productivity rates. You can compare your department's productivity to that of other organizations and/or departments. This was done in Skill Builder 14-1 (page 491). A productivity rate can also be set as the standard, and you can compare your department's productivity to the standard on an ongoing basis. This is done in Applying the Concept 15-5.

Increasing Productivity. Increasing productivity is about working smarter (using our brains), not simply working harder, and doing more with less. Recall that motivating employees has been shown to increase productivity. As a manager, you should work with your employees to measure productivity and continually increase it.

There are three ways to increase productivity:

1. Increase the value of the outputs but maintain the value of the inputs ($\uparrow O \leftrightarrow I$).
2. Maintain the value of the outputs but decrease the value of the inputs ($\leftrightarrow O \downarrow I$).
3. Increase the value of the outputs but decrease the value of the inputs ($\uparrow O \downarrow I$).

In simple terms, you can reduce labor costs, improve outputs, or both.[112] **Alcoa** got employees to make following proper standard procedures a "*habit*" and streamlined production; costs came down, quality went up, and productivity skyrocketed.[113] **Boeing** and **Airbus** are adding more seats per plane (8 and 9) so that airlines, including **Southwest**, can squeeze more passengers in per flight.[114] **McDonald's** is trimming its menu to speed up service and focusing on efficiency to cut expenses.[115] The more technologically advanced farms and manufacturing become, the fewer people they employ as they continue to increase productivity.

The Balanced Scorecard and Dashboards

Is your organization achieving its mission? If you don't have a quick and accurate answer, then, besides financial measures, you need a balanced scorecard (BSC).[116] Researchers **Robert Kaplan** and **David Norton** concluded that financial measures alone were not sufficient to measure performance; other factors in the new economy were missing from traditional financial reporting.[117] And dashboards can help the organization keep a balanced scorecard.

The Balanced Scorecard. The **balanced scorecard (BSC)** *measures financial, customer service, and internal business performance, as well as learning and growth performance.* All four dimensions of the scorecard are equally important, and results relate to one another through the systems effect. Let's face it—you have to make a profit (financial performance), but without customers (customer service performance), you don't have a business, and without employee development (learning and growth performance) and continuously improving

balanced scorecard (BSC) A management tool that measures financial, customer service, and internal business performance, as well as learning and growth performance.

15-5   APPLYING THE CONCEPT

Measuring Productivity

The standard monthly productivity rate in your department is

Outputs of 6,000 units

$$\frac{\text{Outputs of 6,000 units}}{\text{Inputs of \$9,000 cost}} = .67$$

For the first five months of the year, calculate the current productivity rate and show it as a ratio and a percentage. Also, calculate the percentage productivity change, compared to the standard, stating whether it is an increase or a decrease.

23. January: outputs of 6,200, inputs of $9,000
_____ ratio, _____%, increase/decrease of _____%

24. February: outputs of 6,000, inputs of $9,300
_____ ratio, _____%, increase/decrease of _____%

25. March: outputs of 6,300, inputs of $9,000
_____ ratio, _____%, increase/decrease of _____%

26. April: outputs of 6,300, inputs of $8,800
_____ ratio, _____%, increase/decrease of _____%

27. May: outputs of 5,900, inputs of $9,000
_____ ratio, _____%, increase/decrease of _____%

EXHIBIT 15-11   THE BALANCED SCORECARD

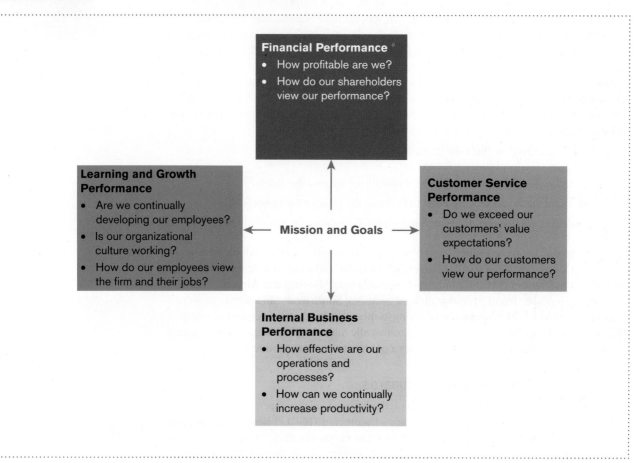

Financial Performance
- How profitable are we?
- How do our shareholders view our performance?

Learning and Growth Performance
- Are we continually developing our employees?
- Is our organizational culture working?
- How do our employees view the firm and their jobs?

Mission and Goals

Customer Service Performance
- Do we exceed our custormers' value expectations?
- How do our customers view our performance?

Internal Business Performance
- How effective are our operations and processes?
- How can we continually increase productivity?

operations (internal business performance), you will not be successful. So you need a multi-measure scorecard. Rather than simply measuring the past, the targets and measures create focus for the future, as the BSC is both a planning and a control method.

If your team is without a BSC, it isn't playing the game; it's only practicing.[118] See Exhibit 15-11 for an overview of the BSC.

As you can see, the BSC plays to the well-known management adage "If you want to manage it, you've got to measure it, and you get what you measure and reinforce."

Dashboards. Digital dashboards can help keep a BSC by monitoring the contribution of the various departments in an organization to measure exactly how well they are performing overall. Dashboards are essentially a visual progress report that measures key performance indicators of objectives or processes and can be used as a tool to increase productivity. Dashboards are usually shown on a web page that is linked to a database, allowing the report to be displayed in real-time.

A manufacturing dashboard can display numbers related to productivity of the number of products and/or parts manufactured and inventories (internal business performance). Frito-Lay is using handheld devices tracking sales at every store (financial performance). Dashboards can administer and report customer satisfaction (customer service performance). HR dashboards can deliver training and track recruitment average days and cost per recruitment (learning and growth performance.[119]

Trends and Issues in Management

It's very challenging to maintain and increase productivity when employees are all over the world.[120] In the *global* economy, using effective operations supply chain resources increases

15-2 SELF-ASSESSMENT

Putting It All Together

For this self-assessment, refer to prior Self-Assessments and Skill Builders; write down a few things you have learned about yourself, focusing on strengths and areas for improvement.

Chapter 1, Self-Assessment 1-1, Management Traits, p. 7

_____

_____

Chapter 2, Self-Assessment 2-1, How Ethical Is Your Behavior? pp. 47–48

_____

_____

Chapter 3, Self-Assessment 3-1, Country of Origin Ownership of Products, p. 70

_____

_____

Chapter 3, Self-Assessment 3-2, Attitudes About Women and Minorities Advancing, p. 81

_____

_____

Chapter 4, Self-Assessment 4-1, Decision-Making Styles, p. 107

_____

_____

Chapter 5, Self-Assessment 5-1, Effective Planning, p. 139

_____

_____

Chapter 5, Self-Assessment 5-2, Time Management Techniques, p. 160

_____

_____

Chapter 6, Self-Assessment 6-1, Entrepreneurial Qualities, p. 191

_____

_____

Chapter 7, Self-Assessment 7-1, Organizational Preference, p. 221

_____

_____

Chapter 7, Self-Assessment 7-2, Personal Priorities, p. 225

_____

_____

Chapter 8, Self-Assessment 8-1, Are You a Team Player?, p. 243

_____

_____

Chapter 8, Skill Builder 8-2, Management Styles in Group Situations, p. 269

_____

_____

Chapter 9, Self-Assessment 9-1, Career Development, p. 287

_____

_____

Chapter 10, Self-Assessment 10-1, Personality Profile, p. 325

_____

_____

Chapter 10, Self-Assessment 10-3, Job Satisfaction, p. 332

_____

_____

Chapter 10, Self-Assessment 10-4, Use of Political Behavior, p. 339

_____

_____

Chapter 10, Self-Assessment 10-5, Personality Type and Stress, p. 350

_____

_____

Chapter 11, Self-Assessment 11-1, What Motivates You?, p. 372

_____

_____

Chapter 11, Self-Assessment 11-2, Acquired Needs, p. 373

_____

_____

Chapter 12, Self-Assessment 12-2, Theory X and Theory Y Leadership Behavior, p. 400

_____

_____

Chapter 13, Self-Assessment 13-1, Listening Skills, p. 441

_____

_____

Chapter 13, Skill Builder 13-4, Analyzing Communication Style, p. 456

_____

_____

Chapter 14, Self-Assessment 14-1, Coaching, p. 479

_____

_____

Based on your review, how can you use this knowledge to help you in your career development?

Develop a plan to apply your self-assessments in both your personal and your professional lives. What specific areas will you work on improving? How will you improve? How will you know if you have improved?

in importance to business success,[121] as increasing productivity is a global issue[122] as logistics 3PL[123] and supply chain management are critical success factors.[124] MNCs will converge on more universal operations standards,[125] as is the goal of the ISO. *Big Data* is improving quality and speed of operations throughout the global supply chain,[126] as it improves inventory, routing, pricing, and staffing productivity.[127] But collecting big data poses *ethical* and *privacy* concerns, as **Bose** is being sued for collecting data on users' music-listening histories from its headphones, and **Genesis Toys** sold a doll that collected recordings of kid's voices.[128]

The future of manufacturing is industrial production equipment (robots), as their cost drops and productivity increases.[129] Americans like to think they are the best at everything, including *technology*, but the U.S. global market share of robots is declining (1995 = 81% vs. 63% in 2015).[130] SCM drones are being developed[131] and used to deliver products,[132] and 3-D printing promises to alter manufacturing.[133] The cloud will continue to grow and drop computer costs,[134] and the Internet of Things (IoT) is projected to grow to 32 billion objects connected by 2020.[135] Will the United States be a leader?

Although technology is important to productivity, don't forget that it's people who develop the technology,[136] and jobs requiring creativity and complex human exchanges are increasing, while those that can be computerized are in decline.[137] Also, even though companies are using algorithmic models for decision making, they generally also use human judgment in the decision making process.[138] Also on the human side, recall that women have been discriminated against in business, but especially in high-tech companies, and they are clearly underrepresented in operations jobs. To increase *diversity*, women are being encouraged to get into the higher-paying operations STEM jobs.

Operations all along the supply chain need to be *ethical* and *socially responsible*. **Anheuser-Bush InBev** tricked Americans into believing that some of its beer, including **Beck's**, was authentic imported German pilsner, when it is really brewed in the United States.[139] **Progress Rail Services** inspectors at railroad cars say they have been pressured to increase business by "green repairs," needlessly replacing parts that work.[140] Would you perform green repairs under pressure? People are now using social media to find plaintiffs for lawsuits, for victims of identity theft, and other unethical and illegal activities.[141]

All types of businesses operations systems are working on *sustainability* but not just because they are altruistic—also because it increases productivity. Decreasing waste benefits everyone. **Amazon** has a North Star program for the minimization of packaging. By making packaging smaller and frustration free to open easily and quickly, time and money are saved by reducing packaging material costs and increasing room on trucks for more packages.[142]

As we bring this chapter to a close, you should understand operations and be able to classify operations systems, know how operations systems are designed, realize how operations and the supply chain are managed, and know how to measure and increase productivity and understand the parts of the balanced scorecard.

Digital Resources

Learning Objective	Digital Resource
15-1. Discuss why operations and products are important, and contrast manufacturing and service operations.	▶ Operations Management

Learning Objective	Digital Resource
15-2. Compare the differences among operations systems with respect to tangibility of products, levels of customer involvement, operations flexibility, and management of resources and technology.	▶ Customer Service
15-3. Explain the four facility layouts in terms of their level of customer involvement and flexibility, and give an example of the type of industry that would use each of the four facility layouts.	▣ Process vs. Product Layout
15-4. Describe the three planning schedules, supply chain management, and quality control.	▶ Management in Action: Supply Chain Management*
15-5. Recall how to measure productivity and list three ways to increase it.	▶ Productivity Measurement*

* premium video available only in the interactive eBook

• • • CHAPTER SUMMARY

15-1. Discuss why operations and products are important, and contrast manufacturing and service operations.

Operations is the function concerned with transforming resource inputs into product outputs. A *product* is a good, a service, or a combination of the two. Operations is important because if a firm doesn't have a good product developed through effective operations that change with the environment, it will not survive. Manufacturing and service operations are similar because they are both used to produce products, but they are also different. *Manufacturing operations* are used to transform inputs into tangible output products, whereas *service operations* use inputs to provide intangible product services, and their transformation is not as clear as with manufactured goods.

15-2. Compare the differences among operations systems with respect to tangibility of products, levels of customer involvement, operations flexibility, and management of resources and technology.

A product can be a tangible good, an intangible service, or a combination of the two. The three levels of customer involvement refer to whether a standard product is made to stock, customer-specific products are made to order, or a standard product with some customized features is assembled to order. Operations flexibility refers to whether the products are produced continuously in nondiscrete units, repetitively on an assembly line for one product, in batches with the same resources used for multiple products, individually to customer specifications at the seller's facilities, or individually over a long time at sites including the customer's facilities. Resources

may be capital intensive (if machines do most of the work), labor intensive (if human resources do most of the work), or a balance of the two.

15-3. Explain the four facility layouts in terms of their level of customer involvement and flexibility, and give an example of the type of industry that would use each of the four facility layouts.

Product layout is associated with make-to-stock and assemble-to-order levels of customer involvement and relatively inflexible repetitive or continuous process operations, and it is commonly used in any manufacturing business. *Process layout* is associated with a make-to-order level of customer involvement and flexible individual process operations, and it is commonly used in retail and health care businesses. *Cellular layout* is associated with make-to-stock and assemble-to-order levels of customer involvement and relatively flexible batch process operations, and it is commonly used in restaurants to prepare food or in office work areas. *Fixed-position layout* is associated with make-to-order and assemble-to-order levels of customer involvement and flexible project process operations, and it is commonly used in any business that must go to the customer to do the work.

15-4. Describe the three planning schedules, supply chain management, and quality control.

The three planning schedules are as follows: *Planning sheets* state an objective and list the sequence of activities required to meet the objective, when each activity will begin and end, and who will complete each activity. *Gantt charts* use bars to graphically illustrate a schedule and progress toward the objective over a period of time. Gantt charts, like planning sheets, are appropriate when independent sequential steps are needed to accomplish the objective. The Gantt chart has an advantage over the planning sheet in that it places progress toward the objective on the chart as a control technique. PERT is a network scheduling technique that illustrates the dependence of activities. When some activities are dependent and some independent, PERT is more appropriate. *Supply chain management* is the process of coordinating all the activities involved in producing a product and delivering it to the customer, with a focus on purchasing and inventory control. *Quality control* is the process of ensuring

that all types of inventory (raw materials, work-in-process, output finished products, and products en route to customers) meet standards.

15-5. Recall how to measure productivity and list three ways to increase it.

Productivity is measured by dividing outputs by inputs. Productivity can be increased by (1) increasing the value of the outputs while maintaining the value of the inputs, (2) maintaining the value of the outputs while decreasing the value of the inputs, or (3) increasing the value of the outputs while decreasing the value of the inputs.

••• KEY TERMS

balanced scorecard (BSC), 521
capacity, 508
critical path, 512
customer involvement, 502
facility layout, 507
Gantt chart, 511
International Organization for
    Standardization (ISO), 517

inventory, 512
inventory control, 512
just-in-time (JIT) inventory, 513
materials requirement planning
    (MRP), 513
operations, 500
operations flexibility, 503
PERT, 511

planning sheet, 510
priority scheduling, 510
product, 500
productivity, 519
quality control, 515
routing, 510
supply chain management, 514
technology, 504

••• KEY TERM REVIEW

Complete each of the following statements using one of this chapter's key terms.

1. _____ is the function concerned with transforming resource inputs into product outputs.

2. A _____ is a good, a service, or a combination of the two.

3. _____ refers to the amount of input from customers, which determines whether operations are make to stock, assemble to order, or make to order.

4. _____ refers to the amount of variety in the products an operation produces, which determines whether the products are produced continuously, repetitively, in batches, or individually.

5. _____ is the process used to transform inputs into outputs.

6. _____ refers to the spatial arrangement of physical resources relative to each other.

7. _____ is the amount of products an organization can produce.

8. _____ is the path and sequence of the transformations of a product into an output.

9. _____ is the continuing evaluation and reordering of the sequence in which products will be produced.

10. A _____ states an objective and lists the sequence of activities required to meet the objective, when each activity will begin and end, and who will complete each activity.

11. A _____ uses bars to graphically illustrate a schedule and progress toward the objective over a period.

12. _____ is a network scheduling technique that illustrates the dependence of activities.

13. The _____ is the most time-consuming series of activities in a PERT network.

14. _____ is the stock of materials held for future use.

15. _____ is the process of managing raw materials, work in process, finished goods, and in-transit goods.

16. _____ is an inventory method in which necessary parts and raw materials are delivered shortly before they are needed.

17. _____ is a system that integrates operations and inventory control with complex ordering and scheduling.

18. _____ is the process of coordinating all the activities involved in producing a product and delivering it to the customer.

19. _____ is the process of ensuring that all types of inventory meet standards.

20. The _____ certifies firms that meet set quality standards.

21. _____ is a performance measure relating outputs to inputs.

22. A _____ measures financial, customer service, and internal business performance, as well as learning and growth performance.

• • • REVIEW QUESTIONS

1. What does the operations department do?

2. Is the level of customer involvement highest with make-to-stock, assemble-to-order, or make-to-order operations? Why?

3. Which type of process operation is the most flexible? Least flexible?

4. Which type of process operation is most commonly used by retailers and service organizations?

5. Are services generally more capital or labor intensive than manufacturing? Why?

6. Why is it important to balance time-based competition and design?

7. Which two facility layouts are the most flexible? Which two layouts are the least flexible?

8. Why is capacity planning so important?

9. Why is scheduling important?

10. What does a Gantt chart show that a planning sheet and a PERT network don't show?

11. When would you use a PERT network rather than a Gantt chart?

12. What are the four types of inventory?

13. What does materials requirement planning integrate?

14. What is the relationship between inventory and quality control?

15. What are the five rules of customer relations?

16. Why should you measure productivity rather than just production?

• • • COMMUNICATION SKILLS

The following critical-thinking questions can be used for class discussion and/or as written assignments to develop communication skills. Be sure to give complete explanations for all questions.

1. Why are some companies (such as Apple) innovative when it comes to changing products and processes, while others (such as Eastman Kodak) are slow to innovate and change?

2. Can a standard make-to-stock product (such as soda) also be made to order? If so, how?

3. Is the trend toward broader product mix with unrelated diversification? Why or why not?

4. Think about your career and the ideal job you are planning to obtain. Use Exhibit 15-2 to classify the operations systems and Exhibit 15-4 to identify the facility layout where you will work.

5. Assume you are planning a major event or project, such as a big wedding. (If you have an actual future event or project, use it rather than selecting an assumed event.) Would you use a planning sheet, a Gantt chart, or PERT to plan and control the event? Why? Identify the major things that you need to plan for and make, and put them on the actual form using either Exhibit 15-5, 15-6, or 15-7 as a guide.

6. Many companies are now using radio-frequency identification (RFID) technology. RFID is revolutionary and is helping businesses improve supply chain management. However, critics are concerned about protecting people's privacy. For example, with RFID, businesses will better know consumers' shopping habits and purchases. Do you want businesses to know where you live and the products you have in your house? Explain.

7. What is your view of the quality of products you have purchased over the past year compared to previous years? Did you have to return and exchange products or have them repaired? Do you think that quality is getting better with time?

8. The balanced scorecard calls for measuring performance in four areas. If a business is making good profits, should it bother with the other three nonfinancing measures? Why or why not?

CASES

• • • Case 15-1   3M

3M was founded by five businessmen as a small-scale mining venture back in 1902. From its humble beginnings more than a century ago, the company has grown to become a diversified technology company headquartered in St. Paul,

Minnesota. The company operates in the following business segments: industrial, safety and graphics, health care, electronics and energy, and consumer. It has achieved more than $30 billion in sales and maintains a workforce of more than 90,000 employees worldwide. The mission of 3M is: "To be committed to actively contributing to sustainable development through environmental protection, social responsibility and economic progress." The vision of the company is: "3M technology advancing every company, 3M products enhancing every home, 3M innovation improving every life."

The core values of the company are:

- Act with uncompromising honesty and integrity in everything we do.

- Satisfy our customers with innovative technology and superior quality, value and service.

- Provide our investors an attractive return through sustainable, global growth.

- Respect our social and physical environment around the world.

- Value and develop our employees' diverse talents, initiative and leadership.

- Earn the admiration of all those associated with 3M worldwide.

In January 2001, 3M started using the Lean/Six Sigma methodology to streamline operations, eliminate variations in processes and outcomes, and enhance its ability to provide competitive advantage for its customers in terms of its product and service offerings. The "Lean" comes from Lean Manufacturing that focuses on maximizing speed, while the "Six Sigma" focuses on quality. The Lean/Six Sigma process used by 3M follows these steps:

Analyze Opportunity -> Plan Improvement -> Focus Improvement -> Deliver Performance -> Improve Performance

The Lean/Six Sigma initiative helped 3M to begin 2005 with more than 30,000 employees who were Six Sigma certified. This initiative resulted in substantial revenue growth and massive savings and benefits. The company's 2003 annual report stated that operating income was increased by more than $500,000 in 2002 alone as a result of the Six Sigma initiatives. In addition, 3M's network continued to expand. It created a program called Six Sigma With Our Customers to provide opportunities for Six Sigma trained teams to work

on projects for customers to enhance their efficiency and quality. To date, they have partnered on more than 250 projects, such as Grainger, DuPont, Ford, Estee Lauder, the Home Depot, Motorola, Procter & Gamble, Land Rover, Toyota, and Walmart.

Despite all of the very positive benefits of the Lean/Six Sigma program at 3M, one challenge that this initiative has created is a tension between efficiency and innovation. In the future, companies will be under tremendous pressure to develop new ideas and be able to translate these ideas into actual products and services, so innovation will be critical to the success of many organizations.

Discussion Questions

1. What were the objectives of the Lean/Six Sigma program at 3M?

2. What are the key elements of the Lean/Six Sigma program at 3M?

3. Evaluate the effectiveness of the Lean/Six Sigma program at 3M.

4. What are the challenges associated with maintaining the success of the Lean/Six Sigma program at 3M?

5. Why do you think that Lean/Six Sigma has grown in popularity in many organizations? Do you think that Lean/Six Sigma will continue to be popular in the future? Why or why not?

6. Do you think the use of Lean/Six Sigma undermines the ability of an organization to be innovative? Why or why not?

References

http://solutions.3m.com/wps/portal/3M/en_US/3M-Company/Information/

http://solutions.3m.com/wps/portal/3M/en_US/3M-Company/Information/Profile/Conduct/

http://solutions.3m.com/wps/portal/3M/en_US/3M-Company/Information/AboutUs/WhoWeAre/

http://solutions.3m.com/wps/portal/3M/en_US/Community-Giving/US-Home/about-us/

http://solutions.3m.com/wps/portal/3M/en_US/CNDDSD/Home/technology-solutions/manufacturing-services/operational-excellence/lean-six-sigma/

https://www.isixsigma.com/community/blogs/3m-six-sigma/

https://www.6sigma.us/case/3m-case-study/

https://www.bloomberg.com/research/stocks/private/snapshot.asp?privcapId=289194

https://6sigma.com/case-study-3m-six-sigma/

Case created by Loren Kuzuhara, University of Wisconsin–Madison.

● ● ● Case 15-2   Zara's Formula to Successful Fast Fashion: Innovative Supply Chain Management

The world's preeminent pop singer takes the stage for the first leg of a month-long tour. Because she is known for her style, the fashion world takes notice of the patterned skirt she's wearing. Within three weeks, a similar skirt is designed, manufactured,

and available in retail stores for purchase. By the end of the tour, fans can be spotted at concerts wearing the same skirt the pop singer wore just a few weeks prior. This is fast fashion, and in this quick-moving industry, Zara is king.

How has Zara become so successful in the competitive retail clothing industry? The answer is in the second industry in which Zara operates that many are not aware of—apparel manufacturing. Zara, unlike many of its competitors, owns much of its supply chain. At the company's headquarters in Arteixo, Spain, thought of as "the brain" of the organization by those who work there,(1) Zara's strategic decisions on what and how to produce its merchandise are made. Store managers place biweekly orders, and exactly two weeks later, inventory arrives at retail stores.(2)

This just-in-time inventory technique affords Zara the opportunity to be nimble enough to respond to demand while minimizing risk.

> Zara achieves an extremely fast turnover by producing every product in small quantities. New designs can arrive in store within 15-days, which means that Zara can respond to its customer demand by producing more of its popular products and disregarding less popular items. Zara's Just in Time inventory procurement is underpinned by a highly developed forecasting system. Essentially, store managers collect sales data and current trends on a daily basis and send it back to head office where the information is analysed by its leading designers, who then update Zara's clothing ranges.(3)

If a new fashion trend is identified from a Paris runway or a pop icon, Zara can manufacture a small batch and distribute it to stores. If demand is high, a larger order can be placed, and manufacturing can be ramped up in a two-week time frame. If it doesn't sell, little harm is done. In fact, Zara's unsold items account for a mere 10% of its inventory in comparison to the industry average 17% to 20%.(4)

> To complement its JIT model, Zara did not follow in the footsteps of many of its rivals, who have based their main manufacturing bases in the far-east. Instead it took the bold step of centralising its textile factories and main logistics centres in Europe. Today, just over fifty per cent of Zara's clothing are produced in Spain, Turkey and North Africa, which means Zara can send garments anywhere in the world within 48 hours.(5)

When in-season adjustments are made to garments, such as a modification on a dress hemline or a new pattern on a blouse, the company's headquarters relies on its in-house manufacturers to produce and deliver inventory back to the warehouse for shipment to stores within its infamous two-week timeframe.(6)

The fast-fashion garments produced in this manner account for half of Zara's inventory.(7) The less trendy, more common wardrobe staples such as T-shirts, jeans, and sweaters account for the other half and are ordered in a similar manner to other traditional retailers: from Asian manufacturers approximately six months in advance.(8) For retail competitors, these long-lead orders typically account for at least 80% of the merchandise they will offer that season.(9) As a result, Zara's in-house factories are freed up to produce the quick-turnaround items ordered by company headquarters.

Zara's in-house manufacturing costs are significantly higher than those of Asia-based factories—wages for European workers were estimated at 8 euros an hour compared to 50 cents an hour abroad.(10) Though the use of overnight shipping to reduce inventory idle time further increases in-house production expenses, the company understands these costs are a necessary part of its supply chain dynamic. The lack of excess inventory means there's less need to discount merchandise. Zara receives full price on 85% of its items sold, while its industry competitors average 60% to 70%.(11)

> Zara also operates an extremely responsive logistics operation. For example, each of its 2,000 stores receives new items eight times a month. For this to happen, garments are picked, packed and ready to leave its distribution centre in Arteixo, Spain, approximately eight-hours after a store manager places an order.(12)

Knowing that inventory is limited and new items are stocked often, Zara customers frequent the company's retail stores more often than customers of other chains, averaging about 17 visits per year over an average of five for Gap customers.(13) As a result of high store traffic, Zara does not advertise,(14) allowing these resources to be allocated to its supply chain management.

Zara's unique core competencies have created a blueprint for other retailers to follow, such as H&M and Forever 21. Step into a Zara store and pick up something off the rack—there's a good chance that garment went from idea to design to production to store to customer within the last two weeks. As for that pop star–inspired patterned skirt mentioned earlier? It's already old news—Zara is working on its replacement.

Case Questions

1. What category does Zara fall under from an operations flexibility perspective?

2. Explain how just-in-time (JIT) inventory affects Zara's pricing strategy.

3. Explain how utilizing both its in-house facilities and external manufacturers maximizes the efficiency of Zara's supply chain. What are the advantages and disadvantages of each form of manufacturing?

4. What other companies utilize Zara's business model? How much control do these companies have over their supply chain?

Cumulative Case Questions

5. Which of Porter's three competitive strategies does Zara utilize (Chapter 5)? Explain why.

6. Is Zara a product innovator or a process innovator (Chapter 6)? Explain why.

7. Discuss the need for a team approach to supply chain management at Zara (Chapter 8).

8. Apply the four stages of the systems process and describe how Zara controls each stage of the process (Chapter 2).

References

(1) Berfield, S., & Baigorri, M. (2013, November 14). Zara's fast-fashion edge. *Bloomberg BusinessWeek*. Retrieved June 14, 2015, from http://www.bloomberg.com/bw/articles/2013-11-14/2014-outlook-zaras-fashion-supply-chain-edge#p1

(2) Ibid.

(3) Wilding, R. (2016, September 2). The secret behind Zara and Uniqlo's supply chain models. *Supply Chain Management* in The Leadership Network. Retrieved February 7, 2017, from https://theleadershipnetwork.com/article/supply-chain-management/zara-uniqlo-supply-chain

(4) Berfield, S., & Baigorri, M. (2013, November 14). Zara's fast-fashion edge. *Bloomberg BusinessWeek*. Retrieved June 14, 2015, from http://www.bloomberg.com/bw/articles/2013-11-14/2014-outlook-zaras-fashion-supply-chain-edge#p1

(5) Wilding, R. (2016, September 2). The secret behind Zara and Uniqlo's supply chain models. *Supply Chain Management* in The Leadership Network. Retrieved February 7, 2017, from https://theleadershipnetwork.com/article/supply-chain-management/zara-uniqlo-supply-chain

(6) Stevenson, S. (2012, June 21). Polka dots are in? Polka dots it is! *Slate*. Retrieved June 14, 2015, from http://www.slate.com/articles/arts/operations/2012/06/zara_s_fast_fashion_how_the_company_gets_new_styles_to_stores_so_quickly_.html

(7) Berfield, S., & Baigorri, M. (2013, November 14). Zara's fast-fashion edge. *Bloomberg BusinessWeek*. Retrieved June 14, 2015, from http://www.bloomberg.com/bw/articles/2013-11-14/2014-outlook-zaras-fashion-supply-chain-edge#p1

(8) Ibid.

(9) Ibid.

(10) Stevenson, S. (2012, June 21). Polka dots are in? Polka dots it is! *Slate*. Retrieved June 14, 2015, from http://www.slate.com/articles/arts/operations/2012/06/zara_s_fast_fashion_how_the_company_gets_new_styles_to_stores_so_quickly.html

(11) Berfield, S., & Baigorri, M. (2013, November 14). Zara's fast-fashion edge. *Bloomberg BusinessWeek*. Retrieved June 14, 2015, from http://www.bloomberg.com/bw/articles/2013-11-14/2014-outlook-zaras-fashion-supply-chain-edge#p1

(12) Wilding, R. (2016, September 2). The secret behind Zara and Uniqlo's supply chain models. *Supply Chain Management* in The Leadership Network. Retrieved February 7, 2017, from https://theleadershipnetwork.com/article/supply-chain-management/zara-uniqlo-supply-chain

(13) Stevenson, S. (2012, June 21). Polka dots are in? Polka dots it is! *Slate*. Retrieved June 14, 2015, from http://www.slate.com/articles/arts/operations/2012/06/zara_s_fast_fashion_how_the_company_gets_new_styles_to_stores_so_quickly.html

(14) Berfield, S., & Baigorri, M. (2013, November 14). Zara's fast-fashion edge. *Bloomberg BusinessWeek*. Retrieved June 14, 2015, from http://www.bloomberg.com/bw/articles/2013-11-14/2014-outlook-zaras-fashion-supply-chain-edge#p1

Case created by Herbert Sherman, Hannah K. Walter, and Naveed Ahmad, Long Island University

● ● ● SKILL BUILDER 15-1: DEVELOPING A PLAN TO OPEN A GAMESTOP

Objective

To develop your skills in planning using a Gantt chart and PERT network.

Skills

The primary skills developed through this exercise are:

1. *Management skill*—decision making (conceptual, diagnostic, analytical, critical-thinking, and quantitative reasoning skills are needed to develop a schedule to open a business)

2. *AACSB competency*—analytic skills

3. Management function—controlling

You have decided to open and manage a GameStop to buy and sell video games on April 1. It is now late December. You plan to move in 1 month before the store opens in order to set up. During March, your assistant will help you set up while you train him or her. Assume that you have decided to use (1) a Gantt chart and (2) a PERT network. Develop both, in whichever order you prefer, following the text guides for their development. Assume that you have identified the activities and completion times listed in what follows (the activities may not be given in sequence) and that you will start to implement the plan on January 2.

a. Lease the fixtures necessary to display your games; it will take 2 weeks to get them.

b. Order and receive games. This will take 1 week.

c. Recruit and select an assistant (3 weeks or less).

d. Install the fixtures, paint, decorate, and so on (2 weeks).

e. Form a corporation (4 weeks).

f. Make arrangements to buy games on credit (2 weeks).

g. Find a store location (6 weeks or less).

h. Unpack and display the games (1 week).

i. Train the assistant (1 week).

j. Select the games you plan to stock (1 week).

k. Determine start-up costs and cash outflows per month through April 30; your rich uncle will lend you this amount (1 week).

Gantt Chart

When developing the Gantt chart, use the following format, based on weeks. You may want to change the letter sequence to match the starting dates.

Gantt Chart				
Activity Letter	January 1 2 3 4	February 1 2 3 4	March 1 2 3 4	April 1
_____				
_____				
_____				
_____				
_____				
_____				
_____				
_____				
_____				
_____				

PERT

When developing the PERT chart, draw arrows from the start to your circles for the independent activities. Place the letter of the activity inside the circle. On the arrow to the activity, place the number of weeks needed to complete it. Then draw an arrow to the end. Also from the start, draw the first dependent activity, followed by the next dependent activity, and so on, until you get to the last one; then draw an arrow to the end. Be sure to put the number of weeks and activity/event letters on your network. After all activities have been listed, determine the critical path and draw the second arrow to indicate it. *Hint:* You should have five arrows to activities coming from the start; you can begin the process with either selecting movies/music or finding a store location.

PERT

(with critical path)

Start   End

Conclusion

Is Gantt or PERT more appropriate for this type of plan?

Apply It

What did I learn from this experience? How can I use this knowledge in the future?

••• SKILL BUILDER 15-2: INCREASING PRODUCTIVITY

Objective

To gain experience in determining ways to increase productivity.

Skills

The primary skills developed through this exercise are:

- *Management skill*—decision making (conceptual, diagnostic, analytical, critical-thinking, and quantitative reasoning skills are needed to develop cost-cutting ideas)
- *AACSB competency*—analytic skills
- *Management function*—controlling
  1. Select a place where you work or have worked. Identify the few critical success factors (Chapter 14) that were/are important for your job/department success.
  2. Determine ways to cut input costs but maintain outputs in order to increase productivity. Identify ways to save time and money. How can things be done more cheaply?
  3. Determine ways to increase outputs but maintain inputs in order to increase productivity. What can be done to produce more? How can things be done quicker and better?

Apply It

What did I learn from this experience? How will I use this knowledge in the future?

••• SKILL BUILDER 15-3: YOUR COURSE SELF-ASSESSMENT

Objective

To review your course self-assessments.

Skills

The primary skills developed through this exercise are:

1. *Management skill*—decision making

2. *AACSB competency*—reflective thinking skills
3. Management function—controlling

Break into groups and discuss your answers to Self-Assessment 15-2, "Putting It All Together." Focus on helping each other improve career development plans.

Apply It

What did I learn from this experience? How will I use this knowledge in the future?

••• SKILL BUILDER 15-4: THE MOST IMPORTANT THINGS I GOT FROM THIS COURSE

Objective

To review your course learning, critical thinking, and skill development.

Skills

The primary skills developed through this exercise are:

1. *Management skill*—decision making

2. *AACSB competency*—reflective thinking skills

3. Management function—controlling

Think about and write/type the three or four most important things you learned or skills you developed through this course and how they are helping or will help you in your personal and/or professional lives.

Apply It

What did I learn from this experience? How will I use this knowledge in the future?

●●● Glossary

acquired needs theory Theory that proposes that employees are motivated by their needs for achievement, power, and affiliation.

acquisition Occurs when one business buys all or part of another business.

adaptive strategies Overall strategies for a line of business, including prospecting, defending, and analyzing.

arbitrator A neutral third party who resolves a conflict by making a binding decision.

assessment centers Places job applicants undergo a series of tests, interviews, and simulated experiences to determine their potential.

attitudes Positive or negative evaluations of people, things, and situations.

attribution The process of determining the reason for someone's behavior and whether that behavior is situational or intentional.

authentic leaders Leaders who develop open, honest, trusting relationships.

authority The right to make decisions, issue orders, and use resources.

balanced scorecard (BSC) A management tool that measures financial, customer service, and internal business performance, as well as learning and growth performance.

BCF statement A statement that describes a conflict in terms of behaviors, consequences, and feelings in a way that maintains ownership of the problem.

behavioral leadership theorists Theorists who attempt to determine distinctive styles used by effective leaders.

behavioral theorists Researchers who focus on people to determine the best way to manage in all organizations.

benchmarking The process of comparing an organization's products and services and processes with those of other companies.

big data The analysis of large amounts of quantified facts to aid in maximizing decision making.

bona fide occupational qualification (BFOQ) An occupational qualification that may be discriminatory but that is reasonably necessary to normal operation of a particular organization.

brainstorming The process of suggesting many possible alternatives without evaluation.

budget A planned quantitative allocation of resources for specific activities.

business plan Written description of a new venture, describing its objectives and the steps for achieving them

business portfolio analysis The corporate process of determining which lines of business the corporation will be in and how it will allocate resources among them.

capacity The amount of products an organization can produce.

capital expenditures budget A projection of all planned major asset investments.

career development The process of gaining skill, experience, and education to achieve career objectives.

career planning The process of setting career objectives and determining how to accomplish them.

centralized authority Important decisions are made by top managers.

change agent The person responsible for implementing an organizational change effort.

charismatic leadership A leadership style that inspires loyalty, enthusiasm, and high levels of performance.

citizenship behavior Employee efforts that go above and beyond the call of duty.

classical theorists Researchers who focus on the job and management functions to determine the best way to manage in all organizations.

coaching The process of giving motivational feedback to maintain and improve performance.

coalition A network of alliances that help achieve an objective.

collaborative conflict resolution model A conflict resolution model that calls for (1) stating the problem in a BCF statement, (2) getting the other party to acknowledge the problem or conflict, (3) asking for and/or presenting alternative resolutions to the conflict, and (4) coming to an agreement.

collective bargaining The negotiation process resulting in a contract between employees and management that covers employment conditions.

command groups Groups that consist of managers and the employees they supervise.

communication The process of transmitting information and meaning.

communication channel The means or medium by which a message is transmitted; the three primary channels are oral, nonverbal, and written.

communication process The process that takes place between a sender who encodes a message and transmits it through a channel to a receiver who decodes it and may give feedback.

compensation The total of an employee's pay and benefits.

competitive advantage Specifies how an organization offers unique customer value.

concurrent control Action taken to ensure that standards are met as inputs are transformed into outputs.

conflict A situation in which people are in disagreement and opposition.

consensus mapping The process of developing group agreement on a solution to a problem.

contemporary leadership theories Theories that attempt to determine how effective leaders interact with, inspire, and support followers.

content motivation theories Theories that focus on identifying and understanding employees' needs.

contingency leadership model A model used to determine if leadership style is task or relationship oriented and if the situation matches the style.

contingency plans Alternative plans to be implemented if uncontrollable events occur.

contingency theorists Researchers who focus on determining the best management approach for a given situation.

contract manufacturing Contracting a foreign firm to manufacture products a company will sell as its own.

control frequency The rate of repetition—constant, periodic, or occasional—of measures taken to control performance.

control systems process (1) Set objectives and standards, (2) measure performance, (3) compare performance to standards, and (4) correct or reinforce.

controlling The process of monitoring progress and taking corrective action when needed to ensure that objectives are achieved.

creative process The approach to generating new ideas that involves three stages: (1) preparation, (2) incubation and illumination, and (3) evaluation.

creativity A way of thinking that generates new ideas.

criteria The standards that an alternative must meet to be selected as the decision that will accomplish the objective.

critical path The most time-consuming series of activities in a PERT network.

critical success factors The limited number of areas in which satisfactory results will ensure successful performance, achieving the objective/standard.

customer involvement The amount of input from customers, which determines whether operations are make to stock, assemble to order, or make to order.

damage control Action taken to minimize negative impacts on customers/stakeholders due to faulty outputs.

decentralized authority Important decisions are made by middle and first-line managers.

decision making The process of selecting a course of action that will solve a problem.

decision-making conditions Certainty, risk, and uncertainty.

decision-making model A six-step process for arriving at a decision that involves (1) classifying and defining the problem or opportunity, (2) setting objectives and criteria, (3) generating creative and innovative alternatives, (4) analyzing alternatives and selecting the most feasible, (5) planning and implementing the decision, and (6) controlling the decision.

decision-making skills The ability to conceptualize situations and select alternatives to solve problems and take advantage of opportunities.

decoding The receiver's process of translating a message into a meaningful form.

delegation The process of assigning responsibility and authority for accomplishing objectives.

departmentalization The grouping of related activities into units.

development Ongoing education to improve skills for present and future jobs.

devil's advocate approach Group members focus on defending a solution while others try to come up with reasons the solution will not work.

direct feedback An OD intervention in which the change agent makes a direct recommendation for change.

direct investment The building or buying of operating facilities in a foreign country.

disability A mental or physical impairment that substantially limits an individual's ability.

discipline Corrective action to get employees to meet standards and standing plans.

discontinuous change A significant breakthrough in technology that leads to design competition and a new technology cycle.

discrimination An illegal practice that gives unfair treatment to diversity groups in employment decisions.

diversity The variety of people with different group identities within the same workplace.

divisional structure Departmentalization based on semiautonomous strategic business units.

empathic listening Understanding and relating to another's feelings.

employee assistance program (EAP) A benefit program staffed by people who help employees get professional assistance in solving their problems.

encoding The sender's process of putting the message into a form that the receiver will understand.

entrepreneur Someone who starts a small-business venture.

equity theory Theory that proposes that employees are motivated when their perceived inputs equal outputs.

ERG theory Theory that proposes that employees are motivated by three needs: existence, relatedness, and growth.

ethics Standards of right and wrong that influence behavior.

ethnocentrism Regarding one's own ethnic group or culture as superior to others.

expatriates Individuals who live and work outside their native country.

expectancy theory Theory that proposes that employees are motivated when they believe they can accomplish a task and the rewards for doing so are worth the effort.

external environment The factors outside of an organization's boundaries that affect its performance.

facility layout The spatial arrangement of physical resources relative to each other—operations use product, process, cellular, or fixed-position layouts.

feedback Information that verifies a message.

financial statements The income statement, balance sheet, and cash flow statement.

forcefield analysis An OD intervention that diagrams the current level of performance, the forces hindering change, and the forces driving toward change.

franchising An entrepreneurial venture in which a franchisor licenses a business to the franchisee for a fee and royalties.

functional conflict A situation in which disagreement and opposition support the achievement of organizational objectives.

functional strategies Strategies developed and implemented by managers in marketing, operations, human resources, finance, and other departments.

Gantt chart A scheduling tool that uses bars to graphically illustrate a schedule and progress toward the objective over a period.

giving praise model A four-step technique for providing feedback to an employee: (1) Tell the employee exactly what was done correctly; (2) tell the employee why the behavior is important; (3) stop for a moment of silence; (4) encourage repeat performance.

glass ceiling The invisible barrier that prevents women and minorities from advancing to the top jobs in organizations.

global sourcing Hiring others outside the organization to perform work worldwide.

global village Refers to companies conducting business worldwide without boundaries.

global virtual teams Teams whose members are physically located in different places but work together as a team.

goal-setting theory Theory that proposes that achievable but difficult goals motivate employees.

grand strategy An overall corporate strategy for growth, stability, or turnaround and retrenchment, or for some combination of these.

grapevine The informal flow of information in any direction throughout an organization.

group Two or more members, with a clear leader, who perform independent jobs with individual accountability, evaluation, and rewards.

group cohesiveness The extent to which members stick together.

group composition The mix of members' skills and abilities.

group performance model Group performance is a function of organizational context, group structure, group process, and group development.

group process The patterns of interactions that emerge as members perform their jobs.

group process dimensions Roles, norms, cohesiveness, status, decision making, and conflict resolution.

group roles Group task roles, group maintenance roles, and self-interest roles.

group structure dimensions Group type, size, composition, leadership, and objectives.

group types Formal or informal, functional or cross-functional, and command or task.

growth strategies Strategies a company can adopt in order to grow: concentration, backward and forward integration, and related and unrelated diversification.

hierarchy of needs theory Theory that proposes that employees are motivated by five levels of needs: physiological, safety, social, esteem, and self-actualization.

horizontal communication The flow of information between colleagues and peers.

human resources management process Planning for, attracting, developing, and retaining employees.

inclusion A practice of ensuring that all employees feel they belong as valued members of the organization.

incremental change Continual improvement that takes place within the existing technology cycle.

innovation The implementation of a new idea.

internal environment Factors that affect an organization's performance from within its boundaries.

international company An organization that is based primarily in one country but transacts business in other countries.

International Organization for Standardization (ISO) An organization that certifies firms that meet set quality standards.

interpersonal skills The ability to understand, communicate, and work well with individuals and groups through developing effective relationships.

intrapreneur Someone who starts a new line of business within a larger organization.

inventory The stock of materials held for future use.

inventory control The process of managing raw materials, work in process, finished goods, and in-transit goods.

job description Identifies the tasks and responsibilities of a position.

job design The process of identifying tasks that each employee is responsible for completing.

job enrichment The process of building motivators into a job to make it more interesting and challenging.

job evaluation The process of determining the worth of each job relative to the other jobs within the organization.

job specifications Identify the qualifications needed by the person who is to fill a position.

joint venture Two or more firms sharing ownership of a new company.

just-in-time (JIT) inventory A method by which necessary parts and raw materials are delivered shortly before they are needed.

knowledge management Involving everyone in an organization in sharing knowledge and applying it continuously to improve products and processes.

labor relations The interactions between management and unionized employees.

large-group intervention An OD technique that brings together participants from all parts of the organization, and often key outside stakeholders, to solve problems or take advantage of opportunities.

leader-member exchange (LMX) leaders Leaders who create in-groups and out-groups based largely on being similar to them and/or competency.

leadership continuum model A model used to determine which of seven styles of leadership, on a continuum from autocratic (*boss centered*) to participative (*employee centered*), is best for a given situation.

Leadership Grid® A model that identifies the ideal leadership style as incorporating a high concern for both production and people.

leadership style The combination of traits, skills, and behaviors managers use in interacting with employees.

leadership trait theorists Theorists who attempt to determine a list of distinctive characteristics that account for leadership effectiveness.

leading The process of influencing employees to work toward achieving objectives.

learning organization An organization with a culture that values sharing knowledge so as to adapt to the changing environment and continuously improve.

levels of authority The authority to inform, the authority to recommend, the authority to report, and full authority.

levels of culture Behavior, values and beliefs, and assumptions.

levels of management Top managers, middle managers, and first-line managers.

licensing The process of a licensor agreeing to give a licensee the right to make its products or services or use its intellectual property in exchange for a royalty.

line authority The responsibility to make decisions and issue orders down the chain of command.

management audit Analysis of the organization's planning, organizing, leading, and controlling functions to look for improvements.

management by objectives (MBO) The process in which managers and their employees jointly set objectives for the employees, periodically evaluate performance, and reward according to the results.

management by walking around (MBWA) A type of supervision in which the three major activities are listening, teaching, and facilitating.

management counseling The process of giving employees feedback so they realize that a problem is affecting their job performance and referring employees with problems to the employee assistance program.

management functions Planning, organizing, leading, and controlling.

management role categories The categories of roles—interpersonal, informational, and decisional—managers play as they accomplish management functions.

management science theorists Researchers who focus on the use of mathematics to aid in problem solving and decision making.

management skills The skills needed to be an effective manager, including technical, interpersonal, and decision-making skills.

manager The individual responsible for achieving organizational objectives through efficient and effective utilization of resources.

manager's resources Human, financial, physical, and informational resources.

materials requirement planning (MRP) A system that integrates operations and inventory control with complex ordering and scheduling.

mechanistic organizations Bureaucratic organizations, focusing on following procedures and rules through tight controls and specialized jobs, with top managers making decisions.

mediator A neutral third party who helps resolve a conflict.

merger Occurs when two companies form one corporation.

message-receiving process A process that includes listening, analyzing, and checking understanding.

message-sending process A process that includes (1) developing rapport, (2) stating your communication objective, (3) transmitting your message, (4) checking the receiver's understanding, and (5) getting a commitment and following up.

micromanagement A management style generally used as a negative term for when a manager closely observes or controls the work of his or her employees.

mission An organization's purpose or reason for being.

motivation The willingness to achieve organizational objectives or to go above and beyond the call of duty (organizational citizenship behavior).

motivation process The process of moving from need to motive to behavior to consequence to satisfaction or dissatisfaction.

multinational corporation (MNC) An organization that has ownership in operations in two or more countries.

networking The process of developing relationships for the purpose of career building and socializing.

new venture A small business or a new line of business.

nominal grouping The process of generating and evaluating alternatives using a structured voting method.

nonprogrammed decisions Significant decisions that arise in nonrecurring and nonroutine situations, for which the decision maker should use the decision-making model.

nonverbal communication Messages sent without words.

norms Expectations about behavior that are shared by members of a group.

objectives Statements of what is to be accomplished that are expressed in singular, specific, and measurable terms with a target date.

OD interventions Specific actions taken to implement specific changes.

one-minute self-sell An opening statement used in networking that quickly summarizes your history and career plan and asks a question.

operating budgets The revenue and expense budgets.

operational planning The process of setting short-range objectives and determining in advance how they will be accomplished.

operations The function concerned with transforming resource inputs into product outputs.

operations flexibility The amount of variety in the products an operation produces, which determines whether products are produced continuously, repetitively, in batches, or individually.

organic organizations Flexible organizations with minimal focus on procedures and rules, broadly defined jobs, and decisions made at lower levels.

organization chart A graphic illustration of an organization's management hierarchy and departments and their working relationships.

organizational behavior The study of actions that affect performance in the workplace.

organizational change Alterations of existing work routines and strategies that affect the whole organization.

organizational culture The values, beliefs, and assumptions about appropriate behavior that members of an organization share.

organizational development (OD) The ongoing planned process of change used as a means of improving performance through interventions.

organizing The process of delegating and coordinating tasks and allocating resources to achieve objectives.

orientation The process of introducing new employees to the organization and their jobs.

paraphrasing The process of restating a message in one's own words.

path-goal model A model used to determine employee objectives and to clarify how to achieve them using one of four leadership styles.

perception The process of selecting, organizing, and interpreting environmental information.

performance Means of evaluating how effectively and efficiently managers utilize resources to achieve objectives.

performance appraisal The ongoing process of evaluating employee performance.

performance formula Performance = ability × motivation × resources.

personality A combination of behavioral, mental, and emotional traits that define an individual.

PERT A network scheduling technique that illustrates the dependence of activities.

planning The process of setting objectives and determining in advance exactly how the objectives will be met.

planning sheet A scheduling tool that states an objective and lists the sequence of activities required to meet the objective, when each activity will begin and end, and who will complete each activity.

policies General guidelines to be followed when making decisions.

politics The process of gaining and using power.

power The ability to influence others' behavior.

preliminary control Action designed to anticipate and prevent possible problems.

priority scheduling The continuing evaluation and reordering of the sequence in which products will be produced.

problem The situation that exists whenever objectives are not being met.

problem solving The process of taking corrective action to meet objectives.

procedure A sequence of actions to be followed in order to achieve an objective.

process consultation An OD intervention designed to improve team dynamics.

process motivation theories Theories that focus on understanding how employees choose behaviors to fulfill their needs.

product A good, a service, or a combination of the two.

productivity A performance measure relating outputs to inputs.

programmed decisions Decisions that arise in recurring or routine situations, for which the decision maker should use decision rules or organizational policies and procedures.

Pygmalion effect The theory that managers' attitudes toward and expectations and treatment of employees largely determine their performance.

quality control The process of ensuring that all types of inventory meet standards.

reciprocity The mutual exchange of favors and privileges to accomplish objectives.

recruiting The process of attracting qualified candidates to apply for job openings.

reflecting responses Responses that paraphrase a message and communicate understanding and acceptance to the sender.

reinforcement theory Theory that proposes that the consequences of their behavior will motivate employees to behave in predetermined ways.

responsibility The obligation to achieve objectives by performing required activities.

rework control Action taken to fix an output.

routing The path and sequence of the transformation of a product into an output.

rules Statements of exactly what should or should not be done.

selection The process of choosing the most qualified applicant recruited for a job.

servant leaders Leaders who focus on helping others by placing their needs ahead of self-interest.

single-use plans Programs and budgets developed for handling nonrepetitive situations.

situation analysis An analysis of those features in a company's environment that most directly affect its options and opportunities.

situational approaches to leadership Theories that attempt to determine appropriate leadership styles for particular situations.

Situational Leadership® model A model used to select one of four leadership styles that match the employees' maturity level in a given situation.

small business A business that is independently owned and operated with a small number of employees and relatively low volume of sales.

social responsibility The conscious effort to operate in a manner that creates a win-win situation for all stakeholders.

sociotechnical theorists Researchers who focus on integrating people and technology.

span of management The number of employees reporting to a manager.

staff authority The responsibility to advise and assist other personnel.

stages of group development Forming, storming, norming, performing, and termination.

stages of the change process Denial, resistance, exploration, and commitment.

stakeholders' approach to ethics Creating a win-win situation for all relevant stakeholders so that everyone benefits from the decision.

standards Measures of performance levels in the areas of quantity, quality, time, cost, and behavior.

standing plans Policies, procedures, and rules developed for handling repetitive situations.

status The perceived ranking of one member relative to other members in a group.

strategic alliance An agreement to share resources that does not necessarily involve creating a new company.

strategic human resources planning The process of staffing the organization to meet its objectives.

strategic planning The process of developing a mission and long-range objectives and determining in advance how they will be accomplished.

strategy A plan for pursuing a mission and achieving objectives.

stress The body's reaction to environmental demands.

substitutes for leadership Characteristics of the task, of subordinates, or of the organization that replace the need for a leader.

supply chain management The process of coordinating all the activities involved in producing a product and delivering it to the customer.

survey feedback An OD intervention that uses a questionnaire to gather data to use as the basis for change.

sustainability Meeting the needs of the present world without compromising the ability of future generations to meet their own needs.

SWOT analysis A determination of an organization's internal environmental strengths and weaknesses and external environmental opportunities and threats.

symbolic leaders Leaders who articulate a vision for an organization and reinforce the culture through slogans, symbols, and ceremonies.

synectics The process of generating novel alternatives through role playing and fantasizing.

systems process The method used to transform inputs into outputs to make and deliver products and services.

systems theorists Researchers who focus on viewing the organization as a whole and as the interrelationship of its parts.

task groups Employees selected to work on a specific objective.

team A small number of members, with shared leadership, who perform interdependent jobs with both individual and group accountability, evaluation, and rewards.

team building An OD intervention designed to help work groups increase structural and team dynamics and performance.

team leaders Empower members to take responsibility for performing the management functions and focus on developing effective group structure and group process and on furthering group development.

technical skills The ability to use methods and techniques to perform a task.

technology The process used to transform inputs into outputs.

total quality management (TQM) The process that involves everyone in an organization focusing on the customer to continually improve product value.

training The process of teaching employees the skills necessary to perform a job.

transactional leadership A leadership style based on social exchange.

transformational leaders Leaders who bring about continuous learning, innovation, and change.

two-dimensional leadership styles Four possible leadership styles that are based on the dimensions of job structure and employee consideration.

two-factor theory Theory that proposes that employees are motivated by motivators rather than by maintenance factors.

types of change Changes in strategy, in structure, in technology, and in people.

types of managers General managers, functional managers, and project managers.

vertical communication The flow of information both downward and upward through the organizational chain of command.

vestibule training Training that develops skills in a simulated setting.

visionary leaders Leaders who create an image of the organization in the future that provides direction for setting goals and developing strategic plans.

••• Notes

Chapter 1

1. R. McCammon, "Do Me a Solid," *Entrepreneur* (March 2014): 32–33.
2. W. L. Bedwell, S. M. Fiore, and E. Salas, "Developing the Future Workforce: An Approach for Integrating Interpersonal Skills Into the MBA Classroom," *Academy of Management Learning & Education* 13, no. 2 (2014): 171–186.
3. M. Kelly, *Rediscovering Catholicism* (New York: Beacon, 2010).
4. A. Meister, K. A. Jehn, and S. M. B. Thatcher, "Feeling Misidentified: The Consequences of Internal Identity Asymmetries for Individuals at Work," *Academy of Management Review* 38, no. 4 (2014): 488–512.
5. S. Sandberg, commencement speech, University of California, Berkeley, May 16, 2016. Speech can be found on YouTube.
6. Booker T. Washington, quote from *Forbes* (December 20, 2016): 112.
7. B. C. Forbes, quote from *Forbes* (December 20, 2016): 112.
8. H. Delehanty, "A Conversation with Sonja Lyubomirsky: Happiness Expert." *AARP Bulletin* (June 2016).
9. A. Styhre, "What David Foster Wallace Can Teach Management Scholars," *Academy of Management Review* 41, no. 1 (2016): 170–183.
10. B. Urstadt, "Perpetually Linked," *Business Week* (July 3, 2014): 74.
11. A. Ruzo, "My Advice," *Fortune* (April 28, 2014): 30.
12. P. Diamandis, "The Future," *Entrepreneur* (January 2015): 34.
13. H. Mintzberg, "Quote," in "From the Guest Editors: Change the World: Teach Evidence-Based Practices!" *Academy of Management Learning & Education* 13, no. 3 (2014): 319.
14. S. J. Creary, B. B. Caza, L. M. Roberts, "Out of the Box? How Managing a Subordinate's Multiple Identities Affects the Quality of a Manager–Subordinate Relationship," *Academy of Management Review* 40, no. 4 (2015): 538–562.
15. A. M. Kleinbaum and T. E. Stuart, "Network Responsiveness: The Social Structural Microfoundations of Dynamic Capabilities," *Academy of Management Perspectives* 28, no. 4 (2014): 353–367.
16. M. Korn and R. Feintzeig, "Is the Old-School, Hard-Nosed Boss Obsolete?" *The Wall Street Journal* (May 23, 2014): B1.
17. L. Weber and M. Korn, "Where Did All the Entry-Level Jobs Go?" *The Wall Street Journal* (August 6, 2014): B6.
18. V. Harnish, "5 Key Trends to Master in 2016," *Fortune* (December 15, 2015): 52.
19. R. E. Boyatzis, "Possible Contributions to Leadership and Management Development From Neuroscience," *Academy of Management Learning & Education* 13, no. 2 (2014): 300–301.
20. S. Rosenbush, "The Key to Facebook's Productivity," *The Wall Street Journal* (February 23, 2015): R8.
21. G. Colvin, "Ignore These Leadership Lessons at Your Peril," *Fortune* (October 28, 2013): 85.
22. N. J. Fast, E. R. Burris, and C. A. Bartel, "Managing to Stay in the Dark: Managerial Self-Efficacy, Ego Defensiveness, and the Aversion to Employee Voice," *Academy of Management Journal* 57, no. 4 (2014): 1013–1034.
23. Netflix History, http://www.fundinguniverse.com/company-histories/netflix-inc-history/, accessed March 25, 2015.
24. B. Stone, "Labor Gets a Foot in the Door at Amazon," *Business Week* (July 3, 2014): 34.
25. G. Colvin, "The Benefit of Baring It All," *Fortune* (December 2015), 34.
26. J. Naisbitt, "On Power," *Forbes* (November 23, 2015), 160.
27. W. F. Smith, "Dynamic Decision Making: A Model of Senior Leaders Managing Strategic Paradoxes," *Academy of Management Journal* 57, no. 6 (2014): 1592–1623; R. B. Briner and N. D. Walshe, "From Passively Received Wisdom to Actively Constructed Knowledge: Teaching Systematic Review Skills as a Foundation of Evidence-Based Management," *Academy of Management Learning & Education* 13, no. 3 (2014): 415–432.
28. M. Sytch and A. Tatarynowicz, "Exploring the Locus of Invention: The Dynamics of Network Communities and Firms' Invention Productivity," *Academy of Management Journal* 57, no. 1 (2014): 249–279.
29. G. Colvin, "Ignore These Leadership Lessons at Your Peril," *Fortune* (October 28, 2013): 85.
30. G. Fisher, S. Kotha, and A. Lahiri, "Changing with the Times: An Integrated View of Identity, Legitimacy, and New Venture Life Cycles, *Academy of Management Review* 41, no. 3 (2016): 383–409; D. J. Teece, "The Foundations of Enterprise Performance: Dynamic and Ordinary Capabilities in an (Economic) Theory of Firms," *Academy of Management Perspectives* 28, no. 4 (2014): 328–352.
31. Q. N. Huy, K. G. Corley, and M. S. Kraatz, "From Support to Mutiny: Shifting Legitimacy Judgments and Emotional Reactions Impacting the Implementation of Radical Change," *Academy of Management Journal* 57, no. 6 (2014): 1650–1680; N. J. Fast, E. R. Burris, and C. A. Bartel, "Managing to Stay in the Dark: Managerial Self-Efficacy, Ego Defensiveness, and the Aversion to Employee Voice," *Academy of Management Journal* 57, no. 4 (2014): 1013–1034.
32. A. Chatterji and A. Patro, "Dynamic Capabilities and Managing Human Capital," *Academy of Management Perspectives* 28, no. 4 (2014): 395–408.
33. *The Wall Street Journal* (November 14, 1980): 33.
34. D. R. Ames and A. S. Wazlawek, "How to Tell If You're a Jerk in the Office," *The Wall Street Journal* (February 23, 2015): R2.
35. E. Holmes, "The Charisma Boot Camp," *The Wall Street Journal* (August 6, 2014): D1, D3.
36. K. Davidson, "Hard to Find: Workers With Good 'Soft Skills'," *The Wall Street Journal* (August 31, 2016), B1, B6.
37. G. Colvin, "Humans Are Underrated," *Fortune* (August 1, 2015), 100–113.
38. G. Colvin, "Heavy Hitters Travel Light," *Fortune* (February 1, 2016), 20; R. Jennings, "Culture Matters: 7 Ways of Great Leaders," *Forbes* (October 20, 2014): 113.
39. W. L. Bedwell, S. M. Fiore, and E. Salas, "Developing the Future Workforce: An Approach for Integrating Interpersonal Skills Into the MBA Classroom," *Academy of Management Learning & Education* 13, no. 2 (2014): 171–186.
40. K. E. Brink and R. D. Costigan, "Oral Communication Skills: Are the Priorities of the Workplace and AACSB-Accredited Business Programs Aligned?" *Academy of Management Learning & Education* 14, no. 2 (2015): 205–221; L. Weber and M. Korn, "Where Did All the Entry-Level Jobs Go?" *The Wall Street Journal* (August 6, 2014): B6.
41. P. Coy, "Job Training That Works," *Business Week* (November 24–30, 2014): 6–7.
42. A. M. Kleinbaum and T. E. Stuart, "Network Responsiveness: The Social Structural Microfoundations of Dynamic Capabilities," *Academy of Management Perspectives* 28, no. 4 (2014): 353–367.
43. J. Ankeny, "The Good Sir Richard," *Entrepreneur* (June 2012): 31–38.
44. K. J. Lovelace, F. Eggers, and L. R. Dyck, "I Do and I Understand: Assessing the Utility of Web-Based Management Simulations to Develop Critical Thinking Skills," *Academy of Management Learning & Education* 15, no. 1 (2016): 100–121.
45. G. Colvin, "Ignore These Leadership Lessons at Your Peril," *Fortune* (October 28, 2013): 85.
46. A. Lim, D. C. J. Qing, and A. R. Eyring, "Netting the Evidence: A Review of On-Line Resources," *Academy of Management Learning & Education* 13, no. 3 (2014): 495–503.
47. AACSB International, *Eligibility Procedures and Accreditation Standards for Business Accreditation* (Tampa, FL: Author, 2016), http://www.aacsb.edu/-/media/aacsb/docs/accreditation/standards/businessstds_2013_update-03oct_final_tracked_changes.ashx?la=en Accessed November 17, 2016.
48. ACBSP (Accreditation Council for Business Schools and Programs). http://www.acbsp.org/, accessed November 17, 2016.
49. IACBE (International Assembly for Collegiate Business Education). http://iacbe.org/, accessed November 17, 2016.
50. R. D. Costigan and K. E. Brink, "Another Perspective on MAB Program Alignment: An Investigation of Learning Goals," *Academy of Management Learning & Education* 14, no. 2 (2015): 260–276.
51. M. Sytch and A. Tatarynowicz, "Friends and Foes: The Dynamics of Dual Social Structures," *Academy of Management Journal* 57, no. 2 (2014): 585–613.
52. H. Mitchell, "What's the Best Way to Stick With a Resolution?" *The Wall Street Journal* (December 23, 2014): D1, D2.
53. M. L. Verreynne, D. Meyer, and P. Liesch, "Beyond the Formal–Informal Dichotomy of Small Firm Strategy-Making in Stable and Dynamic Environments," *Journal of Small Business Management* 54, no. 2 (2016), 420–444.
54. R. Bachman, "The Week Resolutions Die," *The Wall Street Journal* (January 20, 2015): D1, D4.
55. A. Chatterji and A. Patro, "Dynamic Capabilities and Managing Human Capital," *Academy of Management Perspectives* 28, no. 4 (2014): 395–408.
56. J. Hartz, "Design Your Office Around Your Business's Goals," *INC.* (September 2014): 122.
57. R. Lussier and J. Hendon, *Human Resource Management*, 2nd ed. (Thousand Oaks, CA: Sage, 2016).
58. B. R. Spisak, M. J. O'Brien, N. Nicholson, and M. Van Vugt, "Niche Construction and the Evolution of Leadership," *Academy of Management Review* 40, no. 2 (2015): 291–306.
59. CEO Survey, "Bosses Are Creating a New Generation of Leaders," *INC.* (September 2014): 76.
60. R. McCammon, "Do Me a Solid," *Entrepreneur* (March 2014): 32–33.
61. Y. Zhang, D. A. Waldman, Y. L. Han, and X. Li, "Paradoxical Leader Behaviors in People Management: Antecedents and Consequences," *Academy of Management Journal* 58, no. 2 (2015): 538–566; D. A. Waldman and R. M. Balven, "Responsible Leadership: Theoretical Issues and Research Directions," *Academy of Management Perspectives* 28, no. 3 (2014): 224–234.
62. A. Murray, "Should Leaders Be Modest?" *Fortune* (September 15, 2015), 28; C. Hann, "Dedicated to You," *Entrepreneur* (September 2013): 24.

63. R. Krause and G. Brunton, "Who Does the Monitoring?" *Academy of Management Review* 39, no. 1 (2014): 111–112.

64. L. B. Belker, J. McCormick, and G. S. Topchik, *The First-Time Manager* (New York: AMACOM, 2012).

65. Staff, "Jargon," *Entrepreneur* (August 2015), 30.

66. Y. Zhang, D. A. Waldman, Y. L. Han, and X. Li, "Paradoxical Leader Behaviors in People Management: Antecedents and Consequences," *Academy of Management Journal* 58, no. 2 (2015): 538–566.

67. M. Weber, "Culture Matters: 7 Ways of Great Leaders," *Forbes* (October 20, 2014): 113.

68. H. Mintzberg, *The Nature of Managerial Work* (New York: Harper & Row, 1973).

69. F. P. Morgeson, T. R. Mitchell, and D. Liu, "Event System Theory: An Event-Oriented Approach to the Organizational Sciences," *Academy of Management Review* 40, no. 4 (2015): 515–537.

70. D. Ma, M. Rhee, and D. Yang, "Power Source Mismatch and the Effectiveness of Interorganizational Relations: The Case of Venture Capital Syndication," *Academy of Management Journal* 56, no. 3 (2014): 711–734.

71. A. M. Grant, J. M. Berg, and D. M. Cable, "Job Titles as Identity Badges: How Self-Reflective Titles Can Reduce Emotional Exhaustion," *Academy of Management Journal* 57, no. 4 (2014): 1201–1225.

72. C. Fairchild, "Does Levi Strauss Still Fit America," *Fortune* (October 6, 2014): 180–188.

73. N. Li, B. L. Kirkman, and C. O. H. Porter, "Toward a Model of Work Team Altruism," *Academy of Management Review* 39, no. 4, (2014): 541–565.

74. T. A. De Vries, F. Walter, G. S. Van Der Vegt, and P. J. M. D. Essens, "Antecedents of Individuals' Interteam Coordination: Broad Functional Experiences as a Mixed Blessing," *Academy of Management Journal* 57, no. 5 (2014): 1334–1359.

75. G. Guerra and R. Patuelli, "The Role of Job Satisfaction in Transitions Into Self-Employment," *Entrepreneurship Theory and Practice* 40, no. 3 (2016): 543–570.

76. O. Osiyevskyy and J. Dewald, "Inducements, Impediments, and Immediacy: Exploring the Cognitive Drivers of Small Business Managers' Intentions to Adopt Business Model Change," *Journal of Small Business Management* 53, no. 4 (2015): 1011–1032.

77. M. Rowlinson, J. Hassard, and S. Decker, "Research Strategies for Organizational History: A Dialogue Between Historical Theory and Organization Theory," *Academy of Management Review* 39, no. 3 (2014): 250–274.

78. S. Clegg, "Managerialism: Born in the USA," *Academy of Management Review* 39, no. 4 (2014): 567–576.

79. F. W. Taylor, *Principles of Scientific Management* (New York: Harper & Brothers, 1911).

80. H. Fayol, *General and Industrial Management*, trans. by J. A. Conbrough (Geneva: International Management Institute, 1929).

81. F. Roethlisberger and W. Dickson, *Management and the Worker* (Boston: Harvard University Press, 1939).

82. A. Maslow, *Motivation and Personality*, 2nd ed. (New York: Harper & Row, 1970).

83. D. McGregor, *The Human Side of Enterprise* (New York: McGraw-Hill, 1960).

84. H. Koontz, "The Management Theory Jungle Revisited," *Academy of Management Review* 5 (April 1980): 175; D. Katz and R. Khan, *The Social Psychology of Organizations*, 2nd ed. (New York: Wiley, 1978).

85. R. Ackoff, *Creating the Corporate Future* (New York: Wiley, 1981).

86. E. L. Trist and K. W. Bamforth, "Some Social and Psychological Consequences of the Longwall Method of Coalgetting," *Human Relations* 4 (1951): 3–38; F. E. Emery and E. L. Trist, *Socio-Technical Systems*, Vol. 2 of *Management Science: Methods and Techniques* (London: Pergamon, 1960).

87. T. Burns and G. Stalker, *The Management of Innovation* (London: Tavistock, 1961).

88. M. Korn and R. Feintzeig, "Is the Old-School, Hard-Nosed Boss Obsolete?" *The Wall Street Journal* (May 23, 2014): B1.

89. C. L. Pearce, C. L. Wassenaar, and C. C. Manz, "Is Shared Leadership the Key to Responsible Leadership?" *Academy of Management Perspectives* 28, no. 3 (2014): 275–288.

90. GE ad, "Identifying the Leadership Skills That Matter Most Today," *INC.* (December 2014–January 2015): 78.

91. W. Q. Judge, Y. L. Thompkins, J. L. Brown, and C. Pongpatipat, "The Impact of Home Country Institutions on Corporate Technological Entrepreneurship via E R&D Investments and Virtual World Presence," *Entrepreneurship Theory and Practice*, 39, no. 2 (2015): 237–266.

92. R. B. Briner and N. D. Walshe, "From Passively Received Wisdom to Actively Constructed Knowledge: Teaching Systematic Review Skills as a Foundation of Evidence-Based Management," *Academy of Management Learning & Education* 13, no. 3 (2014): 415–432.

93. J. N. Reyt and B. M. Wiesenfeld, "Seeing the Forest for the Trees: Exploratory Learning, Mobile Technology, and Knowledge Workers' Role Integration Behaviors," *Academy of Management Journal* 58, no. 3 (2015): 739–762.

94. M. Sytch and A. Tatarynowicz, "Exploring the Locus of Invention: The Dynamics of Network Communities and Firms' Invention Productivity," *Academy of Management Journal* 57, no. 1 (2014): 249–279.

95. H. Yang, Y. Zheng, and A. Zaheer, "Asymmetric Learning Capabilities and Stock Market Value," *Academy of Management Journal* 58, no. 2 (2015): 356–374.

96. GE ad, "Identifying the Leadership Skills That Matter Most Today," *INC.* (December 2014–January 2015): 78.

97. E. G. R. Barends and R. B. Briner, "Teaching Evidence-Based Practice: Lessons From the Pioneers," *Academy of Management Learning & Education* 13, no. 3 (2014): 476–483.

98. E. N. Gamble and R. B. Jelley, "The Case for Competition: Learning About Evidence-Based Management Through Case Competition," *Academy of Management Learning & Education* 13, no. 3 (2014): 433–445.

99. "From the Guest Editors: Change the World: Teach Evidence-Based Practices!" *Academy of Management Learning & Education* 13, no. 3 (2014): 305–319.

100. Staff, "Best Practicers," *Entrepreneur* (November 2015): 59.

101. K. Morrell and M. Learmonth, "Against Evidence-Based Management, for Management Learning," *Academy of Management Learning & Education* 14, no. 4 (2015): 520–533.

102. S. Kepes, A. A. Bennett, and M. A. McDaniel, "Evidence-Based Management and the Trustworthiness of Our Cumulative Scientific Knowledge: Implications for Teaching, Research, and Practice," *Academy of Management Learning & Education* 13, no. 3 (2014): 446–466.

103. S. D. Charlier, "Incorporating Evidence-Based Management Into Management Curricula: A Conversation With Gary Latham," *Academy of Management Learning & Education* 13, no. 3 (2014): 467–475.

104. G. Colvin, "Humans are Underrated," *Fortune* (August 1, 2015), 100–113.

105. S. D. Parks, *Leadership Can Be Taught* (Boston: Harvard Business School Press, 2005).

106. S. D. Parks, *Leadership Can Be Taught* (Boston: Harvard Business School Press, 2005).

107. AACSB International, *Eligibility Procedures and Accreditation Standards for Business Accreditation* (Tampa, FL: Author, 2016), http://www.aacsb.edu/-/

media/aacsb/docs/accreditation/standards/businessstds_2013_update-03oct_final_tracked_changes.ashx?la=en, accessed November 28, 2016.

108. "From the Guest Editors: Change the World: Teach Evidence-Based Practices!" *Academy of Management Learning & Education* 13, no. 3 (2014): 305–319.

109. R. L. Dipboye, "Bridging the Gap in Organizational Behavior," *Academy of Management Learning & Education* 13, no. 3 (2014): 487–491.

110. Editor, "Introduction: Bringing to Life a Correlation of .14: Teaching Evidence-Based Management Engagingly and Convincingly," *Academy of Management Learning & Education* 13, no. 3 (2014): 102–103.

111. S. Kepes, A. A. Bennett, and M. A. McDaniel, "Evidence-Based Management and the Trustworthiness of Our Cumulative Scientific Knowledge: Implications for Teaching, Research, and Practice," *Academy of Management Learning & Education* 13, no. 3 (2014): 446–466.

112. K. E. Brink and R. D. Costigan, "Oral Communication Skills: Are the Priorities of the Workplace and AACSB-Accredited Business Programs Aligned?" *Academy of Management Learning & Education* 14, no. 2 (2015): 205–221.

113. E. G. R. Barends and R. B. Briner, "Teaching Evidence-Based Practice: Lessons From the Pioneers," *Academy of Management Learning & Education* 13, no. 3 (2014): 476–483.

114. T. Ungaretti, K. R. Thompson, A. Miller, and T. O. Peterson, "Problem-Based Learning: Lessons From Medical Education and Challenges for Management Education," *Academy of Management Learning & Education* 14, no. 2 (2015): 173–186.

115. J. S. Goodman, M. S. Gray, and R. E. Wood, "Bibliographic Search Training for Evidence-Based Management Education: A Review of Relevant Literature," *Academy of Management Learning & Education* 13, no. 3 (2014): 322–353.

116. "From the Guest Editors: Change the World: Teach Evidence-Based Practices!" *Academy of Management Learning & Education* 13, no. 3 (2014): 305–319.

117. S. D. Charlier, "Incorporating Evidence-Based Management Into Management Curricula: A Conversation With Gary Latham," *Academy of Management Learning & Education* 13, no. 3 (2014): 467–475.

118. E. Bernstein, "Beat Back the Self-Doubt," *The Wall Street Journal* (June 14, 2016): D1, D2; E. G. R. Barends and R. B. Briner, "Teaching Evidence-Based Practice: Lessons From the Pioneers," *Academy of Management Learning & Education* 13, no. 3 (2014): 476–483.

119. S. F. Collins, "Success Steps," *Costco Connection* (January 2016): 29.

120. D. R. Ames and A. S. Wazlawek, "How to Tell If You're a Jerk in the Office," *The Wall Street Journal* (February 23, 2015): R2.

121. Dow Jones, http://new.dowjones.com/, accessed March 25, 2015.

122. G. Colvin, "Four Things That Worry Business," *Fortune* (October 27, 2014): 32.

123. A. Wolfe, "Jack and Suzy Welch," *The Wall Street Journal* (February 21–22, 2015): C11.

124. L. M. Leslie, D. M. Mayer, and D. A. Kravitz, "The Stigma of Affirmative Action: A Stereotyping-Based Theory and Meta-Analytic Test of the Consequences for Performance," *Academy of Management Journal* 57, no. 4 (2014): 964–989.

125. O. E. Varela and R. G. Watts, "The Development of the Global Manager: An Empirical Study on the Role of Academic International Sojourns," *Academy of Management Learning & Education* 13, no. 2 (2014): 187–207.

126. From the Editors, "Organizations With Purpose," *Academy of Management Journal* 57, no. 5 (2014): 1227–1234.

Chapter 2

1. D. Albert, M. Kreutzer, and C. Lechner, "Resolving the Paradox of Interdependency and Strategic Renewal in Activity Systems," *Academy of Management Review* 40, no. 2 (2015): 210–234.

2. Editors, "Reputation and Status: Expanding the Role of Social Evaluations in Management Research," *Academy of Management Journal* 59, no. 1 (2016): 1–13.

3. W. Su and E. W. K. Tsang, "Product Diversification and Financial Performance: The Moderating Role of Secondary Stakeholders," *Academy of Management Journal* 58, no. 4 (2015): 1128–1148.

4. V. F. Misangyi and A. G. Acharya, "Substitutes or Complements? A Configurational Examination of Corporate Governance Mechanisms," *Academy of Management Journal* 57, no. 6 (2014): 1681–1705.

5. Definition recommended by a reviewer from Ohio University, March 30, 2015.

6. D. Albert, M. Kreutzer, and C. Lechner, "Resolving the Paradox of Interdependency and Strategic Renewal in Activity Systems," *Academy of Management Review* 40, no. 2 (2015): 210–234.

7. R. Karlgaard, "Peter Drucker and Me," *Forbes* (April 14, 2014): 38.

8. A. M. Carton, C. Murphy, and J. R. Clark, "A (Blurry) Vision of the Future: How Leader Rhetoric About Ultimate Goals Influences Performance," *Academy of Management Journal* 57, no. 6 (2014): 1544–1570.

9. A. Murray, "The Pinnacles and Pitfalls of Corporate Culture," *Fortune* (March 15, 2016): 14.

10. M. Charski, "Your Business, Described," *Costco Connection* (May 2015): 15.

11. N. Roellis, margin note quote, *Business Week* (September 22–28, 2014): 41; M. Charski, "Your Business, Described," *Costco Connection* (May 2015): 15.

12. C. Hann, "Raison d'etre," *Entrepreneur* (March 2015): 32.

13. V. Harnish, "Five Questions to Ponder, for 2015," *Fortune* (December 22, 2014): 36.

14. Information taken from Walmart's corporate website, http://www.corporate.walmart.com, accessed December 1, 2016.

15. Information taken from the Springfield College website, http://www.springfieldcollege.edu, accessed December 1, 2016.

16. Machine Zone quote, *Business Week* (March 9–15, 2015): 72.

17. B. Costa, "The CEO Who Gets to Hand Out World Series Rings," *The Wall Street Journal* (February 23, 2015): R4.

18. Statement read in *The Wall Street Journal* several years ago.

19. J. S. Lublin and J. Jargon, "McDonald's Nears Decision on Real Estate," *The Wall Street Journal* (October 16, 2015): B3.

20. J. Jargon, "McDonald's Lands in a Real Estate Dilemma," *The Wall Street Journal* (August 26, 2015): B1.

21. S. Ovide, "Nadella Pushes for a Leaner Microsoft," *The Wall Street Journal* (July 11, 2014): B1.

22. M. Blumenstein, "IBM Plans to Thrive as a Digital Company," *The Wall Street Journal* (October 27, 2015): R3.

23. C. Q. Trank, "Reading Evidence-Based Management: The Possibilities of Interpretation," *Academy of Management Education & Learning* 13, no. 3 (2014): 381–395.

24. R. Lewis, "My Advice," *Fortune* (December 22, 2014): 34.

25. D. Baden and M. Higgs, "Challenging the Perceived Wisdom of Management Theories and Practice," *Academy of Management Learning & Education* 14, no. 4 (2015): 539–555; F. Wijen, "Means Versus Ends in Opaque Institutional Fields: Trading Off Compliance and Achievement in Sustainability Standard Adoption," *Academy of Management Review* 39, no. 3 (2014): 302–323.

26. R. Karlgaard, "Vivid Vision for Success," *Forbes* (January 19, 2015): 28.

27. A. Murray, "The Pinnacles and Pitfalls of Corporate Culture," *Fortune* (March 15, 2016): 14.

28. A. Canato, "Coerced Practice Implementation in Cases of Low Cultural Fit: Cultural Change and Practice Adaptation During the Implementation of Six Sigma at 3M," *Academy of Management Journal* 56, no. 6 (2013): 1724–1753.

29. A. Murray, "The Pinnacles and Pitfalls of Corporate Culture," *Fortune* (March 15, 2016): 14.

30. S. Sonenshein, "How Organizations Foster the Creative Use of Resources," *Academy of Management Journal* 57, no. 3 (2014): 814–848.

31. D. Albert, M. Kreutzer, and C. Lechner, "Resolving the Paradox of Interdependency and Strategic Renewal in Activity Systems," *Academy of Management Review* 40, no. 2 (2015): 210–234.

32. S. Sonenshein, "How Organizations Foster the Creative Use of Resources," *Academy of Management Journal* 57, no. 3 (2014): 814–848.

33. D. Albert, M. Kreutzer, and C. Lechner, "Resolving the Paradox of Interdependency and Strategic Renewal in Activity Systems," *Academy of Management Review* 40, no. 2 (2015): 210–234.

34. Adapted from Amazon.com 2015 Annual Report, www.amazon.com, accessed December 1, 2016.

35. T. S. Liao, J. Rice, and J. C. Lu, "The Vicissitudes of Competitive Advantage: Empirical Evidence from Australian Manufacturing SMEs," *Journal of Small Business Management* 53 no. 2 (2015): 469–481; W. McKinley, S. Latham, and M. Braun, "Organizational Decline and Innovation: Turnarounds and Downward Spirals," *Academy of Management Review* 39, no. 1 (2014): 88–110.

36. C. Tkaczyk, "How Google Works," *Fortune* (September 24, 2014): 103.

37. D. Korschun, "Boundary-Spanning Employees and Relationships with External Stakeholders: A Social Identity Approach," *Academy of Management Review* 40, no. 4 (2015): 611–629.

38. G. Golvin, "A CEO's Plan to Defy Disruption," *Fortune* (November 17, 2014): 36.

39. Y. Kubota, "Honda CEO Rethinks Car Maker's Priorities," *The Wall Street Journal* (December 3, 2014): B1, B2.

40. J. P. Doh and N. R. Quigley, "Responsible Leadership and Stakeholder Management: Influence Pathways and Organizational Outcomes," *Academy of Management Perspectives* 28, no. 3 (2014): 255–274.

41. D. Chandler, "Morals, Markets, and Values-Based Business," *Academy of Management Review* 39, no. 3 (2014): 396–397.

42. A. H. Bowers, H. R. Greve, H. Mitsuhashi, and J. A. C. Baum, "Competitive Parity, Status Disparity, and Mutual Forbearance: Securities Analysts' Competition for Investor Attention," *Academy of Management Journal* 57, no. 1 (2014): 38–62.

43. W. Su and E. W. K. Tsang, "Product Diversification and Financial Performance: The Moderating Role of Secondary Stakeholders," *Academy of Management Journal* 58, no. 4 (2015): 1128–1148.

44. Regulatory Studies Center, Washington University, reported in *Fortune* (November 1, 2016): 82.

45. D. Roberts, "Flight of Fantasy," *Fortune* (October 1, 2015): 80–84.

46. Y. Zhang, D. A. Waldman, Y. L. Han, and X. Li, "Paradoxical Leader Behaviors in People Management: Antecedents and Consequences," *Academy of Management Journal* 58, no. 2 (2015): 538–566.

47. D. J. Teece, "The Foundations of Enterprise Performance: Dynamic and Ordinary Capabilities in an (Economic) Theory of Firms," *Academy of Management Perspectives* 28, no. 4 (2014): 328–352.

48. M. L. Besharov and W. K. Smith, "Multiple Institutional Logics in Organizations: Explaining Their Varied Nature and Implications," *Academy of Management Review* 39, no. 3 (2014): 364–381.

49. D. Albert, M. Kreutzer, and C. Lechner, "Resolving the Paradox of Interdependency and Strategic Renewal in Activity Systems," *Academy of Management Review* 40, no. 2 (2015): 210–234.

50. R. Ackoff, *Creating the Corporate Future* (New York: Wiley, 1981).

51. S. Banjo, "Wal-Mart Targets Amazon," *The Wall Street Journal* (October 31, 2014): B2.

52. R. Karlgaard, "Amazon and IBM: Whoops!" *Forbes* (November 24, 2014): 36.

53. Exhibit 2-5 is based on systems theory and was designed by Dr. Abbas Nadim of the University of New Haven. The author added the word *culture* in the segment whose label now reads "Management and Culture."

54. R. J. Funk, "Making the Most of Where You Are: Geography, Networks, and Innovation in Organizations," *Academy of Management Journal* 37, no. 1 (2012): 193–222.

55. C. Hardy and D. Tolhurst, "Epistemological Beliefs and Cultural Diversity Matters in Management Education and Learning," *Academy of Management Learning & Education* 13, no. 2 (2014): 265–289.

56. Xerox website, www.xerox.com, accessed March 31, 2015.

57. A. Murray, "The Pinnacles and Pitfalls of Corporate Culture," *Fortune* (March 15, 2016): 14.

58. M. L. Stallard, "Building a Culture of Connections," *Costco Connection* (July 2015): 112.

59. C. Tkaczyk, "How Google Works," *Fortune* (September 24, 2014): 103.

60. C. Rose, "Charlie Rose Talks to Tory Burch," *BusinessWeek* (October 20–26, 2014): 24.

61. B. Costa, "The CEO Who Gets to Hand Out World Series Rings," *The Wall Street Journal* (February 23, 2015): R4.

62. G. Colvin, "Personal Bests," *Fortune* (March 15, 2015): 106–110.

63. Boxed item, "Leading Innovation," *The Wall Street Journal* (February 10, 2016): R3.

64. Marin note, *INC.* (February 2016): 19

65. S. L. Dailey and L. Browning, "Retelling Stories in Organizations: Understanding the Functions of Narrative Repetition," *Academy of Management Review* 39, no. 1 (2014): 22–43.

66. S. Clinebell, "Snapshots of Great Leadership," *Academy of Management Learning & Education* 13, no. 1 (2014): 139–149.

67. S. Shellenbarger, "Believers in the Project Bead and Other Office Rituals," *The Wall Street Journal* (June 28, 2013): D1, D2.

68. M. C. Schippers, "Social Loafing Tendencies and Team Performance: The Compensating Effect of Agreeableness and Conscientiousness," *Academy of Management Learning & Education* 13, no. 1 (2014): 62–81.

69. W. Boston, H. Varnholt, and S. Sloat, "VW Says 'Culture' Flaw Led to Crisis," *The Wall Street Journal* (December 11, 2015): B1.

70. A. Murray, "The Pinnacles and Pitfalls of Corporate Culture," *Fortune* (March 15, 2016): 14.

71. R. C. Liden, S. J. Wayne, C. Liao, and J. D. Meuser, "Servant Leadership and Serving Culture: Influence on Individual and Unit Performance," *Academy of Management Journal* 57, no. 5 (2014): 1434–1452.

72. S. Ovide, "Nadella Pushes for a Leaner Microsoft," *The Wall Street Journal* (July 11, 2014): B1.

73. M. Blumenstein, "IBM Plans to Thrive as a Digital Company," *The Wall Street Journal* (October 27, 2015): R3.

74. W. Beasley, "Listen Up," *Fortune* (December 15, 2015): 12.

75. D. Leonard, "Will Amazon Kill FedEx?" *BusinessWeek* (August 31, 2016): 46–51.

76. C. Bonanos, "The Lies We Tell at Work," *BusinessWeek* (February 4–10, 2013): 71–73.

77. AACSB International, *Eligibility Procedures and Accreditation Standards for Business Accreditation* (Tampa, FL: Author, 2012), www.aacsb.edu/accreditation/standards-busn-jan2012.pdf, accessed March 31, 2015.

78. D. Baden and M. Higgs, "Challenging the Perceived Wisdom of Management Theories and Practice," *Academy of Management Learning & Education* 14, no. 4 (2015): 539–555.

79. K. Leavitt and D. M. Sluss, "Lying for Who We Are: An Identity-Based Model of Workplace Dishonesty," *Academy of Management Review* 40, no. 4 (2015): 587–610.

80. G. K. Stahl and M. S. De Luque, "Antecedents of Responsible Leader Behavior: A Research Synthesis Conceptual Framework, and Agenda for Future Research," *Academy of Management Perspectives* 28, no. 3 (2014): 235–254.

81. S. S. Wiltermuth, "Power, Moral Clarity, and Punishment in the Workplace," *Academy of Management Journal* 56, no. 4 (2013): 1002–1023.

82. D. Ariely, "Why We Lie," *The Wall Street Journal* (May 26–27, 2012): C1–C2.

83. S. D. Levitt and S. J. Dubner, "SuperFreakonomics: Global Cooling, Patriotic Prostitutes, and Why Suicide Bombers Should Buy Life Insurance," *Academy of Management Perspectives* 25, no. 2 (2011): 86–87.

84. K. Leavitt and D. M. Sluss, "Lying for Who We Are: An Identity-Based Model of Workplace Dishonesty," *Academy of Management Review* 40, no. 4 (2015): 587–610.

85. G. O'Brien, "Sparring Partners," *Entrepreneur* (August 2015): 32.

86. S. Bing, "Why Crazy Works," *Fortune* (September 2016): 108.

87. R. Fehr, K. C. Yam, and C. Dang, "Moralized Leadership: The Construction and Consequences of Ethical Leader Perceptions," *Academy of Management Review* 40, no. 2 (2015): 182–209.

88. K. Y. Hsieh, W. Tsai, and M. J. Chen, "If They Can Do It, Why Not Us? Competitors as Reference Points for Justifying Escalation of Commitment," *Academy of Management Journal* 56, no. 1 (2015): 38–58.

89. H. Willmott, "Reflections on the Darker Side of Conventional Power Analytics," *Academy of Management Perspectives* 27, no. 4 (2013): 281–286.

90. D. Ariely, "Why We Lie," *The Wall Street Journal* (May 26–27, 2012): C1–C2.

91. News Story, National Public Radio aired (September 7, 2016).

92. D. Baden, "Look on the Bright Side: A Comparison of Positive and Negative Role Models in Business Ethics Education," *Academy of Management Learning & Education* 13, no. 2 (2014): 154–170.

93. M. Kelly, *Rediscovering Catholicism* (New York: Beacon, 2010).

94. R. McCammon, "So, Here's the Bad News…" *Entrepreneur* (July 2015): 24–25.

95. C. Hann, "Truth Time," *Entrepreneur* (March 2016): 24.

96. G. O'Brien, "Honesty Policies," *Entrepreneur* (October 2014): 34.

97. G. Colvin, "Personal Bests," *Fortune* (March 15, 2015): 106–110.

98. W. L. Bedwell, S. M. Fiore, and E. Salas, "Developing the Future Workforce: An Approach for Integrating Interpersonal Skills Into the MBA Classroom," *Academy of Management Learning & Education* 13, no. 2 (2014): 171–186.

99. C. Carr, "Stress to Impress," *Costco Connection* (February 2015): 13.

100. Bonanos, "The Lies We Tell at Work," *BusinessWeek* (February 4–10, 2013): 71–73.

101. G. K. Stahl and M. S. De Luque, "Antecedents of Responsible Leader Behavior: A Research Synthesis Conceptual Framework, and Agenda for Future Research," *Academy of Management Perspectives* 28, no. 3 (2014): 235–254.

102. G. Colvin, "The Benefit of Baring It All," *Fortune* (December 2015), 34.

103. S. Bing, "Does the Truth Matter?" *Fortune* (May 1, 2016): 136.

104. A. C. Cosper, "Meeting Fear's Antidote: Hope," *Entrepreneur* (January 2016): 10.

105. C. Bonanos, "The Lies We Tell at Work," *BusinessWeek* (February 4–10, 2013): 71–73.

106. S. S. Wiltermuth, "Power, Moral Clarity, and Punishment in the Workplace," *Academy of Management Journal* 56, no. 4 (2013): 1002–1023.

107. D. T. Welsh and L. D. Ordonez, "Conscience Without Cognition: The Effects of Subconscious Priming on Ethical Behavior," *Academy of Management Journal* 57, no. 5 (2014): 723–1109.

108. D. Ariely, "Why We Lie," *The Wall Street Journal* (May 26–27, 2012): C1–C2.

109. D. T. Kong, K. T. Dirks, and D. L. Ferrin, "Interpersonal Trust Within Negotiations: Meta-Analytic Evidence, Critical Contingencies, and Directions for Further Research," *Academy of Management Journal* 57, no. 5 (2014): 1235–1255.

110. R. Whelan, "Lawsuit: Schorsch Told Us to Lie," *The Wall Street Journal* (December 19, 2014): C1.

111. D. Ariely, "Why We Lie," *The Wall Street Journal* (May 26–27, 2012): C1–C2.

112. From the Editors, "Organizations With Purpose," *Academy of Management Journal* 57, no. 5 (2014): 1227–1234.

113. L. J. Christensen, A. Mackey, and D. Whetten, "Taking Responsibility for Corporate Social Responsibility: The Role of Leaders in Creating, Implementing, Sustaining, or Avoiding Socially Responsible Firm Behavior," *Academy of Management Perspectives* 28, no. 2 (2014): 164–178.

114. L. Daskal, "4 Pieces of Advice Most People Ignore," *INC.* (July/August 2016): 8.

115. P. Jackson, "Conversation With Phil Jackson," *AARP Bulletin* (January–February 2014): 10.

116. D. Crilly, M. Hansen, M. Zollo, "The Grammar of Decoupling: A Cognitive-Linguistic Perspective on Firms' Sustainability Claims and Stakeholders' Interpretation," *Academy of Management Journal* 59, no. 2 (2016): 705–729.

117. M. Langley, "The Many Stakeholders of Salesforce.com," *The Wall Street Journal* (October 27, 2015): R2.

118. Contents page Statement, *BusinessWeek* (September 7–13, 2015): 3.

119. D. Ariely, "Why We Lie," *The Wall Street Journal* (May 26–27, 2012): C1–C2.

120. "World's Most Ethical Companies," http://ethisphere.com, accessed April 2, 2015.

121. E. Grijalva and P. D. Harms, "Narcissism: An Integrative Synthesis and Dominance Complementarity Model," *Academy of Management Perspectives* 28, no. 2 (2014): 108–127.

122. D. T. Welsh and L. D. Ordonez, "Conscience Without Cognition: The Effects of Subconscious Priming on Ethical Behavior," *Academy of Management Journal* 57, no. 5 (2014): 723–1109.

123. R. Fehr, K. C. Yam, and C. Dang, "Moralized Leadership: The Construction and Consequences of Ethical Leader Perceptions," *Academy of Management Review* 40, no. 2 (2015): 182–209.

124. L. J. Christensen, A. Mackey, and D. Whetten, "Taking Responsibility for Corporate Social Responsibility: The Role of Leaders in Creating, Implementing, Sustaining, or Avoiding Socially Responsible Firm Behavior," *Academy of Management Perspectives* 28, no. 2 (2014): 164–178.

125. D. Ariely, "Why We Lie," *The Wall Street Journal* (May 26–27, 2012): C1–C2.

126. S. S. Wiltermuth, "Power, Moral Clarity, and Punishment in the Workplace," *Academy of Management Journal* 57, no. 3 (2014): 849–868.

127. D. A. Waldman and R. M. Balven, "Responsible Leadership: Theoretical Issues and Research Directions," *Academy of Management Perspectives* 28, no. 3 (2014): 224–234.

128. C. C. Manz, "Taking the Self-Leadership High Road: Smooth Surface or Potholes Ahead?" *Academy of Management Perspectives* 29, no. 1 (2015): 132–151.

129. I. Filatotchev and C. Nakajima, "Corporate Governance, Responsible Managerial Behavior, and Corporate Social Responsibility: Organizational Efficiency Versus Organizational Legitimacy," *Academy of Management Perspectives* 28, no. 3 (2014): 289–306.

130. C. L. Pearce, C. L. Wassenaar, and C. C. Manz, "Is Shared Leadership the Key to Responsible Leadership?" *Academy of Management Perspectives* 28, no. 3 (2014): 275–288.

131. M. Washburn and P. Bromiley, "Managers and Analysts: An Examination of Mutual Influence," *Academy of Management Journal* 56, no. 4 (2013): 1002–1023.

132. S. Schaefer, "The Just 100: America's Best Corporate Citizens," *Forbes* (December 20, 2016): 82.

133. C. Q. Trank, "Reading Evidence-Based Management: The Possibilities of Interpretation," *Academy of Management Learning & Education* 13, no. 3 (2014): 381–395.

134. T. Hahn, L. Preuss, J. Pinkse, and F. Figge, "Cognitive Frames in Corporate Sustainability: Managerial Sensemaking with Paradoxical and Business Case Frames," *Academy of Management Review* 39, no. 4 (2014): 463–487.

135. R. M. Kanter, "Why Global Companies Will Behave More and More Alike," *The Wall Street Journal* (July 8, 2014): R8.

136. M. E. Porter and M. R. Kramer, "Profiting the Planet," *Fortune* (September 1, 2015): 64–65.

137. D. S. Siegel, "Responsible Leadership," *Academy of Management Perspectives* 28, no. 3 (2014): 221–223.

138. J. P. Doh and N. R. Quigley, "Responsible Leadership and Stakeholder Management: Influence Pathways and Organizational Outcomes," *Academy of Management Perspectives* 28, no. 3 (2014): 255–274.

139. S. Schaefer, "The Just 100: America's Best Corporate Citizens," *Forbes* (December 20, 2016): 82.

140. S. Berfield, "The Clutter in Kip Tindell," *BusinessWeek* (February 23–March 1, 2015): 41–45.

141. A. Kroeger and C. Weber, "Developing a Conceptual Framework for Comparing Social Value Creation," *Academy of Management Review* 39, no. 4 (2014): 513–540.

142. J. Battilana, M. Sengul, A. C. Pache, and J. Model, "Harnessing Productive Tensions in Hybrid Organizations: The Case of Work Integration Social Enterprises," *Academy of Management Journal* 58, no. 6 (2015): 1058–1685.

143. B. Mycoskie, *Start Something That Matters* (New York: Spiegel & Grau, 2012): 193.

144. V. Harnish, "5 Key Trends to Master in 2016," *Fortune* (December 15, 2015), 52; B Corp website www .bcorporation.net, accessed December 12, 2016.

145. D. J. Jones, C. R. Willness, and S. Madey, "Why Are Job Seekers Attracted by Corporate Social Performance? Experimental and Field Tests of Three Signal-Based Mechanisms," *Academy of Management Journal* 57, no. 2 (2014): 383–404.

146. D. A. Waldman and R. M. Balven, "Responsible Leadership: Theoretical Issues and Research Directions," *Academy of Management Perspectives* 28, no. 3 (2014): 224–234.

147. D. J. Jones, C. R. Willness, and S. Madey, "Why Are Job Seekers Attracted by Corporate Social Performance? Experimental and Field Tests of Three Signal-Based Mechanisms," *Academy of Management Journal* 57, no. 2 (2014): 383–404.

148. Staff, "Corporate Social Responsibility: Good Citizenship or Investor Rip-off?" *The Wall Street Journal* (January 9, 2006): R6.

149. D. Bennet and D. Gambrell, "How CVS Quit Smoking," *BusinessWeek* (December 29, 2014–January 11, 2015): 58.

150. R. Karlgaard, "Society's Lottery Winners," *Forbes* (June 15, 2015): 30.

151. K. Cole, "A Social Agenda at the Office," *Fortune* (September 15, 2016): 36.

152. L. Buchanan, "Call to Action: Make a Profit, Change the World," *INC.* (October 2014): 46–50.

153. Bridgespan Group, "Philanthropy: Change Agents," *Forbes* (December 14, 2015): 40.

154. D. Seetharaman and A. Das, "Zuckerberg to Give Away Fortune," *The Wall Street Journal* (December 2, 2015): B1, B8.

155. R. Rubin, L. Saunders, and D. Seetharaman, "Zuckerberb Tests New Philanthropic Model," *The Wall Street Journal* (December 3, 2015): B1, B10.

156. P. Schreck, "Reviewing the Business Case for Corporate Social Responsibility: New Evidence and Analysis," *Journal of Business Ethics* 103, no. 2 (2011): 167–188.

157. J. Welch and S. Welch, "Giving in an Unforgiving Time," *BusinessWeek* (June 1, 2009): 80.

158. Staff, "Briefs," *BusinessWeek* (December 15–21, 2014): 23.

159. Definition developed by the Brundtland Commission.

160. A. A. Marcus and A. R. Fremeth, "Green Management Matters Regardless," *Academy of Management Perspectives* 23, no. 3 (2009): 17–26.

161. C. L. Pearce, C. L. Wassenaar, and C. C. Manz, "Is Shared Leadership the Key to Responsible Leadership?" *Academy of Management Perspectives* 28, no. 3 (2014): 275–288.

162. A. Nadim and R. N. Lussier, "Sustainability as a Small Business Competitive Strategy," *Journal of Small Strategy* 21, no. 2 (2012): 79–95.

163. D. S. Siegel, "Responsible Leadership," *Academy of Management Perspectives* 28, no. 3 (2014): 221–223.

164. D. Baden, "Look on the Bright Side: A Comparison of Positive and Negative Role Models in Business Ethics Education," *Academy of Management Learning & Education* 13, no. 2 (2014): 154–170.

165. C. L. Pearce, C. L. Wassenaar, and C. C. Manz, "Is Shared Leadership the Key to Responsible Leadership?" *Academy of Management Perspectives* 28, no. 3 (2014): 275–288.

166. R. Karlgaard, "Riches From the Disruptive Dozen," *Forbes* (October 19, 2015): 38.

167. Ad "Green Building U.S.A." *Fortune* (November 1, 2015): n.p.

168. T. Hahn, L. Preuss, J. Pinkse, and F. Figge, "Cognitive Frames in Corporate Sustainability: Managerial Sensemaking With Paradoxical and Business Case Frames," *Academy of Management Review* 39, no. 4 (2014): 463–487.

169. R. M. Kanter, "Why Global Companies Will Behave More and More Alike," *The Wall Street Journal* (July 8, 2014): R8.

170. L. Lorenzetti, "Southwest Airlines Is Flying High," *Fortune* (October 27, 2014): 38.

171. D. Crilly, M. Hansen, and M. Zollo, "The Grammar of Decoupling: A Cognitive-Linguistic Perspective on Firms' Sustainability Claims and Stakeholder' Interpretation," *Academy of Management Journal* 59, no. 2 (2016): 705–729.

172. M. E. Porter and M. R. Kramer, "Profiting the Planet," *Fortune* (September 1, 2015): 64–65.

173. J. A. A. Correa, A. Marcus, and N. H. Torres, "The Natural Environmental Strategies of International Firms: Old Controversies and New Evidence on Performance and Disclosure," *Academy of Management Perspectives* 30, no. 1 (2016): 24–39.

174. A. Nadim and R. N. Lussier, "Sustainability as a Small Business Competitive Strategy," *Journal of Small Strategy* 21, no. 2 (2012): 79–95.

175. B. Johansen, "The Future," *Entrepreneur* (January 2015): 34.

176. C. P. Withorn, "Thanks, Jeff Bezos!" *Forbes* (August 17, 2015): 36–38.

177. C. Helman, "Everyday Renewable Energy," *Forbes* (November 25, 2014): 66–68.

178. G. Colvin, "From High-Minded to High Value," *Fortune* (December 22, 2014): 38.

179. Dow Jones website, http://www.sustainability-indices.com, accessed December 8, 2016.

180. M. P. Johnson and S. Schaltegger, "Two Decades of Sustainability Management Tools for SMEs: How Far Have We Come?" *Journal of Small Business Management* 54 no. 4 (2016): 481–505.

181. Information taken from Wikipedia's entry on chief sustainability officers at http://en.wikipedia.org/wiki/Chief_sustainability_officer, accessed April 3, 2015.

182. F. Wijen, "Means Versus Ends in Opaque Institutional Fields: Trading Off Compliance and Achievement in Sustainability Standard Adoption," *Academy of Management Review* 39, no. 3 (2014): 302–323.

183. C. Hardy and D. Tolhurst, "Epistemological Beliefs and Cultural Diversity Matters in Management Education and Learning," *Academy of Management Learning & Education* 13, no. 2 (2014): 265–289.

184. I. Filatotchev and C. Nakajima, "Corporate Governance, Responsible Managerial Behavior, and Corporate Social Responsibility: Organizational Efficiency Versus Organizational Legitimacy," *Academy of Management Perspectives* 28, no. 3 (2014): 289–306.

185. W. L. Bedwell, S. M. Fiore, and E. Salas, "Developing the Future Workforce: An Approach for Integrating Interpersonal Skills Into the MBA Classroom," *Academy of Management Learning & Education* 13, no. 2 (2014): 171–186.

186. C. Mims, "Huge Touch-Screen Tablets Sneak Into the Workplace," *The Wall Street Journal* (November 28, 2016): B1, B4.

187. H. Ganahl, "My Advice," *Fortune* (March 15, 2015): 42.

188. S. Banjo, G. Bensinger, and J. Nicas, "By Bike and by Air, Amazon Preps Faster Delivery," *The Wall Street Journal* (December 9, 2014): B1, B4.

189. N. Leiber, "A Different King of Ride-Sharing," *BusinessWeek* (July 13–19, 2015): 30–31.

190. C. L. Pearce, C. L. Wassenaar, and C. C. Manz, "Is Shared Leadership the Key to Responsible Leadership?" *Academy of Management Perspectives* 28, no. 3 (2014): 275–288.

191. From the Editors, "Organizations With Purpose," *Academy of Management Journal* 57, no. 5 (2014): 1227–1234.

192. G. K. Stahl and M. S. De Luque, "Antecedents of Responsible Leader Behavior: A Research Synthesis Conceptual Framework, and Agenda for Future Research," *Academy of Management Perspectives* 28, no. 3 (2014): 235–254.

193. S. S. Wiltermuth, "Power, Moral Clarity, and Punishment in the Workplace," *Academy of Management Journal* 57, no. 3 (2014): 849–868.

194. I. Filatotchev and C. Nakajima, "Corporate Governance, Responsible Managerial Behavior, and Corporate Social Responsibility: Organizational Efficiency Versus Organizational Legitimacy," *Academy of Management Perspectives* 28, no. 3 (2014): 289–306.

195. T. Hahn, L. Preuss, J. Pinkse, and F. Figge, "Cognitive Frames in Corporate Sustainability: Managerial Sensemaking With Paradoxical and Business Case Frames," *Academy of Management Review* 39, no. 4 (2014): 463–487.

196. M. Peters and R. E. Silverman, "Big Business Speaks Up on Social Issues," *The Wall Street Journal* (April 18, 2016):

197. M. L. Ram, "John Deere, Modern Farmer," *Fortune* (December 1, 2015): 67–70.

198. J. Bunge, "On the Farm: A Bountiful Harvest of Data," *The Wall Street Journal* (September 1, 2015): B1, B2.

199. M. L. Ram, "Can We Drink the Ocean," *Fortune* (July 1, 2015): 10–12.

200. A. Narayan, "Innovation: Smog Eater," *BusinessWeek* (October 19–25, 2015): 40.

Chapter 3

1. A. Murray, "The Hard Truths of Globalization," *Fortune* (August 1, 2016): 6.

2. M. L. Turner, "Remote Control," *Entrepreneur* (January 2016): 75–79.

3. R. J. Reichard, S. A. Serrano, M. Condren, N. Wilder, M. Dollwet, and W. Wang, "Engaging in Cultural Trigger Events in the Development of Cultural Competence," *Academy of Management Learning & Education* 14, no. 4 (2015): 461–481.

4. Information taken from the FedEx website, www.fedex.com, accessed January 5, 2017.

5. O. E. Varela and R. G. Watts, "The Development of the Global Manager: An Empirical Study on the Role of Academic International Sojourns," *Academy of Management Learning & Education* 13, no. 2 (2014): 187–207.

6. Amazon website, www.amazon.com, accessed January 5, 2017.

7. PepsiCo website, www.pepsico.com, accessed January 5, 2017.

8. E. Sylvers, "Fiat-Chrysler Faces Bend in the Road," *The Wall Street Journal* (found at www.fca.com), accessed April 7, 2015.

9. R. J. Reichard, S. A. Serrano, M. Condren, N. Wilder, M. Dollwet, and W. Wang, "Engaging in Cultural Trigger Events in the Development of Cultural Competence," *Academy of Management Learning & Education* 14, no. 4 (2015): 461–481.

10. D. Antons and F. T. Piller, "Opening the Black Box of 'Not Invented Here': Attitudes, Decision Biases, and Behavioral Consequences," *Academy of Management Perspectives* 29, no. 2 (2015): 193–217.

11. BP website, www.bp.com, accessed January 5, 2017.

12. PVH Corp., www.pvh.com, accessed January 5, 2017.

13. N. Chaichalearmmgkol and J. Beckerman, "A Merger in the Tuna Fish Business," *The Wall Street Journal* (December 20–21, 2014): B1.

14. J. Hagerty and J. Bennett, "Wages Drop as Foreign Parts Invade American Cars," *The Wall Street Journal* (March 24, 2015): A1, A2.

15. J. R. Hagerty, "'Made in America' Has Its Limits," *The Wall Street Journal* (November 23, 2012): B1.

16. K. Stock, "Briefs," *BusinessWeek* (January 26–February 1, 2015): 25.

17. L. Shaw with C. Rahn, "Netflix Looks to the Old World for New Growth," *BusinessWeek* (September 15–21, 2014): 25–26.

18. A. Narayan and B. Shrivastava, "Facebook's Fight to Be Free," *BusinessWeek* (January 18–24, 2016): 33–34.

19. S. Forbes, "Free Trade Means More Jobs," *Forbes* (June 15, 2015): 11–12.

20. A. Murray, "The Fight for the Future of Business," *Fortune* (September 1, 2016): 6.

21. Ibid.

22. I. Talley and W. Mauldin, "Globalization on the Skids," *The Wall Street Journal* (October 7, 2016): A1, A5.

23. Staff, "Trump's Trade War With … Boeing?" *BusinessWeek* (December 6–11, 2016): 36.

24. Abstract, "The WTO Ruled … *The Wall Street Journal* (September 23, 2016): A1, Story B3.

25. Information taken from the WTO's website, www.wto.org, accessed January 5, 2017.

26. M. Campbell and J. Simmons, "Move Over, BRICs; 2015 Is All About the USA," *BusinessWeek* (January 19–25, 2015): 51.

27. J. Immelt, "After Brexit, Global Is *Local*," Fortune (August 1, 2016).

28. Abstract, "China Is Set," *The Wall Street Journal* (November 12–13, 2016): A1, story A10.

29. B. Einhorn with I. Arkhipov, "Russia, Japan, and China Fill the Trade Gap," *BusinessWeek* (December 5–11, 2016): 22–23.

30. B. Einhorn with I. Arkhipov, "Russia, Japan, and China Fill the Trade Gap," *BusinessWeek* (December 5–11, 2016): 22–23.

31. L. Hoffman, "Pound's Drop Cost AB InBev $13 Billion," *The Wall Street Journal* (October 8–9, 2016): B1.

32. J. Ward and L. Mnyanda, "A Serious Pounding," *BusinessWeek* (October 31–November 6, 2016): 17–18.

33. L. Hoffman, "Pound's Drop Cost AB InBev $13 Billion," *The Wall Street Journal* (October 8–9, 2016):

34. A. Murray, "The Hard Truths of Globalization," *Fortune* (August 1, 2016): 6.

35. K. Stock, "Brief," *BusinessWeek* (September 28–October 4, 2015): 25.

36. The IMF website, www.imf.org, accessed January 7, 2017.

37. *Economist* website, www.economist.com/content/big-mac-index, accessed January 7, 2017.

38. J. Immelt, "After Brexit, Global Is *Local*," *Fortune* (August 1, 2016).

39. S. Forbes, "Free Trade Means More Jobs," *Forbes* (June 15, 2015): 11–12.

40. G. D. Bruton, M. W. Peng, D. Ahlstrom, C. Stan, and K. Xu, "State-Owned Enterprises Around the World as Hybrid Organizations," *Academy of Management Perspectives* 29, no. 1 (2015): 92–114.

41. A. Musacchio, S. G. Lazzarini, and R. V. Aguilera, "New Varieties of State Capitalism: Strategic and Governance Implications," *Academy of Management Perspectives* 29, no. 1 (2015): 115–131.

42. D. Gambrell, "Trade Give and Take," *BusinessWeek* (October 21–27, 2016): 18.

43. P. Krugman and R. Wells, *Microeconomics*, 4th ed. (New York: Macmillan, 2016).

44. G. Colvin, "Humans are Underrated," *Fortune* (August 1, 2015), 100–113.

45. C. Mims, "Automation Actually Can Lead to More Job Creation," *The Wall Street Journal* (December 12, 2016): B1, B4.

46. S. Forbes, "Free Trade Means More Jobs," *Forbes* (June 15, 2015): 11–12.

47. P. Coy, "Donald and the Dollar," *BusinessWeek* (December 8–18, 2016): 15.

48. Staff, "Trump's Trade War With … Boeing?" *BusinessWeek* (December 6–11, 2016): 36.

49. Abstract, "The IMF Signaled…." *The Wall Street Journal* (September 2, 2016): A1, Story of page A12.

50. I. Talley and W. Mauldin, "Globalization on the Skids," *The Wall Street Journal* (October 7, 2016): A1, A5.

51. B. Einhorn with I. Arkhipov, "Russia, Japan, and China Fill the Trade Gap," *BusinessWeek* (December 5–11, 2016): 22–23.

52. O. E. Varela and R. G. Watts, "The Development of the Global Manager: An Empirical Study on the Role of Academic International Sojourns," *Academy of Management Learning & Education* 13, no. 2 (2014): 187–207.

53. L. M. Leslie, D. M. Mayer, and D. A. Kravitz, "The Stigma of Affirmative Action: A Stereotyping-Based Theory and Meta-Analytic Test of the Consequences for Performance," *Academy of Management Journal* 57, no. 4 (2014): 964–989.

54. R. Feintzerg, "More Firms Say Targets Are the Key to Diversity," *The Wall Street Journal* (September 30, 2015): R3.

55. Call for papers, *Academy of Management Review* 40, no. 4 (2015): 669–670.

56. M. L. Besharov, "The Relational Ecology of Identification: How Organizational Identification Emerges When Individuals Hold Divergent Values," *Academy of Management Journal* 57, no. 5 (2014): 1485–1512.

57. F. A. Miller and J. H. Katz. *The Inclusion Breakthrough: Unleashing the Real Power of Diversity* (San Francisco: Berrett-Koehler, 2002).

58. National Public Radio, "News," aired April 9, 2015.

59. M. C. Hyter and J. L. Turnock, *The Power of Inclusion: Unlock the Potential and Productivity of Your Workforce* (New York: Wiley, 2006).

60. G. Colvin, "Humans are Underrated," *Fortune* (August 1, 2015), 100–113.

61. Ibid.

62. O. E. Varela and R. G. Watts, "The Development of the Global Manager: An Empirical Study on

the Role of Academic International Sojourns," *Academy of Management Learning & Education* 13, no. 2 (2014): 187–207.

63. U.S. Census Bureau website, www.census.gov, accessed January 6, 2017.

64. J. Adamy and P. Overberg, "Population of Nonwhites Grows," *The Wall Street Journal* (June 23, 2016): A3.

65. S. Y. Lee, M. Pitesa, S. Thau, and M. M. Pillutla, "Discrimination in Selection Decisions: Integrating Stereotype Fit and Interdependence Theories," *Academy of Management Journal* 58, no. 3 (2015): 789–812.

66. A. Joshi, J. Son, and H. Roh, "When Can Women Close the Gap? A Meta-Analytic Test of Sex Differences in Performance and Rewards," *Academy of Management Journal* 58, no. 5 (2015): 1516–1545.

67. L. M. Leslie, D. M. Mayer, and D. A. Kravitz, "The Stigma of Affirmative Action: A Stereotyping-Based Theory and Meta-Analytic Test of the Consequences for Performance," *Academy of Management Journal* 57, no. 4 (2014): 964–989.

68. L. M. Little, V. S. Major, A. S. Hinojosa, and D. L. Nelson, "Professional Image Maintenance: How Women Navigate Pregnancy in the Workplace," *Academy of Management Journal* 58, no. 1 (2015): 8–37.

69. S. Y. Lee, M. Pitesa, S. Thau, and M. M. Pillutla, "Discrimination in Selection Decisions: Integrating Stereotype Fit and Interdependence Theories," *Academy of Management Journal* 58, no. 3 (2015): 789–812.

70. M. Kelly, *The Four Signs of a Dynamic Catholic* (New York: Beacon, 2012).

71. M. Kelly, *Rediscovering Catholicism* (New York: Beacon, 2010).

72. O. E. Varela and R. G. Watts, "The Development of the Global Manager: An Empirical Study on the Role of Academic International Sojourns," *Academy of Management Learning & Education* 13, no. 2 (2014): 187–207.

73. R. J. Reichard, S. A. Serrano, M. Condren, N. Wilder, M. Dollwet, and W. Wang, "Engaging in Cultural Trigger Events in the Development of Cultural Competence," *Academy of Management Learning & Education* 14, no. 4 (2015): 461–481.

74. Call for papers, *Academy of Management Review* 40, no. 4 (2015): 669–670.

75. S. Sandberg, "When Women Get Stuck, Corporate America Gets Stuck," *The Wall Street Journal* (September 30, 2015): R3.

76. M. L. Besharov, "The Relational Ecology of Identification: How Organizational Identification Emerges When Individuals Hold Divergent Values," *Academy of Management Journal* 57, no. 5 (2014): 1485–1512.

77. Y. R. F. Guillaume, D. Van Knippenberg, and F. C. Brodbeck, "Nothing Succeeds Like Moderation: A Social Self-Regulation Perspective on Cultural Dissimilarity and Performance," *Academy of Management Journal* 57, no. 5 (2014): 1284–1308.

78. G. Bensinger, "Airbnb, Under Fire, Promotes Diversity," *The Wall Street Journal* (September 9, 2016): B1.

79. O. E. Varela and R. G. Watts, "The Development of the Global Manager: An Empirical Study on the Role of Academic International Sojourns," *Academy of Management Learning & Education* 13, no. 2 (2014): 187–207.

80. S. Y. Lee, M. Pitesa, S. Thau, and M. M. Pillutla, "Discrimination in Selection Decisions: Integrating Stereotype Fit and Interdependence Theories," *Academy of Management Journal* 58, no. 3 (2015): 789–812.

81. P. G. Lee and C. Hymowitz, "No Place for Old Waiters at Texas Roadhouse," *BusinessWeek* (September 28 to October 4, 2015): 23–24.

82. S. Pinker, "Slower and Wiser: How Intelligence Shifts with Age," *The Wall Street Journal* (August 1–2, 2015): C2.

83. C. Hymowitz, "Where Retirement Isn't Job One," *BusinessWeek* (March 14–20, 2016): 25–26.

84. "Margin Note," *Forbes* (April 13, 2015): 102.

85. G. Ip, "The World's New Population Time Bomb: Too Few People," *The Wall Street Journal* (November 23, 2015): A1, A14.

86. Staff, "The First World Is Aging," *Fortune* (October 1, 2015): 16.

87. G. Ip, "The World's New Population Time Bomb: Too Few People," *The Wall Street Journal* (November 23, 2015): A1, A14.

88. R. Reuteman, "Millennials Are Taking Over the Work Force at a Rapid Clip: What's an Older Leader to Do?" *Entrepreneur* (March 2015): 43–48.

89. S. Hess and J. Katz, "We're Finally Done Talking About Millennials Because Here Comes GenZ," *Entrepreneur* (December 2016): 40.

90. S. Bing, "Millennials Rule!" *Fortune* (June 1, 2016): 96.

91. I. Frisch, "The Generation Z Consultants," *BusinessWeek* (December 5–11, 2016): 86–87.

92. S. Hess and J. Katz, "We're Finally Done Talking About Millennials Because Here Comes GenZ," *Entrepreneur* (December 2016): 40.

93. I. Frisch, "The Generation Z Consultants," *BusinessWeek* (December 5–11, 2016): 86–87.

94. Survey Results, "The Case for the Enlightened Schedule," *INC.* (December 2016/January 2017): 64–65.

95. S. Hess and J. Katz, "We're Finally Done Talking About Millennials Because Here Comes GenZ," *Entrepreneur* (December 2016): 40.

96. K. Lanaj and J. R. Hollenbeck, "Leadership Over-Emergence in Self-Managing Teams: The Role of Gender and Countervailing Biases," *Academy of Management Journal* 58, no. 5 (2015): 1476–1494.

97. J. Bercovici, "Inside the Mind of Sheryl Sandberg," *INC.* (October 2015): 78–80.

98. S. Sandberg, "When Women Get Stuck, Corporate America Gets Stuck," *The Wall Street Journal* (September 30, 2015): R3.

99. U.S. Census data, www.census.gov, accessed April 10, 2015.

100. Census, NPR news, aired April 7, 2014.

101. Staff, "The Gender Wage Gap," *Fortune* (September 15, 2015): 16.

102. J. Adamy and P. Overberg, "Pay Gap Widest for Elite Jobs," *The Wall Street Journal* (May 18, 2016): A1, A10.

103. A. Joshi, J. Son, and H. Roh, "When Can Women Close the Gap? A Meta-Analytic Test of Sex Differences in Performance and Rewards," *Academy of Management Journal* 58, no. 5 (2015): 1516–1545.

104. C. Suddath, "Can Women Ever Win at Work?" *BusinessWeek* (July 28–August 3, 2014): 62.

105. L. Weber and R. L. Ensign, "Promoting Women Is Crucial," *The Wall Street Journal* (September 28, 2016): B1.

106. B. Waber, "Gender Bias by the Numbers," *BusinessWeek* (February 3–9, 2014): 8–9.

107. A. Murray, "Lessons From the Fortune 500," *Fortune* (June 15, 2016): 14.

108. S. Sandberg, "When Women Get Stuck, Corporate America Gets Stuck," *The Wall Street Journal* (September 30, 2015): R3.

109. R. Feintzeg and J. S. Lublin, "Female CEOs, a Rarity, Face Extra Pressures," *The Wall Street Journal* (August 10, 2016): B1, B8.

110. J. Reingold, "The Disappeared," *Fortune* (September 15, 2016): 101–103.

111. E. O. Wright and J. Baxter, "The Glass Ceiling Hypothesis: A Reply to Critics," *Gender & Society* 14 (2000): 814–821.

112. J. Adamy and P. Overberg, "Pay Gap Widest for Elite Jobs," *The Wall Street Journal* (May 18, 2016): A1, A10.

113. K. Rockwood, "Companies Reevaluate Their Hiring Practices," *Entrepreneur* (December 2016): 35.

114. W. Buffett, "Warren Buffett Is Bullish … on Women," *Fortune* (May 20, 2013): 121–124.

115. Staff, "Gender and GDP," *BusinessWeek* (October 5–11, 2025): 20.

116. J. Reingold, "Women Inch Into the Boardroom," *Fortune* (September 15, 2016): 26.

117. C. Post and K. Byron, "Women on Board and Firm Financial Performance: A Meta-Analysis," *Academy of Management Journal* 58, no. 5 (2015): 1546–1571.

118. C. Howard, "The First Women of Women," *Forbes* (December 14, 2015): 97–98.

119. D. M. Ewalt, "The Modest Tycoon," *Forbes* (June 15, 2015): 77–80.

120. J. Bercovici, "Inside the Mind of Sheryl Sandberg," *INC.* (October 2015): 78–80.

121. Lean In website, https://leanin.org, accessed January 11, 2016.

122. W. Mosseberg, "After Leaning In," *The Wall Street Journal* (June 3, 2013): D1.

123. G. Nagesh, "The View From Detroit," *The Wall Street Journal* (September 30, 2015): R7.

124. S. Kolhatkar, "Lean Back," *Business Week* (September 28 to October 4, 2015): 92.

125. E. Bernstein, "In Two-Career Marriages, Women Still Do More of the Work at Home," *The Wall Street Journal* (September 3015, 2015): B1.

126. J. Eidelson, "If You Are Anti Same Sex Marriage, Are You Anti Women?" *Business Week* (February 22–29, 2016): 23–24.

127. J. Bussey, "Gay Rights, Money and Morals at Play," *The Wall Street Journal* (March 20, 2014): B1, B7.

128. NPR, "News," aired April 9, 2015.

129. U.S. Census data, www.census.gov, accessed April 10, 2015.

130. K. Rockwood, "Companies Reevaluate Their Hiring Practices," *Entrepreneur* (December 2016): 35.

131. S. Y. Lee, M. Pitesa, S. Thau, and M. M. Pillutla, "Discrimination in Selection Decisions: Integrating Stereotype Fit and Interdependence Theories," *Academy of Management Journal* 58, no. 3 (2015): 789–812.

132. V. Vara, "Black Workers Still Make Less Than Whites With the Same Degrees," *Business Week* (September 19–25, 2016): 54.

133. A. M. Carton and A. S. Rosette, "Explaining Bias Against Black Leaders: Integrating Theory on Information Processing and Goal-Based Stereotyping," *Academy of Management Journal* 54, no. 6 (2011): 1141–1158.

134. L. M. Little, V. S. Major, A. S. Hinojosa, and D. L. Nelson, "Professional Image Maintenance: How Women Navigate Pregnancy in the Workplace," *Academy of Management Journal* 58, no. 1 (2015): 8–37.

135. L. Gellman, "Exploring the Racial Gap," *The Wall Street Journal* (September 30, 2015): R2.

136. A. Murray, "Lessons From the Fortune 500," *Fortune* (June 15, 2016): 14.

137. Staff, "Three S&P 500 CEOs Are Black," *Business Week* (August 1–7, 2016): 18.

138. A. Murray, "Lessons From the Fortune 500," *Fortune* (June 15, 2016): 14.

139. D. M. Ewalt, "The Modest Tycoon," *Forbes* (June 15, 2015): 77–80.

140. V. Vara, "Black Workers Still Make Less Than Whites With the Same Degrees," *Business Week* (September 19–25, 2016): 54.

141. Fortune website www.fortune.com/diversity, accessed January 10, 2016.

142. V. Vara, "Black Workers Still Make Less Than Whites with the Same Degrees," Business Week (September 19–25, 2016): 54.

143. ADA website, www.ada.gov, accessed January 10, 2017.

144. S. S. Wang, "Companies Find Autism Can Be a Job Skill," *The Wall Street Journal* (March 28, 2014): B1, B2.

145. Y. R. F. Guillaume, D. Van Knippenberg, and F. C. Brodbeck, "Nothing Succeeds Like Moderation: A Social Self-Regulation Perspective on Cultural Dissimilarity and Performance," *Academy of Management Journal* 57, no. 5 (2014): 1284–1308.

146. M. L. Stallard, "Building a Culture of Connections, *Costco Connection* (July 2015): 112.

147. Y. Chung, H. Liao, S. E. Jackson, M. Subramony, S. Colakglu, and Y. Jiang, "Cracking but Not Breaking: Joint Effects of Faultline Strength and Diversity Climate on Loyal Behavior," *Academy of Management Journal* 58, no. 5 (2015): 1495–1515.

148. Box item, "Three Diversity Strategies That Work," Fortune.com, accessed January 3, 2017.

149. Company Spotlight, Cadence, *Fortune* (December 1, 2015): 45.

150. Box item, "Three Diversity Strategies That Work," Fortune.com, accessed January 3, 2017.

151. G. Bensinger, "Airbnb, Under Fire, Promotes Diversity," *The Wall Street Journal* (September 9, 2016): B1.

152. Staff, "The Best Advice," *Fortune* (October 1, 2015): 109.

153. N. Waller and J. Lublin, "What's Holding Women Back in the Workplace?" *The Wall Street Journal* (September 30, 2015): C1, C2.

154. B. Waber, "Gender Bias by the Numbers," *Business Week* (February 3–9, 2014): 8–9; M. L. McDonald and J. D. Westphal, "Access Denied: Low Mentoring of Women and Minority First-Time Directors and Its Negative Effects on Appointments to Additional Boards," *Academy of Management Journal* 56, no. 4 (2013): 1169–1198.

155. S. Y. Yousafzai, S. Saeed, and M. Muffatto, "Institutional Theory and Contextual Embeddedness of Women's Entrepreneurial Leadership: Evidence From 92 Countries," *Journal of Small Business Management* 53, no. 3 (2015): 587–604.

156. Company Spotlight, Cadence, *Fortune* (December 1, 2015): 45.

157. Frito-Lay website, www.fritolay.com, accessed January 3, 2017.

158. A. Chuang, R. S. Hsu, A. C. Wang, and T. A. Judge, Does West Fit With East? In Search of a Chinese Model of Person-Environment Fit," *Academy of Management Journal* 58, no. 2 (2015): 480–510.

159. C. Hardy and D. Tolhurst, "Epistemological Beliefs and Cultural Diversity Matters in Management Education and Learning," *Academy of Management Learning & Education* 13, no. 2 (2014): 265–289.

160. Call for papers, *Academy of Management Review* 40, no. 4 (2015): 669–670.

161. W. L. Bedwell, S. M. Fiore, and E. Salas, "Developing the Future Workforce: An Approach for Integrating Interpersonal Skills Into the MBA Classroom," *Academy of Management Learning & Education* 13, no. 2 (2014): 171–186.

162. G. Colvin, "Humans are Underrated," *Fortune* (August 1, 2015), 100–113.

163. G. Hofstede, "Motivation, Leadership, and Organizations: Do American Theories Apply Abroad?" *Organizational Dynamics* (Summer 1980): 42–63.

164. A. Engelen, T. C. Flatten, J. Thalmann, and M. Brettel, "The Effect of Organizational Culture on Entrepreneurial Orientation: A Comparison between Germany and Thailand," *Journal of Small Business Management* 52, no. 4 (2014): 732–752.

165. Adapted from M. Javidon and R. J. House, "Cultural Acumen for the Global Manager: Lessons from Project GLOBE," *Organizational Dynamics* 29, no. 4 (2001): 289–305.

166. D. Baden and M. Higgs, "Challenging the Perceived Wisdom of Management Theories and Practice," *Academy of Management Learning & Education* 14, no. 4 (2015): 539–555.

167. H. G. Barkema, X. P. Chen, G. George, Y. Luo, and A. S. Tsut, "West Meets East: New Concepts and Theories," *Academy of Management Journal* 58, no. 2 (2015): 460–479.

168. J. R. Ramsey and M. P. Lorenz, "Exploring the Impact of Cross-Cultural Management Education on Cultural Intelligence, Student Satisfaction, and Commitment," *Academy of Management Learning & Education* 15, no. 1 (2016): 79–99.

169. R. J. Reichard, S. A. Serrano, M. Condren, N. Wilder, M. Dollwet, and W. Wang, "Engaging in Cultural Trigger Events in the Development of Cultural Competence," *Academy of Management Learning & Education* 14, no. 4 (2015): 461–481.

170. B. M. Cole, "Lessons From a Martial Arts Dojo: A Prolonged Process Model of High-Context Communication," *Academy of Management Journal* 58, no. 2 (2015): 567–591.

171. W. L. Bedwell, S. M. Fiore, and E. Salas, "Developing the Future Workforce: An Approach for Integrating Interpersonal Skills Into the MBA Classroom," *Academy of Management Learning & Education* 13, no. 2 (2014): 171–186.

172. M. L. Besharov, "The Relational Ecology of Identification: How Organizational Identification Emerges When Individuals Hold Divergent Values," *Academy of Management Journal* 57, no. 5 (2014): 1485–1512.

173. W. L. Bedwell, S. M. Fiore, and E. Salas, "Developing the Future Workforce: An Approach for Integrating Interpersonal Skills Into the MBA Classroom," *Academy of Management Learning & Education* 13, no. 2 (2014): 171–186.

174. O. E. Varela and R. G. Watts, "The Development of the Global Manager: An Empirical Study on the Role of Academic International Sojourns," *Academy of Management Learning & Education* 13, no. 2 (2014): 187–207.

175. R. J. Reichard, S. A. Serrano, M. Condren, N. Wilder, M. Dollwet, and W. Wang, "Engaging in Cultural Trigger Events in the Development of Cultural Competence," *Academy of Management Learning & Education* 14, no. 4 (2015): 461–481.

176. P. C. Godart, W. W. Maddux, A. V. Shipilov, and A. D. Galinsky, "Fashion With a Foreign Flair: Professional Experiences Abroad Facilitate the Creative Innovations of Organizations," *Academy of Management Journal* 58, no. 1 (2015): 195–220.

177. R. J. Reichard, S. A. Serrano, M. Condren, N. Wilder, M. Dollwet, and W. Wang, "Engaging in Cultural Trigger Events in the Development of Cultural Competence," *Academy of Management Learning & Education* 14, no. 4 (2015): 461–481.

178. U.S. Census, www.census.gov, accessed January 10, 2017.

179. D. Hinshaw, "African Baby Boom Brings Hope and Fear," *The Wall Street Journal* (November 28–29, 2015): A1, A10.

180. M. Schuman, "Emerging Markets Are Still the Future," *Business Week* (September 7–13, 2015): 8–9.

181. J. Bussey, "Leadership Lessons From the Generals," *The Wall Street Journal* (December 12, 2014): R10.

182. A. Wolfe, "Jack and Suzy Welch," *The Wall Street Journal* (February 21–22, 2015): C11.

183. R. M. Kanter, "Why Global Companies Will Behave More and More Alike," *The Wall Street Journal* (July 8, 2014): R8.

184. P. Elkind, "Panasonic's Power Play," *Fortune* (March 15, 2015): 67–68.

185. G. Colvin, "In the Future," *Fortune* (June 2, 2014): 193–202.

186. Renault-Nissan Alliance website, www.nissan-global.com/EN/COMPANY/PROFILE/ALLIANCE/RENAULT03, accessed January 4, 2017.

187. J. Corman, R. N. Lussier, and R. Baeder, "Global Strategies for the Future: Large vs. Small Business," *Journal of Business Strategies* 8, no. 2 (1991): 86–93.

188. W. F. Smith, "Dynamic Decision Making: A Model of Senior Leaders Managing Strategic Paradoxes," *Academy of Management Journal* 57, no. 6 (2014): 1592–1623; I. Filatotchev and C. Nakajima, "Corporate Governance, Responsible Managerial Behavior, and Corporate Social Responsibility: Organizational Efficiency Versus Organizational Legitimacy," *Academy of Management Perspectives* 28, no. 3 (2014): 289–306.

189. C. Palmeri with G. Turk, "Rethinking Disneyland for the Chinese Family," *Business Week* (July 13–19, 2015): 18–19.

190. J. Immelt, "After Brexit, Global Is *Local*," *Fortune* (August 1, 2016).

191. P.J. Buckley and R. Strange, "The Governance of the Global Factory: Location and Control of World Economic Activity," *Academy of Management Perspectives* 29, no. 2 (2015): 237–249.

192. Staff, "31.Outsourcing," *BusinessWeek* (December 8–14, 2014): 78.

193. Ryder Ad, "Outsourcing Solves Business Problems," *INC.* ryder.com, accessed January 4, 2017.

194. I. King, "Apple Plus Samsung Equal Terror for Rivals," *BusinessWeek* (May 18–24, 2015): 33–34.

195. J.D. Stoll and G. Nagesh, "GM to Sell Chinese SUV's in America," *The Wall Street Journal* (November 13, 2015): A1.

196. Amazon website, www.amazon.com, accessed January 4, 2017.

197. V. Harnish, "Five Reasons to Escape Overseas," *Fortune* (August 11, 2014): 34.

198. Boxed item, "Greg Creed, CEO, Yum! Brands," *BusinessWeek* (November 9 to January 5, 2016): 64.

199. Subway website, www.subway.com, accessed January 4, 2017.

200. J. Jargon, "Yum Extends Global Reach," *The Wall Street Journal* (October 12, 2016): B1.

201. K. Chu and B. Davis, "A Nation of 1.4 Billion Faces a Labor Shortage," *The Wall Street Journal* (November 24, 2015): A1, A10.

202. Ad, "Made in India," Fortune (October 1, 2015): 29.

203. M. Ayyagari, L.A. Dau, and J. Spencer, "Strategic Responses to FDI in Emerging Markets: Are Core Members More Responsive Than Peripheral Members of Business Groups?" *Academy of Management Journal* 58, no. 6 (2015): 1869–1894.

204. J.D. Stoll, "Volvo Aims to Open Plant in the U.S." *The Wall Street Journal* (March 30, 2015): B1.

205. T. Mann and L Burkett, "GE Deal Long in Coming for Haier," *The Wall Street Journal* (January 16–17, 2016): B1, B4.

206. A. Wexler "Africa's Ikea Buys Owner of Sleepy's," *The Wall Street Journal* (August 8, 2016): B1, B2.

207. D.J. Teece, "The Foundations of Enterprise Performance: Dynamic and Ordinary Capabilities in an (Economic) Theory of Firms," *Academy of Management Perspectives* 28, no. 4 (2014): 328–352.

208. O.E. Varela and R.G. Watts, "The Development of the Global Manager: An Empirical Study on the Role of Academic International Sojourns," *Academy of Management Learning & Education* 13, no. 2 (2014): 187–207.

209. W. Plank and C.A. Tovar, "Who Are Facebook's Biggest Friends?" *The Wall Street Journal* (April 9, 2015): B5.

210. Company Spotlight, "Striving for More Diversity in Tech," *Fortune* (December 1, 2015): 90.

211. S. Marlow and M. McAdam, "Incubation or Induction? Gendered Identity Work in the Context of Technology Business Incubation," *Entrepreneurship Theory and Practice* 39, no. 4 (2015): 791–816.

212. L. Gellman and G. Wells, "Progress Is Hampered for Women in Tech Jobs," *The Wall Street Journal* (March 23, 2016): B1, B7.

213. J. Bussey, "Leadership Lessons From the Generals," *The Wall Street Journal* (December 12, 2014): R10.

214. J. Palazzolo, "Is It a Bribe … or Not?" *The Wall Street Journal* (July 22, 2013): R3.

215. C. Rauwald and C. Reiter, "Reinventing These Wheels," *BusinessWeek* (December 19–25, 2015): 19–20.

Chapter 4

1. J.D. Power, "My Advice," *Fortune* (July 1, 2015): 30.

2. K. Davidson, "Hard to Find: Workers With Good Soft Skills," *The Wall Street Journal* (August 31, 2016): B1, B6; J. Rodkin and F. Levy, "Recruiting Preferred Skills," *BusinessWeek* (April 13–19, 2015): 43.

3. H. Mintzberg, "Quote," in "From the Guest Editors: Change the World: Teach Evidence-Based Practices!" *Academy of Management Learning & Education* 13, no. 3 (2014): 319.

4. N. Brodsky, "The Good News About the Bad News," *INC.* (February 2016): 52.

5. E.E. Jervell and S. Germano, "Lagging in U.S., Adidas Aims to Be Cool Again," *The Wall Street Journal* (March 23, 2015): A1, A10.

6. NBA website, www.nba.com, accessed April 14, 2015.

7. E.N. Gamble and R.B. Jelley, "The Case for Competition: Learning About Evidence-Based Management Through Case Competition," *Academy of Management Learning & Education* 13, no. 3 (2014): 433–445.

8. M.T. Wolfe and D.A. Shepherd, "Bouncing Back From a Loss: Entrepreneurial Orientations, Emotions, and Failure Narratives," *Entrepreneurship Theory and Practice* 39 no. 3 (2015): 675–700.

9. D. Horowitz, "When Customer Service Goes Wrong," *Costco Connection* (October 2014): 15.

10. J. Shotter and H. Tsoukas, "In Search of Phronesis: Leadership and the Art of Judgment," *Academy of Management Learning & Education* 13, no. 2 (2014): 224–243.

11. R. Hennessey, "Decisions, Decisions," *Entrepreneur* (March 2015): 50.

12. J. Cheng and J.D. McKinnon, "Samsung Recall's Fatal Flaw," *The Wall Street Journal* (October 24, 2016): A1, A12.

13. J. Cheng and E.Y. Jeong, "Samsung Recall Takes Toll," *The Wall Street Journal* (October 27, 2016): B1, B4.

14. L. Iacocca, "Thoughts on Risk," *Forbes* (April 19, 2016): 150.

15. J. McGregor, "Smart Management for Tough Times," *BusinessWeek* (March 12, 2009): 30–34.

16. G. Colvin, "The Benefit of Baring It All," *Fortune* (December 10, 2015): 34.

17. T. Monahan, "Revving Up Your Corporate RPMs," *Fortune* (February 1, 2016): 43.

18. M. Esterl, "Keurig Kills Its Kold Soda Maker," *The Wall Street Journal* (June 8, 2016): B1, B2.

19. J.S. Goodman, M.S. Gray, and R.E. Wood, "Bibliographic Search Training for Evidence-Based Management Education: A Review of Relevant Literature," *Academy of Management Learning & Education* 13, no. 3 (2014): 322–353.

20. E.G.R. Barends and R.B. Briner, "Teaching Evidence-Based Practice: Lessons From the Pioneers," *Academy of Management Learning & Education* 13, no. 3 (2014): 476–483.

21. V. Harnish, "Finding the Route to Growth," *Fortune* (May 19, 2014): 45.

22. A. Erez and A.M. Grant, "Separating Data From Intuition: Bringing Evidence Into the Management Classroom," *Academy of Management Learning & Education* 13, no. 1 (2014): 104–119.

23. E.N. Gamble and R.B. Jelley, "The Case for Competition: Learning About Evidence-Based Management Through Case Competition," *Academy of Management Learning & Education* 13, no. 3 (2014): 433–445.

24. R.L. Dipboye, "Bridging the Gap in Organizational Behavior," *Academy of Management Learning & Education* 13, no. 3 (2014): 487–491.

25. K. Morrell and M. Learmonth, "Against Evidence-Based Management, for Management Learning," *Academy of Management Learning & Education* 14, no. 4 (2015): 520–533.

26. W.F. Smith, "Dynamic Decision Making: A Model of Senior Leaders Managing Strategic Paradoxes," *Academy of Management Journal* 57, no. 6 (2014): 1592–1623.

27. P.C. Nutt, "Expanding the Search for Alternatives During Strategic Decision-Making," *Academy of Management Executive* 18, no. 4 (2004): 13–28.

28. M.T. Wolfe and D.A. Shepherd, "Bouncing Back From a Loss: Entrepreneurial Orientations, Emotions, and Failure Narratives," *Entrepreneurship Theory and Practice* 39, no. 3 (2015): 675–700.

29. D.W. Williams and M.S. Wood, "Rule-Based Reasoning for Understanding Opportunity Evaluation," *Academy of Management Perspectives* 29, no. 2 (2015): 218–236.

30. R.L. Hoefer and S.E. Green, "A Rhetorical Model of Institutional Decision Making: The Role of Rhetoric in the Formation and Change of Legitimacy Judgments," *Academy of Management Review* 41, no. 1 (2016): 130–150; J. Shotter and H. Tsoukas, "In Search of Phronesis: Leadership and the Art of Judgment," *Academy of Management Learning & Education* 13, no. 2 (2014): 224–243.

31. R.G. Lord, J.E. Dinh, and E.L. Hoffman, "A Quantum Approach to Time and Organizational Change," *Academy of Management Review* 40, no. 2 (2015): 263–290.

32. L. Weber and K. Mayer, "Transaction Cost Economics and the Cognitive Perspective: Investigating the Sources and Governance of Interpretive Uncertainty," *Academy of Management Review* 39, no. 3 (2014): 344–363.

33. M.T. Wolfe and D.A. Shepherd, "What Do You Have to Say About That?" *Entrepreneurship Theory and Practice* 39, no. 4 (2015): 895–925.

34. E.G.R. Barends and R.B. Briner, "Teaching Evidence-Based Practice: Lessons From the Pioneers," *Academy of Management Learning & Education* 13, no. 3 (2014): 476–483.

35. R. Hennessey, "Decisions, Decisions," *Entrepreneur* (March 2015): 50.

36. Staff, "Building a Culture of Connection," *Costco Connection* (July 2015): 12.

37. L. Alexander and D. Van Knippenberg, "Teams in Pursuit of Radical Innovation: A Goal Orientation Perspective," *Academy of Management Review* 39, no. 4 (2014): 423–438.

38. A. Stuart, "Damage Control," *INC.* (March 2015): 72–73.

39. G. Colvin, "Humans Are Underrated," *Fortune* (August 1, 2015): 100–113.

40. P.M. Picone, G.B. Dagnino, and A. Mina, "The Origin of Failure: A Multidisciplinary Appraisal of the Hubris Hypothesis and Proposed Research Agenda," *Academy of Management Perspectives* 28, no. 4 (2014): 447–468.

41. T. Hahn, L. Preuss, J. Pinkse, and F. Figge, "Cognitive Frames in Corporate Sustainability: Managerial Sensemaking With Paradoxical and Business Case Frames," *Academy of Management Review* 39, no. 4 (2014): 463–487.

42. E. Bernstein, "Decide to Be Happy," *The Wall Street Journal* (October 7, 2014): D1, D2.

43. I. Deligianni, P. Dimitratos, A. Petrou, and Y. Aharoni, "Entrepreneurial Orientation and International Performance: The Moderating Effect of Decision-Making Rationality," *Journal of Small Business Management* 54, no. 2 (2016): 462–480.

44. O. Osiyevskyy and J. Dewald, "Inducements, Impediments, and Immediacy: Exploring the Cognitive Drivers of Small Business Managers' Intentions to Adopt Business Model Change," *Journal of Small Business Management* 53, no. 4 (2015): 1011–1032.

45. E. Bernstein, "Decide to Be Happy," *The Wall Street Journal* (October 7, 2014): D1, D2.

46. M. Kelly, *The Four Signs of a Dynamic Catholic* (New York: Beacon, 2012).

47. L. Alexander and D. Van Knippenberg, "Teams in Pursuit of Radical Innovation: A Goal Orientation Perspective," *Academy of Management Review* 39, no. 4 (2014): 423–438.

48. Editors, "From the Guest Editors: Change the World: Teach Evidence-Based Practices!" *Academy of Management Learning & Education* 13, no. 3 (2014): 305–319.

49. N.J. Fast, E.R. Burris, and C.A. Bartel, "Managing to Stay in the Dark: Managerial Self-Efficacy, Ego Defensiveness, and the Aversion to Employee Voice," *Academy of Management Journal* 57, no. 4 (2014): 1013–1034.

50. M. Cerne, C. G. L. Nerstad, A. Dysvik, and M. Skerlavaj, "What Goes Around Comes Around: Knowledge Hiding, Perceived Motivational Climate, and Creativity," *Academy of Management Journal* 57, no. 1 (2014): 172–192.

51. I. Sager, "Sam Polmisano," *BusinessWeek* (May 1, 2014): 56.

52. S. Sonenshein, "How Organizations Foster the Creative Use of Resources," *Academy of Management Journal* 57, no. 3 (2014): 814–848.

53. P. Lencioni, "Innovation Won't Get You Very Far," *INC.* (December 2014/January 2015): 102.

54. M. Cerne, C. G. L. Nerstad, A. Dysvik, and M. Skerlavaj, "What Goes Around Comes Around: Knowledge Hiding, Perceived Motivational Climate, and Creativity," *Academy of Management Journal* 57, no. 1 (2014): 172–192.

55. N. J. Fast, E. R. Burris, and C. A. Bartel, "Managing to Stay in the Dark: Managerial Self-Efficacy, Ego Defensiveness, and the Aversion to Employee Voice," *Academy of Management Journal* 57, no. 4 (2014): 1013–1034.

56. S. H. Harrison and D. T. Wagner, "Spilling Outside the Box: The Effects of Individuals' Creative Behaviors at Work on Time Spent With Their Spouses at Home," *Academy of Management Journal* 59, no. 3 (2016): 841–859.

57. A. C. Cosper, "The Creative Brief," *Entrepreneur* (June 2015): 14.

58. Ibid.

59. S. Bing, "How to Kill a Good Idea," *Fortune* (April 1, 2016): 116.

60. D. Hayes, "Take Time to Ruminate," *Entrepreneur* (April 2015): 57.

61. S. H. Harrison and E. D. Rouse, "Let's Dance! Elastic Coordination in Creative Group Work: A Qualitative Study of Modern Dancers," *Academy of Management Journal* 57, no. 5 (2014): 1256–1283.

62. S. H. Harrison and D. T. Wagner, "Spilling Outside the Box: The Effects of Individuals' Creative Behaviors at Work on Time Spent With Their Spouses at Home," *Academy of Management Journal* 59, no. 3 (2016): 841–859.

63. 3M website, www.3m.com, accessed January 11, 2017.

64. Teradata, Ad, *Forbes* (February 9, 2015): 24.

65. B. Simmons, "Data Wimps," *Forbes* (February 9, 2015): 34.

66. B. Hope, "Computers Trawl Sea of Data for Stock Picks," *The Wall Street Journal* (April 2, 2015): A1, A12.

67. J. Kell, "Nike," *Fortune* (June 15, 2015): 276–277.

68. P. Lencioni, "When Less Is More," *INC.* (June 2015): 69.

69. S. Harvey, "Creative Synthesis: Exploring the Process of Extraordinary Group Creativity," *Academy of Management Review* 39, no. 3 (2014): 324–343.

70. E. E. Powell and T. Baker, "It's What You Make of It: Founder Identity and Enacting Strategic Responses to Adversity," *Academy of Management Journal* 57, no. 5 (2014): 1406–1433.

71. M. Kohanzo, "Chance the Scene," *Entrepreneur* (April 2015): 59.

72. C. Tate, "Work Simply," *BusinessWeek* (December 22–28, 2014): 71.

73. Staff, "Building a Culture of Connection," *Costco Connection* (July 2015): 12.

74. S. H. Harrison and E. D. Rouse, "An Inductive Study of Feedback Interactions Over the Course of Creative Projects," *Academy of Management Journal* 59, no. 3 (2016): 841–859.

75. Microsoft website, www.microsoft.com, accessed April 15, 2015.

76. S. Johnston, "The Benefits of Walking Meetings," *Costco Connection* (October 2014): 13.

77. S. Fowler, "Improve Your Motivation," *Costco Connection* (January 2015): 15.

78. *Professional Artist* website, www.professionalartistmag.com, accessed January 11, 2017.

79. A. Lim, D. C. J. Qing, and A. R. Eyring, "Netting the Evidence: A Review of On-Line Resources," *Academy of Management Learning & Education* 13, no. 3 (2014): 495–503.

80. J. Rodkin and F. Levy, "Recruiting Preferred Skills," *BusinessWeek* (April 13–19, 2015): 43.

81. E. E. Jervell and S. Germano, "Lagging in U.S., Adidas Aims to Be Cool Again," *The Wall Street Journal* (March 23, 2015): A1, A10.

82. W. Amos, "Accept the Change," *Costco Connection* (April 2014): 13.

83. D. Huston, "Side Bar," *Fortune* (November 17, 2014): 132.

84. E. N. Gamble and R. B. Jelley, "The Case for Competition: Learning About Evidence-Based Management Through Case Competition," *Academy of Management Learning & Education* 13, no. 3 (2014): 433–445.

85. E. N. Gamble and R. B. Jelley, "The Case for Competition: Learning About Evidence-Based Management Through Case Competition," *Academy of Management Learning & Education* 13, no. 3 (2014): 433–445.

86. B. Costa, "Bill and Billy Discuss Big Data in Baseball," *The Wall Street Journal* (September 22, 2015): D6.

87. D. Gage, "What Do Scientists Do All Day at Work?" *The Wall Street Journal* (March 14, 2016): R6.

88. Staff, "The Meaning of Big Data," *Fortune* (June 16, 2014): 232.

89. J. Ma, "CEO Wisdom," *BusinessWeek* (October 19–25, 2015): 31.

90. R. Charan, "The Algorithmic CEO," *Fortune* (January 22, 2015): 45–46.

91. V. Harnish, "5 Ways to Turn Precision Into Profits," *Fortune* (July 1, 2015): 32.

92. Teradata, Ad, *Forbes* (February 9, 2015): 24.

93. M. E. Belicove, "Can I Use Big Data Without Going Broke?" *Entrepreneur* (June 2016): 52.

94. B. Simmons, "Data Wimps," *Forbes* (February 9, 2015): 34.

95. V. Harnish, "5 Ways to Turn Precision Into Profits," *Fortune* (July 1, 2015): 32.

96. M. E. Belicove, "Can I Use Big Data Without Going Broke?" *Entrepreneur* (June 2016): 52.

97. J. Roth, "Hair Cult for Men," *BusinessWeek* (March to April 3, 2016): 82.

98. J. Daley, "Driven by Data," *Entrepreneur* (January 2016): 133–134.

99. D. Gage, "What Do Scientists Do All Day at Work?" *The Wall Street Journal* (March 14, 2016): R6.

100. C. Giammona, "Taco Bell App Is a Fix for the Munchies," *BusinessWeek* (July 14–19, 2015): 20–21.

101. D. Wakabayashi and A. Barr, "Apple and Google Race to Predict What You Want," *The Wall Street Journal* (August 4, 2015): B1, B6.

102. A. White, "Sidebar," *Forbes* (September 29, 2014): 26.

103. S. Yagan, "Book Review," *Fortune* (December 1, 2015): 20.

104. R. Blumenstein, "The Mistakes Firms Make With Big Data," *The Wall Street Journal* (February 10, 2016): R1.

105. R. E. Silverman, J. S. Lublin, and R. Feintzeig, "CEOs Put Less Stock in Predictions," *The Wall Street Journal* (July 13, 2016): B6.

106. S. Yagan, "Book Review," *Fortune* (December 1, 2015): 20.

107. A. Stuart, "4. Do a Cost-Benefit Analysis," *INC.* (March 2015): 23.

108. E. N. Gamble and R. B. Jelley, "The Case for Competition: Learning About Evidence-Based Management Through Case Competition," *Academy of Management Learning & Education* 13, no. 3 (2014): 433–445.

109. O. Osiyevskyy and J. Dewald, "Inducements, Impediments, and Immediacy: Exploring the Cognitive Drivers of Small Business Managers' Intentions to Adopt Business Model Change," *Journal of Small Business Management* 53, no. 4 (2015): 1011–1032.

110. C. Q. Trank, "Reading Evidence-Based Management: The Possibilities of Interpretation," *Academy of Management Learning & Education* 13, no. 3 (2014): 381–395.

111. G. Colvin, "Four Things That Worry Business," *Fortune* (October 27, 2014): 32.

112. I. Deligianni, P. Dimitratos, A. Petrou, and Y. Aharoni, "Entrepreneurial Orientation and International Performance: The Moderating Effect of Decision-Making Rationality," *Journal of Small Business Management* 54, no. 2 (2016): 462–480; J. Shotter and H. Tsoukas, "In Search of Phronesis: Leadership and the Art of Judgment," *Academy of Management Learning & Education* 13, no. 2 (2014): 224–243.

113. J. Faveau, taken from a quote, *Fortune* (October 1, 2015): 111.

114. J. Bussey, "Leadership Lessons From the Generals," *The Wall Street Journal* (December 12, 2014): R10.

115. P. Lencioni, "Innovation Won't Get You Very Far," *INC.* (December 2014/January 2015): 102.

116. A. P. Petkova, A. Wadhwa, X. Yao, and S. Jain, "Reputation and Decision Making Under Ambiguity: A Study of U.S. Venture Capital Firms' Investments in the Emerging Clean Energy Sector," *Academy of Management Journal* 57, no. 2 (2014): 422–448.

117. A. Chatterji and A. Patro, "Dynamic Capabilities and Managing Human Capital," *Academy of Management Perspectives* 28, no. 4 (2014): 395–408.

118. R. Karlgaad, "Vivid Vision for Success," *Forbes* (January 19, 2015): 26.

119. J. Shotter and H. Tsoukas, "In Search of Phronesis: Leadership and the Art of Judgment," *Academy of Management Learning & Education* 13, no. 2 (2014): 224–243.

120. Y. Zhang, D. A. Waldman, Y. L. Han, and X. Li, "Paradoxical Leader Behaviors in People Management: Antecedents and Consequences," *Academy of Management Journal* 58, no. 2 (2015): 538–566.

121. R. L. Hoefer and S. E. Green, "A Rhetorical Model of Institutional Decision Making: The Role of Rhetoric in the Formation and Change of Legitimacy Judgments," *Academy of Management Review* 41, no. 1 (2016): 130–150.

122. H. Drummond, "Escalation of Commitment: When to Stay the Course," *Academy of Management Perspectives* 28, no. 4 (2014): 430–446.

123. K. Y. Hsieh, W. Tsai, and M. J. Chen, "If They Can Do It, Why Not Us? Competitors as Reference Points for Justifying Escalation of Commitment," *Academy of Management Journal* 56, no. 1 (2015): 38–58.

124. H. Drummond, "Escalation of Commitment: When to Stay the Course," *Academy of Management Perspectives* 28, no. 4 (2014): 430–446.

125. P. Ziobro and R. Trichur, "Target Bails Out of Canada," *The Wall Street Journal* (January 16, 2015): B1, B4.

126. G. Colvin, "The Art of Doing the Unpopular," *Fortune* (June 15, 2016): 32.

127. M. T. Wolfe and D. A. Shepherd, "Bouncing Back From a Loss: Entrepreneurial Orientations, Emotions, and Failure Narratives," *Entrepreneurship Theory and Practice* 39, no. 3 (2015): 675–700.

128. World Economic Forum, "The Global Competitive Report," http://www3.weforum.org/docs/gcr/2015-2016/Global_Competitiveness_Report_2015-2016.pdf accessed January 12, 2017.

129. I. Sager, "Sam Polmisano," *BusinessWeek* (May 1, 2014): 56.

130. H. Ersek, "Sidebar," *Fortune* (November 17, 2014): 132.

131. Editors, "Rethinking Governance in Management Research," *Academy of Management Journal* 57, no. 6 (2014): 1535–1543.

132. M. R. Hass, P. Criscuolo, and G. George, "Which Problems to Solve? Online Knowledge Sharing and Attention Allocation in Organizations," *Academy of Management Journal* 58 no. 3 (2015): 680–711.

133. M. R. Hass, P. Criscuolo, and G. George, "Which Problems to Solve? Online Knowledge Sharing and Attention Allocation in Organizations," *Academy of Management Journal* 58 no. 3 (2015): 680–711.

134. I. Sager, "Sam Polmisano," *BusinessWeek* (May 1, 2014): 56.

135. M. Esterl, "Pepsi Tries to Fix Diet Cola Stumble," *The Wall Street Journal* (June 28, 2016): A1, A10.

136. J. Brustein, "RadioShack Sold Its Stores. Can It Sell You?" *BusinessWeek* (April 6–12, 2015): 25–26.

137. E. N. Gamble and R. B. Jelley, "The Case for Competition: Learning About Evidence-Based Management Through Case Competition," *Academy of Management Learning & Education* 13, no. 3 (2014): 433–445.

138. I. Filatotchev and C. Nakajima, "Corporate Governance, Responsible Managerial Behavior, and Corporate Social Responsibility: Organizational Efficiency Versus Organizational Legitimacy," *Academy of Management Perspectives* 28, no. 3 (2014): 289–306.

139. S. Clegg, "Managerialism: Born in the USA," *Academy of Management Review* 39, no. 4 (2014): 567–576.

140. Staff, "Lies, Damned Lies, and More Statistics," *BusinessWeek* (March to April 3, 2016): 12.

141. J. Alsever, "Is Software Better at Managing People Than You Are?" *Fortune* (March 15, 2015): 41–42.

142. T. Hahn, L. Preuss, J. Pinkse, and F. Figge, "Cognitive Frames in Corporate Sustainability: Managerial Sensemaking With Paradoxical and Business Case Frames," *Academy of Management Review* 39, no. 4 (2014): 463–487.

143. S. S. Wiltermuth, "Power, Moral Clarity, and Punishment in the Workplace," *Academy of Management Journal* 56, no. 4 (2014): 1002–1023.

144. G. K. Stahl and M. S. De Luque, "Antecedents of Responsible Leader Behavior: A Research Synthesis Conceptual Framework, and Agenda for Future Research," *Academy of Management Perspectives* 28, no. 3 (2014): 235–254.

145. C. Larson, "China Turns to the Sea for Fresh Water," *BusinessWeek* (April 13–19, 2015): 13–14.

146. A. Satariano and A. Bjerga, "Farming Big Data," *BusinessWeek* (July 13–26, 2016): 29–30.

Chapter 5

1. A. Chen, "More Rational Resolutions," *The Wall Street Journal* (December 31, 2013): D1.

2. R. N. Lussier and C. E. Halabi, "A Three-Country Comparison of the Business Success Versus Failure Prediction Model," *Journal of Small Business Management* 48, no. 3 (2010): 360–377.

3. M. L. Verreynne, D. Meyer, and P. Liesch, "Beyond the Formal-Informal Dichotomy of Small Firm Strategy-Making in Stable and Dynamic Environments," *Journal of Small Business Management* 54, no. 2 (2016), 420–444.

4. A. Handley, "Having a Plan," *Entrepreneur* (December 2014): 41.

5. W. F. Smith, "Dynamic Decision Making: A Model of Senior Leaders Managing Strategic Paradoxes," *Academy of Management Journal* 57, no. 6 (2014): 1592–1623.

6. Staff, "Controllers," *Entrepreneur* (November 2015): 63.

7. R. Karlgaad, "Vivid Vision for Success," *Forbes* (January 19, 2015): 26.

8. E. Sylvers, "Fiat Set to Spin Off Ferrari in IPO," *The Wall Street Journal* (October 30, 2014): B3.

9. J. Rodkin and F. Levy, "Recruiting Preferred Skills," *BusinessWeek* (April 13–19, 2015): 43.

10. V. Harnish, "Five Questions to Ponder for 2015," *Fortune* (December 22, 2014): 36.

11. D. Albert, M. Kreutzer, and C. Lechner, "Resolving the Paradox of Interdependency and Strategic Renewal in Activity Systems," *Academy of Management Review* 40, no. 2 (2015): 210–234.

12. A. C. Cosper, "Creating Relevance," *Entrepreneur* (May 2015): 10.

13. D. W. Williams and M. S. Wood, "Rule-Based Reasoning for Understanding Opportunity Evaluation," *Academy of Management Perspectives* 29, no. 2 (2015): 218–236; R. Myers, "That Sounds Like a Plan," *INC.* (June 2014): 90–92.

14. R. Karlgaad, "Vivid Vision for Success," *Forbes* (January 19, 2015): 26.

15. L. Stevens, "UPS Campaigns to Redefine Itself," *The Wall Street Journal* (March 9, 2015): B3.

16. R. Karlgaad, "Vivid Vision for Success," *Forbes* (January 19, 2015): 26.

17. Y. Koh and K. Grind, "Twitter CEO Costolo Struggles to Define Vision," *The Wall Street Journal* (November 7, 2014): B1, B2.

18. A. Murray, "Lessons From the Fortune 500," *Fortune* (June 15, 2016): 14; L. Weber and K. Mayer, "Transaction Cost Economics and the Cognitive Perspective: Investigating the Sources and Governance of Interpretive Uncertainty," *Academy of Management Review* 39, no. 3 (2014): 344–363.

19. C. Tkaczyk, "How Google Works," *Fortune* (September 24, 2014): 103.

20. D. Albert, M. Kreutzer, and C. Lechner, "Resolving the Paradox of Interdependency and Strategic Renewal in Activity Systems," *Academy of Management Review* 40, no. 2 (2015): 210–234; A. Chatterji and A. Patro, "Dynamic Capabilities and Managing Human Capital," *Academy of Management Perspectives* 28, no. 4 (2014): 395–408.

21. M. Porter, "How Competitive Forces Shape Strategy," *Harvard Business Review* 57, no. 2 (1979): 137–145.

22. L. Stevens, "UPS Campaigns to Redefine Itself," *The Wall Street Journal* (March 9, 2015): B3.

23. Staff, SWOT Analysis," *Fortune* (June 15, 2015): 12.

24. D. W. Williams and M. S. Wood, "Rule-Based Reasoning for Understanding Opportunity Evaluation," *Academy of Management Perspectives* 29, no. 2 (2015): 218–236.

25. Staff, SWOT Analysis," *Fortune* (June 15, 2015): 12.

26. R. L. Weinberger, "Surviving Shark Tank," *Costco Connection* (September 2014): 13.

27. M. L. Verreynne, D. Meyer, and P. Liesch, "Beyond the Formal-Informal Dichotomy of Small Firm Strategy-Making in Stable and Dynamic Environments," *Journal of Small Business Management* 54, no. 2 (2016), 420–444.

28. J. M. Ross and D. Sharapov, "When the Leader Follows: Avoiding Dethronement Through Imitation," *Academy of Management Journal* 58, no. 3 (2015): 658–679.

29. A. Chatterji and A. Patro, "Dynamic Capabilities and Managing Human Capital," *Academy of Management Perspectives* 28, no. 4 (2014): 395–408.

30. K. Dziczek, "Sidebar," *BusinessWeek* (February 23–March 1, 2015): 22.

31. J. Jargon, "TGI Fridays Won't Run Restaurants Anymore," *The Wall Street Journal* (September 27–28, 2014): B3.

32. F. Alsever, "Yes, There's an Uber for That," *Fortune* (June 15, 2015): 62.

33. J. Chaussee, "Briefs," *BusinessWeek* (June 29 to July 5, 2015): 26.

34. R. Hastings, "Margin Note," *Forbes* (March 23, 2015): 56.

35. P. Burrows, "I Just Feel Like I Can't Get Out of This Box," *BusinessWeek* (May 18–24, 2015): 32–33.

36. R. Reuteman, "Accentuate the Negative," *Entrepreneur* (February 2015): 44–45.

37. S. F. Collins, "Success Steps," *Costco Connection* (January 2016): 29.

38. C. Hann, "Always BE Closing," *Entrepreneur* (August 2015): 30.

39. Staff, "CEO Survey," *INC.* (September 2014): 78.

40. H. Mitchell, "What's the Best Way to Stick With a Resolution?" *The Wall Street Journal* (December 23, 2014): D1, D2.

41. Staff, "No. 6 McDonald's," *Entrepreneur* (January 2016): 106.

42. D Wakabayashi, "Apple Sets 2019 Goal to Build an Auto," *The Wall Street Journal* (September 22, 2015): A1.

43. Staff, "Trending," *Forbes* (February 8, 2016): 52.

44. T. Mickle, "AB InBev Sets Lofty Goal," *The Wall Street Journal* (April 2–3, 2016): B1.

45. D. Hull, "Testla," *BusinessWeek* (August 31–September 6, 2015): 20–21.

46. J. Chaussee, "Briefs," *BusinessWeek* (August 3–9, 2015): 25.

47. C. Rogers, "Ford Sets Plans for Cars Without Steering Wheels," *The Wall Street Journal* (August 17, 2016): B1.

48. H. Mitchell, "What's the Best Way to Stick With a Resolution?" *The Wall Street Journal* (December 23, 2014): D1, D2.

49. T. Mandoza, "Culture Matters: 7 Ways of Great Leaders," *Forbes* (October 20, 2014): 113.

50. D. T. Welsh and L. D. Ordonez, "Conscience Without Cognition: The Effects of Subconscious Priming on Ethical Behavior," *Academy of Management Journal* 57, no. 5 (2014): 723–1109.

51. A. Von Tobel, "Where Money Meets Morale," *INC.* (April 2014): 48–49.

52. H. Ibarra, "The Way to Become a Strategic Executive," *The Wall Street Journal* (February 23, 2015): R7.

53. M. Kelly, *The Four Signs of a Dynamic Catholic* (New York: Beacon, 2012).

54. R. Clough, "General Electric Wants to Act Like a Startup," *BusinessWeek* (August 11–24, 2014): 22–24.

55. Based on the author's experience using MBO at Springfield College.

56. G. Colvin, "The Benefit of Baring It All," *Fortune* (December 2015), 34.

57. A. Von Tobel, "Where Money Meets Morale," *INC.* (April 2014): 48–49.

58. R. Hatman, "Re-event Yourself," *Costco Connection* (April 2016): 29.

59. D. S. Siegel, "Responsible Leadership," *Academy of Management Perspectives* 28, no. 3 (2014): 221–223.

60. D. Wakabayashi, "Apple Seeks New Growth Beyond the iPhone," *The Wall Street Journal* (September 10 2015): B1, B4.

61. Staff, "No. 10 Anytime Fitness," *Entrepreneur* (January 2016): 114.

62. WD-40 website, www.wd40.com, accessed January 24, 2017.

63. W. McKinley, S. Latham, and M. Braun, "Organizational Decline and Innovation: Turnarounds and Downward Spirals," *Academy of Management Review* 39, no. 1 (2014): 88–110.

64. A. Vandermey, "Keeping a Sparkle, as Soda Fizzles," *Fortune* (May 19, 2014): 30.

65. C. Fairchild, "Does Levi Strauss Still Fit America?" *Fortune* (October 6, 2014): 180–188.

66. J. Jargon, "Burned by Rivals, Woes Abroad, McDonald's Vows Fresh Thinking," *The Wall Street Journal* (October 22, 2014): B1, B2.

67. J. Jargon, "Sbarro Looks Beyond the Food Court," *The Wall Street Journal* (October 3–4, 2015): B1, B4.

68. J. Wieczner, "The New Geek Squad," *Fortune* (November 1, 2015): 143–148.

69. I. Boudway, "Briefs," *BusinessWeek* (January 25–31, 2016): 23.

70. S. Kapner, "Gap to Close a Quarter of Its U.S. Stores," *The Wall Street Journal* (June 16, 2015): B1.

71. S. Kapner, "Squeezed Sears Sheds Craftsman," *The Wall Street Journal* (January 6, 2017): B1, B2.

72. Staff, "Should They Stay, or Should They Go?" *Fortune* (June 15, 2016): 176.

73. Y. Onaran, "Shrinking Footprint," *BusinessWeek* online, accessed January 25, 2017.

74. Staff, "Franchise 500," *Entrepreneur* (January/February 2017): 72.

75. M. Esterl, "Coke Tries Asset Light Formula," *The Wall Street Journal* (March 22–23, 2016): B1, B2.

76. W. Su and E. W. K. Tsang, "Product Diversification and Financial Performance: The Moderating Role of Secondary Stakeholders," *Academy of Management Journal* 58, no. 4 (2015): 1128–1148.

77. J. Jargon, "General Mills to Buy Annie's," *The Wall Street Journal* (September 9, 2014): B1.

78. Virgin website, www.virgin.com, accessed January 25, 2017.

79. Staff, "Google Income Statement," *BusinessWeek* (December 12–18, 2016): Cover.

80. C. Dulaney, "Jarden Makes Nostalgic Buy," *The Wall Street Journal* (October 15, 2015): B8.

81. A. Gasparro, "Mars Takes Bigger Bite Out of Pet-Care Industry," *The Wall Street Journal* (January 10, 2017): A1, A2.

82. J. T. Campbell, D. G. Sirmon, and M. Schijven, "Fuzzy Logic and the Market: A Configurational Approach to Investor Perceptions of Acquisition Announcements," *Academy of Management Journal* 59, no. 1 (2016): 163–187.

83. J. M. Brown, "Will a Stock Bust Follow the M&A Boom?" *Fortune* (January 1, 2016): 39–40.

84. R. Ragozzino and C. Moschieri, "When Theory Doesn't Meet Practice: Do Firms Really Stage Their Investments?" *Academy of Management Perspectives* 28, no. 1 (2014): 22–37.

85. J. Greene, "Microsoft Places a Big Bet on LinkedIn," *The Wall Street Journal* (June 14, 2016): A1.

86. K. Stock, "Bid/Ask," *BusinessWeek* (November 23–29, 2015): 43.

87. S. Finkelstein, "How to Avoid Four Common Problems in Mergers," *The Wall Street Journal* (February 22, 2016): R7.

88. Staff, "Cutting Waste—or Creating Monopolies?" *BusinessWeek* (September 15–21, 2015): 31–32.

89. R. Ragozzino and C. Moschieri, "When Theory Doesn't Meet Practice: Do Firms Really Stage Their Investments?" *Academy of Management Perspectives* 28, no. 1 (2014): 22–37.

90. S. Carey, "New Airline Boss Starts With an Apology," *The Wall Street Journal* (October 1, 2015): A1, A8.

91. M. Gurman, "Mac Pro Users Want Updates?" *BusinessWeek* (December 26, 2016, to January 8, 2017): 33–34.

92. I. S. Nam, "Can Kia Escape Hyundai's Shadow?" *The Wall Street Journal* (August 29, 2014): B5.

93. R. J. Funk, "Making the Most of Where You Are: Geography, Networks, and Innovation in Organizations," *Academy of Management Journal* 37, no. 1 (2012): 193–222.

94. C. E. Pollard and M. Morales, "Exploring the Impact of Aligning Business and IS Strategy Types on Performance in Small Firms," *Journal of Small Business Strategy* 25 no. 1 (2015): 26–32.

95. D. W. Williams and M. S. Wood, "Rule-Based Reasoning for Understanding Opportunity Evaluation," *Academy of Management Perspectives* 29, no. 2 (2015): 218–236.

96. Staff, "Data Champions," *Entrepreneur* (November 2015): 63.

97. Groupon website, www.groupon.com, accessed January 25, 2017.

98. J. M. Ross and D. Sharapov, "When the Leader Follows: Avoiding Dethronement Through Imitation," *Academy of Management Journal* 58, no. 3 (2015): 658–679.

99. Ibid.

100. M. Porter, *Competitive Strategy: Techniques for Analyzing Industries and Competitors* (New York: Free Press, 1980).

101. M. Cerne, C. G. L. Nerstad, A. Dysvik, and M. Skerlavaj, "What Goes Around Comes Around: Knowledge Hiding, Perceived Motivational Climate, and Creativity," *Academy of Management Journal* 57, no. 1 (2014): 172–192.

102. C. Clifford, "My Advice," *Fortune* (August 11, 2014): 32.

103. H. Ibarra, "The Way to Become a Strategic Executive," *The Wall Street Journal* (February 23, 2015): R7.

104. L. Lorenzetti, "Southwest Airlines Is Flying High," *Fortune* (October 27, 2014): 38.

105. J. Bachman, "Southwest Hangs Up Its Low-Cost Jersey," *BusinessWeek* (September 15–21, 2015): 27–28.

106. Asics website, www.asicsamerica.com, accessed May 6, 2015.

107. S. Reddy, "Why Are You Always Late? It Could Be the Planning Fallacy," *The Wall Street Journal* (February 3, 2015): D1, D4.

108. T. Robbins, "Money Masters," *Costco Connection* (December 2014): 35.

109. O. Schilke, "Second-Order Dynamic Capabilities: How Do They Matter?" *Academy of Management Perspectives* 28, no. 4 (2014): 366–380.

110. M. Priesemuth, M. Schminke, M. L. Ambrose, and R. Folger, "Abusive Supervision Climate: A Multiple-Mediation Model of Its Impact on Group Outcomes," *Academy of Management Journal* 57, no. 5 (2014): 1513–1534.

111. Dialogue, "Is Decoupling Becoming Decoupled From Institutional Theory? A Commentary on Wijen," *Academy of Management Review* 40, no. 2 (2015): 307–313.

112. D. J. Jones, C. R. Willness, and S. Madey, "Why Are Job Seekers Attracted by Corporate Social Performance? Experimental and Field Tests of Three Signal-Based Mechanisms," *Academy of Management Journal* 57, no. 2 (2014): 383–404.

113. F. Wijen, "Means Versus Ends in Opaque Institutional Fields: Trading Off Compliance and Achievement in Sustainability Standard Adoption," *Academy of Management Review* 39, no. 3 (2014): 302–323.

114. A. Chatterji and A. Patro, "Dynamic Capabilities and Managing Human Capital," *Academy of Management Perspectives* 28, no. 4 (2014): 395–408.

115. G. Di Stefano, M. Peteraf, and G. Verona, "The Organizational Drivetrain: A Road to Integration of Dynamic Capabilities Research," *Academy of Management Perspectives* 28, no. 4 (2014): 307–327.

116. G. Di Stefano, M. Peteraf, and G. Verona, "The Organizational Drivetrain: A Road to Integration of Dynamic Capabilities Research," *Academy of Management Perspectives* 28, no. 4 (2014): 307–327.

117. Editors, "Putting Communication Front and Center in Institutional Theory and Analysis," *Academy of Management Review* 40, no. 1 (2015): 10–27.

118. C. Hann, "Caught in the Cookie Jar," *Entrepreneur* (December 2014): 41.

119. B. A. Scott, A. S. Garza, D. E. Conlon, and Y. J. Kim, "Why Do Managers Act Fairly in the First Place? A Daily Investigation of Hot and Cold Motives and Discretion," *Academy of Management Journal* 57, no. 6 (2014): 1571–1591.

120. M. J. Waller, Z. Lei, and R. Pratten, "Focusing on Teams in Crisis Management Education: An Integration and Simulation-Based Approach," *Academy of Management Learning & Education* 13, no. 2 (2014): 208–221.

121. L. Weber and K. Mayer, "Transaction Cost Economics and the Cognitive Perspective: Investigating the Sources and Governance of Interpretive Uncertainty," *Academy of Management Review* 39, no. 3 (2014): 344–363.

122. S. Shellenbarger, "Put a Dollar Value on Your Time, With Help From New Tools," *The Wall Street Journal* (July 22, 2015): D1, D2.

123. M. Adams, "There Is Never Enough Time," *The Wall Street Journal* (October 26, 2015): R4.

124. S. Bing, "Productivity Now!" *Fortune* (January 1, 2016): 100.

125. R. G. Lord, J. E. Dinh, and E. L. Hoffman, "A Quantum Approach to Time and Organizational Change," *Academy of Management Review* 40, no. 2 (2015): 263–290.

126. V. Harnish, "Five Ways to Get Organized," *Fortune* (September 1, 2014): 42.

127. R. Abrams, "Gain an Hour a Day," *Costco Connection* (September 2016): 14.

128. J. Bercovici, "How Dick Costolo Keeps His Focus," *INC.* (March 2015): 48–57.

129. NPR, "News," aired January 12, 2015.

130. J. Robinson, "Pay Attention!" *Entrepreneur* (September 2014): 60–65.

131. A. Handley, "Detox Your Inbox," *Entrepreneur* (November 2014): 34.

132. J. Bercovici, "How Dick Costolo Keeps His Focus," *INC.* (March 2015): 48–57.

133. V. Shmidman, "Advise," *Fortune* (October 1, 2015): 111.

134. M. Whelan, "Productivity Hack," *Fortune* (October 1, 2015): 114.

135. J. Krasny, "The Latest Thinking About Time," *INC.* (March 2015): 44–45.

136. J. Robinson, "Pay Attention!" *Entrepreneur* (September 2014): 60–65.

137. V. Harnish, "5 Crucial Performance Metrics," *Fortune* (August 1, 2016): 32.

138. J. Wang, "A Delicate Balance," *Entrepreneur* (September 2014): 136.

139. J. Krasny, "The Latest Thinking About Time," *INC.* (March 2015): 44–45.

140. J. Bercovici, "How Dick Costolo Keeps His Focus," *INC.* (March 2015): 48–57.

141. S. S. Wang, "Never Procrastinate Again," *The Wall Street Journal* (September 1, 2015): D1, D2.

142. Staff, "When Good Habits Go Bad," *AARP Magazine* (January 2015): 19.

143. M. Kelly, *Rediscovering Catholicism* (New York: Beacon, 2010).

144. J. Robinson, "Pay Attention!" *Entrepreneur* (September 2014): 60–65.

145. D. Meyer, "One Thing at a Time," *Entrepreneur* (September 2014): 64.

146. J. Robinson, "Pay Attention!" *Entrepreneur* (September 2014): 60–65.

147. F. Feiberbaum, "Forget-Me-Nots," *Costco Connection* (June 2016): 37.

148. A. J. Lombardi, "Tech Neck," *Strength & Conditioning* online, accessed January 27, 2017.

149. Staff, "Self-Improvement Through Data," *Fortune* (March 15, 2016): 28.

150. R. Abrams, "Gain an Hour a Day," *Costco Connection* (September 2016): 14.

151. J. Bercovici, "How Dick Costolo Keeps His Focus," *INC.* (March 2015): 48–57.

152. G. Mark, "One Thing at a Time," *Entrepreneur* (September 2014): 64.

153. J. Robinson, "Pay Attention!" *Entrepreneur* (September 2014): 60–65.

154. W. McKinley, S. Latham, and M. Braun, "Organizational Decline and Innovation: Turnarounds and Downward Spirals," *Academy of Management Review* 39, no. 1 (2014): 88–110.

155. J. Shotter and H. Tsoukas, "In Search of Phronesis: Leadership and the Art of Judgment," *Academy of Management Learning & Education* 13, no. 2 (2014): 224–243.

156. D. L. Gamache, G. McNamara, M. J. Mannor, and R. E. Johnson, "Motivated to Acquire? The Impact of CEO Regulatory Focus on Firm Acquisitions," *Academy of Management Journal* 58, no. 4 (2015): 1261–1282.

157. W. K. Smith, "Dynamic Decision Making: A Model of Senior Leaders Managing Strategic Paradoxes," *Academy of Management Journal* 57, no. 6 (2014): 1592–1623.

158. V. Harnish, "Five Questions to Ponder for 2015," *Fortune* (December 22, 2014): 36.

159. R. Bachman, "The Week Resolutions Die," *The Wall Street Journal* (January 20, 2015): D1, D4.

160. R. Reuteman, "Accentuate the Negative," *Entrepreneur* (February 2015): 44–45.

161. R. G. Lord, J. E. Dinh, and E. L. Hoffman, "A Quantum Approach to Time and Organizational Change," *Academy of Management Review* 40, no. 2 (2015): 263–290.

162. H. Yang, Y. Zheng, and A. Zaheer, "Asymmetric Learning Capabilities and Stock Market Value,"

Academy of Management Journal 58, no. 2 (2015): 356–374.

163. S. Pulvirent, "Google Is Acting More Like a Phone Maker," *BusinessWeek* (October 5–11, 2015): 38–39.

164. J. D. Stoll, "GM to Expand Its Lineup of Trucks," *The Wall Street Journal* (June 15, 2015): B1, B2.

165. K. Naughton and D. Welch, "Detroit Has Valley Envy," *BusinessWeek* (May 2–8, 2016: 21–22.

166. N. Davis, "How I Turned Big Data Into Viral Marketing," *INC.* (September 2014): 134.

167. Teradata, "Data-Driven Businesses Outperform," *Forbes* (February 9, 2015): 24.

168. Staff, "Controllers," *Entrepreneur* (November 2015): 63.

169. M. Glassman, "Drinks the World's Top 10 Beers," *BusinessWeek* online, accessed January 28, 2017.

170. D. T. Welsh and L. D. Ordonez, "Conscience Without Cognition: The Effects of Subconscious Priming on Ethical Behavior," *Academy of Management Journal* 57, no. 3 (2014): 723–742.

171. Staff, No. 5 Subway, *Entrepreneur* (January 2016): 104.

172. P. Romano, "Ingredients for a Successful Business," *Fortune* (April 1, 2015): 32.

173. J. P. Doh and N. R. Quigley, "Responsible Leadership and Stakeholder Management: Influence Pathways and Organizational Outcomes," *Academy of Management Perspectives* 28, no. 3 (2014): 255–274.

174. T. Hahn, L. Preuss, J. Pinkse, and F. Figge, "Cognitive Frames in Corporate Sustainability: Managerial Sensemaking With Paradoxical and Business Case Frames," *Academy of Management Review* 39, no. 4 (2014): 463–487.

175. G. Colvin, "From High-Minded to High Value," *Fortune* (December 22, 2014): 38.

Chapter 6

1. G. B. Shaw, "Disrupt This," *Entrepreneur* (November 2015): 10.

2. A. Murray, "Lessons From the Fortune 500," *Fortune* (June 15, 2016): 14.

3. J. Ankeny, "20/20 Visions," *Entrepreneur* (January 2015): 32–36.

4. J. Rodkin and F. Levy, "Recruiting Preferred Skills," *BusinessWeek* (April 13–19, 2015): 43.

5. M. Cerne, C. G. L. Nerstad, A. Dysvik, and M. Skerlavaj, "What Goes Around Comes Around: Knowledge Hiding, Perceived Motivational Climate, and Creativity," *Academy of Management Journal* 57, no. 1 (2014): 172–192.

6. J. Ankeny, "20/20 Visions," *Entrepreneur* (January 2015): 32–36.

7. M. Cerne, C. G. L. Nerstad, A. Dysvik, and M. Skerlavaj, "What Goes Around Comes Around: Knowledge Hiding, Perceived Motivational Climate, and Creativity," *Academy of Management Journal* 57, no. 1 (2014): 172–192.

8. J. Raffiee and J. Feng, "Should I Quit My Day Job? A Hybrid Path to Entrepreneurship," *Academy of Management Journal* 57, no. 4 (2014): 936–963.

9. National Center for the Middle Market, "Take Smart Risks for Sure Growth," *INC.* (April 2015): 49.

10. F. D'Souza, "CEO 101," *Fortune* (November 17, 2014): 130.

11. K. Plank, "CEO Wisdom," *BusinessWeek* (April 27–May 3, 2015): 23.

12. M. Cerne, C. G. L. Nerstad, A. Dysvik, and M. Skerlavaj, "What Goes Around Comes Around: Knowledge Hiding, Perceived Motivational Climate, and Creativity," *Academy of Management Journal* 57, no. 1 (2014): 172–192.

13. "50 Most Powerful Women," *Fortune*, http://fortune.com/most-powerful-women, accessed May 11, 2015.

14. A. von Tobel, "Adapting to Your Company's Growth," *INC.* (December 2014/January 2015): 34.

15. D. Albert, M. Kreutzer, and C. Lechner, "Resolving the Paradox of Interdependency and Strategic

Renewal in Activity Systems," *Academy of Management Review* 40, no. 2 (2015): 210–234.

16. Y. Zhang, D. A. Waldman, Y. L. Han, and X. Li, "Paradoxical Leader Behaviors in People Management: Antecedents and Consequences," *Academy of Management Journal* 58, no. 2 (2015): 538–566.

17. Anonymous reviewer of this eighth edition suggested this addition.

18. D. G. Cosh and J. McNish, "BlackBerry Will Stop Making Its Phones," *The Wall Street Journal* (September 29, 2016): B1, B4.

19. R. D. Costigan and K. E. Brink, "Another Perspective on MAB Program Alignment: An Investigation of Learning Goals," *Academy of Management Learning & Education* 14, no. 2 (2015): 260–276.

20. A. Page, "Google Creates Parent in Shake-Up," *The Wall Street Journal* (August 11, 2015): A1, A2.

21. A. Murray, "What Do Millennials Want?" *Fortune* (March 15, 2015): 14.

22. G. Colvin, "Four Things That Worry Business," *Fortune* (October 27, 2014): 32.

23. M. M. Moya and J. L. M. Aleman, "The Differential Effect of Development Speed and Launching Speed on New Product Performance: An Analysis in SMEs," *Journal of Small Business Management* 54, no. 2 (2016): 750–770.

24. E. Van Oosten and K. E. Kram, "Coaching for Change," *Academy of Management Learning & Education* 13, no. 2 (2014): 295–298.

25. Staff, "Self-Improvement Through Data," *Fortune* (March 15, 2015): 28.

26. G. Colvin, "Ignore These Leadership Lessons at Your Peril," *Fortune* (October 28, 2013): 85.

27. C. Sandler, "Business Lessons From *The Art of War*," *Costco Connection* (May 2014): 15.

28. Y. Zhang, D. A. Waldman, Y. L. Han, and X. Li, "Paradoxical Leader Behaviors in People Management: Antecedents and Consequences," *Academy of Management Journal* 58, no. 2 (2015): 538–566; S. Harvey, "Creative Synthesis: Exploring the Process of Extraordinary Group Creativity," *Academy of Management Review* 39, no. 3 (2014): 324–343.

29. L. Alexander and D. Van Knippenberg, "Teams in Pursuit of Radical Innovation: A Goal Orientation Perspective," *Academy of Management Review* 39, no. 4 (2014): 423–438.

30. C. Fuzzell, "We're All Connected—and That Will Change Everything," *The Wall Street Journal* (February 28, 2015): R8.

31. G. Colvin, "A CEO's Plan to Defy Disruption," *Fortune* (November 17, 2014): 36.

32. Staff, "Shifting Gears," *BusinessWeek* (January 11–17, 2016): 19.

33. J. Muskus, "78. Smartphone," *BusinessWeek* (December 8–14, 2014): 16–17.

34. D. Hughes, "Better to Be the Disrupter Than the Disrupted," *The Wall Street Journal* (February 23, 2015): R4.

35. H. W. Jenkins, "Tesla: Just Another Car Company," *The Wall Street Journal* (March 25, 2015): A13.

36. D. Hughes, "Better to Be the Disrupter Than the Disrupted," *The Wall Street Journal* (February 23, 2015): R4.

37. G. Colvin, "Lead a Revolution From Within," *Fortune* (August 1, 2016): 22.

38. G. Colvin, "Four Things That Worry Business," *Fortune* (October 27, 2014): 32.

39. G. Colvin, "Lead a Revolution From Within," *Fortune* (August 1, 2016): 22.

40. D. Hughes, "Better to Be the Disrupter Than the Disrupted," *The Wall Street Journal* (February 23, 2015): R4.

41. G. Colvin, "Lead a Revolution From Within," *Fortune* (August 1, 2016): 22.

42. A. Murray, "We Are All Technology Companies Now," *Fortune* (December 1, 2015): 8.

43. Ad, "84% of Global Executives," *Fortune* (December 15, 2015): S5.

44. D. W. Williams and M. S. Wood, "Rule-Based Reasoning for Understanding Opportunity Evaluation," *Academy of Management Perspectives* 29, no. 2 (2015): 218–236.

45. M. Blumenstein, "IBM Plans to Thrive as a Digital Company," *The Wall Street Journal* (October 27, 2015): R3.

46. D. Antons and F. T. Piller, "Opening the Black Box of "Not Invented Here: Attitudes, Decision Biases, and Behavioral Consequences," *Academy of Management Perspectives* 29, no. 2 (2015): 193–217.

47. A. Murray, "We Are All Technology Companies Now," *Fortune* (December 1, 2015): 8.

48. L. Alexander and D. Van Knippenberg, "Teams in Pursuit of Radical Innovation: A Goal Orientation Perspective," *Academy of Management Review* 39, no. 4 (2014): 423–438.

49. B. R. Spisak, M. J. O'Brien, N. Nicholson, and M. Van Vugt, "Niche Construction and the Evolution of Leadership," *Academy of Management Review* 40, no. 2 (2015): 291–306.

50. D. Antons and F. T. Piller, "Opening the Black Box of "Not Invented Here: Attitudes, Decision Biases, and Behavioral Consequences," *Academy of Management Perspectives* 29, no. 2 (2015): 193–217.

51. A. C. Cosper, "The Accidental Tourist," *Entrepreneur* (September 2015): 16.

52. T. Monahan, "Revving Up Your Corporate RPMs," *Fortune* (February 1, 2016): 43.

53. Ad, "84% of Global Executives," *Fortune* (December 15, 2015): S5.

54. L. Alexander and D. Van Knippenberg, "Teams in Pursuit of Radical Innovation: A Goal Orientation Perspective," *Academy of Management Review* 39, no. 4 (2014): 423–438.

55. Google website, www.google.com, accessed May 12, 2015.

56. R. C. Liden, S. J. Wayne, C. Liao, and J. D. Meuser, "Servant Leadership and Serving Culture: Influence on Individual and Unit Performance," *Academy of Management Journal* 57, no. 5 (2014): 1434–1452.

57. A. Murray, "We Are All Technology Companies Now," *Fortune* (December 1, 2015): 8.

58. G. Colvin, "Where Disrupters Meet Aristocrats," *Fortune* (December 1, 2015): 28.

59. A. Engelen, T. C. Flatten, J. Thalmann, and M. Brettel, "The Effect of Organizational Culture on Entrepreneurial Orientation: A Comparison Between Germany and Thailand," *Journal of Small Business Management* 52, no. 4 (2014): 732–752.

60. Cadence, "Company Spotlight," *Fortune* (March 15, 2015): 225.

61. A. Canato, "Coerced Practice Implementation in Cases of Low Cultural Fit: Cultural Change and Practice Adaptation During the Implementation of Six Sigma at 3M," *Academy of Management Journal* 56, no. 6 (2013): 1724–1753.

62. A. C. Cosper, "The Creative Brief," *Entrepreneur* (June 2015): 14.6.

63. S. Sonenshein, "How Organizations Foster the Creative Use of Resources," *Academy of Management Journal* 57, no. 3 (2014): 814–848.

64. T. Mandoza, "Culture Matters: 7 Ways of Great Leaders," *Forbes* (October 20, 2014): 113.

65. Ad, "84% of Global Executives," *Fortune* (December 15, 2015): S5.

66. C. Tkaczyk, "How Google Works," *Fortune* (September 24, 2014): 103.

67. Google website, www.google.com, accessed May 12, 2015.

68. T. Daniels, "Starbucks Sponsors the Betacup Challenge to Spur Challenge Problem-Solving," *BetaCup*, http://www.thebetacup.com/2010/03/15/starbucks-sponsors-the-betacup-challenge-to-spur-creative-problem-solving, accessed May 12, 2015.

69. N. Brodsky, "The Good News About the Bad News," *INC.* (February 2016): 52.

70. A. Murray, "We Are All Technology Companies Now," *Fortune* (December 1, 2015): 8.

71. A. Satariano, "Apple Gets More Bang for Its R&D Buck," *BusinessWeek* (November 3–December 6, 2015): 38–39.

72. L. Alexander and D. Van Knippenberg, "Teams in Pursuit of Radical Innovation: A Goal Orientation Perspective," *Academy of Management Review* 39, no. 4 (2014): 423–438.

73. M. L. Verreynne, D. Meyer, and P. Liesch, "Beyond the Formal-Informal Dichotomy of Small Firm Strategy-Making in Stable and Dynamic Environments," *Journal of Small Business Management* 54, no. 2 (2016), 420–444.

74. A. H. Bowers, H. R. Greve, H. Mitsuhashi, and J. A. C. Baum, "Competitive Parity, Status Disparity, and Mutual Forbearance: Securities Analysts' Competition for Investor Attention," *Academy of Management Journal* 57, no. 1 (2014): 38–62.

75. O. Osiyevskyy and J. Dewald, "Inducements, Impediments, and Immediacy: Exploring the Cognitive Drivers of Small Business Managers' Intentions to Adopt Business Model Change," *Journal of Small Business Management* 53, no. 4 (2015): 1011–1032.

76. M. Bloomberg, "Leadership Secrets of the Great CEOs," *BusinessWeek* (December 15–21, 2014): 10.

77. GE ad, "Identifying the Leadership Skills That Matter Most Today," *INC.* (December 2014/January 2015): 78.

78. P. Sellers, "Fortune's Most Powerful Women 2014," *Fortune* (October 6, 2014): 94.

79. C. Rahn, "Innovation Duds," *BusinessWeek* (March 2–8, 2015): 35.

80. M. Ulman, "Margin Quote," *Fortune* (December 1, 2015): 28.

81. M. Rosenwald, "Bound by Habit," *BusinessWeek* (March 19–25, 2012): 106–107.

82. S. Bing, "How to Kill a Good Idea," *Fortune* (April 1, 2016): 116.

83. E. Bernstein, "The Smart Path to a Transparent Workplace," *The Wall Street Journal* (February 23, 2015): R5.

84. S. Bing, "How to Kill a Good Idea," *Fortune* (April 1, 2016): 116.

85. M. Rosenwald, "Bound by Habit," *BusinessWeek* (March 19–25, 2012): 106–107.

86. T. Laamanen, J. A. Lamberg, and E. Vaara, "Explanations of Success and Failure in Management Learning: What Can We Learn From Nokia's Rise and Fall?" *Academy of Management Learning & Education* 15, no. 1 (2016): 2–25.

87. S. Bing, "How to Kill a Good Idea," *Fortune* (April 1, 2016): 116.

88. M. Rosenwald, "Bound by Habit," *BusinessWeek* (March 19–25, 2012): 106–107.

89. "Disrupt This," adapted from a quote from G. B. Shaw, *Entrepreneur* (November 19, 2015): 10.

90. A. Murray, "We Are All Technology Companies Now," *Fortune* (December 1, 2015): 8.

91. M. Rosenwald, "Bound by Habit," *BusinessWeek* (March 19–25, 2012): 106–107.

92. A. Lockett, G. Currie, R. Finn, G. Martin, and J. Waring, "The Influence of Social Position on Sensemaking About Organizational Change," *Academy of Management Journal* 57, no. 4 (2014): 1102–1129.

93. T. Mandoza, "Culture Matters: 7 Ways of Great Leaders," *Forbes* (October 20, 2014): 113.

94. M. Kelly, *The Four Signs of a Dynamic Catholic* (New York: Beacon, 2012).

95. Staff, "The World's Most Admired Companies," Fortune.com, accessed January 30, 2017.

96. K. Hultman, *The Path of Least Resistance* (Austin, TX: Learning Concepts, 1979).

97. Q. N. Huy, K. G. Corley, and M. S. Kraatz, "From Support to Mutiny: Shifting Legitimacy Judgments and Emotional Reactions Impacting the Implementation of Radical Change," *Academy of Management Journal* 57, no. 6 (2014): 1650–1680.

98. A. Lockett, G. Currie, R. Finn, G. Martin, and J. Waring, "The Influence of Social Position on Sensemaking About Organizational Change," *Academy of Management Journal* 57, no. 4 (2014): 1102–1129.

99. A. Gasparro, "McDonald's Puts Its Plan on Display," *The Wall Street Journal* (May 4, 2015): B2.

100. Suggestion from sixth-edition reviewer S. Giura, SUNY Oneonta, April 2015.

101. Suggestion from seventh- and eighth-edition reviewer C. Blencke, University of Central Florida, reviewer suggestion, added February 3, 2017.

102. A. Von Tobel, "Where Money Meets Morale," *INC.* (April 2014): 48–49.

103. R. King, "Companies Want to Know: How Do Workers Feel?" *The Wall Street Journal* (November 14, 2015): R3.

104. Margin note, "98 Percent," *INC.* (June 2016): 107.

105. Suggestion from seventh- and eighth-edition reviewer C. Blencke, University of Central Florida, added February 3, 2017.

106. A. S. Amezcua, M. G. Grimes, S. W. Bradley, and J. Wiklund, "Organizational Sponsorship and Founding Environments: A Contingency View on the Survival of Business-Incubated Firms, 1994–2007," *Academy of Management Journal* 56, no. 6 (2013): 1628–1654.

107. J. S. Gordon, "Entrepreneurship in American History," *Imprimis* (February 2014): 1.

108. A. Rauch and W. Hulsink, "Putting Entrepreneurship Education Where the Intention to Act Lies," *Academy of Management Learning & Education* 14, no. 2 (2015): 187–204.

109. "CEO Survey: How Dreamers Become Doers," *INC.* (September 2016): 44–46.

110. R. Clough, "General Electric Wants to Act Like a Startup," *BusinessWeek* (August 11–24, 2014): 22–24.

111. B. Costa, "The CEO Who Gets to Hand Out World Series Rings," *The Wall Street Journal* (February 23, 2015): R4.

112. D. Courpasson, F. Dany, and I. Marti, "Organizational Entrepreneurship as Active Resistance: A Struggle Against Outsourcing," *Entrepreneurship Theory and Practice* 40, no. 1 (2016): 131–160.

113. R. P. Garrett and J. G. Covin, "Internal Corporate Venture Operations Independence and Performance: A Knowledge-Based Perspective," *Entrepreneurship Theory and Practice* 39, no. 4 (2015): 763–790.

114. Ad, "84% of Global Executives," *Fortune* (December 15, 2015): S5.

115. A. Rauch and W. Hulsink, "Putting Entrepreneurship Education Where the Intention to Act Lies," *Academy of Management Learning & Education* 14, no. 2 (2015): 187–204.

116. SBA website, www.sba.gov, accessed February 9, 2017.

117. U.S. DOL website, www.bls.gov, accessed February 9, 2017.

118. SBA website, www.sba.gov, accessed February 9, 2017.

119. SBA, "Small Business Is Booming," *Costco Connection* (February 2015): 13.

120. G. Guerra and R. Patuelli, "The Role of Job Satisfaction in Transitions Into Self-Employment," *Entrepreneurship Theory and Practice* 40, no. 3 (2016): 543–570.

121. Ad, "84% of Global Executives," *Fortune* (December 15, 2015): S5.

122. J. Rodkin and F. Levy, "Recruiting Preferred Skills," *BusinessWeek* (April 13–19, 2015): 43.

123. I. Deligianni, P. Dimitratos, A. Petrou, and Y. Aharoni, "Entrepreneurial Orientation and International Performance: The Moderating Effect of Decision-Making Rationality," *Journal of Small Business Management* 54, no. 2 (2016): 462–480.

124. R. P. Garrett and J. G. Covin, "Internal Corporate Venture Operations Independence and Performance: A Knowledge-Based Perspective," *Entrepreneurship Theory and Practice* 39, no. 4 (2015): 763–790.

125. J. Rodkin and F. Levy, "Recruiting Preferred Skills," *BusinessWeek* (April 13–19, 2015): 43.

126. Staff, "Decoding the DNA of the Entrepreneur," *INC.* (December 2015/January 2016): 53–59.

127. J. Ankeny, "20/20 Visions," *Entrepreneur* (January 2015): 32–36.

128. "CEO Survey: How Dreamers Become Doers," *INC.* (September 2016): 44–46.

129. J. Raffiee and J. Feng, "Should I Quit My Day Job? A Hybrid Path to Entrepreneurship," *Academy of Management Journal* 57, no. 4 (2014): 936–963.

130. K. Inskeep, "Margin Quote," *Entrepreneur* (January 2016): 49.

131. M. Macinnis, "What I Learned From Steve Jobs," *INC.* (September 2014): 129.

132. P. Berkhout, J. Hartog, and M. van Praag, "Entrepreneurship and Financial Incentives of Return, Risk, and Skew," *Entrepreneurship Theory and Practice* 39, no. 4 (2015): 763–790.

133. J. Raffiee and J. Feng, "Should I Quit My Day Job? A Hybrid Path to Entrepreneurship," *Academy of Management Journal* 57, no. 4 (2014): 936–963.

134. J. Chew, "Be Better!" *Fortune* (January 1, 2016): 16.

135. The White Lion Brewing Company information was written by Founder Ray Berry and edited by the author.

136. M. M. Gielnik, M. Spitzmuller, A. Schmitt, D. K. Klemann, and M. Frese, "I Put in Effort, Therefore I Am Passionate: Investigating the Path From Effort to Passion in Entrepreneurship," *Academy of Management Journal* 58, no. 4 (2015): 1012–1031.

137. R. N. Lussier, J. Corman, and D. C. Kimball, *Entrepreneurial New Venture Skills* (New York: Routledge, 2015).

138. I. Deligianni, P. Dimitratos, A. Petrou, and Y. Aharoni, "Entrepreneurial Orientation and International Performance: The Moderating Effect of Decision-Making Rationality," *Journal of Small Business Management* 54, no. 2 (2016): 462–480.

139. M. D. Foo, M. A. Uy, and C. Murniek, "Beyond Affective Valence: Untangling Valence and Activation Influences on Opportunity Identification," *Entrepreneurship Theory and Practice* 39, no. 2 (2015): 407–431.

140. P. Diamandis, "The Future of … Scaling and Strategy," *Entrepreneur* (January 2015): 34.

141. Staff, "CEO Survey," *INC.* (September 2014): 126.

142. J. Schneuer, "Are We on to Something?" *Entrepreneur* (November 2014), www.entrepreneur.com, accessed August 22, 2017.

143. F. D'Souza, "CEO 101 Quote," *Fortune* (November 17, 2014): 130.

144. S. Ramoglou and E. W. K. Tsang, "A Realist Perspective of Entrepreneurship: Opportunities as Propensities," *Academy of Management Review* 41, no. 3 (2016): 410–434.

145. L. Stevens, "Technology Bubble? Ask Waffle House," *The Wall Street Journal* (February 24, 2015): B1.

146. S. Gerber, "Interview With Sandy Lerner," *INC.* (October 2015): 156.

147. R. Abrams, "Rules for Success," *Costco Connection* (April 2016): 13.

148. Ibid.

149. M. Malmstrom, J. Johansson, and J. Wincent, "Cognitive Construction of Low-Profit and High Profit Business Models: A Repertory Grid Study of Serial Entrepreneurs," *Entrepreneurship Theory and Practice* 39, no. 5 (2015): 1083–1109.

150. Staff, "Decoding the DNA of the Entrepreneur," *INC.* (December 2015/January 2016): 53–59.

151. B. Chesky, "Quote," *BusinessWeek* (January 30–February 5, 2017): 1.

152. W. Amos, "Don't Quit, Part 2," *Costco Connection* (May 2015): 15.

153. T. Kautonen, M. van Gelderen, and M. Fink, "Robustness of the Theory of Planned Behavior in Predicting Entrepreneurial Intentions and Actions," *Entrepreneurship Theory and Practice* 39, no. 3 (2015): 655–647.

154. A. C. Cosper, "Creating Relevance," *Entrepreneur* (May 2015): 10.

155. R. N. Lussier, "A Three-Country Comparison of the Business Success Versus Failure Prediction Model," *Journal of Small Business Management* 48, no. 3 (2010): 360–377.

156. E. Schurenberg, "Born Leaders or Idea Machines," *INC.* (March 2015): 14.

157. V. Harnish, "Five Not-to-Be-Missed Books," *Fortune* (November 17, 2014): 45.

158. E. Kasabov, "Start-Up Difficulties in Early-Stage Peripheral Clusters: The Case of IT in an Emerging Economy," *Entrepreneurship Theory and Practice* 39, no. 4 (2015): 727–761.

159. R. Abrams, "Rules for Success," *Costco Connection* (April 2016): 13.

160. Business Plan Pro website, http://www.businessplanpro.com, accessed February 13, 2017.

161. Enloop website, http://www.enloop.com, accessed February 13, 2017.

162. L. Blakely, "Pitch Perfect," *INC.* (December 2015/January 2016): 24–25.

163. A. Zissu, "How to Win at *Shark Tank*," *Entrepreneur* (October 2016): 18.

164. J. Robinson, You're Going to Love Sales," *Entrepreneur* (February 2016): 40–44.

165. G. Fisher, S. Kotha, and A. Lahiri, "Changing With the Times: An Integrated View of Identity, Legitimacy, and New Venture Life Cycles," *Academy of Management Review* 41, no. 3 (2016): 383–409.

166. D. J. Cunning, J. A. Pandes, and M. J. Robinson, "The Role of Agents in Private Entrepreneurial Finance," *Entrepreneurship Theory and Practice* 39, no. 2 (2015): 345–374.

167. "CEO Survey. How Dreamers Become Doers," *INC.* (September 2016): 44–46.

168. L. Buchanan, "Wired for Success," *INC.* (September 2014): 26–52.

169. R. Abrams, "Rules for Success," *Costco Connection* (April 2016): 13.

170. V. Harnish, "Five Not-to-Be-Missed Books," *Fortune* (November 17, 2014): 45.

171. L. Buchanan, "Wired for Success," *INC.* (September 2014): 26–52.

172. M. Mustache, "Dump That Debt," *Costco Connection* (January 2016): 26.

173. V. Harnish, "Five Not-to-Be-Missed Books," *Fortune* (November 17, 2014): 45.

174. D. Seetharaman, "Facebook Investors Press Suit on Shares," *The Wall Street Journal* (December 10, 2016): B1, B2.

175. SBA, sba.gov/tools/linc Accessed February 20, 2017.

176. L. Buchanan, "Wired for Success," *INC.* (September 2014): 26–52.

177. W. Isaacson, "The Ultimate Icon," *INC.* (October 2014): 82–84.

178. K. Stock, "Margin Note," *Business Week* (January 30–February 5, 2017): 11.

179. "Apple Is Nearing," *The Wall Street Journal* (January 26, 2017): A1, B4.

180. Ad, "84% of Global Executives," *Fortune* (December 15, 2015): S5.

181. P. C. Godart, W. W. Maddux, A. V. Shipilov, and A. D. Galinsky, "Fashion With a Foreign Flair: Professional Experiences Abroad Facilitate the Creative Innovations of Organizations," *Academy of Management Journal* 58, no. 1 (2015): 195–220.

182. A. Engelen, T. C. Flatten, J. Thalmann, and M. Brettel, "The Effect of Organizational Culture on Entrepreneurial Orientation: A Comparison Between Germany and Thailand," *Journal of Small Business Management* 52, no. 4 (2014): 732–752.

183. G. Guerra and R. Patuelli, "The Role of Job Satisfaction in Transitions Into Self-Employment," *Entrepreneurship Theory and Practice* 40, no. 3 (2016): 543–570.

184. A. Rauch and W. Hulsink, "Putting Entrepreneurship Education Where the Intention to Act Lies," *Academy of Management Learning & Education* 14, no. 2 (2015): 187–204.

185. K. Frieswick and K. Lenz, "The New Startup Math," *INC.* (October 2014): 20–21.

186. R. Simon, "Women Make Strides in Business Ownership," *The Wall Street Journal* (August 20, 2015): B1, B4.

187. E. McGirt, "Google Searches Its Soul," *Fortune* (February 1, 2017): 49–56.

188. K. Weisul, "Will the Next Steve Jobs Be a Woman?" *INC.* (October 2015): 71–74.

189. C. Dawson and A. Henley, "Gender, Risk, and Venture Creation Intentions," *Journal of Small Business Management* 53, no. 2 (2015): 501–515.

190. S. Y. Yousafzai, S. Saeed, and M. Muffatto, "Institutional Theory and Contextual Embeddedness of Women Entrepreneurial Leadership: Evidence From 92 Countries," *Journal of Small Business Management* 53, no. 3 (2015): 587–604.

191. E. Schurenberg, "The Next Iconic Founders Will Be Women," *INC.* (October 2015): 14.

192. D. Whitford, "Why Would Anyone Want to Kill Brianna Wu?" *INC.* (April 2015): 87–90.

193. D. M. Ewalt, "The Modest Tycoon," *Forbes* (June 15, 2015): 77–80.

194. C. Suddath, "Music for the One Percent," *BusinessWeek* (April 13–19, 2015): 78.

195. Staff, "Beyoncé," *Entrepreneur* (December 2014): 52.

196. A. Murray, "What Do Millennials Want?" *Fortune* (March 15, 2015): 14.

197. Staff, "Picture Perfect," *Forbes* (September 2014): 20.

198. Staff, "Survey," *INC.* (September 2014): 78.

199. D. Leonard, "Young Buns," *BusinessWeek* (July 28–August 3, 2014): 42–47.

200. G. Wong, "Alibaba Strives to Think Younger," *The Wall Street Journal* (May 8, 2015): B1.

201. A. C. Cosper, "The Accidental Tourist," *Entrepreneur* (September 2015): 16.

202. J. Daily, "Frontiers in Franchising," *Entrepreneur* (October 2015): 97–101.

203. R. Karlgaard, "Riches From the Disruptive Dozen," *Forbes* (October 19, 2015): 38.

204. C. Mims, "Apps Tell Boss What Workers Really Think," *The Wall Street Journal* (June 22, 2015): B1, B2.

205. S. Nicola, with R. Penty and J. Ainger, "Spread Your Wings and Fly, Penguin," *BusinessWeek* (January 30–February 5, 2017): 17–18.

206. R. Stevens, N. Moray, and J. Bruneel, "The Social and Economic Mission of Social Enterprises: Dimensions, Measurement, Validation, and Relation," *Entrepreneurship Theory and Practice* 39, no. 5 (2015): 1051–1082.

207. R. Yitshaki and F. Kropp, "Motivation and Opportunity Recognition of Social Entrepreneurs," *Journal of Small Business Management* 54, no. 2 (2016): 546–565.

208. A. Kroeger and C. Weber, "Developing a Conceptual Framework for Comparing Social Value Creation," *Academy of Management Review* 39, no. 4 (2014): 513–540.

209. L. Buchanan, "Call to Action," *INC.* (October 2014): 48.

210. B. Mycoskie, *Start Something That Matters* (New York: Spiegel & Grau, 2012).

211. M. Bedat, "Call to Action," *INC.* (October 2014): 48.

212. I. M. Thomas, "Sal Khan Is a Can-Do Guy," *Costco Connection* (August 2013): 30–31.

213. Ad, "Energizer," *INC.* (April 2015): 25.

Chapter 7

1. B. R. Spisak, M. J. O'Brien, N. Nicholson, and M. Van Vugt, "Niche Construction and the Evolution of Leadership," *Academy of Management Review* 40, no. 2 (2015): 291–306.

2. M. Brettel, C. Chomik, and T. S. Flatten, "How Organizational Culture Influences Innovativeness, Proactiveness, and Risk-Taking," *Journal of Small Business Management* 53, no. 4 (2015), 868–885.

3. G. Fisher, S. Kotha, and A. Lahiri, "Changing With the Times: An Integrated View of Identity, Legitimacy, and New Venture Life Cycles," *Academy of Management Review* 41, no. 3 (2016): 383–409.

4. M. L. Verreynne, D. Meyer, and P. Liesch, "Beyond the Formal-Informal Dichotomy of Small Firm Strategy-Making in Stable and Dynamic Environments," *Journal of Small Business Management* 54, no. 2 (2016), 420–444.

5. J. Robinson, "Up, Down and Sideways," *Entrepreneur* (December 2015): 59.

6. M. L. Verreynne, D. Meyer, and P. Liesch, "Beyond the Formal-Informal Dichotomy of Small Firm Strategy-Making in Stable and Dynamic Environments," *Journal of Small Business Management* 54, no. 2 (2016), 420–444.

7. B. R. Spisak, M. J. O'Brien, N. Nicholson, and M. Van Vugt, "Niche Construction and the Evolution of Leadership," *Academy of Management Review* 40, no. 2 (2015): 291–306.

8. M. L. Besharov and W. K. Smith, "Multiple Institutional Logics in Organizations: Explaining Their Varied Nature and Implications," *Academy of Management Review* 39, no. 3 (2014): 364–381.

9. M. Brettel, C. Chomik, and T. S. Flatten, "How Organizational Culture Influences Innovativeness, Proactiveness, and Risk-Taking," *Journal of Small Business Management* 53, no. 4 (2015), 868–885.

10. Staff, "Best Practicers," *Entrepreneur* (November 2015): 59.

11. M. Brettel, C. Chomik, and T. S. Flatten, "How Organizational Culture Influences Innovativeness, Proactiveness, and Risk-Taking," *Journal of Small Business Management* 53, no. 4 (2015), 868–885.

12. S. Leibs, "The Micromanager's Guide to Delegation," *INC.* (March 2014): 19.

13. R. C. Liden, S. J. Wayne, C. Liao, and J. D. Meuser, "Servant Leadership and Serving Culture: Influence on Individual and Unit Performance," *Academy of Management Journal* 57, no. 5 (2014): 1434–1452.

14. C. Mims, "Data Is Now the New Middle Manager," *The Wall Street Journal* (April 20, 2015): B1, B2.

15. V. Harnish, "5 Key Trends to Master in 2016," *Fortune* (December 15, 2015), 52.

16. E. Lehoczky, "Get Out of the Way," *INC.* (July/August 2015): 24.

17. E. Bernstein, "The Smart Path to a Transparent Workplace," *The Wall Street Journal* (February 23, 2015): R5.

18. T. A. De Vries, F. Walter, G. S. Van Der Vegt, and P. J. M. D. Essens, "Antecedents of Individuals' Interteam Coordination: Broad Functional Experiences as a Mixed Blessing," *Academy of Management Journal* 57, no. 5 (2014): 1334–1359.

19. T. Hahn, L. Preuss, J. Pinkse, and F. Figge, "Cognitive Frames in Corporate Sustainability: Managerial Sensemaking With Paradoxical and Business Case Frames," *Academy of Management Review* 39, no. 4 (2014): 463–487.

20. W. K. Smith, "Dynamic Decision Making: A Model of Senior Leaders Managing Strategic Paradoxes," *Academy of Management Journal* 57, no. 6 (2014): 1592–1623.

21. R. P. Garrett and J. G. Covin, "Internal Corporate Venture Operations Independence and Performance: A Knowledge-Based Perspective," *Entrepreneurship Theory and Practice* 39, no. 4 (2015): 763–790.

22. B. R. Spisak, M. J. O'Brien, N. Nicholson, and M. Van Vugt, "Niche Construction and the Evolution of Leadership," *Academy of Management Review* 40, no. 2 (2015): 291–306.

23. E. Bernstein, "The Smart Path to a Transparent Workplace," *The Wall Street Journal* (February 23, 2015): R5.

24. E. Bernstein, "Don't Apologize So Fast," *The Wall Street Journal* (July 15, 2014): D1, D4.

25. S. Shellenbarger, "It's Not My Fault! A Better Response to Criticism at Work," *The Wall Street Journal* (June 18, 2014): D1, D4.

26. S. F. Collins, "Success Steps," *Costco Connection* (January 2016): 29.

27. Y. Zhang, D. A. Waldman, Y. L. Han, and X. Li, "Paradoxical Leader Behaviors in People Management: Antecedents and Consequences," *Academy of Management Journal* 58, no. 2 (2015): 538–566.

28. S. H. Harrison and E. D. Rouse, "Let's Dance! Elastic Coordination in Creative Group Work: A Qualitative Study of Modern Dancers," *Academy of Management Journal* 57, no. 5 (2014): 1256–1283.

29. J. Gaines, "Play With the Big Boxes," *Entrepreneur* (February 2015): 15.

30. G. B. Ryan, "More Happiness, More Revenues: Ryan's Story," *Fortune* (March 15, 2015): 20.

31. S. F. Collins, "Success Steps," *Costco Connection* (January 2016): 29.

32. B. M. Galvin, D. Lange, and B. E. Ashforth, "Narcissistic Organizational Identification: Seeing Oneself as Central to the Organization's Identity," *Academy of Management Review* 40, no. 2 (2015): 163–181.

33. Q. N. Huy, K. G. Corley, and M. S. Kraatz, "From Support to Mutiny: Shifting Legitimacy Judgments and Emotional Reactions Impacting the Implementation of Radical Change," *Academy of Management Journal* 57, no. 6 (2014): 1650–1680.

34. F. Aime, S. Humphrey, D. S. Derue, and J. B. Paul, "The Riddle of Heterarchy: Power Transitions in Cross-Functional Teams," *Academy of Management Journal* 57, no. 2 (2014): 327–352.

35. J. R. Hollenbeck and B. B. Jamieson, "Human Capital, Social Capital, and Social Network Analysis," *Academy of Perspectives* 29, no. 3 (2015): 370–365.

36. Staff, "Best Practicers," *Entrepreneur* (November 2015): 59.

37. J. J. Reuer and S. V. Devarakonda, "Mechanisms of Hybrid Governance: Administrative Committees in Non-Equity Alliances," *Academy of Management Journal* 59, no. 2 (2016): 510–533.

38. T. Hahn, L. Preuss, J. Pinkse, and F. Figge, "Cognitive Frames in Corporate Sustainability: Managerial Sensemaking With Paradoxical and Business Case Frames," *Academy of Management Review* 39, no. 4 (2014): 463–487.

39. C. Mims, "Data Is Now the New Middle Manager," *The Wall Street Journal* (April 20, 2015): B1, B2.

40. Y. Zhang, D. A. Waldman, Y. L. Han, and X. Li, "Paradoxical Leader Behaviors in People Management: Antecedents and Consequences," *Academy of Management Journal* 58, no. 2 (2015): 538–566.

41. R. Lowenstein, "Forget Buffett the Investor. Follow Buffett the Manager," *Fortune* (April 21, 2015): 67–68.

42. J. Jargon, "McDonald's Hacks at Its Bureaucracy," *The Wall Street Journal* (October 31, 2014): B1.

43. K. Safdar, "Gaps Analytical CEO Bets on Data," *The Wall Street Journal* (November 28, 2016): A1, A12.

44. Staff, "Controllers," *Entrepreneur* (November 2015): 63.

45. S. Leibs, "The Micromanager's Guide to Delegation," *INC.* (March 2014): 18–19.

46. J. Robinson, "Up, Down and Sideways," *Entrepreneur* (December 2015): 59.

47. D. Albert, M. Kreutzer, and C. Lechner, "Resolving the Paradox of Interdependency and Strategic Renewal in Activity Systems," *Academy of Management Review* 40, no. 2 (2015): 210–234.

48. D. Courpasson, F. Dany, and I. Marti, "Organizational Entrepreneurship as Active Resistance: A Struggle Against Outsourcing," *Entrepreneurship Theory and Practice* 40, no. 1 (2016): 131–160.

49. A. M. Kleinbaum and T. E. Stuart, "Network Responsiveness: The Social Structural Microfoundations of Dynamic Capabilities,"

Academy of Management Perspectives 28, no. 4 (2014): 353–367.

50. Staff, "Best Practicers," *Entrepreneur* (November 2015): 59.

51. C. L. Pearce, C. L. Wassenaar, and C. C. Manz, "Is Shared Leadership the Key to Responsible Leadership?" *Academy of Management Perspectives* 28, no. 3 (2014): 275–288.

52. S. J. Creary, B. B. Caza, L. M. Roberts, "Out of the Box? How Managing a Subordinate's Multiple Identities Affects the Quality of a Manager–Subordinate Relationship," *Academy of Management Review* 40, no. 4 (2015): 538–562.

53. M. Berman, "The No-Boss Company," *The Wall Street Journal* (October 27, 2015): R3.

54. T. A. De Vries, F. Walter, G. S. Van Der Vegt, and P. J. M. D. Essens, "Antecedents of Individuals' Interteam Coordination: Broad Functional Experiences as a Mixed Blessing," *Academy of Management Journal* 57, no. 5 (2014): 1334–1359.

55. P. Lencioni, "When Less Is More," *INC.* (June 2015): 69.

56. SAGE website, www.sagepub.com, accessed May 20, 2015.

57. B. M. Firth, J. R. Hollenbeck, J. E. Miles, D. R. Ilgen, and C. M. Barnes, "Same Page, Different Books: Extending Representational Gaps Theory to Enhance Performance in Multiteam Systems," *Academy of Management Journal* 58, no. 3 (2015): 813–835.

58. R. M. Kanter, "Why Global Companies Will Behave More and More Alike," *The Wall Street Journal* (July 8, 2014): R8.

59. Staff, "The M-Form Style," illustration in *BusinessWeek* (November 24–30, 2014): 61.

60. PepsiCo website, www.pepsico.com, accessed March 1, 2017.

61. D. Cameron, "Gun Maker Bets on Sporting Goods," *The Wall Street Journal* (January 20, 2016): B1.

62. R. Lowenstein, "Forget Buffett the Investor. Follow Buffett the Manager," *Fortune* (April 21, 2015): 67–68.

63. A. Barr, "Google Creates Parent in Shake-Up," *The Wall Street Journal* (August 11, 2015): A1, A2.

64. S. Higginbotham, "A Look at Google's Plan B …and C and D," *Fortune* (September 2015): 10.

65. A. Barr, "At Google, Breathing Room for Ideas," *The Wall Street Journal* (October 2, 2015): B1, B4.

66. D. Antons and F. T. Piller, "Opening the Black Box of 'Not Invented Here': Attitudes, Decision Biases, and Behavioral Consequences," *Academy of Management Perspectives* 29, no. 2 (2015): 193–217.

67. S. Karim, T. N. Carroll, and C. P. Long, "Delaying Change: Examining How Industry and Managerial Turbulence Impact Structural Realignment," *Academy of Management Journal* 59, no. 3 (2015): 791–817.

68. T. Monahan, "Revving Up Your Corporate RPMs," *Fortune* (February 1, 2016): 43.

69. Ibid.

70. J. Jargon, "McDonald's Hacks at Its Bureaucracy," *The Wall Street Journal* (October 31, 2014): B1.

71. C. Rose, "Despite the Rhetoric I Hear, Thank God Employers Are Still in the Health-Care System," *BusinessWeek* (March 4–10, 2013): 32.

72. V. Harnish, "Finding the Route to Growth," *Fortune* (May 19, 2014): 45.

73. M. Berman, "The No-Boss Company," *The Wall Street Journal* (October 27, 2015): R3.

74. B. M. Firth, J. R. Hollenbeck, J. E. Miles, D. R. Ilgen, and C. M. Barnes, "Same Page, Different Books: Extending Representational Gaps Theory to Enhance Performance in Multiteam Systems," *Academy of Management Journal* 58, no. 3 (2015): 813–835.

75. J. Clegg, "And the Oregon Ducks Prefer to Avoid It," *The Wall Street Journal* (January 8, 2015): D6.

76. J. Clegg, "And the Oregon Ducks Prefer to Avoid It," *The Wall Street Journal* (January 8, 2015): D6.

77. R. J. Funk, "Making the Most of Where You Are: Geography, Networks, and Innovation in Organizations," *Academy of Management Journal* 57, no. 1 (2014): 193–222.

78. A. Shipilov, R. Gulati, M. Kilduff, S. Li, and W. Tsai, "Relational Pluralism Within and Between Organizations," *Academy of Management Journal* 57, no. 2 (2014): 449–459.

79. M. Sytch and A. Tatarynowicz, "Exploring the Locus of Invention: The Dynamics of Network Communities and Firms' Invention Productivity," *Academy of Management Journal* 57, no. 1 (2014): 249–279.

80. Ohio State University, ad, *Fortune* (September 22, 2014): S7.

81. R. M. Kanter, "Why Global Companies Will Behave More and More Alike," *The Wall Street Journal* (July 8, 2014): R8.

82. K. J. Lovelace, F. Eggers, and L. R. Dyck, "I Do and I Understand: Assessing the Utility of Web-Based Management Simulations to Develop Critical Thinking Skills," *Academy of Management Learning & Education* 15, no. 1 (2016): 100–121.

83. D. Antons and F. T. Piller, "Opening the Black Box of 'Not Invented Here': Attitudes, Decision Biases, and Behavioral Consequences," *Academy of Management Perspectives* 29, no. 2 (2015): 193–217.

84. G. F. Davis, "Can an Economy Survive Without Corporations? Technology and Robust Organizational Alternatives," *Academy of Management Perspectives* 30, no. 2 (2015): 129–140.

85. E. Dexheimer, "Visa Fends Off Usurpers by Joining Apple in Pay System," *BusinessWeek* (October 2, 2014), http://www.bloomberg.com/news/articles/2014-10-02/visa-fends-off-usurpers-by-joining-apple-in-pay-system, accessed August 30, 2015.

86. M. R. Barrick, G. R. Thurgood, T. A. Smith, and S. H. Courtright, "Collective Organizational Engagement: Linking Motivational Antecedents, Strategic Implementation, and Firm Performance," *Academy of Management Journal* 58, no. 1 (2014): 111–135.

87. A. M. Grant, J. M. Berg, and D. M. Cable, "Job Titles as Identity Badges: How Self-Reflective Titles Can Reduce Emotional Exhaustion," *Academy of Management Journal* 57, no. 4 (2014): 1201–1225.

88. J. P. J. de Jong, S. K. Parker, S. Wennekers, and C. H. Wu, "Entrepreneurial Behavior in Organizations: Does Job Design Matter?" *Entrepreneurship Theory and Practice* 39, no. 4 (2015): 981–995.

89. C. Tate, "Work Simply," *BusinessWeek* (December 22–28, 2014): 71.

90. G. Colvin, "The Art of Doing the Unpopular," *Fortune* (June 15, 2016): 32.

91. J. P. J. de Jong, S. K. Parker, S. Wennekers, and C. H. Wu, "Entrepreneurial Behavior in Organizations: Does Job Design Matter?" *Entrepreneurship Theory and Practice* 39, no. 4 (2015): 981–995.

92. T. A. De Vries, F. Walter, G. S. Van Der Vegt, and P. J. M. D. Essens, "Antecedents of Individuals' Interteam Coordination: Broad Functional Experiences as a Mixed Blessing," *Academy of Management Journal* 57, no. 5 (2014): 1334–1359.

93. J. Price, "If You Leave Me Now …," *INC.* (January 2015): 20–21.

94. M. R. Barrick, G. R. Thurgood, T. A. Smith, and S. H. Courtright, "Collective Organizational Engagement: Linking Motivational Antecedents, Strategic Implementation, and Firm Performance," *Academy of Management Journal* 58, no. 1 (2014): 111–135.

95. R. Hackman and G. Oldham, *Work Redesign* (Reading, MA: Addison-Wesley, 1980).

96. J. Robinson, "The Refueling Principle," *Entrepreneur* (October 2014): 67–70.

97. M. Whelan, "Productivity Hack," *Fortune* (October 1, 2015): 114.

98. Ad, "More Happiness, More Revenue: Ryan's Story," *Fortune* (March 15, 2015): 20.

99. Suggestion from reviewer G. Desa, San Francisco State University, added May 22, 2015.

100. J. Shotter and H. Tsoukas, "In Search of Phronesis: Leadership and the Art of Judgment," *Academy of Management Learning & Education* 13, no. 2 (2014): 224–243.

101. S. Leibs, "Just Trust," *INC.* (March 2015): 18–19.

102. J. Krasny, "The Latest Thinking About Time," *INC.* (March 2015): 44–45.

103. J. Buchanan, "Wired for Success," *INC.* (September 2014): 26–52.

104. M. Whelan, "Productivity Hack," *Fortune* (October 1, 2015): 114.

105. J. Krasny, "The Latest Thinking About Time," *INC.* (March 2015): 44–45.

106. J. Wang, "A Delicate Balance," *Entrepreneur* (September 2015): 136.

107. This section and Skill Builder 7-1 are adapted from Harbridge House training materials (Boston).

108. J. Bercovici, "How Dick Costolo Keeps His Focus," *INC.* (March 2015): 48–57.

109. L. Welch, "A CEOs Job," *INC.* (May 2015): 49–50.

110. G. Rometty, "Most Powerful Women Advice," *Fortune* (November 17, 2014): 149.

111. M. Adams, "There Is Never Enough Time," *The Wall Street Journal* (October 26, 2015): R4.

112. G. Rometty, "Most Powerful Women Advice," *Fortune* (November 17, 2014): 149.

113. J. Fried, "Leading by Letting Go," *INC.* (December 2014–January 2015): 128.

114. S. Leibs, "Just Trust," *INC.* (March 2015): 18–19.

115. J. Buchanan, "Wired for Success," *INC.* (September 2014): 26–52.

116. S. Leibs, "Just Trust," *INC.* (March 2015): 18–19.

117. C. K. Lam, X. Huang, and S. C. H. Chan, "The Threshold Effect of Participative Leadership and the Role of Leader Information Sharing," *Academy of Management Journal* 58, no. 3 (2015): 836–855.

118. R. Abrams, "Gain an Hour a Day," *Costco Connection* (September 2016): 14.

119. P. Andruss, "What to Delegate," *Entrepreneur* (January 2014): 74–83.

120. Staff, "Decoding the DNA of the Entrepreneur," *INC.* (December 2015/January 2016): 53–59.

121. S. F. Collins, "Success Steps," *Costco Connection* (January 2016): 29.

122. M. Villano, "Creative Genius," *Entrepreneur* (April 2015): 56–60.

123. R. McCammon, "I'm Going to Need a Bit More Time," *Entrepreneur* (September 2014): 28–30.

124. G. F. Davis, "Can an Economy Survive Without Corporations? Technology and Robust Organizational Alternatives," *Academy of Management Perspectives* 30, no. 2 (2016): 129–140.

125. M. Brettel, C. Chomik, and T. S. Flatten, "How Organizational Culture Influences Innovativeness, Proactiveness, and Risk-Taking," *Journal of Small Business Management* 53, no. 4 (2015), 868–885.

126. G. D. Bruton, M. W. Peng, D. Ahlstrom, C. Stan, and K. Xu, "State-Owned Enterprises Around the World as Hybrid Organizations," *Academy of Management Perspectives* 29, no. 1 (2015): 92–114.

127. R. Albergotti, "At Facebook, *Boss* Is a Dirty Word," *The Wall Street Journal* (December 26, 2014): B1, B2.

128. D. Harris, "How Ford Quantifies Its Future," *Fortune* (October 1, 2015): 58.

129. A. Vance and B. Stone, "Global Tech Issue," *Business Week* (June 13–26, 2016): 55–61.

130. J. Alsever, "Startups … Inside Giant Companies," *Fortune* (May 1, 2015): 33–35.

131. Teradata, "Data-Driven Businesses Outperform," *Forbes* (February 9, 2015): 24.

132. C. Mims, "Data Is Now the New Middle Manager," *The Wall Street Journal* (April 20, 2015): B1, B2.

Chapter 8

1. L. M. Maruping, V. Venkatesh, S. M. B. Thatcher, and P. C. Patel, "Folding Under Pressure or Rising to the Occasion? Perceived Time Pressure and the Moderating Role of Team Temporal Leadership," *Academy of Management Journal* 58, no. 5 (2015): 1313–1333.

2. A. Joshi and A. P. Knight, "Who Defers to Whom and Why? Dual Pathways Linking Demographic Differences and Dyadic Deference to Team Effectiveness," *Academy of Management Journal* 58, no. 1 (2015): 59–84.

3. R. D. Costigan and K. E. Brink, "Another Perspective on MBA Program Alignment: An Investigation of Learning Goals," *Academy of Management Learning & Education* 14, no. 2 (2015): 260–276.

4. AACSB website, www.aacsb.edu, accessed April 10, 2017.

5. K. Davidson, "Hard to Find: Workers With Good Soft Skills," *The Wall Street Journal* (August 31, 2016): B1, B6; J. Rodkin and F. Levy, "Recruiting Preferred Skills," *BusinessWeek* (April 19, 2015): 43.

6. N. M. Lorinkova, M. J. Pearsall, and H. P. Sims, "Examining the Differential Longitudinal Performance of Directive Versus Empowering Leadership in Teams," *Academy of Management Journal* 56, no. 2 (2013): 573–596.

7. J. Dorsey, "CEO Wisdom," *BusinessWeek* (October 12–18, 2015): 24.

8. Staff, "Margin Note," *INC.* (June 2016): 106.

9. J. Hu and R. C. Liden, "Making a Difference in the Teamwork: Linking Team Prosocial Motivation to Team Processes and Effectiveness," *Academy of Management Journal* 58, no. 4 (2015): 1102–1127.

10. N. M. Lorinkova, M. J. Pearsall, and H. P. Sims, "Examining the Differential Longitudinal Performance of Directive Versus Empowering Leadership in Teams," *Academy of Management Journal* 56, no. 2 (2013): 573–596.

11. R. D. Costigan and K. E. Brink, "Another Perspective on MBA Program Alignment: An Investigation of Learning Goals," *Academy of Management Learning & Education* 14, no. 2 (2015): 260–276.

12. S. H. Harrison and E. D. Rouse, "Let's Dance! Elastic Coordination in Creative Group Work: A Qualitative Study of Modern Dancers," *Academy of Management Journal* 57, no. 5 (2014): 1256–1283.

13. L. Jia, J. D. Shaw, A. S. Tsue, and T. Y. Park, "A Social-Structural Perspective on Employee–Organization Relationships and Team Creativity," *Academy of Management Journal* 57, no. 3 (2014): 869–891.

14. M. Sytch and A. Tatarynowicz, "Exploring the Locus of Invention: The Dynamics of Network Communities and Firms' Invention Productivity," *Academy of Management Journal* 57, no. 1 (2014): 249–279.

15. F. Aime, S. Humphrey, D. S. Derue, and J. B. Paul, "The Riddle of Heterarchy: Power Transitions in Cross-Functional Teams," *Academy of Management Journal* 57, no. 2 (2014): 327–352.

16. Suggestion from seventh- and eighth-edition reviewer C. Blenche, University of Central Florida, added April 10, 2017.

17. J. Bussey, "Leadership Lessons From the Generals," *The Wall Street Journal* (December 12, 2014): R10.

18. L. Alexander and D. Van Knippenberg, "Teams in Pursuit of Radical Innovation: A Goal Orientation Perspective," *Academy of Management Review* 39, no. 4 (2014): 423–438.

19. M. L. Turner, "Remote Control," *Entrepreneur* (January 2016): 75–79.

20. Staff, "Self-Improvement Through Data," *Fortune* (March 15, 2016): 28.

21. S. Marikar, "Tools for Your Remote Team," *INC.* (December 2015/January 2016): 88–89.

22. Suggestion from seventh- and eighth-edition reviewer C. Blenche, University of Central Florida, added April 10, 2017.

23. R. Karlgaard, "Think (Really!) Small," *Forbes* (April 13, 2015): 32.

24. P. Lencioni, "When Less Is More," *INC.* (June 2015): 69.

25. C. Clifford, "My Advice," *Fortune* (August 11, 2014): 32.

26. C. C. Manz, "Taking the Self-Leadership High Road: Smooth Surface or Potholes Ahead?" *Academy of Management Perspectives* 29, no. 1 (2015): 132–151.

27. Staff, "Leader Board: Business Library," *Forbes* (November 23, 2015): 32.

28. R. Karlgaard, "Think (Really!) Small," *Forbes* (April 13, 2015): 32.

29. Staff, "Leader Board: Business Library," *Forbes* (November 23, 2015): 32.

30. S. Yagan, "Book Review," *Fortune* (December 1, 2015): 20; R. Karlgaard, "Diversity's Central Paradox," *Forbes* (May 4, 2015): 34.

31. Editors, "Call for Papers," *Academy of Management Review* 40, no. 4 (2014): 664–665; A. M. Grant, J. M. Berg, and D. M. Cable, "Job Titles as Identity Badges: How Self-Reflective Titles Can Reduce Emotional Exhaustion," *Academy of Management Journal* 57, no. 4 (2014): 1201–1225.

32. A. Joshi and A. P. Knight, "Who Defers to Whom and Why? Dual Pathways Linking Demographic Differences and Dyadic Deference to Team Effectiveness," *Academy of Management Journal* 58, no. 1 (2015): 59–84.

33. A. Joshi and A. P. Knight, "Who Defers to Whom and Why? Dual Pathways Linking Demographic Differences and Dyadic Deference to Team Effectiveness," *Academy of Management Journal* 58, no. 1 (2015): 59–84.

34. C. Rose, "Charlie Rose Talks to … Tory Burch," *BusinessWeek* (October 20–26, 2014): 24.

35. L. Alexander and D. Van Knippenberg, "Teams in Pursuit of Radical Innovation: A Goal Orientation Perspective," *Academy of Management Review* 39, no. 4 (2014): 423–438.

36. C. L. Pearce, C. L. Wassenaar, and C. C. Manz, "Is Shared Leadership the Key to Responsible Leadership?" *Academy of Management Perspectives* 28, no. 3 (2014): 275–288.

37. N. M. Lorinkova, M. J. Pearsall, and H. P. Sims, "Examining the Differential Longitudinal Performance of Directive Versus Empowering Leadership in Teams," *Academy of Management Journal* 56, no. 2 (2013): 573–596.

38. C. C. Manz, "Taking the Self-Leadership High Road: Smooth Surface or Potholes Ahead?" *Academy of Management Perspectives* 29, no. 1 (2015): 132–151; C. L. Pearce, C. L. Wassenaar, and C. C. Manz, "Is Shared Leadership the Key to Responsible Leadership?" *Academy of Management Perspectives* 28, no. 3 (2014): 275–288.

39. L. M. Maruping, V. Vewnkatesh, S. M. B. Thatcher, and P. C. Patel, "Folding Under Pressure of Rising to the Occasion? Perceived Time Pressure and the Moderating Role of Team Temporal Leadership," *Academy of Management Journal* 58, no. 5 (2015): 1313–1333; C. L. Pearce, C. L. Wassenaar, and C. C. Manz, "Is Shared Leadership the Key to Responsible Leadership?" *Academy of Management Perspectives* 28, no. 3 (2014): 275–288.

40. M. Sytch and A. Tatarynowicz, "Friends and Foes: The Dynamics of Dual Social Structures," *Academy of Management Journal* 57, no. 2 (2014): 585–613.

41. M. Sytch and A. Tatarynowicz, "Exploring the Locus of Invention: The Dynamics of Network Communities and Firms' Invention Productivity," *Academy of Management Journal* 57, no. 1 (2014): 249–279.

42. L. M. Maruping, V. Vewnkatesh, S. M. B. Thatcher, and P. C. Patel, "Folding Under Pressure of Rising to the Occasion? Perceived Time Pressure and the Moderating Role of Team Temporal Leadership," *Academy of Management Journal* 58, no. 5 (2015): 1313–1333; N. Li, B. L. Kirkman, and C. O. H. Porter, "Toward a Model of Work Team Altruism," *Academy of Management Review* 39, no. 4 (2014): 541–565.

43. T. A. De Vries, F. Walter, G. S. Van Der Vegt, and P. J. M. D. Essens, "Antecedents of Individuals' Interteam Coordination: Broad Functional Experiences as a Mixed Blessing," *Academy of Management Journal* 57, no. 5 (2014): 1334–1359.

44. A. Lockett, G. Currie, R. Finn, G. Martin, and J. Waring, "The Influence of Social Position on Sensemaking About Organizational Change," *Academy of Management Journal* 57, no. 4 (2014): 1102–1129.

45. J. N. Reyt and B. M. Wiesenfeld, "Seeing the Forest for the Trees: Exploratory Learning, Mobile Technology, and Knowledge Workers' Role Integration Behaviors," *Academy of Management Journal* 58, no. 3 (2015): 739–762.

46. J. Hu and R. C. Liden, "Making a Difference in the Teamwork: Linking Team Prosocial Motivation to Team Processes and Effectiveness," *Academy of Management Journal* 58, no. 4 (2015): 1102–1127.

47. N. Li, B. L. Kirkman, and C. O. H. Porter, "Toward a Model of Work Team Altruism," *Academy of Management Review* 39, no. 4 (2014): 541–565.

48. N. Li, B. L. Kirkman, and C. O. H. Porter, "Toward a Model of Work Team Altruism," *Academy of Management Review* 39, no. 4 (2014): 541–565.

49. B. M. Galvin, D. Lange, and B. E. Ashforth, "Narcissistic Organizational Identification: Seeing Oneself as Central to the Organization's Identity," *Academy of Management Review* 40, no. 2 (2015): 163–181.

50. H. Delehanty, "A Conversation With S. Lyubomirsky," *AARP Bulletin* (June 2016): 30.

51. M. Sytch and A. Tatarynowicz, "Friends and Foes: The Dynamics of Dual Social Structures," *Academy of Management Journal* 57, no. 2 (2014): 585–613.

52. B. R. Spisak, M. J. O'Brien, N. Nicholson, and M. Van Vugt, "Niche Construction and the Evolution of Leadership," *Academy of Management Review* 40, no. 2 (2015): 291–306.

53. D. Chandler, "Morals, Markets, and Values-Based Business," *Academy of Management Review* 39, no. 3 (2014): 396–397.

54. G. Di Stefano, A. A. King, and G. Verona, "Sanctioning in the Wild: Rational Calculus and Retributive Instincts in Gourmet Cuisine," *Academy of Management Journal* 58, no. 3 (2015): 906–931.

55. R. C. Liden, S. J. Wayne, C. Liao, and J. D. Meuser, "Servant Leadership and Serving Culture: Influence on Individual and Unit Performance," *Academy of Management Journal* 57, no. 5 (2014): 1434–1452.

56. Y. R. F. Guillaume, D. Van Knippenberg, and F. C. Brodbeck, "Nothing Succeeds Like Moderation: A Social Self-Regulation Perspective on Cultural Dissimilarity and Performance," *Academy of Management Journal* 57, no. 5 (2014): 1284–1308.

57. R. Durand and P. A. Kremp, "Classical Deviation: Organizational and Individual Status as Antecedents of Conformity," *Academy of Management Journal* 59, no. 1 (2016): 65–89.

58. A. Meister, K. A. Jehn, and S. M. B. Thatcher, "Feeling Misidentified: The Consequences of Internal Identity Asymmetries for Individuals at Work," *Academy of Management Review* 38, no. 4 (2014): 488–512.

59. A. Bitektine and P. Haack, "The Macro and the Micro of Legitimacy: Toward a Multilevel Theory of the Legitimacy Process," *Academy of Management Review* 40, no. 1 (2015): 49–75.

60. Staff, "Self-Improvement Through Data," *Fortune* (March 15, 2016): 28.

61. R. C. Liden, S. J. Wayne, C. Liao, and J. D. Meuser, "Servant Leadership and Serving Culture: Influence on Individual and Unit Performance," *Academy of Management Journal* 57, no. 5 (2014): 1434–1452.

62. M. L. Turner, "Remote Control," *Entrepreneur* (January 2016): 75–79.

63. E. Frauenheim, "Lessons From the Warriors," *Fortune.com*, accessed April 12, 2017.

64. Ibid.

65. S. J. Creary, B. B. Caza, L. M. Roberts, "Out of the Box? How Managing a Subordinate's Multiple Identities Affects the Quality of a Manager–Subordinate Relationship," *Academy of Management Review* 40, no. 4 (2015): 538–562.

66. A. G. Pollock and A. G. Acharya, "Shoot for the Stars? Predicting the Recruitment of Prestigious Directors at Newly Public Firms," *Academy of Management Journal* 56, no. 5 (2013): 1396–1419.

67. F. Aime, S. Humphrey, D. S. Derue, and J. B. Paul, "The Riddle of Heterarchy: Power Transitions in Cross-Functional Teams," *Academy of Management Journal* 57, no. 2 (2014): 327–352.

68. J. C. Marr and S. Thau, "Falling From Great (and Not-So-Great) Heights: How Initial Status Position Influences Performance After Status Loss," *Academy of Management Journal* 57, no. 1 (2014): 233–248.

69. R. Durand and P. A. Kremp, "Classical Deviation: Organizational and Individual Status as Antecedents of Conformity," *Academy of Management Journal* 59, no. 1 (2016): 65–89.

70. J. C. Marr and S. Thau, "Falling From Great (and Not-So-Great) Heights: How Initial Status Position Influences Performance After Status Loss," *Academy of Management Journal* 57, no. 1 (2014): 233–248.

71. D. Ma, M. Rhee, and D. Yang, "Power Source Mismatch and the Effectiveness of Interorganizational Relations: The Case of Venture Capital Syndication," *Academy of Management Journal* 56, no. 3 (2014): 711–734.

72. S. J. Creary, B. B. Caza, L. M. Roberts, "Out of the Box? How Managing a Subordinate's Multiple Identities Affects the Quality of a Manager–Subordinate Relationship," *Academy of Management Review* 40, no. 4 (2015): 538–562.

73. Y. R. F. Guillaume, D. Van Knippenberg, and F. C. Brodbeck, "Nothing Succeeds Like Moderation: A Social Self-Regulation Perspective on Cultural Dissimilarity and Performance," *Academy of Management Journal* 57, no. 5 (2014): 1284–1308.

74. A. Joshi and A. P. Knight, "Who Defers to Whom and Why? Dual Pathways Linking Demographic Differences and Dyadic Deference to Team Effectiveness," *Academy of Management Journal* 58, no. 1 (2015): 59–84.

75. R. L. Hoefer and S. E. Green, "A Rhetorical Model of Institutional Decision Making: The Role of Rhetoric in the Formation and Change of Legitimacy Judgments," *Academy of Management Review* 41, no. 1 (2016): 130–150.

76. L. R. Weingart, K. J. Behfar, C. Bendersky, G. Todorova, and K. A. Jehn, "The Directness and Oppositional Intensity of Conflict Expression," *Academy of Management Review* 40, no. 2 (2015): 235–262.

77. M. Sytch and A. Tatarynowicz, "Friends and Foes: The Dynamics of Dual Social Structures," *Academy of Management Journal* 57, no. 2 (2014): 585–613.

78. C. Blencke, University of Central Florida, review suggestion to add the name, added April 12, 2017.

79. N. M. Lorinkova, M. J. Pearsall, and H. P. Sims, "Examining the Differential Longitudinal Performance of Directive Versus Empowering Leadership in Teams," *Academy of Management Journal* 56, no. 2 (2013): 573–596.

80. N. Li, B. L. Kirkman, and C. O. H. Porter, "Toward a Model of Work Team Altruism," *Academy of Management Review* 39, no. 4 (2014): 541–565.

81. N. M. Lorinkova, M. J. Pearsall, and H. P. Sims, "Examining the Differential Longitudinal Performance of Directive Versus Empowering Leadership in Teams," *Academy of Management Journal* 56, no. 2 (2013): 573–596.

82. R. D. Costigan and K. E. Brink, "Another Perspective on MBA Program Alignment: An Investigation of Learning Goals," *Academy of Management Learning & Education* 14, no. 2 (2015): 260–276.

83. E. Whitford, "Management Playbook," *INC.* (April 2014): 46–47.

84. R. D. Costigan and K. E. Brink, "Another Perspective on MBA Program Alignment: An Investigation of Learning Goals," *Academy of Management Learning & Education* 14, no. 2 (2015): 260–276.

85. R. E. Silverman, "Going Bossless Backfires at Zappos," *The Wall Street Journal* (May 21, 2015): A1, A10.

86. J. Reingold, "The Zappos Experiment," *Fortune* (March 15, 2016): 207–214.

87. T. C. Bednall, K. Sanders, and P. Runhaar, "Stimulating Informal Learning Activities Through Perceptions of Performance Appraisal Quality and Human Resource Management System Strength: A Two-Wave Study," *Academy of Management Learning & Education* 13, no. 1 (2014): 45–61.

88. W. L. Bedwell, S. M. Fiore, and E. Salas, "Developing the Future Workforce: An Approach for Integrating Interpersonal Skills Into the MBA Classroom," *Academy of Management Learning & Education* 13, no. 2 (2014): 171–186.

89. AACSB website, www.aacsb.edu, accessed April 12, 2017.

90. R. E. Silverman, "Going Bossless Backfires at Zappos," *The Wall Street Journal* (May 21, 2015): A1, A10.

91. A. Von Tobel, "Where Money Meets Morale," *INC.* (April 2014): 48–49.

92. R. E. Silverman, "Going Bossless Backfires at Zappos," *The Wall Street Journal* (May 21, 2015): A1, A10.

93. W. L. Bedwell, S. M. Fiore, and E. Salas, "Developing the Future Workforce: An Approach for Integrating Interpersonal Skills Into the MBA Classroom," *Academy of Management Learning & Education* 13, no. 2 (2014): 171–186.

94. B. Lussier, Indeed employee information, given April 12, 2017.

95. N. M. Lorinkova, M. J. Pearsall, and H. P. Sims, "Examining the Differential Longitudinal Performance of Directive Versus Empowering Leadership in Teams," *Academy of Management Journal* 56, no. 2 (2013): 573–596.

96. R. E. Silverman, "Going Bossless Backfires at Zappos," *The Wall Street Journal* (May 21, 2015): A1, A10.

97. W. Amos, "Agent of Change," *Costco Connection* (August 2015): 15.

98. R. E. Silverman, "Going Bossless Backfires at Zappos," *The Wall Street Journal* (May 21, 2015): A1, A10.

99. Ibid.

100. J. D. Power, "My Advice," *Fortune* (July 1, 2015): 30.

101. R. E. Silverman, "Going Bossless Backfires at Zappos," *The Wall Street Journal* (May 21, 2015): A1, A10.

102. Suggestion from seventh- and eighth-edition reviewer C. Blenche, University of Central Florida, added April 17, 2017.

103. A. Dizol. "Meeting Overload," *Fortune* (May 1, 2015): 68–70.

104. R. McCammon, "Zap! Session," *Entrepreneur* (February 2014): 32–33.

105. A. Dizol, "Meeting Overload," *Fortune* (May 1, 2015): 68–70.

106. J. Libert, "Secrets of Effective Meetings," *Fortune* (May 1, 2015): 67.

107. A. Dizol, "Meeting Overload," *Fortune* (May 1, 2015): 68–70.

108. S. Bing, "Productivity Now!" *Fortune* (January 1, 2016): 100.

109. J. Libert, "Secrets of Effective Meetings," *Fortune* (May 1, 2015): 67.

110. A. Gogo, Productivity Hack, *Fortune* (October 1, 2015): 114.

111. A. Dizol, "Meeting Overload," *Fortune* (May 1, 2015): 68–70.

112. C. Tate, "Work Simply," *BusinessWeek* (December 22–28, 2015): 71.

113. S. Shellenbarger, "Stop Wasting Everyone's Time," *The Wall Street Journal* (December 3, 2014): D1, D3.

114. S. Shellenbarger, "Stop Wasting Everyone's Time," *The Wall Street Journal* (December 3, 2014): D1, D3.

115. A. Dizol, "Meeting Overload," *Fortune* (May 1, 2015): 68–70.

116. S. Shellenbarger, "Stop Wasting Everyone's Time," *The Wall Street Journal* (December 3, 2014): D1, D3.

117. B. Lanks, "You Can't Beat the Clock," *BusinessWeek* online, accessed May 28, 2015.

118. M. Whelan, Productivity Hack," *Fortune* (October 1, 2015): 114.

119. R. McCammon, "Zap! Session," *Entrepreneur* (February 2014): 3233.

120. A. Dizol, "Meeting Overload," *Fortune* (May 1, 2015): 68–70.

121. S. Shellenbarger, "Don't Be Late or You'll Be a Schedule-Wrecker," *The Wall Street Journal* (July 8, 2015): D1, D3.

122. R. McCammon, "Zap! Session," *Entrepreneur* (February 2014): 32–33.

123. S. Shellenbarger, "Stop Wasting Everyone's Time," *The Wall Street Journal* (December 3, 2014): D1, D3.

124. R. D. Schatz, "How to Make Off-Sites Pay Off," *INC.* (December 2014/January 2015): 82.

125. R. E. Silverman, "Going Bossless Backfires at Zappos," *The Wall Street Journal* (May 21, 2015): A1, A10.

126. R. McCammon, "Zap! Session," *Entrepreneur* (February 2014): 32–33.

127. A. Dizol, "Meeting Overload," *Fortune* (May 1, 2015): 68–70.

128. A. Webb, "Don't Forget to Meet," *INC.* (December 2015/January 2016): 90.

129. R. Karlgaard, "Diversity's Central Paradox," *Forbes* (May 4, 2015): 34.

130. J. Libert, "Secrets of Effective Meetings," *Fortune* (May 1, 2015): 67.

131. A. Dizol. "Meeting Overload," *Fortune* (May 1, 2015): 68–70.

132. J. P. Pullen, "A Better Brainstorm," *Entrepreneur* (April 2015): 63.

133. A. Dizol, "Meeting Overload," *Fortune* (May 1, 2015): 68–70.

134. V. Harnish, "5 Ways to Get More From Your PR," *Fortune* (March 1, 2015): 38.

135. S. Shellenbarger, "Don't Be Late or You'll Be a Schedule-Wrecker," *The Wall Street Journal* (July 8, 2015): D1, D3.

136. Suggestion from reviewer Professor Lynn Klein, Chabot College, added May 28, 2015.

137. S. Shellenbarger, "Don't Be Late or You'll Be a Schedule-Wrecker," *The Wall Street Journal* (July 8, 2015): D1, D3.

138. B. Lanks, "You Can't Beat the Clock," *BusinessWeek,* online, accessed May 28, 2015.

139. A. Dizol, "Meeting Overload," *Fortune* (May 1, 2015): 68–70.

140. S. Shellenbarger, "Stop Wasting Everyone's Time," *The Wall Street Journal* (December 3, 2014): D1, D3.

141. N. J. Fast, E. R. Burris, and C. A. Bartel, "Managing to Stay in the Dark: Managerial Self-Efficacy, Ego Defensiveness, and the Aversion to Employee Voice," *Academy of Management Journal* 57, no. 4 (2014): 1013–1034.

142. A. Joshi and A. P. Knight, "Who Defers to Whom and Why? Dual Pathways Linking Demographic Differences and Dyadic Deference to Team Effectiveness," *Academy of Management Journal* 58, no. 1 (2015): 59–84.

143. M. Sytch and A. Tatarynowicz, "Friends and Foes: The Dynamics of Dual Social Structures," *Academy of Management Journal* 57, no. 2 (2014): 585–613.

144. R. E. Silverman, "Going Bossless Backfires at Zappos," *The Wall Street Journal* (May 21, 2015): A1, A10.

145. D. Eng, "How to Get Over Yourself," *Fortune* (March 1, 2015): 36.

146. R. E. Silverman, "Going Bossless Backfires at Zappos," *The Wall Street Journal* (May 21, 2015): A1, A10.

147. C. Hann, "Dedicated to You," *Entrepreneur* (September 2013): 24.

148. S. Shellenbarger, "Meet the Meeting Killers," *The Wall Street Journal* (May 16, 2012): D1, D3.

149. B. Lanks, "You Can't Beat the Clock," *BusinessWeek,* online, accessed May 28, 2015.

150. D. Eng, "How to Get Over Yourself," *Fortune* (March 1, 2015): 36.

151. R. McCammon, "Put Down the Phone!" *Entrepreneur* (August 2014): 44–45.

152. Ibid.

153. S. Shellenbarger, "Meet the Meeting Killers," *The Wall Street Journal* (May 16, 2012): D1, D3.

154. A. Joshi and A. P. Knight, "Who Defers to Whom and Why? Dual Pathways Linking Demographic Differences and Dyadic Deference to Team Effectiveness," *Academy of Management Journal* 58, no. 1 (2015): 59–84.

155. N. J. Fast, E. R. Burris, and C. A. Bartel, "Managing to Stay in the Dark: Managerial Self-Efficacy, Ego Defensiveness, and the Aversion to Employee Voice," *Academy of Management Journal* 57, no. 4 (2014): 1013–1034.

156. C. C. Manz, "Taking the Self-Leadership High Road: Smooth Surface or Potholes Ahead?" *Academy of Management Perspectives* 29, no. 1 (2015): 132–151.

157. Suggestion from seventh- and eigth-edition reviewer C. Blenche, University of Central Florida, added April 17, 2017.

158. N. Li, B. L. Kirkman, C. O. H. Porter, "Toward a Model of Work Team Altruism," *Academy of Management Review* 39, no. 4 (2014): 541–565.

159. R. McCammon, "I'm Going to Need a Bit More Time …," *Entrepreneur* (September 2014): 28–30.

160. Y. R. F. Guillaume, D. Van Knippenberg, and F. C. Brodbeck, "Nothing Succeeds Like Moderation: A Social Self-Regulation Perspective on Cultural Dissimilarity and Performance," *Academy of Management Journal* 57, no. 5 (2014): 1284–1308.

161. A. Joshi and A. P. Knight, "Who Defers to Whom and Why? Dual Pathways Linking Demographic Differences and Dyadic Deference to Team Effectiveness," *Academy of Management Journal* 58, no. 1 (2015): 59–84.

162. K. Lanaj and J. R. Hollenbeck, "Leadership Over-Emergence in Self-Managing Teams: The Role of Gender and Countervailing Biases," *Academy of Management Journal* 58, no. 5 (2015): 1476–1494.

163. R. E. Silverman, "Do Men and Women Like Working Together," *The Wall Street Journal* (December 16, 2014): B1.

164. R. McCammon, "Put Down the Phone!" *Entrepreneur* (August 2014): 44–45.

165. J. Samuel, "Cantabrigian Investing Hopes to Get an Ethical Edge," *The Wall Street Journal* (May 19, 2015): C1.

Chapter 9

1. R. L. Dipboye, "Bridging the Gap in Organizations Behavior," *Academy of Management Learning & Education* 13, no. 3 (2014): 487–491.

2. L. Jia, J. D. Shaw, A. S. Tsue, and T. Y. Park, "A Social-Structural Perspective on Employee-Organization Relationships and Team Creativity," *Academy of Management Journal* 57, no. 3 (2014): 869–891.

3. A. Chatterji and A. Patro, "Dynamic Capabilities and Managing Human Capital," *Academy of Management Perspectives* 28, no. 4 (2014): 395–408.

4. B. R. Dineen and D. G. Allen, "Third Party Employment Branding: Human Capital Inflows and Outflows Following Best Places to Work Certifications," *Academy of Management Journal* 59, no. 1 (2016): 90–112.

5. L. Goler and J. de Baubigny, "What Employees Want," *The Wall Street Journal* (March 7, 2017): R1, R2.

6. P. White, Independence University, reviewer; this section added at her suggestion.

7. I. Sager, "Career Services," *BusinessWeek* (May 1, 2014): 56.

8. Based on personal knowledge of the person.

9. R. W. Robertson, Independence University, and C. M. Littlefield, Peirce College—reviewers; this section added at their suggestion.

10. Exhibit 9-2 changes for this edition recommended by Dr. Callie Burnley, Cal State University Polytechnic Pomona.

11. EEOC website, www.eeoc.gov, accessed June 1, 2015.

12. M. B. Watkins, A. N. Smith, and K. Aquino, "The Use and Consequences of Strategic Sexual Performance," *Academy of Management Perspectives* 27, no. 3 (2013): 173–186.

13. EEOC website, www.eeoc.gov, accessed June 2, 2015.

14. Ibid.

15. L. A. Mainiero and K. J. Jones, "Sexual Harassment Versus Workplace Romance: Social Media Spillover and Textual Harassment in the Workplace," *Academy of Management Perspectives* 27, no. 3 (2013): 187–203.

16. M. B. Watkins, A. N. Smith, and K. Aquino, "The Use and Consequences of Strategic Sexual Performance," *Academy of Management Perspectives* 27, no. 3 (2013): 173–186.

17. G. O'Brien, "Dipping One's Pen in the Company Ink," *Entrepreneur* (May 2015): 28.

18. L. A. Mainiero and K. J. Jones, "Sexual Harassment Versus Workplace Romance: Social Media Spillover and Textual Harassment in the Workplace," *Academy of Management Perspectives* 27, no. 3 (2013): 187–203.

19. J. Smith, "With Cupid at the Office, Rules Can Reduce Hazards," *The Wall Street Journal* (February 11, 2013): B1, B7.

20. Staff, "Decoding the DNA of the Entrepreneur," *INC.* (December 2015/January 2016): 53–59.

21. B. R. Dineen and D. G. Allen, "Third Party Employment Branding: Human Capital Inflows and Outflows Following Best Places to Work Certifications," *Academy of Management Journal* 59, no. 1 (2016): 90–112.

22. J. R. Hollenbeck and B. B. Jamieson, "Human Capital, Social Capital, and Social Network Analysis," *Academy of Perspectives* 29, no. 3 (2015): 370–365.

23. J. C. Molloy and J. B. Barney, "Who Captures the Value Created With Human Capital? A Market-Based View," *Academy of Perspectives* 29, no. 3 (2015): 309–325.

24. G. O'Brien, "Safety First," *Entrepreneur* (September 2015): 36.

25. R. Lussier and J. Hendon, *Human Resource Management,* 2nd ed. (Thousand Oaks, CA: Sage, 2016).

26. Bain & Company, "Survey," reported in *INC.* (October 2014): 112–113.

27. R. Myers, "That Sounds Like a Plan," *INC.* (June 2014): 90–92.

28. V. Harnish, "Five Questions to Ponder for 2015," *Fortune* (December 22, 2014): 36.

29. CEO Survey, "How Fast-Growing Companies Innovate," *INC.* (September 2014): 126.

30. K. Stock, "Brief," *BusinessWeek* (May 11–17, 2015): 23.

31. P. K. Thompson, "Help With Hiring," *Costco Connection* (December 2014): 13–14.

32. L. Weber and M. Korn, "Where Did All the Entry-Level Jobs Go?" *The Wall Street Journal* (August 6, 2014): B6.

33. C. Hann, "Go Get 'Em," *Entrepreneur* (July 2014): 34.

34. L. Adler, "4 Big Hiring Mistakes—and How to Avoid Them," *INC.* (March 2015): 10.

35. S. Frier and A. Satariano, "Big IPO," *BusinessWeek* (December 21–27, 2015): 29–30.

36. R. Lussier and J. Hendon, *Human Resource Management,* 2nd ed. (Thousand Oaks, CA: Sage, 2016).

37. L. Adler, "4 Common Leadership Fears and How to Avoid Them," *INC.* (April 2015): 10.

38. C. Blencke, University of Central Florida, review recommendation added May 8, 2017.

39. A. M. Grant, J. M. Berg, and D. M. Cable, "Job Titles as Identity Badges: How Self-Reflective Titles Can Reduce Emotional Exhaustion," *Academy of Management Journal* 57, no. 4 (2014): 1201–1225.

40. DOL, The Occupational Information Network (O*Net) website, https://www.onetonline.org, accessed June 2, 2015.

41. Survey, "The HR Guide to the Galaxy," *Forbes* (May 25, 2015): 90.

42. CEO Survey, "Bosses Are Creating a New Generation of Leaders," *INC.* (September 2014): 76.

43. Staff, "Company Spotlight: First American," *Fortune* (March 15, 2016): 59.

44. Staff, "Reader Poll," *Costco Connection* (April 2015): 13.

45. Y. Liu, G. R. Ferris, J. Xu, B. A. Weitz, and P. L. Perrewe, "When Ingratiation Backfires: The Role of Political Skill in the Ingratiation–Internship Performance Relationship," *Academy of Management Learning & Education* 13, no. 4 (2014): 569–586.

46. J. C. Marr and D. M. Cable, "Do Interviewers Sell Themselves Short? The Effects of Selling Orientation on Interviewers' Judgments," *Academy of Management Journal* 57, no. 3 (2014): 624–651.

47. A. Handley, "Get Outta Here!" *Entrepreneur* (January 2016): 26.

48. ADP Research reported in *Forbes* (November 23, 2015): 102–103.

49. K. Rockwood, "Tip Sheet Corporate Culture: Beyond Fitting In," *INC.* (December 2015/January 2016): 112–113.

50. R. Lussier and J. Hendon, *Human Resource Management,* 2nd ed. (Thousand Oaks, CA: Sage, 2016).

51. M. Bidwell and J. R. Keller, "Within or Without? How Firms Combine Internal and External Labor Markets to Fill Jobs," *Academy of Management Journal* 57, no. 4 (2014): 1035–1055.

52. Y. Liu, G. R. Ferris, J. Xu, B. A. Weitz, and P. L. Perrewe, "When Ingratiation Backfires: The Role of Political Skill in the Ingratiation–Internship Performance Relationship," *Academy of Management Learning & Education* 13, no. 4 (2014): 569–586.

53. M. Bidwell and J. R. Keller, "Within or Without? How Firms Combine Internal and External Labor Markets to Fill Jobs," *Academy of Management Journal* 57, no. 4 (2014): 1035–1055.

54. Scripps Health, "Company Spotlight," *Fortune* (March 15, 2015): 70.

55. A. Von Tobel, "Where Money Meets Morale," *INC.* (April 2014): 48–49.

56. A. Gumbus and R. N. Lussier, "Career Development: Enhancing Your Networking Skill," *Clinical Leadership & Management Review* 17 (2003): 16–20.

57. L. A. Mainiero and K. J. Jones, "Sexual Harassment Versus Workplace Romance: Social Media Spillover and Textual Harassment in the Workplace," *Academy of Management Perspectives* 27, no. 3 (2013): 187–203.

58. R. E. Silverman, "Going Bossless Backfires at Zappos," *The Wall Street Journal* (May 21, 2015): A1, A10.

59. ADP Research reported in *Forbes* (November 23, 2015): 102–103.

60. S. Y. Lee, M. Pitesa, S. Thau, and M. M. Pillutla, "Discrimination in Selection Decisions: Integrating Stereotype Fit and Interdependence Theories," *Academy of Management Journal* 58, no. 3 (2015): 789–812.

61. T. Monahan, "Revving Up Your Corporate RPMs," *Fortune* (February 1, 2016): 43

62. G. Anders, "Nice Guys Hire Better," *Forbes* (May 25, 2015): 54.

63. A. Von Tobel, "Where Money Meets Morale," *INC.* (April 2014): 48–49.

64. A. Lashinsky, "Larry Page Interview," *Fortune* (February 6, 2012): 98–99.

65. G. Anders, "Nice Guys Hire Better," *Forbes* (May 25, 2015): 54.

66. R. Hogan, "Find Out if Your Personality Fits Your Job," *Time* (June 22, 2015): 45.

67. EEOC website, www.eeoc.gov, accessed June 3, 2015.

68. L. Weber, "Drug Use Is on the Rise Among Workers in U.S.," *The Wall Street Journal* (June 3, 2015): B1, B7.

69. Y. Liu, G. R. Ferris, J. Xu, B. A. Weitz, and P. L. Perrewe, "When Ingratiation Backfires: The Role of Political Skill in the Ingratiation–Internship Performance Relationship," *Academy of Management Learning & Education* 13, no. 4 (2014): 569–586.

70. L. Weber, "To Get a Job, New Hires Are Put to the Test," *The Wall Street Journal* (April 15, 2015): A1, A10.

71. L. Weber and E. Dwoskin, "As Personality Tests Multiple, Employers Are Split," *The Wall Street Journal* (September 30, 2014): A1, A12.

72. L. Weber, "To Get a Job, New Hires Are Put to the Test," *The Wall Street Journal* (April 15, 2015): A1, A10.

73. A. Von Tobel, "Where Money Meets Morale," *INC.* (April 2014): 48–49.

74. ADP Research reported in *Forbes* (November 23, 2015): 102–103.

75. A. Von Tobel, "Where Money Meets Morale," *INC.* (April 2014): 48–49.

76. P. Lencioni, "Being Smart Is Overrated," *INC.* (October 2014): 128.

77. J. C. Marr and D. M. Cable, "Do Interviewers Sell Themselves Short? The Effects of Selling Orientation on Interviewers' Judgments," *Academy of Management Journal* 57, no. 3 (2014): 624–651.

78. G. O'Brien, "Honesty Policies," *Entrepreneur* (October 2014): 34–35.

79. S. Y. Lee, M. Pitesa, S. Thau, and M. M. Pillutla, "Discrimination in Selection Decisions: Integrating Stereotype Fit and Interdependence Theories," *Academy of Management Journal* 58, no. 3 (2015): 789–812.

80. S. Boyd, "CEO 101," *Fortune* (November 17, 2014): 150.

81. S. McGregor, "CEO 101," *Fortune* (November 17, 2014): 133.

82. M. Bidwell and J. R. Keller, "Within or Without? How Firms Combine Internal and External Labor Markets to Fill Jobs," *Academy of Management Journal* 57, no. 4 (2014): 1035–1055.

83. B. Shoot, "HR Made Easier," *Entrepreneur* (June 2015): 80.

84. G. Colvin, "From High-Minded to High Value," *Fortune* (December 22, 2014): 38.

85. Y. Dong, M. G. Seo, and K. M. Bartol, "No Pain, No Gain: An Affect-Based Model of Developmental Job Experience and the Buffering Effects of Emotional Intelligence," *Academy of Management Journal* 57, no. 4 (2014): 1056–1077.

86. G. Colvin, "Ignore These Leadership Lessons at Your Peril," *Fortune* (October 28, 2013): 85.

87. G. Jones, "Sports Wisdom in the Office," *INC.* (April 2014): 47.

88. M. Voronov and K. Weber, "The Heart of Institutions: Emotional Competence and Institutional Actorhood," *Academy of Management Review* 41, no. 3 (2016): 456–478.

89. G. O'Brien, "Putting Everyone at Ease," *Entrepreneur* (July 2015): 30.

90. R. Lussier and J. Hendon, *Human Resource Management,* 2nd ed. (Thousand Oaks, CA: Sage, 2016).

91. "Profile iCracked," *Entrepreneur* (November 2015): 59.

92. S. Liu, M. Wang, P. Barmberger, J. Shi, and S. B. Bacharach, "The Dark Side of Socialization: A Longitudinal Investigation of Newcomer Alcohol Use," *Academy of Management Journal* 58, no. 2 (2015): 334–355.

93. L. Jia, J. D. Shaw, A. S. Tsue, and T. Y. Park, "A Social-Structural Perspective on Employee–Organization Relationships and Team Creativity," *Academy of Management Journal* 57, no. 3 (2014): 869–891.

94. R. Lussier and J. Hendon, *Human Resource Management,* 2nd ed. (Thousand Oaks, CA: Sage, 2016).

95. A. Von Tobel, "Where Money Meets Morale," *INC.* (April 2014): 48–49.

96. C. Hann, "Go Get 'Em," *Entrepreneur* (July 2014): 34.

97. A. Von Tobel, "Where Money Meets Morale," *INC.* (April 2014): 48–49.

98. R. Miller, "How Productive Is the U.S.?" *BusinessWeek* (March 2–8, 2015): 16–17.

99. I. Nooyi, "CEO 101," *Fortune* (November 17, 2014): 129.

100. T. C. Bednall, K. Sanders, and P. Runhaar, "Stimulating Informal Learning Activities Through Perceptions of Performance Appraisal Quality and Human Resource Management System Strength: A Two-Wave Study," *Academy of Management Learning & Education* 13, no. 1 (2014): 45–61.

101. L. W. Chen and P. Thompson, "Skill Balance and Entrepreneurship Evidence From Online Career Histories," *Entrepreneurship Theory and Practice* 40, no. 2 (2016): 289–304.

102. CEO Survey, "Bosses Are Creating a New Generation of Leaders," *INC.* (September 2014): 76.

103. G. Colvin, "From High-Minded to High Value," *Fortune* (December 22, 2014): 38.

104. R. Clough, "General Electric Wants to Act Like a Startup," *BusinessWeek* (August 11–24, 2014): 22–24.

105. Cadence, "Company Spotlight," *Fortune* (March 15, 2015): 225.

106. Information added based on reviewer David Biemer, Texas State University, suggestion May 9, 2017.

107. Y. Dong, M. G. Seo, and K. M. Bartol, "No Pain, No Gain: An Affect-Based Model of Developmental Job Experience and the Buffering Effects of Emotional Intelligence," *Academy of Management Journal* 57, no. 4 (2014): 1056–1077.

108. L. W. Chen and P. Thompson, "Skill Balance and Entrepreneurship Evidence From Online Career Histories," *Entrepreneurship Theory and Practice* 40, no. 2 (2016): 289–304.

109. B. L. Rau, "The Oxford Handbook of Evidence-Based Management," *Academy of Management Learning & Education* 13, no. 3 (2014): 485–487.

110. L. Kolodny, "A New Way to Train Workers, One Small Bite at a Time," *The Wall Street Journal* (March 14, 2016): R6.

111. E. Van Oosten and K. E. Kram, "Coaching for Change," *Academy of Management Learning & Education* 13, no. 2 (2014): 295–298.

112. ADP Research reported in *Forbes* (November 23, 2015): 102–103.

113. P. Jacquart and J. Antonakis, "When Does Charisma Matter for Top-Level Leaders? Effect of Attributional Ambiguity," *Academy of Management Journal* 58, no. 4 (2015): 1051–1074.

114. R. E. Silverman, "Going Bossless Backfires at Zappos," *The Wall Street Journal* (May 21, 2015): A1, A10.

115. C. Hann, "Looking Back," *Entrepreneur* (October 2014): 36.

116. E. Van Oosten and K. E. Kram, "Coaching for Change," *Academy of Management Learning & Education* 13, no. 2 (2014): 295–298.

117. A. Choen, "When Do You Do Your Best Thinking?" M. Buckley response, *BusinessWeek* (Mary 14, 2015): 78.

118. Company Spotlight, "More Happiness, More Revenue: Ryan's Story," *Fortune* (March 15, 2015): 20.

119. S. Marikar, "Tools for Your Remote Team," *INC.* (December 2015/January 2016): 88–89.

120. P. B. Whyman and A. I. Petrescu, "Workplace Flexibility Practices in SMEs Relationship With

Performance via Redundancies, Absenteeism, and Financial Turnaround," *Journal of Small Business Management* 53, no. 4 (2015): 1097–1126.

121. E. Bernstein, "The Smart Path to a Transparent Workplace," *The Wall Street Journal* (February 23, 2015): R5.

122. S. Shellenbarger, "It's Not My Fault! A Better Response to Criticism at Work," *The Wall Street Journal* (June 18, 2014): D1, D4.

123. M. Houlihan and B. Harvey, "You Won't Learn This in Business School," *Costco Connection* (April 2014): 13.

124. Staff, "Nearly Departed," *Forbes* (May 4, 2015): 24.

125. R. King, "Companies Want to Know: How Do Workers Feel?" *The Wall Street Journal* (November 14, 2015): R3.

126. D. Roberts, "A Latticework of Workers," *Fortune* (March 5, 2015): 130–134.

127. L. Gallagher, "Why Employees Love Marriott," *Fortune* (March 15, 2015): 113–118.

128. R. E. Silverman, "At Zappos, 14% of Workers Elect to Leave," *The Wall Street Journal* (May 8, 2015): B3.

129. G. Colvin, "Personal Bests," *Fortune* (March 15, 2015): 106–110.

130. S. Marikar, "All Hail the King," *INC.* (June 2015): 30.

131. A. Von Tobel, "Where Money Meets Morale," *INC.* (April 2014): 48–49.

132. G. Colvin, "Personal Bests," *Fortune* (March 15, 2015): 106–110.

133. R. Feintzeig, "When the Annual Raise Isn't Enough," *The Wall Street Journal* (July 16, 2014): B1, B5.

134. J. Worth, "Bonus, Baby!" *Entrepreneur* (December 2014): 84.

135. M. Houlihan and B. Harvey, "You Won't Learn This in Business School," *Costco Connection* (April 2014): 13.

136. A. Von Tobel, "Where Money Meets Morale," *INC.* (April 2014): 48–49.

137. S. Nassauer, "Wal-Mart Broadens Pay Increases," *The Wall Street Journal* (January 21, 2016): B1, B2.

138. ADP Research reported in *Forbes* (November 23, 2015): 102–103.

139. A. W. Mathews, "Cost of a Family Health Plan Tops $17,000," *The Wall Street Journal* (September 23, 2015): B3.

140. E. Schurenberg, "What Do You Owe Your Employees," *INC.* (November 2015): 12.

141. S. Simone, "Stick With Contractors," *INC.* (November 2015): 74.

142. L. Weber, "The End of Employees," *The Wall Street Journal* (February 3, 2017): A1, A10.

143. L. Weber, "Some Bosses Reclassify Employees to Cut Costs," *The Wall Street Journal* (July 1, 2015): B1, B7.

144. G. Colvin, "Personal Bests," *Fortune* (March 15, 2015): 106–110.

145. C. Zillman, "Outdoor Adventures on the Job," *Fortune* (May 1, 2015): 24.

146. M. Bloomberg, "Leadership Secrets of the Greatest CEOs," *BusinessWeek* (December 15–21, 2014): 10.

147. ADP Research reported in *Forbes* (November 23, 2015): 102–103.

148. A. Von Tobel, "Get Financially Fit Before 2015," *INC.* (October 2014): 104.

149. T. Cettina, "Retirement Comes First," *Costco Connection* (January 2016): 27.

150. C. Flavelle, "Facing America's Other Middle-Class Squeeze," *BusinessWeek* (October 20–26, 2014): 43–44.

151. K. Kristof, "Take Risks When You're Young," *INC.* (March 2017): 56.

152. T. Cettina, "Retirement Comes First," *Costco Connection* (January 2016): 27.

153. K. Kristof, "It's Not About a Rocking Chair," *INC.* (March 2017): 56.

154. J. N. Reyt and B. M. Wiesenfeld, "Seeing the Forest for the Trees: Exploratory Learning, Mobile Technology, and Knowledge Workers' Role Integration Behaviors," *Academy of Management Journal* 58, no. 3 (2015): 739–762.

155. J. Alsever, "Take It Easy. That's An Order!" *Fortune* (December 15, 2015): 46.

156. M. M. Butts, W. J. Becker, and W. R. Boswell, "Hot Buttons and Time Sinks: The Effects of Electronic Communication During Nonwork Time on Emotions and Work-Nonwork Conflict," *Academy of Management Journal* 58, no. 3 (2015): 763–788.

157. L. Weber, "Overtime Pay for Answering Late-Night Emails," *The Wall Street Journal* (May 21, 2015): B1, B6.

158. T. L. Stanko and C. M. Beckman, "Watching You Watching Me: Boundary Control and Capturing Attention in the Context of Ubiquitous Technology Use," *Academy of Management Journal* 58, no. 3 (2015): 712–738.

159. J. J. Ladge, B. K. Humberd, M. B. Watkins, and B. Harrington, "Updating the Organization Man: An Examination of Involved Fathering in the Workplace," *Academy of Management Perspectives* 29, no. 1 (2015): 152–171.

160. N. Waller and J. Lublin, "What's Holding Women Back in the Workplace?" *The Wall Street Journal* (September 30, 2015): C1, C2.

161. W. Mosseberg, "After Leaning In," *The Wall Street Journal* (June 3, 2013): D1.

162. P. B. Whyman and A. I. Petrescu, "Workplace Flexibility Practices in SMEs Relationship With Performance via Redundancies, Absenteeism, and Financial Turnaround," *Journal of Small Business Management* 53, no. 4 (2015): 1097–1126.

163. S. Leibs, "Perks That Work," *INC.* (November 2014): 64–65.

164. K. Rockwood, "Blowing Up the Workweek," *INC.* (December 2016/January 2017): 84–85.

165. Company Spotlight, "More Happiness, More Revenue: Ryan's Story," *Fortune* (March 15, 2015): 20.

166. Staff, "Trends: Idea Home Work," *Forbes* (September 29, 2014): 52.

167. Staff, "Companies/Industries," *BusinessWeek* (August 10–23, 2015): 21–23.

168. S. Leibs, "Perks That Work," *INC.* (November 2014): 64–65.

169. OSHA, "42. Workplace Safety," *BusinessWeek* (December 8–14, 2014): 62.

170. A. Levin, "The Perils of Flying," *BusinessWeek* (May 18–24, 2015): 26–27.

171. S. Grobart, "Daimler Veers Into Maximum Overdrive," *BusinessWeek* (May 18–24, 2015): 34–35.

172. R. King, "Companies Want to Know: How Do Workers Feel?" *The Wall Street Journal* (November 14, 2015): R3.

173. Added as suggested by reviewer Feresheeh Mofidi, Merritt College, May 9, 2017.

174. Company Spotlight, "At Employee-Owned PCL Construction," *Fortune* (March 15, 2015): 197.

175. Bureau of Labor Statistics website, www.bls.gov, accessed June 5, 2015.

176. J. Eidelson, "Politics/Policy, *BusinessWeek* (February 20 to March 5, 2017): 25–26.

177. M. Trottman, "Union Membership Stagnates Around 11%," *The Wall Street Journal* (January 24–25, 2014): A3.

178. J. Eidelson, "Unions Try to Get Between Banks and Their Customers," *BusinessWeek* (March 21–April 5, 2015): 50–51.

179. J. Eidelson, "Politics/Policy, *BusinessWeek* (February 20 to March 5, 2017): 25–26.

180. J. Bennett and C. Ross, "Car Maker, UAW Weigh Class of Hires," *The Wall Street Journal* (May 11, 2015): B1, B2.

181. C. Ross, "Cadillac Tax Imperils UAW's Health Benefits," *The Wall Street Journal* (March 25, 2015): B1, B6.

182. M. L. Call, A. J. Nyberg, R. E. Ployhart, and J. Weekley, "The Dynamic Nature of Collective Turnover and Unit Performance: The Impact of Time, Quality, and Replacements," *Academy of Management Journal* 58, no. 4 (2015): 1208–1232.

183. B. R. Dineen and D. G. Allen, "Third Party Employment Branding: Human Capital Inflows and Outflows Following Best Places to Work Certifications," *Academy of Management Journal* 59, no. 1 (2016): 90–112.

184. J. Hu and R. C. Liden, "Making a Difference in the Teamwork: Linking Team Prosocial Motivation to Team Processes and Effectiveness," *Academy of Management Journal* 58, no. 4 (2015): 1102–1127.

185. R. Hennessey, "Decisions, Decisions," *Entrepreneur* (March 2015): 50.

186. Survey, "The HR Guide to the Galaxy," *Forbes* (May 25, 2015): 90.

187. C. McCain Nelson, "Poll: Most Women See Bias in the Workplace," *The Wall Street Journal* (April 12, 2013): A4.

188. L. M. Leslie, D. M. Mayer, and D. A. Kravitz, "The Stigma of Affirmative Action: A Stereotyping-Based Theory and Meta-Analytic Test of the Consequences for Performance," *Academy of Management Journal* 57, no. 4 (2014): 964–989.

189. G. Colvin, "Personal Bests," *Fortune* (March 15, 2015): 106–110.

190. A. Murray, "What Do Millennials Want?" *Fortune* (March 15, 2015): 14.

191. R. Reuteman, "Generation Gaps," *Entrepreneur* (March 2015): 43–48.

192. R. Albergotti, "At Facebook, Boss Is a Dirty Word," *The Wall Street Journal* (December 26, 2014): B1, B2.

193. J. Kruse, "With Big Data, HR Departments Too Often Get Short Shrift," *The Wall Street Journal* (February 23, 2015): R6.

194. J. Alsever, "Is Software Better at Managing People Than You Are?" *Fortune* (March 15, 2016): 41–42.

195. W. Leitch, "Isn't Google Awesome?" *BusinessWeek* (April 6–12, 2015): 64.

196. L. Weber, "To Get a Job, New Hires Are Put to the Test," *The Wall Street Journal* (April 15, 2015): A1, A10.

197. Staff, "This Time, It's HR Getting Fired," *BusinessWeek* (May 25–31, 2015): 32–33.

198. R. E. Silverman and N. Waller, "Thinking of Quitting? The Boss Knows," *The Wall Street Journal* (March 14–15, 2015): A1, A2.

199. G. Hayes, "The Meaning of Big Data," *Fortune* (June 16, 2014): 232.

200. S. Grobart, "Daimler Veers Into Maximum Overdrive," *BusinessWeek* (May 18–24, 2015): 32–33.

201. L. A. Mainiero and K. J. Jones, "Sexual Harassment Versus Workplace Romance: Social Media Spillover and Textual Harassment in the Workplace," *Academy of Management Perspectives* 27, no. 3 (2013): 187–203.

202. E. Dwoskin, "Data Privacy: Test Your Knowledge," *The Wall Street Journal* (April 20, 2015): R6.

203. Staff, "Not Ready," *The Wall Street Journal* (March 14, 2016): R8.

204. Staff, "Walmart Is Always Watching," *BusinessWeek* (November 30–December 6, 2015): 52.

205. A. Bluestein, "Get Ready for Your Robot," *INC.* (June 2015): 92.

206. A. Murray, "Lessons From the Fortune 500," *Fortune* (June 15, 2016): 14.

207. G. Colvin, "Humans are Underrated," *Fortune* (August 1, 2015): 100–113.

208. G. O'Brien, "Honesty Policies," *Entrepreneur* (October 2014): 34–35.

209. L. Weber, "Some Bosses Reclassify Employees to Cut Costs," *The Wall Street Journal* (July 1, 2015): B1, B7.

210. Staff, "Briefing," *Fortune* (March 1, 2017): 16.

211. A. Chuang, R. S. Hsu, A. C. Wang, and T. A. Judge, Does West Fit With East? In Search of a Chinese Model of Person-Environment Fit," *Academy of Management Journal* 58, no. 2 (2015): 480–510.

Chapter 9 Appendix

1. A. Gumbus and R. N. Lussier, "Career Development: Enhancing Your Networking Skill," *Clinical Leadership & Management Review* 17 (2003): 16–20.

2. MyPerfectResume, www.MyPerfectResume.com, accessed May 10, 2017.

3. College Recruiter, www.collegerecruiter.com, accessed May 10, 2017.

4. Career Rookie, www.CareerRookie.com, accessed May 10, 2017.

5. This section is adapted from A. Gumbus and R. N. Lussier, "Career Development: Enhancing Your Networking Skill," *Clinical Leadership & Management Review* 17 (2003): 16–20.

Chapter 10

1. S. D. Charlier, "Incorporating Evidence-Based Management Into Management Curricula: A Conversation With Gary Latham," *Academy of Management Learning & Education* 13, no. 3 (2014): 467–475.

2. W. L. Bedwell, S. M. Fiore, and E. Salas, "Developing the Future Workforce: An Approach for Integrating Interpersonal Skills Into the MBA Classroom," *Academy of Management Learning & Education* 13, no. 2 (2014): 171–186.

3. L. Weber and M. Korn, "Where Did All the Entry-Level Jobs Go?" *The Wall Street Journal* (August 6, 2014): B6.

4. P. Harvey, K. Madison, M. Martinko, T. R. Crook, and T. A. Crook, "Attribution Theory in the Organizational Sciences: The Road Traveled and the Path Ahead," *Academy of Management Perspectives* 28, no. 2 (2014): 128–146.

5. E. Bernstein, "The Year in Relationship Troubles, and How Talk Can Help," *The Wall Street Journal* (December 30, 2014): D1, D2.

6. A. Lawrence, "A Racing Champ's High-Octane Encore," *Fortune* (June 15, 2015): 67–71.

7. D. L. Ferris, H. Lian, D. J. Brown, and R. Morrison, "Ostracism, Self-Esteem, and Job Performance: When Do We Self-Verify and When Do We Self-Enhance?" *Academy of Management Journal* 58, no. 1 (2015): 279–297.

8. G. O'Brien, "It's All Your Fault!" *Entrepreneur* (February 2015): 30.

9. A. S. DeNisi, "Some Further Thoughts on the Entrepreneurial Personality," *Entrepreneurship Theory and Practice* 39, no. 5 (2015): 997–1003.

10. D. Sterling, "Advice to My 20-Year-Old Self," *Fortune* (October 1, 2015): 116.

11. M. S. Cardon and C. P. Kirk, "Entrepreneurial Passion as Mediator of the Self-Efficacy to Persistence Relationships," *Entrepreneurship Theory and Practice* 39, no. 5 (2015): 997–1003.

12. P. M. Picone, G. B. Dagnino, and A. Mina, "The Origin of Failure: A Multidisciplinary Appraisal of the Hubris Hypothesis and Proposed Research Agenda," *Academy of Management Perspectives* 28, no. 4 (2014): 447–468.

13. A. S. DeNisi, "Some Further Thoughts on the Entrepreneurial Personality," *Entrepreneurship Theory and Practice* 39, no. 5 (2015): 1027–1050.

14. E. Bernstein, "Beat Back the Self-Doubt," *The Wall Street Journal* (June 14, 2016): D1, D2.

15. M. Kelly, *Rediscovering Catholicism* (New York: Beacon, 2010).

16. J. Gaines, "Playing With the Big Boxes," *Entrepreneur* (February 2015): 15.

17. R. Lewis, "My Advice," *Fortune* (December 22, 2014): 34.

18. S. Shellenbarger, "When the Only Thing Holding You Back Is Self-Doubt," *The Wall Street Journal* (April 15, 2015): D3.

19. C. Rose, "Charlie Rose Talks to Tory Burch," *BusinessWeek* (October 20–26, 2014): 24.

20. E. Bernstein, "Beat Back the Self-Doubt," *The Wall Street Journal* (June 14, 2016): D1, D2.

21. F. P. Morgeson, T. R. Mitchell, and D. Liu, "Event System Theory: An Event-Oriented Approach to the Organizational Sciences," *Academy of Management Review* 40, no. 4 (2015): 515–537.

22. S. F. Collins, "Success Steps," *Costco Connection* (January 2016): 29.

23. M. Kelly, *Rediscovering Catholicism* (New York: Beacon, 2010).

24. W. Amos, "Agent of Change," *Costco Connection* (August 2015): 15.

25. M. Rosenwald, "Bound by Habit," *BusinessWeek* (March 19–25, 2012): 106–107.

26. E. Bernstein, "Beat Back the Self-Doubt," *The Wall Street Journal* (June 14, 2016): D1, D2.

27. C. Kenny, "The Economic Power of Positive Thinking," *BusinessWeek* (January 12–18, 2015): 8–9.

28. B. Cohen, "The Power of Ohio State's Positive Thinking," *The Wall Street Journal* (January 9, 2015): D6.

29. L. Holtz, "Setting a Higher Standard," *Success Yearbook* (Tampa, FL: Peter Lowe International, 1998): 74.

30. Staff, "4 Habits of Truly Resilient People," *INC.* (March 2016): 10.

31. New, *National Public Radio (NPR)*, aired November 23, 2015.

32. E. Bernstein, "Self-Talk, or a Heart-to-Heart With Your Closest Friend," *The Wall Street Journal* (May 6, 2014): D1, D2.

33. Ziglar, www.ziglar.com, accessed May 17, 2017.

34. V. Williams, "Top Videos," *INC.* (December 2016/January 2017): 10.

35. E. Bernstein, "Beat Back the Self-Doubt," *The Wall Street Journal* (June 14, 2016): D1, D2.

36. Staff, "What's on Entrepreneur.com?" *Entrepreneur* (December 2014): 12.

37. M. Rosenwald, "Bound by Habit," *BusinessWeek* (March 19–25, 2012): 106–107.

38. E. Bernstein, "We Actually Get Nicer With Age," *The Wall Street Journal* (April 22, 2014): D1, D2.

39. E. Grijalva and P. D. Harms, "Narcissism: An Integrative Synthesis and Dominance Complementarity Model," *Academy of Management Perspectives* 28, no. 2 (2014): 108–127.

40. T. Hahn, L. Preuss, J. Pinkse, and F. Figge, "Cognitive Frames in Corporate Sustainability: Managerial Sensemaking With Paradoxical and Business Case Frames," *Academy of Management Review* 39, no. 4 (2014): 463–487.

41. A. S. DeNisi, "Some Further Thoughts on the Entrepreneurial Personality," *Entrepreneurship Theory and Practice* 39, no. 5 (2015): 1027–1050.

42. E. Bernstein, "We Actually Get Nicer With Age," *The Wall Street Journal* (April 22, 2014): D1, D2.

43. Ibid.

44. T. A. Judge and C. P. Zapata, "The Person-Situation Debate Revisited: Effect of Situation Strength and Trait Activation on the Validity of the Big Five Personality Traits in Predicting Job Performance," *Academy of Management Journal* 58, no. 4 (2015): 1149–1179.

45. L. Weber and E. Dwoskin, "As Personality Tests Multiply, Employers Are Split," *The Wall Street Journal* (September 30, 2014): A1, A12.

46. L. Weber, "To Get a Job, New Hires Are Put to the Test," *The Wall Street Journal* (April 15, 2015): A1, A10.

47. R. Karlgaad, "Do Jerks Always Win?" *Forbes* (December 29, 2014): 44.

48. E. Grijalva and P. D. Harms, "Narcissism: An Integrative Synthesis and Dominance Complementarity Model," *Academy of Management Perspectives* 28, no. 2 (2014): 108–127.

49. S. Bing, "Why Crazy Works," *Fortune* (September 2016): 108.

50. A. S. DeNisi, "Some Further Thoughts on the Entrepreneurial Personality," *Entrepreneurship Theory and Practice* 39, no. 5 (2015): 1027–1050.

51. T. Georgens, "Trust Your People to Innovate, Take Risks," *Forbes* (October 29, 2014): 113.

52. L. Buchanan, "Wired for Success," *INC.* (September 2014): 26–52.

53. V. Bamiatzi, S. Jones, S. Mitchelmore, and K. Nikoogpulos, "The Role of Competencies in Shaping the Leadership Style of Female Entrepreneurs," *Journal of Small Business Management* 53, no. 3 (2015): 627–644.

54. K. Tindell, "Top Videos," *INC.* (March 2016): 10.

55. J. Robinson, "Where There's Willpower, There's a Way," *Entrepreneur* (July 2015): 50–54.

56. J. Ankeny, "The Six Entrepreneurial Profiles," *Entrepreneur* (February 2015): 37.

57. B. M. Galvin, D. Lange, and B. E. Ashforth, "Narcissistic Organizational Identification: Seeing Oneself as Central to the Organization's Identity," *Academy of Management Review* 40, no. 2 (2015): 163–181.

58. S. Shellenbarger, "Ever Thought, How Did He Get Promoted? Here's How," *The Wall Street Journal* (July 9, 2014): D1, D2.

59. L. Tomkins and E. Ulus, "Is Narcissism Undermining Critical Reflection in Our Business Schools?" *Academy of Management Learning & Education* 14, no. 4 (2015): 595–606.

60. J. Ankeny, "The Six Entrepreneurial Profiles," *Entrepreneur* (February 2015): 37.

61. T. A. Judge and C. P. Zapata, "The Person-Situation Debate Revisited: Effect of Situation Strength and Trait Activation on the Validity of the Big Five Personality Traits in Predicting Job Performance," *Academy of Management Journal* 58, no. 4 (2015): 1149–1179.

62. B. Antoncic, T. B. Kregar, G. Singh, and A. F. DeNoble, "The Big Five Personality-Entrepreneurship Relationship: Evidence from Slovenia," *Journal of Small Business Management* 53, no. 3 (2015): 819–841.

63. L. Welch, "A CEO's Job Is to Continually Find Ways of Getting Other People to Do Their Best Work," *INC.* (May 2015): 49–50.

64. J. Ankeny, "A Winning Personality," *Entrepreneur* (March 2015): 37–41.

65. Ibid.

66. T. A. Judge and C. P. Zapata, "The Person-Situation Debate Revisited: Effect of Situation Strength and Trait Activation on the Validity of the Big Five Personality Traits in Predicting Job Performance," *Academy of Management Journal* 58, no. 4 (2015): 1149–1179.

67. K. Lanaj and J. R. Hollenbeck, "Leadership Over-Emergence in Self-Managing Teams: The Role of Gender and Countervailing Biases," *Academy of Management Journal* 58, no. 5 (2015): 1476–1494.

68. E. Grijalva and P. D. Harms, "Narcissism: An Integrative Synthesis and Dominance Complementarity Model," *Academy of Management Perspectives* 28, no. 2 (2014): 108–127.

69. T. A. Judge and C. P. Zapata, "The Person-Situation Debate Revisited: Effect of Situation Strength and Trait Activation on the Validity of the Big Five Personality Traits in Predicting Job Performance," *Academy of Management Journal* 58, no. 4 (2015): 1149–1179.

70. K. Lanaj and J. R. Hollenbeck, "Leadership Over-Emergence in Self-Managing Teams: The Role of Gender and Countervailing Biases," *Academy of Management Journal* 58, no. 5 (2015): 1476–1494.

71. O. Ybarra, E. Kross, and J. S. Burks, "The Big Idea That Is Yet to Be: Toward a More Motivated, Contextual, and Dynamic Model of Emotional Intelligence," *Academy of Management Perspectives* 28, no. 2 (2014): 93–107.

72. H. Lian, D. J. Brown, D. L. Ferris, L. H. Liang, L. M. Keeping, and R. Morrison, "Abusive Supervision and Retaliation: A Self-Control Framework," *Academy of Management Journal* 57, no. 1 (2014): 116–139.

73. S. Shellenbarger, "Ever Thought, How Did He Get Promoted? Here's How," *The Wall Street Journal* (July 9, 2014): D1, D2.

74. A. Murray, "Should Leaders Be Modest?" *Fortune* (September 15, 2015): 28.

75. S. Bing, "Why Crazy Works," *Fortune* (September 2016): 108.

76. E. Grijalva and P.D. Harms, "Narcissism: An Integrative Synthesis and Dominance Complementarity Model," *Academy of Management Perspectives* 28, no. 2 (2014): 108–127.

77. D. Roberts, "The Rock," *Fortune* (November 17, 2014): 146.

78. Staff, "Margin Note," *BusinessWeek* (July 20–26, 2015): 21.

79. J. C. Molloy and J. B. Barney, "Who Captures the Value Created With Human Capital? A Market-Based View," *Academy of Perspectives* 29, no. 3 (2015): 309–325.

80. K. Lanaj and J. R. Hollenbeck, "Leadership Over-Emergence in Self-Managing Teams: The Role of Gender and Countervailing Biases," *Academy of Management Journal* 58, no. 5 (2015): 1476–1494.

81. D. Brady, "Dave Goldberg," *BusinessWeek* (April 23–29, 2012): 96.

82. S. H. Harrison and D.T. Wagner, "Spilling Outside the Box: The Effects of Individuals' Creative Behaviors at Work on Time Spent With Their Spouses at Home," *Academy of Management Journal* 59, no. 3 (2016): 841–859.

83. T. A. Judge and C. P. Zapata, "The Person-Situation Debate Revisited: Effect of Situation Strength and Trait Activation on the Validity of the Big Five Personality Traits in Predicting Job Performance," *Academy of Management Journal* 58, no. 4 (2015): 1149–1179.

84. B. P. Owens and D. R. Hekman, "How Does Leader Humility Influence Team Performance? Exploring the Mechanism of Contagion and Collective Promotion Focus," *Academy of Management Journal* 59, no. 3 (2016): 1088–1111.

85. HumanMetrics website, www.humanmetrics.com/cgi-win/jtypes2.asp, accessed May 17, 2017.

86. D. X. H. Wo, M. L. Ambrose, and M. Schminke, "What Drives Trickle-Down Effects? A Test of Multiple Mediation Processes," *Academy of Management Journal* 58, no. 6 (2015): 1848–1868.

87. R. Fehr, K. C. Yam, and C. Dang, "Moralized Leadership: The Construction and Consequences of Ethical Leader Perceptions," *Academy of Management Review* 40, no. 2 (2015): 182–209.

88. O. Ybarra, E. Kross, and J. S. Burks, "The Big Idea That Is Yet to Be: Toward a More Motivated, Contextual, and Dynamic Model of Emotional Intelligence," *Academy of Management Perspectives* 28, no. 2 (2014): 93–107.

89. A. Meister, K. A. Jehn, and S. M. B. Thatcher, "Feeling Misidentified: The Consequences of Internal Identity Asymmetries for Individuals at Work," *Academy of Management Review* 38, no. 4 (2014): 488–512.

90. T. Hahn, L. Preuss, J. Pinkse, and F. Figge, "Cognitive Frames in Corporate Sustainability: Managerial Sensemaking With Paradoxical and Business Case Frames," *Academy of Management Review* 39, no. 4 (2014): 463–487.

91. M. R. Barrick, G. R. Thurgood, T. A. Smith, and S. H. Courtright, "Collective Organizational Engagement: Linking Motivational Antecedents, Strategic Implementation, and Firm Performance," *Academy of Management Journal* 58, no. 1 (2015): 111–135.

92. A. C. Peng, J. M. Schaubroeck, and Y. Li, "Social Exchange Implications of Own and Coworkers' Experience of Supervisory Abuse," *Academy of Management Journal* 57, no. 5 (2014): 1385–1405.

93. G. Colvin, "What Really Has the 99% Up in Arms," *Fortune* (November 7): 87.

94. P. Harvey, K. Madison, M. Martinko, T. R. Crook, and T. A. Crook, "Attribution Theory in the Organizational Sciences: The Road Traveled and the Path Ahead," *Academy of Management Perspectives* 28, no. 2 (2014): 128–146.

95. A. C. Peng, J. M. Schaubroeck, and Y. Li, "Social Exchange Implications of Own and Coworkers' Experience of Supervisory Abuse," *Academy of Management Journal* 57, no. 5 (2014): 1385–1405.

96. P. Jacquart and J. Antonakis, "When Does Charisma Matter for Top-Level Leaders? Effect of Attributional Ambiguity," *Academy of Management Journal* 58, no. 4 (2015): 1051–1074.

97. V. Desai, "Learning Through the Distribution of Failures Within an Organization," *Academy of Management Journal* 58, no. 4 (2015): 1032–1050.

98. J. C. Marr and D. M. Cable, "Do Interviewers Sell Themselves Short? The Effects of Selling Orientation on Interviewers' Judgments," *Academy of Management Journal* 57, no. 3 (2014): 624–651.

99. P. Harvey, K. Madison, M. Martinko, T. R. Crook, and T. A. Crook, "Attribution Theory in the Organizational Sciences: The Road Traveled and the Path Ahead," *Academy of Management Perspectives* 28, no. 2 (2014): 128–146.

100. D. Antons and F.T. Piller, "Opening the Black Box of 'Not Invented Here': Attitudes, Decision Biases, and Behavioral Consequences," *Academy of Management Perspectives* 29, no. 2 (2015): 193–217.

101. D. Ariely, "Ask Ariely," *The Wall Street Journal* (September 27–28, 2014): D4.

102. B. M. Firth, J. R. Hollenbeck, J. E. Miles, D. R. Ilgen, and C. M. Barnes, "Same Page, Different Books: Extending Representational Gaps Theory to Enhance Performance in Multiteam Systems," *Academy of Management Journal* 58, no. 3 (2015): 813–835.

103. B. P. Owens and D. R. Hekman, "How Does Leader Humility Influence Team Performance? Exploring the Mechanism of Contagion and Collective Promotion Focus," *Academy of Management Journal* 59, no. 3 (2016): 1088–1111.

104. E. Grijalva and P.D. Harms, "Narcissism: An Integrative Synthesis and Dominance Complementarity Model," *Academy of Management Perspectives* 28, no. 2 (2014): 108–127.

105. H. Willmott, "Reflections on the Darker Side of Conventional Power Analytics," *Academy of Management Perspectives* 27, no. 4 (2013): 281–286.

106. A. Meister, K. A. Jehn, and S. M. B. Thatcher, "Feeling Misidentified: The Consequences of Internal Identity Asymmetries for Individuals at Work," *Academy of Management Review* 38, no. 4 (2014): 488–512.

107. E. Grijalva and P.D. Harms, "Narcissism: An Integrative Synthesis and Dominance Complementarity Model," *Academy of Management Perspectives* 28, no. 2 (2014): 108–127.

108. D. M. Ames and A. S. Wazlawek, "How to Tell If You're a Jerk in the Office," *The Wall Street Journal* (February 23, 2015): R2.

109. Ibid.

110. L. Daskal, "4 Pieces of Advice Most People Ignore (But Great Entrepreneurs Don't)," *INC.* (July/August 2016): 8.

111. D. M. Ames and A. S. Wazlawek, "How to Tell If You're a Jerk in the Office," *The Wall Street Journal* (February 23, 2015): R2.

112. P.M. Picone, G. B. Dagnino, and A. Mina, "The Origin of Failure: A Multidisciplinary Appraisal of the Hubris Hypothesis and Proposed Research Agenda," *Academy of Management Perspectives* 28, no. 4 (2014): 447–468.

113. D. Antons and F.T. Piller, "Opening the Black Box of 'Not Invented Here': Attitudes, Decision Biases, and Behavioral Consequences," *Academy of Management Perspectives* 29, no. 2 (2015): 193–217.

114. M. E. Chan and D. J. McAllister, "Abusive Supervision Through the Lens of Employee State Paranoia," *Academy of Management Review* 39, no. 1 (2014): 44–66.

115. D. X. H. Wo, M. L. Ambrose, and M. Schminke, "What Drives Trickle-Down Effects? A Test of Multiple Mediation Processes," *Academy of Management Journal* 58, no. 6 (2015): 1848–1868.

116. M. E. Chan and D. J. McAllister, "Abusive Supervision Through the Lens of Employee State Paranoia," *Academy of Management Review* 39, no. 1 (2014): 44–66.

117. S. Diestel, J. Wegge, and K. H. Schmidt, "The Impact of Social Context on the Relationship Between Individual Job Satisfaction and Absenteeism: The Roles of Different Foci of Job Satisfaction and Work-Unit Absenteeism," *Academy of Management Journal* 57, no. 2 (2014): 353–382.

118. B. P. Owens and D. R. Hekman, "How Does Leader Humility Influence Team Performance? Exploring the Mechanism of Contagion and Collective Promotion Focus," *Academy of Management Journal* 59, no. 3 (2016): 1088–1111.

119. A. Lashinsky, "Larry Page Interview," *Fortune* (February 6, 2012): 98–99.

120. A. Kirkman, "It's All About Attitude," *Fortune* (November 17, 2014): 34.

121. N. Waller and J. Lublin, "What's Holding Women Back in the Workplace?" *The Wall Street Journal* (September 30, 2015): C1, C2.

122. R. McCammon, "I'm Sure You're Wondering Why I've Called You All Here," *Entrepreneur* (March 2015): 28–29.

123. A. Kirkman, "It's All About Attitude," *Fortune* (November 17, 2014): 34.

124. T. Gimbel, "CEO 101," *Fortune* (November 17, 2014): 147.

125. D. Antons and F.T. Piller, "Opening the Black Box of 'Not Invented Here': Attitudes, Decision Biases, and Behavioral Consequences," *Academy of Management Perspectives* 29, no. 2 (2015): 193–217.

126. A. C. Peng, J. M. Schaubroeck, and Y. Li, "Social Exchange Implications of Own and Coworkers' Experience of Supervisory Abuse," *Academy of Management Journal* 57, no. 5 (2014): 1385–1405.

127. T. Gimbel, "CEO 101," *Fortune* (November 17, 2014): 147.

128. P. Harvey, K. Madison, M. Martinko, T. R. Crook, and T. A. Crook, "Attribution Theory in the Organizational Sciences: The Road Traveled and the Path Ahead," *Academy of Management Perspectives* 28, no. 2 (2014): 128–146.

129. A. C. Peng, J. M. Schaubroeck, and Y. Li, "Social Exchange Implications of Own and Coworkers' Experience of Supervisory Abuse," *Academy of Management Journal* 57, no. 5 (2014): 1385–1405.

130. S. J. Creary, B. B. Caza, L. M. Roberts, "Out of the Box? How Managing a Subordinate's Multiple Identities Affects the Quality of a Manager-Subordinate Relationship," *Academy of Management Review* 40, no. 4 (2015): 538–562.

131. M. E. Chan and D. J. McAllister, "Abusive Supervision Through the Lens of Employee State Paranoia," *Academy of Management Review* 39, no. 1 (2014): 44–66.

132. E. Bernstein, "Train Your Brain to Be Positive, and Feel Happier Every Day: It Only Sounds Corny," *The Wall Street Journal* (August 28, 2012): D1, D2.

133. S. Bing, "Why Crazy Works," *Fortune* (September 2016): 108.

134. M. Korn and R. Feintzeig, "Is the Old-School, Hard-Nosed Boss Obsolete?" *The Wall Street Journal* (May 23, 2014): B1, B2.

135. S. Shellenbarger, "Ever Thought, How Did He Get Promoted? Here's How," *The Wall Street Journal* (July 9, 2014): D1, D2.

136. D. X. H. Wo, M. L. Ambrose, and M. Schminke, "What Drives Trickle-Down Effects? A Test of Multiple Mediation Processes," *Academy of Management Journal* 58, no. 6 (2015): 1848–1868.

137. L. Tomkins and E. Ulus, "Is Narcissism Undermining Critical Reflection in Our Business Schools?" *Academy of Management Learning & Education* 14, no. 4 (2015): 595–606.

138. H. Willmott, "Reflections on the Darker Side of Conventional Power Analytics," *Academy of Management Perspectives* 27, no. 4 (2013): 281–286.

139. Q. N. Huy, K. G. Corley, and M. S. Kraatz, "From Support to Mutiny: Shifting Legitimacy Judgments and Emotional Reactions Impacting the Implementation of Radical Change," *Academy of Management Journal* 57, no. 6 (2014): 1650–1680.

140. J. D. Westphal and G. Shani, "Psyched-Up to Suck-Up: Self-Regulated Cognition, Interpersonal Influence, and Recommendations for Board Appointments in the Corporate Elite," *Academy of Management Journal* 59, no. 2 (2016): 479–509.

141. I. Sutherland, J. R. Gosling, and J. Jelinek, "Aesthetics of Power: Why Teaching About Power Is Easier Than Learning for Power, and What Business Schools Could Do About It," *Academy of Management Learning & Education* 14, no. 4 (2015): 607–624.

142. L. Tomkins and E. Ulus, "Is Narcissism Undermining Critical Reflection in Our Business Schools?" *Academy of Management Learning & Education* 14, no. 4 (2015): 595–606.

143. D. Ma, M. Rhee, and D. Yang, "Power Source Mismatch and the Effectiveness of Interorganizational Relations: The Case of Venture Capital Syndication," *Academy of Management Journal* 56, no. 3 (2014): 711–734.

144. A. A. Cannella, C. D. Jones, and M. C. Withers, "Family-Versus Lone-Founder-Controlled Public Corporations: Social Identity Theory and Boards of Directors," *Academy of Management Journal* 58, no. 2 (2015): 436–459.

145. N. W. Biggart and R. Delbridge, "Systems of Exchange," *Academy of Management Review* 29, no. 1 (2004): 28–49.

146. D. Ma, M. Rhee, and D. Yang, "Power Source Mismatch and the Effectiveness of Interorganizational Relations: The Case of Venture Capital Syndication," *Academy of Management Journal* 56, no. 3 (2014): 711–734.

147. J. Robinson, "Your Brain on Power," *Entrepreneur* (March 2014): 61.

148. D. Eng, "How to Get Over Yourself," *Fortune* (March 1, 2015): 36.

149. P. M. Picone, G. B. Dagnino, and A. Mina, "The Origin of Failure: A Multidisciplinary Appraisal of the Hubris Hypothesis and Proposed Research Agenda," *Academy of Management Perspectives* 28, no. 4 (2014): 447–468.

150. C. L. Pearce, C. L. Wassenaar, and C. C. Manz, "Is Shared Leadership the Key to Responsible Leadership?" *Academy of Management Perspectives* 28, no. 3 (2014): 275–288.

151. F. Aime, S. Humphrey, D. S. Derue, and J. B. Paul, "The Riddle of Heterarchy: Power Transitions in Cross-Functional Teams," *Academy of Management Journal* 57, no. 2 (2014): 327–352.

152. N. M. Lorinkova, M. J. Pearsall, and H. P. Sims, "Examining the Differential Longitudinal Performance of Directive Versus Empowering Leadership in Teams," *Academy of Management Journal* 56, no. 2 (2013): 573–596.

153. F. Aime, S. Humphrey, D. S. Derue, and J. B. Paul, "The Riddle of Heterarchy: Power Transitions in Cross-Functional Teams," *Academy of Management Journal* 57, no. 2 (2014): 327–352.

154. F. Sobral and G. Islam, "He Who Laughs Best, Leaves Last: The Influence of Humor on the Attitudes and Behavior of Interns," *Academy of Management Learning & Education* 14, no. 4 (2015): 500–518.

155. H. Lian, D. J. Brown, D. L. Ferris, L. H. Liang, L. M. Keeping, and R. Morrison, "Abusive Supervision and Retaliation: A Self-Control Framework," *Academy of Management Journal* 57, no. 1 (2014): 116–139.

156. D. Wescott, "Field Guide to Office Bullies," *BusinessWeek* (November 26–December 2, 2012): 94–95.

157. B. M. Galvin, D. Lange, and B. E. Ashforth, "Narcissistic Organizational Identification: Seeing Oneself as Central to the Organization's Identity,"

158. A. Bitektine and P. Haack, "The Macro and the Micro of Legitimacy: Toward a Multilevel Theory of the Legitimacy Process," *Academy of Management Review* 40, no. 1 (2015): 49–75.

159. D. J. Harmon, S. E. Green, G. T. Goodnight, "A Model of Rhetorical Legitimation: The Structure of Communication and Cognition Underlying Institutional Maintenance and Change," *Academy of Management Review* 40, no. 1 (2015): 76–95.

160. S. S. Wiltermuth, "Power, Moral Clarity, and Punishment in the Workplace," *Academy of Management Journal* 56, no. 4 (2013): 1002–1023.

161. J. Naisbitt, "Thoughts: On Power," *Forbes* (November 23, 2015): 160.

162. A. Joshi and A. P. Knight, "Who Defers to Whom and Why? Dual Pathways Linking Demographic Differences and Dyadic Deference to Team Effectiveness," *Academy of Management Journal* 58, no. 1 (2015): 59–84.

163. P. Lencioni, "Being Smart Is Overrated," *INC.* (October 2014): 128.

164. M. Berman, "The No-Boss Company," *The Wall Street Journal* (October 27, 2015): R3.

165. L. Hann, "Long-Distance Leadership," *Entrepreneur* (March 2015): 19.

166. Y. Liu, G. R. Ferris, J. Xu, B. A. Weitz, and P. L. Perrewe, "When Ingratiation Backfires: The Role of Political Skill in the Ingratiation–Internship Performance Relationship," *Academy of Management Learning & Education* 13, no. 4 (2014): 569–586.

167. D. R. Soriano, "Political Skills in Organizations: Do Personality and Reputation Play a Role?" *Academy of Management Perspectives* 22, no. 1 (2008): 66–68.

168. D. Seetharaman, "Facebook Investors Press Suit on Shares," *The Wall Street Journal* (December 10, 20160: B1, B2.

169. Y. Liu, G. R. Ferris, J. Xu, B. A. Weitz, and P. L. Perrewe, "When Ingratiation Backfires: The Role of Political Skill in the Ingratiation–Internship Performance Relationship," *Academy of Management Learning & Education* 13, no. 4 (2014): 569–586.

170. R. McCammon, "Do Me a Solid," *Entrepreneur* (March 2014): 32–33.

171. C. H. Chang, C. C. Rosen, and P. E. Levy, "The Relationship Between Perceptions of Organizational Politics and Employee Attitudes, Strain and Behavior: A Meta-Analytic Examination," *Academy of Management Journal* 52, no. 4 (2009): 779–801.

172. A. C. Peng, J. M. Schaubroeck, and Y. Li, "Social Exchange Implications of Own and Coworkers' Experience of Supervisory Abuse," *Academy of Management Journal* 57, no. 5 (2014): 1385–1405.

173. S. J. Creary, B. B. Caza, L. M. Roberts, "Out of the Box? How Managing a Subordinate's Multiple Identities Affects the Quality of a Manager-Subordinate Relationship," *Academy of Management Review* 40, no. 4 (2015): 538–562.

174. R. McCammon, "Do Me a Solid," *Entrepreneur* (March 2014): 32–33.

175. Ziglar website, www.ziglar.com, accessed May 18, 2017.

176. G. Di Stefano, A. A. King, and G. Verona, "Sanctioning in the Wild: Rational Calculus and Retributive Instincts in Gourmet Cuisine," *Academy of Management Journal* 58, no. 3 (2015): 906–931.

177. S. Shellenbarger, "Ever Thought, How Did He Get Promoted? Here's How," *The Wall Street Journal* (July 9, 2014): D1, D2.

178. S. Shellenbarger, "Leader? No, Be a Follower," *The Wall Street Journal* (September 30, 2015): D1, D3.

179. R. McCammon, "I'm Going to Need a Bit More Time …," *Entrepreneur* (September 2014): 28–30.

180. S. Shellenbarger, "Ever Thought, How Did He Get Promoted? Here's How," *The Wall Street Journal* (July 9, 2014): D1, D2.

181. S. Shellenbarger, "Leader? No, Be a Follower," *The Wall Street Journal* (September 30, 2015): D1, D3.

182. M. Selman, "Manipulate Creative People," *BusinessWeek* (April 11, 2013): 92.

183. R. McCammon, "How to Own the Room," *BusinessWeek* online, accessed May 18, 2017.

184. E. Bernstein, "Don't Apologize So Fast," *The Wall Street Journal* (July 15, 2014): D1, D4.

185. Staff, "The Reconciliation Game," *The Wall Street Journal* (November 17, 2015): D1.

186. S. Fisher, "How to Turn Foes Into Friends," *Costco Connection* (April 2016): 13.

187. R. D. Costigan and K. E. Brink, "Another Perspective on MBA Program Alignment: An Investigation of Learning Goals," *Academy of Management Learning & Education* 14, no. 2 (2015): 260–276.

188. W. L. Bedwell, S. M. Fiore, and E. Salas, "Developing the Future Workforce: An Approach for Integrating Interpersonal Skills Into the MBA Classroom," *Academy of Management Learning & Education* 13, no. 2 (2014): 171–186.

189. K. Leavitt and D. M. Sluss, "Lying for Who We Are: An Identity-Based Model of Workplace Dishonesty," *Academy of Management Review* 40, no. 4 (2015): 587–610.

190. N. Brodsky, "Shut Up and Listen," *INC.* (March 2015): 58.

191. D. T. Kong, K. T. Dirks, and D. L. Ferrin, "Interpersonal Trust Within Negotiations: Meta-Analytic Evidence, Critical Contingencies, and Directions for Further Research," *Academy of Management Journal* 57, no. 5 (2014): 1235–1255.

192. S. Raice, S. E. Ante, and E. Glazer, "In Facebook Deal, Board Was All but Out of Picture," *The Wall Street Journal* (April 18, 2012): A1, A2.

193. G. Colvin, "Where Disrupters Meet Aristocrats," *Fortune* (December 1, 2015): 28.

194. D. T. Kong, K. T. Dirks, and D. L. Ferrin, "Interpersonal Trust Within Negotiations: Meta-Analytic Evidence, Critical Contingencies, and Directions for Further Research," *Academy of Management Journal* 57, no. 5 (2014): 1235–1255.

195. S. D. Charlier, "Incorporating Evidence-Based Management Into Management Curricula: A Conversation With Gary Latham," *Academy of Management Learning & Education* 13, no. 3 (2014): 467–475.

196. R. Lussier, "The Negotiation Process," *Clinical Leadership & Management Review* 14, no. 2 (2000): 55–59.

197. A. Coombs, "The Biggest Mistakes Executives Make When Negotiating a Retirement Package," *The Wall Street Journal* (June 13, 2016): R1, R2.

198. N. Brodsky, "Shut Up and Listen," *INC.* (March 2015): 58.

199. A. Coombs, "The Biggest Mistakes Executives Make When Negotiating a Retirement Package," *The Wall Street Journal* (June 13, 2016): R1, R2.

200. Ibid.

201. C. Hann, "Always Be Closing," *Entrepreneur* (August 2015): 30.

202. N. Brodsky, "Shut Up and Listen," *INC.* (March 2015): 58.

203. G. Colvin, "Humans Are Underrated," *Fortune* (August 1, 2015): 100–113.

204. D. Horowitz and A. Horowitz, "When Customer Service Goes Wrong," *Costco Connection* (October 2014): 15.

205. A. Coombs, "The Biggest Mistakes Executives Make When Negotiating a Retirement Package," *The Wall Street Journal* (June 13, 2016): R1, R2.

206. N. Brodsky, "Shut Up and Listen," *INC.* (March 2015): 58.

207. A. Coombs, "The Biggest Mistakes Executives Make When Negotiating a Retirement Package," *The Wall Street Journal* (June 13, 2016): R1, R2.

208. D. T. Kong, K. T. Dirks, and D. L. Ferrin, "Interpersonal Trust Within Negotiations: Meta-Analytic Evidence, Critical Contingencies, and Directions for Further Research," *Academy of Management Journal* 57, no. 5 (2014): 1235–1255.

209. C. Hann, "Fair Pay," *Entrepreneur* (May 2016): 23.

210. S. Shellenbarger, "To Fight or Not to Fight? When to Pick Workplace Battles," *The Wall Street Journal* (December 17, 2014): D1, D2.

211. E. Bernstein, "The Year in Relationship Troubles, and How Talk Can Help," *The Wall Street Journal* (December 30, 2014): D1, D2.

212. E. Bernstein, "I'm Sorry, I'm Allergic to You," *The Wall Street Journal* (July 1, 2014): D1, D2.

213. M. Sytch and A. Tatarynowicz, "Friends and Foes: The Dynamics of Dual Social Structures," *Academy of Management Journal* 57, no. 2 (2014): 585–613.

214. E. Bernstein, "Don't Apologize So Fast," *The Wall Street Journal* (July 15, 2014): D1, D4.

215. S. Shellenbarger, "To Fight or Not to Fight? When to Pick Workplace Battles," *The Wall Street Journal* (December 17, 2014): D1, D2.

216. E. Bernstein, "You Can Do It! Be a Motivator," *The Wall Street Journal* (June 16, 2016): D1, D3.

217. R. McCammon, "I'm Sure You're Wondering Why I've Called You All Here," *Entrepreneur* (March 2015): 28–29.

218. D. X. H. Wo, M. L. Ambrose, and M. Schminke, "What Drives Trickle-Down Effects? A Test of Multiple Mediation Processes," *Academy of Management Journal* 58, no. 6 (2015): 1848–1868.

219. R. McCammon, "Can We Talk," *Entrepreneur* (May 2015): 25–26.

220. D. X. H. Wo, M. L. Ambrose, and M. Schminke, "What Drives Trickle-Down Effects? A Test of Multiple Mediation Processes," *Academy of Management Journal* 58, no. 6 (2015): 1848–1868.

221. P. Lencioni, "Innovation Won't Get You Very Far," *INC.* (December 2014/January 2015): 102.

222. K. Clark, "Why the Seahawks Like Confrontation," *The Wall Street Journal* (January 8, 2015): D6.

223. T. Perrotta, "The Secret Power of Twins: Amnesia," *The Wall Street Journal* (May 27, 2014): D6.

224. B. Benmosche with P. Marks, *Good for the Money: My Fight to Pay Back America* (St. Martin's Press, 2016).

225. S. Shellenbarger, "To Fight or Not to Fight? When to Pick Workplace Battles," *The Wall Street Journal* (December 17, 2014): D1, D2.

226. Ibid.

227. D. Horowitz and A. Horowitz, "When Customer Service Goes Wrong," *Costco Connection* (October 2014): 15.

228. E. Bernstein, "I'm Sorry, I'm Allergic to You," *The Wall Street Journal* (July 1, 2014): D1, D2.

229. L. R. Weingart, K. J. Behfar, C. Bendersky, G. Todorova, and K. A. Jehn, "The Directness and Oppositional Intensity of Conflict Expression," *Academy of Management Review* 40, no. 2 (2015): 235–262.

230. S. D. Charlier, "Incorporating Evidence-Based Management Into Management Curricula: A Conversation With Gary Latham," *Academy of Management Learning & Education* 13, no. 3 (2014): 467–475.

231. T. Robbins, "Robbins' Rules," *Fortune* (November 17, 2014): 131.

232. E. Bernstein, "The Year in Relationship Troubles, and How Talk Can Help," *The Wall Street Journal* (December 30, 2014): D1, D2.

233. R. McCammon, "Can We Talk," *Entrepreneur* (May 2015): 25–26.

234. Ibid.

235. S. Shellenbarger, "To Fight or Not to Fight? When to Pick Workplace Battles," *The Wall Street Journal* (December 17, 2014): D1, D2.

236. L. R. Weingart, K. J. Behfar, C. Bendersky, G. Todorova, and K. A. Jehn, "The Directness and Oppositional Intensity of Conflict Expression," *Academy of Management Review* 40, no. 2 (2015): 235–262.

237. R. McCammon, "Can We Talk," *Entrepreneur* (May 2015): 25–26.

238. S. Fisher, "How to Turn Foes Into Friends," *Costco Connection* (April 2016): 13.

239. A. Kirkman, "It's All About Attitude," *Fortune* (November 17, 2014): 34.

240. The term *eustress* was added at the suggestion of reviewer Carl Blencke, University of Central Florida, added on May 23, 2017.

241. Y. Zhang, J. A. Lepine, B. R. Buckman, and F. Wei, "It's Not Fair … Or Is It? The Role of Justice and Leadership in Explaining Work Stressor-Job Performance Relationships," *Academy of Management Journal* 57, no. 3 (2014): 675–697.

242. E. Agnvall, "Stress: Don't Let It Make You Sick," *AARP Bulletin* (November 2014): 26–27.

243. S. Reddy, "Why Are You Always Late? It Could Be a Planning Fallacy," *The Wall Street Journal* (February 3, 2015): D1, D2.

244. Y. Zhang, J. A. Lepine, B. R. Buckman, and F. Wei, "It's Not Fair … Or Is It? The Role of Justice and Leadership in Explaining Work Stressor-Job Performance Relationships," *Academy of Management Journal* 57, no. 3 (2014): 675–697.

245. S. S. Wang, "Never Procrastinate Again," *The Wall Street Journal* (September 1, 2015): D1, D2.

246. J. Fried, "In Praise of Deadlines," *INC.* (December 2015/January 2016): 128.

247. L. M. Maruping, V. Vewnkatesh, S. M. B. Thatcher, and P. C. Patel, "Folding Under Pressure of Rising to the Occasion? Perceived Time Pressure and the Moderating Role of Team Temporal Leadership," *Academy of Management Journal* 58, no. 5 (2015): 1313–1333.

248. A. J. Lombardi, "Tech Neck," *Strength & Conditioning* online, accessed May 23, 2017.

249. J. Schramm, "Manage Stress, Improve the Bottom Line," *HR Magazine* (February 2013): 80.

250. H. Mitchell, "Does Being Stressed Out Make You Forget?" *The Wall Street Journal* (March 17, 2015): D1.

251. Staff, "Worship Positive for Health and Happiness," *afaJournal* (October 2016): 8.

252. D. Ariely, "Better Off Bed," *INC.* (March 2015): 52.

253. S. Reddy, "Sleep Experts Close in On the Optimal Night's Sleep," *The Wall Street Journal* (July 22, 2015): D1, D2.

254. G. D. Redford, "Why Sleep Is Precious," *AARP the Magazine* (December 2014/January 2015): 22.

255. E. Bernstein, "Changing the Clock Wasn't Good for Your Relationship," *The Wall Street Journal* (March 10, 2015): D1, D2.

256. M. Gulati, "The Higher Your Stress, the Higher Your LDL," *The Wall Street Journal* (February 9, 2016): D1, D2.

257. Staff, "Drinking Diet Soda," *AARP the Magazine* (December 2014/January 2015): 19.

258. M. Gulati, "The Higher Your Stress, the Higher Your LDL," *The Wall Street Journal* (February 9, 2016): D1, D2.

259. S. Shellenbarger, "Are You Hard-Wired to Boil Over From Stress?" *The Wall Street Journal* (February 13, 2013): D3.

260. M. Gulati, "The Higher Your Stress, the Higher Your LDL," *The Wall Street Journal* (February 9, 2016): D1, D2.

261. A. J. Lombardi, "Tech Neck," *Strength & Conditioning* online, accessed May 23, 2017.

262. M. Gulati, "The Higher Your Stress, the Higher Your LDL," *The Wall Street Journal* (February 9, 2016): D1, D2.

263. S. S. Wang, "Never Procrastinate Again," *The Wall Street Journal* (September 1, 2015): D1, D2.

264. Ibid.

265. M. Gulati, "The Higher Your Stress, the Higher Your LDL," *The Wall Street Journal* (February 9, 2016): D1, D2.

266. L. M. Leslie, D. M. Mayer, and D. A. Kravitz, "The Stigma of Affirmative Action: A Stereotyping-Based Theory and Meta-Analytic Test of the Consequences for Performance," *Academy of Management Journal* 57, no. 4 (2014): 964–989.

267. E. Bernstein, "Don't Apologize So Fast," *The Wall Street Journal* (July 15, 2014): D1, D4.

268. G. James, "Avoid These 4 Toxic Thought Patterns," *INC.* (December 2015/January 2–16): 10.

269. G. Colvin, "Humans Are Underrated," *Fortune* (August 1, 2015): 100–113.

270. R. Karlgaard, "Riches From the Disruptive Dozen," *Forbes* (October 19, 2015): 38.

271. R. E. Silverman, "Bosses Tap Big Data to Flag Workers' Ills," *The Wall Street Journal* (February 17, 2016): B1, B7.

272. M. Villano, "Prognosis: Better Health," *Entrepreneur* (May 2015): 68.

273. E. Dwoskin and D. Wakabayashi, "Apple's Next Big Focus: Your Health," *The Wall Street Journal* (September 6–7, 2014): B1, B4.

274. J. Alsever, "Electrify Your Mind," *Fortune* (December 1, 2015): 41–44.

275. E. Bernstein, "Honey, You Never Said …," *The Wall Street Journal* (March 24, 2015): D1, D4.

276. C. Bonanos, "The Lies We Tell at Work," *BusinessWeek* (February 4–10, 2013): 71–73.

Chapter 11

1. R. Fehr, K. C. Yam, and C. Dang, "Moralized Leadership: The Construction and Consequences of Ethical Leader Perceptions," *Academy of Management Review* 40, no. 2 (2015): 182–209.

2. General Electric ad, "Identifying the Leadership Skills That Matter Most Today," *INC.* (December 2014–January 2015): 78.

3. P. Wahba, "She Thanks You for Not Smoking," *Fortune* (September 15, 2015): 125–130.

4. S. Shellenbarger, "Leader? No, Be a Follower," *The Wall Street Journal* (September 30, 2015): D1, D3.

5. J. Rodkin and F. Levy, "Recruiting Preferred Skills," *BusinessWeek* (April 13–19, 2015): 43.

6. M. E. Chan and D. J. McAllister, "Abusive Supervision Through the Lens of Employee State Paranoia," *Academy of Management Review* 39, no. 1 (2014): 44–66.

7. N. Li, B. L. Kirkman, and C. O. L. H. Porter, "Toward a Model of Work Team Altruism," *Academy of Management Review* 39, no. 4 (2014): 541–565.

8. C. Hann, "Dedicated to You," *Entrepreneur* (September 2013): 24.

9. R. K. Ross, "Recognizing Employee Disengagement … and Taking Steps to Re-Engage," *Costco Connection* (December 2014): 13–14.

10. K. Rockwood, "Tracking the Mood of Your Employees," *INC.* (January 2016): 106–107.

11. R. King, "Companies Want to Know: How Do Workers Feel?" *The Wall Street Journal* (October 14, 2015): R3.

12. N. Li, B. L. Kirkman, and C. O. L. H. Porter, "Toward a Model of Work Team Altruism," *Academy of Management Review* 39, no. 4 (2014): 541–565.

13. Nationwide, "Company Spotlight," *Fortune* (March 15, 2015): 38.

14. B. M. Galvin, D. Lange, and B. E. Ashforth, "Narcissistic Organizational Identification: Seeing Oneself as Central to the Organization's Identity," *Academy of Management Review* 40, no. 2 (2015): 163–181.

15. A. C. Peng, J. M. Schaubroeck, and L. Li, "Social Exchange Implications of Own and Coworkers' Experiences of Supervisor Abuse," *Academy of Management Journal* 57, no. 5 (2014): 1385–1405.

16. F. K. Matta, B. A. Scott, J. Koopman, and D. E. Conlon, "Does Seeing Eye to Eye Affect Work Engagement and Organizational Citizenship Behavior? A Role Theory Perspective on LMX Agreements," *Academy of Management Journal* 58, no. 6 (2015): 1686–1708.

17. C. K. Lam, X. Huang, and S. C. H. Chan, "The Threshold Effect of Participative Leadership and the Role of Leader Information Sharing," *Academy of Management Journal* 58, no. 3 (2015): 836–855.

18. O. Ybarra, E. Kross, and J. S. Burks, "The Big Idea That Is Yet to Be: Toward a More Motivated, Contextual, and Dynamic Model of Emotional Intelligence," *Academy of Management Perspectives* 28, no. 2 (2014): 93–107.

19. T. Mitchell, "Victory Dance," *INC.* (April 2014): 47.

20. W. Buffett and M. Barra, "Most Powerful Women Advice!" *Fortune* (November 17, 2014): 149.

21. R. C. Liden, S. J. Wayne, C. Liao, and J. D. Meuser, "Servant Leadership and Serving Culture: Influence on Individual and Unit Performance," *Academy of Management Journal* 57, no. 5 (2014): 1434–1452.

22. B. Johansen, "The Future of … the Consumer Experience," *Entrepreneur* (January 2015): 36.

23. E. Bernstein, "You Can Do IT! Be a Motivator," *The Wall Street Journal* (June 16, 2016): D1, D3.

24. Y. Zhang, D. A. Waldman, U. L. Han, and X. B. Li, "Paradoxical Leaders Behaviors in People Management: Antecedents and Consequences," *Academy of Management Journal* 58, no. 2 (2015): 538–566.

25. A. Maslow, "A Theory of Human Motivation," *Psychological Review* 50 (1943): 370–396; *Motivation and Personality* (New York: Harper & Row, 1954).

26. R. L. Dipboye, "Bridging the Gap in Organizational Behavior," *Academy of Management Learning & Education* 13, no. 3 (2014): 487–491.

27. C. Alderfer, "An Empirical Test of a New Theory of Human Needs," *Organizational Behavior and Human Performance* (April 1969): 142–175; *Existence, Relatedness, and Growth* (New York: Free Press, 1972).

28. F. Herzberg, "One More Time: How Do You Motivate Employees?" *Harvard Business Review* (January/February 1968): 53–62.

29. S. Diestel, J. Wegge, and K. H. Schmidt, "The Impact of Social Context on the Relationship Between Individual Job Satisfaction and Absenteeism: The Roles of Different Foci of Job Satisfaction and Work-Unit Absenteeism," *Academy of Management Journal* 57, no. 2 (2014): 353–382.

30. A. Liveris, "CEO 101," *Fortune* (November 17, 2014): 129.

31. P. Diamandis, "The Future of … Technology," *Entrepreneur* (January 2015): 36.

32. Camden, "Company Spotlight," *Fortune* (March 15, 2015): 176.

33. P. Keegan, "The New Rules of Engagement," *INC.* (December 2014/January 2015): 86–132.

34. D. McClelland, *The Achieving Society* (New York: Van Nostrand Reinhold, 1961); D. McClelland and D. H. Burnham, "Power Is the Great Motivator," *Harvard Business Review* (March/April 1978): 103.

35. J. Rodkin and F. Levy, "Recruiting Preferred Skills," *BusinessWeek* (April 13–19, 2015): 43.

36. M. Mursthorn, "More Brokers Say No to Being Boss," *The Wall Street Journal* (online), accessed June 18, 2015.

37. G. O'Brien, "It's All Your Fault!" *Entrepreneur* (February 2015): 30.

38. D. T. Kong, K. T. Dirks, and D. L. Ferrin, "Interpersonal Trust Within Negotiations: Meta-Analytic Evidence, Critical Contingencies, and Directions for Further Research," *Academy of Management Journal* 57, no. 5 (2014): 1235–1255.

39. B. A. Scott, A. S. Garza, D. E. Conlong, and Y. J. Kim, "Why Do Managers Act Fairly in the First Place? A Daily Investigation of Hot and Cold Motives and Discretion," *Academy of Management Journal* 57, no. 6 (2014): 1571–1591.

40. D. T. Kong, K. T. Dirks, and D. L. Ferrin, "Interpersonal Trust Within Negotiations: Meta-Analytic Evidence, Critical Contingencies, and Directions for Further Research," *Academy of Management Journal* 57, no. 5 (2014): 1235–1255.

41. A. C. Peng, J. M. Schaubroeck, and L. Li, "Social Exchange Implications of Own and Coworkers' Experiences of Supervisor Abuse," *Academy of Management Journal* 57, no. 5 (2014): 1385–1405.

42. J. S. Adams, "Toward an Understanding of Inequity," *Journal of Abnormal and Social Psychology* 67 (1963): 422–436.

43. G. O. Trevor, G. Reilly, and B. Gerhart, "Reconsidering Pay Dispersion's Effect on the Performance of Interdependent Work: Reconciling Sorting and Pay Inequality," *Academy of Management Journal* 55, no. 3 (2012): 585–610.

44. K. Leavitt, S. J. Reynolds, C. M. Barnes, P. Schilpzan, and S. T. Hannah, "Different Hats, Different Obligations: Plural Occupational Identities and Situated Moral Judgments," *Academy of Management Journal* 55, no. 6 (2012): 1316–1333.

45. News, National Public Radio (NPR), aired November 18, 2015.

46. S. F. Collins, "Success Steps," *Costco Connection* (January 2016): 29.

47. D. Baden and M. Higgs, "Challenging the Perceived Wisdom of Management Theories and Practice," *Academy of Management Learning & Education* 14, no. 4 (2015): 539–555.

48. J. Fried, "In Praise of Deadlines," *INC.* (December 2015/January 2016): 128.

49. V. Harnish, "5 Crucial Performance Metrics," *Fortune* (August 1, 2016): 322.

50. E. Locke, "Guest Editor's Introduction: Goal-Setting Theory and Its Applications to the World of Business," *Academy of Management Executive* 18, no. 4 (2004): 124–125.

51. S. D. Charlier, "Incorporating Evidence-Based Management Into Management Curricula: A Conversation With Gary Latham," *Academy of Management Learning & Education* 13, no. 3 (2014): 467–475.

52. O. Ybarra, E. Kross, and J. S. Burks, "The Big Idea That Is Yet to Be: Toward a More Motivated, Contextual, and Dynamic Model of Emotional Intelligence," *Academy of Management Perspectives* 28, no. 2 (2014): 93–107.

53. C. L. Pearce, C. L. Wassenaar, and C. C. Manz, "Is Shared Leadership the Key to Responsible Leadership?" *Academy of Management Perspectives* 28, no. 3 (2014): 275–288.

54. C. Duhigg, "Smarter Faster Better," *Fortune* (March 15, 2016): 28.

55. C. Ricketts, "Hit List: Lou Holtz," *The Wall Street Journal* (December 23, 2006): P2; L. Holtz, "Setting a Higher Standard," *Success Yearbook* (Tampa, FL: Peter Lowe International, 1998): 74.

56. L. M. Maruping, V. Venkatesh, S. M. B. Thatcher, and P. C. Patel, "Folding Under Pressure or Rising to the Occasion?" *Academy of Management Journal* 58, no. 5 (2015): 1313–1333.

57. G. Colvin, "Humans Are Underrated," *Fortune* (August 1, 2015): 100–113.

58. J. Hu and R. C. Liden, "Making a Difference in the Teamwork: Linking Team Prosocial Motivation to Team Processes and Effectiveness," *Academy of Management Journal* 58, no. 3 (2015): 836–855.

59. L. Alexander and D. Van Knippenberg, "Teams in Pursuit of Radical Innovation: A Goal Orientation Perspective," *Academy of Management Review* 39, no. 4 (2014): 423–438.

60. V. Vroom, *Work and Motivation* (New York: John Wiley & Sons, 1964).

61. N. J. Fast, E. R. Burris, and C. A. Bartel, "Managing to Stay in the Dark: Managerial Self-Efficacy, Ego Defensiveness, and the Aversion to Employee Voice," *Academy of Management Journal* 57, no. 4 (2014): 1013–1034.

62. B. F. Skinner, *Beyond Freedom and Dignity* (New York: Alfred A. Knopf, 1971).

63. S. D. Levitt and S. J. Dubner, "SuperFreakonomics," *Academy of Management Perspectives* 25, no. 2 (2011): 86–87.

64. N. Pasricha, "The Happiness Equation," *Fortune* (March 15, 2016): 28.

65. H. Geffen, "36. Laffer," *BusinessWeek* (December 8–14, 2014): 70–71.

66. A. Lashinsky, "The Right Watchman," *Fortune* (March 17, 2014): 68.

67. E. L. Weber, "Nowhere to Hide for Dead Wood Workers," *The Wall Street Journal* (August 22, 2017): A1, A10.

68. N. Li, B. L. Kirkman, and C. O. L. H. Porter, "Toward a Model of Work Team Altruism," *Academy of Management Review* 39, no. 4 (2014): 541–565.

69. M. E. Chan and D. J. McAllister, "Abusive Supervision Through the Lens of Employee State Paranoia," *Academy of Management Review* 39, no. 1 (2014): 44–66.

70. N. Li, B. L. Kirkman, and C. O. L. H. Porter, "Toward a Model of Work Team Altruism," *Academy of Management Review* 39, no. 4 (2014): 541–565.

71. S. F. Collins, "Success Steps," *Costco Connection* (January 2016): 29.

72. L. Daska, "4 Pieces of Advice Most People Ignore (but Great Entrepreneurs Don't)," *INC.* (July/August 2015): 8.

73. M. Rosenwald, "Bound by Habit," *BusinessWeek* (March 19–25, 2012): 106–107.

74. N. Li, B. L. Kirkman, and C. O. L. H. Porter, "Toward a Model of Work Team Altruism," *Academy of Management Review* 39, no. 4 (2014): 541–565.

75. M. R. Barrick, G. R. Thurgood, T. A. Smith, and S. H. Courtright, "Collective Organizational Engagement: Linking Motivational Antecedents, Strategic Implementation, and Firm Performance," *Academy of Management Journal* 58, no. 1 (2015): 111–135.

76. Y. Zhang, D. A. Waldman, U. L. Han, and X. B. Li, "Paradoxical Leader Behaviors in People Management: Antecedents and Consequences," *Academy of Management Journal* 58, no. 2 (2015): 538–566.

77. N. J. Fast, E. R. Burris, and C. A. Bartel, "Managing to Stay in the Dark: Managerial Self-Efficacy, Ego Defensiveness, and the Aversion to Employee Voice," *Academy of Management Journal* 57, no. 4 (2014): 1013–1034.

78. M. Cerne, C. G. L. Nerstad, A. Dysvik, and M. Skerlavaj, "What Goes Around Comes Around: Knowledge Hiding, Perceived Motivational Climate, and Creativity," *Academy of Management Journal* 57, no. 1 (2014): 172–192.

79. R. C. Liden, S. J. Wayne, C. Liao, and J. D. Meuser, "Servant Leadership and Serving Culture: Influence on Individual and Unit Performance," *Academy of Management Journal* 57, no. 5 (2014): 1434–1452.

80. R. L. Dipboye, "Bridging the Gap in Organizational Behavior," *Academy of Management Learning & Education* 13, no. 3 (2014): 487–491.

81. S. J. Creary, B. B. Caza, and L. M. Roberts, "Out of the Box? How Managing a Subordinate's Multiple Identities Affects the Quality of a Manager-Subordinate Relationship," *Academy of Management Review* 40, no. 4 (2015): 538–562.

82. G. Colvin, "Personal Bests," *Fortune* (March 15, 2015): 106–110.

83. P. Keegan, "The New Rules of Engagement," *INC.* (December 2014/January 2015): 86–132.

84. Staff, "Beyond the Cash Bonus," *INC.* (November 2016): 42–43.

85. I. Filatotchev and C. Nakajima, "Corporate Governance, Responsible Managerial Behavior, and Corporate Social Responsibility: Organizational Efficiency Versus Organizational Legitimacy," *Academy of Management Perspectives* 28, no. 3 (2014): 289–306.

86. L. Jia, J. D. Shaw, A. S. Tsue, and T. Y. Park, "A Social-Structural Perspective on Employee-Organization Relationships and Team Creativity," *Academy of Management Journal* 57, no. 3 (2014): 869–891.

87. S. Leibs, "Perks That Work," *INC.* (November 2014): 64–65.

88. L. Vanderkam, "Work/Life Integration Is the New Normal," *Fortune* (March 15, 2015): 139.

89. R. Feintzeig, "More Family Time Can Give Dad's Career Lift," *The Wall Street Journal* (February 5, 2015): D2.

90. L. Vanderkam, "Work/Life Integration Is the New Normal," *Fortune* (March 15, 2015): 139.

91. R. Feintzeig, "When the Annual Raise Isn't Enough," *The Wall Street Journal* (July 16, 2014): B1, B5.

92. T. Demos, "Motivate Without Spending Millions," *Fortune* (April 12, 2010): 37–38.

93. Ibid.

94. Ibid.

95. C. L. Pearce, C. L. Wassenaar, and C. C. Manz, "Is Shared Leadership the Key to Responsible Leadership?" *Academy of Management Perspectives* 28, no. 3 (2014): 275–288.

96. R. McCammon, "Words of Encouragement," *Entrepreneur* (October 2015): 26.

97. E. Bernstein, "The Hidden Benefits of Chitchat," *The Wall Street Journal* (August 13, 2013): D1, D2.

98. D. M. Ames and A. S. Wazlawek, "How to Tell if You're a Jerk in the Office," *The Wall Street Journal* (February 23, 2015): R2.

99. E. Bernstein, "If You Want to Persuade People, Try Altercasting," *The Wall Street Journal* (September 5, 2016): D1, D2.

100. Based on the author's consulting experience.

101. O. E. Varela and R. G. Watts, "The Development of the Global Manager: An Empirical Study on the Role of Academic International Sojourns," *Academy of Management Learning & Education* 13, no. 2 (2014): 187–207.

102. M. Javidan, P. W. Dorfman, M. S. de Luque, and R. J. House, "In the Eye of the Beholder: Cross Cultural Lessons in Leadership From Project GLOBE," *Academy of Management Perspectives* 20, no. 1 (2006): 67–90.

103. I. Filatotchev and C. Nakajima, "Corporate Governance, Responsible Managerial Behavior, and Corporate Social Responsibility: Organizational Efficiency Versus Organizational Legitimacy," *Academy of Management Perspectives* 28, no. 3 (2014): 289–306.

104. S. Leibs, "Perks That Work," *INC.* (November 2014): 64–65.

105. G. Colvin, "Personal Bests," *Fortune* (March 15, 2015): 106–110.

106. P. Keegan, "The New Rules of Engagement," *INC.* (December 2014/January 2015): 86–132.

107. A. Murray, "What Do Millennials Want?" *Fortune* (March 15, 2015): 14.

Chapter 12

1. S. Clinebell, "Snapshots of Great Leaders," *Academy of Management Learning & Education* 13, no. 1 (2014): 139–149.

2. J. Rodkin and F. Levy, "Recruiting Preferred Skills," *BusinessWeek* (April 13–19, 2015): 43.

3. B. R. Spisak, M. J. O'Brien, N. Nicholson, and M. Van Vugt, "Niche Construction and the Evolution of Leadership," *Academy of Management Review* 40, no. 2 (2015): 291–306.

4. L. Hann, "Long-Distance Leadership," *Entrepreneur* (March 2015): 19.

5. S. D. Charlier, "Incorporating Evidence-Based Management Into Management Curricula: A Conversation With Gary Latham," *Academy of Management Learning & Education* 13, no. 3 (2014): 467–475.

6. R. Lowenstein, "Forget Buffett the Investor. Follow Buffett the Manager," *Fortune* (April 21, 2015): 67–68.

7. I. Boudway, "Holy Cow! It's a Business Plan," *BusinessWeek* (April 1–12, 2015): 40–45.

8. J. S. Lublin and S. Kapner, "A Boot at Men's Wearhouse," *The Wall Street Journal* (June 20, 2013): B2.

9. R. Hennessey, "Decisions, Decisions," *Entrepreneur* (March 2015): 50.

10. B. R. Spisak, M. J. O'Brien, N. Nicholson, and M. Van Vugt, "Niche Construction and the Evolution of Leadership," *Academy of Management Review* 40, no. 2 (2015): 291–306.

11. D. Collinson and D. Tourish, "Teaching Leadership Critically: New Directions for Leadership Pedagogy," *Academy of Management Learning & Education* 14, no. 4 (2015): 576–594.

12. Based on the suggestion of reviewer David Biemer, Texas State University, added June 1, 2017.

13. I. Sager, "Career Services," *BusinessWeek* (May 1, 2014): 56.

14. G. Colvin, "From High-Minded to High Value," *Fortune* (December 22, 2014): 38.

15. G. Colvin, "Four Things That Worry Business," *Fortune* (October 27, 2014): 32.

16. B. O'Keefe, "The Chosen One," *Fortune* (June 15, 2015): 134–139.

17. A. C. Peng, J. M. Schaubroeck, and Y. Li, "Social Exchange Implications of Own and Coworkers' Experience of Supervisory Abuse," *Academy of Management Journal* 57, no. 5 (2014): 1385–1405.

18. M. D. Baer, R. K. D. Kahlon, J. A. Colquitt, J. B. Rodell, R. Outlaw, and D. M. Long, "Uneasy Lies the Head That Bears the Trust: The Effects of Feeling Trusted on Emotional Exhaustion," *Academy of Management Journal* 58, no. 6 (2015): 1637–1657.

19. G. Colvin, "Ignore These Leadership Lessons at Your Peril," *Fortune* (October 28, 2013): 85.

20. C. Hann, "Dedicated to You," *Entrepreneur* (September 2013): 24.

21. R. Karlgaad, "Do Jerks Always Win?" *Forbes* (December 29, 2014): 44.

22. R. L. Dipboye, "Bridging the Gap in Organizations' Behavior," *Academy of Management Learning & Education* 13, no. 3 (2014): 487–491.

23. N. M. Lorinkova, M. J. Pearsall, and H. P. Sims, "Examining the Differential Longitudinal Performance of Directive Versus Empowering Leadership in Teams," *Academy of Management Journal* 56, no. 2 (2013): 573–596.

24. GE ad, "Identifying the Leadership Skills That Matter Most Today," *INC.* (December 2014–January 2015): 78.

25. D. Wakabayshi, "Tim Cook's Vision for His Apple Emerges," *The Wall Street Journal* (July 8, 2014): B1, B5.

26. A. Lashinsky, "Being Tim Cook," *Fortune* (April 1, 2015): 60–63.

27. D. Collinson and D. Tourish, "Teaching Leadership Critically: New Directions for Leadership Pedagogy," *Academy of Management Learning & Education* 14, no. 4 (2015): 576–594.

28. C. K. Lam, X. Huang, and S. C. H. Chan, "The Threshold Effect of Participative Leadership and the Role of Leader Information Sharing," *Academy of Management Journal* 58, no. 3 (2015): 836–855.

29. C. L. Pearce, C. L. Wassenaar, and C. C. Manz, "Is Shared Leadership the Key to Responsible Leadership?" *Academy of Management Perspectives* 28, no. 3 (2014): 275–288.

30. J. Clegg, "And the Oregon Ducks Prefer to Avoid It," *The Wall Street Journal* (January 8, 2015): D6.

31. R. E. Boyatzis, "Possible Contributions to Leadership and Management Development From Neuroscience," *Academy of Management Learning & Education* 13, no. 2 (2014): 300–301.

32. B. R. Spisak, M. J. O'Brien, N. Nicholson, and M. Van Vugt, "Niche Construction and the Evolution of Leadership," *Academy of Management Review* 40, no. 2 (2015): 291–306.

33. T. A. Judge and C. P. Zapata, "The Person–Situation Debate Revisited: Effect of Situation Strength and Trait Activation on the Validity of the Big Five Personality Traits in Predicting Job Performance," *Academy of Management Journal* 58, no. 4 (2015): 1149–1179.

34. A. C. Cosper, "O Captain! My Captain!" *Entrepreneur* (March 2015): 14.

35. K. Lanaj and J. R. Hollenbeck, "Leadership Over-Emergence in Self-Managing Teams: The Role of Gender and Countervailing Biases," *Academy of Management Journal* 58, no. 5 (2015): 1476–1494.

36. E. Grijalva and P. D. Harms, "Narcissism: An Integrative Synthesis and Dominance Complementarity Model," *Academy of Management Perspectives* 28, no. 2 (2014): 108–127.

37. R. Karlgaad, "Do Jerks Always Win?" *Forbes* (December 29, 2014): 44.

38. E. Ghiselli, *Explorations in Management Talent* (Santa Monica, CA: Goodyear, 1971).

39. GE ad, "Identifying the Leadership Skills That Matter Most Today," *INC.* (December 2014–January 2015): 78.

40. G. Colvin, "From High-Minded to High Value," *Fortune* (December 22, 2014): 38.

41. A. Bornstein and J. Bornstein, "What Makes a Great Leader?" *Entrepreneur* (March 2016): 36–44.

42. R. Fehr, K. C. Yam, and C. Dang, "Moralized Leadership: The Construction and Consequences of Ethical Leader Perceptions," *Academy of Management Review* 40, no. 2 (2015): 182–209.

43. D. A. Waldman and R. M. Balven, "Responsible Leadership: Theoretical Issues and Research Directions," *Academy of Management Perspectives* 28, no. 3 (2014): 224–234.

44. A. Murray, "The Moral Imperative for Leaders," *Fortune* (December 1, 2016): 6.

45. Edgewalkers International website, https://edgewalkers.org, accessed June 1, 2017.

46. J. Saraceno, "Conversation With Phil Jackson," *AARP Bulletin* (January–February 2014): 10.

47. Zig Ziglar website, www.ziglar.com, accessed June 1, 2017.

48. Y. Zhang, D. A. Waldman, Y. L. Han, and X. Li, "Paradoxical Leader Behaviors in People Management: Antecedents and Consequences," *Academy of Management Journal* 58, no. 2 (2015): 538–566.

49. K. Lewin, R. Lippert, and R. K. White, "Patterns of Aggressive Behavior in Experimentally Created Social Climates," *Journal of Social Psychology* 10 (1939): 271–301.

50. R. Likert, *New Patterns of Management* (New York: McGraw-Hill, 1961).

51. R. M. Stogdill and A. E. Coons, eds., *Leader Behavior: Its Description and Measurement* (Columbus: Ohio State University Bureau of Business Research, 1957).

52. R. Blake and J. Mouton, *The Leadership Grid III: Key to Leadership Excellence* (Houston: Gulf Publishing, 1985); R. Blake and A. A. McCanse, *Leadership Dilemmas—Grid Solutions* (Houston: Gulf Publishing, 1991).

53. P. Harvey, K. Madison, M. Martinko, T. R. Crook, and T. A. Crook, "Attribution Theory in the Organizational Sciences: The Road Traveled and the Path Ahead," *Academy of Management Perspectives* 28, no. 2 (2014): 128–146.

54. C. L. Pearce, C. L. Wassenaar, and C. C. Manz, "Is Shared Leadership the Key to Responsible Leadership?" *Academy of Management Perspectives* 28, no. 3 (2014): 275–288.

55. M. L. Besharov, "The Relational Ecology of Identification: How Organizational Identification Emerges When Individuals Hold Divergent Values," *Academy of Management Journal* 57, no. 5 (2014): 1485–1512.

56. B. Temple, "On Being in Charge," *INC.* (March 2015): 10.

57. A. S. Amezcua, M. G. Grimes, S. W. Bradley, and J. Wiklund, "Organizational Sponsorship and Founding Environments: A Contingency View on the Survival of Business-Incubated Firms, 1194–2007," *Academy of Management Journal* 56, no. 6 (2013): 1628–1654.

58. O. Ybarra, E. Kross, and J. S. Burks, "The Big Idea That Is Yet to Be: Toward a More Motivated, Contextual, and Dynamic Model of Emotional Intelligence," *Academy of Management Perspectives* 28, no. 2 (2014): 93–107.

59. Y. Zhang, D. A. Waldman, Y. L. Han, and X. Li, "Paradoxical Leader Behaviors in People Management: Antecedents and Consequences," *Academy of Management Journal* 58, no. 2 (2015): 538–566.

60. T. L. Stanko and C. M. Beckman, "Watching You Watching Me: Boundary Control and Capturing Attention in the Context of Ubiquitous Technology Use," *Academy of Management Journal* 58, no. 3 (2015): 712–738.

61. M. Whitman, "Most Powerful Women Advice," *Fortune* (November 17, 2014): 149.

62. F. Fiedler, *A Theory of Leadership Effectiveness* (New York: McGraw-Hill, 1967).

63. R. Tannenbaum and W. Schmidt, "How to Choose a Leadership Pattern," *Harvard Business Review* (May/June 1973): 166.

64. R. House, "A Path-Goal Theory of Leadership Effectiveness," *Administrative Science Quarterly* 16, no. 2 (1971): 321–329.

65. V. H. Vroom, "Leadership and the Decision-Making Process," *Organizational Dynamics* 28, no. 4 (2000): 82–94.

66. Ibid.

67. P. Hersey and K. Blanchard, "Life-Cycle Theory of Leadership," *Training and Development Journal* (June 1979): 94–100.

68. S. Kerr and J. Jermier, "Substitutes for Leadership: The Meaning and Measurement," *Organizational Behavior and Human Performance* 22 (1978): 375–403.

69. A. C. Cosper, "O Captain! My Captain!" *Entrepreneur* (March 2015): 14.

70. B. B. Baekgaard, "My Advice," *Fortune* (September 15, 2015): 40.

71. R. Greenfield, "The Future Is Bossless," *BusinessWeek* (July 13–18, 2015): 63.

72. C. C. Manz, "Taking the Self-Leadership High Road: Smooth Surface or Potholes Ahead?" *Academy of Management Perspectives* 29, no. 1 (2015): 132–151.

73. Added at the suggestion of reviewer David Diemer, Texas State University, added June 4, 2017.

74. S. Shellenbarger, "Leader? No, Be a Follower," *The Wall Street Journal* (September 30, 2015): D1, D3.

75. Harvard University website, https://www.hks.harvard.edu/about/faculty-staff-directory/barbara-kellerman, accessed June 4, 2017.

76. S. Shellenbarger, "Leader? No, Be a Follower," *The Wall Street Journal* (September 30, 2015): D1, D3.

77. A. C. Peng, J. M. Schaubroeck, and Y. Li, "Social Exchange Implications of Own and Coworkers' Experience of Supervisory Abuse," *Academy of Management Journal* 57, no. 5 (2014): 1385–1405.

78. F. K. Matta, B. A. Scott, J. Koopman, and D. E. Conlon, "Does Seeing 'Eye to Eye' Affect Work Engagement and Organizational Citizenship Behavior? A Role Theory Perspective on LMX Agreements," *Academy of Management Journal* 58, no. 6 (2014): 1686–1708.

79. S. J. Creary, B. B. Caza, and L. M. Roberts, "Out of the Box? How Managing a Subordinate's Multiple Identities Affects the Quality of a Manager–Subordinate Relationship," *Academy of Management Review* 40, no. 4 (2015): 538–562.

80. Ad, "Lynne Doughtie," *Fortune* (June 15, 2015): n.p.

81. D. L. Shapiro, P. Hom, W. Shen, and R. Agarwal, "How Do Leader Departures Affect Subordinates' Organizational Attachment? A 360-Degree Relational Perspective," *Academy of Management Review* 41, no. 3 (2015): 479–502.

82. S. Berfield, "The Clutter in Kip Tindell," *BusinessWeek* (February 23–March 1, 2015): 41–45.

83. E. Frauenheim, "Lessons From the Warriors," *Fortune.com* accessed June 2, 2017.

84. A. Wolfe, "Jack and Suzy Welch," *The Wall Street Journal* (February 21–22, 2015): C11.

85. D. L. Gamache, G. McNamara, M. J. Mannor, and R. E. Johnson, "Motivated to Acquire? The Impact of CEO Regulatory Focus on Firm Acquisitions," *Academy of Management Journal* 58, no. 4 (2015): 1261–1282.

86. D. Collinson and D. Tourish, "Teaching Leadership Critically: New Directions for Leadership Pedagogy," *Academy of Management Learning & Education* 14, no. 4 (2015): 576–594.

87. A. C. Cosper, "O Captain! My Captain!" *Entrepreneur* (March 2015): 14.

88. R. Ackoff, *Creating the Corporate Future* (New York: Wiley, 1981).

89. A. M. Carton, C. Murphy, and J. R. Clark, "A (Blurry) Vision of the Future: How Leader Rhetoric About Ultimate Goals Influences Performance," *Academy of Management Journal* 57, no. 6 (2014): 1544–1570.

90. E. Grijalva and P. D. Harms, "Narcissism: An Integrative Synthesis and Dominance Complementarity Model," *Academy of Management Perspectives* 28, no. 2 (2014): 108–127.

91. R. Fehr, K. C. Yam, and C. Dang, "Moralized Leadership: The Construction and Consequences of Ethical Leader Perceptions," *Academy of Management Review* 40, no. 2 (2015): 182–209.

92. A. M. Carton, C. Murphy, and J. R. Clark, "A (Blurry) Vision of the Future: How Leader Rhetoric About Ultimate Goals Influences Performance," *Academy of Management Journal* 57, no. 6 (2014): 1544–1570.

93. Mars company M&M's website, http://www.mymms.com, accessed June 2, 2017.

94. A. Pasztor, "Musk Offers Vision of Mars Flights," *The Wall Street Journal* (September 28, 2016): B1.

95. D. L. Gamache, G. McNamara, M. J. Mannor, and R. E. Johnson, "Motivated to Acquire? The Impact of CEO Regulatory Focus on Firm Acquisitions," *Academy of Management Journal* 58, no. 4 (2015): 1261–1282.

96. M. A. LePine, Y. Zhang, E. R. Crawford, and B. L. Rich, "Turning Their Pain to Gain: Charismatic Leader Influence on Follower Stress Appraisal and Job Performance," *Academy of Management Journal* 59, no. 3 (2016): 1036–1059.

97. E. Grijalva and P. D. Harms, "Narcissism: An Integrative Synthesis and Dominance Complementarity Model," *Academy of Management Perspectives* 28, no. 2 (2014): 108–127.

98. W. Isaacson, "Steve Jobs: The Biography …His Rivalry With Bill Gates," *Fortune* (November 7, 2011): 97–112.

99. J. Antonakis, M. Fenley, and S. Liechti, "Can Charisma Be Taught? Test of Two Interventions," *Academy of Management Learning & Education* 10, no. 3 (2011): 374–396.

100. Y. Zhang, J. A. Lepine, B. R. Buckman, and F. Wei, "It's Not Fair … Or Is It? The Role of Justice and Leadership in Explaining Work Stressor-Job Performance Relationships," *Academy of Management Journal* 57, no. 3 (2014): 675–697.

101. B. R. Spisak, M. J. O'Brien, N. Nicholson, and M. Van Vugt, "Niche Construction and the Evolution of Leadership," *Academy of Management Review* 40, no. 2 (2015): 291–306.

102. S. J. Creary, B. B. Caza, and L. M. Roberts, "Out of the Box? How Managing a Subordinate's Multiple Identities Affects the Quality of a Manager–Subordinate Relationship," *Academy of Management Review* 40, no. 4 (2015): 538–562.

103. D. Collinson and D. Tourish, "Teaching Leadership Critically: New Directions for Leadership Pedagogy," *Academy of Management Learning & Education* 14, no. 4 (2015): 576–594.

104. C. Dieterich and B. Eisen, "Amazon Stock Breaches $1,000," *The Wall Street Journal* (June 3–4, 2017): B1.

105. F. K. Matta, B. A. Scott, J. Koopman, and D. E. Conlon, "Does Seeing 'Eye to Eye' Affect Work Engagement and Organizational Citizenship Behavior? A Role Theory Perspective on LMX Agreements," *Academy of Management Journal* 58, no. 6 (2014): 1686–1708.

106. S. J. Creary, B. B. Caza, and L. M. Roberts, "Out of the Box? How Managing a Subordinate's Multiple Identities Affects the Quality of a Manager–Subordinate Relationship," *Academy of Management Review* 40, no. 4 (2015): 538–562.

107. M. Kelly, *Rediscovering Catholicism* (New York: Beacon, 2010).

108. B. M. Galvin, D. Lange, and B. E. Ashforth, "Narcissistic Organizational Identification: Seeing Oneself as Central to the Organization's Identity," *Academy of Management Review* 40, no. 2 (2015): 163–181.

109. R. C. Liden, S. J. Wayne, C. Liao, and J. D. Meuser, "Servant Leadership and Serving Culture: Influence on Individual and Unit Performance," *Academy of Management Journal* 57, no. 5 (2014): 1434–1452.

110. A. C. Cosper, "O Captain! My Captain!" *Entrepreneur* (March 2015): 14.

111. J. Clemmer, "Leadership Strategies," *Costco Connection* (April 2015): 13.

112. I. Berkovich, "Between Person and Person: Dialogical Pedagogy in Authentic Leadership Development," *Academy of Management Learning & Education* 13, no. 2 (2014): 245–264.

113. M. Kelly, *Rediscovering Catholicism* (New York: Beacon, 2010).

114. I. Berkovich, "Between Person and Person: Dialogical Pedagogy in Authentic Leadership Development," *Academy of Management Learning & Education* 13, no. 2 (2014): 245–264.

115. A. McConnon, "To Be a Leader, Watch Your Body Language," *The Wall Street Journal* (October 3, 2016): R8.

116. B. M. Galvin, D. Lange, and B. E. Ashforth, "Narcissistic Organizational Identification: Seeing Oneself as Central to the Organization's Identity," *Academy of Management Review* 40, no. 2 (2015): 163–181.

117. R. McCammon, "Faking It Right," *Entrepreneur* (December 2015): 15–16.

118. J. Saraceno, "Conversation With Phil Jackson," *AARP Bulletin* (January–February 2014): 10.

119. J. Bussey, "Leadership Lessons From the Generals," *The Wall Street Journal* (December 12, 2014): R10.

120. A. Wolfe, "Jack and Suzy Welch," *The Wall Street Journal* (February 21–22, 2015): C11.

121. J. Shotter and H. Tsoukas, "In Search of Phronesis: Leadership and the Art of Judgment," *Academy of Management Learning & Education* 13, no. 2 (2014): 224–243.

122. P. Jacquart and J. Antonakis, "When Does Charisma Matter for Top-Level Leaders? Effect of Attributional Ambiguity," *Academy of Management Journal* 59, no. 4 (2015): 1051–1074.

123. R. J. Reichard, S. A. Serrano, M. Condren, N. Wilder, M. Dollwet, and W. Wang, "Engaging in Cultural Trigger Events in the Development of Cultural Competence," *Academy of Management Learning & Education* 14, no. 4 (2015): 461–481.

124. M. Javidan, A. Bullough, and R. Dibble, "Mind the Game: Gender Differences in Global Leadership Self-Efficacies," *Academy of Management Journal* 30, no. 1 (2016): 59–73.

125. N. Waller and J. Lublin, "What's Holding Women Back in the Workplace?" *The Wall Street Journal* (September 30, 2015): C1, C2.

126. K. Lanaj and J. R. Hollenbeck, "Leadership Over-Emergence in Self-Managing Teams: The Role of Gender and Countervailing Biases," *Academy of Management Journal* 59, no. 5 (2015): 1476–1494.

127. A. Ruzo, "My Advice," *Fortune* (April 28, 2014): 30.

128. B. Stone, "Valley of the Boys," *BusinessWeek* (March 23–April 5, 2015): 14–16.

129. "The World's 50 Greatest Leaders," *Fortune* (April 1, 2015): 59–90.

130. Ad, "Lynne Doughtie," *Fortune* (June 15, 2015): n.p.

131. B. Stone, "Valley of the Boys," *BusinessWeek* (March 23–April 5, 2015): 14–16.

132. E. Mcgirt, "Google Searches Its Soul," *Fortune* (February 1, 2017): 49–56.

133. N. Waller and J. Lublin, "What's Holding Women Back in the Workplace?" *The Wall Street Journal* (September 30, 2015): C1, C2.

134. G. Colvin, "Personal Bests," *Fortune* (March 15, 2015): 106–110.

135. R. Reuteman, "Generation Gaps," *Entrepreneur* (March 2015): 43–48.

136. A. Wolfe, "Jack and Suzy Welch," *The Wall Street Journal* (February 21–22, 2015): C11.

137. Teradata, "Data-Driven Businesses Outperform," *Forbes* (February 9, 2015): 24.

138. A. V. Mey, "Publishing Discovers the Age of Disruption," *Fortune* (May 1, 2015): 26.

139. M. Ramsey, "Tesla's Model S Gets an Upgrade," *The Wall Street Journal* (April 9, 2015): B3.
140. C. L. Pearce, C. L. Wassenaar, and C. C. Manz, "Is Shared Leadership the Key to Responsible Leadership?" *Academy of Management Perspectives* 28, no. 3 (2014): 275–288.
141. R. Karlgaad, "Do Jerks Always Win?" *Forbes* (December 29, 2014): 44.
142. C. C. Manz, "Taking the Self-Leadership High Road: Smooth Surface or Potholes Ahead?" *Academy of Management Perspectives* 29, no. 1 (2015): 132–151.
143. G. O'Brien, "Safety First?" *Entrepreneur* (September 2015): 36.

Chapter 13

1. R. D. Costigan and K. E. Brink, "Another Perspective on MBA Program Alignment: An Investigation of Learning Goals," *Academy of Management Learning & Education* 14, no. 2 (2015): 260–276.
2. L. Tomkins and E. Ulus, "Is Narcissism Undermining Critical Reflection in Our Business Schools?" *Academy of Management Learning & Education* 14, no. 4 (2015): 595–606.
3. GE ad, "Identifying the Leadership Skills That Matter Most Today," *INC.* (December 2014–January 2015): 78.
4. D. M. Ames and A. S. Wazlawek, "How to Tell If You're a Jerk in the Office," *The Wall Street Journal* (February 23, 2015): R2.
5. K. E. Brink and R. D. Costigan, "Oral Communication Skills: Are the Priorities of the Workplace and AACSB-Accredited Business Programs Aligned?" *Academy of Management Learning & Education* 14, no. 2 (2015): 205–221.
6. K. Davidson, "Hard to Find: Workers With Good 'Soft Skills,'" *The Wall Street Journal* (August 31, 2016), B1, B6.
7. J. Robinson, "Up, Down and Sideways," *Entrepreneur* (December 2015): 59.
8. GE ad, "Identifying the Leadership Skills That Matter Most Today," *INC.* (December 2014–January 2015): 78.
9. F. P. Morgeson, T. R. Mitchell, and D. Liu, "Event System Theory: An Event-Oriented Approach to the Organizational Sciences," *Academy of Management Review* 40, no. 4 (2015): 515–537.
10. GE ad, "Identifying the Leadership Skills That Matter Most Today," *INC.* (December 2014–January 2015): 78.
11. N. J. Fast, E. R. Burris, and C. A. Bartel, "Managing to Stay in the Dark: Managerial Self-Efficacy, Ego Defensiveness, and the Aversion to Employee Voice," *Academy of Management Journal* 57, no. 4 (2014): 1013–1034.
12. B. Snyder, "Tech's Next Disruption: The Org Chart," *Fortune* (June 15, 2015): 90.
13. Ibid.
14. G. Colvin, "The Benefit of Baring It All," *Fortune* (December 2015), 34.
15. J. Naisbitt, "On Power," *Forbes* (November 21, 2015): 160.
16. G. F. Davis, "Can an Economy Survive Without Corporations? Technology and Robust Organizational Alternatives," *Academy of Management Perspectives* 30, no. 2 (2016): 129–140.
17. G. Colvin, "Humans Are Underrated," *Fortune* (August 1, 2015): 100–113.
18. M. R. Hass, P. Criscuolo, and G. George, "Which Problems to Solve? Online Knowledge Sharing and Attention Allocation in Organizations," *Academy of Management Journal* 58, no. 3 (2015): 680–711.
19. A. Rosenbush, "At the Helm of the Digital Transformation," *The Wall Street Journal* (February 10, 2016): R1.
20. M. R. Hass, P. Criscuolo, and G. George, "Which Problems to Solve? Online Knowledge Sharing and Attention Allocation in Organizations," *Academy of Management Journal* 58, no. 3 (2015): 680–711.
21. R. Blumenstein, "The Mistakes Firms Make With Big Data," *The Wall Street Journal* (February 10, 2016): R1.
22. J. Ankeny, "20/20 Visions," *Entrepreneur* (January 2015): 32–36.
23. Staff, "The Meaning of Big Data," *Fortune* (June 16, 2014): 232.
24. B. O'Keefe, "The Chosen One," *Fortune* (June 15, 2015): 134–144.
25. M. Schlangenstein, "Southwest Tries to Squash Its Tech Bugs," *BusinessWeek* (August 8–16, 2016): 23–24.
26. N. O. Giles, "Which Devices Rule the Workplace?" *The Wall Street Journal* (March 14, 2016): R6.
27. J. Tyrangiel, "Introduction to Code," *BusinessWeek* (June 15–28, 2015): 13.
28. Staff, "Pinning Down the Cloud," *Forbes* (July 20, 2015): 86–87.
29. H. J. Wilson and P. R. Daugherty, "Remember When We Used to Look at Screens?" *The Wall Street Journal* (October 14, 2015): R3.
30. M. E. Belicove, "The New New Thing," *Entrepreneur* (May 2015): 84.
31. S. Higginbotham, "The Cloud Is Dead. Long Live the Cloud," *Fortune* (May 1, 2015): 58.
32. C. Mims, "The Internet of Things Isn't About Things—It's About Services," *The Wall Street Journal* (August 22, 2016): B1, B6.
33. K. Stock, "Briefs: Look Sharp!" *BusinessWeek* (April 6–12, 2015): 23.
34. Staff, "Retail Bailout," *Forbes* (June 13, 2017): 94–98.
35. R. Charan, "The Algorithmic CEO," *Fortune* (January 22, 2015): 45–46.
36. R. Winkler, "Google Pushes Its Own Content," *The Wall Street Journal* (August 19, 2014): B1, B5.
37. M. Villano, "The Sharing Economy 2.0," *Entrepreneur* (December 2014): 58.
38. L. Rao, "Money for Nothing," *Fortune* (January 1, 2016): 36.
39. J. Alsever, "Managing on the Go," *Fortune* (April 2015): 42.
40. ComScore, "The Stat," *Entrepreneur* (July 2015): 60.
41. K. Noyes, "To the Cloud?" *Fortune* (November 17, 2014): 52.
42. N. O. Giles, "Which Devices Rule the Workplace?" *The Wall Street Journal* (March 14, 2016): R6.
43. Ad, "The Connected Cloud," *Fortune* (January 1, 2016): 44–45.
44. L. Weber, "Overtime Pay for Answering Late-Night Emails," *The Wall Street Journal* (May 21, 2015): B1, B6.
45. M. M. Butts, W. J. Becker, and W. R. Boswell, "Hot Buttons and Time Sinks: The Effects of Electronic Communication During Nonwork Time on Emotions and Work-Nonwork Conflict," *Academy of Management Journal* 58, no. 3 (2015): 763–788.
46. T. L. Stanko and C. M. Beckman, "Watching You Watching Me: Boundary Control and Capturing Attention in the Context of Ubiquitous Technology Use," *Academy of Management Journal* 58, no. 3 (2015): 712–738.
47. C. Zakrzewski, "The Key to Getting Workers to Stop Wasting Time Online," *The Wall Street Journal* (March 14, 2016): R4.
48. C. Hann, "Goofing Off Online," *Entrepreneur* (November 2014): 36.
49. L. Weber, "No Personal Calls on the Job? No Thanks," *The Wall Street Journal* (May 9, 2012): B10.
50. E. Dwoskin, "Data Privacy: Test Your Knowledge," *The Wall Street Journal* (April 20, 2015): R6.
51. B. Stone and S. Frier, "Facebook's Next Decade," *BusinessWeek* (February 3–9, 2014): 44–49.
52. Survey, "Greatest Challenge?" *Fortune* (June 15, 2015): 16.
53. R. Hackett, "Tech," *Fortune* (May 1, 2015): 53.
54. R. Hackett, "Briefing," *Fortune* (January 1, 2017): 16.
55. J. Shin, "Malware Creeps Into Apple Apps," *The Wall Street Journal* (September 21, 2015): B1, B6.
56. Ad, "4 Ways Your Company Could Be Vulnerable," *Fortune* (May 1, 2015): 241.
57. D. Lawrence, "Tracking the Enemy Within," *BusinessWeek* (March 16–22, 2015): 39–41.
58. Ad, "Know the Threat," *Fortune* (May 1, 2015): 15.
59. R. Khasandv, "Spy Tech That Reads Your Mind," *Fortune* (July 1, 2016): 73–75.
60. M. L. Turner, "Remote Control," *Entrepreneur* (January 2016): 75–79.
61. K. Kokalitcheva, "The Bloodstream of the Enterprise," *Fortune* (November 1, 2015): 105.
62. Ad, "Riverbed," *BusinessWeek* (May 25, 2015): 23.
63. Staff, "Pinning Down the Cloud," *Forbes* (July 20, 2015): 86–87.
64. J. Rodkin and F. Levy, "Recruiting Preferred Skills," *BusinessWeek* (April 13–19, 2015): 43.
65. L. Weber and M. Korn, "Where Did All the Entry-Level Jobs Go?" *The Wall Street Journal* (August 6, 2014): B6.
66. E. Bernstein, "The Hidden Benefits of Chitchat," *The Wall Street Journal* (August 13, 2013): D1, D2.
67. B. M. Cole, "Lessons From a Martial Arts Dojo: A Prolonged Process Model of High-Context Communication," *Academy of Management Journal* 58, no. 2 (2015): 567–591.
68. E. Bernstein, "Honey, You Never Said …," *The Wall Street Journal* (March 24, 2015): D1, D4.
69. W. L. Bedwell, S. M. Fiore, and E. Salas, "Developing the Future Workforce: An Approach for Integrating Interpersonal Skills Into the MBA Classroom," *Academy of Management Learning & Education* 13, no. 2 (2014): 171–186.
70. N. Brodsky, "Shut Up and Listen," *INC.* (March 2015): 58.
71. J. Robinson, "Pay Attention!" *Entrepreneur* (September 2014): 60–65.
72. Ibid.
73. J. Bussey, "Leadership Lessons From the Generals," *The Wall Street Journal* (December 12, 2014): R10.
74. B. M. Cole, "Lessons From a Martial Arts Dojo: A Prolonged Process Model of High-Context Communication," *Academy of Management Journal* 58, no. 2 (2015): 567–591.
75. Niki's Int'l Ltd. website, https://nilservices.com/, accessed June 8, 2017.
76. Suggestion of reviewer Charles Mambula, Langston University, added June 8, 2017.
77. W. L. Bedwell, S. M. Fiore, and E. Salas, "Developing the Future Workforce: An Approach for Integrating Interpersonal Skills Into the MBA Classroom," *Academy of Management Learning & Education* 13, no. 2 (2014): 171–186.
78. Niki's Int'l Ltd. website, https://nilservices.com/, accessed June 8, 2017.
79. Editors, "Putting Communication Front and Center in Institutional Theory and Analysis," *Academy of Management Review* 40, no. 1 (2015): 10–27.
80. W. L. Bedwell, S. M. Fiore, and E. Salas, "Developing the Future Workforce: An Approach for Integrating Interpersonal Skills Into the MBA Classroom," *Academy of Management Learning & Education* 13, no. 2 (2014): 171–186.
81. K. E. Brink and R. D. Costigan, "Oral Communication Skills: Are the Priorities of the Workplace and AACSB-Accredited Business Programs Aligned?" *Academy of Management Learning & Education* 14, no. 2 (2015): 205–221.
82. S. Dembling, "Should I Stay or Should I Go?" *Entrepreneur* (August 2014): 28.
83. L. Hochwald, "The Personal Touch," *Entrepreneur* (December 2014): 96.
84. Ad, "Mutual of America," *INC.* (June 2017): 95.
85. S. Sandberg, quote in *Fortune* (October 1, 2015): 114.
86. A. Gogo, "Productivity Hack," *Fortune* (October 1, 2015): 114.
87. I. Khrennikov, "Now the Boss Can Monitor Your Phone," *BusinessWeek* (June 27 to July 3, 2016): 31–32.

88. J. Queenan, "Speak No Evil," *The Wall Street Journal* (June 14–15, 2014): C1, C2.

89. D. Eng, "How to Get Over Yourself," *Fortune* (March 1, 2015): 36.

90. S. Shellenbarger, "Raise a Glass, Give a Speech, Without a Stumble," *The Wall Street Journal* (December 23, 2015): D3.

91. A. McConnon, "To Be a Leader, Watch Your Body Language," *The Wall Street Journal* (October 3, 2016): R8.

92. W. L. Bedwell, S. M. Fiore, and E. Salas, "Developing the Future Workforce: An Approach for Integrating Interpersonal Skills Into the MBA Classroom," *Academy of Management Learning & Education* 13, no. 2 (2014): 171–186.

93. R. McCammon, "Zap! Session," *Entrepreneur* (February 2014): 32–33.

94. S. Shellenbarger, "You Really Look Smart," *The Wall Street Journal* (January 4, 2015): D1, D2.

95. S. Shellenbarger, "You Really Look Smart," *The Wall Street Journal* (January 4, 2015): D1, D2.

96. S. Reddy, "Walk This Way: Acting Happy Can Make It So," *The Wall Street Journal* (November 18, 2014): D3.

97. S. Dembling, "Should I Stay or Should I Go?" *Entrepreneur* (August 2014): 28.

98. C. Hann, "Keep a Level Head," *Entrepreneur* (January 2016): 23.

99. R. K. Ross, "Recognizing Employee Disengagement … and Taking Steps to Re-engage," *Costco Connection* (December 2014): 13–14.

100. S. Reddy, "Walk This Way: Acting Happy Can Make It So," *The Wall Street Journal* (November 18, 2014): D3.

101. A. McConnon, "To Be a Leader, Watch Your Body Language," *The Wall Street Journal* (October 3, 2016): R8.

102. S. Shellenbarger, "You Really Look Smart," *The Wall Street Journal* (January 4, 2015): D1, D2.

103. A. C. Cosper, "Creating Relevance," *Entrepreneur* (May 2015): 10.

104. Survey, "CEO Survey," *INC.* (September 2014): 78.

105. A. Handley, "Words of Wisdom," *Entrepreneur* (October 2014): 38.

106. S. Shellenbarger, "Stop Wasting Everyone's Time," *The Wall Street Journal* (December 3, 2014): D1, D3.

107. A. Handley, "Before You Hit Send," *Entrepreneur* (January 2015): 28–29.

108. A. Handley, "Detox Your Inbox," *Entrepreneur* (November 2014): 34.

109. R. McCammon, "So, Here's the Bad News …" *Entrepreneur* (July 2015): 24–25.

110. J. R. Hollenbeck and B. B. Jamieson, "Human Capital, Social Capital, and Social Network Analysis," *Academy of Perspectives* 29, no. 3 (2015): 370–365.

111. E. Griffith, "Facebook's Video Invasion," *Fortune* (June 15, 2015): 149–151.

112. Editors, "Putting Communication Front and Center in Institutional Theory and Analysis," *Academy of Management Review* 40, no. 1 (2015): 10–27.

113. W. L. Bedwell, S. M. Fiore, and E. Salas, "Developing the Future Workforce: An Approach for Integrating Interpersonal Skills Into the MBA Classroom," *Academy of Management Learning & Education* 13, no. 2 (2014): 171–186.

114. B. B. Baekgaard, "My Advice," *Fortune* (September 15, 2015): 40.

115. S. Pinker, "When Being Too Smart Ruins Writing," *The Wall Street Journal* (September 27–28, 2014): C3.

116. R. McCammon, "I'm Sure You're Wondering Why I've Called You All Here," *Entrepreneur* (March 2015): 28–29.

117. D. M. Ames and A. S. Wazlawek, "How to Tell If You're a Jerk in the Office," *The Wall Street Journal* (February 23, 2015): R2.

118. Ibid.

119. S. H. Harrison and E. D. Rouse, "An Inductive Study of Feedback Interactions Over the Course of Creative Projects," *Academy of Management Journal* 59, no. 3 (2016): 841–859.

120. T. Robbines, "Questions Are the Answer," *Fortune* (November 17, 2014): 140.

121. E. Bernstein, "You Can Do It! Be a Motivator," *The Wall Street Journal* (June 16, 2016): D1, D3.

122. E. Bernstein, "The Hidden Benefits of Chitchat," *The Wall Street Journal* (August 13, 2013): D1, D2.

123. J. Lauder, "Most Powerful Women Advice," *Fortune* (November 17, 2014): 149.

124. E. Bernstein, "How Well Are You Listening?" *The Wall Street Journal* (January 13, 2015): D1, D4.

125. F. Feiberbaum, "Forget-Me-Nots," *Costco Connection* (June 2016): 37.

126. Ibid.

127. J. Steinberg, "Advice Quote," *Fortune* (October 1, 2015): 116.

128. R. B. Pollock, "CEO 101," *Fortune* (November 17, 2014): 130.

129. H. Ersek, "CEO 101," *Fortune* (November 17, 2014): 132.

130. N. Brodsky, "Shut Up and Listen," *INC.* (March 2015): 58.

131. Ibid.

132. F. Feiberbaum, "Forget-Me-Nots," *Costco Connection* (June 2016): 37.

133. Ibid.

134. W. L. Bedwell, S. M. Fiore, and E. Salas, "Developing the Future Workforce: An Approach for Integrating Interpersonal Skills Into the MBA Classroom," *Academy of Management Learning & Education* 13, no. 2 (2014): 171–186.

135. E. Bernstein, "How Well Are You Listening?" *The Wall Street Journal* (January 13, 2015): D1, D4.

136. Ibid.

137. R. McCammon, "Don't Pop Your Top," *Entrepreneur* (May 2016): 15–16.

138. E. Bernstein, "You Can Do It! Be a Motivator," *The Wall Street Journal* (June 16, 2016): D1, D3.

139. Ibid.

140. B. Murphy, "4 Habits of Exceptional Bosses," *INC.* (June 2016): 12.

141. E. Bernstein, "You Can Do It! Be a Motivator," *The Wall Street Journal* (June 16, 2016): D1, D3.

142. Ibid.

143. E. Bernstein, "How Well Are You Listening?" *The Wall Street Journal* (January 13, 2015): D1, D4.

144. S. Fowler, "Improve Your Motivation," *Costco Connection* (January 2015): 15.

145. R. McCammon, "Can We Talk," *Entrepreneur* (May 2015): 25–26.

146. A. Chen, "More Rational Resolutions," *The Wall Street Journal* (December 31, 2013): D1, D2.

147. B. Murphy, "4 Habits of Exceptional Bosses," *INC.* (June 2016): 12.

148. D. Goleman, *Emotional Intelligence* (New York: Bantam, 1995) and *Working With Emotional Intelligence* (New York: Bantam, 1999).

149. C. Sandler, "Business Lessons From *The Art of War*," *Costco Connection* (May 2014): 15.

150. G. Colvin, "What Really Has the 99% Up in Arms," *Fortune* (November 7, 2011): 87.

151. J. Robinson, "Where There's Willpower, There's a Way," *Entrepreneur* (July 2015): 50–54.

152. S. Shellenbarger, "To Fight or Not to Fight? When to Pick Workplace Battles," *The Wall Street Journal* (December 17, 2014): D1, D2.

153. S. Shellenbarger, "Find Out What Your Boss Really Thinks About You," *The Wall Street Journal* (June 29, 2016): D1, D2.

154. R. McCammon, "Can We Talk," *Entrepreneur* (May 2015): 25–26.

155. E. Bernstein, "Venting Isn't Good for Us," *The Wall Street Journal* (August 11, 2015): D1, D4.

156. J. Whalen, "Angry Outbursts Really Do Hurt Your Health, Doctors Find," *The Wall Street Journal* (March 24, 2015): D1, D4.

157. E. Bernstein, "Thou Shalt Not Send in Anger," *The Wall Street Journal* (October 21, 2014): D1.

158. C. Sandler, "Business Lessons From *The Art of War*," *Costco Connection* (May 2014): 15.

159. R. McCammon, "Don't Pop Your Top," *Entrepreneur* (May 2016): 15–16.

160. R. McCammon, "How to Own the Room," *BusinessWeek* online, accessed May 18, 2017.

161. S. Shellenbarger, "Relax? Don't You Tell Me to Relax!" *The Wall Street Journal* (August 17, 2016): D1, D2.

162. E. Bernstein, "You Can Do It! Be a Motivator," *The Wall Street Journal* (June 16, 2016): D1, D3.

163. S. Shellenbarger, "Relax? Don't You Tell Me to Relax!" *The Wall Street Journal* (August 17, 2016): D1, D2.

164. E. Bernstein, "Venting Isn't Good for Us," *The Wall Street Journal* (August 11, 2015): D1, D4.

165. E. Bernstein, "To Be a Friend in a Time of Need, Talk Less, and Listen More," *The Wall Street Journal* (August 24, 2014): D1, D2.

166. M. Korn and R. Feintzeig, "Is the Old-School, Hard-Nosed Boss Obsolete?" *The Wall Street Journal* (May 23, 2014): B1, B2.

167. G. Colvin, "Employers Are Looking for New Hires With Something Extra: Empathy," *Fortune* (September 4, 2014): 55.

168. I. Berkovich, "Between Person and Person: Dialogical Pedagogy in Authentic Leadership Development," *Academy of Management Learning & Education* 13, no. 2 (2014): 245–264.

169. B. Murphy, "4 Habits of Exceptional Bosses," *INC.* (June 2016): 12.

170. R. McCammon, "So, Here's the Bad News …" *Entrepreneur* (July 2015): 24–25.

171. H. Ersek, "CEO 101," *Fortune* (November 17, 2014): 132.

172. E. Bernstein, "How Well Are You Listening?" *The Wall Street Journal* (January 13, 2015): D1, D4.

173. K. Clark, "Why the Seahawks Like Confrontation," *The Wall Street Journal* (January 8, 2015): D6.

174. R. Feintzeig, "When Nice Is a Four-Letter Word," *The Wall Street Journal* (December 31, 2015): D1, D3.

175. S. Shellenbarger, "It's Not My Fault! A Better Response to Criticism at Work," *The Wall Street Journal* (June 18, 2014): D1, D4.

176. M. Kelly, *Rediscovering Catholicism* (New York: Beacon, 2010).

177. R. Feintzeig, "When Nice Is a Four-Letter Word," *The Wall Street Journal* (December 31, 2015): D1, D3.

178. E. Bernstein, "Venting Isn't Good for Us," *The Wall Street Journal* (August 11, 2015): D1, D4.

179. R. Feintzeig, "When Nice Is a Four-Letter Word," *The Wall Street Journal* (December 31, 2015): D1, D3.

180. S. Shellenbarger, "Find Out What Your Boss Really Thinks About You," *The Wall Street Journal* (June 29, 2016): D1, D2.

181. L. Adler, "4 Common Leadership Fears and How to Avoid Them," *INC.* (April 2015): 10.

182. S. Shellenbarger, "Find Out What Your Boss Really Thinks About You," *The Wall Street Journal* (June 29, 2016): D1, D2.

183. N. J. Fast, E. R. Burris, and C. A. Bartel, "Managing to Stay in the Dark: Managerial Self-Efficacy, Ego Defensiveness, and the Aversion to Employee Voice," *Academy of Management Journal* 57, no. 4 (2014): 1013–1034.

184. S. Shellenbarger, "It's Not My Fault! A Better Response to Criticism at Work," *The Wall Street Journal* (June 18, 2014): D1, D4.

185. R. McCammon, "How to Own the Room," *BusinessWeek* online, accessed May 18, 2017.

186. G. Anders, "The Other Social Network," *Forbes* (July 16, 2012): 76–84.

187. J. Tarmy, "Facebook at Work Is Late to the Office," *BusinessWeek* (January 26–February 1, 2015): 33–34.

188. J. Hempel, "The Second Coming of Facebook," *Fortune* (April 29, 2013): 73–78.

189. J. H. McWhorter, "What the World Will Speak in 2115," *The Wall Street Journal* (January 3–4, 2015): C1, C2.

190. B. M. Cole, "Lessons From a Martial Arts Dojo: A Prolonged Process Model of High-Context Communication," *Academy of Management Journal* 58, no. 2 (2015): 567–591.

191. E. Bernstein, "How Well Are You Listening?" *The Wall Street Journal* (January 13, 2015): D1, D4.

192. Staff, "Crying at Work," *Entrepreneur* (October 2014): 16.

193. J. Lipman, "Women at Work: A Guide for Men," *The Wall Street Journal* (December 13–14, 2014): C1, C2.

194. J. Levitz, "When It Comes to Office Technology, Millennials Are Boss," *The Wall Street Journal* (June 23, 2015): A1, A10.

195. G. Colvin, "Employers Are Looking for New Hires With Something Extra: Empathy," *Fortune* (September 4, 2014): 55.

196. Staff, "Is Technology Making People Less Social," *The Wall Street Journal* (May 11, 2015): R4.

197. G. Colvin, "Humans Are Underrated," *Fortune* (August 1, 2015): 100–113.

198. E. Griffith, "Empathy, Thanks to Algorithms," *Fortune* (June 15, 2015): 88–90.

199. L. A. Mainiero and K. J. Jones, "Sexual Harassment Versus Workplace Romance: Social Media Spillover and Textual Harassment in the Workplace," *Academy of Management Perspectives* 27, no. 3 (2013): 187–203.

200. J. Bercovici, "Social Media's New Mad Men," *Forbes* (November 2014): 71–82.

201. D. Seetharaman, "Facebook's Female Engineers Claim Bias," *The Wall Street Journal* (May 3, 2017): B1.

202. E. Griffith, "The Ugly Unethical Underside of Silicon Valley," *Fortune* (January 1, 2017): 73–77.

203. T. L. Stanko and C. M. Beckman, "Watching You Watching Me: Boundary Control and Capturing Attention in the Context of Ubiquitous Technology Use," *Academy of Management Journal* 58, no. 3 (2015): 712–738.

Chapter 14

1. D. J. Teece, "The Foundations of Enterprise Performance: Dynamic and Ordinary Capabilities in an (Economic) Theory of Firms," *Academy of Management Perspectives* 28, no. 4 (2014): 328–352.

2. M. R. Barrick, G. R. Thurgood, T. A. Smith, and S. H. Courtright, "Collective Organizational Engagement: Linking Motivational Antecedents, Strategic Implementation, and Firm Performance," *Academy of Management Journal* 58, no. 1 (2015): 111–135.

3. A. Murray, "Should Leaders Be Modest?" *Fortune* (September 15, 2015): 28.

4. V. Harnish, "5 Crucial Performance Metrics," *Fortune* (August 1, 2016): 32.

5. V. Harnish, "5 Ways to Stay Ahead of Rising Costs," *Fortune* (April 28, 2014): 32.

6. E. Grijalva and P. D. Harms, "Narcissism: An Integrative Synthesis and Dominance Complementarity Model," *Academy of Management Perspectives* 28, no. 2 (2014): 108–127.

7. R. L. Hoefer and S. E. Green, "A Rhetorical Model of Institutional Decision Making: The Role of Rhetoric in the Formation and Change of Legitimacy Judgments," *Academy of Management Review* 41, no. 1 (2016): 130–150.

8. R. Krause and G. Brunton, "Who Does the Monitoring?" *Academy of Management Review* 39, no. 1 (2014): 111–112.

9. V. F. Misangyi and A. G. Acharya, "Substitutes or Complements? A Configurational Examination of Corporate Governance Mechanisms," *Academy of Management Journal* 57, no. 6 (2014): 1681–1705.

10. Editors, "Rethinking Governance in Management Research," *Academy of Management Journal* 57, no. 6 (2014): 1535–1543.

11. Added at the suggestion of reviewer C. Blencke, University of Central Florida, June 14, 2017.

12. R. P. Garrett and J. G. Covin, "Internal Corporate Venture Operations Independence and Performance: A Knowledge-Based Perspective," *Entrepreneurship Theory and Practice* 39, no. 4 (2015): 763–790.

13. L. Weber, "Nowhere to Hide for 'Dead Wood' Workers," *The Wall Street Journal* (August 22, 2016): A1, A10.

14. B. Haislip, "There Is Never Enough Time," *The Wall Street Journal* (October 26, 2015): R4.

15. R. Reuteman, "Accentuate the Negative," *Entrepreneur* (February 2015): 44–45.

16. R. Bachman, "The Week Resolutions Die," *The Wall Street Journal* (January 20, 2015): D1, D4.

17. E. Van Oosten and K. E. Kram, "Coaching for Change," *Academy of Management Learning & Education* 13, no. 2 (2014): 295–298.

18. Dialogue, "Is Decoupling Becoming Decoupled From Institutional Theory? A Commentary on Wijen," *Academy of Management Review* 40, no. 2 (2015): 307–313.

19. C. Carr, "Stress to Impress," *Costco Connection* (February 2015): 13.

20. D. A. Waldman and R. M. Balven, "Responsible Leadership: Theoretical Issues and Research Directions," *Academy of Management Perspectives* 28, no. 3 (2014): 224–234.

21. V. Harnish, "5 Crucial Performance Metrics," *Fortune* (August 1, 2016): 32.

22. C. Hann, "Dedicated to You," *Entrepreneur* (September 2013): 24.

23. A. Stuart, "Metrics Sell Doughnuts and More," *The Wall Street Journal* (December 22, 2015): B6.

24. A. Canato, "Coerced Practice Implementation in Cases of Low Cultural Fit: Cultural Change and Practice Adaptation During the Implementation of Six Sigma at 3M," *Academy of Management Journal* 56, no. 6 (2013): 1724–1753.

25. S. S. Wiltermuth, "Power, Moral Clarity, and Punishment in the Workplace," *Academy of Management Journal* 56, no. 4 (2013): 1002–1023.

26. E. Bernstein, "The Smart Path to a Transparent Workplace," *The Wall Street Journal* (February 23, 2015): R5.

27. L. Jia, J. D. Shaw, A. S. Tsue, and T. Y. Park, "A Social-Structural Perspective on Employee-Organization Relationships and Team Creativity," *Academy of Management Journal* 57, no. 3 (2014): 869–891.

28. J. Tozzi, "What Does Good Medical Look Like?" *BusinessWeek* (May 5–11, 2015): 28–29.

29. B. Dummett, "Costs Cuts Narrow BlackBerry's Loss," *The Wall Street Journal* (September 27–28, 2014): B3.

30. D. Chandler, "Morals, Markets, and Values-Based Business," *Academy of Management Review* 39, no. 3 (2014): 396–397.

31. E. Grijalva and P. D. Harms, "Narcissism: An Integrative Synthesis and Dominance Complementarity Model," *Academy of Management Perspectives* 28, no. 2 (2014): 108–127.

32. Dialogue, "Is Decoupling Becoming Decoupled From Institutional Theory? A Commentary on Wijen," *Academy of Management Review* 40, no. 2 (2015): 307–313.

33. T. S. Liao, J. Rice, and J. C. Lu, "The Vicissitudes of Competitive Advantage: Empirical Evidence From Australian Manufacturing SMEs," *Journal of Small Business Management* 53, no. 2 (2015): 469–481.

34. V. Harnish, "5 Crucial Performance Metrics," *Fortune* (August 1, 2016): 32.

35. D. A. Waldman and R. M. Balven, "Responsible Leadership: Theoretical Issues and Research Directions," *Academy of Management Perspectives* 28, no. 3 (2014): 224–234.

36. E. Bernstein, "Don't Apologize So Fast," *The Wall Street Journal* (July 15, 2014): D1, D4.

37. R. L. Hoefer and S. E. Green, "A Rhetorical Model of Institutional Decision Making: The Role of Rhetoric in the Formation and Change of Legitimacy Judgments," *Academy of Management Review* 41, no. 1 (2016): 130–150.

38. M. T. Wolfe and D. A. Shepherd, "Bouncing Back From a Loss: Entrepreneurial Orientations, Emotions, and Failure Narratives," *Entrepreneurship Theory and Practice* 39, no. 3 (2015): 675–700.

39. E. Bernstein, "The Smart Path to a Transparent Workplace," *The Wall Street Journal* (February 23, 2015): R5.

40. G. O'Brien, "It's All Your Fault!" *Entrepreneur* (February 2015): 30.

41. E. Whitford, "Management Playbook," *INC.* (April 2014): 46–47.

42. E. Bernstein, "The Smart Path to a Transparent Workplace," *The Wall Street Journal* (February 23, 2015): R5.

43. M. E. Chan and D. J. McAllister, "Abusive Supervision Through the Lens of Employee State Paranoia," *Academy of Management Review* 39, no. 1 (2014): 44–66.

44. Added at the suggestion of reviewer Professor David Biemer, Texas State University, June 15, 2017.

45. R. P. Garrett and J. G. Covin, "Internal Corporate Venture Operations Independence and Performance: A Knowledge-Based Perspective," *Entrepreneurship Theory and Practice* 39, no. 4 (2015): 763–790.

46. H. Lian, D. J. Brown, D. L. Ferris, L. H. Liang, L. M. Keeping, and R. Morrison, "Abusive Supervision and Retaliation: A Self-Control Framework," *Academy of Management Journal* 57, no. 1 (2014): 116–139.

47. W. E. D. Creed, B. A. Hudson, G. A. Okhuysen, and K. S. Crowe, "Swimming in a Sea of Shame: Incorporating Emotion Into Explanations of Institutional Reproduction and Change," *Academy of Management Review* 39, no. 3 (2014): 275–301.

48. C. C. Manz, "Taking the Self-Leadership High Road: Smooth Surface or Potholes Ahead?" *Academy of Management Perspectives* 29, no. 1 (2015): 132–151.

49. M. Berman, "The No-Boss Company," *The Wall Street Journal* (October 27, 2015): R3.

50. R. C. Liden, S. J. Wayne, C. Liao, and J. D. Meuser, "Servant Leadership and Serving Culture: Influence on Individual and Unit Performance," *Academy of Management Journal* 57, no. 5 (2014): 1434–1452.

51. C. C. Manz, "Taking the Self-Leadership High Road: Smooth Surface or Potholes Ahead?" *Academy of Management Perspectives* 29, no. 1 (2015): 132–151.

52. Y. Zhang, D. A. Waldman, Y. L. Han, and X. Li, "Paradoxical Leader Behaviors in People Management: Antecedents and Consequences," *Academy of Management Journal* 58, no. 2 (2015): 538–566.

53. V. Harnish, "5 Ways to Stay Ahead of Rising Costs," *Fortune* (April 28, 2014): 32.

54. W. Su and E. W. K. Tsang, "Product Diversification and Financial Performance: The Moderating Role of Secondary Stakeholders," *Academy of Management Journal* 58, no. 4 (2015): 1128–1148.

55. I. Filatotchev and C. Nakajima, "Corporate Governance, Responsible Managerial Behavior, and Corporate Social Responsibility: Organizational Efficiency Versus Organizational Legitimacy," *Academy of Management Perspectives* 28, no. 3 (2014): 289–306.

56. Editors, "Rethinking Governance in Management Research," *Academy of Management Journal* 57, no. 6 (2014): 1535–1543.

57. Staff, "Data Champions," *Entrepreneur* (November 2015): 62.

58. T. Cettina, "Dump That Debt!" *Costco Connection* (January 2016): 26.

59. B. Greeley, "The Incredible Stickiness of Wages," *BusinessWeek* (September 22–28, 2014): 22–23.

60. "R. Spaeth, "CEO Wisdom," *BusinessWeek* (November 23–29, 2015): 25.

61. M. Colias and J. D. Stoll, "GM Takes Exit From Global Rush," *The Wall Street Journal* (March 7, 2017): B1, B2.

62. G. Nagesh and J. D. Stoll, "GM CEO: Focus on Margins Is Paying Off," *The Wall Street Journal* (September 25, 2015): B1, B2.

63. M. Colias and J. D. Stoll, "GM Takes Exit From Global Rush," *The Wall Street Journal* (March 7, 2017): B1, B2.

64. Staff, "The Two Keys to Profits," *INC.* (December 2014/January 2015): 80.

65. V. Harnish, "5 Ways to Stay Ahead of Rising Costs," *Fortune* (April 28, 2014): 32.

66. Amazon website, www.amazon.com, accessed June 15, 2017.

67. Staff, "Cutting Waste—or Creating Monopolies?" *BusinessWeek* (September 15–21, 2015): 31–32.

68. S. Berfield and N. Buhayar, "Things Are About to Get Ugly at Kraft," *BusinessWeek* (August 24–30, 2015): 18–19.

69. J. Worth, "Best-Laid Plans," *Entrepreneur* (June 2015): 72–73.

70. M. T. Wolfe and D. A. Shepherd, "Bouncing Back From a Loss: Entrepreneurial Orientations, Emotions, and Failure Narratives," *Entrepreneurship Theory and Practice* 39, no. 3 (2015): 675–700.

71. S. Russolillo, "LeBron Deal Won't Foul Nike," *The Wall Street Journal* (December 21, 2015): C1.

72. A. Chatterji and A. Patro, "Dynamic Capabilities and Managing Human Capital," *Academy of Management Perspectives* 28, no. 4 (2014): 395–408.

73. D. Sax, "How Finance Ruined Business," *BusinessWeek* online, accessed June 15, 2017.

74. D. J. Cumming, J. A. Pandes, and M. J. Robinson, "The Role of Agents in Private Entrepreneurial Finance," *Entrepreneurship Theory and Practice* 39, no. 2 (2015): 345–374.

75. J. Lahart, "Profiting From Spending More," *The Wall Street Journal* (June 24, 2016): C1.

76. S. Soper, "Amazon Sorts Itself Out for the Holidays," *BusinessWeek* (December 29, 2014–January 11, 2015): 33–34.

77. C. Fairchild, "Winning the Ground Game," *BusinessWeek* (April 28, 2014): 22.

78. J. Bennett, "GM to Raise Spending on New Cars," *The Wall Street Journal* (January 15, 2015): B8.

79. L. Shaw with C. Rahn, "Netflix Looks to the Old World for New Growth," *BusinessWeek* (September 15–21, 2014): 25–26.

80. S. Russolillo, "LeBron Deal Won't Foul Nike," *The Wall Street Journal* (December 21, 2015): C1.

81. N. Brodsky, "Don't Fear the Numbers," *INC.* (December 2015/January 2016): 80.

82. J. Worth, "Mr. Finance Fix-It," *Entrepreneur* (August 2015): 62–63.

83. Associated Press, "News Release," Charter.net, posted on homepage news August 10, 2011.

84. V. Harnish, "Five Questions to Ponder for 2015," *Fortune* (December 22, 2014): 36.

85. J. Worth, "Mr. Finance Fix-It," *Entrepreneur* (August 2015): 62–63.

86. T. Cettina, "Dump That Debt!" *Costco Connection* (January 2016): 26.

87. Staff, "Data Champions," *Entrepreneur* (November 2015): 62.

88. D. J. Cumming, J. A. Pandes, and M. J. Robinson, "The Role of Agents in Private Entrepreneurial Finance," *Entrepreneurship Theory and Practice* 39, no. 2 (2015): 345–374.

89. D. Seetharaman, "Facebook Investors Press Suit on Shares," *The Wall Street Journal* (December 10, 2016): B1, B2.

90. A. Von Tobel, "Get Financially Fit Before 2015," *INC.* (October 2014): 104.

91. Y. Zhang, D. A. Waldman, Y. L. Han, and X. Li, "Paradoxical Leader Behaviors in People Management: Antecedents and Consequences," *Academy of Management Journal* 58, no. 2 (2015): 538–566.

92. M. R. Barrick, G. R. Thurgood, T. A. Smith, and S. H. Courtright, "Collective Organizational Engagement: Linking Motivational Antecedents, Strategic Implementation, and Firm Performance," *Academy of Management Journal* 58, no. 1 (2015): 111–135.

93. E. Van Oosten and K. E. Kram, "Coaching for Change," *Academy of Management Learning & Education* 13, no. 2 (2014): 295–298.

94. C. Hann, "Goofing Off Online," *Entrepreneur* (November 2014): 36.

95. R. C. Liden, S. J. Wayne, C. Liao, and J. D. Meuser, "Servant Leadership and Serving Culture: Influence on Individual and Unit Performance," *Academy of Management Journal* 57, no. 5 (2014): 1434–1452.

96. L. Jia, J. D. Shaw, A. S. Tsue, and T. Y., Park, "A Social-Structural Perspective on Employee-Organization Relationships and Team Creativity," *Academy of Management Journal* 57, no. 3 (2014): 869–891.

97. Staff, "Decoding the DNA of the Entrepreneur," *INC.* (December 2015/January 2016): 53–59.

98. M. Weber, "Culture Matters: 7 Ways of Great Leaders," *Forbes* (October 20, 2014): 113.

99. A. Von Tobel, "Where Money Meets Morale," *INC.* (April 2014): 48–49.

100. Staff, "The Micromanager's Guide to Delegation," *INC.* (March 2014): 19.

101. E. Van Oosten and K. E. Kram, "Coaching for Change," *Academy of Management Learning & Education* 13, no. 2 (2014): 290–292.

102. A. L. Kenworthy, "Introduction; Coaching and Positive Emotions," *Academy of Management Learning & Education* 13, no. 2 (2014): 295–298.

103. L. Weber, "Nowhere to Hide for 'Dead Wood' Workers," *The Wall Street Journal* (August 22, 2016): A1, A10.

104. A. Von Tobel, "Where Money Meets Morale," *INC.* (April 2014): 48–49.

105. B. L. Rau, "The Oxford Handbook of Evidence-Based Management," *Academy of Management Learning & Education* 13, no. 3 (2014): 485–487.

106. M. Selman, "Manipulate Creative People," *BusinessWeek* (April 11, 2013): 92.

107. P. Lencioni, "Innovation Won't Get You Very Far," *INC.* (December 2014/January 2015): 102.

108. D. M. Ames and A. S. Wazlawek, "How to Tell If You're a Jerk in the Office," *The Wall Street Journal* (February 23, 2015): R2.

109. Added at the suggestion of reviewer Professor David Biemer, Texas State University, June 15, 2017.

110. S. Johnston, "The Benefits of Walking Meetings," *Costco Connection* (October 2014): 13.

111. F. Feiberbaum, "Forget-Me-Nots," *Costco Connection* (June 2016): 37.

112. Walmart website, www.walmart.com, accessed July 8, 2015.

113. J. Reingold, "Angela Ahrendts," *Fortune* (September 15, 2015): 101–118.

114. C. Hann, "Dedicated to You," *Entrepreneur* (September 2013): 24.

115. M. E. Chan and D. J. McAllister, "Abusive Supervision Through the Lens of Employee State Paranoia," *Academy of Management Review* 39, no. 1 (2014): 44–66.

116. R. McCammon, "The Worst of Times," *Entrepreneur* (February 2016): 15–16.

117. Added at the suggestion of reviewer C. Blencke, University of Central Florida, June 16, 2017.

118. P. Keegan, "The New Rules of Engagement," *INC.* (December 2014/January 2015): 86–132.

119. C. Hann, "Caught in the Cookie Jar," *Entrepreneur* (December 2014): 41.

120. J. A. Clair, "Procedural Injustice in the System of Peer Review and Scientific Misconduct," *Academy of Management Learning & Education* 14, no. 2 (2015): 159–172.

121. S. Shellenbarger, "You Don't Have to Be Loved at Work," *The Wall Street Journal* (October 14, 2015): D1, D3.

122. C. Hann, "Goofing Off Online," *Entrepreneur* (November 2014): 36.

123. E. Grijalva and P. D. Harms, "Narcissism: An Integrative Synthesis and Dominance Complementarity Model," *Academy of Management Perspectives* 28, no. 2 (2014): 108–127.

124. S. Y. Lee, M. Pitesa, S. Thau, and M. M. Pillutla, "Discrimination in Selection Decisions: Integrating Stereotype Fit and Interdependence Theories," *Academy of Management Journal* 58, no. 3 (2015): 789–812.

125. A. Canato, "Coerced Practice Implementation in Cases of Low Cultural Fit: Cultural Change and Practice Adaptation During the Implementation of Six Sigma at 3M," *Academy of Management Journal* 56, no. 6 (2013): 1724–1753.

126. B. M. Galvin, D. Lange, and B. E. Ashforth, "Narcissistic Organizational Identification: Seeing Oneself as Central to the Organization's Identity," *Academy of Management Review* 40, no. 2 (2015): 163–181.

127. C. M. Barnes, L. Lucianetti, D. P. Bhave, and M. S. Christian, "You Wouldn't Like Me When I'm Sleepy: Leaders' Sleep, Daily Abusive Supervision, and Work Unit Engagement," *Academy of Management Journal* 58, no. 5 (2015): 1419–1437.

128. M. E. Chan and D. J. McAllister, "Abusive Supervision Through the Lens of Employee State Paranoia," *Academy of Management Review* 39, no. 1 (2014): 44–66.

129. C. Hann, "Caught in the Cookie Jar," *Entrepreneur* (December 2014): 41.

130. L. A. Mainiero and K. J. Jones, "Sexual Harassment Versus Workplace Romance: Social Media Spillover and Textual Harassment in the Workplace," *Academy of Management Perspectives* 27, no. 3 (2013): 187–203.

131. R. Hennessey, "Decisions, Decisions," *Entrepreneur* (March 2015): 50.

132. S. Reddy, "Why Are You Always Late? It Could Be a Planning Fallacy," *The Wall Street Journal* (February 3, 2015): D1, D2.

133. C. Hann, "Caught in the Cookie Jar," *Entrepreneur* (December 2014): 41.

134. E. Bernstein, "You Can Do It! Be a Motivator," *The Wall Street Journal* (June 16, 2016): D1, D3.

135. R. McCammon, "So, Here's the Bad News …" *Entrepreneur* (July 2015): 24–25.

136. S. Painter, "Scott Painter's Tips on Surviving Screwups," INC. (November 2014): 32.

137. R. McCammon, "We Hear You," *Entrepreneur* (April 2014): 30–31.

138. P. Keegan, "The New Rules of Engagement," *INC.* (December 2014/January 2015): 86–132.

139. R. Hennessey, "Decisions, Decisions," *Entrepreneur* (March 2015): 50.

140. R. McCammon, "We Hear You," *Entrepreneur* (April 2014): 30–31.

141. R. McCammon, "The Worst of Times," *Entrepreneur* (February 2016): 15–16.

142. C. Hann, "Fair Pay," *Entrepreneur* (May 2016): 23.

143. S. Painter, "Scott Painter's Tips on Surviving Screwups," INC. (November 2014): 32.

144. Staff, "You Won't Learn This in Business School," *Costco Connection* (April 2014): 13.

145. S. Painter, "Scott Painter's Tips on Surviving Screwups," INC. (November 2014): 32.

146. Ibid.

147. I. Filatotchev and C. Nakajima, "Corporate Governance, Responsible Managerial Behavior, and Corporate Social Responsibility: Organizational Efficiency Versus Organizational Legitimacy," *Academy of Management Perspectives* 28, no. 3 (2014): 289–306.

148. R. M. Kanter, "Why Global Companies Will Behave More and More Alike," *The Wall Street Journal* (July 8, 2014): R8.

149. G. Colvin, "Heavy Hitters Travel Light," *Fortune* (February 1, 2016): 20.

150. J. Alsever, "Is Software Better at Managing People Than You Are?" *Fortune* (March 15, 2016): 41–42.

151. N. Vardi, "Math-Stress of the Universe," *Forbes* (October 19, 2015): 110–118.

152. Ad, "Data Driven," *Fortune* (September 15, 2015): 28.

153. R. Reuteman, "Generation Gaps," *Entrepreneur* (March 2015): 43–48.

154. P. Keegan, "The New Rules of Engagement," *INC.* (December 2014/January 2015): 86–132.

155. J. S. Lubin and J. R. Hagerty, "Why the New Boss Is Younger Than You Are," *The Wall Street Journal* (July 8, 2015): B1, B6.

156. R. Feintzeig, "More Firms Say Targets Are the Key to Diversity," *The Wall Street Journal* (September 30, 2015): R3, R7.

157. G. Jasen, "Male Investors vs. Female Investors: How Do They Compare?" *The Wall Street Journal* (May 4, 2015): R1, R2.

158. R. Holt and M. Zundel, "Understanding Management, Trade, and Society Through Fiction: Lessons From *The Wire*," *Academy of Management Review* 39, no. 4 (2014): 576–585.

159. T. Shumsky and T. Francis, "Accounting Blurs Profit Picture," *The Wall Street Journal* (June 28, 2016): B1, B6.

160. E. Pfanner and M. Fujikawa, "Toshiba Overstated Profits by $1.9 Billion," *The Wall Street Journal* (September 8, 2015): B1.

161. S. Schechner, "Snap Changes Tack on Overseas Taxes," *The Wall Street Journal* (January 1, 2017): B1, B4.

162. T. L. Stanko and C. M. Beckman, "Watching You Watching Me: Boundary Control and Capturing Attention in the Context of Ubiquitous Technology Use," *Academy of Management Journal* 58, no. 3 (2015): 712–738.

163. Staff, "Anonymity Is a Threat to E-Commerce," *BusinessWeek* (November 2–8, 2015): 14.

164. D. A. Waldman and R. M. Balven, "Responsible Leadership: Theoretical Issues and Research Directions," *Academy of Management Perspectives* 28, no. 3 (2014): 224–234.

165. J. Follain, "Pope Urges Drastic Cut in Fossil Fuels to Protect Climate," *BusinessWeek* (June 18, 2015), http://www.bloomberg.com/news/articles/2015-06-18/pope-urges-drastic-fossil-fuel-emission-cut-to-protect-climate, accessed September 21, 2015.

166. J. F. F. Rotondi, "Pope Francis to Congress: Capitalism Must Change," *BusinessWeek* (May 13, 2015): http://www.bloomberg.com/news/articles/2015-05-13/pope-francis-to-congress-capitalism-must-change, accessed September 21, 2015.

Chapter 15

1. P. Lencioni, "Being Smart Is Overrated," *INC.* (October 2014): 128.

2. Apple website, www.apple.com, accessed July 16, 2015.

3. M. Sytch and A. Tatarynowicz, "Exploring the Locus of Invention: The Dynamics of Network Communities and Firms' Invention Productivity," *Academy of Management Journal* 57, no. 1 (2014): 249–279.

4. D. J. Teece, "The Foundations of Enterprise Performance: Dynamic and Ordinary Capabilities in an (Economic) Theory of Firms," *Academy of Management Perspectives* 28, no. 4 (2014): 328–352.

5. K. Weise and J. Lorin, "Arne vs. the Students," *BusinessWeek* (June 1–7, 2015): 26–27.

6. K. Weise, S. Soper, and E. Dexheimer, "Apple Tries to Work Its Magic on Money," *BusinessWeek* (September 15–21, 2014): 45–46.

7. B. R. Dineen and D. G. Allen, "Third Party Employment Branding: Human Capital Inflows and Outflows Following Best Places to Work Certifications," *Academy of Management Journal* 59, no. 1 (2016): 90–112.

8. J. Lahart, "U.S.'s Forgotten Economic Engine," *The Wall Street Journal* (December 1, 2014): C1.

9. J. Alsever, "Smaller Businesses Struggle to Make It in the U.S.A." *Fortune* (November 17, 2014): 29–32.

10. B. Tita, "After a Long Decline, Manufacturing Is Returning to the U.S." *The Wall Street Journal* (June 8, 2016): C1.

11. J. Alsever, "Smaller Businesses Struggle to Make It in the U.S.A.," *Fortune* (November 17, 2014): 29–32.

12. J. R. Hagerty and M. Magnier, "Companies Tiptoe Back Toward Made in the USA," *The Wall Street Journal* (January 14, 2015): A1, A12.

13. J. Alsever, "Smaller Businesses Struggle to Make It in the U.S.A." *Fortune* (November 17, 2014): 29–32.

14. Ad, "Built in America, Beloved Worldwide," *BusinessWeek* (June 9–15, 2015): S1–S10.

15. W. L. Bedwell, S. M. Fiore, and E. Salas, "Developing the Future Workforce: An Approach for Integrating Interpersonal Skills Into the MBA Classroom," *Academy of Management Learning & Education* 13, no. 2 (2014): 171–186.

16. P. Coy, "Solving the Mystery of the Service Sector," *BusinessWeek* (July 28–August 3, 2014): 14–15.

17. J. Miller, "The Meaning of Big Data," *Fortune* (June 16, 2014): 232.

18. Ibid.

19. Bureau of Economic Analysis, "The Data Trade," *BusinessWeek* (May 18–24, 2015): 18.

20. S. Jakab, "GameStop Has More Lives Left," *The Wall Street Journal* (May 28, 2015): C1.

21. S. Hedgecock, "Pill Pusher," *Forbes* (May 4, 2015): 40–41.

22. C. Carr, "Stress to Impress," *Costco Connection* (February 2015): 13.

23. GE ad, "Identifying the Leadership Skills That Matter Most Today," *INC.* (December 2014–January 2015): 78.

24. P. J. Buckley and R. Strange, "The Governance of the Global Factory: Location and Control of World Economic Activity," *Academy of Management Perspectives* 29, no. 2 (2015): 237–249.

25. V. Taft, "Protesters Aren't Going to Like How McDonald's Is Reacting to Their Minimum Wage Concerns," *Independent Journal* (May 26, 2015), http://www.ijreview.com/2015/05/330129-guy-wont-taking-mickey-ds-order-much-longer-might-surprised-reasons/, accessed June 7, 2015.

26. J. Jargon, "McDonald's Hacks at Its Bureaucracy," *The Wall Street Journal* (October 31, 2014): B1.

27. S. J. Creary, B. B. Caza, L. M. Roberts, "Out of the Box? How Managing a Subordinate's Multiple Identities Affects the Quality of a Manager–Subordinate Relationship," *Academy of Management Review* 40, no. 4 (2015): 538–562.

28. W. Su and E. W. K. Tsang, "Product Diversification and Financial Performance: The Moderating Role of Secondary Stakeholders," *Academy of Management Journal* 58, no. 4 (2015): 1128–1148.

29. J. Reingold, "Kent Is Leaving, but Coke's Problems Remain," *Fortune* (January 1, 2017): 16.

30. L. Rupp, "Resuscitating Gap," *BusinessWeek* (April 25–May 1, 2016): 23–24.

31. K. Stock, "Briefs," *BusinessWeek* (February 29–March 6, 2016): 27.

32. A. Gasparro, "Kraft, Heinz Brands Need Some Catching Up," *The Wall Street Journal* (March 26, 2015): B1, B6.

33. D. Leonard, "Fall So Hard," *BusinessWeek* (June 1–7, 2015): 48–53.

34. S. Ovide, "Microsoft's Misdial Cost $7.6 Billion," *The Wall Street Journal* (July 9, 2015): B1, B4.

35. J. Jargon, "McDonald's Menu Problems: It's Supersized," *The Wall Street Journal* (October 31, 2014): B1, B2.

36. J. Jargon and A. Hufford, "Burger Giant's New Bet: Burgers," *The Wall Street Journal* (March 2, 2017): B1.

37. B. Tita, "After a Long Decline, Manufacturing Is Returning to the U.S.," *The Wall Street Journal* (June 8, 2016): C1.

38. Staff, "The Two Keys to Profits," *INC.* (December 2014–January 2015): 80.

39. K. Stock, "Briefs," *BusinessWeek* (December 29–January 11, 2015): 24.

40. A. Satariano, "Apple's First Responders," *BusinessWeek* (September 8–14, 2014): 31–32.

41. T. Monahan, "Revving Up Your Corporate RPMs," *Fortune* (February 1, 2016): 43.

42. J. Daley, "New Frontiers in Franchising," *Entrepreneur* (October 2015): 96–101.

43. M. M. Moya and J. L. M. Aleman, "The Differential Effect of Development Speed and Launching Speed on New Product Performance: An Analysis in SMEs," *Journal of Small Business Management* 54, no. 2 (2016): 750–770.

44. K. Stock, "Briefs," *BusinessWeek* (February 29–March 6, 2016): 27.

45. Y. Lee and M. J. Lee, "Samsung's $2 Billion Mistake," *BusinessWeek* (September 26–October 7, 2016):

46. J. Cheng and E. Y. Jeong, "Samsung Recall Takes Toll," *The Wall Street Journal* (October 27, 2016): B1, B4.

47. M. Gurman and S. Kim, "Samsung Would Love to Talk About This Phone," *BusinessWeek* (April 3–9, 2017): 36–37.

48. Staff, "Growing Demand," *The Wall Street Journal* online, accessed June 22, 2017.

49. J. Hartz, "Design Your Office Around Your Business Goals," *INC.* (September 2014): 122.

50. R. Myers, "Location, Location, Frustration," *INC.* (October 2014): 120–121.

51. J. Jargon, "New Plan at Hostess: Cupcakes Everywhere," *The Wall Street Journal* (September 18, 2015): B1, B5.

52. K. Stock, "Briefs," *BusinessWeek* (April 6–12, 2015): 23.

53. L. Rad, "Out of the Box," *Fortune* (December 1, 2016): 23.

54. Staff, "Cars: Overcapacity Is China's New Normal," *BusinessWeek* (December 9, 2015–January 5, 2016): 67–68.

55. B. Fritz, "At Disney, Park Price May Swing With the Season," *The Wall Street Journal* (October 5, 2015): B1.

56. W. Su and E. W. K. Tsang, "Product Diversification and Financial Performance: The Moderating Role of Secondary Stakeholders," *Academy of Management Journal* 58, no. 4 (2015): 1128–1148.

57. C. Smith, "Setting Your Lineup for Success," *Costco Connection* (April 2015): 13.

58. F. Feiberbaum, "Forget-Me-Nots," *Costco Connection* (June 2016): 37.

59. L. Stevens, "UPS Set Ambitious Targets for Profit Growth," *The Wall Street Journal* (November 14, 2014): B3.

60. C. Hann, "Stocking UP," *Entrepreneur* (September 2014): 27.

61. A. Roberts, "Car Discounts Take Toll," *The Wall Street Journal* (March 2, 1027): B3.

62. S. Pettypiece and M. Townsend, with L. C. Lochner, "Now, Suppliers Are Wal-Mart's Main Squeeze," *BusinessWeek* (September 21–27, 2015): 24–25.

63. S. J. Kahl, "Associations, Jurisdictional Battles, and the Development of Dual-Purpose Capabilities," *Academy of Management Perspectives* 26, no. 4 (2014): 381–394.

64. C. Hann, "Stocking UP," *Entrepreneur* (September 2014): 27.

65. Ad, "Supply Chain Management," *Fortune* (September 22, 2014): S1.

66. Ad, "Help Wanted," *Fortune* (September 22, 2014): S5.

67. S. Leibs, "Think Before You Link," *INC.* (October 2014): 118.

68. Ad, "From Redefining Supply Chain Management," *Fortune* (September 22, 2014): S7.

69. J. Bennett, "A Supply Chain, Reinvented," *The Wall Street Journal* (October 14, 2015): R5.

70. S. Soper, "So Many Boats, So Little Cargo," *BusinessWeek* (February 15–21, 2016): 12–13.

71. Ad, "The Logic of Logistics," *Fortune* (June 15, 2015): S1.

72. Ad, "UPS," *INC.* (April 4, 2015): 49.

73. Ad, "The Strategic Supply Chain," *Fortune* (January 1, 2017): 54.

74. C. Bjork, "Zara Builds Its Business Around RFID," *The Wall Street Journal* (September 17, 2014): B1, B2.

75. A. G. Acharya and T. G. Pollock, "Shoot for the Stars? Predicting the Recruitment of Prestigious Directors at Newly Public Firms," *Academy of Management Journal* 56, no. 5 (2013): 1396–1419.

76. Staff, "The Two Keys to Profits," *INC.* (December 2014–January 2015): 80.

77. V. Harnish, "5 Ways to Tone Your Operations," *Fortune* (October 27, 2014): 46.

78. D. Gilbert and S. Kent, "BP to Pay Out $18.7 Billion to Settle Spill," *The Wall Street Journal* (July 3, 2015): A1.

79. M. Spector and M. Colias, "Takata Pleads Guilty in Air-Bag Case," *The Wall Street Journal* (February 28, 2017): B3.

80. J. Plungis and M. Mittelman, "The Longest Recall," *BusinessWeek* (May 16–22, 2016): 27–28.

81. Motley Rice website, http://www.motleyrice.com/case/takata-airbag-recall-lawsuits?gclid=CO-toq-x4MYCFcsXHwodVcoGmA, accessed July 16, 2015.

82. National Public Radio, "News" (June 26, 2017), http://www.npr.org/2017/06/26/534365579/takata-files-for-bankruptcy-protection-over-air-bag-troubles, accessed August 30, 2017.

83. Staff, "Mary Barra," *Entrepreneur* (December 2014): 46.

84. K. McDonald, "Quote," *BusinessWeek* (April 13–19, 2015): 18.

85. R. Clough, "General Electric Wants to Act Like a Startup," *BusinessWeek* (August 11–24, 2014): 22–24.

86. A. Canato, "Coerced Practice Implementation in Cases of Low Cultural Fit: Cultural Change and Practice Adaptation During the Implementation of Six Sigma at 3M," *Academy of Management Journal* 56, no. 6 (2013): 1724–1753.

87. R. Clough, "General Electric Wants to Act Like a Startup," *BusinessWeek* (August 11–24, 2014): 22–24.

88. A. VanderMey, "Smarter Faster Better," *Fortune* (March 15, 2016): 28.

89. A. Murray, "Lessons From the Fortune 500," *Fortune* (June 15, 2016): 14.

90. T. Monahan, "Revving Up Your Corporate RPMs," *Fortune* (February 1, 2016): 43.

91. S. Bing, "Productivity Now!" *Fortune* (January 1, 2016): 100.

92. J. Chew, "Be Better!" *Fortune* (January 2016): 18.

93. S. Olster, "Is Happiness Just a Lie We Tell Employees?" *Fortune* (June 15, 2015): 24.

94. J. Robinson, "The Refueling Principle," *Entrepreneur* (October 2014): 67–70.

95. D. K. Berman, "Why Aren't Smartphones Making Us More Productive?" *The Wall Street Journal* (May 1, 2013): B1, B2.

96. J. Chew, "Be Better!" *Fortune* (January 2016): 18.

97. Added at the suggestion of reviewer C. Blencke, University of Central Florida, June 23, 2017.

98. E. Fry, "We Were Promised a 20-Hour Workweek," *Fortune* (April 1, 2016): 18.

99. R. Miller, "How Productive Is the U.S.?" *BusinessWeek* (March 2–8, 2015): 16–17.

100. R. Foroohar, "Hard Math in the New Economy," *Time* (March 16, 2015): 32.

101. S. Forbes, "Free Trade Means More Jobs," *Forbes* (June 15, 2015): 11.

102. M. Philips and P. Coy, "Look Who's Driving R&D Now," *BusinessWeek* (June 8–14, 2015): 18–20.

103. S. Forbes, "Free Trade Means More Jobs," *Forbes* (June 15, 2015): 11.

104. Staff, "U.S. Productivity Fell," *The Wall Street Journal* (August 10, 2016): A1.

105. J. Sparshott, "Weakening Productivity Augurs Ill for Wages," *The Wall Street Journal* (June 5, 2015): A2.

106. A. Murray, "Lessons From the Fortune 500," *Fortune* (June 15, 2016): 14.

107. J. Sparshott, "Weakening Productivity Augurs Ill for Wages," *The Wall Street Journal* (June 5, 2015): A2.

108. E. Fry, "We Were Promised a 20-Hour Workweek," *Fortune* (April 1, 2016): 18.

109. S. Rosenbush, "The Key's to Facebook's Productivity," *The Wall Street Journal* (February 23, 2015): R8.

110. J. Bennett, "GM Caps Tough Year With a Profit," *The Wall Street Journal* (February 5, 2015): B1, B2.

111. J. Sparshott, "Weakening Productivity Augurs Ill for Wages," *The Wall Street Journal* (June 5, 2015): A2.

112. D. K. Berman, "Why Aren't Smartphones Making Us More Productive?" *The Wall Street Journal* (May 1, 2013): B1, B2.

113. M. Rosenwald, "Bound by Habit," *BusinessWeek* (March 19–25, 2012): 106–107.

114. D. Leonard, "Your Knees Will Soon Ache Even More," *BusinessWeek* (July 28–August 3, 2014): 22–23.

115. S. Berfield, "McDonald's Revamp Has Missing Ingredients," *BusinessWeek* (May 11–17, 2015): 21.

116. A. Gumbus and R. N. Lussier, "Entrepreneurs Use a Balanced Scorecard to Translate Strategy Into Performance Measures," *Journal of Small Business Management* 44, no. 3 (2006): 407–425.

117. R. Kaplan and D. P. Norton, "Using the Balanced Scorecard as a Strategic Management System," *Harvard Business Review* (January–February 1996): 75–85.

118. A. Gumbus and R. N. Lussier, "Entrepreneurs Use a Balanced Scorecard to Translate Strategy Into Performance Measures," *Journal of Small Business Management* 44, no. 3 (2006): 407–425.

119. Added at the suggestion of reviewer C. Blencke, University of Central Florida, June 23, 2017.

120. M. L. Turner, "Remote Control," *Entrepreneur* (January 2016): 75–79.

121. D. J. Teece, "The Foundations of Enterprise Performance: Dynamic and Ordinary Capabilities in an (Economic) Theory of Firms," *Academy of Management Perspectives* 28, no. 4 (2014): 328–352.

122. W. Q. Judge, Y. L. Thompkins, J. L. Brown, and C. Pongpatipat, "The Impact of Home Country Institutions on Corporate Technological Entrepreneurship via R&D Investments and Virtual World Presence," *Entrepreneurship Theory and Practice*, 39, no. 2 (2015): 237–266.

123. Ad, "The New Logistics Challenge: Globalization," *INC.* (December 2015–January 2016): S1.

124. Ad, "The Strategic Supply Chain," *Fortune* (January 1, 2017): 54.

125. R. M. Kanter, "Why Global Companies Will Behave More and More Alike," *The Wall Street Journal* (July 8, 2014): R8.

126. Teradata, "Data-Driven Businesses Outperform," *Forbes* (February 9, 2015): 24.

127. V. Harnish, "5 Ways to Turn Precision Into Profits," *Fortune* (July 1, 2015): 32.

128. J. J. Roberts, "When Your Stuff Spies on You," *Fortune* (June 1, 2017): 26.

129. J. Alsever, "Is This Robot a Friend—or a Foe?" *Fortune* (March 15, 2017): 22–24.

130. D. Michaels, "Driving U.S. Factories: Foreign Robotics," *The Wall Street Journal* (March 27, 2017): A1, A10.

131. R. Mac, H. Shao, and F. Bi, "Drone Wars," *Forbes* (May 25, 2015): 130–131.

132. J. P. Pullen, "A Fresh Perspective," *Entrepreneur* (June 2015): 65–66.

133. C. Mims, "3-D Printing Promises to Alter Manufacturing," *The Wall Street Journal* (February 29, 2016): B1, B6.

134. R. Karlgaard, "Riches From the Disruptive Dozen," *Forbes* (October 19, 2015): 38.

135. Staff, "Pinning Down the Cloud," *Forbes* (July 20, 2015): 86–87.

136. G. Colvin, "Humans Are Underrated," *Fortune* (August 1, 2015): 100–113.

137. McKinsey, "Wanted: Skills of Human Interaction," *Fortune* (June 2, 2014): 200.

138. L. Scism, "Humans Still Rule Machines in Insurance," *The Wall Street Journal* (May 24, 2017): B1, B2.

139. J. Gershman and T. Mickle, "Trouble Brews for Imported Beer Made in America," *The Wall Street Journal* (June 25, 2015): A1, A6.

140. J. R. Hagerty and B. Tita, "Workers Say Train Repairs Were Often Bogus," *The Wall Street Journal* (July 21, 2014): B1, B6.

141. D. Bloomfield, "Lawsuits: Your Likes May Mark You as a Victim," *BusinessWeek* (June 1–7, 2015): 32–33.

142. L. Rad, "Out of the Box," *Fortune* (December 1, 2016): 23.

●●● Author Index

••• Company Index

••• Subject Index